Understanding American Politics and Government

Understanding American Politics and Government

JOHN COLEMAN
University of Wisconsin, Madison

KENNETH GOLDSTEIN
University of Wisconsin, Madison

WILLIAM G. HOWELL
University of Chicago

PEARSON
Longman

New York San Francisco Boston
London Toronto Sydney Tokyo Singapore Madrid
Mexico City Munich Paris Cape Town Hong Kong Montreal

Editor-in-Chief: Eric Stano
Development Manager: David Kear
Executive Marketing Manager: Ann Stypuloski
Supplements Editor: Brian Belardi
Production Manager: Stacey Kulig
Project Coordination, Text Design, and Electronic Page Makeup: Electronic Publishing
    Services Inc.
Cover Designer/Manager: John Callahan
Photo Researcher: Linda Sykes
Manufacturing Manager: Mary Fischer
Printer and Binder: Hamilton Printing Co.
Cover Printer: Phoenix Color Corp.

For permission to use copyrighted material, grateful acknowledgment is made to the copyright holders on pp.   –   , which are hereby made part of this copyright page.

Library of Congress Cataloging-in-Publication Data

Please visit us at www.ablongman.com

ISBN 13: 978-0-205-65054-5

ISBN 10: 0-205-65054-6

1 2 3 4 5 6 7 8 9 10—HPC—10 09 08

Dear student,

I want to tell you how delighted I am that you are helping the authors and the staff at Pearson Longman with the development of *Understanding American Government and Politics*. Creating a new textbook is a project that involves a great many people. No one, however, is more important than you, the student who will actually be using the book in your course. This preliminary edition of *Understanding American Government and Politics* has been created with the goal of collecting and using your feedback to inform the shape of the final book, which is scheduled to publish in December. Your input will make the final book an even more effective learning tool and resource for future students!

On the next page, you will find a questionnaire about the book. If you complete it and give it to your instructor at the end of the semester, we will be able to use your suggestions in the final draft of the text.

As your instructor may have told you, we are sending you this edition before photos have been selected or a final pass of proofreading completed. We have nonetheless tried to keep this preliminary edition error-free. However, if you find any typos, please don't hesitate to let us know!

The authors and everyone at Pearson Longman join me in wishing you success with this book and in your course. We hope you find it to be a helpful resource as you study American politics and government.

Good luck in your studies!

Sincerely,

Eric Stano
Editor in Chief
Pearson Longman

Student Questionnaire

Dear Student: Having read through *Understanding American Politics and Government*, please take a few minutes to respond to these questions. Please return the sheet to your instructor when you are finished. Thank you for your feedback.

Your Name (Please Print): _____

Email Address: _____

School Name: _____

State: _____

Instructor Name: _____ Your Major: _____

1. Please rate the following statements about this book:

	STRONGLY AGREE	AGREE	NEUTRAL	DISAGREE	STRONGLY DISAGREE
"This text is enjoyable to read."	☐	☐	☐	☐	☐
"This text uses relevant examples."	☐	☐	☐	☐	☐
"This text explores interesting political questions."	☐	☐	☐	☐	☐
"This text gives me a good understanding of cause and effect in our political system."	☐	☐	☐	☐	☐
"This text illustrates how political scientists approach the study of politics."	☐	☐	☐	☐	☐
"This text does a good job of showing how our political system compares to those of other countries."	☐	☐	☐	☐	☐
"I like this text's page design and illustrations."	☐	☐	☐	☐	☐

2. How effective were the following features in helping you to understand and think critically about the material?

	VERY HELPFUL	SOMEWHAT HELPFUL	NEUTRAL	NOT VERY HELPFUL	NOT HELPFUL
Chapter opening examples	☐	☐	☐	☐	☐
"How Do We Know?" boxes	☐	☐	☐	☐	☐
Case Studies	☐	☐	☐	☐	☐

3. Please tell us what you liked most about the book.

_____

_____

4. Based on your reaction to this book, would you recommend this text to your instructor?
☐ Yes   ☐ No

5. May we quote you in the promotional materials for this text?
☐ Yes   ☐ No

Signature:_____   Date: _____

Thank you for your feedback!

Instructor Questionnaire

Dear instructor: Longman Publishers would like to thank you for taking the time to use *Understanding American Politics and Government*, and providing us with valuable feedback.

Name: _____

School: _____

City, State, Zip: _____

Email Address: _____

Your Current Text (Author, Title): _____

1. What would you most like to see changed about your current Intro American Government text?

   _____

   _____

2. How does the book compare to your current text in the following areas:

	SUPERIOR	SOMEWHAT BETTER	ABOUT THE SAME	NOT QUITE AS GOOD	NOT AS GOOD
Readability/Clarity of Explanations	☐	☐	☐	☐	☐
Scholarship	☐	☐	☐	☐	☐
Use of Examples	☐	☐	☐	☐	☐
Emphasis on Social Science Techniques	☐	☐	☐	☐	☐
Comparative Perspective (flagged)	☐	☐	☐	☐	☐
Political Culture Emphasis	☐	☐	☐	☐	☐
Design / Photos & Illustrations	☐	☐	☐	☐	☐

3. How effective do you think the following features would be in helping your students understand and think critically about American politics?

	VERY HELPFUL	SOMEWHAT HELPFUL	NEUTRAL	NOT VERY HELPFUL	NOT HELPFUL
Chapter opening examples	☐	☐	☐	☐	☐
"How Do We Know?" boxes	☐	☐	☐	☐	☐
Case Studies	☐	☐	☐	☐	☐

4. What did you think of the book overall?

   _____

   _____

   _____

   _____

5. Based on your reaction to this preliminary edition, how likely would you be to consider adopting this text when it publishes in December 2008 (after the Presidential election)?

☐ Very Likely ☐ Somewhat Likely ☐ Not Likely

If "Not Likely," what would need to occur for this to become a text you would consider?

_____

_____

_____

6. May we acknowledge your contribution to this project in the Preface of the printed text?

☐ Yes ☐ No

7. May we quote you in our promotional materials for this text?

☐ Yes ☐ No

Please mail completed instructor and student questionnaires to:

Ann Stypuloski
Pearson Publishers
51 Madison Ave.
New York, NY 10010

Thank you for your feedback!

Brief Contents

Detailed Contents

CHAPTER 3

The Constitution   51

CHAPTER 4

Federalism   85

Deciding End-of-Life Issues in a Federalist System   86

CHAPTER 7

Public Opinion   193

CHAPTER 8

Political Participation   223

CHAPTER 9

Voting, Elections, and Campaigns 255

CHAPTER 10

Media and Politics 293

CHAPTER 11

Political Parties   327

The Difficulty of Being Different   328

xx

Preface

Overview

Have you ever been convinced that your favorite team loses only because *you* show up at the game? Ever think that it rains *because* you've just washed your car? While these are tongue-in-cheek examples, they are nonetheless questions of causality, and you face important and consequential ones every day in your life and in your job. They also abound in American politics.

Did John Kerry lose in 2004 because gay marriage was on the ballot in 11 states—driving conservatives to the polls—as many pundit (and even a former president) suggested? Or was it because more people trusted Republicans to keep us safe in a time of terror. Did Barack Obama win the Democratic party's nomination because his message of "change" simply resonated with voters more or did Hillary Clinton lose the Democratic nomination because she was a woman and did not get a fair shake from voters and the media?

This book examines these and numerous other causal questions in American politics, and it gives students the critical thinking tools they need to go behind the headlines and the simplistic theories often espoused by both politicians and pundits. This book helps students dig down to the core of causes and consequences of politics in America.

By empowering students with these skills, we hope to brace them with some armor against the hyperbole that we hear from so many of our leaders and members of the press. While still teaching them the basics of our government, in what we hope is a highly engaging and accessible presentation, this book will help students engage in American politics and explore for themselves some of the most interesting and provocative questions in our political world.

Why We Wrote this Book?

The introductory course in American politics is the first class that most students take in political science. For a significant number of students American politics may be the only course they take in political science specifically or the social sciences more generally. With that in mind, what should this class—this book - accomplish? Fundamentally, we hope this book will help spark students' interest in politics. Instructors of the American government course always hope it will encourage their students to participate in the political process, but exhortation only goes so far. We believe that an approach to American politics that treats students not only as students and citizens but also investigators in search of answers can spark their interest in understanding and participating in the political system.

Rather than assuming that political science is settled fact kept within the dusty covers of an old textbook, we hope the discussions found here will show students a discipline very much alive with questions. Students will see that scholars often struggle to analyze politics and that new knowledge is created through their efforts. These discussions will help students, with guidance from instructors, think about how they might study political questions of interest to them—what data they would need, how they might collect it, what problems they might confront in analyzing it, what explanatory factors they would include, and so on.

Of course, the primary goal of this first class in American politics is to first teach students substantive material about U.S. government and politics. Making sure students understand the basic principles, institutions, behaviors, and debates in American politics is critically important to any introductory American politics class. This substantive foundation will also benefit students in other courses as well as in their role as citizens, and we have served those basics up in each chapter in prose, photos, and graphs we hope readers will find both clear and interesting. In addition to presenting the foundations, and—in fact—to help present them even more effectively, this book weaves two major themes throughout the chapters: the importance of understanding the actual causal factors behind political developments and, , the importance of understanding those factors and American politics in a comparative perspective.

Our Approach

Causality. From the very first chapter the book trains students to distinguish between the concepts of "correlation" and "causation" as they examine political phenomena, helping turn them into good critical thinkers, more thoughtful citizens, and more effective investigators. Each chapter begins with a story that explores a causal question, and then other causal questions are explored further in the chapter. The **"How Do We Know?"** feature in every chapter hooks students with a provocative, important political question related to that chapter's topic and then schools them in the techniques political scientists use to answer it. Each box provides context for—and underscores the importance of—the question, highlights the means and challenges of answering it, and ends with a summary on what conclusions social scientists have or have not—cached.

Comparative Perspective. Understanding how politics and political institutions in the United States differ from those in other democracies can shed light on our own system of government. For students who wonder "why don't we do this" or "what are the alternatives," the comparative discussions help answer those questions. Knowing the alternatives is a crucial part of political involvement, and helps answer causal questions as well. Substantive comparative examples throughout the text deepen students' understanding of American politics.

Political Culture. Because political culture can also shed a light on causal questions, Chapter 2 sets the stage for the book's emphasis on how Americans' shared political culture–our prizing of individualism, democracy, and liberty, respect for property, and religious rights–influences our politics and government. Values and beliefs motivate participants in the political process, and they also make some policy paths more likely than others in American politics. When students do become involved in politics, it is ideas, values, and beliefs that to a large degree will influence their position on issues and their political activity.

Real World Emphasis. Whether the topic is lobbying, elections, political communication, or something else

entirely, an emphasis on the real world of politics can maintain student interest, provide concrete examples of the arguments being made in the text, and teach students how to assess evidence. We've provided real-world examples throughout the text to help connect the concepts to the student's world, and show students how it is relevant to them. Each chapter opens with a story of a recent event or situation, exploring a causal question, to set the context for the chapter. The Case Study in each chapter is also taken from recent major events, and is used to expand on major concepts in the chapter. Integrated throughout, these high-interest, in-depth examples apply the ideas developed in the book to real world events, bringing abstract concepts to life and making them concrete. Each Case Study concludes with "Thinking Critically" questions, helping students understand, apply, and synthesize key points.

Our separate experiences teaching thousands of students in introductory classes at elite private universities, major public research and teaching institutions, and community colleges convinces us that giving students a story line that pays attention to the real world of politics, teaches students how to evaluate evidence, talks about values and beliefs, and presents the American political experience in a comparative perspective can be an effective way to engage students in the most current research questions and interest them in the most important puzzles that define political science. Most texts we have seen present knowledge about American politics as a closed book where the important questions have all been answered. The student reader would never guess that there is lively and interesting debate raging about many of the issues that are presented in the standard texts as "givens" about US politics and government. Our aim is to spark students' curiosity and, we hope, produce more involved and participatory citizens. The themes that drive this text are oriented more to those goals than to convincing students—or instructors—of any particular normative world view that we might have. Our approach is less about telling students "here is what you should believe about American politics" and more about telling them "here are interesting questions and puzzles in American politics and some ways you can go about investigating them."

About the Authors

JOHN J. COLEMAN
The University of Wisconsin at Madison

John J. Coleman is Chair of the political science department at The University of Wisconsin at Madison. His teaching and research interests center on the evolution of the American state and the relationship between changes in the political economy of the United States and its party structure. Professor Coleman is the author of *Party Decline in America: Policy, Politics, and the Fiscal State* (Princeton University Press, 1996) and numerous articles on party organizations, elections, Congress, the presidency, campaign spending, and international trade. His current research includes projects on campaign spending, congressional political parties, and the politics of income distribution.

KENNETH M GOLDSTEIN
The University of Wisconsin at Madison

Ken Goldstein is a Professor of political science at the University of Wisconsin-Madison and Director of the University of Wisconsin Advertising Project. He is the author of Interest Groups, Lobbying, and Participation in America (Cambridge University Press, 1999) and Campaign Advertising and American Democracy (Temple University Press, 2007) as well as over 30 journal articles and book chapters on political communication, voter turnout, campaign finance, survey methodology, Israeli politics, presidential elections, and news coverage of health issues. Professor Goldstein is currently a consultant for the ABC News elections unit and a member of their election night decision team. He has worked on network election night coverage in every U.S. federal election since 1988.

WILLIAM HOWELL
The Harris School at The University of Chicago

William Howell is an Associate Professor at the Harris School of The University of Chicago. Professor Howell has written widely on separation-of-powers issues and American political institutions, especially the presidency. Howell is the co-author (with Jon Pevehouse) of While Dangers Gather: Congressional Checks on Presidential War Powers (Princeton University Press, 2007); author of Power without Persuasion: The Politics of Direct Presidential Action (Princeton University Press, 2003); co-author (with Paul Peterson) of The Education Gap: Vouchers and Urban Schools (Brookings Institution Press, 2002); and editor of Besieged: School Boards and the Future of Education Politics (Brookings Institution Press, 2005). His research also has appeared in numerous professional journals and edited volumes. His current research examines the impact of war on presidential policymaking.

CHAPTER

1 Thinking About American Politics

On the third day of February 2004, two weeks after John Kerry's surprise victory in the Iowa caucuses and one week after the New Hampshire primary had secured his status as frontrunner in the Democratic race for president, the Massachusetts Supreme Court temporarily stole the national spotlight. On this day, the court instructed the Massachusetts state legislature to recognize by law the right of gays and lesbians in the state to marry.

This decision climaxed an effort begun in 2001 by seven gay and lesbian couples. When they were denied marriage licenses by their local city and town councils, they sued the Massachusetts Department of Public

Health, the agency responsible for administering the state's marriage laws. These couples ultimately prevailed in the Massachusetts Supreme Court, a victory that was sealed when the U.S. Supreme Court declined to review the case. Though the legal machinations had come to an end, the Massachusetts decision launched a political discussion that continued throughout the 2004 political season. After all, Massachusetts was the home state of John Kerry, the man who had locked up the Democratic nomination.

The question naturally arose: Did Kerry support gay marriage? The candidate gave a typically, well, vague response, saying that although he was personally opposed to same-sex marriages, he thought the issue was best decided by individual states. One very important state, California, had already decided the question. By law, the Golden State had defined marriage as a covenant between a man and a woman. But the recently elected mayor of San Francisco, Gavin Newsom, wanted to extend marriage rights

to same-sex couples. Accordingly, on February 12, 2004, little more than one week after the Massachusetts court decision, the City of San Francisco began granting marriage licenses to gay and lesbian couples.

At this point, President George W. Bush entered the fray. At a press conference held on February 24, 2004, he announced a strategy designed to stop the gay marriage movement in its tracks: "If we are to prevent the meaning of marriage from being changed forever, our nation must enact a constitutional amendment to protect marriage in America."[1]

In addition, in a number of states, defenders of traditional marriage worried that unless their own state constitutions clearly prohibited same-sex marriage, their courts might follow the Massachusetts example and declare a right to same-sex marriage. They worked, therefore, to put constitutional prohibitions against gay marriage on the ballot in Oregon, Arkansas, Georgia, Kentucky, Michigan, Mississippi, Montana, North

▼ **GAY COUPLES IN LINE TO GET MARRIED**

When Mayor Newsom granted marriage licenses to gay and lesbian couples, hundreds of gay couples lined up to get married, and shock waves reverberated through the political world as a presidential election loomed. What role might scenes like this have played in the national debate and in the way people voted?

Source: Terry Schmidt/UPI/Landov

Dakota, Oklahoma, Ohio, and Utah. On Election Day—November 3, 2004—each of these 11 states passed a constitutional amendment banning gay marriage. The measure won handily everywhere. The smallest still margin of victory was in Oregon, which passed its ban by a comfortable 14 percentage point margin.[2]

There were, of course, other contests on the ballot that day, one of which was the presidential race. In 9 of the 11 states with gay marriage amendments on the ballot—including, critically, Ohio—George W. Bush won the presidential vote. Had Bush lost Ohio—or Georgia and Montana, or Missouri and Arkansas, or a number of other two-state combinations—he would have lost the presidency. But most of the states that frowned on gay marriage smiled on George W. Bush and he won reelection, earning the right to lead the country, act as commander-in-chief, and nominate Supreme Court judges among other things for the next four years.

In the aftermath of the election, various analysts and pundits suggested that Bush had won 9 of the 11 marriage-ban states, and therefore the presidency, *because* gay marriage had been on the ballot there. No less a political authority than former President Bill Clinton subscribed to this theory: "Gay marriage was an overwhelming factor in the defeat of John Kerry," he said. The presence of the gay marriage issue on state ballots, said

Clinton, led to "an astonishing turnout among evangelical Christians who were voting on the basis of moral values."[3] In fact, a recent book by a prominent campaign operative claims that Clinton tried to persuade Kerry to support the gay marriage ban in the months leading up to the election.

Politics makes strange bedfellows, so it was not particularly surprising to see conservatives join Clinton in his assessment. Richard Cizik, government affairs director for the National Association of Evangelicals, echoed the former president's comments:

> Five judges in Massachusetts and the mayor of San Francisco may have done more to help George W. Bush's campaign than anything else. Evangelicals turned out as much to vote for these amendments as they did to vote for President Bush. It got them to the polls.[4]

Even individuals without a "dog in the fight," sized up the election in light of the gay marriage issue. According to Walter Shapiro, columnist for *USA Today*:

> In 2000, the U.S. Supreme Court helped put George W. Bush in the White House. On Tuesday, Bush again won a presidential election with the aid of a state supreme court. This time, it was the ruling by

the Massachusetts Supreme Court legalizing gay marriage in that state that may have been the decisive factor in granting Bush a second term.[5]

It appears, then, that if one were to ask informed political observers why George W. Bush was reelected in 2004, many of them would answer with two words: gay marriage. Did the presence of the gay marriage ban really make the difference in reelecting George W. Bush? If so, how? Did it bring out Republican voters who otherwise would not have come to the polls? Did it increase the prominence of "moral values" issues, and therefore encourage people to vote for Bush, the more socially conservative candidate? Did it lower the electorate's estimation of John Kerry, a Massachusetts Democrat whom voters may have associated with the cause of gay rights? Or was it a wash? Did the ballot measures encourage just as many liberals to vote who ended up voting for John Kerry? Or, was all of this irrelevant, with the war on terror easily trumping gay marriage as the deciding issue in 2004?

As explained below, such questions are called *causal questions*. We will be examining such questions throughout this text. This chapter will outline the framework this book will use to explain American politics, and answer such questions.

THIS CHAPTER WILL EXAMINE:

- ▶ challenges that researchers face when trying to study politics and answer causal questions
- ▶ American government in comparative and historical context and how unique aspects of American

culture determine what is possible in American politics

- ▶ some general characteristics of government and why government is necessary

causal question a question regarding the factors responsible for a particular outcome in the political world.

Thinking About Politics

As indicated previously, **causal questions** are concerned with "what *causes* what." Such questions address the roots or origins of particular events or behaviors. They attempt to explain which factor or factors made a particular outcome occur. You deal with causal questions every day. Did I get a "C" on that exam because I didn't study hard enough, or because I didn't study the right material? Which major gives me the best chance of getting into law school—political science or economics? Which will improve my job prospects more—taking extra classes during the summer, or working in an unpaid internship? In all of these cases, you are trying to understand an actual or potential outcome—getting a "C," getting into law school, getting a good job—in terms of factors that may bring it about. In this sense, you are always asking causal questions, and coming up with answers, as you seek to understand your world.

Answering causal questions—in the realm of politics and government—is what political science is all about and is what this book is all about. The question of gay marriage and its impact on the 2004 election is a particular causal question. However, before we are able to tackle this sort of question and identify what factors determine different sorts of political behaviors or outcomes, we must first be able to describe and measure the basic characteristics and organization of American government and society. Furthermore, the particular case of gay marriage also leads to larger questions of why government should be involved in some areas and not others. Why is government involved in marriage at all? Why are there certain tax benefits and legal advantages for married couples?

Public officials, political activists, journalists, and pundits often have simple answers to such questions. Sorting out fact from fiction in the hurly-burly of political debate can be difficult and can make citizens wary about getting involved in political arguments or political activity. While you do not need to run for office or get involved in every political campaign, knowing the fundamentals of your political system and the fundamentals of good thinking allows you to keep your leaders—not to mention your friends and family—accountable. How health care will be funded, what sorts of taxes you will pay, the shape of your retirement are all major issues that will surely be debated in the coming years. The war in Iraq will surely not be the last war debated by public officials and political activists.

> **"You are always asking causal questions, and coming up with answers, as you seek to understand your world."**

This book provides you with the tools to see through simplistic answers that often get put forward in political debates, cable talk shows, and dinner-table conversations and to help you become a more informed and active citizen. This book will talk a lot about power and how it is wielded. The authors of this book want to give you the confidence to be able to take part in politics and influence how power is wielded in America's democracy. As you study each topic, pay close attention to the different ways researchers gather and analyze evidence as they try to understand politics and political decisions.

In this introduction to American politics, we will concentrate on five main aspects: (1) the political, cultural, and historical background of American government; (2) politics at the level of the individual citizen; (3) mechanisms and groups that link citizens to their leaders; (4) political institutions and the ways in which they generate policies; and (5) how all of these factors come together in the making of public policy.

Throughout this text, we will present political scientists' answers to important questions in American politics in each of these areas. Whatever the topic, we will encourage you to take a critical view of how arguments are framed and made. This will not only enable you to make sense of class material, but also it can give you the confidence to evaluate research and make arguments in other settings—academic, political, professional, or even social.

We will certainly discuss topics like which factors influence presidential election outcomes—the questions that concluded the vignette about gay marriage and the 2004 election. Other examples of causal questions we will tackle include

- Why do some people become Democrats, others Republicans, and others independents?
- Why does the United States have low rates of voter turnout?
- Do the major media in this country give preferential treatment to one political party or the other?
- Why are members of Congress reelected at such high rates?
- Why do views of the president fluctuate so much over the course of a term in office?

All of these questions have outcomes that political scientists try to explain: party attachments, voter turnout, media bias, congressional election outcomes, and presidential approval. In addressing these questions and explaining these outcomes, the first step for researchers is identifying which factors could influence or cause change in the particular outcome they are studying. So, if the president's approval rating is the outcome to be studied, one of the explanatory causes would be the state of the national economy. This is just another way of saying that the performance of the U.S. economy is one factor that affects presidential job approval.

There are rarely simple solutions.

Most good studies, however, associate more than one causal or explanatory factor with each outcome. Political scientists tend to believe, for example, that while the state of the economy has an important influence on presidential approval, it is not the *only* relevant factor. The percentage of the electorate that has an attachment to the political party of the president (Republican or Democrat) is another factor that influences presidential approval. Another would be whether the nation is at war or at peace or whether the president is perceived as responding well to a natural disaster like Hurricane Katrina.

Where political scientists see a world in which more than one factor contributes to an outcome, journalists and politicians often focus on one major cause, even claiming it is *the* sole cause of something. If the economy is bad, it is because taxes are too high. If a candidate loses an election, it is because he ran a poor campaign. If the president suffers a legislative defeat, it is because the media covered his proposal in negative ways. If a political protest evolves into a riot, it is because the police failed to keep order. Simple answers make the journalist's job and the politician's job much easier.

Often these single-cause explanations flow from a particular viewpoint or partisan posture, or even the need to explain something in a quick sound bite. Generally, they do not represent good theory or good social science research, or even the whole story. Political scientists see the world as complex, with most conditions having not just one but a variety of causes. One of our goals in this book is to help you get beyond the tiring shouting matches on cable television news shows and give you the tools to make, interpret, and evaluate arguments on your own and thus to be a critical and informed citizen, one who can question the black-and-white world of sound bites and television talk shows and see the world in more realistic, more complex terms.

Correlation does not equal causation.

There are challenges that arise when conducting research on politics. One challenge occurs with such frequency that it needs special attention as you learn about others' research and possibly come up with your own answers: Correlation is not the same as causation. Consider a fairly silly example from outside the world of politics. Imagine that when ice cream sales went up, so too did residential burglaries. Likewise, when ice cream sales went down, residential burglaries went down as well. What would you conclude from this? One conclusion would be that the increase in ice cream sales was somehow causing the rise in burglaries. Perhaps when criminals eat ice cream, they get a sudden rush of carbohydrate energy and break into the nearest house they can find. Or, maybe it works the other way. Criminals who have just broken into a home have more money to spend. With more money to spend, they buy more of all the things they normally buy—including ice cream. Most likely, however, neither of these scenarios is correct. Instead, it is probably the case that during the summer, ice cream sales go up, and so do home burglaries. Why? In summertime, people buy more ice cream in order to cool down. Also during the summer, people tend to go on vacation, leaving their homes empty. These homes then become attractive targets for burglars.

Thus, ice cream sales and residential burglaries move up and down together; they are **correlated** and therefore are associated with one another. But, in this case, correlation does not necessarily mean **causation**; that is, increased ice cream sales do not *cause* increased burglary; they are not *responsible for* increased burglary.

Consider another example. It is a fact that the more firefighters who respond to a fire, the worse the damage and the injuries. Again, stop and think for a moment. First, what possibly could be happening here? More firefighters get in the way of each other and cause injuries? Not likely. A more likely explanation is that this is another case of two factors that occur together—they are related but their relationship is not causal. Political scientists call this a **spurious relationship**. The more serious the fire, the more firefighters that respond. Of course, the more serious the fire, the more likely it

correlation a relationship between two or more factors such that change in one is accompanied by change in the other(s).

causation a relationship between two or more variables such that change in the value of one variable is directly responsible for change in the value of the other(s).

spurious relationship a relationship between two or more variables that reflects correlation but not causation.

is that damage and injuries will occur. The same factor that is influencing the number of firemen sent is also influencing the amount of damages and injuries that result.

The concept of a relationship that is correlated but not causal is illustrated in the simple "sideways V" diagram in Figure 1-1. It illustrates how a third factor is influencing both of the other two outcomes. In this case, the seriousness of the fire influences both the number of firefighters who are called to the fire and the amount of damage from the fire.

Now, consider an example from the world of politics. Congressional studies show that politicians tend to vote in ways consistent with the preferences of the interest groups that contribute to their campaigns. Politicians who receive funds from the National Rifle Association (NRA), for example, reliably vote against gun control legislation and in support of an expansive interpretation of the Second Amendment to the Constitution, which guarantees citizens the right to bear arms.

You could conclude from this that the NRA is buying votes—that the correlation between their campaign contributions and the votes of members of Congress is actually evidence of causation. This is precisely the sort of case, however, in which one must exercise caution. Perhaps causation is working in reverse here. Maybe the NRA supports those candidates who vote in favor of its issue positions. Rather than the NRA buying votes with its contributions, maybe members of Congress are attracting NRA contributions with their votes. Again, what at first appears to be a case of correlation *and* causation is not so straightforward. Something else may be happening. There may be another more complex, more realistic explanation.

**Figure 1-1.
Correlation does not equal causation.**

When you hear people make causal arguments, make sure there is not some other factor at work. A small fire will probably cause less damage and injuries, but not just because there are fewer fighters.

Source: David McNew/Getty (left); Tom Carter/Alamy (right)

Size of Fire

Number of Firefighters Responding

Severity of Damage

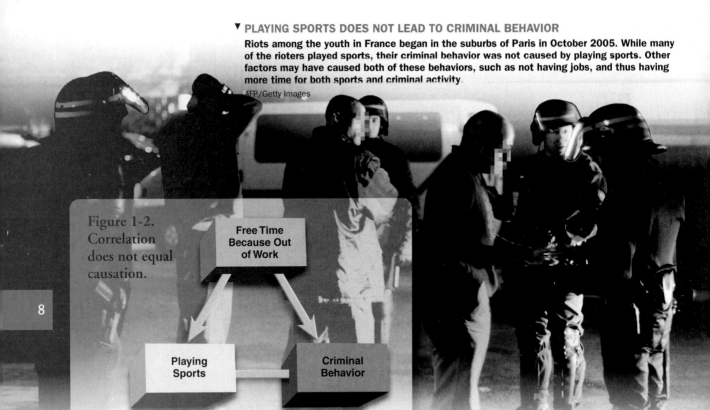

Riots among the youth in France began in the suburbs of Paris in October 2005. While many of the rioters played sports, their criminal behavior was not caused by playing sports. Other factors may have caused both of these behaviors, such as not having jobs, and thus having more time for both sports and criminal activity.

AFP/Getty Images

Figure 1-2. Correlation does not equal causation.

Free Time Because Out of Work

Playing Sports

Criminal Behavior

8

So, how do you sort through such issues? First, for a change in a particular factor or situation to cause a change in an outcome, the situation must precede the outcome. World War II could not have caused World War I. If you want to assert a causal relationship between two factors, make sure that any change in the value of the one precedes a change in the value of the other. Second, try to rule out the possibility of outside factors that may be responsible for the movement or change. For example, a researcher in France found a strong, positive correlation between young men who play sports and those who took part in riots in the suburbs of France's biggest cities. The argument was that playing sports made young men more aggressive and prone to violence. Still, this finding seems surprising since conventional wisdom and the rationale behind the funding of many sports programs is that they instill discipline and keep kids off the streets—helping to decrease crime. The positive correlation between playing sports and violent behavior could be driven by a third factor. We know that those without jobs are more likely to engage in crime. Perhaps those without jobs also have more time to play sports? (Figure 1-2)

This example reinforces a point made earlier: the world is complex, and there is rarely a single cause for any observed effect. One should always be careful, therefore, to consider *all* variables that might be driving a relationship they have observed. Throughout this text we will be examining causal relationships. Such discussions will be highlighted by a marginal causation flag like the one in the margin here.

THINKING ABOUT CAUSALITY

How do we know we got it right?

So how do political scientists arrive at answers that they can be confident are better than the simple, single-cause answers? What techniques do they use and what techniques can you use to be a more informed citizen and make better arguments? The explanations in this book are based on the findings of the most recent research in our field. But, instead of just presenting you with the results of that research and expecting you to accept it, we want to help you understand how such research is done and how you can employ good research and good thinking both in and out of the classroom. First of all, it's interesting stuff, but, more importantly, it will help you see beyond the simplistic explanations about government and politics that you see and hear in the media. Hence, each chapter contains a feature that we have called "How Do We Know?"

The "How Do We Know?" features begin with an important research question, puzzle, or serious methodological challenge relevant to the material in the chapter and to being a good citizen. For example, when we study political participation we will examine how we know how to calculate voter turnout and when we study elections we will examine the challenges involved in determining the effect of campaign money on election outcomes. We describe each question, puzzle, or challenge in some detail, and tell you why political scientists consider it important. We then explain how scholars have tried to answer the question, solve the puzzle, or meet the challenge—often using the methods and principles discussed in this chapter. Through the "How Do We Know?" features, we hope you will see how political scientists approach their work, and maybe even begin to use some of those methods as you observe the activities of American government and the coverage of those events in the media.

We also want you to see how many of the concepts we discuss in the book have tangible, real-world consequences. We study politics and tackle causal questions because we find issues revolving around elections, presidential power, congressional decisions, and public policy debates to be interesting and important. Put another way, we enjoy following current politics and political battles. Accordingly, throughout this book we will illustrate important concepts and arguments with up-to-date and—we think—exciting examples of politics and political decision making. Every chapter will begin with a short story that illustrates a key puzzle for the subject at hand. In addition, each chapter will have a Case Study section that will examine in more depth how citizens or our leaders went about making political decisions or how a particular political event played itself out.

Contexts for Studying American Government and Politics

Understanding the answers to—and how to answer—fundamental questions in American politics and government is a main goal of this book. That said, we also want to help you begin to think logically and carefully in investigating important causal questions related to American government. In addition, you will learn about American politics in light of two important contexts: the comparative context and the cultural context.

The presidential system and rights are central to American government.

Democracy, a word derived from ancient Greek, means "rule by the many" (in contrast to its opposite, **autocracy**, which means "rule by a single person," such as a king or emperor). The defining principle in a democracy is that government is based on the consent of the governed. In other words, democratic government operates at the pleasure or will of the people.

democracy a form of government in which the people rule. This can take place directly, through participation by the people in actual law-making, or indirectly, through free elections in which the people choose representatives to make laws on their behalf.

autocracy a form of government in which a single person rules with effectively unlimited power.

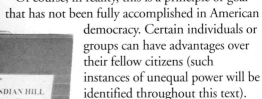

direct democracy a form of democracy in which the people themselves make the laws and set the policies adopted by the government.

representative democracy a form of democracy in which the people, through free elections, select representatives to make laws on their behalf and set policies adopted by the government.

Democracy in its purest form is known as **direct democracy**. In a direct democracy, the people vote directly on laws. Many U.S. states have a form of direct democracy, in which citizens can both initiate and vote on ballot measures to change state law. (Examples are the state initiatives to amend their constitutions to ban gay marriage, referred to above.)

The U.S. federal government, however, has no such mechanism. It is organized entirely as a **representative democracy**. In a representative democracy, people vote for their leaders through elections. But those leaders, not the people themselves, make the laws. Whether direct or representative, democracy implies more than just providing avenues for individuals to influence government. American democracy, for example, is also characterized by the following principles:

- *Political equality.* All adult Americans (with some narrow exceptions) have the right to vote, and each American's vote counts equally. Furthermore, all adult Americans have an equal right to participate in politics at every level.

- *Plurality rule and minority rights.* Plurality rule means that whoever or whatever gets the most votes wins, and in American politics the will of the plurality of people usually prevails. Whoever gets the most votes wins elective office; bills pass with a plurality vote in the legislature; Supreme Court decisions must command a plurality in order to have the force of law. In any of these settings, however, pluralities may not use their dominant status to trample the rights of those in the minority. Specific minority rights are guaranteed in state and federal law, in state and federal constitutions, in state and federal court decisions, and in the operating rules at various levels of government. Thus, even if one group could muster a winning margin for the proposition that a smaller group be denied the right to vote, state and federal constitutions would prevent this from happening.

- *Equality before the law.* With only a few exceptions, every American has the same legal rights and obligations as all other Americans. Every American is subject to the laws as every other. And every American must be treated the same by government. In other words, American government is not permitted to discriminate arbitrarily among groups or individuals. Of course, in reality, this is a principle or goal that has not been fully accomplished in American democracy. Certain individuals or groups can have advantages over their fellow citizens (such instances of unequal power will be identified throughout this text).

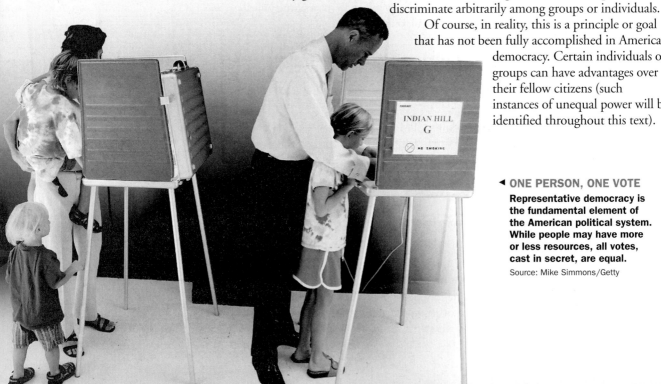

◀ **ONE PERSON, ONE VOTE**
Representative democracy is the fundamental element of the American political system. While people may have more or less resources, all votes, cast in secret, are equal.
Source: Mike Simmons/Getty

America is a **constitutional democracy**. This means that there is a document with the force of law that defines and constrains government's exercise of power. The U.S. Constitution, for example, expressly identifies the responsibilities of each branch of government, ensuring that the president, Congress, or the courts will not overreach. The Constitution also makes clear, through the Bill of Rights, that the government must do certain things and may not do certain things. For example, it must ensure that criminal defendants receive a speedy and fair trial. And it must not limit freedom of speech, religion, or assembly.

Politics in America is not the only model for politics or democracy.

America is one among a number of the world's democracies. It shares some common features with all of them, such as a commitment to majority rule through elections. It also differs in many respects as well. The U.S. Constitution, for example, is rightly seen as a limiting document, one intended by the founders as a bulwark against the possibility of governmental tyranny. Not all democracies set such limits on themselves at their founding, however. For example, when Israel became a state, major political interests there were unable to agree on a constitution. In place of a single constitutional document, therefore, Israel has a series of "basic laws" and court decisions that have accumulated over the years. These define the contours of government responsibility. Similarly, the United Kingdom has no single, limiting document like the U.S. Constitution. Instead, it has an evolving set of laws, judicial decisions, customs, and practices that are the rough equivalent of American constitutional law.

American democracy also differs from others in that it is a federal system. This means that there is a national government with responsibility for the affairs of the nation as a whole, and 50 separate state governments, each with responsibility for affairs within state borders. Thus, as we will discuss in Chapter 4, much of the federal governing apparatus—a president, a Congress, and federal courts—is duplicated at the state level, with governors, state legislatures, and state courts.

Federalism is not the only structure by which a democracy can be organized. France, Japan, and Uruguay, for example, have only one layer of decision-making authority—at the national level. In these countries, there are no equivalents to American governors or state legislatures. Canada, Germany, and India, on the other hand, are organized as federal systems—with a national government and regional governments, just as in the United States.[6]

Finally, the United States differs from most other democracies in being a presidential system rather than a parliamentary one. In a **presidential system**, the voters select separately their chief executive and their legislators. In 2004, for example, a voter living in North Carolina could have "split their ticket," casting one vote for Republican presidential candidate George W. Bush, and a separate vote for Democratic senatorial candidate Erskine Bowles.

In a **parliamentary system**, this kind of split-ticket voting in which one votes for one party for president and another for Congress would be impossible. In fact, in the United Kingdom, voters do not cast a ballot for the chief executive at all. Instead, they vote for representatives to the national legislative assembly (the

constitutional democracy a form of democracy in which there is a foundational document (such as the U.S. Constitution) that describes the structure, powers, and limits of government.

THINKING ABOUT COMPARISON

presidential system a political system in which the head of the executive branch is selected by some form of popular vote and serves a fixed term of office. The United States has a presidential system.

parliamentary system a political system in which the head of the executive branch is selected by members of the legislature rather than by popular vote.

House of Commons). The House of Commons then chooses the chief executive from among their ranks, typically referred to as the prime minister.

On occasion, this book will make these sorts of comparisons, contrasting American politics and government with the corresponding processes and institutions in other countries. These sorts of comparisons will clarify the unique features of American government. These comparative or cross-national comparisons can also shed light on underlying causal processes here in the United States. In other words, cross-national comparisons can help us make causal arguments about the roles of parties, elections, culture, and other aspects of American politics. As with discussions of causation, discussions of comparisons will be indicated by a marginal flag, as this one was.

political culture the values and beliefs of citizens toward the political system and toward themselves as actors in it.

Unique values and attitudes define politics in America.

American politics and government are continually shaped by the uniquely American **political culture**. Political culture refers to the orientation of citizens toward the political system and toward themselves as actors in it—the basic values, beliefs, attitudes, predispositions, and expectations that citizens bring to political life.

The United States has a dominant political culture, sometimes referred to as the American Creed. Chapter 2 will explain the American political culture in detail. The main ideas and values that make up the creed are individualism, democracy, equality, and liberty, as well as respect for private property and religion. Most Americans strongly embrace these concepts in the abstract, and often in specific cases as well. Often these values, however, can clash with one another. For example, doesn't equality dictate that everyone in America should have equal access to health care? Not necessarily. When Americans express their belief in the value of equality, they generally mean equality of opportunity—everyone having an equal chance to rise as high as their talents will carry them. This is not the same, however, as everyone enjoying equal outcomes. That is an idea that most Americans do *not* embrace.

American political culture gives a sense of what is politically possible in this country: what the American people demand, expect, and will tolerate from government; which public policy undertakings are likely to be viewed favorably, and which negatively; which political messages are consistent winners and losers with American voters; and which social, political, and demographic trends are likely to put pressure on government.

The American political culture is not a perfectly harmonious set of beliefs. When it comes to specific cases, some values and ideas in the culture clash, and others give way to more practical considerations. Although it establishes some clear boundaries for American political discourse and governmental action, those boundaries are fairly expansive. Chapter 2 will explain the American political culture in comparative and historical contexts, and this text throughout will periodically invoke American political culture as a useful lens through which to view U.S. politics and government.

▲ **THE ROLE OF GOVERNMENT**
Debates about the role of government in issues like health care continue to rage in American politics. While many other industrialized democracies provide health care for their citizens, health care and health insurance are generally in private hands in America. How might this result from the political culture of the United States?
Source: Douglas Menuez/Getty

Government and Why It Is Necessary

When this book refers to **government**, it means the institutions that create and enforce rules for a specific territory and people. As we noted previously, there are many governments in the United States. Although this book focuses almost exclusively on the central or national government based in Washington, D.C., a citizen of the United States is also subject to the authority of many other governments. These include state government; county government; city and town councils; local school boards; and special entities that cross the boundaries of local governments, such as water, tourism, and transportation authorities. Although each of these governments is distinctive, all are related in that, as the definition states, they consist of institutions that create and administer public policies for a particular territory and the people within it. All may have particular direct relevance to you and your family as they determine the amount of local taxes you pay, the quality of your schools, and the size of your community's police force.

government the institutions that have the authority and capacity to create and enforce public policies (rules) for a specific territory and people.

◄ **EQUAL AT THE STARTING LINE, BUT A WINNER EMERGES**
Most Americans hold that citizens should have equal opportunities, but—like runners in a race—understand that our society, economy, and politics will generate both winners and losers. Are there any areas where you think there should be an equal outcome?
Source: David Madison/Getty (left); Robert Michael/Corbis (right)

Citizens in a democracy make a fundamental bargain with their government.

Government is distinct from other institutions in society in that it has a broad right to use force. To put the matter bluntly, government can make citizens do things that they otherwise might not do (such as pay taxes, educate their children, carry car insurance, and pay for lost library books). If citizens refuse to do these things, or insist on doing things that are prohibited by law, government can take action against them—imposing financial or other penalties, including extreme penalties, such as life imprisonment or death.

No other segment of society has such wide-ranging authority or ability to enforce its rules. Even corporations and wealthy individuals, which many Americans think of as very powerful, ultimately must use the court system—i.e., the government—to get others to do what they want.

Why do people willingly grant government this monopoly on force and compulsion? Because, as people often say about getting older, it beats the alternative. The alternative to a government monopoly on force is a collection of individuals trying to impose their will on each other. Imagine, for example, that you and your neighbor enter into a dispute over where your property ends and hers begins. Without a government available to mediate the dispute, you would be left to resolve it on your own. If you could not resolve it on peaceful, mutually agreeable terms, one or both of you might seek to enforce your will through force or even violence.

Or imagine that your neighbor was hungry, while you had abundant food. If you did not wish to share, your neighbor might attempt to steal some of your food

▼ WHOSE JOB IS IT?

One of the core definitions of government is that it has the sole authority to enforce laws. On the U.S.-Mexican border, some citizens and groups like the Minutemen are taking the law into their own hands to discourage illegal immigration. What should citizens do if they feel the government is not providing essential services?

Source: Dario Lopez-Mills/AP (right); Norm Dettlaff/Las Cruces Sun-News/AP (left)

Government:
U. S. Border Patrol

Authority

Civilian:
Minutemen

Senor Fox, The King of England Didn't like the Minuteman either

◄ **A WAR OF ALL AGAINST ALL**

Thomas Hobbes, shown here with the cover of his famous treatise *Leviathan*, popularized the idea of a social contract which people enter into with one another to create and give authority to government.

Source: Time Life Pictures/Getty (both images)

in order to feed his family. Without government, the only way to stop this would be to take matters into your own hands. You would have to forcibly prevent your neighbor from stealing and probably leave him with a lump on his head as a token of your displeasure. He, of course, would try to resist all of this, perhaps resulting in a lump on your head. Now imagine these scenarios multiplied tens of thousands of times per day, as men and women pursued their own self-interest without any restrictions, regulations, or protection provided by a governing authority. This sort of arrangement would obviously be unacceptable. In the words of Thomas Hobbes, a famous political thinker writing during the English Civil War in the 1600s in his treatise *Leviathan*, it would soon lead to "a war of all against all," and a world in which life was "solitary, poor, nasty, brutish, and short."[7]

Governments arise or must arise because individuals do not wish to live in such a world. Accordingly, they enter into a **social contract** with one another to create, and give authority to, a governing body with a legal monopoly on power or force. Under this arrangement, individuals give up any claim to use force to get what they want. They give the instruments of compulsion—laws, courts, police, prosecutors, and prisons, for example—to the arms of government. In exchange for this, individuals get to enjoy life, liberty, and property without constant fear of outside interference. In the United States, the social contract is the Constitution. In Chapter 3, we will discuss in great depth the nature and logic behind this document that has defined the relationship between the people and their leaders in the United States for over two hundred years.

social contract an agreement among members of a society to form and recognize the authority of a centralized government that is empowered to make and enforce laws governing the members of that society.

▲ **WHO'S GOING TO CLEAR THE ROAD?**
Although it is certainly in every motorist's best interest to have the road cleared, there is no incentive for any car owner to clear the road on their own. This is one such public good that government can provide to all residents.
Source: Corbis

This is the essence of the idea that government is a social contract, an idea popularized by its main proponents—the political thinkers Thomas Hobbes, John Locke, and Jean-Jacques Rousseau.[8] Notice that in this idea government receives its authority from the people. It is decidedly *not* the case that government grants rights. Rather, the reverse is true—the people decide, through their contract with one another, which rights and authorities they will give over to government, and which they will retain for themselves.

Because in a democracy governmental authority rests on an agreement among the governed, that authority can be modified. In the United States, for example, the people can change government's authority by changing or amending the Constitution. Or if they wish, the people can revoke the authority of government altogether. This is one check against the possibility of government overstepping its bounds in the social-contract agreement. In **authoritarian systems**, where one person or group enjoys total power, there are no such checks.

Government provides public goods and services.

Government is not only about protecting us from each other. Government also provides its citizens with **public goods**. Public goods are products or services that are enjoyed by all citizens and unlikely to be provided by anything other than government. Non-governmental institutions generally cannot, or will not, provide public goods because

- it would be too difficult for them to marshal sufficient resources to provide the good; and
- it is difficult, if not impossible, to exclude non-payers from receiving the good.

The best example of a public good is national defense. The United States currently spends more than $400 billion per year on various elements of its national defense. This kind of investment, year in and year out, is simply beyond the reach of any private sector institution.

National defense is also difficult to exclude from those unwilling to pay for it. Imagine that U.S. national defense was provided by a private company, and that individual consumers could choose whether they wished to pay to be defended. Now imagine that only half of the homeowners in a particular neighborhood decided to pay for this service. If a missile were headed toward this neighborhood,

authoritarian (or totalitarian) system a political system in which a single individual or political party has absolute control over the apparatus of government, and in which popular input in government is minimal or non-existent.

public goods goods (and services) that are enjoyed by all citizens and unlikely to be provided by any organization other than government.

there would be no way for the defense company to protect only those homeowners who had paid its services. Instead, the company would have to defend all of the neighborhood's residents.

Such a scenario is problematic in two respects. First, the company is providing a service and not being compensated by everyone benefiting from it. Why would the company want to stay in this business? Second, homeowners who *did* pay for the service would quickly begin to feel like they were being taken advantage of. Why should they continue to pay for the service if others will receive the service for free? Obviously, either the company will get out of the business, or individuals who are currently paying for defense will stop doing so. Either way, national defense will not be provided.

Government overcomes such problems by providing the service itself and then compelling everyone to contribute by paying taxes. Any situation that has the characteristics of a public good will be a prime area for government involvement.

Although government's primary responsibilities are to keep order, protect individual rights, and provide public goods, in practice, government's activities extend well beyond these areas. One of the federal government's largest areas of responsibility, for example, is providing retirement security for workers and their families through the Social Security system. The government does this even though provision of Social Security is unrelated to ensuring public order or preserving individual rights. Furthermore, government provides Social Security even though it is not a public good—private companies *do* sell retirement securities, and it is a simple matter to provide them only to those willing to pay.

▼ **BILLIONS OF DOLLARS IN MILITARY HARDWARE**

The funding of the military is a classic example of a public good. Everyone shares in the benefits of advanced national defense. No single citizen could fund it, and those who might choose to not contribute to it cannot be excluded from its benefits.

Source: Claude Paris/AP

17

politics individual and collective efforts to influence the workings of government.

Politics is about influencing decisions.

Of course, exactly which goods and services are public and how they are provided can vary significantly by who gets to decide how and which public goods and services are provided. In the context of this book, **politics** refers to individual and collective efforts to influence the workings of government. Engaging in politics, therefore, means trying to influence

- who will lead government;
- how government will operate and make decisions;
- what the nature and substance of government decisions will be; and
- how government enforces its decisions.

To consider specific examples, politics means working to elect a particular person as mayor, or state senator, or judge, or president. Politics means collecting signatures to put on the ballot a requirement that raising taxes would need more than a majority in the state legislature. Politics means testifying at a public hearing to voice concerns about proposed federal regulations. Politics means forming a group to demonstrate outside of a prison as a way to protest the death penalty. And politics means participating in an organized effort for higher minimum wage, increased student loan programs, bringing American troops home from a war, job training, small business assistance, and agricultural subsidies.

Often, politics is referred to in a negative manner—"it was all about politics," or so and so "was just playing politics." But there is nothing inherently negative in the definition of politics. Certainly, politics can in some ways be distasteful to people. But efforts to influence the workings of government can also be noble and high-minded.

Furthermore, although one might cringe at times at the way politics is conducted—petty partisanship, shrill language, naked appeals to selfish interests, broken promises, and so on—again, it is surely better than the alternative. Without politics, many differences would be settled violently, outside of the accepted processes of government. Americans experienced that most clearly in the Civil War, when differences over slavery were settled on the battlefield and at the cost of hundreds of thousands of lives.

One of the differences Americans have with each other is over which issues are appropriate for government consideration. For example, is the content of movies, music, and video games a purely private matter, or is it a public concern? Some would say that this matter can be dealt with appropriately by individual businesses and consumers. Others say that government should have the right to require that movies, music, and video games come with a rating label.

And, finally, consider as another example the case of gay marriage. We began this chapter with a discussion of the debate over gay marriage in the 2004 elections. The debate was really about whether marriage would be a purely private concern or a public concern. Should the decision to marry and the enjoyment of certain benefits be a public matter decided by the government? Or should it be a private matter to be decided by consenting adults, their families, and their community and religious leaders.

Clearly, then, politics "starts" even before an issue makes it to the governmental agenda. As this book will frequently note, much of the substance of politics is devoted to wrangling over which issues belong on that agenda in the first place.

▲ **MAKING YOUR VOICE HEARD**

Protests are one of the many ways you have of influencing policy and politics.

Source: Spencer Platt/Getty

CHAPTER SUMMARY

▶ Political science focuses on politics and government and how government leaders and citizens behave. Political scientists typically try to determine what factor, or combination of factors, produce a particular outcome. Political scientists strive to be rigorous, thorough, and scientific researchers. To be good citizens and understand how your government and society work, students of American politics should also understand some basic rules of rigorous thinking. One important rule, often violated by politicians and pundits alike, is the fact that correlation does not equal causation. Just because two factors may move together—ice cream sales and burglaries, firefighters and fire damage—does not mean that one is causing the other.

▶ The American model of government is one sort among many. America is a democracy and like all democracies is committed to majority rule through elections. Differences in governmental structure and the core values of citizens influence the path of politics in different democracies. Understanding the major features of American politics, and the major factors that drive political decisions and outcomes, can be made easier by comparing our system to government systems in other countries. Decisions made throughout our history also influence the path of politics today. We can learn much about how American leaders and citizens behave today by looking at how previous situations were dealt with and how that affects decisions and outcomes in today's politics. American politics and government are influenced by the uniquely American, dominant political culture, some-

times referred to as the American Creed. The main ideas and values that make up the creed are individualism, democracy, equality, and liberty as well as respect for private property and religion.

▶ Government is necessary because only government has the broad right to force citizens to do things that they otherwise might not do. Citizens grant government this monopoly on force and coercion in order to gain public goods such as roads, military defense, clean water, and education and to protect themselves against fellow citizens trying to enforce their wills through coercion or violence. Individuals give up any claim to use force to get what they want, and, in return, get security for themselves, their families, and their property. Still, in a democracy, government receives its power from the people—citizens decide, through a social contract with their leaders, which rights and authorities they will relinquish to government, and which they will retain for themselves. Politics in America is a competition about which rights and authorities are best handled by government and what government will do with its authority. America is a constitutional democracy in which the U.S. Constitution identifies the responsibilities of each branch of government, executive, legislative, and judicial. The Constitution also makes clear, through the Bill of Rights, that the government may not do certain things—abridge freedom of speech, religion, or assembly, for example—and that it must do certain things, such as ensure that criminal defendants receive a speedy and fair trial.

KEY TERMS

authoritarian (or totalitarian) system, p. 16
autocracy, p. 9
causal question, p. 4
causation, p. 6
constitutional democracy, p. 11
correlation, p. 6
democracy, p. 9
direct democracy, p. 10
government, p. 13

parliamentary system, p. 11
political culture, p. 12
politics, p. 18
presidential system, p. 11
public goods, p. 16
representative democracy, p. 10
social contract, p. 15
spurious relationship, p. 6

SUGGESTED READINGS

Levitt, Steven and Stephen Dubner. *Freakonomics: A Rogue Economist Explores the Hidden Side of Everything*. An economist and a journalist team up to examine a

number of different puzzles in current American society, providing a good illustration of how one social science method can help us understand vexing social issues.

2 Political Culture

Abortion, Faith, and Campaign Politics

Campaigning for the presidency in 1960, Democratic nominee John F. Kennedy found himself addressing issues of faith and politics. Critics charged that Kennedy, a Roman Catholic, would be guided in his decision making by the pope in Rome. In a speech before Protestant ministers in September 1960, Kennedy rejected the accusation and emphasized his belief in the separation of church and state. "I do not speak for my church on public matters—and the church does not speak for me," he stated. His faith, though, did matter to him: "I do not intend to apologize for these views . . . nor do I intend to disavow either my views or my church in order to win this election." In one of the closest presidential elections in American history, Kennedy became the first Catholic president.

Forty-four years later, Catholic politicians found themselves criticized not for being too close to the church but for not adhering closely enough to church doctrine. The controversy erupted when some Catholic bishops announced that they would refuse communion to politicians who took a pro-choice position on abortion, and a Vatican cardinal supported that stance. Many of the targeted politicians stated that they opposed abortion personally but thought it was inappropriate in public policy to impose their religious views on non-Catholics. This response raised an immediate strategic concern for these

politicians, many of whom were running for election. Should they avoid taking communion to prevent any incident? Or would avoiding communion itself become a major news story?

The flip side of the controversy was whether the church should so directly insert itself into politics. Pro-choice Catholic politicians complained that the bishops were being highly selective, by threatening to withhold the sacrament of communion only from Catholic politicians who veered from church teachings on the issue of abortion but not on other issues. They further charged the bishops were being highly partisan in their stance, because Democrats were more likely than Republicans to be pro-choice. However, on issues like capital punishment, social services spending, and the Iraq war, critics argued, it would more likely be Republican politicians who were out of step with church doctrine.

In mid-June, the bishops issued a statement that allowed individual bishops to deny communion to pro-choice politicians, but did not require them to do so. They also declared that Catholic institutions should not in any way give preference or a platform to Catholics acting "in defiance of our fundamental moral principles."

The standoff raised larger questions. During the colonial period, many came to American shores seeking religious freedom, and religious

belief has always been an important part of American political culture. But where are the lines to be drawn? To what degree, if at all, should a public official attempt to square the beliefs of personal faith with public policy positions? What makes justifying a position based on one's faith any more problematic than any other justification? Should religious leaders take actions during a campaign that might have direct political consequences? In a country of diverse religious beliefs, is it appropriate or desirable for politicians to base part of their electoral appeal on their faith?

Religion is only one aspect of American political culture, a set of beliefs that guides the behavior of the public and politicians alike. Beliefs in individualism, liberty, property rights, and democracy also influence how people think about politicians and political issues. Such beliefs guide people in how they vote, how they want the government to spend their tax dollars, and who should benefit from such spending. These beliefs are also reflected in the institutional structure of American government and the framework for governance provided by the Constitution (see Chapter 3). And as they did for Catholic candidates in 2004, these beliefs often present individuals and the larger political community with difficult choices.

This chapter will focus on the nature of political culture and its role in American politics.

THIS CHAPTER WILL EXAMINE:

▶ the meaning of political culture and the presence of shared political ideals in a country of remarkable diversity

▶ the key values and beliefs of the American creed

▶ the political consequences and implications of American political culture

▶ the major challenges and alternatives to the dominant political culture

Political Culture in America

Culture refers to a way of thinking or mode of behavior. **Political culture** refers to the basic values, beliefs, attitudes, predispositions, and expectations of citizens toward the political system and toward themselves as participants in it. Take, for example, the value of freedom of speech. Survey results over a long period of time suggest that freedom of speech is a bedrock value in the United States, with 90 percent or more of the public agreeing with statements such as "I believe in free speech for all no matter what their views might be." When evaluating an issue concerning speech, most Americans start from the premise that free speech is important and should be encouraged and that they have a right to speak their minds. Clearly, then, freedom of speech is part of American political culture.

Political culture is not the same as public opinion. Public opinion focuses more on the issues of the day and is more susceptible to change, even over relatively short periods. It reveals, for example, how the public feels about a particular candidate or issue. Political culture is a broader, more permanent set of beliefs. Which candidate the public will vote for in the next presidential election is the realm of public opinion; that competitive elections are central to Americans' sense of democracy is the realm of political culture.

The American creed is the dominant political culture in the United States.

The dominant political culture in the United States consists of beliefs in individualism, democracy, liberty, property, and religion, all tied together by the value of equality. This set of beliefs has been labeled with many terms; we will call it the **American creed**.[1] It provides the frame of reference most Americans use to evaluate candidates and specific issues. For that reason, politicians make heavy use of this frame of reference to reach Americans, which then reinforces its importance. President George W. Bush provided an example in his State of the Union address in 2008, framing his remarks with a recurring theme of trusting and empowering individuals to be self-responsible.

These beliefs are ideals, and as such they are general rather than specific. To say there is a widely shared political culture is *not* to say that Americans agree on all the specifics about politics and that there is no conflict in the United States. It is also not to say that these beliefs always describe the political reality for all groups. Even a passing glance at American political history reveals that not all groups have had full property rights, or access to democratic politics, and so on. Instead, to say that there is a strong, widely held political culture is to say that most Americans start with this set of beliefs and predispositions, in a general way, when they think about issues. It is to say that most Americans share a set of general presumptions about politics and that most political debates operate within those general boundaries. The debate within those boundaries, however, can be intense. Rivals to the American creed have also had a significant place in American politics, and they will be discussed later in this chapter.

In many countries, including those with far less diverse populations than the United States, competing political cultures are at the core of politics. There might be competition between a capitalist orientation and a socialist orientation, between a secular and religious outlook, between one language and another, or even between one region of the country and others. European countries such as Spain and France regularly pit evenly matched socialist parties against capitalist

24

parties. Canada has weathered deep regional splits based in language and cultural differences between French-speaking Quebec and the remaining provinces. These different perspectives offer fundamentally different beliefs to guide citizens and politicians.

The population of the United States is among the most diverse of any country in history. Although less so around the time of the Revolution, the population of the United States became gradually more varied as waves of immigration reshaped the demographic landscape. In the 2000 U.S. Census, when Americans were asked to identify their ancestry, they named over one hundred countries and tribes. In some parts of the country, notably California, the terms "minority" and "majority" are becoming outmoded as non-Hispanic whites become a minority of the population, a development that is likely to be mirrored elsewhere.[2] This remarkable diversity makes American political culture all the more interesting. One might expect that this demographic diversity would lead to sharply competing sets of basic political values and beliefs—competing political cultures—but that has not been the case.

Considering the varied backgrounds of the American population, the agreement in the United States around a set of general political beliefs is remarkable. Other beliefs, discussed at the end of this chapter, have played an important role in American politics, but there is nonetheless a widespread adherence in spirit, if not always in day-to-day politics, to the general ideals embodied in the American creed. However, that agreement has not been without significant racial, ethnic, and religious strife. Through all the waves of immigration there have been charges that new immigrants were too "different" to fit into American life. Furthermore, second- and third-generation immigrants who have grown up in the United States have often found themselves culturally at odds with their first-generation ancestors. Efforts to "Americanize" immigrants through instruction in values, culture, language, childrearing, household management, and dress were explicit in past immigration waves and implicit in more recent attempts to make English the official language of the United States. One argument has been that without knowledge of the dominant language, immigrants cannot fully partake of political and economic liberty, democracy, or equality, which will set them apart from the American creed and corrode American social cohesion. Those who offer this argument believe that a highly diverse country requires a shared identity of some sort, and that in the United States this identity has been based on fundamental beliefs of political culture.

American creed beliefs became dominant for several possible reasons.

Why would one particular set of values and beliefs become dominant? One explanation is that Americans hear numerous messages from politicians, economic leaders, and educators that reinforce and tout the superiority of those beliefs. Other messages that reinforce political culture come from outside politics, for example, the entertainment media. Popular culture, whether fictional or based on actual events, tends to embrace the individualistic ideals and wants of Americans, celebrating the self-reliant individual who overcomes the odds. Self-help and self-improvement books are a huge market. Popular music extols the individual pursuing what he or she wants without the interference of society, family, or friends.

There have been other explanations for the dominance of the American creed. Addressing the question "why is there no socialism in the United States?" one scholar offered three reasons.[3] First, because voting rights spread early to white men, the political system in the United States was relatively more open to working-class influence than in other countries. It did not take a socialist movement or party for workers to gain these rights. Second, prosperity in the United States made it difficult for competing political cultures to take firm root; the creed seemed to work. And last, the United States did not experience the same history of class relations as did European countries, and that history, with its very strict and hierarchical relationships between classes, may have been necessary for an alternative to the creed to take root.[4] Other scholars have been less optimistic, arguing that government use of repressive tactics and judicial rulings played a stronger role in thwarting opposition to the creed than this interpretation suggests. They point to examples ranging from nineteenth-century labor activists being beaten and jailed, to investigations like those launched by Senator Joseph McCarthy in the 1950s to root out suspected communists in government, entertainment, and other industries, to dissident groups being infiltrated and monitored by government agents, as evidence that the government has often taken action to chill dissent against the American creed.[5]

In sum, it is reasonable to describe American political culture as one based in the American creed, but as this chapter will show, consensus does not eliminate conflict. First, there is substantial conflict in American politics within the confines of the creed. The weight to place on each belief and the meaning of the beliefs themselves are often up for debate. And second, other competing beliefs have had important impacts on American political life. These alternative approaches have mixed and mingled with the beliefs of the creed in American politics, proving that American political culture is not fixed and unchanging.

The Beliefs of the American Creed

The central value of the American creed is **equality**. A sense of equality underlies each of the specific beliefs of the creed—individualism, democracy, liberty, property, and religion.[6] Americans value people being treated the same under law, being able to influence government, and having equal opportunity to succeed in life. This does not mean that everyone will or should have equal results, but that all people should "play by the same rules." The perception that some individuals have advantages not based on merit severely violates this norm of equality. Clearly, the American experience has fallen short of these ideals many times in many places, and these shortfalls will be discussed in this and other chapters. For now, however, as you read the descriptions below, remember that the emphasis in this part of the chapter is on the general ideals to which Americans say they aspire and how they affect the ways Americans think about politics and government.

Individualism: People should choose their own path through life.

For Americans, individuals—not groups or classes—are the fundamental political unit. Americans believe in **individualism**, meaning that all individuals should be able to succeed to the maximum extent possible given their talents and abilities. Individuals should be treated equally, regardless of group membership or other characteristics. Many years ago, the U.S. Army ran a series of television commercials on the theme of "be all you can be." This is precisely what Americans think of when they think about individualism—which is, of course, why savvy marketers would tap into this message. The leading example of what Americans mean by freedom is the ability of individuals to choose their own path in life (see Table 2-1). The notion that the individual is entitled to a sphere of unfettered freedom is much less established in other countries than in the United States.[7]

Equal opportunity versus equal outcomes Americans generally prefer that individuals have an equal chance for success rather than a guarantee that all Americans will have equal results. A recent survey found that more than 90 percent of adult Americans agreed that "our society should do what is necessary to make sure that everyone has an equal opportunity to succeed." Only about 30 percent, however, agreed that "we should make every possible effort to improve the position of blacks and other minorities, even if it means giving them preferential treatment." To most Americans, treating a group "preferentially," even to rectify past injustices, is inconsistent with equal opportunity. And most Americans—by a margin of 3 to 1—placed the responsibility for failure to succeed on the individual rather than on society. This disparity holds by nearly the same margin even when considering only the opinions of former or current welfare recipients.[8] When asked to choose which is a more important role for government, many more Americans select creating "as much opportunity as possible" rather than creating "a greater equality of income."[9] These views do not mean that Americans oppose helping those in need, or that they do not believe in private charity for the poor, but they show that Americans place a strong emphasis on individual responsibility.

Different perspectives on individualism across countries In preferring equality of opportunity over equality of outcome, the United States is unique. A 1999 survey of several countries found that about 80 percent of the respondents in Italy, Austria, and Hungary believed that reducing income inequality was a major task of government, while in the Netherlands and Great Britain support was around 60–70 percent. About 45 percent of the citizens in Australia and Switzerland agreed. In the United States, barely 30 percent thought that reducing income inequality was an important task for government. Examining surveys across a broader time period produces the same result: Americans are just as likely to think that income inequality is a problem, but they are less likely than citizens of other

Table 2-1. What Freedom Means to Americans (in percentages)

CHARACTERISTICS OF FREEDOM	ONE OF THE MOST IMPORTANT THINGS ABOUT FREEDOM	EXTREMELY IMPORTANT	VERY IMPORTANT	MODERATELY, SOMEWHAT, OR NOT TOO IMPORTANT
Having the power to choose and do what I want in life	44.7	27.1	21.9	6.3
Being able to express unpopular ideas without fearing for my safety	39.9	29.0	23.6	7.4
Having a government that doesn't spy on me or interfere in my life	29.8	25.7	32.3	12.2

Source: General Social Survey 2000

Note: Percentages add across each row. Survey respondents were asked for each characteristic of freedom whether it was one of the most important things about freedom, extremely important, very important, or moderately, somewhat, or not too important an aspect of freedom.

Table 2-2. Public Perceptions of the Causes of Income Inequality

Survey Question: Next, we'd like to know why you think it is, that in America today, some people have better jobs and higher incomes than others do. I'm going to read you some possible explanations, and I want you to tell me how important you think each is. Because . . .	Very important	Somewhat important	Not important
Some people don't get a chance to get a good education	54.6%	34.9%	9.3%
Some people just don't work as hard	44.6	41.8	12.7
Some people have more in-born ability to learn	33.0	43.0	23.4
Discrimination holds some people back	25.7	50.3	23.0
Government policies have helped high-income workers more	24.8	38.6	34.5
Some people just choose low-paying jobs	18.9	38.4	40.6
God made people different from one another	22.2	26.1	49.1

Source: Questions and wording from the National Election Study, 2002; data presented in Larry Bartels, "Homer Gets a Tax Cut: Inequality and Public Policy in the American Mind," paper presented at the annual meeting of the American Political Science Association, Philadelphia, August 2003.

Note: Percentages add across rows.

countries to believe that government has an obligation to reduce income differences.[10] And Americans are more likely to see economic inequality as something created by personal opportunities rather than by fate or the actions of others (see Table 2-2).

Democracy: Government actions should reflect the will of the people.

The second belief of the American creed is that government should adhere to democratic principles. Democracy, as described in Chapter 1, is a form of government in which the people rule. This rule can take place directly, through participation by the people in actual law making, or indirectly, through free elections in which the people choose representatives to make laws. Between elections, people have indirect input in democracy through a variety of means—hearings, writing to public officials, signing petitions, and lobbying, for example. Because voting and these other activities are not participated in equally by all segments of American society, many political observers are highly critical of the performance of American democracy compared to the ideal. To Americans, the ideal suggests four criteria in particular.

The will of the people First, government actions should reflect the will of the people. The people's wishes are not always easy to identify, but the general principle is that government should be guided by them as much as possible.[11] Periodic elections allow the people to remove officials that have not lived up to this standard.

The consent of the governed Second, and closely related, power granted to public officials is done so by the consent of the governed. In this view, power that is exercised by a public official is always an extension of the public will and can potentially be reclaimed by the people. At its most extreme, the notion of consent means that citizens have a right to abolish the government altogether if they conclude that it is using power inappropriately.[12]

Equal opportunity to influence government Third, to Americans, democracy also means an equal opportunity to influence government. This includes not only the opportunity to vote, but also access to government by citizens from all walks of life. Americans are uneasy with the idea—while recognizing it is the reality—that some individuals or groups may appear to have "inside connections" with government officials, so that their views are more influential than that of the "average" person. In the 1990s, between 75 and 80 percent of Americans agreed, "there is too much power concentrated in the hands of a few big companies."[13] Saying a group has "too much" power reflects a worry that the equal opportunity to influence government has been undermined.

Equal treatment by the law Fourth, to Americans democracy means equal treatment by the law. Laws, regulations, and penalties should be enforced regardless of the social stature of the individual. This does not mean that judges, juries, or public officials should ignore circumstances when determining penalties or benefits. Rather, it means that the same actions taken under the same set of circumstances should result in equal penalties or benefits, regardless of the social status, religion, ethnicity, race, income, or other characteristics of the individuals involved. Of course, Americans recognize and lament that these ideals are violated in everyday life. For example, wealthier individuals can hire more talented lawyers and thus increase the odds of a case working out to their advantage. The fact that Americans are troubled by such inequities is a sign of the potency of the idea of equal treatment.

Liberty: Government restraint on individual behavior should be minimal.

The third belief in the American creed is liberty, which was the dominant demand of the American Revolution. Americans often define **liberty** as freedom from government restraint over the exercise of one's rights; that is, whenever possible, government should leave people to do as they please.

Natural rights Associated with this belief is the conviction that government does not grant rights. Rather, rights are inherent, part of what makes people human: these are **natural rights**. Americans consider the rights to free speech, to associate in groups, and to hold and practice religious faith to be effectively sewn into human beings upon birth, not rights that government *gives* us. The Declaration of Independence provides a clear statement of this idea: "we hold these truths to be self-evident, that all men are created equal, that they are endowed by their Creator with certain unalienable rights, that among these are life, liberty, and the pursuit of happiness." You can choose not to exercise your rights, but that does not mean that the right itself is any less real.

Government's role in securing liberty To Americans, government secures liberty either by not restricting rights or by restricting them only when their expression imposes excessively on the rights of other individuals. Freedom of speech and assembly are considered fundamental rights, but even these are commonly restricted by government. Slanderous and libelous speech can lead to punishment. Marching and demonstrating without a permit can result in fines or other sanctions. And when they believe national security is threatened, Americans often tolerate what would be considered unacceptable infringements on liberty at other times. All these limitations can be a matter of great political controversy.

Individuals in other countries view liberty in somewhat different ways. In Scandinavian countries, for example, liberty requires being given something by government in order to thrive fully as a human being. This may mean health care, or education, or housing, or any number of other services. In this view, the freedom to speak, to earn a living, and the like are weak unless citizens are given the tools to use these freedoms effectively. For example, without a health care system to provide for all citizens, the promise of "life" or the "pursuit of happiness" is empty. Or, without high quality education for all, "free speech" quickly becomes the province of a relatively small elite. Without both of these, one's opportunities to pursue success, whether in one's career or elsewhere, are sharply limited.

In the United States, the perspective is different. Many or even most Americans may agree that universal health care and quality education are important goals for government. However, relatively few would say that liberty is absent if these government services are not provided.

Property: Individuals should be free to acquire, own, and use goods and assets.

Americans believe in extensive **property rights**—the idea that people should be able to acquire, own, and use goods and assets free from government constraints, as long as their acquisition and use does not interfere with the rights of other individuals. Property rights are therefore twofold: freedom to acquire property and freedom to use property.

Freedom to acquire property. First, people should have the right to acquire private property without limitations. This means that individuals should be paid whatever they can command in the economic marketplace for their goods or their work. You may feel uneasy that a professional athlete or movie star makes $10 million or $20 million a year, but few Americans believe that this should be prohibited. With their talents or resources, individuals should be able to obtain property—goods, services, real estate, stocks—with minimal meddling by society or government.

Freedom to use property. Second, individuals should be free to use property with few restrictions. Some acceptable restrictions protect the property of others or protect some societal interest. You cannot drive your car through a neighbor's front door or use your property in a manner designed to deceive other people out of their property. Nor can you build your house on sensitive wetlands.

Ironically, political scientists have noted that property rights in the form of activities such as shopping might lead some individuals to be skeptical about government, as they might see the free market as ultimately more democratic and equal than the political system. Not everyone can afford every product, but there is a sense that the only thing standing between you and that purchase is the price tag. You are like everyone else: if you can gain sufficient resources through hard work or luck, you have the same opportunity to obtain that item as anyone else. By contrast, the political system might not seem nearly so open and accessible. For many Americans, freedom to purchase is akin to freedom of speech and equally valuable.[14]

Religion: Individuals should be free to practice their religious faith.

Finally, Americans believe in **religious freedom**, the idea that individuals should be free to choose and practice their religious faith and that government should not establish any particular religion as the official or preferred religion.[15]

Freedom of religious expression Americans view the freedom to practice one's religion as akin to the right to free speech. Early in the nation's history, so-called "dissenting Protestants" emigrated to the colonies in part as a way to practice their faith. They fled societies, England in particular, where official government religions made it difficult for individuals with other religious beliefs to practice their faith. The idea that government should remain neutral among religions was therefore closely linked to the idea of freedom of religious practice. In this perspective, freedom of religious expression was likely only if government did not take sides. Such freedom was more easily stated than accomplished, however, and religious intolerance in the colonies was common. Favoring a particular religion—and effectively discriminating against others—was also a practice of many local and state governments into the twentieth century. Anti-Catholicism, in particular, was a strong force in many areas. The twin beliefs in freedom of expression and non-interference by government, although not common at the time of the American Revolution, were enshrined in the Constitution and have grown gradually over time.

Importance of religion in American political life Religious belief has been central to American political discourse. Major causes such as the anti-slavery, civil rights, and anti-abortion movements relied on religious language and principles. Presidents of both parties, including Presidents Clinton and Bush, have historically sprinkled religious language in their speeches and ended major addresses with the exhortation "God Bless America." Faced with the issue of whether to allow stem-cell research on frozen embryos—a process that destroys the embryos—Bush leaned heavily on his faith in disallowing the development of any new stem-cell lines and later vetoed an attempt to change his policy.[16]

Recent survey results provide a sense of just how important religion is to Americans today. Close to 90 percent of Americans said they completely or mostly agree that they never doubt the existence of God, that prayer is an important part of their daily life, that divine miracles still happen, and that everyone will have to answer to God for their sins.[17] Over two-thirds of Americans said it was important for a president to have strong religious beliefs, and only one-quarter thought politicians expressed their religious faith too much.[18]

This degree of religiosity is unusually high (see Figure 2-1). The general pattern around the globe is that countries that are wealthier, more developed, and industrialized tend to place less emphasis on religious belief. Perhaps scientific and rationalistic reasoning have moved people away from faith-based beliefs or the vast entertainment and leisure options of the modern world draw attention away from spiritual matters. The United States, however, bucks the trend. The exceptionally diverse scope of religious denominational choices in the United States may be one reason—this competitive marketplace draws attention to religion, while also providing many niches that can satisfy Americans' differing spiritual needs.

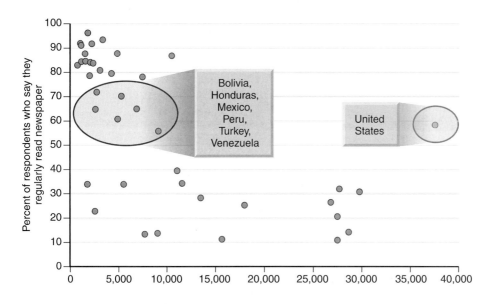

Figure 2-1. **Relationship Between Religion's Importance in People's Lives and Economic Development.** High percentages of Americans state that religion is a very important part of their daily lives. Countries with similar levels of belief tend to be much poorer than the United States.

Note: Survey question asked in 44 countries, 2002. "How important is religion in your life—very important, somewhat important, not too important, or not at all important?"

Sources: Survey data: Pew Center for the People and the Press, http://people-press.org/reports/display.php3?ReportID=167. Income data (Gross national income per capita, 2003): World Bank, http://siteresources.worldbank.org/DATASTATISTICS/Resources/GNIPC.pdf.

The American creed provides a starting point for most Americans to evaluate issues, candidates, and government actions.

The five beliefs of the American creed have endured despite the fact that they are ideals that have not always been honored in practice. For much of the nation's history, not all groups have shared equally in the promises and benefits of creedal beliefs or the overarching value of equality. During the Revolutionary era, only about 15 to 30 percent of the adult population could take full advantage of the promises of life, liberty, and the pursuit of happiness. Laws and customs made sure that women, blacks, white indentured servants, and non-propertied adult white males could not.

Widespread belief in the creed Despite this widespread exclusion, the remarkable fact is that these groups still believed in the promise of the American creed. They did not argue that this set of beliefs should be discarded. Instead, women, white men without property, blacks, and other racial and ethnic minorities demanded to be let in to the club. These groups engaged in massive social movements for individual rights, liberty, property, and participation in the democratic process, a testament to just how powerful these beliefs were to those on the outside looking in. By championing the equality promised by the American creed, these movements had a strong impact on public opinion about the

Figure 2-2. Support for Women's Equal Role, 1972-2000. In 1972, nearly half the population held neutral views or believed women's place was in the home, but by 2000 only about one-fifth of the population held those views.

Note: Answers to the question: "Some people feel that women should have an equal role with men in running business, industry and government. Others feel that women's place is in the home. Where would you place yourself on this [7-point] scale or haven't you thought much about this?" "Equal role" indicates respondent chose point 1, 2, or 3 on the 7-point scale; "Neutral" is point 4; "In the home" is point 5, 6, or 7. Remaining percentage had no opinion.

Source: National Election Study. Question not asked in 1986.

inequality of opportunity, as Figure 2-2 shows in the case of equal roles for women. Equality as defined by the women's rights movement has gained support from the American public.

Abstract belief versus practical reality Political culture does not necessarily explain how Americans will respond to every situation. For instance, earlier we noted that consistently over 90 percent of Americans say they believe in free speech for all, regardless of their views. But when pushed, Americans will sometimes back

Table 2-3. Support for Free Speech in Specific Difficult Circumstances (percentages)

YEAR OF SURVEY			
Allow book in library that . . .	**1974**	**1984**	**1994**	**2004**
States blacks are genetically inferior	62.1	65.1	67.9	67.2
Is against churches and religion	61.4	65.3	71.3	74.8
Allow someone to teach in college who . . .				
Believes blacks are genetically inferior	42.0	42.2	44.1	52.9
Is against churches and religion	43.3	47.4	54.3	61.4
Allow someone to make a speech in your community who . . .				
Believes blacks are genetically inferior	62.0	58.7	62.6	64.2
Is against churches and religion	62.6	68.6	73.6	77.5

Source: General Social Survey.

Note: First year for questions about race issues is 1976.

away from this commitment. In one survey taken about a decade after World War II, for example, less than 15 percent of Americans were willing to allow fascists and communists to hold meetings and express their political views. Table 2-3 gives other examples of Americans' support for free speech in specific circumstances. The table presents hard cases: racist and anti-religious speech that most Americans would find offensive and hateful. Even though support for free speech has been increasing in recent decades, many Americans find their principles wavering in certain scenarios.

Framework for political evaluation Clearly there are significant inconsistencies when moving from abstract beliefs to concrete decisions and issues. But abstract principles still matter. Most of you would agree with the old saying that "honesty is the best policy." You likely also believe that people should obey the law, that laws should be enforced, and that enforcement of the law should be done fairly. Yet few people think being brutally honest is right if it would needlessly hurt someone. And most of you who drive have probably found yourself, on occasion, driving over the posted speed limit when there were no police watching (we plead guilty).

Does that inconsistency mean that your general belief that honesty is the best policy is a farce? No. You start there when you evaluate what to do. The belief provides a framework for decision making. The sign that beliefs and values matter is that, even when we violate them, we feel compelled to understand and justify why we do so.

Political culture works the same way. It provides a general framework and a starting point to evaluate issues, candidates, and the actions of public officials. It can also be exploited by politicians or political activists looking to score a victory. They know that these themes and beliefs resonate with the public and so will adjust their language accordingly.

Consequences and Implications of the American Creed

Political scientists ask the "so what" question: Why does all this matter anyway? The American creed matters because its consequences and implications are far-reaching. A brief survey of some of these consequences and implications will demonstrate the important influence of political culture on American life.

Americans prefer government to be limited in the scope of its activities.

One consequence of the American creed is a preference for **limited government** rather than a large, active government. This means a government is seen as a last resort to solving problems. Americans tend to rely first on other arenas—families, churches, the marketplace, nonprofit institutions, self-improvement—and turn to government only when these alternatives fail or are overwhelmed by the scope of a problem. Individuals who favor government activism typically must demonstrate that these other arenas are insufficient to the task, leaving government as the only viable alternative. People do not need to be convinced that it is appropriate for real estate developers to build houses, but they may need to be convinced that it is appropriate for government to build housing, to subsidize mortgages for home-buyers, or to pay part of the costs for certain people to rent housing.

"Government as last resort" does not mean that Americans do not look to government to solve many problems and provide many services. Clearly they do, and the policy areas in which Americans expect government to act have grown significantly during recent history. Retirement pensions; health insurance for seniors; grants and loans for college students; and money to assist those who lose their jobs are just a few things Americans today routinely expect government to provide. A look at Figure 2-3 shows that the American public was reluctant to cut federal government spending even during an era when reducing the federal budget deficit was considered a high priority by the public. Nothing close to a majority favored cuts in any of the policy areas listed, despite frequent skepticism about government efficiency and effectiveness.[19]

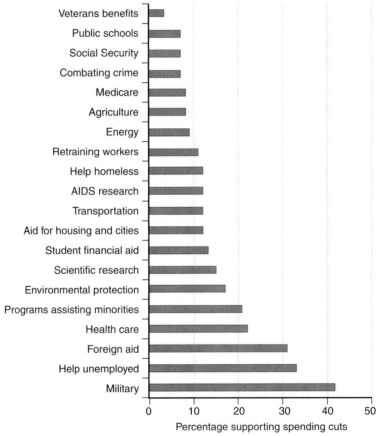

Figure 2-3. Highest Level of Public Support for Cutting Federal Government Spending, 1987-2002 (percent). Americans generally support the idea of a small, efficient government. But when asked about spending, they find it difficult to identify areas they would like to see cut. At no time across the fifteen-year period does a majority express support for cutting any of these programs.

Note: Not every policy area was asked about in each survey. Surverys were typically about three to four years apart.

Source: Data from Pew Center on the People and the Press, various surveys 1987-2002. Not every policy area was asked about in each survey. Surveys were typically about three to four years apart.

The dedication to limited government is stronger in the United States than in other industrialized democracies. In general, governments in these countries are larger and have more control over society and the economy than is true in the United States. When comparing the size of government to the size of the economy, the United States regularly falls at the low end of the list. The unique history of the United States compared to other industrialized democracies accounts for some of these differences. Although groups in all countries seek to use government to promote their causes, groups in the United States who have had an expansive vision of government power, such as some labor unions and political parties in the nineteenth century, have not had the same control over government here that they have had elsewhere.

There is a weak sense of sovereign power in the United States.

A second consequence of the American creed, related closely to the idea of limited government, is that there is a weak sense of sovereign power in the United States. **Sovereign power** suggests a final authority, a final decision maker. In the United States, it is difficult to think of any truly "final" authority. American government is structured so that one part of government can challenge and check other parts of government. For example, Congress can pass legislation, but the president can veto it. With enough votes, Congress can then override that veto. The Supreme Court can declare unconstitutional the actions of both Congress and the president. Congress and the states can pass constitutional amendments that will guide future Court decisions or the president can nominate and the Senate can approve new Supreme Court justices who might render different decisions. There is no ultimate seat of power in the system at the national level—there is always some other way to try to dislodge a prior decision.

And there are some policy areas in which the federal and state governments battle for primacy. The issue of same-sex marriage is being fought and defined at many different levels and in many different institutions of government, including state courts and legislatures, voter referenda on state constitutional amendments, national legislation such as the Defense of Marriage Act, and a proposed national constitutional amendment, which would have to go to the states for approval. If an amendment was added to the U.S. Constitution, then the Supreme Court would likely address cases over how precisely to interpret that amendment, and those interpretations could shift as new justices are nominated and confirmed by future presidents and senators.

American political culture fits well with, and has shaped, this sense of weak sovereign power. The major branches of government are in a competitive arrangement that limits their pretensions to be the final decision maker, and neither the national nor state governments are the sole location for sovereign power.

But what about the claim that the American people are sovereign? In the abstract, this is true. Their opinion influences policy makers. And the people reserve the ultimate right to push for a rewriting of the Constitution or to enter into a revolution. But on a practical, day-to-day level it is a limited sovereignty. This is not an accident but an intended result of the Constitution. American government is designed to hear the voice of the people, but not to translate that voice into immediate action. When the American people are dissatisfied, the strongest practical recourse they have is to replace members of government. But there is never a time when Americans can vote out all members of government in a single election. And members of the federal judiciary and bureaucracy, who are unelected, are never up for direct public removal. Thus, sovereign power of the people is limited, providing only indirect control over some parts of government and involving a lengthy process.

Competing ideas are viewed with suspicion.

A third consequence of the American creed is that competing ideas are often viewed with suspicion. In general, the American people and their leaders tend to assume the superiority of the creed's values. For a long time in the United States, one way to discredit an idea—without necessarily analyzing it in any detail—was to suggest that the idea was "socialistic." The medical industry used the term "socialized medicine" to great effect in its campaigns to prevent the adoption of national health insurance in the United States. Only rarely do U.S. policy makers, at least publicly, seriously talk about the policies and programs of other countries as examples to be followed, the assumption being that the underlying values and beliefs guiding these programs would not be relevant in the American context.

"Un-American" beliefs Competing ideas not only challenge the American creed, but also are sometimes deemed "un-American." Throughout U.S. history, ideas that have challenged the creed were often seen as infections on the body politic caused by outsiders. In few countries is a set of political beliefs so inter-twined with national identity that to oppose or challenge the beliefs can sometimes be perceived as a challenge to the nation itself.

In the 1950s, the House Un-American Activities Committee investigated a large number of individuals suspected of holding or being sympathetic to "un-American" ideas, chiefly socialism and communism. At other points in American history, efforts to remove immigrants and to restrict the future flow of immigration were based on the idea that these individuals brought disruptive beliefs and values to the United States. At one time or another in American history, Catholics, Irish, Chinese, Japanese, Eastern and Southern Europeans, Jews, and others were seen as dangerous because of the cultural practices and the disruptive ideas they might import into the United States.

Appeals to social class Also often considered a danger to national harmony are attempts to appeal to Americans as members of social classes. With the exception of references to "the middle class"—which is widely used and tends to be defined in very broad terms—directly appealing to class interest is often denounced. When presidential candidates in 2008 charged that President George W. Bush's tax cuts were a "giveaway to the rich," the president and his supporters charged these critics with advocating "class warfare," a term that conjures up images of socialism and communism. These fears of disharmony are often sincerely held. But the charge that the rich are warring on the poor or the poor are warring on the rich can also be a strategy for halting serious discussion about a particular policy.

Other countries have been more comfortable talking about class and challeng-ing individualistic political culture. Socialism, which views society through the lens of social class and envisions an expansive role for government, has had a much more sympathetic reception elsewhere, particularly in the form of strong labor unions and a Labour Party (Australia, Ireland, New Zealand, United Kingdom), Social Democratic Party or New Democrat Party (Canada, Germany, Sweden), or Socialist Party (France). Although in the early twentieth century, socialist parties had some success in industrial cities in the United States, they have made little impact on the national scene.

Appeals to the public interest are difficult in an individualistic political culture.

A fourth consequence of the American creed is that it can be difficult for politicians and the public to act in the public interest or even to define it. Because American political culture has such a strong emphasis on individual freedom, opportunity, and rights, how do you convince people to focus on the public interest instead of self-interest? When advocating policies, politicians and political activists continually wrestle with the tension between appealing to the interests of the community and the interests of the individual. In his famous *Democracy in America* (1835), Alexis de Tocqueville suggested that Americans engaged in "self interest rightly understood." In Tocqueville's view, one way Americans reconciled the conflict between self-interest and public interest was by recognizing how engaging in benevolent acts toward others and being concerned about the public interest could also serve their self-interest. If you vote in favor of a school referendum that will "help the children" and the community, your property value will likely increase because communities with good schools are attractive to home-buyers. If you help others and provide them with valuable assistance, you will also feel good about yourself and believe you are being consistent with your religious or moral beliefs. Volunteer for community service and do good things, and you will have another impressive line on your résumé.

Political conflict emerges from tension among the creed's beliefs and from debate over the meaning of the beliefs.

A very important and ironic final consequence of the widely-shared American creed is that it also produces much of the political conflict in the United States. The creed creates political tension because, first, its beliefs are often in conflict, and second, the meaning of the individual beliefs is open to debate.[20] Both of these sources of tension have led to significant amounts of political debate and struggle in the United States. Much of the conflict between the two major political parties, for example, may be attributed to the differential emphasis they place on American creed beliefs when these beliefs—for example, property versus democracy—are in conflict, or the different meaning they may attach to a belief such as liberty.

Tension among the creed's beliefs Consider a poor high-school student. She is an excellent student, qualified for admission at a prestigious university. Her ability to maximize her potential depends on her going to college, the most prestigious one for which she is qualified. Being poor, however, she cannot afford such a university. Her situation poses a conflict between two beliefs. According to the belief in individualism, this girl should be able to achieve all she can achieve without any artificial barriers, certainly not the barrier of her parents' income. On the other hand, according to the belief in property, your property is your property; when you work hard to earn income, that money is yours. If you want to donate voluntarily to a scholarship fund, you can do that, but you should not be forced by government to give your money to someone else.

As a society, Americans have resolved this particular conflict between American creed beliefs by deemphasizing property rights to elevate individual opportunity. That is, we have created federal financial aid programs that take tax dollars and redistribute them to individuals like this student. The government takes property from one group and gives it to another. This example reinforces the point made earlier that beliefs can prevail at the abstract level but weaken in specific circumstances. Americans do believe that, on the whole, people should be able to do with their property as they wish, but when this belief collides with the belief in individual opportunity, Americans, through government, have to decide how heavily to weigh each belief to reach a decision in a specific case.

Cultural differences across regions When the beliefs of the American creed are in conflict, there is no balance that is inherently right or wrong. Instead, there is a balance that can gain the strongest political support nationally at a particular moment in time. At the same time, in different parts of the country that balance might differ, leading to either more or less restrictive laws than are present at the national level. Most states, for example, have their own student financial aid programs, ranging from modest to generous.

This regional variety has led some political scientists to suggest that the balance among creedal beliefs varies systematically from region to region, state to state, and even within states. One famous classification speaks of moralistic, traditionalistic, and individualistic subcultures that dominate or mix in different parts of the United States.[21] The traditionalistic subculture has been most present in the southern states, the individualistic through the middle tier of states and in California, and the moralistic in the northern states and the Pacific Northwest. The moralistic culture views government as a positive force and tends to place heavy emphasis on the needs of the community and government's ability to satisfy those needs. A more active government is welcomed and popular participation is encouraged. A traditionalist culture favors limited government that works to sustain the social hierarchy and values already dominant in society and the economy. Popular participation is not strongly encouraged and historically was actively discouraged for some groups. Individualistic culture sees politics neither as a means to transform society (like moralism) nor to preserve society (like traditionalism), but a mechanism through which private interests are advanced and in which government is expected to encourage, enable, and support private initiative. Political scientists have used these regional cultural differences as one factor among many to try to explain differences in voting turnout, election outcomes, and social policy across states.

CaseStudy: Defining Democracy When Drawing District Lines

Political tension results not only from the conflict between beliefs, but also from different interpretations of beliefs in the American creed.[22] For example, consider the process of redistricting, the drawing of boundaries around legislative districts. Each district elects one legislator.[23] Prior to 1964, congressional and state legislative district boundaries often followed county lines. They were redrawn for U. S. House districts only when the U.S. Census, taken every ten years, indicated that a change in a state's share of the national population meant it should have more or fewer House members than it currently had. If the census showed no need to change the state's number of seats in Congress, the state could go a very long time without changing the congres-

sional district boundaries. For state legislatures, whose size would not change because of the census—a state can have as many members in its own legislature as it wishes—there was even less reason to redraw the lines. Under this system, districts could vary enormously in population from one House district to another or one state legislative district to another, yet each would have the same number of legislators: one.

What does a seemingly technical matter like redistricting have to do with the American creed or beliefs in democracy? A lot, as it turns out. In 1964 the Supreme Court, in two famous decisions, concluded that democracy hinges on the principle of "one person, one vote," the idea that every citizen has one vote, each voter is equally powerful in selecting legislators, and each voter is equally represented in the legislature. If one district had 1,000 potential voters and another had 600,000, the power of each voter in selecting a representative in the first district would be 600 times greater than in the second. The 1,000 voters of the first district would have one vote in the legislature, as would the 600,000 voters in the second district. Such unequally sized districts, which were common around the country, violated constitutional norms of equality that were fundamental to the American democratic process.

The Court's one person, one vote principle provides no explicit guidance about how to draw the lines that separate districts. Every ten years, states need to redraw their district lines to be sure that population is approximately equal in the House districts (if the state has more than one representative in the U.S. House) and in state legislative districts. Which way of drawing the lines would most enhance democracy? Is democracy better served if lines are drawn in a way that some districts are likely to be heavily Republican and others heavily Democratic? The individuals elected to the legislature in these districts are apt to represent their citizens very well because they tend to share common viewpoints. However, competitive elections will be rare in these districts—the weaker party is unlikely to have any chance to win, so voters might not have much real choice, which some consider an important aspect of

democracy. If the lines are drawn with an intent to spread Democratic and Republican voters about equally across the two districts, elections may be more competitive—considered by many people to be a fundamental sign of a healthy democracy—but large numbers of people in the districts may feel they share few beliefs and values with the elected officials who represent them in the legislature. They might feel unrepresented, and that hardly seems democratic.

Every decade, after the census is finished, there are bitter battles to draw up district lines. In most states, the job falls to the legislature. And, most often, the pattern is predictable. First, lines are drawn in a way to protect incumbents of both major parties. Then, the majority party seeks to draw lines around remaining districts in such a way as to maximize the number of seats the party will win. This process, known as gerrymandering, often produces districts with contorted, convoluted boundaries. And last, the minority party might file suit against the new district lines, usually to no avail. In a split decision in 2004, the U.S. Supreme Court declined to intervene in a case involving partisan bias in congressional redistricting in Pennsylvania (Figure 2-4 shows one of the disputed districts). The Court concluded it had no clear standard to apply to determine how much partisan bias is "too much" and is contrary to democratic principles and equality. But it did not rule out the possibility that it might determine such a standard in the future.[24]

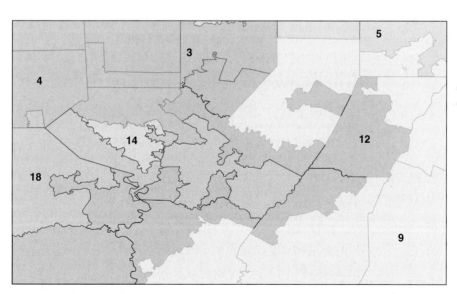

Figure 2-4. Contested Congressional District 12 in Pennsylvania Partisan Redistricting Case, 2004.
The boundaries of Pennsylvania's 12th congressional district, located in the state's southwest corner, were carefully crafted to advantage the candidates of one political party. In an effort to build a safe Democratic seat, the district's boundary twists and turns, picking up disparate pockets of neighborhoods along the way and almost completely surrounding portions of the adjacent district 18. The Supreme Court concluded that it did not have any clear standard to determine whether partisan bias in drawing the boundary of this district violated norms of democracy and equality.
Source: http://www.jenner.com/practice/practice_news.asp?ID=19&AssetID=000000029001&ParentID=&ParentName=

The most widely publicized dispute in recent years over district lines occurred in Texas. Following the 2000 census, the Texas legislature, with one house controlled by each party, was unable to agree on a new districting plan and, under state law, the districting process went before a panel of federal judges. The judges drew new lines that kept in place a Democratic majority in the Texas delegation to the U.S. House. In the 2002 Texas state legislative elections, however, Republicans gained control of the legislature and in 2003 passed a new district map to replace the judge-drawn lines. These new lines were drawn to be much more favorable to Republican candidates, and—predictably—in the 2004 U.S. House election the Republicans won 21 seats, compared to 15 in 2002.

Challenges to the new Texas district lines landed in the U.S. Supreme Court in 2006, arguing two points.[25] First, Democrats charged that there was no lawful reason to change the lines that had just been established in 2001. The mid-decade redrawing, the suit argued, was done solely for partisan advantage. Rather than treating individuals equally under the law, the suit alleged that the redistricting targeted and discriminated against Democratic voters for their political viewpoints. Second, minority groups claimed that the Texas legislature illegally sought to distribute Latino and black voters across districts in order to decrease the likelihood of electing Democrats to the House. Since the late 1980s, the Supreme Court has frowned on using race as a primary factor in drawing district lines, including deliberate attempts to weaken the vot-ing clout of minority groups. In 2006, the Court concluded that the critics of the plan had not established that the partisan rearrangement was inherently unequal or undemocratic, but it did strike down one district for unconstitutionally weakening minority voting power.

These conflicts show again that Americans believe in democracy in general, but they can disagree on precisely what that belief requires them to do in the specific case of drawing district lines. And in the real world of politics, ideals about democratic principles and values often jostle head and shoulder with very hardheaded aspirations for political power. Americans may generally believe in democracy, or liberty, or the other beliefs of the American creed, but their understanding of what those terms mean will always be a battleground for public officials, political activists, and other citizens. Most Americans share the general ideals of the American creed, but the tension inherent in the creed leaves plenty of room for political debate, conflict, and struggle.

ThinkingCritically

1. In your view, what are the considerations line drawers should have in mind if they want to draw the most democratic, equal district lines?

2. In a democracy, should district lines be drawn to maximize the competitiveness of elections, even if that means about one-half of the residents will by definition not believe their elected officials represent their policy viewpoints?

Challenges to the American Creed

Although the American creed has had strong allegiance, alternative beliefs have also influenced American politics. At times, people might profess the creed's beliefs while also agreeing with some of the alternatives. This may seem logically impossible, but individuals often put ideas together in surprising combinations. Even within a society like the United States where one set of general beliefs generally predominates, the mosaic of cultural beliefs and values can be incredibly rich and complex because of the way that American creed ideals are mixed and mingled with other beliefs. American political culture is dynamic, not fixed and unchanging.

Communitarianism emphasizes the contributions and interests of the community.

Whereas the American creed gives primacy to the individual in society, **communitarianism** focuses on society and the community.[26] In the communitarian view, individuals are not self-made: society makes us and we owe something to society in return. In the words of Revolutionary leader Samuel Adams, "A citizen owes everything to the Commonwealth."[27] The communitarian approach does not dispute that individuals are personally responsible and need to work hard and diligently. But it would point out that we all depend on the resources provided by others and by the community, whether education, transportation, an array of commercial and cultural choices, or the bounty of the earth and water. These resources do not determine whether we will reach our goals, but they influence our ability to reach them, and we rely on others to provide them.

Communitarianism also suggests that the goal of self-improvement should not focus only on the self, but on how self-improvement serves the community and society more broadly. This way of thinking suggests that it is not an inherently bad thing for an individual to make a lot of money, but asks whether society is served in the process.

Communitarian beliefs in American history Communitarianism has been influential throughout American history. In the colonial and revolutionary eras, this was the dominant mode of thought.[28] The political language during those eras emphasized communitarian themes along with individualistic ones. It was common practice for government to regulate wages, prices, and the entry of new businesses into the marketplace, all to maintain social order. Gradually, individualistic beliefs gained ascendancy. Communitarian ideals survived, but in a less prominent position than previously.

Periodically, these ideals flourished in the advocacy of social, political, or economic reform. Populists from 1875 through 1900 expressed deep concern about the disruption of communities by industrial capitalism and proposed many reforms to rectify the perceived exploitation of government by private interests. Communitarian ideas alone were not enough to lead to reform—political activists and politicians needed to organize people who held these views. Major reform movements like the Progressives (1904–1918), the New Deal (1930s), and the Great Society (1960s), were successfully infused with the idea that politics or economics needed to be reformed for the greater interest of the community. Proposed reforms such as income taxes, retirement and social welfare programs, and extensive regulation of business practices were denounced by opponents as signs of socialism. Right up to today, campaign language condemning a politics of "the people versus the powerful" resonates with Americans.

Private interest and the public good To communitarians, the rights of individuals and the interests of the community are not necessarily in conflict. But when they are, the public good should trump private interest.[29] For example, in some states and municipalities, police set up sobriety checkpoints, where police stop drivers at random to screen them for drunk driving. These checkpoints bypass the normal requirement that police can stop drivers only if they believe they have probable cause to investigate them. Sobriety checkpoints are clearly an infringement on the privacy rights of individuals, but the checkpoints have been defended as serving the community's interests. If drivers realize they might get pulled over even when they are not driving erratically, they will be more cautious about drinking and driving, thereby enhancing everyone's safety and reducing the social costs involved with car crashes, injuries, and loss of life.[30]

Refining the American creed One way to look at communitarianism is that it refines the American creed without necessarily rejecting it.[31] On their own, creedal beliefs about individualism can appear harsh, advocating a "sink or swim" society in which individuals either succeed or fail, with little compassion for those who fall behind. Communitarian ideas remove this harsh edge by supporting government programs to provide social resources and services for individuals who are struggling, if that is in the community's interest. Consider unemployment compensation. Whereas a strict application of the creed's emphasis on individual responsibility would see unemployment compensation as unnecessary—someone could land another job quickly if they moved or accepted lower wages—communitarianism would view such

continued on page 45 ▶

Why Is There No National Health Insurance in the United States?

The Question

In nearly all industrialized countries, health care coverage for every individual is guaranteed by the national government, either by the government paying for private health care services, the government directly providing services, or some combination of these two. In the United States, government has not provided this guarantee, despite serious efforts to do so, most recently by President Bill Clinton in 1994.[33] Private expenditures are a far larger share of the total spent on health care than is true elsewhere (Figure 2-5). Why is there no national health insurance in the United States? How do we know?

Why It Matters

Nearly 46 million Americans, or about 16 percent of the population, have no health insurance. Among the unemployed, the poor, and racial and ethnic minorities, the rate is even higher. Many Americans drop into and out of heath care coverage for short periods of time, meaning that the proportion of the population falling into the hole of uninsurance over a two- or three-year period is even higher than 16 percent. In public opinion surveys, Americans frequently express fears that they will lose their insurance and will not be able to afford their medical expenses.[32] Whether you believe that national health insurance is crucially important to individuals' health and

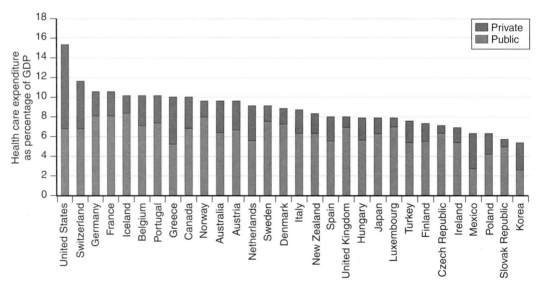

Figure 2-5. Public and Private Health Care Expenditures as Percentage of Gross Domestic Product, 2004. The United States devotes a much larger share of its economy to health care expenditures than other countries and has a much larger role for the private sector. American national and state governments also spend substantial sums on health care.

Source: Organization for Economic Cooperation and Development, Health Data 2006. Internet update October 17, 2006.
http://www.oecd.org/document/16/0,3343,en_2649_34631_2085200_1_1_1_1,00.htm

life opportunities, or you believe that national health insurance would harm medical care more than help it, the answer to the question matters. By understanding what has blocked previous efforts at national health insurance, you learn what would be necessary to achieve it or defeat it in the future.

For political scientists, explaining why something did not happen is similar to explaining why something did happen: a researcher needs to come up with an idea that connects the outcome to factors that might explain the outcome. The outcome we are interested in is the absence or presence of national health insurance that covers all individuals. The possible cause we are especially interested in is political culture. The hunch is that the American creed's emphasis on individualism, liberty, and property is incompatible with the idea that health care should be considered a federal government responsibility. Individualism demands personal responsibility. Liberty means allowing choices, and if some people choose not to have insurance, why force it upon them? Moreover, in the American free enterprise economy, health insurance has been a benefit offered by employers to entice prospective employees and retain their current workers. This competition might give employers the incentive to offer more generous insurance packages as they compete for employees. And if different jobs provide different levels of benefits, workers have choices. They might trade off health insurance for higher income, or more flexible work schedules, or overtime opportunities.

The most straightforward way to test this idea is through examining public opinion. Regarding health insurance, surveys show that Americans express some communitarian views. Depending on the survey, half to three-quarters of Americans say they favor "providing health care coverage for all," even if it means raising taxes. American political culture is rooted predominantly in the American creed, however, and we see its influence in public opinion also. In one survey, a majority said they favored national health insurance provided by government, but support dropped off if the program would limit one's choice of doctors or if there were waiting lists for non-emergency treatments. Adding these new opponents to those who initially opposed a universal health insurance program makes opposition the majority view.[34]

Overall, American political culture seems like it might be a deterrent to national health insurance. The idea that there is no support for national health insurance certainly is not correct. But support for a national plan is vulnerable to political arguments—and survey question wording—about service quality, availability, and choice. So it is fair to say that American political culture does not prohibit national health insurance, but it also does not lend clear support for it if advantages of the current system might be lost. So is it that simple? Case closed?

The answer, in fact, is not so simple. The United States does not have national health insurance, but it does have the Medicare and Medicaid programs, which provide insurance for the elderly and the poor, respectively. U.S. national and state governments spend huge sums on health care, even more than in many other countries (Figure 2-5). If American political culture simply would not allow any form of national health insurance, the existence of these two programs and all that spending would be a real puzzle. What if the explanation was modified to say that Americans will oppose government-funded health insurance except for those individuals who are unable to provide for themselves? That seems to fit Medicare. But what about Medicaid? American creedal beliefs in individualism might argue that low-income persons, unlike the elderly, are in a position to better their financial standing and acquire health care, so government should not provide it. But government does.

Given the mixed public opinion results and the presence of these two partial forms of national health insurance in the United States, how might we further try to explain the lack of universal national health insurance? Remember from Chapter 1 that there are rarely simple solutions. So one possibility is to add another factor: American political institutions.[35] For something as massive as national health insurance—which would entail changes throughout the entire health care industry—the president, Congress, different parts of the federal bureaucracy, state governments, and possibly even the Supreme Court would be involved in the policy-making process. The health care industry is huge and well established, so efforts to change it will be long and complicated, requiring a great deal of political dedication throughout multiple levels of political power. The passage of Medicare, for example, was highly contested by opposing policy makers. The task is even more daunting when you add a political culture that is only partly supportive of national health insurance and a highly complex institutional dispersion of power. This intersection of culture and institutions poses significant hurdles for national health insurance.

The political activity of "special interests" is another factor to consider.[36] Adding this factor further helps explain the complexity in this area of public policy. Many parts of the health care industry are likely to oppose movements toward national health insurance because they fear bureaucratic oversight of their business practices, interference with patient care, and depression of prices and salaries that would make the industry less efficient economically and less desirable as a career.[37] The interests opposed to national health insurance are likely to be already very well organized and very persistent on the issue because they have a lot at stake financially. Those individuals or groups in favor of national health insurance, on the other hand, will need to get organized to fight this battle and they may not have as intense an interest in creating national health insurance as opponents will have in stopping it. For one thing, Americans are generally satisfied with their own health care. Add to this the complication that, even among supporters, opinion is split over which of the many methods of achieving national health insurance is best and how acceptable the alternative methods would be.[38] A battle between a movement divided across several different plans and groups relatively unified to protect their turf will usually be won by the latter, even if there are more people in the former.

The Bottom Line

Political culture, institutional features of American government, and the politics of special interests together form a thicket of obstacles to the adoption of national health insurance. In 2008, several candidates in the presidential primaries and caucuses were promoting national health insurance. Language during the campaign about health care being an individual's "right" spoke to American creed beliefs. What would change the long losing streak for national health insurance? Considering political culture, advocates for change would need to argue convincingly that their idea is truer to the American creed than is current practice; redefine the meaning of the beliefs; propose a different balance among the beliefs; or convince people to emphasize communitarianism more than their American creed beliefs. For example, some advocates argue not about individual rights, but that quality health care for all members of the community is a moral imperative. Overcoming the obstacles requires public officials and powerful interests to substantially recalculate the economic and political desirability of national health insurance. A growing worry that health care costs had become economically unsustainable for businesses, governments, and individuals and were severely harming U.S. global competitiveness could prod such a recalculation. A belief that there would be a severe political price to pay if health insurance were not adopted would further it.

compensation as necessary, at least for a few months, to prevent the social disruption of unpaid rent and mortgages, delinquent bills, and families in disarray. Similar beliefs motivate some of the advocates for national health insurance (see *How Do We Know? Why Is There No National Health Insurance in the United States?*).

Public support for communitarianism Public opinion reveals the persistence of communitarian ideals today. For example, nearly two-thirds of Americans believe that "business corporations make too much profit." The very notion of "too much profit" is telling. In the creedal beliefs of property, liberty, and individualism, the idea of "too much" profit makes no sense. If an individual or business is clever enough to make a product for which there is high demand, how can we say "too much" profit is being made? Assuming you have choices, you are not forced to buy the product. If you believe the price is too high, you should not purchase it. While the creedal view holds that substantial profit indicates a good business plan, communitarianism worries that businesses may be taking advantage of customers individually and society more generally. Many Americans share the communitarian belief that it is wrong for businesses to "exploit" certain situations—such as shortage of a key resource—and increase their profit. This attitude is consistent with communitarianism's focus on the interest of the community.

Discrimination stresses that not all groups deserve equal treatment.

Another challenge to the American creed, particularly the value of equality, is **discrimination**. According to this view, society is a hierarchy where not all groups deserve all the rights and benefits the American creed can offer—some groups are favored and others are disfavored. The most glaring example of discrimination in American history was the treatment of racial minorities, especially blacks. Those holding hierarchical ideas considered blacks inherently inferior to whites. The language used to describe blacks in comparison to whites was degrading and offensive, depicting blacks as anything from children to savages. Racism was so pervasive in American history that even many of those who opposed slavery, for example, did not consider blacks fully equal and fully deserving of the same rights as whites.

Discrimination cannot be dismissed as an inconvenient blip on history, or an unpleasant set of ideas held by relatively few people on the bottom rungs of society, or the distorted worldview of just a few white supremacist organizations such as the Ku Klux Klan. Political, educational, and business leaders believed in these ideas. Well into the twentieth century, American public policy at the national and state levels was greatly influenced by the racist, anti-equality premises of discrimination, denying minorities equal access to the opportunities in America's society, economy, and polity. University researchers of the late nineteenth and early twentieth centuries measured the brain size of blacks and whites to demonstrate "objectively" the innate superiority of whites. The research lent an air of scientific justification to the denial of economic, social, and political rights to blacks. Across the country businesses refused to hire minorities, paid them less when they did, and often refused to serve them as customers. And public officials pandered to racist views held by the public.

The same group-inferiority and social-hierarchy arguments used to limit the individual rights of blacks were also historically used against other ethnic groups, Native Americans, and women. The derogatory labels questioning the maturity, character, intelligence, and emotional stability of blacks were applied to these groups as well. Some today would say that homosexuals have faced some of the same kinds of unequal treatment in American history. In 1974, for example, only half of Americans said they would be willing to allow homosexuals to teach in colleges, compared to over four-fifths in 2004. Visions of the United States as a social hierarchy are still part of the mixture of American political culture, but not in the same bold, public, and widespread manner as in previous eras.[39]

Multiculturalism questions the desirability of a common American political culture.

Multicultural thought began sweeping through the United States in the 1980s, particularly on college campuses and in popular culture. The defining characteristics of **multiculturalism** are a belief that American society consists of multiple cultures and a focus on group identity rather than on the individualism strongly emphasized in the American creed. Advocates of multiculturalism are skeptical about the notion of any common American political culture or, if there is such a culture, it is seen as reflecting the domination of one group in society—white men of European descent in particular—over other groups. Rather than bringing people together in social cohesion, the notion that there is *an* American political culture to which most individuals subscribe is seen as an exercise of power by dominant groups in society over weaker groups. In this view, as groups become more aware of how the dominant culture has cemented their subordinate position in society, they become more determined to protect and advocate their separate group identity and culture. They may interact with "mainstream" American society, but they also wish to preserve their distinctive language, customs, and beliefs.[40] "Identity politics" is a recent term used to describe such political activity.

Recognition and tolerance of diversity In its least controversial version, multiculturalism simply calls for a recognition that the United States is composed of many different ethnic, racial, religious, sexual preference, class, gender, and nationality groups with distinctive contributions to bring to American society. Viewed this way, it is possible to conceive of the American creed as a national political culture, even while acknowledging that many other aspects of culture and behavior might differ from one group to another. It is from this version of multiculturalism that frequent calls for toleration, diversity, and "embracing our differences" are heard in public discourse.

Rejection of a common culture In a more controversial version, multiculturalism means that any concept of a unified national political culture is false and is inherently an attempt by dominant groups to exert their power. Some multiculturalists contend not only that national political culture is highly diverse rather than unified, but also that individuals themselves reflect multiple cultural beliefs. Because of unique histories and life experiences, people look at the world differently. People "carry" a culture with them based on their group identity, but usually people have a collection of identities based on race, gender, ethnicity, and other characteristics, so the mix of beliefs may differ markedly from person to person.

Conflict with the American creed This approach can lead to direct conflicts with beliefs in the American creed. One area that has been especially controversial and delicate is how multiculturalism intersects with the focus on equality and individualism in the American creed. For example, the nature of gender relations in some cultures has led to the rise of "cultural defenses" in court cases.[41] The cases are inherently inflammatory and controversial. The most successful have involved men charged with kidnap and rape who defend their actions as part of a particular marriage custom in their culture; and men who explained their murder of their wives as a culturally-sanctioned response to their wives' adultery or mistreatment. In other cases, mothers who killed their children have explained their actions as instigated by the shame of a husband's infidelity and as part of a cultural practice of mother–child suicide. In cases of these types, expert testimony about the defendant's cultural background has sometimes led to dropped or reduced charges or reduced sentences.[42]

Cases like these raise very difficult and challenging questions. Advocates of the American creed would ask whether equality is better served by emphasizing the equal and free status of each individual or by emphasizing the equal status of different cultural beliefs, which might differentiate between the rights accorded to men and women. Advocates of multiculturalism would ask whether these defenses are any different from those offered earlier in American history by individuals whose cultural heritage was European. For a long time in the United States, they note, legal rights were sharply different for men and women, largely because of Western cultural understandings about gender relations.

Libertarianism argues for a very limited government role.

Libertarianism argues that individuals are responsible for their own lives, and society is best off with individuals maximally free from government restraints. Government's responsibilities should be very limited and should not intrude on individual property rights or liberties. Its fundamental duties are to defend the country militarily, to protect individuals from crime, and to ensure that people fulfill contracts entered into freely. Beyond those duties, individual choice, the market, and voluntary action are what drive society, and government should not interfere. Outside these core responsibilities, each and every act of government compromises individual freedom.

In the United States, many citizens and politicians of both major political parties profess to hold some libertarian beliefs. This pick-and-choose method is usually unsatisfactory to libertarians: limited government activity and the primacy of the individual and the market are core principles that should apply across all policy areas, not just be applied when politically convenient. The American creed prizes individualism and limited government, but to libertarians, the creed tolerates too big a role for government.

American political culture is a mosaic of beliefs.

The beliefs of the American creed have been powerful guides for public thinking about politics. As noted above, these beliefs are ideals that mark out the starting point for most Americans when they think about political issues. Americans may be convinced to change their understanding of the meaning of these beliefs, or they may find the beliefs in severe tension and have to determine the acceptable balance between them. They may in some cases simply choose to ignore, or be persuaded to ignore, one of the beliefs that they profess to support.

For some Americans, American creed beliefs may be displaced by alternative sets of beliefs. More common, however, is for Americans to hold many of these beliefs simultaneously and in some tension—supporting the American creed's beliefs, for example, but also holding strong communitarian beliefs or even views supportive of discrimination. And, perhaps, some hold beliefs from all three of these streams—American creed, communitarianism, discrimination—simultaneously. Or it could be the joining of other beliefs like multiculturalism or libertarianism with the American creed beliefs. The beliefs of the American creed are powerful touchstones in American politics that guide the way most individuals think about politics and government, but they do not preclude other beliefs and ideals holding important places in the mosaic of American political culture.

SUMMARY

▶ Political culture consists of the basic values, beliefs, attitudes, predispositions, and expectations within which politics operates. It is where citizens start as they process and assess issues, causes, groups, parties, candidates, and public officials. Political culture provides a language used by politicians in speaking to the public.

▶ At the heart of American political culture is the American creed. The creed is built around beliefs in individualism, democracy, liberty, and respect for property rights and religious freedom, all tied together by the value of equality. These beliefs are frequently discussed during the formation of public policy. One of the key storylines of American history is that over time additional groups, such as racial minorities and women, demanded that they, too, be able to receive the benefits of the creed.

▶ Several consequences emerge from the creed's dominance in American political culture, including a preference for limited government, a weak sense of sovereign power, tension between private and public interest, and concern about the impact of competing beliefs. One important consequence is the tension inherent in the American creed. The beliefs of the creed can sometimes conflict. The belief in liberty might lead toward one policy solution, but the belief in democracy might lead toward another. Tension also arises because the beliefs themselves may be defined differently or might change over time. A term like "democracy" or "liberty" might mean somewhat different things to different people. Tension between beliefs and over the definition of each belief creates much of the debate in American politics.

▶ Throughout American history other views have challenged the creed. Alternative modes of thinking about political life have had important effects in the United States. Communitarianism emphasized the role of society or community rather than the centrality of the individual. Communitarianism was prominent during the colonial and revolutionary periods and it continues to influence politics today. Discrimination also has had a profound influence on American politics. Justification and defense of social hierarchy and inequality, particularly those based on race and gender, have had a long place in American history. Multiculturalism questions the desirability of a consensus in political culture, arguing that any such consensus is more likely the imposition of the values and beliefs of dominant groups upon groups that are weaker politically. Last, libertarianism tolerates only the most minimal role for government.

KEY TERMS

American creed, p. 23
communitarianism, p. 40
discrimination, p. 45
equality, p. 25
individualism, p. 25
libertarianism, p. 47

liberty, p. 28
limited government, p. 33
multiculturalism, p. 45
natural rights, p. 28
political culture, p. 23
property rights, p. 29
religious freedom, p. 30
sovereign power, p. 35

SUGGESTED READINGS

Jim Cullen. *The American Dream: A Short History of an Idea That Shaped a Nation.* New York: Oxford University Press. 2003. The history of the "American dream" and its continuing power in American thought today.

Alexis de Tocqueville. *Democracy in America.* Originally published 1835. Still a remarkably perceptive and insightful analysis of the nature of American society, politics, and identity and how they differ from other countries.

Richard J. Ellis. *American Political Cultures.* New York: Oxford University Press. 1993. Challenges the idea of a consensus in American political culture, contending instead that American politics has featured an ongoing contest between five political cultures.

Samuel P. Huntington. *American Politics: The Promise of Disharmony.* Cambridge: Harvard University Press. 1981. An argument that American politics has been cyclically driven by gaps that emerge between the ideals of the American creed and the reality of American institutions, and that the timing of the cycle is related to the rise and fall of religious "great awakenings."

Jennifer L. Hochschild. *What's Fair: American Beliefs about Distributive Justice.* Cambridge: Harvard University Press. 1981. The author analyzes what Americans mean by equality, finding that support for equality thrives in political and private life, but that there is less support for equality in economic matters.

Calvin C. Jillson. *Pursuing the American Dream: Opportunity and Exclusion Over Four Centuries.* Lawrence: University Press of Kansas. 2004. A sweeping overview of the idea of opportunity in American thought and its institutionalization in social, economic, and political life.

Seymour Martin Lipset. *American Exceptionalism: A Double-Edged Sword.* New York: W. W. Norton. 1996. Examines whether America is distinctive from other societies in culture, economics, and politics, and concludes that overall it is.

Richard M. Merelman. *Partial Visions: Culture and Politics in Britain, Canada, and the United States.* Madison: University of Wisconsin Press. 1991. Examines how embedded political messages and values in popular culture weaken and distort democratic participation.

James A. Morone. *The Democratic Wish: Popular Participation and the Limits of American Government.* New York: Basic Books. 1990. Explores the interplay between Americans' fear of political power and government, their desire for democracy, and how the two combine to thwart the resolution of important public problems.

Michael Sandel. *Democracy's Discontent: America in Search of a Public Philosophy.* Cambridge: Harvard University Press. 1996. An accessible discussion of American political culture, noting particularly the strain between individualism and communitarianism.

political culture the basic values, beliefs, attitudes, predispositions, and expectations of citizens toward the political system of their society and toward themselves as participants in it.

American creed the dominant political culture in the United States, marked by a set of beliefs in individualism, democracy, liberty, property, and religion, tied together by the value of equality.

equality the value advocating that all Americans should be treated the same under the law, be able to influence government, and have equal opportunity to succeed in life.

individualism a belief that all individuals should be able to succeed to the maximum extent possible given their talents and abilities, regardless of race, religion, or other group characteristics.

liberty the belief that government should leave people free to do as they please and exercise their natural rights to the maximum extent possible.

natural rights rights inherent in the essence of people as human beings; government does not provide these rights, but it can restrict the exercise of them.

property rights the belief that people should be able to acquire, own, and use goods and assets free from government constraints, as long as their acquisition and use does not interfere with the rights of other individuals.

religious freedom a belief that individuals should be free to choose and practice their religious faith and that government should not establish any particular religion as the official or preferred religion.

limited government the idea that the scope of government activities should be narrow and that government should act only when the need is great and other sectors of society are unable to meet the need.

sovereign power the individual or institution in a political system whose decisions are binding and unable to be overturned by other individuals or institutions.

communitarianism a view on politics that the needs of the community are of higher priority in government than the needs of the individual, even if the result is a restriction of individual liberties.

discrimination a view on politics that not all groups in society are deserving of equal rights and opportunities.

multiculturalism a view of politics that group identity influences political beliefs and, because groups are naturally diverse in their beliefs, the idea of a shared or dominant political culture merely reflects the imposition of a dominant group's beliefs on subordinate groups.

libertarianism a view of politics that emphasizes the importance of individual choice and responsibility, the private sector, and the free market, in which government's primary obligations are to defend the country militarily, protect individuals from crime, and ensure that people fulfill contracts entered into freely.

3 The Constitution

"We will direct every resource at our command—every means of diplomacy, every tool of intelligence, every instrument of law enforcement, every financial influence, and every necessary weapon of war—to the disruption and to the defeat of the global terror network." President George W. Bush spoke these words before Congress in a nationally televised address on September 20, 2001. In his speech, the president promised bold, aggressive action against those responsible for terrorist activity.

In the heat of the immediate aftermath of the terrorist attacks on the United States, the president's words garnered wide support and approval. Four years later, however, the president's vision had become more controversial. What does "every resource at our command" mean? What are the limits to the resources and to the president's command? The United States Constitution provides for a government of carefully balanced legislative, executive, and judicial powers, centered chiefly in Congress, the president, and the courts, respectively. How far could the president go and remain faithful to this constitutional principle?

In December 2005, the New York Times revealed the existence of a program in which the National Security Agency, without authorization from the courts, monitored communications that the administration said involved individuals and members of terrorist organizations in the United States. Under the 1978 Foreign Intelligence Surveillance Act (FISA), the government is normally expected to obtain a warrant from the Foreign Intelligence Surveillance Court to eavesdrop on the international communication of individuals in the United States when at least one party to the communication is suspected of having ties to terrorism. The revela-

tion that the government had been conducting surveillance without requesting warrants prior to intercepting messages provoked a firestorm of protest. In emergencies, FISA allowed surveillance to be done, with three days allowed to obtain a warrant after the surveillance, but the administration had not obtained these warrants. Moreover, although a few members of Congress had been informed about the program, they were not permitted to divulge any information with their colleagues, so Congress as an institution had no knowledge of the surveillance. Those who criticized the program charged that the president was taking unilateral, unchecked action in a manner inconsistent with the Constitution.

To many critics, the failure to obtain warrants or advise Congress about the surveillance program indicated that the president had taken a far too expansive view of the executive branch's power, threatening the constitutional balance between the branches. The president's most severe critics had complaints about other executive branch actions that paralleled their complaints about the surveillance program, but even many Republicans in Congress raised concerns about the newly-revealed program. Even after months of publicity, the scope of the program and the precise nature of the surveillance were unknown. In March 2006 three Republican senators introduced a bill that they believed would, one senator noted, "bring the NSA's surveillance program out of the shadows by reasserting the necessary constitutional checks and balances that both the legislative and judicial branches government have over the Executive."[1]

The administration, on the other hand, argued that Congress's authorization of military action to root out terrorism after September 11, 2001,

implicitly gave the president wartime authority to order the National Security Agency to monitor e-mail and telephone calls in which one of the persons in the communication— either in the United States or abroad—might have terrorist links. As commander in chief, the administration argued, the president needed the flexibility to respond to military threats with actions such as the Terrorist Surveillance Program, the administration's label for the surveillance program. Administration officials also pointed out that they continued to obtain warrants for communications that were entirely domestic.

In July 2006, Senator Arlen Specter, a Pennsylvania Republican who chaired the Senate Judiciary Committee, announced that he and the White House had reached agreement on a bill concerning the surveillance program. The bill clearly was a work of compromise between the senator and the administration. For the first time, the president consented to allow the program to be reviewed by the Foreign Intelligence Surveillance Court. His consent, however, was voluntary—the president refused to agree to the bill if it mandated that he get approval for the program. The president agreed to submit the program to the court for review, but for a one-time review on its constitutionality—he was not agreeing to obtain warrants for each individual target of surveillance. The bill extended the three-day grace period for obtaining a warrant to seven days, but did not require the president to seek such warrants. Any lawsuits challenging the president's program would also have to go to the Foreign Intelligence Surveillance Court rather than through the federal courts, eliminating the prospect of conflicting opinions in different cases. The bill specifically acknowledged the president's constitutional authority to conduct intelligence operations and stated the Foreign Intelligence Surveillance Act should not be considered the exclusive statute concerning the type of surveillance program in question. Within the administration, this language was read approvingly as leaving open the possibility that the president could order other surveillance without needing to go through the warrant requirements of the existing law. The president's critics, disapprovingly, read it the same way. Whether the agreement would ultimately trim or expand the president's power, whether it would defuse or exacerbate the constitutional concerns that originally led to the agreement was, therefore, not at all clear.[2]

Although the Framers of the U.S. Constitution could not have foreseen the precise issue leading to the battle over wiretapping, the questions raised by the controversy are the same kinds the Framers wrestled with nearly 220 years earlier. Where should power be located in government? What are the responsibilities of the different branches? What is the appropriate balance of power between the branches? How can the Constitution ensure that no one part of American government becomes too powerful or too unchecked in its exercise of power? In this chapter, we explore how the Framers answered these questions as they wrote the Constitution. Based on their experience with Great Britain, as well as their experience in governing the new country after the Revolution in 1776, the Framers were deeply concerned with power—its use, abuse, extent, and proper exercise.

THIS CHAPTER WILL EXAMINE:

▶ the meaning of the American Revolution, the events leading up to it, and the country's first constitution

▶ the governing problems the Framers of the Constitution attempted to resolve

▶ the opposing sides in the battle to ratify the Constitution

▶ the process by which the Constitution can be amended

From Revolution to Constitution

Momentous in its impact, the American Revolution has been difficult for historians to classify. Unlike other revolutions, it was not a revolt of one social class against another or a replacement of one economic system by another. If it was not a revolution in these ways, then what was it?

The American Revolution changed ideas about governance.

One answer provided by political scientists and historians is that the American Revolution was an "ideological" revolution, which is to say a revolution most notably in ideas and philosophy of government. With this answer, scholars agree with former president John Adams, who wrote in 1818 that the "radical change in the principles, opinions, sentiments, and affections of the people was the real American Revolution."[3]

It was a revolution about ideas, particularly ideas about governing.[4] To colonial leaders, power, because of human corruption, tended to be too aggressive, to extend beyond its legitimate boundaries. The victim of power was liberty. To defend liberty and thwart excessive power required vigilance and virtue from ordinary people. The colonists drew insights from their own experience and borrowed liberally from various political theorists and writers. British political theorist John Locke's ideas on limited government and social contracts were especially influential. The idea of the social contract was that the relationship between the governed and those in power was equivalent to a business contract in which each side had obligations to fulfill or the contract would become void.[5] The governed were not bound indefinitely to corrupt or dysfunctional political institutions.

From this basis, the colonists built a new understanding of politics based on the concepts of representation, constitutional rights, and sovereignty. During the decade prior to the colonists' formal declaration of independence, the language of democratic representation was a key rallying cry to build enthusiasm for the prospect of a separation from Great Britain. The expression "no taxation without representation" highlights one of the most famous demands from the American Revolution and has been learned by every school child since as a key to what the revolution was about. British government officials attempted to convince the colonists they were "virtually represented"—even though the colonists did not elect members of Parliament, members of Parliament in effect represented their interests because they tended to the interests of the British Empire in general, and these two sets of interests were the same. The colonists, instead, touted the concept of direct representation: the job of the representative was to reflect faithfully the opinions of the constituents who elected him or her. Citizens should send representatives to the legislature with specific instructions about how to vote. In addition, constitutions should mark the boundaries of legitimate government power. People had natural, inherent rights that preceded any government action, and written constitutions were needed to protect these rights. Lastly, the colonists challenged the dominant view of sovereignty. In Britain, the idea that there could only be one final, ultimate authority—sovereignty—was undisputed. The colonists, however, argued that sovereignty could be divided. Authority could be located in different geographical locations, for example at the local and national levels, as well as in different institutions, such as the executive and legislative branches.

The combination of these beliefs generated a radical view of the people as self-governing. The concept of "the people" as a positive, active force, rather than just passive subjects of government, became a touchstone for much of the oratory of the period.[6] The people's role had been transformed from occasional watchdog to participant: the people were not only a check on government, they in effect *were* the government. In this new conceptual understanding of how politics should work, the active and continuous consent of the governed was necessary.[7]

The colonists rebelled against taxes imposed unilaterally by the British government.

The immediate impetus for the revolution was a series of economic and political events, many of which received prominent billing in the Declaration of Independence. The causal forces are difficult to disentangle. Would the events have had such resonance in the absence of new ideas about the right of the people to self-government? For decades the colonists had been out of practical reach of British rulers and had been allowed to operate with extensive freedom. This experience built their confidence in their ability to self-govern. So we can flip the question and ask: Would those ideas about self-government have flourished as thoroughly in the absence of a set of provocative events? After all, the revolutionary leaders were not simply dreamily concocting new political ideas from the sidelines—they were very practical and strategic politicians whose ideas about government were forged in the political battles within the colonies and with Britain.

The best resolution to these questions is to see the events and ideas as mutually reinforcing. When Britain began to clamp down on the colonies, the colonists believed the freedom they had already achieved was being threatened, and this threat strengthened the ideas of self-governance. To them, the revolution was an attempt to maintain their freedom, not to create it. As they saw it, an orchestrated campaign was afoot to demolish American liberty. These causal factors—ideas and events—cannot be completely separated, as each furthered the other and both in turn fostered sentiment for revolution.

The two most influential economic groups of the day were New England merchants and Southern planters. These two groups had long been fiercely loyal to the British government and, by controlling key positions of power in the colonies, they prevented more radical elements in the colonies from pushing toward conflict with the mother country. Now, however, they were agitated by recent changes in British policies, particularly tax policies. For seven years Britain had been engaged in the French and Indian War, an engagement that depleted the British treasury. Believing that many of its costs were related to maintaining the safety of the American colonists, that the colonists had had a free ride for some time, and that British citizens had subsidized the colonies extensively, the British government instituted new policies designed to extract some revenue from this growing part of its empire.

Stamp Act One new law was the Stamp Act, passed by Parliament in 1765. This law required all legal documents, licenses, commercial contracts, newspapers, and pamphlets to obtain a tax stamp. The colonists rebelled. Stamp agents were attacked by mobs, and many had their property destroyed. Several colonial assemblies passed resolutions of protest against the act. The Stamp Act Congress sent a protest to the king and Parliament. A boycott of British goods finally led Parliament to repeal the tax. But Parliament then passed the Declaratory Act, stating the right of the British government to pass laws that would be binding on the colonists. The British government wanted to send a clear message that the colonies were indeed part of the British Empire and subject to its edicts.

Townshend Acts That message would soon be reinforced with the Townshend Acts. Passed in 1767, one of these acts suspended the New York legislature because that colony had not complied with a law requiring that British soldiers be quartered in (that is, reside in) housing owned by the colonists. The Revenue Act, the second of the Townshend Acts, imposed customs duties on colonial imports of glass, lead, paint, paper, and tea. Generally, the cost of these fees was passed along to the colonists by raising the price tag on these products. Resistance to the Revenue Act was considerable. The Massachusetts Assembly, indicating its unwillingness to enforce the law, was disbanded by the British in 1768. Tensions rose over the next 18 months, culminating with the Boston Massacre in March 1770. British soldiers, enduring another day of taunting from a crowd gathered at the Customs House, killed five colonists. The event and the subsequent acquittals further agitated the colonists. Ultimately, boycotts and merchants' refusal to import goods led to the repeal of all the Townshend duties except that on tea.

Tea Act Following a three-year lull, the British government enacted a particularly controversial new economic policy in 1773, the Tea Act. Tea was an extremely important industry in that era. Much like high technology today or automobiles 20 years ago, leaders of the economically advanced countries of the day believed that tea stimulated the national economy. Nearly every country wanted a piece of this industry. Competition was brisk, but the profit potential was enormous. The Tea Act allowed the British-controlled East India Company to export its tea to America without paying the tea duty that had been imposed by the Townshend Acts. This made the British tea cheaper than the Dutch tea, which dominated the

American market and was sold by colonial merchants. The colonial merchants were squeezed out by the new law, because the East India Company would use its own British agents, not colonial merchants, to sell the tea.

The colonists' response was the incident known as the Boston Tea Party. Inflammatory language unmistakably threatened death to anyone who assisted the East India Company in unloading its tea. In December 1773, protesters prevented the unloading of the East India Company tea, and threw the tea in the harbor. The British government viewed the Tea Party as an act of terrorism—random violence and property damage coupled with random threats designed to intimidate colonists and British officials alike, all to prevent a company from carrying out its legal activities.

When the Boston Town Meeting refused Parliament's demand for compensation for the tea, the British government retaliated with what colonists referred to as the Intolerable Acts. These acts closed the port of Boston, restricted the power of the Massachusetts Assembly and local town meetings, quartered troops in private houses, and exempted British officials from trial in Massachusetts. In response, 12 of the 13 colonies banded together to establish the First Continental Congress in September and October 1774.[8] The Congress issued demands to the king in the form of a Declaration of Rights and Grievances and developed plans for colonial resistance to what they deemed as an overbearing imperial government.

The colonists had traveled a long way in a remarkably short time. Only ten years earlier, most colonists still saw the British political system as an ideal. The balance that the British system aimed to achieve between different social classes in the two houses of Parliament and the monarchy was praised as an especially effective form of government. And rather than seeking independence, many colonial leaders emphasized that they simply wished to have the same rights as Englishmen. They had believed they were part of "the people" of Britain. After an eventful decade, however, the colonists had now reached a new crossroads.

The Declaration of Independence aimed to build a nation.

The Continental Congress met again from May 1775 through December 1776 in a charged atmosphere. Communications within and between the colonies about the trouble with the British government were frequent and impassioned, with writers like Thomas Paine using pamphlets (and in January 1776, his book Common Sense) to arouse opposition to the royal government. In April skirmishes had broken out in Lexington and Concord, Massachusetts. Parliament had rejected the Declaration of Rights and Grievances, which set out complaints about economic policies, lack of representation, British domination of the colonial judicial system, and disbanding of colonial legislatures.

Recognizing the drift of events and opinion, the Second Congress began the process of building a new government by creating an army, approving the issuance of currency, and establishing diplomatic and trade relations with other countries. Influenced by experience, their reading of history, the lessons of the republics of antiquity in Greece and Rome, and the ideas of a range of writers, political leaders were building the intellectual framework necessary to justify revolution. On July 4, 1776, their efforts bore fruit, as the Second Congress approved the **Declaration of Independence** drafted by Thomas Jefferson.

The Declaration asserted that rights of life, liberty, property, and the pursuit of happiness were "unalienable," meaning they cannot be given away. Similarly, these rights were natural, born in people as an essential part of their being. Government did not provide these rights—the most it could do was restrict them. When it restricted them arbitrarily and unjustly, then revolution was an appropriate response. The Declaration was also an attempt to find common ground that would join the colonists as "Americans." Although "nation" is often used as synonymous with "country," from a political science perspective, a **nation** is a distinctive concept. It refers to a shared sense of understanding among a people, a shared sense that they are different and separate from other peoples, and that there are basic principles, values, and outlooks that unite a certain people. The Declaration attempted to inspire that sense of nationhood.

The Articles of Confederation aimed to build a government.

The next step was to build a set of government institutions infused by fundamental principles, rules of operation, values, and beliefs.[9] A government enhances a population's sense of nationhood. Constructing a government that can rule effectively and is consistent with a population's sense of nationhood was a significant challenge in 1776, just as it is in emerging democracies today. Rules and procedures guide how governments operate. And rules laid down early can be very difficult to change later. The stakes, therefore, are high.

The first attempt to devise governing principles and draft a national constitution was the **Articles of Confederation**. The Articles were approved in November 1777 by the Third Continental Congress, which had begun meeting in December 1776. Each of the former colonies, now called states, had to ratify the document. The ratification process was completed in March 1781, and the Articles remained in effect until 1789. The Revolutionary War, which had begun in April 1775, ended in April 1783.[10]

The challenge facing the authors of the Articles of Confederation was to create a government that embraced the sense of nationhood expressed in the Declaration of Independence, while also recognizing that Americans primarily identified themselves by the individual states in which they lived. The Articles of Confederation reflected a deep fear of centralized political power, born out of the Americans' experience with Parliament and British royalty and expressed in the Declaration. It also provided a leading role for the states. For both these reasons, it seemed a reasonable fit for the new country.

Under the Articles, the central government was based in Congress. Members of Congress were selected by state legislatures, paid by the states, and able to be recalled and removed from office by the states. Laws were to be implemented by the individual states. There was neither an executive branch nor a judiciary. It was difficult for Congress to pass legislation. Although state legislatures typically sent three representatives to Congress, each state cast only one vote. For a bill to pass, a simple majority of seven of the thirteen states was not enough. Instead, a supermajority—a set amount that is more than a simple majority—of nine states had to agree. Changing the Articles required the approval of all thirteen states.

Congress's powers were limited. It could declare war—but there was no standing national army. It could regulate trade with Native Americans—but it could not regulate trade between the states. It could borrow money or coin money—but it could not institute taxes. Effectively, the system of government built under the Articles made the central government almost entirely dependent on the voluntary cooperation of the states. There was little this government controlled and little it could do to force action.

Problems with the Articles as a governing framework Difficulties set in almost immediately. First, the United States had no coherent way to deal with other countries. Economic treaties were a free-for-all, with states making their own arrangements with foreign countries. Under the Articles, Congress would have had no way to enforce international treaties even if it had been able to negotiate them. Although Congress could declare war and could name senior army officers, any military action required pulling together the disparate state militias.

Second, politicians, merchants, and creditors were shaken by this domestic upheaval. During the Revolutionary War, political and economic leaders had used the rallying cry of democracy to mobilize opposition to Britain. In part, this may have simply been good political strategy to build up support for what was the dangerous venture of challenging the British army. As the 1780s wore on, however, political and economic leaders lamented what they saw as a citizenry motivated by self-interest rather than civic good and public virtue. No doubt they were also concerned that their own political power might be slipping.

Many events during the 1780s worried politicians and businessmen. For example, Rhode Island printed paper money for use in repaying debts, but creditors considered it worthless. Some states instituted one-year terms for legislators, to limit their power and make them more responsive to public opinion. However, to leaders in government and business, democracy had degenerated into rule by the mob, or "mobocracy." In their view, all that was wrong under the Articles surfaced in the incident known as **Shays's Rebellion** in 1786–1787. Daniel Shays was a former army officer angered by the growing number of people being thrown off their land in western Massachusetts, mostly for inability to pay land taxes. To prevent further foreclosures, Shays joined and then—perhaps reluctantly—led likeminded men from August 1786 through February 1787. Bearing firearms, they assembled outside courthouses to prevent the courts from opening. In the view of political and business leaders, Shays was holding Massachusetts government hostage at gunpoint. Punctuating the incident, his supporters attempted to raid the federal arsenal in Springfield, where weapons were stockpiled. Massachusetts officials asked the Continental Congress for assistance, but the national government was ill-equipped to pull together either financial resources or military personnel. The state itself had no permanent militia. To displace Shays and his supporters, Boston businessmen raised private money to fund the state militia. Although Massachusetts then successfully put down the rebellion within a few days, the incident sent shockwaves around the country. The political system created by the Articles of Confederation seemed unable to manage either international or domestic affairs. As a result, the political and economic leaders concluded that the new nation's first constitution had already failed.

Frustration with the Articles led to the writing of a new Constitution.

The 1780s were unsettling. Schooled in the communitarian belief that concern for the public good should outweigh personal interests, many political leaders worried that the people's capacity for restrained self-government had failed. Self-government required that the people use their power cautiously and not to advantage one group at the expense of another. In the view of these leaders, a critical juncture had been reached. Not everyone agreed that the experience of the 1780s was so dire—the real concern of political leaders, they suggested, was the erosion of their political power. But those who did share a sense of worry over the country's direction concluded that change was necessary.[11]

The first attempt to repair the Articles had occurred before Shays's Rebellion. In the fall of 1786, accepting an invitation from the Virginia legislature, delegates from five states met in Annapolis, Maryland, to discuss the problems facing the young national government. The delegates approved a resolution drafted by Alexander Hamilton that called for possible revision of the Articles. Hamilton had been an assistant to George Washington in the Revolutionary War, and would later play a large role in the ratification of the Constitution and as Secretary of the Treasury in Washington's administration.[12] His resolution called for Congress to send delegates to Philadelphia at some future date to make the Articles more effective in managing domestic and international affairs.

Soon, Congress did just that. Shocked by Shays's Rebellion, Congress called on each state to send delegates to Philadelphia in May 1787 to discuss revision of the Articles (every state except Rhode Island participated). They met with a sense of crisis in the air: the national government appeared to be unable to manage international affairs, establish civility and cooperation between the states, or react to domestic insurrection. The delegates quickly concluded that revision of the Articles was pointless. They decided to start over and establish a new set of ground rules for an effective American government.[13]

Those efforts would culminate in the Constitution, the young country's second attempt to build a government that would rule effectively and unify the new American nation. The delegates were still concerned about threats to personal liberty posed by the concentration of too much power in a central government, but they now believed that too weak a national government was just as severe a threat. As they struggled to devise a new set of rules for the national government, the Framers would need to find a way to blend power with liberty, freedom with order, and national authority with state sovereignty.

Crafting the Constitution

America's constitutional structure has held remarkable legitimacy. Although Americans may often be skeptical about the individuals in power, they tend to be proud of their Constitution and the system of government, liberties, and responsibilities it created. Indeed, for many Americans, government in the American form essentially defines democracy. People may be critical of politicians, but they believe that the constitutional system works fairly and effectively. If a system of rules is legitimate, people will agree to challenge policies and actions through constitutionally-established procedures. In its perceived protection for liberty, property, religion, democracy, and equality, the Constitution adheres to beliefs deeply held by most Americans across many diverse groupings, which enhances the esteem in which it is held.

For the most part, this satisfaction is reasonable. The U.S. Constitution is now the oldest national written constitution in the world, and the vast majority of countries have followed the American model of a written constitution. Great Britain is the primary example of an unwritten constitution. The British constitution might be thought of as "an understanding" that has emerged from statutes and traditions. In the United States and other countries with written constitutions, such as Canada, Mexico, France, and Germany, the interpretation of the text might change, but "the constitution" is a well-defined, explicit document. Similarly, the means to amend it is precisely stated, normally requiring a procedure that differs from the one used to pass legislation.

Fashioning a constitution is an exercise in problem-solving that reflects the particular circumstances present at the document's creation. This was no less true for Americans in 1787 than it was for constitution writers in West Germany after World War II or those attempting to construct a constitution in Iraq in 2005. In their problem-solving, the Germans prohibited political parties based on Nazism. The drafters of Iraq's constitution sought ways to give different ethnic and religious groups a stake in the broader sense of nationhood, and to determine the balance between central and regional authority that would be best for governing and most practical for the political task of ratifying the constitution.

Constitutions are complex. The resolution of one problem might well create new problems and unintended consequences. The more detailed and complicated the document, the higher the risk that it may institutionalize ideas that have only passing or temporary allegiance. This criticism has been lodged against state constitutions in the United States. Too thin a framework, however, runs the risk that the document will not be taken seriously as a guide to behavior or a limit on the abuse of power. As they worked on the draft, the Framers of the new American constitution were well aware of these considerations.[14]

There are many ways to think about and categorize the results of the deliberations of the convention. Table 3-1 lists the seven articles of the Constitution. Rather than review the Constitution article by article, however, we will discuss the crafting of the new constitution as an exercise in problem-solving. In particular, the Framers had four major objectives:

- overcoming fundamental disputes over representation in the new government
- encouraging public input while limiting both "excessive" democracy and concentrated power
- protecting commerce and property
- creating legitimacy for the new system.

The Great Compromise and Three-Fifths Compromise resolved fundamental splits over representation.

Two issues facing the delegates absolutely had to be resolved if the convention were to succeed. Both involved the distribution of political power. The delegates' solutions did not guarantee success, but without them, failure was assured.

More so than many of us can understand or appreciate today, the delegates were oriented toward their individual states. Political history, tradition, and loyalty, as they knew it, had much more to do with their colonies, now states, than with the American nation at large. In their view, the creation of the Union was less a union of disparate individuals and more a union of sovereign states.

The name of the new country—the United States—is quite significant in that regard. Indeed, it was not until Abraham Lincoln would try to rebuild the Union in the Civil War that Americans would routinely refer to the "United States" in the singular rather than the plural—"the United States is" rather than "the United States are." We see this conception directly reflected in Article III of the Constitution: "Treason against the United States, shall consist only in levying War against them, or in adhering to their Enemies."

The large state–small state split Given this strong allegiance to the states, the relative influence of the various states in the new system rose immediately as a contentious issue. The first split was the division between large and small states. If

Table 3-1. The Constitution

ARTICLE 1: THE LEGISLATIVE BRANCH
Bicameral legislature
Nature of election
Powers and duties

ARTICLE 2: THE EXECUTIVE BRANCH
Nature of election
Qualifications
Powers and duties

ARTICLE 3: THE JUDICIAL BRANCH
Nature of appointment and tenure
Creation of Supreme Court
Types of cases

ARTICLE 4: NATIONAL UNITY
"Full faith and credit" to acts of other states
All "privileges and immunities" to be same whether or not a state's citizen
Guarantee of republican government
Admitting new states

ARTICLE 5: THE AMENDING PROCESS
Procedures to amend Constitution

ARTICLE 6: NATIONAL SUPREMACY
Constitution to be "supreme law" of the land
No religious test for public office

ARTICLE 7: RATIFICATION PROCESS
Procedure to ratify Constitution

the new system was to be based at least in part on a representative legislature, how would states be represented in that body? Should representation be based on a state's population or should each state have equal representation? The battle lines were predictable. Large states gravitated around the **Virginia Plan** offered by Virginia governor Edmund Randolph.[15] This plan called for state representation in the national legislature to be based on state population: the larger a state's population, the more representatives it would send to the legislature. The so-called lower house would be elected by the people; in turn it would select the members of the upper house, based on lists of candidates provided by state legislatures.

Delegates from small states saw this plan as an unacceptable formula for large-state domination of the new political system. Their response was the **New Jersey Plan**, introduced by William Paterson. Like the Virginia Plan, the New Jersey Plan concerned more than just the issue of representation, but it was on this issue that the two competing visions of the new government were especially divided.[16] The New Jersey Plan called for equal state representation in a single-house legislature. Regardless of a state's population, it would send the same number of representatives to the legislature as any other state.

With the two plans on the table, each side staked out strong stances. If the small states wanted to destroy the union, the large-state delegates opined, then so be it. If the large states wanted to throw their power around, declared the small states, any number of foreign countries would be more than happy to create a new government with the small states. The convention and the task of writing a new constitution faced a deep fracture, but returning to what nearly all concluded was a defunct and ineffective status quo was not a reassuring prospect for either side, so they were open to compromise.

Although sometimes in politics there is an obvious compromise or consensus position when developing rules, policies, or institutions, often this position is not reached until rounds of bargaining and negotiation have been conducted. There may even be a solution no one offered at the outset. With regard to the big state–small state split, the solution came in the form of the Connecticut Plan, also known as the **Great Compromise**. Under this plan, representation in the House of Representatives would be based on population, as the large states preferred, and legislators would be elected by the people. A second legislative body, the Senate, would have equal representation of all the states, as the small states preferred, and be elected by the state legislatures. The idea of a bicameral, or two-house, legislature itself was not new: Great Britain had a House of Commons and House of Lords, and two legislative houses was the norm in the colonies and then in the states.

The vote for the Great Compromise was close: five states voted in favor, four were opposed, two others did not vote, and two more were not in attendance. Although the plan was not entirely satisfactory to either side, it did prevent either group of states from dominating the new system of government. Bicameral arrangements are a common feature of political systems in which power is shared by governments at the national and sub-national levels. As in the Great Compromise model, typically the upper house represents geographical units and the lower house represents "the people."

The slave state–free state split Similar calculations drove the other critical division between political leaders. The split was between states where slavery was forbidden and states where slavery was allowed, which geographically meant a split between northern and southern states, respectively. If representation in the House of Representatives was to be determined by a state's population, how would population be determined? In particular, do slaves count as part of the population? Southern states argued that slaves should count. Delegates from northern states saw this as hypocrisy. Slave states certainly did not consider slaves to be citizens and it was doubtful whether they even considered them persons, northerners charged.

Once again, both sides were concerned with the balance of power in the new legislature. There were more free states than slave states, so the South was disadvantaged in the Senate. And the population of the North exceeded that of the South, so the South faced the prospect of being outvoted in the House also. Southern delegates made it clear that this was a make-or-break issue: either include slaves in the population count, or the convention ends.

A resolution was reached through the **Three-fifths Compromise**. Under this plan, each slave would count as three-fifths of a person in the population count for each state. Sixty percent was chosen not as a philosophical statement, but because this number would balance representation between the North and South in the House. Neither side could dominate the other.[17]

It was clear that the issue of slavery could destroy the convention. On the surface, therefore, it might appear that the delegates avoided the issue, but in reality they were strategically accommodating competing points of view in order to produce a constitution. The Framers were engaged in a huge project that could have failed in many different ways at many different times. To make failure less likely, the Framers engaged in a series of bargains.

Although the terms slave and slavery do not appear in the Constitution, three provisions directly concerned slavery. The first is the Three-fifths Compromise, which boosted Southern representation in the House of Representatives. Second, the Constitution forbade Congress from prohibiting the importation of slaves prior to 1808. And third, any slave escaping to a free state would have to be returned to his or her master. Those who opposed slavery and saw it as a violation of the tenets of the Declaration of Independence were frustrated by these provisions, but they also realized that no new government would be formed if they pressed the issue. Their hope was that the new government would, over time, devise a way to deal with this problem. Bargains in the first half of the nineteenth century gradually confined slavery to the southern states, but they were unable to resolve the issue, which exploded in the calamity of the Civil War.

The Framers wanted public officials to hear the voice of the people but prevent both "excessive" democracy and concentrated power.

The Framers believed that the people should have a voice in government. How should that be accomplished? One option would be to allow the people to rule directly, which is the classic definition of democracy. The Framers had experience with that kind of government, because many municipalities in America did much of their important business in town meetings where citizens directly voted on matters of public policy. Despite that experience, or perhaps because of it, they did not believe that the people's voice should dictate the behavior of public officials. The people's input should influence the decisions of government, they concluded, but there must be a buffer between the people's demands and the government's actions. They feared that a government that was too close to the people would get swept up in the people's passions and impulsive decisions; that government would weaken the rights of the minority, particularly the minority that owned significant amounts of property. To the Framers, those were the risks of democracy. The political system needed to be structured in a way that took account of the people's views, but also allowed for a "cooling off" of those views. At the same time, the people's voice would be impotent if government were weak. Power and authority needed to be both encouraged and restrained.

For these reasons, the Framers did not create a democracy in the technical sense, in which the people themselves directly rule. Rather, they created a **republic**, in which the people select representatives who are entrusted to make the laws.[18] Preventing excessive democracy meant not only protecting government from the people's passions, but also protecting citizens from each other—preventing groups from using government to oppress other groups. The Framers accomplished these goals in several ways.

Selection of public officials The Constitution provided for staggered terms of office for elected officials (Articles I, II). House members would serve two-year terms; senators would serve six-year terms, with one-third of the senators up for election in any given election year; and the president would serve a four-year term. This arrangement means that Americans can never dismiss all government officials at once because all officials are never up for election in the same year. Americans can "clean house" in government, but it is always only a partial cleaning: in any given election year, two-thirds of the senators will not be up for election, while the president will be up for election only every other election year. Regardless of the passions that may be stirring the public, it would take six years before they could completely replace all the elected officials in the national government. And the public has no direct way to choose federal judges. Once nominated by the president and confirmed by the Senate, federal judges—unlike judges in many states—have lifetime tenure and do not face elections. This provision again provides a buffer between the people's voice and the government's actions. And should the people try to change the system to make it more immediately responsive to the people's demands, they would have to work through a process of amending the Constitution that makes change difficult. The Framers did not want the people to be able to easily rewrite the rules. Such a process was not just for the Framers' benefit, however—it reduced the likelihood that one group would amend the Constitution in a manner to reject or restrict the rights of another group.

In the Constitution as ratified, the people directly elected only the members of the House of Representatives. Senators were selected by state legislatures. The people voted for state legislators, and they in turned selected the state's U.S. senators, a process known as **indirect election**. Not until the passage of the Seventeenth Amendment in 1913 would the people directly elect their U.S. senators. Presidents were also elected indirectly in the new constitution. The public in a state voted for electors (in some states, the state legislature selected the electors), and these electors then met in their states in the Electoral College to cast ballots for president and vice president. The candidate who received a majority of the electoral vote would be the president. Even today, although ballots list the presidential candidates, voters are technically voting for a group of electors that have pledged to cast their electoral vote for the particular candidate. The logic was that the people could select the electors, but the electors, presumably individuals who were wise, knowledgeable, and distinguished, would evaluate the presidential candidates more carefully.

Separation of powers The Framers most famously attempted to protect against the effects of excessive democracy with separation of powers and checks and balances. The idea of balancing power was not new. In the colonists' eyes prior to 1763, this had been the defining achievement of British politics and a source of great pride. The colonies, too, relied on the idea of balancing power against power, with legislators checking the power of the governor, who served on the behalf of Britain.

Recall that in the Articles of Confederation, the legislature was the national government, albeit a weak one. By contrast, in the Constitution the Framers provided for three independent centers of authority in a legislature, executive, and judiciary (in Articles I, II, and III, respectively). **Separation of powers** means that the major branches of government would have different primary functions and responsibilities—the legislature would make law; the executive would implement law; and the judiciary would interpret law (see Figure 3-1). The separation would be reinforced by alternative methods of selecting the leadership of each branch—legislators were directly and indirectly elected (House and Senate, respectively); the president was indirectly elected; and judges were appointed. In practice, the divi-

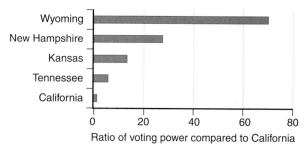

Figure 3-1. Ratio of Residents' Voting Power in U.S. Senate. As a result of the Great Compromise, each state has equal voting power in the Senate. However, because populations differ among states, people who live in states with smaller populations like Wyoming effectively have greater voting power per person than people who live in states with large populations, like California. This chart shows the ratio of state residents' voting power in the Senate, compared to California residents. Equal state representation in the Senate was seen by the Framers as a way to protect the interests of the various states.

sion in functions has not been quite this neat and tidy, so some observers suggest that a better description of separation of powers is "separated institutions sharing powers." Rather than rigid demarcation between branches, this formulation suggests that each institution trespasses somewhat on the jurisdiction of the others.

Checks and balances The system of **checks and balances** provides the main set of mechanisms through which the branches monitor each other. Checks and balances means that each branch of government has a way to affect and, in some instances to stop, the actions of the others. Many of the checks- and-balances techniques are likely familiar; they are listed in Figure 3-2. They reinforce the idea of separated institutions sharing power. Lawmaking, for example, is not the province of Congress alone. The president has to approve any bills before they can become law. And because of legislative bicameralism—Congress is divided into two houses, each of which must approve the same version of a bill before it can be sent to the president for approval—Congress has internal checks and balances. In some areas, notably approval of treaties and confirmation of judges, the Framers wanted the people involved, but only through their indirectly elected representatives in the Senate. Lastly, although the judiciary's power was only thinly described in the Constitution, this branch soon asserted the power of **judicial review**, meaning it would decide whether the laws and other actions of government officials were or were not constitutional. This meant the judiciary could strike down a federal or state law altogether, and overturn non-legislative actions such as a policy or procedure implemented by an executive branch agency. Thus, the judiciary has the power to determine what the text of the Constitution means. As for checks on this branch, Congress and the president can counteract the judiciary's power through constitutional amendments, new appointments to the courts, and restructuring of the courts.

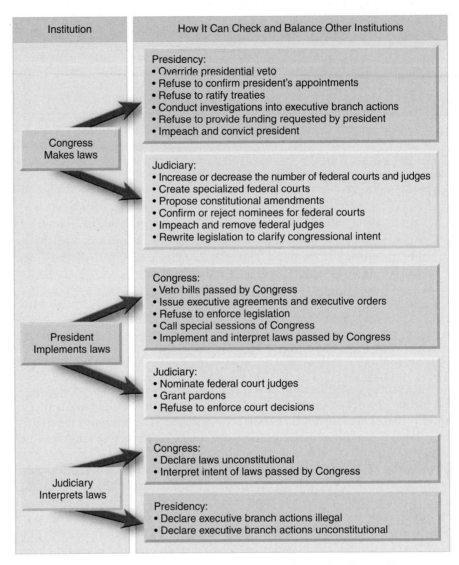

Institution	How It Can Check and Balance Other Institutions
Congress Makes laws	**Presidency:** • Override presidential veto • Refuse to confirm president's appointments • Refuse to ratify treaties • Conduct investigations into executive branch actions • Refuse to provide funding requested by president • Impeach and convict president **Judiciary:** • Increase or decrease the number of federal courts and judges • Create specialized federal courts • Propose constitutional amendments • Confirm or reject nominees for federal courts • Impeach and remove federal judges • Rewrite legislation to clarify congressional intent
President Implements laws	**Congress:** • Veto bills passed by Congress • Issue executive agreements and executive orders • Refuse to enforce legislation • Call special sessions of Congress • Implement and interpret laws passed by Congress **Judiciary:** • Nominate federal court judges • Grant pardons • Refuse to enforce court decisions
Judiciary Interprets laws	**Congress:** • Declare laws unconstitutional • Interpret intent of laws passed by Congress **Presidency:** • Declare executive branch actions illegal • Declare executive branch actions unconstitutional

Figure 3-2. "Separation of Powers" and "Checks and Balances." With separation of powers and checks and balances, each branch of government has distinct but overlapping responsibilities.

There were competing views early in the convention on how to check and balance power. In the Virginia Plan, the president and judiciary, who had been selected by the legislature, would form a Council of Revision that could veto legislative acts. However, the legislature could override those vetoes, and would also have the authority to veto state laws. The New Jersey Plan called for a single-chamber Congress in which each state had one vote. Congress would appoint a multi-person Executive, who would in turn appoint the judiciary. The New Jersey Plan declared that the Constitution and federal laws would supersede state constitutions and laws, but given that state governors were given the power to remove the Executive, this "supremacy" was effectively conditional on the states' acceptance.

Both these plans gave the legislature the strongest position in American government, as Congress selected the members of the other branches. The Framers ultimately did choose to prioritize Congress—it is Article I in the Constitution and the institution with the most detailed list of responsibilities and duties—but they dispersed power and increased the independence of the other branches more than either the Virginia or New Jersey plans.[19] The Framers wanted to make sure that any pressure from the people was heard by government, but that it was diffused across the three branches. If one branch reached too far in pushing a new policy demanded by the people, the other branches could slow it down or stop it altogether. Moreover, the Framers wanted a strong national government, but they also wanted to be sure that it would not become so powerful as to threaten liberty and property. The proposed government was designed to thwart the power-grabbing tendencies of human nature, according to James Madison. "If men were angels, no government would be necessary," he wrote. "If angels were to govern men, neither external nor internal controls on government would be necessary."[20]

The checks and balances system was one aspect of the careful balancing act between government power and personal freedom. Each seemed necessary, yet each could dominate the other. The task of the Framers was to keep the two in balance. As they saw it, disaggregating power this way both protected against abuse of the people by government and made it more difficult for any one part of the public to capture all of the power centers in government. Madison referred to this system, in combination with federalism (described in the following section), as a "double security" against tyrannical government.[21]

Federalism Despite differences concerning the relative power and authority of the national and state governments, delegates agreed that federalism would be an underlying principle of the new system. **Federalism** is a governing arrangement that provides multiple levels of government with independent ruling authority over certain policy areas, and guarantees the survival of these different levels of government. As noted, resolving the distribution of power between the states and the national government was a key practical concern. At the level of principle, however, federalism was a bulwark against the risk of concentrated power and excessive democracy. The states check the power of the national government, but the national government checks the power of the states. We will have much more to say about federalism in Chapter 4 (Federalism).

The parliamentary system as an alternative distribution of power
The choices made by the Constitutional Convention delegates differ significantly from the choices made in later years in other parts of the world. In Europe, especially, the **parliamentary system** was the structure of choice for those constructing governments. In a parliamentary system, the prime minister, who serves as the chief executive, is selected from Parliament (the legislature) by other members. Although voters are usually well aware of the candidates for prime minister, they do not vote on the position nationally or directly. The prime minister then selects department heads from among his fellow partisans in the legislature. Typically in a parliamentary system, the legislature ultimately determines what the constitution means (even if the constitution is unwritten, as in Great Britain). In this system, the legislature is supreme and the notions of checks and balances and separation of powers are not particularly relevant.

Opponents of the parliamentary system charge that it puts too much power in the hands of the majority party. Unlike in the American system, control of the executive branch and the legislature cannot be split between two parties, even if that would be the voters' preference. In the view of these critics, parliamentary systems leave voters who do not support the majority party powerless. Advocates of the parliamentary system respond that it is a government that is not at cross-purposes with itself. Rather than checking and balancing power, parceling power out to different parts of government, having branches of government intentionally frustrate each other and the majority's will, the ideal behind the parliamentary system is to gather power in the leading party in the legislature to enable swift action. The Framers of the American Constitution were wary of giving any entity, including the majority of the population, so much power.

Numerous constitutional provisions were designed to protect commerce and property.

Events in the states in the 1780s, such as Shays's Rebellion and the printing of currency of questionable worth, panicked New England merchants, Southern planters, and the entire spectrum of businesspeople in between. Therefore, one chief concern of the Framers was to protect commerce and property from the designs of the national government, the state governments, and states pitted against states.

Delegates included many provisions in the Constitution to do this. First, they established that the national government would have primary regulatory control over commerce and finance. The national government would regulate commerce between the states and with other countries, be responsible for producing coinage and currency, establishing bankruptcy laws, and creating protections for copyrights and patents (Article I in the Constitution). This arrangement still allowed differences between the states—for example, states could have different insurance or banking regulations—but it prevented states from creating alliances with each other or with another country that harmed the commercial or property interests of citizens in other states. It also prevented states from inflating currency or devising other schemes to make it easy for their citizens to escape from debt obligations.

Second, the Constitution's **supremacy clause** declared that national laws and treaties would have supremacy over state laws and treaties (Article VI). State laws could differ from the national law, but they had to be consistent with it. For example, states can enact anti-pollution laws more stringent than the federal government requires, but not more relaxed. Federal law can, however, preempt the states from deviating from federal standards. For example, the Federal Cigarette Labeling and Advertising Act imposes national rules on cigarette advertising and prohibits state governments from imposing additional advertising regulations.[22]

States were also to be nondiscriminatory toward each other (Article IV). Through the **full faith and credit** clause, states are to honor the official acts of other states, such as public records and the results of judicial proceedings. Under the **equal privileges and immunities** clause, states are to treat their citizens and citizens of other states similarly. Congress and the president can override these provisions if they choose to do so. This happened in 1996 with the passage of the Defense of Marriage Act, which stipulated that states need not honor same-sex marriages performed in other states.

The Constitution included additional protections for commerce and property. Article VI stipulated that any contracts entered into before the Constitution must still be honored after the Constitution was ratified: the adoption of a new political system did not negate ongoing economic commitments. This provision was motivated chiefly by concern that debts incurred during the Revolutionary War be paid, but it applied to debts incurred after the war also. The national government also guaranteed each state a republican—that is, representative—form of government and pledged to protect the states against domestic violence, a reaction to Shays's Rebellion. Lastly, the Framers provided for a president who would be a counterweight to Congress. As the Framers saw it, representatives would often allow the narrow interests of their districts to guide their decisions, while senators would have the somewhat broader but still biased self-interests of their states in mind. Only the president would represent the country as a whole and have an ongoing commitment to the national interest rather than to any special interest of a state or district.

Certain measures and principles were emphasized to enhance the proposed system's legitimacy.

Legitimacy is about trust. When you believe that an arrangement is legitimate, you believe it is fair and reasonable. You may not trust individual officials, but you trust the system. Americans had come to see the British government, or at least its control over the colonies, as illegitimate. The idea that the colonies were "virtually represented" though not actually directly represented in Parliament struck many Americans as folly. Americans then placed their trust in the new governmental system of the Articles of Confederation, but many saw that, too, as a failure. To the Framers, establishing legitimacy for the new government was critical, and they addressed the challenge in three ways.

First, they emphasized the representativeness of the new government. In the House, Senate, and presidency, they noted, distinct parts of society were represented—parts of states, states, and the country, respectively. Direct popular election of the House of Representatives was another legitimacy-building feature. The House would be the "people's house." Its members would have shorter terms than any other part of government, giving the people frequent input into its composition. And because of the system of checks and balances, relatively little could be done that did not have to pass through the people's House.

Second, the Framers built the case for legitimacy around the notion that the new government would not be dominating. It would have more power than under the Articles, but constrained power. The checks-and-balances system would prevent government from acting recklessly. With its concept of federalism, the Constitution delegated specific powers to the federal government and left others to the states. Public officials would take the Constitution seriously. Article VI required public officials to swear to uphold the Constitution—not the wishes of a monarch, church, or select group. The Constitution, the Framers noted, was a "social contract" between rulers and ruled (see Chapter 1 for more on the social contract). If the rulers violated this contract, the people had a right to remove them, and if the violations were extensive, the people had a right to scrap the contract and construct a new system of government. Further, the Framers promised that a "bill of rights" guaranteeing personal liberties would be added to the Constitution as the first order of business after ratification.

Third, they created an enduring but flexible framework for government. They wanted the people to believe that the Constitution had roots—that its meaning and content would have some stability—but they also wanted the people to believe that the system could be changed if necessary. By providing for amendments, the Framers created a document that would be flexible. By making the amending process difficult, they created a document that would be enduring. We discuss the amendment process in detail below.

Balancing stability and flexibility was also achieved by writing a Constitution that provided a basic framework for government and politics. The Constitution lays down the essential rules of how government will work and how officials will be selected. It also indicates the responsibilities of government officials. It presents a general outline for how public policy will be made, but it contains very little actual policy.

For example, it gives Congress the power to regulate interstate commerce, declare war, and establish currency, but it does not set in stone any particular policy about interstate commerce or when declarations of war should and should not occur. Nothing in the Constitution states how much should be spent on national defense, how many roads should be built, and so on. The Framers left that kind of detail to the branches of government to work out in the form of laws. They realized that preferences about particular issues would change over time, so enshrining them in the Constitution would be problematic in two respects. If the Constitution were difficult to change, citizens would be stuck with policies they no longer agreed with. If the Constitution were made easy to change, it would lose the sense that it had permanency and was above competitive politics.

The Civil War provides the most glaring exception to the rule that Americans believe their political differences can be worked out through constitutional provisions. The Constitution could not contain the depth of division between North and South. And for much of American history the Constitution was seen as compatible with discrimination of the rankest sort against racial, ethnic, and religious minorities and women. Americans today, however, are more likely to fault the people and the politicians in power during those times rather than the Constitution itself, because the Constitution also provided the means to change these patterns.

The Battle for Ratification

Sending the Constitution to the states for ratification was a risky gambit. The Framers could not look to other countries to see how a national ratification effort would fare, or what the risks and rewards were of giving the people this much influence. The experience of other countries in later years shows just how risky it was. In France, popular ratification failed in 1789, 1791, 1793, and 1830. Canadian leaders chose not to risk a popular ratification process for its constitution. Britain's unwritten constitution was similarly not subject to a ratification process. Among English-speaking countries, only Australia followed the U.S. ratification model, more than a century later.[23] In the American context, however, supporters of the Constitution believed that ratification in the states was a political necessity. It was also, they realized, an opportunity for opponents to derail the document.

Battle lines over ratification of the Constitution were drawn between the **Federalists**, who supported ratification, and the **Antifederalists**, who opposed it.[24] Problems with the Articles of Confederation were evident, but this did not necessarily mean everyone agreed that the proposed Constitution was the best solution to the crisis. The central debate concerned not democracy, which might be the center-stage issue today, but liberty: What kind of governmental arrangement would best preserve liberty? See How Do We Know? What Motivated the Framers of the Constitution? for analysis of how political scientists have examined the Framers' motivations.

Antifederalists argued that the Constitution threatened liberty.

Antifederalists argued that the proposed Constitution was a direct threat to the people's liberty because it established a centralized national government that would be distant from the people. This kind of government might begin to tax heavily, override state court decisions, have a permanent army at its disposal, or absorb functions performed by the states. Legendary patriots such as Patrick Henry, a stalwart supporter of the Revolution, saw the proposed Constitution as a counterrevolution, pushing back toward more central authority, reducing democratic influence on government, and protecting the interests of political and economic leaders.

To the Antifederalists, a different kind of government was needed. Their ideal was, like in the New Jersey Plan, a government more along the lines of the one established by the Articles of Confederation. The loose union of states that characterized the Articles was the ideal arrangement to protect liberty—the central government's powers were so limited, it lacked the means to restrict liberty, even if public officials were so inclined.[25]

Given the public's apparent preference for a stronger national government, the Antifederalists offered some principles to guide its development. They argued that such a government should have many restrictions on its power. For example, they suggested reducing the range of cases the Supreme Court could hear; creating a council to review all presidential decisions; leaving military affairs to state militias; enlarging the House of Representatives, which would mean creating smaller districts so that representatives would feel more closely bound to their constituents; and adding a Bill of Rights to protect individual freedoms.

Only on this last item were the Antifederalists successful. Supporters of the Constitution initially argued that a Bill of Rights was unnecessary—unless the Constitution gave Congress the right, for example, to establish an official religion, then government should not be presumed to have that right. And a listing of rights or liberties could become effectively a limitation on rights and liberties if misinterpreted as a comprehensive list or a list of the truly important rights. In the climate of the ratification debate, however, a strong symbolic statement was needed, so the proponents of ratification agreed to a Bill of Rights. They did not want to send the document to states and have states begin revising it. They knew their best chance of success would be if states were forced to make an up-or-down vote—this document or nothing. Agreeing to offer the Bill of Rights in the future was a way to close off revision of the Constitution during the ratification process, but it opened up the risk that other pre-ratification concessions might be demanded by the Constitution's opponents. As ultimately ratified by the states, the **Bill of Rights** refers to the first ten amendments to the Constitution, which focus on preserving individual freedoms.

Madison responded that a large republic is the best defense for liberty.

The argument between Federalists and Antifederalists was fought out in speeches, handbills, and newspaper columns. The most famous of all these was a set of newspaper opinion columns penned under a pseudonym by James Madison, Alexander Hamilton, and John Jay. Collectively, these columns would come to be called the Federalist Papers. These columns discussed the many nuances of the proposed government. They presented the theoretical basis of American government, discussing such concepts as federalism, the separation of powers, and checks and balances. Although it is unlikely that the columns were widely read, those who did read them were likely to be opinion leaders—individuals who, because of their status, could shape the opinions of others.

The Antifederalist argument about the desirability of democracies and small republics was rejected in the most famous of the Federalist Papers, number 10. In Federalist 10, James Madison argued that liberty is actually most at risk in direct democracies and small republics. It is safest in precisely the kind of large republic being proposed in the Constitution.

Madison begins by stating that the most severe threat to liberty is the presence of factions. To Madison, factions are defined by having some self-interest or common passion that threatens the rights of other citizens, and they can be either a majority or minority of the population. Factions are natural, Madison argues, as people naturally cluster with like-minded individuals. Trying to prevent the emergence of factions would require authoritarian and conformist measures that would be a "cure worse than the disease." The real question, therefore, is how to control factions and their effects, especially, for Madison, their effects on property rights.

Could democracy cure the effects of factions? Madison says no. In a democracy, a majority faction has no check on its behavior—it would be quite easy for a majority of the population to deny rights or otherwise oppress a minority.

The proposed republic, on the other hand, could control excessive factional influence. First, in Madison's view, having a relatively small number of representatives increases the likelihood that voters are selecting individuals of honor, merit, and virtue for public office. Second, larger, more diverse districts will send mixed policy messages to representatives, encouraging them to sift out the bad ideas and keep the good. Representatives with large districts are less likely to be "captured" by any one interest, because they will try to represent a broader cross-section of their constituency. Third, in a geographically large political system, more opposing interests will be vying for attention, and as interest battles interest, a majority faction is less likely to form. Madison thought it unlikely that the same dangerous idea would arise in far-flung parts of the country, and if it did, it would be difficult logistically to organize a majority faction over a large area, which again protects liberty.

The bottom line of Madison's argument was a remarkable rejection of the conventional wisdom of his day. Rather than holding onto communitarian hopes about civic virtue—selfless political participants concerned only for the common welfare—Madison suggested the country allow self-interest to serve public ends. Each individual's self-interest, he reasoned, gives that person an incentive to ensure that other individuals do not abuse power, thus producing precisely the best outcome for society. Madison took this argument one step further in Federalist 51, where he noted that governmental power would be distributed across the national and state governments and across the three major branches of government, whose officials would challenge each other and thus prevent the monopolization of power.

Today's easy geographical mobility and ubiquitous high-technology communications might be seen as a threat to the Madisonian vision. Individuals anywhere in the United States can communicate with others rapidly and frequently. Pressure can be placed on members of Congress very quickly. National political figures—politicians, media commentators, interest group leaders—can build followings and organizations that are truly national in scope. On the other hand, as Madison noted, power remains dispersed across branches and levels of government, which may not be equally responsive to public desires. And as Madison also noted, the more interests that are brought into politics, the more likely it is that other interests will seek to participate, reducing the likelihood of any interest having a monopoly on what legislators hear. The relationship between the people and government is much tighter and potentially more immediate today than Madison would likely recommend, but on the whole his vision about parceling out power remains compelling.

Belief that change was necessary assisted the Federalists' ratification campaign.

Citizens in the states voted for delegates to attend state ratifying conventions. Nine states needed to approve the Constitution for it to be in effect. The first state to ratify was Delaware, in December 1787. Seven months later, when New Hampshire became the ninth state to approve, the Constitution was ratified. In eight states, the Constitution received the support of at least 65 percent of the delegates. In the remaining five states, support ran from about 51 to 55 percent. One state, North Carolina, had originally voted against the Constitution but voted to support it after the Constitution had been ratified.

In the end, the Federalists won the debate. The main causes are straightforward. In part, this victory appears due to the Federalist arguments being more convincing. In part, it owes to the absence of a comprehensive Antifederalist alternative. Many who voted for the Constitution might well have shared some of the Antifederalists' fears about a strong central government, but they also feared domestic disturbances and foreign threats.[26] The foreign threats were significant. Britain controlled the territory around the Great Lakes, while Spain controlled Florida and areas to the west. Skirmishes with Native American tribes were frequent. The Constitution provided the promise of executive and legislative leadership and coordination to respond to these challenges. At bottom, the decision became whether to adopt the Constitution, stick with the Articles, or start over again. Given the sense that the young country faced both foreign and domestic challenges, the appeal of continuing with the Articles or renewing the debate was limited. Change was needed, most people believed, and the Constitution provided that change. The Constitution was also politically attractive because it incorporated the beliefs of the American creed. Liberty, religious freedom, property, and democracy were the focus of many constitutional rules and principles. And although the historical reality would often prove glaringly different, underlying many of these constitutional principles were the belief in individual opportunity and the value of equality.

What Motivated the Framers of the Constitution?

The Question

The men sent to the Constitutional Convention in Philadelphia in 1787 had risen to prominence in their respective states. Overall, however, the U.S. Constitution reduced the autonomy of the states. For political scientists, this raises a research puzzle: why would ambitious, intelligent political leaders agree to a system that might reduce the power of the states in which they had been politically influential? What motivated the Framers of the Constitution? How do we know?

Why It Matters

Why should anyone care what motivated the Framers of the Constitution so long ago? The reason is simple: if Americans wish to know whether contemporary American politics and government live up to founding ideals, they must know why the system was designed the way it is.

Investigating the Answer

One answer, offered by economist Charles Beard early in the twentieth century, is that the Constitution reflected the economic self-interest of those drafting and voting for it.[27] Beard complained that previous accounts of the Constitution had been based on ideals and wishful thinking. He called for social scientists to conduct hardheaded, systematic analyses of the world as it was. Politics, including the writing of the Constitution, was about the political will, conflict, and interests of people or groups of people in power.

Beard wanted to explain the votes of delegates at the Constitutional Convention. Assuming that political action is guided by self-interest, Beard hypothesized that delegates' financial self-interest determined how they voted on the Constitution. By analyzing the financial holdings and economic interests of the delegates, he concluded that the Framers protected their commercial interests, including currency, public securities, manufacturing, and trade and shipping. Opponents in the convention, he argued, were also influenced by their self-interest, and were mostly farmers who had land holdings, those without property, and those in debt. Knowing the economic interests of those who supported or opposed the document, he argues, reveals the motivations of the document's writers. He did not suggest the Framers should be indicted on this account, however. If it had not been one group's interests that were primarily served with the crafting of the document, it would have been another's.[28]

Beard's critics offer a different answer to the question about the Framers' motivations, and a different approach to political investigation. They took more interest in the convention delegates' ideas and rhetoric. They saw the Framers' actions as grounded more in their practical political assessment of what was necessary to keep the country united and afloat, or in their sincere interest in the political ideals they were espousing.[29] To the critics, Beard mistakenly assumed that correlation equals causation: the fact that delegates' financial self-interest and their votes in the convention were correlated did not prove that the interests caused the votes.

Having also analyzed the delegates' financial interests, the critics pointed out that Beard did a poor job of identifying them. Reanalysis of Beard's data showed that the delegates in favor of the Constitution also had substantial land ownership, which was a prime characteristic Beard identified among the opponents. In fact, those favoring the Constitution had more land ownership than ownership of commercial interests.[30] If landholders had a self-interest in opposing the Constitution, then even the supporters of the Constitution should have opposed it because they had a larger financial stake in land than in commerce.

Beard may have been too quick to leap from correlation to causation. But by assuming that the ideals of those who supported the Constitution were unified and that therefore their motives were the same, the critics may also have erred. For example, James Madison and Alexander Hamilton wrote the bulk of *The Federalist Papers*, but within a few years it was clear that their political ideologies were radically different.[31] They may have both supported the Constitution, but their motivations were likely not identical.

Rather than looking at a political outcome and then assuming that the result reflects some group's motives, political scientists can look to the historical record—memoirs, journals, interviews, and other sources—to determine what drove individuals to take particular actions. Individuals may not be completely aware of or candid about their motivations, but this approach can reveal important insights. In a study of the crafting of the Constitution, for example, one political scientist concluded that the final document was a defeat for some of its most ardent proponents, such as Madison.[32] The most successful bloc in the convention sought to preserve the states' autonomy within an environment of international and domestic uncertainty that was leading many to call for a strong national government. Throughout the convention, Madison unsuccessfully pushed for a more powerful national government than created in the final document. Careful analysis of the day-by-day proceedings shows Madison to be frequently on the defensive. Rather than Madison's rhetoric in the *Federalist Papers* being a completely clear signal of his true preferences, he shaped his argument around the Constitution that was approved by the convention.

Such analysis highlights the importance of sequence and timing in explaining political outcomes. Early decisions, even small decisions, can have tremendous impact because they begin a process that influences future decisions. Once the delegates decided on an elected presidency, for example, that decision affected their votes on other aspects of the Constitution, and rethinking that decision would have been very difficult because everything else afterward depended on it. Some decisions become "locked in" and shape future decisions. The document was created by a series of decisions. This sequence produced a document much more deferential toward the states than Madison and many others wanted. Scholars have also shown that the voting rules at the convention—each state's delegation would cast a single vote—gave disproportionate influence to certain delegates. A different set of rules where, for example, each delegate voted individually, would have likely produced a different Constitution.[33] And yet, after the Constitutional Convention sent the document to the states for ratification, Madison strongly supported the document, and scholars ever since, influenced by that strong support, have inaccurately seen the Constitution as a victory for him.

The Framers of the Constitution were motivated by a number of factors, including political ideals and principles, a belief that the status quo was unacceptable, concerns about what would be politically palatable to the states, and likely some political and economic self-interest as well. But simply correlating the convention votes with economic self-interests and assuming that this was the primary motivation behind the Constitution is faulty social science. In political analysis, it is important to consider multiple causal factors and to realize that the sequence and timing of decisions, as well as the rules for making decisions, affect the outcome. These factors can even lead an individual to support something he or she believes falls short. Just as Madison vigorously supported a document that did not entirely reflect his preferences, a president must sometimes sign legislation that does not reflect his or hers.

The Bottom Line

Amending the Constitution

The structure of the constitutional system sometimes frustrates Americans. Features usually thought of as strengths can sometimes be seen as negatives. The separation of powers and checks and balances can be seen as protectors of liberty, but they can also slow government responses to important national problems. The American system is designed for the cautious use of power, consistent with the American creed, but Americans often get upset when government does not act. Federalism allows for diversity and innovation, but it can frustrate those who believe that national standards in some area are necessary. Thus, the structure of the Constitution can lead to some frustration, but on the whole this frustration is outweighed by a belief among Americans that the system works.

Part of the process of establishing legitimacy for the Constitution, however, was providing a procedure by which it could be revised. With the Constitution established as a broad framework for government, the Framers were free to create amending procedures that were difficult but not impossible. The underlying premise of the Constitution's amendment process is that any change in the Constitution has to have broad consensus throughout society. The consensus required is not as extensive as that in the Articles of Confederation, however, which required the congressional representatives of every state to agree to any proposed change.

Amendments should have broad societal acceptance.

The introduction of amendments is essentially a national-level process, while the ratification of amendments is a state-level process (see Figure 3-3). Moreover, supermajorities are a requirement of all four paths to amendment. Amendments will not be added to the Constitution unless they receive supermajority support at two stages; three stages, if we consider that a proposed amendment must have supermajority support separately in the House and in the Senate. (The president

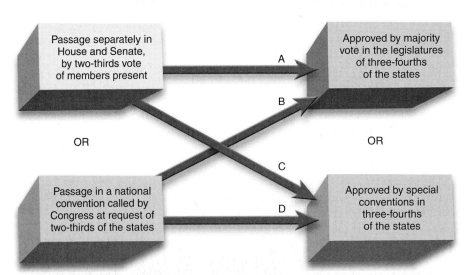

Figure 3-3. Paths to Amending the Constitution. The amending process is based on supermajorities at both the proposal and ratification stages.

Note: Congress chooses which path is used. Path A: Used for 26 Amendments. Path B: Never used. Path C: Used for one amendment (21st). Path D: Never used.

has no formal role in the amending process.) The premise that amendments should have broad social acceptance is therefore built into the process, and the degree of acceptance is often a chief point of debate, as in the discussion of a proposed amendment banning same-sex marriage.[34]

In the two paths used for the introduction of all amendments to date (paths A and C in Figure 3-3), it is not enough to get the support of just over half the members of Congress, a "simple majority." Rather, two-thirds of the members of the House and two-thirds of the members of the Senate who are present and voting are needed to approve a proposed constitutional amendment. Echoing the Great Compromise, the process in paths A and C ensures that two-thirds of the representatives of the entire population—House members—must agree to the amendment, as well as two-thirds of the representatives of the states—U.S. senators.

The constitutional rules for introduction of an amendment using paths B and D are less clear, as this method has never been used. The Constitution does not indicate whether or not votes at a national convention would need to be supermajorities. Most likely, given that the Constitution gives Congress the power to call the convention if two-thirds of the states request it, Congress would set the rules for how the convention would be run. Some observers worry that a convention could become a "runaway convention," proposing amendments on any number of issues. The Constitution seems to imply that Congress could prevent this possibility by establishing ground rules for the convention.

At the ratification level, we again see the Framers' desire that constitutional changes have broad societal acceptance. Three-quarters of the states, or 38 today, either in the state legislature or specially convened state conventions, are needed to ratify an approved amendment. Table 3-2 lists all the constitutional amendments that passed Congress but did not receive the necessary support in the states. Table 3-3 lists potential amendments since 1980 that had supermajority support in at least one house of Congress but foundered in the other house or in the states. Just as few amendments have been added to the Constitution, few have made it through Congress and then foundered in the states. This makes sense if we assume that Congress would be unlikely to approve a proposed amendment that seemed to lack sufficient support in the states to be ratified. On some occasions, however, initial supportive conditions can deteriorate as opponents mobilize against the proposal. After a rapid string of state ratifications, the proposed Equal Rights Amendment (ERA) in the 1970s proved susceptible to the arguments of opponents in some states that its implications were vague and its interpretation so uncertain that extensive litigation would be a likely result.[35] Opponents thwarted societal consensus enough to prevent its ratification. What looked like a relatively easy victory at the outset turned into defeat.

Table 3-2. Proposed Amendments Rejected by the States

AMENDMENT	YEAR APPROVED BY CONGRESS
Regulate size of House	1789
U.S. citizens cannot accept titles of nobility	1810
Prohibit any amendments that would interfere with slavery	1861
Give Congress power to limit child labor	1926
Equal rights of men and women	1972
Grant District of Columbia residents full voting rights	1978

Note: Years indicate when these proposed amendments passed the second house of Congress.

Table 3-3. Failed Attempts to Amend the Constitution Since 1980

AMENDMENT	YEAR
Equal Rights Amendment*	1982
No right to abortion	1983
School prayer allowable	1984
District of Columbia voting representation*	1985
Term limits for Congress	1995
Prohibit flag "desecration"	1995, 2006
Require supermajority to increase taxes	1996
Require balanced budget (multiple attempts)	1982–97

*Amendment was rejected by the states. In all other cases, amendment passed one house of Congress only.

Congress has the responsibility to decide which ratification path a proposed amendment will take. Congress also determines whether proposed amendments have any time limits attached to their ratification. The most recent amendment, the Twenty-seventh, was actually introduced at the same time as the Bill of Rights but did not gather enough state support to be ratified—mostly because it had been forgotten—until 1992. This amendment states that a congressional pay raise cannot take effect until after the next election. On the other hand, the ERA fell just short of receiving the support of three-fourths of the states and died with the expiration of its 10-year time limit, which Congress had already extended from the original 7 years.

CaseStudy: Lowering the Voting Age to 18

The uniform adoption of an 18-year-old voting age across the United States was accomplished through the ratification of the Twenty-sixth Amendment in 1971. A handful of states had lowered their voting age before this, at least for some elections. Most states, however, still had 21 as the legal age for voting entering the 1970s. This was consistent with the societal consensus that 21 was the age of maturity. This consensus would need to shift to lower the voting age.[36]

War provided one key catalyst to changing thoughts about the age of maturity. Eighteen-to twenty-year-olds were dying in the Vietnam War in large numbers, but did not have the right to vote. Similar pressure had arisen following previous wars. During World War II, Republican Senator Arthur Vandenberg joined Democratic Representative Randolph Jennings to introduce a constitutional amendment in 1942 to lower the voting age. Large numbers of the military forces were not of voting age—one-half of the Marines, one-third of the Navy, and one-quarter of the Army. The proposal, however, did not make it out of committee. Only one state, Georgia, lowered its voting age during World War II.

Some organizations continued the pressure after World War II. The National Education Association argued that the national increase in high-school graduates suggested that 18-year-olds were more ready to assume the duties of citizenship than ever before. Veterans' organizations like the American Legion and youth organizations also argued for the change. Primarily, these groups focused their energy on changing state laws rather than a national constitutional amendment. Only Alaska, Hawaii, and Kentucky agreed to lower the age to vote.

At the national level, Republican President Dwight Eisenhower, who had a long military history, supported the idea of a constitutional amendment in 1954, right on the heels of the Korean War. Some prominent legislators, including future Democratic Vice President Hubert Humphrey, agreed with Eisenhower.

Although by this time a majority of Americans favored a lower voting age, the voting age amendment went nowhere. In part, this was because the support was not overwhelming, and many Americans saw the ages of 18–20 as those of rebellion, uncertainty, and susceptibility to emotional appeals and rabble rousing rather than sober and thoughtful citizenship. In addition, it was not a strongly felt issue for most Americans who believed the voting age should be lowered, and most legislators who supported the idea also had higher-priority concerns.

Vietnam changed everything. Unlike the previous conflicts, this one became tremendously controversial and highly unpopular among large, though not always majority, parts of the population. It was especially unpopular among younger Americans, at least in part because of the military draft. Youth protested in unconventional ways rather than through the ballot box, because they could not vote. The contradiction between eligibility for military service and ineligibility to vote was more pronounced, at least symbolically, under these circumstances. States began to reconsider their laws and support grew again at the national level for an amendment. In addition to the organizations that had supported the idea for decades, a number of the youth organizations that emerged during the war pressed for the 18-year-old vote, as did labor unions, some church groups, and organizations linked to the civil rights movement. The societal consensus for an 18-year-old voting age had grown.

The path to an amendment was accelerated in 1970, with the addition of a provision in the Senate's renewal of the Voting Rights Act (originally passed in 1965) that lowered the age for all elections to 18. Although many members of the House suspected the provision was unconstitutional, they agreed to it so that the renewal of the Voting Rights Act would not be derailed. President Nixon, similarly skeptical about the provision's constitutionality, nonetheless signed the bill.

A challenge to the provision quickly reached the Supreme Court. Four members of the Court believed the provision was constitutional, and that Congress could legislate the voting age for all elections. Four others argued that it was up to the states to decide the voting age for all elections. The final justice, Hugo Black, concluded that Congress could set the age for federal elections but not state elections. Therefore, the country was now faced with an 18-year-old voting age for federal elections (president, U.S. House, U.S. Senate) and whatever age each state set for its own elections.[37]

This scenario promised a very difficult election in 1972. Many states would have to monitor different voting ages for different parts of the ballot. Even if they wanted to change their voting age to 18, in many states that change required voter approval of a proposed state constitutional amendment at two subsequent elections. The national consensus was now nearly complete that lowering the voting age uniformly was right, whether on policy grounds or because of the horrors facing election administration without a uniform age.

Congress moved quickly. Within a month of the Supreme Court decision, Randolph Jennings, who had proposed the first constitutional amendment on the issue in 1942, introduced another constitutional amendment to lower the voting age. The amendment was approved unanimously in the Senate, with fewer than twenty dissenting votes in the House, and sent to the states for ratification. The amendment needed quick passage to be in effect for 1972. In the states, ratification was accomplished in record time. A little over three months after being sent to the states, the Twenty-sixth Amendment had been ratified and added to the Constitution.

The quick response across the states marks this amendment as unusual—ratification looked much the same in every state. In the importance of causal factors such as societal consensus, interest-group pressure, and politicians who believed in the proposal for reasons of good policy or electoral advantage, or both, however, the story of the Twenty-sixth Amendment looks like those of other successful amendments.[38]

ThinkingCritically

1. Some activists have proposed that the voting age be lowered to 16. What criteria would you use to decide if this is a good idea?

2. In your view, what are the valid reasons, if any, to deny someone the ability to vote?

3. War was a key causal factor in lowering the voting age to 18. Should we generally expect war to lead to social change or instead to preserve the status quo?

Twenty-seven amendments have been added to the Constitution.

The proof that the federal amending process is difficult is in the numbers. Since 1789, over 10,000 proposals for constitutional amendments have been introduced in Congress. Of these, only 27 have been ratified. Ten were ratified almost immediately, as part of the Bill of Rights. Since 1791, there have been only 17 amendments added to the Constitution, less than one per decade on average. In practice, the country can go long periods without any amendments—over sixty years elapsed between the Twelfth and Thirteenth Amendments, and over forty between the Fifteenth and Sixteenth Amendments—and then have a number of amendments over a short period. Between 1961 and 1971, four amendments were added to the Constitution.[39]

As Table 3-4 shows, amendments have followed the logic of the articles of the Constitution, emphasizing the basic framework of government, the powers of government, the size of the electorate, and the relationship between people and government. The amendments have generally not dealt with matters of social or economic policy, with three exceptions: the elimination of slavery, the approval of a federal income tax, and the prohibition—and then repeal of the prohibition—of alcohol production and sales. Slavery and taxation were issues addressed in the Constitution, implicitly and explicitly, respectively, so these amendments did not address new areas. The failure of Prohibition is often considered a prime example why specific social policy should not be included in the Constitution.[40]

Table 3-4. Amendments to the Constitution

AMENDMENT	PURPOSE	YEAR ADOPTED
	Relationship of People and Government	
1st	Freedom of religion, speech, press, assembly, petition	1791
2nd	Right of people to keep arms	1791
3rd	No housing of militia without due process	1791
4th	Restrictions on search and seizure	1791
5th–8th	Rights in judicial proceedings	1791
9th–10th	Non-enumerated rights reserved to the states or people	1791
13th	Slavery prohibited	1865
14th	Civil liberties and civil rights protections extended to states	1865
	Government Structure	
12th	Changes in Electoral College process	1804
17th	Direct election of U.S. senators	1913
20th	Starting dates for terms; procedure when president-elect dies	1933
22nd	Presidents limited to two terms	1951
25th	Succession in cases of president's death or disability	1967
27th	Congressional pay raises require intervening election	1992
	Size of the Electorate	
15th	Extend voting rights to all races	1870
19th	Extend voting rights to women	1920
23rd	Extend voting rights to residents of District of Columbia	1961
24th	Eliminate payment of "poll tax" as requirement to vote	1964
26th	Extend voting rights to citizens 18 years of age and over	1971
	Powers of Government	
11th	Restricts federal courts role in cases involving states	1795
16th	National income tax	1913
18th	Prohibition of sale, manufacture, and transportation of intoxicating liquor	1919
21st	Repeal of 18th Amendment	1933

The Constitution can be "amended" through judicial interpretation.

Although the amending process does provide some flexibility to the Constitution that enhances system legitimacy, it is, as we have seen, infrequently successful, and the country can go long periods without any formal change to the Constitution. The formal amending process, however, is not the only means of constitutional change: interpretation of the Constitution can also lead to change.

When the Supreme Court interprets what the Constitution means, it can change the meaning of the Constitution. In the Plessy v. Ferguson decision of 1896, for example, the Supreme Court declared that racial segregation was legally permissible under the Constitution. Nearly sixty years later, however, in the Brown v. Board of Education decision, the Court concluded precisely the opposite. The language of the Constitution had not changed in the meantime with regard to this issue, yet the Court, with different members, in a different time, read the meaning of the Constitution differently.

Think of the formal amending process as producing "hard amendments" to the Constitution: they actually change the text of the document. Constitutional interpretation as performed by the courts produces what might be considered "soft amendments": the constitutional text remains the same, but the meaning of that text is read differently. To some observers of American politics, this practice creates the risk of allowing judges to insert their policy preferences into the Constitution, by decreeing the Constitution requires or prohibits something that had previously been left to elected officials to decide. In this view, far too much power is placed in the hands of unelected federal judges, rather than the elected officials who would have to pass constitutional amendments. On the other hand, soft amendments undeniably provide additional adaptability to the system, which was a goal of the Framers. Most likely, it would have proved impossible to pass a constitutional amendment between 1896 and 1954 stating that segregation was unconstitutional, but through a change in interpretation, the Constitution was, in effect, amended.

SUMMARY

▶ Although scholars still debate the causes and effects of the American Revolution, we can safely say that ideas about liberty and democracy were prominent rallying cries of the colonists. After a series of acts by the British government led to support for independence, the Americans turned their attention to building a structure of governance. The first attempt at a constitution, the Articles of Confederation, proved to be insufficient in building a national government with sufficient power and authority over the states.

▶ Convinced that the Articles were defective, and disillusioned with what they considered "mobocracy," the states sent delegates to Philadelphia to revise the document. The delegates soon concluded that the Articles needed to be replaced. As they wrote a new constitution, the Framers sought to meld power, liberty, freedom, order, national authority, and state sovereignty. They focused on resolving four problems: overcoming fundamental disputes on representation in the new government; allowing for public input while limiting "excessive" democracy and concentrated power through election procedures, separation of powers, checks and balances, and federalism; protecting commerce and property; and creating legitimacy by constructing an adaptable but stable governing framework.

▶ The Constitution went to the states for ratification. The battle lines were drawn between the Federalists and the Antifederalists. The Antifederalists favored a system closer to that provided by the Articles of Confederation—a loose union of the states in which the national government was clearly subordinate. At the very least, they wanted a national government that was very close to the people and had many checks on its power. The Federalists argued that the best protection for liberty would be a stronger national government, a large republic rather than a small democracy, and a system with some distance between the people and government power, so that any "passions" that swept through the population would not immediately find their way into law.

► The amending process involves two stages: the introduction or proposal of an amendment, which happens at the national level, and the ratification of a proposed amendment, which happens at the state level. Through this two-level process, and through the use of supermajorities in Congress and the states, the Framers hoped to ensure that only those amendments with broad societal approval would be added to the Constitution. To date, only 27 out of more than 10,000 amendments proposed have made it through both levels of the amending process. The Constitution does not change only when the text is changed, however. When judges interpret the Constitution, they give it specific meaning. And when those interpretations change, the meaning of the Constitution changes also, even though the text remains unchanged.

KEY TERMS

Antifederalists, p. 68
Articles of Confederation, p. 55
Bill of Rights, p. 69
checks and balances, p. 63
Declaration of Independence, p. 54
equal privileges and immunities, p. 66
federalism, p. 64
Federalists, p. 68
full faith and credit, p. 66
Great Compromise, p. 60
indirect election, p. 62

judicial review, p. 64
nation, p. 55
New Jersey Plan, p. 59
parliamentary system, p. 65
republic, p. 61
separation of powers, p. 62
Shays's Rebellion, p. 56
supremacy clause, p. 66
Three-fifths Compromise, p. 60
Virginia Plan, p. 59

SUGGESTED READINGS

Catherine Drinker Bowen. Miracle at Philadelphia: The Story of the Constitutional Convention. Boston: Little, Brown. 1966. A popular and easy-to-read account of the events prior to the Constitutional Convention and the competing ideas and individuals at the convention.

Robert A. Dahl. How Democratic Is the American Constitution? New Haven: Yale University Press. 2002. A comparison of the U.S. Constitution to others around the world.

James A. Gardner. Interpreting State Constitutions: A Jurisprudence of Function in a Federal System. Chicago: University of Chicago Press. 2005. A sophisticated analysis of the place of state constitutions within the national constitutional framework.

Alexander Hamilton, John Jay, and James Madison. The Federalist Papers. 1787–88, any edition. Considered by many political scientists to still be the single best distillation of American political philosophy, The Federalist Papers presented arguments in favor of the proposed Constitution.

Merrill Jensen. The Articles of Confederation: An Interpretation of the Social-Constitutional History of the American Revolution, 1774–1781. Madison: University of Wisconsin Press. 1959. A lively review of the political and economic factions among the colonists as they debated independence from Great Britain and the form of the new American government.

Edmund S. Morgan. The Birth of the Republic: 1763–89. Chicago: University of Chicago Press. 1992. A classic overview of the separation from Great Britain and the struggles to build a national government following independence.

David Brian Robertson. The Constitution and America's Destiny. New York: Cambridge University Press. 2005. An account of the Constitutional Convention that emphasizes the practical politics as well as principles involved in shaping the Constitution, profiling the defeats suffered by James Madison to delegates wary of national government power.

Herbert J. Storing. What the Anti-Federalists Were For: The Political Thought of the Opponents of the Constitution. Chicago: University of Chicago Press. 1981. A brief overview of the philosophy and principles that drove the Antifederalists and gave them lasting relevance in American politics.

Gordon S. Wood. The Creation of the American Republic, 1776–1787. New York: W.W. Norton. 1969. A beautifully written account of the events between independence and the Constitution, focusing especially on the significance of the classical republican, communitarian vision in America.

Declaration of Independence
the document announcing the intention of the colonies to separate from Great Britain based on shared grievances about the treatment of the colonists by the British government.

nation a shared sense of understanding and belonging among a people, a shared sense that they are different and separate from other peoples with particular characteristics.

Articles of Confederation the first constitution of the United States, which based most power in the states.

Shays's Rebellion a protest by farmers in western Massachusetts in 1786–87 to stop foreclosures on property by state courts, it convinced many political leaders that the Articles of Confederation were insufficient to govern the United States.

Virginia Plan one of the alternative plans during the Constitutional Convention, it argued for a two-house legislature, with representation to be based on a state's population; the lower house would be elected directly by the people, and that house would in turn select the members of the upper house.

New Jersey Plan one of the rival plans at the Constitutional Convention in 1787, it called for, among other things, equal representation of the states in a single-house legislature.

Great Compromise the agreement between small states and large states that representation in the Senate would be equal for each state, as small states preferred, and representation in the House would be based on population, as large states preferred.

Three-fifths Compromise an agreement between slave states and free states that a state's slave population would be counted at 60 percent for purposes of determining a state's representation in the House of Representatives.

republic a system in which people elect representatives to make policy and write laws, in contrast to direct democracy in which the people do these activities themselves.

indirect election an election in which voters select other individuals who directly vote for candidates for a particular office; U.S. Senate and presidential elections were of this type in the Constitution, but Senate elections are now direct elections.

separation of powers the principle that the executive, legislative, and judicial functions of government should be primarily performed by different institutions in government.

checks and balances the principle that each branch of the federal government has the means to thwart or influence actions by other branches of government.

judicial review the power of the courts to declare laws and other actions of government officials unconstitutional.

federalism a governing arrangement that provides multiple levels of government with independent ruling authority over certain policy areas and guarantees the survival of these different levels of government.

parliamentary system a system of government in which power is concentrated in the legislative branch, and important executive and judicial branch officials may be simultaneously members of the legislature.

supremacy clause a clause in the Constitution that declares that national laws and treaties have supremacy over state laws and treaties.

full faith and credit a clause in the Constitution stating that states are to honor the official acts of other states.

equal privileges and immunities a clause in the Constitution stating that states are to treat equally their citizens and the citizens of other states.

Federalists individuals who supported the proposed Constitution and favored its ratification.

Antifederalists individuals opposed to the proposed Constitution, fearing it concentrated too much power in the national government.

Bill of Rights the first ten amendments to the U.S. Constitution, intended to protect individual liberties from federal government intrusion.

4 Federalism

Deciding End-of-Life Issues in a Federalist System

On March 31, 2005, Terri Schiavo died at the age of 41. Fifteen years earlier, on February 25, 1990, Terri had collapsed at her home in Florida. A potassium imbalance temporarily induced cardiac arrest and stopped the flow of oxygen to her brain. Doctors declared her to be in a vegetative state and a feeding tube was inserted to deliver hydration and nutrition. Without the tube, she would die.

In November 1990, an experimental treatment at a clinic in California failed to bring her out of a "persistent vegetative state." Over the next few years, Terri was examined by numerous specialists, who all came to the same conclusion—her condition had not improved and was not likely to improve.

In November 1992, Terri's husband, Michael, won a malpractice suit against doctors for their failure to diagnose her chemical imbalance. Of the approximately $1 million awarded after fees and other costs, about 70 percent was dedicated to provide for her care. By July 1993, her parents filed a lawsuit to have her husband removed as her legal guardian, but their case was dismissed. The family, once close-knit, had now become torn with mistrust and accusations concerning Terri and her care. In March 1994, a guardian appointed by the court determined that Michael had acted appropriately regarding his wife's care.

Michael petitioned in May 1998 to have the feeding tube removed, stating that before the 1990 incident Terri had told him that she would never wish to live in such a debilitated condition. She had not prepared a "living will," which states in writing what an individual wants done in the case of extreme medical and health emergencies. Without a written document, states vary in how to proceed. In Florida, the decision is left to the guardian; the husband, in this case. Her parents objected to Michael's request, and petitioned the court to appoint another legal guardian. This guardian concluded in December 1998 that Terri's condition would not improve, but also suggested her husband's judgment might be influenced by the potential to inherit Terri's estate.

From February 2000 through October 2003, Terri's case wound an extensive path through the Florida county and state courts, the Florida Supreme Court, and a federal district court. Her feeding tube was removed for two days in April 2001 and six days in October 2003. At this point, the Florida House of Representatives and Senate entered the fray and passed a bill known as "Terri's Law," which gave the governor authority to "stay" (suspend) a court order in certain instances. Governor Jeb Bush signed the bill and ordered the feeding tube reinserted. Terri's Law provided for a third guardian to be appointed by the Florida courts. That guardian concluded in December 2003 that Terri had no chance for improvement. In May 2004, a Florida court determined that Terri's Law violated Florida's Constitution; the Florida Supreme Court unanimously agreed in September 2004. Governor Bush filed a petition for the U.S. Supreme Court to review the decision. The Court declined in January 2005. On February 25, 2005, after all appeals had been exhausted, county judge George Greer declared that the feeding tube be removed on March 18. The Florida courts rejected Governor Bush's bid to make the state Terri's guardian.

The battle over Terri's health dominated headlines, mobilized political activists, and split typical political alliances. Especially among conservative Christian groups, Terri's plight led to demands for federal government involvement. Responding to the concerns of these groups and to their own values, legislators and the president crafted a response to the most recent developments. In Washington, on March 21, three days after the tube was removed, Congress passed, and President Bush signed, a "private bill"—an act concerned with only one situation that creates no precedent—to allow a federal court to review the Schiavo case. The next day, a federal district judge refused to order reinsertion of the tube. A federal appeals court upheld the district court decision one day later. On March 24, after petitions from Terri's parents and members of Congress, the U.S. Supreme Court declined to enter the case. Governor Bush declared, "I cannot violate a court order. I don't have power from the U.S. Constitution, or the Florida Constitution for that matter that would allow me to intervene after a decision has been made."[1] The case returned to the federal appeals court, but it declined to hold another hearing, and on March 30, the U.S. Supreme Court again refused to overturn this ruling. Terri died the next day.

After her death, federal lawmakers, recovering from a harsh political and emotional battle, continued to spar. Some charged that the federal courts had failed. Others said it was Congress and the president who failed, by involving themselves improperly in the case. Another group wondered whether federal standards should be established for end-of-life issues, although this had traditionally been an area left to state law. Public opinion was strongly negative: three quarters of the public believed the federal government should have stayed out of Terri's case.[2] A slim majority agreed that Terri's feeding tube should have been removed, thinking it an act of mercy.

At one time simply a tragic medical condition, Terri Schiavo's situation ultimately became a riveting tale about federalism and the Constitution. Her story illuminated the fault lines in American politics between different levels of government and between different institutions. It raised issues that, to some observers, were profoundly personal and not the province of government, while to others, they were life and death matters of deep societal and governmental concern. It raised questions about where the responsibilities of the state governments end and the federal government begins, or whether one can even think of any clear line on profound issues of life and death. Some citizens were outraged by how the federal constitutional system performed and could not believe government had allowed Terri Schiavo to die. Others saw the case as a success of the American federal system, with decisions ultimately being made in their proper place and multiple opportunities provided to challenge previous decisions. The principles and practice of American federalism, they believed, had worked well.

This chapter explores those principles and practices of federalism and the controversies surrounding them.

THIS CHAPTER WILL EXAMINE:

▶ the Constitution as a framework for federalism

▶ the principles of dual federalism and the support for these principles in the Supreme Court's traditional understanding of interstate commerce

▶ the evolution from dual to cooperative federalism, the linkage of a new interpretation of the concept

of interstate commerce to the rise of cooperative federalism, and the methods and techniques of cooperative federalism

▶ the nature of federalism today, after changes initiated by elected officials and the Supreme Court beginning in the 1990s.

The Nature of the Union

Although the Schiavo case was unusually dramatic and emotional, the issues about federalism that it raised have been central to political debates in the United States for over two centuries. When the Constitution was written and sent to the states for ratification, the debate between Federalists and Antifederalists was not only about liberty. As the names of the two sides suggest, it was also about federalism. And it was about the interaction of liberty and federalism.

What was the appropriate relationship between the state governments and the national government? The question was important not in the dry sense of deciding who should do what. Individuals on the two sides of the debate believed it was important mainly because it had significant implications for liberty, a key element of American political culture embodied in the proposed new government. To the Antifederalists, a system with a powerful, remote national government was likely to lead to the erosion of individual liberty. State governments could be better monitored and controlled by the people and, thus, were less a danger to liberty. Many Federalists agreed that the states should have an important role, but they argued that a strong national government could help protect liberty by preventing control by factions, as James Madison explained in *Federalist 10* (see Chapter 3). Other Federalists, such as Alexander Hamilton, took a much more aggressive view and desired the formation of a strong central government that would be very active in the economy and build a powerful military to rival those in Europe.

Under the Articles of Confederation, American government was similar to the structure we see today in the United Nations (UN), along with its attendant problems. UN decisions can be difficult to enforce because they often depend on countries to comply voluntarily. Resources can be hard to come by because members can choose to withhold their contribution to the organization. Member countries are frequently in competition, trying to best or disadvantage each other, especially economically. Most countries have strong norms of independence, and ambitious politicians might rail against outsiders dictating their country's policies. As explained in Chapter 3, these governing difficulties of a **confederation** were paralleled in the United States under the Articles of Confederation.

The Framers did not share the Antifederalists' enthusiasm for a confederal arrangement that gave more power to the states, but neither did they construct a **unitary system** that would make the states dependent on the national government. In a unitary system, lower levels of government are subordinate to the national government and have little, if any, independent governing authority. The central government is free to create, combine, or disband lower level governments. Lower levels of government typically have very limited ability to raise funds on their own. In the United States, the District of Columbia is an example of this type of arrangement. Washington, D.C., does have its own city government, but that government's independent authority is limited by Congress, which can revoke laws passed by the city government and controls the city budget. Although there have been movements and proposed constitutional amendments to give the District a representative in the U.S. House and two senators, like the states, these attempts have so far been unsuccessful.

State governments are essentially unitary systems with respect to local municipalities. Typically they allow substantial independence to the localities within their borders, but this arrangement is at the convenience of the state government. The Constitution makes no mention of cities and counties or other sub-state governments, nor does it guarantee their existence: their creation is up to the states.

Around the world, the unitary system of government is the norm. France, Great Britain, The Netherlands, Japan, Spain, and Italy are unitary systems, and South America and Africa are dominated by unitary systems. The amount of independence granted to lower-level governments is determined by the central government. In some cases, central governments have granted increasing authority to their sub-national governments. Regions in Italy, for example, have governing units that have been given increasing freedoms since the establishment of the 1948 constitution. And over the past decade, the United Kingdom has allowed more autonomy for Scotland and Wales, including the establishment of their own parliaments. In the United States, by contrast, a functioning set of state governments already existed when the Constitution was being debated. This made a move to a unitary form of government difficult.

The Constitution provides the framework for intergovernmental relations.

The Framers steered a middle course between a confederation and a unitary government, building instead a federal governing arrangement. **Federalism** is a system that distributes political power across a national government and sub-national governments. In the United States, these sub-national governments are the states. Federalism ensures that the sub-national units can make some final decisions and have their existence protected. In addition to the United States, other federal systems include Austria, Australia, Brazil, Canada, Germany, India, Mexico, Spain, and Tanzania. As discussed in Chapter 3, it is important to recognize that the Framers were not unified in their vision. Some would have favored a unitary system, with power centralized at the national level. Some preferred a confederal arrangement, in which the states were supreme. Some preferred federalism, in which the national and state governments shared power. Federalism was a middle-ground position between the unitary and confederal extremes.

The Constitution distributed power and decision-making between the national government and the states. According to the *supremacy clause*, when the two are in conflict, national laws overrule state laws. And powers delegated to the national government are not available to the states. On the other hand, the Tenth Amendment provides that powers not delegated to the national government by the Constitution, and not prohibited for state governments, are reserved for the states. States also are guaranteed equal voting rights in the United States Senate, protection against domestic insurrection and foreign invasion, and the preservation of a representative form of government. Existing states, via their representation in the U.S. Congress, have a role in the admission of new states, and existing states can not have their territory shifted to a new state without their consent.

The Constitution also mandates fair play between the states with three crucial provisions that are intended to prevent states from discriminating against one another or cutting special deals that would aggravate relations with other states or potentially other countries. The *full faith and credit clause* requires states to honor the official acts of other states, such as public records and the results of judicial proceedings. The *equal privileges and immunities clause* requires states to treat similarly their citizens and citizens of other states. And the *commerce clause* places the regulation of interstate commerce and foreign economic trade in the federal government, not the individual states. The evolution of interstate commerce has played a key role in the evolution of federalism, and so is discussed at length later in this chapter.

The appropriate balance of national and state power creates significant debate.

Ratification of the Constitution did not end disputes over the nature of the new system. From the start, the question of precisely how much control the national government had over the states was a matter of contention. Sovereignty was a key point of difference. **Sovereignty** refers to a government having the ultimate authority to make decisions about what happens within its borders, free from interference by other governments. Advocates of a limited national role preferred a **compact theory** of federalism, which suggested the states were sovereign entities that joined together. The Constitution was an instrument for these sovereign states to coordinate and pursue their interests. The states gave up some limited and specific powers, but they retained their sovereignty. The national government could make no other demands upon state governments beyond those in the Constitution, nor could it intrude into relations between these sovereign states and their citizens. Except in ways that they explicitly consented to, the states were to be left alone. Although individuals supporting the compact theory did not agree on all the details, the idea that the states were sovereign was a powerful idea held by important figures such as Thomas Jefferson.

This approach to understanding federalism was particularly prominent in the South, where it led to the doctrine of **nullification**—the idea that states could nullify national government laws with which they disagreed and which they believed violated the letter or spirit of the U.S. Constitution. Identified most strongly with Vice President John Calhoun of South Carolina (1825–1832), nullification was frequently and controversially employed in the decades prior to the Civil War, especially with regard to the slavery issue, but it had been present in political circles long before that.[3]

In later years, the compact theory would sometimes be referred to as the "states' rights" position. This became a controversial term in the 1950s and 1960s when it was most commonly invoked to thwart the push of the national government to end racial segregation, particularly in southern states. The compact view of federalism, however, should not be seen as limited to issues concerning civil rights, nor does it inherently advocate a limited, minimalist government. State governments could be quite active within the compact framework.

The **nationalist theory**, more prominent in northern states, provided an alternative to the compact theory. This approach stressed that the Constitution was intended to be a departure from the limited government of the Articles of Confederation. Rather than a joining together of states, the Constitution represented "the people" coming together. The preamble to the Constitution is instructive. It could have begun "We the states" or "We the people of the states," but it did not. The very language "We the people," according to the nationalist view, indicates that the Constitution's purpose is to provide the institutions and rules by which a nation of people, rather than a collection of states, can be governed. This does not mean abusing the states or ignoring their independence, but it does mean that national needs override states' wishes. At times, states will have to accept national direction and demands, regardless of their approval or disapproval of those demands, especially if the national action can be portrayed as promoting the general well-being of the country.

Strongly identified with this view is Alexander Hamilton, Secretary of the Treasury under President Washington. Among executive branch officials in the early years of the republic, Hamilton had the most expansive vision for national government power, especially with regard to establishing the national government as the clear leader in economic matters. He proposed that the national government establish a bank and that it invest heavily in building the roads, canals, and other infrastructure that would help unite the new country and advance economic development. Given the unhappy experience of centralized British power during the colonial era, how could Hamilton go about creating the political coalition to support such a plan? His answer was to mastermind a deal in which the federal government assumed all the debt that state governments had incurred in fighting the Revolutionary War. To Hamilton, this plan would link wealthy individuals and institutions in financial arrangements with the national government rather than the states, and the stability, power, and authority of the national government would become critical in their eyes. To many who subscribed to the compact theory, however, Hamilton's nationalist vision veered toward monarchy.

Across the course of American history, debate has flourished concerning the appropriate balance of power between the national and state governments. And the debate matters in very concrete ways. Issues as diverse as slavery, punishing violence against women, regulation of business, environmental protection, minimum wages, end-of-life decisions, and enforcement of antidiscrimination statutes, among many others, are influenced heavily by interpretations of federalism. People who care about these issues need to care about federalism, because in the American political system, prevailing interpretations of federalism will strongly shape what if anything can or should be done about these matters by government and which level of government should do it.

Dual Federalism

Federalism has evolved over the course of U.S. history and is still evolving. Dual federalism would give way to cooperative federalism. Over time, cooperative federalism would develop different variants. And today's federalism features a mix of a renewed dual federalism along with continuing elements of cooperative federalism.

Distinct lines separating the national and state governments are the hallmark of the system of **dual federalism**, which dominated American politics through the mid-1930s. This model of federalism embraces the ideas of dual sovereignty and dual citizenship. Sovereignty refers to a final say—the sovereign power is the one who speaks last and most authoritatively. In dual federalism, the national government is sovereign in some areas and the state governments are sovereign in others. Described sometimes as "layer-cake federalism," with one layer representing national government responsibilities and the other representing state government responsibilities, the essence of dual federalism is the idea of a constitutional division of labor between the national and state governments.

Dual sovereignty provides separate areas of authority for the national and state governments.

In dual federalism, the two levels of government have separate functions and areas of authority. They are both dominant over their respective areas of concern in this system of **dual sovereignty**. Each has policy responsibilities in which it has the final say, the defining aspect of sovereignty. In the nineteenth century, the federal government—the terms federal government and national government are used interchangeably in American politics—was primarily involved in internal improvements, such as building canals and roadways and opening new public lands and territories to development; setting tariffs on foreign goods; granting patents and copyright protection; managing the country's currency; establishing agreements with other countries; and providing defense and postal services. States in the nineteenth century were concerned with pretty much everything else: banking and insurance law; family and morals regulation; public health; education; criminal law; construction codes; water use; health, safety, and environmental regulations; and so on. Collectively, this is often referred to as the **police power** reserved to state governments in the Tenth Amendment—protection of public safety, health, welfare, and morality. For ambitious politicians, a career in state politics might well have been more satisfying than a career in national politics, simply because of the broader range of activity afforded to state governments.

Citizens of the United States are also citizens of a state.

If you are a U.S. citizen, you are also a citizen of a state.[4] Under dual federalism, this is known as **dual citizenship**. As a citizen of the United States, you have the same rights as other citizens of the United States. As a citizen of your state, you will have rights and responsibilities that may be different from citizens of another state. For example, in many states, citizens have a constitutional guarantee of a "uniform" or "equal" or "suitable" education system, or similar words. This difference in language has led to lawsuits charging that students have a right to equal education funding across districts. In seven states, your right to hunt or fish is constitutionally protected; more than a dozen others are considering similar amendments. The ability to purchase alcohol legally, to be married, to drive a car, and so on, varies from state to state. Responsibilities regarding jury duty, an obligation to help strangers, or the process by which life support can be terminated, as in the Terri Schiavo case, also vary across the states.

The case of *Barron v. Baltimore* (1833) illustrates the principle of dual citizenship under dual federalism. John Barron operated a commercial wharf in Baltimore. During construction projects, the city began dumping dirt and fill in the harbor. With ships facing great difficulty navigating in or out of the area near Barron's wharf, his business collapsed. Barron sued the city, arguing that the Fifth Amendment to the U.S. Constitution guarantees that citizens will be compensated when government takes their property for public purposes (known as the *takings clause*). Barron won his case, but the city appealed and won in the Maryland appeals court. Barron appealed that decision to the U.S. Supreme Court. The Court agreed that Barron was injured by the city's actions, but he was not entitled to any compensation. In the Court's view, the Fifth Amendment—indeed, the Bill of Rights as a whole—applies only to Barron as a citizen of the United States, not as a citizen of Maryland. In this case, Barron was not injured by the U.S. government—he was injured by a state government. If the Maryland constitution had a "takings" clause, then Barron would have recourse through the Maryland courts.

What would cause the Court to reach this conclusion? The distinction between Barron's rights as a state citizen and a national citizen may seem odd, but it is consistent with the forces that led to the Bill of Rights. Recall that the Federalists agreed to add a Bill of Rights to respond to the charge that the Constitution did not sufficiently protect the people from the national government. Antifederalist agitation for the Bill of Rights was based not on the premise that the people needed to be protected from state governments—the Antifederalists surely would have said that citizens worried about state government power should work through the state legislature to rectify their concern—but on the premise that the national government needed to be constrained. Had it been the U.S. government rather than a state government that had taken Barron's property, he would have a valid claim as a citizen of the United States.

For reasons discussed in Chapter 5 (Civil Liberties), the Supreme Court would decide Barron's case differently today. Nonetheless, the concept of dual citizenship remains an important part of American federalism.

Interpretation of the commerce clause affects national government power.

Interstate commerce has been a central battleground on which the meaning of federalism has been fought. Consistent with dual federalism, the Constitution marks out the regulation of interstate commerce as within the realm of federal government authority. The Constitution's **commerce clause**, in Article 1, section 8, gave Congress the power to "regulate commerce with foreign nations, and among the several states, and with the Indian tribes." Intrastate commerce was, implicitly, under the jurisdiction of the states.

Regarding interstate commerce, the Supreme Court confirmed the national government's primacy in this policy area in its decision in *Gibbons v. Ogden*

(1824). The state of New York granted exclusive rights to two individuals to operate steamboats on the state's waters. This policy created problems because the water flowed into and from other states—New York required boats entering from another state to obtain a permit to navigate on New York waters. A steamboat owner whose business required him to travel between New Jersey and New York challenged this law. In its decision, the Court concluded that, because of the Constitution's supremacy clause, New York's licensing requirement was overridden by a federal law that regulated coastal trade. Chief Justice John Marshall's opinion made it clear that, in addition to the buying and selling of goods and services, commerce included navigation on interstate waterways, and thus was an arena solely for federal government regulation.

Gibbons v. Ogden was a victory for national commercial authority over the states. Subsequent decisions refined and limited the federal government's control over interstate commerce. The Sherman Antitrust Act of 1890 was a response to the growth of huge corporations that monopolized sales in their particular industries. For many Americans, the sheer size of these corporations brought into question the promises of equality and democracy in the American creed, particularly because corporations were treated as "persons" as far as law was concerned. For others, these corporations were seen as a threat to property rights as embodied in the creed. As monopolies or nearly so, they could price their products excessively high to gain extra profit, or they could price excessively low to drive out any remaining competitors. In response, the antitrust act prohibited contracts, mergers, or conspiracy that restrained trade or commerce between states or with other countries.

By 1892, the E. C. Knight Company, through stock purchases of other sugar refining companies, controlled about 98 percent of the sugar-refining business in the United States. In a blow to the federal government's regulation over interstate commerce, however, the Supreme Court ruled in 1895 that "commerce" did not include manufacturing and that the Sherman Act only applied to commerce, the actual moving of goods from one location to another, not to monopolies in manufacturing.[5] In the Court's view, manufacturing was a local activity that preceded commerce, regardless of the fact that E. C. Knight controlled firms in more than one state. Although the Court recognized that monopoly over manufacturing might be linked to restraint of commerce, it sought to keep the two separate in the interests of dual federalist principles. States, but not the federal government, could regulate manufacturing; the federal government, but not the states, could regulate commerce.[6]

The Court's interpretation of interstate commerce was reiterated in other controversial cases. For example, the Keating-Owen Child Labor Act prohibited the interstate shipment of goods produced by child labor.[7] A father challenged the law on behalf of his two sons, one younger than 14 and one younger than 16. Both children worked in a cotton mill in Charlotte, North Carolina. The Court ruled that the law was unconstitutional because the regulation of manufacturing, which was not part of commerce, was reserved to the states by the Tenth Amendment.[8] If states wanted to limit child labor, they could, but the federal government could not use its commerce powers to do so.

Although this definition of interstate commerce placed limits on what the federal government could do, it did not leave that government powerless. In the early twentieth century the government expanded its reach into economic matters. The Pure Food and Drug Act of 1906 gave the federal government the regulatory authority to monitor food and drug safety and, in particular, to ensure that labeling of these products was accurate. Regulating misleading information was acceptable because such information could affect commercial transactions. The agency responsible for these tasks was later named the Food and Drug Administration. Prior to the 1906 law, most regulation of this type had been at the state level. The Federal Trade Commission (FTC) is another example of increased federal power under the traditional definition of commerce. Created in 1914 in the Federal Trade Commission Act, the FTC monitors false and deceptive advertising as well as corporate mergers with implications for commerce.

Cooperative Federalism

Dual federalism's sharp line of separation between national and state responsibilities was blurred by **cooperative federalism**, which rose to prominence beginning in the 1930s. In this form of federalism, the national and state governments share many functions and areas of authority. Cooperative federalism diminished the notion of separate spheres of state and national authority that was embodied in dual federalism. (Changes in the application of dual citizenship are discussed in Chapter 5.) Accordingly, rather than a layer cake, cooperative federalism has been described as "marble-cake federalism," with the swirls of vanilla and chocolate in a marble cake representing the intersecting areas of state and federal involvement, rather than strict demarcation between the two levels of government.

Many of the new social programs adopted by the national government during the 1930s, including welfare, unemployment insurance, and jobs programs, were jointly financed and administered by the national and state governments. Why would this be? This was often and perhaps usually done for practical political reasons rather than for reasons of grand philosophy. The New Deal, as the collection of new programs in the 1930s was known, called for a significant expansion of the role of the national government in American life. Although the misery of the Great Depression pushed politicians toward supporting this new federal role, state officials were sure to be reluctant to give up power. So a joint program might have been necessary in some instances to ensure passage through Congress. In some cases, the support of local officials seemed to hinge on whether they would have a piece of the action in administering the new program. If benefits were to be distributed to their constituents, they wanted some say in the matter and some of the political credit. In other cases, if a program seemed likely to have significant and possibly disruptive social and economic effects, state officials would want to have some flexibility in managing the program. For example, the new national minimum wage law was crafted in a way to omit agricultural workers, meaning that a large proportion of blacks in southern states fell outside the protection of the national minimum wage.[9] This design was motivated by southern political leaders' dual goals of holding down costs in agriculture and maintaining racial order. For northern politicians, this was the price they had to pay to get a minimum wage. They also recognized that southern support for a range of other New Deal policies might hinge on the negotiations over the minimum wage.

In practice, cooperative federalism has sometimes been referred to as "picket-fence federalism." The idea is that each horizontal band of the fence represents a level of government: federal, state, and local. Each vertical picket represents a separate policy area, such as transportation, health care, or education. The vertical pickets run across the three horizontal pickets in each policy area. The intersection signifies the joint efforts of officials across these three government levels in their particular policy area. Although these joint efforts may be beneficial by pulling together national, state, and local officials, one implication of the picket-fence metaphor is that within each level of government, officials may be relatively unaware of the practices and needs of officials in the other areas (see Figure 4.1). For example, transportation officials in the federal government might have much closer connections with state and local transportation officials than they do with federal officials in energy or housing or environmental affairs, even though the issues concerning these areas overlap in important ways. For the president and Congress, this pattern can make it more difficult to coordinate policy across different issue areas.

As noted above, minimum wage legislation is one example among many of cooperative federalism in action. Originally enacted at the federal level in the 1930s, minimum wage policy has been consistently cooperative. The national government sets minimum-wage standards that states have to meet. States, however, are free to exceed those wages if they so choose, and may establish minimum wages for workers not covered under federal law. Figure 4-2 shows how states vary on the minimum wage. About 40 percent of the states have adopted minimum wage levels higher than required by federal law. Where the map indicates the state level is lower, the federal rate prevails except for workers who are not covered by the federal minimum wage law—the state minimum wage for those workers is less than the standard federal minimum wage.[10]

The practice in minimum wage is similar to that in other contentious policy areas, such as welfare. Prior to 1996, the national government had specific programs designed to address the needs of poor families with children. The states, however, had substantial leeway in administering these programs, most notably in the benefit levels. After the passage of welfare reform legislation in 1996, state-by-state variation became even more pronounced. National law set a few guidelines for states to work within, but the programs themselves were entirely the creation of

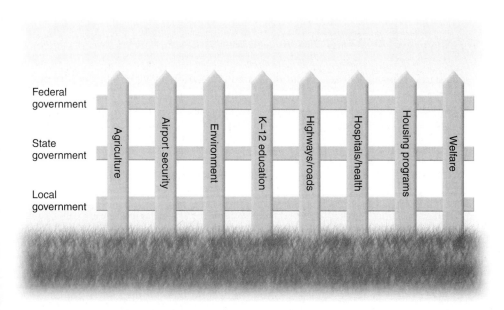

Figure 4.1. Picket Fence Federalism. The vertical pickets of the fence overlap each level of government, indicating that officials at these three levels work jointly in these example policy areas. Officials in one policy area, however, might be relatively uninformed regarding what is happening in other policy areas at their same level of government.

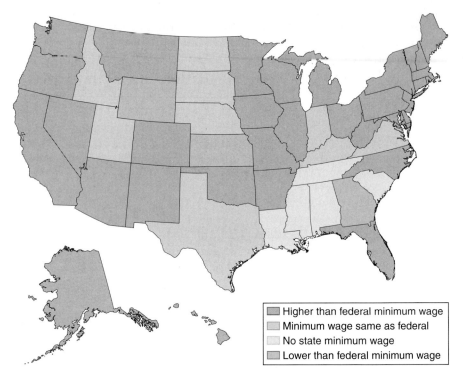

Figure 4.2. Differences in State Minimum Wages, 2008. States can set minimum wages that match or exceed the federal wage. For work categories not covered by the federal law, states can have a minimum wage below the wage assigned for categories that are federally covered, or can choose to have no minimum wage.

the states. Prior to 1996, states administered one national program but in fifty different ways; now states are administering fifty different state programs within broad national guidelines. Each of these two approaches is an example of cooperative federalism.

Implied powers increased the scope of permissible federal government activity.

Changes in constitutional interpretation were necessary to facilitate the evolution from dual federalism to cooperative federalism. One important step happened early in American history, in the case of *McCulloch v. Maryland*.

The Supreme Court's decision in *McCulloch v. Maryland* (1819) expanded Congress's ability to interlope on policy areas previously considered to be the province of the states. The case involved the Second Bank of the United States. The bank, chartered by Congress, had a branch in Baltimore, Maryland. Traditionally, states had chartered banks, so this new national role was eyed warily by the states. In response, Maryland taxed the bank. The United States government challenged this tax and filed suit against Maryland in the Supreme Court.

The Court had to resolve two questions. Could Congress charter a national bank? The Court's answer was yes. Its justification was twofold. First, Chief Justice John Marshall, the author of the Court's decision, argued against the compact theory of the Constitution in favor of the nationalist theory. Maryland presented the argument that the states had created the federal government and owed no deference to it in banking. Marshall responded that it was not the states, but the people, who had formed the national government, and the national government therefore did not require the consent of the states to carry out its powers, nor was it subordinate to the states.

Second, the Court pointed to the **necessary and proper clause**, sometimes referred to as the *elastic clause*. Article 1, section 8, of the Constitution gives Congress the authority "to make all laws which shall be necessary and proper for carrying into execution the foregoing powers, and all other powers vested by this Constitution in the Government of the United States, or in any Department or Officer thereof." The "foregoing powers" refers to a list of duties prescribed in Article 1 as the responsibilities of Congress. These listed duties, specifically mentioned in the Constitution, are known as Congress's **enumerated powers**.

What the Court said in *McCulloch* is that the necessary and proper clause gave Congress **implied powers**, meaning it could make laws needed to carry out its enumerated powers. It was reasonable, in the Court's view, for a Congress given the power to pay debts, borrow money, regulate commerce, and coin money, to create a bank to facilitate the performance of these duties. The creation of the bank was an implied power that resulted from Congress's need to carry out its enumerated powers.

Having answered the first question by ruling that the bank was constitutional, the Court now had to answer the second question—whether Maryland could tax the bank. The Court's answer was no. The power to tax, the Court famously stated, is the power to destroy. Under a federal system, a single state government has no right to destroy an entity of the national government. Maryland could not force the national government out of banking by onerous taxation.

The *McCulloch* decision opened the door for Congress to expand the reach of the national government and chip away some of the wall separating state and national government functions and responsibilities. The decision certainly broadened the scope of what could be considered legitimate federal government activity. Congress did not rush out to move the national government onto the policy turf of the state governments, but the precedent was established that Congress potentially could do so.

Redefining interstate commerce expands federal government power.

If the door to cooperative federalism cracked open in 1819, it swung fully open in 1937. In *National Labor Relations Board v. Jones & Laughlin Steel Corporation* (1937), the Supreme Court expanded the scope of what was meant by interstate commerce. Jones & Laughlin had fired workers for labor union activity. The recently enacted National Labor Relations Act (1935) prohibited employers engaged in interstate commerce from taking such actions. The act declared that labor-management relations were an aspect of commerce and thus subject to federal government regulation. When challenged by the National Labor Relations Board, which was created by the 1935 law, the steel company argued that labor-management relations were not part of commerce and therefore not subject to federal regulation. Traditionally, the Supreme Court interpreted interstate commerce to mean not what happened inside a factory—that was manufacturing, not commerce but what was involved in the transfer of products from one state to another. The national government could regulate shipping rates, for example, and it could regulate the entry of firms into the business of shipping steel, but what happened inside a steel plant was not in and of itself interstate commerce. Using this definition of commerce, Jones & Laughlin argued that the National Labor Relations Act was an invalid federal intrusion into its business practices.

In its decision in *Jones & Laughlin*, the Supreme Court concluded that this conception was too narrow. Instead, a company that uses any interstate products in its business or sells any product interstate is part of the stream of interstate commerce, and the stream involves the company's entire operations. Poor labor-management relations can lead to industrial strife, and this strife can affect the stream of commerce. In the Court's view, the fundamental principle was that some activities may appear to be intrastate when considered alone, but if they had a close relationship to interstate commerce, then Congress must be given the authority to regulate those activities to prevent obstructions to commerce.

The *Jones & Laughlin* decision meant, in effect, that national government action on issues such as worker safety, environmental controls, health codes, work hours and conditions, and overtime pay were justified by the government's responsibility to regulate interstate commerce. Everything in the stream of commerce was now ripe for federal involvement. Once solely under the purview of the states, these responsibilities would now be shared. And, in accordance with the Constitution's premise of the supremacy of national laws, it would be the states that would have to conform with federal standards in these areas, not the other way around.

Although the Court cautioned that its new definition of interstate commerce must be "a matter of degree," the principle of the stream of interstate commerce provided a nearly limitless range to congressional action. Anything in the stream or any action or practice that might affect the stream was now open to national government involvement. The Court declared that it was up to Congress to decide the appropriate use of its newly expanded interstate commerce powers.[11] The constitutional basis of cooperative federalism was now firmly in place and the scope of federal government activity in society and economy grew accordingly.

CaseStudy: Federalism and the Regulation of Native American Casinos

Long before the Founding Fathers led a revolution and crafted a constitution, Native Americans governed territory in what would come to be the United States. This history created a particularly difficult problem for governance in the United States: How would these Native American, or Indian, nations be incorporated into the American political system?

The answer was to grant tribes some degree of sovereignty within the United States and within the states. The tribes, in other words, are part of the American system of federalism. The Supreme Court has upheld this principle, noting that the tribes hold "attributes of sovereignty over both their members and their territory."[12] In the Constitu-

tion's commerce clause (Article 1, section 8), Indian tribes are made the equivalent of other sovereign entities: Congress is responsible "To regulate Commerce with foreign Nations, and among the several States, and with the Indian Tribes." In an executive memorandum in April 1994, President Clinton reaffirmed that federal government agencies are to operate on a "government to government" basis with Indian tribes.[13]

The questions raised by tribal sovereignty are similar to those raised by the relationship between states and the national government in American federalism. In what areas does the national government prevail? What areas are the province of tribal law and regulation rather than the U.S. government? How do the states fit in?

In recent years, the status of Indians in the federal system has been particularly salient because of gambling and the revenues it generates. Prior to 1988, casinos on Indian reservations were rare, but by 2008, about 230 tribes ran over 400 casinos in 30 states. The world's largest casino is the tribal-owned Foxwoods Resort in Connecticut. And casino gambling has generated huge revenues for tribes. From 1987 to 2008, revenues from tribal-owned casinos increased from barely $100 million to more than $20 billion.[14]

One of the federalism controversies raised by Indian gaming is the ability of state governments to regulate tribal-run casinos. In 1987, the Supreme Court ruled that a state could not enforce its gaming laws within tribal reservations, unless Congress had specifically given the states that authority.[15] Overall, federal, not state, authority prevails when it comes to the tribes. In this case, the Court believed that state restrictions on Indian gaming conflicted with the federal government's attempt to further tribal self-sufficiency and economic development through tribal gaming. Other Court decisions confirmed that American federalism made Indian tribal sovereignty subordinate to the federal, not state, government.[16]

Recognizing the difficult political issues that might arise with the expansion of tribal gaming in the states, the federal government provided a role for the states in regulating this gambling. The Indian Gaming Regulatory Act (IGRA), signed into law in 1988, established three classes of Indian gambling activity: (1) social and traditional games with stakes or prizes of minimal value, commonly associated with tribal customs or celebrations; (2) bingo and other games played against other players, not against "the house;" and (3) any games not in the first two groups, such as slot machines, blackjack, and roulette. Tribes are essentially free to offer the first two classes of games; the third requires the tribes to negotiate a "compact" with a state that would determine casino size, games, hours, and the share of the profits that would go to the state.

Intended to regulate gambling on Indian reservations, the IGRA also gave the states some incentive to encourage, or at least not discourage, Indian gaming, because now states would receive a portion of the profits. Because they are sovereign entities, Indian tribes cannot be taxed directly by the federal or state governments.[17] This means that the tribes are not sources of tax revenue in the states. Under IGRA, states were assured part of the financial windfall from casino gambling. The law also provided for a mediator to choose between the final offers of tribes and states if a tribe could convince a federal court that a state

was not negotiating in good faith. Knowing the mediator might agree with the tribe and leave the states with a smaller share of the profit, states had a strong financial incentive to reach agreements with the tribes.[18]

To its critics, IGRA was a disaster. They describe it as reckless—in effect establishing a national policy that encourages loose affiliations of Native Americans to petition the Bureau of Indian Affairs to be declared tribes in order to enter into casino gambling operations. Once acknowledged as tribes, sovereignty leaves them free to develop their lands without being subject to state environmental, safety, zoning, or other ordinances. As the critics see it, the control of states over their own future development is imperiled.

States seemed to regain some leverage in 1996. The Seminole tribe in Florida filed suit in federal court, complaining that the state had violated IGRA by not bargaining in good faith to establish a gaming compact. In *Seminole Tribe v. Florida*, the Supreme Court rejected the tribe's case. The Court concluded in a 5-4 decision that the Eleventh Amendment gave states, as sovereign bodies, immunity from lawsuits in federal courts without their consent. Just as a sovereign body can be undermined if another entity taxes it, it can be undermined if another entity encourages lawsuits against it. In the Court's view, Congress did not have the constitutional authority to remove the state's immunity simply because of its interstate commerce powers to regulate the tribes and states.[19]

As it turns out, with significant financial resources likely to flow from gambling, states did not use the *Seminole* decision to prevent Indian casinos. Instead, they used the decision as leverage to negotiate more lucrative agreements with the tribes. Suffering from revenue shortfalls, states saw casino gambling on reservations as a potential windfall, now that they could force better deals. By 2004, states were collecting $900 million in profit sharing from the casinos.[20] And at the same time, they could continue to prohibit commercial casino gambling outside the reservations.[21]

The sovereign status of Indian tribes intersects American federalism at both the national and state levels. Although states sometimes complain that Indian sovereignty compromises their own sovereignty, they have been able to use the *Seminole* decision—itself based on state sovereignty—to wrest more profitable deals with the casinos in difficult budgetary times. At the same time, states without casinos or with less attractive gaming options see their citizens and other tourists pouring into neighboring states to gamble at Indian casinos, which gives some negotiating power back to the tribes. Within states, Indian casino gambling has emerged as a political football, as governors and legislatures battle to determine who has the authority to negotiate and sign the gaming compacts.

ThinkingCritically

1. Should states or the federal government have the primary regulatory role regarding Native American tribes?

2. Should tribes have to negotiate with states or should they, as sovereign entities, be free to determine how they will run their gaming enterprises?

3. Consider the case of tribes that have members scattered around geographically and do not control any land as a group. Are these the equivalent of tribes on reservations? Should these individuals, due to tribal sovereignty, have a right to receive land from the federal and state governments for the purpose of establishing casino operations?

Cooperative federalism uses multiple methods.

The regulation of Indian gaming indicates the complexity involved when multiple levels of government are involved in the same policy area. The national–state relationship in cooperative federalism similarly can take on different forms: collaboration, mandates, and persuasion.

Collaboration To understand collaboration, consider environmental policy. State governments and the national government collect and share significant amounts of data and information on the environment. They work together to identify and create rules to protect endangered species. State offices often provide personnel who implement at the state level programs that are created at the national level, such as water and air pollution control. Sometimes, these agreements and sharing of information and personnel involve multiple states in a region in addition to the federal government.

As a form of collaboration, the national government may set standards and then allow states to exceed those standards, as is the case in air pollution control. A provision added to the Clean Air Act in 1967 allowed California to seek exemptions from federal air pollution rules. If these exemptions were granted, other states then had the option of following the federal or California standards, whichever were more stringent. The Environmental Protection Agency granted about fifty of these waivers over four decades before, but for the first time, denied a California exemption request in 2007. That request concerned new standards for automobile emissions. By early 2008, 16 other states had decided they would adopt the California standards if the state was ultimately successful in obtaining an exemption.

Ideally, officials at all levels of government have shared environmental goals, so these collaborations are considered mutually beneficial. Freedom for states to tailor policy to fit their needs, while still falling within federal guidelines, increases the likelihood of mutually beneficial collaboration.[22]

Even while collaborating, the state and national governments will often still have separate areas of responsibility, the hallmark of dual federalism. For example, states are responsible for noise pollution and non-endangered wildlife management policy within their borders. The national government, on the other hand, controls the management and disposal of nuclear waste generated by national defense needs. Both of these are environmental concerns, but the two levels of government work on them independently. Similarly, the federal government sets policy on which pesticides can be made, but a state, or a city if allowed by the state, can decide which of these allowable pesticides can be used within its borders and in what ways.

Mandates Another possibility is for the national government to issue a **mandate** that orders the state governments to take certain actions. Beginning in the 1960s, the volume of federal government mandates upon the states increased sharply. For example, in the area of education, states must follow the rules established by the national government in the Individuals with Disabilities Education Act. This law sets out the kinds of services that states and localities must provide to students with learning or other disabilities. Here "cooperative" federalism need not mean that there is harmony and agreement between the two levels of government. Instead, the national government may set the rules that states are required to follow, regardless of the view of the states toward these rules. Some analysts referred to this practice as "coercive federalism."

Federal mandates have rankled state officials for two reasons. First, the mandates may force states to do things they would prefer not to do or for which there is only modest support from state residents. Second, mandates impose demands upon the states but often do not provide federal financial assistance to carry out the demands. States long complained that they were spending far too much to meet the policy demands and policy preferences of federal government officials and politicians, draining money from policies of more interest to state politicians and residents. Columbus, Ohio, reported it would need to raise $1 billion from 1991 through 2000 to meet federal environmental mandates. Danville, Virginia, complained in 1993 that federal mandates absorbed 16 percent of its local revenue. The state of Texas estimated it would need to spend $11.4 billion in 1994–95 to accommodate mandates. Examples like these made the elimination of **unfunded mandates** a major priority of the Republican Party when it gained control of the U.S. House and Senate following the 1994 election. Unfunded mandates are federal requirements that states take some action, but without provision of sufficient resources to take the action.

The result, after lengthy controversy, was the 1995 Unfunded Mandates Reform Act. The bill required congressional committees to get estimates of the cost of proposed legislation that would mandate new expenses on states, localities, or businesses. If the cost exceeded $50 million on states and localities or $100 million on the private sector, legislators could then be required to vote that the benefits of the bill exceeded the costs. These figures were adjusted for inflation, reaching $67 million and $134 million, respectively, in 2008. The act did not apply to existing unfunded mandates and did not apply to mandates that protected the constitutional rights of individuals, prohibited discrimination, or were labeled emergency legislation.

Unfunded mandates seemingly declined after the act was passed. By one accounting, only five new mandates had been passed during the decade after the law's enactment, and the law had changed the way Congress interacted with the states. However, this correlation may be misleading. Evidence on the effectiveness of the act has been mixed. Another accounting argues the law had fallen short because its exemptions allowed major new unfunded mandates that simply were not labeled as such, including education reforms in the No Child Left Behind Act, education services for disabled children, Medicaid, and a requirement after 2000 that states meet standards for voting technology.[23] The National Conference of State Legislatures (NCSL) discontinued its Mandate Monitor in 1995 but restarted it in 2004 because of state complaints about a renewed escalation of unfunded mandates. The NCSL estimated that unfunded mandates, interpreted more broadly than the federal law, totaled approximately $100 billion from 2004 through 2007.[24] These data suggest that some of the "success" of the federal law has been more in labeling what counts as an unfunded mandate than in actually reducing the fiscal burdens imposed on the states.

Persuasion through fiscal federalism In addition to collaboration and mandates, cooperative federalism can work through persuasion. The national government might try to influence or persuade a state government to take some action in the area of education, the environment, or some other policy area, but not require it. Typically, this will involve providing some incentive for states to agree to take the desired action.

One of the best incentives is money. **Fiscal federalism** refers to the national government's use of its financial resources to persuade the states to take particular actions. The restrictions on the use of the money might be specific or general. With a **categorical grant**, the federal government provides money that is to be used for very specific purposes. For example, funds might be provided for a particular form of science instruction for children in grades one through three who attend schools with a large proportion of low-income students. To receive the funds, the state or locality would have to agree to these and any other restrictions on their use. For example, as of 2006, states are required to include pet evacuation in their emergency preparedness plans in order to receive aid from a federal disaster relief and emergency assistance program.

Block grants, which began during the presidency of Richard Nixon (1969–1974), are more general and provide greater flexibility to the states. These grants are for broad categories of spending: transportation funds, welfare program funds, and so on. States are free to spend those funds more or less as they please, within those particular policy areas. Block grants can come with conditions, however. For example, in 1984, a new federal law required a portion of transportation block grants to be withheld from any state that did not raise its legal drinking age to 21. Similarly, states that do not comply with portions of the federal Clean Air Act will also lose some of their highway funding.

From its inception in 1972 through 1987, **revenue sharing** was a significant source of federal assistance to states, cities, and counties. Under revenue sharing, the federal government provided funds to the states based on a formula that considered population, per capita income, and the property tax base. The idea was for the federal government to provide assistance to those localities that could not raise sufficient revenues through their tax systems, especially the property tax, which was the major source of revenue at the local level. In practice, however, revenue sharing was spread to all states and nearly all cities and counties—nearly 40,000 governments received these funds in 1984. The funds could be spent however those governments wished. President Ronald Reagan, however, believed the program had become too expensive, especially as the federal budget deficit grew. States were dropped from the program in 1981 and revenue sharing was completely eliminated in 1987.

Since 1987, the federal government has provided funds to state and local governments through block grants and categorical grants that comprise about 25 to 30 percent of state and local expenditures.[25] The most rapidly growing area of federal aid to states and localities has been assistance for medical expenses, which increased from about $44 billion to nearly $209 billion between 1990 and 2007. Over half of the additional $314 billion transferred from the federal government to states and localities since 1990 has been devoted to medical care. Medical care expenses have substantially affected other areas of federal aid (see Figure 4-3). Although the percentage of state and local budgets financed by federal aid has stayed about the same since 1990, much more of that aid is now dedicated to medical expenses. As most medical care expenses are funneled through state governments, one hidden story in Figure 4-3 is that federal assistance directly to the nation's urban areas has declined over the past two decades.

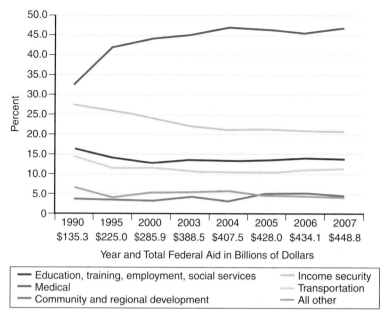

Figure 4.3. Federal Aid to States and Cities by Function. Federal grants and medical expenses have been an increasing share of all federal aid provided to states and cities.

To state governments, fiscal federalism is attractive. It provides states with funding to do things they otherwise would be unable to do. If politics often concerns "who gets what" and "who will pay for it," fiscal federalism is a prime example. Whenever an elected official can provide a benefit to his or her constituents but have someone else's constituents pay the cost, it is an attractive proposition. Fiscal federalism gives members of Congress reasons to join together, even across party lines, to provide more funds for the folks back home.

But fiscal federalism creates problems as well. One problem is that these cash infusions may come with strings attached, so that the state may be creating some programs or services primarily because there is money available to do so, rather than because it is a priority of the state government or the people of the state. Programs can mean jobs and an infusion of cash to the state economy, however, and those can be difficult to refuse.

Another problem with fiscal federalism is that states may find themselves battling each other to get a larger share of federal funds. The criteria that the federal government uses to distribute aid become tremendously important and the focus of great political conflict, because one set of criteria might advantage some states in the competition for money while another might advantage other states. States pay acute attention to how much their citizens pay into the federal government per person and how much the state receives back per person. Generally, over the past two decades, states that are more rural have fared better than those that are more urban, and southern and western states have fared better than eastern and northern states (see Figure 4-4).

A final problem with fiscal federalism is the difficulty of a state or city in speaking with one voice. Officials at the highest levels of state and local government, such as governors or mayors, typically prefer the flexibility of block grants and lobby the federal government for more. Officials in state and city agencies, however, as well as organized interest groups, are often equally determined to

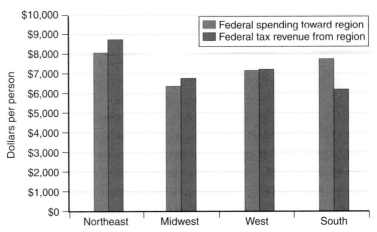

Figure 4.4. Federal Spending Versus Federal Tax Revenue, by Region, 2005. States in the West and South receive as much or more money from the federal government as they contribute. Northeast and Midwest states pay in more than they receive.

obtain categorical grants that they know will be used for a defined purpose. In addition, states and city officials can have different political incentives. In particular, to the extent that federal grants go directly to cities, state political leaders will not receive political credit for new programs and spending. Moreover, the funds being received by the city might, in the view of state officials, be put to better use elsewhere. This view might be based on an assessment that competing needs in the state should have higher priority, or it might be based on a calculation that spreading resources to other constituents will be more politically beneficial for the state official, or both of these. One of the reasons federal officials sometimes wish to funnel funds directly to cities is precisely because they are concerned that states will shortchange the cities. City officials, of course, have just the opposite incentive as state officials, hoping to receive federal funds directly so they can claim full credit for this success.

Members of Congress, even if they philosophically believe in the principle of block grants, gravitate toward the more defined grants because they can claim more credit for obtaining them. For members of Congress, there is little better than a grateful constituent who can thank them for a specific program or service that came about through the initiative of the federal government. Despite the wishes of some politicians at both the federal and state levels, categorical grants have continued to grow more rapidly than block grants.

Federalism can create both problems and solutions.

So which are better—categorical grants or block grants? Categorical grants reveal the national government's priorities. These may not necessarily be the same as a state's priorities, but, like most of us, states will rarely turn down what appears to be "free" money. With block grants, the national government has money spent where it wants, but the states decide how they want to spend it. Thus, national lawmakers can be less sure that funds are being spent in a way they would desire. For federal lawmakers, the tradeoff is between the close control of categorical grants, and the efficiency and effectiveness of block grants, which encourage states to try different policy solutions and spend money where it is most needed.

The more general question raised by the choice between categorical grants and block grants is what type of relationship one desires between the national and state governments. For those who favor more national standards and control, the concerns are multiple. States may simply not have access to the same expertise available to the federal government. One state's solutions may create problems for bordering states. If states are not required to meet high national standards, there may be a "race to the bottom" in which states try to provide minimal services and cut taxes and regulation in an attempt to attract business (see *How Do We Know? Are States Engaged in a Race to the Bottom?*). And political power is a factor as well. If particular ideas and politicians dominate national politics—whether conservative or liberal—why not use that opportunity to implement uniform conservative or liberal policies, respectively, across the country?

For those who favor allowing states more flexibility and leeway, the advantages are also multiple. Allowed flexibility in solving problems, the states become "laboratories of democracy," a phrase coined by Supreme Court Justice Louis Brandeis early in the twentieth century to describe an environment in which numerous policy proposals can be implemented and tested. States vary tremendously in the substance of their policies in areas such as education, welfare, consumer protection, health care, and many more. States also vary in their political processes. The veto power of governors, the making of state budgets, the length of legislative sessions, voter registration laws, access of minor parties to election ballots, campaign finance laws, lobbying regulations, and many other aspects of the political process are quite different from one state to another. Ultimately, the nation gains because other states can borrow those policy reforms that prove to be effective and efficient. Citizens also have the advantage of choice—they can choose where to live based on a number of factors, including the different styles and roles of government across the states.[26]

States also serve as laboratories for individuals who wish to ultimately enter into politics on the national level. For example, since 1977, four presidents—Jimmy Carter, Ronald Reagan, Bill Clinton, and George W. Bush—had served as governors. Many members of Congress first served as state or local officials. Indeed, political scientists have found that candidates for the U.S. House and Senate who have served at other levels of government have a decided electoral advantage. States can also serve as training grounds for individuals who move to positions in executive branch agencies and departments. Although the scope of the job at the national level will often far exceed that at the state level, the federal system allows officials to enter the federal government with practical governing experience.

Advocates of federalism also note that societies with potentially deep divisions are best governed with federal arrangements. Federalism is not a cure-all, they concede—the tortured history of conflict between Catholics and Protestants in Northern Ireland provides one example; the mixed record of federalism in Africa provides another—but it provides the ingredients for sharing power and thwarting separatism.[27] Countries with distinctive clusters of ethnic groups or groups that see themselves as "nations," such as the French-speaking population in Canada, might particularly benefit from this mode of government. Critics reply that the record is not nearly so clear-cut. Federalism, for example, might help prevent conflict, but because it gives rival groups competing bases of power, it also might perpetuate conflict once it emerges. And even in Canada, federalism did not discourage separatists from seeking Quebec's independence.

Political scientists' research into this question has produced mixed results. Overall, research suggests federalism tends to mitigate conflict, but that in certain contexts—for example, Eastern Europe—it may have contributed to conflict. It may also be that federalism works best in societies where the economic pie provides ample slices to share. In very poor countries, federalism may spawn, or at least not deter, violent conflict.[28]

Part of the reason for mixed results in studies of federalism and domestic conflict relates to the difficulties inherent in researching these questions: The term "federalism" embraces a vast spectrum of systems, and the term "conflict" is equally difficult to pin down. Moreover, some societies prone to conflict may choose federalism precisely for that reason; if these societies continue to be fractious, is federalism really the "cause" of that conflict? Researchers also must make judgments based on time spans. Does federalism in the United States prevent conflict? One answer might be yes, with the Civil War being the exception that proves the rule. That is, however, a very large exception.[29]

Are States Engaged in a Race to the Bottom?

The Question

Critics of welfare policy argue that states with generous welfare benefits risk becoming "magnets" that attract the poor. Furthermore, the higher taxes resulting from these policies may be a disincentive to businesses looking to locate in the state. Defenders of these policies worry that this logic leads states to compete economically by decreasing welfare benefits to the level of neighboring states, which they refer to as a "race to the bottom." Are states engaged in a race to the bottom? How do we know?

Why It Matters

The race-to-the-bottom question is one of the most contentious in the study of federalism. The policy consequences are significant for welfare recipients, taxpayers, and economic development. Philosophically, the question engages the very strong and competing points of view researchers may have about the desirability of welfare programs for individuals. And the concern about magnets and policy "races" in American federalism appears in other policy areas. School districts and states express concern at the financial pressures that may result if, for example, excellent special education services attract out-of-district and out-of-state parents seeking particular services for their children. Advocates for parents of these children worry that states and districts will reduce their services because of this fear of becoming a magnet.[30]

Investigating the Answer

The premise of the race to the bottom debate is that states offering generous welfare policies put themselves at risk by becoming "welfare magnets." With more generous policies, there will be an influx of welfare recipients because of higher benefits and an outflow of business because of higher taxes. States respond to this dilemma by reducing welfare benefits, which prompts surrounding states to do the same. The result is a downward spiral in which states follow each other toward low benefits. Federalism allows differences in state benefits; if the national government simply set a fixed benefit across all states, the "race" could not occur. This is the case in a program like Social Security, where states do not set benefit levels.

The basic approach in studies of the race to the bottom is twofold. One group of studies focuses on state government behavior. The outcome to be explained is whether surrounding states adjust their level of welfare benefits in reaction to changing levels of benefits by their neighbors. The causal relationship being tested is whether lower benefits in one state leads to lower benefits in surrounding states. This requires tracking benefit levels over time.

These researchers may also seek to determine whether a state is a "welfare magnet" by looking at states that make benefits more generous and then seeing whether the poverty level in those states changes. The logic is that if increased benefits lure the poor, then at least initially a state's poverty rate would increase after benefits were raised because poor residents from other states will have migrated to the generous state.

Any investigation of state government welfare benefits needs to take account of a number of factors other than the actions of other states that might affect a state's benefit levels. Wealthier states can more easily afford higher benefits per person, because they have a smaller percentage of their population receiving benefits than poorer states. States with more liberal public opinion might also be expected to have higher spending. On the other hand, states with declining wages might reduce welfare benefits to discourage workers from leaving jobs to enter the welfare system.

A second set of studies focuses on the behavior of individuals rather than state governments. These studies seek to determine why low-income individuals move from one state to another and, in particular, whether welfare benefits are part of that decision. Researchers tracking the movement of individuals from one state to another need to consider other factors that may lead individuals to move, particularly family concerns and greater work opportunities in another state. The latter is particularly important. A low-income individual might move to a higher-benefit state not because of the higher benefits, but because that state is more likely to be prosperous and have more jobs available. Thus, the increased economic opportunity, not the generous welfare policy, would be the magnet. Although there would be a correlation between welfare benefits and migration, the benefits would not actually be causing the migration.

Research on the race-to-the-bottom thesis faces other complications. Most studies, for example, assume that neighboring states are the relevant set of states— these are the states that a government is "competing" with in terms of welfare benefits and also the states from which migration is most likely. However, this assumption is not always accurate. California, for example, has more migrants from Texas, New York, Illinois, and Florida than from neighboring Oregon. Also, what if state officials set their benefits not in reaction to actual reductions in other states but in anticipation that other states will reduce their benefits? As a result, the cause of their behavior may well be behavior in other states that has not even happened yet and thus would be hard to demonstrate by a researcher. A similar problem is that states may reduce their welfare benefits to be more in line with nearby states even if individuals do not behave in the manner presumed by the welfare magnet thesis. State government officials might *assume* that individuals will migrate for benefits and therefore reduce their state welfare expenditures to preempt migration. In this scenario, state policy makers are influenced by the threat of movement, rather than by any demonstrated fact that individuals do move for welfare reasons.

The Bottom Line

Despite these research challenges, political scientists have reached some conclusions on the race-to-the-bottom theory. Overall, research has found support for the notion that states compete on benefit levels. States tend to follow each other as benefits are lowered, but they do not seem to follow each other if benefits are increased. The size and speed of the "copying" behavior, however, is not clear. In some studies, states match nearly dollar for dollar what other states do, while in other studies the matching is modest, adjusting state benefits only a few cents to every dollar in a competing state.

There have been fewer studies on whether individuals move to welfare magnets, but these generally conclude that factors other than welfare benefits are more important in determining the location decisions of low-income individuals. Once cost-of-living is factored in, some studies suggest, state-to-state differences in welfare benefits are not as large as it would seem initially and, thus, are less an incentive to move from one state to another. On the other hand, for policy makers, it may not matter whether welfare benefits are the only reason an individual moves or a major reason: what might matter is simply whether welfare benefits influence location decisions to any degree.[31]

Federalism Today

Since the early 1990s, American federalism has changed. "Revolutionary" is probably too strong a term to describe the change, but certainly there has been a significant departure from previous decades in the way federalism is interpreted and implemented.

Elected officials have initiated changes in federalism.

Congress and the president instigated part of the shift. After Republicans won control of the House and Senate in the 1994 congressional elections, they pushed an agenda of devolution and block grants. **Devolution** refers to the transfer of authority over program details and implementation from the federal government to the states. The federal government remains involved, but it allows the states to use more discretion in deciding how programs will be run. The most famous example is the reform of the national welfare system in 1996. The environment is another example. By the end of the 1990s, the federal Environmental Protection Agency had shifted the authority for nearly 760 federal environmental programs to the states. Over 80 percent of the programs related to the Clean Air Act are now run by state governments. In other policy areas as well, block grants have been used more extensively to give states more flexibility in spending federal funds.

The Supreme Court has redefined contemporary federalism.

Even more dramatic than the changes initiated by elected officials were the changes produced by the Supreme Court. In a series of decisions starting in the mid-1990s, the Court began to redraw the boundaries between federal and state responsibilities and authority. It did this by scaling back Congress's use of the interstate commerce clause to justify legislation and by reasserting dual sovereignty ideals. In these efforts, the Court majority believed it was breathing new life into the Tenth Amendment—powers not delegated to the United States are reserved for the states or the people—and the Eleventh Amendment—the federal judicial power does not extend to cases of private individuals against states.

Reining in Congress's use of the commerce clause Following the Supreme Court's 1937 decision in *National Labor Relations Board v. Jones & Laughlin Steel Corporation* (described earlier), Congress used the court's new interpretation of the interstate commerce clause to move the federal government into areas previously relegated to the states. Until 1995, the Supreme Court acceded to this expansion of federal power. That year, however, in *United States v. Lopez*, the Supreme Court signaled a change in direction. The Gun-Free School Zones Act of 1990 prohibited the possession of firearms within 1,000 feet of a school. Congress justified its intervention in this area by arguing that guns were an item of interstate commerce, but the Court struck down the law.[32] In the Court's view, Congress was improperly involving itself in matters of local policing and using the interstate commerce clause as a thin and unconvincing rationale for its action. If states and localities wished to pass such restrictions on firearm possession, they were free to do so, but this was not a matter for federal government involvement. For the first time in nearly six decades, the Court refused to agree to Congress's use of the interstate commerce clause to expand federal power.

In 2000, the Court's decision in *United States v. Morrison* confirmed this new direction. In the Violence Against Women Act, part of President Clinton's 1994 package of anti-crime legislation, Congress allowed women to file civil suits in federal courts against their attackers. Congress supported its action on interstate commerce grounds, noting that fear of violence suppressed women's full participation in economic life. The Court struck down the law, determining once again that Congress did not have authority over local criminal activity and that Congress's interstate commerce justification for its action was not credible. Although the Court majority agreed that the violence in the case—a rape of a college student—was reprehensible, it argued that the proper remedy was to be found through the laws of Virginia, not the United States.

Reasserting dual sovereignty Another issue in the Court's new federalism offensive was whether states could be sued by private parties, such as individuals or organizations, in federal court. In a set of controversial decisions, the Court concluded that under the Eleventh Amendment, states had **sovereign immunity** against these suits—in essence, the states could not be sued unless they chose to allow themselves to be sued or Congress made a compelling case that it should be able to override this immunity.[33] The Court majority in these decisions added that even without the Eleventh Amendment, the states were sovereign entities prior to the creation of the Constitution and had not given up that status. This view restates the compact theory explained earlier in this chapter.

Under this framework, the Court restricted the use of federal courts to sue states. For example, the Court ruled that the states could not be sued in federal courts by employees complaining that they had not received overtime pay required under the federal Fair Labor Standards Act. States were not subject to age discrimination suits arising from the Age Discrimination in Employment Act or some suits arising from the Americans with Disabilities Act. As mentioned above in the *Seminole* case, the Court also struck down the ability of Indian tribes to sue states for their failure to negotiate in good faith regarding gambling compacts.[34] Only under certain specific conditions, the Court concluded in these cases, could Congress subject the states to suit by private parties in federal courts.

Other decisions reasserted principles of dual sovereignty and were designed to limit the federal government's ability to impose its will on the states. In *Printz v. United States* (1997), the Court declared that the federal government could not require state officials to perform federal functions. The issue in this case was background checks for handgun purchasers, a function that the law known as the Brady Bill had assigned temporarily to local law enforcement officials until a federal system was in place. The Court concluded that the Constitution's "necessary and proper" clause did not entitle Congress to compel state or local law enforcement officials to perform federal tasks without their consent. In *City of Boerne v. Flores* (1997), the Court concluded that Congress had exceeded its power in the Religious Freedom Restoration Act by attempting to impose restrictions on local zoning, health, and other regulations in order to prevent perceived threats to religious freedom. The case concerned a complaint by the archbishop in San Antonio over the city's historic preservation zoning regulations. He charged that regulations prohibiting him from expanding his church violated his religious freedom.[35] And in *Gonzales v. Oregon* (2006), the Court concluded that the federal government did not have the authority, under the Controlled Substances Act, to prohibit the use of regulated but legal drugs for physician-assisted suicide in Oregon. The Court majority reasoned that Congress had intended to prevent physicians from engaging in the sale and distribution of what the federal government considered legal drugs, not to define standards of medical practice, an arena traditionally left to state governments.

The cumulative effect of the Court's jurisprudence in this era was to send Congress and the president stark messages that they had to tread carefully in their attempts to intervene in states' relationships with their citizens and other areas traditionally established as matters of state concern. It was a clear attempt to restore the influence of dual federalist principles and to restore the ideas of the compact theory, described earlier in this chapter.

State officials have implemented significant new policy.

As law and constitutional interpretation shifted at the federal level, policy innovation in the states expanded in the 1990s and the first decade of the twenty-first century. In areas as diverse as the minimum wage, greenhouse gas emissions, health care coverage, prescription drug imports, and embryonic stem-cell research, state governments enacted significant legislation. By 2007, California, Illinois, Connecticut, and New Jersey had dedicated funding to promote new types of stem-cell research that were generally disallowed under federal funding. Even though President Bush's policy did not allow federal funds to be used for the development of new embryonic stem-cell lines for research purposes, the research was not illegal, so there was no usurpation of national supremacy.[36]

In most of these areas, states acted because of their dissatisfaction with national government policies. In other areas, the federal government's involvement had waned as government officials' concerns were focused elsewhere. Other factors were tight budgets that forced legislative innovation and the increased demands placed on state governments by advocacy groups.

Has there been a revolution in federalism?

Given these strong moves by Congress, the president, the Supreme Court, and the states, why consider the change in federalism to be anything short of a revolution? One reason is that the federal government still remained involved in those policy areas known for devolution, such as welfare. States are free to design their programs as they wish, but they are not free to eliminate those programs. And federal involvement in new policy areas is possible. Complaining about "frivolous" and "junk" lawsuits, President Bush and many members of Congress argued strongly for national limits on non-economic damages—factors such as pain and suffering, loss of companionship—in cases concerning matters such as medical malpractice and injuries received from using a product. Traditionally, this issue has been regulated by the states, but with an increasingly globalized economy and for purposes of efficiency and competitiveness, business interests may push more strongly for nationalized standards to replace 50 separate state standards. More aggressively, the federal government can pass **preemption legislation** that declares certain actions off-limits for state governments (just as state governments can pass this kind of legislation to restrict localities within their borders). For example, federal law passed in 2005 prohibits certain kinds of liability suits from being filed against firearms manufacturers in state courts.[37]

One example of the pull and tug of federalism links terrorism and driver's licenses—two seemingly distinct areas of federal and state responsibility, respectively. Congress, in the Real ID Act of 2005, sought as an antiterrorism measure to require all states to demand proof of permanent residency before issuing driver's licenses; ten states had no such requirements. In addition, licenses were to be standardized in certain ways across the states, such as the information stored on the machine-readable cards, and state license databases would need to be linked to a national database. If a state's licenses were not consistent with the federal standard, individuals holding those licenses would not be able to use them for identification purposes with federal agencies, such as the Transportation Security Administration, which handles security at the nation's airports. Proponents of the law argued it would make it more difficult for terrorists to operate in the United States and more difficult for illegal immigrants to get legal employment. Some of the hijackers involved in the September 11, 2001, attacks had acquired driver's licenses and been able to board planes, despite being in the United States illegally.

Opposition to the Real ID Act spread through states in early 2007. Legislators in many states objected to this federal intervention in traditional state responsibility, its perceived threats to privacy, and the cost imposed on state governments. State governments estimated the cost to them to be $11 billion nationwide, but the federal government had allocated only $40 million to implement the law.[38] Quickly, a majority of states passed resolutions objecting to the law and pledging not to implement it. By the end of 2007, the federal government had softened its demands in an attempt to increase support from state officials, and the original May 2008 deadline to meet the act's requirements was extended by ten years.[39]

Similarly, in other areas the federal government's role has become more pronounced in recent years. In the conduct of elections, which were once considered completely the province of the states, national norms have emerged over time, including who can vote. States have not been allowed to place term limits on members of Congress. The federal "Motor Voter" law of 1993 mandated that voting registration be made available at government offices such as motor vehicle bureaus. Following the problems in the 2000 presidential election, the Help America Vote Act (HAVA) of 2002 mandated changes in state's voting technology—eliminating punch card ballots, for example.[40]

The most notable recent example of an expanded federal role has been in education, long a bastion of state and local governments. The No Child Left Behind Act championed by President Bush and passed by Congress in 2002 required school districts to test each child in grades three through eight and specified penalties for schools whose students do poorly and are not improving. The federal role has also increased with regard to marriage, another traditional state concern. The Defense of Marriage Act in 1996 declared that marriage for federal purposes is between one man and one woman and that states cannot impose other marriage arrangements upon the other states.[41] During George W. Bush's presidency, the national government and the states were in frequent conflict over their appropriate roles in environmental policy. This increased federal role across policy areas had multiple causes—partisan goals, interest group activism, reactions to crises, similarity of goals among federal and state officials, and disorganized state officials outmaneuvered by unified legislators at the national level.[42]

Another reason not to overstate the extent of the new federalism "revolution" is that the Court did not completely defer to the states in its decisions about sovereign immunity from lawsuits. When cases involved Fourteenth Amendment issues of equal protection (see Chapter 6), particularly in the areas of race and gender, the Court allowed states to be subject to federal authority. For example, the Court concluded that an individual could sue a state in federal court for that state's alleged gender-based discrimination in implementing the Family Medical Leave

Act, and that these suits were consistent with Congress's intent when it passed the act.[43]

This idea, that Congress could respond to widespread and persistent discrimination, was also at the core of *Tennessee v. Lane* (2004). The case concerned a paraplegic who could not attend a court case because of a lack of elevators in the court building. To the Supreme Court, the fundamental importance of citizen access to the courts overrode the state's claim to immunity from a discrimination lawsuit. Congress was right to allow an exception to sovereign immunity, in the Court's view, because it had amassed evidence of recurrent, extensive violations of equal access by the states. If the Court believes a right is of special gravity, it will give Congress more leeway to force states to comply with federal rules that might otherwise be seen as exceeding federal constitutional authority.[44]

The Supreme Court also has been willing to trim state power. The Court rejected a California law that allowed Holocaust survivors to pursue insurance claims through lawsuits, rather than through international diplomacy as called for by federal foreign policy. The California statute, in the Court's view, interfered with the federal government's authority over foreign policy.[45] And in *Gonzales v. Raich* (2005), Congress's power to prohibit the personal growing and possession of marijuana for medical use was upheld, superseding a California law that allowed such use. The federal Controlled Substances Act did not allow exemptions for medical use of marijuana and the federal government could regulate those products involved in interstate commerce. Although growth for personal medicinal use might appear to be entirely local and thus not an area for congressional regulation, the Court concluded that it affected supply and demand and was in effect a part of the national marijuana market. Therefore, it was subject to the national government's interstate commerce power.

So where does federalism stand today? Entering the second decade of the twenty-first century, federalism continues to evolve. It has not returned to the dual federalism of the nineteenth century, as the federal government's intervention into areas like education, traditionally thought of as a local and state responsibility, makes clear. But it is also not simply the cooperative federalism of much of the twentieth century. It is neither strictly layer cake nor marble cake. Today's federalism remains cooperative in many respects but does so within dual federalism boundaries that are being reasserted by elected officials and by the Supreme Court.

Rather than a cake, perhaps a better metaphor today would be a pie. Dual federalism is the crust that prevents cooperative federalism from spilling too far outside the constitutional pan. Rather than the open-ended cooperative federalism in place from the mid-1930s to mid-1990s, today's is a constrained cooperative federalism, restricted and limited by the Court's enforcement of dual federalist principles via the Tenth and Eleventh Amendments.

SUMMARY

▶ The Constitution defines the framework within which American federalism operates, identifying areas where the national government is supreme to the states. But disputes about the role of the states in the federal system have never gone away. Differing interpretations of the formation of the United States contribute to the dispute. To some, the union was a joining together of "the people," which weakens the primacy that states should have in federalism. To others, the union was a joining together of the states in which states reserved a substantial amount of the sovereignty they held prior to creating the United States.

▶ The two major forms of federal–state relations in American history have been dual federalism and cooperative federalism. Dual federalism delineates separate and independent spheres of function and responsibility for the federal and state governments. All citizens have dual citizenship, being a citizen of both their state and the country. Prevailing Supreme Court interpretation of Congress's power to regulate interstate commerce reinforced dual federalism.

▶ Rather than strict spheres, cooperative federalism allows for many areas of overlapping responsibilities for these two layers of government. Redefining interstate commerce played a significant role in expanding the scope of federal government responsibility and moving the country from dual to cooperative federalism. Collaboration, mandates, and persuasion in the form of fiscal federalism are types of federal–state interaction in cooperative federalism. Generally, the federal government was the more powerful in this "cooperative" arrangement, thus, cooperative did not always mean harmonious. Mandates are sometimes described as coercive federalism, and fiscal federalism can apply pressure on state officials to follow federal government wishes.

▶ Over the past two decades, the relationship between the federal and state governments has shifted. State officials became more active in policy areas where they had previously deferred to national leadership. At the national level, elected officials sought to provide states with more flexibility and responsibility over some policies. And in a number of important decisions, the Supreme Court clamped down on Congress's use of the interstate commerce justification, concluded that the federal government had become improperly involved in areas of state government responsibility, and asserted the argument that the sovereignty of state governments shielded them from some federal government regulation. Not everything has moved in the direction of more state authority, however. In few policy areas has the federal government fully withdrawn, and it has inserted itself into new areas that had traditionally been the purview of the states.

KEY TERMS

block grant, p. 000
categorical grant, p. 000
commerce clause, p. 000
compact theory, p. 000
confederation, p. 000
cooperative federalism, p. 000
devolution, p. 000
dual citizenship, p. 000
dual federalism, p. 000
dual sovereignty, p. 000
enumerated powers, p. 000
federalism, p. 000
fiscal federalism, p. 000

implied powers, p. 000
mandate, p. 000
nationalist theory, p. 000
necessary and proper clause, p. 000
nullification, p. 000
police power, p. 000
preemption legislation, p. 000
revenue sharing, p. 000
sovereign immunity, p. 000
sovereignty, p. 000
unfunded mandate, p. 000
unitary system, p. 000

SUGGESTED READINGS

Samuel H. Beer. 1993. *To Make A Nation: The Rediscovery of American Federalism*. Cambridge: Harvard University Press. A thorough analysis of the principles and philosophy of American federalism.

Martha N. Derthick. 2001. *Keeping the Compound Republic: Essays on American Federalism*. Washington, DC: Brookings Institution Press. The evolution of federalism in the United States and an analysis of a range of issues concerning federalism and intergovernmental relations.

Morton Grodzins. 1966. *The American System.* Chicago: Rand McNally. Makes the argument that the idea of a distinct division of labor between the federal and state governments has been exaggerated.

Paul Manna. 2006. *School's In: Federalism and the National Education Agenda.* Washington, DC: Georgetown University Press. Shows how the increased role of the federal government in education was a result of building upon state-level fiscal and administrative capacities created by education reformers in previous decades.

Paul E. Peterson. 1995. *The Price of Federalism.* Washington, DC: Brookings Institution Press. An exploration of the ways in which federalism works well and the political pressures that can push legislators away from it.

Paul L. Posner. 1998. *The Politics of Unfunded Mandates: Whither Federalism?* Washington, DC: Georgetown University Press. Examines the political struggle between national and state officials over paying for programs required by the national government.

Deloria Vine Jr. and Clifford M. Lytle. 1998. *The Nations Within: The Past and Future of American Indian Sovereignty.* Austin: University of Texas Press. Through a close accounting of the politics surrounding an important bill, the book explores the complexity of tribal sovereignty in the American federal system.

confederation a loose grouping of independent political units, such as states or countries, whose main purpose is to govern the relationship between those units.

unitary system a form of government in which government at the highest level has the power to create, combine, or disband lower-level governments and determine what powers will be allowed at the lower levels.

federalism a form of government that distributes power across a national government and sub-national governments and ensures the existence of the sub-national governments.

sovereignty having the ultimate authority to make decisions within one's borders, without interference by other governments.

compact theory a theory of the founding of the American government that argued that the states were sovereign units that joined together in the new national government but did not give up their status as sovereign, independent governments.

mandate an order from the federal government that requires state governments to take a certain action.

fiscal federalism a technique of persuasion in which the federal government offers resources to states that agree to take certain actions.

nullification the suggestion that states had the right to nullify national laws to which they objected and believed violated the U.S. Constitution.

nationalist theory a theory of the founding of the American government that sees the Constitution as the joining together of the people as much as or more so than the joining together of the states.

cooperative federalism a form of federalism in which the national and state governments share many functions and areas of authority.

necessary and proper clause a provision in the U.S. Constitution that gives Congress the authority to make the laws needed to carry out the specific duties assigned to Congress by the Constitution.

enumerated powers a list of specifically listed duties that the U.S. Constitution assigns to Congress.

implied powers
functions and actions that Congress could perform in order to implement and exercise its enumerated powers.

categorical grant
funds provided by the federal government to a state or local government for a specific, defined purpose.

dual federalism a form of federalism in which the national and state governments have distinct areas of authority and power, and individuals have rights as both citizens of states and citizens of the United States.

dual sovereignty the idea that both the national and state governments have sovereignty, but over different policy areas and functions.

police power the protection of public safety, health, welfare, and morality by a government.

commerce clause a provision in the U.S. Constitution that gives Congress the power to regulate commerce with other countries, among the states, and with Indian tribes.

dual citizenship the idea that an individual is a citizen of both his or her state and the United States. Rights and responsibilities can vary from state to state and can be different on the state and national levels.

unfunded mandate federal requirements that states take some action, but without provision of sufficient resources to take the action.

block grant funds provided by the federal government to a state or local government in general support of a broad government function such as education or transportation.

revenue sharing federal government funds provided to state, cities, and counties to use for whatever purposes these governments chose.

devolution a process in which the authority over a government program's rules and implementation is largely transferred from the federal government to the state governments.

sovereign immunity the principle that state governments are immune from being sued by private parties in federal court unless they consent to the suits or under particular circumstances in which Congress may constitutionally override this immunity.

preemption legislation laws that prohibit a lower-level government from taking a specific action.

5 Civil Liberties

Pledge of Allegiance

I pledge allegiance to the Flag of the United States of America, and to the Republic for which it stands, one Nation, under God, indivisible, with liberty and justice for all.

Since the 1950s, millions of American school children have recited the Pledge of Allegiance as they started their school day. Should they?

Michael Newdow believed they should not. Newdow's daughter attended school in Elk Grove, California, where teachers led students in the recitation of the Pledge. Newdow, an atheist, protested that this practice imposed religion on his daughter and infringed on his rights as a parent to guide his daughter's religious beliefs. In 2000 he filed a federal court case challenging the Pledge as an unconstitutional establishment of religion.

Many Americans may think the Pledge of Allegiance was born along with the American Revolution, but it did not exist until 1892, when Francis Bellamy wrote it to help celebrate Columbus Day. It was sent to schools around the country and quickly caught on as part of the typical school day. The language recited today is Bellamy's, with one exception: Congress's 1954 addition of the words "under God" to the Pledge.[1] The addition was intended to separate the United States from its primary Cold War rival, the Soviet Union, where there was no official tolerance of religion.

The Pledge raises two immediate issues. First, in a country in which free speech is treasured, can children be compelled to recite the Pledge? The Supreme Court's answer is that they cannot. Not even the purpose of national unity, of building in children a love of their country, can be allowed to infringe on freedom of speech. In a 1943 decision, the Court struck down a West Virginia law that required teachers and students to begin the school day with a salute and pledge to the flag.[2] The Court's majority concluded that if "there is any fixed star in our constitutional constellation, it is that no official, high or petty, can prescribe what shall be orthodox in politics, nationalism, religion, or other matters of opinion or force citizens to confess by word or act their faith therein."

The second issue is whether, in a country in which freedom of religion is treasured, the presence of the phrase "under God" in the Pledge is equivalent to government endorsement of religion. Does it impose religious views on children? Would disallowing this language restrict the free speech rights of those individuals who are fully prepared to say the Pledge as written? Although children cannot be forced to recite the Pledge, the reality is that in many schools the Pledge is recited. Technically, students can simply remain silent or leave the room, but in its school prayer decisions, the Court has typically considered this impractical given the age of the children and the social dynamics of the school environment. The pressure to conform, the Court has concluded, would be large. Is "under God" in the Pledge different?

Newdow's initial lawsuit, filed in March 2000 in federal district court, argued that his daughter was injured when compelled to "watch and listen as her state-employed teacher in her state-run school leads her classmates in a ritual proclaiming that there is a God, and that ours is 'one nation under God.'"[3] His suit was dismissed, but in 2002 a federal appeals court decided in his favor, ruling that public school recitation of the Pledge's "under God" was the equivalent of a government- endorsed religious act and was therefore unconstitutional.[4]

Political leaders denounced the decision, arguing that it ignored the importance of religion in American political culture and did not impose religion on anyone. The Senate voted 99-0 to keep the words "under God" in the Pledge; the House concurred by a 416-3 vote. On June 14, 2004—Flag Day, an irony lost on no one—the Supreme Court overturned the appeals court decision on technical, not constitutional, grounds.[5] The Court ruled that Newdow should not have been allowed to file the case on his daughter's behalf because his ex-wife, the girl's mother, did not object to her daughter hearing the Pledge, and the girl lived with her mother. To many political scientists and legal analysts, the Court took the safest way out of a difficult bind. Politically, overturning the Pledge would have resulted in widespread condemnation, but legally, the Court's previous decisions lent support to Newdow's position. Although public opinion and political leaders of both parties clearly support allowing "under God" to be part of the Pledge, it will be up to a future Court to decide whether the Pledge with that language is constitutionally acceptable.

The case of the Pledge is not unique in American civil liberties history. Constitutional guarantees such as freedom of speech, freedom of religion, and the right to assemble are general principles, but politics is also about specifics. Few people, for example, would argue that speech that is deliberately untrue and defames someone should be allowed without any consequence. Few people would find it appropriate for a group to hold a loud and raucous protest rally at 3:00 a.m. in the middle of a quiet residential neighborhood. It is a frequent aspect of civil liberties that one

person's liberty might infringe on another's, or that one form of civil liberties, such as the right to assemble, might conflict with another individual's right to enjoy his property, or his right to privacy. And sometimes an individual right might be in conflict with an important governmental or societal interest. In these conflicts, choices must be made, either through law, executive action, or court decision, each of which are examined in this chapter. Some people will be unhappy that the Supreme Court will not allow a mandatory Pledge of Allegiance. Others will complain that even a voluntarily spoken Pledge infringes on their freedom of speech and violates the separation of church and state. If the words "under God" were removed from the Pledge, other individuals would believe that *their* religious freedom was infringed upon. In this chapter, you will note a number of Supreme Court decisions that were decided by votes of 5-4, suggest-

ing just how deep the conflict over defining proper protections for civil liberties can be, and how a change in the members of the Court can lead to significant changes in these definitions.

In addition to tension and conflict, another constant of civil liberties is change: What is considered appropriate at one time might not be considered so at another. This chapter will emphasize how the scope of civil liberties protections has changed across time. Historically, three paths have led to this change in scope. First, the civil liberties restrictions placed on the federal government by the United States Constitution were gradually applied to state governments. Second, as membership in the Supreme Court changes, interpretation of the Constitution's meaning can also change. And third, Supreme Court decisions have established individual rights that are not specifically mentioned in the Constitution.

THIS CHAPTER WILL EXAMINE:

▶ the guarantees of civil liberties in the Constitution and the process by which these guarantees became binding on state governments

▶ the different standards by which the Supreme Court has determined whether restrictions on freedom of speech are acceptable

▶ how the Supreme Court has interpreted cases regarding government establishment of religion and cases concerning the right of individuals to practice their faith, and how Congress has reacted to the Court's actions

▶ the expansion since the 1960s in the rights accorded to those accused of crimes, and how the Supreme Court has attempted to balance the rights of defendants with the need for police and prosecutors to investigate potential criminal activity

▶ the methods by which participants in judicial proceedings have attempted to establish that Americans have rights other than those specifically listed in the Constitution.

Civil Liberties in American Politics and the Constitution

Civil liberties are another name for individual rights. The Declaration of Independence makes eight references to a "right" or "rights." Equality, another important principle in the American governmental framework, is mentioned only twice. Even "the people," a staple of revolutionary thought and language, appears less frequently than rights. And this rights language is not just a thing of the past.

The 2004 Democratic Party platform mentions rights 36 times. The Republican platform goes even further, mentioning rights 51 times. (See Table 5-1.) The parties' references range from very general mentions of rights to more specific notions such as the right to not join a union or the right to health care.

Table 5-1. Number of References to Rights in the Republican and Democratic Party Platforms, 2004

REFERENCE	REPUBLICAN PLATFORM	DEMOCRATIC PLATFORM
Human rights, foreign	5	7
Civil rights	3	5
Voting rights	3	4
Right of U.S. territories to self-determination	4	2
Own guns	4	1
Join labor union	1	2
Protect rights	1	1
Individual rights	1	1
Israel's self defense	1	1
Victims' rights	1	1
To be free	1	
Property rights	5	
Educational rights	3	
Right to life	2	
Equal rights	2	
Workers' rights	2	
Property rights, foreign	1	
Religious freedom	1	
Rights of families (no international abortion funds)	1	
Cuban refugees	1	
Equal rights, foreign	1	
Right to vote, foreign	1	
Right to choose government, foreign	1	
Plaintiff's right to speedy trial	1	
Right to not join union	1	
Prohibit flag "desecration"	1	
Religious organizations freedom in hiring	1	
Right of states to ignore same-sex marriages	1	
Workers' rights, foreign		3
Right to choose abortion		2
Military families' Bill of Rights		1
Health care		1
Patients' Bill of Rights		1
Constitutional rights		1
Immigrants		1
Equal rights for District of Columbia residents		1

Compiled by the authors.

Note: Each entry indicates references to a "right" or "rights" in the party platforms.

We can safely say that very few words are more important to Americans' understanding of their political system than *rights*. Political rhetoric in America is full of references to rights, whether individual rights, like the right to speak freely, or collective rights, such as the right of the people to assemble. American political culture, with its emphasis on individual independence, liberty, property ownership, religious freedom, and democratic government, is infused throughout with individual rights. Some rights might be expressed from a more communitarian perspective, such as the idea that it is in the community's interest and not only the individual's interest that everyone in the community has a right to an equal quality of education.

To declare something as a right is significant because it implies that government has an obligation to protect it or provide it. If you believe that freedom of speech is a right, for example, you most likely do not want government to interfere with speech. If you believe that health care is a right, you most likely want government to play some role in providing health care either through direct provision or by giving individuals the financial resources to purchase it in the private market.

Civil liberties identify areas where government should not interfere.

In the United States, **civil liberties** focus on individual rights that government is obliged to protect, normally by standing back and not interfering. When Americans talk about civil liberties, they are typically talking about places government should not go: speech, the press, religious expression, organizing for political purposes, and so on.[6] With civil liberties, the call is usually for government to be passive and not intrude when, for example, individuals speak, worship, or engage in political action. As discussed in Chapter 2, American political culture suggests that these rights are not *granted* to us or *given* to us by government—they are inherent in us as people. What government can do is protect or restrict the exercise of these rights.[7]

In some instances, Americans will tolerate limits on certain rights to preserve public safety, order, or other important societal goals. For example, Americans have the right to assemble, but that does not extend into a right to assemble in the middle of a city street and stop traffic. Government has to be concerned with the conflicting rights of both the assemblers and those needing to go about their lives and go to work, school, or wherever they might need to travel. Part of civil liberties protection, therefore, is that when government restricts the exercise of rights, it does so with **due process**. This means that there are procedural safeguards in place prior to the restriction of rights. Government officials exercising due process have followed clear guidelines and established procedures. In the case of gathering in the street, for example, there are procedures by which a group can get a permit to assemble in the street. Or if government takes your real estate property so it can build a new road, it cannot simply take the land but must compensate you for taking your private property for a public use. As with many terms in the Constitution, "public use" can be defined broadly or narrowly. In 2005, for example, a divided 5-4 Supreme Court upheld New London, Connecticut's desire to take private property for economic development, which in practice meant building private office space and a conference hotel.[8] In effect, property was transferred from one private party to another as a "public use." In the wake of that controversial decision, laws were passed around the country to prohibit this kind of government action.

On the whole, civil liberties protections are strong in the United States. Although Americans often think of the United States as unique in this regard, the

United States is 1 of 52 countries judged in 2008 to have the strongest protection for civil liberties among all 193 independent countries by Freedom House, an international political rights and civil liberties watchdog group. Freedom House describes these countries as having freedom of expression, assembly, association, education, and religion; having an established and equitable rule of law; and enjoying free economic activity. In general, civil liberties protections are strongest in Europe and the Americas and weakest in Asia and Africa. These patterns correlate roughly with the distribution of prosperity around the globe, leading social scientists to examine whether civil liberties result from prosperity or create prosperity. Research suggests that both processes are present: civil liberties encourage economic growth, and economic growth encourages civil liberties.[9] Figure 5-1 shows the countries Freedom House considers to be free, partly free, and not free.[10]

The Constitution protects civil liberties.

When Americans think about the constitutional protection of civil liberties, they think first of the Bill of Rights, the first ten amendments to the Constitution. But this is only one of the Constitution's protections of liberty. To the Framers, the structural principles in the articles of the Constitution—separation of powers, checks and balances, federalism, and limited government—all worked to enhance the general protection of the people's liberty. The Framers also included specific civil liberties protections in the articles of the Constitution. For example, to protect the integrity of "due process," the Constitution declares that only courts and juries—not the legislature—can determine whether an individual is guilty of a crime. The intent is to ensure that, before any rights are restricted, the proceedings that might lead to that outcome are fair, impartial, proper, and not subject to the political pressures that exist in a legislature. Both the federal and state governments are prohibited from passing a bill of attainder, which is legislation that declares a person guilty of a crime and establishes punishment, all without a trial.

The articles of the Constitution protect civil liberties in other ways. Religious tests or oaths for federal employment are prohibited. The writ of *habeas corpus*, which gives an accused individual the right to appear in court to hear the formal charges against him, cannot be suspended except to enhance public safety during times of rebellion or invasion. And an individual cannot be tried based on *ex post facto* ("after the fact") laws passed by state governments or the federal government, meaning that you cannot be tried for an act that was not illegal at the time you committed it.

Freedom of expression and the rights of the accused are the two main areas of civil liberties protection in the Bill of Rights.

The Bill of Rights is at the heart of constitutional civil liberties protections. The first eight of these ten amendments protect specific rights. The Ninth Amendment states that the failure to list rights in the preceding amendments should not be presumed to mean that the people do not have additional rights. The Tenth Amendment declares that powers not given to the federal government are reserved for the states or the people.[11]

The Federalists believed that a Bill of Rights was unnecessary (see Chapter 3). In their view, the articles of the Constitution itself contained specific guarantees of liberty, its general structure was designed to protect liberty, and state constitutions had bills of rights. The risk of specifying rights was that government might be presumed free to ignore all rights not mentioned. But the Federalists quickly saw that the promise of additional specific protections would increase the likelihood of ratification.

The protections in the first eight amendments of the Bill of Rights can be categorized into three groups, according to whether the amendment appeared geared primarily toward law making (legislative branch), the execution and administration of law (executive branch), or the interpretation of law (judicial branch). Table 5-2 shows that the protections were also overwhelmingly in two categories: freedom of expression and the rights of those accused of crime. A final category consists of

Table 5-2. Specific Civil Liberties Protections in the Bill of Rights

PRIMARY GOVERNMENT BRANCH TARGETED	CATEGORY OF SPECIFIC CIVIL LIBERTIES PROTECTED (AMENDMENT NUMBER IN PARENTHESES)		
	FREEDOM OF EXPRESSION	RIGHTS OF DEFENDANTS	OTHER PROTECTIONS
Legislative	Freedom of religion exercise		
	No establishment of religion (I)		
	Freedom of speech (I)		
	Freedom of assembly (I)		
	Freedom to petition government (I)		
	Freedom of the press (I)		
Executive		Cannot search for or seize evidence without court warrant and probable cause (IV)	Right of people to keep and bear arms (II)
			Cannot use citizen homes to house soldiers without due process (III)
			Property cannot be taken for public use without fair compensation (V)
Judicial		Right to grand jury hearing in criminal cases (V)	
		Right to jury trial in criminal and civil cases (VI and VII)	
		Right to speedy trial (VI)	
		Right to hear charges against oneself (VI)	
		Right to confront witnesses and offer own witnesses (VI)	
		Cannot be forced to incriminate oneself (VI)	
		Cannot be tried for the same crime more than once (VI)	
		Right to legal counsel (VI)	
		Bail and punishment cannot be excessive (VIII)	

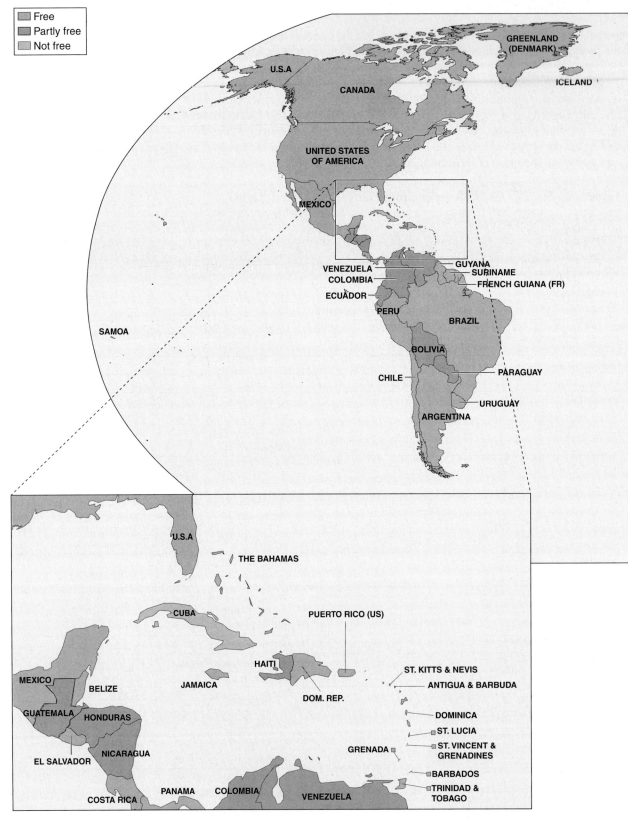

Figure 5-1. Freedom Around the Globe, 2008. The number of free or partly free countries has increased since 1997, but there is still significant re-

gional variation in the spread of political rights and civil liberties around the globe.

three provisions that do not fit in the previous two categories. One of these, the quartering of troops in homes, has not been especially significant since its ratification into the Constitution, but the other two—the right to keep and bear arms and the compensation for public appropriation of one's property—have been the subject of extensive political and legal debate.

Nationalization of the Bill of Rights protected individuals against the actions of state governments.

Despite its importance in the constitutional ratification debate and despite the reverence with which it is held today, the Bill of Rights had a more limited effect on American politics during the nineteenth century than it does today. During that time, government was much more active on the state level. Many states had their own bills of rights to protect their citizens from state government actions, but the U.S. Constitution's Bill of Rights was considered to apply only to the actions of the national government. After all, the words "Congress shall make no law" in the First Amendment seem pretty clearly to apply to the national level of government and not the states. Recall the case of *Barron v. Baltimore* (see Chapter 4), in which the Supreme Court declared that Barron was not entitled to compensation under the Constitution's Fifth Amendment because it was the city of Baltimore, not the federal government, that took Barron's property without compensation.

The nationalization of the Bill of Rights is the first of three paths by which the scope of civil liberties protection has been changed. Beginning in 1897, as explained below, the Supreme Court began to see the Bill of Rights as limiting the actions of state governments as well as the national government. This revolutionary shift opened the door for increased federal government authority.[12]

Incorporation and the Fourteenth Amendment The Supreme Court used the **incorporation process** to apply the Bill of Rights to the states. The Fourteenth Amendment was key to this process. Stated technically, the Bill of Rights was incorporated into the Fourteenth Amendment and through this inclusion, became binding on the states.

The Fourteenth Amendment has been profoundly important to American life. The amendment was ratified in July 1868 as part of the post–Civil War reconstruction of American government and society. It was the first amendment to limit state action directly, declaring that no state may "deprive any person of life, liberty, or property, without due process of law." Considering the battle over state versus national power during the framing of the Constitution, and the many protections for state sovereignty, this was a remarkable turnabout. Why the change? Given that the collapse of a unified nation contributed to the descent into a horrific war, it is understandable that a majority of politicians and the public supported constitutional provisions that could prevent states from straying too far from fundamental protections of life, liberty, and property.

Specifically, this "due process clause" of the Fourteenth Amendment brings protection from state government intrusions on life, liberty, and property into the U.S. Constitution.[13] But what exactly does that mean? This is what the Supreme Court began to determine in a series of decisions. The Court needed to decide precisely what life, liberty, and property referred to.

Selective incorporation The Court began the process with a decision concerning property. In 1897, the Court decided that in order for the Fourteenth Amendment's general protection of property to be a meaningful concept, it required compensation when property was taken for public use. The Fifth Amendment's "takings clause," which states that private property cannot be taken for public use unless the property owner is compensated, was thus incorporated into the Fourteenth Amendment and, therefore, now applied to the states.

Over a quarter-century would pass before the Court took another incorporation step. In 1925, the Court decided that the Fourteenth Amendment's protection of "liberty" must include a guarantee of free speech. The First Amendment's free speech guarantee was thus incorporated into the Fourteenth Amendment's protection for "liberty" and now it, too, applied to the action of state governments.[14]

Notice that these two cases incorporated only part of the Bill of Rights guarantees into the Fourteenth Amendment. In practice, the Supreme Court has proceeded through **selective incorporation**, meaning that it incorporated civil liberties guarantees in bits and pieces. The Supreme Court has not simply declared that the entire Bill of Rights applied to the states. Rather, the Court has worked with the issues in the cases before it. As cases raised issues concerning particular parts of the amendments that comprise the Bill of Rights, the Court would decide whether that particular right was fundamental enough to the Fourteenth Amendment's protection of life, liberty, and property that it should now apply to the states.

Over time, the Court declared that additional portions of the Bill of Rights beyond these first two would apply to state governments. This spread of selective incorporation was due mainly to changing perspectives brought by new justices on the Court, as well as the cumulative process of incorporation itself. As one part of the Bill of Rights was incorporated, the logic of future decisions pushed toward incorporating similar constitutional provisions. Table 5-3 shows that selective incorporation has been a lengthy process. For a long time, selective incorporation was essentially limited to the First Amendment. Then, in the 1960s, the Court addressed many issues concerning the rights of defendants. Before the year indicated in the table, it would have been possible for a state to engage in the behavior mentioned. For example, prior to 1961, a state or local government could allow its police to conduct searches and seize evidence without a warrant. This does not mean that all states allowed such searches, because the state constitution or state law might have prohibited it. But there would have been no federal constitutional prohibition on states conducting such searches as they investigated alleged violations of state or local law.

Right to keep and bear arms Even today, there are sections of the Bill of Rights that have not been incorporated and so are not binding on the states. Of the unincorporated portions of the Bill of Rights, the Second Amendment right to keep and bear arms has been the most politically significant. The National Rifle Association (NRA), a group that advocates for the interests of gun owners, has been one of the most visible political organizations in American politics at the national level for decades, and politicians have scrambled to avoid being seen as anti-gun. The NRA relies heavily on the individualism and distrust of government authority present in American political culture when it appeals to the public for support.

There is a disconnect, however, between the public debate and the courts' interpretation of the Second Amendment. The Second Amendment states, "a well regulated Militia, being necessary to the security of a free State, the right of the people to keep and bear Arms, shall not be infringed." The Supreme Court has considered this to be a collective guarantee of the self-defense of the states, rather than a guarantee of individual ownership. Militias were called into action by state

Table 5-3. Selective Incorporation of the Bill of Rights into the Fourteenth Amendment

AMENDMENT	ISSUE	YEAR	KEY CASE
Amendments Fully Incorporated			
I	Freedom of speech	1925	*Gitlow v. New York*
I	Freedom of the press	1931	*Near v. Minnesota*
I	Freedom of assembly	1937	*De Jonge v. Oregon*
I	Freedom of religious exercise	1940	*Cantwell v. Connecticut*
I	No establishment of religion	1947	
I	Freedom of association	1958	*NAACP v. Alabama*
I	Right to petition	1963	*NAACP v. Button*
IV	No unreasonable search and seizure	1949	*Wolf v. Colorado*
IV	No search and seizure without warrant	1961	*Mapp v. Ohio*
VI	Right to counsel in capital punishment cases	1932	*Powell v. Alabama*
VI	Right to public trial	1948	*In re Oliver*
VI	Right to counsel in felony cases	1963	*Gideon v. Wainwright*
VI	Right to confront witnesses	1965	*Pointer v. Texas*
VI	Right to impartial jury	1966	*Parker v. Gladden*
VI	Right to speedy trial	1967	*Klopfer v. North Carolina*
VI	Right to compel supportive witnesses to appear in court	1967	*Washington v. Texas*
VI	Right to jury trial for serious crimes	1968	*Duncan v. Louisiana*
VI	Right to counsel for all crimes involving jail terms	1972	*Argersinger v. Hamlin*
Amendments Partially Incorporated			
V	Compensation for public taking of private property	1897	*Chicago, Burlington, and Quincy Railroad v. Chicago*
V	No compulsory self-incrimination	1964	*Malloy v. Hogan*
V	No forced confession	1964	*Escobedo v. Illinois*
V	Right to remain silent	1966	*Miranda v. Arizona*
V	No double jeopardy	1969	*Benton v. Maryland*
V	Right to grand jury hearing in criminal cases	NA	
VIII	No cruel and unusual punishment	1962	*Robinson v. California*
VIII	No excessive bail or punishment	NA	
Amendments Not Incorporated			
II	Right to keep and bear arms	NA	
III	Limits on quartering of soldiers	NA	
VII	Right to jury trial in civil cases	NA	

governments to repel threats to public order. As long as the Supreme Court considers constitutionally protected gun ownership to be connected to state militias rather than individual ownership, it is unlikely that it will conclude that gun control laws violate the Second Amendment.[15] The Court was prepared to rule on this issue in 2008 in a case involving the prohibition of handgun ownership in the District of Columbia.

Denationalization allows variation in states' protection of civil liberties.

Nationalization of civil liberties means that most of the Bill of Rights guarantees now also apply to state governments. But in some areas, the Supreme Court has allowed denationalization. This does not mean literally that federal constitutional protection has been eliminated, but that the Supreme Court allows variation in the exercise of a right from one state to another.

Consider freedom of religious practice. The freedom to practice one's religion is fundamentally the same in New Hampshire as it is in New Mexico, the same in Oregon as Ohio, the same in Texas as Tennessee. That is because the Supreme Court considers freedom of religious practice a fundamental right, such that liberty is unthinkable as a concept without it—religious freedom is part of the very essence of liberty.

The Court has made it clear that other rights, although undeniably of value and importance, do not rise to that level.[16] With fundamental rights, the Supreme Court tolerates very little variation from state to state. With qualified rights, however, the Court allows states more flexibility. Abortion is the most politically charged example of denationalization. Freedom to obtain an abortion does not fall into the category of fundamental rights, so the Court has allowed significant variation in states' restriction of its exercise. The ability of a minor to obtain an abortion, for example, varies widely across the states (see Table 5-4).

Freedom of Speech

As noted at the beginning of this chapter, nationalization of the Bill of Rights, which gradually applied most of the protections in the Bill of Rights to the actions

Table 5-4. Requirements for Abortion Access by Minors

REQUIREMENT	STATES
Consent of both parents or judge	Mississippi, North Dakota
Consent of one parent or judge	Alabama, Alaska*, Arizona, Arkansas, California*, Idaho*, Indiana, Kentucky, Louisiana, Massachusetts, Michigan, Missouri, New Mexico*, Pennsylvania, Rhode Island, Tennessee, Texas, Virginia, Wyoming
Consent of one parent, judge, or other relative	Maine, North Carolina, South Carolina, Wisconsin
Notification to both parents	Utah
Notification to both parents or judge	Minnesota
Notification to both parents, judge, or relative	Colorado
Notification to one parent or judge	Florida, Georgia, Kansas, Maryland, Montana*, Nebraska, Nevada*, New Hampshire*, New Jersey*, Ohio, Oklahoma, South Dakota, West Virginia
Notification to one parent, judge, or relative	Delaware, Illinois*, Iowa
No consent or notification requirement	Connecticut, Hawaii, New York, Oregon, Vermont, Washington, Washington, D.C.

*Laws not enforced due to legal or constitutional issues.

Source: Planned Parenthood, "Laws Requiring Parental Consent or Notification for Minors' Abortions," http://www.plannedparenthood.org/pp2/portal/files/portal/medicalinfo/abortion/fact-parental-consent.xml

Note: States also vary on many additional details, such as whether the rules apply to age 16 and under or age 18 and under; which relatives, under what conditions can give consent or receive notice; whether a mental health professional can give consent or receive notice; and how to proceed when both parents are no longer married or one or both parents cannot be located or are deceased.

of state governments, is one of three paths by which the scope and reach of civil liberties protections has changed over time. A second path is when the Supreme Court or Congress expands or restricts the protections for rights and liberties listed in the Constitution as they develop new interpretations of what the Constitution requires and forbids. Political scientists have shown that a change in membership in these institutions can lead to dramatic changes in the constitutional interpretation of individual rights.[17] The following sections will explore this path by examining the changing scope of civil liberties protection in the areas of speech, freedom of religion, and rights of the accused.

To Americans, freedom of speech is the most prized of all the rights guaranteed by the Constitution and perhaps the most definably *American* right. The freedom to speak one's mind is a hallmark of America's political and popular culture.

Government can attempt to limit speech before and after its utterance.

Government action limiting speech is of two types. Action that prevents speech from being uttered is referred to as **prior restraint**. This is censorship in its truest form: preventing certain speech from being expressed by requiring some kind of permission or pre-clearance from government that the content of the speech was acceptable, or by simply forbidding the speech. Most often this kind of restraint has concerned the news media. The Supreme Court today is reluctant to tolerate restraint of this type. The Court first established its position in *Near v. Minnesota* (1931), in which a Minnesota law that allowed government to prevent the publication of malicious material was struck down as a violation of the First Amendment. The most famous prior restraint case is *New York Times v. United States* (1971). The U.S. government attempted to prevent the newspaper from printing the "Pentagon Papers," a history of the Vietnam War based on State Department documents that had been leaked to the *Times* and the *Washington Post* by a former State Department official. Despite the government's argument that publishing the documents threatened national security, the Court agreed with the newspaper's contention that the public had a right to the information.[18]

After speech has been uttered, government may punish individuals by equating the speech with a crime. In practice, this can have the same censoring effect as prior restraint. One of the most controversial examples of this type of speech restriction concerns "hate speech."

Beginning in the 1990s, hate speech emerged as a major concern on college campuses and in society more broadly. Over 300 institutions of higher education adopted speech codes that punished the use of derogatory speech based on group characteristics such as race, gender, and ethnicity.[19] Some cities did the same. In 1992, the Court considered a case in which a cross was burned on the lawn of a black family.[20] The defendant was charged under St. Paul, Minnesota's Bias Motivated Crime Ordinance, which prohibited the display of a symbol that was known to arouse "anger, alarm or resentment in others on the basis of race, color, creed, religion or gender." The Court struck down St. Paul's law, concluding that it violated the First Amendment by criminalizing speech based on a particular viewpoint.[21] The Court determined that hate speech cannot be considered a crime simply because of its hatefulness.

A decade later, the Court refined its stance. The case concerned a Virginia law prohibiting cross burning on someone's property, along a highway, or in any public place "with the intent of intimidating any person or group."[22] In its decision, the Court ruled that a state could constitutionally ban cross burning, because of that symbol's historical use to intimidate and terrorize targeted groups. The fact that Virginia's law automatically *assumed* that the intent of cross burning was to intimidate, however, made that aspect of the law unconstitutional. Cross burning, even though hateful, was constitutionally protected if it was not designed to be intimidating and make particular targets fear for their safety. Following these Court decisions, some colleges continued to adopt the equivalent of speech codes by including them in more general codes of conduct.[23]

The "presumed reasonableness" standard assumed government restriction on speech was necessary.

The evolution of the Supreme Court's perspective on speech as criminal conduct shows how, over time, the scope of free speech rights has generally expanded in the United States. This might be considered the strongest test for freedom of speech: Can speech that appears to be supportive of criminal actions be tolerated? The Court is often faced with balancing the need for free speech with the need for social order. How has the Court handled this difficult question?

Up until 1919, the Supreme Court was guided by the **standard of presumed reasonableness**. Using this standard, the Court sided with government, assuming that government restrictions on speech were reasonable unless proven otherwise. If certain acts were criminal, then speech that seemed to advocate such conduct was itself criminal. The burden, therefore, fell on the individual to demonstrate that the government's speech restriction was in some way unreasonable or that the speech in question was not actually supportive of illegal conduct.

The "clear and present danger" standard made it more difficult for government to justify restricting speech.

The reasonableness standard was replaced in 1919 by the **clear and present danger standard**. Charles Schenck and Elizabeth Baer mailed pamphlets to men drafted to serve in World War I, arguing that the draft was motivated by the needs of Wall Street financial interests and was illegal. They encouraged draftees to "assert your rights" and "do not submit to intimidation" but did not advocate any violent or illegal activity, suggesting instead actions such as organizing petition drives to repeal the draft. The Espionage Act of 1917 prohibited actions that would cause insubordination in the military or would hinder recruiting. Schenck and Baer were found guilty of violating the Espionage Act and were sentenced to prison.

In *Schenck v. United States* (1919), the Supreme Court upheld the convictions. Although speech is technically not action, the Court concluded that it can effectively be the same thing. If speech brings about a clear and present danger that prohibited actions will take place, then that speech itself can be considered a criminal act. Chief Justice Oliver Wendell Holmes, writing for the Court, noted that speech that is constitutional in one circumstance might be unconstitutional in another. In *Schenck*, the distinction between wartime and peacetime was key. Words could be prohibited under the clear and present danger standard if there was a risk they would encourage the kinds of actions that government is constitutionally authorized to prevent—for example, actions that hinder the war effort. Public support for restrictions on speech and civil liberties may also vary between times of war and peace (see *How Do We Know? Did the Public's Response to 9/11 Lead to Civil Liberties Restrictions?*).

Did the Public's Response to 9/11 Lead to Civil Liberties Restrictions?

The Question

Are Americans their own worst enemies when it comes to civil liberties? As discussed in Chapter 2, American political culture includes a strong belief in liberty—at least in the abstract. Public opinion polls consistently show high levels of support among the American public for basic free speech principles, as shown in the top section of Table 5-5. But note the bottom section of Table 5-5, indicating the level of support for free speech when survey respondents are provided with specific situations. Support for free speech plummets when individuals feel threatened by certain ideas or lifestyles or are worried about their physical security. Following the terrorist attacks of September 11, 2001, Americans indicated greater support for measures that infringed on civil liberties. Did the public's response to 9/11 lead to civil liberties restrictions? How do we know?

Why It Matters

Extensive protection for civil liberties is a central part of the American experiment in democracy. To most Americans, freedom is synonymous with civil liberties. Therefore it is critical to understand when civil liberties can be restricted and for what reason. Civil liberties restrictions are particularly likely during wartime, but when war ends or ebbs, those restrictions are eventually repealed, overturned by the courts, or weakened substantially.[24] For this reason, many observers are concerned about current restrictions on civil liberties as the country pursues a war on terrorism. Unlike traditional war, the conclusion of such a war—because of the very nature of terrorism—will be difficult to define.

Investigating the Answer

Americans' commitment to civil liberties appears to weaken—alarmingly—when put to the test in specific cases. Using public opinion research, one study of public support for civil liberties after September 11, 2001, examined individuals' depth of support for civil liberties. The analysis considered a number of possible factors that might explain an individual's depth of support for civil liberties. The researchers found that the greater the perceived sense of threat to oneself or the country, the more willing individuals were to sacrifice civil liberties. Trust in government played an important role also. Regardless of whether people perceived a great or modest terrorist threat, people with less trust of government were less willing to give government more power to reduce civil liberties. People who were more trusting toward government were more willing to make the tradeoff.[25]

To civil liberties advocates, Americans fortunately give little indication of wanting to act on their attitudes regarding a reduction in civil liberties, or of demanding immediate action from public officials that would be consistent with these attitudes. This line of argument still leaves open one possibility—Americans might not push for civil liberties restrictions, but perhaps they will accept them when politicians initiate them. Studies of support for civil liberties show that the manner in which an issue is framed—whether it is free speech or security at stake—can influence public support for civil liberties.[26] For example, in 2005, whereas 29 percent of the public expressed a willingness to allow government to monitor telephone calls and e-mail messages of "ordinary Americans on a regular basis," 56 percent would allow such monitoring of "Americans that the government is suspicious of."[27]

Table 5-5. Americans' Support for Liberty

GENERAL PRINCIPLES	AGREE
No matter what a person's political beliefs are, he is entitled to the same legal rights and protections as anyone else.	93%
People in the minority should be free to try to win majority support for their opinions.	89%
I believe in free speech for all no matter what their views might be.	85%
People who hate our way of life should still have a chance to be heard.	82%
Nobody has a right to tell another person what he should and should not read.	81%

SPECIFIC CASES	AGREE
People ought to be allowed to vote, even if they can't do so intelligently.	48%
People should be allowed to say things in public that might be offensive to racial groups.	35%
Books that preach the overthrow of the government should be made available by the library, just like any other book.	32%
Members of the Ku Klux Klan should be allowed to run for public office.	23%
A community should allow its civic auditorium to be used by atheists who want to preach against God and religion.	17%

Source: Herbert McClosky and Alida Brill, *Dimensions of Political Tolerance: What Americans Believe About Civil Liberties* (New York: Russell Sage, 1983), 203; Herbert McClosky and John Zaller, *The American Ethos: Public Attitudes Toward Capitalism and Democracy* (Cambridge: Harvard University Press, 1984), 25, 37, 38, 74, 75; Pew Center for the People and the Press surveys.

HOW DO WE KNOW?

What if government instituted restrictions on civil liberties with the rationale that war or other international threats demanded such action? Given the public's fears of terrorism, might people simply view these initiatives, passively, as an acceptable tradeoff for security? They might. Absent an intensely hostile public attitude against civil liberties restrictions, politicians have some leeway to act. The correlation between public support for civil liberties restrictions and public policy might be just that—a correlation, not necessarily a causal link from beliefs to policy. The public may not cause politicians to restrict civil liberties but it may tolerate restrictions when they happen.[28]

The historical record indicates that the public may well be willing to sacrifice some liberty if it is given a convincing security rationale. This is not isolated to September 11. In fact, study of similar historical cases suggests it would have been puzzling if Americans had *not* been supportive of civil liberties restrictions following the 2001 terrorist attacks.[29] Throughout American history, particularly when war or foreign disruption of American life was feared, the national government has imposed restrictions on civil liberties that usually received at least passive support from the majority or large segments of the public:

- The Sedition Act of 1798, enacted while Americans believed their young country was vulnerable to the world's major powers and to deepening political divisions at home, made it illegal to say or write anything that might encourage hostile actions by other countries or that might bring disrepute or disfavor to the government, the president, or Congress.
- During the Civil War, President Abraham Lincoln suspended the writ of habeas corpus, meaning prisoners could be held without charges.
- The Espionage Act of 1917, passed during World War I, restricted speech or action that might be perceived as contributing to insubordination in the military or a hindrance to recruiting.
- The Alien Act of 1918 promised deportation to any alien belonging to a group that advocated the overthrow of the U.S. government, while the Sedition Act of 1918 cracked down on criticism that might affect the country's military operations.

- The Smith Act of 1940, passed while World War II was raging in Europe, prohibited any speech, action, or organization that supported the overthrow of the U.S. government.
- During World War II President Franklin Roosevelt ordered Japanese-Americans to be relocated and held in detention camps.
- At the outset of the Cold War, the Internal Security Act of 1950 stated that membership at any time in the Communist Party or other totalitarian party was grounds to deny an alien admission to the United States; that communist organizations needed to register with the federal government; and that individuals and groups considered threats could be ordered into detention camps.
- As part of the "war on terror" after September 11, 2001, "enemy combatants" were indefinitely detained at Guantanamo Bay, Cuba; the National Security Agency engaged in surveillance without judicial approval; "extraordinary rendition" led to suspects being sent to other countries for potentially harsh interrogation techniques; and the Patriot Act allowed the government to engage in searches and investigations without the judicial approval typically required for other investigations.

Looking across this list, war or the fear of war were primary motivations for the actions. The stress of these times led Americans to distinguish between their abstract preference for civil liberties and their perceived needs for the country's safety under specific circumstances.[30] Certainly support was not unanimous, as these actions did arouse determined opposition. But overall the public tolerated restrictions that seemed to fit a particular context. If public opinion polling was available during World War I, for example, it might have shown strong support for government investigations of German-Americans based on their ethnic background. But asking that same question today would likely provoke very little support for such an idea.

The Bottom Line

Did the public's response to September 11 lead to civil liberties restrictions? Research shows that the public certainly is willing to veer from its general principles in support of civil liberties, especially during times of war. But the evidence suggests it is more likely that public opinion responds to restrictive actions taken by the government or provides a supportive environment for government actions rather than directly causing those actions.

The "gravity of the danger" standard allowed restrictions on speech if its subject matter was sufficiently "evil."

Schenck guided Court decisions until the late 1960s, but through the 1950s and 1960s clear and present danger proved less useful as a standard as every word—*clear, and, present, danger*—was up for debate and interpreted with great variation around the country.[31] The Court turned then to the **gravity of the danger standard**. Here, the Court asserted it would consider the potential "evil" advocated by someone's speech when deciding whether government could punish that speech.[32] The case introducing this standard concerned the Smith Act, which made it illegal to advocate overthrowing the U.S. government by force. Although such attempts were highly unlikely to be successful, and thus the "clear and present danger" low, the Court approved convictions under the Smith Act, using the gravity of the danger standard. If the evil of the potential outcome from speech—in this case, the overthrow of the government—was great enough, the improbability of it actually happening need not deter government from restricting it. On the other hand, something that posed a danger, but of a lesser significance, would need a higher level of probability of it happening for government to restrict it. In effect, the Court was inversely moving two sliders—the significance of the danger and the probability of the danger happening—as it determined whether speech restrictions were constitutionally acceptable.

Throughout the 1950s and 1960s, the Supreme Court used the gravity of the evil standard to evaluate convictions based on individuals' membership in groups deemed dangerous by a government entity. Given the Cold War era in which the standard emerged, government actions against individuals with communist affiliations were especially likely to be upheld.[33]

The "preferred position" standard presumes the unreasonableness of restrictions on speech.

Change in membership on the Court in the 1960s led to the strongest support yet for the protection of free speech rights and abandonment of the gravity of the danger standard. The Court had held for decades that the First Amendment held a "preferred position" among the amendments, and that free speech itself held a preferred position within the amendment.[34] A **preferred position** means that freedom of speech should be abridged only with great reluctance, and that if speech is in conflict with other rights, speech should be protected more than those other rights. But only in the late 1960s, in *Brandenburg v. Ohio* (1969), did the Court explicitly adopt preferred position as its primary free speech standard.

Clarence Brandenburg, a speaker at a Ku Klux Klan rally in 1964, was convicted under an Ohio law—similar to laws in many states—that made it illegal to advocate or assemble with those who promote criminal behavior in the pursuit of political or economic reform. The Court concluded that Ohio's law was unconstitutional. The decision established a two-part rule to determine whether speech acts could be considered criminal: First, was the speech "directed at inciting or producing imminent lawless action"? Second, was the speech "likely to incite or produce such action"? If the answer was yes to both, then government could restrict the speech. The Court concluded that the Ohio law ignored the second part of this test. Given the preferred position of free speech, unless a speech was extremely likely to produce immediate lawless behavior, it could not be restricted or considered illegal itself. Advocating that people commit illegal acts was not in and of itself an illegal act, unless it was highly likely to result imminently in that lawbreaking.

With its strong statement in *Brandenburg*, the Court had effectively reversed the burden of proof in free speech cases. Under the standard of reasonableness, prior to 1919, it was up to the individual charged with a crime related to speech to prove that a governmental restriction on speech was unreasonable. Under the clear and present danger standard and the gravity of the danger standard, up through the 1960s, the Court pushed more of the burden toward government. And with the preferred position standard, the Court had moved to a benchmark that assumed that government restrictions on speech were likely to be inherently unreasonable and that it was the government's burden to show, through a stringent two-part test, that limiting speech was desirable and constitutionally acceptable.

The Supreme Court determines which categories of speech merit constitutional protection.

Restrictions on several categories of speech have been regularly upheld by the Supreme Court. These include "fighting words," defamation, commercial speech, student speech by minors, and obscenity. Fighting words or inflammatory words that create an immediate threat to public safety are not constitutionally protected.[35] The person who uses such words could, for example, be validly charged with disturbing the peace. Defamation means speaking (slander) or writing (libel) a false statement that is heard or read by a third party and harms the target's reputation.[36] For public figures—public officials and others, such as celebrities who are frequently in the public's attention—defamation also requires that the person who spoke or wrote the offensive words did so knowing they were false.[37] Commercial speech has gained growing protection from the courts, as it, like political speech, transmits information, but unlike political speech, the government can regulate commercial speech to be sure it is accurate and not misleading.[38] Minors have generally not been accorded the same speech rights as adults. In 2007, the Court upheld a school principal's right to suspend a student for holding up a banner reading "Bong Hits 4 Jesus" during a school-sponsored event, because the message contradicted the school's anti-drug policy.[39]

Governments have passed numerous laws attempting to thwart the distribution of obscene materials, and challenges to these laws have generated a lengthy trail of court decisions. In 1973, a 5-4 Court ruling revised the definition of obscenity and, in the process, increased the range of speech protected by the Constitution. The ruling retained the "community standards" provision from an earlier decision, which stated that material was obscene if, by average community standards, the material mainly appealed to prurient interest.[40] The Court now added that, to be obscene and thus subject to government restrictions, a work also must depict or describe sexual conduct "in a patently offensive way" and have no serious literary, artistic, political, or scientific value. Federal law and court rulings have established that any sexually explicit depictions of children or depictions of children in sexual acts inherently violate these guidelines and are not constitutionally protected.[41] The difficulty of defining obscenity in other instances was most famously reflected in the comment of Justice Potter Stewart when he wrote that although he could not easily define hard-core pornography, "I know it when I see it."[42]

With the advent of the Internet, controlling the spread of obscene materials has become very difficult. The Communications Decency Act (CDA) of 1996 prohibited making available to minors online any obscene or indecent material that show or describe "sexual or excretory activities or organs" in a way that would be considered offensive by community standards. In 1997, however, the Supreme Court strongly declared the law to be an unconstitutional limit on free speech.[43] Including "indecent" materials, the Court ruled, made the law overly broad and intruded too far on the speech rights of adults. Congress responded with the Children's Online Protection Act of 1998, which required websites to provide age-verification systems (for example, providing credit card information) to keep harmful content from minors.[44] Dissatisfied, the Court suspended enforcement of the act unless Congress could demonstrate that there were no other methods available to achieve its goals that would be less intrusive on personal privacy. This time, Congress responded with a law far more modest in scope than either of the previous laws. The Children's Internet Protection Act of 2000 required public libraries that received federal funds to install filtering software on their publicly accessible computers. The Supreme Court upheld the law, concluding that it did not violate patrons' First Amendment rights.[45]

The legal treatment of pornography has varied across countries. One particularly interesting case is Canada. Rather than following the U.S. model, which places individual freedom of expression at its core, Canada has followed a communitarian approach (see Chapter 2). Although the 1982 Canadian Charter of Rights and Responsibilities guarantees protection of free speech, the protection is qualified by the need to promote gender equality and to consider what should be acceptable in a democratic society. In a key case, the Canadian Court rejected a challenge to Canada's criminalization of the possession and distribution of obscene materials. The Court concluded that degrading materials that place women in subordinate, servile, or humiliating positions violate principles of equal human dignity. This type of material, the Canadian Court ruled, would be prohibited not for moral reasons, but because public opinion considers it harmful to the community.[46]

Freedom of Religion

As with speech, the First Amendment sets out the Constitution's basic principles regarding freedom of religion.[47] The amendment states, "Congress shall make no law respecting an establishment of religion, or prohibiting the free exercise thereof." "Respecting an establishment of religion" is referred to as the **establishment clause**. Government is not to designate any official religion, appear to embrace some religions at the expense of others, become involved in religious teaching, or, as interpreted by some scholars and justices, favor religion over non-religion. "Prohibiting the free exercise thereof" is referred to as the **free exercise clause**. This clause declares that government should not interfere with the individual practice of religious beliefs. Because of incorporation, the establishment and free exercise clauses also apply to the states.

Like with speech, the seemingly unconditional text of the First Amendment has not been interpreted by the Supreme Court to mean that there can be no restrictions on religious freedom. And regulating church–state relations also follows the speech example in that over time the courts have altered the scope of the right to freedom of religion. What Americans would now consider violations of religious freedom were common from the colonial era, when official churches were not unusual, through the 1960s. Evangelical Christians, members of nontraditional denominations, and individuals whose worldview was guided more by science and reason were particularly active in urging church–state separation, and the

Constitution represented a victory for these groups.[48] But even though the Constitution avoids religious references, and an early treaty declared that the United States was not founded specifically upon Christianity, Supreme Court decisions sometimes referred to the United States as a Christian nation as part of their reasoning.[49] Prior to the nationalization of the Bill of Rights, religious oaths for holding office were present in some states and members of specific religions, most commonly Catholics and Jews, were prohibited from holding public office. In other states, attending Catholic parochial school was illegal. Government intrusion into religious practice and some forms of establishment did not simply disappear after the colonial era.

Establishment clause cases have been decided using the Lemon test.

The Court's current standard on establishment clause issues is provided by the **Lemon test,** drawn from its decision in *Lemon v. Kurtzman* (1971). In this ruling, the Court used standards from previous cases and applied a three-part test to determine whether a government action was permissible. First, the law or action must have a plausible secular—i.e., non-religious—purpose. Second, its primary effect must not be to either advance or inhibit religion. Third, it must not foster "excessive government entanglement with religion." A law or action violating any of these three precepts would be considered unconstitutional under this test. In the laws under review in 1971, the Court concluded that providing financial subsidies to private schools for non-religious subject instruction excessively entangled government and religion and were therefore unconstitutional. Because the schools were religious, the Court was concerned that the need for ongoing government surveillance of church financial records involved government too intimately in church affairs.

Relaxation of the Lemon test The *Lemon* test continues to guide establishment clause decisions, but many political scientists who study constitutional law believe the Court may be ready to formulate a new approach to these cases. For example, in 1985 the Court considered New York's deployment of public-school remedial education teachers to parochial schools to be in violation of the establishment clause because of excessive entanglement.[50] In 1997, however, the Court directly overturned this decision and concluded that New York's program was constitutional. The Court majority did not discard the *Lemon* test, but noted that its view toward "excessive entanglement" had begun to shift over the previous decade. There was no reason to assume that public employees would advocate a religion simply because they were in religious schools, so the "pervasive monitoring" of teachers was not necessary to avoid excessive entanglement.[51]

Another sign of the Court's more lenient view toward establishment clause cases appeared in its 2002 decision regarding educational vouchers. Vouchers are public funds that provide parents or guardians with a stipend to use for a child's tuition at non-public schools. One such program provided need-based assistance to parents in the Cleveland school district. Ninety percent of the funds were used to send children to religious schools. The Court, by a narrow 5-4 vote, concluded that the program did not constitute establishment of religion. The program was secular on its face, and if parents used the funds to send their children to religious schools, that was their decision, not the government's.

Establishment clause cases Many issues test the establishment clause. Three important ones are school prayer, the faith-based initiative, and public religious displays. In a long line of cases, the Court has ruled that public school prayer or similar activities constitute establishment of religion if they rely on public resources or imply the sponsorship or endorsement of the school.[52] Individual student decisions such as wearing religious symbols to public school or praying privately while in school are not considered establishment. Not yet tested is President Bush's faith-based initiative, which allows religious organizations to provide government-funded social services without having to abandon their religious nature. For example, these organizations would not have to abide by federal regulations that prohibit discrimination in the hiring process based on religious beliefs. Cases concerning the faith-based initiative will likely reach the Supreme Court in the near future. And regarding religious displays, the Court has granted states and cities leeway to display religiously oriented symbols, as long as these displays can pass the *Lemon* test.

Evaluating two displays in 2005, the Court concluded by a 5-4 vote that a Ten Commandments display in Austin, Texas, was constitutional because it had a valid secular purpose, was part of a large number of statues, and had been on display for over forty years without complaint that it was advocating a particular religion. It determined that a courthouse display in Kentucky was unconstitutional because it had clearer religious intent, having been posted initially in courtrooms without any other historical documents and being modified later only after complaints were lodged by the American Civil Liberties Union.[53]

The placement of religious symbols in public places has been controversial in other countries as well. In 1991, parents of elementary school children challenged a Bavarian law that required a crucifix to be placed in every public school. Based on Germany's constitution, the Basic Law, which declares freedom of faith to be "inviolable," the parents successfully argued that the Christian crucifix infringed on their religious freedom. In the Court's view, religious freedom demanded that government be neutral in matters of faith, especially because students were mandated to be in school.[54] In 2004, France went even further by banning students from wearing "conspicuous" religious symbols in public schools. Prohibited items include Muslim veils or headscarves, Sikh turbans, Jewish yarmulkes, and Christian crucifixes. By contrast, U.S. federal courts have made it clear that students must be allowed to wear religious symbols to school.

The balancing test carved out a zone of protection for religious free expression.

In addition to prohibiting any establishment of religion, the First Amendment also guarantees the free exercise of religion. Are restrictions on free exercise ever permissible? If so, when and why?

As with establishment cases, the Court has answered these questions with standards that it then applied to subsequent cases. From 1963 through 1990, the Court relied on the **balancing test**, introduced in *Sherbert v. Verner* (1963). Adeil Sherbert, a Seventh-day Adventist, lost her job when she refused to work on Saturday, her Sabbath Day. After she was unable to find other work for the same reason, she applied to the state of South Carolina for temporary unemployment benefits. The state denied her any benefits, because the state believed she could have taken a job requiring Saturday work.

The Supreme Court applied a two-part test to resolve the dispute. First, did the government law or policy impose a significant burden on religious exercise? The Court concluded in this instance that South Carolina's eligibility requirements for unemployment compensation did significantly burden Sherbert's ability to practice her faith. With that established, the Court turned to the second part of the test: was a compelling government interest served by this burdensome law or policy? If it was, then the policy or law would be constitutional despite its interference with religious expression. Here, the Court determined that there was no compelling state interest that justified the burden on Sherbert's religious practice. On the basis of the two-part test, the Court ruled in favor of Sherbert.

The neutrality standard narrows the scope of religious free expression.

The two-part balancing test survived for nearly three decades before being demoted in favor of a new test.[55] The new standard made it surprisingly more difficult to carve out space for religious expression. The case establishing the new standard involved Alfred Smith and Galen Black, who participated in Native American church ceremonies that involved the ingestion of peyote, an illegal hallucinogen. Unlike many other states, Oregon law provided no exception for use of the drug for sacramental purposes. Smith and Black were fired from their jobs at a private drug rehabilitation center because their drug use was considered work-related misconduct. They were denied state unemployment benefits on those grounds.

In *Employment Division v. Smith* (1990), the Supreme Court upheld Oregon's refusal to provide unemployment benefits. In a striking shift away from the balancing test established in *Sherbert*, the decision introduced the Court's **neutrality test** for free-exercise cases: a neutral law applied in a neutral way can validly impose a burden on religious practice, even if there is no compelling government interest at stake. If a law was not neutral in intent and application, the Court would employ the balancing test. The Court would want to be convinced that such a law was justified by a compelling government interest, and that it was as narrowly constructed, meaning as minimally invasive on rights as possible, in its quest to advance that interest.

In the Court's view, the law prohibiting peyote and other drugs validly regulated something that government is allowed to regulate, and it did so in a neutral way. Its enactment was not targeted at any one group and it was applied equally across groups. Restriction of religious expression was an "incidental effect" of the law, not an intentional goal. There is no religious exemption from the law, just as there is no religious exemption if one believes one's taxes support causes that one finds spiritually repugnant.[56]

A notable example of the Court's application of the neutrality test concerned the issue of animal sacrifice. The city of Hialeah, Florida, passed several laws to forbid the practice of animal sacrifice or slaughter, but exempted state-licensed activities from the new regulation, including slaughterhouses, food establishments, and some hog and cattle slaughter that did not occur in areas zoned for slaughterhouses. In its decision in *Church of the Lukumi Babalu Aye v. Hialeah* (1993), the Supreme Court struck down the city's ordinances as an undue burden on the religious practice of the Santeria religion, which used animal sacrifice. Had the laws been designed neutrally and applied neutrally, they could have been upheld even though burdening religion. They were not neutral, however. The Court concluded that the city could have found other ways to protect public health and prevent animal cruelty without targeting one group's religious practice.[57]

Given this new standard, future free exercise cases may be based more on free speech grounds than on religious practice. Challenges to laws or government actions that neutrally impinge on religious exercise might fare better if these laws or actions can be characterized as violating free speech rights.

Protest over the Court's neutrality standard in free exercise cases prompted Congress to respond with legislation.

Responding to a massive outcry among religious groups, Congress responded to the Court's new neutrality test by passing the Religious Freedom Restoration Act (RFRA) of 1993. Referring directly to the Court's *Smith* decision, RFRA attempted to erase the Court's use of the neutrality test by prohibiting the federal and state governments from restricting an individual's free exercise of religion unless such restriction served a compelling government interest and was narrowly tailored to meet that interest. In short, with RFRA Congress was telling the Court that balancing, not neutrality, was the standard by which to judge religious practice cases. Congress passed follow-up legislation in 1994, the American Indian Religious Freedom Act Amendments, which specifically protected Native American use of peyote.

In 1997, the Supreme Court invalidated the underlying premise of RFRA and declared its applicability to the states to be unconstitutional.[58] Regarding the underlying premise, the Court majority concluded that RFRA went too far into the judiciary's responsibilities in the American separation of powers system. Regarding the states, the Court decided the law was far too extensive and intrusive in its impact and could not be imposed on state governments. RFRA could, however, apply to the federal government because Congress has the authority to set the guidelines by which federal agencies make decisions. The Court unanimously reiterated in 2006 that federal agencies needed to abide by the balancing requirements imposed by Congress in RFRA.[59]

Rather than try to tell the Court how to interpret the Constitution and apply it to the states, supporters of RFRA passed the Religious Land Use and Institutionalized Persons Act of 2000. This time, using its power of fiscal federalism (see Chapter 4), Congress required states that chose to receive certain federal funds to use the balancing test when deciding how to accommodate religion for institutionalized persons. In June 2005, the Supreme Court, which tends to be very deferential toward Congress's spending power, ruled unanimously that Congress was free to set conditions on the receipt of federal funds.[60] Overall, through RFRA as imposed on federal agencies, state enactment of their own versions of RFRA, and Congress's use of fiscal federalism with the states, elected officials were able to ensure a prominent place for balancing, even if the Supreme Court would no longer consider it to be the primary constitutional standard by which it evaluated free exercise cases.

Rights of the Accused

As with freedom of speech and freedom of religion, the scope of rights accorded to individuals accused of a crime has changed significantly over the past 50 years. Much of what Americans now take for granted as "standard operating procedure" in police procedures and criminal prosecutions in fact marked a stark change from previous practice. This procedure was mandated during the 1960s by the Supreme Court led by Chief Justice Earl Warren. Americans, although acknowledging generally the need for procedural safeguards for defendants, can nonetheless be frustrated when criminals go free because of what appear to be "technicalities."

The rights of the accused concern the behavior of police and government prosecutors and processes related to trials. Today Americans may wonder why the system is so concerned with the rights of those accused of crimes, even to the point where the guilty sometimes go free. But it makes perfect sense that the framers of the Constitution, especially the Antifederalists who demanded a Bill of Rights, were eager to protect the rights of defendants. Remember their experience with the British government. They feared a powerful government that could fabricate charges or corrupt the legal process to get the results it desired. They chose to err on the side of caution and crafted a series of safeguards that they hoped would prevent government from imprisoning the innocent, even if sometimes letting the guilty go free. Table 5-6 lists these rights, ordered from initial investigation to subsequent trial and sentencing.

The Supreme Court has established guidelines for the constitutional gathering of evidence.

The job of the police and prosecutors depends fundamentally on uncovering evidence that links an individual with a crime. This means that the gathering of evidence is absolutely critical. It also means, as the framers of the Constitution feared, that investigators might be overzealous in their attempts to unearth damaging information. At the extreme, investigators might even manufacture evidence in

Table 5-6. Rights of the Accused from Investigation to Sentencing

• No unreasonable or unwarranted searches and seizures (4th Amendment)
• No arrest without probable cause (4th)
• No entrapment (4th)
• Must be informed of rights (to remain silent, to counsel) (5th)
• No coerced confession and no illegal interrogation (5th)
• No self-incrimination during arrest or trial (5th)
• Be informed of charges (6th)
• Prompt arraignment (6th)
• Legal counsel (6th)
• No excessive bail (8th)
• Grand jury hearing to determine if case is viable (5th)
• Trial before a judge (Article I, Section 9)
• Speedy and public trial before an impartial jury (6th)
• Trial atmosphere free from prejudice and external interference (6th)
• Evidence obtained by illegal search not admissible during trial (4th)
• Right to confront witnesses (6th)
• No double jeopardy (5th)
• No cruel and unusual punishment (8th)
• Opportunity to appeal verdicts (8th)

order to obtain a conviction. The protections in the Bill of Rights are designed to minimize that threat.

Central to these protections is the nature of the search-and-seizure process. The Fourth Amendment of the Constitution protects citizens against "unreasonable" searches and seizures, noting that people are to be "secure in their persons, houses, papers, and effects." The amendment mandates that prior to any search, police obtain warrants specifically indicating the place to be searched and the items to be seized. To obtain a warrant, police must have probable cause—that is, they must have enough information suggesting that a crime has taken place and that an individual or location is linked to the crime. Police must also obtain a warrant before engaging in wiretaps of phone and electronic communication, but for obvious reasons, these need not be shown to the target of the investigation. Originally these provisions protected individuals from federal government action. Later, through incorporation, they became binding on the states as well.

The Fourth Amendment prohibits unreasonable searches, but it does not specify what is reasonable or what should happen if police overstep "reasonable" boundaries. For example, can police look through your trash without a warrant? They can. According to the Supreme Court, individuals cannot assume that trash placed by public streets is covered by any expectation of privacy.[61] Can police stop you while driving even if you are not suspected of wrongdoing? They can. The Court has confirmed that police are allowed to conduct "sobriety checkpoints," in which motorists are stopped without cause in order to deter drunk driving, because the government's compelling interest in public safety outweighs the minor intrusion on personal liberty.[62] On the other hand, police cannot stop vehicles without cause or traffic violations and search them for drugs or other contraband—with no immediate safety issue, the intrusion on liberty outweighs the government's interest in regulating the contraband.[63]

Convictions may not be based on illegally obtained evidence.

In 1914, the Supreme Court prohibited federal courts from basing decisions on evidence obtained improperly—a principle known as the **exclusionary rule**. According to this rule, evidence that is gathered during an illegal search cannot be introduced in a trial, even if that evidence is absolutely necessary to obtain a conviction. In 1961, the Supreme Court applied the rule to the states also.[64] Even after a trial, a conviction can be overturned if a defendant can convince an appeals court that the evidence used for conviction was obtained improperly and should not have been introduced at trial.

Over time, the Court has become flexible in its enforcement of the exclusionary rule. The general principle stands, but the Court has allowed for introduction of questionably obtained evidence in specific circumstances. For example, the Court has concluded that it is acceptable to introduce evidence obtained illegally if police can show that they would have eventually obtained the evidence through legal means. If evidence is mobile, in an automobile for example, courts may conclude that the time that would elapse prior to a warrant being issued is too extensive a period for the police to wait. The Court has also allowed evidence that was technically collected improperly, but which police exercised "good faith" to collect properly. In addition, if a person agrees to a search even without a warrant, these searches are legal as long as the individual did not feel intimidated into complying with the police request. Police do not need to obtain warrants to seize illegal goods that are in open view—firearms, for example.

The Constitution protects defendants during investigations and trials.

Individuals accused of crimes have a number of rights during the process of investigation and litigation (see Table 5-6). These rights leave much leeway for interpretation by the courts. What is "excessive" bail? What is a "speedy" trial? What is "cruel and unusual" punishment? Questions like these have spawned a long line of judicial clarifications of what the Constitution requires.

Informing suspects of their rights As any viewer of television dramas knows, police are required to read suspects their rights when placing them under arrest. One of these rights is the right to remain silent. The basic idea is that individuals should not be coerced or intimidated into offering a confession and that, before confessing, individuals must be informed that they are not required to speak to the police except to respond to basic questions of identification; that anything they say can be used against them in court; that they have a right to have an attorney present during questioning; and that an attorney would be provided if they could not afford one. Confessions made in the absence of these conditions would be inadmissible in court. This procedure is known as the **Miranda warning** or Miranda rule, based on the Court's 1966 decision in the case of *Miranda v. Arizona*. Prior to *Miranda*, whether a confession was voluntary had been the Court's chief concern, but the Court concluded that defendants needed to be explicitly informed of their rights prior to making any confession. Over time the Court has made the burden on the police less restrictive—for example, unless individuals explicitly request to speak to an attorney, police need not assume that they would like to do so—but, despite occasional congressional attempts to overturn it, the *Miranda* warning remains binding on police during investigations.[65]

The right not to incriminate oneself stretches back well before the United States Constitution. English courts honored this right by the seventeenth century, and the Supreme Court pointed to this English legal tradition in *Miranda*. English courts and Parliament, however, neither require English police to offer Miranda-like warnings nor require prosecutors to exclude evidence obtained from improper searches. As of 1995, an act of the British Parliament allows judges and prosecutors to assume the guilt of anyone who refuses to testify in his or her defense. Other major European countries are more consistent with the American model. Germany, France, and Italy all exclude statements from trial if the police failed to inform defendants of their right to remain silent, but the time at which suspects must be informed differs. Italy's practice is closest to that of the United States, with expectations that suspects will be informed of their right to remain silent at the time of arrest.

The right to counsel One of the rights guaranteed by the Constitution and mentioned in the *Miranda* warning is the right to have the advice of legal counsel during questioning and trial. As it selectively incorporated the Sixth Amendment, the Court increasingly broadened the range of cases that fit within the right to counsel (see the entries for Article VI in Table 5-3). Moreover, the Court made the individual's right to counsel an obligation upon governments to *provide* counsel for defendants who could not afford an attorney. The defining case was *Gideon v. Wainwright* (1963). Clarence Earl Gideon, not entitled to public counsel under Florida law unless he faced the death penalty, defended himself at trial and was convicted and sentenced. Gideon appealed to the Supreme Court, and the Court unanimously concluded that individuals in all felony cases must be provided with legal assistance if they cannot afford their own. Lawyers in criminal cases, the

Court ruled, are not a luxury but, rather, a necessity for a fair trial. The broad right to counsel established in this case was extended even further in subsequent years, with defendants able to challenge convictions based on the poor quality of publicly provided legal representation they received.

Cruel and unusual punishment Once a defendant is found guilty, a judge or jury must declare an appropriate sentence. The Constitution forbids "cruel and unusual" punishment, and the Supreme Court has focused on the "and." A punishment can be cruel but not unusual, or unusual but not cruel; the Supreme Court is most concerned when it is both.

Capital punishment—the death penalty—is the area that most often reaches the Supreme Court for review under the Eighth Amendment's prohibition against cruel and unusual punishment. Though opponents of the practice decry it as inhumane, the Court has never declared the death penalty in general to constitute cruel and unusual punishment. It has, however, decided in recent years that it constitutes cruel and unusual punishment for the mentally retarded and for minors.[66] For individuals outside these two categories, the Court has sought to ensure that defendants' due process rights were adhered to rigorously. Although it is uncommon, the Court will, for example, overturn death sentences if it believes a defendant received a defense so inadequate that it violates the constitutional right to counsel.[67] The Court also considers whether the method of execution is cruel and unusual. In April 2008, the Supreme Court ended its eight-month moratorium on the death penalty when it decided that death by lethal injection—the primary method used in 35 of the 36 capital punishment states—did not constitute cruel and unusual punishment.

The current system of regulating capital punishment began with the Supreme Court's decision in *Furman v. Georgia* (1972). In that ruling, the justices struck down three death penalty sentences, concluding that the use of capital punishment was impermissibly arbitrary. The decision did not eliminate capital punishment, but led to a five-year hiatus in its use. States needed to reexamine their procedures for imposing the penalty. This meant, first, being specific about which crimes might justify capital punishment, so that a jury could not impose the death penalty arbitrarily. Second, cases would be two-staged, with a jury first determining guilt or innocence and then, if guilty, determining whether the death penalty is warranted. Today, the federal law and the law in 36 states allow the use of the death penalty under this procedure, with nearly all executions taking place at the state level.[68]

The death penalty is a highly charged emotional and moral issue. To opponents, it is morally wrong, applied inconsistently across racial and ethnic groups, and no more effective than other deterrents to crime. Opponents also point to the elimination of capital punishment in many countries around the world as evidence that it is widely considered inhumane. By 2008, 133 countries had either eliminated the death penalty in law or eliminated it in practice, including Mexico and Canada, while 62 countries allowed it, including India, China, Japan, and the United States.[69] To supporters, capital punishment is justified on individualistic grounds as an appropriately harsh response to the destruction of the liberty of other individuals, and on communitarian grounds as an appropriate protection of the community's safety and sense of justice, which outweigh the life and liberty interest of the convicted criminal.

CaseStudy: The USA PATRIOT Act

Few events truly "shock the world," but the terrorist attacks of September 11, 2001, clearly belong in that category. Americans were stunned by their country's vulnerability, saddened at the tragic loss of life, and angered by those responsible for the acts. President Bush needed to respond to strengthen the country's security. And he also needed to act for political reasons: in times of crisis a president needs to respond with strength and authority or risk a sharp drop-off in public support. Among President Bush's responses was organizing an international effort to attack Afghanistan, the suspected home of Osama bin Laden, mastermind of the September 11 attacks.

Inside the United States, the president's response was four-fold. First, foreigners in the United States who were suspected of possibly having knowledge about terrorist acts were indefinitely detained and questioned. Second, the government began interviewing thousands of young Middle Eastern men to get possible leads on future terror attacks. Third, military tribunals, which do not have many of the civil liberties safeguards of civilian courts, were formed to put some suspected terrorists on trial. Each of these tactics raised concerns about possible civil liberties violations. But it was the fourth part of the president's domestic response to the attacks that proved to be the most controversial: the Uniting and Strengthening America by Providing Appropriate Tools Required to Intercept and Obstruct Terrorism Act—the USA PATRIOT Act—typically referred to as the Patriot Act.

Defying the usually slow legislative process, the Patriot Act was passed overwhelmingly by both chambers of Congress six weeks after the September 11 attacks.[70] Although many of its provisions were uncontroversial, some aspects of the bill raised alarms among groups, such as the American Civil Liberties Union, that see themselves as defenders of civil liberties. Many of the complaints about these provisions centered around the federal government's ability to investigate individuals and obtain records without probable cause or a judge's approval. Supporters of the law responded that in most cases these controversial changes simply allowed law enforcement to use tactics for detecting terrorism that they had been allowed to use for other criminal activity.

Controversial provisions of the Patriot Act included the following:

- a definition of "domestic terrorism" that seems to encompass activism designed to "influence the policy of a government by intimidation or coercion"

- authorization of searches and wiretaps without having to show probable cause to a judge to justify a search warrant
- restricted entry into the United States of individuals who have engaged in speech that "undermines" American efforts to reduce terrorism
- expanded ability to search personal records held by a third party such as a bank or insurance company
- ability to obtain information on reading and viewing habits from bookstores, libraries, and video stores
- ability to install software to track all forms of Internet activity
- ability to detain immigrants without charges for up to seven days and indefinitely if any immigration violations are discovered

The Patriot Act has been under constant attack from its critics since its inception. In September 2004, a federal judge struck down a provision in the law that allowed the Federal Bureau of Investigation to require Internet service providers to turn over subscriber information without informing the subscriber or being able to challenge the order in court. This was the first time that a court had limited the government's surveillance powers under the act. A handful of states and over one hundred cities, towns, and counties voted not to cooperate with any provisions of the Patriot Act that officials believed violated civil liberties or civil rights. Over time public support for the act diminished. A Harris Poll survey compared public opinion in late September 2001 and mid-June 2005, when Congress was considering reauthorizing the Patriot Act, and found decreased support for a number of the act's more aggressive measures—stronger document and physical security checks for travelers, expanded undercover activities to investigate suspicious groups, closer monitoring of banking and credit card transactions, adoption of a national ID system for all U.S. citizens, expanded camera surveillance on streets and public places, and monitoring of Internet chat rooms and other forums. Despite the drop in support, however, each of these investigatory activities still retained majority support in 2005, some overwhelmingly. In times of uneasiness, Americans tend to tilt the scales more toward security and somewhat away from liberty. In only one area addressed by the survey did majority support in 2001 become minority support in 2005—expanded government monitoring of e-mail and cell phones.[71]

Sixteen provisions of the Patriot Act were set to expire at the end of 2005. During the spring and summer of 2005, Congress was engaged in hearings concerning the renewal of these provisions. President Bush strongly urged

Congress to continue and strengthen these parts of the Act.[72] Despite the president's urging, objections from many members of Congress prevented a permanent reauthorization of the Patriot Act in 2005. The road to reauthorization looked rocky enough, given the concerns of many legislators about encroachments upon civil liberties. But the road became impassable in late 2005, when it was revealed that President Bush, separately from the Patriot Act, had authorized the National Security Agency (NSA) to intercept the conversations of Americans without court approval. Democrats and some Republicans denounced the president's action as being in direct violation of a 1978 law concerning domestic wiretapping for intelligence purposes. In the ensuing uproar, a filibuster stalled reauthorization and Congress resorted to temporary extensions of the Patriot Act through March 2006.

Negotiations in early 2006 between the White House and members of Congress produced concessions from the president and swung enough votes to reauthorize 14 of the 16 main provisions permanently. The concessions allowed recipients of subpoenas to challenge, after one year, a requirement that they not discuss their case publicly. They also prevented the Federal Bureau of Investigation from demanding the names of lawyers consulted by individuals who received secret government requests for information. And they excluded most libraries from having to turn over records on their patrons.

The revised version of the Patriot Act passed overwhelmingly in both the House and Senate. Some members of Congress who voted for it, such as the chairman of the Senate Judiciary Committee, Republican Arlen Spector of Pennsylvania, remained troubled by it and hinted they might try to pass additional legislation to amend aspects of the bill. Outright opponents declared the compromise to be insufficient in its defense of civil liberties. Russell Feingold, a Democratic senator from Wisconsin who was the only senator to vote against the Patriot Act in 2001 and was instrumental in leading the filibuster in late 2005, spent most of a day reading the Constitution aloud on the Senate floor to express his displeasure.[73] Despite this discontent, large majorities of legislators cast their support for the bill. In March 2006, the president had achieved his long-sought goal and signed the Patriot Act extension into law.

ThinkingCritically

1. Select one of the Patriot Act provisions identified above and make the strongest argument you can for it and against it.

2. Considering both the Framers' vision and your own analysis, to what degree should public opinion about the tradeoff between civil liberties and security guide policy makers?

3. Devise and defend guidelines for the federal government's surveillance of e-mail and instant messages during wartime.

Discovering New Rights That Are Protected by the Constitution

As explained above, the scope of civil liberties has changed with nationalization and denationalization. The scope has also been revised by a second path, as judicial interpretations of the Constitution with regard to freedom of speech and religion and the rights of the accused have all undergone expansion and contraction at different times in American history. The scope of civil liberties can also change by a third path, by the discovery of new rights that are protected by the Constitution.

The identification of new rights happens by two methods that are examined below. First, lawyers and Supreme Court justices may use the Ninth Amendment, which states that rights not specifically mentioned in the Constitution are reserved to the people. The second method for the identification of new rights is through the Fourteenth Amendment, and particularly through the due process clause discussed earlier in this chapter.

The right to privacy has revolutionized the law concerning birth control, abortion, and same-sex relationships.

Some of the most momentous civil liberties decisions of the past four decades have been based on a right that is not even explicitly guaranteed in the Constitution, the right to privacy. Court decisions concerning birth control, abortion, and homosexual behavior have all focused on individuals' privacy rights. These rights connect deeply to Americans' political culture beliefs in individualism and liberty. The Court used the Ninth Amendment to discover this right.

Birth control From 1873 through 1938, the federal government criminalized the distribution of birth control material across state lines.[74] Many states, following the federal government's lead, also restricted the use of birth control within their borders. In the early 1960s, 28 states still prohibited married couples from using contraceptive devices. Challenges to such laws made only limited headway. Federal courts initially struck down state laws that were not flexible enough to allow physicians to prescribe contraceptives to protect patients' health, but the courts otherwise left the contraception bans in place.

In 1961, the Planned Parenthood League of Connecticut opened a birth control clinic in defiance of state law. The clinic provided information and instruction on contraceptive use to married couples. Ten days after opening the clinic, Estelle Griswold, the league's executive director, and Charles Lee Buxton, the medical director, were arrested and convicted for violating Connecticut's law barring the dissemination of information about birth control devices and techniques. Four years later, in *Griswold v. Connecticut* (1965), the U.S. Supreme Court overturned the convictions and declared by a 7-2 majority that there was a constitutional right to privacy for married couples, later extended to unmarried heterosexual couples.[75] The Court's majority concluded that even though the word *privacy* does not appear in the Constitution, the Ninth Amendment, combined with provisions of the First, Third, Fourth, and Fifth Amendments, implicitly suggested that the Constitution contained a right to privacy.[76] Protections in these amendments create "zones of privacy" in the Constitution. The dissenting justices in *Griswold* argued unsuccessfully that by declaring a general right to privacy beyond the specific privacy protections mentioned in the Constitution, the unelected justices of the Supreme Court were displacing the appropriate role of elected officials in the states and of the voters who elected them.

Abortion *Roe v. Wade* (1973) demonstrated the extensive impact of the *Griswold* decision. Abortion had been illegal by law in Texas since 1854, unless medical personnel determined it was necessary to save the life of the mother. Similar laws existed in almost every state by the 1950s; in most cases these dated back to the latter half of the nineteenth century. During the 1960s, several states liberalized their abortion statutes, but a majority still had laws similar to that in Texas. Norma McCorvey—known as "Jane Roe"—wishing to terminate her pregnancy legally, filed a challenge to Texas's law in 1970. Building from the *Griswold* decision, the suit contended that the statute violated McCorvey's right to privacy.

The Supreme Court, by a 7-2 majority, agreed. A woman's privacy right was not absolute, however. The Court determined that the right to privacy in the abortion decision could be conditional upon important government interests in health, medical standards, and protecting potential life. The privacy interest dominates at first, but as pregnancy advances, these government interests begin to balance the woman's privacy interest. Based on this framework and on what it took to be generally consensual understandings of fetal development, the Court established a trimester arrangement. During the first three months of pregnancy, women were free to obtain abortions. During the second trimester—after the first three months but before fetal viability (i.e., before the fetus can potentially live outside the mother's womb)—*Roe* allowed the state to regulate abortion in a manner consistent with its interest in protecting maternal health. During the final trimester, a state could regulate or prohibit abortion, consistent with its interest in protecting potential human life.[77]

In later years, the Court would allow states to adopt some first-trimester restrictions consistent with their interest in protecting potential life, but none that could put an undue burden on a woman's right to obtain an abortion.[78] The Court defined an undue burden as a "substantial obstacle in the path of a woman seeking an abortion before the fetus attains viability." By this standard, in *Planned Parenthood v. Casey* (1992) the Court accepted a mandatory 24-hour waiting period before an abortion procedure could be performed, requiring doctors to counsel women on alternatives to abortion, and requiring minors to get parental consent or a judge's approval as reasonable and constitutional restrictions on abortion access. Requiring a woman to notify her husband before obtaining an abortion was struck down as an undue burden. No state can deny access to abortion completely, but some have made it more difficult to exercise this right than others.

In 2006, the strongest challenge yet to *Roe v. Wade* came from South Dakota, where a bill outlawing all abortions except those necessary to save the life of the mother was signed into law. The law was passed soon after Samuel Alito joined the Supreme Court, replacing former justice Sandra Day O'Connor, who had been pivotal in upholding abortion rights during her tenure. Pro-life forces believed that with the change in personnel on the Court, the time was ripe for a full-fledged challenge to *Roe* that would return decisions about abortion to the states, and they expected that pro-choice advocates would challenge the law in court. This pro-life strategy was derailed when opponents of the South Dakota law instead forced a referendum that put the law up for a statewide vote in November 2006. In that balloting, 56 percent of South Dakota voters rejected the new law, meaning that there was now no need for pro-choice advocates to bring a case to court.

At the national level, the most significant restriction on abortion rights came in 2003, when President George W. Bush signed into law the Partial Birth Abortion Ban Act, which prohibited one specific type of abortion procedure. The Supreme Court upheld the constitutionality of the law in 2006.

Sexual activity *Griswold* and *Roe* were landmark decisions with significant social implications. The Supreme Court's 2004 decision in *Lawrence v. Texas* added a third milestone privacy decision, this time concerning homosexual activity. Nearly twenty years earlier in *Bowers v. Hardwick* (1986), a case involving an anti-sodomy law in Georgia, the Court concluded that there was no right to privacy for homosexual conduct. But in *Lawrence* the Court sharply repudiated its previous decision, declaring that the previous court, by defining the issue as the "right to engage in sodomy," minimized the liberty at stake. Liberty, the Court concluded, demanded that homosexuals not lose "their dignity as free persons" because of their sexual behavior in the confines of their own home. The right to privacy trumps the state's interest in controlling this behavior unless the state can show a strong, compelling reason why this behavior should be criminalized.

Implications of the right to privacy Privacy need not be a constitutional right for government to protect it. Government can choose legislatively or administratively to protect aspects of privacy if it wishes. For example, the Privacy Act places restrictions on how government agencies use personal information about individuals. The Family Educational Rights and Privacy Act protects the privacy of students' educational records. The Financial Modernization Act governs how financial institutions collect and disclose personal financial information and how individuals can limit that disclosure. The national "do not call" registry allows phone customers to prohibit calls from telemarketers. Even if privacy had not been established as a constitutional right, Congress and the president could have, and have, chosen to protect privacy in various ways.

The constitutional right to privacy will remain contentious because it implies a much broader scope of privacy than these legislative enactments provide, and a scope that will be determined not by elected officials but by judges. Scholars, activists, and justices who see no general right to privacy argue that the Constitution prohibits some specific violations of privacy but is silent on others. Where the Constitution is silent, they argue, it should be up to legislatures, not judges, to determine whether to extend privacy protections. And just how far does a *general* right to privacy go, they ask? Does a general right to privacy require that euthanasia be legal? Suicide? Assisted suicide? What about bigamy or polygamy? Must laws prohibiting prostitution be struck down?

The Court has ruled on each of these issues. In some cases, such as upholding state or federal laws restricting bigamy, polygamy, and prostitution, the decisions came before the privacy right was fully established, but the Court today might see a compelling government interest at stake that would justify limiting privacy. In end-of-life issues, the Court's decisions have been more recent. In *Cruzan v. Director, Missouri Department of Health* (1990), the Court declared that a patient can refuse unwanted medical treatment. If the patient is incompetent and unable to articulate his or her wishes, a state is constitutionally allowed to require that there be "clear and convincing" evidence that the patient would have refused the treatment. The case of Terri Schiavo, described in Chapter 4, riveted national attention in 2005 as her husband and parents fought over whether to discontinue a feeding tube that was keeping her alive. Ultimately, the consensus of the courts was that Schiavo had made her intent clear enough to her husband and that he could order her feeding tube discontinued.

If an individual has a privacy right to reject treatment, which can passively result in death, does an individual also have a specific privacy right to end his or her life deliberately? In 1997, the Court upheld the state bans on physician-assisted suicide in Washington and New York, firmly and unanimously rejecting the idea that liberty includes a right to suicide. In 2006, however, the Court let stand Oregon's law that allowed physician-assisted suicide.[79] Because the Court does not see suicide as a right, but has not concluded that it is constitutionally prohibited, it appears to be allowing states latitude to either prohibit or allow physician-assisted suicide.

To defenders of the Court's discovery of a general right to privacy, these decisions show that there need be no "slippery slope" that leads to potentially problematic social outcomes in areas like prostitution, suicide, and marriage between multiple partners. They argue that—as with other liberties—privacy is outweighed when government can show that it has a compelling need to restrict it.

Substantive due process discovers new rights by applying specific guarantees to the Fourteenth Amendment's general guarantee of life, liberty, and property.

The federal courts have established that the Constitution protects many rights other than those specifically listed in the document. There is, for example, a right of association, a right against compelled association and compelled speech, a right to supervise the education of one's children, a right to an attorney being present while being questioned about a crime, and a right to procreate.[80]

Where does protection for these rights come from? The answer is through the second method for the discovery of new rights, the concept of substantive due process. Due process is normally thought of as procedural—did a government official follow the specified rules and accord an individual all the rights and appeals allowed before restricting some aspect of the person's life, liberty, or property? Were the rules clear so that individuals did not inadvertently fail to defend a right because the process was unclear? Were they clear enough that the individual knew the consequence of taking certain actions? Procedural due process, then, is doing the "right thing" by way of process.

Substantive due process, on the other hand, is doing the "right thing" by way of substance. It is saying that "life, liberty, and property," mentioned in the Fourteenth Amendment, has particular substantive meaning that must be protected by the courts because of their fundamental nature or their place in American tradition.[81] Substantive due process has had a large impact on civil liberties interpretation. The right to privacy was discussed above as an example of discovering new rights through the Ninth Amendment. It has alternatively been justified as an aspect of substantive due process by some judges, participants in legal proceedings, and political scientists.[82] Opponents of Connecticut's birth control restrictions, for example, did not claim that the state of Connecticut was violating *procedural* due process when it arrested individuals who distributed birth control materials—the state followed the law and proper procedures. The claim, instead, was that privacy to use birth control must be protected as part of the *substance* of the "liberty" protected by the Fourteenth Amendment's due process clause.

Substantive due process was at its height in the 1960s and 1970s. Since then, the Supreme Court has been reluctant to read new rights into the Constitution via this method. For example, in the 1990s, the Court ruled unanimously against a substantive due process claim that workers have a right to be free from "unreasonable risk of harm," or that the public has a right to safety that is violated when innocent bystanders are injured during high-speed pursuit of criminal suspects by the police.[83] However, the Court has tended to uphold rights established by substantive due process in previous decisions.[84]

SUMMARY

▶ Civil liberties touch upon individualism, property, liberty, and religion—rights that Americans believe are inherent and should not be interfered with by government. Civil liberties are guaranteed in the U.S. Constitution—in the articles and in the Bill of Rights. Through selective incorporation, the Bill of Rights gradually became binding upon the states.

▶ Freedom of speech holds a preferred position among Americans' civil liberties. Over time, the Court has adopted a series of standards that has expanded the right of free speech, even in difficult cases where the speech might lead to illegal acts. The Court's interpretation of particular categories of speech, such as obscenity, has also shifted over time.

▶ The Constitution's religious freedom guarantee is two-fold. Individuals are to be free to exercise their religion, and government is not to establish religion. Since 1990, the Court has employed a neutrality standard, which is less likely to provide legal exemptions for religious practice as long as a law is conceived and implemented neu-

trally. Establishment cases since the 1970s have been decided by the three-prong *Lemon* test.

▶ The Supreme Court in the 1960s added significant safeguards to protect the rights of the accused in the evidence gathering stage, through investigations and trials, and during sentencing. Well-known features of the legal system such as the *Miranda* warning and the obligation of government to provide counsel were introduced during this era. Over the past two decades, the Supreme Court has given police more leeway in their investigations.

▶ The discovery of new rights that are protected by the Constitution has come about in two ways, through the Ninth Amendment and through the Fourteenth Amendment. Many significant new rights have been established by one or the other of these means. The most far-reaching of these rights in terms of its social impact has been the right to privacy, which is the basis most notably for dramatic changes in government regulation of birth control, abortion, and sexual behavior.

KEY TERMS

balancing test, p. 000
civil liberties, p. 000
clear and present danger standard, p. 000
due process, p. 000
establishment clause, p. 000
exclusionary rule, p. 000
free exercise clause, p. 000
gravity of the danger standard, p. 000
incorporation process, p. 000

Lemon test, p. 000
Miranda warning, p. 000
neutrality test, p. 000
preferred position, p. 000
prior restraint, p. 000
selective incorporation, p. 000
standard of presumed reasonableness, p. 000
substantive due process, p. 000

SUGGESTED READINGS

Richard Delgado and Jean Stefancic. 1997. *Must We Defend Nazis? Hate Speech, Pornography, and the New First Amendment.* New York: New York University Press. The authors argue for the constitutionality of restrictions on hateful speech.

Garrett Epps. 2001. *To an Unknown God: Religious Freedom on Trial.* New York: St. Martin's Press. An examination of *Employment Division of Oregon v. Smith*, the case concerning sacramental use of peyote that ushered in the Court's neutrality standard in free exercise cases.

Amitai Etzioni. 1999. *The Limits of Privacy.* New York: Basic Books. Writing from a communitarian perspective, the author argues that there are times when com-

munity interests need to trump the privacy concerns of individuals.

Jon B. Gould. 2005. *Speak No Evil: The Triumph of Hate Speech Regulation.* Chicago: University of Chicago Press. Examines the rise of hate speech codes and other forms of hate speech regulation.

Frank Lambert. 2003. *The Founding Fathers and the Place of Religion in America.* Princeton, NJ: Princeton University Press. An accessible overview of the politics and growth of religion during the colonial era and the early years of the United States.

Anthony Lewis. 1964. *Gideon's Trumpet.* New York: Random House. A classic account of the individuals and events leading to *Gideon v. Wainwright*, in which the Court declared that government was obliged to provide an attorney for individuals charged with a felony who could not afford legal representation.

Herbert McClosky and Alida Brill. 1983. *Dimensions of Political Tolerance: What Americans Believe About Civil Liberties*. New York: Russell Sage. An analysis of the civil liberties beliefs of Americans in general and in specific circumstances.

Herbert McClosky and John Zaller. 1984. *The American Ethos: Public Attitudes Toward Capitalism and Democracy*. Cambridge: Harvard University Press. A classic account of the variety of public attitudes about topics such as individualism, property, equality, and success.

John Durham Peters. 2005. *Courting the Abyss: Free Speech and the Liberal Tradition*. Chicago: University of Chicago Press. Examines whether an absolutist support for free speech makes sense in the present age.

David M. Rabbins. 1999. *Free Speech in its Forgotten Years, 1870–1920*. New York: Cambridge University Press. The author shows when and how free speech issues emerged on the judicial or political agenda during the era when government restrictions on speech were difficult to defeat.

Geoffrey R. Stone. 2004. *Perilous Times: Free Speech in Wartime from the Sedition Act of 1798 to the War on Terrorism*. New York: W. W. Norton. Focuses on six periods of war and social stress in American history and analyzes the restrictions on civil liberties in those years.

Cass R. Sunstein. 1995. *Democracy and the Problem of Free Speech*. New York: Free Press. Argues that the Supreme Court should add democratic concerns for justice and equality to its concerns for individualistic freedom when it decides free speech cases.

civil liberties individual rights and freedoms that government is obliged to protect, normally by not interfering in the exercise of these rights and freedoms.

due process procedural safeguards that government officials are obligated to follow prior to restricting rights of life, liberty, and property.

incorporation process the application, through the Fourteenth Amendment, of the civil liberties protections in the Bill of Rights to state governments.

selective incorporation the process by which protections in the Bill of Rights were gradually applied to the states, as the Supreme Court issued decisions on specific aspects of the Bill of Rights.

prior restraint the attempt by government officials to prevent speech prior to its utterance or publication.

standard of presumed reasonableness a free speech standard which took as its starting point a presumption that government restrictions on speech were reasonable and constitutional, thus leaving the burden of proof to those who objected to the restriction.

clear and present danger standard used in free speech cases, this standard permitted government restrictions on speech if public officials believed that allowing the speech created a risk that some prohibited action would result from the speech.

gravity of the danger standard a free speech standard in which the Supreme Court allowed restrictions on speech if the danger espoused by the speech was sufficiently evil, even if that evil was unlikely to occur.

preferred position the idea, endorsed by the Supreme Court, that the First Amendment predominates over the other amendments and that, within the amendment, free speech predominates over the other protections of rights, meaning that speech restriction should be done narrowly and reluctantly and speech generally should prevail when in conflict with other rights.

establishment clause a clause in the First Amendment that prevents government from establishing an official religion, treating one religion preferably to another, proselytizing, or promoting religion over non-religion.

free exercise clause a clause in the First Amendment that prohibits government from interfering with individuals' practice of their religion.

***Lemon* test** a three-part establishment clause test used by the Supreme Court that states that, to be constitutional, a government action must have a plausible non-religious purpose; its primary or principal effect must be to neither advance nor inhibit religion; and it must not foster excessive government entanglement with religion.

balancing test used by the Supreme Court in free exercise of religion cases, this two-part test first determined whether a government action or law was a burden on religious practice and, if it was, whether a compelling government interest was at stake that would make the burden constitutionally acceptable.

neutrality test the Supreme Court's most recent approach to deciding free exercise of religion cases, this test declares that a government law or action with a neutral intent and application is constitutional, even if it burdens religion and there is no compelling government interest at stake.

exclusionary rule principle established by the Supreme Court, according to which evidence gathered illegally cannot be introduced into trial and convictions cannot be based on this evidence.

***Miranda* warning** ruling that requires police, when arresting suspects, to inform them of their rights, including the right to remain silent and have an attorney present during questioning.

substantive due process an interpretation of the due process clause in the Fourteenth Amendment that says the clause's guarantee of "life, liberty, and property" provides a means to discover new rights not mentioned elsewhere in the Constitution, and that these rights would exist at both the national and state levels of government.

6 Civil Rights

Presumed Suspicious: Japanese-American Internment in World War II

On December 7, 1941, Japan's air force attacked the U.S. military base at Pearl Harbor, Hawaii. Now World War II was on American soil. Immediately, Japanese Americans found themselves the targets of suspicion and hostility, not for anything they had done, but for who they were. Two months later, in February 1942, President Franklin D. Roosevelt directed the Secretary of War to move citizens purportedly vulnerable to enemy sabotage or spying to detention centers away from military zones on the West Coast—specifically the entire western halves of California, Washington, and Oregon, and the southern third of Arizona. Everyone knew that meant Japanese Americans. A month later, Congress passed a law making it a crime to violate the president's directive.

Over 120,000 Japanese Americans were relocated, and most remained in the detention centers for more than two years. They were forced to leave behind their belongings, homes, and careers. About one-third were given a conditional release—to work in selected factories or farms, engage in military spying, or to serve in a segregated Japanese-American army unit. Families lost property that in today's dollars would be valued in the billions. Also devastating was that the detainees were considered un-American and were not treated equally as citizens, simply because of their identity. In 1944 the Supreme Court ruled that excluding individuals from the military zone was constitutional, but it did not rule directly whether the subsequent relocation to detention centers was constitutional. The Court's decision went to great lengths to paint the case as one of executive authority in wartime, not one about racial prejudice. In a time of national emergency, the Court concluded it needed to defer to Congress, the president, and the assessment of military commanders.[1]

The victims remained silent for decades. But in the 1970s, inspired by the successes of the black civil rights movement, the Japanese American Citizens League (JACL), an organization that lobbied on issues of interest to Japanese Americans, began to act. Under considerable pressure, President Gerald Ford issued a proclamation that rescinded President Roosevelt's order, expressing regret for this "setback to fundamental American principles." JACL passed resolutions calling for financial reimbursement for those who had been sent to the detention camps. Japanese Americans were split over whether asking for financial reparations cheapened the principles of liberty and equal treatment under the law. Many were also concerned that strong demands would lead to public backlash. Despite these concerns, by the end of the 1970s JACL agreed on a specific proposal, calling for $25,000 for each person held in the centers and a trust fund to support Japanese-American organizations.

JACL and its allies had considered several possible paths to achieve their goal. Establishing a federal commission to publicize and investigate the issue, with the hope of influencing public opinion and pressuring Congress, was one possibility. Introducing legislation immediately in Congress was another. A third strategy was bypassing the elected branches by seeking compensation through a class-action lawsuit representing all the internees. Because the 760,000 Japanese Americans in the United States were concentrated in Hawaii and California and unlikely to be much of a political force in elections elsewhere, some advocates for Japanese-American compensation believed a judicial rather than legislative strategy would be more successful. Consultations with civil rights groups and members of Congress, however, suggested that this third possibility faced an uphill climb against lingering racism and a possible perception that the lawsuit was simply a financially motivated special-interest handout. JACL did not pursue this approach.

Instead, JACL pushed for Congress to create a federal investigatory commission, with the hope that compensation legislation would follow the commission's report. The Commission on Wartime Relocation and Internment of Civilians began work in 1981 and issued a report in 1983. In harsh terms, the report labeled the internment "a grave injustice" directly linked to racial prejudice. The commission called for a federal apology, $20,000 for each surviving detainee, and funds for research and education about the relocation of Japanese Americans.

After the report was issued, the four Japanese-American members of Congress introduced a bill that would implement the commission's recommendations. Debate continued in Congress for over five years. To many members of Congress, the internment had been a reasonable response during a time of crisis and called for neither an apology nor financial compensation. The four members of Congress who introduced the bill played a critical role in the discussions, convincing their colleagues to support the bill and the resulting compensation. JACL also developed a sophisticated lobbying plan to influence Congress, implementing a plan for Japanese Americans and their advocates to express support for the legislation through letter writing and personal testimony. In August 1988, President Ronald Reagan signed the bill that provided funds for research and education, a $20,000 payment for each internee or a descendant, and a national apology for the relocation and detention of Japanese Americans.[2]

The experience of the Japanese-American internees mirrors the political courses of action often seen throughout the history of American civil rights activism. A group—based on its race, gender, or any other category—is singled out and treated differently from the rest of the population. Through shared memories, the group starts to think about its shared interests, and it seeks action to correct past or present wrongs. But having shared memories and interests is not enough—the group must determine how to influence the political process. Is the group unified enough to present a clear argument for its case? Should it focus on the courts, Congress, or the president? The national government, or the state governments? What specific strategies and tactics might it use? What is the right timing for their efforts? Can the group draw upon beliefs in the American creed to make its case, or does it need to change people's thinking? These kinds of questions are common in the area of civil rights.

THIS CHAPTER WILL EXAMINE:

▶ advances and setbacks in black civil rights in the nineteenth century, including the doctrine of *separate but equal*

▶ the demise of the separate-but-equal doctrine in the twentieth century, and the creation of new laws and regulations to address racial inequalities

▶ political opportunities and challenges faced by the movement for black civil rights

▶ legal and legislative actions to extend equal protection guarantees to other groups.

Equality and Civil Rights

Civil rights are the guarantees of government to provide equal opportunities, privileges, and treatment under the law for all individuals. President Lyndon Johnson, in a speech in June 1965, provided a concise definition of civil rights as the freedom "to share fully and equally in American society—to vote, to hold a job, to enter a public place, to go to school. It is the right to be treated in every part of our national life as a person equal in dignity and promise to all others." This description reflects the value of equality that is basic to American political culture. Civil rights are about being fully granted the equal rights, responsibilities, and opportunities of citizenship. Civil rights are about being truly part of the American nation.

When Americans claim that civil rights have been violated, they usually mean that the government needs to defend the rights of an individual or group that has been denied some form of access or opportunity based on their race, ethnicity, color, gender, religion, sexual orientation, or other group characteristic. When a group or individual asserts their civil rights, they are telling government that it needs to act on behalf of those receiving unequal treatment in society.

In American politics, discriminatory treatment toward different groups has led to deep and sometimes bloody conflict over civil rights. Angry words, violence, and even riots have often been the result. This experience has torn through the history of many groups. The experience of black Americans has been a particular touchstone for civil rights. Most civil rights laws and court decisions arose originally in the area of black–white relations and set the framework for the legal status of other groups. The black civil rights movement was also the earliest to be extensively organized, thus providing a historical example that has played a key role in the evolution of American civil rights for further groups.

Slavery was not prohibited in the Constitution.

The framers of the Constitution faced a dilemma. Controversy over slavery was already substantial. After independence, several northern states prohibited slavery, while southern states retained it. Addressing slavery in any direct way during the Constitutional Convention might well have been a deal breaker, ending the possibility of crafting a constitution to unite the 13 colonies. But the issue could not be entirely avoided.

Although the word *slavery* did not appear in the Constitution, three provisions in the document concerned the subject. First, the Three-Fifths Compromise determined that three-fifths of a state's slave population would be added to its headcount for purposes of allocating representatives in the House of Representatives. Second, the importation of slaves was to cease after 1808. And third, fugitive slaves were to be returned to their owners.[3] The net result of these provisions was that slavery, by not being prohibited, was accepted as constitutional.

For the 70 years following ratification of the Constitution, slavery repeatedly flared up as an issue. Political leaders tried to keep the nation together through legislative compromises, especially concerning the place of slavery in America's westward expansion. Throughout the period, as with the adoption of the Three-Fifths Compromise during the Constitutional Convention, an important political goal was to keep the power of slave states and free states as nearly equal as possible.

Dred Scott rejects black citizenship.

One particularly dramatic development brought the issue to the Supreme Court. Dred Scott, a slave from Missouri, traveled with his owner to Illinois, a free state, and to other free territories north of the line established by the Missouri Compromise of 1820. The compromise had established in which territories and states slavery would be legal. Scott and his owner lived in these free areas for seven years, ultimately returning to Missouri, a slave state. When his owner died, Scott filed a lawsuit in Missouri, arguing that he should be considered a free man because he had been living on free soil.[4] Scott's petition was opposed by the owner's widow. After a series of court decisions in Scott's home state of Missouri, Scott brought the case to federal court. To file a federal lawsuit, however, Scott had to demonstrate that he was a citizen.

In one of the most notorious opinions in its history, the Supreme Court ruled in **Dred Scott v. Sandford** (1857) that Scott could not bring his case to federal court. To Chief Justice Roger Taney, the question was straightforward: "Can a negro, whose ancestors were imported into this country, and sold as slaves, become a member of the political community formed and brought into existence by the Constitution of the United States, and as such become entitled to all the rights, and privileges, and immunities, guaranteed by that instrument to the citizen?" Taney's answer was "no": Slaves could not be citizens, and neither could the descendants of slaves, whether free or not. When the Constitution was written, the Court concluded, blacks were considered "subordinate and inferior" to the "dominant race." Therefore, they could not possibly be considered citizens or part of "the people" as understood by the authors of the Constitution.

The Civil War amendments bring civil rights into the Constitution.

The *Dred Scott* decision also declared the Missouri Compromise an unconstitutional use of congressional power because it deprived slaveholders of their property without due process of law. The political firestorm it triggered was one of the contributing factors to the country's descent into civil war. By late 1865, when the Civil War ended, a nation disassembled by war needed to be put back together—not on its old terms, but recast, with African Americans as citizens. From 1865 through 1877, this process, known as Reconstruction, repeated the efforts of the revolutionary and constitutional eras to build both a sense of shared nationhood and a government capable of delivering the war's hard-won gains to blacks. It was, in effect, the third time the young country would try to lay a new foundation for itself.

Following the Civil War, the Thirteenth, Fourteenth, and Fifteenth Amendments—commonly referred to as the Civil War amendments—were added to the Constitution. All concerned civil rights for blacks. Congress included a section in each amendment giving it the authority to enforce the amendment by "appropriate legislation." This was Congress's attempt to prevent the Supreme Court from saying Congress did not have constitutional authority to act, as the Court had ruled in the *Dred Scott* decision. For a country imbued with a political culture of limited government, the addition of that power-expanding language was a remarkable move by Congress. The Thirteenth Amendment, ratified in December 1865, made slavery unconstitutional anywhere within the United States. The Fifteenth Amendment, ratified in March 1870, made it unconstitutional for the national government or state governments to deny someone the right to vote based on race, color, or whether the individual had previously been a slave or was descended from a slave.

The Fourteenth Amendment, ratified in July 1868, has had an extraordinary impact on American politics and life, as discussed in Chapter 5. It establishes that anyone born or naturalized in the United States is a citizen of the United States and also the state in which he or she lives. This made it clear that former slaves were fully citizens. It then declares that no state shall "deny to any person within its jurisdiction the equal protection of the laws." This **equal protection clause** would be the basis of much of the subsequent legislation and court decisions concerning civil rights.

Congress passed civil rights legislation to bring blacks into American life.

In addition to the Civil War amendments, Reconstruction included other legislation that assisted the efforts to gain black civil rights. The Freedmen's Bureau, created in 1865, provided food, clothing, and fuel; established schools; supervised labor–management relations; and created a system by which blacks could become landowners. The Civil Rights Act of 1866 was a response to so-called Black Codes passed by southern states in 1865 and 1866. The Black Codes restricted the rights and abilities of African Americans in a number of areas—parental and employment rights, occupation choices, property ownership, firearms, curfews, land rental, and the ability to serve on a jury or testify if a white was a party to a case. The Civil Rights Act guaranteed blacks the same property and legal rights as whites.[5] It also provided for the punishment of those who violated an individual's rights because of race or color.[6] The Civil Rights Act of 1875 was the last federal civil rights legislation until 1957. Unlike previous civil rights laws, this act concerned the private sector. It promised blacks the "full and equal enjoyment" of hotels, transportation, and places of entertainment such as theaters.

Several laws, known as enforcement acts, were passed to make sure these promises were implemented. They provided protection for black voters, ensured access to office holding and jury duty for blacks, and monitored equal treatment under the law. As a result of this legislation, blacks, running as Republicans, were elected to state governments and to Congress. They began attending schools and entering professions in large numbers. The means to reach these ends were controversial, however, including the creation of five military governing districts to enforce these new laws across the former Confederate states.[7] Especially during the administration of President Andrew Johnson (1865–1969), civil rights laws often had to override a presidential veto and pass by two-thirds of the House and Senate. Public response to the laws spanned the extremes. Whites in the North were divided between those who thought the laws did not go far enough and those that thought they had gone too far. In the South, the laws provoked violent responses, including the rise of the Ku Klux Klan, a secretive group that terrorized blacks.

"Equal protection of the laws" does not prohibit private discrimination.

The Civil Rights Act of 1875 seemed to mark the end of a decade of civil rights action that promised substantial equality and integration for blacks. But reality proved otherwise. By 1877, federal troops had been removed from the South, and the former Confederate states were essentially on their own. Southern state governments came under the control of whites who had been unhappy with the changes since 1865. And the Supreme Court interpreted civil rights laws and amendments in a narrow way that significantly hampered black equality with whites.

One major stumbling block was whether the Civil War amendments covered actions in the private sector. The Court ruled they did not. *Strauder v. West Virginia* (1880) was the first case in which the Court was asked to apply the equal protection clause to black civil rights. The Court struck down a West Virginia law that limited jury duty to white males. The Court thus clearly saw the Fourteenth Amendment as applicable to the actions of state governments, known as the doctrine of **state action**. But what about private sector action? In the *Civil Rights Cases* (1883), the Court consolidated five cases from California, Kansas, Missouri,

New Jersey, and Tennessee, in which blacks had been denied service in private establishments—seemingly a violation of the Civil Rights Act of 1875. The Court declared the act to be unconstitutional because it concerned discriminatory private, as opposed to government, action.[8] The Fourteenth Amendment, in the Court's view, applied to the actions of governments: it did not apply to discriminatory private behavior between individuals.[9] This "state action" view of the Fourteenth Amendment has remained a binding standard for Court decisions.

The Supreme Court declares that segregating the races does not violate equal protection.

In these decisions, the Court established that government actions which discriminated against blacks violated equal protection, but that private discrimination was not unconstitutional. Working within these guidelines, some state governments would prove to be creative in their attempts to perpetuate a society in which whites dominated. Beginning in the late 1880s, southern states enacted laws that required blacks and whites to be separated when they used public accommodations. Referred to as **Jim Crow** laws, the statutes covered a wide range of circumstances. From parks to schools, hotels, restaurants, hospitals, prisons, funeral homes, cemeteries, sporting events, restrooms, entrances, exits, transportation, and more, the laws required separate facilities for blacks and whites. Blacks were prohibited from eating at whites-only restaurants, attending whites-only state universities, or riding in the front of public buses. African Americans had separate and usually unequal hospital systems and educational systems. In 1890, Louisiana passed a law requiring all railway companies to provide "equal but separate accommodations" for blacks and whites.

Homer Plessy was arrested in June 1892 after he boarded a train in New Orleans and refused to leave the car reserved for whites.[10] In **Plessy v. Ferguson** (1896), the Supreme Court ruled 8-1 that Louisiana's law was constitutional. Separate accommodations were not a "badge of servitude" akin to slavery, the Court ruled, so the Thirteenth Amendment did not apply. As for the Fourteenth Amendment, there was nothing inherently discriminatory in separating the races, the Court concluded, so long as each race was accommodated. The amendment was intended to create equality before the law, not to abolish racial distinctions or enforce social integration. Indeed, the Court noted, Congress had passed acts requiring separate schools for blacks in the District of Columbia, so it would not likely disapprove of similar acts in the states. The Court interpreted Louisiana's law as a reasonable attempt to promote the public good as legislators saw it, not an attempt to oppress any group and not a violation of equal protection of the laws.

With these late nineteenth century decisions, national authority over race relations was extremely limited. Neither members of Congress nor the president were likely to address racial discrimination seriously. For southern politicians, such action would be career-ending. For northern politicians, there were few constituencies pushing actively for integration. And segregation itself was constitutionally protected by the Supreme Court. According to the **separate but equal** doctrine, it was constitutional to require separate facilities for the races, so long as the facilities were substantially equal, even though not identical.

Equal Protection of the Laws Gains Meaning

Segregation proved to be separate, but certainly not equal. Facilities and services provided to blacks were notably inferior in quality, quantity, and convenience. For nearly half a century after the *Plessy* decision, federal politicians did little to improve the political, economic, social, or legal status of blacks in the United States. Jim Crow continued unabated and black voters in the South dwindled to just a very small percent of all blacks, because of voting restrictions that were technically color-blind but were very color-aware in practice. Leaders of black civil rights organizations, however, continued to press for government action. After a long period, these efforts began to succeed. In fits and starts, the legal underpinning for segregation eroded. And in 1954, the separate-but-equal doctrine came crashing down. Soon after, a wave of legislative and administrative change would follow and advance civil rights.

Presidents bypass Congress to chip away at racial discrimination.

Black political activists knew that elected officials needed to see the protection of civil rights as in their own political interests, especially given the Supreme Court's blunt acceptance of segregation. Over the first four decades of the twentieth century, activists formed organizations to represent black political interests, place pressure on politicians, and form a legal strategy for use in the courts. The most important of these organizations was the National Association for the Advancement of Colored People (NAACP), formed in 1909. The organization focused largely on legal strategies in its first two decades and began deeper consideration of legislative and administrative strategies in the 1930s. At the time of the NAACP's founding, white southern Democrats dominated Congress and thwarted any attempts to pass civil rights legislation. For this reason, the NAACP primarily concentrated its lobbying efforts on the president and the executive branch, and this strategy began to bear fruit during the presidency of Franklin Roosevelt (1933–1945).

Roosevelt used his unilateral executive powers to make some progress in civil rights. He appointed more blacks to his administration than any previous president. In June 1941, in part to forestall a massive March on Washington by blacks, but also because of the impending acceleration in military production brought on by U.S. involvement in World War II, President Roosevelt signed an executive order—a presidential proclamation with the force of law that does not require congressional approval—creating the Fair Employment Practices Committee (FEPC).[11] The order mandated an end to employment discrimination based on race, creed, color, or national origin in companies and U.S. government agencies involved in defense production, and it authorized the committee to punish offenders. The FEPC expired in 1946 when Congress refused to extend funding.

Following Roosevelt's death, President Harry Truman (1945–1952) continued the use of executive orders to advance civil rights in the face of congressional opposition. Truman took his most dramatic civil rights action by integrating the armed forces through Executive Order 9981. Issued in July 1948, the order declared that regardless of race, color, national origin, or religion, there would be "equality of treatment and opportunity" for all members of the military. A companion order, 9980, created the Fair Employment Board and forbade all racial discrimination in federal government hiring. By October 1954, the last all-black military unit had been disbanded, and the military had become the most fully integrated institution in American society.

Court decisions began to challenge separate but equal.

Supreme Court decisions after 1937 began to challenge racial discrimination. Why this change at this time? In large part, the new perspective coincided with a major change in Court membership. Between 1937 and 1943, President Roosevelt appointed eight new justices; between 1945 and 1949, President Truman appointed three.

Civil rights for blacks began to make some progress in education. Although the Court did not challenge the separate but equal doctrine during this period, it did become more demanding in ensuring that conditions for black students and white students were somewhat comparable. In 1938, the Court struck down Missouri's practice of paying blacks' tuition at out-of-state law schools rather than enrolling them at the University of Missouri Law School.[12] This decision did not result in integration of the law school—Missouri established a separate law school for minorities—but it did indicate that the Court was looking more carefully at how "equal" conditions between the races really were. Clearly, forcing students of one race to leave their state to attend school elsewhere was not comparable treatment. Following this victory, blacks in other states won similar victories at professional schools.

Engaging in lawsuits that challenged the system of segregation in American education was the strategy of the newly-created legal arm of the NAACP, the NAACP Legal Defense and Educational Fund, which was formed in 1940. The organization sought first to win victories at specific schools around the idea of what "equal" meant. With successes in those cases on the state level, and in federal courts if those decisions were appealed, the organization could then move to challenge separate but equal as a principle.

Victories in important cases convinced the organization that the time had come to challenge the *Plessy* decision. In 1950, the Supreme Court ruled that an alternative Texas law school for black students did not provide "substantial equality," and it ruled that a black student in the University of Oklahoma School of Education could not be separated from white students in classrooms, libraries, or cafeterias.[13] For the first time, the Court hinted that separation itself was likely to damage the quality of a student's education.[14]

Segregation is declared unconstitutional in *Brown v. Board of Education.*

With these victories, the stage had been set for an assault on the separate-but-equal doctrine. Four cases in 1951 and 1952, from Kansas, South Carolina, Virginia, and Delaware, challenged the doctrine in education. The Supreme Court consolidated these cases and considered them together as **Brown v. Board of Education** *of Topeka, Kansas* (1954). The lead case was prompted when Oliver Brown attempted to enroll his daughter for third grade in an all-white school and was turned away. Arguing the case on behalf of Brown was Thurgood Marshall of the NAACP, who later became the first black Supreme Court justice.

Under the leadership of Chief Justice Earl Warren, the Court unanimously struck down the separate-but-equal doctrine. Avoiding any definitive stand on what the Fourteenth Amendment required in public education, the Court instead emphasized the importance of education in modern society and asked whether segregating the races provided equal opportunity for black children. In the Court's view, the answer was no. Referring to psychological studies, the Court concluded that segregation could generate a permanent "feeling of inferiority as to their status in the community." In public education, the Court famously ruled, "the doctrine of 'separate but equal' has no place. Separate educational facilities are inherently unequal."

The *Brown* decision was an earthquake, bringing down the legal and constitutional edifice of enforced segregation. It struck down the laws of 21 states.[15] In practical terms, however, change was not as swift. Aware of the potential explosiveness of its decision, the Court did not set any timetable in *Brown*. In a follow-up opinion in 1955, referred to as *Brown II*, the Court stated that school districts should move with "all deliberate speed" to desegregate their schools.[16]

Massive resistance, especially in the South, blunted the speed of change. Many school boards preferred to go to court rather than voluntarily abide by the Court's ruling. Others districts sought to disband their public schools. Incidents of violence and intimidation to keep blacks from white schools were common. A decade after *Brown*, barely 3 percent of southern black children were in schools where a majority of students were white.

In response to this foot dragging, the federal government began threatening to initiate lawsuits and withhold federal funds from states and districts that were not making progress in implementing desegregation. These tactics were effective. By 1970, about one-third of southern black children were in majority-white schools and 90 percent were in schools with at least some white students.[17]

Civil rights activists sought to extend *Brown*'s reach to cases of *de facto* segregation.

Activists in the black civil rights movement pushed courts to address instances both of **de jure segregation** and **de facto segregation**. *De jure* segregation refers to segregation explicitly written into laws and regulations. It was the kind of segregation outlawed by the *Brown* decision and was common in southern states. *De facto* segregation occurs because of residential patterns. If residential patterns are highly skewed racially and all children attend the school nearest to them, then schools would automatically remain highly segregated. This pattern was common in the North. The issue became whether schools were required to desegregate, which could be achieved by repealing *de jure* segregation, or whether they were required to integrate, which would also entail challenging *de facto* segregation.

The Court's early decisions leaned toward integration.[18] "Busing" was an especially controversial remedy. This called for students to be bused from one part of a school district to another in order to achieve a particular racial balance, even if there had been no history of *de jure* segregation in the district. A later Court decision scaled back this remedy. In 1974, by a 5-4 vote, the Supreme Court concluded that the Fourteenth Amendment's equal protection guarantee did not extend to *de facto* segregation if there was no evidence that a school district intended to discriminate (see Table 6-1).[19] This meant that courts could not easily order school districts to use busing to remedy *de facto* segregation in the schools.

Nonetheless, school districts could voluntarily devise busing and other integration plans in order to achieve more diversity at their schools or to thwart potential lawsuits. Many districts did precisely that. In *PICS v. Seattle* (2007), however, the Supreme Court struck down such plans in Seattle, Washington, and Louisville, Kentucky, as an unconstitutional violation of equal protection.[20] In each city, white parents whose children were denied admission to a school on racial grounds brought the lawsuit against the school districts. The decision allowed districts to continue to find ways to make their schools more diverse, through the drawing of

Table 6-1. Significant Supreme Court Decisions on School Desegregation

CASE	YEAR OF DECISION	DECISION
Brown v. Board of Education of Topeka, Kansas	1954	Segregated "separate but equal" schools are inherently unequal and unconstitutional.
Green v. County School Board of New Kent County	1968	Integration and not simply repeal of discriminatory laws and practices is necessary to comply with the "unitary system" of schools implied by Brown. Examination of student assignments, faculty assignments, staff assignments, transportation, physical facilities, and extracurricular activities will determine whether a school system is unitary or dual and separate.
Swann v. Charlotte-Mecklenburg Board of Education	1971	Busing is acceptable as a remedy to desegregate schools, as are quotas. The racial balance at a school need not be identical to the overall district balance. A school district's intent to discriminate by law or practice must be proven before a court imposes a desegregation plan.
Milliken v. Bradley	1974	Court-imposed busing cannot cover multiple school districts such as a city and its suburbs, unless intentional segregation is demonstrated in each district.
Freeman v. Pitts	1992	Federal courts can gradually withdraw from oversight of school districts as they are convinced that specific aspects of a desegregation plan are being met.
Parents Involved in Community Schools v. Seattle School District No. 1	2007	Denying students enrollment in particular schools on the basis of their race, as part of a school district's voluntary integration or diversity plan, is unconstitutional.

school boundaries, magnet schools, open enrollment, and other such plans. School districts could not, however, make an individual student's enrollment in a school dependent on his or her race. Wrote Chief Justice John Roberts, "the way to stop discrimination on the basis of race is to stop discriminating on the basis of race." But as critics saw it, the decision effectively overturned *Brown* and would accelerate the resegregation of schools in the United States.[21]

The debate over how best—or whether—to achieve racial integration in education will continue as districts devise plans they hope will meet the Supreme Court's approval. In its *PICS* decision, the Court did not rule out using income and other socioeconomic factors as a basis for enrollment. Because minority status is often correlated with income and wealth, this approach achieves racial integration by increasing socioeconomic diversity (see Figure 6-1). One challenge for architects of even the most creative integration and diversity plans will remain finding public support for their efforts. Public opinion data consistently show that people of all races are more concerned about the quality of education than about the racial diversity of students in schools.

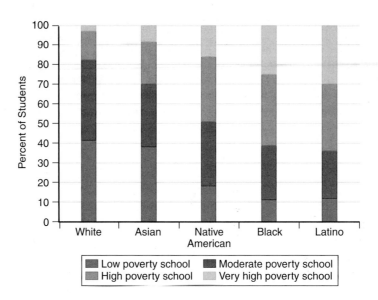

Figure 6-1. **Type of Public School Attended by Race and Ethnic Group, 2002–03.** Minority students are more likely than white students to attend schools with high or very high numbers of students from poor families. Only a small percentage of white students attend schools with very high poverty levels, compared to about 25–30 percent of black and Latino students.

Note: Low poverty schools: 0–20% of students attending are poor; Moderate: 21–50%; High: 51–80%; Very high: 81–100%.

Source: Gary Orfield and Chungmei Lee, "Why Segregation Matters: Poverty and Educational Inequality," The Civil Rights Project at Harvard University, January 2005, Table 7.

New laws and executive orders expand civil rights protection.

During the 1960s, civil rights also advanced in other spheres of public and private life. As with the education system, public officials employed both legislation and executive orders in this process.

Legislation The Civil Rights Act of 1964 is the centerpiece of American antidiscrimination law. Work on the law began under President Kennedy and, following his assassination, was completed by President Johnson. The law prohibited discrimination in public accommodations and in private employment on the basis of race, color, religion, sex, and national origin.

On the surface, this sounds similar to the 1868 Civil Rights Act that was struck down in the *Civil Rights Cases*. (Recall that decision ruled that the Fourteenth Amendment gave Congress the authority to regulate only government action, not private behavior.) Significantly, however, Congress justified the Civil Rights Act of 1964 not in terms of the equal-protection guarantee of the Fourteenth Amendment, but by linking the law to Congress's power to regulate commerce. As noted in Chapter 4, the Supreme Court in 1937 established a generous definition of interstate commerce that vastly expanded the power of the federal government. As a result, if Congress could link discrimination to the flow of commerce, it could regulate discriminatory actions in the private sector.

Grounding Congress's action in an established constitutional power like regulation of interstate commerce was a dramatically consequential idea, opening new horizons for civil rights legislation. The Civil Rights Act of 1964 also set the mold in another way: it denied federal funds to any program or activity that discriminated. After 1964, all civil rights legislation that affected the private sector was justified either on interstate commerce grounds or as an extension of Congress's control over federal spending.[22] Through these means, Congress bypassed the restrictions of the state-action doctrine. The Civil Rights Act of 1968, which prohibited discrimination in the sale, rental, financing, or advertising of housing on the basis of race, color, religion, or national origin, is one significant example.

Another signal legislative achievement was the Voting Rights Act of 1965. Earlier Civil Rights Acts in 1957 and 1960 had provided for more federal oversight of elections in the southern states. The bills were modest steps, largely because they faced considerable opposition from southern members of Congress. The 1965 act was much stronger, permanently prohibiting the use of discriminatory methods, such as literacy tests, to intentionally weaken the voting power of blacks (see Chapter 8). States or parts of states that had a history of such methods were required to clear any changes in their voting laws with the Department of Justice. The same pre-clearance regulations applied to laws that might have impact on the electoral power of minorities. For example, pre-clearance would be necessary if a city with a significant minority population wished to annex neighboring suburbs that were almost completely white. The pre-clearance requirement is subject to periodic reauthorization by Congress and the president and remains in place today.[23]

Black access to voting was also enhanced with the abolition of poll taxes. A **poll tax** was a per-person charge to vote in an election. These were introduced in southern states after the passage of the Fifteenth Amendment and were often designed to deny the vote to blacks or recent immigrants. For example, if your father or grandfather had been able to vote in elections prior to the Thirteenth Amendment, you were "grandfathered" in and did not need to pay the tax. Clearly, only whites would meet that standard. In some states, poll taxes were cumulative, so you not only had to pay the fee for this year's election but all the previous elections you had not voted in. The Twenty-fourth Amendment, ratified in 1964, outlawed use of the poll tax in federal elections. The Supreme Court subsequently ruled in 1966 that poll taxes in state elections violated the equal protection clause of the Fourteenth Amendment.[24]

Executive orders As noted earlier, Presidents Roosevelt and Truman began using executive orders to advance civil rights—a practice continued by later presidents. Presidents Eisenhower and Kennedy, for example, used executive orders to send National Guard units in Arkansas, Mississippi, and Alabama to enforce school desegregation. President Kennedy ordered the creation of compliance mechanisms for nondiscriminatory employment policies by federal contractors. Orders by later presidents enhanced these mechanisms. Additional categories of protection were added as well, including discrimination based on sex (President Johnson), disability and age (President Carter), and sexual orientation and status as a parent (President Clinton).[25]

Affirmative action Despite becoming one of the most controversial civil rights policies, **affirmative action** started out quietly in executive orders issued by Presidents Kennedy, Johnson, and Nixon in the 1960s to combat discrimination in federal hiring and contracts.[26] On its face, affirmative action calls for aggressive outreach efforts targeted to groups traditionally underrepresented in particular jobs and college admissions. Concerned that outreach might not be enough to satisfy the Supreme Court, many employers, colleges, and government administrators interpreted affirmative action to require setting guidelines, such as quotas, for the recruitment of minorities. Black civil rights leaders in the 1960s had been luke-warm to the idea of fixed quotas, fearing a backlash among white, working class voters.[27] For leaders like Martin Luther King Jr., this was a dangerous risk. And to the extent that "affirmative action" was thought of strictly as "quotas," it was in fact highly unpopular among white voters (see *How Do We Know? Is White Opposition to Affirmative Action Racist?*).

Since 1989, the Supreme Court has been reining in the scope of these plans. In *Richmond v. Croson* (1989), the Court struck down "set-aside" programs that required contractors on city projects to subcontract 30 percent of the business to minority businesses. The Court declared that state and local affirmative action like that in Richmond could not be initiated as a response to racism in general: there had to be a specific discriminatory practice in a specific location to justify the need for the affirmative action policy. The Court further narrowed the scope of affirmative action programs in its 5-4 decision in *Adarand v. Pena* (1995), a case concerning extra payments supplied by the federal government to contractors who hired minority firms. The decision decreed that all racial classifications at all levels of government would be subject to strict scrutiny, meaning the Court would have to be convinced that the classification was absolutely necessary to meet a compelling government interest, and that this interest was being achieved in the least intrusive, narrowest manner possible ("narrowly tailored").

Outside of employment and contracts, college admissions have been another hotbed of controversy over affirmative action. The Court's first major ruling in this area was **Regents of the University of California v. Bakke** (1978), in which the Court prohibited racial quotas for admissions but concluded that race could be a "plus" factor considered along with many other factors as admissions criteria. More recently, the Supreme Court in *Grutter v Bollinger* (2003) upheld in a 5-4 vote the University of Michigan Law School's "holistic" use of race to foster viewpoint diversity at the school, which the Court had established in *Bakke* was a compelling interest for a public academic institution. In *Gratz v. Bollinger* (2003), however, the Court rejected the undergraduate affirmative action admissions policy of the university's largest college. In the interest of achieving a diverse student body, the college awarded 20 points—one-fifth of the total needed to guarantee admission—to every African American, Hispanic, and Native American applicant. While again confirming that student diversity is a compelling government interest, the Court concluded that the college's automatic point system had not created, as its *Bakke* decision called for, a narrowly tailored solution.

HOW DO WE KNOW ?

Is White Opposition to Affirmative Action Racist?

The Question

There is no doubt that the opinions of whites and blacks are often far apart on programs like affirmative action, school desegregation, and spending on social programs. Such a gap could be explained by genuine principled opposition among whites to certain roles for government. It could also be explained by white racism. If whites hold inherently negative and generalized views toward racial minorities they might be more likely to oppose policies that seem to disproportionately benefit minorities. Is white opposition to affirmative action and similar programs racist? How do we know?

Why It Matters

Whether white opposition to policies benefiting minorities is based on bigotry or other factors matters for at least two reasons. First, as discussed in Chapter 2, political culture is negotiable. Advocates for a policy can try to convince people to balance beliefs in a new way, or redefine what they mean by particular beliefs. If policy opposition is based on political culture, there is some prospect that opponents can be convinced to change their minds. On the other hand, if policy opposition is based on racism, that more deep-seated resistance will be hard to change. Second, if bigotry, rather than different weighting on beliefs in the American creed, is the primary reason for opposition to certain policies, then the prospects for civil rights and racial and ethnic harmony would seem to be dim. The answer tells us something about how far the United States has evolved from the days of acute, public racism.

Investigating the Answer

Political scientists have explored this question largely through research on black and white public opinion, so that is the focus here.[28] The outcome analyzed is white opposition to affirmative action. The two competing factors that may explain the outcome are racist beliefs and general philosophical beliefs about government's appropriate role.

Public opinion data show substantial differences between whites and blacks. White and black public opinion are working at cross-purposes on matters related to race, with whites often opposing the adoption of policies favored by blacks. The differences between the races' attitudes toward race-related policies, income redistribution programs, and the fairness of American life are often larger than those of class, gender, and religion.[29]

Exploring the extent to which racial considerations drive white opinion has been a large, complex, and heated area of debate in political science research.[30] One group of scholars points to the significance of what they call racial resentment.[31] Traditional racism was cruel and blunt and built around an explicitly stated belief in white racial superiority. The success of the civil rights movement, however, blocked that kind of racism from entering public discourse. Its public legitimacy evaporated; things that were once commonly said could now no longer be said.

In its place, however, arose a more subtle racism in which blacks were not seen as inherently inferior, but were critiqued for not making the best of the opportunities given to them. This racism blends traditional beliefs of American political culture, especially individualism, with disaffection for blacks or what is considered to be "black behavior." Discrimination, in this view, is not a significant problem and is used as an excuse by blacks. Black progress is stunted by blacks themselves—their failure to work and study hard and their expectation that government should take care of people even if they make poor choices in life. This racism is polite and hard to detect in surface behavior, but underneath lies suppressed racist views—the old racism dressed up in the language of traditional American values. Extensive analysis of survey research has led scholars in this school to conclude that white attitudes toward affirmative action and similar programs are strongly determined by this racial resentment.

Another group of scholars believes the racial resentment argument goes too far in blaming racism for white opposition to programs like affirmative action. This view claims that the impact of any white racism on policy attitudes has been overstated and is less important than general ideological predispositions about government. Whites are not averse to assistance for blacks, but they are, on average, less likely than blacks to support the types of assistance policies and programs favored by liberals. Opposition to certain programs would exist because of ideological positions favoring limited government, regardless of whether the beneficiaries were white or black. To the extent that the racial resentment argument presumes that liberal positions favor racial equality and conservative positions do not, white public opinion will be wrongly interpreted as racist when in fact whites are simply more ideologically conservative, on average, than blacks.

One technique employed to test this possibility is to change the wording of a public opinion survey question and compare responses. This is called a survey experiment. For example, in one study whites were split into two groups. The first group was asked if, because of past discrimination, blacks should be given preference in college admissions. Only 26 percent of whites supported this idea. The second group was asked instead whether an extra effort should be made to ensure that qualified blacks applied for college admission. About 65 percent of whites supported this form of affirmative action specifically aimed toward blacks. This softer form of affirmative action might fit more easily within the beliefs of American political culture.

Another experiment divided respondents into three groups. All three were asked about government assistance for those born into poverty. For the first group, the program was said to help blacks as a matter of racial justice for past wrongs: 31 percent of whites approved of such a program. For the second group, the program was said to help blacks, but the justification was equal opportunity rather than racial justice: 42 percent of whites supported this program. And for the third group, the program was said to help poor people, with no race indicated: 49 percent of whites supported this program. This suggests that programs that are justified by reference to American creed beliefs and that do not single out particular groups receive greater support from whites.

Finally, an experiment dividing respondents into two groups asked one group about blacks and the other about new immigrants from Europe. Whites were equally likely to say these two groups should "work their way up without special favors"— white views appeared more driven by ideology than by who benefited from government help.

The debate over the concept of racial resentment has been extensive and deeply felt among political scientists. The perceived stakes are high. Studies continue to support each side in the argument.[32] Virtually all scholars agree that racism remains a potent force in American society. There is no doubt that bigotry remains an everyday problem facing blacks and other minorities. Although it is complicated to measure and analyze, clear and incontrovertible evidence that racism is the predominant driver of white public opinion is lacking. Evidence in some studies shows that white public opinion is open to persuasion and appeals to principle, which seems unlikely if racism thoroughly dominated white opinion on racially oriented policies.

The Bottom Line

Civil rights policies vary across countries.

The United States is not the only country to struggle with racial and ethnic conflict. European countries have faced tremendous internal electoral and policy tensions due to the diversity of an increasing immigrant population. The European Union in 2000 called for an end to discrimination in education, employment, housing, social welfare, and training, along the lines of American antidiscrimination law and policy. Countries remained free to add preference policies for groups long discriminated against. Progress has been uneven across Europe in implementing the decree.

Each country's particular context of political culture has shaped the extent to which it emphasizes antidiscrimination laws and government programs. Compared to other countries, the United States has stronger antidiscrimination laws but less generous government services and benefits. Generous benefits do not ensure non-discrimination, but they may reduce the economic inequality between groups. On the other hand, those paying for these programs may resent the beneficiaries.

Two of America's allies have handled the civil rights challenge differently from each other and from the United States. Britain and France have sizable minority populations, both native and immigrant. Britain has leaned toward American-style antidiscrimination laws, but enforcement has been modest. Britain also has a more generous set of government services and benefits than the United States, some tailored to particular groups. France offers generous benefits, but generally not targeted toward particular minority groups. It has not focused as strongly as the United States or Great Britain on antidiscrimination law. Affirmative action has been most deeply embedded in the United States, while Britain has allowed affirmative action but not quotas, and France has prohibited any kind of affirmative action. Assimilation and colorblindness have been key themes in France. Racial divisiveness is highly monitored and frequently punished. For example, the wearing of religious symbols in public schools was outlawed in 2004 as divisive, Holocaust denial is illegal, convicted racists are stripped of some civil rights, and collection of racial and ethnic data is sharply limited, much more so than in the United States and Britain.[33]

The Politics of Civil Rights

By the end of the 1960s, the United States had been through a civil rights revolution that reverberates to this day. The equal protection clause of the Fourteenth Amendment had been used to challenge discrimination in laws and regulations. Congress had used its commerce-clause powers and its spending power to advance civil rights in the private sector. And presidents had used their power as the head of the executive branch to further civil rights in government and among those who did business with or received services from the federal government. Segregation had fallen in schools and public accommodations. Voting rights had been significantly expanded and protected. Employment discrimination was prohibited. Although inequities in quality of life remained and still remain today, there is no doubt that the country had changed radically in a relatively short time.

How did all this happen? To understand, we need to explore the politics of civil rights in greater detail. Some political scientists argue that the success of civil rights resulted from political opportunities that created the possibility for change. Others focus on effective appeals to American creedal beliefs. Still others emphasize overcoming the difficulties in organizing people for political action. All of these factors are important, and their reversals featured prominently in the struggles civil rights advocates continued to face after these major successes.[34]

The civil rights movement led to civil rights successes for blacks.

The pressure created by the civil rights movement contributed to the legal, legislative, and administrative successes gained by blacks. As mentioned earlier, organizations advocating for black civil rights led to significant legal victories in the first half of the twentieth century, culminating in the dramatic victory in *Brown v. Board of Education* in 1954. In December 1955, the NAACP encouraged a year-long boycott of the bus system in Montgomery, Alabama, to protest segregation of public buses. The boycott drew national attention. The name of NAACP member Rosa Parks, who like Homer Plessy refused to change her seat, became a household word. Martin Luther King Jr. the Baptist minister, similarly became nationally known. King, and the organization he would soon head, the Southern Christian Leadership Conference (SCLC), advocated a strategy of **civil disobedience**. This practice used nonviolent tactics such as marches and demonstrations to sway public opinion and pressure public officials. Prior to the late 1950s, mass protests had been infrequent. Inequalities and injustice were severe, but organizing and encouraging mass participation in the face of entrenched and powerful opponents was not easy. Participants risked their jobs and even their lives. Each victory was important, and each victory gave future participants the sense that direct political action could succeed. Mass political activity for the right to vote and for the repeal of Jim Crow restrictions did not become widespread until the 1960s, by which time the country became filled with these forms of political action (see Figure 6-2).

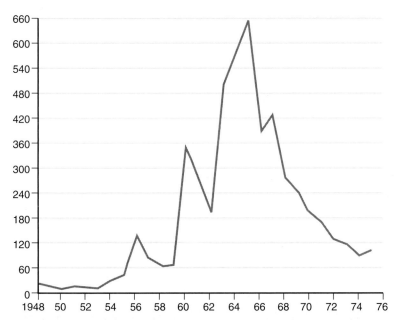

Figure 6-2. Number of Civil Rights Movement Marches, Speeches, Protests, Sit-ins, and Related Events Annually. The number of events initiated by civil rights movement groups and organizations peaked from 1963 to 1965 and declined swiftly after that as the movement won major legislative victories and then splintered over goals and tactics.

Source: Doug McAdam. *Political Process and the Development of Black Insurgency 1930–1970* (Chicago: University of Chicago Press, 1982), p. 121.

One of the most important of these protests occurred in Alabama in 1963. That spring, the SCLC decided to target Birmingham—a center of segregation—for a series of protests and boycotts. The goal of these protests and boycotts was not only to force downtown stores to desegregate and end discriminatory hiring practices, but to focus national attention on similar situations throughout the South. Sheriff Bull Connors and his deputies quickly obliged civil rights leaders on the latter goal. The notorious chief of the Birmingham police unleashed fire hoses and police dogs on the peaceful protestors and jailed thousands. Many of the protesters were high-school and even elementary-school students. These harsh actions were widely covered by the national press and the broadcast networks.

King and his deputies skillfully capitalized on the publicity and the images that were being transmitted to the rest of the country, by raising money and galvanizing support in the North.[35] Their efforts even encouraged some Northern whites, mostly college students and religious leaders, to come to the South and help organize voter registration drives and other acts of protest.

In retrospect, the success of the civil rights movement and the important role that mass protest played in breaking down barriers and winning African Americans the right to vote suggests that these activities were the obvious course for African Americans in the South and their supporters in the North. But why would someone risk their livelihood, if not their life, to register to vote or to get others to register to vote? Why would someone face police dogs to win the right to sit at a department store lunch counter or ride a bus? Why would individuals in the North bother to write letters to legislators and send contributions in support of the protests in the South?

The answers are complex and have been studied at great length by political scientists. Clearly, some individuals sincerely believed their actions could make a difference. Among those key political entrepreneurs and patrons were the foundations that provided financial support to civil rights organizations, the interest groups that focused on civil rights, the ministers who motivated congregations to act, and the government officials who promoted policy change. Others participated to express their support for a cause and for the benefit of feeling like a contributor to something important. And movements can have a cumulative effect—as successes mount, as more individuals have participated, and as public awareness grows, the incentives to participate, to be part of a winning cause, can grow.[36]

Changes in the Democratic Party aided the civil rights movement.

A wave of political action by supporters of civil rights is part of the explanation of the civil rights success in the 1960s. But why did public officials respond to the movement as they did? The answer lies largely in the transformation of the Democratic Party.

In the period following the Civil War, politics in the South had been dominated by the Democratic Party. The Republican Party, considered the party of the North and of Lincoln, was almost invisible in the South, especially at the state and local levels. In many respects the region had a one-party system. Most outcomes were essentially decided in the Democratic Party's primary election. Often, until outlawed in 1944 by the Supreme Court, this was a **white primary**, in which—as the name implies—only white voters were allowed to cast ballots.[37] So even in the rare instances when African Americans were allowed to register and vote in general elections, there were usually no contested races and no meaningful choices on the ballot.

Just as the Democratic Party dominated southern politics, so the South dominated Democratic Party politics. Democratic Party politicians had to tread carefully around issues of race or risk disrupting the party coalition. At the national level, this power of the South over the Democratic Party played out in two ways. First, the Democrats required their presidential nominee to receive two-thirds of the delegate votes at the presidential nominating convention. This rule ensured that the South could thwart an undesirable contender for the Democratic nomination. A candidate who made civil rights a major goal would have no way to win the nomination. Second, in the Senate, the ability of a minority of senators to block action on bills—known as a filibuster (discussed further in Chapter 13)—meant that civil rights legislation would face a difficult road to passage. Moreover, by the middle of the twentieth century, committee chairs were awarded almost exclusively on the basis of seniority. With no serious two-party competition in the South, Democrats from that region tended to be the committee chairs. Because chairs had great influence over when, if, and in what form bills would leave a committee and go to the full House or Senate, it was difficult to move civil rights legislation through Congress.[38]

The grip of the South over the Democratic Party began to weaken in the 1930s but was still formidable. The Great Migration of blacks from the South, where they typically could not vote, to the North, where they could, gave northern Democratic politicians increased interest in cultivating the black vote. But they had to proceed cautiously, because many northern Democratic constituencies did not embrace civil rights as an issue. After the Democrats swept through the country with a massive election victory in 1932, President Franklin Roosevelt was able to have the two-thirds rule removed in 1936. As a result, the South no longer had a veto over the Democratic presidential nomination. Recognizing that the party's geographical center was increasingly moving north, every Democratic presidential nominee after 1936 expressed support for civil rights. Democratic Presidents Roosevelt, Truman, Kennedy, and Johnson all used executive orders and other unilateral powers to advance civil rights. For each, the calculation may have involved principle, but it certainly included a substantial amount of political pragmatism as well, as the path to passing civil rights legislation was still strewn with obstacles.

Southern Democrats' grip on Congress slowly weakened as well. With the northern share of congressional Democrats growing, and with this share dominated by urban, liberal representatives, support for civil rights was increasing. And even though southern Democratic senators were still able to impede civil rights reforms by threatening or carrying out filibusters, the rule governing the termination of filibusters was modified in the mid-1960s to make filibusters easier to defeat. Subcommittees also gained additional independence to work around some of the tight control exerted by conservative southern committee leaders. All these factors combined to push the civil rights and voting rights acts through Congress in the 1960s.[39]

Obstacles slowed the momentum of the civil rights movement.

The civil rights achievements of the 1960s were monumental. But as the decade wore on, the politics of gaining additional civil rights advances grew daunting. Three causes contributed to this trend. First, unity in the civil rights movement disintegrated. Second, new issues raised by the movement threatened many whites who had supported, or at least not opposed, the breakthroughs of the early 1960s. And third, blacks had the support of the Democratic Party, and the party had the support of black voters, and this mutual support created challenges as well as opportunities. The intersection of these three factors created particular problems for the civil rights agenda.[40]

Collapse of unity in the black civil rights movement

By the late 1960s, the black civil rights movement appeared to have peaked. Participation in civil disobedience events had dwindled, as had the number of events. The ability of leaders like Martin Luther King Jr. to maintain nonviolent civil disobedience as the movement's central strategy came under increasing pressure after 1964. In the summer of 1964, massive violence directed at blacks and white civil rights activists in Mississippi shocked the country and inflamed black public opinion—80 civil rights workers beaten; 35 shot at; 4 killed; 70 black homes, businesses, and churches burned; 1,000 activists jailed.[41] Similar scenes elsewhere shook faith in the effectiveness of nonviolent appeals. Riots sprang up in Los Angeles in 1965 and in many cities across the country following the assassination of King in April 1968. Some in the civil rights movement, such as the members of the Black Panther party, believed that the violent resistance to civil rights should be met with a violent response. Black leaders including Malcolm X argued for a black nationalism that sought to advance black equality by withdrawing from white society and developing the black community, rather than by focusing on integration.

The rupture in the movement was evident in 1966 when the Student Nonviolent Coordinating Committee (SNCC, founded 1960) and the Congress of Racial Equality (CORE, founded 1942) embraced this notion of separationist black power. Two other prominent civil rights groups, the NAACP and the Urban League (founded 1910) rebuked this goal. In part, these debates echoed those stretching back to the early twentieth century, when black leaders such as Booker T. Washington and W.E.B. Du Bois argued over the extent to which black advancement was in the control of self-improvement by blacks and to what extent it depended on major changes in white society. In the latter half of the 1960s, the consensus over strategy that was present in the early part of the 1960s had evaporated.

Challenging issues in the late 1960s

Once the legal and political infrastructure of segregation and denial of voting rights had fallen, civil rights activists moved onto issues of social and economic equality. These issues were more difficult for many whites to support. As contentious as the issues of political equality were, they stood firmly within a political culture framework that was familiar to Americans and mostly consistent with their values. Equal treatment under the law, equal opportunity, the freedom to hold a job and earn a living, the chance to go as far as one's talents allowed, to be judged "not on the color of [one's] skin, but on the content of [one's] character," as King preached, echoed familiar themes.

For many, newer issues presented a greater challenge and a range of possible solutions. Some activists advocated reparations, the idea that blacks who were descendants of slaves needed to be compensated financially for the harsh deprivations imposed by slavery. Others advocated strong outreach efforts to bring minorities into colleges and the workforce, including racial quotas if necessary. Yet others called for redistribution of wealth to address economic inequality. In the eyes of many, these policies called quite directly for taking something from one group and giving it to another—always a controversial proposition. Many labor unions struggled with civil rights issues due to the fear and opposition of their white members. By the late 1960s, a white backlash to the demands of the civil rights movement had set in.

Consolidation of black political pressure in one party Once the Democratic Party became the champion of black civil rights, black voter support for that party surged. In presidential elections, 90 percent or more of blacks typically voted for the Democrat. Black support for Democratic candidates at other levels was similarly high. Some scholars have suggested that this situation created a dilemma for black political power.[42] On the one hand, unified voting made blacks an important constituency for the Democratic Party and often an indispensable part of a winning coalition. On the other hand, such unified support can also be taken for granted by Democratic candidates, who might minimize blacks' concerns in order to avoid antagonizing white voters. The more candidates highlight issues of particular interest to blacks, this argument suggests, the greater the risk of losing the votes of moderate whites and thus losing elections. And Republican candidates, given black voting patterns, might conclude they have relatively little to gain by making a strong pitch for the African-American vote, which would risk alienating other factions who do not favor expanding the scope of government spending, taxation, or redistribution. Thus, according to this argument, black political interests tend to be systematically underrepresented in electoral politics.

As the black vote became increasingly identified as Democratic, there were feedback effects on the party. Support for Democrats in the white South, which had once been unshakable, began to wobble. Republican candidates began winning in the South, and the region became a key part of Republican Party presidential election strategy. This created a dilemma for Democrats. The more they conceded the South to Republicans, the more difficult it would be to win the presidency. Republicans sought to link Democratic candidates to plans to redistribute wealth, bus students long distances, and base hiring on racial and minority quotas. From 1968 through 2004, only two Democrats won the presidency, both from the South and both considered relatively conservative or moderate compared to the party nationwide. They did not disavow civil rights, but they did not prominently campaign on these issues.

Debate continues over how to enhance minority electoral power.

One question facing minority groups is how best to enhance their political power. Would an effective strategy be to spread minority voters out across districts so that they are a sizable and potentially influential block but not necessarily a majority of the district population? Or would minority interests be better served by concentrating minority voters in a small number of districts and virtually ensuring that a minority candidate will be elected who will then be able to negotiate on behalf of minority interests in the legislature? Districts where boundaries are drawn to ensure that a majority of potential voters are minority—meaning a historically disadvantaged racial or ethnic minority group—are known as **majority-minority districts**. Starting in the late 1980s, the U.S. Supreme Court issued decisions in a series of cases that challenged the constitutionality of creating district lines for the express purpose of creating a majority-minority district. The conclusion of these decisions was that race or ethnicity could not constitutionally be the predominant factor in drawing district lines, but could be taken into account as one of several factors.[43]

Whether the creation of majority-minority districts assists minority political influence has become hotly debated. The answer depends in part on the behavior of white voters.[44] One study suggests that spreading minority voters across districts had not been an optimal strategy for minority political influence in the 1970s or 1980s, but had become so by the 1990s. In part, less white bloc voting meant that even in districts where the minority population is 40 to 50 percent rather than a majority, a minority candidate can win about two out of three times.[45] Even if a minority does not win, this argument suggests, their strong share in the electorate may influence their legislator's voting behavior.

Extension of Equal Protection to Other Groups

In a country founded on the ideal of the equality of all people, discrimination strikes a discordant note. The benefits of individualism, property ownership, liberty, and democracy, all central to the American creed, were out of reach to Americans whose civil rights were denied. In the civil rights experience, we see the power of ideas directly contrary to the American creed: that some groups were simply not deserving of full citizenship and equality. As noted in Chapter 2, these ideas were not just blips on the American political culture radar, but significant beliefs for large parts of the population.

It is inevitable that governments classify individuals into groups and use these classifications to make decisions. Federal education assistance programs, for example, classify individuals as students and non-students. They classify students by full-time or part-time status, by the expense of the institution they are attending, by the ability of their family to provide financial support, by whether or not they have a high school diploma or the equivalent, and whether they are independent or dependent on their parents. The government uses all these classifications to make decisions about who can receive a grant or loan and for what amount. Not everyone qualifies and not everyone gets the same amount. In short, the program discriminates between groups, and most people have no problem with that.

Other discrimination is different. Most Americans consider different treatment between individuals based on race, gender, or other factors offensive. How do the federal courts determine which kinds of group classifications that result in differential treatment are acceptable and which are not? The courts divide these cases into three types.

The first type concerns "suspect categories," namely race and ethnicity. Due to the country's struggle with slavery and the origin and history of the Fourteenth Amendment, the courts pay particularly close attention to laws and policies involving race and ethnicity. Selecting applicants for employment or government contracts on the basis of race or ethnicity would be an example. The courts employ "strict scrutiny," meaning government officials would need to prove that there was a *compelling* governmental interest at stake that *required* the distinction between racial or ethnic groups. This is normally very difficult to prove.[46]

A second type of case involves most other classifications, such as age, income, and disability. They are evaluated on what the courts call a "rational basis" standard; that is, does the classification have some rational connection that contributes to the goal of the law or policy?[47] This is an easier test for government officials to meet, and the courts will be more easily convinced that these classifications were necessary than they will for race and ethnicity. For example, the courts allow the federal government to impose higher tax rates on wealthier individuals in order to fund programs and redistribute income across income levels, but it would not allow higher tax rates to be imposed on the basis of race.

The third type of case falls in-between the first two and involves "quasi-suspect categories." Cases involving classification on the basis of sex are the prime example. Government would have to show that classifying by sex had a substantial relationship to an important government interest.[48] Overall, then, the courts demand the strongest justification from government officials for classifying by race and ethnicity and next so by sex.

Many of the political and social accomplishments of the black civil rights movement had benefits for other groups. In addition to race and color, the legislative and administrative actions of the 1960s have been applied to religion, national origin, sex, disability, age, and sexual orientation. The three mechanisms to advance black civil rights—equal-protection clause cases, Congress's use of its commerce clause and spending powers, and the president's authority over the executive branch—were also used to advance the civil rights of other groups that have been victims of discrimination.

Pervasive sex discrimination in law has eroded.

The movement for women's equality had two distinct phases. The early phase culminated in 1920 with the Nineteenth Amendment, which gave women the right to vote. An extensive array of legal restrictions on women remained, however, and these became the focus of women's rights organizations in the second phase, beginning in the 1960s.

Like the civil rights movement, the women's movement used legal and legislative strategies to challenge laws and policies that differentiated between men and women. The women's movement also engaged in "consciousness raising" designed to help women understand their identity and their status in law and society. Sometimes criticized as being geared toward the needs of white upper middle class women, this self-awareness and its call for "women's liberation" likely generated important organizational benefits by contributing to fundraising and support for the efforts of women's rights organizations. These funds would be instrumental in filing court cases and lobbying for legislative changes. One of the key organizations involved in these efforts, the National Organization for Women (NOW), was founded in 1966.

Supreme Court rulings Prior to the 1970s, the Supreme Court had tended to uphold gender-based distinctions in law. It had sustained laws that denied women the right to vote prior to 1920, restricted their working hours to "protect the weaker sex," and prohibited admission to trades and professions. Fundamental rights and responsibilities of citizenship, such as participating on juries, were often denied to women.[49] After 1970, the Court overturned many gender-based state laws. Examples of the kinds of gender distinctions in law that the Court rejected included different treatment of men and women when calculating Social Security benefits, different ages for consuming alcohol, and permitting unwed mothers but not unwed fathers to withhold consent on the adoption of their children.

Most of the Court's discrimination-based decisions since the mid-1980s have been justified on the interpretation of civil rights statutes—what did laws mean and what did they require—rather than on Fourteenth Amendment equal-protection grounds. For example, the Court ruled in 1986 that the Civil Rights Act of 1964 prohibited not only sex discrimination in hiring and firing, but also sexual harassment on the job.[50] Sexual harassment includes unwanted sexual attention, advances, or comments. The harassment can be directed toward a person or can be a part of the culture or environment of a workplace. A hostile environment on the job, whether general or targeted to a particular person, threatens the full participation in American commerce that is at the base of Congress's commerce-clause justification for laws regulating discriminatory actions in the private sector.

While striking down most sex distinctions, the Court has upheld those that furthered important government interests. It has upheld limiting the military draft to men, for example. It has also supported regulations and policies that do not formally distinguish between men and women but in practice will have the effect of doing so. Giving preferences to veterans in state and federal government employment will tend to advantage men disproportionately, but the Court has upheld these as furthering an important government interest. Job screening that requires the ability to lift large weights will tend to favor men, but if this skill is related to the job being performed, the Court has accepted the practice. However, the Court may also examine whether there is any prospect for restructuring the job to eliminate the need for heavy-lifting skill, so that these skill filters are not simply indirect ways to discriminate on the basis of sex.

Actions by Congress and the president Congress and the president have also addressed sex discrimination issues. The 1963 Equal Pay Act required equal pay for equal work. The Civil Rights Act of 1964 prohibited employers, employment agencies, and labor unions from discriminating on the basis of sex. Amendments to the Higher Education Act in 1972, specifically that portion of the act known as Title IX, denied federal funds to universities that discriminated against women in any respect, including admissions, course availability, athletics, and advising.

Women's rights activists have argued that full equality sometimes needs to take account of differences. For example, pregnancy, childrearing, and homemaking responsibilities continue to fall disproportionately on women. Expanded government support for child care, for example, has been advocated on gender equality grounds, so that women can more fully enter the workforce. In the United States, the need to accommodate the special demands placed on women inspired the Family and Medical Leave Act of 1993, which provides women with 12 weeks unpaid leave following childbirth. New fathers can take this time off also, as can individuals needing to care for a sick family member. France, Denmark, Austria, Spain, Germany, and India provide from 12 to 26 weeks of leave with 100% of wages paid. The United Kingdom, Italy, Greece, and Japan offer from 14 to 22 weeks at 60–90 percent of one's wages. And Australia offers unpaid leave, like the United States, but for a one-year period.[51]

Equal Rights Amendment Like the black civil rights movement, the women's rights movement splintered over time. Some political scientists saw the movement as geared toward the interests of well-off white women rather than poor or minority women. Others noted that after many successes, it is difficult for any movement to maintain strong momentum—many of the issues that motivated early supporters had been addressed. A third factor is that after its early, widely-appealing successes, the movement may have suffered by becoming too narrowly focused on upholding the Supreme Court's 1973 decision in *Roe v. Wade*, which struck down anti-abortion laws around the country. The rise of a strong conservative Christian spiritual and political movement by the late 1970s raised the question of whether the women's movement only allowed for a single, narrow identity for women—pro-choice on abortion, career-oriented, in the workforce, seeking jobs traditionally held by men, believing that male–female distinctions were socially perpetuated rather than biological. Although often agreeing with the women's movement on economic and legal equality issues, women holding more conservative views did not necessarily accept the other liberal views propounded by the major women's rights organizations or share the same aspirations.

The difficulties facing the women's movement became apparent in the battle over adding an Equal Rights Amendment (ERA) to the U.S. Constitution. Proposed annually since 1923, the ERA finally passed both houses of Congress in 1972 after heavy lobbying by NOW and the National Women's Political Caucus. The proposed amendment stated, "Equality of rights under the law shall not be denied or abridged by the United States or by any State on account of sex." It was sent to the states for ratification, with 1979 set as the deadline. Twenty-two states ratified the amendment in the first year. By 1978, the amendment was three states short of the 38 needed for ratification. Congress controversially extended the ratification period through 1982. But by 1982, the amendment was still three states short, and five states that had approved the amendment rescinded their approval (see Figure 6-3). The constitutionality of the decisions to revoke a prior approval was unclear; nevertheless, the proposed amendment was never able to obtain enough state approval to add it to the Constitution.

Two key factors explain what had happened. First, the ERA faced concerted opposition by religious and conservative groups, which had used this issue to build very effective political organizations. These groups may have actually benefited

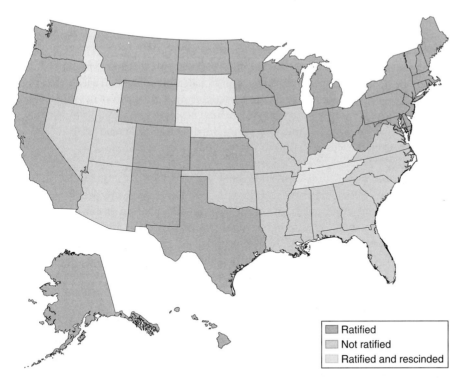

Figure 6-3. Ratification of the Equal Rights Amendment. The Equal Rights Amendment failed to be ratified before the ratification period expired in 1982. Ratification by 38 states was necessary for the amendment to be added to the Constitution, but only 35 ratified the proposed amendment and five of those sought to rescind their ratification. Opposition was strongest in the South but also present elsewhere.

from the quick approval of the ERA in 35 states. Rather than a national battle, they were able to concentrate their resources and lobbying on the remaining states.[52] Second, division among women meant the pro-amendment forces were unable to marshal the same focused intensity as the opponents. Some women thought the amendment did not go far enough. Others thought women would lose some rights in the workplace—for example, accommodations for pregnancy— or would not be able to obtain support from ex-husbands. Others believed that much of what the amendment was intended to achieve had already been accomplished by law, unilateral presidential action, and Supreme Court application of the Fourteenth Amendment's equal-protection guarantee and its interpretation of civil rights laws.

Age and disability discrimination are subject to standards of review different from race and sex.

Not considered suspect classifications requiring strict scrutiny by the Supreme Court, the use of an age or disability classification in law must have some rational connection to the goal of the law. If it does not, the law will be struck down as inconsistent with equal protection. If it does, the law can stand. For example, the Court upheld Missouri's mandatory requirement that public officials retire at age 70.[53] Similarly, certain rights, such as voting, are limited to adults.

Laws passed by Congress and executive orders issued by presidents have also addressed discrimination based on age and disability. The Age Discrimination in Employment Act of 1967 prohibits employment discrimination against individuals between the ages of 40 and 70—the time when discrimination is considered more likely.[54] Two major laws have advanced civil rights for the disabled. The Rehabilitation Act of 1973 prohibited discrimination in federal employment on the basis of physical or mental disability, required the federal government to make reasonable accommodations for disabilities, and mandated affirmative action in hiring. The act also played a significant role in igniting the disability rights movement.[55] A key concern for the movement has been that disability law be presented as a civil rights issue and not a welfare or benefits issue.

Years of lobbying, litigation, and protest led to the Americans with Disabilities Act (ADA) of 1990. This act placed the same requirements on the private sector as the Rehabilitation Act had placed on the government. The law prohibits discrimination in employment, in all programs and services of state and local governments, and in public accommodations. Unlike in racial and gender discrimination, disability antidiscrimination remedies can be avoided if they are too costly or would impose an "undue hardship." For example, a store owner who would face prohibitive costs to redesign a store for wheelchair access might be exempted from the law's demands. Because of this possible exemption, and because "accommodation" and "disability" are subject to different interpretations, many cases have reached the courts in an attempt to sort out what is and is not reasonable with regard to accommodations and what type and severity of disability leaves a person qualified or unqualified for a particular job.

The transformation of law concerning the disabled from a welfare and assistance orientation to a civil rights orientation—integrating the disabled as full participants in the economy and society—has occurred around the world since the passage of the ADA. Australia and Great Britain enacted laws prohibiting employment discrimination and calling on employers to make efforts to accommodate the disabled. Several European countries have required quotas to move disabled people into the workforce. In Germany, employers who do not meet their quotas are fined, and the funds raised from these fines go to employers who meet or exceed their quotas. Generally, quota systems have yielded disappointing results. Some were not well enforced, while in others like Germany's, the fine proved insufficient to motivate employers. The American ADA antidiscrimination model has become more attractive to many advocates for the disabled in countries with quota systems and has been endorsed by the European Union.[56]

Latinos, Asians, and Native Americans have experienced different histories of discrimination.

Severe discrimination faced other racial and ethnic groups throughout U.S. history. Many states and municipalities enacted laws specifically targeting groups for differential treatment. When these laws have been challenged on constitutional grounds, the Supreme Court has generally applied reasoning similar to that in cases involving black civil rights. Segregation, until 1954, was acceptable. Laws that treated groups differently, however, were suspect. For example, in 1886 the Court struck down a San Francisco law that, despite appearing neutral on its face, the Court interpreted as intended to drive Chinese laundries out of business. The Fourteenth Amendment's guarantees of equal protection, the Court declared, "are universal in their application."[57] Similarly, legislation and presidential orders enacted as a result of the black civil rights movement in the 1960s benefited other groups as well.

Each group has had its own particular history and specific issues, as well as its own interest groups to represent its concerns. Ethnic groups such as Latinos—the largest minority group in the country—and Asians are not randomly distributed throughout the country. As a consequence, laws targeting Latinos were more common in the Southwest, while laws targeting Asians were more common on the West Coast.

Because of the ways their histories differ from that of blacks—most notably the absence of slavery—the umbrella terms *Latino* or *Asian* may mean less for individuals in these categories than do national identities such as Mexican, Argentinean, Cuban, Japanese, Korean, or Chinese. "Latino" and "Asian" have not provided the same kind of common identity and widely shared political outlook that has been prevalent among African Americans. That circumstance has made political organization of these groups more difficult, and cross-ethnic group coordination—black, Latino, Asian—has been minimal. On some issues, such as immigration and language accommodation, individuals in these three groups often see more conflict than commonality among their interests.[58]

The experience of Native Americans has its own distinctive features. Prior to the passage of the Indian Citizenship Act in 1924, Native Americans were not considered U.S. citizens. As members of sovereign nations, they had to go through the same citizenship application procedures as individuals from other countries. Attempts to use the Fifteenth Amendment as a basis for the right to vote failed because of this lack of citizenship.[59] With the passage of the act, Native Americans were considered U.S. citizens without any special procedure required. This status entitled Native Americans to the rights and responsibilities of U.S. citizenship, but as with other groups, rights did not instantly materialize. They required political action.

The case of Native Americans differs from the other groups in that they are considered U.S. citizens and also members of sovereign nations that exist within the United States. Native Americans are protected by the antidiscrimination statutes and regulations that cover other groups. They also have tribal rights and responsibilities that differ among the various tribes and are determined by tribal authorities. Tribes have been actively involved in court cases and legislation seeking to preserve and restore their interests in land, mineral, and water resources, and defending traditional customs even if they conflict with state or national law.

Gay and lesbian equality has involved both civil liberties and civil rights.

Rights campaigns for gays and lesbians have concerned both civil liberties and civil rights. Regarding civil liberties, many states had prohibitions against homosexual sexual activity. The Supreme Court upheld these restrictions in 1986, but overturned them as invasions of privacy in the *Lawrence v. Texas* decision of 2003 (see Chapter 5).

At the national level, one of the most prominent issues concerns homosexuals serving in the military. Under the present "don't ask, don't tell" policy, individuals are not, as a matter of privacy, to be asked about their sexual orientation. However, revealing that one is homosexual can lead to dismissal from the military. While this policy allows gays and lesbians to serve in the military, it does not allow them to do so openly. The policy remains highly controversial.

Regarding civil rights, most states, many cities, and the federal government have adopted antidiscrimination hiring policies that include sexual orientation. These cover government employees and companies doing business with the government. Which aspects of federal civil rights law apply to homosexuals has been handled by the Supreme Court on an issue by issue basis. For example, the Supreme Court ruled in 1998 that same-sex sexual harassment is forbidden by the 1964 Civil Rights Act.[60] On the other hand, the Court in 2000 upheld the Boy Scouts of America's right to prohibit homosexuals from serving as troop leaders because it conveyed a message contrary to the organization's beliefs.[61]

CaseStudy: Marriage as a Civil Rights Issue

Among the issues that gay and lesbian civil rights groups currently see as fundamental to equality, the most publicly prominent has been same-sex marriage. The issue is characteristic of many civil rights battles: the struggle between tradition and change; the appeals to American political culture and its embrace of equality; strategic calculations about whether to seek change via legislatures or courts; and political activity at both the state and national levels.

Marriage confers favorable treatment in a range of areas—inheritance, taxation, health care, child custody, immigration, property rights, hospital visitation, and Social Security survivor benefits. Over 1,000 federal laws include reference to marital status. Activists for gay and lesbian equal rights have argued that prohibition of same-sex marriage is a civil rights violation. Because they are prohibited from marrying their preferred partners and are thus shut out of the benefits and status that accrue to marriage, homosexuals as a group, they argue, are prevented

from fully participating as equals to heterosexual married couples in society.

Marriage has typically been a legal status determined by state law. The issue of same-sex marriage first entered national political conversation in the mid-1990s when it appeared the state of Hawaii might—though ultimately it did not—legalize this type of marriage. The 1996 Defense of Marriage Act signed by President Clinton was the federal response. This act stipulates that, for the purpose of federal programs and benefits, marriage consists of "the legal union between one man and one woman as husband and wife." As the Constitution allows, the law also creates an exemption to the usual requirement that states honor the official acts of other states, by specifying that they need not honor same-sex marriages that are legal in another state.

Because marriage has traditionally been a state-level issue, and because the chances for success have been greater in the states than at the federal level, gay and lesbian civil rights organizations have focused most of their attention on this issue at state government. Court cases have asserted that the guarantee of equality under state constitutions means that prohibitions on same-sex marriages are unconstitutional. So far, these cases have failed, except in Massachusetts. In 2004, the Massachusetts Supreme Judicial Court declared that prohibiting same-sex marriage violated the Massachusetts Constitution's guarantee of equal protection under the law. To date, the Massachusetts legislature has resisted efforts to put a constitutional amendment before voters that would outlaw same-sex marriages in that state. There have been other victories for the pro-same-sex-marriage forces. Vermont, Connecticut, California, New Hampshire, New Jersey, and Hawaii all have a form of "civil union" or "domestic partnership," either as a result of legislation or court decisions. Unions or partnerships are a legal status that can provide some or nearly all of the benefits of marriage. Unlike marriage, however, civil unions and domestic partnerships have no meaning outside the state in which they were created; other states do not acknowledge them. In September 2005, California Governor Arnold Schwarzenegger vetoed a bill passed by the state legislature—the first such bill passed by a state legislature—that legalized same-sex marriage, but at the same time signed four bills that strengthened California's domestic partnership law.

Although marriage is usually a state issue, the Supreme Court has upheld the federal government's authority to pass laws banning certain state-approved marriage arrangements, such as polygamy. It has also struck down some state marriage restrictions. In *Loving v. Virginia* (1967), the Court declared Virginia's ban on interracial marriage to be a violation of the U.S. Constitution's promise of equal protection of the laws. In the Court's view, the law had no purpose outside of "invidious racial discrimination." Gay and lesbian civil rights activists point to the ban on same-sex marriage as presenting precisely the same discriminatory issues as *Loving*. Opponents of same-sex marriage reject this parallel, saying the two situations are worlds apart—banning interracial marriage was purely discrimination, while banning same-sex marriage is about the basic definition of a social institution. Whether based on religious or other grounds, they see marriage as the fundamental social unit in society, a unit that has for centuries across societies joined men and women together for reproduction and the nurturing of children. They charge that same-sex marriage is not consistent with those concepts.

Accordingly, these critics led a countermovement designed to stop the legal recognition of same-sex mar-

riages. Part of the strategy has been passage of laws and constitutional amendments in the states to prohibit same-sex marriage. These efforts have been extremely successful. Another part of the strategy has been the proposal of an amendment to the U.S. Constitution to prohibit same-sex marriage. This effort has not been successful. The proposed Marriage Protection Amendment states that "Marriage in the United States shall consist only of the union of a man and a woman. Neither this Constitution, nor the constitution of any State, shall be construed to require that marriage or the legal incidents thereof be conferred upon any union other than the union of a man and a woman." Thus, the amendment states that neither at the federal nor state level should "equal protection" be interpreted to require the recognition of same-sex marriage.

Gay and lesbian rights advocates argue against the proposed amendment on substantive grounds and on federalism grounds. Substantively, they claim same-sex marriage is a matter of civil rights and equality. Regarding federalism, they note that nearly every state by 2005 had either a law or constitutional amendment explicitly prohibiting same-sex marriage. Therefore, they suggest, there is little need for a federal constitutional amendment. The main task for the gay and lesbian rights movement at the national level is avoiding an amendment to the U.S. Constitution. Like the supporters of such an amendment, they realize that once added, an amendment would be very difficult to dislodge.

Politically, the issue is delicate for both sides. Those opposed to same-sex marriage seem to have public opinion on their side, but public opinion is not necessarily supportive of a constitutional amendment or of prohibiting civil unions. The majority of the public also recoils from appeals that appear to be hostile to homosexuals.[62] Meanwhile, those who see same-sex marriage as a civil rights issue recognize that they are working in an environment in which the public overall does not support same-sex marriage and votes against it when given the chance. That makes it hard to achieve gains on this issue through legislative means.

ThinkingCritically

1. To what degree should legislators or judges consider public opinion when they are deciding what to do about same-sex marriage?

2. Which factors should determine whether a member of Congress votes for or against a proposed constitutional amendment prohibiting same-sex marriage?

Who bears the burden of proof in discrimination cases is controversial.

Across all these various population groups, one of the issues considered by the Supreme Court and Congress is whether each individual who believes he or she has been discriminated against has to prove discrimination. In a 1989 decision, the Supreme Court declared that the burden of proof was on the person alleging discrimination to show how an employment practice was, on its own, directly discriminatory toward that particular person.[63] If each individual must prove intentional discrimination, rather than rely on statistical patterns that show disparity between groups, for example in pay, these cases would be much more difficult to win.

Congress responded to the Supreme Court in the Civil Rights Act of 1991. The act returned the burden of proof to the employer—the employer would have to defend a questionable pattern in employment and explain why it was not problematic. In 1993, a Court decision divided the burden of proof, concluding that each individual need not prove the employer set out to discriminate against him or her, but would still need to demonstrate that any discriminatory impact between groups was intentional and unreasonable.[64]

SUMMARY

▶ Amendments to the Constitution during and following the Civil War, as well as legislation enacted during the period known as Reconstruction, began the process of national recognition of civil rights for blacks. The Fourteenth Amendment's guarantee of equal protection of the laws was interpreted by the Supreme Court to limit government discrimination, not private discrimination. And the Supreme Court concluded that mandating separate facilities for blacks and whites did not violate equal protection as long as the facilities were substantially equal.

▶ In the twentieth century, black civil rights organizations began to challenge discriminatory laws in court, with some success. Presidents also bypassed Congress to promote civil rights through executive orders and other unilateral actions. The rejection of the separate-but-equal doctrine by the Supreme Court in *Brown v. Board of Education* prompted a broader movement to press for civil rights. Major legislation challenging discrimination in the private sector and government, significant executive orders introducing affirmative action policies, and a constitutional amendment prohibiting use of the poll tax produced a civil rights revolution in the United States. Congress used its interstate commerce powers and spending powers to bypass Supreme Court concerns that the Fourteenth Amendment did not apply to the private sector.

▶ These civil rights successes depended on several factors. These included the rise of a strategically effective civil rights movement, appeals to key beliefs in the American creed, and changes in the Democratic Party that focused the party more on its growing northern, urban, and minority constituency. The push for civil rights encountered difficulty when the movement splintered, policies and ideas became more controversial, and white backlash worried Democratic politicians about their chances to win the presidency.

▶ The same laws, court decisions, and presidential actions that aided black civil rights helped other groups also. The doctrine of equal protection extends to these groups, although the Supreme Court does not treat every classification the same. Race and ethnic classifications in laws and regulations are reviewed the most strictly, followed by gender classifications. Although covered by the broad civil rights accomplishments of the black civil rights movement, groups based on ethnicity, religion, age, and sexual orientation, among other categories, have each faced distinctive issues and formed their own organizations to challenge discriminatory laws and practices.

KEY TERMS

affirmative action, p. 000
Brown v. Board of Education, p. 000
civil disobedience, p. 000
civil rights, p. 000
de facto segregation, p. 000
de jure segregation, p. 000
Dred Scott v. Sandford, p. 000
equal protection clause, p. 000

Jim Crow, p. 000
majority-minority districts, p. 000
Plessy v. Ferguson, p. 000
poll tax, p. 000
Regents of the University of California v. Bakke, p. 000
separate but equal, p. 000
state action, p. 000
white primary, p. 000

SUGGESTED READINGS

Ward Connerly. 2002. *Creating Equal: My Fight Against Race Preferences*. New York: Encounter Books. A memoir by the chief architect of the campaign to outlaw racial preference in California state government and universities.

Paul Frymer. 1999. *Uneasy Alliances: Race and Party Competition in America*. Princeton: Princeton University Press. Argues that the American party system was built on racial considerations and inevitably marginalizes the interests of black Americans.

Ira Katznelson. 2005. *When Affirmative Action Was White: An Untold History of Racial Inequality in Twentieth Century America*. New York: W. W. Norton. An accessible account of mid-twentieth century social programs and how they were structured to advantage whites.

Matthew Frye Jacobsen. 1999. *Whiteness of a Different Color: European Immigrants and the Alchemy of Race*.

Cambridge: Harvard University Press. An exploration of immigration and the changing meaning of who is considered "white" across American history.

Jane J. Mansbridge. 1986. *Why We Lost the ERA.* Chicago: University of Chicago Press. Highlights the organizational, ideological, and strategic reasons the Equal Rights Amendment was not ratified.

Abagail M. Thernstrom. 1987. *Whose Votes Count? Affirmative Action and Minority Voting Rights.* Cambridge: Harvard University Press. Highlights the successful struggle for voting rights that culminated in the Voting Rights Act of 1965, but argues that the implementation of the law since then has undermined the law's original purpose.

Richard M. Valelly. 2004. *The Two Reconstructions: The Struggle for Black Enfranchisement.* Chicago: University of Chicago Press. Examines movements for black enfranchisement, offering an explanation of why these efforts were successful in the twentieth century but failed in the nineteenth century.

C. Vann Woodward. 1957. *The Strange Career of Jim Crow.* New York: Oxford University Press. A classic account of the system of Jim Crow laws that prevailed throughout the southern states until the 1960s.

Dred Scott v. Sandford
Supreme Court decision in 1857 that ruled that neither slaves nor the descendants of slaves could be United States citizens.

equal protection clause clause in the Fourteenth Amendment stating that states were not to deny any person equal treatment under the law.

state action Supreme Court interpretation of the equal protection clause that said the clause prohibited unfair discriminatory actions by government, not by private individuals.

Jim Crow system of laws that separated the races in schools, public accommodations, and other aspects of daily life.

Plessy v. Ferguson Supreme Court decision in 1896 that upheld the constitutionality of laws and government policies that required segregated facilities for blacks and whites.

separate but equal Supreme Court doctrine that laws or policies requiring segregated facilities for the races are constitutionally acceptable as long as the facilities were of equal quality.

Brown v. Board of Education
Supreme Court decision in 1954 that determined that in public education mandatory separation of children by race resulted in inherently unequal education. The decision overturned the separate but equal doctrine.

de jure segregation racial segregation that occurs because it is written into law, policy, or government procedures.

de facto segregation racial segregation that results not because of explicit law, policy, or procedures, but because residential housing patterns result in different races living disproportionately in different areas.

poll tax fee assessed on each person who wished to vote; prohibited by the Twenty-fourth Amendment in 1964.

affirmative action efforts to reach and attract applicants for jobs, college admissions, and business contracts from traditionally underrepresented groups, ranging from extensive publicity and outreach to quota plans.

Regents of the University of California v. Bakke Supreme Court decision in 1978 that ruled that a rigid quota plan for admissions violated the Constitution's equal protection guarantee, but that race could be considered a "plus factor" in college admissions to increase student body diversity.

civil disobedience strategy of breaking law nonviolently in order to protest a law one considers unjust and draw attention to one's cause.

white primary primary elections in southern states in which only white voters were allowed to participate.

majority-minority districts legislative districts in which district boundaries are drawn in a manner to ensure that a majority of the district residents are members of minority groups, intended to increase the probability of minorities being elected.

civil rights guarantees of equal opportunities, privileges, and treatment under the law that allow individuals to participate fully and equally in American society.

7 Public Opinion

One day in the fall of 1906, British scientist Francis Galton left his home in the town of Plymouth and headed for a country fair. As he walked through the exhibition that day, Galton came across a weight-judging competition. A fat ox was on display, and members of a gathering crowd were lining up to place wagers on the weight of the ox.

Eight hundred people tried their luck. They were a diverse lot. Many of them were butchers and farmers, who were presumably expert at judging the weight of livestock, but there were also quite a few people who had no special knowledge of cattle. "Many non-experts competed," Galton later wrote in the scientific journal *Nature*, "like those clerks and others who have no expert knowledge of horses, but who bet on races, guided by newspapers, friends, and their own fancies."

When the contest was over and the prizes had been awarded, Galton borrowed the tickets from the organizers and ran a series of statistical tests. He undoubtedly thought that the average guess would be way off the mark. After all, mix a few very informed people who may be expert at guessing weights of livestock with a slew of less well informed folks, and it seems likely the result would be a wrong answer. But Galton was wrong about getting a wrong answer. The crowd as an average had guessed that the ox, after it had been slaughtered and dressed, would weigh 1,197 pounds. After it had been slaughtered and dressed, the ox weighed 1,198 pounds. In other words, the crowd's judgment was essentially perfect.[1]

What Galton discovered that day was something of a paradox: a group of people, many of whom have little interest or expertise in a particular subject matter, can still, collectively, make appropriate judgments about it.

This chapter will consider this paradox as applied to American politics. Although the great mass of Americans have no great interest or expertise in politics or policy, somehow they tend to make appropriate, reasonable, and logical judgments about political life. These judgments fall under the heading of "public opinion," one of the most commonly used phrases in any discussion of politics and policy. During the 2004 presidential campaign, for example, one could read or hear all of the following:

> [P]ublic opinion as expressed in polls is carefully scrutinized by administrations, whether openly as with Bill Clinton, or while denying the fact as with George Bush. Thus, if these polls do in fact skew hard to the right, they make very bad tools for designing actual policy—at least if we still care to pretend that it matters at all what the majority of Americans want.
>
> Kevin Drum, writing in *The Washington Monthly*[2]

> The advertising they produce is meant to communicate an emotion or feeling, and what we do is move public opinion.
>
> Steve McMahon, strategist for Democratic presidential candidate Howard Dean, comparing business advertising to political advertising[3]

Political leaders focus on public opinion and strategists focus on influencing the content and direction of what people think and know. The fact that public opinion has an important role in American politics comes from our political culture and the value it places on democracy, representation, and civil liberties. Compared to other political systems (even other Democratic ones), Americans seem to have a greater opportunity for their opinions to matter.

The Nature of Public Opinion

Public opinion is one of the most commonly used phrases in the discussion of politics and policy. **Public opinion** can be measured, obeyed, manipulated, ignored, and even misunderstood. But, what, in fact, is public opinion? A simple and useful definition is "the preferences of the adult population on matters of relevance to government."[4] Another definition provides a broader perspective: "public opinion is the collective political beliefs and attitudes of the public, or groups within the public, about issues, candidates, officials, parties, and groups." This second definition makes clear that although public opinion typically refers to the collective opinion of the public, it can also refer to opinions of groups within the public. Both types of public opinion are useful to examine.

Public opinion has four basic traits: salience, stability, direction, and intensity. **Salience** indicates an issue's importance to a person, or to the public in general. The public can feel strongly about an issue but yet not rate that issue as particularly salient in their lives or political calculations. Similarly, the public might mildly favor or mildly oppose an issue, but that issue might be quite salient to many people.

For example, in a December 2004 survey, 38 percent of Americans took the most extreme positions on abortion—it should be legal in all circumstances or illegal in all circumstances. Fifty-nine percent had more moderate opinions—it should be legal in most circumstances or illegal in most circumstances. Asked how

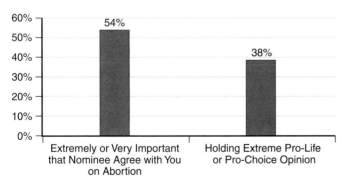

Figure 7-1. More People Likely to Say Abortion Matters in Supreme Court Choice Than Have Intense Pro-Life or Pro-Choice Views. There's a disconnect on public opinion and abortion. Although a majority of Americans say that the abortion positions of a Supreme Court nominee are very important to them, less than four in ten Americans hold intense views on the issue.

important it was that the next nominee to the Supreme Court agree with their view on abortion, 54 percent said it was extremely or very important to them. Comparing this 54 percent to the 38 percent in the extreme positions indicates that at least some of the people for whom this issue has high salience have relatively moderate views on abortion.[5]

When politicians decide whether to attempt to change public opinion or whether to follow the message the public appears to be sending, they need to consider the **stability** of public opinion. Is public opinion on an issue likely to change and, if so, is change likely to be gradual or rapid? Once changed, is opinion likely to solidify around that new position, or is this an issue on which one might expect changes to be frequent? These are crucial questions for politicians. Are attitudes, for example, about gay marriage likely to change significantly in the short term? And, if they do, is that change likely to endure?

Along with salience and stability, direction and intensity round out the four basic traits of public opinion. The **direction** of the public's opinion about something refers to whether the public favors or opposes it. Any indication of agreement or disagreement, approval or disapproval, favor or opposition, is an example of direction.

The **intensity** of the public's opinion measures the strength of the direction. For example, some people strongly favor or oppose abortion, while others may not harbor such strong feelings on the issue. Some will favor abortion in most cases, but not strongly; some will oppose abortion in most cases, but not strongly.

For politicians, it is crucial to understand the nature of public opinion. A politician has to ask, "do I follow public opinion now, only to find that it soon will shift in another direction?" "Do I attempt to move public opinion in a new direction, or make it more intense or salient, when I can see that opinion on this issue tends to have great stability and is very difficult to alter?" Answering these questions about stability, and trying to gauge the direction, intensity, and salience of public opinion can be very challenging for public officials.

Politicians do not always base their actions on public opinion and representative democracy does not demand that officeholders always follow public opinion. Still, in a well functioning representative democracy, policymaking should generally follow the contours of public opinion on most issues. Furthermore, most politicians like to be on the "80 side of 80-20 issues." In other words, officeholders who are too often on the wrong side of public opinion risk great political cost and face electoral danger. We have much more to say about this in our chapter on Congress.

Can Surveys Accurately Gauge the Opinions of Almost 300 Million Americans?

The Question

Discussions of American public opinion are a routine part of American political life. During election season, scores of polls report who is ahead and behind virtually every day. At other times, news reports frequently mention the public's perception of the president's job performance and whether the country is heading in the right direction. If the president or a member of Congress makes a significant policy proposal, major media outlets survey Americans for their reactions. Politicians seldom rely on media polls; they conduct their own surveys. Presidents have extensive polling operations. Typically they take the pulse of the nation before, during, and after a campaign, an important speech, or the introduction of a major policy initiative. Political scientists, too, use surveys to gauge the collective consciousness of the American people.

Not all surveys are created equal, however. A well-designed survey can provide accurate information on public opinion, but a poorly done one can lead to false conclusions and be essentially useless. The question is: Can surveys accurately gauge the opinions of almost 300 million Americans? How do we know?

Why It Matters

Agreement between public opinion and government action is one measure of a democratic government. However, it is not always a good one. Sometimes the opinion "snapshot" in a survey obscures important momentum—at the time of the survey, government may be in the process of moving toward the public's position, or vice versa. And sometimes what the public wants may be unconstitutional or otherwise ill-advised. However, a critical starting point is understanding how surveys work.

Investigating the Answer

Imagine you are making a pot of soup for some friends. You add water, chicken, vegetables, and spices, and let the soup simmer for a couple of hours. Before serving it, you want to make sure it tastes good, so you take a small spoonful. If you took the spoonful from the top, you might think the soup needed more seasoning. If you took a spoonful from the bottom, you might think the soup needed more water. A good cook mixes the soup before taking a sample spoonful to make sure all parts are represented.

The same logic applies to survey **sampling**, the process of choosing a small group of people to interview for a survey. A survey sample should represent all elements of the population—men, women, young, old, Democrats, Republicans, and other groups—in rough proportion to their population percentages. This is accomplished by using a **random sample**, a sample of the population in which every member of the population has an equal chance of ending up in the sample.

Particularly with large populations, the sampling procedures for a random sample can become very complex. But consider this simple example. We begin with a population of 100 people, half men, half women. We want to take a random sample of 20. To do this, we give each man and woman a slip of paper with a number, 1 through 100. Each number is used only once. Then we have a computer generate 20 random numbers between 1 and 100. As the computer generates each number, the person holding the number is asked to step forward. Once the computer has provided 20 numbers, we have our random sample.

This sample should end up with roughly half men and half women, and in that respect be representative of the total population of 100, because every man and woman in our population had an equal probability, or chance, of being sampled. We can then have some confidence that if we pose questions to members of the sample, their answers will be very similar to the ones we would get if we posed them to the entire population.

Even in perfectly drawn samples, unavoidable **sampling error** occurs because no sample is an exact match for the population. Sampling error is reported in most surveys as the **margin of error**. To understand what this means, suppose that 55 percent of respondents in a survey approved of the president's job performance and the survey claims a margin of error of plus or minus 5 percentage points. This means that if we had talked to the entire population, we would have found that somewhere between 50 percent and 60 percent approved of the president's performance—55 percent plus or minus 5 percentage points. So, the result from interviewing a random sample is close to what we would get if we spoke with the entire population.

One influence on sampling error is the size of the sample. The larger the sample, the smaller the sampling error. If you flipped a coin several times, you should get a roughly equal proportion of heads and tails, but you could get all heads or all tails. The more times you flip the coin, the more likely the proportion of heads to tails will be nearly equal. The same applies to survey samples. If researchers picked just 1 person at random, or 10, or even 100, to represent the entire U.S. population, the sampling error would be enormous. But if they picked 1,000 people at random, the sampling error would be 3 or 4 percentage points, a margin most researchers are comfortable with. With 1,000 people in the sample, there would likely be a fair mix of men, women, young, old, Democrats, Republicans, whites, non-whites, and so on. In other words, 1,000 people are a large enough group to be broadly representative of the entire U.S. population.

Sampling error also can result from the diversity of the population studied. To take an extreme example, suppose you knew everyone in a state had the same opinion on every issue. If you wanted to measure public opinion on an issue in that state, you would need to ask only one person. Now suppose everyone had a slightly different opinion on every issue. If you were to interview just one person, your sampling error would be unacceptably large; one person's opinion could not possibly capture the diversity of thinking within the population. So, the greater the diversity of opinion, the more people a researcher needs to survey to be confident of results.

Surveys can contain other sorts of errors. For example, questions can be poorly written or structured to encourage a particular response. Consider the following questions:

> Given the recent series of murders in our state, some people say the state should reinstate the death penalty. Do you agree or disagree?

> Given the recent cases of police misconduct and the freeing of inmates who had been wrongly convicted, do you agree or disagree that the state should reinstate the death penalty?

The first question is structured to elicit pro–death penalty responses, while the second question is structured to elicit anti–death penalty responses. Even if a question is asked in a straightforward manner—"Do you support or oppose the death penalty for convicted murderers?"—*where* that question appears in a survey also matters. If it followed a long series of questions on crime, a pro–death penalty result would be more likely. If, on the other hand, it followed a series of questions on police misconduct, one might expect more anti–death penalty responses.

The demographic characteristics of interviewers can also introduce error. Evidence shows that men reply differently to male interviewers than to females on issues such as abortion and birth control, and answers to questions about race are influenced by the race of the interviewer.

Another source of error is **non-response bias**. Even though a researcher may have drawn a reliable sample, not everyone in that sample may agree to participate in the survey. If those who participate have attitudes different from those who decline, the results will be biased. In a survey on Social Security, for example, young workers would be expected to have opinions different from older workers and retired individuals. If the refusal rate for the younger group was much higher than for the older group, the survey would contain disproportionate input from older individuals and inadequate input from younger.

The Bottom Line

Surveys can be an incredibly useful tool for journalists, political scientists, and politicians. However, understanding good survey methods and how particular surveys are conducted are highly useful skills for citizens as well. Those skills will serve you well in other courses as well as enabling you to be a good consumer of polls.

Political Socialization

What is the source of public opinion? How do individuals acquire their political values and attitudes in the first place? The process takes place through what political scientists call **political socialization**. Political socialization is a learning process, one in which individuals absorb information about the political world and add it, selectively, to their stock of knowledge and understanding of politics and government.

This learning tends to be governed by two important principles: primacy and persistence. **Primacy** means that what is learned first is learned best, that is, it is lodged most firmly in one's mind. **Persistence** means that political lessons, values, and attitudes learned early in life tend to structure political learning later on in life. In keeping with these two principles, what children learn about politics at a young age becomes an important determinant of the values, attitudes, and beliefs they will hold in later life.

The most common expression of values, attitudes, and beliefs is the identification of an individual's ideology—and the two most commonly used ideological categories are "liberal" and "conservative." Ideology can be described as a consistent set of ideas about a given set of issues. While there are no hard-and-fast definitions for what makes an individual "liberal" or "conservative," certain beliefs are generally associated with one ideology or the other. A liberal would generally favor a government that is active in promoting social equality and economic welfare. A conservative would generally favor a smaller government that interferes minimally in the economic sphere but actively promotes social morality. Further, liberals are often said to fall to the "left" of the political spectrum, while the "right" is occupied by political conservatives. Of course, there may be many people who do not fall squarely in either of the two camps. People who favor a smaller government that interferes minimally in the economy and does not interfere in social morality are often call "libertarians." Those who support an active government role in both the economy and social morality are sometimes dubbed "populists."

Political sophistication grows as children grow up.

Political socialization plays a crucial role in determining which ideology an individual will support. Children begin learning about politics and government surprisingly early. In their preschool years, the first representative of government that they become familiar with is often the police officer. Preschoolers generally consider the police officer a helpful, benevolent authority figure.[6] Most preschool-aged children are unfamiliar with the president, but this changes in the early grade-school years.[7] As with the police officer, grade schoolers typically see the president in a positive light, believing him to be an honest, trustworthy, virtuous figure.

In the later grade-school years, children's political thinking becomes substantially more sophisticated. In the first place, the child's awareness of political figures begins to expand. To the short list of police officer and president, many children add figures such as mayor, governor, fireman, and soldier.[8] At the same time, the child begins to think of government not just in terms of political figures, but in terms of institutions and activities as well. These may include Congress and the political parties, for example, and activities such as voting.[9]

The child also begins to distinguish more clearly among different individuals and institutions. During the later grade-school years, children come to understand the differences in the roles played by, for example, the president, the Supreme Court, and members of Congress.[10] They also begin to view some political figures more favorably than others. For example, grade schoolers tend to find the president more likeable than the police officer, and both of these more likeable than the senator.[11] Overall, positive feelings toward various authority figures begin to decline during the late childhood period, however. Though children still maintain generally favorable assessments of political figures and institutions, during the grade-school years they transition toward a more realistic, less heroic view of specific political figures.[12] During these years children also begin to gain a basic understanding of the concept of "policy," of conflict over specific issues, and of the idea of competition between the political parties.[13]

Beyond basic political knowledge, grade schoolers also develop a concept of the elements of good citizenship. Their earliest thoughts on the subject consist primarily of being a "good person." In later years, children expand the concept of good citizenship to include showing an interest in governmental affairs, and participating in politics by voting.[14] As for *how* one should vote, children tend to think that good citizens should support those who will perform well in office, regardless of their partisanship.[15] Even so, particularly in the later grade-school years, most children are able to express a preference for one political party or the other, though they often have a hard time understanding the differences between the two parties.[16]

Further political maturity comes with adolescence. High-school-aged students begin to understand major policy issues and take sides on them. They also gain an understanding of the place of interest groups in the political process, and of which groups are involved with which issues.[17] In the high-school years, too, children make significant progress in understanding differences between the two major political parties.[18]

The adolescent's concept of good citizenship does not change measurably during high school. It remains centered on the ideas of attention to public affairs, participation in the political process, and obedience to the laws.[19] One thing that does change, however, is the adolescent's sense of trust in the political system. Just as young children's views evolve from highly trusting to more guarded and realistic, in the high-school years, idealistic views begin to give way to some distrust and cynicism. Even so, high-school seniors tend to be less cynical about politics and government than their parents.[20]

What are the sources of these attitudes that children have toward the political world? Political scientists tend to think in terms of *agents* of socialization, that is, individuals or institutions that help confer political knowledge, and *events* that help socialize people to politics.

Family The single most important socialization agent is the family, particularly parents. Children spend a tremendous amount of time with their parents, and the bonds between parent and child are usually very close. Furthermore, parents are likely to reveal their own political beliefs in front of their children more frequently and openly than other socializing agents—teachers and peers, for example.[21]

The political attitudes of parents and their children are not always in agreement, however. A variety of factors explain the disparity. Chief among these is the communication between parents and children about politics—the quantity, clarity, and importance of that communication. If parents spend little time talking about politics in front of children, watching (and reacting to) political programming on television, or trying to teach children political values, the mechanisms of political socialization do not work as well. Therefore, if public affairs do not seem especially significant to parents, then children will also be likely to view them this way. Further, if a child does not receive a clear, consistent message about politics from his or her parents, either because the parents' views seem to be in frequent flux or because the parents in a two-parent home do not share the same beliefs, it is inevitable that the children will not fully adopt either parent's political views. Lastly, children have their own minds, and can sort through information about the political world and arrive at conclusions different from those of their parents. This is particularly true when they are exposed to events or influences that are unique to their generation. For example, young people of college or draft age were more influenced by the Vietnam War than their parents and grandparents were. In addition, children—especially teenagers—sometimes take pride in small acts of rebellion against their mother and/or their father. These may include adopting divergent positions on the hot political topics of the day.

The most reliable area of transmission from parent to child is identification with a political party, that is, whether one considers oneself a Democrat, Republican, independent, or something else.[22] One reason that partisanship tends to be "inherited" more easily than specific issue positions is that a parent's partisanship is much easier for a child to grasp than a parent's position on, say, Social Security reform. (Consider: "My mom's a Republican," versus, "My mom thinks that if the government stopped indexing retiree earnings to account for increases in average wages, the financial problems with Social Security would be much more manageable.") Finally, partisanship is often deeply held and highly salient to adults. Such core beliefs tend to be transmitted most reliably.[23]

Religious institutions and traditions Family religious traditions may also influence a child's political learning. Religious teachings are, of course, dedicated to the spiritual realm rather than the political. But different religions and denominations also teach different values with respect to punishment and mercy, social justice, the importance of law and authority, equality, and so on. These values, adopted by the child in a religious context, can also play an important role in thinking about politics.

Furthermore, adherents of different religious traditions have historic affiliations with different parties and socioeconomic groups.[24] Jews, for example, tend to be Democrats, while evangelical Christians are more likely to be Republicans. In cases such as these, parents who pass their religion on to their children also may pass along part of their politics. Of course, and as we will discuss in a subsequent chapter on voting (Chapter 9), such loyalties are not set in stone. One excellent historical example of change is the movement of white evangelical Christians in the South from the Democratic Party to the Republican Party.

Peer groups The child's peer group (the friends that a child most closely associates with) will likely have a significant impact on the development of political views. This influence is particularly strong during adolescence, when children begin the transition to adulthood, and spend more time with their friends, away from their parents. The salience of politics to adolescents is generally low, and is largely unrelated to a child's status within peer groups.[25] Accordingly, therefore, political communication among adolescents is, in general, expected to be relatively limited, and the resulting peer-to-peer socialization similarly limited.[26]

Educational system Another potentially important socialization agent is the educational system. Public schools actively seek to inculcate students with a respect for the law, authority, and democratic values; an appreciation of the American political system; a sense of the meaning and import of active democratic citizenship; and the political knowledge necessary for active, effective political participation. They also teach some of the rituals and symbolism of politics—flying the flag, reciting the Pledge of Allegiance, voting in student elections, writing to elected officials, and so on. Because schools are often homogenous, with children from similar backgrounds attending the same school, it is difficult to separate the impact of the education system from other socialization agents. Still, schools seem a very likely contributor to children's stance toward the American political system and the idea of good citizenship.[27] On the other hand, contrary to the claims of some partisans that teachers indoctrinate students with their own views, there is little evidence that school has a significant impact on partisan or issue attitudes.

The media Political socialization depends on politically relevant information, often provided by the media. What the media choose to cover, how they choose to do so, and the accessibility of their coverage are all important political socialization questions. We will discuss the media and its effects in Chapter 10.

Considering this brief overview of political socialization, think again about the primacy and persistence principles. Although the period from preschool through young adulthood brings dramatic change in political knowledge and sophistication, children are socialized to have generally positive predispositions toward the political system. Later in life, these positive orientations will erode somewhat, but most individuals will enter adulthood with a reservoir of support for American democratic government, and, as discussed in Chapter 2, the "American Creed." This contributes to the relatively smooth functioning and stability of the U.S. political system.

These generally positive sentiments are by no means universal, however. There are certain sub-groups of children who do not view political authority as favorably as the general population—African Americans; Latinos; and the low-income, white children of Appalachia, for example.[28]

Events that socialize can have generational, period, or life-cycle effects.

Events as well as agents contribute to political socialization. Whereas socialization by agents typically revolves around the socialization of children and young adults, events can influence the political learning of older individuals as well.

Generational effects One kind of effect that political events can exert on public opinion is a **generational effect**. When a generational effect occurs, younger members of the body politic are influenced by events in a way that makes their attitudes and beliefs different from those of older generations. Consider the tumultuous political period of the 1960s and early 1970s, for example. For many young people coming of age in these years, the defining political events were the Vietnam War and the protest movement surrounding it. Not surprisingly, in general, those who lived through this era as young men and women, and particularly those who participated in protest politics, ended up with a distinctive—and more liberal—set of political beliefs.

One research study found that college-educated war protesters in the 1960s did, in fact, take on a distinctive political character.[29] Because the researchers had information about the people before they went to college and knew that protesters and non-protesters had similar backgrounds, they were able to conclude that participation in protests inspired a particular set of political attitudes, even though everyone in this generation lived through the same tumultuous time.

For example, in 1965, the war protesters were quite similar to their college-educated, non-protesting peers on a number of demographic and attitudinal measures. But by 1973, on the down slope of the war protest movement, the protesters differed sharply from non-protestors in a number of ways:

- protesters were much stronger Democratic partisans than non-protesters;
- protesters showed much higher support for civil liberties than non-protesters;
- protesters showed much less support for conservative groups, and much more support for women, the poor, and minorities than did non-protesters; and
- protesters espoused significantly more liberal issue positions than the non-protesters.

A follow-up study in 1982 concluded that differences between the two groups were still present. Thus, those who received their "political baptism" via the Vietnam War protests maintained the distinctive set of political beliefs learned during that period. Again, because these researchers had information on the attitudes and behavior of these students before they protested, we know that "protesting" was a decisive factor and we can be confident that there was a causal relationship.

Period effects Political events affect not only younger generations. Sometimes, events exert a noticeable impact across political generations and affect the political socialization of citizens young and old. This is known as a **period effect**. Consider, for example, responses to the following survey question:

> There is much discussion as to the amount of money the government in Washington should spend for national defense and military purposes. How do you feel about this? Do you think we are spending too little, too much, or about the right amount?

Figure 7-2 presents the public's answers to this question during the period from 1971 through 1981.[30] Consider only the "too little" responses given in Figure 7-2. Note that in the early 1970s, only a small percentage of Americans thought that the country was spending too little on national defense. But by the mid-

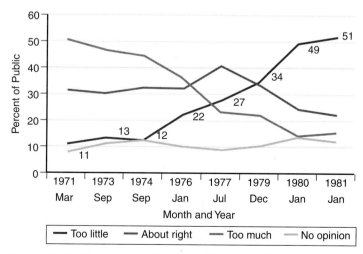

Figure 7-2. Support for Defense Spending Shows a Strong Surge, 1971–1981. After reaching a low point at the end of the Vietnam War, support for defense spending surged through the late 1970s and early 1980s with the election of Ronald Reagan.

1970s, the number of Americans who held that belief doubled once, and then, surprisingly, doubled again. What caused this dramatic shift? One political scientist suggests it was a combination of two factors: First, this period saw a substantial decline in defense spending, as a percentage of the federal budget, and as a percentage of gross domestic product. Second, a series of disturbing foreign policy events rocked the world—the fall of South Vietnam, Cambodia, and Nicaragua to communist forces; the Soviet military build-up and takeover of Afghanistan; and the hostage crisis at the American embassy in Iran.[31] To produce such substantial shifts in public opinion, these events must have pushed virtually every age group in the same direction—toward support of more defense spending. This is a clear illustration of period effect.

Life cycle effects   Finally, one event that can have an impact on political opinions is less an event than a process—the process of getting older. In the **life cycle effect**, just as common understanding suggests, individuals tend to get more conservative as they grow older and more secure in their political beliefs. Consider again the study of Vietnam War protesters and their non-protesting peers. As mentioned above, the impact of the war and protest politics appears to have made the protesters a substantially more left-leaning group than non-protesters of the same age. Even so, the study found *both* groups moving in a more conservative direction, with the protestors doing so at a more rapid pace. In other words, while protestors remained more liberal, the groups grew more alike, and more conservative, as they aged.

The same basic phenomenon can be observed in Americans' description of themselves as "liberal" or "conservative." As they age, survey respondents are more likely to declare themselves conservative—a classic life cycle effect.[32] Americans also grow more secure in their partisan attachments as they grow older: they are increasingly likely to side with the Democratic or Republican parties and less likely to say that they are politically independent.[33]

Attitudes About the American Political System

As we discuss in Chapter 2 on political culture, public opinion in America is more than just collective thought about policy issues, parties, and political figures. It also consists of people's attitudes toward their government, their role as citizens in a democracy, and their support for the freedoms that government is supposed to protect. These attitudes are highly important to the healthy functioning of a democratic government. As U.S. Circuit Court Judge Learned Hand reminded us,

> Liberty lies in the hearts of men and women; when it dies there, no constitution, no law, no court can save it; no constitution, no law, no court can even do much to help it. While it lies there it needs no constitution, no law, no court to save it.[34]

In more colloquial terms, Hand means that the American public is the ultimate guardian of its own rights and freedoms. As long as Americans believe in their democratic system and are willing to engage in it, there can be no serious threat to liberty or democratic stability. If Americans, however, lose faith in the system, fail to hold it accountable, or abandon the democratic values that support it, the very concepts of self-rule and liberty may be at risk.

There has been a long-term decline in political trust.

The American public's trust and confidence in government and in their ability to influence policy has been declining for some time. In 1960, three in four Americans (73 percent) believed that they could trust the government to do what is right most of the time or all of the time. In 2004, fewer than half (47 percent) believed that they could trust the government to do what is right most of the time or all of the time.[35]

What might explain this decline? To some degree, no doubt, it is linked to a succession of demoralizing events in American politics—Vietnam, Watergate, the protracted period of "stagflation" in the 1970s, the Iran-Contra affair in the late 1980s, and the Iraq war in the more recent times.

It would be nice if there were a single, "silver bullet" explanation. As we have cautioned, though, political life tends to be complicated. Thus, political scientists have proposed a variety of factors, each with some validity:

- Trust was artificially inflated in the post–World War II years. In other words, the anomaly is not the low levels now, but the high levels in the 1960s.

- American politics at the elite level has become more polarized, a trend that has been amplified through negative coverage of politics in the media.

- In recent decades, American economic life has become less secure and traditional morals have eroded; government has been unwilling or unable to do much to reverse these trends.

- There has been declining respect for *all* large institutions, not simply government.[36]

America is not alone among industrial democracies in its declining levels of trust in government. Surveys in other countries have uncovered a "wide-scale erosion of trust in government across the advanced industrial democracies during the later third of the twentieth century."[37] This finding suggests that "America-specific" explanations for the decline in political trust are too limited. A broader explanation points to increasing expectations of government and democracy among younger citizens and individuals of high social status. In the 1950s these groups were relatively satisfied with government, but now they expect more of government, and find fewer satisfying solutions in the traditional structures and processes of democracy. Although they still support democratic principles, they are not strong supporters of the way democracy functions in their particular countries.

So why does it matter that trust in government has declined? Although American democracy is not in mortal peril, a more modest but still important concern is that lower levels of trust may translate into lower approval ratings for both the president and the Congress.[38] Governing within the American system of separation of powers and checks and balances has never been easy. But with lower levels of public support for the main political actors and institutions, it becomes an even greater challenge. Can the government make tough decisions about foreign policy, energy policy, and Social Security when few people trust it? Declining trust in government has also led, some argue, to declining interest and participation in civic life.[39]

Political leaders and the public keep democracy safe in different ways.

Democratic freedoms seem relatively secure in America, but not necessarily because they are widely supported by the American public. Instead, it appears that whereas the American public merely frowns on oppression of disfavored groups, political elites intensely favor protecting against it. In addition to adequate levels of trust and confidence in government, and in the people's belief in their own ability to influence government, a functioning democracy requires a commitment to democratic values. By democratic values, we mean those values that define the liberal consensus, or the American creed (see Chapter 2). Primarily, this means a belief in the values of equality, individualism, majority rule, minority rights, and protection of personal freedoms.

Some of the drop-off in support for democratic values in the mass public is a result of competing values within the liberal consensus. For example, nearly four out of five Americans recognize the importance of teaching children that all people are equal. This reflects the American belief in the idea of equality. It should not be surprising, then, that the public objects to the idea of allowing speech that would be offensive to racial groups—presumably because such speech would suggest racial *in*equalities.

The problem here is obvious. If people are allowed to speak freely, they may do so in a manner that offends Americans' beliefs about equality. If people are not allowed to speak freely, however, that undermines Americans' beliefs about freedom of speech. There is no win-win solution here; something has to give and what gives in this case is free speech rights. This is not, however, because the public is anti-democratic. It is because two democratic values are coming into conflict in this case.

Second, given the arguments in this chapter about the nature of public opinion, it would be surprising if most Americans held their anti-democratic attitudes with any considerable degree of intensity or certitude. Similarly, Americans give little indication of wanting to act on their anti-democratic attitudes by demanding action from public officials.

Consider a roughly analogous case. Imagine, for example, that the questions above were not about civil rights and liberties, but about government price support for sugar-producers. That support is estimated to cost American sugar consumers as much as $2 billion per year.[40] Huge majorities of the public would undoubtedly favor a repeal of price supports, and a free market in sugar. But this is not an important issue for the vast majority of Americans. As a result, sugar prices stay where they are.

So it is, too, with civil liberties. With regard to the public opinion traits introduced earlier in this chapter, many issues appear not to be particularly *salient* to Americans, nor are Americans' opinions on those issues especially *intense*. Without active, insistent demands by the American public, it is unlikely that policymakers will take to heart the public's anti-democratic opinions.

However, what if a demagogic leader were to *incite* the public to clamor for change? What if some charismatic, highly effective communicator ran for president, for example, on a platform that threatened the rights of American Muslims? Given fears of terrorism and the ease with which Americans appear to adopt anti-democratic attitudes, might not such an appeal work?

The relative infrequency with which such campaigns succeed suggests that it would not. There are, of course, prominent examples of minorities being persecuted in modern American history—the internment of Japanese Americans during World War II, the crackdown on communists in public and private life during the McCarthy period, and the systematic denial of civil rights to blacks up through the 1960s—but these cases are noteworthy because they are exceptional. They are also receding further and further into the American past.

One protection against the recurrence of such episodes may be the strong commitment to democratic values among those Americans most deeply involved in politics. A number of studies have shown this small but highly important segment of Americans to be generally more politically tolerant and more likely to embrace democratic values than the broader public.[41] A number of competing studies, however, have called these results into question.[42] We are left to conclude

that, either because of the importance that influential political elites place on tolerance and civil liberties, or because the American public in general shows little support for oppression of disfavored groups, democratic freedoms seem relatively
secure in America.

Political Knowledge and Ideology

The term "public opinion" contains the word "opinion" for a good reason: democratic governance requires the public to have opinions, or preferences, regarding
candidates and policy decisions. Only by developing such opinions can the public
express its will at the ballot box and through other forms of direct political action.
And, only by expressing these preferences can the public guide policymakers in
their day-to-day decision-making, and ultimately hold political leaders accountable
for the choices they make and the consequences of those choices.

Developing an informed opinion about matters of government, politics, and
public policy requires some basic knowledge. For example, before deciding on a
preferred presidential candidate, a citizen must at least know who is running, and
in general terms, how the candidates will govern if elected. Without this basic
information, a voter will be unable to make an informed choice among presidential candidates.

Americans possess less political knowledge than they should, but more than is alleged.

Unfortunately, at least from the perspective of democratic theory, American adults
have generally low levels of knowledge regarding American politics and government. For example, in response to the question, "Can you tell me the name of the
person George W. Bush has nominated to replace Colin Powell as Secretary of
State?" respondents replied as shown in Figure 7-3.

Consider a few other specifics that are detailed in Table 7-1: In 2004, roughly
two-thirds of the American public had essentially no knowledge of the PATRIOT
Act, the Medicare prescription drug benefit, or the partial-birth abortion ban,
despite the prominence of these items in media coverage of politics that year.
Almost one-third of the public was unable in 2003 to name the vice president, and
in 2002 only about one-third of the public knew that Republicans controlled the
House of Representatives, despite the fact that there was a Congressional election
that year.

These numbers are certainly eye-opening, but not sufficiently comprehensive
to determine the extent of political knowledge and ignorance within the American
electorate. A more thorough study of American knowledge of politics and government was based on more than 50 years' worth of survey questions. To excerpt the
conclusions:

> Only 13 percent of the more than 2,000 political questions examined could be
> answered correctly by 75 percent or more of those asked, and only 41 percent
> could be answered correctly by more than half the public. Many of the facts
> known by relatively small percentages of the public seem critical to understand-
> ing—let alone effectively acting in—the political world: fundamental rules of the
> game; classic civil liberties; key concepts of political economy; the names of key
> political representatives; many important policy positions of presidential
> candidates or the political parties; basic social indicators; and significant public
> policies.[43]

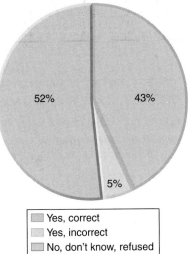

52%   43%

5%

Yes, correct
Yes, incorrect
No, don't know, refused

Figure 7-3. Percent of the Public Able to Identify Condoleezza Rice as President Bush's Nominee to Replace Colin Powell as Secretary of State. A bare majority of Americans were able to name the person nominated to one of the most influential jobs in the president's administration.

This pessimistic finding is not the whole story, however. This study also found that a significant proportion of the American public is aware of key governmental institutions and processes, civil liberties, and economic terms. The public could also identify the politicians at the very top of government along with the policies endorsed by prominent politicians—both historic and contemporary.[44] To characterize these contrasting conclusions, then, one might say that while Americans do not know as much about politics as one would wish, nor as much as they should in order to be highly effective democratic citizens, they do possess some substantial political knowledge—more, in fact, than is often alleged.

How does Americans' political knowledge stack up in comparative terms? It's a mixed picture, although one in which the United States does not fare particularly well. For example, an eight-nation survey conducted in 1994, which tested knowledge of international affairs, finds Americans finishing in the bottom three countries, ahead of only Mexico and Spain (Table 7-2). Thirty-seven percent of Americans were unable to answer correctly any of the five survey questions—the highest percentage among the participating countries.

Americans fared somewhat better when the task was limited to naming world leaders. In a 1986 survey that inquired about the heads of government in the U.S., the U.K., France, West Germany, Italy, and Japan, Americans scored at the top in terms of their ability to name their own president (compared to, say, Italians' ability to name the Italian prime minister). Americans generally lagged behind the other countries in their ability to name European heads of state, but did as well as or better than all but one country (Italy) in naming the prime minister of Japan (Table 7-3).

Americans are ideologically innocent.

Having examined *what* Americans know about politics, the next logical question is: How well are they able to use their knowledge to form political opinions?

Table 7-1. Basic Political Knowledge Among American Adults

YEAR	QUESTION	KNOW	DON'T KNOW/ REFUSED/INCORRECT
2004	Know at least "some" information about the USA PATRIOT Act?	39%	61%
2004	Know that Congress recently passed a Medicare prescription drug benefit?	31%	69%
2004	Know that Congress recently passed a bill banning "partial birth" abortions?	36%	64%
2004	Know approximate number of U.S. troops killed in Iraq?	40%	60%
2003	Two of the three branches of the U.S. government are called the Executive and the Legislative branches. What is the third branch called?	57%	43%
2003	How many U.S. senators are there from each state?	59%	41%
2003	What are the first 10 amendments to the U.S. Constitution called?	47%	53%
2003	Who is the current Vice President of the United States?	69%	31%
2003	Who is the current Chief Justice of the U.S. Supreme Court?	17%	83%
2002	Which party controls the United States House of Representatives?	32%	68%
2000	Know that the post held by Janet Reno is U.S. Attorney General?	55%	45%
2000	Which party controls the United States Senate?	50%	50%
2000	Which candidate is more supportive of abortion rights: Gore or Bush?	46%	54%
2000	Know that the U.S. crime rate decreased between 1992 and 2000?	37%	63%
2000	Which party controls the United States House of Representatives?	55%	45%
2000	Correctly name at least one candidate for House of Representatives in respondent's district?	15%	85%
2000	Know that post held by Trent Lott is Senate Majority Leader?	9%	91%

Source: George H. Gallup Jr., "How Many Americans Know U.S. History?, Part I," The Gallup Organization, October 21, 2003, available online at http://www.gallup.com/poll/content/print.aspx?ci=9526; and Ilya Somin, "When Ignorance Isn't Bliss: How Political Ignorance Threatens Democracy," Cato Institute, *Policy Analysis* Number 525, September 22, 2004

Although written over 40 years ago, the seminal study of this question was published in 1964 by University of Michigan scholar Philip Converse. Converse's research is still the starting point in any discussion of the sophistication of political thinking among the public at large.

The 1964 study painted a fairly gloomy picture of Americans' political sophistication. Converse concluded Americans lacked the capacity for well-developed, informed political thought. He went on to declare most of the American public "innocent" of organized, logical, structured political thinking.[45] Converse argued that Americans' political beliefs often had little internal logic, and sometimes appeared to be arrived at without any application of forethought or reasoning. Not only, said Converse, do Americans not think about politics with anywhere near the sophistication of politicians and political journalists, they probably are largely *incapable* of doing so.

Table 7-2. Knowledge of Foreign Affairs in Comparative Perspective (Percentage Correct)

	CANADA	FRANCE	GERMANY	ITALY	MEXICO	SPAIN	UNITED KINGDOM	UNITED STATES
President of Russia?	59	61	94	76	42	65	63	50
Country threatening to withdraw from nonproliferation treaty	12	7	45	26	6	5	11	22
Who is Boutros Boutros Ghali?	26	32	58	43	14	15	22	13
Ethnic group that has conquered much of Bosnia	42	55	77	51	12	24	46	28
Name of group with whom Israelis recently reached peace accord	51	60	79	56	21	29	59	40
Answered four or five correctly	19	25	58	34	8	10	18	15
Answered none correctly	27	23	3	18	41	32	22	37
Mean number correct	1.92	2.13	3.55	2.49	1.22	1.35	2.01	1.53

Source: Michael X. Delli Carpini and Scott Keeter, *What Americans Know About Politics and Why it Matters* (New Haven, CT: Yale University Press, 1996), pp. 89–90

Converse proposed a "black and white" model of public opinion. According to this model, some particularly attentive citizens have stable and coherent attitudes, but most people change attitudes on issues almost with the same frequency that one would get if they were flipping a coin to determine what they thought.

When asked to offer opinions on specific policy issues, large proportions of the public simply had no substantively meaningful opinions to offer. This absence of opinions did not stop the public from offering answers to survey questions. In a

Table 7-3. Knowledge of Political Leaders in Comparative Perspective (Percentage Correct)

	WEST GERMANS	FRENCH	BRITISH	ITALIANS	AMERICANS
President of United States	94	94	93	95	99
Prime Minister of United Kingdom	80	89	96	77	74
President of France	64	99	55	76	34
Chancellor of West Germany	95	59	17	37	16
Prime Minister of Italy	39	18	2	89	6
Prime Minister of Japan	19	17	4	23	19

Source: Michael X. Delli Carpini and Scott Keeter, *What Americans Know About Politics and Why it Matters* (New Haven, CT: Yale University Press, 1996), p.91

separate publication, Converse referred to such hollow answers as an expression of "non-attitudes."

Many argue that the American public may not be politically ignorant.

One possible response to Converse is that he did his research at a particularly quiet time in American politics—the late 1950s and the early 1960s. Converse had completed his analysis over fifty years ago—before the Kennedy assassination and Vietnam, before the major race riots of the 1960s, before Watergate and stagflation, before the Reagan Revolution of 1980 and the terrorist attacks of September 11, 2001. Perhaps if he had undertaken his analysis a few years later, in a more turbulent or ideologically charged period, he would have found Americans more engaged in issues of politics and government.

Another response challenging Converse's argument is that, inevitably, survey responses are flawed. The apparent flip-flopping of opinions over time, and the failure of respondents' answers to "hang together" in logical ways, may result as much from poorly worded questions as from genuine randomness of respondent opinions. The instability and lack of logical groupings one sees in survey responses are, as one commentator put it, a product of "fuzzy measures *and* fuzzy citizens."[46]

Another line of criticism relates to Converse's treatment of the concept of ideology. Specifically, critics have complained that a simple left/right, liberal/conservative concept of ideology is far too narrow. Americans are capable of ideological thinking, this line of argumentation goes, but only ideological thinking that can be captured in the limited terms typically used by political leaders. Furthermore, these critics argue, surveys typically are not well designed to capture the complexity of Americans' thinking about politics. How can a format that forces respondents into a limited choice among one- or two-word responses accurately capture the fullness of an opinion, or the processing of ideas and information that took place in order to arrive at that opinion?

Another interesting possibility about the nature of individual Americans' opinions on specific policy issues also has a bearing on Converse's claims. Perhaps people do not have perfectly formed attitudes that correspond to the specific answers required by survey questions. Instead, they possess a mix of considerations.[47] Think of a bunch of ping pong balls in your head each with a competing thought about a particular issue.

For some people, that mix of ideas might be more or less a 50-50 proposition. One person, for example, might have a head full of competing ideas on abortion, about half of which suggest that abortion should remain legal, and the other half of which suggest it should be outlawed. Another person on another issue, though, might have a more lopsided mix. For example, most of what he or she knows might suggest the wisdom of tougher gun control laws, but he or she might also recognize instances in which gun laws are fine as-is (or perhaps even too restrictive).

What happens when someone with a head full of different, sometimes inconsistent ideas is asked a question in a survey? The survey respondent answers by making reference to whatever considerations happen to be most accessible at the moment—that is, by giving an answer based on those ideas that, at that moment, are at the forefront of his or her mind.

Think again about the person with a head full of ideas on abortion, half of which could be classified as "pro-choice," and half, "pro-life." One morning, that person reads a newspaper article about pro-life activists blocking access to a family planning clinic. This action strikes her as inappropriate—as long as abortion is legal, she thinks, people should have access to clinics. That afternoon, she receives a call from a pollster. The pollster asks a question about abortion rights. Most salient in the respondent's mind is a vague feeling of unease with pro-lifers, based on her reading of the morning's newspaper article. Accordingly, she tells the pollster that she supports abortion rights and would describe herself as pro-choice, even though her enduring opinion is not so black-and-white.

Consider, too, the case of the person with predominantly pro-gun control ideas, but also a handful of ideas sympathetic to the gun rights movement. Under normal circumstances, we would expect this person to answer a survey question about gun control in a sympathetic fashion. Most of her ideas, after all, are supportive of more gun control, so it is likely that one of those ideas will be at the top of her head when the pollster calls. But what if she has just heard a story from a neighbor who successfully defended his home against a break-in by brandishing a handgun? The burglar fled, and the neighbor and his family were safe. This kind of story does not fit with most of the ideas about gun control that our hypothetical citizen has in her head. But if a pollster should call while this story is still fresh in her mind, she might very well give an answer supportive of more gun rights. Why? Because those considerations happened to be at the top of her head when the survey interviewer telephoned.

Over time, then, the same respondent might give very different answers to the same questions, depending on what considerations or ideas happened to be at the forefront of his or her mind at the time of the survey. This would produce the very thing that Converse found in his study—a high level of response instability.

This instability could suggest that many people were simply "making up" a response, on the fly, in order to accommodate the interviewer, meaning that respondents had no substantive thoughts on the issue. Although survey respondents very often do not have complete, fully formed attitudes on public policy issues, this is not the same as saying that they have "non-attitudes" and simply invent answers to satisfy survey interviewers. Instead, they have a variety of ideas about a specific issue. Yet, those ideas typically do not form a cohesive, stable stance that mirrors ideological categories—either with respect to one particular issue, or from one issue to the next.

CaseStudy: An Experiment in Non-Attitudes

The phrase "non-attitudes" refers to the hastily concocted, largely baseless opinions that some people offer when asked to comment on political topics of which they have little or no genuine knowledge. In 1978, some enterprising researchers carried the concept of the non-attitude to its logical extreme. If people are willing to essentially fabricate opinions on real political issues, they wondered, might they do the same if asked about an *imaginary* one?[48]

To answer this question, the researchers asked a random sample of survey respondents about a completely fictitious piece of legislation, the "1975 Public Affairs Act." Specifically, respondents were asked this question: "Some people say that the 1975 Public Affairs Act should be

repealed. Do you agree or disagree with the idea that the 1975 Public Affairs Act should be repealed?"

In one version of the survey, the researchers found that one-third of respondents were willing to offer an opinion on the repeal of the imaginary legislation. Rather than volunteering the fact that they had never heard of the 1975 Public Affairs Act, respondents politely gave the pollsters an opinion. (About 16 percent supported repeal, and about 18 percent opposed it.)

The researchers then decided to make it somewhat easier for respondents to admit they had never heard of the 1975 Public Affairs Act. They asked the question somewhat differently: "Some people say that the 1975 Public

Affairs Act should be repealed. Have you been interested enough in this to favor one side over the other?" Though survey respondents were given an easy out, 7 percent *still* insisted that they had heard of, and had an opinion on, the wholly fictitious legislation.

ThinkingCritically

1. Think of several reasons why American citizens seem to be so poorly informed politically. Should we be concerned or is this predictable and benign?

2. What implications does this study have for researchers crafting survey questions?

Making Public Opinion Work in a Democracy

Although political knowledge and sophistication among Americans may be somewhat lacking, there are certain reassuring regularities in the ebb and flow of public opinion. For example, when a president performs poorly in office, the public usually recognizes this, reduces its collective approval of his job performance, and ultimately denies him reelection. Likewise, when a president performs well in office, the public recognizes this, too, and typically rewards him with high job approval numbers and another term. Similarly, the public will often react in orderly, predictable ways to shifts in public policy.

The miracle of aggregation can compensate for low levels of information among the mass public.

Recall the example presented at the beginning of this chapter, with common men and women accurately guessing the weight of an ox. It illustrates a paradox that has often been referred to as the **miracle of aggregation**. The "miracle" is that, even though a group of individuals can be largely ignorant of a particular phenomenon, when their opinions are aggregated, their collective opinion tends to make sense.

Here is how it works. Imagine an American public in which only 30 percent of the people paid close attention to politics, and the other 70 percent were completely ignorant. And now imagine, for example, that politicians are looking for guidance from the public on whether or not to undertake a dramatic reform of the Social Security program. According to the terms of our example, 70 percent of the public has no real opinion on the matter. But let's assume that, of the other 30 percent, two-thirds want reform, and one-third do not. So, now we have 20 percent of the electorate that wants reform, 10 percent that does not, and 70 percent that have no idea.

As shown above, even completely ignorant members of the public will often give answers to survey questions just to be polite, or perhaps not to seem as ignorant of a particular issue as they really are. Let us assume, then, that the 70 percent split equally on the Social Security question—between the pro-reform and no reform options. (There is no reason to believe that individuals essentially inventing their answers to a survey question should favor one side more than the other.)

Now the picture of public opinion on the issue looks like this: 55 percent support reform, and 45 percent do not. Notice what has happened: Opinion from the public as a whole, including the great mass of ignorant individuals, conveys the same message to policymakers as opinion from only the informed 30 percent: Americans want Social Security reform. A miracle!

As long as the random opinions of uninformed members of the public cancel each other out, policymakers will get a clear, meaningful signal that accurately reflects the wishes of those who are paying attention. This result may cause some anguish for those who would like the entire public to be aware, interested, and informed. However, the miracle of aggregation at least provides a way for the truly interested and informed to see their policy preferences accurately represented to decision-makers.

Opinion leaders shape what the public thinks about and what they think about it.

Studies of public opinion typically divide the American public into three segments: those who pay very close attention to politics, those who are generally indifferent to politics but pay attention sporadically, and those who pay no attention to politics at all. There are debates over the relative size of these different segments, but the most-attentive group is likely to be a small one, and on particularly obscure issues, extremely small.

That this group is small, however, does not mean that it lacks significant influence. In fact, many of the members of this group can be considered "opinion leaders." **Opinion leaders** are people who can legitimately claim high levels of interest and expertise in politics, and who seek to communicate their political beliefs to others. This group may include political writers and journalists; politicians; political professionals (lobbyists, pollsters, campaign consultants, association executives); bloggers; academic political scientists; community activists; and the garden-variety "political junkie."

Opinion leaders make it their business to send strong signals to the public regarding which political issues are important, and what the public ought to think about them. An opinion leader can communicate with a member of the public as impersonally as through the television, or as intimately as over a cup of coffee. Either way, the mass public can become informed quickly and easily through the efforts of opinion leaders.

One can see an example of opinion leadership by looking at results of the Gallup Poll's "most important problem" question over the years. Periodically, Gallup has asked the American public the following question: "What do you think is the most important problem facing the country today?" In December of 2004, only 2 percent of the public identified "Social Security/ Medicare issues" as America's most important problem. A mere two months later, however, in February of 2005, that number had risen to 13 percent.[49] Clearly, the financial health of the Social Security and Medicare programs had remained unchanged in those two months. What *had* changed, however, was that President George W. Bush began to discuss the urgent need for reform in these programs. The media carried that message from the president through television and newspaper coverage of his speeches, and through commentary and editorials of their own. Various opinion leaders continued this "trickle down" process, discussing the issue in community meetings and personal conversations. The Gallup data indicate that at least part of the public ultimately got the message that the president intended. As we discuss in greater depth in other chapters, one of the biggest influences elites can have is by setting the agenda—deciding what gets talked about. Consider one other case—global warming. Gallup asked the American public six times between 1992 and 2004 how well it thought it understood the issue of global warming. In 1992, when Gallup first asked the question, 22 percent responded "not at all." By 2004, however, that number was down to 6 percent.[50] Clearly, in that 12-year interim the

American public got the message from opinion leaders—most obviously the media and the president—that they ought to be paying attention to this issue.[51]

Beyond giving the public cues about what issues it should be thinking about, opinion leaders also help shape *how* the public thinks about certain issues. In one scholarly study, for example, researchers identified 80 different questions that were asked at least twice on a variety of surveys during the period 1969 to 1983. In many cases, opinion had changed noticeably between the first time the question was asked and the second. In explaining these changes, the researchers found that changes in public opinion corresponded significantly with television news commentary—in other words, messages from opinion leaders.[52]

Partisanship simplifies political judgments.

Unlike many other aspects of public opinion, most voters have a self-defined, stable affiliation with a political party. In making judgments about the political world, then, they can use partisanship as a cue.[53] The partisan affiliation of a political candidate communicates a tremendous amount of information. If you are a Democrat, for example, you know that you are much more likely to agree with the policy preferences of Democrats than Republicans, without having to sort through each and every position of a particular candidate. If you vote strictly along party lines, you may regret your choice occasionally, but for the most part, a vote for your party versus the other party will tend to be consistent with your preferred outcome. Similarly, if you are a Republican, you know that most of the policy proposals from your party's leaders are likely to be more acceptable to you than proposals from the Democrats. Knowing that your party proposed them provides you with some assurance that the ideas make sense.[54]

The same basic logic applies to your approval or disapproval of the job performance of policymakers, from the president on down. If they share your partisan affiliation, it is likely that you will agree, on the whole, with the policy choices they are making. You may not know the details of those choices, but because you are members of the same party, you know that you probably share the same broad set of beliefs. With that knowledge, you can have some confidence that if time permitted you to follow their performance closely, you would likely approve of the job they were doing.[55] We will have much more to say about partisanship and party identification in Chapter 9.

Moderately politically attentive "scorekeepers" cause most aggregate public opinion change.

One political scientist proposes that the middle stratum of Americans referred to above—the group that is only moderately attentive to politics—serves an important "scorekeeping" function.[56] This group has little passion for politics, and does not think about the political world in ideological terms. It pays just enough attention to politics to pick up on signals indicating big changes—for example, a change from peace to war, from recession to recovery, from bipartisan cooperation to acrimony and scandal, or from a conservative bent in social policy to a liberal one. The scorekeepers, in other words, keep a running tally of "how things are going" in very broad, very general policy areas. When they pick up a signal that a noticeable change has occurred, they change their opinions accordingly. According to this view, those changes account for most of the movement in aggregate public opinion. Furthermore, they are connected to real-world events in a fairly logical, orderly fashion that results in government accountability.

These are just some of the shortcuts that help the public arrive at collectively rational opinions about politics and government. Certainly, these shortcuts help mitigate some of the potential consequences of low voter sophistication and keep policymakers aware of, and generally accountable to, the public. But American public opinion remains a very mixed picture, full of attitudes and non-attitudes; contradictory beliefs; loosely and fleetingly held considerations; authentic opinions; strong value commitments; vast stretches of ignorance and indifference; and isolated oases of knowledge, all mixed together.

SUMMARY

- Public opinion is a subject at the heart of democratic theory, and it has four basic traits: salience, stability, direction, and intensity. It is challenging but crucial for leaders to know and understand public opinion in terms of all these traits and patterns.

- Political socialization is the process by which citizens acquire the values and attitudes that shape their thinking about politics. It tends to be governed by two important principles: primacy and persistence, both of which point to the importance of early childhood learning. There are several phases of socialization from early childhood all the way through young adulthood, and the development of ideological thinking demonstrates increased political sophistication. Socialization occurs through specific agents of socialization and socializing events. Although the family is foremost among agents of socialization, socializing events include generational effects, period effects, and life cycle effects.

- In the realm of support for the American political system, there has been declining trust among Americans over the past few decades. Though these trends are unlikely to threaten the stability of American government, they result in lower levels of participation and civic engagement. In terms of democratic values, although Americans embrace the American creed in the abstract, their opinions are often strikingly undemocratic

in specific cases. Even so, those opinions do not appear to be particularly intense, and political leaders have expressed robustly democratic views. Accordingly, democratic governance, the free enterprise system, and civil liberties in America are probably safe for now.

- Political knowledge among the American public is somewhat lacking. Large proportions of the public simply have no substantively meaningful opinions to offer when faced with political survey questions. Not surprisingly, Americans' capacity to translate their knowledge into opinions is also less than desirable. Political scientist Philip Converse's work was particularly important to these discoveries. While much subsequent research has taken issue with Converse's findings and not all of the conclusions hold today, a large proportion of what we know about public opinion has come about as scholars have addressed and often challenged the findings from the original work.

- Despite the above, American public opinion *collectively* makes sense in many cases. That is, despite the lack of political knowledge and sophistication at the individual level, collective opinion is often rational, ordered, and predictable. A number of shortcuts and devices enable the American public to communicate to policymakers a collectively ordered, rational set of preferences.

KEY TERMS

direction, p. 000
generational effect, p. 000
intensity, p. 000
life cycle effect, p. 000
margin of error, p. 000
miracle of aggregation, p. 000
non-response bias, p. 000
opinion leaders, p. 000
period effect, p. 000

persistence, p. 000
political socialization, p. 000
primacy, p. 000
public opinion, p. 000
random sample, p. 000
salience, p. 000
sampling, p. 000
sampling error, p. 000
stability, p. 000

SUGGESTED READINGS

Robert Erickson and Kent Tedin. 2005. *American Public Opinion: It's Origins, Content, and Impact.* New York: Longman. This is an excellent text that covers a wide range of information about the measurement, nature, and importance of public opinion.

Morris Fiorina. 2006. *Culture War? The Myth of a Polarized America.* New York: Longman. The author argues that

Americans are not nearly as divided on major political issues as many pundits and commentators claim.

Paul M. Sniderman, Richard A. Brody, and Philip E. Tetlock. 1991. *Reasoning and Choice: Explorations in Political Psychology.* Cambridge: Cambridge University Press. This book argues that ordinary citizens who pay little attention to politics can still make reasonable decisions based on particular shortcuts.

James Stimson. 2004. *Tides of Consent: How Public Opinion Shapes American Politics*. Cambridge: Cambridge University Press. The author argues that while the public rarely engages in politics, when public opinion is aroused, major changes in policy result.

Herbert Weisberg, Jon Krosnick, and Bruce Bowen. 1996. *An Introduction to Survey Research, Polling, and Data Analysis*. Thousand Oaks: Sage Publications. This text gives the basics of how to conduct and analyze survey research with information on sampling, question writing, and interviewing techniques.

John Zaller. 1992. *The Nature and Origins of Mass Opinion*. New York: Cambridge University Press. The author devises and tests a model of public opinion formation in which people sample from a mix of political considerations in their head when confronted with the need to make political decisions or share political attitudes.

public opinion the collective political beliefs and attitudes of the public, or groups within the public, on matters of relevance to government.

salience an issue's importance to a person, or to the public in general.

stability the likelihood that public opinion will change, the speed with which the change would occur, and the likelihood that the new opinion would endure.

direction in public opinion, the tendency for or against some phenomenon.

sampling taking a small fraction of something that is meant to represent a larger whole—e.g., a group of people that represents a larger population.

intensity the strength of the direction of public opinion.

random sample a population sample in which it is equally likely that each member of the population will be included in the sample.

sampling error the difference between the reported characteristics of the sample and the characteristics of the larger population that result from imperfect sampling.

margin of error the range surrounding a sample's response within which researchers are confident the larger population's true response would fall.

non-response bias a non-random error that occurs when people who choose to participate in a survey have different attitudes from those of people who decline to participate.

political socialization the learning process in which individuals absorb information and selectively add it to their knowledge and understanding of politics and government.

primacy the principle that what is learned first is learned best and lodged most firmly in one's mind.

persistence the principle that political lessons, values, and attitudes learned early in life tend to structure political learning later on in life.

generational effect the situation in which younger citizens are influenced by events in such a fashion that their attitudes and beliefs are forever rendered distinct from those of older generations.

period effect an event that influences the attitudes and beliefs of people of all ages.

life cycle effect attitudes or physical characteristics that change as one ages no matter the time period or generation. One's hair turning grey is a life cycle effect.

miracle of aggregation the phenomenon that occurs when a group consists of individuals who are largely ignorant of a particular issue, but their collective opinion tends to makes sense.

opinion leaders individuals who can legitimately claim high levels of interest and expertise in politics, and who seek to communicate their political beliefs to others.

8 Political Participation

Literacy Tests

Political participation is the effort to influence what happens in the political world—either by voting or by doing things like writing letters, signing petitions, or attending a demonstration to influence political officials or the public at large. Now, imagine that you wanted to participate in politics by voting in an election for president, governor, Congress, or a local office, but you are required to answer the following questions:

1. The only laws which can be passed to apply to an area in a federal arsenal are those passed by ___ provided consent for the purchase of the land is given by the _____.
2. Appropriation of money for the armed services can be only for a period limited to ____ years.
3. A United States senator elected at the general election in November takes office the following year on what date?

_____.

These are actual questions from a test given to African Americans attempting to vote in Alabama in the late 1950s and early 1960s.[1] The questions varied from state to state, but these are fairly typical of the obscure facts that African Americans were required to know in order to vote in many southern states. Known as literacy tests, they were merely a sham created primarily to bar blacks from voting. Literacy tests and other hurdles such as the poll tax (which required one to pay a fee to register to vote) were, in fact, relatively tame compared to the violence and intimidation that black Americans faced when they tried to exercise their rights to participate in American democracy.

For black Americans, freedom and the ability to participate in American politics was obtained piecemeal. The Civil War and the Emancipation Proclamation freed blacks from slavery. The Fourteenth Amendment to the U.S. Constitution, passed in 1868, conferred citizenship upon African American men and, through protection of civil liberties, further guaranteed blacks' political liberty. Although you might assume that citizenship included the right to vote, southern states nonetheless systematically turned blacks away at the polls. Pressure mounted to provide a constitutional guarantee of black voting rights. Accordingly, in 1870, the Fifteenth Amendment was passed. It stated, "the right of citizens of the United States to vote shall not be denied by the United States or by any state on account of race, color, or previous condition of physical servitude."

Despite the amendment, many barriers to voting remained, including physical intimidation, literacy tests, and poll taxes. The results of these measures were striking. In 1960, nearly 100 years after the end of the Civil War, the number of African Americans registered to vote in some southern states was around one-tenth of the number of eligible voters. In Mississippi, for example, only 5.2 percent of African Americans were registered. The figure was 13.7 percent in Alabama and 12.7 percent in South Carolina. The comparable figures for white citizens in those states were 63.9 percent in Mississippi, 63.6 percent in Alabama, and 57.1 percent in South Carolina. Overall, 29.1 percent of African Americans were registered in the 11 southern states that had formerly comprised the Confederacy, compared to 61.1 percent of white citizens.[2] The differential between blacks and whites shrank only when the 1965 Voting Rights Act gave the federal government new powers to enforce the promises made in the Fifteenth Amendment.

The history of African-American voting in this country is an extreme but instructive example of how legal factors influence who participates in our democracy. Political scientists tend to believe that political participation depends on an individual's perception of the costs and benefits associated with it. Historically, African Americans who wished to register and vote faced some severe costs—including physical violence. At the same time, if they somehow managed to cast a ballot, their expected benefits were meager. In the racially segregated South, politicians were white, and they did not stay in office by lavishly awarding government benefits to former slaves or their descendants. Although these specific examples are extreme, more generally, the cost/benefit perspective can help explain who participates in American politics, and under what circumstances.

The Paradox of Political Participation

If you have ever voted on Election Day, volunteered for a political campaign, or written a letter to a public official advocating a certain position, you had to make a decision *before* you determined which candidate to vote for, which campaign was worth your commitment, or which side of the issue your letter would support. You first had to decide whether it was worth the effort to vote, volunteer, or write a letter in the first place.

Many people in America engage in these sorts of activities, but just as many—and usually more—choose not to. In fact, as we will see in the next section, about half of Americans engage only in voting, and most do not vote in all the elections available to them.[3] Political scientists have studied why some people get involved in politics and others do not, borrowing language and ideas from another discipline—economics. These political scientists believe that decisions about whether or not to participate in politics depend in large part on individual evaluations about the costs and benefits of political activity.

Citizens weigh costs and benefits in deciding whether to vote.

While we will illustrate the cost/benefit concept with the most common kind of political participation—voting—the basic logic we outline here holds for others sorts of political activities. Assume that an individual's decision about whether or not to vote depends on his or her weighing the relative costs and benefits of voting. First, consider the costs of voting. These costs include the time and effort required to register to vote or update your registration, to travel to a polling place, to wait in line, and to cast your vote. The costs also include the time spent determining how to register or re-register, finding out where your polling place is, and, perhaps the most time-consuming, learning enough about the different candidates and issues to make educated choices.

Now, consider the benefits of voting. If your vote helps elect your preferred candidate, some or all of his or her policies—policies that you support—will be adopted. Depending on your political preferences, some of the benefits you would receive from voting might include lower taxes, more money for student loans, a new federal highway near your hometown, increased Social Security benefits for your grandparents, or other policy changes the candidate has promised.

The final element in your decision about whether or not to vote involves a comparison of the costs and benefits of voting. If the benefits to you outweigh the costs, you will vote. If they do not, you will stay at home.

It is unlikely that a single individual will influence an election outcome or political decision.

Initially, the potential benefits of voting would seem to outweigh the costs and you would decide to vote. For example, even if you have to spend a half-hour on the Internet figuring out how to register, or use a lunch break or hire a babysitter in order to be able to cast a ballot, those costs are minor compared to the benefits of more generous student loans, expanded health care, lower payroll taxes, and the other policy changes your candidate favors. But that assumes that your candidate needs your vote in order to win.

What if your candidate could win without your vote? Then you could enjoy all of the benefits of voting—specifically, the policy changes that your candidate will bring about when he or she wins—without experiencing any of the "costs" of voting. And if that were true, why would you bother voting? The only cases in which your vote would be decisive are if your vote causes or breaks a tie. In only those two cases, the candidate for whom you cast your vote becomes the winner or ties his or her opponent by one vote, your vote. In all other cases, whether you vote or not, the winner will be the same.

Looking at the history of elections, even local elections with very few voters involved, it is exceedingly rare that an election is decided by a single vote. In fact, for all intents and purposes, you can assume before any particular election that your vote will not decide the outcome. Whether you stay home or cast your ballot, the election result will be the same. From this perspective it makes no sense for you to vote *ever*. And yet, every election day Americans vote by the millions. That they do so, even though they could enjoy the benefits of voting without bearing the costs of casting a ballot, is the paradox of voting.

This paradox applies to other types of political participation, too. For this reason, the paradox of voting really can be considered a paradox of *participation*. Suppose, for example, that the president of your college or university has proposed a tuition increase. Student leaders decide to organize a letter-writing campaign to oppose the proposal. They hope to get 5,000 students to send letters to the president's office, demanding that tuition not be raised. You are not surprised when you receive a phone call from an organizer asking you to join the letter-writing campaign.

Faced with this situation, you could think through costs and benefits as described above. Before you even began to do so, however, you might think to yourself: What if the student leaders succeed in getting the other 4,999 people to write a letter? Is my one letter, making it an even 5,000, really going to matter? Probably not. There is really no difference between 4,999 letters and 5,000 letters. On the other hand, what if the student leaders are able to get only 100 letters from other people? If I write a letter, then there will be 101. But there is no real difference between 100 and 101, either. Whether or not I write a letter will not likely be critical.

Your logic here would be exactly the same as the logic about whether or not to vote. The effect of your participation is unlikely to make any meaningful difference in the outcome either way, so why bother? If the president is going to raise tuition whether you write a letter or not, then you should not bother. But if the president is going to decide *not* to raise tuition whether you write a letter or not, not writing looks even better. You get to enjoy the benefit of the lower tuition without putting forward any effort.

There are a number of possible solutions to the paradox of participation.

As you probably realize, people *do* put forward the effort of political participation every day, in all walks of life, and in many different kinds of activities. This leaves political scientists to resolve the paradox of participation—the fact that people participate in politics, even though the impact of their individual participation would seem far too small to matter. How have they attempted to resolve this paradox?

One argument is that citizens worry about other individuals making the same decision they make. That is, individuals might recognize that it is possible for them to collect benefits without paying the costs of participation, but they also recognize that if all citizens were to make the same calculation, then democracy would be threatened because no one would participate. Not wanting democracy to collapse, at least some citizens decide to participate.[4]

There is another possible resolution of the paradox: individuals may think about benefits of voting other than the immediate election outcome, that is, other than the victory or defeat of their preferred candidate. A candidate's victory or defeat is what political scientists call a **collective benefit**—everyone gets to enjoy it, whether they vote or not. But political scientists have also identified what can be called **selective benefits** of voting—benefits that only voters get to enjoy.[5]

What might such a selective benefit be? The one most frequently mentioned by political scientists is that only those who vote get to experience the satisfaction of having fulfilled their civic duty. Importantly, you do not have to believe that you will be the deciding vote in order to receive this benefit, nor does it matter to you whether other individuals vote. For those who actually show up to vote on Election Day, this benefit is enough to outweigh the costs associated with voting. For those who do not show up, the benefit is not large enough to outweigh the costs of voting.[6]

Cost-benefit analysis can help us understand who participates.

The cost-benefit approach can be extremely useful in understanding why some people participate in politics and others do not. The argument is not that individuals are "computers" who put precise figures on costs and benefits and calculate expected outcomes. Still, there is evidence that people behave *as if* they are taking into account, if not making precise calculations, about costs and benefits in their heads, even if political scientists do not quite understand how or why this works. For example, in a large-scale survey of Americans who regularly participate in a variety of political activities, 61 percent said that one of the reasons they vote is "the chance to influence government policy."[7] To political scientists, it is absurd to think that one vote can influence government policy, when more than 100 million votes may be cast in a given election. But if that idea makes sense to Americans who participate in politics, then political scientists need to take it seriously.

People are more likely to participate when expected costs are low. For example, it is easy to register to vote because registration deadlines are now closer to Election Day. In these circumstances, potential voters need not do much advanced planning. People are also more likely to vote when they can easily absorb the costs of voting and afford the cost of the time it takes to become informed; for example, when they can afford to hire a babysitter so that they can get to the polls, or can afford to pay for magazines or cable television programming that help them understand election issues.

As for expected benefits, participation in elections (typically dubbed *voter turnout*) is likely to be higher when the collective benefits are greater, and lower when they are smaller. When, for example, the election is for the county registrar of deeds, then the expected benefit of one candidate or the other winning is unclear to many potential voters. As a result, turnout will likely be lower. If candidates seem very close on many issues, the expected benefit of voting will also be more difficult to discern, because regardless of which candidate wins, the policy outcomes would likely be quite similar. Or, if a particular candidate is running for office unopposed, the selective benefits derived from voting are negligible. Why? The sense of civic duty a voter feels, and the satisfaction from doing one's duty, are probably not as strong when the election has effectively been decided before Election Day.

The Nature and Extent of Political Participation in America

How many Americans participate in politics? The answer to that question varies, depending on the type of participation. In any mention of political participation, the activity that first comes to mind is voting. Although voting is the most common type of political activity, there are many other ways that citizens can participate in politics. Whereas voting involves the direct choice of political leaders, the goal of non-voting activities is to try to influence leaders who have already been selected.

Much political participation goes on outside the voting booth.

Each year Americans typically participate in a variety of political activities other than voting (see Table 8-1). These include signing petitions, attending demonstrations, organizing or attending community meetings, joining political organizations, contacting government officials, and volunteering for political

Table 8-1. Participation in Politics Among American Adults Varies Widely by Type of Activity

TYPE OF ACTIVITY	PERCENTAGE OF AMERICANS PARTICIPATING IN ACTIVITY LAST YEAR
Discuss politics with family or friends	80
Serve as member of a community organization	42
Volunteer	42
Campaign-related activities (attend meeting, put up signs, etc.)	31
Work at/join organization to deal with community problem	29
Attend community meeting about school or community issue	27
Campaign contributions to party, candidate, or other group	25
Contact public officials	21
Attend campaign meetings, rallies, speeches, etc.	8
Participate in protest	4

Source: The American National Election Studies, "2004 American National Election Study," University of California Berkeley Survey Documentation and Analysis, http://sda.berkeley.edu/cgi-bin/hsda?harcsda+nes2004p

campaigns. In addition, about one-quarter of Americans contribute money to political campaigns. No more than one-fifth of Americans are engaged in any of the other activities. The least common activities are participating in political protests and serving as a member of a public board, such as a school board or zoning commission.

Another form of non-voting political participation is the social movement. Social movements are made up of informal alliances of groups or individuals for the purpose of enacting or resisting social change. They often include several other types of the non-voting behavior discussed previously, such as joining and attending meetings of political organizations, contacting government officials, and participating in political protests. The civil rights movement of the 1950s and 1960s and the anti–Vietnam War movement of the 1960s and early 1970s are famously influential social movements. These examples demonstrate the potential power of this type of political participation; however, social movements no longer play as notable a role in American politics. While the civil rights movement led to sweeping changes including federally enforced desegregation and employment rights, little in the way of such influential social change is being enacted today. Perhaps the immigrant and/or anti–Iraq war movements (or some other soon to emerge) will become similarly powerful in the future, but there are no current movements that match those of the 1950s to 1970s. Social movements are something of a "sleeping giant" of non-voting political participation.

Still, although Americans have the reputation of being relatively inactive in politics, that reputation may be largely undeserved. Figure 8-1 compares levels of participation in various political activities across several countries. Only in voting do Americans lag substantially behind their peers in industrialized democracies. (We will have more to say about that later). In the remaining four activities, American rates of participation either exceed or are roughly equivalent to those seen in other industrial democracies.

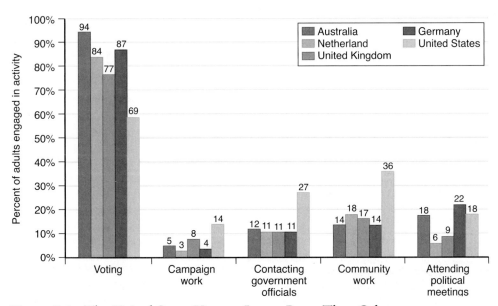

Figure 8-1. **The United States Votes at Lower Rates Than Other Countries but Has Higher Rates of Other Types of Political Participation.**

Source: Sidney Verba, Kay Shlozman, and Henry Brady, *Voice and Equality* (Boston: Harvard University Press, 2006), p. 70

Why Is It So Difficult to Determine How Many People Vote on Election Day?

The Question

The success of democracy depends in part on popular participation in politics and government. Knowing how many people vote on Election Day gives an indication of whether the United States is thriving as a democracy or is struggling or even failing to live up to its democratic ideals. Because of the importance of this question, political scientists ask after every national election: How many people voted? How do we know?

Why It Matters

Voting is the most fundamental, most important act of democratic citizenship. That is because for government to be truly accountable to its citizens, those citizens must vote; they must express approval for policies and policymakers they like, and disapproval for those they do not. When voter turnout is high, we can be satisfied that this important part of American democracy is working as intended. When turnout is low, we may wish to consider reforms designed to stimulate registration and voting. Before considering the merits of any of these reforms, however, we need to construct a valid, reliable measure of voter turnout in order to assess our progress—a far more challenging task than it seems.

Investigating the Answer

We want a measure of turnout that accurately tells us how many people voted on Election Day, that is consistent, and that produces comparable results from one election to the next, regardless of the particular characteristics of each election. Political scientists usually measure not the absolute number of voters who show up on Election Day (e.g., 125 million), but rather the turnout *rate* (for example, 50 percent). Calculating the turnout rate for an election entails dividing the number of people who voted in the election by the number of people who could have voted:

Turnout Rate = Actual Voters divided by Potential Voters

So, for example, if 100 people could have voted in an election, but only 50 people actually did vote, the turnout rate would be 50 percent.

Although a seemingly straightforward exercise, several problems arise in performing a real-world calculation of turnout based on this formula. We have to decide whether potential voters are: (a) only those people who were registered to vote and therefore could have cast a ballot on Election Day, or (b) this first group, *plus* those people who failed to register and so were ineligible to vote, but nonetheless met all of the other legal requirements for voting. Most political scientists prefer to use the latter definition. If we were to use the registered voter measure, a situation could arise in which, say, only 30 percent of the eligible voting population was registered to vote, but 90 percent of those who were registered actually showed up on Election Day. In this case, turnout would be 90 percent—the kind of number we would like to see in a democracy. In actuality, though, only 27 percent of individuals eligible to vote would have shown up to cast a ballot (30 percent multiplied by 90 percent)—an unhealthy number. In addition, as we have seen in this chapter, the population of registered voters has historically been subject to political manipulation. African Americans in particular were denied opportunities to register under the pre-1965 political system in the South. This means that if we used a registered- voter measure to calculate turnout in, say, the 1960 presidential election, we would be obscuring the fact that large numbers of Americans were effectively *prohibited* from turning out.

Finally, using a measure based on registered voters makes it difficult to compare U.S. turnout rates with those in other countries. Why? In the United States, individuals who wish to vote are responsible for registering themselves, and then keeping their registration status up to date. In most other democracies, however, the government assumes responsibility for registering legal voters. In those countries, therefore, all individuals who are eligible to vote are registered. If we wish to compare turnout in these countries to U.S. turnout, we must make the comparison among equivalent groups. The registered voter population in other countries is more or less equivalent to the entire eligible U.S. voter population, whether registered or not. For purposes of comparing U.S. turnout to foreign turnout, therefore, it makes sense to use the entire eligible U.S. voter population.

There are also problems, however, with using the eligible-voter population. How do we know how many members of the U.S. population are eligible to vote? In the voter turnout calculations that you are probably familiar with, statisticians estimate the number of eligible voters using census data on the "voting-age population," that is, the number of individuals 18 years of age or older living in the United States. But not everyone who lives in the U.S. is eligible to vote—citizens of other countries, for example, whether living in the U.S. legally or illegally, cannot vote in American elections. Furthermore, in some states convicted felons are legally prohibited from voting. But these groups, along with others who for one reason or other cannot vote, are all lumped into the pool of the voting-age population. At the same time, legally eligible American citizens living overseas are *not* counted as members of the voting-age population, because they do not live in the U.S.

Despite these problems, many researchers—including most political scientists—typically rely on some measure of the U.S. voting-age population to determine the number of potential voters. In recent years, though, researchers have begun to refine their measures of the legally eligible voting population.[8] The Census Bureau, for example, has prepared an alternate measure that seeks to exclude non-citizens from the pool of potentially eligible voters.

To this point, we have addressed only half of the problem—how to measure the number of potential voters. But what about measuring the number of people who actually vote? The most common way of doing this is simply to count up all of the ballots that are cast on Election Day. With one ballot per person, the number of ballots cast would represent the number of voters. It is surprisingly difficult, however, to get an accurate count of the number of ballots cast. As we learned in the 2000 presidential election in Florida, all the ballots cast are not counted. This can result from voter error, machine error, mistakes by poll workers, or some combination. Though Florida attracted most of the attention in 2000, uncounted ballots are a problem nationwide. Across the country in 2000, for example, researchers have estimated that between four million and six million ballots were uncounted.[9]

Political scientists and assorted media outlets have pursued one other avenue in estimating the number of voters: public opinion surveys. In fact, surveys can be used to determine both parts of the turnout equation. For example, survey researchers could ask a nationally representative sample of voting-age adults: (a) whether they met the legal requirements to vote, and (b) whether they did, in fact, vote. Then, they could estimate turnout on the basis of the survey as follows:

Turnout Rate = Number of Survey Respondents Who Report Having Voted divided by Number of Survey Respondents Legally Eligible to Vote

Unfortunately, as with all survey data, there are risks using this approach. First, many surveys fail to draw a representative sample of the voting-age population. For example, if a survey is conducted by telephone, it will not include individuals without phones. Such people are likely to have lower incomes, and are less likely to vote. If such individuals are omitted from telephone surveys, the resulting turnout calculations may be inflated. Similarly, surveys typically exclude dormitories and those who exclusively use cell phones, thus excluding younger people, who are less likely to vote. Accordingly, excluding students from a survey sample could result in an overestimate of the turnout rate. Surveys also may overstate the number of people who actually cast a ballot. Studies comparing survey responses to actual voting records show that many survey respondents report having voted when they did not—perhaps because they were embarrassed to admit to interviewers that they had not done their "civic duty."

The combination of these two problems—excluding low- turnout voters from the denominator and overstating the number of voters in the numerator—tends to result in an inflated turnout estimate. Even so, surveys are still among the best tools for studying turnout. While turnout rates based on survey data may be inflated, political scientists are able to use even inflated rates to compare behavior among different demographic groups and to compare rates of turnout over time. For example, assume that a standard, nationally representative survey will overstate turnout by roughly 20 percentage points every year. If a turnout calculation based on survey data shows a turnout rate of 70 percent in one year, and then 75 percent four years later, we can be confident that turnout rose by about 5 percentage points. It does not matter that the overall turnout rates are overstated, as long as they are overstated by the same amount in each survey. Similarly, an individual survey might show that self-described "strong Democrats" and "strong Republicans" turned out at a rate of 85 percent in a particular presidential election, while independents turned out at a rate of only 50 percent. Though these individual figures might be inflated, we can still be confident that strong partisans turned out at a rate roughly 35 percentage points higher than political independents.

The Bottom Line

Even something as seemingly straightforward as measuring how many people vote in American elections presents difficult methodological issues. Nonetheless, recent work that takes into account the number of eligible voters—the voting- eligible population—makes us more confident that we are assessing the actual proportion of voters who turn out to vote in any particular election. Furthermore, although surveys almost definitely overstate turnout in any one election, they are a useful way to look at trends over time and how particular groups behave, such as the young, old, rich, poor, strong partisans, or weak partisans.

Factors That Influence Participation

Political scientists have identified a number of factors that affect individuals' perceptions of the costs and benefits of participation, and therefore the likelihood that they will participate when presented with the opportunity. These include personal factors, legal factors, the political environment, and mobilization. Many of the factors we discuss below are related, and it is important for political scientists to take all into account when attempting to determine the impact of each.

Personal factors have a critical impact on participation.

By a wide margin, the most important personal factor influencing political participation is **socioeconomic status** (SES). This factor has turned up as a highly significant predictor of participation in study after study, election after election. SES influences participation directly, but also through its impact on other factors that influence participation.

Socioeconomic status SES is usually measured as a combination of an individual's occupation, income, and education levels. Someone with a high-ranking professional position, a high income, and an advanced education has a high socioeconomic status. Someone who has a low socioeconomic status has a poor education, minimal specialized skills, and a job with low earnings.

Why should occupation level have an impact on political participation? In a high-level professional position, one normally cultivates the skills of writing, speaking, analyzing, and organizing. These skills translate quite handily into the political arena, where political activists often have to speak, write, persuade others, think on their feet, and organize events and individuals. To someone with these **civic skills**, the costs of political participation will seem lower. So, the more advanced one's occupational level, the more likely one is to have the skills that make participation easier, and the more likely one is to participate in politics, other things being equal.

A large income clearly makes one type of political participation less costly—contributing money to political campaigns. Moreover, a substantial income also may bring one in contact with certain institutions—philanthropies, social clubs, and civic organizations—in which discussion of and participation in politics are common. Being steeped in politics in this fashion can lower the cost of participation, both by making it easier to understand the political world and by helping to develop the skills that make political participation seem less daunting.

Education is not only the most important component of SES, it is one of the most important determinants of political participation generally. For one thing, education tends to give people access to better jobs and to more income. And, as shown, those kinds of jobs, coupled with more money, can help increase participation by lowering its costs. The classroom also provides instruction and practice in the skills critical for taking part in political life—reading, writing, speaking, organizing, and critical thinking. So the better educated an individual is, the better developed these skills usually are, and the less costly participation seems. Lastly, a more advanced education level increases the likelihood that an individual has gained enough understanding of politics and government to believe that he or she can influence what happens in the political world, developing a sense of **political efficacy**.[10]

These qualities affect one's perception of the costs and benefits of political participation. Greater interest in politics results in more satisfaction from political activity. This is just another way of saying that more education brings greater benefit from political participation than less education. A sense of political efficacy also raises an individual's assessment of the benefits of participation. The more effective and influential you feel, the more likely you are to believe that your participation will result in some collective benefit you value. Finally, the knowledge about politics that education brings can help reduce the costs of getting involved. If your education has made you conversant in political and policy issues, you can more readily participate in politics than someone with less education.

Personal factors and voting behavior In addition to socioeconomic status, civic skills, political efficacy, political interest, and political knowledge, a few other personal qualities can affect political participation. These include strength of political partisanship, age, and having intense feelings on particular issues, such as abortion or the death penalty.

The particular case of voting behavior demonstrates just how important some of these personal factors can be in determining who gets involved in politics and who does not. Table 8-2 indicates rates of voter turnout in 2004 among groups of individuals with varying personal characteristics. The first characteristic, education, is among the most important determinants of participation, because it has both direct and indirect effects. Notice that someone with a college diploma or an advanced degree is about twice as likely to vote as someone with less than a high-school education. Income also shows a strong relationship with an individual's propensity to vote. From the lowest income group to the next income group, the

Table 8-2. Older, More Educated, and More Partisan Voters Were More Likely to Vote in 2004

PERSONAL QUALITIES OR CHARACTERISTICS	PERCENT WHO REPORTED VOTING IN 2004
Education	
Grade School/Some High School	51
High School Diploma	61
Some College, No Degree	80
College Diploma or Advanced Degree	93
Income	
0 to 16 percentile	56
17 to 33 percentile	68
34 to 67 percentile	82
68 to 95 percentile	90
96 to 100 percentile	89
Age	
29 and under	65
30–45	74
46–61	83
62–77	85
78 and over	71
Partisanship	
Democrats (incl. leaners)	76
Independents and Apoliticals	48
Republicans (incl. leaners)	84
Ideology	
Liberals	82
Moderates	76
Conservatives	85
Region	
South	69
Non-south	80

Source: The American National Election Studies, "The ANES Guide to Public Opinion and Electoral Behavior," The American National Election Studies, http://www.electionstudies.org/nesguide/2ndtable/t6a_2_2.htm (accessed April 27, 2008)

probability of voting jumps by almost 20 percentage points. And among those in the highest income groups, nearly 90 percent turn out to vote on Election Day.

Note also the significance of political efficacy. In assessing political efficacy, political scientists ask about an individual's agreement with statements such as the following: "Sometimes politics and government seem so complicated that a person like me can't really understand what's going on." Through a series of such questions, individuals can demonstrate low, medium, or high political efficacy. Those levels of efficacy tend to affect voter turnout. As Table 8-2 illustrates, in the 2004 election, individuals with a medium level of political efficacy were about 12 percentage points more likely to vote than those with a low level of efficacy. Similarly, individuals with high political efficacy were roughly 8 percentage points more likely to vote than those with medium political efficacy. Related to efficacy is citizen interest in politics. Individuals who reported that they were interested in politics and government "most of the time" were nearly 50 percent more likely to vote than those who were interested "hardly at all."

Finally, note in Table 8-2 the importance of party identification, or party ID, the strength of one's attachment to one of the two major political parties. Citizens who strongly identify with either the Democratic or Republican parties are 33 percentage points more likely to vote than citizens who consider themselves pure independents. In between these two groups are individuals who say they are independent but tend to lean toward one of the parties, and individuals who say that they identify with one of the two parties, but only weakly. Thus, according to these statistics, turnout increases across the spectrum from pure independents, to independent leaners, to weak partisans, to strong partisans. Citizens with strong partisan attachments are more likely to believe that they will enjoy meaningful benefits if their candidate wins, or that they will lose such benefits if their candidate loses. Therefore, the stronger the partisanship, the greater the perceived benefits, and the greater the likelihood of voting on Election Day.

Legal factors affect the cost of participation.

As the description of literacy tests at the outset of this chapter demonstrated, legal factors can make it more or less costly to participate in politics, particularly to vote. In the United States, **suffrage**, the right to vote, has become available to all citizens relatively recently. At various points in U.S. history, wealth, gender, race, age, and property ownership have all served as voting qualifications. Until the 1820s most men who did not own land, regardless of their race or ethnicity, were prohibited from voting. Although allowed to vote in some states before its passage, women were not allowed the right to vote by federal law until passage of the Nineteenth Amendment in 1920. Many African Americans were effectively barred from voting in a large segment of the country until passage of the **Voting Rights Act of 1965**. Young people in the 18- through 20-year-old age range were not allowed to vote until passage of the Twenty-sixth Amendment in 1970.[11] Today, convicted felons and non-citizens are the only remaining groups of adults to whom voting rights have been denied. Thirty-two states maintain some manner of prohibition on the casting of ballots by felons, and non-citizens are universally excluded from the franchise, with the exception of a limited number of municipal and school-board elections.[12]

Even for adults who can vote, however, the United States is rare among democracies in that voting is a two-step process. All states except North Dakota require that citizens register to vote before they cast a ballot. Registration requirements vary from state to state. In some states, citizens can register at the polls on

Election Day. In those states, turnout rates tend to be higher. But in those places where an individual has to register 10, 20, or 30 days before an election, a voter who becomes interested late in the campaign—the point when most campaigns actually *get* interesting—will be unable to cast a ballot. States that allow early voting or make it easier to vote absentee by mail when a voter cannot make it to the polls will also tend to see higher turnout.

In general, over time the movement has been toward a reduction in the legal barriers to registration and voting. For example, thanks to the efforts of political parties, civic groups, and the courts, registration offices are now required to stay open during standard business hours. Also, since the passage of Motor Voter legislation in 1993, citizens are allowed to register by mail and at many different government offices (including motor vehicle agencies, which gave the law its nickname). Furthermore, the maximum number of days before an election that one must register is now 30 days, rather than 60 or 90 days, which had been the deadlines in some states.

CaseStudy: Did Motor Voter Work?

On May 20, 1993, President Clinton signed into law the National Voter Registration Act, more commonly known as "Motor Voter." The legislation had been delayed for years by Republicans in Congress, and was even vetoed once by President George H.W. Bush. But with the change in administrations in 1993, the long-delayed bill became the law of the land.

The Motor Voter law stipulated that in addition to their existing registration methods, states were required to allow voters to register for federal elections:

- at the same time they applied for an original or renewal driver's license;
- at all offices that provide public assistance or services to persons with disabilities; and
- by mail, using a standardized form provided by the Federal Election Commission.

In lieu of making these changes, a handful of states were allowed to adopt procedures in which people could register to vote on the day of an election.

The Motor Voter law became effective January 1, 1995. The first federal election in the wake of Motor Voter took place in 1996. In opposing Motor Voter, Republicans had argued that making registration easier was an invitation to vote fraud. Critics of the GOP, however, saw a less civically minded motivation. They argued that Republicans feared the consequences of expanding the registration rolls to new voters, particularly to low-income and disabled voters, who would be expected to support the Democratic Party. If this was what Republicans were afraid

of, the 1996 election did not give them much cause for alarm. Although President Clinton was reelected, turnout in 1996 was down substantially from 1992—49 percent, versus 55.2 percent just four years earlier and reaching a new modern low.

These statistics do not necessarily mean that Motor Voter failed to work. Ease of registration is only one among a variety of factors that can influence individuals' decisions about whether or not to vote. It may be that Motor Voter actually did bring new voters to the polls, but that other factors acted to suppress collective turnout.

We do know for certain that there was a substantial increase in voter *registration* between the 1992 and 1996 elections. More than 41 million registration applications were processed in 1995 and 1996. By the time of the presidential vote in 1996, the overall registration rate for the voting-age population had reached 73 percent, the highest level ever. State motor vehicle agencies were responsible for about one-third of the increase in voter registration applications.[13]

An increase in voter registration, however, does not necessarily bring new voters to the polls on Election Day. This could happen, for example, if the new voters who were registered were those whose personal characteristics, or whose political environment or likelihood of mobilization, made them highly unlikely to show up on Election Day. In fact, the decline in turnout in 1996 would suggest that the actual effects of Motor Voter were minimal.

Two studies employing sophisticated statistical techniques confirm this conclusion. At most, the influence of

Motor Voter was to make the decline in turnout about 3 percentage points smaller than it otherwise would have been. The lower estimate is that it had no effect at all.[14] Furthermore, if the Motor Voter law did have any impact, it was not through the availability of voter registration at state agencies. The federal government gave states the option of implementing Election Day registration at polling places rather than offering agency-based registration. The states that did so were the ones primarily responsible for limiting the turnout decreases.[15] Election Day registration, therefore, may be a more promising reform than the broader "Motor Voter" changes.

Finally, both studies show that Republicans' concerns about a change in the composition of the electorate favoring the Democrats were unfounded. If anything, the electorate became somewhat more supportive of Republicans than one would have expected in the absence of Motor Voter.

Note, however, that three presidential elections and three midterm elections have been held since the two research studies described above were completed. Thus, it remains to be seen whether Motor Voter will have more significant long-run effects than it did in the first election following implementation.

ThinkingCritically

1. Looking forward, how do you expect the costs of political participation to change in the next 10, 20 or 30 years? What impact will this have on political participation?

2. Identify reforms that federal and local government should enact in order to increase political participation. Explain how your reforms will accomplish your goal.

The political environment also influences voter turnout decisions.

In addition to personal and legal factors, the nature of the candidates, campaigns, and issues in an election year can also influence who turns out to vote. As noted above, people who have stronger attachments to one of the parties are more likely to participate in politics. Imagine, for example, that one of the issues in a political campaign is a proposed reduction in state and federal student loan funds. No doubt many students would have intense feelings about this issue, mostly in opposition. Those students would perceive a substantial benefit, then, in making sure this reduction did not take place. That benefit would give them added incentive to cast a ballot.

A similar phenomenon takes place every election year, primarily at the state level. About half of the states have a process for putting issues directly on the ballot for consideration and approval or rejection by voters. In November of 1996, for example, California voters approved Proposition 209, which prohibited government agencies, colleges, and public schools from using affirmative action procedures when making purchasing, hiring, or admissions decisions. And as noted in Chapter 1, in 2004 11 states had measures on their ballots that sought to ban same-sex marriage. Research has shown that states with this kind of referendum tend to have higher turnout than those without such a process.[16] The presence of specific issues on the ballot apparently can induce some citizens to perceive benefits in participation that they might not otherwise see.

Similarly, the presence on the ballot of more interesting or important races and candidates can also boost turnout. A race for president, governor, or U.S. Senate tends to increase turnout.[17] The potential benefits of a victory or defeat for George W. Bush or John Kerry in the 2004 contest for president apparently seem larger than in a race for, say, state mine inspector (an elective position in Arizona). Having appealing, attractive, or even "star quality" choices on the ballot also appears to elevate turnout.[18] Voters seem to find politics more interesting, and therefore more worth their time, when they can vote for a candidate with the "star power" of Arnold Schwarzenegger or John F. Kennedy.

Some research has shown, too, that elections that are perceived to be close will boost turnout.[19] Close elections stimulate more intense campaign activity and media coverage, which provides voters with more information about the campaign. Furthermore, citizens are more likely to discuss politics among themselves when an election is close. In the months preceding the 2004 presidential contest, newspapers, Internet sites, and news broadcasts were full of stories about the battle between Bush and Kerry as ads saturated the airways and as the candidates barnstormed around the country. Citizens who typically do not talk about politics told various survey organizations that they were interested and engaged in the presidential election. This was especially the case in competitive or "battleground" states. These states, which drew most of the candidates' attention, produced higher turnout than states that were not as close and crucial to the respective campaigns. With all the attention and conversation about the race, especially in battleground states, citizens could more easily access the information they needed and wanted in order to vote. Close elections can also convince voters that their individual vote will "count," increasing their perception that their vote may influence the outcome and, thus, determine whether they receive benefits.

Mobilization efforts increase turnout.

Mobilization efforts, often dubbed **GOTV (get-out-the-vote)** are activities by candidates, political parties, activists, interest groups, friends, and co-workers to induce others to participate in politics. These efforts can include phone calls, personal visits, mailings, and even transportation to the polls on Election Day. If you have ever been called the night before an election and urged to vote, or had someone stop you outside the library and ask you to sign a petition, you have been the target of mobilization efforts. In the 2000 election, those who reported being contacted by a party or campaign worker were 29 percentage points more likely to cast a ballot than those who were not contacted.[20]

Mobilization can increase participation in three ways. First, mobilization efforts tend to provide information about the relevant candidates and issues, making it easier for people to learn what they need to know in order to get involved. For example, in addition to simply asking you to help organize a community meeting on local crime, a neighbor would probably give you some background on the issue and tell you what a local meeting might accomplish. Second, mobilization efforts lower the costs of participation by providing information to individuals on exactly how to carry out the activity—where and when to vote, how to get to the rally, how to sign up to be heard at the committee hearing, and so on. In states with early and absentee voting, mobilizers can arrange for ballots to be sent to citizens at home. Third, mobilization brings implicit social rewards for those who agree to participate, and possibly negative consequences for those who do not. Individuals who get involved in politics at the behest of others will enjoy the gratitude and esteem of those who asked them to participate.[21] This benefit can be very important, considering that these individuals are often co-workers, neighbors, or fellow parishioners.

Typically, the mobilization efforts of Democrats and Republicans have taken different directions, based on their assumptions about their voters. Democrats have usually focused efforts on voters with somewhat lower SES, whereas Republicans have tended to mobilize suburbanites, church members, and hunters. In the 2004 election, both parties and their supporters were engaged in massive mobilization and GOTV efforts along these lines. Typically, Democrats have focused more of their energies on mobilizing their voters with the assumption that their voters—

Table 8-3 Contacting Government Officials Tops List of Non-Voting Political Behavior

ACTIVITY	PERCENTAGE ASKED	PERCENTAGE OF THOSE ASKED WHO SAY YES
Campaign work	12	48
Campaign contribution	22	27
Contact government officials	29	57
Protest	11	28
Community activity	19	50

Source: Sidney Verba, Kay Shlozman, and Henry Brady, *Voice and Equality* (Boston: Harvard University Press, 2006), p. 135

who, on average, have lower SES than Republican voters—needed more of a push to get to the polls. And in 2004 groups supporting John Kerry, such as Americans Coming Together, spent tens of millions of dollars in a handful of battleground states like Ohio. But the Republicans also put together an extensive field organization to identify, register, and mobilize their likely voters.

How common an occurrence is mobilization in American political life? In a typical year, between 10 and 30 percent of American adults will be asked by someone else to participate in some non-voting form of political activity (see Table 8-3). Of those who are asked, anywhere between 27 and 57 percent actually agree to participate.

Where people are asked to participate is also interesting. You might expect requests to come primarily from those who interact regularly—co-workers, for example. Survey data indicate, however, that the workplace is actually the *least* common setting for mobilization. Membership organizations and churches tend to be the more common location of choice for political mobilizers.

Finally, how close a relationship usually exists between two people in order for one to ask the other to get involved in a political issue? Figure 8-2 addresses that

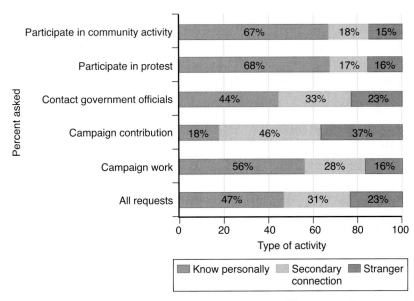

Figure 8-2. Personal Connections Are Most Effective in Encouraging Political Participation.

Source: Sidney Verba, Kay Shlozman, and Henry Brady, *Voice and Equality* (Boston: Harvard University Press, 2006), p. 135

question. For adult Americans who report having been asked to participate in various political activities, note the percentage of requests that came from: someone they knew personally; a secondary connection, that is, a "friend of a friend," or someone they did not know but whose name they recognized; or a complete stranger.

The higher effectiveness of contacts from people with a personal connection was demonstrated in the 2004 election. The Democratic Party and its allies in the labor unions largely relied on paid staff to conduct GOTV efforts. The Republican Party and the Bush campaign relied on volunteers. After the election, many Democrats admitted that they were surprised by the effectiveness of the GOP efforts, and one union head praised the "neighbor-to-neighbor" voter mobilization program that the GOP ran in 2004 and contrasted it with the "stranger-to-stranger" program run by Democratic allies.

Finally, note that mobilization efforts tend to add to the already substantial influence of socioeconomic status in determining participation. If you wanted to have someone help advance a political issue you cared about, you would be smart to pick someone with developed civic skills and a high-prestige job; someone with substantial amounts of money to give to the cause; someone with access to clubs and charities full of other people with money; and someone with a good education and all of the knowledge, skills, and confidence that education brings with it. In other words, you would ask a high-SES individual. In fact, high-SES individuals are the ones most likely to be asked to participate in political activities. So, even though individuals who enjoy high socioeconomic status are more likely to participate in politics in the first place, they are also prime targets for mobilization campaigns.

Comparative and Historical Puzzles of Voter Turnout

American rates of voter turnout lag behind those in a handful of Western European countries (see Figure 8.1). Expanding the list of countries to include Canada, Japan, New Zealand, and Iceland yields the same result. Among the 21 countries that would be included in this list, American voter turnout would rank next-to-last in recent years. Only the Swiss vote at lower levels.

Voter registration requirements top the list of reasons for America's low voting rate.

Why does America's voter turnout lag so far behind other democracies? Answering this question is somewhat of a challenge because comparable data on some variables are unavailable from one country to the next. Still, some important explanations are obvious.

Registration regulations First, as explained, voter registration requirements in the United States significantly depress turnout in comparison with other countries, where voter registration is a government responsibility and the registration process is effortless and cost-free.[22] The United States has a personal registration requirement, meaning that Americans are responsible for registering themselves to vote. Like buying a car, this is something most people do infrequently and so are less likely to know how to do it. Some Americans, therefore, forget to register or do not realize that they need to; others attempt to do so but fail to comply with state regulations; and others try to register but give up in frustration over the process. As a result, tens of millions of Americans who are otherwise eligible to vote cannot do so, simply because they have not registered.

The personal registration requirement has significant consequences for voter turnout. Fully 30 percent of Americans who could register to vote have not done so and are thus not eligible to cast ballots. Among registered voters in the United States, turnout is about 85 percent in presidential election years, a rate that is respectable in comparison with other western democracies.[23] But in midterm elections this percentage drops to 69 percent. On the basis of this comparison, then, it appears that if the United States were to adopt a European-style voter registration system, participation in American elections would come closer to matching that in other countries.

Election scheduling Another legal factor with implications for U.S. voter turnout is the way elections are conducted. In America, elections are held on a single day—a Tuesday—during which voters are expected to find time to participate amidst their other personal and professional activities. In other democracies, elections are sometimes held over a multi-day period, or on weekends. Election days in other countries may also be declared national holidays, so that voters have the time they need to attend to their civic obligations. All of these considerations may affect participation.

Some political scientists believe that Americans suffer voting fatigue, based on the frequency with which they are asked to go to the polls. If citizens are required to vote too often, they may see less urgency in each election and be less inclined to turn out. In many democracies, voters go the polls no more than two or three times over a four-year period. In the United States, by contrast, national elections are held every two years, and state, city, county, school-related, and special elections may be held in between. Furthermore, each election campaign may consist of both a party-level (primary) and a general election. Complicating matters, Americans also must vote on many more offices and issues than their counterparts in other countries. Some European countries, for example, do not have or do not frequently use the ballot initiative process in which citizens vote directly on legislation (instead of just leaving such votes to elected legislators). Furthermore, many democracies have far fewer elected offices and far more appointed offices than the United States. As a result of both the frequency and the complexity of U.S. elections, then, the investment required to be an active voter in the United States is substantially more than in other countries.

Plurality decisions The way votes are counted and apportioned in America also may depress voter turnout. Elections in the United States are predominantly plurality, or winner-take-all, affairs. Decision by plurality means that the candidate who receives the most votes wins the seat being contested; all other candidates lose. Imagine that you are a liberal Democrat living in Orange County, California, a bastion of conservative politics. In election after election, your district sends Republicans to Congress. You show up faithfully to vote in every election, but your candidate, the Democrat, always loses. Under the circumstances, it would not be surprising if you concluded, "Why bother?"

Many foreign countries have a proportional representation system in which a party's share of legislative seats is proportionate to its share of votes. In such a system, even if the party you vote for finishes in second place or worse, it will likely win some seats in the legislature. As a voter, this system gives you an incentive to vote; at least some candidates of the party you favor can win seats, even if your party does not get the most votes. The net effect of this procedure is to increase the benefits of voting.

The two-party system Finally, the U.S. system has only two major political parties, and two relatively centrist parties at that, both of them battling within the confines of the American creed. This situation may also result in lower rates of voter turnout. In multi-party parliamentary systems, the parties have more narrowly focused agendas and closer links to population groups. For example, in many European countries, environmentalists can find a comfortable home in various Green parties, which are devoted almost exclusively to environmental issues. In the United States, by contrast, voters who are very environmentally conscious have to choose between Republicans and Democrats, neither of which places environmental politics at the center of their agendas. Thus, in a multi-party system, voters may feel that their vote can help deliver the specific kinds of collective benefits that interest them most. Naturally, this perception gives them a greater incentive to turn out on Election Day.

The 2004 national elections in the United States and in Spain illustrate this phenomenon. In the United States, the leadership of both the Democratic and Republican parties had agreed that the U.S. military must stay in Iraq and "finish the job," that is, ensure that stability and democracy had taken hold. In the Spanish election, however, the two major parties differed dramatically on this issue. The Partido Popular, a center-right party not unlike the Republican Party in the United States, committed to keeping Spanish troops in Iraq to help usher in a new Iraqi government. But the Partido Socialista Obrero Español (PSOE), the Spanish socialist party, vowed to quit Spain's current Iraq policy and bring home Spanish troops immediately. PSOE consistently trailed in the pre-election polling and few thought they had any chance of winning the contest in Spain. Still, when Islamic terrorists struck a central Madrid train station just days before the election, voter turnout surged and Spanish voters handed an unexpected victory to the PSOE. Within a matter of weeks, all of Spain's troops serving in Iraq were brought home.

A variety of other factors might explain the turnout differential between the United States and other countries. Just remember two main points: First, the structure of America's government and election system tends to make casting a ballot more costly here than in other democracies. Second and specifically, the single largest determinant of the relatively low rate of American turnout in comparison with other countries is America's uniquely onerous voter registration system.

Despite increases in education and the legal ease of voting, turnout has dropped since 1960.

In the close and hotly contested 1960 presidential race between Richard Nixon and John F. Kennedy, over three-fifths of eligible Americans cast their ballots. In an equally competitive presidential race in 2000 between George W. Bush and Al Gore, only about half of all eligible Americans voted. In the 40 years between those two elections, voter turnout declined (see Figure 8-3). While there were rises in the 1992 and 2004 elections, a smaller proportion of Americans vote now than did 40 years ago. The low point in this time period came in 1996, when fewer than half of those who could cast a ballot chose to do so.

A similar voter-turnout pattern emerges in midterm elections. Although there is no presidential race in midterm elections, all 435 House of Representatives seats

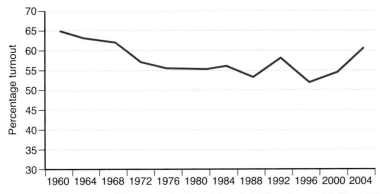

Figure 8-3. Voter Turnout in Presidential Elections, 1960–2004. Voter
turnout in presidential elections declined after 1960, but has shown an
upturn in recent years.

Source: John Woolley and Gerard Peter. American Presidency Project. "Voter Turnout in
Presidential Elections." http://www.presidency.ucsb.edu/data/turnout.php accessed April 28,
2008

are up for election, along with one-third of Senate seats and more than thirty state
governorships. Turnout in these contests has declined by 11 percentage points in
the last 40 years (see Figure 8-4).

This decline in voter turnout has been one of the most intensely studied puzzles in American politics. What makes the decrease particularly curious is that two
factors that are strongly correlated with turnout—education and legal restrictions—have changed in ways that should have boosted turnout.

Americans have higher levels of education now than they did 40 years ago. In
1960, for example, only 41 percent of Americans had a high-school education. In
2000, the proportion of Americans who had graduated high school had increased
to 84 percent.[24] Furthermore, as noted earlier, legal restrictions on voting have
become less burdensome. The poll tax was abolished by the Twenty-fourth
Amendment to the Constitution in 1964, and literacy tests were eliminated via the
Voting Rights Act of 1965 and its revisions in 1970. Finally, the passage of the

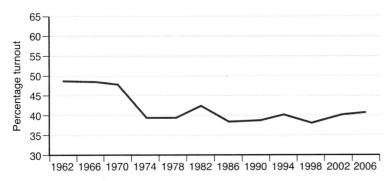

Figure 8-4. Midterm Election Turnout, 1962–2006. Midterm election
turnout has also declined over the last forty years. In the 1962 midterm
elections, 47 percent of eligible Americans cast ballots. In the 2002
midterm elections, only 36 percent cast a ballot.

Source: Curtis Gans, "Bush, Iraq Propel Modest Turnout Increase Ending 12-Year Republican
Revolution. Dems Higher than GOP for First Time Since 1990," American University News,
November 9, 2006, http://www.american.edu/ia/cdem/csae/pdfs/csae061109.pdf

Motor Voter Act in 1993 made voter registration forms available in scores of government offices and agencies, and in recent years, restrictions on voter registration and use of mail-in and absentee ballots were eased to make registration and voting a simpler, more inclusive process.

According to one study, given the increase in levels of education and the easing of registration and voting laws, turnout should have risen by close to 5 percentage points. Instead, turnout declined by 14 percentage points from 1960 to 1988.[25] How, then, can we explain the 14 percentage point drop in turnout at the same time it was expected to increase?

Many reasons work in concert to explain the drop in turnout.

One explanation for the drop in turnout is that the electorate expanded with the ratification of the Twenty-sixth Amendment in 1970. The net impact of enfranchising millions of 18- to 20-year-olds—granting them the right to vote—was to decrease the proportion of Americans voting. Why? Because the electorate was expanded to include young people, and because young people are less likely to vote than older people, the net effect of the Twenty-sixth Amendment was to decrease voter turnout. Some scholars have calculated that the enfranchisement of 18- to 20-year-olds caused a 3-percentage-point decline in turnout rates.[26] Others have argued that the turnout rate in the United States is measured incorrectly (an argument we discussed in *How Do We Know?*). If you correct for this, these scholars argue that the lowering of the voting age explains almost all the drop in turnout that we have seen since the early 1970s.

Other factors that relate to voting, such as the political attitudes and attachments discussed above, can also explain part of the decline in turnout. As shown in Figures 8-5, Americans have lower levels of political efficacy, lower levels of trust in

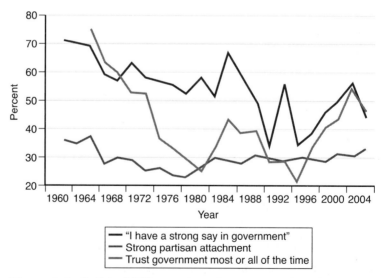

Figure 8-5. Political Efficacy, Attachment to Political Parties and Trust in Government Have Declined over the Last 40 Years, 1960–2004.

Source: The American National Election Studies, "The NES Guide to Public Opinion and Electoral Behavior," http://www.electionstudies.org/nesguide/ gd-index.htm#6

government, and are less attached to political parties today than they were 40 years ago. Taken together, these factors may account for as much as three-quarters of the decline in turnout since 1960.[27]

Another study invokes the mobilization factor and argues that fewer people are voting because fewer are being urged to vote. However, National Election Studies data presented in two different studies indicate that, on the whole, mobilization by political parties increased between 1960 and 1982, and increased again after 1992.[28]

If levels of party mobilization have not declined noticeably in the past four decades, perhaps something about the nature of mobilization has changed. Scholars have speculated, for instance, that the quality of mobilization may have declined in recent decades. Whereas in the past mobilization meant friends, neighbors, and committed volunteers canvassing in person, today voter mobilization operations are often conducted by professional consultants and phone banks. It seems reasonable to believe that a contact from a friend, neighbor, or volunteer was likely to be more effective than a computerized phone call from an anonymous telemarketer at a phone bank. More research needs to be done on this theory, but the initial research shows strong potential.[29]

One final, and promising, explanation for the decline in voter turnout is that over time, Americans have been interacting with each other less and less outside of work. This steady decrease in "social connectedness" is manifested in declining church attendance, declining participation in civic and membership organizations, the sharp decrease in labor union membership, and the drop-off in social activities with families and friends.

Several arguments suggest how social connectedness plays into decisions about voting. First, the more connections an individual has with others, the more likely he or she is in a position to mobilize and to be mobilized. Second, social connectedness may help individuals see greater meaning and consequence in the outcome of an election, which is another inducement to vote.[30] Third, social involvement can also reduce information costs by facilitating the sharing of information relevant to politics.[31]

Scholars disagree about the extent to which social connectedness might affect turnout. In addition, there is little consensus about how to measure social connectedness, or about the precise mechanisms whereby connectedness influences political behavior. As with the study of the quality of political mobilization, these questions remain fertile areas of inquiry.

Who Gets Heard? Does It Matter?

Just below the surface of this discussion lies an important and disconcerting fact of American political life: participation in the political process is not equal among American citizens. As we well know, income, education, political attitudes, and opportunities for mobilization are not uniformly distributed across the demographic spectrum. Men and women; young and old; black, white, and Hispanic; wealthy and poor; and Republicans and Democrats all differ among the factors that help determine participation. The result is that these groups participate in American politics to very different degrees.

Political participation differs considerably across demographic categories.

Consider the different rates of participation according to race (see Figure 8-6). Whites tend to participate to a greater extent than both blacks and Latinos, except in campaign work, protests, and community activity. Latinos, on the other hand, are not the most involved group in any of the activities indicated in the figure. They are second to whites in terms of their frequency of serving as board members. Except for that category, however, they show the lowest rates of participation among the three groups.

Expanding this analysis to other demographic categories, it would quickly become clear that those who participate in American politics tend to be whiter, older, wealthier, better educated, more likely male, and more conservative than the populace at large. This fact has led some observers to complain that the American political system does not live up to its ideals—for example, that all have an equal say in government—and that it caters disproportionately to the needs and demands of an unrepresentative portion of the population.

Considering broad demographic categories, some of those needs and demands would appear to differ significantly from one group to the next. Table 8-4 compares opinions between whites and blacks on a variety of policy issues. The opinion difference between blacks and whites in each issue area is substantial—between 24 and 36 percentage points. Thus, if blacks are being under-represented in the political process and whites are being over-represented, that difference may have significant implications for which opinions are being aired among policymakers.

Political participation also differs considerably according to another demographic category, age (see Table 8-5). Note substantial differences in the participation and the opinions of Americans under the age of 30 and those 55 and older. In all political activities, seniors participate at significantly higher rates than younger cohorts. And in virtually every issue, older Americans support the more conserva-

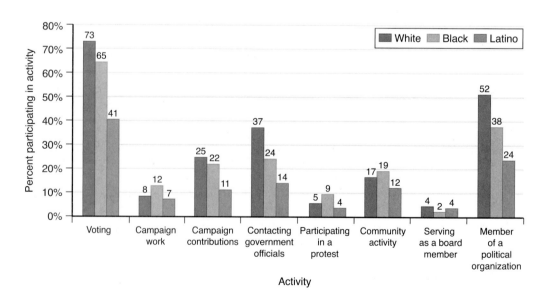

Figure 8-6. Across the Board, White Americans Are More Likely to Take Part in Political Activity

Source: Sidney Verba, Kay Shlozman, and Henry Brady, *Voice and Equality* (Boston: Harvard University Press, 2006), p. 233

Table 8-4. The Opinions of Black and White Americans Differ Significantly on Important Issues

ISSUE	WHITES	BLACKS	DIFFERENCE
Government should make every effort to improve the economic and social condition of blacks and other minorities	17%	47%	30%
Due to past discrimination blacks should be given preferences in hiring and promotion	11%	44%	33%
Affirmative action programs needed "as long as there are no rigid quotas"	43%	79%	36%
Government should provide more services and increase spending	47%	65%	18%
Government should guarantee food and shelter	62%	80%	18%
Favor death penalty for those convicted of murder	77%	45%	32%
War in Iraq was not worth fighting	38%	74%	36%
Government collects too much information about people like me	54%	74%	20%

Source: Robert S. Erikson and Kent L. Tedin, *American Public Opinion* (New York: Pearson Education, 2005), p. 201–03

tive position. In the most extreme example, older Americans support increased student loans at a rate 23 percentage points lower than their younger counterparts.

One could expand this analysis to other groups—the working class and the upper class, different religious groups, and so on. It would likely become obvious that different demographic groups sometimes hold very different opinions on policy issues. This fact, combined with differential rates of political participation,

Table 8-5. Younger and Older Americans Have Differing Attitudes on Various Issues

ISSUE	UNDER 30	55 AND OVER	DIFFERENCE
Government should provide more services, even if it means increased spending	63%	45%	18%
Favor government versus private medical insurance	57%	40%	17%
Favor allowing Social Security funds invested in stock market	74%	49%	25%
Increase spending on student loans	70%	42%	28%
Homeowners should not refuse to sell home to someone because of race	79%	54%	25%
Marijuana should be made legal	35%	17%	12%
Allow same-sex marriage	50%	22%	28%
Allow abortion for any reason	40%	28%	12%
U.S. should decrease military spending	27%	12%	15%
War in Iraq was not worth the cost	67%	58%	9%
Liberal	39%	21%	18%
Moderate	37%	33%	4%
Conservative	24%	46%	22%

Source: Robert S. Erikson and Kent L. Tedin, *American Public Opinion* (New York: Pearson Education, 2005), p. 208

raises the concern that not all voices and positions get the hearing they deserve in America.

If demographic groups participated in proportion to their percentage in the population, *collective* opinion would change little.

A number of researchers have attempted to determine the message that policymakers would hear from the American public if various demographic groups were to participate in proportion to their percentage of the population. They have analyzed, for example, the extent to which the message communicated to policymakers would differ if African Americans, who constitute approximately 12 percent of the population, also constituted 12 percent of the individuals engaged in various forms of political participation. Researchers have extended this analysis to all major population groups, and have compared opinions among those who actually participate in politics with those who would participate if all groups participated at rates equal to their population percentages.

When researchers construct a hypothetical public such as this, equal in its proportions to the demographic groups in the population at large, that public holds only a mildly more liberal set of beliefs than the actual participating public. But how can this be, given the very sharp differences in opinion shown above? In general, the groups that tend to be most under-represented also tend to be small. African Americans and the poor, for example, each constitute no more than about one-seventh of the American public. Thus, even if they were to participate at full strength, it would be hard for them to change *collective* opinion considerably. However, they certainly could gain influence at the margin in some very competitive congressional districts and states.

Other groups are under-represented as well, such as women. However, their opinions tend to align more closely with the groups that are over-represented. So again, even if women were to participate in politics at rates equivalent to their population percentages, they would not dramatically change opinion.

The most persuasive critique of this conclusion comes from those who argue that comparing responses to survey questions between political participants and non-participants is not the best approach. After all, one does not write a letter to a public official requesting "more services and increased spending," which would be a typical survey question. Usually, an individual's interests in policy are very specific. When it comes to these more specific policy preferences, the distortion created by under-representation of some groups may be far more significant than the survey data indicate.

Another difficulty with opinion comparisons based on surveys is that they fail to indicate the different issue agendas that different groups might bring before government. Imagine that the wealthy and the poor had precisely the same opinions on school voucher programs—programs that provide government funds for parents to send their children to private school. This might provide some comfort to those who worry that the poor are under-represented in politics and the wealthy over-represented. But imagine further that a federal voucher program is the number-one priority for the poor, and at the bottom of the list for the wealthy. The wealthy are unlikely to bring this issue to the attention of policymakers, while the poor would do so if they were actively participating. In politics, as we discuss in chapters on public opinion and interest groups, who controls the agenda is a vitally important question.

Does participation matter?

This discussion about differential participation rates is entirely academic if participation does not influence the decisions that policymakers make. Does participation matter?

Considered at the level of the individual, it would be hard to argue that participation matters much. As noted above, the impact of an individual's participation in politics is minimal. Someone engaging in a one-person protest outside of the offices of a business guilty of polluting the environment, or a clinic that provides free contraceptives, or a school that does a poor job educating its students, would be fighting a lonely battle unlikely to succeed. Being the one hundred-thousandth marcher in a demonstration will not materially affect its impact. One would expect these behaviors to have no effective impact. This is part of the paradox of participation.

The collective actions of individuals, though, whether coordinated or not, clearly do have an impact on political outcomes. In the 1932 presidential election, for example, a surge in voter turnout ousted the conservative Herbert Hoover and swept in the progressive New York governor, Franklin D. Roosevelt. This vote was largely a response to the dire economic conditions gripping the country in 1932, the height of the Great Depression. The coalition that came together to support Roosevelt dramatically changed the shape of American public policy in ways that continue to affect the country today through programs such as Social Security, welfare, unemployment compensation, housing assistance, and labor union protections.

Perhaps a less momentous, but equally dramatic, result of participation can be seen in the presidential elections of 2000 and 2004 and the midterm contest in 2006. The result in Florida, and therefore the outcome of the presidential election in 2000, came down to slightly more than 500 votes. If a relative handful of people had voted differently that day, or decided not to vote at all, the result of the election—and perhaps of American history—would have been different. Furthermore, the voting behavior of those few hundred people may have been influenced by others' participation—mobilizing them to vote, for example, or to vote one way rather than the other. Although in 2004 the margin was more decisive, the presidential election again came down to one state and George W. Bush won Ohio and the presidency by a little more than 130,000 votes. Again, the impact of citizen participation in the election was unmistakable and decisive. In 2006, the Democrats took control of the Senate by narrow victories in two states, Virginia (where Democrat James Webb won by about 9,000 votes) and Montana (where Democrat Jon Tester won by 3,500 votes).

The impact of voter participation is also apparent from the election-year activities of political parties and organized interests. For example, the Democratic and Republican parties, as well as their interest group allies, spent tens of millions of dollars on voter mobilization efforts in the 2004 election. The parties and the groups that support them obviously believe that who shows up on Election Day, and how they vote when they show up, can determine an election outcome. Otherwise, why invest such significant resources in get-out-the-vote efforts?

Measuring the impact of non-voting forms of participation, such as contacting elected officials or joining a protest, is more difficult. Often, evidence concerning the impact of such participation is less systematic. That does not necessarily make it less persuasive, however. For example, we know that the Clinton health care plan went down in defeat in 1994. We also know that in the battle leading up to that defeat, opponents of the Clinton plan were much more likely to contact Congress than supporters of the believed plan were. Moreover, many of those active in the fight over Clinton's plan believed that this **grassroots lobbying** was decisive. One key architect of President Clinton's health care policy claimed, "the most effective tactic against our program was grassroots lobbying and phone banks in selected districts."[32]

If grassroots mobilization and phone banks—selectively used—are not effective tactics, that means that the tens of millions of dollars that interest groups spent on those tactics did not work. More broadly speaking, if non-electoral forms of political participation do not matter, we have to ask why millions of individuals and organized interests spend countless dollars and hours participating in politics, and why political insiders routinely report that these non-electoral forms of participation do have an impact. Either participation matters, or those who act as if it matters and those who report that it matters are simply fooling themselves.

Two key examples demonstrate how much participation matters.

We can find examples, of course, in which the impact of non-voting forms of participation is undisputed. As we noted at the beginning of the chapter, extension of the franchise to women and minorities is a relatively new development in this country. Women were not guaranteed a constitutionally protected right to vote until 1920. It took the women's rights movement, which was launched with a convention at Seneca Falls, New York, in 1848, roughly 70 years to achieve this outcome.

In the second half of the nineteenth century, women volunteered in the anti-slavery movement, the temperance movement (advocating the abolition of liquor), the settlement house movement (which provided educational, health, and cultural programs for the urban poor), and assorted organizations promoting better working conditions for women and children. In the course of this work, they came to see the franchise as indispensable in promoting their concerns on a broader scale.

In 1869, therefore, two organizations promoting women's suffrage were founded: The National Woman Suffrage Association (NWSA) and the American Woman Suffrage Association (AWSA). After two decades of pursuing separate agendas, the groups merged in 1890. The new organization was named the National American Woman Suffrage Association (NAWSA). Its leader was Susan B. Anthony.

The suffrage movement was greatly aided by the skills and relationships its female members had built in their fight for prohibition, abolition of slavery, and improved living and working conditions for the poor, women, and children. Women's participation in social clubs, too, strengthened their ties to other women and helped create an organizational base for the movement. Like a snowball rolling downhill, as the suffrage movement began growing in size and success through its victories in securing the franchise at the state level, it was joined by other women's groups. These included the General Federation of Women's Clubs and assorted professional organizations. Eventually, both the size of the movement and its success in securing the franchise at the state level created an irresistible momentum for a constitutional amendment guaranteeing women the right to vote. Congress proposed that amendment in 1919, and it was ratified by the required 36 states in 1920.[33]

The story of the civil rights movement is similar in many respects to the women's suffrage movement. In 1963, there were essentially no federal protections for the voting rights of African Americans. As a result, there was not a single African-American member of the House of Representatives from the South, and only a handful of state and local officials such as mayor or sheriff. In Birmingham, Alabama, thousands hit the streets to protest. By the year 2001, thanks to civil rights legislation and court decisions protected the voting rights of African-Americans, 39 members of the U.S. House of Representatives were African-American, and thousands of black elected officials served at the state and local level. In Birmingham, Alabama, site of the original clashes to attain equality, both the mayor and the sheriff are African Americans. Although there is currently only one black U.S. senator (Barack Obama, from Illinois), African-American votes have been crucial in electing Democratic governors and senators throughout the South. The civil rights movement, a form of mass, non-electoral participation, created irresistible pressure on policymakers to guarantee voting rights to African Americans. With those voting rights in place, African Americans have changed the American political landscape.

Finally, participation also matters in a broader sense than the outcomes it produces on a particular issue. The health of representative democracy demands that citizens choose their leaders, monitor their work, and provide feedback both at the ballot box and through non-electoral forms of participation. This is how Americans must act as responsible stewards of democratic government. Furthermore, the act of citizen participation can be beneficial to the individual citizen. It can provide skills, experience, knowledge, and a sense of efficacy that will enable individuals to play a more active, constructive role in the workplace, the church, and the community—or even in politics.

SUMMARY

- Political participation is the effort to influence what happens in the political world—either by voting or through non-voting activities like joining a political organization or contacting a government official. Many Americans vote even though a rational analysis suggests they will not—this is the paradox of participation. Citizens weigh costs and benefits in deciding whether to vote. As the incremental benefit of one vote is often quite small, a confusing situation arises in which the costs seem to outweigh the benefits of voting. While the paradox of voting remains unresolved, it seems likely that the satisfaction voters receive from performing their civic duty plays some role in encouraging voting.

- The number of Americans participating in politics depends on the activity. Although voting is the type of participation that first comes to mind, citizens can participate in politics in many other ways. Signing petitions,

attending demonstrations, organizing community meetings, joining political membership organizations, volunteering for political campaigns, and contacting elected officials are examples of other sorts of political activity. While Americans tend to vote at lower rates than citizens in other countries, we do tend to engage in these other activities at higher rates.

- Personal factors, legal factors, the political environment, and mobilization efforts are key elements that influence political participation. By a wide margin, the most important personal factor influencing political participation is socioeconomic status. The civic skills it implies make the costs of political participation seem lower, and levels of political efficacy are generally higher for those with higher socioeconomic status. Legal factors, like poll taxes and literacy tests, also played an important role in participation decisions. The twentieth century brought an end to a number of legal barriers that prevented women and African Americans from voting. Further, Motor Voter legislation made voter registration more convenient. The competitiveness of a race, as well as the efficacy of mobilization efforts, also affect participation. The more competitive the race and the more effective the mobilization, the higher the levels of political participation.

▶ There are many comparative and historical puzzles of political participation. One comparative puzzle is the fact that America's voter turnout lags far behind other democracies. Reasons may include America's personal registration requirement—which makes it inconvenient for citizens to register to vote. Other factors may include voter fatigue (due to the relative frequency of American elections), plurality decisions, and the two-party system. On the other hand, the United States has high levels of non-voting political participation relative to other advanced democracies. Historically, the United States is in a puzzling situation: both the costs and levels of participation in the United States have decreased with time.

Participation should increase as costs decrease, but other reasons, including younger eligible voters, decreases in political trust and efficacy, and ineffective mobilization, may explain the puzzle.

▶ Questions of whether political participation matters and whether it affects the decisions of government are particularly important because participation in the political process is not equal across demographic groups. Whites, men, and upper-class individuals tend to have higher levels of participation than their counterparts in nearly every category. Interestingly, however, if demographic groups participated in proportion to their percentage in the population, collective opinion would change very little. This would likely occur because under-represented groups are either relatively small or have opinions similar to the over-represented groups. Finally, while individual participation is unlikely to cause great change, political participation collectively can change the American political landscape in vast and meaningful ways. The women's suffrage movement, the election of FDR, and the civil rights movements are just a few such examples.

KEY TERMS

civic skills, p. 000
collective benefit, p. 000
get-out-the-vote (GOTV), p. 000
grassroots lobbying, p. 000
political efficacy, p. 000

selective benefits, p. 000
socioeconomic status, p. 000
suffrage, p. 000
Voting Rights Act of 1965, p. 000

SUGGESTED READINGS

Steve Rosenstone and Mark Hansen. *Mobilization, Participation, and Democracy in America.* New York: Longman Classics. 2002.

Sidney Verba, Kay Shlozman, and Henry Brady. *Voice and Equality.* Boston: Harvard University Press. 2006.

collective benefit a benefit everyone enjoys, regardless of whether or not they contributed to its attainment.

selective benefits benefits that only those who contributed to their attainment get to enjoy (compare to collective benefits).

socioeconomic status a combination of an individual's occupation, income, and education levels.

civic skills the skills of writing, speaking, analyzing, and organizing that reduce the cost of political participation.

political efficacy an individual's belief that he or she can influence what happens in the political world.

suffrage the right to vote.

Voting Rights Act of 1965 legislation that abolished literacy tests as a requirement to register to vote.

get-out-the-vote (GOTV) term used by campaign professionals to describe the various activities candidates, political parties, activists, and interest groups use to make sure their likely supporters go to the polls on Election Day.

grassroots lobbying efforts to persuade citizens to contact their elected officials regarding a particular issue or piece of legislation.

9 Voting, Elections, and Campaigns

When Americans woke up on the day after the 2000 election, they did not know who their next president would be. The identity of the 43rd president would only become clear more than a month later, when Democratic Vice President Al Gore conceded victory to Republican George W. Bush. Gore's concession speech came 36 days after Election Day. It occurred only after a deeply divided Supreme Court denied Gore a statewide vote recount in Florida.

After all was said and done, a number of people had a lot of explaining to do. Television network executives had to explain why they made not one, but two, mistaken calls in Florida (first calling the state for Gore, then for Bush) before finally saying it was too close to call. Voting machine manufacturers and election officials had to explain the high number of spoiled (uncountable) ballots across the entire country, especially in Florida. The Democratic election supervisor in Palm Beach County, Florida, had to explain the confusing butterfly ballot design, which many voters claimed had caused them to vote unwittingly for independent candidate Pat Buchanan rather than for Democrat Al Gore.

Supreme Court justices had to explain their controversial ruling, which ended the Democrats' legal challenges. And Al Gore had to explain why he had not won the election in a landslide, given his association with eight years of peace and prosperity under the Clinton administration.

Lost among the errant network calls, confusing ballots, and novel legal rulings was another embarrassing fact—embarrassing, at least, for political scientists. Using analysis that had proved to be highly reliable in previous presidential elections, a panel of political scientists at an American Political Science Association conference had uniformly predicted that Gore would beat Bush. Their estimates of Gore's share of the two-party vote (that is, the total number of votes cast for either the Republican or the Democrat, but not for third-party candidates like Ralph Nader) ranged between 53 percent and 60 percent.[1]

Although political scientists had predicted a sizeable Gore popular-vote victory, Gore's actual share of the vote was 49.7 percent, only about half a percent more than George W. Bush.[2] "It's not even going to be close," one had confidently proclaimed.[3] Furthermore, since the popular vote does not decide presidential elections, the election ended with an exceedingly narrow Gore defeat. Obviously, political scientists had some explaining to do as well.

So, what went wrong? The types of analysis used to predict elections differ in some minor ways, but most share some basic characteristics. First, they assume that party identification determines individual vote choice. Citizens tend to identify with one of the two major political parties. When more voters go into an election identifying with one party than another, that party will have an advantage. This helps explain why the political scientists' models predicted a Gore victory in 2000. In that election year, more members of the electorate identified themselves as Democrats than as Republicans.

Second, the models also assume that voters cast their ballots with a retrospective perspective, selecting candidates based on their or their party's past performance, rather than comparing what each candidate would do if elected. The 2000 election came after nearly a decade of robust economic growth, presided over by a Democratic administration. Since voters' retrospective judgments of the Democrats' performance were generally positive, according to political theory, that should have been reflected more widely in the popular vote.

So what happened? Did Al Gore "blow" the election? Or did political scientists "blow" their predictions? In order to answer these questions, this chapter will examine the factors that determine individual vote choice and collective election outcomes—not just party identification and incumbent performance, but also the nature of the candidates' campaigns, their issue positions, and voter assessments of them as individuals, as well as the rules that structure and finance campaigns and elections.

The Basic Rules Governing American Elections

The choices available to voters in America, and the decisions voters ultimately make about who they want their leaders to be, are strongly shaped by the rules governing elections. To understand individual vote choice and collective election outcomes, then, one must understand the rules of American elections. If presidential elections were decided on the basis of the popular vote rather than an Electoral College majority, presidential candidates would probably conduct their campaigns much differently. Furthermore, the rules that govern U.S. elections are different from those in most other democracies around the world. Most parliamentary democracies, for example, employ a system known as proportional representation. In this system, seats in the legislative body are assigned according to each party's vote share. Therefore, a party whose candidates ran a consistent second in every race would still be allocated a significant number of seats in the legislature. Also, in many countries, party leaders or party committees choose the nominees to run in the general election. In Great Britain, for example, if an individual wants to run for Parliament under the Labour Party banner, his or her candidacy must be approved by a small committee of Labour Party leaders or members. Not so in the United States, where a different set of rules decide party nominations for president and other elected offices.

The first objective of a candidate running for office is to receive his or her party's nomination.

Only one candidate can be listed on state ballots as *the* Democratic candidate for president, or a House or Senate seat, and only one as *the* Republican candidate.[4] That is the candidate who receives the party nomination. As a result of running under the party label, that candidate will receive "built-in" support from the party's members in the electorate, and may also get substantial financial and logistical help from the state and national party organizations.

How does a candidate receive the nomination of his or her party? In the presidential race, the candidate does so by successfully accumulating a majority of **delegates**—representatives of the voters—at the party's nominating convention in the summer before the November election. Candidates earn delegates' support primarily by competing in state primaries and caucuses. Virtually all of the primaries and caucuses for presidential elections are held during a five-month period of each election year, from late January or early February through May. By tradition, Iowa always holds the country's first caucuses, and New Hampshire always holds the country's first primary.

In a **caucus** system, registered members of each political party are invited to get together in small meetings around their state. At these meetings, party members select delegates to attend regional and state-level conventions. These conventions then choose delegates to send to the national conventions. The delegates who attend the national conventions are usually pledged to specific presidential candidates.

A primary system is considerably simpler. A **primary** election is conducted just like a regular election, with voters casting ballots for the candidate of their choice. However, the voter may choose only from candidates of one party. In some primaries, delegates are assigned to candidates in proportional fashion. This means that a state's delegates are assigned to each candidate based on his or her proportion of the primary vote.

In the 2008 New Hampshire Democratic presidential primary, for example, Hillary Clinton received 39 percent of the vote; Barack Obama, 36 percent; and John Edwards, 16 percent. Bill Richardson received 5 percent of the vote and Dennis Kucinich got 1 percent. All Democratic primary delegates are allocated in proportional fashion. Under the Democratic Party's rules, a candidate must receive at least 15 percent of the primary vote in order to receive a proportional share of that primary's delegates.[5] With rounding, Clinton and Obama each ended up with nine delegates and Edwards with four.

In Republican presidential primaries, by contrast, delegates can be allocated according to the **winner-take-all** rule, which means that coming in second—even if one loses by only one vote—means that the losing candidate gets no delegates. The choice between proportional and winner-take-all allocation is left up to the party in individual states. In 2008, for example, Arizona Senator John McCain received 50 percent of the Virginia Republican primary vote, while Mike Huckabee garnered a solid 40 percent. Because Virginia's Republican primary system is winner-take-all, however, McCain was awarded all of Virginia's 63 delegates to the Republican Party's national convention. Although Huckabee had received almost half of the Virginia vote, he got none of the state's delegates.[6]

Rules governing primaries may differ from state to state. In an **open primary**, a voter can participate in either party's primary (but not both), regardless of his or her party registration. In a **modified open primary**, registered voters who are not affiliated with either party can vote in either party's primary. A registered Democrat, however, cannot "cross over" and vote in a Republican primary, or vice versa. Finally, in a **closed primary**, only registered Democrats can participate in the Democratic primary, and only registered Republicans can participate in the Republican primary.

Most states have closed primaries and caucuses. The logic of this system is obvious: only registered members of the party should have a voice in selecting the party's nominee. But if party voters have more extreme views than members of the general electorate, they may end up selecting a nominee who will not have broad appeal in the general election. An open primary helps address this problem, by allowing voters outside of the party to have a say in choosing the party's nominee. In the 2008 campaign, because Barack Obama did better with independents, Hillary Clinton often did better in closed primary states.

The process for securing the nomination for a House or Senate seat is different from that for the presidential race and much more straightforward. A congressional candidate must win the party's primary election in order to run as the party's candidate in the fall election. But unlike presidential primary contests, which contests occur over a series of months as candidates attempt to secure delegates, congressional primaries are conducted like a typical election in which the plurality winner receives his or her party's nomination.

The nomination process has changed significantly in American history.

The allocation of convention delegates by presidential caucuses and primaries is a relatively new phenomenon that has come about in the last 30 years. Until 1972, state delegations were chosen not by voters but by powerful party leaders and elected officials within the states. Some states did have primaries prior to 1972, but they were usually not binding and did not actually choose delegates. Instead, they were "beauty contests," so-called because candidates ran in order to demonstrate to party leaders their appeal to voters. For example, John F. Kennedy made a strong effort in the West Virginia primary in 1960. He did not do so to win a large numbers of delegates to the national convention—West Virginia had few delegates, and they were not bound to support the state's primary winner. Instead, Kennedy campaigned strongly to prove to party leaders around the country—the ones who would actually choose and control the delegates at the party convention—that the Catholic Kennedy could win votes in an overwhelmingly Protestant state.

The watershed year of 1968 Party primaries began to take on much greater importance after the tumultuous Democratic nomination campaign of 1968. In that year, after a weaker-than-expected victory over Minnesota Senator Eugene McCarthy in the New Hampshire primary, incumbent Democratic President Lyndon Johnson decided not to seek reelection. With the once formidable Johnson out of the way, two other prominent Democrats joined the race—New York Senator Robert Kennedy, younger brother of John F. Kennedy, and Vice President Hubert Humphrey. McCarthy and Kennedy competed in a number of primaries and mobilized many young voters who were adamantly opposed to the continuing war in Vietnam. After Senator Kennedy was assassinated on the night of his victory in the California primary, the field was left to Humphrey, who supported President Johnson's Vietnam War policy, and McCarthy, who had become the standard-bearer for the anti-war movement.

Even though Humphrey did not campaign in any of the Democratic primaries, party leaders supported his candidacy. Thus, Humphrey arrived at the 1968 Democratic convention in Chicago with a sufficient number of delegates to win the nomination. To anti-war activists and supporters of McCarthy and Kennedy, this meant a continuation of the current Vietnam policy, which they strongly opposed. Their anger boiled over into the streets of Chicago, where violent demonstrations and clashes with the police ensued. All of this was captured on live television and broadcast to the entire country. Ultimately, Humphrey lost a close election in November to Republican Richard Nixon, while independent candidate George Wallace picked up 13 percent of the popular vote and 46 electoral votes.

Democratic reforms Aware of the damage that the convention had done to their party's nominee, the Democratic Party appointed a commission to study ways to give rank-and-file party members a greater voice in the choice of the party's nominee. South Dakota Senator George McGovern, who would become the Democratic Party's nominee for president in 1972, chaired the commission. The recommendations of the McGovern commission led to the system of delegate selection described above—one in which candidates accumulate delegates chiefly through primary and caucus votes, rather than through the back-room dealings of party leaders.

The Democratic reforms led to a proliferation of presidential primaries (see Table 9-1). In 2004, 38 states held Democratic primaries, and 34 states held Republican primaries. In 1968, by contrast, the numbers were 17 and 16, respectively. The remainder of the delegates were chosen in caucuses. All of these delegates chosen by voters in primaries and caucuses are dubbed "pledged delegates" and are committed to voting for the candidate they pledged to on the first ballot at the nominating convention.

Super-delegates and brokered conventions One exception to the trend toward the increasing importance of primaries is the creation of Democratic "super-delegates." Since the 1980s the Democratic Party—though not the Republican Party—has selected a bloc of about one-fifth of its convention delegates outside of the primary and caucus process. These so-called super-delegates include:

• members of the Democratic National Committee (DNC),

• members of the U.S. House and Senate,

• sitting Democratic governors, and

• other distinguished party leaders, such as former presidents, vice presidents, and DNC chairmen.

Super-delegates may vote for whomever they choose at the convention, but they are typically expected to follow the preferences expressed by voters during the primary and caucus season. If a single candidate does not emerge with a majority of the delegates, however, there would be a "brokered convention," in which party leaders would have to choose a candidate to carry their party's banner in the fall

Table 9-1. Number of Presidential Primaries and Percentage of Convention Delegates from Primary States, 1960–2004

	DEMOCRATIC[a]		REPUBLICAN	
	NUMBER OF PRIMARIES	PERCENTAGE OF DELEGATES FROM PRIMARY STATES[b]	NUMBER OF PRIMARIES	PERCENTAGE OF DELEGATES
1960	16	38.3	15	38.6
1964	17	45.7	17	45.6
1968	17	37.5	16	34.3
1972	23	60.5	22	52.7
1976	29[b]	72.6	28[b]	67.9
1980	31[b]	74.7	35[b]	74.3
1984	26	62.9	30	68.2
1988	34	66.6	35	76.9
1992	39	78.8	38	80.4
1996	35	70.9	43	85.9
2000	39	65.6	42	82.7
2004	38	n.a.	34[c]	n.a.

[a]Includes party leaders and elected officials chosen from primary states.

[b]Does not include Vermont, which holds non-binding presidential preference votes but chooses delegates in state caucuses and conventions.

[c]In 2004 the Republicans held party conventions in 11 states and caucuses in 5.

Source: Stephen J. Wayne, *The Road to the White House, 1996* (New York: St Martin's Press, 1996), table 6.2. Data for 1996 from Harold W. Stanley and Richard G. Niemi, *Vital Statistics on American Politics 2003–4* (Washington, DC: Congressional Quarterly Press, 2003), table 1.23, p. 66. Data for 2004 from the US Federal Election Commission

election. In such a situation, the super-delegates would be expected to support the most electable candidate, and would probably induce other convention delegates to follow their lead. This brokered convention scenario, while a perennial favorite of political journalists, political scientists, and other political junkies, has not occurred since the 1968 Democratic reforms were instituted. In 2008, with Barack Obama having a lead in the primaries, but not a majority of pledged delegates, the battle for the Democratic nomination was actually decided by the super-delegates. Both Hillary Clinton and Obama fought hard to convince these Democratic Party leaders that they were the most deserving and most electable.

More primaries, earlier primaries As the number of primaries has increased over the past 30 years, primaries have also been occurring earlier in the year. In 1972, for example, the New Hampshire primary took place on March 7. In 2008, the New Hampshire primary occurred on January 8. Other states, seeing the attention and money that flow to the early contests in Iowa and New Hampshire, have moved up their contests as well. In fact, there has been a general tendency toward "front-loading"—the scheduling of primaries earlier in the election year—because a state that holds its primary toward the end of the primary season runs the risk that the nomination will have been largely determined before its voters have a chance to express their preferences. In 1968, for example, fewer than 10 percent of states holding primaries had done so by the end of March. In 2008, that number was nearly 75 percent. In 2008, the states of Florida and Michigan moved up their primary days to January to get more attention. This resulted in the Democratic Party penalizing the two states and taking away their delegates. Ironically, primaries late in the season that few thought would matter—Ohio and Texas on March 3, Pennsylvania on April 22, and North Carolina and Indiana on May 7—became crucial and received immense attention from the campaigns and the media.

As the primary calendar has shortened, many states now hold primaries on the same day. In the 1980s, Democrats in southern states sought to turn this situation to their advantage. Concerned about what they considered to be the liberal tilt of the national Democratic Party, and eager to avoid a repeat of Walter Mondale's 49-state loss to Ronald Reagan in 1984, southern Democrats united to create a regional primary, called Super Tuesday. The first Super Tuesday primary was held on March 9, 1988. The results of that contest were mixed, with the Reverend Jesse Jackson, Senator Albert Gore, Governor Michael Dukakis, and Representative Richard Gephardt each taking at least one state.

Although the nomination went to Governor Dukakis, who represented the liberal wing of the Democratic Party, Super Tuesday also gave a boost to the candidacy of moderate Democrat Al Gore. In the next Super Tuesday contest in 1992, the consummate Democratic centrist, Arkansas Governor Bill Clinton, swept the day's primaries and became unstoppable in his quest for the nomination.

Figuring out the winner in general elections for Congress is easy.

Determining the winner in U.S. congressional elections is easy; the person who gets the most votes wins. Congressional elections operate by winner-take-all rules. Supporters of the proportional representation system argue that it produces a legislature that more accurately represents the various opinions of voters. In the U.S. system, they argue, the winner-take-all format leads to two major parties rather than multiple parties, creating conditions where large minorities can feel unrepresented in Congress. However, supporters of the winner-take-all system note that it avoids the factionalism caused by having too many competing parties in the legislature. Moreover, they note, in parliamentary systems smaller parties often have to form coalitions after the election in order to create a governing majority. In the United States, by contrast, the major parties themselves represent coalitions, so voters know the coalition they are voting for prior to the election rather than after.

Congressional and most other U.S. elections are also conducted according to the plurality rule. The **plurality rule** means that a candidate wins office by getting more votes than his or her opponent, even if that candidate does not receive an absolute majority. There are some exceptions to the plurality rule in the United States, however. Some local elections have two rounds of voting. If no candidate receives a majority of the vote in the first round, the contest goes to a second round, or runoff election, in which the top two candidates face off against each other. In 2002, for example, Louisiana Senator Mary Landrieu received 46 percent of the vote on Election Day, making her the top vote-getter in a nine-person field. But because she failed to receive an absolute majority of the vote, she and the second- place finisher—Republican Suzanne Terrell—had to face each other in a runoff election. In that contest, Landrieu outpolled Terrell and so was able to keep her Senate seat.

Presidential election rules are more complicated.

In a presidential election, determining winners and losers tends to be substantially more complicated than in congressional races. In the fall general election for president, the winner of the popular vote may or may not win the presidency. In 2000, for example, Al Gore won the national popular vote, but he lost the presidential election to George W. Bush. That is because in order to win the presidency, a candidate must win a majority in the Electoral College—regardless of his popular vote total.

The decision to select the president via the Electoral College rather than by popular vote resulted from a compromise during the Constitutional Convention in Philadelphia in 1787. Delegates at the convention considered two options for selection of the president—popular vote, and selection by members of the House of Representatives. The popular vote was not favored by representatives of smaller states, who imagined their states' influence in the presidential election would be overwhelmed by the larger states.[7] At the same time, some convention members worried about whether the largely uneducated populace could be counted on to make a wise choice for president. Yet others worried about logistical issues involved in holding a single nationwide election on a specific day.[8]

The alternative to popular election—selection of the president by the House of Representatives—was more strongly favored by convention members, but it also raised concerns. The chief worry was that the president would be beholden to the legislature that had selected him, violating the principles of separation of powers and checks and balances. This scenario might lead to the very tyranny that the new system was intended to prevent.[9]

The convention reached a compromise solution, the **Electoral College,** which addressed a number of these concerns, albeit imperfectly. Small states received disproportionately high representation in the Electoral College relative to their population. Each state was granted an elector for each member it sent to the House of Representatives. But each state, regardless of size, was also granted an elector for each of its two senators. This helped boost the representation of small states relative to larger ones. Because the Constitution needed to be ratified by 9 of the 13 states, with each state counting equally, this compromise was likely necessary to receive adequate support from small states.

For those who worried about the capacity of the people to pick an appropriate president, the Electoral College was thought of as an assembly of "wise men" who would choose a president more carefully than the masses. The electors from each state would meet in their respective states about a month after Election Day and vote for the presidential and vice presidential candidates of their choosing. If no candidate received a majority of the delegates' votes, then the House of Representatives would determine the president.[10] On Election Day, therefore, though they may not realize it, voters in presidential elections are casting their ballots for a party's slate of electors to the Electoral College. A New Yorker who voted for George W. Bush in 2004, for example, was actually voting for a group of New York electors committed to casting their electoral votes for President Bush.

With only two exceptions, states assign their electoral votes on a winner-take-all basis. (Maine and Nebraska allocate their electors somewhat differently.) First, the winner of a state's popular vote as a whole receives two electoral votes. Then, the remainder of the electoral votes is allocated by congressional district, with the popular vote winner in each district receiving one electoral vote. Although this creates the possibility that a state could split its electoral votes between two candidates, this has never happened in practice.[11]

The modern Electoral College consists of 538 electors, representing the 50 states and the District of Columbia. Each state's number of electors is equivalent to its combined number of House and Senate members. (The District of Columbia does not have voting representatives in the House or Senate, but is allocated three electors in the Electoral College.) In 2000, for example, Florida had 23 members in the House of Representatives and, like every other state, two senators. Thus, Florida had 25 votes in the Electoral College. In the 2000 presidential election, with every state except Florida counted, George W. Bush had earned 246 electoral votes, and Al Gore had earned 266. (One elector abstained in protest.) Thus, the Florida race was crucial because the candidate who won would have more than the 270 electoral votes needed to win a majority of the Electoral College, and therefore the presidency. In 2004, although John Kerry lost the national popular vote by 2.5 percentage points or about three million votes, only 130,000 votes separated Bush and Kerry in Ohio—and if Kerry would have won Ohio's 20 electoral votes, he would have won the presidency.

The evolution of the modern party system—dominated by two political parties, the Democrats and the Republicans—has changed at least one aspect of the Electoral College in a way America's founders did not envision. Local political parties and the presidential campaigns now select the electors who will participate in the Electoral College vote. Selection is based not necessarily on wisdom or experience, but on service to the party, political contributions, and other demonstrations of party loyalty. Thus, the Electoral College no longer serves as a deliberative body, consisting of wise men and women who will choose the best-qualified candidate. Instead, electors are expected to vote for their party's nominee for the presidency— whether or not they believe that nominee is the best-qualified person. In fact, in most states, they are required to do so or they face a fine.

Understanding Individual Vote Choice

In a presidential election, voters generally have two chances to cast a vote for a candidate—once in the primaries, and once in the general election. Once the campaigns are over, the advertisements have been aired, the debates have come and gone, and the media have made their endorsements, the voters must make a choice and cast a ballot. And because the processes are different in the primary election and the general election, the factors that determine those choices may be different.

Presidential primary voting is less studied and understood than general election voting.

No single aspect of political behavior in America has been examined more often or more closely than the individual vote. Interestingly, however, although political scientists know a great deal about individual vote choice during the November presidential election, they know relatively little about individual decision-making among presidential primary voters. There are two reasons for this discrepancy. First, the general election determines who will be president, and that, in turn, usually has major consequences in terms of domestic policy, the economy, and international affairs. But who wins a particular party's nomination may end up being little more than a historical footnote. How many Americans remember that Gary Hart was Walter Mondale's chief competition in the 1984 Democratic primary? Not many. But virtually *everyone* knows who won the general election match-up in 1984 between Mondale and Reagan. Naturally, political scientists gravitate toward the more compelling research question—why did voters choose *this* person to be their president rather than *that* one?

The second reason for political scientists' greater attention to presidential elections is that one critical factor in understanding voting behavior in the general election is not a factor in primary elections—party identification (or party ID). An individual voter's party identification is the single most important influence on vote choice in the general election. In the 2004 general election for example, 89 percent of Democrats voted for John Kerry, and 93 percent of Republicans voted for George W. Bush.[12]

In a primary, though, all of the candidates are of the same party. Political scientists, therefore, cannot explain the primary vote choice as well as they can explain the general election vote. We do, however, have some understanding of the outcome of the primary process as a whole—why a particular candidate ends up being the party's nominee. Accordingly, we will address primary election results in more detail in the section on election outcomes.

Partisanship can both influence and be influenced by the general election vote.

In the 1950s, a pioneering study established enduring theories on the role of partisan identification in the behavior of individual voters. In their seminal work, *The American Voter*, Angus Campbell, Philip Converse, Warren Miller, and Donald Stokes argue that in their pre-adult years, most voters adopt a partisan affiliation that becomes a psychological attitude akin to the attachment one has to a religion or racial identity. Therefore, it tends to be highly stable over time (although slow change could occur), and is the predominant force in determining most other

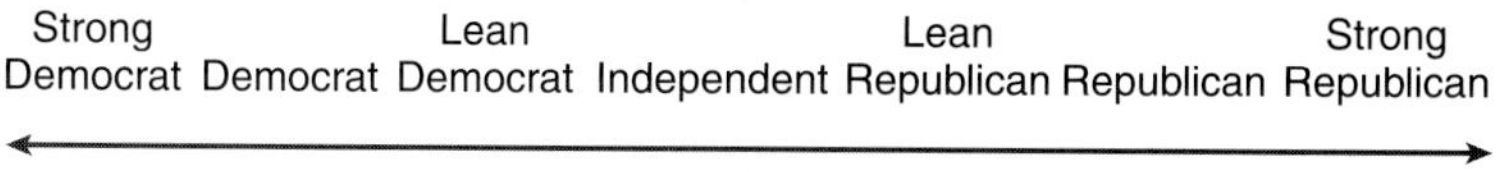

| Strong | Lean | | | Lean | | Strong |
| Democrat | Democrat | Democrat | Independent | Republican | Republican | Republican |

←——————————————————————————————————————→

Figure 9-1.   Partisan Identification on a Seven-Point Scale.
Source: American National Election Study, Cumulative File.

political attitudes and behaviors—including voting. This view has come to be known as the "traditional" view of partisan affiliation.

Direction and strength of partisan identification   *The American Voter*
identified two components in an individual's partisan attachment: direction and strength. Direction refers to whether a person identifies more with the Republican Party or the Democratic Party. Strength refers to the intensity of that attachment. Accordingly, researchers typically measure partisan identification using a series of questions and a seven-point scale which captures both direction and strength, like the one in Figure 9-1.

Since the 1950s there have been relatively few party ID panel studies that track the same group of individuals over many years. Those few suggest that partisan affiliation is a stable attachment. For example, a panel study that looked at the same group of adults at three different times—1965, 1973, and 1982—found that nearly 80 percent of these individuals maintained the same partisan status from one time period to the next. A majority of the rest only moved into or out of the independent category.[13]

Differing views of party identification   The traditional view of partisanship sensibly emphasized party ID as a factor that determined *other* beliefs and behaviors, that is, a causal factor. Because the average citizen pays little attention to the fine points of politics, the voter needs some way to simplify and make sense of the political world. Partisan affiliation is a highly effective mechanism for this. Supporting one's party and opposing the other party is a relatively simple way to organize the political world. Thus, it makes sense to think of partisanship as a lens through which one sees the political world, and a handy shortcut for arriving at opinions about specific political figures and issues.

Not all political scientists are completely satisfied with this view of party ID, however. In the "revisionist" view embraced by some scholars, while party affiliation can certainly influence vote choice, issue stands, and evaluations of candidates, the reverse is also true; those same opinions about issues and candidates can influence party identification. Consistent with this view, political scientist Morris Fiorina has argued that party identification is less a "standing decision" than a mental "running tally" of party performance. Ronald Reagan, a Democrat who became a Republican in the 1950s, reflected this aspect of party identification when he stated, "I didn't leave the Democratic Party. The Democratic Party left me."

Which view of partisan attachment makes more sense—the traditional or the revisionist? Consider that each explains some of the puzzle of partisan attachment. Due to political socialization, most voters develop a partisan attachment long before they would be capable of assessing the parties' performance in office. Furthermore, there is little evidence of individuals switching from one party to another in reaction to party performance (with limited movement to the independent category).

Partisan change and instability At the same time, partisan affiliation is not always permanent or perfectly stable, nor need it be seen only as a causal agent. Partisans, especially weaker ones, sometimes do "switch sides" and affiliate with the other party particularly when extraordinary political events upset existing political arrangements. During the civil rights movement of the 1960s, for example, the national Democratic Party adopted an agenda of federal intervention to promote political, social, and economic equality for African Americans—leaving many white southern Democrats disenchanted (see Figure 9-2).

Another example of political attitudes affecting partisan affiliation instead of the reverse is the emergence in the 1980s of a group of voters known as "Reagan Democrats." These were generally white, working-class voters who had tradition-ally considered themselves Democrats but began to identify with the Republican Party on social issues. Accordingly, many of these individuals voted for Ronald Reagan in 1980 and 1984 and ultimately registered as Republicans. But as the tra-ditional theory would suggest, these conversions were not a simple calculation that it suddenly made more sense to identify with the Republican Party. These individ-uals had to overcome their strong, lifelong attachment to the Democrats.

Other scholars have pointed to the weakening of partisan attachments in the electorate as a whole as evidence that partisanship is not as stable as indicated by the traditional view. As Figure 9-3 shows, the direction and intensity of partisan attachments *have* changed noticeably since the 1960s.

In the 1960s, pure independents constituted only about 10 percent of the electorate; independents and right or left "leaners" added up to about 25 percent. The 1970s witnessed a further drop in the number of Americans identifying with one of the two major parties—particularly the Democrats.

The defection of previous partisans to the independent and "leaner" cate-gories, as shown in Figure 9-3, might raise some doubts about the traditional view of partisan stability. However, research into the dynamics of the de- alignment sug-gests that two other factors have been more influential than partisan defections.

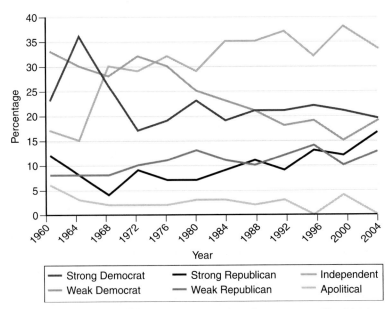

Figure 9-2. Partisan Affiliation Among Southerners, 1960–2000.

Source: American National Election Study, Cumulative File.

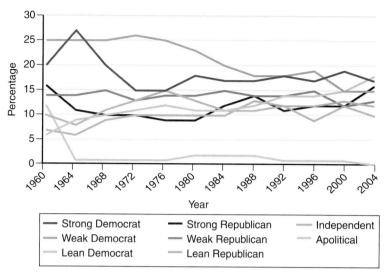

Figure 9-3. Partisan Affiliation Among American Adults, 1960–2000.
Source: American National Election Study, Cumulative File.

First, individuals who came of political age in the late 1950s and early 1960s entered adulthood with weaker partisan attachments than their parents. Second, some individuals who typically would be expected to grow stronger in their partisan attachments over time—a "life cycle" effect of the sort we discussed in Chapter 7—did not do so. Therefore, only a minority of the de-alignment—perhaps 30 to 40 percent—can be accounted for by defections among former Republicans and Democrats.[14]

Despite these examples of partisan change and instability, one is generally safe in assuming the overall durability of partisan attachments. Any change tends to occur slowly, and is more likely to appear in the *strength* of attachment rather than the *direction* of attachment.

Regardless of one's precise view of partisanship, there is no question that partisan affiliation remains a singularly important predictor of the presidential vote. In recent presidential elections, typically 90 percent or more of "strong" Democratic and Republican partisans have voted for their party's candidate. Among individuals who identify themselves as Democrats and Republicans, though not strongly, the loyalty rate is somewhat lower but still impressive—generally in the range of 70 to 85 percent.[15] Thus, knowing voters' partisan affiliations would yield a tremendous insight into their probable vote choice.

Not all partisans are loyal to their party's candidate in every election, however. Furthermore, not every voter considers himself or herself a Democrat or Republican. Two other factors are thought to have an important influence on the individual vote—issue and policy preferences and candidate evaluations.

Issue and policy preferences have a complex and uncertain impact on voter choice.

Most political scientists agree that voters' opinions on specific issues and their preferences for certain policies can and do affect their presidential vote. The shorthand phrase for this phenomenon in the research literature is **issue voting**. It makes sense intuitively. For example, if you are a strong supporter of universal, government-paid health care, you will likely be inclined to vote for a candidate who also supports that concept rather than one who opposes it (other things being equal). Political scientists also agree on certain preconditions that prevail in order for a voter to engage in issue voting:

- the voter must be aware of the issue and have an opinion concerning it,

- the issue must be at least minimally important to the voter,

- the voter must be able to identify the candidates' positions on the issue accurately, and

- the voter must believe that one party or candidate represents the voter's own position better than the other party or candidate.16

Beyond these basics, political scientists disagree about the relative importance of issues in the voting decision, the precise mechanisms by which voters compare their issue positions to those of presidential candidates, the kinds of issues that are relevant to voters, and the best ways to study issue voting.

Consistency between issue preference and voter choice
Other researchers viewed voters' capabilities more optimistically. In *The Responsible Electorate*, for example, V.O. Key argued that on highly salient campaign issues, voters were capable of developing meaningful issue positions and voting in part on the basis of them. Using a body of survey data, Key looked at the behaviors and attitudes of individuals in consecutive presidential elections. The most interesting data came from "party switchers"—individuals who voted for different parties in consecutive elections. In comparison with individuals who voted for the same party in both elections, Key found the party switchers much more likely to have disagreements with their previous party on major campaign issues, such as Social Security or U.S. involvement in World War II. From this data, Key inferred that those issue disagreements were the *cause* of the party switchers' vote changes.

Key's research methods were not without problems, however. Imagine, for example, that you as a voter find a particular candidate personally appealing for reasons having nothing to do with his issue stances. Because you like the candidate so much, you may also come to embrace his issue positions, seeing them in the "reflected glow" of his personal characteristics. This logic would suggest that your preference for the candidate *led to* your support of his issue positions, rather than the opposite.

Later generations of political scientists, using much more comprehensive voter databases and sophisticated analytical techniques, have addressed this and other shortcomings in Key's analysis. For example, a now-classic article by Gregory Markus and Philip Converse acknowledged and adjusted for the fact that the congruence between voters' policy preferences and their vote choices, demonstrated by Key, may be a simple result of voters adopting the issue positions of candidates they prefer. Having made the appropriate statistical corrections for this possibility, Markus and Converse found that voters' ultimate evaluations of candidates were significantly affected by their policy preferences in five different issue areas—social welfare, school desegregation and busing, treatment of minority groups, women's rights, and tax reform (all salient issues in the 1970s, when the study was conducted). Voters' evaluation of candidates, in turn, also had a significant effect on their ultimate vote choice. Thus, voters' issue positions affected the vote indirectly, by contributing to voters' evaluation of candidates.

Retrospective and prospective voting Scholars also introduced another insight on issue voting. Voters do not only try to project how candidates will perform on important issues in the future—a process known as **prospective voting**. Rather, issue voting can also be **retrospective**; voters simply assess the performance of the party that has held the presidency for the past four years. If the party has performed well on the issues the voter cares about, she will reward that party's candidate with her vote. According to this logic, presidential elections are considered more of a referendum on the incumbent party's stewardship of the country than a judgment about the relative strengths and weaknesses of two competing candidates. Key summed up the essence of this idea in fairly dramatic terms, describing the voter as "a rational god of vengeance and reward."[17]

Support for Key's argument can be seen in a number of twentieth-century presidential elections. Presidents who presided over periods of recession or slow economic growth, or who found themselves mired in serious scandal or controversy, or who were associated with conspicuous foreign policy failures, did not win reelection—Herbert Hoover, Gerald Ford, and Jimmy Carter, among others. Other presidents have served during eras of peace and general prosperity, and so have been rewarded with reelection—Dwight Eisenhower, Ronald Reagan, and Bill Clinton, for example. This same logic applies even when an incumbent president is not up for reelection. In 1988, for example, because of the peace and prosperity of the Reagan years, Reagan's vice president—George W. Bush—had a relatively easy path to the presidency. In 1968, on the other hand, when Lyndon Johnson's vice president, Hubert Humphrey, ran for the presidency, he was defeated—a victim in part of the late-1960s inflation combined with growing public disenchantment with the Vietnam War.

One reason for the intuitive appeal of the retrospective voting model is that making retrospective judgments about whether a particular party deserves to be rewarded or punished is a much easier, more reasonable task than making prospective judgments based on candidate issue positions. Prospective judgments require one to learn what the two presidential candidates say they will do on various issues if elected, and then compare the candidates' positions with one's own. Retrospective voting, on the other hand, simply requires the voter to observe the results of the incumbent presidential party's policies. Furthermore, retrospective judgments require the voter to observe and pass judgment on only those things that the incumbent party has actually *done*—not what they *say* they will do.

As noted, voters tend to make retrospective judgments on the basis of "big" issues—for example, the state of the national economy, whether the country is at peace or at war, and if the latter, whether or not that war is being executed successfully. Furthermore, whether making retrospective or prospective judgments, one should expect issue voting to take place with respect to issues that voters, not researchers, consider important. This point may seem obvious, but in early research on issue voting, researchers often specified the issues that *they* considered important in national affairs. This approach had a tendency to understate the relevance of issues in determining the vote.

Developing positions and making voting decisions Some issues are relatively easy for voters to develop opinions on—and therefore to incorporate into their voting decisions—while others are much more difficult, technical, and complex. For example, compare and contrast two issues: gay marriage, and the military action in Iraq after the 9/11 terrorist attacks. With respect to the gay-marriage issue, there are only two options: for or against. Developing a well-informed position on this issue might require nothing more than thinking through one's own existing beliefs and values. With respect to the Iraq situation, however, there were a number of policy options available:

- maintain the status quo,
- attempt to strengthen the existing economic sanctions against Iraq,
- seek to overthrow Saddam Hussein's regime through covert action,
- support Iraqi forces seeking to overthrow Hussein,
- launch a renewed weapons inspection program,
- seek U.N. approval to invade Iraq,
- invade Iraq unilaterally, without U.N. approval, or
- some combination of these steps.

Although many Americans had opinions, developing a well-informed position on the appropriate Iraq policy would involve a thorough consideration of all these options and their potential costs and benefits—an expertise beyond the reach of the vast majority of Americans. In general, one should expect a greater incidence of issue voting on issues that are relatively easy for the mass electorate to consider.[18]

Perhaps the "easiest" issues of all are so-called **valence issues**—issues on which virtually everyone agrees. Almost all voters agree, for example, that less crime is better than more, that peace is better than war, and that lower unemployment is better than higher unemployment. On these issues, voters cannot be said to have conflicting positions. However, voters *do* have distinct beliefs about which party is better able to handle such valence issues.[19] One voter might believe, for example, that the Democratic Party is more likely to help achieve low unemployment than the Republicans. Another voter might believe precisely the opposite. Such voters may not be able to explain *how* the parties would handle the issue, or what the voters themselves would like to see done on that issue, but party ID simplifies their evaluation.

Some evidence suggests that voters do cast ballots in part on the basis of judgments about the parties' potential handling of valence issues.[20] When this occurs, it does not necessarily mean that voters can explain why or how one party would do a better job managing the issue than the other. In fact, many voters would be unable to offer any such explanation. It does mean, though, that voters are engaged in issue voting of a sort. They care about a particular set of issues, and they will vote for the party that they believe would be more capable of addressing those issues.

Beyond these generalities, it is difficult to draw conclusions on the circumstances under which a particular issue will affect a given election outcome. This does not stop journalists, campaign consultants, and even political scientists from claiming that a specific issue—say, abortion, gun control, or "moral values"—influenced or even determined an election. When assessing such claims, keep in mind the prerequisites for issue voting identified above. When these circumstances do not hold, or when their applicability is open to debate, then any talk about issue voting is just that—so much talk.

Voters appraise candidates in three "big" ways.

A final factor that many political scientists consider important in influencing individual vote choice is candidate evaluation. This term does *not* refer to which candidate has the most winning smile, the most engaging wit, or the most photogenic family. Although democratic theorists worry that such superficial characteristics may influence the vote, little political science research indicates that they do. Rather, political scientists have measured candidate evaluations in ways that are typically considered more relevant to an informed, meaningful vote choice. The different approaches to measuring voter evaluations of candidates have included:

- voter descriptions of candidate ideology, such as "liberal" or "conservative," or in some cases, "too liberal" or "too conservative";

- voter assessment of candidates in terms such as "moral," "knowledgeable," "inspiring," "provides strong leadership," and "really cares about people like me";[21]

- open-ended voter comments about aspects they like and dislike about specific candidates;[22]

- voter assessments of whether particular presidential candidates have "the kind of personality a president ought to have";[23] and

- "feeling thermometer" ratings of presidential candidates, in which voters are asked to assign a number to a candidate on a zero-to-100 scale, with zero indicating "very cold or unfavorable" and 100 indicating "very warm or favorable."[24]

Despite many studies regarding the effects of candidate evaluations on vote choice[25]—some large, some very modest—no consensus has evolved on the best ways to measure candidate evaluations, or on the relative importance of candidate evaluations among other factors that influence the vote. Even so, it is reasonable to consider candidate evaluations, alongside party ID and issue voting, one of the "big three" determinants of vote choice.

Party ID, issues, and candidate appraisals come together to produce a vote choice.

How exactly do these three elements combine to produce an individual vote decision? This is a difficult question, for two reasons. First, individual decision-making inevitably includes elements of random, idiosyncratic behavior that are very hard to identify and describe—even for voters themselves. Second, the three elements of voter choice interact with each other in complex ways. Party identification can affect candidate evaluations, which in turn can affect a voter's thinking about the candidate's issue positions. Other things being equal, a Republican voter is more likely to evaluate a Republican candidate favorably and then to project his preferred issue positions onto that candidate. For example, "I like everything about John McCain, I'm sure I agree with him on most of the important issues." And, the reverse is true as well—the voter's understanding of the candidate's issue positions can affect her evaluation of the candidate.

Despite the complexity of these interactions and the degree of randomness inherent in human decision-making, a good, general "rule" that describes most presidential voting behavior might be:

> The voter canvasses his likes and dislikes of the two candidates involved in the election. He or she then votes for the candidate for whom he or she has the greatest net number of favorable attitudes. If no candidate has such an advantage, the voter votes consistently with his or her partisan affiliation, if he or she has one.[26]

One can test the accuracy of the rule by generating vote predictions from it using voter survey data. This basic rule, relying on candidate evaluation and party ID, can generate a correct prediction nearly 85 to 90 percent of the time (depending on the election). Thus, it would seem to be a good approximation of the way that voters actually arrive at a final decision.[27]

You may have noticed, however, that the rule includes only two of the "big three" vote determinants: candidate evaluations and party identification. What about voter issue positions? Issue positions influence the vote by way of candidate evaluations. Specifically, the voter's assessment of candidates' issue positions affects the voter's candidate evaluation, which in turn affects the vote. Not surprisingly, party identification also affects voter evaluations of candidates. Because of this, party ID influences the vote *through* candidate evaluation, and not just as a tie-breaker, as the rule given above would seem to indicate. Finally, party identification also affects voter issue positions, which provides another avenue through which party ID can affect the vote indirectly.[28]

Understanding Election Outcomes

The winners and losers of public office in the United States emerge from the interaction of three factors: the laws governing how elections are conducted, how candidates wage their campaigns, and how voters decide whom to support. How do rules and campaigns and choices and decisions all come together to determine election outcomes and the leaders who govern us?

Frontrunners have a great advantage in presidential nomination contests.

Even if political scientists do not understand all the ins and outs of vote choice, they *do* understand the primary-election process and how it produces a particular nominee. This understanding has changed significantly over the past generation, however.

The pre-primary season A candidate hoping to win his party's nomination needs to be prepared to make a credible run in multiple states *before* the primary season even begins. The candidates best equipped to do this begin the primary season having raised the most money, having already achieved frontrunner status in pre-primary polls, or both. Candidates who have reached one or both of these success milestones—who have won the "**invisible primary**"—almost always go on to win their party's nomination. This principle holds over most of the previous 11 contested nomination battles, as shown in Table 9-2. (A contested nomination is one in which there is no incumbent president seeking his party's nomination.)

Note several things in particular in Table 9-2. First, in most cases the pre-primary season *does* produce a clear winner of the invisible primary, that is, a candidate who leads in both fund-raising and pre-primary polling. The two exceptions are 1980 and 1988. Second, when there is a clear invisible-primary winner, that individual goes on to win his party's nomination, with the exception of 2004. Finally, in no case does someone win the nomination *unless* at the end of the invisible-primary period he led the field in public opinion polls, in fund-raising, or in both.

Importance of momentum in past primaries Until the early 1980s, the key to understanding the primary process was one word: **momentum**. Thirty years ago, primary contests were few in number and spaced far enough apart that even

Table 9-2. Pre-Primary Leaders in Fund-Raising and Opinion Poll Preference Among Party Identifiers, 1980–2004

YEAR	PARTY	CANDIDATE WITH LEAD IN LAST POLL BEFORE IOWA CAUCUSES	CANDIDATE RAISING MOST MONEY PRIOR TO THE YEAR OF THE ELECTION	CLEAR INVISIBLE PRIMARY WINNER?	EVENTUAL NOMINEE
1980	Republican	Reagan	Connally	*None*	Reagan
1980	Democratic	Carter	Carter	Carter	Carter
1984	Democratic	Mondale	Mondale	Mondale	Mondale
1988	Republican	Bush	Bush	Bush	Bush
1988	Democratic	Hart	Dukakis	*None*	Dukakis
1992	Republican	Bush	Bush	Bush	Bush
1992	Democratic	Clinton	Clinton	Clinton	Clinton
1996	Republican	Dole	Dole	Dole	Dole
2000	Republican	Bush	Bush	Bush	Bush
2000	Democratic	Gore	Gore	Gore	Gore
2004	Democratic	Dean	Dean	Dean	Kerry

long-shot candidates had time to build a credible campaign over the course of a primary season. An early success in Iowa or New Hampshire gave them a coveted shot of momentum, indicated by a boost in media coverage, name recognition, fund-raising, and perceptions of electability. They could convert these assets into a successful campaign in the next primary, and the benefits going forward would compound. In this way, by exceeding expectations in an early caucus or primary, a long-shot candidate like George McGovern in 1972 or Jimmy Carter in 1976 could leverage the primary process itself to become a formidable candidate for the nomination.[29]

With front-loaded primaries, those days are over. The crowded primary calendar leaves very little time to raise money, organize local volunteers, attend campaign events, and develop and implement state-specific media strategies while the campaign is in progress. A candidate who attempts to run a credible campaign in only one or two early states, hoping to turn that into success in the next round of contests, probably will not have adequate time to make this strategy work. In 2004, for example, North Carolina Senator John Edwards devoted most of his pre-primary resources to the Iowa caucuses, and finished a surprisingly strong second there. Pre-election polls predicted Edwards would finish farther back, and the novelty of his over-performing in Iowa led to increased and favorable attention from the press. But the New Hampshire primary was just one week later, and Edwards finished fourth with 12.1 percent of the vote—receiving no delegates. In 2008, he followed the identical strategy, but came in a close but disappointing third in Iowa.

Emergence of the frontrunner As demonstrated above, the pre-primary period usually creates a clear frontrunner for the nomination. And in general, though he or she must first compete in a gamut of primaries that inevitably produce twists, surprises, tension, and drama, that individual goes on to win his or her party's nomination. Why should this be? As we have noted, the compressed primary calendar rewards candidates who can run a credible campaign in multiple states in a very short span of time. The candidate best equipped to do this is the one who has abundant resources and support in place before the primaries begin. He or she will be prepared to win from day one. And when all is said and done, he or she usually will win.

Despite the relative accuracy of this claim, there is still something unsatisfying about it. Note that it says nothing about how or why a particular individual comes to win the invisible primary in the first place. The reason we have neglected this topic is that political scientists do not fully understand invisible-primary dynamics—specifically, how one builds momentum in the *pre*-primary period. We do know that early fund-raising success leads to favorable media coverage, which in turn leads to greater name recognition and a higher standing in the polls, which can then lead to more successful fund-raising, and so on. But this simply raises the question, why are some candidates more successful than others at raising money?[30] And why do some candidates who raise large sums of money—such as businessman Steve Forbes in 1996 and 2000, or former Texas Governor John Connally, who raised the most money among Republicans in 1980—*not* succeed? Yet, even if political scientists could answer these questions, they almost certainly would find it difficult to predict winners of the invisible primary. Those kinds of predictions, however, are the hallmark of good political science theory.

Beyond this gap in our understanding of the invisible primary, the evolution of the Internet as a political tool and communications medium may be changing some of the basic logic of the primary process. Thanks to the World Wide Web, candidates can now raise and immediately spend large sums of money as fast as interested supporters can type their credit card numbers into a digitized form. Furthermore, websites and e-mail make 'round-the-clock' mass communication and campaign coordination possible at an extremely low cost. The Web has also changed the news cycle significantly. Stories that used to be updated once a day, when the morning paper was delivered or the evening news came on, are now updated continuously, online. Twenty-four-hour news channels and the proliferation of nationwide talk-radio programming have also contributed to this phenomenon. The result of all this is that candidates who need to raise money, communicate with millions of supporters, recruit volunteers, raise media awareness, and get their message out *in a hurry* now have tools that were not available to them even 15 years ago. Eventually, these factors may change the existing primary season dynamic in which candidates who start behind almost always end behind as well.

Key factors allow political scientists to accurately forecast election results.

As noted, political scientists have developed election forecasting models that are both surprisingly simple and surprisingly accurate. In 2004, for example, the American Political Science Association solicited election forecasts from seven different scholars or teams of scholars. These scholars completed their forecasts several months before the fall election. In each case, they predicted that George W. Bush would be reelected. On average, the forecasters predicted that President Bush would receive 54 percent of the two-party vote.[31] In actuality, the president received just over 51 percent of the vote. Thus, although the forecasters were slightly more optimistic about Mr. Bush's electoral prospects than actual events warranted, they clearly got the basic storyline correct.

Factors in forecasting In predicting presidential election outcomes, the political scientists' models generally take into account four different kinds of factors:

- the partisan orientations of the electorate,
- the job approval rating of the incumbent party president,
- the performance of the economy during the first half of the election year, and
- incumbency, that is, whether an incumbent president is running for reelection, and if so, how long his party has held the presidency.

Inclusion of these factors should make sense in light of the earlier discussion about partisan orientations, which are obviously a critical influence on individual electoral choices. The incumbent president's job approval gives a rough sense of what kind of retrospective judgments voters will make about the performance of the party in power, about voters' comfort level with that party's issue positions, and about their personal feelings toward the party's leader (the president). Whether or not the incumbent president is running for reelection, all of these factors can influence voters' evaluation of the party's candidate in the general election. Inclusion of an economic performance variable reflects the fact that the strength of the economy has proved to be the single most important issue to voters in election after election. When the economy is performing well, the party in power tends to win. When it is not, the party in power tends to lose. Finally, the incumbency factor captures the generally greater name recognition and voter comfort with an incumbent president in comparison with a lesser-known challenger. However, incumbency can operate in reverse; the longer the same party holds the presidency, the more likely the voters will become disenchanted with its candidates and policies and vote for a change.

From one election to the next, the factors that are most likely to change sharply, and thus exert decisive effects on election outcomes, are presidential approval ratings and economic performance. Anyone wishing to predict an election outcome, or to understand why an election turned out the way it did, would do well to study one or both of these factors. Looking at presidential elections since 1952, for example, when the incumbent party's president has an average approval rating of 49 percent or better during April, May, and June of the election year, that party's candidate wins the general election. When that number is 46.7 percent or lower, on the other hand, the incumbent party's candidate loses.[32] In between these two numbers is a sort of "no man's land," an area of uncertainty. George W. Bush was dangerously near this no man's land in 2004, barely achieving an approval rating of 49 percent during the second quarter of the election year. Thus, predictions based solely on his approval ratings would have considered him vulnerable, but with a slightly better chance of winning than losing.

Looking at economic performance as a predictor between 1952 and 2004, when gross domestic product (GDP) grows at an annualized rate of at least 2.6 percent in the second quarter of the election year, the incumbent party wins. When growth is 1.5 percent or less, the incumbent party loses. Growth rates in between are inconclusive. Looking again at 2004, GDP grew by 3 percent during the second quarter of the year. This should have put George W. Bush in a relatively good position to earn reelection, though not as strong as some of his predecessors. Richard Nixon, for example, saw 6.9 percent GDP growth in 1972 and was reelected overwhelmingly. Ronald Reagan and Bill Clinton benefited from growth rates of 5.3 percent and 4.6 percent, respectively, during their reelection years. Both were rewarded with a second term.[33]

Party attachments in the electorate typically change at a snail's pace, and party attachments in this country were essentially even in 2000 and 2004. By 2008 however, the Democrats had a healthy advantage in party identification. Furthermore, with the economy in trouble and the war in Iraq moving into its fifth year, as well as presidential approval numbers in record low territory, all the fundamental factors seem to be with the Democrats in 2008.

Still, these fundamental advantages that the Democrats enjoy in 2008 do not mean that a Democrat will definitely win. Swing voters still have to reach a threshold level of comfort with a presidential candidate. In 1980, the fundamental factors advantaged the Republicans, but it was not until late in the campaign that Ronald Reagan achieved credibility with key blocks of voters and was able to win the election. In 2004, even with President Bush's approval level in a dangerous zone for an incumbent, John Kerry was not quite able to reach a threshold level of credibility with key swing voting blocks.

CaseStudy: Election 2000: Failed Forecast

We return now to the question posed at the beginning of the chapter: In light of forecasting models that predicted a big win for Al Gore in the 2000 presidential election, did Gore blow the election, or did political scientists blow their predictions? The answer is *both*. On the one hand, Gore did not receive the normal boost expected from having served under a president with job approval ratings as high as those of Bill Clinton. Why? One explanation is that the Gore campaign sought to distance its candidate from President Clinton, perhaps fearing that disapproval of Clinton's moral behavior might hurt Gore, and/or wanting Gore to emerge from Clinton's shadow and be his own man. Whatever the reason, Gore avoided running as the candidate of "four more years of good times, without the scandal"—a fact that was noted during the 2000 campaign, and that drew criticism from Democrats. As a result, Gore appears not to have received the full benefit of the Clinton administration's strong economic record.[34]

As for evaluation of the candidate as a man and a potential president, Gore did not suffer from a significant "likeability deficit" with the electorate—despite his admittedly stiff and occasionally prickly manner. He also got relatively high marks from voters for competence and experience, and for his positions on specific issues. However, he appears to have paid a price for voters' perceptions that he was too liberal—more liberal, in fact, than George W. Bush was conservative, and more liberal than the president (Clinton) with whom Gore had served.[35] The Gore campaign has to take some blame for running him as a left-leaning populist, rather than a centrist in the Clinton tradition.

And what about the political scientists? As noted above, their forecasting models do not take into account the unique aspects of a particular campaign, including candidates and their campaign strategies. To the extent that there were particular campaign effects in 2000, as suggested, they worked to Al Gore's disadvantage. This was one reason the political scientists' predictions were overly optimistic about Gore's election prospects. Also as noted, Gore did not attempt what admittedly would have been a difficult straddle—openly embracing the successful record of the Clinton administration, while distancing himself from Clinton's behavior in the Lewinsky scandal. But political scientists, too, failed to make a necessary straddle—one that would have been much easier than Gore's. Although they included Clinton's job approval ratings in their models, they did not include voters' assessments of his personal behavior. Historically, these two measures have tended to track one another fairly closely. In Clinton's case, though, his personal ratings were substantially lower than his job approval. This disconnect appears to have hurt Al Gore in the election.[36] In that respect, Gore got the worst of both worlds. He failed to get full credit for his association with the economic prosperity of the Clinton years, and he was weighed down by the judgments of voters disenchanted with Clinton's behavior. It may have been no consolation to Gore, but this split embarrassed political scientists too. By failing to take into consideration Clinton's low personal ratings and include them in their models, they wrongly predicted a Gore win—and a fairly handy one at that.

ThinkingCritically

1. Suppose you had been an advisor to Barack Obama or John McCain in 2008, how would you have explained to them the fundamentals of American presidential elections?

2. Given what you have learned, what campaign message would you have recommended that each try to convey to voters? How would you have communicated the message, in order to achieve the objectives of a successful campaign?

The reward/punishment equation. What all of this suggests is that a basic "reward/punishment" or retrospective voting model, combined with a recognition of the importance of partisanship, is a sensible way to think about and understand election outcomes. Every election year starts with the electorate divided into three camps—Republicans, Democrats, and independents. There will be some movement among these groups during the year, but their proportions should remain fairly stable. Naturally, the vast majority of strong partisans vote loyally. Some of the weaker partisans, though, and most of the independents will likely decide on the basis of comparative candidate evaluations that are heavily influenced by the performance and leadership of the party in power. In terms of the political scientists' predictive models, if voters are generally pleased with the incumbent party and its president—as indicated in presidential approval ratings—they will be inclined to look favorably on the party's candidate for president. Likewise, if the economy has performed well with the incumbent party in charge, that party's candidate for president is likely to receive favorable voter evaluations and be rewarded with the presidency.

Those who are not political scientists tend to be uncomfortable with this logic, and with political scientists' predictive models, because they seem to omit so much. In 2004, for example, the news was full of stories on the Iraq war. Had George W. Bush misled the country about the presence of weapons of mass destruction in Iraq? Was deposing Saddam Hussein worth the cost in American lives and tax dollars? While it might seem that the forecasting models do not take into account such important voter concerns, they do—by way of presidential approval. To the extent these concerns were important to voters, they were included in the president's job approval ratings. And as noted above, President Bush's second quarter approval ratings were hardly in a comfortable range for him. In fact, when the president's Gallup poll rating dropped to 46 percent in early May of 2004, Frank Newport of Gallup said, "Looking at [his approval rating] in context, Bush is following the trajectory of the three incumbents who ended up losing rather than the trajectory of the five incumbents who won."[37]

The Presidential Campaign

The foregoing discussion has mentioned nothing about the impact of the campaign itself on the outcome of presidential elections. What about the hundreds of millions of dollars that were spent on television advertising between Labor Day and November 2, 2004? What about the national conventions, debates, and visits to key states like Florida, Ohio, and Pennsylvania? Did none of this matter at all?

The short answer is yes, it did matter. In fact, considered from one perspective, it mattered greatly. Imagine a hypothetical election year in which one party decided to mount an election campaign, but the other party did not. One party ran television and radio advertisements; conducted a **direct mail** campaign; organized get-out-the-vote efforts (GOTV) in important states; showed up for the debates; traveled around the country to motivate and mobilize local party activists; and held a national convention. Now, imagine that the other party did none of these things. Would it matter? Almost certainly. The party that had run a campaign could expect a higher turnout rate among partisans than the party that had done nothing. The party that had run a campaign could expect higher loyalty among its partisans—that is, fewer voter "defections" to the other party's candidate—than the party that had done nothing. Finally, the party that had run a campaign could expect a higher vote among weak partisans and independents than the party that had done nothing.

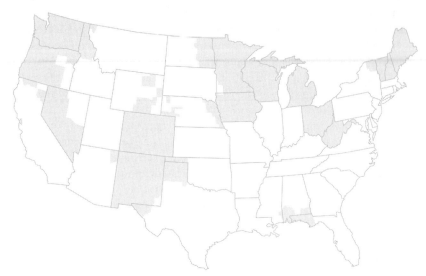

Figure 9-4. Map of Advertising Buys in 2008. Advertising in the presidential race in 2004 was highly focused with a handful of states getting the great majority of all advertising dollars.
Source: To Come.

In the real political world, though, both parties run very active, aggressive presidential campaigns. In one sense, then, the parties' efforts offset one another. But the parties' and candidates' efforts are not always equally effective. In a close race, a particularly good campaign or a particularly inept one might budge the vote just enough to make a difference between winning and losing. After all, had 250 votes in Florida gone for Al Gore rather than George Bush in 2000, Gore would have won the presidency. Thus, though political scientists do not think of the campaign as routinely decisive, they recognize that it can be—particularly when the country is closely divided politically. They also freely admit that their forecasting models, which do not explicitly account for campaign effects, often miss the mark in their predictions by a few percentage points. These misses clearly could be a result of unmeasured campaign effects—and as noted, in a close election, those effects can be the difference between winning and losing.

Turnout, loyalty, defection, and persuasion are the ingredients of a successful campaign.

Consistent with the arguments presented above, candidates and their campaign managers know that to win a presidential election they must successfully achieve as many as possible of the following objectives:

- achieve high turnout among their own party's identifiers,
- win a large share of the vote from their own party's identifiers,
- encourage some of the other candidate's partisans to "defect,"
- reduce turnout among the other candidate's identifiers, and win independents.

A winning campaign equation based on these objectives would look something like this:

Turnout + Loyalty + Defection + Persuasion = Victory

The equation begins with turnout—getting large numbers of your own partisans to show up on Election Day, and if possible, demoralizing the other candidate's partisans so that they do not vote. Loyalty is next—ensuring that the highest possible percentage of your partisans vote for your party's candidate. Defection is the reverse of loyalty—getting some of the other party's voters to cast their ballots for your party's candidate. Last comes persuasion—convincing independent voters that they should vote for your candidate rather than the other party's. Put all of these elements together, and they add up to victory.

Campaign messages are meticulously researched and targeted.

How do campaigns pursue the elements of victory? First, by developing messages or themes beneficial to their candidate. When constructed properly, these messages may induce voters to view one candidate more favorably; may generate enthusiasm among partisans, inspiring them to vote; and may demoralize the other party's voters, discouraging them to vote. Messages and themes that have these qualities are repeated endlessly in debates, campaign appearances, and television and radio advertising.

The fundamental factors mentioned above—the state of the economy and presidential approval—render some messages more plausible and effective than others. A shaky economy, for example, set the stage for Bill Clinton's successful campaign to unseat George Bush in 1992. With its mantra of "it's the economy, stupid," the Clinton team continually reminded voters of the country's sluggish employment situation, placing the blame squarely on George Bush's shoulders. The substantial rise in welfare caseloads under President Bush also opened the door to the memorable Clinton pledge to "end welfare as we know it."

In other cases, the political environment significantly constrains the message options available to candidates. Consider 1980, when Jimmy Carter's reelection bid was hindered by an election-year recession and a series of foreign-policy crises, including a protracted hostage standoff at the U.S. embassy in Tehran, Iran. A "You've never had it so good" campaign did not fit the facts or the national mood. Thus, Carter sought to raise serious doubts about his opponent, Ronald Reagan, and the conservative Republicans that Reagan spoke for:

> The Republican nominee advocates abandoning arms control policies which have been important and supported by every Democratic President since Harry Truman, and also by every Republican President since Dwight D. Eisenhower. This radical and irresponsible course would threaten our security and could put the whole world in peril. You and I must never let this come to pass.[38]

How do campaigns develop such messages? Using information gathered from research on their opponents and the positions of their own candidate, they identify the most persuasive arguments for their side and against their opponent, and the most compelling language with which to couch their message. Among the methods they use toward this end are surveys and **focus groups**—in-depth interviews with a small number of people representing important voter constituencies (undecided voters, for example). Consider, for example, this excerpt from a 2004 focus group report prepared by Democracy Corps, a not-for-profit political consulting firm founded by Democratic campaign professionals:

> In our discussions with voters, we explored attitudes toward George W. Bush and John Kerry, [and] views on major issues impacting the vote. . . . We also compared Bush's current message with a Kerry message centered on American priorities,

and looked at voters' responses to some of the candidates' television commercials.

. . .Key observations include:

- Attitudes toward Bush remained unchanged from the many other focus groups we have conducted since 9/11. Positive feelings still revolve around his moral character, Christianity, strong family, leadership, decisiveness, and patriotism. The only policy related area where he received credit was 9/11 and his strong response during the nation's crisis. As usual, the doubts about Bush were wrapped in his close ties to big business, spending too much overseas at the expense of our problems at home, and for some, a go-it-alone foreign policy.

- Perceptions of Kerry are forming and most participants had some opinion of him, frequently reflecting the messages delivered in the Bush and Kerry television commercials. A dominant attitude was that Kerry changes his position on issues and tells people what they want to hear; he will also raise their taxes. And while people recognize his military service, for now, negative perceptions driven by the media dominate the positive ones.

- Despite the even division among the number of [2000] Gore voters and Bush voters within the focus groups—which, as usual, played out with highly polarized views on Bush and the parties—the Kerry message of prioritizing and creating a strong America, and going in a new direction was far better received than Bush's message of steady leadership demanded by these times. This held true in all groups regardless of gender, income, or education.39

Once campaign messages are developed and tested, they need to be delivered. Television advertising is one major way that political campaigns deliver their messages. In the 2004 presidential campaign, over $800 million was spent on television advertising. (Tens of millions more were spent on radio and direct mail ads.) Because the Electoral College ultimately chooses the president, candidates have a strong incentive to focus their advertising on states that are expected to be especially competitive in the fall campaign because they have many Electoral College votes. With winner-take-all rules for assigning the vast majority of electoral votes, it makes little sense for candidates to invest resources in states that they can safely expect to win or lose. There is no "extra credit" for an especially large victory margin, and no credit at all for coming in second. Campaigns spend advertising dollars accordingly.

In the 2004 election, for example, the Bush and Kerry campaigns bought no political advertising at all in the country's three largest states: California, New York, and Texas. Both camps were confident that Kerry would win California and New York, and Bush would win Texas. Thus, neither had any reason to advertise there. But the Bush and Kerry campaigns both invested heavily in television advertising in three states that were vote-rich and thought to be competitive—Ohio, Florida, and Pennsylvania. (Bush ended up winning Ohio and Florida. Kerry won Pennsylvania.)

In recent years, the list of such competitive or **battleground states**, along with those that are reliably Republican or Democrat, has been fairly stable. In 2004 the Republican states came to be known as "**red states,**" because of media graphics that used the color red to indicate these states on election maps. For the same reason, reliably Democratic states have come to be called "**blue states.**" Competitive, "swing," or battleground states are usually indicated with white, yellow, or gray. Figure 9-5 offers one picture of the states thought to be red, blue, and competitive, respectively, prior to the 2004 election. Figure 9-6 shows the actual results of the 2004 election.

Field operations encourage voting and make it more convenient to vote.

To help achieve their objectives, presidential campaigns pursue one final type of campaign tactic, known as **field operations**. If television advertising constitutes the "air war" in a political campaign, then field operations are the "ground war." Field operations are intended to produce high turnout among party loyalists, particularly in battleground states. Specific tactics include phone calls, letters, e-mail, and personal visits, encouraging supporters to vote and offering resources to help them do so. For example, Democrats know that African Americans in most cases will overwhelmingly support their party's nominee. The Democratic Party has, therefore, traditionally invested significant resources in get-out-the-vote efforts targeted at African-American neighborhoods in large cities within competitive states. Republicans, by contrast, invest considerable energy in turning out white, evangelical Christians, who have become core supporters of the GOP.

Campaign finance laws govern the way campaigns raise and spend money.

Running a modern campaign for the presidency or for Congress is extremely expensive. In the 2004 election, the incumbent president George W. Bush spent more than $345 million on his reelection campaign. His Democratic opponent,

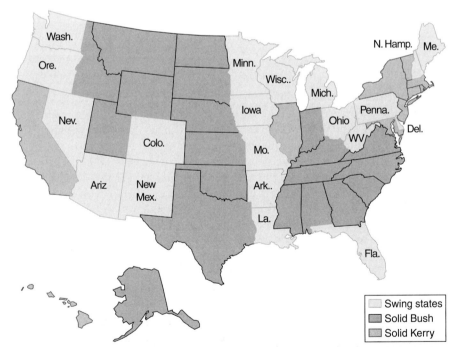

Figure 9-5. **Classification of States According to Their Pre-Election Status: Pro-Bush, Pro-Kerry, or Competitive.** Kerry and Bush could each count on the support of about one in three states. The campaign would be fought out in fewer than 20 states along the Mississippi River and the upper Midwest.
Source: To Come.

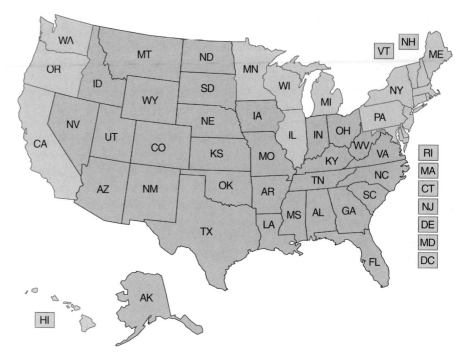

Figure 9-6. **State-by-State Results from the 2004 Election.** In 2004, Democrat John Kerry was strong in the Northeast, upper Midwest, and along the West Coast. Republican George Bush dominated in the South, the Plains, and in the Mountain West.
Source: To Come.

Massachusetts Senator John Kerry, spent more than $310 million.[40] Races for the Senate in 2004 averaged about $2.6 million; races for the House of Representatives, more than $530,000.[41] These averages include many races that were not competitive; in competitive races spending is much higher.

In order to spend money, of course, campaigns first have to raise it. The rules governing campaign fund-raising are very complex, and have changed considerably in recent years. To understand campaign finance, one must begin with the three kinds of monies used to fund federal campaigns: hard money, soft money, and public money. **Hard money** refers to funds designated for the express purpose of running an election campaign, or advocating for or against the election of a specific candidate. **Soft money** refers to funds designated for political purposes other than running a campaign—voter registration and get-out-the-vote efforts, for example, or political advertising that does not expressly advocate the election or defeat of a specific candidate. **Public money** refers to taxpayer funds designated to help finance presidential campaigns, both in the primary season and in the general election. The laws and regulations governing these three kinds of monies differ substantially.

Hard money. For each political campaign, individuals are currently permitted to contribute up to $2,300 in hard money. The primary election and general election are considered separate elections, so an individual can contribute $4,600 per year to the same campaign. This amount is indexed to inflation, so it will rise to keep pace with future price increases.

To each of the national political parties (the Democratic National Committee and the Republican National Committee), an individual each year may contribute up to $26,700 in hard money—an amount that is also indexed for inflation. In addition, an individual may contribute up to $5,000 to any federal **political action committee (PAC)**. A political action committee is an organization funded by 50 or more people, usually affiliated with a corporation, labor union, or some other special interest group. The PAC combines individual contributions to funnel campaign funds to federal candidates. It exists, in part, as a way to allow corporations and labor unions to make campaign contributions under tight regulations: these groups are prohibited by law from contributing directly from their corporate or union treasuries to a political campaign. Political action committees also allow individuals to pool their resources, thereby having greater influence on a campaign than they could exert on their own.

Political parties are also able to make **coordinated expenditures** on behalf of political candidates. A coordinated expenditure, as the name suggests, is one made in coordination with a campaign. If, for example, a political party were to pay for a voter survey at the request of a particular candidate, that would be considered a coordinated expenditure. In House races, coordinated expenditures by parties were limited to a total of roughly $35,000 in 2004, which will rise along with prices in future years. In Senate races, the allowable total is determined by an inflation-adjusted formula, based on the voting-age population of the state. In the largest state, California, the allowable figure amounted to nearly $2 million in 2004. According to a similar formula—based on the voting-age population of the United States, and adjusted for inflation—each party was also able to make about $16 million in coordinated expenditures on behalf of their presidential candidates in 2004.[42]

The parties and interest groups are also able to make unlimited **independent expenditures**. These are expenditures on behalf of a candidate, but without any coordination between the party and the candidate's campaign. For example, the party might wish to pay for a campaign advertisement in a local newspaper. If it checks with the candidate's campaign on the wording of the ad, that would be a coordinated expenditure. If the party places the ad completely independently of the candidate's campaign, however, that would be considered an independent expenditure.

Table 9-3 summarizes the amounts of hard money that can be given directly to a campaign, national party, or political action committee, by an individual, political action committee, or national party, respectively.

Table 9-3. Hard Money Contribution Limits

	TO ANY CANDIDATE CAMPAIGN	TO A NATIONAL PARTY	TO A POLITICAL ACTION COMMITTEE
An individual can give...	$2,300 per election, indexed to inflation	$26,700 per year, indexed to inflation	$5,000 per year
A PAC can give...	$5,000 per election	$15,000 per year	$5,000 per year
A national party can give...	$5,000 per election in the House; up to $37,300 for a Senate campaign	Not applicable	$5,000 per year

Can Congressional Candidates Buy Victory with Campaign Spending?

Running a campaign for Congress can be very expensive. In 2006, for example, the two candidates for senator in Pennsylvania, Rick Santorum and Bob Casey, spent a total of $36 million on their race. In the same year, in a single House district in Florida, candidates Vern Buchanan and Christine Jennings spent a total of more than $11 million.[43] Looking at all of the 2006 House and Senate races together, the Federal Election Commission reported that spending on congressional campaigns reached an all-time high: $2.6 billion. That figure was nearly 20 percent higher than the amount spent just four years earlier, in the 2002 congressional election.[44] The magnitude of these dollar amounts raises serious concern about the cost of congressional campaigns. Some critics have charged that candidates are simply buying their way into the House or Senate, using vast sums of donated campaign cash. This claim is precisely the sort of issue that political scientists study. Specifically, they ask: Can congressional candidates buy victory with campaign spending? How do we know?

Why it Matters

The growing chorus of concerned observers calling for campaign finance reform stresses the need to "get money out of politics." Their argument is that as campaigns become more costly, candidates must increasingly rely on private donations to get elected. The successful candidate may then feel beholden to his or her financial supporters, making decisions that favor their narrow interests. Those interests may conflict with the broader interests of the candidate's legislative district, state, or even the nation as a whole. One way to reduce candidates' reliance on private donors is to limit the amount of money that can be spent on a campaign. But such a restriction will likely have an adverse effect on one group of candidates in particular—challengers. Challengers rely on campaign spending to level the playing field with incumbents, who enter the election season with a number of advantages. Thus, any reform designed to reduce the amount of money that candidates can spend on their election campaigns may reduce the competitiveness of congressional elections, and increase the already sky-high reelection rates of incumbent members of the House and Senate.

A basic way to investigate this question is to determine whether, in fact, candidates who spend more money than their opponents actually win their elections. Most of the time, they do. In 2004, for example, the candidate who spent the most money won 415 of 435 House races, and 31 of 34 Senate races.[45] Clearly, then, there is a correlation between the amount of campaign spending and the probability of an election victory. But a political scientist would ask whether that correlation reflects *causation*—that is, whether candidates who spend more win *because* they spend more. As we noted in Chapter 1, very few political phenomena can be explained by a single cause. Instead, most events in the political world have multiple causes. Accordingly, a political scientist seeking to determine the impact of campaign spending on election outcomes would need to build a model that takes into account not just the impact of campaign spending, but all of the other variables that affect the election result.

Political scientists have, in fact, constructed such models of the electoral process, using various statistical techniques. In these models, the outcome is typically a measure of the incumbent candidate's share of the two-party vote in the election. The two causes or variables are: (a) the amount of money the incumbent candidate spent on the campaign, and (b) the amount of money the challenger spent on the campaign. Together, these two causes represent the campaign-spending variable. The purpose is to determine the extent to which campaign spending affects the election outcome, given the other variables known to influence election results, such as the party ID composition of the electorate, the challenger's political positions, the incumbent candidate's past performance, and so on. To ensure the most accurate results, all variables must be considered.

So, what have political scientists learned about the impact of campaign spending on election outcomes? To date, the results have been inconclusive on whether, or how much, incumbent spending affects the outcome of an election. However, challenger spending does appear to exert a large and consistent impact on election results. Specifically, the more the challenger spends on an election campaign, the higher his or her vote percentage tends to be, other things being equal. Even though the results on incumbent spending are inconclusive, let us assume for the moment that challenger spending does matter. Why would this be? An incumbent is usually well-known and well-liked, and has the benefits of office to help preserve and promote his or her standing with the electorate—for example, mailing privileges, political experience, the respect enjoyed by high-ranking public officials, the ability to do favors for constituents and bring federal dollars back to the state or district, easy access to local and national media, and so on. Under these circumstances, campaign spending does not help an incumbent much, precisely because the incumbent does not need much help. Because he or she starts the electoral cycle in a highly favorable position, spending money on a campaign can improve that position to a very limited extent.

Unlike incumbents, challengers often begin the election cycle with little name recognition among voters, and none of the incumbent's advantages of office. At the outset of a campaign, therefore, they can be at a distinct disadvantage. Yet, by spending large amounts of money during the campaign, chiefly on radio and television advertising, challengers can raise their name recognition dramatically, and help create a favorable impression among voters. Put simply, money can help challengers buy some of the familiarity, respect, and good will that incumbent officeholders get for free. That familiarity, respect, and good will can translate into votes for the challenger on Election Day.

These arguments make sense intuitively, and political science research supports them in most circumstances. However, imagine that an incumbent officeholder is facing a very strong challenger who is well-known and well-liked, and who has managed to raise a significant amount of money, or who has a large personal fortune available to finance a campaign. With a challenger of this quality, the campaign will be hard-fought, and the election will probably be close. When an incumbent officeholder expects an election to be close, he or she will usually raise and spend significant sums of money to fend off the challenge. Even so, because the challenger is strong and has also raised large sums of money, the race usually ends up being close anyway. In other words: Incumbent expects close race, incumbent spends heavily, outcome is close.

If, on the other hand, the incumbent faces an unknown challenger waging a largely symbolic campaign with little or no money to spend, the incumbent has every reason to expect an easy victory. Under those circumstances, he or she usually will raise and spend relatively little money. Ultimately, because the challenger is so weak, the incumbent usually wins handily. In other words: Incumbent expects easy win, incumbent spends little, incumbent wins big.

It is often the case that the more an incumbent spends, the closer the race ends up, and the less he or she spends, the greater the margin of victory. This is somewhat counterintuitive; one might expect that when incumbents spend a lot of money, they should win big, and when they spend only a little money, the race will be close. This paradoxical result occurs, however, because the same factors—the strength, experience, and quality of the challenger—influence both how much money the incumbent spends *and* the closeness of the outcome on Election Day.

There is not an easy answer to the question of whether money buys elections. In fact, the topic is a classic example of a point we have made throughout this book—namely, that correlation does not equal causality. That said, a variety of studies demonstrate that challenger spending is likely to matter more than incumbent spending and that even incumbent spending can matter at the margin—which can make all the difference in a close election.

The Bottom Line

Soft money Funds used for purposes other than the election or defeat of a specific candidate are known as soft money. The role of soft money in American politics has changed considerably since President Bush signed into law the Bipartisan Campaign Reform Act (BCRA) in 2002. BCRA is also known by the shorthand "McCain-Feingold," named for the two U.S. senators who worked for years to get the legislation passed: Republican John McCain, from Arizona, and Democrat Russell Feingold, from Wisconsin.

Prior to passage of the McCain-Feingold law, individuals, corporations, labor unions, and other groups were permitted to make unlimited soft money contributions to the national political parties. The American Federation of State, County, and Municipal Employees (AFSCME), a public employee union, generously wrote a check to the Democrats for $6.6 million. Showing that the union has a sense of humor, AFSCME also gave $500 to the Republicans. Some soft money contributions, however, were lopsided in the other direction: the Pharmaceutical Research and Manufacturers of America gave $3.3 million to the national Republican Party, but only $133,000 to the Democrats.[46] In general, Democrats were able to raise larger soft money contributions than Republicans—offsetting the Republicans' advantage in raising hard money.

Two concerns about soft money resulted in a change to the law in 2002. First, there was widespread concern about the possible corrupting influence on American politics of such large contributions. Senator McCain made the case as follows in a *Washington Post* editorial in January of 2000:

> Soft money's practical effect on the legislative process is to elevate both parties' allegiance to their chief donors above our ideological distinctions and our responsibility to address pressing national priorities. Indeed, partisan deference to core supporters of both parties is a less significant cause of legislative gridlock than is our gratitude to the chief underwriters of our campaigns in elections that are less a battle of ideas than a test of political treasuries.[47]

Aside from the allegation of corruption, there was also concern about the uses to which the parties were putting soft money. The McCain-Feingold law prohibited the use of soft money for explicitly promoting the election or defeat of a specific candidate. The political parties, however, often used soft money to pay for advertisements that were largely undistinguishable from regular campaign ads. Consider the following example, paid for by the Republican National Committee during the 1996 election.[48]

Under the terms of the law, this advertisement was not considered a campaign ad, because it did not specifically encourage people to vote against President Clinton or for his Republican opponent in the 1996 election, Kansas Senator Bob Dole. Plainly, though, the advertisement was intended to encourage negative feelings toward the president, which in turn could raise the probability of a vote for Senator Dole. But unlike hard money, there were no limits on soft money expenditures for this sort of advertising. As long as the advertisements avoided specific wording—such as "vote for" or "vote against"—they were considered issue ads rather than candidate advocacy, and could be funded by soft money without limit.

This loophole around the limits on hard money expenditures, coupled with the concerns about corruption, led to the prohibition in McCain-Feingold of soft money contributions to the political parties. However, just as soft money issue ads provided a way around the limits on hard money expenditures, campaign contributors found a new way to circumvent the ban on soft money contributions to the parties. That way was the "**527 committee**," or just "527," named for the relevant section of the Internal Revenue Code. A 527 is a tax-exempt, non-party group that

---

Sample Advertisement

"Pledge"

Clinton: I will not raise taxes on the middle class

Announcer: We heard this a lot.

Clinton: We gotta give middle class tax relief, no matter what else we do.

Announcer: Six month later, he gave us the largest tax increase in history. Higher income taxes, income taxes on Social Security benefits, more payroll taxes. Under Clinton, the typical American family now pays over $1,500 more in federal taxes. A big price to pay for his broken promise. Tell President Clinton you can't afford higher taxes for more wasteful spending.

Figure 9-7. **Sample "Issue Ad" Paid for by the Republican Party.** This ad did not use any "magic" words that explicitly advocated for a vote against Bill Clinton. Thus, the Republican party was able to air the ad with funds raised outside of campaign finance regulations.
Source: To Come.

can raise and spend money on political activities and advertising, including the kind of issue ad just described.

Public money and matching funds In addition to hard money and soft money, public money has been a major source of funding in presidential campaigns. The funding structure in the primary election process is different from that in the fall general election.

During the primary season, candidates for their party's nomination can qualify for **matching funds,** which are public monies given to candidates to match a certain percentage of the funds they have raised from private donors. In order to receive matching funds, a candidate must raise at least $5,000 in individual contributions of $250 or less in at least 20 states. The candidate must also agree to adhere to both state-specific and total spending limits during the primary season. Finally, should the candidate fail to receive at least 10 percent of the vote in two successive primaries, he or she loses eligibility for matching funds.

Candidates who can clear the fund-raising hurdle, agree to the spending limits, and continue to get at least 10 percent of the vote in party primaries will receive matching funds. Specifically, the federal government will provide a dollar-for- dollar match for each individual contribution received by the candidate up to certain limits.[49]

Candidates are not required to receive public money. If they accept public money, however, they must abide by the spending limits. If they do not accept public money, they are free to spend what they wish. This format is consistent with the Supreme Court's rulings on campaign finance, namely that spending limits on campaigns are unconstitutional unless they are voluntary. Government, therefore, has to offer something to get candidates to agree to limit their spending. In determining whether or not to participate in the matching fund system, then, candidates have to assess their ability to win the nomination within the confines of the federal spending limits, and also their ability to raise the funds without the help of public financing. Furthermore, candidates often want to spend money *after* the primary season is over—to keep their names on voters' minds before the national conventions and fall campaigns take place. If a candidate believes that the federal spending limits will leave inadequate dollars to fund a post-primary media campaign, he or she may opt out of the public funding system.[50]

In recent years, some candidates have shunned public financing during the primaries. In 2000, for example, George W. Bush became the first eventual party nominee to refuse matching funds. In 2004 he refused again, as did Democratic Senator John Kerry, who went on to become his party's nominee. In 2008, none of the major candidates accepted matching funds in the primaries. On the Democratic side, Hillary Clinton and Barack Obama raised massive amounts of money—over $200 million for Clinton and over $250 million for Obama. The campaigns raised their money in significantly different ways, however. The majority of Clinton's contributions came from donors giving the maximum amount. Obama relied on many more contributors—over one and a half million—who gave smaller amounts, often online.

Once the parties have selected their nominees, the federal government provides financing for the fall general election campaign. In 2004, the Democratic and Republican presidential nominees each received about $75 million to spend on the presidential campaign. As a condition of receiving this money, however, the candidates had to agree that (a) their campaigns would not seek to raise or spend any additional funds from private individuals; and (b) they would not spend any more than $50,000 of their own personal funds on the campaign. If they agree to these terms, the candidates are able to spend the campaign funds largely as they see fit, with no state-specific limits on spending. In other words, if a candidate wished to spend all $75 million in, say, Hawaii or California or New York, he or she could do so. In 2008, Barack Obama, is unlikely to take public funds while the Republican nominee, John McCain, will.

Third parties—that is, parties other than the Democrats and Republicans—can qualify for full general election campaign funding only if they receive at least 25 percent of the vote in the previous presidential election. If a party accomplished this, it would retroactively receive the same amount received by the two major parties in that year, and it would be given an equal share in the next presidential election, just like the two major parties. And just like the major parties, it would receive these funds at the outset of the general election campaign, not after the election. No third party has received full public funding, but third parties can receive *some* public funds by receiving at least 5 percent of the national vote in the preceding election. For example, based on the performance of presidential candidate Ross Perot in 1992 and 1996, the Reform Party qualified for partial general election funding in 1996 and 2000.[51]

SUMMARY

▶ The first objective of a candidate running for office is to receive his or her party's nomination. In the presidential race the candidate does so by winning a majority of delegates to the party's nominating convention during the state primary elections. The Electoral College and the "winner-take-all" system do much to define the American political landscape.

▶ Certain key factors determine how voters make electoral choices. Primary among these are "the big three" determinants—party identification, issue voting (including the retrospective vote), and candidate evaluations. A voter's party ID is the single most important influence on vote choice in the general election. Other influences are voters' opinions on specific issues and retrospective voting, in which voters judge candidates based on their, or their party's, past performance. Despite idiosyncratic voter behavior and the complex interaction of "the big three," vote prediction forecasting models are highly accurate.

▶ In order to succeed in presidential primaries, it is crucial to win the invisible primary. This includes leading the field in public opinion polls, in fund-raising, or in both at the end of the pre-primary period. Candidates who begin the heavily front- loaded primary season in the lead often go on to win. Primaries follow each other too rapidly for underdog candidates to devote resources to multiple races and build the momentum necessary to win the nomination. In general elections, presidential approval ratings and economic performance are the two variables most often included in election forecasting models—and have excellent predictive power. The partisan orientations of the electorate, whether there is an incumbent president running for reelection, and how long his party has held the presidency are also significant factors. Not to be forgotten, however, is the significance of campaign effects at the margin in close races.

▶ Understanding the "victory equation" and its components, turnout, loyalty, defection and persuasion, is crucial to understanding how presidential candidates wage a campaign. The main ways candidates attempt to secure these components are by developing messages or themes beneficial to the campaign, and by effectively managing field operations. The messages and field operations are carefully planned and are targeted almost exclusively to battleground states. Forecasting models and candidates are not perfect, however, as demonstrated by the failed forecasts of the 2000 presidential election. Ultimately, the Al Gore campaign and political scientists failed to appropriately manage and account for Bill Clinton's negative association—and both suffered the consequences.

▶ Finally, running a modern campaign for the presidency or for Congress is extremely expensive and campaign finance laws dictate how money may be raised and spent by candidates. Campaign finance laws further distinguish between hard, soft, and public money, and are responsible for the recent proliferation of 527 organizations to circumvent restrictions on these monies.

KEY TERMS

527 committee, p. 000
battleground states, p. 000
blue states, p. 000
caucus, p. 000
closed primary, p. 000
coordinated expenditures, p. 000
delegates, p. 000
direct mail, p. 000
Electoral College, p. 000
field operations, p. 000
focus groups, p. 000
hard money, p. 000
independent expenditures, p. 000
invisible primary, p. 000
issue voting, p. 000

matching funds, p. 000
modified open primary, p. 000
momentum, p. 000
open primary, p. 000
plurality rule, p. 000
political action committee (PAC), p. 000
primaries, p. 000
prospective voting, p. 000
public money, p. 000
red states, p. 000
retrospective voting, p. 000
soft money, p. 000
valence issues, p. 000
winner-take-all, p. 000

SELECTED READINGS

Paul Abramson, John Aldrich and D. Rohde. 2007. *Change and Continuity in the 2004 and 2006 Elections*. Washington, DC: CQ Press.

Gary Jacobson. 2008. *Politics of Congressional Elections*. New York: Longman.

Richard G. Niemi and Herbert F. Weisberg (eds.). 2007. *Controversies in Voting Behavior*. Washington, DC: CQ Press.(Ann Arbor, MI: University of Michigan Press, 1998), 8.

delegates individuals who represent a state's voters in the selection of a political party's presidential candidate.

caucus a small meeting at which registered political party members select delegates to attend the national party convention and nominate a presidential candidate.

primaries elections in which voters choose the candidate that will represent their political party in the general election.

electoral college a body of presidential electors who act as representatives of the 50 states and the District of Columbia.

winner-take-all election in which the candidate who gets the most votes wins, while any other candidate(s) loses and receives nothing.

open primary an election in which a voter can participate in either party's primary (but not both), regardless of his or her party registration.

modified open primary an election in which registered voters who are not affiliated with either party can vote in either party's primary.

closed primary an election in which only registered members of a political party can participate in the party's primary election.

plurality rule rule by which a candidate wins office by getting more votes than his or her opponent, even if that candidate does not receive an absolute majority of the votes.

issue voting voting style in which the voter judges candidates based on the voter's and the candidates' opinions on specific issues and preferences for certain policies.

prospective voting voting style in which voters judge a candidate based on their assessment of what the candidate will do in office, if elected.

retrospective voting voting style in which voters judge candidates based on the candidates', or their party's, performance rather than issue stands and assessments of what each candidate would do if elected.

valence issues issues on which virtually everyone agrees.

invisible primary the race to raise the most money and achieve frontrunner status before the primary season begins.

momentum the boost in media coverage, name recognition, fund-raising, and perceptions of electability that accompanies unexpected and repeated primary success.

direct mail political advertising in which messages are sent directly to potential voters in the form of mail or e-mail, rather than using a third-party medium.

focus group in-depth interview with a small number of people representing important voter constituencies.

battleground states competitive states in which no candidate has an overwhelming advantage, and therefore whose Electoral College votes are in play.

red states largely uncontested states in which the Republican candidate for president is very likely to win.

independent expenditures legally unlimited purchases or payments made by a political party on behalf of, but without coordination with, a specific campaign.

blue states largely uncontested states in which the Democratic candidate for president is very likely to win.

field operations the "ground war" intended to produce high turnout among party loyalists, particularly in battleground states.

hard money funds to be used for the express purpose of running an election campaign, or advocating for or against the election of a specific candidate.

soft money funds to be used for political purposes other than running a campaign, for example, get-out-the-vote efforts.

public money taxpayer funds used to help finance presidential campaigns.

political action committee (PAC) an organization funded by 50 or more people, affiliated with a special-interest group that makes contributions to federal candidates.

coordinated expenditures legally limited purchases or payments made by a political party on behalf of, and in coordination with, a specific campaign.

527 committee a tax-exempt, non-party group that can raise and spend unlimited sums of money on political activities and advertising, but cannot engage in express advocacy.

matching funds public monies given to qualifying candidates to match a certain percentage of the funds they have raised from private donors.

10 Media and Politics

In November of 1968, 25-year-old Yale graduate John Kerry began a four-month tour of combat duty in Vietnam. Kerry was given the command of a Patrol Craft-Fast boat (PCF), more commonly known as a swift boat. Swift boat duty was among the most dangerous assignments in the war, and Kerry was wounded several times (and won three Purple Hearts). After receiving his third wound in March of 1969, he was granted permission to return to the United States.

Kerry's Vietnam service made a profound impression on him. Witnessing the conduct of the war and sharing information with fellow Vietnam veterans, he came to believe that the war was immoral. He also believed that the day-to-day conduct of some soldiers serving in Vietnam was so barbaric as to be criminal. He testified before Congress to that effect in 1971.

When Kerry ran for president 23 years later, a group of some other swift boat veterans vehemently objected to what they called Kerry's "phony war crimes charges," and to what they alleged were exaggerations of Kerry's heroism during the war. In early May of 2004, a group of these veterans held a press conference in Washington, D.C. Calling themselves "Swift Boat Veterans for Truth," they offered to the assembled reporters personal testimony and their strong objections to a Kerry presidency. The leader of the group, John O'Neill, spoke on behalf of over 250 Swift Boat Veterans saying, "We believe, based on our experience with him, that he is totally unfit to be commander-in-chief."[1]

Despite the extraordinary nature of this charge, the event drew little attention. Only a handful of major newspapers ran stories, and none gave it prominent placement. Among the big three broadcast networks, only CBS covered the charge and anchorman Dan Rather suggested a partisan motivation by describing the group as "allied with the Bush campaign."[2]

To O'Neill, all of this indicated blatant media bias: "The establishment media was very pro-Kerry. They were opposed to any story that was critical of Kerry, and I believe that they were captured by their own bias."[3] Convinced that the mainstream media would never cover the story, the Swift Boat group adopted an alternative, two-fold strategy: they published a book about Kerry, *Unfit for Command*; and they raised funds for an anti-Kerry advertising campaign. These activities, of course, took a few months. During this time, alternative media sources began picking up on the Swift Boat Vets' story. These included talk radio hosts Sean Hannity, Rush Limbaugh, and Laura Ingraham. Matt Drudge, operator of the immensely popular Web site The Drudge Report, also began covering the Swift Boat Vets' allegations. Thus, although the story had not yet broken through in the mainstream media, the charges were gaining traction in alternative venues.

August of 2004 was a decisive month for the Swift Boat story. Using contributions by many people who had also contributed to the Bush campaign, the Swift Boat Vets placed their first anti-Kerry advertisement on 20 television stations in seven small media markets in Wisconsin, West Virginia, and Ohio.[4] The Kerry campaign threatened the television stations with legal action if they broadcast the advertisement. The stations aired the ad anyway, claiming that they were well within their legal rights to do so. In addition to the limited viewing audiences of these stations, an additional 1.5 million people downloaded the advertisement from the Internet for their own private viewing.[5]

As more people bought the Swift Boat Vets' book, saw their advertisement, and visited their Web page (http://www.swiftvets.com/), the group's fund-raising picked up dramatically. The additional funds enabled the group to plan additional advertisements, the second of which began running on August 20. On the eve of the appearance of that ad, Kerry himself publicly denounced the Swift Boat Vets, accusing them of trading in false charges and serving as a front for the Bush campaign.[6]

All of this opened the floodgates on the Swift Boat Vets story. Coverage increased dramatically—television networks and newspapers that had not previously reported the story began to do so, and talk radio and Internet weblogs made the Swift Boat Vets' allegations a staple of their daily discussion. A debate about their accuracy raged in the media. One news program, *Nightline*, even sent a production crew to Vietnam to try to dig up new evidence on the allegations.

Not surprisingly, all of this activity captured the public's attention. A Gallup poll taken in late August revealed that 43 percent of Americans had seen the Swift Boat Vets' ads.[7] This figure indicated the extent to which the ads were being re-broadcast by the mainstream media and downloaded off the Internet, as only a tiny fraction of Americans lived in the media markets where the ads actually appeared. The Gallup poll also found that an additional 38 percent of Americans had heard about the allegations in the ads. In total, then, more than 80 percent of Americans had become aware of the Swift Boat Vets' charges, either by viewing the advertisements directly or by hearing about them second-hand.

Did these ads contribute to or even cause Kerry's defeat? Many factors shape presidential election outcomes, and pinpointing how many votes Kerry lost because of the actions of the Swift Boat Vets would be impossible. What is certain, however, is that they did not help Kerry. For most of August, Kerry had held a slim lead over incumbent President Bush. In late August he relinquished that lead and never regained it. Moreover, the percentage of Americans saying that Kerry's Vietnam service made them more likely to vote for him declined from 42 percent to 21 percent during the time the Swift Boat story was gaining traction.[8]

Whatever its effect on the 2004 presidential race, the Swift Boat Veterans for Truth campaign raises a number of interesting themes and questions relevant to the place of media in American politics.

THIS CHAPTER WILL EXAMINE:

▶ the unique role that the media play in American politics and society

▶ the legal constraints on American media

▶ the types of media that exist today

▶ the nature of media coverage of politics and government

▶ the question of whether the media are biased

▶ the effect of the media on attitudes and behaviors.

The Unique Role of the American Mass Media

The **mass media** are the various modes of communication designed to reach a mass audience. These include television, radio, newspapers, newsmagazines, and the Internet. The term also refers to the individuals responsible for producing the content disseminated through various communications media. Thus, when this chapter refers to "the media," it may be referring to the actual communications media themselves (newspapers, for example), or to the people who are responsible for their content (for example, newspaper reporters and editors). In many respects, the mass media occupy a position in American political life different from that in most other countries. We shall examine several of these differences in this section.

American mass media are largely privately owned.

First, unlike other industrialized democracies, the largest media outlets in the United States are owned and operated in the private sector, rather than by the government. The U.S. government does not own any major television networks or cable news outlets. Public broadcasting in the United States receives only a small share of its funding from the government and accounts for about 2 percent of the total television audience share.[9] By contrast, in the vast majority of European countries and the democratic countries of Asia and the Pacific, the government owns at least one major television outlet.[10] Government-owned outlets in these areas typically have at least a 30 to 40 percent audience share.[11] In the United Kingdom, for example, the various channels of the government-owned and -operated British Broadcasting Company (BBC) dominate the airwaves.[12]

Newspapers are a different story. In the industrialized democracies, including the United States, government ownership of print media is highly unusual. However, many other countries have a print tradition that is not well established in the United States—that of the national newspaper. Most American newspapers are tied to a particular city, state, or region—the *San Francisco Chronicle*, the *New York Post*, the *Des Moines Register*, and the *Rocky Mountain News* are examples. In other countries, though, some of the oldest, most respected, and most widely read newspapers are national in scope. These include the *Sun* in the United Kingdom, *Le Monde* in France, and *Die Zeit* in Germany.

American mass media stress objective political coverage.

A second difference lies in the American media's effort to be objective and non-partisan in covering the news. This means that reporters and editors generally seek to present all sides completely, fairly, and accurately. Journalists usually refrain from advocating particular views or suggesting who or what is right and wrong. They also operate independently of government and the political parties, refusing to become spokespeople for any particular party or government administration.

Media in other countries do not always follow these standards. In Western Europe, for example, newspapers frequently assume an advocacy role, presenting the news in ways that support a particular political party or ideology.[13] In 1997, for example, the British *Daily Mirror* newspaper openly supported the election of Labour Party candidate for prime minister Tony Blair. Topless models, so-called "Blair babes," appeared in the paper every day, giving their reasons for supporting Blair.[14] Similarly, if less provocatively, with its first edition in the 1970s, the Italian newspaper *La Republica* announced:

> This newspaper is a bit different from others: It is a journal of information that
> doesn't pretend to follow an illusory political neutrality but declares explicitly
> that it has taken a side in the political battle. It is made by men who belong to
> the vast arc of the Italian left.[15]

In the United States, such open advocacy for a party, candidate, or philosophy by a mainstream newspaper would be unthinkable. (So, too, would the appearance of topless models.)

Journalists in other countries also hold different views of the *meaning* of objectivity. American journalists are more likely than others to see their role as limited to reporting opposing sides' positions (see Figure 10-1). In a multinational survey, for

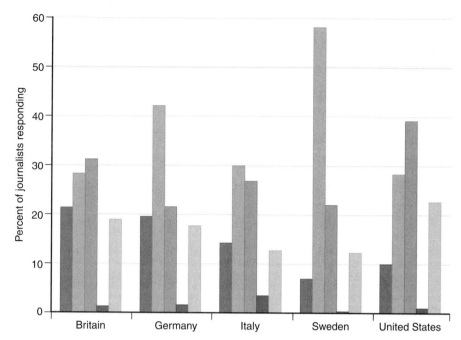

Legend:
- An equally thorough questioning of the position of each side in a political dispute
- Going beyond the statements of the contending sides to the hard facts of a political dispute
- Expressing fairly the position of each side in a political dispute
- Making clear which side in a political dispute has the better position
- Not allowing your own political beliefs to affect the presentation of the subject

Figure 10-1. American journalists are more likely to support presenting both sides of an issue than are colleagues in other countries.

Source: Thomas E. Patterson "Political Roles of the Journalist." In *The Politics of News* eds. Doris Graber, Denis McQuail, and Pippa Norris (Washington, D.C.: Congressional Quarterly Press), p. 22, table 1.1.

example, only 28 percent of American journalists said that "objectivity" meant "going beyond the statements of the contending sides to the hard facts of a political dispute." In Sweden, this definition was supported by 58 percent of journalists. Moreover, 39 percent of American journalists defined objectivity as "expressing fairly the position of each side in a political dispute," while only 21 percent of German journalists said that this definition closely reflected their understanding of "objectivity."[16]

These differing views of objectivity have practical implications. Journalists in Sweden and Germany act not only as reporters of information but also as analysts and social critics. They attempt to reveal the "hard facts" behind and beyond what political figures say and do. Many American journalists would consider this stepping into the middle of a political debate, which would violate their objectivity standard. But foreign journalists see it merely as delivering a truthful version of events to audiences—a version of events not typically available from politicians.[17]

American mass media play a "watchdog" role in government and politics.

The job of the American journalist is sometimes described as "comforting the afflicted and afflicting the comfortable."[18] When they "afflict the comfortable," journalists are serving in a **watchdog** role. They keep a close eye on government and politics, watching for signs of dishonesty, corruption, unfair dealing, and broken promises, and investigating aggressively when they have found such evidence. In other words, they often seek to "uncover" news, that is, to present stories and information that politicians might not willingly reveal to the media.

This watchdog role marks a third respect in which American journalists differ from some of their foreign counterparts. In Italy, Germany, and the United Kingdom, for example, print and broadcast media are more passive in their coverage of politics. Rather than actively patrolling the political arena for signs of foul play, journalists in these countries tend to take their cues from political actors on which stories deserve news coverage.[19]

American mass media operate largely unfettered by government restriction.

A fourth difference is that the American media are largely unrestrained by government interference. Most significantly, U.S. media are allowed to publish or broadcast free from the threat of **prior restraint**—that is, government intervention to stop the publication of material it finds objectionable. This freedom has never been absolute, however. The Supreme Court has ruled that if publication of certain information "will surely result in direct, immediate, and irreparable harm to our nation or its people," then prior restraint can be exercised.[20] For instance, the government often tries and sometimes succeeds in exercising prior restraint in cases involving national security. A broadcast or print outlet could be restrained from publishing the secret locations of U.S. armed forces in enemy territory, or the names and addresses of intelligence agents overseas. Significantly, however, the Supreme Court has made it clear that the burden rests with government to demonstrate that publication would be harmful, rather than with the media to show why the information merits a public airing.

This principle grew out of the Pentagon Papers case in June of 1971. During the early summer of 1971, the *New York Times*, the *Washington Post*, and the *Boston Globe* published excerpts of a top-secret government study of U.S. involvement in Vietnam. The excerpts were provided by Daniel Ellsberg, a former government employee who had worked on the study and who had become disenchanted with the Vietnam War. Initial excerpts cited repeated examples of poor presidential decision-making and failures to deal honestly with both Congress and the American public. Claiming a threat to national security, the Nixon administration sought an injunction to prevent publication of further installments. The administration won an injunction but the victory was short-lived; the U.S. Supreme Court ultimately ruled in favor of the newspapers and argued that the government did not meet the extraordinarily high burden of proof necessary to justify such a restraint.

There are, however, instances when the media will voluntarily hold off publishing or broadcasting information. This was the case in 2005 when the *New York Times* learned of a covert program in which American scientists and special forces helped guard Pakistani nuclear material. Due to the fear of adverse reaction in Pakistan and the Muslim world if word got out about the top-secret program, the Bush administration asked the *New York Times* not to reveal its existence. The paper agreed and held the information for more than two years. In this case, the key point was that the paper's restraint was voluntary. There was virtually nothing the Bush administration could have done to prevent the paper publishing the information.

Constraints on American Media Freedom

The press's ability to publish what it deems appropriate without government restriction has come a long way over the course of American history. Members of the modern media face very few of the restraints faced by their earliest forebears. However, contemporary political journalists in the United States do face some significant constraints on what they can air or publish.

The freedom the American press enjoys was not won quickly.

The relative freedom that characterizes U.S. media operations today was not established by the adoption of the First Amendment in 1791. At the time of its passage, the First Amendment was thought to guarantee freedom of the press only from prior restraint by government. Expansions of freedom were won through ongoing battles between the press, the government, and public figures, many of which the press lost.

Early restrictions on the press The most famous early restriction on the press was the Sedition Act, a federal law passed in 1798. The act effectively criminalized criticism of Congress and the president:

> . . . if any person shall write, print, utter or publish . . . any false, scandalous and malicious writing or writings against the government of the United States, or either house of the Congress of the United States, or the President of the United States, with intent to defame the said government, or either house of the said Congress, or the said President, or to bring them, or either of them, into contempt or disrepute; or to excite against them, or either or any of them, the hatred of the good people of the United States . . . then such person, being thereof convicted before any court of the United States having jurisdiction thereof, shall be punished by a fine not exceeding two thousand dollars, and by imprisonment not exceeding two years.[21]

Ostensibly, the act was designed for national security purposes—to silence American supporters of France, a country with which President John Adams feared the United States might soon be at war.[22] Critics argued, however, that the act was intended instead to quiet the critics of President Adams and his Federalist Party allies in Congress.[23] And, in fact, all 14 individuals indicted under the act (10 of whom were convicted) were members of the Antifederalist opposition—mostly editors of opposition newspapers.[24]

When Thomas Jefferson, leader of the Antifederalists, was elected president in 1800, he freed those still serving prison sentences because of Sedition Act convictions. The Sedition Act itself was allowed to expire in 1801, but the struggle for a free press was far from over. During the Civil War, the federal government limited telegraph transmissions from Washington, D.C., that it argued might compromise the successful planning and prosecution of the war. During the post–Civil War era, the federal government jailed reporters who were critical of the program of southern Reconstruction. Reporters also were cited for contempt of court for describing pending legal cases, particularly if they criticized presiding judges.

By the turn of the twentieth century, press outlets were being sued, successfully, for printing photographs of and intimate gossip about figures of interest to the public.

Legislation was enacted to restrict the ability of the press to "invad[e] the sacred precincts of private and domestic life."[25] Further restrictions on the press were enacted during World War I. The Espionage Act, passed in 1917 and expanded in 1918, made illegal any "seditious expression"—in particular, publications that might undermine military recruitment or weaken support for the military draft. Nearly one thousand individuals ultimately were convicted for engaging in such expression.[26] A similar law, the Smith Act, was passed as World War II loomed. Though it was rarely enforced during the war, it was used in the early post-war years to prosecute American communists.

Establishment of press freedoms in the twentieth century A counter-vailing trend began to appear during the 1930s, when the Supreme Court started to develop a more expansive interpretation of the First Amendment. The trend took decades to reach maturity, but, by the end of the 1970s, the press freedoms that we recognize today had largely been established in case law and federal statute. Eventually, the press—and private individuals who wished to publish information for mass distribution—won important decisions expanding their freedom to criticize the government and public officials; guaranteeing their right to cover criminal trials and aspects of individuals' private lives; setting highly restrictive limits on prior restraint in cases related to national security; and granting access to government information that was once off-limits. Thus, the twenty-first century American press operates with substantially more latitude than it did in the first 200 years of the nation's history—and with much more freedom than the mass media in most other countries.

The media can be both forbidden and compelled to provide certain information.

There are other sorts of restrictions or standards that the media must follow. For example, defamation refers to a false or unsubstantiated attack on someone's good name or reputation. To be considered defamation, an attack must be *false.* If the press calls the president a liar and a thief and he can be shown to be a liar and a thief, laws against defamation do not apply. Even if he is not a liar and a thief, however, defamation can be very difficult to prove. As the case law has evolved, the courts have stated that actual malice by the media must be demonstrated in order to prove defamation of a public figure. This means that the media outlet must have reported the defamatory information "with knowledge that it was false or with reckless disregard of whether it was false or not."[27] Furthermore, defamation cases are civil lawsuits that can be appealed endlessly. Given the difficulty of meeting this standard, public figures must rely on journalists' integrity and self-policing by media outlets, as much as on anti-defamation laws, to protect their reputations.[28]

If the government cannot actively restrain the American media from disseminating content, can the media be compelled to publish or broadcast certain information? With respect to print media, the answer is *no.* The courts have ruled that no individual or institution has a *right* to coverage of an opinion or pet issue in the print media. The broadcast media, on the other hand, are treated differently. The broadcast spectrum is considered a public asset; unlike a newspaper or magazine, no one owns it. And while the broadcast spectrum can carry only a limited amount of programming, the number of potential print outlets is unlimited. The broadcast media, therefore, are considered semi-monopolies.

For both of these reasons, the federal government takes a more active role—through the Federal Communications Commission—in regulating broadcasters. One regulation relevant to political programming is the equal time provision. Under this rule, if a television station gives time to a candidate for office, it must give all other candidates for that office equal access. Because national debates, news, and public affairs programming are exempt from this rule, its primary impact is on campaign advertising. If a local television or radio station runs a 30-second advertisement by a candidate for governor, for example, the station must offer to sell the same amount of time to the candidate's opponent(s) at equal cost. When Arnold Schwarzenegger ran for governor of California for the first time in 2003, California TV stations did not dare to air any of his movies during his election campaign for fear that it would trigger the equal time provision.

Reporters may be compelled by the federal government to reveal their sources.

Despite their resistance to the idea, reporters can be compelled to reveal the names of confidential sources. This can become an issue when the information provided by a source is germane to a legal matter. In 2003, for example, *Time* magazine published an article revealing the name of CIA officer Valerie Plame. The reporters involved in the story did nothing illegal by revealing Plame's identity, but it is illegal for a government official with authorized access to a covert agent's identity to deliberately reveal that information to a reporter. Accordingly, a federal grand jury was assembled to determine whether any criminal wrongdoing had taken place.

At the heart of the investigation was one question: Who revealed Valerie Plame's identity to reporters? Two reporters involved in the story, Matthew Cooper of *Time* magazine and Judith Miller of the *New York Times*, were called to testify. Having received permission from his source to reveal his name, Cooper named presidential adviser Karl Rove. But Miller either received no such permission from her source or chose not to exercise it; she would not reveal her source in testimony before the grand jury. For her refusal, she was sentenced to remain in jail until the grand jury was dismissed. She eventually revealed her source—Lewis Libby, Vice President Richard Cheney's chief of staff—when he released her from her pledge of confidentiality. But this happened only after she spent 85 days in jail.

In order to avoid the choice between jail and revealing a confidential source, reporters have advocated shield laws. These laws grant them certain exemptions from having to testify in legal matters. Just as a priest cannot be compelled to testify against a penitent, or a husband against a wife, shield laws protect journalists from having to reveal the name of a confidential source in a legal proceeding. Most states have adopted shield laws of varying leniency, but the federal government has not. However, both federal and state courts have recognized limited exemptions from the normal requirement that a reporter testify when subpoenaed—even when no explicit statutory exemption exists. In summary, then, reporters have some protections against compelled testimony, but those protections are far from absolute. Reporters argue they need this protection—without it, sources would fear to come forward and reveal crimes.

Despite these various restrictions, American mass media are still among the most free in the world. By way of comparison, consider working conditions for the media in Russia, ostensibly a democratic country:

> The Kremlin gained "nearly total control" of broadcast media in 2003 through legislation and financial pressure. While the print media provide some dissenting viewpoints, broadcast media has denied coverage to opposition parties and ideas. Although the Russian Supreme Court did curtail some government censorship legislation, many editors and journalists had already turned to self-censorship. Most unfortunately for those who have not, "independent journalists continue to be harassed, assaulted, kidnapped, and killed."[29]

According to Reporters without Borders, the United States ranked 22nd out of 167 countries on the index of press freedom.[30] Though American journalists sometimes complain about government restrictions on their activities, one can see that in comparative terms, they operate with tremendous latitude.

Types of Media and Patterns of Media Use

The mass media in this country began to develop long before modern technology was imaginable. Inexpensive, daily, mass-circulation newspapers—which are still available today—first appeared in the United States in the 1830s. Mass-circulation magazines devoted to political news and opinion began to appear roughly 35 years later. (*The Nation*, which is still published today, was launched in 1865.)[31]

Regularly scheduled, continuous commercial radio broadcasts began in the United States in 1920.[32] By 1933, 63 percent of Americans had radios.[33] The radio boom was short-lived, however, because of the development of television. Just after World War II, televisions and television programming began to proliferate. By 1955, half of American homes had a television set.[34] (Both radio and television ownership are now nearly universal in the United States.) Cable television was developed during this era for consumers who could not receive a strong, clear broadcast signal. It was not until the late 1970s, however, that cable began to appear in significant numbers of American homes.[35] Finally, in the mid-1990s the World Wide Web emerged as an everyday tool for the mass dissemination and consumption of information.

In the late 1950s, TV supplanted newspapers as Americans' primary information source.

Americans do not rely equally on these media forms to get their news about the world. The dominance of television over other forms of media is part of a long-term trend. Until the late 1950s, newspapers topped television as Americans' primary source of information about politics and government.[36] Since that time, however, newspaper readership has been in decline. In 1960, for example, combined circulation for morning and evening newspapers in the United States was about 59 million. By 2003, that number had fallen to 55 million—despite a nearly 60 percent increase in the U.S. population.[37]

Figure 10-2 provides additional detail on this trend, illustrating the declining percentage of Americans who report reading a newspaper "regularly."

What caused the decline in newspaper readership and the ascendancy of television? Whereas reading a newspaper requires effort, attentiveness, and energy, watching television is largely passive—even relaxing. Furthermore, print media cannot compete with the sights, sounds, emotions, and attractive personalities available on television—and, increasingly, the Internet. The mass movement of women into the workforce in the second half of the twentieth century also played a role in declining newspaper readership. Women found they had less time to read newspapers. Finally, the growth of American suburbs and exurbs increased commute times for many Americans, which also reduced the amount of leisure time available to read a daily paper.[38]

Americans are moving away from broadcast television and national network news.

Despite the dominance of television as a news source, its control has begun to weaken in recent years—particularly in broadcast television and the network news programs. Note the percentage of Americans who reported getting their news from the listed sources on a daily basis in 1995 and 2006, as shown in Figure 10-3. Local television remains the most common source of news for Americans, but cable network news, radio talk shows, and news on the Internet have become increasingly popular sources of information in the past decade. The comparison also indicates the sharply declining power of the networks as news sources. That reality is reinforced by the decline in the absolute number of viewers of the networks' nightly news programming over the same period, as shown in Figure 10-4.

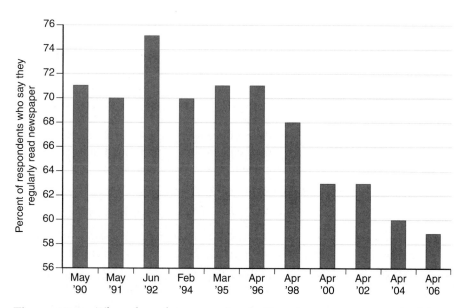

Figure 10-2. There have been massive declines in newspaper readership over the last 20 years.

Source: http://www.people-press.org/reports/questionnaires/282.pdf

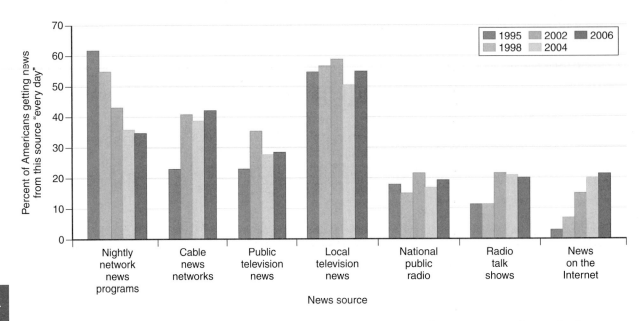

Figure 10-3. Local news continues to dominate as an "everyday" source of news.

Source: http://www.galluppoll.com/content/default.aspx?ci=260538.pg=1

Where have these viewers gone? Not to daily newspapers, as we have already noted. Some have turned to cable television. CNN, MSNBC, and the Fox News Channel all offer news programming in direct competition with the networks. Some former network viewers appear to be tuning in to talk radio for their news. Two broadcasters alone—Rush Limbaugh and Sean Hannity—each attract more than ten million listeners per week.[39] Local television news has also managed to fill part of the role the networks used to fill (see Figure 10-4). Satellite technology now makes it possible for local news stations to cover national and international stories that formerly only the "big three" networks could cover.[40] As mentioned above, more Americans get their news from local news than from any other source.

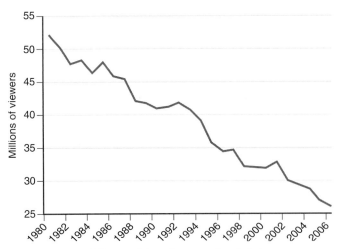

Figure 10-4. Viewership of network nightly news broadcasts is on the decline.

Source: http://www.stateofthemedia.org/2007/chartland.asp?id=211&ct=line&dir= &sort= &coll_box=1

The World Wide Web is becoming an increasingly important source of information.

An increasingly large percentage of the population is getting its news from the Internet or, more accurately, the World Wide Web (the Internet is the infrastructure and the World Wide Web is the content). In 1995, the World Wide Web was still unfamiliar to most Americans. By 2006, however, roughly one-quarter of the U.S. population was getting news from the Web on a daily basis.

When we talk about getting news on the Web, we can mean a number of different things. Almost all of the national broadcast networks, cable networks, and local television stations have a presence on the Web. Networks and most affiliates post articles, community information, and streaming video on their Web sites. Often, these television news operations use the Web to post materials or provide information that cannot be shown on their broadcasts because of limited time or the difficulty of conveying the information on television. For example, ABC News might conduct a poll about attitudes toward the economy and the president. Only a few seconds of time could be devoted to the poll on one of the network's traditional broadcasts, but ABC News could post additional analysis, commentary, and a full copy of the poll itself on its Web site. Similarly, investigative reporters might post additional analysis or the source documents they used in a particular story on the Web.

In addition, most newspapers have online editions. However, the decision to develop one is a difficult choice for newspaper owners. Unlike television stations, newspapers not only earn money from advertising but also charge for their papers as well. People may be reluctant to buy a paper if the material is available for free on the Web. Furthermore, online editions often compete with the print editions of the same newspaper. Should an editor post a story immediately when it is completed or wait until the next morning when the paper comes out? If the editor holds the story until the next day, the story may be scooped by other news outlets. At the same time, posting it on the Web decreases any incentive for buying the print edition of the paper. Nonetheless, while newspapers struggle to survive, they have little choice but to put their material on the Web.

An increased number of news and information platforms reside solely on the World Wide Web. These can include big computer service companies such as Yahoo. Yahoo both creates news content and serves as a portal to thousands of other news sources. The Yahoo homepages attempt to organize the vast amount of data available on the Web. In addition, services like "Google News" track news sources around the world.

Finally, weblogs or "blogs" are becoming an increasingly important source of information in political life—particularly for those who are politically engaged. Blogs are online journals or diaries that invite users to comment on and add content to postings on various topics. Blogs often have links to other blogs, Web sites, and sources of information. They are typically specialized by subject and tend to cater to those with particular political leanings. In other words, information on blogs typically flows to those who already agree with the "blogger." For example, liberals follow the Daily Kos and conservatives visit the Hugh Hewitt site. Some blogs have even become more professional with paid staff and slick graphics paid for by sponsors and advertisers. Most, however, are managed by individuals who simply want to use the power of the Web to get commentary out to the world.

CaseStudy: The Blogosphere Bags an Elephant

On September 8, 2004, the CBS program *60 Minutes Wednesday* aired a story on George W. Bush's service in the Texas Air National Guard during the Vietnam War era. The CBS story featured four documents purportedly taken from the files of Lieutenant Colonel Jerry B. Killian, the commander of then-Lieutenant Bush's squadron. The documents appeared to indicate that Bush had defied Killian's order to submit to a required flight physical and was suspended from flight status, as a result. They also showed that during his suspension, Bush traveled to Alabama to work on a Senate campaign. Though he had received permission to do so, the documents indicated that Lieutenant Colonel Killian was not pleased with Bush's transfer.

The CBS News story was a potential bombshell. George W. Bush's opponent in the 2004 presidential election was Massachusetts Senator John F. Kerry. Kerry had served with distinction in Vietnam, suffering combat wounds on three separate occasions. George W. Bush, on the other hand, had secured a coveted Texas Air National Guard slot that allowed him to avoid combat service in Vietnam.

One could only imagine the response to the CBS story. It was bad enough, Bush opponents would say, that he had used family political connections to get into the Guard (a charge that the CBS story also made). To make matters worse, he had not even kept up with his service commitment. He had defied a direct order to get a physical, was suspended from flight status as a result, and went to work on a political campaign. All the while, men like John Kerry were fighting and dying in Vietnam.

This response, as damning as it would have been, never came. Why not? Within hours after the story appeared on CBS, Internet bloggers and their readers began to question the authenticity of the documents used in the CBS story. Among others, sites such as LittleGreenFootballs.com, FreeRepublic.com, Powerlineblog.com, Instapundit.com, and The Drudge Report were instrumental in raising questions, posting reader comments and e-mails, and spreading the word that the CBS story might not be all that it appeared. Excerpts from the early Internet posts and comments on September 8 and 9, 2004, included the following:

- *. . . every single one of these memos to file is in a proportionally spaced font, probably Palatino or Times New Roman. . . . In 1972 people used typewriters for this sort of thing, and typewriters used monospaced fonts. . . .*

- *I am saying these documents are forgeries, run through a copier for 15 generations to make them look old.*[41]
- *This forger was a fool. This fake document actually does have the tiny "th" in "187th" and there is simply no way this could have occurred in 1973. There are no keys on any typewriter in common use in 1973 which could produce a tiny "th."*[42]
- *I opened Microsoft Word, set the font to Microsoft's Times New Roman, tabbed over to the default tab stop to enter the date "18 August 1973," then typed the rest of the document purportedly from the personal records of the late Lieutenant Colonel Jerry B. Killian. And my Microsoft Word version, typed in 2004, is an* exact match *for the documents trumpeted by CBS News as "authentic."*[43]
- *The signatures on the CBS documents do not appear to be authentic. . . . The one on the left is an actual signature of Lt. Col. Jerry Killian. The one on the right is from one of the CBS documents. It's not even close; in fact, it doesn't even look like the person who signed it made any attempt to copy Killian's signature.*[44]

These doubts soon made their way from Internet weblogs to the online version of the *Weekly Standard* magazine, to Fox News, to the Associated Press, and to ABC News—all within 24 hours of the initial airing of the story.[45] Within those same 24 hours, CBS issued its first response: "As is standard practice at CBS News, each of the documents broadcast on *60 Minutes* was thoroughly investigated by independent experts, and we are convinced of their authenticity."[46] By the next day, however, stories raising questions about the documents' authenticity appeared in the *Washington Post* and the *New York Times*, two papers with extraordinary influence among policymakers and members of the media. There was blood in the water, and the media sharks were hungry.

CBS was buffeted by bad news over the next week and a half. Both the mainstream media and the blogosphere consulted document experts, re-interviewed sources on which the CBS story had been based, talked with typewriter technicians, spoke with Lt. Col. Killian's family, and for good measure, picked the brains of amateur typewriter collectors, font aficionados, and computer geeks. The evidence all pointed in one direction—toward forgery.

At first, CBS refused to give an inch. Various officials, including CBS news anchor Dan Rather, who had introduced the controversial *60 Minutes Wednesday* report, continued to vouch for the documents. CBS also aired additional stories purporting to support the documents' authenticity. The network, however, was like a sapling trying to stand against a hurricane; the force of evidence from other media outlets was simply overwhelming. On September 20, 2004, CBS News president Andrew Heyward finally made the inevitable concession: "Based on what we now know, CBS News cannot prove that the documents are authentic, which is the only acceptable journalistic standard to justify using them in the report. We should not have used them. That was a mistake, which we deeply regret."[47]

How could CBS make such a mistake? Many influential conservatives denied that a "mistake" had been made. Instead, they claimed that CBS had been driven by an anti-Republican agenda. Dan Rather had long been suspect within the American right. He had had a contentious relationship with two Republican presidents, Richard Nixon and George H.W. Bush. A former Rather colleague at CBS, Bernard Goldberg, had written a book called *Bias*, in which he accused Rather and CBS of tilting the news to the left. There was even a Web site called Ratherbiased.com, which listed hundreds of Rather quotes that purported to reveal his bias against Republicans and conservatives.

Yet, when CBS appointed an independent panel to investigate how the fatally flawed story had made it to air, the panel report denied that political bias was a factor: ". . . (we) cannot conclude that a political agenda at *60 Minutes Wednesday* drove either the timing of the airing of the segment or its content."[48] How, then, had CBS made such a mistake? The panel acknowledged that it had difficulty answering this question itself:

> CBS News has a historic and deep-seated commitment to accurate and fair reporting, and the Panel was impressed by the fact that so many of its personnel have been with CBS News for many years and appear fully committed to the standards of accuracy and fairness that CBS News has articulated. That makes it all the more difficult for the Panel to understand how this breakdown could have occurred.
> . . . More than a few of the staff members interviewed by the Panel likened this breakdown in the production of the September 8 segment to a "perfect storm," in which a confluence of factors came together and led to the failures. The Panel believes that there is some basis for this analogy, as the combination of a new *60 Minutes Wednesday* management team, great deference given to a highly respected producer and the network's news anchor, competitive pressures, and a zealous belief in the truth of the segment seem to have led many to disregard some fundamental journalistic principles . . .[49]

Specifically, the CBS production team had failed to

- establish the chain of custody for the suspect Killian documents;

- fully understand the document authentication process and the implications of the testimony of document experts interviewed by CBS;
- corroborate critical, allegedly factual information in the documents themselves; and
- have the documents inspected by Lt. Col. Killian's commanding officer, Major General Bobby Hodges.

Thus, in their fervor to get a sensational story to air before their competitors could, CBS either missed or deliberately ignored red flags indicating that there *was* no story to be told.

The bloggers, however, did not. The new technology of the Internet made it possible to raise questions about the CBS story before it could gain any traction, and, ultimately, earn a retraction from CBS. The network itself posted the alleged Killian documents on the World Wide Web. There they could be printed, downloaded, and inspected by anyone who was interested. Without the ability to examine the documents, it would have been impossible for the blogosphere to challenge the story. With the documents widely available, they were subject to close scrutiny and questioning by literally thousands of readers and writers.

Those readers and writers acted, in effect, like a single, giant group of journalists working on the same story, 'round the clock, in different parts of the country (and, in some cases, the world). Granted, much of what appeared later on the Internet turned out to be inaccurate—some early 1970s typewriters could, for example, produce a superscript "th." Furthermore, much of the Internet coverage of the story was rumor, speculation, and debate to begin with, making no pretense of factual accuracy. But the amateur Internet sleuths who contributed to the story got enough right, brought enough new and accurate information to bear, and raised enough legitimate questions that the mainstream media had to pay attention. Once they did, they found that the National Guard story had more holes than a tin can on a Texas rifle range (as Dan Rather might say).

Sites that allow users to post and share video clips entered the scene with a bang during the 2006 elections. In past elections, much of what a candidate had to say—at least in non-presidential races and early in the primary season—went unrecorded by television news cameras. Now, with inexpensive video cameras and digital cameras with video capability—not to mention cell phones—every word a candidate says seems to be recorded by supporters and, more importantly, by opponents. Virginia Senator George Allen lost his bid for reelection largely because he was caught on a cell phone video directing a racial slur at a minority student working for his opponent Jim Webb. The student posted the slur on YouTube, where it was viewed by millions and made its way to national press outlets.

2. Do blogs and the freedom of the Internet create any professional or ethical dilemmas for journalists?

ThinkingCritically

1. Can you think of some other instance where non-mainstream media had such a huge influence?

The Nature of Media Coverage of Politics and Government

What kind of information do Americans get from their news sources? Because of the diversity of the media, the kinds of stories they cover, and the high variance in quality of news information, the answer is not simple. One significant problem is that most of what political scientists know about media content concerns media coverage of elections rather than day-to-day politics and governance. Nonetheless, there are a few general trends. We'll examine both the subjects that are covered and how the media covers them.

The media devote most of their attention to explaining and interpreting the president's actions.

When covering national politics, the media focus primarily on the president, the White House staff, and the executive branch. Collectively, they are the subject of about 70 percent of government news coverage by national and local newspapers and about 80 percent of the government news coverage on the network news.[50] Congress receives the next highest level of coverage, with about "one-in-four discussions of government in the print press and one-in-six on television."[51] The judiciary receives so little coverage as to be almost an afterthought. Clearly, the Congress and the judiciary cannot compete with the amount of attention the president and the executive branch receive.

Reporters receive much more air time than candidates.

The second trend in media coverage is that in presidential election coverage on television, reporters tend to get substantially more camera time than the actual candidates. In the 2000 presidential election campaign, for example, reporters accounted for 74 percent of spoken air time; Al Gore and George W. Bush accounted for 11 percent, and other sources 15 percent.[52] In 2000, Al Gore received a cumulative total of 53 minutes of speaking time and George Bush received 42 minutes. The reporters who covered the candidates, on the other hand, were shown speaking for nearly 10 hours.

These numbers indicate that reporters assume a prominent mediating role in election coverage. That is, they report and analyze what candidates say.[53] In the 1992 election, for example, the CBS *Evening News* broadcast a brief statement by Bill Clinton regarding the proposed North American Free Trade Agreement:

> I'm reviewing it carefully, and when I have a definitive opinion, I will say so.
> It's a very long and complex document; it was negotiated over a long period of time. And I think we have to go through it, and check it all off.

Rather than letting the matter rest there, CBS reporter Eric Enberg added:

> Time out! Clinton has a reputation as a committed policy wonk who soaks

up details like a sponge. But on an issue which will likely cost him votes no matter what side he takes, the one-time Rhodes scholar is a conveniently slow learner.[54]

Since Vietnam and Watergate, TV coverage of politics has become conspicuously cynical.

The third media trend is that media coverage of politics and government has assumed an increasingly skeptical—even cynical—tone.[55] Most media historians date this trend to the late 1960s and early 1970s, coincident with the Vietnam War and the Watergate scandal.[56] The two events convinced many reporters that government officials were capable of dishonesty and corruption on a scale previously unthinkable and the media had let them get away with such behavior for too long.

To this day, journalists frequently cast politicians in a negative light or quote sources who do. Based on ABC, CBS, and NBC network news coverage of government during 1993 and 2001, Table 10-1 shows the percentage of negative, positive, and neutral stories on the federal government.

Although not overwhelmingly negative in either year, in both samples the stories reflect a tendency to portray the workings of government, and specific politicians, in a negative light.

As an example, a 2001 ABC News assessment of the contentious budget battle by John Cochran painted both Congressional Democrats and President Bush in a negative light: "Back in Washington, Mr. Bush's Democratic opponents were launching their 'bash him on Social Security campaign' that they will push all through this fall. House Democratic leader Dick Gephardt accusing the president of using an accounting gimmick to transfer money from a Social Security Trust Fund to pay for other programs, including Mr. Bush's tax cut.[57] NBC *Nightly News* reporter Lisa Myers offered a similarly negative comment about President Clinton in the summer of 1993: "The president already had a reputation on the Hill for making contradictory promises and not keeping commitments. Now House members say even if he tells them the truth, they can't trust the president not to cave later under pressure."[58]

While coverage in 2001 is both less negative and more neutral in 2001 than in 1993, it must be noted that the war on terrorism dominated government news in 2001. It accounted for four times as many network news stories and twice as many print stories as any other topic, even though the coverage was compressed into the last four months of the year.[59] Therefore, the 2001 sample represents a momentary blip with less negative and more neutral coverage than expected.

TV coverage generally focuses on strategy over substance.

Yet another trend is that television coverage of elections tends to neglect substantive matters, such as the content of policy proposals, candidates' posi-

Table 10-1. **Evaluative Content of Network News Stories on the U.S. Government, 1993 and 2001.** News coverage of government concentrates on the negative.

	1993	2001
Negative	59%	41%
Positive	36%	23%
Neutral	5%	36%

tions on issues, and politicians' voting records. Instead, the focus often is on the **horse race**—who is up or down in the latest polls, what is happening behind the scenes, who has committed the latest gaffe or landed a rhetorical blow, and which candidates are winning a competitive advantage. Such reporting is also referred to as "strategy frame coverage" because it sometimes treats elections purely as a competitive game for power or a contest of political strategies rather than policy ideas.

The following are a few examples of "horse-race" and campaign strategy coverage from recent campaigns:

- After falling behind in the Iowa polls, Senator Clinton, who earlier condemned attacks by other Democrats, turned negative on Obama. Fair enough. Except her attacks were neither focused nor effective. . . . It's a good bet that Clinton, encouraged by her husband, is weighing a shakeup, such as bringing in former White House Chief of Staff John Podesta to direct the overall campaign. The question is whether it's too late and too awkward before those first contests, which are to be held in 3 1/2 weeks.

  —Al Hunt of Bloomberg, December 10, 2007[60]

- After a series of blows, many of them self-inflicted, [Bush] aides acknowledge their message has been muffled.

  —Bill Whitaker of CBS, September 17, 2000[61]

- . . . the first *real* political battle is shaping up across the country in New Hampshire where, with the primary only nine days away, Arkansas Governor Bill Clinton's lead in the Democratic race appears to be shrinking, and the other candidates have suddenly found themselves in a horse race.

  —Forrest Sawyer of ABC, February 9, 1992[62]

Why do television reporters prefer this kind of coverage? It may simply be that reporters, and viewers, find such stories more entertaining than the dry stuff of policy papers and voting records.[63] Such coverage may also reflect the cynicism referred to above.[64] Reporters may believe stories on strategies, tactics, and behind-the-scenes discussions shed light on what is *really* driving a campaign (as opposed to what candidates and their handlers *say* is driving the campaign). Furthermore, candidates' issue positions and policy proposals do not change from day to day, but poll numbers, political tactics, and politicians' behavior can change on a daily basis, so they get reported as news.

Evidence on the quality of *print* media reporting is limited and mixed. In some studies, national newspapers and newsweeklies appear just as prone to adopt a "mediating" role; they are just as negative and cynical, and just as likely to focus on the competitive elements of elections as the television networks. Much more research needs to be done, however, before one can reach any definitive conclusions.

Television coverage focuses on the game of politics.

A research institute recently studied network news coverage of the Democrats' primary campaign in the 2004 presidential election. In the 26 days before the New Hampshire primary, ABC, NBC, and CBS ran 173 stories on the Democratic race. Of these, only 17 percent addressed candidates' issue positions or voting records. The remainder focused on the horse race, campaign strategies and tactics.[65]

Similarly, a 2004 study from the University of Wisconsin Newslab found that presidential coverage dominated local election coverage in 2002, when there was no presidential race. Fifty-five percent of the broadcasts contained a presidential story. By contrast, just 8 percent contained a story about a local race. Local election coverage was so slight that "eight times more coverage went to stories about accidental injuries, and 12 times more coverage to sports and weather, than to coverage of all local races combined."[66] Additional studies conducted by the University of Wisconsin Newslab in 2004, 2006, and 2007, both during and outside of elections cycles, found that stories on strategy vastly outnumbered those focusing on substantive issues.

Are the Media Biased?

One enduring debate among observers of American politics is whether media coverage of politics and government exhibits **bias**. Certain aspects of the American media are decidedly and unapologetically partisan. Radio hosts Rush Limbaugh and Sean Hannity, for example, are openly conservative, and are far more critical of Democrats than Republicans in their daily radio monologues. On the other hand, the editorial page of the most influential newspaper in America, the *New York Times*, is clearly left-of-center, and often criticizes Republican politicians. These are not, however, instances of media bias. The media's objectivity ethic—that is, its stated commitment to avoid partisan or political bias—applies only to hard news reporting, not to commentaries or editorials.

But what about journalists, television programs, newspapers, newsmagazines, radio programs, Internet sites, and other news outlets that are supposedly devoted primarily to reporting the basic facts of the news in an objective matter? Do the media favor some politicians, groups, positions, and political outcomes over others? Some media critics argue that the media favor Republicans and conservatives at the expense of Democrats and liberals, while others argue just the opposite.

What would a biased media mean for American politics? First, it could create a distorted democratic process—one in which the public made up its mind on certain issues on the basis of incomplete and possibly misleading information. Second, it might contribute to a climate in which the public was less informed about matters of politics and government than it could be. A public suspecting that mainstream media outlets were providing biased coverage might avoid such outlets, seeking alternative sources of information in talk radio, cable television talk shows, and Internet weblogs. Alternatively, or in addition, they might switch to more entertainment-oriented "news light" programs, such as the early morning network offerings (e.g., *Good Morning America*). Third, like the public, politicians might migrate away from media outlets they believed to be biased, and provide information and access only to friendlier, more specialized media. The potential significance of such developments makes it all the more important that political scientists continue to study the true extent of media bias.

Anecdotal evidence of bias in the media is mixed.

In the debate over media bias, much of the evidence is anecdotal, meaning it is based on a few isolated examples that may or may not represent overall media coverage. An organization called Fairness and Accuracy in Reporting (FAIR), for example, has produced studies indicating that conservative think tanks are cited more often in the media than left-leaning ones.[67] On the other hand, the Center for Media and Public Affairs found that in the 2004 election, John Kerry received the most favorable coverage of any general election candidate for the presidency since 1980.[68]

Little conclusive evidence of media bias has been found in examinations of media content.

Obviously, by choosing issues, media outlets, and time periods selectively, one can produce evidence of both liberal and conservative media bias. The question, however, is whether a comprehensive analysis across a broad range of issues, a wide variety of media outlets, and a substantial time period would indicate systematic bias. Ultimately, the proof is in the actual content of media reporting.

Self-assessment One way to assess the content is to ask journalists themselves what they think of it. In a survey of more than 1,700 newspaper journalists, the American Society of Newspaper Editors asked the following question: "Thinking about how your newspaper tends to cover particular social or political groups, is that coverage sometimes too favorable or sometimes unfavorable?" The results for particular groups relevant to the debate over media bias are presented in Table 10-2.

At first glance, the figure suggests a bias against conservatives; the reporters indicated that they report less favorably on conservatives than on liberals. This finding is not consistent throughout, however. For example, the same reporters indicated that the military and the wealthy, two groups usually associated with the American right, received overly *favorable* coverage. Similarly, poor people and labor union members, groups usually associated with the left, appeared to receive disproportionately *unfavorable* coverage. Then again, gun owners—another group associated with political conservatives—*also* seem to receive unfavorable coverage.

More generally, a series of surveys conducted over more than 40 years have shown journalists to be more liberal than conservative, and to be more liberal than the average American.[69] Perhaps most famously, a survey of Washington, D.C.-based reporters indicated that 89 percent had voted for Democrat Bill Clinton in the 1992 election—compared with only 42 percent of the American public. That survey has been criticized for its low response rate and allegedly unrepresentative sample.[70] The survey findings on the general ideological leanings of journalists have been replicated often enough, however, to leave little doubt that liberals outnumber conservatives substantially in American newsrooms. For example, a 2004 survey indicated that, despite an increased percentage of self-described "moderates" in newsrooms, liberal journalists still outnumbered conservative ones by a significant margin, and that journalists were much more liberal in their political orientations than the public as a whole.

Advocates of the survey approach argue that reporters' political predispositions inevitably make their way into news stories, leading to biased reporting. Others argue that there is no correlation between journalists' personal beliefs and the content of

Table 10-2. Newspaper Journalists' Self Assessments. Journalists are more likely than the general public to call themselves liberal.

IDEOLOGICAL SELF-RATING	GENERAL PUBLIC*	NATIONAL PRESS	LOCAL PRESS
Liberal	20%	34%	23%
Moderate	41%	54%	61%
Conservative	33%	7%	12%
Don't know	6%	5%	4%
	100%	100%	100%

*Public figures from May 2004 Pew Media Believability Study (N=1800)

Source: http://www.stateofnewsmedia.org/prc.pdf, p. 24

their reporting. First, they note that journalists are trained to set aside their personal predispositions when reporting on politics and government. A Democratic journalist reporting on a Republican administration, they say, is no different from a Democratic doctor operating on a Republican patient. Second, they say that the economics of the media industry are designed to drive out biased coverage. Newspapers, television and radio programs, and newsmagazines that allowed bias to enter their coverage of politics and government would risk offending paying customers and advertisers who did not share their opinions. If for no other reason than the "bottom line," then, the media must work to keep their product bias-free. Third, though reporters may exhibit liberal tendencies, publishers and owners of radio, television, and print media outlets, being businesspeople, are presumed to exhibit more conservative ones. Somewhere, then, in the balance between reporters' and owners' politics, the media get the story right.

Content analysis Fortunately, given the mixed nature of these findings, political scientists and other researchers have moved beyond examination of survey data into actual content analysis of media reporting. Content analysis is a technique for identifying themes, categories, and logical groupings in written material or material that can be converted into a written transcript. This could include television programming, newspaper and magazine reporting, and radio broadcasts. The methods of content analysis, therefore, can be applied to the study of media bias.

Because presidential elections are the great spectator sport of American politics, scholars have studied media bias primarily in the context of presidential election coverage. A 2000 study examined 59 studies of media bias in presidential election coverage from 1948 to 1996 that included analysis of television, newspaper, and newsweekly magazine reporting on the presidential election. They investigated three kinds of bias:

- Gatekeeping bias: presenting news stories that cast a favored party or politician in a positive light, while ignoring stories that would cast the party or politician in a negative light;
- Coverage bias: providing more news coverage to a favored party or politician, and less to opponents; and
- Statement bias: making positive statements about a favored party or politician, and negative ones about opponents.

In analyzing the results of the 59 studies addressing these three kinds of bias, the authors concluded: "In short, the results indicate an aggregate, across all media and all elections, of zero overall bias."[71]

This conclusion does *not* indicate that every media outlet was bias-free in every presidential election conducted between 1948 and 1996. First, the number of studies of gatekeeping bias in newspaper and television news coverage of presidential elections was too small to draw any definitive conclusions.[72] Second, bias in one medium in one election can be offset by an opposing bias in another medium. For example, the study identified small pro-Democratic coverage and statement biases in television news covering presidential elections, and even smaller pro-Republican statement and coverage biases in newsweekly reporting of the same elections. These two results effectively canceled each other, leading to a finding of zero "net" bias.

Recall, however, that Americans' consumption of the news tends to come disproportionately from television. Thus, "a little" bias in television news coverage could have a big impact on viewer beliefs. The researchers recognized that possibility but found it irrelevant. Specifically, they acknowledged that Democratic candidates received just over 10 percent more television coverage than Republican candidates, but they claimed this difference was "almost certainly undetectable by the audience."[73] (Were they right? We discuss the impact of the mass media on public opinion in the next section.)

Presidential elections, as interesting and exciting as they can be, are not the only setting in which biased media coverage might occur. What about the day-to-day media coverage of Congress, the presidency, and current events? Is that coverage biased, and, if so, in what direction? Among political scientists, there are no consensus answers to these questions. The existing studies are too few, too limited in scope, and too contradictory in their conclusions to provide any definitive conclusions. Perhaps after another generation of scholarship, it will be possible to conduct a "meta-analysis" of the sort described above in the context of election coverage. Until then, the jury is out.

Media Effects on Public Opinion

To what extent does the content of mass media coverage affect public opinion? The early research on this subject was prompted by startling demonstrations of the power of mass media in the 1920s, 1930s, and 1940s. An early instance was the panic following news of the stock market crash in 1929. Next was the rise of the fascist dictators, Benito Mussolini in Italy and Adolf Hitler in Germany. Both cultivated popular support through radio addresses and newsreels that carried their fiery speeches to enraptured crowds. Then came Orson Welles's 1938 radio broadcast of H. G. Wells's book *War of the Worlds*, which set off a panic among a million Americans who mistook the dramatization for an actual news broadcast of an alien invasion.[74]

Observing these events, scholars worried that clever use of the mass media could enable leaders to "inject" the masses with supportive attitudes, in the same way a hypodermic needle injects a patient with medicine. One researcher warned that "one persuasive person could, through the use of mass media, bend the world's population to his will."[75]

Early research into the impact of media pointed to its "minimal effects."

Researchers in the United States first investigated the effects of the mass media on voting behavior. These seminal voting studies conducted in the 1940s and 1950s revealed an electorate surprisingly unaffected by media coverage. The studies found most voters were party loyalists whose votes could not be swayed by media messages. A host of group and personal characteristics—particularly religion, social status, and place of residence—also strongly dictated political predispositions. Partisanship and other political predispositions were so strong, in fact, that large majorities of voters in the 1950s and 1960s decided for whom they would vote before the general election campaign and the related media coverage even *began*.[76] Thus, changes in voting intent as a result of mass media exposure were relatively rare.

This finding in the early literature came to be referred to as **minimal effects**. For years, media scholars accepted the minimal effects conclusion, although many found it unsatisfying. One researcher explained the scholars' dilemma as follows:

> The mass media have been a source of great frustration to social scientists. On one hand, citizens in modern democracies routinely develop opinions about political events and personalities far beyond their direct experience. It is hard to imagine where many of these opinions come from if not from the mass media. And yet it

has proven maddeningly difficult to demonstrate that the mass media actually produce powerful effects on opinion.[77]

Ultimately, scholars were able to demonstrate that the media's effect is more than minimal. But to do so, they had to overcome certain assumptions about the kinds of effects they should be looking for and how such effects might work.

The media may exert influence through agenda-setting and priming.

Early researchers into media effects focused on persuasion, or changing someone's mind about an issue, person, or group. But the media can also play a role in political socialization; in educating the public with basic information about politics, government, issues, groups, and candidates; in stimulating or discouraging political participation among the public; in helping to "crystallize," or reinforce, existing beliefs and predispositions; and in determining which issues the public and policymakers consider important, or **agenda-setting**.

Of these topics, agenda-setting is particularly important because it has been highly influential in shaping political scientists' thinking about media effects. The issues that the media cover the most extensively are in turn the issues that the public considers most important. Conversely, the public considers the issues that the media neglect less important. In short, by covering some issues and ignoring others, the media help determine which issues the public considers important.

Do People React to Coverage of Events or to the Events Themselves?

The Question

When it comes to measuring the agenda-setting power of the media, how do we know that people are reacting to media coverage of events rather than to events themselves? In times of economic recession, for example, many people will lose a job or know someone who has lost a job, or witness local companies going out of business. They have an understanding of the problems in the economy through direct, personal experience. At the same time, they are exposed to media coverage of the recession. So, when people tell researchers that they believe the performance of the economy is an important issue, are they reflecting their own experience, or are they responding to media coverage of the issue? In other words, the relationship between media coverage and public attention to certain issues might reflect *reverse* agenda-setting. Being profit-oriented businesses, media outlets need to appeal to a broad audience in order to sell advertising and subscriptions. A good way to ensure audience appeal is to cover issues the audience considers important. Therefore, the media may cover certain problems because the audience considers them important, rather than the audience thinking certain problems are important because the media cover them. In addition to difficulties in identifying causality, scholars have also struggled with how to measure accurately who has been exposed to what sorts of media content.

Why It Matters

The ultimate question in studying the various media in this country and the professional norms and legal frameworks that determine their content is whether the media influence political behavior. Even though most people and politicians assume that the media have extraordinary power to shape mass opinions and behavior, scholars have had a hard time finding evidence of significant effects. The failure to find media effects has been described by one scholar as "one of the most notable embarrassments of modern social science."[78]

Investigating the Answer

Fortunately, experiments can be designed to disentangle the sort of "chicken or egg" causal puzzle that exists when examining the potential agenda-setting power of the media. The 1987 book *News That Matters* offered an experimental research approach that addressed concerns about both determining causality and accurately measuring exposure to particular media sources.[79] The researchers recruited hundreds of volunteers to participate in their experiment. They asked participants to complete a questionnaire covering a variety of topics relevant to politics and current events. Participants were then randomly divided into different groups.

Over the next four days, the different groups gathered and watched what they were told were videotaped recordings of the previous evening's network news. The researchers, however, had manipulated the news broadcasts to emphasize certain issues. For example, one group of participants saw broadcasts with a few added stories on American defense preparedness. Another group saw broadcasts with extra stories on pollution; another saw additional stories on inflation. Because the groups were kept separate, they did not realize they were watching slightly different versions of the news. All simply assumed that they were watching the same newscast.

To make the experience of watching the television news more realistic, the researchers sought to create a comfortable, home-like atmosphere for participants. They provided newspapers, magazines, and refreshments and asked questions in the survey that were designed to mask the true goal of their research.

After the groups had watched the manipulated broadcasts on four consecutive nights, the researchers again administered a questionnaire to participants. Answers to this second questionnaire revealed that individuals who had seen the broadcasts with added stories on defense preparedness considered that issue much more important than they had before the experiment began. The same held true for pollution, though not for inflation. (The authors argued that participants considered inflation such an important issue before the experiment that there was little room for them to show *more* concern after the experiment.) Thus, the agenda-setting hypothesis was largely supported; media emphasis on an issue could elevate the salience of that issue in the public mind.

The Bottom Line

The finding that media emphasis could elevate the salience of an issue was important. But just as important was the fact that this hypothesis was supported in an experimental setting. Because this controlled group could not in any way influence what the researchers' media people were reporting, it was clear that media coverage itself was driving the change in perceptions of issue salience. Therefore, it could not be argued that the media coverage reflected audience concerns. Given the difficulties in systematically measuring what the media are covering and what people are exposed to in the real world, experiments such as this have become a useful way for scholars to study media effects.

Researchers have also demonstrated a media effect called **priming**, which refers to the process by which the public assesses the performance of the president, or presidential candidates, in terms of the issues that the public considers most important. Imagine, for example, that the media devote extensive coverage to the issue of welfare fraud. If the public begins to consider welfare fraud an important problem because of this media coverage, that is evidence of agenda-setting. But if the public also begins to evaluate the performance of the president in terms of what he is doing (or not doing) about welfare fraud, that is evidence of priming. The experiments described in How Do We Know? demonstrated that people exposed to extra stories on defense preparedness tended to evaluate the president more heavily in terms of his performance in addressing defense preparedness. The same held true for the pollution and inflation issues. Thus, the media appear to have a priming effect on public opinion as well.

Agenda-setting effects do not stop with the public, however. The media draw the attention of policymakers as well. For example, studies have shown that policymakers' attention to the issues of global warming, the North American Free Trade Agreement, and the Clinton administration's Whitewater scandal was increased in part by intensive media coverage of these issues.[80] The research in this area has not been as thorough, and the conclusions not as strong, as studies of the effect that the media have on what gets on the public's policy agenda. Furthermore, the research often suggests a two-way relationship: media coverage affects policymakers' agendas, but policymakers' agendas also affect what the media cover. Still, most of the research on the agenda-setting power of the media among policymakers, and particularly the most recent research, indicates that the media can exhibit a strong influence on the issues that policymakers choose to pay attention to.[81]

Three primary phenomena may limit the media's influence on attitudes and behaviors.

The early media-effects research tended to assume that with enough exposure to a particular media message, individuals would eventually accept it. But this assumption was inconsistent with theories and findings from the fields of communications and psychology. Three phenomena limit the ability of media to influence attitudes and behaviors. In the first, *selective exposure*, people tend to expose themselves to information that is in accord with their beliefs. Thus, the conservative gets her news from Rush Limbaugh and the liberal gets his information from the Daily Kos. In so doing, they avoid information and arguments that might upset their belief system—and potentially change their opinions. This phenomenon has an important impact on the effect of Web-based communications or talk radio. Unlike an advertisement on television, individuals deliberately expose themselves to or actively seek out information from the Web or from a talk radio station. While these sources may mobilize and energize base supporters (Republicans when it comes to talk radio and Democrats on liberal blogs), because people probably already agree with the source they engage, the persuasive effects are likely to be severely limited.

The second phenomenon is *selective perception*, the tendency of individuals to interpret information in ways consistent with their beliefs. Imagine, for example, a television news story depicting President George W. Bush comforting the victims of Hurricane Katrina in Louisiana. A Bush supporter likely would see this as evidence of the president's compassionate nature and rapport with everyday people. A Bush detractor, on the other hand, might see it as a politician seeking to score political points from a tragedy. Or, consider the debates held during presidential election campaigns. Republicans and Democrats both watch the very same debates, but Republicans inevitably conclude that the Republican candidate performed better, and Democrats conclude that the Democrat performed better. In part, this is a consequence of selective perception.

Finally, there is *selective retention*, the tendency of individuals to recall information that is consistent with existing beliefs and to discard information that runs counter to them. An admirer of President Ronald Reagan and his supply-side economics, for example, would recall the significant tax cuts enacted in Reagan's first and second terms but might well forget the substantial tax *increases* that were also enacted during Reagan's first term.

Note that there is a common element in these phenomena that limits the ability of the media to influence attitudes and behaviors. All represent efforts by individuals to avoid or reduce cognitive dissonance. Cognitive dissonance is a state in which some of one's attitudes, beliefs, or understandings are inconsistent with others. This dissonance leads to psychological discomfort, which people normally try to avoid or remedy.[82] The effect of selective exposure, selective perception, and selective retention is to render the information inside one's head more internally consistent, or consonant.

Think again about the example of selective exposure. If the conservative reader suddenly stopped listening to Rush Limbaugh and started reading the Daily Kos, she would be exposed to a number of arguments and ideas that were inconsistent with her existing worldview. This exposure might force her to question some of her beliefs. She might end up having doubts about matters on which she had held a settled opinion for years. On some issues, she might even be forced to change her mind. All of this could cause psychological discomfort. A sure way to avoid that discomfort, however, would be not to read the Daily Kos in the first place.

However, selective exposure, selective perception, and selective retention all limit the impact that the mass media can have on individual attitudes. If people are inclined to see, hear, interpret, and retain only information that reinforces their existing beliefs, it becomes more difficult for the media to produce a large-scale attitude change.

Exposure, comprehension, and receptivity are preconditions for media effects.

Discovering the consequences of selective exposure, perception, and retention led political scientists to approach the study of media effects differently. Rather than simply assuming a direct link between the content of media messages and public opinion, they began studying the necessary preconditions for a message to change opinion. One of these is **exposure**—whether a person actually sees, hears, or reads a particular media message. Another is **reception**, understanding a message to which one has been exposed. A third is **acceptance**, which refers to an individual's openness to accepting a message communicated through the media.

Without exposure, reception, and acceptance, an individual cannot be influenced by a media message. If we look for media effects on public opinion among the public at large, we will probably be disappointed because many people, perhaps most, will not have been exposed to a particular media message and, even if they have, will not have comprehended it. But if we look for effects among individuals who have been exposed to a message, who have comprehended it, and who are at least potentially receptive to it, then our search is likely to be more fruitful.

Moderately attentive and predisposed individuals are most likely to feel media influence.

Political scientist John Zaller has been the foremost proponent of this way of thinking about media impact on public opinion. In *The Nature and Origins of Mass Opinion*, Zaller argues that the likelihood of exposure to and comprehension of a media message depends largely on **political attentiveness**, an individual's general attention to and knowledge of politics.[83] An individual who is highly attentive to and knowledgeable about politics is likely to be exposed to, and understand, most politically oriented media messages. On the other hand, someone who pays little attention to politics and understands little of the political world will either miss most political messages in the media or fail to understand them if he or she should happen to come across them.

Accepting a message or being persuaded by a message also depends on one's **political predispositions**—the interests, values, and experiences that help organize one's thinking about politics.[84] Someone who has very strong political predispositions is unlikely to be receptive to media messages that contradict those predispositions. For example, someone who is firmly convinced that U.S. troops should be used only to guard America's borders is unlikely to be receptive to media messages indicating the need for a deployment of troops to, say, the Middle East.

These insights have many interesting implications. Since data indicate that the most politically attentive individuals also tend to have the strongest political predispositions, individuals who are *most* likely to be exposed to and comprehend media messages (people who are most politically attentive) are *least* likely to be persuaded by them (because they have the strongest predispositions). The reverse is also true—the least politically attentive individuals tend to have the weakest political predispositions.[85] While they are most likely to be persuaded by media messages (because they have the weakest political predispositions), they are least likely to be exposed to and comprehend media messages (because they are least politically attentive). Figure 10-5 illustrates these relationships.

Who, then, are the *most* likely candidates for political persuasion by the media? People right in the middle—that is, individuals with a medium level of

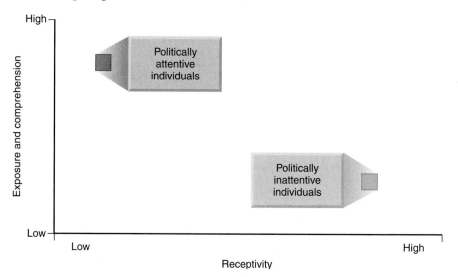

Figure 10-5. Those most likely to be influenced by the media are less likely to be exposed to and understand media messages.

Source: John Zaller. 1992. *The Nature and Origins of Mass Opinion.* Cambridge University Press.

political attentiveness and political dispositions of medium strength. They will not be exposed to and comprehend *every* message that comes through the media, but they will encounter and understand many of them. And when they do, their political predispositions will be flexible enough to accept many of these messages. These realities suggest that part of the failure by political scientists to find strong media effects in the past was a failure to focus the search on this middle group.

Zaller does not argue that this middle group is the only one that can be influenced by the media or that the media always influence this middle group. In some cases, when a message is particularly prominent (such as the coverage of Anna Nicole Smith's death), even the least attentive person will be unable to miss it. The massive increase in President George W. Bush's job approval ratings after the September 11, 2001, terrorist attacks reflected the fact that *everyone*—from the most politically attentive to the least—had gotten the message about the attacks and the administration's strong response.

If a message is relatively "quiet," opinion change can still take place, but it will bypass all except the most politically attentive. Between 1964 and 1966, for example, press coverage of the Vietnam War became more negative. During that same time period, some highly politically attentive individuals—but *only* highly politically attentive individuals—grew less supportive of the war. Why? Because only the highly attentive were exposed to, and were able to comprehend, the change in the tone of media coverage. Individuals of middling and low attentiveness missed this shift, so their support for the war remained strong.[86]

Thinking in these terms, it becomes relatively easy to identify areas in which the media can have a large impact, and those in which the impact is likely to be limited. For example, we know now that predispositions limit people's receptivity to media messages. If we want to look for media effects, then, we should look for cases in which predispositions are weak. Think, for example, about primary elections in which no incumbent is running—the 2008 Republican and Democratic presidential primaries, for example. In these races, all of the primary candidates were of the same party. Party identification, therefore, was useless as a tool for judging candidates. Furthermore, many of the candidates were unfamiliar to the public at large when the primary season began. Without partisanship and previous information about the candidates to draw on, voter predispositions toward candidates were weak. Accordingly, the potential for media influence was greatly enhanced. And, in fact, research has shown that the media *do* exert a strong influence on voter judgments during the presidential primary process.[87]

On the other hand, consider a case in which policymaker and media discussions of an issue are largely balanced between a "pro" side and a "con" side. The general election between Republican and Democratic candidates for president usually fits this model. The campaigns and their supporters have roughly equal amounts of money to spend on their message, and the mainstream media present broadly balanced coverage of the campaigns. (See the discussion above on the absence of media bias in presidential election campaigns.) Under these circumstances, even if there were universal exposure to "the message," a balanced message would not challenge anyone's political predispositions because it would not convey a strong point of view. It would be unlikely, therefore, to result in large-scale opinion change.[88] (Note, however, that in a country as closely politically divided as the United States, even small shifts in public opinion can have significant consequences. Thus, even if the "minimal effects" perspective still were considered accurate, "minimal" would not necessarily mean "inconsequential.")

Media effects can be found if you look in the right places.

Scholars may have failed to find large media effects because they have been looking in the wrong places. We now know that, to find media effects, one should look for opinion change among people with moderate levels of political attentiveness and only moderately strong political predispositions. These people are likely to be exposed to most media messages, to have at least some comprehension of them, and to be somewhat receptive to them, even if the messages contradict their beliefs.

Second, opinion change occurs most often when the message is "loud," that is, when it is covered thoroughly, by a number of media outlets, for a long period of time. This maximizes the chances of broad exposure to the message, which in turn maximizes the chances of broad-based opinion change. Recall the example of media coverage of the 9/11 terrorist attacks and the Bush administration's response.

Third, a media message that carries a largely one-sided point of view is more likely to lead to opinion change than balanced coverage. During the 1992 general election campaign, for example, 90 percent of network news references to the economy were negative.[89] This kind of coverage can shift public opinion. On the other hand, coverage that is balanced—"some believe the economy remains weak, while others point to signs that it is in recovery"—would be unlikely to change opinions because it does not convey a particular point of view.

Fourth, opinion change occurs when media messages do not fit neatly with existing political predispositions. Recall the example of media coverage of presidential primary elections, in which partisanship and thorough knowledge of the candidates are generally not available to bolster predispositions. Another example would be media coverage of new or particularly complex issues, such as stem-cell research. The public can have difficulty determining how new or complex issues fit with their predispositions. With predispositions less of a factor, the chances for media influence on opinion are greatly enhanced.

Fifth, opinion change results from media messages to which people are most likely to be exposed. Recall that most Americans get their news from local television stations (see Figure 10-4). And yet, most studies of media influence focus on messages delivered by network news and major newspapers, such as the *New York Times* and *Washington Post*. Why? Network news and newspaper content are monitored by various archiving and indexing services that are accessible online. Similar technology for archiving and tracking local news content is only beginning to be put in place. But Figure 10-4 suggests that local television news content holds the most promise for demonstrating the influence of media messages.

Sixth, opinion change takes two forms—gross *and* net. In an extreme example, imagine a society divided into two equal-sized groups—Group A and Group B. One hundred percent of Group A approves of the job the president is doing, while zero percent of Group B approves. This puts the president's overall job approval at 50 percent. Imagine, though, that in a moment of weakness the president reveals to reporters that he finds members of Group A annoying and unattractive but finds members of Group B delightful and easy on the eyes. The media provide blanket coverage of the president's verbal indiscretion and the president's job approval falls to zero in Group A, but rises to 100 percent in Group B. The president's overall approval rating remains at 50 percent, so there has been no *net* change, but there has been massive *gross* change, that is, change within Group A and Group B. By concentrating solely on net change, researchers can miss large but offsetting gross changes in opinion within sub-groups of the population.

Finally, if a media message is particularly "quiet" or largely balanced between two sides, look for opinion change only among the most politically attentive. This is the only group likely to pick up on a quiet message in the first place, and the only group sophisticated enough to notice any subtle cues amidst the largely balanced coverage that might induce a change in opinion.

SUMMARY

▶ The U.S. mass media differ from the media in other countries in several key ways, including largely private ownership of American media; different views about objectivity and "taking sides"; the American media's "watchdog" role; and the relative freedom with whi ch the U.S. media operate. Freedom from prior restraint is a particularly noteworthy characteristic of the U.S. media.

▶ Despite their relative press freedom, the American media do operate under some constraints, including laws against defamation; the "equal time" rule; and the limited protection of shield laws. These limits are minor compared to those faced by American journalists in the eighteenth, nineteenth, and early twentieth centuries, when the media operated under much stricter government control. Beginning in the 1930s, this situation changed dramatically with a series of U.S. Supreme Court decisions expanding press freedoms.

▶ Americans acquire information on politics and government from various types of media. Whereas newspapers once dominated, they were supplanted by broadcast television in the second half of the twentieth century. However, broadcast news has been in decline in recent years, with cable television, talk radio, and the World Wide Web gaining popularity as alternate news sources.

▶ A few principles govern broadcast media's coverage of American politics and government. These include the tendency to focus on the president to the exclusion of Congress and the courts; the mediating role played by

reporters in news coverage of elections; the negative tone of much television news coverage; and the tendency of television news to focus on the "horse race" and campaign strategies and tactics rather than candidates' policy positions and voting records. It is more difficult to make generalizations about the print media.

▶ Several kinds of evidence—anecdotal, survey data on journalists' beliefs, and the actual content of reporting—can be brought to bear on whether the media are biased. The best available evidence indicates a lack of bias in press reporting of presidential elections, but there is insufficient information to draw conclusions about other kinds of coverage.

▶ The question of whether and to what extent the media affect public opinion has drawn an enormous amount of attention from political scientists. Early studies of media influence focused on voting behavior and produced evidence of only minimal effects. However, once political scientists began to wrestle with the concepts of exposure, reception, and acceptance, they could better evaluate media influence. Applying these concepts to research in appropriate ways, it became possible to uncover the large media effects that political scientists expected were there all along but could never demonstrate. The media also have considerable influence in the agenda-setting process, that is, in helping to set the policy priorities of the public and politicians. Studies of agenda-setting and priming have also revealed the media's influence.

KEY TERMS

acceptance, p. 000
agenda setting, p. 000
bias, p. 000
exposure, p. 000
horse race, p. 000
mass media *or* media, p. 000
minimal effect, p. 000

political attentiveness, p. 000
political predisposition, p. 000
priming, p. 000
prior restraint, p. 000
reception, p. 000
watchdog, p. 000

SUGGESTED READINGS

Shanto Iyengar and Donald R. Kinder. 1989. *News That Matters: Television and American Opinion.* University of Chicago Press.

John Zaller. 1992. *The Nature and Origins of Mass Opinion.* Cambridge University Press.

mass media *or* **media** various modes of communication intended to reach a mass audience—including television, radio, newspapers, newsmagazines, and the Internet.

watchdog the media's role in keeping a close eye on politicians and presenting stories and information that politicians might not willingly reveal to the media on their own.

prior restraint government intervention to prevent the publication of material it finds objectionable.

horse race a focus in election coverage on who and what are up or down in the latest poll numbers.

bias favorable treatment to certain politicians, policy positions, groups, and political outcomes.

minimal effect the belief that change in voting intent as a result of mass media exposure was relatively rare.

agenda-setting the media role in determining which issues the public considers important, by covering some issues and ignoring others.

priming the tendency of the public to assess the performance of the president, or presidential candidates, in terms of the issues that the media have emphasized as most important.

exposure the act of seeing, hearing, or reading a particular media message.

reception understanding a message to which one has been exposed.

acceptance an individual's openness to being persuaded by a message communicated through the media.

political attentiveness an individual's general attention to and knowledge of politics.

political predisposition the interests, values, and experiences that help organize one's thinking about politics.

Joe Lieberman was elected to the U.S. Senate from Connecticut in 1988. Over the years, he compiled a record as a moderate Democrat and won reelection handily. He served—as had Bill Clinton—as a chair of the Democratic Leadership Council, a group concerned with moving the Democratic Party more to the center on a range of economic, social, and foreign policy issues. He won reelection convincingly with about two-thirds of the vote in 1994 and 2000. Tapped by Democratic nominee Al Gore to be his running mate in the 2000 presidential election, Lieberman broke a barrier by being the first Jew named to a major party ticket.

In many respects, Lieberman's positions during his Senate terms were conventional for Democrats. He did, however, take positions over the years that put him on the more conservative side of the Democratic spectrum. And in 1998, he was among the first Democrats to criticize President Clinton for his inappropriate relationship with a White House intern.

The Iraq War that would prove to be Lieberman's undoing among Democratic supporters. Lieberman was a staunch supporter of the war prior to its onset in 2003, as were many other Democrats. Over time, however, as the war dragged on and criticism of it mounted, this support waned. But not for Lieberman. He remained convinced that the war was correct and was a key battle in the fight against terrorism, and urged Democrats to work closely with President Bush to secure victory in Iraq, positions that had become anathema to liberal political activists. Lieberman's support for the war also earned public rebukes by Harry Reid and Nancy Pelosi, the leaders of the Senate and House Democrats, respectively.

2006 proved to be a flashpoint in Lieberman's struggles with his party. Although endorsed at the Connecticut Democratic convention, he received only a third of the delegate votes, forcing a primary election. Declaring that his loyalty to his state and country exceeded that to his party, Lieberman declared that if he was defeated, he would run in the general election on the Connecticut for Lieberman "party" line. Democra-

tic National Committee chair Howard Dean criticized Lieberman's position as disrespectful to Democrats and the Democratic Party. After a harsh campaign, Lieberman was beaten in the primary 52% to 48% by Ned Lamont, a candidate heavily supported by Moveon.org, a prominent political group pushing the Democratic Party to move in a more liberal direction. After having spent more than $17 million in his primary and general election contests, Lieberman won a three-way race against Lamont and the Republican nominee in November with 50% of the vote. Only one-third of Democrats supported him, but nearly three-fourths of Republicans and over half of Independents did.

Lieberman returned to the Senate as an Independent and, as he had promised, caucused with the Democrats. This gave the Democrats the support of 51 senators, which was critical. Had Lieberman caucused with the Republicans, the balance would have been 50-50 and given majority control the Republicans, because Vice President Dick Cheney would have been able to cast tiebreaking votes.

The man who was 537 votes away from being elected a Democratic Vice President in 2000—the amount by which Gore and Lieberman lost Florida—was by the end of 2006 unable to win his party's primary and no longer even a Democrat. In 2008, he announced his support for Republican John McCain for president, largely because of McCain's views on terrorism and the war. In response, the Democratic Party removed Lieberman as a delegate to its national convention. The senator, for his part, indicated that he would be pleased to speak at the Republican Party national convention in support of McCain.[1]

Although many Americans might appreciate Joe Lieberman's independent streak, political activists that support the Democrats and Lieberman's Democratic colleagues did not. In part, this different response reflects Americans' skittishness toward concentrated political power, which grows directly from American political culture. Political parties and their activist supporters, on the other hand, are without apology trying to concentrate power within the hands of their public officials in order to enact public policy. That, as they see it, is precisely the point of a political party.

THIS CHAPTER WILL EXAMINE:

▶ the basic functions performed by political parties and their benefit to individual politicians and the functioning of American politics and government

▶ why American political competition is dominated by two political parties rather than multiple political parties

▶ the relative electoral success of the parties over time, their chief differences over public policy, and why party coalitions are politically difficult to manage and maintain

▶ the evolution of American party organizations and their increase in activity in recent decades.

The Functions of Political Parties

Americans' views of parties have changed over time from fearful, to supportive, to skeptical. President George Washington, in his Farewell Address, warned Americans about the dangers of political parties. By the late 19th century, however, partisanship was a central aspect of Americans' identity, mentioned right alongside one's ethnicity, region, and religion. Today, Americans still have strong attachments to parties and they do not fear them, but there is a pervasive skepticism that parties confuse issues more than clarify them and do not stand up for principle—or alternately, that they are too polarized and stubborn and refuse to work with the other party. What has provoked these strong reactions? What are political parties and what do they do?

Political parties are organized groups that seek to gain office and exercise political power through legislation, executive action, and control of government agencies, among other means. They aim to elect officeholders who identify themselves by the group's common label and who consider themselves to be associated with that group. To get elected, candidates rally voters to their side based on some sense of shared perspectives, values, or loyalty based on other factors.[2] Connection to parties occurs at all levels in American politics, from the individual voters who feels close to a party, to candidates at the local, state, and national level, and through the processes of decision-making by public officials in government.

While candidates for public office and the formal party organizations are the most visible representatives of parties, parties should be considered more broadly as networks of peoples and groups who share common ideals. The leadership of labor unions, environmental groups, teachers, pro-choice groups, and the liberal blogosphere align with the Democratic Party. Major trade associations, Christian organizations, veterans, pro-life groups, and radio talk show hosts align with the Republicans. Dozens of other issue advocacy groups have close ties with one or the other of the two major parties and actively seek to help the party's candidates win. These groups also expect that their voice will be heard within the party as it debates policy options. Delegates to state and national party conventions frequently include members from these political action groups. The party network thus involves the intersection and conversations and mutual support between the party organizations, elected officials and party candidates, and political activists. In thinking of "the Republican Party" or "the Democratic Party," it is useful to keep this entire party network of influence and conversation in mind.[3]

Parties perform many roles in American politics, reflecting their construction as networks, and their activity at all levels of politics. These roles serve the self-interest of party members, but they also produce benefits for the operation of American government and politics and for the public.

Political parties provide legitimacy for American government and politics.

Legitimacy implies consent and acceptability. When citizens believe a political system is legitimate, they believe that people in power deserve to be in power. In various political systems, legitimacy might be conferred through heredity, through connections with the church or other important institutions, through force, or through the election process. The United States relies mainly on the electoral process to confer legitimacy on leaders.

The Constitution provided the basic structure for the selection of public officials. Elections, either direct or indirect, would determine the president, members of the House of Representatives, and U.S. senators. State constitutions, similarly, provided for a series of elections.

But the Constitution stopped there. To say that elections are the selection mechanism is one thing—it was now up to candidates and voters to make it work. Somehow potential officeholders would need to emerge and voters would need to participate in elections. For the system established by the Constitution to gain credibility and legitimacy, processes needed to be developed to staff the offices of government and involve the public.

Political parties filled this void. They were created by ambitious, hard-headed politicians to solve particular problems of candidate recruitment, increasing the likelihood of winning debates in the legislature, and mobilizing enough voter support to win elections.[4] They also serve these purposes for political advocates who represent groups in the public—for example, the leadership of a group advocating for more solar energy development and another advocating for more drilling for oil—and are pushing a particular point of view. In serving these self-interested purposes of politicians and political activists, parties also contribute to legitimizing the political system by contributing to a functioning system of electoral politics beyond that specified by the Constitution.

Parties recruit candidates into the electoral process and nominate them for office.

Nationally and in most states, political parties take a very active role in identifying promising individuals and recruiting them to run for office. In the course of doing this, the party will assist the candidate with the various aspects of running a campaign. These would include raising money, dealing with the media, identifying potential supporters, developing positions on issues, and putting together a campaign organization to contact citizens and research opponents. All these tasks can be daunting for first-time candidates, as well as more seasoned candidates. Parties can help these candidates compete. Parties also provide a ladder of opportunity up which candidates can climb: this helps sort out the potentially competing ambitions of many individual candidates by providing them with various offices to run for and a structure for moving up the party rungs to the next level of offices.

Parties are engaged in finding candidates so that the party can increase its power. The party has the incentive to run as many candidates as it can to try to win control of as many offices as it can. But this self interest also serves a social interest. Parties provide voters with choices, which are key to generating a sense of legitimacy for American politics. Elections without choices do not make voters feel empowered. The Constitution could appear an empty promise if there were indeed elections but few real choices for voters between candidates.

After recruiting candidates, parties nominate them as the party's standard-bearer, thus putting the candidate on the ballot. Around the world, control of the nomination process is considered as perhaps the single most important power of political parties: the power to filter who is elected to public office. In the United States, the nomination of candidates was first controlled by party leaders, then expanded to selection by delegates at party conventions, and now is determined in most cases by the results of primary elections (see Chapter 9).

The public exerts leverage over public officials through use of the party label.

Parties benefit from the attachments and loyalty of the public. Democratic candidates and Republican candidates know they can count on 80 to 90 percent, or more, of their loyalists to vote for them. They will need to spend some time energizing these loyalists and convincing them to vote, but they can devote much of their time, resources, and effort to appealing to undecided voters who do not have strong partisan leanings. Thus, party candidates benefit from having the party label.

Voters, in turn, can also use the party label to increase their leverage over public officials. The party label is a powerful tool. If voters believe that the parties are substantially different from each other in their policy priorities and preferences, they can take this into account when voting. This means that voters are freed from having to know extensive information about each candidate on the ballot.

Voters can use the party label to sweep one party out of office and put the other party in. This happened in 1994, when voters put Republicans in control of the U.S. House and Senate simultaneously for the first time in 40 years. No Republican incumbents were defeated. And Republicans won all the way down to the state and local level, picking up state legislatures, governorships, and mayoral positions. In 2006, the tables were turned and the Democrats swept into control of the U.S. House and Senate and picked up many new seats on the state and local level. The party label provides Americans with the simplest and most practical tool they have to make wide-ranging changes in the personnel of government.

Parties bridge constitutional gaps between institutions.

The Constitution deliberately spread power across institutions, across two houses of the legislature, across elected and unelected offices, and across the federal and state governments. It created a governing system that made the abuse of power difficult. This diffusion of power is consistent with the limited government ethos of the American creed, as we saw in Chapter 2.

Political parties create bridges across these gaps between institutions by providing incentives for officials to cooperate with each other, as shown in Figure 11.1. Officials who share a party label share a "brand name." When a president does well, members of his party in Congress enjoy some of the glow of that success. If he suffers from low approval ratings, the public's critical view can carry over to his fellow partisans in Congress. When George Bush's public approval struggled in 2006, his party struggled with him, losing 30 seats in the House, 6 in the Senate, and the majority in both. The effects were felt at the state level as well, where Republicans lost 6 governorships and control of 5 state legislatures. Officials who share a party's brand name have a self interest in seeing fellow partisans do well.

This common bond does not undermine the Constitution's separation of powers, checks and balances, or federalism, but it does increase the ability to get things done. Members of a party will usually share general goals and approaches, so they start from a base of support when trying to enact policy. In that way, political parties contribute to governing by reducing some of the challenges to lawmaking in the American system. While members of a party do not always agree, the shared party label increases the probability of cooperation. Because this cooperation increases the government's ability to act, the legitimacy of American government and politics is likely enhanced in the eyes of the public. Without the connecting glue of partisanship, government might be even more hamstrung in acting.

A. Institutional walls of separation in the Constitution

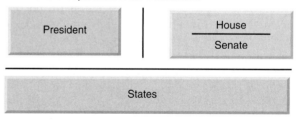

B. The party brand name provides incentives for coordination and cooperation across the constitutional walls

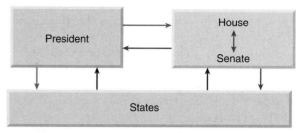

Figure 11-1. Political Party Assistance to Governance. The Constitution created a set of institutions that would be involved in policymaking and focused on the way these institutions could check each other's use of power. Left unstated was how the individuals in these institutions might work together. A political party provides common "brand name" that encourages cooperation across institutional boundaries. Politicians know that when other members of their party are successful, the party brand name is enhanced and public approval increases.

This logic would seem to suggest that government gets more "big things" done when one party controls Congress and the presidency—**unified government**—rather than having different parties control each of these branches—**divided government**. In fact, many other factors could lead to more or less being accomplished by government. A sense of crisis might inspire action; a shortage of revenue might discourage it. Public opinion may be calling for government to be active, or it might be calling for government to pull back. Studies by political scientists that account for these and other factors have shown predominantly that unified government tends to increase the number of important laws enacted and reduces delay in various facets of legislative activity.[5] Whether that is a good thing or not is a matter of one's personal political philosophy.

Political parties bring citizens into the electoral process.

Political parties involve citizens in the electoral process, a very practical need of parties to suit their self interest. To assert power, parties need to win offices. To win offices, they need to win elections. And to win elections, they need more votes on Election Day than their opponents. Parties therefore have an incentive to get voters involved, and they do in a number of ways.

Educate and inform voters Historically, political parties played a very significant role educating voters about the party's candidates. In the 19th century, parties distributed large books of policy positions, and staged parades, festivals, and other events to attract a crowd. Given the much more limited entertainment options in the 19th century, these events were often a very big deal for a small town or city neighborhood. Voters would be entertained but they would also listen to speeches detailing the party's superiority over its opponents.

In addition, political parties controlled much of the mass media of that era, newspapers in particular. So the view of the party and its candidates on issues were very prominently available for most citizens. Every day they were reminded about the party's positions.

Parties today do not have the same kind of monopoly on information about their candidates. Nonetheless, they still do attempt to educate voters through campaign advertisements, brochures and other literature, websites and blogs, and frequent appearances by party officials and important party members on television and radio shows. They may coordinate messages across the country, so that, for example, an advertisement on health care reform can be used in multiple districts, simply replacing the candidate's name.

Deliver people to the polls Parties deliver people to the polls in two ways. Parties work hard to convince supportive voters that something is at stake in the election, that the benefits of voting are so important that the voter best not stay at home. And more directly, with their get-out-the-vote (GOTV) efforts, party supporters—or sometimes hired telemarketing firms—make phone calls, send email, and go door-to-door to remind people to vote and ask if they need assistance getting to the polling place.

An individual voter might get a number of these reminders. Does any of this matter? Individuals who are contacted by political parties, or by other groups, are more likely to say they voted than individuals who were not contacted. This correlation is not proof of causation, however, because it is also the case that parties target their contacts to those individuals who they have reason to believe are more likely to vote. Thus it could be a prior history of voting, or some other expression of strong interest, that led to the individual being contacted in the first place. Research controlling for this possible reverse causation suggests that the contacts do still have an effect on driving up turnout.[6]

Integrate new social groups Political parties have an incentive to bring new groups into the political process, but are selective about which groups to reach out to. With the goal of winning elections, parties will not invest resources in bringing in new voters who will hurt their chances. They may even invest resources in keeping a group out of politics, as southern Democrats did regarding blacks up through the mid-1960s. In cases like this, the logic of competition suggests that the other major party would have an interest at integrating a new group into American politics, especially if it can do so without unduly alarming groups that already support the party. Up through the 1950s, the Republican Party benefited from its legacy as the party that ended slavery and seemed more open to integrating blacks into the country's political life. Other groups already in the United States but newly enfranchised, like women after 1920 and young voters after 1971, were also seen as opportunities by the parties who then reached out to these groups.

This process is also seen with immigrant groups. In the waves of immigration across American history, the two major parties have vied with each other to bring members of these groups into the electoral process and make them feel that the party represents them and cares about them. German immigrants tended to be more strongly courted by Republicans. Irish immigrants, on the other hand, were targeted for attention by the Democratic Party. Various Latino groups have been courted by the two parties, with Cuban immigrants tending toward the Republicans and Mexicans toward the Democrats. When it has suited their purpose, parties have also sought to make it hard for immigrant groups to enter politics. For example, in the 1890s, virtually every state enacted some form of personal voter registration. Often, these at first only applied to urban areas, where immigrant groups were concentrated. Although this could make good policy sense—perhaps the risk of voter fraud is greater in areas of higher population—it was also seen by reformers as a way to reduce immigrant influence in elections.[7] Today, some observers lodge the same charge at efforts to require photo identification prior to voting. Although reducing fraud is undoubtedly a good thing, these observers argue that part of the goal of photo ID is to discourage voting by immigrants wary of U.S. legal authorities.

The Two-Party System

American electoral competition is usually between two major political parties. A major party is one that has a large following, has endured over time, and has a perception that it can feasibly win elections. Minor parties, or "third parties," lack these features. They are usually small, have not been around long, and are not perceived as having a serious chance at winning office.

To say that the United States has a **two-party system** does not mean that only two parties compete but, rather, than it is a system of electoral competition in which two parties are consistently seen as the most likely to win office and gain power. If you were to predict who was going to win an election, and you predicted it would be either a Democrat or Republican, you would be right nearly every time.

This is not generally true in electoral systems elsewhere. In multi-party systems based on proportional representation, as discussed below, more than two parties are seen as plausibly able to win. In those systems, this is in part because a party need not finish in first place to win seats in a legislature. Therefore, even smaller parties can be seen as genuine contenders for power.

Hundreds of political parties have competed over the years in the United States, but competition nationally has almost always been between two major parties. Across American history there have been five major political parties: Federalists (1789–1816); the Democratic-Republicans (1790–1824); the Democrats (1828 to the present); the National Republicans, later Whigs (1824–1854); and the Republicans (1854 to the present). Third parties have included a wide array, including parties organized around ideology (Socialist Party, Progressive Party, Green Party, Libertarian Party), predominantly single issues (Prohibition Party, Greenback Party), defection from a major party (States' Rights, also known as Dixiecrats), and parties built initially around a single presidential candidacy (American Independent Party for George Wallace in 1968; National Unity Party for John Anderson in 1980; United We Stand/Reform Party for Ross Perot in 1992 and 1996). At its very beginning, the Republican Party was a third party, but it quickly rose to ascendancy over the Whigs, which disbanded.

Third parties are rarely successful electorally, but may have influence in other ways.

The electoral performance of American third parties can be summed up in one word: dismal. Third party candidates rarely win elections and usually do not garner a significant share of the vote. Over the past fifty years, they rarely, as a group, have garnered more than a few percent of the total national congressional vote. Never strong, their performance was stronger in the nineteenth century, with about 5% of House seat in the period from 1830–1870 being held by third party members. Over the past half century, by contrast, there have only been 9 times when a third-party candidate held a seat in the House, and 8 of these are accounted for by the same representative (Bernard Sanders, Socialist Party, Vermont).[8]

Similarly, in presidential elections, third party candidates rarely win states. No state has sided with a third-party candidate since 1968, when five southern states backed Alabama's Democratic governor George Wallace, who was running as an independent candidate with the newly-created American Independent Party.

Although third parties do not often win elections, they can still play significant roles in elections. Probably the most important of these roles is that third party candidates, or independent candidates more generally, can introduce ideas and issues into the campaign that the major party candidates might be neglecting or avoiding. Ross Perot in 1992, for example, brought attention to the issue of international trade, an area on which Republican President George Bush and his Democratic rival, Bill Clinton, largely agreed. If a third party candidate raises issues that are popular with the public, often one of the major party candidates will be able to adopt that issue as their own. In 1992, Clinton increased his focus on the budget deficit after that issue had proved to be a popular one for Perot. Some analysts believe Democrat Al Gore struck a more populist tone in 2000 because of the solid showing of Green Party candidate Ralph Nader in polls.[9] Given this ability to introduce new ideas, one positive sign for third parties is that more voters today have the opportunity to hear from them in congressional

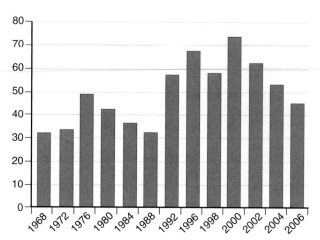

Figure 11-2. **Percent of U.S. House Districts with a Minor Party or Independent Candidate Running.** Since 1992, voters in U.S. House elections have been more likely to see a third party or independent candidate on the ballot than was true previously. Since 1992, usually over half of all districts feature a third party or independent candidate. Prior to 1992, the proportion was more typically around 30 to 35 percent.

Source: Christian Collett and Martin P. Wattenberg, "Strategically Unambitious: Minor Party and Independent Candidates in the 1996 Congressional Elections," in John C. Green and Daniel M. Shea, eds., *The State of the Parties: The Changing Role of Contemporary American Parties* nham, MD: Rowman and Littlefield, 1999); authors' calculations.

elections (Figure 11-2), due in large part to ballot access lawsuits filed by Perot in 1992.

Another possible but controversial role for third parties is to alter the election outcome between the major parties. It was easy for Democrats in 1968 and Republicans in 1992 to blame George Wallace and Ross Perot for the defeat of Hubert Humphrey and George Bush, respectively, based on the argument that Wallace and Perot diverted votes from these two major party candidates. Many Democrats remain angry at Ralph Nader for his run in 2000, believing he cost Al Gore the presidency.

However, these are usually cases where correlation is mistaken for causality. These third party candidates emerged and did well because of the weakness with the major party and its candidate, rather than creating that weakness. Strong major party candidates will deflate third party performance. And the idea that third party candidates deliberately employ a spoiler strategy—seeking to cause the defeat of the major party they are ideologically closer to—is not well supported by political science research, including the Nader candidacy in 2000.[10] Nader's main goal seemed to be to reach 5% of the national vote to qualify the Green Party for public campaign financing, not to deny Gore the presidency.

Single-member districts with plurality elections favor two party competition.

Certainly there is no constitutional prohibition on significant third parties. Indeed, the Constitution does not mention political parties at all. Why would America's electoral competition tend to feature two major parties as serious competitors?

In U.S. House elections, as with most American elections, **single-member districts** are the norm: one candidate is elected to represent each congressional district. In addition, the candidate with the most votes wins: these are **plurality elections**. To Americans, these points are so obvious, they are hardly worth stating, but they have significant consequences. Only one candidate, and thus one party, can win. Assume that politicians are ambitious and want to increase their chances of consistently winning office. What would be the best strategy: to remain in a small party that has the support of 5% of the population, or to join together with other factions into a larger party that can potentially obtain majority support? Joining together is the likely answer, and two large, roughly evenly-sized parties are the likely result.[11]

An alternative to the single-member plurality model is a system of **proportional representation**, common in many other countries. In this system, many representatives are elected from the same district. The district, in fact, might be the entire country. The number of representatives elected from a particular party will depend on that party's percentage of the vote on election day. If a party receives 40% of the vote in a district, it will send roughly 40% or more of the legislators from that district.[12] What this means is that the second or third place finishing parties, or even more, may also be sending representatives to the legislature. Thus in a proportional system, an ambitious politician can conclude that he or she can remain in a smaller party and still have a chance to be elected to the legislature. And because there is a significant likelihood that no party will win a majority of the legislative seats, a majority coalition will need to be forged, and this further empowers smaller parties.

There is good reason to believe that single-member districts with plurality elections reinforce tendencies toward two-party competition. But it is not necessarily the case they cause it. One study of the adoption of proportional representation systems found that these systems were adopted in countries that had a prior history of diverse political competition between multiple groups. In other words, the proportional representation system was adopted because of what was effectively multiparty competition.[13] In the United States, on the other hand, political scientists have suggested that early political discourse and the American creed was strongly oriented around basic, fundamental debates about the proper role of government, and these debates tended to feature two competing views, a liberal and conservative view. A system like single-member districts with plurality elections could work well in such an environment, reflecting rather than creating the nature of political competition between two predominant opposing viewpoints.[14]

The winner-take-all system in presidential elections favors two major parties.

Presidential elections pose a similar challenge to third parties. With the exception of Maine and Nevada, all states allocate their electoral votes on a **winner-take-all** basis. This means that the popular vote winner of the presidential contest in the state wins all the electoral votes from the state, no matter what the size of the popular vote victory. For a third-party candidate, this system makes it difficult to win electoral votes. By its very nature, a third-party is not likely to be the leading votewinner in a state, meaning it will win no electoral votes. With the winner of the presidency needing to win a majority of the electoral vote, the third party path to the presidency is very challenging.

The structure of the presidential election process benefits third parties with strong regional appeals while hurting those with substantial national appeal. George Wallace in 1968 won 13 percent of the popular vote nationally, but won enough in five southern states to win their electoral votes over Republican Richard Nixon and Democrat Hubert Humphrey. In 1992, Ross Perot won 19% of the popular vote nationally, but did not win a single electoral vote. He had broad national appeal, but not a strong enough appeal in any single state or region to win electoral votes.

Legal and behavioral features of American elections reinforce two party competition.

In addition to the basic structural features of American politics already discussed, statutes affecting elections, as well as the behavior of voters, politicians, and the media, reinforce the tendencies toward two-party politics.

Anti-fusion laws Anti-fusion laws prohibit third parties from practicing **fusion** with a major party. Fusion, a common and successful strategy until banned in nearly all states around the turn of the twentieth century, allowed voters to vote for a candidate either under the third-party label or under the major-party label. The logic was to make voters comfortable voting for a third-party candidate and to increase the leverage the third party could exert on the candidates once in office.[15] Currently, only seven states allow fusion in its traditional form, most notably in New York where it is known as cross-filing. In 1997, the Supreme Court rejected a challenge to the constitutionality of anti-fusion laws.[16]

Ballot access laws Prior to the 1880s, ballot access was not an issue. Parties printed their own ballots, which voters took to the polling place and dropped into the ballot box. Ballots could be a variety of shapes, sizes, and colors, and it was often easy to identify which party's ballot a voter was casting. Over a short period of time in the 1880s and 1890s, nearly every state adopted what is known as the **Australian ballot**, for its country of origin. This is the ballot as we know it today—an official ballot printed by the government, provided at the polling place, listing all the candidates for every office, and cast secretly.

As soon as the ballot became an official, standardized government document, questions emerged. Would every candidate from every party, no matter how small, be listed? Or would a limited set of candidates be listed to prevent "ballot clutter"? In every state, the limited, clutter-free version was adopted. States had to set rules for being listed on the ballot. Minor parties would face a hurdle, usually the collection of a large number of signatures, in putting their candidates in front of the voters. States often made it very difficult for third parties to qualify by placing onerous rules on the signature collection and submission process. Over time, these restrictions have relaxed somewhat, usually as a direct result of lawsuits filed by third party candidates.

Campaign finance laws Running for office is expensive. Third party candidates suffer from the fact that donors are usually not interested in contributing money to candidates they perceive as having no chance of winning. But the system of public financing for presidential candidates is also geared toward the major party candidates (see chapter 9). Parties whose candidate received at least 25 percent of the vote in the prior presidential election get a full share of public financing for the general election in the fall. If a candidate received between 5 and 25% in the previous election, his or her party is entitled to a proportional share of public financing in the current election. Candidates falling below 5%, which is nearly always the case for third-party candidates, do not earn their party any share of public financing. Thus, third parties rarely qualify for public financing in presidential campaigns. In addition, if a third party candidate does receive more than 5% in the current election, he will not receive federal funds for this election until after it is over. The major party candidates receive their funds at the start of the campaign.

Voter, media, and candidate behavior The ways in which voters, the media, and candidates respond to the incentives created by these structural and legal aspects of American politics reinforces the tendency toward two-party politics. Voters unhappy with major party candidates often choose not to vote rather than vote for a third-party candidate that is likely to lose. Other voters fear that voting for a third party candidate amounts to throwing their vote away and helping the least favored of the two major party candidates by denying his opponent a vote. Third parties face a very difficult time breaking through the psychology of nonvoting and the fear of the wasted vote.

Media coverage is also problematic for third parties. Third party officials often complain that if the media paid more attention to third parties, they would do better electorally. Media representatives respond that if third parties did better electorally, the news media would pay more attention to them. Each side is right. As businesses, media companies have to be aware of their customers, and the reality is that most news consumers are more interested in hearing about the candidates they are likely to choose between—the major party candidates—than about minor party candidates. A media outlet that focuses a lot of attention on relatively obscure candidates may well find its readers, viewers, or listeners, drifting to other media outlets. But more attention from the media would, overall, be at least marginally helpful for third party candidates.

Ambitious, qualified candidates are much more likely to run for office as a Democrat or Republican than as a third-party candidate. Someone wanting to maximize her probability of winning, certainly someone who would like to make a career of elective office, is highly likely to affiliate with one of the major parties. Most voters are reluctant to vote for third party candidates and are guided by their party identification with one of the major parties (see chapter 9). Further, each major party has a network of supporters, consultants, expertise, and fundraisers to draw upon. There are huge built-in advantages to running as a major party candidate.

Occasionally, third parties overcome these difficulties. Third party candidates who have already become nationally visible as a member of a major party or in some other way will often be talented, strong candidates, as Table 11.1 indicates. Teddy Roosevelt, George Wallace, and Ralph Nader all had significant name recognition. For some candidates, like Ross Perot in 1992 and 1996, campaign finances are not an obstacle.[17]

Alternative voting rules have been proposed to assist third-party electoral fortunes.

This occasional success is only a matter of degree, because the reality remains that it is almost always a Democrat or Republican that wins an election. Supporters of an enhanced role for third parties argue that changes in voting rules could give these parties a better chance of winning elections. Whether this is accurate is diffi-

Table 11-1. Most Successful Third Party Presidential Candidates, 1900-2008

YEAR	CANDIDATE	PARTY	PERCENT OF POPULAR VOTE	NUMBER OF ELECTORAL VOTES
1912	Theodore Roosevelt	Progressive	27.4	88
1992	Ross Perot	Independent/ United We Stand	18.9	0
1924	Robert La Follette	Progressive	16.6	13
1968	George Wallace	American Independent	13.5	46
1996	Ross Perot	Reform	8.4	0
1980	John Anderson	Independent	6.6	0
1912	Eugene Debs	Socialist	6.0	0
1920	Eugene Debs	Socialist	3.4	0
1916	Allan Benson	Socialist	3.2	0
1904	Eugene Debs	Socialist	3.0	0
1908	Eugene Debs	Socialist	2.8	0
1948	Henry Wallace	Progressive	2.8	0
2000	Ralph Nader	Green	2.7	0
1948	Strom Thurmond	States' Rights	2.4	39
1932	Norman Thomas	Socialist	2.2	0

Source: Dave Leip's Atlas of U.S. Presidential Elections, www.uselectionatlas.org

Note: Includes all third party presidential candidates who received at least 2% of the national vote.

cult to determine because these alternative rules are not in wide use in the United States. Moreover, it may be the case that these reforms tend to be enacted in places already friendly to third parties—that is why they are enacted—rather than leading to support for third parties. Nonetheless, it seems plausible they would have some minor benefit for third parties. Each of the rules is targeted at overcoming voter psychology that reinforces the two-party system by discouraging casting a vote for a third-party candidate.[18] Rather than proportional representation, which would require the dismantling of single-member districts, we focus on two voting systems that would work within the American single-member district format.[19]

Preference voting In American elections, voters select their favored candidate among those on the ballot. An alternative arrangement would allow voters to rank their choices, indicating which candidate is their first pick, second, third, and so on. The idea is that voters could express support for a third party candidate, but would not be forced to indicate support for only that candidate.

There are several varieties of preference voting arrangements. One that has received some attention in the United States and has been adopted in a handful of cities, including San Francisco, is instant runoff voting. In this system, voters rank their choices. If no one receives a majority of the first place votes, the candidate receiving the fewest first place votes is eliminated, and the votes cast for him are redistributed to other candidates based on the preference ranking indicated by his voters. If a candidate now has a majority, she wins. If not, the last place candidate is again eliminated and his votes redistributed.

Approval voting Rather than ranking candidates, approval voting allows voters to indicate all candidates of which they approve. The candidate receiving the most votes wins. As with preference voting, the logic is that voters might be interested in a third party candidate but, because of their fear of wasting their vote, would not want to commit their only vote to that candidate. Instead, with approval voting, they could vote for a third party candidate and other candidates of their choosing.

The Evolution of Party Competition and Party Coalitions

Key issue concerns and the relative strength of the two major parties have changed over time. Political scientists refer to the switch from one period of competition to another as **electoral realignment**—the shuffling of support groups between the parties, the integration of new groups, and the rise of a new set of issues to prominence. Political scientists dispute the process by which electoral realignment occurs and whether the most important change is sudden and dramatic in the form of a "critical election" or slow-building and gradual.[20] That there are some roughly demarcated periods of competition, labeled party systems, is more widely accepted.

American parties have evolved through six periods of party competition.

A common perspective among political scientists is that the United States has gone through six periods of party competition. Briefly, these are:

1800–1828 The Federalist Party of the 1790s, including John Adams and Alexander Hamilton, advocated a larger, more active national government. Its support was strongest in the Northeast, among business people, and those of higher income. The Democratic-Republican Party, represented by Thomas Jefferson and James Madison, pushed to protect states' rights and limit national power. It prospered in the South and Mid-Atlantic states. The Democratic-Republicans were the dominant party and effectively the only major party for much of this period (see Table 11.2).

Table 11-2. Party Control of Congress and the Presidency, 1801-2008

	PRESIDENT		HOUSE		SENATE	
	DEMOCRATIC-REPUBLICANS	FEDERALISTS	DEMOCRATIC-REPUBLICANS	FEDERALISTS	DEMOCRATIC-REPUBLICANS	FEDERALISTS
1801-1828	28	0	26	2	26	2
	DEMOCRATS	NATIONAL REPUBLICANS/ WHIGS	DEMOCRATS	NATIONAL REPUBLICANS/ WHIGS	DEMOCRATS	NATIONAL REPUBLICANS/ WHIGS
1829-1860	24	8	24	8	28	4
	DEMOCRATS	REPUBLICANS	DEMOCRATS	REPUBLICANS	DEMOCRATS	REPUBLICANS
1861-1896	8	28	6	30	14	22
a. 1861-1876	0	16	2	14	0	16
b. 1877-1896	8	12	4	16	14	6
1897-1932	8	28	10	26	6	30
1933-1968	28	8	32	4	32	4
1969-2008	12	28	28	12	23	17
a. 1969-1980	4	8	12	0	12	0
b. 1981-2008	8	20	16	12	11	17

Source: Marjorie Randon Hershey, *Party Politics in America*, 13th ed. (New York: Pearson Longman, 2009), p. 119

1828–1860 The Democratic-Republican Party split in two. The Democratic Party, represented by Andrew Jackson, continued the tradition of representing rural, low-income, and southern voters, but also added support among the urban working class. The National Republican Party, which would become the Whig Party, argued for an expansion of the national government's economic powers. John Quincy Adams was a major figure in this party, which was supported predominantly by wealthier voters. The Democrats dominated in this party system.

1860–1896 The Whig party collapsed, unable to heal its internal divisions over the slavery issue. In 1854, the Republican Party, represented by Abraham Lincoln, emerged and quickly moved to major party status as the Whigs disappeared. As slavery and its aftermath became the central issue, party competition was strongly regional, with Democrats prevailing in the South and Republicans in the Northeast and Midwest. The national government's role in economic development, and particularly its promotion of industrial capitalism through tariffs and other measures, also strongly divided the parties, with Republicans advocating a stronger government role and Democrats arguing for the primacy of states' rights and local economic development. Republicans dominated up through 1876, when the Southern states were fully incorporated back into the Union. After that, party competition was evenly divided.

1896–1932 In the 1890s, the Democratic Party adopted some of the populist economic views of the People's Party, most notably its views about the monetary system and how it affected farmers and agricultural workers. The Democratic presidential candidate in 1896, Williams Jennings Bryan, was also endorsed by the People's Party as a fusion ticket. The 1896 presidential election was widely viewed at the time as a referendum on industrial capitalism. Would the United States continue down that path, with increasingly large and national corporations? The Republican Party and its candidate William McKinley, supporter of the view that industrial capitalism should be promoted and encouraged by the national government through its policies, prevailed. Democrats remained the dominant, virtually the only, party in the South, and did well in many rural western states. They did well in some northern cities as well, especially among immigrant Catholic voters. Their only presidential victories were in 1912, when Woodrow Wilson benefited from the Progressive party candidacy of former Republican president Theodore Roosevelt, and Wilson's reelection in 1916. Although the majority, the Republican Party wrestled internally with the question of how best to regulate the increasingly large and dynamic private sector.

1932–1968 The Democratic Party was the majority party for most of this period, winning most presidential elections and controlling Congress for all but four years. Galvanized by the Great Depression, Democrats argued for a stronger federal role in social programs that provided a safety net for those who were struggling to make ends meet or those who were not able to provide for themselves. Republicans initially opposed these programs, arguing they risked sapping the individualist strength prized in American history. Dwight Eisenhower, a war hero who was the only Republican to win the presidency in this era, argued that his party needed to accept the popularity of these assistance programs and make sure they were administered as fiscally responsibly as possible. By the latter part of this era, Republicans were split over whether to continue the Eisenhower path or, as with the selection of Barry Goldwater as the party's presidential nominee in 1964, offer a strong conservative alternative. Democrats were split over the Vietnam War and various issues related to the civil rights, women's, and antiwar movements.

1968-the present Political competition in this period was closely fought. Neither major party could claim the mantle of the undisputed majority party. Divided control of government was very common, occurring in 30 of the 40 years between 1969 and 2008. Rather than an electoral realignment, some analysts described this period as one of **dealignment**, with voters splitting tickets, feeling less attachment to the parties, and increasingly identifying themselves as Independents. These behaviors peaked in the mid-1980s. After that, ticket splitting dropped—though there remains more split ticket voting than was true in the early through mid twentieth century—and voters who identified as Democrats were increasingly likely to support the Democratic candidate for the House, Senate, or president, and similarly for Republicans. Generally, the Democrats were stronger in the Northeast and Pacific coast, Republicans prevailed in the Mountain and western states and the South, and the Midwest was a battleground between the two parties. By 2006, the advantage in this era of closely balanced party competition had swung to the Democrats.

The Democratic New Deal coalition dominated electoral politics for over forty years.

The coalition brought together by Democratic presidential candidate Franklin Roosevelt in 1932 proved to be remarkably resilient. For over forty years, this coalition produced victories in the House, Senate, and the presidency. Galvanized by Roosevelt's promise that he would actively respond to the economic stress of the Great Depression, the Democratic supporters agreed that economic recovery was the first and most important priority of government. The coalition included southern whites, agricultural workers, unionized labor, lower to low-middle income workers, big-city public officials and urban ethnic group supporters, Catholics, Jews, and industries pleased by Roosevelt's free trade approach. These constituencies strongly supported the array of new government services, programs, and entitlements created by Roosevelt and the Democrats in response to the Depression.

Over time, the Democratic coalition shifted. Blacks, who voted in small numbers in the 1930s and were favorable toward the Republicans—the party of Lincoln—were not initially a major part of the coalition. With the civil rights achievements of Democratic presidents in the 1960s, however, blacks moved firmly into the Democratic column. Support among white southerners began to decline. Moving further away from the Great Depression, the centrality of the economy as the glue holding together the coalition began to fracture. New concerns based on civil rights, women's rights, environmentalism, lifestyle issues, and the use of American military power became more prominent. Upper-middle-class professionals, particularly in government, the nonprofit sector, law, the media, and academia, became a larger share of the party coalition. Support for Democrats began to wane among the original members of the New Deal coalition.[21] Although these traditional groups still supported Democratic candidates in solid numbers, those numbers were no longer enough to assure Democrats of victories.[22] The 2008 nomination contest between Barack Obama and Hillary Clinton highlighted the split between these two wings of the party.

The coalition crafted by Ronald Reagan brought the Republicans to national parity.

With Democrats in the ascendancy after the 1930s, Republicans scrambled to put together a competitive coalition. One key element tapped into by Republican candidates was a growing resentment of what was perceived as the cultural elitism of the evolving Democratic coalition—a sense of being "talked down to" and mocked by political activists associated with the Democrats. This uneasiness in some parts of the population was exacerbated by the civil rights, women's, and antiwar movements. Richard Nixon, in his successful presidential bids of 1968 and 1972, capitalized on this sentiment.[23] In the 2008 Democratic presidential nomination contest, Senator Barack Obama's comment about frustrated voters "clinging to" guns and religion received widespread attention from conservatives as an example of liberal cultural elitism.

Ronald Reagan in 1980 built a coalition that brought the Republicans to parity with Democrats nationally. In the wake of bad economic times and struggling U.S. foreign policy, Reagan encouraged new identities for disgruntled groups. Middle class and working class voters were asked to think of themselves not as the beneficiaries of government programs, but as the taxpayers paying the heavy cost of supporting them. Blue collar workers were asked to focus not merely on their economic concerns, but their patriotic concerns for the United States. These "Reagan Democrats" were added to conservative white southerners, conservative Christians, businesses frustrated by high taxes and regulation, and the Republicans' traditional support groups such as middle to high income individuals and small town and rural residents.[24]

This coalition produced several Republican presidential victories. Table 11.3 shows Republican President George W. Bush's support among various groups in the 2004 presidential election. In 1994, the coalition gave Republicans control of the House and Senate for the first time in forty years. This majority lasted until 2006 when Republicans lost their control of both the House and Senate.[25] Table 11.4 shows the Democratic support groups in the 2006 House races.

Democrats and Republicans today have significant differences over public policy.

Third party candidates often deride the differences between the two major parties. Green Party presidential candidate Ralph Nader, in 2000, proclaimed that the Democratic and Republican parties were just two peas in a corporate pod. Libertarian party candidates see both parties as willing to bloat the size of government and intrude on personal freedom. Citizens with strong liberal or conservative views who lean toward one of the two major parties nonetheless are often harshly critical of their party for failing to distinguish itself from its rival. Anti-Iraq War liberals rebuked congressional Democrats for not shutting off funding for the war in 2007 and 2008. Republican 2008 presidential nominee John McCain faced strong criticism from many conservatives for working with Democrats on issues such as campaign finance reform, immigration, and nomination of federal judges.

Despite this critique, the two parties do differ significantly on many policy issues. Indeed, if this were not so, it would be difficult to understand why the two parties have different voting coalitions, different alliances of interest groups that support them, and different profiles of their campaign contributors. Presumably, voters support candidates in part for their issue stances. And even if voters support party candidates for reasons of group affiliation—a sense that the party is friendly to "people like us" and that others of your group support that party—that, too, is rooted in some sense that the party will behave in a way that you will tend to approve.

Party differences are more noticeable at the national level than at the state level. Within a particular state, parties may adjust their position to be competitive. Republicans in the Northeast, for example, are generally more liberal than Republicans in the Southwest. Democrats in the South are generally more conservative than Democrats in the Pacific Northwest. Though the parties in a state may offer genuinely different positions, they may not mirror the differences present at the national level. Nationally, for example, Democrats are more likely to support stronger gun control regulations, but in many states with widespread gun ownership, that would not be a viable position to take.

Table 11-3. Strongest Support Groups for George W. Bush in 2004

GROUP (SIZE IN ELECTORATE)	PERCENT VOTING FOR BUSH	PERCENT VOTING FOR KERRY	PRO-BUSH GAP (% POINTS)
Republican (37%)	93%	6%	87
Terrorism is country's most important problem (19%)	86%	14%	72
Conservative (34%)	84%	15%	69
Moral values are country's most important problem (22%)	80%	18%	62
White evangelical/born-again (23%)	78%	21%	57
Abortion should be always illegal (16%)	77%	22%	55
Abortion should be mostly illegal (26%)	73%	26%	47
No legal recognition for same-sex couples (37%)	70%	29%	41
White men (36%)	62%	37%	25
Weekly church attendance or more (41%)	61%	39%	22
Protestant (54%)	59%	40%	19
Married with children (28%)	59%	40%	19
White (77%)	58%	41%	17
Income $100,000 or more (18%)	58%	41%	17
Have served in military (18%)	57%	41%	16
South (32%)	58%	42%	16
Married (63%)	57%	42%	15
Live in rural area or small town (25%)	57%	42%	15
Taxes are country's most important problem (5%)	57%	43%	14
Income $50-75,000 (23%)	56%	43%	13
Have not lost job (83%)	56%	44%	12
Male (46%)	55%	44%	11
White women (41%)	55%	44%	11
No union members in household (76%)	55%	44%	11
Income $75-100,000 (14%)	55%	45%	10

Source: Voter News Survey exit polls, 13,660 respondents. Data available at http://www.cnn.com/ELECTION/2004/pages/results/states/US/P/00/epolls.0.html

Table 11-4. Strongest Support Groups for House Democratic Candidates in 2006

GROUP (SIZE IN ELECTORATE)	PERCENT VOTING FOR DEMOCRAT	PERCENT VOTING FOR REPUBLICAN	PRO-DEMOCRATIC GAP (% POINTS)
Democrat (38%)	93%	7%	86
African-American (10%)	89%	10%	79
Liberal (20%)	87%	11%	76
Jewish (2%)	87%	12%	75
Disapprove of Iraq War (56%)	80%	18%	62
Non-White Women (11%)	78%	21%	57
Non-White Men (9%)	75%	23%	52
No religious affiliation (11%)	74%	22%	52
Gay, lesbian, or bisexual (3%)	75%	24%	51
Family falling behind financially (17%)	74%	23%	51
Latino (8%)	69%	30%	39
Someone in household in union (23%)	64%	34%	30
Single (32%)	64%	34%	30
Northeast (22%)	63%	35%	28
Asian (2%)	62%	37%	25
Immigrants should be offered legal status (57%)	61%	37%	24
Live in urban area (30%)	61%	37%	24
Attend church occasionally or never (53%)	61%	37%	24
Age 18-29 (12%)	60%	38%	22
Income below $50,000 (40%)	60%	38%	22
Moderate (47%)	60%	38%	22
Economy extremely important factor in vote (39%)	59%	39%	20
Independent (26%)	57%	39%	18
Postgraduate (18%)	58%	41%	17
Female (51%)	55%	43%	12
High school graduate (21%)	55%	44%	11
Catholic (26%)	55%	44%	11
West (21%)	54%	43%	11
No children under 18 (66%)	54%	44%	11

Source: Voter News Survey exit polls, 13,251 respondents. Data available at http://www.cnn.com/ELECTION/2006/pages/results/states/US/H/00/epolls.0.html

Nationally, Democrats tend to argue for a more expansive use of government in addressing social and economic problems. They are more inclined to define these problems as ones requiring a government solution. Republicans will tend to argue for a market-based, private sector solution to the problem: can individuals and businesses be given incentives that will lead them to take the desired behavior? On social issues such as abortion, however, Democrats are less inclined to involve government in individual decisionmaking, while Republicans support government restrictions on this behavior. Democrats are more supportive of tax arrangements that take larger shares of one's income as income rises, while Republicans argue that increased tax rates of that type amount to a penalty for individual hard work and success. In foreign policy, Republicans have generally supported a more aggressive use of military force to obtain desired goals, while Democrats have expressed more reluctance in this area.[26] Democratic rhetoric will more often invoke equality and fairness, while Republicans will refer to individual opportunity and freedom. Although cultural and social issues like abortion or same-sex marriage receive significant attention in public discussion of parties and candidates, the contrasting agendas of the parties focus much more on economic, financial, and regulatory matters, including economic growth, prices, employment, taxes, regulating business, health care, retirement, and other issues such as education that can be defined as having economic significance.[27]

Across history, the two major parties have catered to different groups with competing views on public policy and basic values. In recent times, this has been depicted as the clash between red America and blue America, or red states (Republican) and blue states (Democratic). Politicians like former Republican presidential candidate Patrick Buchanan and media commentators like Bill O'Reilly refer to it as a culture war. To other observers, though, the nature of American public opinion and the breadth of party coalitions means there is at best a culture skirmish rather than a culture war (see *How Do We Know? Is America a Polarized Red/Blue Country?*)

Is America a Polarized Red/Blue Country?

| The Question |

In the eyes of many Americans, politics in the United States has become nasty, bitter, and rife with conflict. In 2008, both Barack Obama and John McCain criticized the nature of political debate in the United States, with Obama deriding it "do-anything, say-anything, divisive politics" and McCain labeling it as "mindless, paralyzing rancor."[28] Terms like two Americas, the 50/50 nation, red and blue America, and the culture war have been used to define current American politics.[29] Is America a Polarized Red/Blue Country? How do we know?

| Why It Matters |

Both for citizens and politicians looking to influence the policy process, it matters whether Americans are in two different worlds politically or have political differences that are modest in degree. If the country is polarized, then political success will depend on high-charged mobilization based on strong rhetoric. If the country is not, then success will depend more on mobilizing the support of those whose views are relatively moderate. One's analysis of American democracy might also be influenced by the level of difference. Parties offering strongly different views might be considered the lifeblood of democracy, and therefore polarization a sign of a healthy political system. Or high degrees of partisanship might be seen as an obstacle to solving problems and a blot on democracy by others.

| Investigating the Answer |

The idea that Americans live in polarized worlds politically, with a vast gulf in their cultural values and political preferences, was popularized as the red state/blue state difference when television election result maps in those colors showed the country divided sharply into regions of Democratic support and Republican support. The map of the 2004 presidential election results, for example, showed the Democratic blue states of the Northeast, upper Midwest, and Pacific Coast aligned against the remainder of the red Republican country (Figure 11.3).

Closer examination, however, shows that the maps were misleading. Some red states were barely red, and some blue states barely blue. Maps colored at the county level and shaded for their degree of support for Republican George Bush and Democrat John Kerry show much of the country was closer to purple rather than distinctly red or blue. Moreover, an examination of a map of state legislative party control shows that the red-blue distinction does not carry over very well to that level (Figure 11.4).

Perhaps the place to look for polarization is not in the pattern of party victories, but in public opinion. Does public opinion show more polarized views among the public?

One prominent study examines public issues on a range of "hot button" issues like abortion and gay rights. The authors find that, when given the option, most Americans place themselves toward the middle of the scale rather than taking a position on the far left or far right. And even where opinion has become more polarized over time, the difference is not that great. For example, the National Election Study asks survey respondents to place themselves on a series of 7-point issue scales. The average difference between Democrats and Republicans increased since the early 1970s, when it was 0.5 points, but only to about 1 point. By that measure,

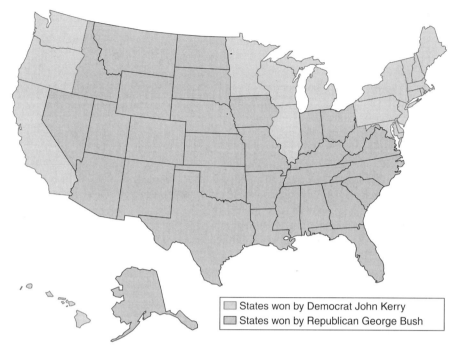

Figure 11-3. Red and Blue America in the 2004 Presidential Election.

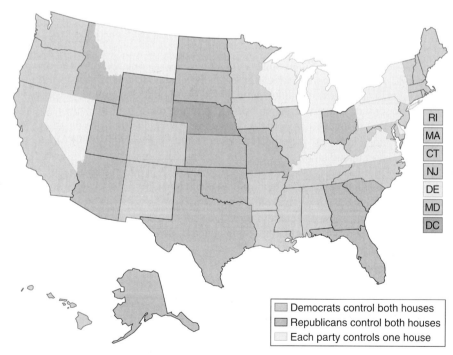

Figure 11-4. Party Control of State Legislatures, 2008.

Note: Nebraska has a unicameral, nonpartisan legislature.

Source: Data obtained from http://www.ncsl.org/statevote/statevotemaps2008.htm.

public opinion among Democrats and Republicans is distinctive, but they are separated on average by 1 point on the 7-point scale.[30]

Another study confirms that differences between Democrats and Republicans have grown—and uniquely so. The authors looked at public opinion on 35 issue areas since 1972. They found that by every measure—age, education, race, religious affiliation, region, and gender—there had been convergence rather than divergence of opinion between groups. The groups (old versus young, for example) did differ on their opinions, but the degree of difference had not grown. Except one: partisans had grown further apart.[31] This suggests that there might not be much more polarized opinion in America, but that the issue differences that do exist are now better reflected in the political parties. Political scientists refer to this as ideological sorting, meaning that the correlation between one's ideology and one's party identification is stronger today than previously: liberals are increasingly likely to identify with Democrats and conservatives with Republicans.

Partisans at the elite level have also moved further apart. Studies of roll call voting in Congress show Democrats and Republicans in Congress are more ideologically distinct now than previously (see Chapter 15). Even more than the public, liberals in Congress are now much more consistently in the Democratic Party and conservatives in the Republican Party—they are better sorted than previously. The opinion of party activists, as measured by delegates to the two parties' national conventions in 2004, is also strongly divergent, more so than among the public. The opinion of Republican and Democratic delegates was 56 percentage points apart on whether abortion should be permitted in all cases and 70 points apart on whether the federal government should increase regulation of businesses' safety and environmental practices. The differences between Republicans and Democrats in the public was 24 and 26 points, respectively.[32]

So both elites and the public are better sorted ideologically into parties. That is the correlation. But what is the causality—what led to what? Did liberal and conservative voters start sorting themselves out better in the two parties, and then candidates had to respond to this by taking stronger views? Or did candidates take stronger views, and the public responded to that?

Political scientists have attempted to answer these questions. Although the data are mixed, overall it appears that elites led and the public followed. Political activists that are part of the party network—representatives of business groups, advocacy groups, nonprofits, unions—became better organized, more involved politically, and more important to candidates, and candidates took positions that would garner the support of these activists. With this happening in both parties, the public was faced with candidates taking stronger ideological stances, and individual voters sorted themselves into the party closer them ideologically. With a more ideologically unified base of support in the public, candidates then had further reason to distance themselves from the candidates in the other party. These trends were reinforced by the two-party transformation of Southern politics since the 1960s (conservatives could now support Republican candidates), redistricting of U.S. House districts into safer partisan seats (allowing representative to vote more ideologically in Congress), and other factors.[33]

| The Bottom Line | Public opinion overall is not dramatically more polarized now than previously. What has changed is that opinion differences are now more sharply reflected in the political parties. Ideological sorting has led to more difference between Democratic and Republican elites and, to a lesser degree, Democrats and Republicans in the public. Some observers decry these trends, arguing that this change artificially creates more political conflict and leaves moderate voters with unappealing choices.[34] But others counter that ideological sorting has led to party competition that gives voters real choices on Election Day and gives them a reason to vote. |

Successful party coalitions are broad and diverse.

The discussion so far shows that American political parties are coalitions of various interests, groups, and policy perspectives. Coalitions are the basic building block of political parties and are essential for victory. The story of party competition in U.S. history is the story of competing coalitions. What are the stresses and strains on building and maintaining coalitions?

With two major parties in the United States, winning an election means getting more votes than the opponent, typically more than 50%. American parties, therefore, are large coalitions that bring together, or aggregate, a wide range of interests under the same umbrella. This is useful for these groups, in that latching on with a winning party increases the likelihood that action will be taken on issues they care about. It is useful for governing, in that it forces some compromise among these groups because not every interest can be the top priority of the president and legislators. And it is useful for parties, because it helps them win.

Aggregating interests does pose challenges, however. The larger the party, the more factions it is likely to have. For a while, these can be held in peaceful coexistence, but as groups in the coalition begin to believe that their interests are being marginalized, the coalition comes under strain. The Republican Party during the presidency of George W. Bush and after, for example, had pulled together social conservatives, foreign policy conservatives, economic conservatives, and libertarians. Increasingly, these groups found it harder to support each other's causes or to want to defer to let the other group's priorities be the party's main focus. In the Republican presidential nomination of 2008, this division in the party helps explain why neither John McCain, Mike Huckabee, Mitt Romney, Ron Paul, or any of the other candidates seemed "just right" to Republicans. A candidate might be the darling of one of these groups while being unacceptable to other groups.

If a party knows that its success depends on serving the members of its coalition, what might prevent it from doing that? There are several possible factors. New events might push the concerns of one group aside in favor of another. The federal budget might simply not allow attending to every group's wishes. One group's interests might clash with the interests of other groups in the coalition. A group may be too small to get consistent attention from the party. Or a group might be so loyal to the party that it seems to have no serious options politically and is thus held "captive" by the party.[35] The party might also be looking ahead to its strategy in the next election and believe that emphasizing certain positions might be problematic for electoral success in November.

The fact that American party coalitions need to be large has been the basis for a longstanding debate about American parties. Some analysts have called for American parties to run as a team of candidates offering a very clear platform of proposals and to work in a highly unified, disciplined fashion to enact them. This is called the **responsible party model**. Alternatively, some analysts have said the broad nature of American party coalitions makes this kind of party behavior unlikely in the long run because parties constantly need to adjust their positions to either become the majority or maintain it. And some positions might sell better in one part of the country than another, so candidates of the same party will differ from place to place.[36]

Coalitions are dynamic, not static.

"The party coalition" is a general term that obscures the complicated nature of holding together a coalition. Party coalitions are always changing and facing strains. A victorious party might wish for time to stand still—its coalition intact and the party a national majority. This is impossible. Like tectonic plates, the factions within a party shift and collide, sometimes creating minor rumbles, sometimes earthquakes.

Americans do not vote directly for parties—they vote for candidates who happen to have a party label. The constellation of voting groups that tends to support a party may not be equally relevant for each candidate. Some groups that may be strong components of a party's national coalition—blacks in the Democratic Party, for example—might simply not be present in significant numbers in all the districts represented by party members. Therefore, the pressure to serve the interests of these groups are likely to be less strong for some party members than for others.

One of the challenges facing parties is to keep the common concerns of the coalition members upfront. Coalitions come together in a wave of optimism—and perhaps in a wave of relief from removing the other party from power—because their members believe that their interests will be better served by joining forces. In general, they believe the party's approach to issues will advance their cause. They might even be willing to defer pressing their cause for a while as other coalition members take their turn.

Over time, however, this unity tends to fracture. Waiting becomes less palatable, and the various parts of a coalition want their issues to be the party's primary concerns. Groups that are especially loyal to a party might come to believe they are always last in line, because the party believes it can take them for granted. Leaders of black and labor organizations have had such complaints about the Democratic Party, while leaders of conservative Christian groups have had similar criticisms of the Republican Party.

In addition to competing priorities among its members, a party must also monitor how addressing one group's issues might alienate other members of the coalition. Some of the desires of the Republican Party's conservative Christian followers, for example, would be objectionable to those Republicans who define themselves as libertarians and argue that government needs to stay out of individual decisions as much as possible. Some of the desires of the more liberal, populist wing of the Democratic Party directly clash with those Democrats who argue the party needs to maintain a centrist, business-friendly approach to economic issues. Party leaders may wish to keep these coalition- busting issues off the table for as long as possible. The Whig Party tried to do this with slavery. Congressional Democratic leaders did likewise with civil rights in the 1940s and 1950s.

Parties perceiving themselves as frequent losers will have different internal interpretations about what lessons should be learned from these defeats. The winning interpretation will favor some factions more than others. Following five Democratic Party defeats in the six presidential elections from 1968 through 1988, for example, the Democratic Leadership Council, a group of Democratic elected officials and political activists, successfully argued that the party's losses were due to it being perceived as too liberal economically and socially and too dominated by traditional powerhouses like organized labor, and that its path to success meant deemphasizing these elements.[37]

Groups themselves can change and prompt coalitional shifting. As a social group becomes more affluent, for example, its members might find the policy appeals of a conservative political party more to their liking. As one particular social group becomes better represented within a political party, other groups might gradually pull out. Political scientists have suggested that both these developments have occurred over the past few decades. For example, as Catholics moved steadily into the middle class, they became less reliably Democratic. As blacks gained a louder voice in the Democratic Party, whites, especially southern whites, increasingly supported Republicans. As religious and social conservatives played an increasing role in the Republican Party, Republican moderates found themselves increasingly likely to vote Democratic.

Changing demographics can also require responses from the parties. As the population of the white working class has shrunk relative to college-educated whites and to blacks and other minorities, the policy interests of the Democratic Party have shifted as well to the interests of those groups. And as these groups received more attention from the party, many white working class voters, in fact a majority, shifted their voting allegiance to the Republican Party.

Political scientists refer to flips in party positioning as **issue evolution**. An issue evolution has occurred when a policy position switches from one party to another. This might happen because voters supporting the new position are now supporting the party's candidates. Or it might be an effort by an entrepreneurial officeholder to attract new supporters to the party rather than treat the coalition as static. Some examples of issue evolution are the Democratic Party advocating civil rights laws in the 1960s, a stance previously taken by Republicans; the Republicans moving to a free-trade position after 1970, after having been the party more supportive of protectionism since its founding in 1854; the Republicans adopting a pro-life position in the late 1970s, which had been more predominant in the formerly Democratic South; and Democrats advocating for the importance of a balanced budget in the 1990s, long a staple of Republican policy but not a central concern of Republican economic policy after Ronald Reagan.

Party Organization

American political parties are sometimes described as the three legs on a stool. There is the party in the electorate. This refers to the attachment of the public to the parties, known as party identification, changes in this attachment over time, and the influence of this attachment on political behavior. Party in the electorate is discussed in detail in chapters 8 and 9. A second leg of the stool is party in government. This refers to the role of political parties in structuring the behavior, influence, and success of the president, Congress, the courts, and bureaucracy. Party in government is discussed at various points in chapters 11 through 14.

The third leg of the stool is party organization, the focus of this section. Party organization is defined in different ways, but generally it refers to the formal structure of political parties that set rules for party operations and provide services for various party units and for candidates.

Party organization in the nineteenth century was informal.

Political parties were not strongly rule based in the nineteenth century. Prominent elected officials like governors or members of Congress usually held great sway over party activities. They would meet informally in informal caucuses to select the party's candidates. Later, parties adopted nominating conventions to select candidates, which included larger numbers of participants, but the delegates to the convention were still often hand-picked by elected officials.

These officials had a strong interest in selecting candidates who would fit well with the rest of the ticket, would feel some obligation to help promote the party's agenda, and would provide benefits for the county, district, or state. Thinking of parties as a brand label, during this era the control was relatively tight over who could claim the label as a candidate. Because these officials expected the election of a fellow partisan to be to their benefit, they were very involved in organizing parades, rallies, marches, and other events to motivate voters to get involved and support the ticket. These efforts had the feel of "us against them" military campaigns. It worked tremendously well, as turnout rates in the nineteenth century, especially the latter decades, were often in the range of 80 percent or more.[38]

Party machines provided organization in urban areas.

The era from 1870 to 1920 was the heyday of the local **party machine**. They did not disappear entirely after that point, but they became less common and less powerful. One of the latest and best known survivors was that of Mayor Richard Daley of Chicago from 1955–1976. Daley combined his roles as mayor and chair of the Cook County Democratic party to wield tremendous influence on city affairs.

Although best known for their legacy in large cities, machines were common in smaller cities as well and even some rural areas. There were Democratic machines and Republican machines, and they were very active in mobilizing immigrants into the local political system.

The word machine gives some hint as to their nature. Unlike the somewhat informal party organization common earlier in the nineteenth century and at the state and national level, machines were disciplined organizations that selected candidates, got out the vote, and provided benefits to loyal constituencies. Usually the leader of the machine was an elected official, typically a mayor, but not always. Machines were organized hierarchically and were spread all over a city, so that each precinct (usually a few blocks) had a machine representative in charge, who reported to a ward boss. They were intensely local in focus: the issues animating state and national partisans were often a distant focus to machine politicians. On the other hand, they would be willing to offer the backing of the machine and its supporters to a state or national politician who could return the favor in some way.

The machine spread benefits broadly. As a candidate or office holder, you knew that affiliation with the machine increased your likelihood of victory. Kicking back a portion of your salary to the machine might be considered an acceptable price to pay—it beat losing. As a worker, the promise of a city job awarded to you for your loyalty to the machine, known as **patronage**, made the machine a path to upward mobility. This was especially true for immigrants who might otherwise find it difficult to advance in the American economy. Businessmen, lawyers, and bankers knew their business would prosper through government contracts and favorable regulation if the machine was electorally successful. And individual voters were catered to by precinct captains who would provide them with groceries, legal assistance, help renting a facility for a wedding, or any other kind of help that would cement the voter's loyalty to the machine.

Party organizations were reformed at the beginning of the twentieth century.

Despite building deeply personal alliances with their supporters and serving important social service functions, machines were not without their problems. Fiscal discipline was not one of their hallmarks, nor were open and fair bids for contracts. The patronage system rewarded loyalty more than competence.

With the rise of professions and the middle class at the turn of the twentieth century, machines came under strong political attack. Businesses who were not favored by the machines, rival politicians, and middle class reformers joined forces in the Progressive movement to change civil-service laws, first at the national level and then in states and cities. These reforms protected government workers from being removed when a new party came into power.

Parties at the state and local level were the subject of a wide range of **progressive reforms** during the first two decades of the twentieth century. The reforms varied from city to city, but included the introduction of nonpartisan elections; at large rather than ward based elections to city councils; the development of special governing districts for services such as water, transportation, and schooling; and the hiring of city managers by city councils to run much of the day to day finance and business of the city, taking that job away from elected mayors. At the state level, reforms included the widespread adoption of personal registration requirements for voting and requirements that party nominations be determined by primary elections. For reformers, all these changes were designed to weaken political parties, or at least to weaken the control of their opponents over the parties and government. Individually and collectively they had the effect of depressing turnout by raising the cost of voting and decreasing the benefit. After the mid-twentieth century, the "party of nonvoters" was larger than either of the two major parties, though this was caused by multiple factors, not solely the Progressive reforms. Voting turnout became much more class-skewed than it had been previously.[39]

Because it was ardently pursued by reformers, the adoption of the primary election has usually been thought of by political scientists as an assault on a party's most defining power—control over nominations. And certainly, primaries do present challenges, as they force the party to be very publicly sparring within itself and risk the nomination of weak candidates. There is also the curious fact of having a public process to select the candidates of a private organization—it is as if the Board of Directors of the Sierra Club was a matter of a public vote rather than being determined by the Sierra Club membership. The correlation of the support of reformers and the adoption of the reform, however, is misleading. More recent research shows that major party officials welcomed the primaries in part because they had increasingly struggled to maintain control over their growing organizations and the conflicts about who "deserved" a nomination. Factional disputes were becoming very common. It was easier to sort out the disputes in primaries—which major powers in the party assumed they would be well positioned to win.[40]

The adoption of primaries as the dominant form of party nomination was part of a broader trend of state regulation of political parties. As one political scientist has put it, political parties at this time began to be treated as the equivalent of public utilities.[41] Just like gas, electric, and phone companies were regulated by the state government, so too were the political parties.

As a result, party organizations became much more formal. There were many different types of rules across the country, but some features were common. County committees and state party committees were established, with their officer selection process, membership, and length of term often set out in state law. States enacted a range of rules, including how money could be raised by parties and what it could be spent on. Rules determined in what ways parties could assist their candidates. States agreed to pay for party primaries at public expense, but this also meant that parties had to abide by state rules on how these primaries were conducted—who could vote in them, who qualified to be on the ballot, and when they would be held. The proliferation of primaries coincided with and contributed to the rise of the candidate-centered campaign, in which candidates built their own campaign organization, became less reliant on the services and resources of the formal party organization, and deemphasized their link to their political party.

Party organizations have become more active in recent decades.

For decades after the introduction of the progressive reforms, party organizations were criticized for being ineffective and inactive. The organizations were threadbare, rarely had a headquarters, and seemed to disappear between elections. Party functions such as recruiting, training, and assisting candidates fell by the wayside as candidate-centered campaigning emerged. Voter mobilization lagged in many areas.

Since the 1970s, however, state and national political party organizations have become more active, particularly in campaigns and fundraising. In part, this increased activity was the result of a more competitive political environment across the country and a more evenly matched balance of power between the two major parties after 1970. And as one party became more active, the other was obliged to respond in order to remain competitive.

State party organizations Two problems faced state party organizations. First, they were heavily regulated by government. Second, as candidate-centered campaigning grew, an election industry of fundraisers, strategists, media advisers, and pollsters emerged and challenged the parties' traditional dominance in these areas.[42]

State parties responded in two ways. They challenged their legal status by arguing that, rather than being quasi-public utilities, they were in fact private associations that were entitled to set their own rules. In a series of decisions beginning in the late 1980s, the Supreme Court agreed and granted state party organizations more autonomy from government regulations. For example, state government could not force parties to have open primaries—open to all voters—if parties wished to keep their parties closed to registered party members, or vice versa. The blanket primary, in which voters can choose office by office which primary to participate, was also struck down. The right of parties to spend unlimited sums in independent spending on behalf of candidates was upheld.[43]

To respond to the competitors for some of their key functions, state party organizations increased their professionalism, hiring new staff and experts. They created headquarters and maintained their operations between elections. Fundraising operations increased, and party organizations became more involved in recruiting and training promising candidates for office. Parties worked more closely with interest group political action committees, providing guidance about where their contributions would do the most good, and with the new web of pollsters, consultants, and media advisers. In state legislatures, the parties' campaign committees—each party typically has a campaign committee in the lower and upper house in each state—also became more active and involved in developing strategy and issue messages for candidates across districts and raising funds.

National party organizations The national party organizations include the Democratic and Republican national committees and the campaign committees for each party in the House and Senate, referred to as the Hill committees (Democratic Congressional Campaign Committee; National Republican Congressional Committee; Democratic Senatorial Campaign Committee; National Republican

Senatorial Committee). The national committees and congressional committees were formed in the mid-nineteenth century; the senatorial committees emerged in 1913 when senators began being popularly elected. As candidates increasingly built their own organizations, as incumbents felt increasingly safe about their reelection, and as new services such as polling and media consulting were available in the private market, the national party organizations became less visible. They had never been particularly prominent, even less so than the state party organizations, but their role and purpose increasingly seemed unclear in the years after World War II.

Crises pushed the parties to action. For the Republicans, it was a crisis of competition as the party was becoming less and less a force on the national scene from the mid-1950s through mid-1970s, especially in Congress. For the Democrats, the crisis in their presidential nomination process (see chapter 9) and, following that, their frequent defeats in presidential elections, were central.

Beginning in the mid-1960s, but even more so in the mid-1970s, the Republican National Committee began to modernize its operations and become more active in presidential campaigning. Innovations like targeted direct mail fundraising were a boon for the party treasury, intersecting with a widespread sense among donors that the country was at an important crossroads. Democrats and the Hill committees soon followed suit.

Both parties engaged in expanding their funding and staff. Voter contact, polling, advertising, candidate recruitment and training, opposition research, internal party communications, and fund transfer arrangements between the national and state parties, all increased markedly. Parties benefited from the complexity of campaigning in an era of high technology, constant media, large fundraising demands, and intense demand from issue activists. Some candidates simply cannot assemble on their own the necessary money and expertise needed to run a new style campaign, thus opening the door to party involvement.

In addition to contributing funds and providing services to their candidates, the national party organizations also acted independently, spending millions of dollars on campaign advertising. In election years from 2004 through 2008, the national party committees spent anywhere from three to fifteen times as much money overall in their independent spending than in their contributions to the party's candidates.[44] And in competitive congressional races, it was not unusual for the party organizations to spend more on a campaign than either of the candidates.

The national party organizations have also created "coordinated campaigns" with state party organizations, in which the national party provides financial resources, expertise, and staff to help a state party's effort to win a congressional seat. These activities could also be expanded to benefit other party candidates as well, rather than having each candidate go through the expense and difficulty of handling these tasks individually. Howard Dean, chairman of the Democratic National Committee in 2006, adopted the "50- State Strategy" to signal to state party organizations that this kind of national assistance was possible across the country, not just in traditional Democratic strongholds. The DNC paid for national staff to be provided for all fifty states. The plan created a great deal of dissension. Rahm Emmanuel, the head of the Democratic Congressional Campaign Committee and a member of Congress from Illinois, blasted the plan as squandering resources rather than focusing them on turning out the vote in the most competitive races.

CaseStudy: Getting to Know Voters, One by One

One feature of the party machine praised by political scientists was their tight connections with voters. Machine precinct leaders knew each supporter in their area, checked in on them, helped them navigate through city government, and provided services such as legal assistance, finding a doctor, and arranging for groceries during tough times. The machines were, in part, social service or welfare agencies. In exchange, the machines sought votes. They knew their voters.

Party organizations today are also trying to know their voters. They do not have the kind of deep personal connection with voters as the machine did. Nor are they providing social services. But they are trying to understand voters one by one to target messages to them. The hope is to persuade the unpersuaded to support the party's candidate and to motivate the already persuaded to get out to vote. Instead of predominantly a local party activity, this microtargeting has been initiated by the Republican and Democratic national party organizations.

Microtargeting consists of building huge databases of information about voters. This data can then be used to send messages to a voter that touch upon that voter's key interests. The voter's interests may be inferred from various demographic or consumer characteristics. Or, phone or direct contact from a party staffer or volunteer—known as party canvassing—might extract some information that can be added to the database. Information can be acquired through voter visits to the party's website and pages at social networking sites such as Facebook. The more information that can be acquired about the voter, the better. Like the party machine precinct leader, the party organizations want to know their voters.[45]

Microtargeting was first used in a systematic way in 2002 and became prominent in 2004. The Republican National Committee, in coordination with the Bush campaign and Republican state and local party organizations, purchased commercial databases that held hordes of information on individuals. The party also purchased or received from supporters the membership information from organizations that might be expected to lean toward the party's positions, including membership groups like the National Rifle Association, churches, and clubs. The data could include purchasing habits, brand of car owned, television networks watched, magazine subscriptions, gun ownership, sports preferred, type of musical preference, and much more. These preferences could then be connected to voting preferences—by linking the voter's individual information about which party primary they voted in, for example, or their self-reported vote to a party canvasser—to these characteristics. Republicans found, for example, that viewers of Fox News or the Golf Channel, BMW drivers, health club visitors after work hours, and bourbon or Coors beer drinkers were more likely to support Republicans than Democrats.[46]

For each potential voter, hundreds of bits of information are entered, ranging from neighborhood characteristics available from the U.S. Census to consumer characteristics. Scores are compiled for each individual to estimate their likelihood of supporting the party's candidates. A database of this type can be used for sophisticated and very narrowly targeted advertising, mailings, phone contact, personal contact, and get out the vote drives on behalf of a range of party candidates.[47]

In 2004, the Republican microtargeting effort was used to connect with voters who leaned toward Republican candidates but had not voted regularly. Voter databases are readily available from states, indicating the voter's turnout history and possibly which party primary she voted in and her party registration. The state and federal governments also have databases of campaign contributions. The party targeted 17 million infrequent voters, including 7 million Republicans and 10 million Independents with conservative views.

Merging public opinion data with the demographic information and the voter history, and whatever political preferences the party might have recorded for an individual, allowed the party to send mail or make a phone call about a particular issue that seemed to resonate with similar individuals. Contact with the individual voter could help confirm whether the general relationship between demographics and policy preferences, known as "data mining," were true for this voter as well. Ken Mehlman, the chairman of the Republican National Committee in 2004, called microtargeting neighbor-to-neighbor campaigning.[48]

All this information was entered into the national Republican database known as Voter Vault. The database holds information on approximately 170 million voters. The effects were dramatic. In Ohio, the Republicans recruited 85,000 volunteers. In the three days leading up to the 2004 election, they made 1.8 million phone calls and 750,000 personal visits.

The Democrats have also been involved with microtargeting and used it extensively in their successful bid to win majorities in the House and Senate in 2006. Their database, DataMart, had caught up to the Republicans in size by 2008. The Democrats also had a separate database, DemZilla, that operated on the same microtargeting principles but was designed to raise funds and identify possible volunteers.

Creating microtargeting databases is an example of a job that can be best performed by the national party organizations. For years, the Democrats had a number of different databases at the state and national level of varying quality. Some were destroyed after an election was over, so the party would be starting over again in the next election cycle. By 2008, however, the Democratic National Committee had succeeded in building a national voter database that insiders believed brought the party to parity, or near parity, with Republicans. The national party organizations are in the best position to pull all this information together and to then provide the resources for massive voter contact drives, especially in highly competitive areas that will help the party obtain a majority in Congress or win the presidency.

ThinkingCritically

1. What might be some objections to parties tailoring their messages and appeals to individual voters?

2. Are there circumstances under which you can imagine microtargeting not being an effective mobilization technique?

3. Is the advent of microtargeting a plus or a minus for third parties?

For most Americans, the most visible activity of the national party organizations is running the **national party convention** held every four years to select the party's presidential and vice-presidential nominees. The convention delegates also pass the **party platform**, a statement of the party's principles, goals, and plans. And the convention delegates settle rules controversies within the party. Up through the mid-twentieth century, conventions were the place where rival factions within a party battled for dominance and to select the party's nominees. Multiple ballots would sometimes be needed to determine the nominee; the Democrats famously took 104 ballots to select John Davis in 1924. Today, however, largely because of the reforms to the nominating process after 1968 (see Chapter 9), the nominee is usually known well in advance of the convention. The convention is also a televised spectacle as well, and neither party wants a divisive internal battle to be cast across television screens like a bad reality TV show.

A new federalism of the parties Before the 1970s, the national party organizations had relatively little influence on state and local party organizations. Political scientists referred to the relationship as one of stratarchy—separate, autonomous levels—rather than hierarchy. If anything, it would be the state and local parties that were seen as the lead players, as they would extract promises from presidential and congressional contenders that would benefit the cities and states. If the candidate was cooperative, state or local officials would work to provide the support needed at conventions or in primary elections to aid the candidate.

Today, there is less stratarchy and more hierarchy. This does not mean a strict, top-down control, which is more common in other countries. But there is more influence of the national party organizations on the state organizations now than was true previously. Both parties provide financing and technical assistance for their state parties. Both parties channel contributions to the state parties—when an individual or organization has maxed out on what can be contributed to the national parties—with directions about how these funds are to be employed to benefit candidates for national office.

Both parties, but especially the Democrats, set rules at the national level that must be followed by the state parties. The Democrats have established rules for how delegates are to be apportioned among candidates in presidential primaries and caucuses, the demographic composition of state delegations to the national convention, and the procedures by which caucuses are to be run. The Republicans leave these matters to the state parties to determine.

In the 2008 presidential nomination process, these national rules were a major matter of controversy among Democrats. Both the Democratic and Republican National Committees had passed rules stipulating that states that held primaries or caucuses too early—Iowa, New Hampshire, South Carolina, and Nevada were exempted—would be penalized in their representation at the national convention. Though this had no significant effect on the Republican contest, it became a major matter of dispute between the campaign teams of Barack Obama and Hillary Clinton when Michigan and Florida were penalized for holding their primaries too early.

The growing role of the national party organizations has been beneficial for state party organizations and candidates, particularly in providing resources and expertise. However, the new role has also created some strains. Some candidates in competitive races have felt little in control of their own campaigns because of the overwhelming involvement of the national party. And some state party organization officials have complained that national party organizations have become too heavily involved in identifying candidates in a state to run for office and then supporting those candidates, often leading to rifts within the state party. The national party's main goal is winning the seat, not necessarily supporting the candidate whose "turn" has come, or who pleases the largest number of party supporters, or who is endorsed by the most state officials—all this can create tension with the state party. In 2004 in Pennsylvania, for example, the national Republican Party organizations supported Senator Arlen Spector for reelection, even though he had opposed President Bush on a number of issues and was facing a strong conservative challenger popular among state Republicans. In 2006 in that same state, the national Democratic Party organizations promoted the candidacy of Bob Casey for the Senate. Casey's pro-life stand is the minority position in the Democratic Party, and he was facing a pro-choice candidate. However, this kind of national party involvement is now common.[49]

All these new activities surely breathed new life into the national (and state) party organizations. They helped candidates. But they were not building the kind of party organization, like a party machine, that had a tight relationship with the public and drew large proportions of the public into politics. They were service providers for party candidates, seeking to build a party majority in the House, Senate, and state legislatures, as well as capture governorships and the presidency.[50]

SUMMARY

▶ Political parties play a wide variety of roles. Parties filled the void in the Constitution concerning where candidates would be found to run for office and how citizens would be engaged in the electoral process. These functions, intended mainly to advance the self-interest of the parties and their candidates, also enhanced the legitimacy of American politics and government by bringing to practice the promise of electoral competition that was implicit in the Constitution. Political parties also contribute to American governance by giving public officials in different institutions and at different levels of government incentives to cooperate with each other to make public policy.

▶ American electoral competition has been dominated by two parties since the very beginning. The structure of American government, including especially single-member districts, plurality elections, and winner-take-all electoral votes in presidential elections, push electoral competition toward a two-party model. In addition, a number of laws as well as the behavior of voters, the media, and candidates, reinforce the tendency for two parties to be the serious competitors. Third parties are only rarely successful electorally, but they can make a mark in other ways, such as introducing issues to the campaign that the major party candidates have ignored.

▶ American parties have evolved through six periods of party competition, with different issues and different strength of major parties present across the periods. The coalitions brought together by the Democrats in the 1930s and the Republicans in the 1980s are still important sources of support for the two parties, but each coalition has suffered defeats and internal disputes and tension. Neither party can produce victories today by simply relying on the coalitions of the past. The broad and diverse nature of coalitions necessary to produce a majority and win elections creates a difficult job of political management for party leaders. They play the balancing act of maintaining the coalition while also adapting to new circumstances and trying to keep the coalition growing. As they accommodate new issues and new groups, they risk unraveling the coalition by driving current supporters away.

▶ Party organization has gone through several phases. In early American history, party organization was informal and largely implemented the wishes, especially candidate nomination, of important political leaders in an area. Party machines emerged in the late nineteenth century. Machines thrived by developing a very personal form of politics, but ran afoul of reformers who saw them as bastions of corruption. Party organizations became heavily regulated in the early 20th century, and Progressive reformers passed a series of laws that weakened political parties. In recent decades, party organizations have become much more active, especially by providing campaign services to party candidates.

KEY TERMS

Australian ballot, p. 000
dealignment, p. 000
divided government, p. 000
electoral realignment, p. 000
fusion, p. 000
issue evolution, p. 000
national party convention, p. 000
party machine, p. 000
party platform, p. 000
patronage, p. 000

plurality elections, p. 000
political parties, p. 000
progressive reforms, p. 000
proportional representation, p. 000
responsible party model, p. 000
single-member districts, p. 000
two-party system, p. 000
unified government, p. 000
winner-take-all, p. 000

SUGGESTED READINGS

Mark D. Brewer and Jeffrey M. Stonecash. 2006. *Split: Class and Cultural Divides in American Politics*. Examines the relative contribution of economic and cultural issues to the recent conflicts between Democrats and Republicans and their effects on voters. Washington, DC: CQ Press.

Leon D. Epstein. 1986. *Political Parties in the American Mold*. Thorough explanation of the functions and history of American political parties. Madison: University of Wisconsin Press.

Steven P. Erie. 1988. *Rainbow's End: Irish-Americans and the Dilemmas of Urban Machine Politics, 1840-1985*. Explores the political logic and practical workings of party machines. Berkeley: University of California Press.

Morris P. Fiorina, 2006. *Culture War? The Myth of a Polarized America*, 2nd ed. Refutes the argument that Americans are in the throes of a culture war and blames political elites and the media for fostering the impression that the country is deeply divided. New York: Longman.

John Gerring. 1998. *Party Ideologies in America, 1828-1996*. Thorough account documenting the ideological distinctions between the major political parties across, noting areas of continuity and change in the parties' philosophies. New York: Cambridge University Press.

Lawrence Goodwyn. 1978. *The Populist Moment: A Short History of the Agrarian Revolt in America*. Wonderfully readable account of the rise of one of America's most important social movements and its eventual transformation into the People's Party, a third party with some short-lived success in the mid-1890s.

Norman Mailer. 2008. *Miami and the Siege of Chicago*. Re-release of the classic account of the 1968 Republican and Democratic conventions by the famous novelist. New York: New York Review of Books.

Michael E. McGerr. 1986. *The Decline of Popular Politics: The American North, 1865-1928.* Insightful account of the transformation of American political campaigns from party-centered pageantry and mobilization to candidate-centered advertising. New York: Oxford University Press.

Mark A. Smith. 2007. *The Right Talk: How Conservatives Transformed the Great Society into the Economic Society.* An exploration of how conservatives altered the discussion of key issues into economic terms and sparked the revival of the Republican Party. Princeton, NJ: Princeton University Press.

James Sundquist. 1986. *Dynamics of the Party System: Alignment and Realignment of Political Parties in the United States.* Very readable account of the passage of the United States through various periods of party completion, including what might accelerate or stop these passages. Washington, DC: Brookings Institution Press.

political parties organized groups with public followings that seek to elect officeholders who identify themselves by the group's common label, for the purpose of exercising political power.

unified government a situation where the presidency and both houses of Congress are controlled by the same party.

divided government a situation where the presidency is held by one party and at least one house of Congress is controlled by a different party.

two-party system a system of electoral competition in which two parties are consistently the most likely to win office and gain power.

single-member districts electoral districts in which only one person is elected to represent the district in a representative body.

plurality elections elections in which the candidate with the most votes, not necessarily a majority, wins.

proportional representation an election system in which candidates are elected from multi-member districts, with a party's share of seats from a district being roughly proportional to their share of the popular vote.

winner-take-all the system of awarding all the electoral votes in a state to the presidential candidate who received the most votes.

fusion a strategy in which third parties endorse a major party candidate but list that candidate separately on the ballot so that voters can vote for the candidate under the third-party label.

Australian ballot an official government-produced ballot for elections that lists all offices and all the candidates and parties who have qualified to be on the ballot.

electoral realignment a shift in the composition of party coalitions that produces a new, relatively durable pattern of party competition.

dealignment a substantial reduction in the proportion of the voting consistently for one party and identifying with a party.

responsible party model the idea that political parties should run as unified teams, present a clear policy platform, implement that platform when in office, and run on their record in the subsequent election.

issue evolution a change in the partisan base of support for an issue over time, such that the position of Democrats and Republican switch.

party machine disciplined local party organizations that selected candidates; got out the vote; provided benefits to supporters including government workers, local constituents, and businesses; and served as social service agencies for their followers.

patronage awarding jobs in government on the basis of party support and loyalty rather than expertise or experience.

progressive reforms a set of political and electoral reforms in the early 20th century that had the combined effect of weakening political parties.

national party convention a meeting held over several days at which delegates select the party's presidential nominee, approve the party platform, and consider changes in party rules and policies.

party platform a document expressing the principles, beliefs, and policy positions of the party, as endorsed by delegates at the national party convention.

12 Interest Groups

n 1868 no women anywhere in the United States were allowed to vote. By 1920, however, women in every state had the same voting rights as men. How did this change take place? Primarily through the efforts of the women's suffrage movement. In 1869, after the civil war, two organizations promoting women's suffrage were founded: the National Woman Suffrage Association (NWSA) and the American Woman Suffrage Association (AWSA). After two decades of pursuing their agendas separately, the groups merged in 1890 to form the National American Woman Suffrage Association (NAWSA) with Susan B. Anthony as its leader.

Like a snowball rolling downhill, the suffrage movement grew as it won victories at the state level. NAWSA was soon joined by other women's groups, including the General Federation of Women's Clubs and assorted professional and working women's organizations. This enhanced clout helped secure further victories, which won yet more converts to the cause, creating a positive momentum. Even-

tually, both the size of the movement and its repeated successes at the state level created irresistible momentum for a nationwide policy change. Congress proposed an amendment to the Constitution in 1919 that granted women the right to vote and the amendment was ratified by the required 36 states in 1920.[1]

Admirers of American democracy look to this story with pride. In what other country, they ask, could a disenfranchised group force such dramatic changes in the law in such a short period of time? The success of the women's suffrage movement, they argue, shows the openness of the American political system to influence by groups of all political stripes—regardless of their resources or their previous level of political involvement.

On the other hand, consider the plight of Americans without health insurance. Despite being one of the world's wealthiest nations, the United States is the only industrialized country without universal health care coverage. Most Americans have adequate coverage through the patchwork of state, federal, and employer-based

programs, but substantial numbers lack any insurance—47 million, according to the most recent Census Bureau data.[2] Furthermore, large proportions of Americans believe it is the responsibility of the federal government to ensure that Americans have health care coverage.[3] Even so, only one 20-century president, Bill Clinton seriously promoted the idea of universal health insurance and his proposal went down to decisive, and ignominious, defeat.

These two examples paint very different pictures of the political system in the United States. The story of the women's suffrage movement suggests that American politics is open to influence by any group with a reasonable agenda, even if it lacks the power of the vote to hold as an implicit threat over the heads of policymakers. America's lack of universal health care suggests that certain interests may be largely excluded from meaningful political consideration. Furthermore, media coverage and popular perception of interest groups and lobbying suggests that groups are all powerful and have a largely negative influence on public policy.

These competing narratives lead to a few questions about the place of organized interests, or interest groups, in American politics. Are interest groups active and powerful, or passive and ineffective? Are they a positive or negative influence on American democracy? Do they encourage a healthy, broad-based consideration of a variety of interests, or do they promote the pursuit of narrow self-interest? Guided by these important questions, in this chapter we examine the role of interest groups in America.

The Problem of Factions and the Pluralist Answer

Almost every discussion of group politics in the U.S. begins with one of the most famous pieces of political rhetoric ever written by an American—*Federalist* #10, by James Madison. As we discussed in Chapter 3, this brief essay was part of a broader collection of writings known as *The Federalist Papers*. In *Federalist* #10, Madison noted the capacity of the proposed federal republic "to break and control the violence of faction." Madison's use of the word faction varied somewhat from modern usage. In more familiar language, Madison was referring to a group of individuals who share a belief that, if acted upon, would jeopardize the rights of individuals outside of the group, and/or the interests of the community as a whole. Madison's concern was that factions would be able to exercise their will through the mechanisms of government. If this happened, then individual rights might suffer, along with the long-term, collective interests of the new republic. It was critical, therefore, Madison argued, that government—and by extension, Americans as individuals and the country as a whole—be protected from the influence of faction.

Although Madison clearly worried about the potential influence of factional interests on individual rights and the collective well-being of the country, he also believed that the American system was well designed to mute the influence of such interests.

Political scientists in the 1950s began to re-consider the place of group interests in politics. Like James Madison, scholars generally believed that the tendency toward factions in political life was inevitable (though they generally referred to factions as "groups," "interests," "organized interests," or **interest groups**). However, these scholars were not preoccupied with keeping interest groups away from the corridors of power. Instead, they viewed the competition of groups for influence in American politics as generally healthy, and a legitimate aspect of democratic governance.

This thinking on the place of group interests in America came to be known as **pluralism,** referring to the multiple groups and interests making demands on government (even if the demand was to be left alone). Pluralist theory consisted of a number of core arguments that speak both to the importance of group interests and to their relatively benign, even healthy, influence.

Pluralists assumed that groups and group struggle were the essence of politics. Pluralist thinkers believed that politics can be seen primarily as an organized effort to resolve conflicts between and among competing group interests.[4] Furthermore, they viewed political power and resources as being dispersed widely in society, with some groups being influential and resource-rich in some issue areas, and a completely different set of groups being influential and resource-rich in other issue areas. Because of this dispersion of power and resources, no one group or set of groups can achieve long-term supremacy over others across a significant number of issue areas.

Pluralists also believed that the political system provides multiple access points for influence, consistent with the multiple interests it must accommodate. Groups are free to petition government at the local, state, and national levels, and through the offices of the executive, the legislature, and the judiciary. A group denied its policy preferences in one venue or at one level of government may take its argument to a different venue or to a higher or lower level. Because of this, most every group can expect an opportunity to be heard and be taken seriously somewhere in the political system.[5]

Finally, pluralists argued that even if not organized into a formal group, individuals with a common interest can still have their needs addressed through politics. Policymakers recognize that such **potential groups** can become *actual* groups if their needs are not met, which may upset existing political arrangements. Thus, elected officials have an incentive to take into account the needs of unorganized interests, precisely to keep them from becoming organized.

Critics of Pluralism

Since at least the 1950s, pluralism has been a highly influential framework for thinking about American politics and government. Along with influence, however, comes scrutiny. Thus, as important as pluralism has been in structuring political scientists' thinking about American government, it has also attracted a significant number of criticisms: that the American political system was inherently conservative, that political resources were not distributed equally, that many important issues never made it on to the agenda, and that groups do not automatically form.

The American political system is inherently conservative.

A fundamental critique of pluralism is that the American political system is resistant to change. The checks and balances designed by the framers, coupled with the multiple decision points in the system, make it much more difficult to change the status quo than to defend the status quo. As we will see in more detail in the Congress chapter, an individual or group wishing to defeat a new policy proposal can stop it from:

- being introduced as a bill in the first place;
- being heard in committee;
- being approved in committee;
- being reported out of committee;
- being heard on the House floor;
- being heard on the Senate floor;
- being approved by the House;
- being approved by the Senate.

Even if the bill were to make it over all of these hurdles, an individual or group could still stop:

- the reconciliation of any differences between the Senate and House versions of the bill;

- the House from voting on the reconciled version;
- the Senate from voting on the reconciled version;
- the House from approving the reconciled version;
- the Senate from approving the reconciled version;
- the president from signing the reconciled version.

But even this list does not exhaust the possibilities for defeating a policy proposal. As we shall see in later chapters, programs and initiatives that make it through the legislative process can also be challenged in the court system, denied necessary funding in the appropriations process, or watered down or ignored by bureaucrats and/or state and local officials responsible for implementing them.

The bias against change in the American system should now be clear. Someone wishing to preserve the status quo need only succeed at *one* point to kill a policy initiative, but someone wishing to change the status quo must succeed at *every* point.

Because of this, critics of pluralism argue that the apparent openness of the American political system may not count for much. If a group succeeds in getting its policy preferences adopted, it is difficult for other groups with different preferences to come along later and alter the status quo. Thus, while the complex machinery of American government protects citizens against tyranny and faction, it also makes it hard for organized interests to bring about change.

Political resources are distributed unequally.

As we noted above, pluralism is often viewed as a way of explaining how democracy works despite Americans' low levels of knowledge and competence with respect to politics. The pluralists said that interest groups enable citizens who may not have high levels of political skill and interest to involve themselves in the issues that are most important to them, on which they should most knowledgeable. On issues that are less important, they can leave political participation to others.

Critics argue, however, that some examples of non-participation are less a result of lack of interest than deliberate exclusion from the political system, or insurmountable obstacles to participation. In the pre-civil rights era, for example, participation in politics by blacks was at strikingly low levels. One should not, however, construe this as indicating contentment with the status quo, or blacks' failure to see the relevance of political decision-making to their own interests.[6] In other words, as we discussed in Chapter 6, for much of American history, political participation was effectively foreclosed as an option for blacks in many parts of the United States.

Thankfully, the political history of blacks in America is an unusual case. But other, less extreme cases of political exclusion are quite common. According to the most recent data, for example, more than 36 million Americans are in families with incomes below the poverty line.[7] Many of the impoverished are children, a group toward which the public is very sympathetic. And yet while gun owners, nurses, attorneys, teachers, and the elderly are represented by vocal, highly successful interest groups in Washington, D.C., the poor are not.

There are many reasons for this. One is that effective political organization require resources that the poor often do not have in abundance: money, time, knowledge, education, personal relationships, and political experience and competence, among others. Critics of pluralism argue that since critical political resources are not distributed equally across the population, the interest group system is

Table 12-1. Distribution of Groups by Sector[45]

Citizen Sector	24%
Profit Sector	38%
Nonprofit Sector	33%
Mixed Sector	6%

biased in favor of upper- and middle-class groups, who have relatively easy access to the most important political resources and assets.

Even the pluralists acknowledged that political participation is costly in terms of resources, and that the upper and middle classes are better able to afford those costs: As Schattschneider famously said, "public activity of all kinds is a habit of the middle and upper classes."[8] One political scientist, Jack Walker, determined that among all organized groups with a presence in Washington, D.C., 70 percent represented business interests (Table 12.1). Fewer than five percent represented civil rights groups, minority organizations, social welfare groups, poor people's organizations, and groups advocating on behalf of the elderly, the handicapped, gays, and women. As he concluded, quoting political scientist E.E. Schattschneider, "the flaw in the pluralist heaven is that the heavenly chorus sings with an upper-class accent."[9]

Pluralists ignore issues that policymakers ignore.

A third critique of pluralism begins with the observation that pluralists tend to study issue areas in which policymakers are debating solutions and groups are actively involved in the process. As the pluralists' critics have noted, however, some issues are not discussed or debated in politics; in other words, some issues are not actually *considered* issues by political elites.[10]

Consider poverty as a political issue. In the Great Depression of the 1930s, and then again with Lyndon Johnson's declaration of a War on Poverty in 1964, the plight of the country's poor occupied center stage on the national agenda. But between these two periods—in the 1940s and 1950s—poverty virtually disappeared as a topic on the public policy agenda. Policymakers simply assumed (wrongly, as it turns out) that with the nation's return to prosperity in the 1940s, poverty had been largely vanquished. Thus, the attention of government decision-makers turned to other issues.

This example illustrates the importance of what political scientists call **non-decisions**.[11] A non- decision can be defined as a decision *not* to put a particular issue on the **policy agenda**, which is the set of issues actively under consideration and discussion by policymakers. Whereas the pluralists focused on group participation in the decision-making process, their critics argue that one must take note of non-decisions as well. Quoting E.E. Schattschneider again, "Some issues are organized into politics while others are organized out."[12]

When government shunts some issues aside, the pluralist model breaks down. Group preferences on a particular issue cannot be taken into account if policymakers have chosen not to address that issue.

This page will not be blank in the final book.

Studying Dogs That Don't Bark

The Question

Inspector Gregory: "Is there any point to which you would wish to draw my attention?"

Sherlock Holmes: "To the curious incident of the dog in the night time."

Inspector Gregory: "The dog did nothing in the night time."

Sherlock Holmes: "That was the curious incident."

In this excerpt from the Arthur Conan Doyle story, "Silver Blaze," Sherlock Holmes takes note of a "curious incident": the failure of a guard dog to bark during the theft of a racehorse. From this, Holmes deduces that the thief was not a stranger to the dog. This information ultimately helped Holmes solve the case. Sometimes in politics, as in fiction, things that do not happen are just as important as things that do. However, identifying, quantifying, and studying political fights that did not occur is no easy task. In fact, when we presented this notion of studying non-events in the context of a criticism of pluralism, we also presented the pluralists' response to this criticism. One of the pluralists' rejoinders was that non-events—by definition, things that *do not happen*—are intrinsically difficult to study, if not impossible. Is it possible?

Why It Matters

We have already discussed certain "non-events": specifically, non-decisions and the failure of groups to advance their interests when one might expect them to. In other words, interest groups wield power or fail to wield power by influencing what sorts of issues get talked about or discussed. Understanding power in the United States and the influence that interest groups might wield demands that we pay attention to the "dogs that are not barking."

Investigating the Answer

In *The Un-politics of Air Pollution*, Matthew Crenson. examines why some cities take aggressive action against local pollution, while others neglect the issue? Crenson comes up with several useful ways to explore the failure of some cities to take the pollution issue seriously during the time period. First, he uses the results of a 51-city survey of community leaders to identify the extent to which pollution was considered an important public issue in each city. With these results, he identifies cities that have put the pollution problem on their policy agenda, and those that have largely ignored the issue. Crenson then seeks to develop explanations for these two different outcomes.

One possible explanation is that the cities that take pollution seriously have particularly bad pollution problems. In contrast, the cities that neglect the issue do so because pollution is not a serious problem there. Looking at pollution measures for each city, though, Crenson finds that this is no more than part of the explanation. Next, therefore, he undertakes an intensive study of two cities that exhibited very different responses to their pollution problems: Gary and East Chicago, both cities in Indiana. The former city delayed action in tackling a serious pollution problem, while the latter acted quickly to address the issue. Why? Crenson's intensive study of the two cases led him to believe that the failure of industrial interests in Gary, Indiana to throw their weight behind the issue, or to oppose it outright, left air pollution as an issue in limbo. Other actors in town appeared to be paralyzed by the failure of industry to stake out a clear position.

Based on this finding, Crenson hypothesizes that the greater the relative influence of business interests in a community, the slower that community will be to respond to its air pollution problems. He then marshals survey data from local public figures to gain their assessment of local business influence. He matches that data against survey data indicating how seriously the community takes the issue of air pollution. Crenson finds that, indeed, in high pollution cities, the stronger the perceived influence of the business community, the less likely that city is to elevate the problem of air pollution to the public policy agenda.

In *Power and Powerlessness*, by John Gaventa was occupied with the question of why miners in Middlesboro, Kentucky did not take action in the face of miserable economic inequalities and poor working conditions. Part of Gaventa's explanation for this was that the townsfolk internalized a system of beliefs and values propounded by powerful economic and political interests in their town. These beliefs and values were structured to keep the powerless miners quiet and submissive.

Gaventa has no difficulty demonstrating that the town's mining interests sought to cultivate a value system and ideology that would hold at bay any challenge to their hegemony. What is more difficult to demonstrate, however, is that the townsfolk embraced that value system and ideology, and therefore did not seek to improve their situation when one might have expected them to. Gaventa applies two basic approaches in trying to demonstrate this latter point. First, like Crenson, he also performs a comparative case study. He considers the behavior of miners in nearby communities that are not as dominated by economic interests as the town of Middleboro is. If his argument about Middleboro is correct, then he should find more of a tendency for protests, strikes, and even insurrections in these nearby communities. He finds precisely that.

However, this need not indicate any ideological "brainwashing." Instead, it might simply indicate that miners in Middleboro recognized that the likelihood of a successful protest, strike, or insurrection was negligible, given the pervasive power of the mine-owners. Acknowledging this, Gaventa analyzes the response of the Middlesboro townsfolk when the power of the mining interests weakens. One might expect the miners and their supporters to respond to this weakness with an increasing volumeof demands. On the other hand, if the townsfolk had internalized the idea of subordination as their "natural" role, as Gaventa suspects, they might remain quiet when the power relationship changed. Gaventa finds the truth somewhere in the middle—there are limited challenges and demands for change when the power of the mine owners weakens, but not as numerous or vocal as one would expect if the miners truly recognized their own interests.

By definition, studying non-events or non-decisions is difficult. That said, these two in-depth and creative studies show how it is possible to study political power even when we do not see power being wielded directly. This is crucial because if we just look at who has resources and how they use them on policy or legislative battles that we can see, we may miss a fundamental way that power is wielded.

The Bottom Line

Groups do not automatically form.

In order for the pluralist model of democracy to work in optimal fashion, collections of individuals with interests that can be addressed by government need to come together to form groups. Since the political world is full of groups and associations actively pursuing their agendas at all levels of government, pluralists tend to take for granted that this happens. Pluralists explain the formation of groups through the **disturbance theory**. This holds that when social, political, and economic relationships are upset by some outside force, affected individuals often form a group in response.[13]

In 2004, for example, as the American military position in Iraq steadily eroded, a group of veterans formed Iraq Veterans Against the War, which advocated a withdrawal of all U.S. troops from Iraq, reparations to Iraqis for the damage done to their country, and improved benefits for servicemen and women returning from Iraq.[14]

Groups do not always form, however, when there is a disturbance. In fact, when a potential group consists of a large number of individuals, the obstacles to group formation can be prohibitive. This argument was made most cogently in 1965 by Harvard economist Mancur Olson. Olson argued that "rational, self-interested individuals will not act to achieve their common or group interests"[15] Why? Because an individual's own efforts "will not have a noticeable effect on the situation of his organization, and he can enjoy any improvements brought about by others whether or not he has worked in support of his organization."[16]

Olson's argument is a statement of what is known, variously, as the "public goods problem," the **free rider problem,** the "collective action problem," the "prisoner's dilemma," and the "the tragedy of the commons." Consider a real-world example. College students as a whole may have an interest in increasing the pool of government scholarships available. But an individual student pursuing his or her own interests would just as soon *not* contribute time or money to help convince legislators to increase scholarships or support to higher education. Furthermore, if he or she *did* not work for better funding for higher education, the amount of funds available would hardly suffer. Moreover, and crucially, an individual who failed to contribute time or money to help convince the government to fund higher education would still be eligible for such funding and could still enjoy the benefits of a subsidized college education.

What does this have to do with group formation? An individual who has interests in common with others—interests that might effectively be pursued through group activity—has an incentive to let others do the work of forming and maintaining a group to pursue those interests. Take another example. Imagine that you and your fellow students wish to have the school year shortened by two weeks. This requires a decision by school administrators. The best way of getting the decision you want is to form a group, organize rallies and email campaigns, and **lobby** the relevant decision-makers. From your perspective as an individual, however, it would be ideal if other students did all of the work and left you in peace. If the group consisted of, say, 500 active participants, your individual effort probably would not be missed anyway. Furthermore, if you failed to participate and the group succeeded without you, you would reap all of the benefits without having to give up any of your own time, money, or energy. What a great deal for you!

The obvious problem is that if *everyone* were to think this way, then everyone would leave it to others to do the work and the group would never form, get organized, bring attention to the issue, and lobby decision-makers. The school year would remain two weeks longer than students would like it to be. And this would have happened even though members of the group had a *collective* interest in a shorter school year. Their *individual* interests in letting someone else do the work would have prevailed.

This is a simple statement of the free rider problem. The free rider problem is a shot right at the heart of pluralism. If individuals with a common interest fail to organize to pursue that interest, they can hardly join in the group competition for government attention and benefits that defines pluralism. If this happens often enough, the pluralist model collapses.

Solving the Collective Action Problem: Group Formation and Maintenance

We know, of course, that groups *do* form, get organized for political action, and participate in politics. These groups clearly have found a way to deal with the collective action problem, but the problem persists. In fact, the logic of group formation and maintenance is a central issue in the study of politics.

Groups overcome the collective action problem in a number of ways.

Political scientists have identified a variety of ways groups can overcome the collective action problem. These include: a) selective benefits provided to group members, typically material or monetary , but also social or ideological;[17] b) individual entrepreneurship, which can motivate individuals to get involved in a group's activities and stay involved; and c) patronage from outsiders who support the group's mission.

Selective benefits Groups often provide contributors with **selective benefits**, benefits *not* available to those who don't contribute. Remember, one of the key parts of the collective action problem is "free riding": in certain circumstances, individuals can enjoy the benefits of group activity without having to bear any of the costs of that activity. Providing selective benefits is a way for groups to get around the free rider problem.

The most obvious kind of benefit that groups may provide is a **material benefit.** Benefits of this type can include publications, goods and services, discounts on products, and professional advice. For example, individuals who join the American Associated of Retired Persons (AARP) become eligible for scores of benefits, simply by virtue of their membership. These include:

- discounts on hundreds of consumer products;
- members-only insurance plans (auto, dental, prescription drug, and many more);
- a subscription to AARP's magazine Modern Maturity (which has the highest circulation in the country);
- health and fitness tips;
- exclusive investment products, credit cards, and financial advice;
- an invitation to a national expo with baseball player Cal Ripken as a speaker;
- tax preparation assistance;
- a driver safety course;

and literally dozens of others. The cost of all this? Anyone 50 years old or older can join AARP for as little as $8 per year.

Considering the low cost of membership, there are undoubtedly millions of AARP members who join the group for the benefits alone. In fact, a 1982 survey found that only 17 percent of members had joined primarily because of the group's work on behalf of the elderly. The rest were more interested in the material benefits.[18]

Associations of professionals—doctors, lawyers, teachers, nurses, accountants, social workers, and so on—provide similar material benefits, as well as professional certification and credentialing, which have a direct bearing on various professionals' ability to earn a living. Attorneys, for example, cannot practice law without first being admitted to their state bar and must meet continuing legal education requirements to remain bar members in good standing. State bar associations regulate these processes and charge members a fee for these services. The fees help subsidize the bar organizations' government relations activities, which tend to be considerable. An attorney who doesn't wish to subsidize group political action can refuse to pay the fee but the bar will deny him or her the ability to practice law. A state bar's control over this highly important selective benefit is one way it overcomes the collective action problem, enabling itself to participate actively and effectively in the political process.

A group can provide to its members **social benefits**.[19] Imagine, for example, that you are an avid environmentalist. Joining the Sierra Club, Greenpeace, or the Nature Conservancy would allow you to interact with people who are just as passionate about the environment. If you were the owner of a small business, joining the National Federation of Independent Businesses could put you in touch with individuals who shared many of the same challenges and successes you had.

Such group participation creates opportunities for you to socialize with people who have similar interests. Moreover, a sense of camaraderie can come from associating with others who are like you, and a sense of status from affiliating with people who share certain beliefs or values.[20]

If, for example, you are proud to tell others that you are a member of the College Republicans or a contributor to EMILY's List, you are enjoying a solidary benefit of group membership.

Olson considered material and solidary benefits to be quite powerful motivators of human behavior in a group setting. He even argued that for some groups, pursuit of group interests was a by-product of the group's selective benefits. (Olson called this the **by-product**.) Once the group solved the free rider problem through the use of selective benefits, it could pursue traditional political activities.

Some critics argue that Olson's focus on material and solidary benefits exaggerates the mercenary nature of actual and potential group members. Millions of people join groups because they believe in what the group stands for. Could Olson's theory account for these individuals, too?

Some interest group theorists believe so, arguing that the rewards such people seek are another kind of selective benefit, a **purposive benefit**. Purposive benefits are so called because they are connected to a group's stated purpose.[21]

Enjoying purposive benefits from group membership means that getting satisfaction from contributing to a cause, or purpose, one believes in. For example, consider the following testimonial from a volunteer with Compassionate Action for Animals (CAA), an animal rights advocacy group:

> Through CAA I've come to realize that every little bit I do to end the suffering of animals makes a difference. But my efforts combined with others sets an

example for a whole new generation, offering knowledgeable support in everything from raising positive awareness of farming to maintaining nutrition as a vegan. Through CAA I believe people give animals and our society a brighter, more socially responsible future. CAA has definitely given me hope for a better tomorrow.22

This person clearly derives satisfaction from helping promote animal rights. Of course, individuals need not volunteer or join a group in order to promote a cause that they believe in. Groups, however, make that process easier by creating, structuring, an supporting specific participation opportunities for members and volunteers. This allows members to enjoy unique purposive benefits not available to non-members.

Individual entrepreneurship Selective benefits are an important mechanism for overcoming the collective action problem, but before a group can offer selective benefits, someone has to do significant organizational work to create the group.

Some political scientists have argued that the collective action problem reasserts itself at this point. How do groups get started in the first place? Wouldn't everyone with a potential interest in organizing the group prefer to free ride, letting others bear the burden of group formation? And again, if everyone thought this way, how do groups come into being?

One strain of the interest group literature provides a solution to this apparent problem: **interest group entrepreneurs**. This term refers to someone who launches and manages an interest group.[23]

Consider one of the most effective and well-known interest groups in America, the National Rifle Association (NRA). Though its primary interest today is in promoting and protecting the rights of gun owners, the NRA began with a very different agenda. Two Civil War veterans, William Conant Church and George Wood Wingate, had been alarmed by the poor shooting skills of Union troops.

Church and Wingate did much of the necessary "pushing," seeking a charter from the New York legislature, along with $25,000 with which to purchase land and develop shooting ranges. Church urged New York's "citizen soldiers" to write their legislators and encourage approval of the charter and funding (a strategy the NRA follows to this day). The legislature ultimately obliged, and the NRA was born.[24]

The interest group entrepreneurs in this story were Church and Wingate. They invested the initial time and energy (and some cash) to get the NRA off the ground. Like business entrepreneurs, they gambled that their efforts would pay off, and that their initial investment would be returned, along with some "profit." Had they not done so, an NRA-style organization probably would have emerged at some point. But it would not have happened when it did, or in the form that it did, had Church and Wingate not assumed an entrepreneurial role.

Patronage The decision by the New York state legislature to give the group $25,000 in start-up funds was critical. It may very well have made the difference between the NRA sinking and swimming. If Church and Wingate had tried to raise the same amount of money—about $400,000 in today's dollars—from prospective NRA members in 1871, many would have balked at the price tag and some would have chosen to free ride: "Why should I contribute? Let others pick up the tab, and I'll just enjoy the benefits."

This is where **patrons** come into play. Patrons provide groups with the resources they need to get established. Patrons may work with an interest group entrepreneur to get a group started, or may launch the group themselves but leave it to be managed by others. Either way, they obviate the need for groups to try to cobble together small contributions from potential members, all of whom are susceptible to free-rider thinking.

Sometimes, a patron is a single individual with a passion for an issue, and with resources to share. In 2004, for example, billionaire financier George Soros learned of a new organization called America Coming Together (ACT). The objective of this group was to increase voter turnout in an effort to defeat President George W. Bush's bid for reelection. Soros, who described the defeat of President Bush as "the central focus of my life," was intrigued. He knew that if ACT was to be successful, it would have to make a massive effort, reaching into key electoral battlegrounds across the United States. Accordingly, he pledged $10 million to help get the group up and running, effectively shifting ACT from idle to fifth gear with a stroke of his check-writing pen.[25]

Patrons need not be autonomous individuals. Corporations, units of government, foundations, and even other interest groups can act as patrons, founding new groups or helping start-ups get off the ground. Consider, for example, the National Association of Counties, which represents the interests of the nation's counties "on Capitol Hill and throughout the federal bureaucracy," and which was created with the patronage of county governments.[26]

Or consider the United States Chamber of Commerce, a membership group of businesses, associations, and state, local, and international chambers of commerce. The U.S. Chamber was created in 1912, in part as a result of the patronage of Secretary of Commerce and Labor Charles Nagel. Nagel had brought the idea of a national business organization to the attention of President William Howard Taft. At Nagel's encouragement, Taft publicly expressed his interest in the creation of a commercial group that could speak to Washington policymakers with a single voice. With the president on board, business had a strong incentive to act. But how to bring together diverse businesses from all over the country? Nagel provided the answer through an important act of patronage. He used the resources of his department to convene a national business conference to which approximately 1,000 associations were invited. Nagel and President Taft both spoke at the conference, once again promoting the idea of a consolidated national business group, and encouraging conferees to take advantage of the rare gathering. Taft and Nagel then stepped aside, leaving conference participants to their work. By the time the conference was adjourned, a new, nationwide business organization had been born: the Chamber of Commerce of the United States.[27]

Even the casual observer of American politics knows that one way or another, tens of thousands of groups have succeeded in overcoming the collective action problem and have fended off threats to their survival.

The challenges inherent in this are not the same for all groups, however. Some groups have ready access to desirable selective benefits, or to dynamic entrepreneurs, or to resource-rich patrons. Some have access to all three. Some have access to none. Some groups are very small, and therefore do not have to struggle with the free-rider problem. Some are so large that they must continually work to keep their members engaged. Some are organized around simple, high-profile, ideologically charged issues that naturally incite passions and attract interest. Others are focused on technical, abstruse, nuanced issues that make the general public yawn. In short, different groups face different challenges, and have strengths and weaknesses in different areas. This means that groups must choose among various potential strategies and tactics to achieve their ends. We explore some of the choices in the next section.

What Groups Do, and Why They Do It

The ultimate goal of most politically oriented interest groups is to shape public policy in ways consistent with the group's interests, values, and beliefs. In general, groups use two primary strategies to do this. They attempt to influence either the selection of public officials (an electoral strategy) or the decisions of elected officials, bureaucrats, or members of the judiciary who have already been elected or appointed (a decision strategy).

Of course, groups can pursue both strategies at once. Furthermore, as we will discuss later in the chapter, the two strategies often intertwine.

An electoral strategy consists of a variety of tactics.

In pursuing an electoral strategy, interest groups and their members may employ a number of tactics. The most familiar, and controversial, involve spending money in an effort to get certain candidates elected. Less controversial tactics include endorsements, voter mobilization efforts, voter education, and volunteering.

Political action committees Many groups interested in election outcomes form **political action committees** (PAC), or encourage group members to donate to a PAC created by someone else. A PAC is an organization funded by 50 or more people, usually affiliated with a corporation , labor union, or some other special interest group. The PAC collects donations from individuals, and then turns those donations into contributions to political parties and candidates for election. Among the largest PACs (Table 12.2) in terms of candidate contributions are the following:

- the National Association of Realtors
- the Laborers Union,
- the National Auto Dealers Association,
- the International Brotherhood of Electrical Workers, and
- the National Beer Wholesalers Association.

Table 12-2. Top 10 PAC Contributors to Federal Candidates in 2006[46]

RANK	PAC	TOTAL AMOUNT	DEM %	REP %
1	National Association of Realtors	$3,752,000	49%	51%
2	National Beer Wholesalers Assn	$2,946,500	31%	69%
3	National Assn of Home Builders	$2,900,000	26%	73%
4	National Auto Dealers Assn	$2,821,600	30%	70%
5	Int. Brotherhood of Electrical Workers	$2,796,875	97%	3%
6	Operating Engineers Union	$2,784,435	78%	21%
7	American Bankers Assn	$2,748,299	36%	64%
8	Laborers Union	$2,687,150	85%	15%
9	American Assn for Justice	$2,558,000	96%	3%
10	Credit Union National Assn	$2,412,853	45%	54%

Table 12-3. Summary of Campaign Donation Limits, 2008

INDIVIDUALS CAN GIVE:	
To Candidates:	$2,300
To National Party Committee:	$28,500
To PAC/State or Local Party:	$10,000 to state or local party
	$5,000 to each PAC
Aggregate Total:	$108,200 per two year election circle
	$42,700 to candidates
	$65,500 to all national party committees of which no more than $40,000 per cycle can go to PACs
MULTICANDIDATE PACS CAN GIVE:	
To Candidates:	$5,000
To National Party Committee:	$15,000
To PAC/State or Local Party:	$5,000
Aggregate Total:	No Limit

Other well-known PACs include:

- the Association of Trial Lawyers of America,

- the American Medical Association PAC,

- the United Auto Workers PAC,

- the American Federation of Teachers PAC, and

- the Teamsters Union PAC.

Groups form PACs, rather than contributing directly to a campaign or party, for several reasons. Federal law prohibits labor unions and corporations from contributing directly to political parties or candidates for federal office but these groups may form a PAC and collect and distribute money from individuals sympathetic to their interests. PACs also allow individuals to multiply the effect of a campaign contribution. If you were to contribute, say, $50 directly to a Senate campaign, you might feel that your contribution didn't amount to much. But if you were to donate that same $50 to a PAC supporting your favorite Senate candidate, and that PAC in turn donated $10,000 to the candidate by combining your contribution with many others, you might feel that you had gotten more bang for your buck.

Like individuals, PACs are limited in the amounts of money they can contribute to a political campaign (Table 12.3). PACs may give a maximum of $15,000 per year to a political party and a maximum of $5,000, per election, to any federal election candidate. Because primaries and general elections are considered separate elections, however, a PAC may actually give a total of $10,000 to each federal candidate per election cycle. In the 2006 election, PACs contributed almost $370 million to candidates running for the House and Senate.[28]

This represents about one-quarter of the funds that candidates for Congress raised during the 2005/2006 election cycle. Competitive campaigns for Congress can be extraordinarily expensive, however. In 2006, for example, the most expensive House campaign cost more than $8 million (Vernon Buchanan, R- Florida), and the most expensive Senate campaign cost more than $40 million (Hillary

Clinton, D-New York).[29] In a very costly race, then, the maximum PAC contribution will comprise a trifling amount of the money the campaign will spend.

Other spending options There are ways that groups can get around the legal limits on PAC contributions. Rather than contributing directly to a political campaign, a PAC can make unlimited **independent expenditures,** which are made with the explicit intent of advocating the election or defeat of a candidate. By law, such expenditures may not be coordinated with the candidate's campaign (hence the qualifier "independent"). Aside from that, however, they may serve exactly the same purpose as advertisements placed by candidates themselves.

Groups can also request that members write checks directly to a candidate's campaign. The group can then collect the individual checks and present them to the candidate all at once, a practice known as **bundling** (Table 12.4). Considering that individuals can write candidate checks for up to $2,300 each, a bundle of checks from dozens of well-heeled donors can make quite an impression.

Groups may also form and raise funds for **527 committees**, also called "527s," named for the relevant section of the Internal Revenue Code. A 527 is a tax- exempt, non-party group that can raise and spend money on political activities and advertising with no effective limits. While 527s cannot directly advocate the election or defeat of specific candidates for federal office, these groups often seek to influence election outcomes in other ways. In 2004, for example, three Democratic-leaning 527s—America Coming Together, The Media Fund, and MoveOn.Org—spent almost $160 million during the election cycle.[30] Large chunks of this money came from extremely wealthy donors. George Soros contributed more than $26 million from his personal resources or his company, Soros Fund Management.[31]

This money was spent primarily on two things: producing and running media advertisements supporting the Democratic nominee, John Kerry, or criticizing his Republican opponent, George W. Bush, and orchestrating a massive get-out-the-vote effort among Democrats.

The Bush forces had their own 527 organizations, though they were less well funded. The most prominent anti-Kerry 527s included Progress for America, Swift Boat Veterans and POWs for Truth, the College Republican National Committee,

Table 12-4. Bundles of Money
(Funds contributed to Senate candidates by individuals connected with an organization, their immediate family and contributions from the organization's PAC.)

CONTRIBUTOR	TOTAL	RECIPIENT
Emily's List	$523,538	McCaskill, Claire
Club for Growth	$443,918	Laffey, Stephen
ActBlue	$419,075	Webb, James
Emily's List	$359,700	Klobuchar, Amy
Act Blue	$313,527	Morrison, John
Moveon.org	$251,126	Lamont, Ned
Club for Growth	$242,831	Steel, Michael
Emily's List	$189,375	Stabenow, Debbie
Club for Growth	$187,005	Bouchard, Michael
Club for Growth	$176,352	McGavick, Michael

and the Club for Growth. Together, these groups spent more than $87 million during the 2004 election season.[32]

Many of the advertisements run by these 527s had the same feel as campaign ads run by the candidates themselves. One of the famous "Swift Boat" television ads, for example, included these statements from the wives of former Vietnam POWs:

> *Mary Jane McManus:* Three months after we were married, my husband was shot down over Hanoi.
>
> *Phyllis Galanti:* Paul and I were married in 1963. Two years later he was shot down over North Vietnam.
>
> *McManus:* All of the prisoners of war in North Vietnam were tortured in order to obtain confessions of atrocities.
>
> *Galanti:* On the other hand, John Kerry came home and accused all Vietnam veterans of unspeakable horrors.
>
> *McManus:* John Kerry gave aid and comfort to the enemy by advocating their negotiating points to our government.
>
> *Galanti:* Why is it relevant? Because John Kerry is asking us to trust him.
>
> *McManus:* I will never forget John Kerry's testimony. If we couldn't trust John Kerry then, how could we possibly trust him now?[33]

On the other side, a radio advertisement run by The Media Fund was highly critical of the Bush administration:

> Announcer: After nearly 3,000 Americans were killed, while our nation was mourning the dead and the wounded, the Saudi royal family was making a special request of the Bush White House. As a result, nearly two dozen of Osama bin Laden's family members were rounded up . . .
>
> Not to be arrested or detained, but to be taken to an airport, where a chartered jet was waiting . . . to return them to their country. They could have helped us find Osama bin Laden. Instead the Bush White House had Osama's family flown home, on a private jet, in the dead of night, when most other air traffic was grounded.
>
> We don't know whether Osama's family members would have told us where bin Laden was hiding. But thanks to the Bush White House . . . we'll never find out.[34]

Other electoral tactics While campaign spending is probably the most high-profile and controversial tactic that interest groups use to pursue their electoral goals, it is just the beginning. Groups interested in electoral outcomes have a number of other tactics at their disposal. These include:

> *Endorsements:* groups often publicize their support for a candidate, providing a valuable voting cue to group members, and to non-members who are sympathetic to the group's ends. Just before the 2008 Nevada caucuses, for example, Democratic presidential candidate Barack Obama scored a political coup by winning the endorsement of the local Culinary Workers Union, representing many casino, bar, and restaurant employees in Las Vegas and Reno.
>
> *Voter mobilization:* as noted above, interest groups often dedicate themselves to increasing voter registration and turnout in competitive Congressional races and in the important battleground states that decide presidential elections.

Voter education: sometimes groups seek to influence elections by disseminating educational materials to prospective voters. These materials may discuss a candidate's background, beliefs, or record; compare and contrast competing candidates; or rate a whole slate of candidates according to their votes or positions on various issues. Conservative Christian groups have been among the most active exponents of this approach, distributing voter guides in evangelical churches every election year.

Volunteer work: groups may provide volunteers to do some of the necessary day-to-day work on behalf of candidates they favor. This can include answering phones, preparing campaign mailers, coordinating local meetings, reminding voters to do their civic duty on election day (for the preferred candidate, of course), and even driving voters to the polls.

Lobbying is the key ingredient in a legislative strategy.

As with the electoral strategy, groups that pursue a decision strategy have a variety of tactics at their disposal. The most familiar of these is lobbying. Lobbying and lobbyists are sometimes stigmatized as sleazy, unseemly, and even undemocratic. In his 2008 presidential campaign, for example, Illinois senator Barack Obama said:

> I am in this race to tell the corporate lobbyists that their days of setting the agenda in Washington are over. I have done more than any other candidate in this race to take on lobbyists—and won. They have not funded my campaign, they will not get a job in my White House, and they will not drown out the voices of the American people when I am president.35

When pursued legally and ethically, however, lobbying is a legitimate tactic used to achieve a legitimate democratic end: influencing the deliberations, decisions, and actions of government officials. In fact, the right to lobby is guaranteed by the first amendment , which prohibits Congress from interfering with the right of the people "to petition the government for a redress of grievances." Lobbying takes two general forms, inside lobbying and grassroots lobbying. We shall examine each in some detail.

Inside lobbying and Congress What most people think of as lobbying is technically called **inside lobbying**, and occurs when group representatives meet with public officials and/or their staff members. The lobbyist's job in these meetings is generally two-fold: to present specific, evaluative information to the public official; and to request an action or a decision based on that information.

The lobbyist does not simply say, "We want you to know that our group is pro-environment, and we hope you will be, too." Instead, the lobbyist presents the group's position on a *specific* bill, amendment, nomination, budget item, etc., along with the reasons for that position: "The Sierra Club is opposed to this amendment because we think it will undercut some major provisions of the Clean Air Act that have nearly universal public support." To this, the lobbyist adds his or her request for action by the public official: "Because of that, we are asking that you vote against the amendment."

There are, of course, dozens of variations on this basic information/request-for-action two-step. Lobbyists recognize that public officials have a variety of goals. As discussed in more detail in Chapter 13, members of Congress value good public policy, reelection, and advancement within the institution (chairing a desirable committee, for example, or earning a spot in the party leadership). The information that lobbyists provide to legislators, then, is presented with these goals in mind. In the example above, the Sierra Club presented an evaluation of the hypothetical amendment in terms of its soundness as public policy. Recognizing that members of Congress are interested in reelection, too, the lobbyist might have added: "Furthermore, our research shows that the substance of this amendment is immensely unpopular within your district. If you vote for it, an opponent in the next election may beat you over the head with this issue all the way to November."

The type and amount of information that lobbyists provide will also vary from situation to situation. Some policymakers want to see detailed studies supporting a group's position. Others are more interested in expressly political information on the issue: polling data, communications from voters, activities of opposing groups. Some want to know what recognized experts think. Some simply want a short list of talking points they can use to explain their vote. Others want to know what kind of media coverage the issue has received in national and home-town newspapers. Still others want to talk through hypothetical scenarios: "What if, instead of just voting against the amendment, we sent it back to committee for reconsideration, with some specific suggestions for improving it?"

The lobbyist must be prepared to answer all such questions and provide supporting information when meeting with public officials or soon after. Lobbyists' ability to do so makes them immensely helpful to members of Congress. Faced with dozens of high-profile issues, each of which must pass through a long series of meetings, hearings, decisions, discussions, negotiations, and votes, representatives and senators cannot become experts in more than two or three issue areas. Having lobbyists available to provide information on other issues is like having a public policy encyclopedia at the ready—one that can answer follow-up questions and produce supplemental information upon request.

Unlike an encyclopedia, however, a lobbyist has a point of view—a position that he or she is promoting, and often a broad philosophical orientation on issues of a certain type ("pro-labor," for example, or "pro-business"). This is actually helpful to public officials. They are far too busy to listen to lobbyists who present both sides and leave it up to the official to decide. Instead, they can hear the strongest arguments from the most passionate, well-informed advocates on both sides. This may help them evaluate an issue in ways that they otherwise could not because they lack the lobbyists' information, expertise, and familiarity with the most salient arguments.

The nature of the request for action by a lobbyist can also vary tremendously from situation to situation. Among other things, the lobbyist might ask a member of Congress to sponsor, amend, rewrite, or vote for or against a piece of legislation; talk to colleagues, hold hearings (or decline to hold hearings), or take a stand regarding an issue; support or oppose a nominee; or intervene with an agency.

Members may agree to do such work on behalf of an interest group because it is consistent with their political or policy goals, they are grateful for the lobbyist's or group's support in the past, or they are trying to build goodwill in anticipation of a request for support in the future. Whatever the case, by helping the lobbyist that comes to visit—and by extension, the group the lobbyist represents—the member of Congress generally helps him or herself.

This kind of help is not a one-way street, however. A lobbyist who asks a member to sponsor a piece of legislation often provides a draft bill that the member can use as a starting point. The lobbyist might also volunteer to answer any questions on the legislation from the member's colleagues. If the member has agreed to meet with a regulatory agency, the lobbyist might offer to help a senior set up the meeting and preview the major issues/arguments.

Furthermore, once a lobbyist has established a trusted relationship with a public official, that official may seek out the lobbyist for help. An official working on a pet issue may ask the lobbyist to supply information or suggest a subject-matter expert to provide congressional testimony, or talk to other groups involved with the issue in order to find out their position on a particular sticking point. Lobbyists are normally happy to oblige, knowing that a close, trusting, and mutually supportive relationship will benefit the groups they represent.

Inside lobbying and the executive branch While inside lobbying is most often thought of in relation to members of Congress and their staff, interest group lobbyists also devote resources to the executive branch. In some cases this means the president and White House personnel, but more often lobbying efforts focus on executive branch agencies. As we will see in Chapter 16, these agencies issue regulations, statutory interpretations, and quasi-legal decisions on issues as diverse as endangered species protection, the content of television and radio advertising, business accommodations for individuals with disabilities, and interstate speed limits. They also participate in the executive branch budget process, identifying programs for which they will seek to maintain funding at current levels, increase funding, or reduce or eliminate funding. Furthermore, they are responsible for oversight and administration of major federal programs and tax credits and deductions. Finally, they pursue policy agendas of their own, encouraging the president to promote and fund certain policy initiatives and to abandon others.

Obviously, interest groups and their members can have a significant stake in these executive agency decisions and activities. Some groups, therefore, devote major lobbying resources to the executive branch.

Inside lobbying and the judiciary Inside lobbying of the judicial branch takes two primary forms. In one, an interest group may file briefs on cases that involve an issue in which it has an interest. Such briefs present the group's analysis of legal or factual questions in the hope that judges, justices, or their clerks will take their arguments into account when deciding the case.

One example involves the U.S. Supreme Court case of *Morse v. Fredrick*. Fredrick, a high school senior, had been suspended from school for hanging a banner school officials found offensive. Fredrick claimed that this was a violation of his first amendment rights. When the case made its way to the Supreme Court, a number of groups, including the National Coalition Against Censorship, the Christian Legal Society, and Students for Sensible Drug Policy, filed briefs supporting Fredrick's position. They saw the case as an opportunity to establish important principles regarding freedom of speech in a public school setting. In the end, however, the Supreme Court ruled that Fredrick's first amendment rights had not been violated by school administrators.

The other judiciary-related tactic available to interest groups is litigation. While this is not lobbying *per se*, it can have important policy implications. In July 2004, for example, Wisconsin Right to Life, Inc. (WRTL), an anti-abortion group, began using funds from its general treasury to broadcast television advertisements that mentioned Wisconsin senators Herb Kohl and Russ Feingold by name. Feingold was running in the September 14 primary, and after August 15, 2004, WRTL was in violation of McCain Feingold, legislation prohibiting the use of general treasure funds to pay for advertisements that mentioned a federal candidate within 30 days of a primary election.

Believing these restrictions on political advertising to be unconstitutional, WRTL sued the Federal Elections Commission, the agency responsible for administering McCain-Feingold. The U.S. Supreme Court decided in favor of WRTL, effectively modifying a law enacted by Congress and signed by President Bush. Thus, the suit resulted in fewer legal restrictions not just for the group involved in the litigation, but potentially for hundreds of similar groups around the country.

Grassroots lobbying The other major tactic that groups use in support of a decision strategy is known as **grassroots or outside lobbying**. In this form of lobbying, rather than communicating directly with decision-makers in government, interest groups and their lobbyists seek to influence opinion and stimulate action by the general public, specific groups, and the media. The hope is that public officials will be swayed by what they hear from influenced individuals, groups, and media outlets.

Groups generally begin a grassroots lobbying effort with their own members. Group leaders have established communication channels with their members, and know that most agree on the issues; many will also take action if asked. Thus, leaders may bring new issues to members' attention, try to shape opinions on existing issues, and request phone calls, emails, and letters to policymakers in positions of influence.

Consider the example of LEAnet, a nationwide coalition of special education professionals and school administrators. LEAnet routinely notifies members of pending congressional actions that may affect group members' interests (primarily, the preservation of Medicaid funding for special needs students in public schools). These communications often include a call to action:

> Please send an email to your Congressperson (if a Republican) or call her/his office as soon as possible. You can find the email address and phone numbers of the Congressman you want to contact here or here. If you call, just ask for the staff person handling education or health and tell them you strongly support inclusion of the moratorium language and request their Congressperson's vote.
>
> If you email, include on the subject line your address, which will tell the staff person in charge of reading emails that you are a constituent. Please respond to this call for help immediately. You can make a difference.
>
> An email message as simple as "Please include moratorium language stopping CMS cuts to children's health programs in any appropriate legislation. Thank you."[36]

Some groups go further and encourage, or even arrange for, their members to meet policymakers in person. The American Veterinary Medical Association (AVMA), for example, touts the value of such meetings on its Web site:

> If an AVMA member plans to visit Washington, D.C., we invite them to contact us so we can set up meetings for them at the Washington offices of their representatives to talk about AVMA issues. They are the constituents, and no one can bring an issue home the way a grassroots member can.[37]

However, interest groups know that government officials respond to public opinion broadly, not just to opinions expressed by group members with an interest in a particular issue. They know, too, that policymakers react to what they see, hear, and read in the media. Because of this, a grassroots lobbying campaign may be quite extensive, and multi-faceted.

Consider, for example, a campaign launched in 2005 by Progress for America, a group that often advocated on behalf of President Bush and various Bush administration and Republican candidates and initiatives. Progress for America used grassroots tactics to build support for Samuel Alito, a Bush nominee to the U.S.

Supreme Court. This included putting up a web site and airing about $500,000 in television advertising. The group also hired consultants in 20 swing states to speak with editorial boards and sent over 10 million e-mail messages to Republican party lists. The group also arranged for Judge Alito's former law clerks to visit Washington and lobby senators for their former boss. To generate favorable news stories, the group even sought out people from Judge Alito's past including former teachers, coaches, and neigbors.[38]

This example illustrates many of the hallmarks of a classic grassroots approach to lobbying. Progress for America attempted to influence the general climate of opinion through the use of paid advertising. It sought to educate and mobilize individuals that it thought might be willing to take action on behalf of Judge Alito. It tried to generate favorable stories and friendly interviews about Judge Alito in mass media outlets. It arranged for meetings between lawmakers and former clerks of Judge Alito, rather than meetings between lawmakers and paid professional lobbyists. In short, instead of using Washington-based, lobbyist- centered *inside* tactics, Progress for America tried to create a climate in which senators (who had to vote on Alito's nomination) would sense that there was significant support for Alito *outside* of Washington. Alito was ultimately confirmed. Although PFA's actions were not the reason or the cause for the vote Alito got in the Senate, it is a modern and textbook example of grass roots lobbying.

The logic that drives grass roots lobbying was perhaps best summed up by the former Illinois Senator Everett Dirksen, "When politicians feel the heat," Dirksen said, "they begin to see the light."[39]

CaseStudy: Grassroots Lobbying and the Clinton Health Care Plan

A particularly intense grassroots lobbying campaign occurred during the battle over health care reform during President Bill Clinton's first term. This campaign was focused on three committees: the Ways and Means Committee and the Energy and Commerce Committee in the House, and the Finance Committee in the Senate. These committees were responsible for deciding whether any health care reform would pass, and if so, what shape it would take. Within these committees, lobbying efforts focused on those members (fewer than 20 in the House and 15 in the Senate) who were still undecided on the general issue, and also on a group of moderate Republican and Democratic senators, known as the "mainstream coalition," that was seeking a broadly acceptable compromise.

A notable element in the grassroots lobbying effort against the Clinton proposal was a television commercial financed by the Health Insurance Association of America, a trade organization of health insurance providers. The commercial showed a married couple, Harry and Louise, sitting at a kitchen table covered with papers. The couple were talking about some of the Clinton plan's features— Would it create a government monopoly over health care provision? Would health care involve a huge, intrusive, impersonal federal bureaucracy? Would government

bureaucrats have the power to deny health care? The ad ended by exhorting people to get in touch with their congressional representative or senator if they, too, were worried about the Clinton plan.

"Harry and Louise" proved to be enormously effective. The producers claimed that the campaign "prompted 500,000 phone calls to a toll-free number, turned 50,000 of those callers into activists, and resulted in one-quarter million contacts with members of Congress."[40]

The ad also led to a tremendous amount of coverage of the ad itself in newspapers, on television, and on the radio. Thus, it received much wider exposure than it would have received from paid placements alone. As a result, policymakers and opinion- shapers were forced to address the arguments in the Harry and Louise campaign.

Other radio and TV ads flooded targeted districts. An ad from Citizens for a Sound Economy, a free market/limited government advocacy group, told listeners, "If you don't want government gatekeepers telling you what doctor you can see, call Congressman (name) at (number) and tell him to vote no on the Clinton health care plan." These and similar efforts were directed not at Congress as a whole, but at the districts and states of members of Congress who were expected to be influential or persuadable in the health care debate. Groups also worked to identify *constituents* who were most likely to influence members of Congress.

Unlike a political activity such as voting, the letters or phone calls from different individuals are not equally influential. Letters most likely to influence congressional decision- making are those from local civic, business, or political leaders; from individuals or groups with a particular interest or expertise in an issue; or from individuals known to be highly involved and engaged in politics generally. Thus, interest groups seek to mobilize individuals with the most potential influence with their elected representatives—an approach sometimes referred to as a grasstops strategy.

Data indicate that such a strategy was at work during the Clinton health care debate. The National Federation of Independent Businesses, a key player in defeating the proposed legislation, created Guardian Advisory Council teams consisting of influential businessmen and women,

and college friends, neighbors, and former colleagues of targeted legislators, people who were thought have extraordinary influence with those legislators. The broader media efforts to defeat the Clinton plan were directed toward the "grass tops." Ben Goddard, who produced and placed the "Harry and Louise" ads, explained, "Our media buys were targeted on involved Americans, people who were registered to vote, wrote letters to the editor or public officials, attended meetings and made political contributions."[41] These are the very people most likely to be taken seriously by policymakers.

ThinkingCritically

1. Have new technologies and the internet created news ways for interest groups to stimulate grass roots communications to lawmakers?

2. If you were trying to generate support for an issue in your Congressional district, who would be the most influential people you would try to contact?

The electoral strategy and the legislative strategy intertwine.

As we noted above, groups need not choose between an electoral strategy and a legislative strategy. Many pursue both strategies at once, and one often reinforces the other. A member of Congress who has been elected with the support of a particular group, for example, may be more open to entertaining that group's viewpoints on policy issues. He or she may feel obligated to meet with the group and knows that maintaining a friendly relationship will likely ensure its support in the next campaign. Thus, the group's electoral strategy can support its legislative strategy.

The reverse can be true as well. A group that wants a member of Congress to vote its way on a bill will often note the political appeal of that vote (or the political damage of opposition) in the next election. A group that engages in an outside lobbying strategy by encouraging communications to a legislator is, of course, registering its viewpoints on issues. At the same time, it is showing the kind of muscle it can flex—on behalf of the legislator or an opponent—in the next election.

In a similar vein, an interest group might seek to have legislation introduced on an issue both because it cares about the issue, but also because the legislation causes problems for political opponents. The proposed "partial birth" abortion ban, for example, first introduced by pro-life members of Congress in 1995, was designed in part to force pro-choice legislators to take a public position on a procedure that a large majority of the American public disapproved of. The same logic held with respect the federal assault weapons ban passed in 1994. Most of the public approved of the ban, putting gun rights supporters in an awkward position if they opposed it.

Interest groups have a wide variety of tactics in their toolkits.

As the preceding discussion indicates, interest groups have a wide variety of tactics that they can choose from to try to influence the policy process. Their choice of tactics depends on the goals they are pursuing. All the various tactics try to convey some sort of information to policy makers—either on the substantive merits of the case or on the political consequences of a particular course of action. Table 12.5 summarizes the various tactics and how often they tend to be used.

Table 12-5. Lobbying Techniques and their Prevalence[47]

LEGISLATIVE BRANCH	
Doing favors and/or providing gifts for legislators	–
Meeting personally with legislators and/or their aides	very often
Testifying at legislative hearings	very often
EXECUTIVE BRANCH	
Interacting with special agencies that advise the chief executive	–
Interacting with special liaison offices within the chief executive's office	–
Meeting personally with chief executive and/or aides	seldom
Meeting personally with executive agency personnel	very often
Serving on executive agency advisory boards or committees	occasionally
Submitting written comments on proposed rules or regulations	very often
Testifying at executive agency hearings	–
JUDICIAL BRANCH	
Attempting to influence judicial selections	–
Engaging in litigation	occasionally
Submitting amicus curia "friends of the court" briefs	occasionally
GRASSROOTS	
Arranging face-to-face meetings between group members/supporters and government officials	–
Dispatching a spokesperson to the media	–
Engaging in email, letter, telegram or telephone campaigns	very often
Engaging in demonstrations or protests	seldom
Running advertisements in the media	seldom
DIRECT DEMOCRACY	
Attempting to place an initiative or referendum on the ballot	–
Campaigning for or against an initiative or referendum	–
ELECTORAL	
Campaigning for or against candidates	seldom
Endorsing candidates	seldom
Engaging in election issue advocacy	seldom
Making in-kind contributions to candidates	seldom
Making monetary contributions to political parties	seldom
Making monetary contributions to candidates	occasionally
Mobilizing activists to work on a candidate's behalf	–
Issuing voter guides	seldom
OTHER	
Joining coalitions with other organizations and/or lobbyists	very often

Note: Dashes (–) indicate that there is little evidence with which to judge the frequency of such activities.

Do Groups Matter?

High profile corruption cases have received significant media attention over the last few years. In these cases, interest groups went well beyond the sorts of activities we have outlined here and attempted outright to bribe members of Congress. Randy Cunningham, a former Representative from California received a Rolls Royce and a yacht for steering Defense Department business toward a particular contract. Cunningham is currently biding his time in prison. Jack Abramoff, a well known lobbyist in DC for many years is also serving time in prison for his role in orchestrating bribes to a series of members of Congress.

These sorts of blatant and illegal activities are quite rare and as we have argued, interest groups and lobbying have an important role in our political system and engage in a various and legitimate strategies to influence the policy process. That said, and having examined what groups do and why they do it, we are left with a final question: do groups matter? That is, do group activities influence election results and public policy outcomes in the ways that groups intend? The answer to that question is surprisingly murky.

It is difficult to prove the impact of campaign contributions.

Few researchers doubt that if interest groups were to disappear from the American political landscape, different public officials would be elected and appointed, different issues would appear on the public agenda, different pieces of legislation would be approved, and budget items would be funded at different levels. For political scientists, however, the challenge comes in providing clear evidence that groups would be responsible for these changes. Consider, for example, the case of interest group spending on federal campaigns. The hundreds of millions of dollars that interest groups spend supporting and opposing candidates must surely have some impact, but political scientists cannot say as a general proposition that the more money a candidate spends, the more votes he or she gets.

Why is this? For one thing, candidates facing a highly competitive race tend to raise and spend more money, while candidates who are shoo-ins for reelection typically spend less. This produces counterintuitive results: candidates who spend a lot money often end up in very close races (they *had* to spend a lot of money *because* the race was close); and candidates who spend very little money often end up winning big (they could afford to spend so little because they faced little competition).

Unfortunately, political scientists have not yet found their way out of this methodological thicket, and therefore do not have a complete understanding of the impact of interest group spending on election outcomes.

One finds similar problems, but somewhat more satisfying answers, when looking at the impact of political action committee contributions on legislator behavior. Journalistic accounts of legislator voting sometimes note that legislators who receive large PAC contributions often vote as their donors wish. Members who receive large campaign contributions from tobacco PACs, for example, often cast votes in support of legislation advocated by the tobacco lobby. From this, one might infer that "big tobacco" is buying votes. Political scientists, however, have suggested an alternative explanation: tobacco PACs take note of legislators who support tobacco interests and distribute campaign dollars accordingly.

Which explanation is the right one? Most research finds that PAC contributions do not "buy" the votes of legislators. Again, there are logical reasons for this. First, a floor vote on a piece of legislation comes at the end of the legislative process. Important decisions, hearings, committee votes, negotiations, and coalition-building have to take place before a bill makes it this far. An interest group trying to buy influence after all of this has occurred would be like a football fan paying full price for a Super Bowl ticket...with only two minutes left in the game.

Second, members of Congress face many influences on their vote in addition to campaign contributions. These include their own policy preferences, the preferences of their constituents, the dictates of party leaders, and their voting records. These influences tend to be so strong that most political scientists consider it unlikely that an interest group contribution could override them, turning a "yea" vote into a "nay," or vice versa.

Group influence may be strongest where it is hardest to observe.

If not floor votes, then what sorts of legislative outcomes might interest groups be buying? One insightful study of this question concluded that money buys *time*, that is, legislator participation in the process of incorporating interest group preferences into law. Political scientists Richard Hall and Frank Wayman found that legislators who received campaign funds from an interest group were more likely to engage in the following activities on the group's behalf: "authoring or blocking a legislative vehicle; negotiating compromises behind the scenes, especially at the staff level; offering friendly amendments or actively opposing unfriendly ones; lobbying colleagues; planning strategy; and last and sometimes least, showing up to vote in favor of the interest group's position."[42] Hall and Wayman argued that such activities, rather than floor votes, were most likely to show evidence of group influence.

These activities can result not just in broad pieces of legislation that interest groups favor, but in the provision of "private goods" for specific groups: government contracts, price increases, tax breaks, "earmarked" funds, exemptions from certain statutory provisions, and so on.[43] Private goods of this sort are typically distributed to groups behind the scenes, away from reporters, in private meetings and committee mark-up sessions, and without a formal vote. They are often buried in the fine print of massive appropriations bills, and therefore easily missed . . . even by political scientists.

In part, this is because political scientists tend to study highly contested issues in which the conflict is in plain view.[44] The politics surrounding these issues can be very dramatic. Accordingly, they seem interesting and important, and generate readily available data, which makes them attractive subjects for study.

But groups probably have their *greatest* influence when the outcomes they seek are not contested by anyone; are negotiated or decided in low-profile, largely private settings; do not have a significant impact outside of the group(s) immediately affected; and cannot easily be observed or exposed by casual observers of politics. For obvious reasons, interest group influence is much harder to study in these situations.

Interest group influence is also most likely to be observable in marginal, unresolved cases. For example, if 10 of 11 committee members decided long ago how they would vote, interest groups would likely focus their lobbying efforts on the undecided one. A scholar looking for group influence on all 11 committee members would likely come up empty-handed.

Similarly, in races for the House of Representatives, only a few dozen contests each year (out of 435) are normally competitive. These are the races where one would expect to find interest group influence, if it is to be found at all. Accordingly, a political scientist looking for the impact of groups across the full slate of congressional races would come up with little to show for his or her work.

To conclude, political scientists clearly need to spend more time looking for group influence in less obvious settings than they have been, on lower-profile issues, in obscure but consequential legislative provisions, on decisions that don't require a vote, in discussions that typically take place behind closed doors, and in the marginal cases that tend to be decisive in determining an electoral or policy outcome. Reorienting interest group research in this way would undoubtedly demonstrate group influence in virtually every aspect of executive, legislative, judicial, and electoral activity.

That influence would not show up on all issues, but select ones. It would not be reflected in every decision or in every setting, but in specific cases. In short, extensive interest group influence undoubtedly could be found, if political scientists were looking for it in the right ways and in the right places.

SUMMARY

▶ James Madison was concerned about the negative influence of interest groups, what he termed factions, on individual rights and the collective good. However, he concluded that the American system was well designed to mute the influence of factions, now called interest groups. The pluralists viewed politics as an organized effort to resolve conflicts among competing group interests, and attempted to demonstrate empirically what Madison had argued theoretically. They concluded that political power and resources in the United States were dispersed widely, with some interest groups being influential and resource-rich in some issue areas, and a completely different set being influential and resource-rich in other issue areas.

▶ Critics of pluralism argued that the American system is resistant to change and retards certain issues from getting on the agenda. Furthermore, the collective action problem questions the assumption that groups automatically form and suggests some types of groups are more able to form than others.

▶ Groups pursue a variety of strategies to get around the collective action problem. They provide selective benefits, which members receive in return for joining. They also provide solidary benefits, in which members enjoy the camaraderie of being a part of a group, and purposive benefits, in which those who join get satisfaction from being involved in an important political struggle.

▶ Groups try to influence public policy in two ways. In an election strategy, groups try to influence which leaders achieve power and make public policy. In a legislative strategy, groups try to influence the behavior of elected officials, bureaucrats, and judges who are already in power.

▶ Media coverage and popular coverage of interest groups and lobbying suggests that groups are all powerful and often malevolent. They are neither. While groups and legislators sometimes cross the line, groups play an important role in American politics and are more likely to influence policy making in more small and subtle ways.

KEY TERMS

527 committee, p. 000
bundling, p. 000
by-product, p. 000
disturbance theory, p. 000
free rider problem, p. 000
grassroots lobbying, p. 000
independent expenditures, p. 000
interest group, p. 000
interest group entrepreneur, p. 000
inside lobbying, p. 000
lobby, p. 000

material benefits, p. 000
non-decision, p. 000
patron, p. 000
pluralism, p. 000
policy agenda, p. 000
political action committee (PAC), p. 000
potential groups, p. 000
purposive benefits, p. 000
selective benefits, p. 000
social benefits, p. 000

SUGGESTED READINGS

Berry, Jeffrey and Clyde Wilcox. 2008. *Interest Group Society*. Longman

Walker, Jack L. 1991. Mobilizing Interest Groups in America: Patrons, Professionals and Social Movements. Ann Arbor: University of Michigan Press.

Baumgarnter, Frank and Beth Leech. 1998. *Basic Interests: The Importance of Groups in Politics and in Political Science*. Princcton N.J. Princeton University Press.

interest groups organizations that seek to influence government decisions.

pluralism describes a society in which all groups are well represented and no single interest controls government decisions.

potential groups unorganized groups that may organize if their needs are not addressed.

non-decision a decision not to consider particular issues on the policy agenda.

policy agenda the set of issues under consideration by policymakers.

disturbance theory holds that when social, political, and economic relationships change, individuals form groups in response.

free rider problem a barrier to collective action because people can reap the benefits of group efforts without participating.

lobby refers to communications with government officials intended to persuade them toward a particular policy decision.

selective benefits can only be accessed by those who participate or contribute to group activity.

material benefits include goods and services offered to encourage participation in group activity.

social benefits encourage individuals to join groups in order to enjoy the company of those who share similar opinions and interests.

purposive benefits encourage group participation by connecting individuals to an organization's political purpose.

interest group entrepreneurs overcome the costs of collective action by launching and managing interest groups.

patrons support interest groups by providing the resources groups need to organize and flourish.

political action committee (PAC) collect money from individuals and make donations to political parties and candidates.

independent expenditures funds donated to elect or defeat candidates but not coordinated with any political campaign.

bundling the practice of collecting individual checks and presenting them to a candidate at one time.

527 committee an independent, non-party group that raises and spends money on political activities.

inside lobbying occurs when groups meet directly with public officials to influence political decisions.

grassroots or outside lobbying includes efforts to influence political decisions through constituent contacts.

political parties organized groups with public followings that seek to elect officeholders who identify themselves by the group's common label, for the purpose of exercising political power

unified government a situation where the presidency and both houses of Congress are controlled by the same party

divided government a situation where the presidency is held by one party and at least one house of Congress is controlled by a different party

two-party system a system of electoral competition in which two parties are consistently the most likely to win office and gain power.

single-member districts electoral districts in which only one person is elected to represent the district in a representative body

plurality elections elections in which the candidate with the most votes, not necessarily a majority, wins

proportional representation an election system in which candidates are elected from multi-member districts, with a party's share of seats from a district being roughly proportional to their share of the popular vote

winner-take-all the system of awarding all the electoral votes in a state to the presidential candidate who received the most votes

fusion a strategy in which third parties endorse a major party candidate but list that candidate separately on the ballot so that voters can vote for the candidate under the third-party label

Australian ballot an official government-produced ballot for elections that lists all offices and all the candidates and parties who have qualified to be on the ballot

electoral realignment a shift in the composition of party coalitions that produces a new, relatively durable pattern of party competition

dealignment a substantial reduction in the proportion of the voting consistently for one party and identifying with a party

responsible party model the idea that political parties should run as unified teams, present a clear policy platform, implement that platform when in office, and run on their record in the subsequent election

issue evolution a change in the partisan base of support for an issue over time, such that the position of Democrats and Republican switch

party machine disciplined local party organizations that selected candidates; got out the vote; provided benefits to supporters including government workers, local constituents, and businesses; and served as social service agencies for their followers

patronage awarding jobs in government on the basis of party support and loyalty rather than expertise or experience

progressive reforms a set of political and electoral reforms in the early 20th century that had the combined effect of weakening political parties

national party convention a meeting held over several days at which delegates select the party's presidential nominee, approve the party platform, and consider changes in party rules and policies

party platform a document expressing the principles, beliefs, and policy positions of the party, as endorsed by delegates at the national party convention

13 Congress

Distributing Homeland Security Funds

I n 2005, the least populous states received the largest per capita share of federal antiterrorism funds. Wyoming received funds amounting to $27.80 for each of its half-million residents from the Homeland Security Grant Program.[1] Though not generally considered to be a terrorist target, Wyoming had enough federal homeland security money to buy a bomb-dismantling robot and chemical suits for all of its policemen and firefighters.[2] New York, by contrast, received just $15.54 per resident, in spite of the fact that it was a site of the September 11, 2001 terrorist attacks.[3]

How did Wyoming manage to secure such a large chunk of federal funds to fight terrorism? The answer lies in the U.S.A. Patriot Act, which Congress passed in the aftermath of September 11, 2001. Among other things, the act established a federal grant system to help state and local governments prepare for and respond to terrorist attacks. Eager to demonstrate their resolve to fight terrorism, members of Congress provided money for states to train first respon-

ders, purchase security equipment, and develop plans for emergency situations. However, the act required the State Homeland Security Program (SHSP) to distribute almost 40 percent of its funds evenly among the 50 states, regardless of their population, size, or risk of being a terrorist target.[4]

When Congress passed the act in late October of 2001, no one objected to the funding distribution formula. In fact, members of Congress were eager to offer a swift, bold response to the September 11 attacks. The chairman of the powerful Senate Judiciary Committee, Senator Patrick Leahy of Vermont, included in the state antiterrorism program a distribution formula that would benefit the citizens of the small state he represented, and others just like it.

The Patriot Act met little resistance in Congress. It was introduced in the House of Representatives on October 23, 2001, and passed the very next day by a vote of 357 to 66. While some senators opposed other provisions of the bill, no one spoke out against the formula for distributing antiterrorism funds to states. The Senate approved the bill with all but one vote in favor and the president

signed it into law on October 26, 2001.

As the Department of Homeland Security devoted increasingly large sums of money to helping state and local governments prepare for a possible terrorist attack, the wastefulness of the Patriot Act's fund distribution formula became apparent. Common sense probably tells you that helping North Dakota buy a $200,000 remote-control bomb-disposal robot is not the most effective way of preparing the nation for a terrorist attack. Thomas H. Kean, chairman of the September 11 Commission, agreed: "We've had some of this money spent to air condition garbage trucks. We've had some of the money spent for armor for dogs. This money is being distributed as if it's general revenue sharing."[5] Kean recommended that antiterrorism funds be distributed not evenly among the states, but on the basis of threat and vulnerability.[6] Homeland Security Secretary Michael Chertoff further acknowledged that a uniform distribution of funds across states was not a good policy.[7]

Yet when Representative Christopher Cox of California tried to craft a new law in 2005 that would have distributed antiterrorism funds on the basis of threat and risk, he could not get enough support from members of the Senate. Senators from smaller, less populous states lined up against the proposed measure, hoping to preserve the minimum amount of funding going to their states under the existing law. Senator Leahy argued that distribution based on the degree of terrorist threat would "shortchange rural states."[8] In July 2005, the Senate passed a milder version of the Cox bill, one that would have slightly reduced the guaranteed state minimum of annual SHSP funds. However, the House and Senate were not able to agree on a compromise and the formula was not changed.

The failure of these efforts to address clear inefficiencies in the distribution of federal antiterrorism funds seems to make little sense. When one thinks about the incentives that motivate individual members of Congress, however, their behavior is easier to understand. Opponents of the Cox proposal were representing the interests of the voters who put them into office. While Cox represented an urban district outside of Los Angeles, Leahy spoke for a rural state. By arguing that Vermont *did* need to protect itself from terrorist attacks, he hoped to secure federal funds for improving the state's police and fire protection services. Other members of Congress also wanted to secure funding to please voters who had the power to reelect them, even if it wasn't best for the country as a whole.

As of 2008, SHSP antiterrorism funds continue to be distributed by the same formula established by the Patriot Act, and are likely to be for some time to come.[9] Members of Congress, after all, work hardest on behalf of those who elected them. The laws they write represent compromises between hundreds of individuals fighting on behalf of different districts and states. Sometimes, the final result is legislation that serves the interests of the country as a whole. Often, though, the pressure of pleasing the voters results in laws that do not address problems as effectively, or as efficiently, as many would like.

THIS CHAPTER WILL EXAMINE:

▶ the ways in which Congress does, and does not, represent the nation's citizens

▶ the challenges that emerge when members of Congress set about working together

▶ the resources and structures that define Congress as an institution

▶ the lawmaking process

▶ the appropriations process.

An Institution with Two Chambers and Shared Powers

Congress is a **bicameral** institution—that is, it consists of two chambers, a House of Representatives and a Senate. In the House, the 435 voting members (and the five non-voting delegates) are elected every two years and represent state districts, which are remade every decade to reflect changes in the number of people living in different regions of the country. On average, each member of the House represents roughly 600,000 voters.[10] In the Senate, the 100 members are elected every six years and represent entire states.[11] Obviously, the size of states varies tremendously. As a consequence, senators from larger states like New York, Texas, and California represent tens of millions of voters, whereas senators from smaller states like North Dakota, Wyoming, and Montana represent far fewer.

For the most part, members of the House and Senate do similar things. As discussed in Chapter 3, most powers enumerated in Article II of the Constitution, which concerns Congress, do not differentiate between the Senate and House. Both chambers have the responsibility of overseeing the bureaucracy, declaring war, regulating interstate commerce, raising and supporting armies, and, most importantly, writing "all Laws which shall be necessary and proper for carrying into Execution the foregoing power." Later in this chapter, we will describe the lawmaking process in detail.

There are some important differences, however, between the two chambers. In terms of duties, the Senate has the responsibility of ratifying foreign treaties. When brokering deals with foreign nations, presidents need only anticipate the reactions of senators, not representatives. Additionally, senators are charged with approving major presidential appointments to the federal judiciary and executive branch.

Therefore, before selecting federal judges, ambassadors, and members of their cabinet, presidents try to calculate their chances of securing the necessary approval of the Senate.

As part of the nation's system of checks and balances, Congress has the power to remove from office the president, vice president, and others immediately under their command. The removal process, however, is divided into two separate phases that are assigned to the House and Senate. In the first, members of the House decide whether to **impeach** the president—that is, determine that the charges against him or her are sufficiently credible and meet the standards laid out in the Constitution of "treason, bribery, or other high crimes and misdemeanors." Should the House impeach the president, the case goes before the Senate, where the chief justice of the Supreme Court then presides. For a conviction, two-thirds of the senators must vote against the president. In the nation's history, two presidents (Andrew Johnson in 1868 and Bill Clinton in 1998) have been impeached. The Senate, however, refused to convict either president.

Members of the House and Senate also have different kinds of relationships with the people who they represent. Because representatives are elected every two years and usually face a smaller (and typically more homogenous) group of voters than senators, they tend to maintain closer relationships with the voters and work on behalf of a narrower band of interests. Senators, by contrast, hold office for six-year terms and represent larger (and typically more heterogeneous) populations. Senators, therefore, have more freedom to exercise their own judgment on policy matters, and are less beholden to a small group of people.

This is no accident. The Framers of the Constitution envisioned the House to be the "People's Chamber," where the interests of specific groups would be aired. The Senate was intended to be more deliberative, allowing elected officials to reflect upon issues with national implications. Therefore, senators are more concerned with whether proposed legislation is consistent with long-standing principles of equality and individualism. Senators also reflect on the pros and cons of legislation for longer periods of time. "The use of the Senate," wrote James Madison in *Notes of Debates in the Federal Convention of 1787*, "is to consist in its proceedings with more coolness, with more system and with more wisdom, than the popular branch."[12] By "the popular branch," of course, Madison was referring to the House.

Congress is not the only bicameral legislature around. In fact, 49 of the country's 50 state governments have legislatures with two chambers. (The one exception is Nebraska). Most large democracies around the globe also have bicameral legislatures, which go by many different names. India's Parliament, for instance, consists of the *Lok Sabha* (which translates to "House of the People") and the *Rajya Sabha* ("Council of States"). Japan's Parliament, which is called the *Diet*, contains the House of Representatives and the House of Councillors. And Switzerland's "Federal Assembly" contains the National Council and the Council of States.

To be sure, the U.S. Congress distinguishes itself from other bicameral legislatures in important ways. For instance, the upper chamber of Congress (the Senate) is comprised of elected representatives, whereas the upper chambers of many European legislatures are appointed. Important similarities, nonetheless, persist. In most countries with bicameral legislatures, the lower chamber tends to have more individuals who represent smaller constituencies and who serve for shorter intervals, whereas the upper chamber tends to have fewer individuals who represent larger numbers of constituencies and who serve for longer intervals. The main reason for designing legislatures in this way is to promote competing notions of representation, the topic to which we now turn.

Principles and Dilemmas of Representation

By design, the two chambers of Congress represent the people like no other branch of government. The federal judiciary is not elected—all judges are appointed. The executive branch sponsors just one election (for president and vice president) every four years—and because they can serve only two terms, presidents usually run for reelection at most once. Everyone else in the executive branch is either appointed or a civil servant. Congress, meanwhile, sponsors hundreds of elections. The public has more opportunities to evaluate members of Congress than any other group of politicians in the federal government. It should come as little surprise, then, that members of Congress are always focused on the next election.

Members of Congress share one objective: getting reelected.

Members of Congress are a diverse bunch, coming from all walks of life. But they have one thing in common. As David Mayhew, a political scientist who wrote one of the most influential books on Congress, writes, members are "single-minded seekers of reelection."[13] Every vote they cast, speech they write, argument they advance, favor they offer, and bill they sponsor is with an eye toward the next election—and the one after that, and the one after that.

Of course, members of Congress have other objectives as well. Some want to make a difference by reforming health care or pushing for prayer in public schools or cracking down on illegal immigration. Others want to direct government benefits to a particular population, such as college students, the poor, African Americans, or farmers. Others want to make names for themselves, and still others just enjoy sitting in a position of power. The mix of policy and personal objectives in Congress is as varied as the members.

To attain their individual goals, though, members must first win a seat and then hold onto it. Hence, the motivation to be reelected precedes all other motivations. As Mayhew notes, reelection "has to be the proximate goal of everyone, the goal that must be achieved over and over if other ends are to be entertained."[14]

To improve their reelection prospects, members serve their constituents.

Chapter 9 discusses the elections that determine who serves in Congress. In this chapter, we focus on what members of Congress actually do while they are in office in order to maximize their chances of winning the next election. More than anything else, successful members work hard on behalf of their **constituents**—that is, the individuals who reside within their political jurisdictions. To convince these people to vote for them, members generally support legislation that is popular in their home state or district. Thus, members from the Midwest stand up for farm subsidies, members from Michigan advance the interests of autoworkers, and representatives in Florida attend to the elderly. For each, their political lives depend upon the voting habits of these populations.

Political scientists have shown that members' electoral fortunes critically depend upon how well they represent their constituents. Members who represent liberal populations but who support conservative bills, and vice versa, are more likely to lose the next election than members who faithfully represent the interests of their constituents. The basic lesson: "out of step, out of office."[15]

Although political scientists have documented a clear link between the preferences of voters and the actions of Congress members, the exact nature of this link is less clear. It may be that individuals who share the policy objectives of most people in their districts or states are more likely to run for office; for the same reason, when they run, they are more likely to win. On the other hand, members may adjust their views according to the opinions of those citizens who will shortly decide their political fate.

It stands to reason that **incumbents**—individuals who currently hold office—have more freedom to do as they please. It turns out that over 90 percent of Congress members are reelected, and they are usually reelected by large margins. Incumbents who are confident of reelection might feel less bound by their constituents' views. We need to be careful, however, about the causal interpretations we draw from incumbent reelection rates. After all, does the fact that voters overwhelmingly approve of their representatives free them to do as they please, or are representatives reelected because they reflect the voters' views? If the latter is true, then members do not have that much freedom. When they disagree with large portions of their constituents, members may well face a tough challenge at the next election.

Beyond the positions they take on the issues of the day, members of Congress also serve their constituents through **casework**—direct assistance to individuals and groups within a district or state. The staffs that work for members of Congress will help constituents locate missing social security checks, direct them to federal agencies, and provide procedural support for dealing with these agencies, among other things. Obviously, members of Congress cannot address the individual needs of every constituent. In the House, after all, members serve roughly 600,000 voters; most senators represent many more. Still, by performing casework for at least some of these constituents, members can hope to secure their votes (as well as those of their friends and families) at the next election.

To enhance their reelection prospects, members of Congress also direct federal benefits to their home districts and states. When new legislation is being considered that is intended to clean up the nation's streams, reduce poverty, or provide health insurance to children, members of Congress work hard to ensure that their own constituents reap the benefits of these initiatives. And as we saw at the chapter's outset, this also applies to legislation designed to combat terrorism. Rather than building a comprehensive program that devotes resources to cities in direct proportion to the threat of terrorism, members of Congress built one that ensured that every district and state received a sizable chunk of the federal government's funds.

Serving constituents can mean different things.

The structural differences between the House and Senate reflect two broader conceptions of representation. According to the **delegate model of representation**, successful members of Congress share the same interests as the voters and promise to act upon them. If a majority of constituents supports affirmative action, then so will the Congress member; and if a majority subsequently opposes the same policy, that member will switch his or her position. Delegates must vote according to the expressed interests of their constituents even when their conscience or personal preferences dictate otherwise.

In contrast, according to the **trustee model of representation**, members of Congress are chosen for their judgment, experience, and skill. As Edmund Burke, an eighteenth-century Irish philosopher and member of England's Parliament, put it, voters ought to choose a legislator for "his unbiased opinion, his mature judgment, his enlightened conscience."[16] Rather than simply mirroring their constituents' opinions, trustees reflect deeply on the arguments for and against different policies before taking a position. To be sure, trustees still represent their constituents. They do so, however, by thinking about the longer-term implications that policies have both for their constituents and for the nation as a whole.

Roughly speaking, members of the House tend to act more like delegates, and members of the Senate behave more like trustees. They do so, after all, because of the electoral incentives they face. Because they face more homogenous constituents at more regular intervals, members of the House have stronger incentives to act on behalf of the public's current preferences. And because they face more heterogeneous constituents over longer periods of time, senators can reflect upon the deeper interests of a citizenry.

Not all constituents are represented equally well.

While all members have powerful incentives to represent their constituents, not all constituents are represented equally well. Instead, constituent groups who are likely to have a greater impact on a member's reelection bid tend to receive greater consideration on Capitol Hill.

Some constituents are less important because they cannot vote, and therefore have fewer opportunities to influence the outcome of an election. Consider, for instance, the differences between the elderly and children. Older Americans tend to monitor the behavior of members of Congress quite closely and to vote in high numbers. Children, by contrast, pay little attention to politics. And even if they wanted to, children cannot vote until they officially become adults at age 18. Thus, it is not surprising that members of Congress tend to work harder on behalf of the elderly than they do on behalf of children. For every federal dollar spent to reduce poverty and poor health among children, four dollars are spent to accomplish the same objectives among the elderly.[17]

The citizens who organize, fund, and participate in interest groups—see Chapter 12—also figure prominently in members' reelection strategies.[18] Through financial contributions and endorsements, interest groups can influence both the number of people who come out on Election Day and the candidates they choose. Members of Congress, therefore, have ample reasons to curry their favor. Between 2003 and 2004, interest groups contributed, on average, more than $25 million to each member's reelection campaign, up from roughly $8 million just six years prior.[19] The sheer number of interest groups lobbying Congress has also increased dramatically in the last decade, as shown in Figure 13-1.

With the upsurge in interest group activity, members of Congress have stronger incentives to act on their behalf. Sometimes members do so by voting in ways that support these groups. More often, though, the influence of interest groups is more subtle, affecting which bills Congress considers, the amendments that are made to these bills, and the speed at which members deliberate.[20] Concerns about the undue influence of interest groups have spurred some reform-minded members to push for campaign finance legislation. For more on this topic, see Chapter 9.

Members of Congress also have strong incentives to listen to their core supporters and those who can be persuaded to vote on their behalf. By contrast, members have less incentive to work on behalf of those individuals who would not, under any circumstances, vote for them. Consequentially, a Republican would likely support different kinds of policy proposals than a Democrat who represented

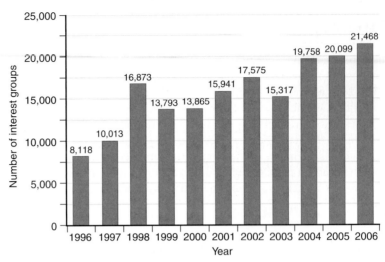

Figure 13-1. Rise in the Number of Interest Groups. The number of interest groups that lobby Congress has nearly tripled in the last decade. In 1996, about 8,000 organizations either had lobbyists of their own or paid outside firms to lobby Congress and the rest of the federal government. By 2006, more than 21,000 interest groups regularly lobbied the federal government.

Note: The figure presents the number of clients of lobbyists or lobbying firms registered with the Senate Office of Public Records under the Lobbying Disclosure Act of 1995. A client is defined as any organization or individual that compensates a person or firm for conducting lobbying activities on its behalf. Organizations that have in-house lobbyists are included. However, organizations that do not spend more than $24,500 on lobbying activities in a 6-month period are not required to register with the Office of Public Records.

Source: Senate Office of Public Records, personal communication, July 12, 2007.

the exact same district two years later, despite the fact that they both technically represented the same people.[21] The Republican representative will tend to support policies that help the district's Republican citizens, and the Democratic representative will generally try to help the district's Democratic citizens. For example, when the Republican Party secured a majority of seats in Congress after the 1994 election, Republican members, many of whom had just won seats held by Democrats, worked to increase federal insurance and loan program funding, a type of government benefit that helps the farmers, entrepreneurs, and small businesses that form the core constituency of the Republican Party.[22]

Political scientists have also examined the ways in which people of different genders, races, and incomes are represented by members of Congress. Some argue that citizens are best represented by members who have much in common with them: women are best represented by women members, African Americans by African American members, and so forth.[23] And there is something to this claim. Female members, for example, are more likely than male members to sponsor laws concerning reproductive rights, women's health, and domestic violence.[24] The composition of members' families also appears to matter. According to one study, male Congress members who have daughters are more likely to support policies that assist women than are male Congress members who have sons.[25]

If the findings from these studies apply more generally, then recent Congresses should be doing a better job than past ones of representing the full spectrum of interests around the country. As Figure 13-2 shows, members of Congress are reasonably diverse. And they are getting more so over time.

How Members Make Group Decisions

Members of Congress do not work alone. To do so, in fact, would be foolhardy. Bills that rally the support of just a handful of other members are unlikely to impress most voters. To stand with confidence before their constituents, members of Congress must find ways to work together. For a variety of reasons, however, working together can be immensely challenging.

Members of Congress often disagree with one another.

Members of Congress hail from different regions of the country. They have wildly different views about the purposes of government. They represent different genders and ethnicities. They even follow different electoral calendars. To understand how Congress functions, it is vital to recognize the diversity of its membership.

Members' different views reflect in part the districts they serve. Members serving districts in Northern California, Massachusetts, New York City, and Chicago are reliably much more liberal than are members serving districts in Eastern Oklahoma, Utah, Orange County in Southern California, and Dallas. The set of issues

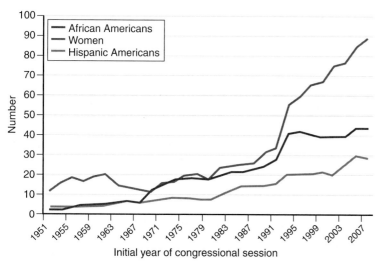

Figure 13-2. African Americans, Women, and Hispanic Americans in Congress, 1951–2007. In 1951, there were just 2 African Americans, 3 Hispanics, and 11 women serving in Congress. Two decades later, 11 African Americans, 6 Hispanics, and 11 women were serving. By 2005, there were 43 African Americans, 29 Hispanics, and 83 women in the House and Senate.

Note: Numbers include non-voting delegates.

Sources: Mildred L. Amer, Congressional Research Service Report for Congress, *Membership of the 109th Congress: A Profile* (Washington, DC: Congressional Research Service, 2005); Mildred L. Amer, CRS Report for Congress, *Black Members of the United States Congress, 1870-2007* (Washington, DC: Congressional Research Service, 2007); and Carmen E. Enciso, *Hispanic Americans in Congress, 1822-1995* (Washington, DC: Library of Congress, 1995). Updated information, through 2007, is available at: http://www.loc.gov/rr/hispanic/congress/chron.html (accessed October 18, 2007).

upon which Barbara Boxer (a Democratic senator from California) and Jim Demint (a Republican senator from South Carolina) agree is small indeed. But even senators representing the same state often disagree about public policy. In the 110th Congress, which served from 2007 to 2008, 17 states had senators from different parties.[26] Even members who represent the same state and come from the same party may disagree about all sorts of issues. For example, Arlen Specter and Rick Santorum, both Republican senators from Pennsylvania who served in the 109th Congress, differed markedly in their views on issues ranging from abortion to the war on terrorism.[27]

Even members who share a common ideological orientation may disagree about what constitutes the most pressing issue of the day. For example, both Zach Wamp and Don Young are conservative Republicans. Wamp, though, represents the third district in Tennessee, whereas Young represents the entire state of Alaska.[28] For Wamp, the key issues are the restoration of the Chickamauga Dam, the ongoing support of the Tennessee Valley Authority (one of the nation's largest government corporations), the support of tobacco farmers, and the introduction of Moccasin Bend into the National Park System. For Young, the protection of the Tongass National Forest, the protection of citizens' rights to bear arms, the regulation of the fishing industry, and the right to drill for oil in the Arctic National Wildlife Refuge stand out as the most important issues. Disagreements between Wamp and Young have considerably less to do with their political outlooks or party affiliations. Rather, they concern the importance of different issues and the legislative priorities of Congress.

There are even differences in members' concerns about reelection—the core issue that supposedly unites them. As previously mentioned, some members come from less competitive states and districts, whereas others expect to face stiffer competition at the next election. In addition, members of Congress come up for reelection at different times. Every two years all House members must face the electorate. Senators, however, serve six-year, staggered terms, with one-third up for election in each election year. Senators from the same state never come up for reelection in the same year. Because they all follow the same electoral calendar, House members therefore find it easier to coordinate their activities with one another. Senators, by contrast, must deal with the fact that every other year one-third of its members are distracted by an election, while the other two-thirds can afford to focus on the obligations of governance.

Members of Congress confront basic challenges.

Although all members of Congress care greatly about their reelection prospects, the things that help one member get reelected are not the same things that help another. Members must find ways of sorting through their differences in order to satisfy their different constituents and thereby retain their seats. Unfortunately, members of Congress—like members of any collective decision-making body—confront a set of problems that make it difficult to work together.

Collecting information Imagine the challenges facing members of Congress each session. They must keep track of changes in everything from the domestic economy to crime to international trade to transportation networks to wars around the world. Having canvassed all of these and many more policy domains, members then must identify the biggest problems facing the country and the best solutions. To do this, they need information–and lots of it.

Take, for example, the minimum wage. On the one hand, this would appear to be a simple issue, requiring members only to figure out whether they think it ought to be increased or decreased. Minimum wage legislation, however, consists of much more than a single line identifying the smallest hourly wage that employers can pay their workers around the nation. It is filled with exemptions and qualifications.[29] To complete the legislation, members must address all kinds of questions: Should there be a different minimum for teenagers and for adults? What about for those who rely on tips for much of their earnings? What about for non-citizens? Should the government provide financial assistance to industries, such as hotels and restaurants, that rely upon large numbers of low-wage workers? If so, then how much and for how long? Should new rates take effect immediately, or be phased in? What kinds of penalties should apply to employers who fail to pay at least a minimum wage? Should the rate depend upon the cost of living? If so, how should it be calculated and how often should it be updated?

There are thousands of issues that must be considered when doing something seemingly as simple as changing the minimum wage. Imagine, then, the challenges of writing laws that address U.S. trade relations with China, immigration reform with Mexico, or urban redevelopment. Individually, members of Congress would appear entirely ill-equipped for the challenge. Though they may have some expertise in a handful of issues—typically ones that directly concern their constituents—members often know very little about most substantive issues they must confront. They must first collect the information they need to write the nation's laws.[30]

Having collected the relevant information, the legislative process has just begun. To enact legislation, members must convince one another about the benefits of their preferred policies. They must bargain and negotiate with one another. And to do this effectively, members need to learn about each other's preferences, which we now know can differ dramatically. Members need to anticipate what others will accept, what they will reject, and what they are willing to compromise over. Lacking this additional information, members of Congress would find it virtually impossible to legislate.

Acting collectively It takes time and money to collect the information needed to write laws and evaluate how they will affect districts, states, and the nation at large. And because they have a relatively short period of time to build a record of accomplishments, members must decide how to allot these scarce resources. Not surprisingly, some would prefer to let other members commit the resources and then take undeserved credit for the solutions.

Though the benefits of lawmaking generalize to all members of Congress, the costs do not. Specifically, the costs fall disproportionately upon those who devote their own manpower to researching an issue, devising possible solutions, and then building the coalitions needed to enact a policy. This, though, creates a basic **collective action problem**, which arises from the mismatch of individual and group incentives. As a group, members of Congress want to devise solutions for the nation's problems; individually, though, members would prefer that others pay the costs of formulating these solutions. And because every member, individually, would prefer that other members pay these costs, there is a substantial risk of inaction.

A simple example serves to illustrate the point. Picture your typical college student housing unit: four students, four bedrooms, a common area, and a very messy kitchen. Each of the students would prefer that the kitchen be cleaned. And if all four students committed to cleaning the kitchen on any given evening, they could complete the job in relatively short order. The trouble is that each one of these students would be even better off if the other three did the work, leaving him free to watch television. Because this basic incentive incompatibility applies to all of the housemates, however, the dishes just pile higher and higher. The collective benefit of a clean kitchen is never realized because the costs fall upon the poor sap who finally rolls up his sleeves and sets to scrubbing. Herein lies the tragedy of collective action problems. All four students would be better off if they all chipped in, but because they would each be even better off if they could reap the rewards without doing the work, the dishes are never done.

So it is with lawmaking. Collectively, members of Congress would be better off if everyone contributed equally; individually, though, each member would be even better off if everyone else did the work, leaving her free to pursue her own agenda. The problem is even more acute than the simple example of a dirty kitchen supposes. Whereas the average dorm houses a handful of students, Congress houses hundreds of members, whose behavior is very difficult to monitor. Some may claim to be working on tax reform, for example, when they are actually focused on projects that will benefit one or two powerful interests in their districts. Without a clear and effective way of monitoring behavior, it is extremely difficult to overcome collective action problems.

Cycling Members have very different ideas about what constitutes good public policy. Consequentially, they often have a difficult time making final decisions about public policy. A majority of members—that is, a group of at least 50 percent—would prefer some alternative to the existing policy. A second majority— that is, a different group that contains at least some members from the first majority—will then prefer a different alternative to the one first proposed. And yet a third majority will prefer still another alternative to the one proposed second. The result, which political scientists refer to as **cycling**, is that members cannot settle upon a single change to existing policy.

In the world of lawmaking, the list of possible policy alternatives is seemingly limitless. And because it is almost always possible to identify another version of a policy that a majority might prefer, debate could go on and on without a decision ever being reached. Members therefore must figure out a way to conclude debates so laws can be written and enacted.

Imposing Structure on Congress

To effectively do their jobs, members of Congress must find ways of collecting information, resolving differences, and making sure everyone does their part. For when members are left to their own devices, too often they work at cross purposes and fail to satisfy their constituents. Rather than relying on their better natures, however, members have devised many structural solutions, making Congress, in many ways, ideally designed to deal with the problems of information, collective action, and cycling.

Committees establish a division of labor.

In both the House and Senate, members are assigned to different committees that oversee distinct policy areas. These committees draft versions of bills, hold hearings about policy issues, and investigate activities in the executive branch. The names of these committees suggest the policy issues that their members focus on: Agriculture; Armed Services; Environment and Public Works; Foreign Relations; Health,

Education, Labor, and Pensions; and Veterans' Affairs, to name but a few in the Senate.

Types of committees In the 110th Congress, there were 16 **standing committees** in the Senate and 20 in the House. Standing committees have well-defined policy jurisdictions, which do not change markedly from Congress to Congress. Standing committees also are the real workhorses of Congress, developing, writing, and updating the most important legislation. Table 13-1 lists all the standing committees in the 110th Congress. **Select committees**, by contrast, are designed to

Table 13-1. Standing Committees of the 110th Congress Committees divide the labor of lawmaking across members of the House and Senate.

HOUSE OF REPRESENTATIVES			SENATE		
COMMITTEE	SUBCOMMITTEES	MEMBERS	COMMITTEE	SUBCOMMITTEES	MEMBERS
Agriculture	6	46	Agriculture, Nutrition, and Forestry	5	21
Appropriations	12	66	Appropriations	12	29
Armed Services	7	61	Armed Services	6	25
Budget	0	39	Banking, Housing, and Urban Affairs	5	21
Education and Labor	5	49	Budget	0	23
Energy and Commerce	6	57	Commerce, Science, and Transportation	7	23
Financial Services	5	70	Energy and Natural Resources	4	23
Foreign Affairs	7	50	Environment and Public Works	6	19
Homeland Security	6	34	Finance	5	21
House Administration	0	9	Foreign Relations	7	21
Judiciary	6	40	Health, Education, Labor, and Pensions	3	21
Natural Resources	5	49	Homeland Security and Governmental Affairs	5	17
Oversight and Government Reform	5	41	Judiciary	7	19
Rules	2	13	Rules and Administration	0	19
Science and Technology	5	44	Small Business and Entrepreneurship	0	19
Small Business	5	31	Veterans' Affairs	0	15
Standards of Official Conduct	0	10			
Transportation and Infrastructure	6	7			
Veterans' Affairs	4	29			
Ways and Means	6	41			

address specific issues over shorter periods of time. Typically, they cease to exist once their members have completed their assigned task. So, for instance, in 2005 the House created the "Select Bipartisan Committee to Investigate the Preparation for and Response to Hurricane Katrina." The committee was to conduct "a full and complete investigation" of the responses of local, state, and federal governments to Hurricane Katrina. One month after filing its report, the select committee was disbanded.

While separate standing and select committees operate in the House and Senate, **joint committees** draw members from both chambers. Similar to select committees, joint committees focus on fairly narrow issues areas; but unlike select committees, joint committees are permanent. For example, the Joint Committee on the Library oversees the Library of Congress; and the Joint Committee on Taxation monitors tax policy. Joint committees tend to be weaker than either standing or select committees. Rather than develop bills that either the House or Senate subsequently considers, a process we describe in greater detail below, joint committees typically act as fact-finding entities. As such, joint committees play an important role in addressing Congress's need to collect information.

Committees consist of smaller, and more specialized, **subcommittees**. For example, the U.S. Senate Committee on Banking, Housing, and Urban Affairs contains five subcommittees: Securities, Insurance, and Investment; Financial Institutions; Housing, Transportation, and Community Development; Economic Policy; and Security and International Trade and Finance. Subcommittees allow for an even greater division of labor, which encourages the production of still more information. Because of their small size, it is easier to monitor members' behavior within subcommittees, improving the chances that all members do their share of the work.

Legislatures in other countries are organized much the same way. The organization of Britain's Parliament, in fact, looks quite a bit like Congress. Parliament consists of two chambers, the House of Commons (akin to the House of Representatives) and the House of Lords (akin to the Senate). Within each chamber are a variety of standing and select committees, whose purposes are defined by the types of policy that they write and oversee. Like Congress, Parliament has committees that focus on education, health, foreign affairs, and public works. They also have committees devoted to issues that are particularly important to the United Kingdom, such as the Northern Ireland Affairs Select Committee and the European Union Select Committee.

Committee membership On average, senators serve on four committees and representatives serve on two. Committee members develop expertise in a handful of policy areas that they can share with their colleagues, who develop expertise in other policy areas. With such a division of labor, Congress as an institution is able to collect more and better information.

Given what we know about members' concerns about reelection, it should not come as a surprise that members of Congress try to serve on committees that oversee policies that their constituents care the most about. Members who have large concentrations of veterans and active military personnel in their districts will often serve on the Veterans' Affairs or Armed Services committees; members from the Midwest who represent farming interests will tend to serve on the Agriculture committees.[31]

Other committees attract members not because of the policies that they oversee, but rather because of the power that they wield. The appropriations committees—Ways and Means in the House and Finance in the Senate—deal with tax and spending issues, which concern all sorts of government programs. Similarly, the Commerce Committee in the House provides members with lots of opportunities to influence a broad array of public policies. Joining these committees gives members prestige and influence that serves them well at the next election.

A chair, who is always from the party with a majority of seats in his or her chamber, oversees each committee and subcommittee. Because they set the agenda, schedule hearings, and call meetings, chairs often exert special influence. For much of the twentieth century, chairs were selected on the basis of **seniority**, that is, the length of time that they served in office. From the perspective of information gathering, this makes perfect sense. The person who served the longest on a committee tended to have the most expertise. Putting them in charge, therefore, would seem the ideal arrangement.

Historically though, the process of selecting chairs has attracted some controversy. For most of the post–World War II period, the Democratic Party retained control of the House and Senate. In part, this was because the South was essentially a one-party region, electing Democrats year in and year out. Because they did not face substantial competition, Southern Democrats tended to hold office for longer periods of time than Northern Democrats. Committee chairs, therefore, were usually Southern Democrats. These Southern Democrats also were much more conservative than their Northern brethren, and they often used their powers as chairs in order to kill bills that they did not like. For example, in 1962 House Rules Committee Chairman Howard W. Smith (D-VA) led a coalition of Republicans and fellow Southern Democrats in undermining legislation that would have created a Department of Urban Affairs. Southerners joined their GOP colleagues in expressing opposition to bigger government. However, the Southerners also appeared to have worried about the possibility that President John F. Kennedy, a Democrat, would nominate an African American for the new Cabinet-level post. Kennedy attempted to create the department with an executive reorganization order, which automatically would have gone into effect if neither chamber had vetoed it within 60 days. The coalition of Republicans and southern Democrats in the House of Representatives, however, swiftly rejected the plan by a vote of 262 to 150.[32]

In response to this kind of obstructionist behavior, Northern Democrats in the late 1960s and early 1970s forced through two reforms. First, the senior committee member of the majority party was no longer guaranteed to be chair, making it possible for Northern Democrats to assume control over some committees. And second, important powers devolved from committees to subcommittees, making it easier to jump-start legislative activity that a committee chair might not support. During this period, the number of subcommittees in Congress rose from roughly 40 to over 300.

Parties impose order on their members.

As the discussion of committee organization makes clear, the two major parties in the United States, Democratic and Republican, provide still more order to Congress. The parties determine who will control the various committees and subcommittees, and thus determine which core issues Congress will consider, which it will disregard, and how the debate will proceed. Through parties, coalitions in favor of one policy or another are formed. And within parties, strategies are developed to promote the policies that best serve their members' reelection prospects. Parties, in short, help to overcome the collective action and cycling problems that otherwise would cripple Congress.

Party leadership At the beginning of each term, congressional Democrats and Republicans gather to select their leadership. For Democrats, the gathering is called the **party caucus**; for Republicans, it is the **party conference**. In the House, the party with most seats elects the **Speaker of the House**, which is the only position in the House that the Constitution specifically mentions. In the Senate, the majority party selects the **majority leader**. In both chambers, the party with fewer seats selects the **minority leader**.

The Speaker of the House and the majority leader of the Senate perform many of the same functions. They preside over their chambers when they are in session, communicate with the White House about the progress of different bills, and act as congressional spokespersons. Because they decide which committees will consider which legislative proposals, they also help set the legislative agenda. And if they strongly oppose a particular proposal, they often find ways of delaying its consideration by Congress as a whole.

For the most part, the Speaker of the House plays a more important role in overseeing affairs in the House than the majority leader does in the Senate. The reason has to do with the differences in the size and culture of the two chambers. Because the House has 435 voting members while the Senate has just 100, it is much more important to have a strong leader in the House overseeing the business of the day. As a result, the majority leader usually does not have as much influence over the legislative agenda as does the Speaker of the House.

Party discipline Second in command in the House is the House majority leader, whose responsibility it is to unify the party caucus and help deliver the party's message to the public. The majority and minority party leaders of both parties have **whips** who deliver messages from the leaders to the rank-and-file members, keep track of their votes, and encourage them to stand together on key issues. The term "whip" comes from "whippers-in," whose job it is to control the dogs in a fox hunt.

The efforts of the House majority leader and whips to get party members to vote together are generally successful. Take a look at Figure 13-3. Over the last half-century, less than 30 percent of Republicans and Democrats have voted against their parties on so-called "party votes," votes on issues that are especially important to their leaders. And the percentage continues to drop. In 2004 less than 10 percent defected on party votes.

Political scientists debate about how party discipline is achieved. Some emphasize the powers of the party leadership to direct their members to vote in certain ways.[33] Leaders have a variety of means by which to punish members for defecting, such as cutting off financial aid to reelection campaigns. And by controlling the legislative agenda, party leaders can keep divisive issues from ever coming up for a vote. Moreover, these scholars argue, members benefit from party discipline, since it helps them achieve their goal of enacting laws that will satisfy constituents.

Other scholars suggest that party leaders have very little to do with the decline of party defections.[34] Instead, party members vote together because they agree with one another. These scholars argue that there is little evidence that members of Congress systematically vote against their constituents' interests in order to toe the party line. Nor should members vote this way. After all, to vote against one's constituents is to reduce one's chances of being reelected. By this account, the correlation between party positions and individual voting behavior is not causal, but simply reflects the shared views of members of the same party.

In the United States, different parties can control the legislative and executive branches of government. In some other systems of government, however, they can-

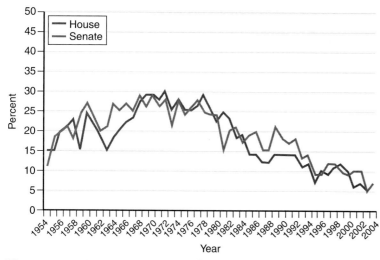

Figure 13-3. **Majority Party Defection on "Party Votes," 1954–2004.**

Since about 1970, both Democrats and Republicans in Congress vote with their party with increasing regularity.

Source: Harold W. Stanley and Richard G. Niemi, *Vital Statistics on American Politics 2007–2008* (Washington, D.C.: CQ Press, 2008), pp. 224–25.

not. In the United Kingdom, for instance, executive and legislative powers are shared by one party. The party holding the majority of seats in the House of Commons (the lower chamber of Parliament) selects the nation's prime minister from within its own ranks, and the prime minister, in turn, often uses valuable positions in his Cabinet to reward loyal party members. Furthermore, the leaders of the Labour and Conservative parties wield substantial control over the distribution of campaign funds and the list of candidates who appear on the ballots. Although individual legislators occasionally defect on party votes, such defections are rare in the United Kingdom.

Party polarization One of the most striking trends in Congress during the past 30 years has been the increase in party polarization. As members have increased their tendency to vote together with their fellow partisans, they, in turn, vote less frequently with members of the opposition party. As Figure 13-4 shows, congressional Republicans in 2004 are significantly more conservative than they were in 1970. Northern congressional Democrats are slightly more liberal than their predecessors and Southern Democrats are much more liberal—largely because conservative Southern Democrats, starting in the mid-1970s, switched parties and became Republicans.[35]

Why are Republican members of Congress more conservative, and Democratic members more liberal, than they were a generation ago? The question is especially puzzling because there is very little evidence that citizens today are any more conservative or liberal than they were in 1970. According to one recent study, the root cause of this phenomenon is the rise in inequality around America.[36] Over the last century, partisan polarization has increased along with income inequality. It remains less clear, though, that inequality and polarization are causally related. Just because the two trends move together does not mean that inequality causes polarization. The authors of this study, in fact, recognize that the opposite might be

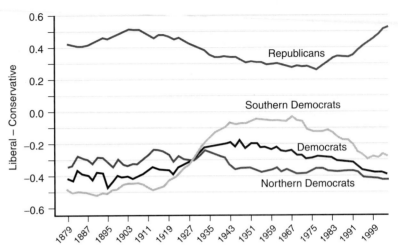

Figure 13-4. Polarization of Democratic and Republican Members of Congress, 1879–2006. The two major parties are more polarized today than they have been in almost a century.

Source: Keith T. Poole and Howard Rosenthal, "House 1879–2006: Party Means on Liberal-Conservative Dimension," November 20, 2006, www.voteview.com (accessed July 17, 2007).

true—polarization might generate inequality. They characterize the relationship between the two phenomena as one of "back and forth causality."

Although the rift between the Republican and Democratic parties in the United States has grown starker in recent years, polarization is not an overarching trend within democracies worldwide. In fact, a number of countries sustain three or more parties, offering different platforms in order to provide representation to diverse opinions about key political issues. The particular mix of parties in these democracies is constantly changing. Israel provides a recent and prominent example. In 2005, amidst disagreements over his proposal to evacuate Jewish settlements in the Palestinian territories, then-prime minister Ariel Sharon withdrew from the conservative Likud Party and, with Shimon Peres of the liberal Labor Party, formed the backbone of a more centrist party called Kadima. Other democracies—such as France, Germany, and Canada—also sustain multi-party systems that offer voters wider options than does the United States.

Staff and support agencies help collect and analyze information.

Members of Congress are assisted by roughly 11,000 staffers who perform all sorts of tasks, many of which concern the collection and analysis of information. On average, each senator has about 40 staffers working for him, and each House member has 17.[37] Some staffers work in a member's Washington, D.C., office, and others work back in the member's district or state. Those in D.C. tend to research public policies, write up briefs, draft proposals, organize hearings, and interact with lobbyists. They also communicate with staffers for other members, helping to build coalitions in support of various policy initiatives. Staffers back home, meanwhile, interact with constituents about their concerns, their interests, and their ideas. These staffers then communicate this information back to the D.C. office.

Members also have access to several administrative agencies that provide vital information about public policy matters. The Congressional Research Service (CRS), established in 1914, handles hundreds of thousands of requests each year from members seeking information. Employees at CRS also take inventory of all the bills introduced in Congress, and track their progress through the legislative process. The Government Accountability Office (GAO) also studies policy issues upon congressional request. Established in 1921, the GAO acts as an investigatory body that members who wish to know more about the spending habits of bureaucratic agencies can use. The Congressional Budget Office (CBO), established in 1974, provides members with information about the costs of policies that they are considering, the economic implications of different budget proposals, and the general state of the economy.

Has Congress Abdicated Its War-Making Authority?

The Question

The Constitution gives most war-making powers to Congress. Article I says that Congress shall have the power to declare war, raise and support armies, appropriate funds for war, and regulate the conduct of ongoing wars. By contrast, the war powers granted to the president are much shorter. Indeed, those Article II passages that refer explicitly to foreign policy merely identify the president as the commander in chief and authorize him to "receive ambassadors and other public ministers."

Today, though, the practice of war would not appear to follow the principles laid out in the Constitution. Most decisions about war are made by the president. And rarely does Congress formally restrict the president's ability to wage war abroad. Has Congress abdicated its war making powers? How do we know?

Why It Matters

There is no greater government power than the ability to send citizens abroad to fight, kill, and perhaps die. And for precisely this reason, the Founders worried a great deal about which branch of government would have the authority to wage war. If they vested such unmatched authority in the president, the Founders worried that the system of checks and balances might one day collapse. As John Jay recognized in *Federalist 5*, "absolute monarchs will often make war when their nations are to get nothing by it, but for purposes and objects merely personal, such as a thirst for military glory, revenge for personal affronts, ambition, or private compacts to aggrandize or support their particular families or partisans." The Founders therefore looked to the legislative branch, which could be expected to better represent the will of the people in making decisions about war.

For much of U.S. history, this is exactly how decisions about whether to go to war were made. From the founding of the Republic to the mid-twentieth century, most major uses of force were approved by Congress. In the last half-century, though, the president has made most decisions involving war, and Congress has been pushed to the sidelines. If the Founders were right that war-making powers should not be entrusted to a president, then citizens ought to be greatly concerned about contemporary practice.

Investigating the Answer

One way to determine whether Congress has abdicated its war-making powers is to examine the declarations and actions of presidents and members of Congress. Who is setting the agenda, and who is following?

The answer appears quite clear: Congress has given up its war-making authority. After all, not since World War II has Congress formally declared war. It has authorized some wars (including the Vietnam, Gulf, and Iraq wars) but not others (including the Korean War and conflicts in Panama, Kosovo, Bosnia, and Haiti).[38] Congress also has been reluctant to exercise its formal legislative and appropriations powers to influence wars that are under way. Though it has the constitutional authority to cut funding for a war, issue regular reports about a war's progress, and demand a withdrawal, Congress rarely takes advantage of these options—even when wars are unpopular.

For example, in 1973, frustrated with the progress of the Vietnam War, members of Congress attempted to reassert their authority by passing the War Powers

Resolution, which gave the president 60 to 90 days to secure formal authorization of a military deployment before troops would have to be withdrawn. Advocates believed the resolution would stop presidential incursions on congressional war powers and put members of Congress back in charge of decisions involving the use of military force. Instead, every president since the resolution was passed has refused to recognize its constitutionality. These presidents have launched one military initiative after another without securing congressional authorization. Only once, for Lebanon in 1983, was the War Powers clock even started; and then the president was granted an 18-month grace period. Rather than re-establishing Congress's constitutional role in matters involving war, says Louis Fisher, the resolution "was a sellout, a surrender."[39]

More recently, political scientists have begun to examine subtle ways in which Congress nonetheless influences decisions about war. Though the president makes the case for war, members of Congress are not altogether silent. During the first three years of the Iraq War, for instance, members gave 5,000 speeches on the floors of the House and Senate. Such speeches, political scientists have shown, can have a profound impact on the ways in which the media covers a war, influencing the tone and content of news stories. And by influencing the media, these speeches also can affect public opinion.[40]

It also is difficult to interpret Congress's apparent reluctance to exercise its formal war-making powers. It could reveal weakness or strength. If presidents recognize that Congress is about to limit their war-making power, they may adjust their actions accordingly. In that case, congressional action may no longer be needed. Rather than demonstrating weakness, then, congressional silence sometimes might testify to the ongoing importance of the legislative branch in matters involving war.

Recent research also demonstrates that the partisan composition of Congress has important implications for the president's ability to wage war. Political scientists have observed the following patterns in military deployments during the post–World War II era: presidents whose party holds a large numbers of seats in the House and Senate tend to wage war more often than those whose party holds relatively few seats; and presidents who enjoy lots of support within Congress tend to take military action more quickly.[41] The checks that Congress places on the president, then, are not constant. Rather, they vary according to the level of support that the president has.

The Bottom Line

The president's power to make decisions involving war has expanded dramatically during the past half-century and congressional involvement in decisions involving war has declined. Congress, however, still represents an important check—arguably the most important check, at least domestically—on presidential war powers. The fact that military deployments tend to vary with the strength of the president's party in Congress says two important things about the domestic politics of war. First, Congress is a collection of diverse individuals with different assessments of the national interest and the value of war. And second, when weighing how presidents conduct war or any other public policy, one must carefully monitor the ways in which they anticipate, and attempt to ward off, efforts by members of Congress to limit their authority.

Lawmaking

Members of Congress perform a variety of functions. As discussed in more detail in Chapter 16, they hold hearings and launch investigations to monitor goings-on in the executive branch. They help educate the public about the major issues of the day. They communicate with constituents and help resolve their problems. The single most important function that Congress serves, however, is to write the nation's laws.

The legislative process is long.

To become a law, a bill must travel a long road, which is outlined in Figure 13-5. To begin the process, a **sponsor** introduces a bill into either the House or Senate. Any member of Congress can serve as a bill's sponsor. A bill can originate in either chamber, and sometimes equivalent bills are introduced simultaneously to both.

Subsequently, the bill must be referred to the appropriate committee for consideration. In the House, the Speaker decides which committee will take up the bill. In the Senate, the bill is assigned to a committee by the chamber's presiding officer, either the vice president or, more commonly, the president pro tempore. The president pro tempore is the most senior member of the majority party.

Bills typically are assigned to the committees that oversee the relevant policy domain. For example, bills on foreign conflicts are generally assigned to the Foreign Relations committee in the Senate and the Foreign Affairs committee in the House. Some bills are assigned to more than one committee—a practice called multiple-referral.[42] In 2005, for example, a proposal to reauthorize the Office of National Drug Control Policy, which oversees federal policy on illicit drug use, manufacturing, and trafficking, was referred to five House committees: Government Reform, Energy and Commerce, Judiciary, Education, and the Permanent Select Committee on Intelligence.

After assignment to one or more committees, a bill then is assigned to one or more subcommittees. The substance of a bill is typically first considered at the subcommittee level. Members of subcommittees carefully review the bill, holding hearings and conducting research on how it will likely affect their constituents and the nation as a whole. In a process called **markup**, members re-write portions of the bill, delete others, and add still more. Once satisfied, the members then report the bill back to the full committee, whose members review the subcommittee's work and offer revisions of their own.

What happens next depends upon which chamber is considering the bill. In the Senate, bills move straight from the committee of origin to the Senate floor, where the entire assembly of senators is given an opportunity to debate the merits of the proposed legislation. In the House, though, most bills coming out of committee are referred to the Rules Committee.[43] The Rules Committee decides how a bill will be debated on the floor by the entire membership of the House. It decides when the bill will go to the floor, how long members will debate the bill, and what kinds of amendments (if any) can be offered. When assigning an **open rule** to a bill, the Rules Committee allows for a wide range of amendments. Under a **closed rule**, the number and types of possible amendments are more restricted. Since bills assigned under an open rule can be altered quite significantly on the floor, supporters typically prefer a closed rule. Having completed its business, the Rules Committee then refers the bill to the House floor.

On the floors of both the House and Senate, members typically give speeches about the bill, offer amendments (rules permitting, at least in the House), and eventually vote. To pass the House, a bill must receive the support of a majority of voting members. In the Senate, though, the threshold is somewhat higher. Technically, only a majority is needed to pass a bill. Any senator, though, may choose to **filibuster** a bill, which allows for indefinite debate. To end a filibuster—a process

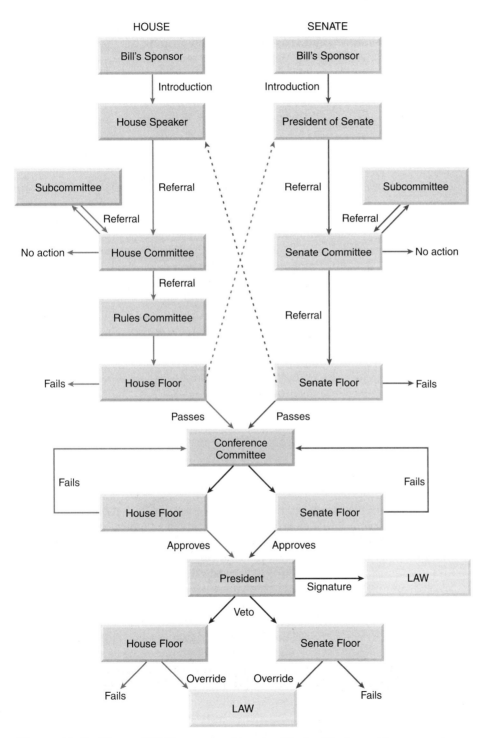

HOUSE SENATE

Bill's Sponsor Bill's Sponsor

Introduction Introduction

House Speaker President of Senate

Subcommittee Subcommittee

Referral Referral

Referral Referral

No action ← House Committee Senate Committee → No action

Referral Referral

Rules Committee

Referral

Fails ← House Floor Senate Floor → Fails

Passes Passes

Conference Committee

Fails Fails

House Floor Senate Floor

Approves Approves

President → Signature → LAW

Veto

House Floor Senate Floor

Fails ← Override Override → Fails

LAW

Figure 13-5. How a Bill Becomes a Law (or Not). The lawmaking process is long, and most introduced bills fail to become laws.

called invoking **cloture**—a supermajority of 60 votes is needed. If a majority of senators, but less than 60, support a filibustered bill, the bill will die.[44]

To become law, a bill must pass both chambers of Congress. But having gone through markups in subcommittees and committees and then having been subject to further amendments on the floor, Senate and House versions of the same bill often look quite different from one another at this stage. During the spring of 2007, for example, Congress considered an appropriations bill that would significantly restrict the president's discretion to wage war in Iraq. The House version included language that would establish a fixed timetable for the withdrawal of U.S. troops, while the Senate version did not. Such differences must be resolved before a bill becomes law.

Often, senators and representatives reconcile their differences informally. Party leaders play an important role in such negotiations, recommending elements of a bill to keep, to discard, and to amend. More formally, appointed members of each chamber serve on a **conference committee**, which has the job of producing a compromise version of the bill. Simple bills may have a relatively small conference committee, while complex and significant legislation may have hundreds of members serving on the conference committee. If conference committee members can come to an agreement—and sometimes they cannot—they send a revised version of the bill to the floors of the House and Senate, where it is subsequently voted on.

If the bill passes the House and Senate, it travels down Pennsylvania Avenue to the White House. The president can sign the bill, in which case it automatically becomes law. Alternatively, the president may **veto**, or reject, the legislation. Members can respond to a veto in three ways. First, they can refuse to reconsider the bill, in which case it dies. Second, they can make concessions to win over the president. In this case, both the House and Senate then vote on a new version of the bill, which is sent back to the president. Third, members can try to override the president's veto by securing the support of two-thirds of both houses. If they fail, the veto is sustained. Members of Congress may also select a combination of approaches. They might first write a revised version of a bill; then, if the president vetoes the bill again, they might try to override him. If this fails, they may simply give up and move on to other issues.

Most bills are not enacted into law.

Traveling down this long legislative road, it is not surprising that bills often hit a pothole and veer onto an embankment. There are, after all, plenty of opportunities for a strategic politician, either working alone or with others, to derail a bill. Committees, minority factions in either the House or Senate, and the president himself can undermine the prospects of even those bills that enjoy the support of congressional majorities.

Let's begin with committees. Committee members who are assigned a bill they oppose could try to tailor the bill more to their liking or could refuse to do anything at all and "table" the bill indefinitely. This **gate-keeping authority** can give committees substantial power over the kinds of bills that come before the floor of either chamber. Despite the fact that a majority of either the House or Senate, presumably, would like to see at least some of these bills enacted, in most congresses, upwards of 80 percent of all introduced bills never make it out of committee.[45]

With just 40 votes in the Senate, opponents can kill a bill—even if 59 senators and all 435 members of the House prefer to see it enacted. The filibuster is a powerful tool for minorities within Congress to check the powers of majorities, and minorities are making increasing use of it. During the first half of the twentieth century, only a handful of bills each congressional session were subject to a filibuster. Beginning in the early 1970s, however, the average number increased to 22; during the 1990s, it increased to over 40.[46] Throughout this period, a filibuster signaled a bill's demise, as supporters almost always failed to invoke cloture.

Historically, the filibuster has been used to forestall congressional action on some of the most important issues the nation has ever faced. During the 1940s and '50s, for example, legislation to protect the political rights of African Americans was virtually impossible to enact because of the filibusters waged by Southern Democrats. Though majorities in both chambers and the president supported such legislation decades prior to passage of the 1964 and 1965 Civil Rights Acts, they could not muster the votes needed to invoke cloture. "The South conquered the Senate on this issue the way Cortez conquered Mexico," said a former legislative aid to Senator Paul Douglas, a vocal supporter of the civil rights movement. "What happened in the Senate was that there was lots of debate, long and prolonged talk, whose purpose was designed to prevent a vote. That was the purpose of the filibuster. It wasn't to educate the public, it was to prevent a vote on Civil Rights."[47] As a consequence, legislative gridlock on the issue persisted across four presidential administrations.[48]

The president can often thwart the general interests of majorities in both chambers of Congress, as well. If either chamber fails to override a presidential veto, a proposed bill fails to become law. During the nation's history, presidents have used this power with greater and greater frequency to influence the content of legislation. During the first half of the nineteenth century presidents tended to use the veto power sparingly, and then only to ward off congressional efforts to usurp executive powers. By the middle of the twentieth century, however, presidents were not at all shy about vetoing bills they objected to on policy grounds. Not surprisingly, the vast majority of these vetoes were sustained. Almost every president has succeeded in having more than 75 percent of his vetoes upheld in Congress.[49]

Clearly, lawmaking is not easy, and most bills are not enacted into law. As Figure 13-6 shows, between 1981 and 2004 roughly 10 percent of bills introduced

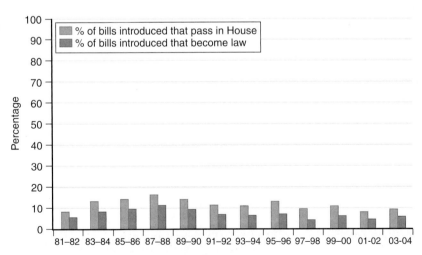

Figure 13-6. Success Rates for Bills Introduced in the House. The vast majority of bills introduced to Congress do not make it through the House; an even lower percentage of bills actually become law.

Source: *Resume of Congressional Activity*, available online at: http://www.senate.gov/pagelayout/reference/two_column_table/Resumes.htm (accessed April 20, 2008).

421

to the House passed; and even fewer were enacted into law. Though the figures fluctuate somewhat, enactment rates peaked at 11.4 percent (in 1987–1988), and bottomed out at 4.8 percent (in 1997–1998). Almost always, the safest bet on a bill's prospects is failure.

CaseStudy: Immigration Reform in 2007

Today the Census Bureau reports more foreign-born residents—33 million—than ever before in its history. Bush administration officials estimate that 12 million are in the country illegally, with that number growing by an average of 400,000 per year. Moreover, over seven million of these illegal immigrants are employed, accounting for nearly 5 percent of the country's civilian labor force and constituting substantial portions of such industries as construction and agriculture.[50]

In his 2007 State of the Union address, President George W. Bush proposed an overhaul of immigration rules, "without amnesty and without animosity," as one of four domestic-policy priorities for the remainder of his second term. Though several previous immigration reform efforts had failed, Bush appeared hopeful that things this time would be different. In the 2006 midterm elections, control of the House and Senate switched to the Democrats, who looked more favorably upon the kinds of immigration reforms that Bush supported. During the spring, Bush sent Commerce Secretary Carlos Gutierrez and Homeland Security Secretary Michael Chertoff to undertake closed-door deliberations with a bipartisan group of senators.

After three months of deliberation, Gutierrez, Chertoff, and members of Congress produced a draft bill. The proposed Comprehensive Immigration Reform Act of 2007 downplayed deportation and instead offered a path to citizenship for illegal immigrants. In an attempt to appease conservatives, the draft also outlined changes in the criteria for processing visa applications, created a business-backed guest worker program, and promised to bolster enforcement of immigration laws.

Senate Majority Leader Harry Reid agreed to introduce the bill directly to the Senate floor, bypassing the Judiciary Committee. Supporters mustered 66 votes in favor of the most controversial portion of the bill, which offered legal status to most illegal immigrants. But Reid pulled the bill from the floor on June 7, after three successive votes for cloture failed and only seven Republicans agreed to close debate. On June 26, the Senate voted 64-35 to reconsider the proposal, but two days later another cloture motion fell short, killing the bill.

Experts generally agree that the current immigration system is broken. Why, then, did the president's and Congress's reform efforts falter? A number of reasons emerge. For starters, the bill's opponents expressed their views more forcefully than did its proponents. As one researcher put it, the bill was "born an orphan in terms of popular support."[51] A substantial portion of Americans did not feel strongly about the issue. Illegal immigrants could not vote, and their American employers, who had much to gain from the legislation, were not a major part of many politicians' voting constituencies. Opponents, by contrast, let their voices be heard, making well over 250,000 contacts with U.S. senators during the run-up to the June 28 vote.[52]

Disagreements between Democrats and Republicans about the immigration issue also made it difficult for Congress to enact needed reform. To make the U.S. economy less of a magnet for undocumented workers, both sides agreed to help employers fill jobs with government approved temporary laborers. However, many Republicans insisted that those workers eventually must leave, while many Democrats wanted to allow them to stay and become citizens. In an effort to strike a deal, the Senate draft outlined a path to citizenship for illegal immigrants as well as a number of hurdles, such as fines, waiting periods, and a merit-based application system. Nonetheless, most Republicans rejected anything that resembled amnesty, while Democrats balked, insisting that the U.S. visa system should do more to keep immigrant families together rather than to attract high-skilled workers.[53]

The immigration debates also revealed divisions within the two major parties. The desire of most Democrats to naturalize immigrants put them at odds with labor unions, while the inclination of most Republicans to send workers home pitted them against business owners. Labor unions maintained that foreign laborers drive down wages for American workers, while businesses argued that sending these laborers home would disrupt operations and increase production costs.[54]

A weakened presidency may also have contributed to the bill's failure. With low approval ratings, a controversial war in Iraq, and poor results in the 2006 midterm elections, President Bush could not overcome the objections of Republican members of Congress. As one moderate Republican dissenter, Representative Steve Pearce of New Mexico, put it: "I trust him, but I'm not going to vote for the bill as it currently stands. Out here, we have a saying, 'Trust your neighbor, but brand your cattle,' and the president will understand that."[55]

Immigration reform, then, ended in collapse rather than compromise. Members of both parties, as well as the executive and legislative branches, bemoaned the failure but were unable to prevent it. Without highlighting his own party's role in killing the bill, President Bush expressed disappointment in Congress's "failure to act."[56]

But Senate Majority Leader Harry Reid may have summarized it best, saying, "The big winner today was obstruction; the big winner today was inaction."[57]

ThinkingCritically

1. How does the fact that illegal immigrants cannot vote figure into the politics of immigration reform?

2. Why were some of the president's strongest critics members of his own party?

Laws, nonetheless, *are* enacted.

Just because lawmaking is difficult does not mean that it is impossible. In a typical year, Congress enacts several hundred laws. Though most of these laws concern rather mundane affairs, at least some have profound policy consequences. According to one study that categorized legislation into four different categories of significance, Congress each year enacts roughly 5 "landmark" laws, 6 "major" laws, 36 "ordinary" ones, and no less than 314 "minor" laws. Most bills may die somewhere along the legislative process, but many make it to the end.

Political scientists have tried to determine the mix of political factors most likely to result in successful legislation. One of the most powerful predictors is the strength of the majority party's control in the House and Senate. When Democrats or Republicans control both chambers of Congress by wide margins, they find it much easier to overcome the various institutional challenges that derail so many bills. The single most productive Congress during the last half-century operated from 1965 to 1966. During this period, when Democrats maintained a whopping 295 seats in the House and 68 in the Senate, Congress enacted such landmark legislation as Medicare and Medicaid, the Immigration Act, the Elementary and Secondary Education Act (ESEA), the Housing and Urban Development Act, the Voting Rights Act, the Freedom of Information Act, and the National Traffic and Motor Vehicle Safety Act, to name but a few.

Some laws come up for reconsideration every few years. And if Congress fails to approve these laws again, they cease to exist. Though most laws live on indefinitely, laws with so-called **sunset provisions** must be re-authorized after a specified number of years. The 2001 No Child Left Behind Act, the enactment of which is described in some detail in Chapter 14, was a re-authorization of the 1965 ESEA Act, which must be reconsidered by Congress every seven years. Given that existing laws maintain programs that are already up and running, that they have received political support in the past, and that they come up for formal consideration in a specified year, they are more likely to pass than other legislation.

The Appropriations Process

The work of Congress is not complete after it enacts a law. Congress subsequently must commit funds so that the law can be set in motion. Every year, Congress uses money from the Treasury Department to fund federal agencies and programs.[58] According to Article I, Section 9, of the Constitution, "no money shall be drawn from the treasury, but in consequence of appropriations made by law." But besides stipulating that "a regular statement and account of receipts and expenditures of all public monies shall be published from time to time," the Constitution has left most of the specifics to the legislature itself.

Spending is a two-step process.

Two steps must be taken for monies to make their way to different agencies and programs. First, these programs and agencies must be **authorized** by the legislation which serves as the legal basis for their continued operation. Subsequently, funds must be **appropriated**, which results in monies being sent to federal agencies and programs. Authorization committees help determine the kinds of programs within their legislative jurisdiction that will be funded; appropriations committees determine the exact amounts of monies to be disbursed.

In principle, authorizations and appropriations are kept separate in order to reduce the chances that members of Congress will use federal monies to alter the actual operations of federal agencies and programs. In practice, though, the distinction between authorizations and appropriations often blurs. In part, this is because appropriations committee members make quite a habit of using limitations on the use of funds as a way to legislate indirectly. The phrase "none of the funds shall be used for . . ." has become an increasingly prominent feature in appropriations bills, effectively changing policy in spite of the prohibition against writing legislation in appropriations committees.[59]

Non-appropriations committees, meanwhile, also use authorizing legislation to grant permanent budget authority to programs and agencies. As a result, a sizeable fraction of each year's federal budget is dedicated to mandatory spending (often called entitlements) on these past obligations. The largest entitlements include such massive programs as Social Security, Medicare, and Medicaid, all of which are discussed at length in Chapter 17. The remainder of the budget—that is, the portion not already promised elsewhere and therefore available for discretionary spending on new obligations—is the subject of deliberations within the appropriations committees.[60] Over time, a rising tide of entitlements has steadily shrunk the discretionary portion of the budget, reducing it to approximately 40 percent in fiscal year 2005.[61] Given that the federal budget is well over $2 trillion, however, this still leaves appropriations committees with a considerable amount of money to disburse.

Members also use **earmarks** to bypass executive agencies altogether and direct funds straight to their constituents. According to one watch-dog organization, Congress disclosed over 11,000 earmarks worth almost $15 billion in the 2008 fiscal year.[62] Texas alone received $2.2 billion in earmarks, including $294,000 for a Houston zoo program and $22 million for an Army gymnasium near El Paso.[63] Facing substantial criticism for funding these "pork barrel" projects, the House in January 2007 passed new rules requiring public lists of every earmark, the recipient's name and address, and the individual who requested it.[64] Nevertheless, the practice is unlikely to disappear in the near future. Earmarks enable members of Congress to deliver benefits directly to their constituents, to take decisions out of the hands of executive officials, and to make bills more popular and passable.

Appropriations come in three forms.

There are three main types of appropriations. "Regular appropriations" are the main source of revenues that are disbursed to agencies and programs. Regular appropriations contain three standard features: an enacting clause that designates the fiscal year for which funds are given, a breakdown of budget authority by accounts, and general provisions that apply to all of the accounts. Small agencies might possess only one account, but larger ones usually are financed by several distinct accounts, designated with names such as "procurement" or "salaries and expenses." In general, agencies can "reprogram" funds (shift budget authority from one activity to another within a single account) by going through the proper notification and oversight channels. However, they cannot "transfer" funds (shift budget authority from one account to another) without statutory authorization.

A second type of appropriations is a **continuing resolution**, which maintains funding when regular appropriations have not been set by the close of the fiscal year on October 1. Continuing resolutions have become quite common. In fact, between 1977 and 2006, Congress and the president completed all of the regular appropriations on schedule only four times.[65] Traditionally, continuing resolutions were brief measures listing the agencies that had not yet received their regular funding and providing temporary assistance at the previous year's level or the president's budget request, whichever was lower. Today, however, continuing resolutions increasingly include omnibus measures that cover several of the regular appropriations bills at once.

Congress also provides **supplemental appropriations** when regular appropriations do not cover certain activities or are deemed insufficient in another respect. In order to evade spending caps, Congress sometimes designates supplements as emergency funds. Much of the Iraq War, in fact, has been funded not through regular defense appropriations, but instead through a series of supplemental appropriations.

The appropriations process resembles, but does not mirror, the legislative process.

The process of appropriating federal funds looks quite a bit like the legislative process. Suggested appropriations are debated and marked up within committees, considered on the floors of the House and Senate, reconciled across chambers, and eventually sent to the president. In two important respects, however, the appropriations process differs from the lawmaking process.

First, appropriations are purposefully streamlined. Whereas a failure to legislate may disappoint key constituencies, a failure to appropriate funds can bring the federal government to a grinding halt. And because appropriations are required every year, members of Congress have a vested interest in minimizing the procedural roadblocks—such as the Senate filibuster—that they are likely to encounter.

Second, the appropriations process is supposed to follow a strict timetable. The president initiates the process by submitting his annual budget proposal to Congress on or before the first Monday in February. The full House and Senate appropriations committees then have the option of conducting overview hearings to discuss the proposal with the Office of Management and Budget. From February to April, agencies meet with the relevant appropriations subcommittees to justify the difference between their newly requested amounts and the previous year's allotments. By April 15, Congress passes a resolution that determines the federal budget for the next five fiscal years and allocates that year's budget among all of its committees.

In May and June, the House chair, subcommittees, and, lastly, the full appropriations committee mark up the proposals, reporting regular bills to the entire House by July. The House debates, considers amendments, passes the bills, and sends them to the Senate, which passes the bills (perhaps with amendments) before the August congressional recess. In September, members of both chambers' appropriations committees hold conferences to resolve any remaining differences. Usually the House considers the conference report first, and the Senate decides whether to accept or reject the House's report. Once the two chambers have settled on the final appropriations bills, they are sent to the president, who has ten days to sign or veto them in their entirety.

In practice, Congress and the president rarely abide by this strict schedule. In some years the legislature does not pass the budget resolution by the April 15 deadline, delaying transmittal of explicit spending ceilings to the appropriations committees. In fact, in fiscal years 1999, 2003, and 2006, Congress did not complete the resolution at all.[66] Rather than responding to the House's passed bills, the Senate sometimes creates its own proposals, which are inserted into the House bills as "amendments." Hampered by the August recess, the chambers might not resolve their differences by October 1. Last but not least, the president could kill the bill, either explicitly or, if Congress has adjourned, by taking no action within the ten-day timeframe. In December 1995, for example, Bill Clinton vetoed the reconciliation bill that would have enacted Republican-backed tax cuts and curtailed spending on social programs. When Congress failed to override the president's veto, portions of the federal government temporarily shut down.

SUMMARY

► Above all, members of Congress want to be reelected. And to be reelected, they must adequately represent the interests of their constituents. It is not always clear, though, what exactly this requires. Depending upon whether members follow a trustee or delegate model of representation, their relationship with their constituents will differ dramatically. Moreover, members do not represent all constituents equally. Depending upon whether they vote, they are organized, they are Democrats or Republicans, and their demographic profile, constituents receive more or less representation by the member of Congress who serves their district or state.

► Members of Congress have different interests, priorities, and world views. To build a record of accomplishments that will serve them well at the next election, members of Congress must effectively navigate these differences. Additionally, they must overcome problems of information, collective action, and cycling that emerge when decisions require the participation of multiple members.

► Fortunately, as an institution Congress is designed to reduce the problems that regularly confront collective decision-making bodies. Members of Congress have staffs that help collect information. They serve on committees and subcommittees that establish a division of labor. And most members belong to one of the two dominant parties, which provide further structure.

► The lawmaking process is long and difficult. To become a law, a bill must pass through multiple committees and subcommittees in both the House and Senate, the floors of both chambers, and a conference committee, before it lands on the president's desk for signature. Even then, though, the president may veto the bill, in which case it returns to Congress for reconsideration. Not surprisingly, most proposed bills fail to become law. Nonetheless, Congress does manage to enact laws on a regular basis—sometimes because its members agree about the solution to a particular problem, and sometimes because the business of the day (appropriations and reauthorizations) requires them to set about finishing the task.

► Because budgets must be approved every year, the authorization and appropriations processes are easier to navigate than the legislative process. Some of the roadblocks to lawmaking are eliminated; the budget has a permanent place on the congressional agenda; and the processes themselves are routinized. Still, delays are common. And increasingly, Congress has had to rely upon continuing and supplemental appropriations to keep the government running.

KEY TERMS

appropriations, p. 000
authorizations, p. 000
bicameral, p. 000
casework, p. 000
closed rule, p. 000
cloture, p. 000
collective action problem, p. 000
conference committee, p. 000
constituents, p. 000
continuing resolution, p. 000
cycling, p. 000
delegate model of representation, p. 000
earmarks, p. 000
filibuster, p. 000
gate-keeping authority, p. 000
impeachment, p. 000
incumbent, p. 000
joint committees, p. 000

majority leader, p. 000
markup, p. 000
minority leader, p. 000
open rule, p. 000
party caucus, p. 000
party conference, p. 000
select committees, p. 000
seniority, p. 000
Speaker of the House, p. 000
sponsor, p. 000
standing committee, p. 000
subcommittees, p. 000
sunset provision, p. 000
supplemental appropriations, p. 000
trustee model of representation, p. 000
veto, p. 000
whips, p. 000

SUGGESTED READINGS

R. Douglas Arnold. 1992. *The Logic of Congressional Action*. New Haven, CT: Yale University Press. Explores how legislation emerges from the individual incentives of members of Congress and the nature of different public policy problems.

Richard Fenno. 2002. *Homestyle: House Members in Their Districts*, new ed. New York: Longman. A classic examination of the relationship between members of Congress and their constituents.

David Mayhew. 2004. *Congress: The Electoral Connection*, 2nd ed. New Haven, CT: Yale University Press. The classic statement on how members' concerns about reelection help explain their behavior in Congress.

Walter Oleszek. 2007. *Congressional Procedures and the Policy Process*, 7th ed. Washington, D.C.: Congressional Quarterly Press. Summarizes the rules and institutions that make up Congress.

Allen Schick. 2007. *The Federal Budget: Politics, Policy, Process*, 3rd Edition. Washington, D.C.: Brookings Institution Press. Provides a comprehensive overview of the appropriations process.

Charles Stewart. 2001. *Analyzing Congress*. New York: W.W. Norton and Company. Surveys the ways in which individual members act strategically to accomplish their objectives within Congress.

bicameral an institution consisting of two chambers.

impeachment performed by the House of Representatives, the act of charging government officials with "treason, bribery, or other high crimes and misdemeanors." The Senate, then, has the responsibility of deciding whether to actually convict and remove the president.

constituents the people who reside within an elected official's political jurisdiction.

incumbent the individual in an election who currently holds the contested office; as distinct from the challenger, who seeks to remove the incumbent from power.

casework the direct assistance that members of Congress give to individuals and groups within a district or state.

delegate model of representation the type of representation by which representatives are elected to do the bidding of the people who elected them; representatives are "delegates" in that they share the same policy positions as the voters and promise to act upon them.

trustee model of representation the type of representation by which representatives are elected to do what they think is best for their constituents.

collective action problem a problem that arises when individuals' incentives lead them to avoid taking actions that are best for the group as a whole, and that they themselves would like to see accomplished.

cycling a phenomenon that occurs when multiple decision-makers must decide among multiple options and cannot agree on a single course of action.

standing committee permanent committees with well defined, relatively fixed policy jurisdictions that develop, write, and update important legislation.

select committees temporary committees that are created to serve a specific purpose.

joint committees committees made up of members of both chambers of Congress to conduct special investigations or studies.

subcommittees smaller organizational units within a committee that specialize in particular segments of the committee's responsibilities.

seniority the length of time a legislator has served in office.

party caucus the gathering of all Democratic members of the House or Senate.

party conference the gathering of all Republican members of the House or Senate.

Speaker of the House the person who presides over the House and serves as the chamber's official spokesperson.

majority leader the individual in each chamber who manages the floor; in the Senate, he or she is the most powerful member in the chamber; in the House, he or she is the chief lieutenant of the Speaker.

minority leader the individual who speaks on behalf of the party that controls the smaller number of seats in each chamber.

whips designated members of Congress who deliver messages from the party leaders, keep track of members' votes, and encourage members to stand together on key issues.

sponsor the member(s) of Congress who introduces a bill.

markup the process by which the members of a committee or a subcommittees re-write, delete, and add portions of a bill.

open rule the terms and conditions applied to a particular bill that allow members of Congress to make a wide range of amendments to it.

closed rule the terms and conditions applied to a particular bill that restrict the types of amendments that can be made to it.

filibuster a procedure by which senators delay or prevent action on a bill by making long speeches and engaging in unlimited debate.

cloture a mechanism by which 60 or more senators can end a filibuster and cut off debate.

conference committee a committee made up of members of both chambers that is responsible for ironing out the differences between House and Senate versions of a bill.

veto the president's rejection of a bill passed by both chambers of Congress, which prevents the bill from becoming law.

gate-keeping authority the power to decide whether a particular proposal or policy change will be considered.

sunset provision a condition of a law that requires it to be reauthorized after a certain number of years.

authorizations the granting of legal authority to operate federal programs and agencies.

appropriations the granting of funds to operate authorized federal programs and agencies.

earmarks federal funds that support specific local projects.

continuing resolution funds used to keep programs up and running when regular appropriations have not been approved by the end of the fiscal year.

supplemental appropriations the process by which Congress and the president can provide temporary funding for government activities and programs when funds fall short due to unforeseen circumstances.

14 The Presidency

You are the president. You are the head of a government in which challenges to your authority seem to erupt from everywhere—from Congress, from the courts, from bureaucratic agencies and departments, from state and local governments. People demand that you manage world affairs and the economy, even though much of what happens in both of those highly complex arenas is not under your immediate control. You can be sure that almost every move you make will be attacked harshly by one segment of the population or another. The media will air critical voices on a daily basis, and late-night talk show hosts and comedians will lampoon you each evening.

You won the presidential election despite receiving fewer popular votes than your opponent. Your victory, in fact, depended on a disputed outcome in one state. To make matters worse, one study suggested that in several recount scenarios you might possibly have lost the state and therefore the election.[1] A series of conflicting court decisions prolonged the vote counting for over a month. Finally, a controversial 5-4 Supreme Court decision ended the vote counting and led your opponent to concede. Only then could you declare victory. Now: Lead.

This is the situation George W. Bush faced on January 20, 2001, when he took the oath of office. Bush's leadership challenge was extreme, but it was by no means unique. All presidents are evaluated on how successful they perform as leaders. The public respects the president as the most important public official in the nation and looks to him to lead them through war and peace, economic hardship or prosperity—whatever the country may face. Because leadership is at the heart of the presidency, political scientists study the question of leadership frequently and systematically.

Stories about individual examples of presidential leadership are the stock in trade of journalists. Although this approach can be illuminating, it can also be potentially misleading, depending on the examples chosen. President Bush, for example, was successful in obtaining the tax cuts he wanted in 2001 and 2003 and achieved some of his goals in education reform, which had been a major priority for him. On the other hand, the president's promotion of Social Security reform, a major campaign theme in 2000, never gained traction. On some issues, such as regulations increasing the level of allowable arsenic in drinking water and proposed oil drilling in the Alaskan National Wildlife Reserve, it is fair to say that the president failed miserably, with members of his own party deserting him in droves.

Rather than focusing on stories, political scientists try to study the president systematically. They have tried to figure out how to measure leadership success and how to determine which factors might contribute to leadership success. In this chapter, we focus on presidential authority and leadership, from the perspective of both the public and political scientists.

Presidential Authority and Leadership

Americans project their hopes on the presidency. They expect their president to develop a legislative program and to convince others to enact it. They expect the president to have, articulate, and defend policy ideas, all while unifying the country. They expect him (someday her), in the most general sense, to provide peace, prosperity, stability, and security. People want to feel that the country's leader has a plan, and they will credit him with good leadership if they believe that events are occurring in line with his plan. They want their leader to convey a firm sense of direction about his goals and priorities and the principles that will govern his decision-making (see Figure 14-1). They want him to use the authority granted by the Constitution and historical precedent as he carries out his plan.

The president performs the roles of statesman and politician.

In efforts to meet the goals of peace, prosperity, stability, and security, the president wears different hats, one as head of state and one as head of government. As

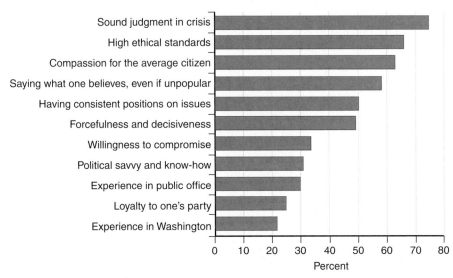

Figure 14-1. "Absolutely Essential" Qualities in a President. This chart shows the qualities the public thinks are "absolutely essential" in a president. The public is more concerned with a president's character and temperament than political or governmental experience.

Source: Harold W. Stanley and Richard G. Niemi, *Vital Statistics on American Politics 2007-2008* (Washington, DC: CQ Press, 2006), p. 345.

head of state, the president is a unifying symbol for the nation. Presidents welcome foreign dignitaries and participates in ceremonies as diverse as honoring the World Series champions and fallen soldiers. They provide support when the nation is suffering. When the *Challenger* space shuttle exploded in 1986, when riots erupted in Los Angeles in 1991, when the federal building in Oklahoma City was bombed in 1995, when terrorists attacked on September 11, 2001, and when Hurricane Katrina devastated New Orleans and the Gulf Coast in 2005, the country turned to the president for reassuring words, for signs that the country was strong and would persevere.

But politics is a contentious business and a "contact sport." As head of government, the president is a politician who attempts to pass his legislative program, representing the views of those who elected him to office. He sides with certain positions and opposes others. He rewards friends, punishes foes. To win political battles, he may discredit opposing viewpoints by portraying them as dangerous to national security, economic prosperity, or important values.

As head of government, the president takes on several specific tasks, including acting as commander-in-chief of the armed forces, being the country's primary diplomat who negotiates with other countries, encouraging Congress to pass particular legislation, and supervising executive branch agencies, departments, and offices. The president may plead for harmony and unity as he carries forth these tasks, but the reality is that he usually faces stern opposition to many of his ideas.

These two roles—head of state and head of government, unifier and hard-nosed politician—can work against each other. During the presidential campaign in 2000, George W. Bush commented that he wanted to be "a uniter, not a divider." But the president must be both. In his head-of-government role, he may be blunt about those opposed to his policies, accusing opponents of working contrary to shared American values. Thus, even if he uses unifying language about "the American people" and "our shared values," as head of government he will inevitably create tension because not everyone will agree with his proposals. The tricky leadership challenge for the president is to unite the country as head of state after having divided it through the rough and tumble of daily politics. Because the head-of-government and head-of-state roles can conflict, in many countries these roles are separated. In Great Britain and the Netherlands, for example, the queen or king plays the head-of-state role, while the prime minister is the head of government.

The president's authority was debated and established at the Constitutional Convention.

The primary source of presidential authority lies in the Constitution. Compared to Congress, however, the role of the president is ill-defined in that document. When the delegates met in Philadelphia in 1787, they agreed on the need for a strong executive. (See Chapter 3.) Beyond that, however, they were sharply divided about the role of executive power in the new government. Having been subject to the rule of the British king and British-appointed governors in the colonies, most of the delegates feared strong executive power. The convention delegates wrestled with precisely what roles, functions, responsibilities, and powers the office should have.

Creating the presidency Wary of giving too much power to one individual, the Framers wrestled with whether one person should hold the office of president or whether an executive committee or council was more appropriate. Some delegates initially lined up behind the Virginia Plan, which called for a congressionally-appointed executive council. The executive would not have any specific powers granted in the Constitution. Members of the council would serve for a single seven-year term. A special body would be created that included the executive council and the Supreme Court. This body, known as the council of revision, could veto (reject) bills passed by Congress, with Congress in turn able to override the veto.

Other delegates argued that accountability would be stronger and more focused if a single individual held the office. These delegates, however, differed among themselves about the relationship between the president and Congress. Some wanted the president to be selected by Congress and have no independent authority. To other delegates, the presidency needed to have its own set of constitutionally enumerated powers. There was general agreement among the delegates that the president would need to be able to check Congress, primarily through veto power.

Selecting the president After deciding that one person would hold the position, the Framers debated how to select that person. Direct election by the public had little support. Instead, indirect election dominated the discussion. With indirect election, the public does not directly elect the president but selects other individuals who, in turn, elect the president. Indirect election was intended to prevent the president from becoming a tool of public passions. One plan called for election of the president by Congress for a single term. He would gain office by appealing not to the public, but to members of Congress. With a one-term limit, his actions would not be geared toward reelection. Most delegates, however, believed this system would make the president too dependent on Congress.

The indirect election plan that prevailed was the **Electoral College**. In the Electoral College system, electors in each state vote for president. Each state legislature could choose how to select its electors. In some states, the state legislatures chose the electors; in others the people voted for them. By 1856, every state allowed the people to vote for electors. Regardless of how the electors were chosen, the key point is that it was the electors who actually voted for the president. This plan increased the president's independence from the legislature by not having Congress vote for the president and by allowing the president to run for reelection. If no individual received a majority of the electoral vote, only then would Congress have a say, with the House of Representatives selecting the president.

The Electoral College was initially thought of as a way for the country's leaders in each state to meet, deliberate, and vote for the president. Thus the selection of the president was insulated from direct public pressure. Rather, the people or the state legislature would be voting for "wise men" who would use their knowledge and wisdom to cast a vote for president. Today this distinction between the electors and the people is meaningless—electors almost always are required by state law to vote for the candidate who won the presidential popular vote in that state. Electors do not in any way today play the role of wise sages that was originally anticipated.

Reaching compromise over the nature of the presidency The American presidency as we know it today was a compromise that left no one at the Constitutional Convention entirely satisfied, but it contained elements that appealed to most delegates. The presidency was limited to individuals at least 35 years of age, born in the United States or born abroad as the child of American citizens, and a resident of the United States for at least 14 years. The office was made more independent of the legislative branch than in earlier proposals. Indirectly elected by the people via the Electoral College, the president would serve a four-year term with the possibility of reelection. The Constitution gave the president some specific duties, including commander-in-chief of the army and navy. As chief executive the president would, however, have to wait for Congress to create executive departments that he could lead, because the Constitution left it up to Congress to draft legislation creating federal departments.

The Constitution granted only limited specific powers to the president, independent of Congress, but it included some open-ended and potentially power-enhancing clauses. One clause directed the president to "from time to time give to the Congress information of the State of the Union, and recommend to their Consideration such Measures as he shall judge necessary and expedient" (Article II, Section 3). The first half of this statement was intended to ensure that the president did not remain aloof and distant from Congress. The second half provided an opening for presidential leadership of Congress. The **necessary and expedient clause**, which echoes the "necessary and proper" clause related to Congress, validates the president as a significant legislator—not merely an executive who is implementing and enforcing the law, but one who is instrumental in the creation and promotion of legislation.[2]

The Constitution also specified the president to "take care that the laws be faithfully executed." This **take care clause** is vague, allowing strong independent action if the president believed laws are being ignored. For example, in 1981 President Ronald Reagan fired all the federal air traffic controllers who had, in violation of their contract, walked off the job.[3] The clause also invites the president to interpret exactly what would be necessary to "faithfully execute" a law passed by Congress, which means he might take much bolder, or much less bold, action than Congress would like.

Presidents have stretched the language of the Constitution to expand their influence in American government.

In addition to the authority granted to the president in the Constitution, presidents have experimented to define the parameters of the office. A comparison of Article I in the Constitution (which concerns Congress) and Article II (which concerns the president) shows that the Framers had a much more detailed sense of the responsibilities and duties of Congress than of the president. Article II was written loosely enough that enterprising presidents have found ways to enlarge the responsibilities of the office.

Put bluntly, presidents had to stretch a few constitutional clauses here and there to see what Congress, the courts, and the public would accept as legitimate exercises of presidential authority. Does being commander-in-chief, for instance, mean that the president could take the country into war? What about a conflict that is not declared as a war? Presidents would push and other institutions would respond, and over time the office would become more clearly defined. The process continues to this day. Through this pushing and prodding of the Constitution, the office eventually became what some early Americans feared—a powerful seat of executive authority. What some in Congress and the public might see as an expansion of presidential power, presidents are inclined to see as a practice of the office's inherent power—the chief executive inherently has certain authority due to the nature of the job that need not be spelled out explicitly in the Constitution.

The early presidency When George Washington took the oath of office as president in 1789, he began with the job as defined in the Constitution. Washington (1789–1797) was determined to protect the president's independence. For example, he was adamant that the Senate's job was to confirm his nominees to the courts, not dictate who those nominees would be. And he immediately established the president's key role as head of state. Indeed, selected for the office primarily because of his enormous reputation throughout the country, Washington was in the eyes of most Americans the one figure to whom the early nurturance of this new political office could be entrusted. Although he was clearly also the head of government during many heated political and legislative battles, his establishment of the symbolic importance of the office as a representative of the nation was highly significant. This objective is clear in his founding of the two-term president tradition. Until 1951, the Constitution did not require a president to step down after a maximum of two terms, but all but one (Franklin Roosevelt) did. Washington began the tradition in part to establish the practice of shifting power, to reassure Americans that no concentrated monarchical powers were contained in the presidency.[4]

The stamp of other early presidents on the office also established the president's independence and made clear that the president would not simply be implementing congressional legislation. Thomas Jefferson (1801–1809) was actively involved in legislative matters. He arranged the Louisiana Purchase, which vastly expanded the geographical reach of the United States, with no congressional consultation. Andrew Jackson (1829–1837) employed aggressive use of vetoes on such politically explosive issues as the re-chartering of the Bank of the United States. Before Jackson, presidential vetoes had been few and had centered on constitutional objections to legislation. Jackson, by contrast, rejected legislation that he found flawed as policy, and in doing so he established the use of the veto as a key tool of presidential power.

During the Civil War, Abraham Lincoln (1861–1865) took an expansive view of the authority of the presidency. To many of his critics, Lincoln's actions assaulted American creed beliefs in liberty and property rights. But in an emergency, Lincoln argued, "executive power," "necessary and expedient," and "take care" had to be given very broad interpretation. Therefore Lincoln initiated measures restricting civil liberties, including eavesdropping on telegraph lines and allowing prisoners to be held without charge.[5] To support the war effort, he launched the first national income tax not only in the absence of any constitutional language allowing such a policy, but, in the eyes of many, directly contrary to constitutional language that seemed to prohibit this tax. It was not until 1913 that the Sixteenth Amendment would specifically allow the federal government to collect an income tax. Lincoln also created a national army that exceeded the size previously approved by Congress, helped found the state of West Virginia, declared a boycott of southern ports, and authorized the construction of warships, all without congressional approval. In most instances, though, Congress ultimately granted its approval after these steps had already been taken.

Creation of the modern presidency Theodore Roosevelt (1901–1909) was the first president to travel abroad during his term in office, cementing the president's role as chief diplomat and representative of the country. He coupled this with a foreign policy that sought to pull the United States more tightly into global politics and economics, including construction of the Panama Canal and declaring the Caribbean and Latin America off-limits to other countries. Roosevelt is considered a pioneer of the tradition of the president communicating directly to the public in easy-to-understand speeches about specific policy and legislative goals. In the nineteenth century, presidential speeches tended to be on broad topics that avoided controversy, rather than on specific legislation. Presidents presented themselves more as the head of state in their speaking tours around the country. Roosevelt, however, wanted to influence public opinion, which he believed would in turn influence members of Congress. He appealed to the public as the head of government.

In the 1930s, crisis again dramatically reshaped the presidency—this time the economic crisis of the Great Depression. "This country wants action, and action now," the new President Franklin Roosevelt declared in 1933, and he had no doubt that he was the one who needed to initiate this action. At one time Americans would have recoiled from a president so determined to promise "action," but by the twentieth century, the idea sat more comfortably in people's minds—indeed, many saw the president's determination to act as a welcome change from previous presidents' refusal to address the problems of the day.

Roosevelt (1933–1945) initiated a vast array of federal programs to deal with the collapse of the economy. He was blunt about his intentions. In his Inaugural Address in 1933, he declared that he was willing to work with Congress, but that if Congress failed to act, he would seek "broad executive power" to address the emergency. Roosevelt put the nation on notice that he intended the presidency to be the leading political institution in the United States and that he intended to experiment in bold ways to redefine the presidency. He did this not only through very active involvement in legislation, but by creating a set of supporting institutions in the Executive Office of the President. With a much larger staff at his disposal, the president could be even more active in policy-making, using government agencies to carry out his wishes, and communicating to the public, legislators, and interest groups.

Several of the laws that Roosevelt pushed through Congress were later declared unconstitutional by the Supreme Court. In response, Roosevelt proposed a plan that would give him a more favorable mix of justices on the Court, but public and congressional outrage at this perceived power grab killed the idea.[6] Despite this setback, the Court shifted course and supported Roosevelt's policy agenda.

The postwar presidency As the United States emerged from World War II as one of the world's superpowers, the president's power grew accordingly. During the Cold War between the United States and the Soviet Union, the president was not only the single most important person in American government, but was commonly seen as the most powerful person in the world. This enormous stock of prestige helped the president domestically. Increasingly his actions were portrayed as connected to and vital for national security. To protect America's national interests, presidents declared that they needed to act swiftly and forcefully around the world. Domestic policy itself became entwined with foreign policy—as the world's economic leader, actions of the U.S. government could have significant repercussions for allies and potential allies.

One area in which all presidents have expanded the boundaries of the office is the control of information, and the postwar presidency continued the trend. The administration of Dwight Eisenhower (1953–1961) in 1958 was the first to use the now common phrase **executive privilege** to refer to the idea that executive branch officials need to be able to advise the president in confidence, and that the president has a right to prevent that advice from becoming public. The withheld information for which presidents invoke executive privilege usually involves discussions in the White House. The argument of the president in these cases is that if he has to fear that members of Congress will have access to every discussion, he and his staff are less likely to be fully forthcoming in conversations. Moreover, if executive privilege is not permitted, Congress can request information merely out of a desire to discredit the president.

The most famous, or infamous, proponent of executive privilege was Richard Nixon (1969–1974). During the investigation of the scandal that became known as Watergate, Nixon claimed that he had the right to withhold from the public his notes, papers, and tapes of discussions in the White House.[7] In *U.S. v. Nixon* (1974), the Supreme Court rejected Nixon's claim of executive privilege. In this first judicial test of executive privilege, however, the Court did agree that presidents had such a privilege, but that it was not absolute and needed to be weighed against the public interest.

Early in his presidency, George W. Bush used the concept of executive privilege when Congress wanted information about the Energy Policy Task Force, headed by Vice President Dick Cheney. The refusal to disclose who the task force had met with in 2001, and what recommendations it had received was the first instance in which an administration used the executive privilege concept to shield its conversations with corporate officials, as opposed to government officials. In December 2002, a U.S. district court sided with the administration, concluding that the doctrine of separation of powers was at stake.[8]

The Bush administration also expanded executive privilege by arguing that it applied broadly throughout the executive branch, not just to the president or vice president. President Bush used the take care clause, in combination with the vesting clause in Article II of the Constitution—"The executive Power shall be vested in a President of the United States of America"—to argue for a view of the presidency known as the unitary executive. This doctrine, which the Bush administration propounded more strongly than other administrations, means that the president is in direct, hierarchical control of all executive power in American government. In this view, congressional control over the executive branch and delegation of authority to executive branch agencies that bypasses the president is limited. In 2007 and 2008, when Congress sought to investigate the firing of nine U.S. attorneys in the Justice Department, the administration wouldn't comply with requests for information that it believed were covered by this broader view of executive privilege.

Despite these signs of increased strength, postwar presidents have faced significant obstacles to exercising power. The country has grown in population and complexity. The political environment contains powerful organized groups with diverse policy concerns. Numerous governmental programs are already in place, and attempts to remove them generate howls of protest. The federal budget is not limitless, nor is the public's willingness to tolerate increasing tax burdens, so presidents are shackled by preexisting policy commitments that they inherit upon taking office. They cannot simply erase decades of history and start fresh. And as members of Congress forge their own power during long careers, presidents confront congressional challenges to their leadership. Unlike members of Congress in the nineteenth century, who were content with one or two terms in Washington, members in more recent eras have been inclined to make Congress a career.

Congress delegates authority to the president.

The president gains some authority from Congress. Often, Congress defers to the president, either explicitly delegating policymaking tasks to him or deferring action until the president takes the initiative. Either way, the effect is to direct more public attention to the president as a leader. Through **delegation** of this sort, the president is given discretion to act in a particular area, presumably within broad parameters of what is acceptable to Congress. If the president goes beyond these boundaries, Congress can find a way to indicate its displeasure. This might include refusing to fund the implementation of the president's plan, setting stricter boundaries around future presidential action in this area, or being less cooperative in considering and passing a bill that is important to the president.

Congress, for instance, has delegated to the president the authority to negotiate foreign trade agreements, agreeing to limit itself to a single vote without the possibility of amending their language or engaging in a filibuster. The process has strict time limits, including how quickly committees must act and the number of hours the proposed trade agreement can be debated on the House or Senate floor. Known as fast-track authority, this is a significant concession of congressional power. Fast-track authority began in 1975, expired in 1994, and was renewed again in 2002.

What would cause legislators to give up their ability to amend trade agreements? Legislators may believe that negotiation with other countries works better when the United States presents a unified voice. Perhaps some fear that other members of Congress would be eager to protect industries in their districts, and the negotiations would unravel if the president then had to go back to other countries with a revised version of the treaty. Some legislators might consider trade to be a controversial subject and want the president to take the criticism. Because some of these reasons put the president at political risk, even a Congress controlled by the opposition party might grant presidents this authority. But if the congressional majority does not trust the president, it may refuse to delegate this authority. Democrat Bill Clinton wanted fast-track authority after its expiration in 1994, but the Republican-majority Congress refused to grant it to him. Similarly, Republican George W. Bush struggled unsuccessfully in 2007 to convince the Democratic-majority Congress to extend fast-track authority for another five years.

Very importantly, Congress also delegated to the president the initiative in the federal budget process. Partly to help the president control executive branch agencies more effectively, and partly to help Congress think more systematically about the budget, Congress after 1921 required the president to submit an overall budget as a framework for congressional deliberation. In practice, this meant that the president set the parameters for the federal budget and Congress worked within these guidelines. The overall budget, as passed by Congress in a series of separate spending bills, typically looked very much like the president's original plan. In 1974, Congress passed the Congressional Budget and Impoundment Control Act to return some of the leverage to Congress. From then on, Congress passed budget resolutions that established targets for revenue and spending across all policy areas. But the president's budget was still the first to reach Congress, so even the budget resolution was a response to the president's plan.

Successful presidential leadership gets people to do what the president wants them to do.

Broadening interpretations of the president's constitutional authority, coupled with the growth in Congress's delegation of power to the president, have increased public expectations about the president's ability to lead. These expectations can be a burden for the president: a president seen as falling short may find a growing proportion of the public disapproving of his performance in office. But public expectations can be a blessing, too. Higher expectations may enhance the president's leadership potential by forcing the president to pressure Congress for cooperation. The president can appeal directly to the public, indicating he wants to meet their expectations but that Congress is obstructing him. Such appeals might generate public pressure on Congress to act and contribute to successful presidential leadership.

Leadership can be evaluated in terms of outcome (Did the president succeed in getting Congress to pass his plan to reduce crime?) or in terms of impact (Did the plan actually reduce the crime rate?).[9] Political scientists tend to focus more on the outcome side of leadership. Thought of this way, leadership involves convincing the public that action is needed and getting a favored piece of legislation passed in Congress. It can also involve stopping action in Congress or influencing the content of legislation. Thus, to political scientists, **leadership** means the ability of a president to influence and guide others to achieve some desired policy or action (see *How Do We Know? Was George W. Bush a Successful Leader?*).

Of course, it is easier to get people to do what they already are inclined to do. In some situations, the president uses his skills to bring people together to do what, in effect, they already want to do but have not quite figured out how to do. When President George W. Bush passed his tax cut package in 2001, he was exercising this type of leadership.

Leadership of this type is challenging, but it is even more difficult to lead while bucking the trend of public and congressional opinion. Here the president tries to push the nation in a new direction and is often criticized for not being responsive to public opinion. Early in President Clinton's first term, he was criticized for ignoring public opinion when he pushed for homosexuals to be able to serve openly in the military.[10]

President Bush's effort in 2003 to engage the United States in military action against Iraq required this second type of leadership. He reassured the public that diplomatic efforts to resolve the crisis were underway, while raising the possibility that military action might be needed and that the United States might have to act alone. Public opinion polls showed that these efforts succeeded. For example, the percentage of Americans believing that the president had laid out a clear and convincing case for military action rose from 37 percent to 52 percent in a one-month period that included a major, highly publicized speech by President Bush to the United Nations.[11]

Was President George W. Bush a Successful Leader?

The Question

In the tense hours after the terrorist attacks on September 11, 2001, Americans waited to hear from President George W. Bush. How would the country respond to the devastation in New York, Washington, D.C., and Pennsylvania? On September 20 the president delivered a solemn, forthright speech to the nation. Soon after, with congressional support, he forged a coalition of allies to attack the Taliban regime in Afghanistan, believed to be a prime sponsor of terrorism and a haven for the perpetrators of the September 11 attacks. To most Americans at that time, Bush's actions after September 11 were the work of a strong, successful leader, someone who took charge of a situation and got things done. Public opinion surveys gave the president high marks for his leadership, and in 2004 the president made a case for his reelection that hinged in large part on his leadership skills. By the beginning of 2006, however, a string of negative news dragged down the president's reputation as a leader to the lowest point of his presidency, and the president limped through 2007 and 2008 with the lowest public approval of his presidency. Was George W. Bush a successful leader? How do we know?

Why It Matters

Most Americans consider the election of the president to be among their most significant political acts. The more clearheaded and accurate we can be when casting these votes, the better. If we as citizens say we want strong and successful leadership, it helps to have standards by which to predict who will be the better leader or to determine whether a president has been a successful leader.

Investigating the Answer

Before researchers can determine whether a president is a strong leader, they first have to determine how to define and measure successful leadership. The public most often tends to think about presidential leadership in terms of impact: Did the president's action alleviate a problem, have no impact, or make things worse? These assessments matter electorally. In November 2004 a majority of voters believed that President Bush had made the country safer than it had been prior to September 11, 2001, and rewarded him with their vote. By November 2006, however, voters swept Democrats to majorities in the House and Senate in part because of their doubt that the president's leadership had been wise and effective on that issue.

To political scientists, however, measuring success by impact is problematic for several reasons. First, whether the impact of a policy has been positive or negative can take a long time to determine and may change over time. Second, drawing the line between success and failure is inherently difficult. What if the economic growth rate increases by 0.1 percent? By 1 percent? By 4 percent? Where does a researcher draw the line between success and failure, and why? Third, measuring presidential leadership by impact can be unreliable because the evaluation may be biased by political ideology. Consider Iraq. Iraq has deposed a dictator, held free elections, and written a constitution. It has also experienced brutal ongoing violence and a surge in terrorist activity that have damaged the image of the United States among our allies. Given the mixed results, one's ideology might dictate whether one judges the president's actions as having an overall positive or negative impact. Lastly, the impact you see may not be the result of presidential action: the correlation of the president's action and a particular outcome does not prove causation.

Therefore, political scientists tend to define presidential leadership in terms of outcome rather than impact. They look at what the president has attempted to accomplish and they evaluate his success in those areas. Some researchers have compared the president's campaign promises with his actual performance. Others have studied the president's State of the Union address as a measure of his highest priorities and tracked what he accomplished legislatively in those areas. Both of these methods are attractive because of the available data on campaign promises or State of the Union addresses across several presidencies. Other researchers have chosen a broader measure, comparing the president's preferences on roll-call votes taken in Congress and calculating how often Congress agreed with the president's position. The focus in these outcome-oriented studies of leadership is not on whether the president's policies "worked," but on whether he was able to persuade Congress to enact them.

The most common political science measure of successful presidential leadership is the frequency with which Congress votes in accord with the president's preferences. The measure is not a perfect indicator of leadership success—the president might not have done much to produce the outcome in Congress, and the final outcome on a vote does not tell us whether the president had to abandon major aspects of his policy in the days or months leading up to the vote. One especially attractive feature of this measure is that there are typically hundreds of congressional roll-call votes on which the president takes a position, so the frequency of presidential success can be calculated across time, across issue areas, and across different presidents, thus aiding political scientists in the kind of systematic analysis they prefer.

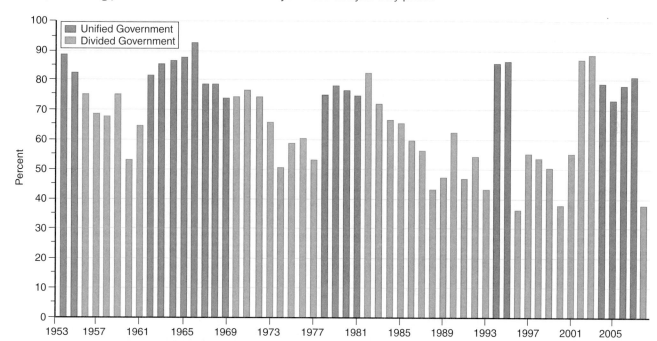

Figure 14-2. **Presidential Victories on Roll-Call Votes, House and Senate, 1953-2007.** Presidential success in Congress is generally higher when the president's party has a majority in both houses of Congress.

Source: Source: Source: Harold W. Stanley and Richard G. Niemi, *Vital Statistics on American Politics 2005-2006* (Washington, DC: CQ Press, 2006), pp. 258-59; Clea Benson, "CQ Vote Studies - Presidential Support: The Power of No," *CQ Weekly,* January 14, 2008, pp. 132-35.

Looking at how often Congress voted the way the president wanted on roll-call votes, President Bush has been a successful leader (see Figure 14-2). In 2005 and 2006, his success rate was higher than any other president in his fifth and sixth year since the Eisenhower administration (1953–1961).[12] His overall success rate from 2001 to 2005 rivaled that of Lyndon Johnson (1964–1968) and John Kennedy (1961–1963). But unlike those two presidents, Bush achieved this result while facing a Senate narrowly controlled by the opposition party for 18 months of his first term; Bush's first-term success rate with the opposition party was substantially higher than that of any president since Richard Nixon.[13] And Senate Democrats voted with the president over half of the time in 2006. With Democrats in control of the House and Senate following the 2006 elections, Bush's success rate has declined, but his first six years show substantial success.

Political scientists focus on outcome rather than impact to analyze presidential leadership systematically. This method avoids the ideological bias that influences the assessments made by political activists and zealous partisans. George W. Bush has taken a position on fewer congressional votes than any other president since Dwight Eisenhower (1953–1961), but overall he has been highly successful on those votes. By this measure, Bush can be considered a successful leader. Measures of other outcomes, such as his inability to get congressional votes on his Social Security and immigration reform initiatives in his second term, might yield different results.

The Bottom Line

Powers of the President

Presidents invoke various powers in their efforts to set policy. Some of these—formal powers—are designated by law or the Constitution. Others—informal powers—derive from the unique advantages of the president as the sole public official in the United States elected by a national constituency. Presidential power is not limitless, however, and its use can be challenged by Congress and the courts.

Formal powers are defined in the Constitution or in law.

The president's **formal powers** are specific grants of authority defined in the Constitution or in laws. Some formal powers, such as making treaties and appointing ambassadors and judges, are shared with the Senate. In these cases, the Senate must approve treaties negotiated by the president or confirm his nominees. As noted above, the Framers were cautious regarding presidential power. This was their way to ensure that the president did not control the judicial branch and, even more importantly, did not compromise the interests of the United States to a foreign power. The president exercises other formal powers independent of Congress. These include the power to commission officers in the military, to grant pardons to those convicted of crimes (or, preemptively, to those who might be charged with a crime), to receive foreign ambassadors, and to convene sessions of Congress.

New legislation The president shares with Congress the role of approving new legislation. In their role as "chief legislator," presidents are engaged in every part of the process. He and his staff can draft bills, although the president cannot himself introduce a bill in Congress; a member of Congress must do that on the president's behalf. During deliberations over the bill, the president and his staff typically contact members of Congress and encourage them to vote with the president. They will also appeal to the media, interest groups, and the public itself to apply pressure on Congress. If the bill passes, the president will need to sign it before it becomes law.[14]

Presidential veto One of the most important formal powers is the **veto**, which, as noted earlier, allows the president to reject bills enacted by Congress: the veto is the president's power to say no. When the president vetoes a bill, Congress can override the veto with a two-thirds vote of each chamber, but this typically proves very difficult to do. In the case of a **pocket veto**, Congress does not even have that opportunity. The Constitution gives the president ten days to either sign or reject a bill. If he does neither, the bill becomes law. If, however, Congress has adjourned during that ten days and the president does not act, the bill is rejected. This is known as a pocket veto—the president kills the bill by keeping it in his pocket. Presidents can use their veto power to extract legislation more to their liking from Congress.[15]

The veto is powerful not merely when it is used, but also when the president threatens its use. When the president threatens to veto a bill, Congress members, particularly those who are not in the president's party, must decide whether they want to revise the bill according to the president's preferences, or to refuse a compromise. If the bill is unchanged, the president will reject it. If they agree to revise the bill, the legislation will pass, but Congress members may be dissatisfied with the compromised version of the original bill. If they decide to allow the president to veto the bill, they are hoping that the public opinion backlash will force the president to reevaluate his stance or, if an election is near, that the president's position might hurt him or his fellow partisans running for office.

The president's threat of using the veto does not necessarily mean that he opposes a bill in that particular policy area, but rather that he does not like some provisions of the particular bill that was put on his desk for his signature. That was frequently true for President Clinton, who made effective use of vetoes and veto threats in his relationship with the Republican Congress beginning in 1995.

President Bush made rare use of the veto power. Presidents from John Kennedy through Bill Clinton vetoed legislation an average of nine times per year, while President Bush had through mid-2008 only issued a total of ten vetoes after nearly eight years in the White House. But he made good use of the veto to achieve his political goals. In 2007, he vetoed a funding bill for the Iraq War that established a timeline for the return of troops. The newly elected Democratic majority was eager to express its displeasure with the war and to hasten its end. The president, however, strongly objected to any efforts by Congress to limit his conduct of the war. Lacking the votes to override the president's veto, the Democrats ultimately relented, sending him a new funding bill stripped of any language about fixed time tables for the return of U.S. troops.

Line-item veto A veto is a big knife, but sometimes what the president really wants is a scalpel. Presidents have long sought a more delicate device for fine-tuning bills in the form of the **line-item veto**, which would allow them to veto portions of bills rather than entire bills. A 1996 law gave this power to presidents, but President Clinton enjoyed it for only a short time. In 1998, the U.S. Supreme Court ruled that the line-item veto unconstitutionally added to the president's powers by, in effect, allowing him to amend proposed legislation—a task limited to Congress in the Constitution. The president could only approve or reject proposed legislation in its entirety: if he wanted the power to approve legislation in part, the Court ruled, a constitutional amendment would be needed.

Commander-in-chief Being commander-in-chief requires the president to work in concert with Congress, but in this role the president tends to lead while Congress follows. The president serves as the commander-in-chief of all the military services—the Army, the Navy, the Marines, the Air Force, and the Coast Guard. As commander-in-chief, the president has the authority to move American troops into combat. This presidential authority is not clearly spelled out in the Constitution; rather, it is one of those areas that presidents claimed over time, often over the vigorous protest of partisan opponents and constitutional scholars.

The commander-in-chief role is one area where presidents historically have argued that they have inherent powers that are not specified in law or the Constitution to respond to emergencies and protect the safety of Americans and the security of the United States. The nature of executive power is to act and use best judgment when emergency strikes, they argue. The Bush administration took controversial actions in response to terrorism, including indefinite detention of enemy combatants, denial of civilian court review of cases involving detainees, and surveillance of communications without prior judicial authorization. In defending these actions, President Bush and his spokespeople frequently argued that they fell squarely within the inherent powers of the president as commander-in-chief.

It does seem that the Framers intended for the president to be in charge of the armed forces and guide their conduct during war, but they intended Congress to declare war. Fearing that the president had become too dominant in this area and had turned a shared power into a presidential power, Congress passed the War

Powers Act in 1973. This act requires the president to notify Congress and receive its approval within 60 days when he deploys American troops militarily. As a practical matter, in most cases, Congress finds that by that time it is too late to change course, and the president's decision stands.

Executive agreement and executive order Two other formal powers available to presidents—the executive agreement and the executive order—enable them to enact public policy without the direct cooperation of Congress. These powers are not found in the Constitution, but instead arise out of presidents' entrepreneurial efforts to expand their base of authority.

With an **executive agreement**, a president can negotiate an arrangement with a foreign government without formal approval by Congress. These agreements cannot require changes in U.S. law—in those instances, Congress must sign off on the change through a treaty. That is why presidents have made much more frequent use of executive agreements than of treaties (see Figure 14-3). Executive agreements are used in a variety of policy areas. In 2002, the Bush administration approved an executive agreement that committed the United States and Russia to specific nuclear arms reductions. In 2003, the United States and Vietnam reached an agreement to raise Vietnamese textile exports to the United States. Executive agreements were also used to end U.S. involvement in the Korean and Vietnam wars.

Executive agreements are not intended to be hidden from Congress and the public, although sometimes presidents have used them that way. A series of executive agreements between the United States and South Vietnam drew the United States more heavily into military involvement in Vietnam. Although the first of these agreements went into effect in the late 1950s under the administration of Dwight Eisenhower and continued through the 1960s under the administrations

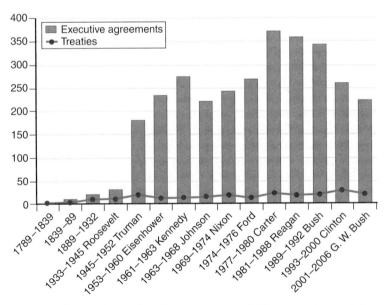

Figure 14-3. **Executive Agreements and Treaties, Annual Average, 1789–2004.** Presidents make much more extensive use of executive agreements than treaties.

Source: Harold W. Stanley and Richard G. Niemi, *Vital Statistics on American Politics 2005–2006* (Washington, DC: CQ Press, 2006), p. 339.

Table 14-1. Examples of Policy Initiatives Implemented Using Executive Orders

EXECUTIVE ORDER	DATE	SUBJECT	ISSUED BY
9066	February 19, 1942	Internment of Japanese-American citizens	F. Roosevelt
9981	July 26, 1948	Segregation in the armed forces ended	Truman
10730	September 23, 1957	Enforcement of school desegregation using National Guard	Eisenhower
10925	March 6, 1961	Affirmative action to be used by government agencies and contractors to ensure nondiscriminatory hiring practices	Kennedy
11615	August 15, 1971	Wage and price controls	Nixon
13158	May 26, 2000	Development of national environmental system of marine protected areas	Clinton
13379	December 12, 2002	More participation by faith-based organizations in federal social programs	G. W. Bush
13435	June 20, 2007	Federally-funded stem-cell research guidelines	G. W. Bush

of John Kennedy and Lyndon Johnson, Congress was unaware of them until 1969. To forestall secret use of executive agreements in the future, Congress passed the Case Act in 1972 to require presidents to inform Congress of an executive agreement within 60 days of its inception (amended to 20 days in 1977).

Executive orders (as well as proclamations, memoranda, and other directives) are presidential commands that have the force of law. Like executive agreements, they do not require Congress's approval; unlike executive agreements, they do not involve a foreign government. Executive orders apply to the executive branch and its employees, so the president, as head of the executive branch of government, is allowed to issue these as would the chief executive of any organization. They can affect the private sector because private organizations interact with government, usually through contracts. For example, an executive order might state that companies wishing to provide goods or services to the government must have certain equal opportunity hiring policies in place. Although most orders are fairly routine matters of administrative procedure, the president can also use this tool to implement a wide range of policies, some of which aid constituencies important for the president's political success (see Table 14-1).[16]

In December 2002, for example, President Bush issued Executive Order 13279, designed to ensure that faith-based organizations—churches, synagogues, mosques, and other religious institutions—could compete for federal financing for programs that provide social services to the local community. Technically, the president was telling executive branch employees that they could not treat these groups differently from any other group applying for federal funding. By issuing the directive as an executive order, the president sidestepped potentially contentious congressional debate about the constitutionality of federal funding for religious organizations. Supporters saw the president's action as a vindication of the cultural support for religious rights and equality; opponents saw it as violating the American creed by forging too close a governmental link with religion.

The president's power to use executive orders can be limited by Congress or by the U.S. Supreme Court. The Supreme Court can declare an executive order void if it finds that the president's action exceeded his authority or is contrary to the

Constitution or federal law. President Nixon's executive orders that closed several federal agencies, for example, were rejected by the Court, because Congress had not abolished these agencies. As with executive agreements, Congress has the power to weaken executive orders by cutting off their funding. Congress could also define areas in which prior congressional approval is required, thus negating the possibility of an executive order.

American presidents' formal powers compared to foreign presidents

Although dozens of countries around the world have systems of government headed by presidents, the exact form of the presidency and its power varies. Compared to other presidential systems, an American president's powers fall around the middle of the range. For example, like the American president, some presidents can issue a unilateral directive similar to an executive order and then veto legislative attempts to repeal it. Although the legislature can check presidential behavior, presidents in these countries are more powerful than those in countries where unilateral action is not possible. On the more powerful end of the range, in some countries presidents have the exclusive right to introduce policy in particular areas. Taiwan and South Korea, among others, constitutionally limit the legislature's ability to refine the president's budgetary allocations.

Other countries have more curbs in place to limit presidential power. In some systems, a president's veto power may be limited to particular forms of legislation. The Mexican president, for example, cannot veto the annual appropriations bill that sets government spending. And the strength of the veto also varies across countries. In Venezuela, for example, an override requires only the same number of votes that originally passed the bill. In other countries, such as Colombia, an absolute majority is necessary. In the United States and Argentina, among others, a two-thirds vote of the legislature is required to override a presidential veto. Although this gives the U.S. president a relatively powerful veto, he does not have the line-item or partial veto available to some other presidents.

Presidents have the power to persuade.

Presidents also have informal powers, meaning powers that are not the result of an established rule, policy mechanism, or constitutional assignment of authority. Most famously in the category of informal powers, presidents have the "power to persuade" in order to accomplish their goals. Some political scientists go so far as to say that the president's power *is* the power to persuade. That is overstating matters, because as described above, presidents do have some unilateral authority. However, it is certainly true that much of what a president does is geared toward persuading others. Some presidents, like Lyndon Johnson and Franklin Roosevelt, had legendary bargaining skills. Others, like Jimmy Carter, struggled more to compromise and understand the political pressures faced by members of Congress.

Persuasion and policymakers

Presidents often need the cooperation of members of Congress, aides and advisors, officials in federal agencies, and fellow politicians on the state and local levels. On some issues, they will be more passionate and involved and less willing to see their plans thwarted. Despite decreasing public and congressional support for the Iraq war, for example, President Bush was determined to defend his strategy.[17] A president may trade success on more peripheral issues to defend his position on the key issue. To secure cooperation, a president tries to persuade other policymakers that his position is right. He may offer them some benefit if they will cooperate—perhaps federal funds for a favorite project, or fund-raising for a legislator facing reelection. He might threaten to withhold something from the legislator's district, or indicate that he will not throw his support behind one of the legislator's priorities. Presidents will also try to put pressure on a recalcitrant member of Congress by appealing directly to his constituents.[18]

Signing statements are one manner of persuading bureaucrats and judges that has received extensive attention during the Bush administration. These are statements issued by the president when signing legislation. Most statements do little more than praise Congress for a job well done or emphasize the importance of the law itself. Increasingly, however, presidents have used these statements to re-interpret legislation in meaningful ways. For example, President Bush argued in signing statements that he retained the option to ignore certain provisions of laws if he concluded they unduly infringed on his constitutional role as commander-in-chief. The statements do not afford the president an opportunity—as some have charged—to actually re-write the content of the law. They are attempts to persuade the bureaucrats who implement laws and the judges who may someday be called upon to interpret them.

Do signing statements change bureaucratic behavior? A congressional investigation in 2007 found some correlation between concerns raised in presidential signing statements and portions of legislation not implemented by federal agencies.[19] Although critics quickly asserted a direct causal relationship between statements and bureaucratic inaction, the facts at hand were more nuanced. It is not clear whether agencies ignored provisions of laws because of the signing statements or whether the statements were simply a convenient justification after the fact. It might also be that the president was more likely to issue a signing statement when an agency had already signaled its predisposition to ignore some aspect of a law. In that case, it would be the agency's planned behavior that caused the signing statement, rather than the other way around. And because the report did not examine laws passed without signing statements, there was no way to know whether bureaucratic inaction was more frequent when signing statements were issued than when they were not.

Persuasion and the American creed One broad informal power is the president's role in the maintenance, perpetuation, and political use of the beliefs of American political culture. Presidents may not wrap themselves in the flag, but they are more than willing to wrap themselves in the powerful beliefs of equality, liberty, individualism, property, democracy, and religion (see Chapter 2). Presidents use these beliefs as touchstones, both to suggest the unity of the United States and to advocate their own particular programs. In his first inaugural address, George W. Bush promised that he would "bring the values of our history to the care of our times." The reference to these beliefs by any president is likely a combination of sincere beliefs and a hard-headed political calculation that wrapping the president's political agenda in the hazy glow of these beliefs might help sell the president's proposals and make opponents look outside the American mainstream. If you oppose my programs, a president says implicitly, are you not opposing these fundamental beliefs that unite Americans?[20]

Congress and the courts can check presidential power.

Both Congress and the courts serve as a check on presidents who try to expand their authority too aggressively. When someone challenges a policy, ruling, or other action taken by the executive branch, the courts might declare it illegal or unconstitutional and therefore void. For example, in June 2004, the Supreme Court ruled in three cases that President Bush had exceeded his constitutional authority by indefinitely detaining non-citizens captured in Afghanistan as part of the U.S. campaign against terrorism. The detainees were held at the U.S. military base at Guantanamo Bay, Cuba, and were prohibited access to attorneys or the courts. The Supreme Court concluded that the detainees had the right to access the federal courts to challenge their incarceration.[21]

Congress can check the president's power through the normal legislative process by not acting on legislation he desires, refusing to approve judicial and other nominees, designing agencies to have some independence from presidential control, and by withholding funding and thereby prohibiting the executive branch from taking certain actions of which Congress disapproves. The threat of these actions often leads presidents to adjust their plans and soothe congressional objections.

The most severe congressional check on presidential power is **impeachment,** a process through which the House of Representatives can vote to initiate a trial conducted by the Senate that can lead to the removal of the president from office.[22] The Constitution allows for the impeachment process to be initiated when a president is accused of "high crimes and misdemeanors," treason, or bribery. The exact meaning of "high crimes and misdemeanors" is left for Congress to decide. Exploration of the discussions among the Framers of the Constitution, study of previous impeachment efforts, and analyses of previous incidences of presidents seeming to exceed their authority all provide Congress with information it can use to decide whether a president has in fact committed high crimes and misdemeanors.

As in most voting situations in Congress, the president's fellow partisans are typically his strongest supporters in the impeachment process. The process begins in the House of Representatives, based on "articles of impeachment" that describe the charges against the president. These articles are usually drafted by leaders in the opposition party, following a long period of strained relations with the president. The case against the president is first heard in the House Judiciary Committee. If that committee votes that there is a credible case against the president on all or some of the charges, it sends those articles to the full House to vote whether to proceed with impeachment. The impeachment trial is then held in the Senate and senators vote whether the president is guilty and must be removed from office. Conviction in the Senate, not impeachment in the House, removes the president from office.

Two presidents, Andrew Johnson in 1868 and Bill Clinton in 1998, have been impeached. In both cases, the Senate acquitted them. Johnson had antagonized congressional Republicans with his too lenient (in their view) approach toward the former Confederate states and with his attempts to derail Republican plans for reconstruction of the South. The impeachment case was based largely on his violation of the Tenure in Office Act, which required the president to receive the Senate's approval before dismissing any officeholders, and which had been passed largely to keep reins on Johnson. The case against Clinton was based largely on the charge that he had lied to a federal grand jury investigating his sexual involvement with White House aide Monica Lewinsky, and that he had obstructed justice by stonewalling when revealing information about the case.

Two other presidents, John Tyler and Richard Nixon, were nearly impeached. Tyler was "censured" in 1843 by the Senate for alleged misuse of power, an option that many Democrats unsuccessfully suggested might be an alternative to impeachment in the case of Bill Clinton.[23] Nixon resigned in 1974 after the House Judiciary Committee voted to send articles of impeachment to the full House. The committee charged the president with obstructing justice in the Watergate investigation and with abuse of power by using agencies such as the Federal Bureau of Investigation and the Internal Revenue Service to intimidate opponents. Technically, then, Nixon was not impeached, but it was all but certain that he would have been both impeached and convicted had he not voluntarily resigned from office.

Public, Electoral, and Contextual Resources for Presidential Leadership

American presidents have varying degrees of success in leading the country, dealing with Congress, and achieving their goals. That success has much to do with the resources that the president brings to the office. These resources for presidential leadership include the president's relationship with the public, electoral factors such as the strength of the president's victory and the size and support of his party in Congress, and historical and policy contexts such as presidential advantages in foreign policy. A president who has an abundant supply of these resources should be more successful with Congress than a president who does not.[24]

High levels of public approval are used to pressure Congress.

One of the most important of a president's resources is his relationship with the public. Since the late 1930s, the public's assessment of the president's job performance has been measured by his public **approval rating**. Public opinion firms conduct surveys and ask respondents whether they approve or disapprove of the job the president is doing. This initial question might be followed by questions relating to distinct policy areas such as the economy, foreign affairs, and the environment. The percentage of the respondents saying they approve of the president's job performance is the president's approval rating.

Approval and its consequences A key reason the president wants to maintain a positive relationship with the public is to exert pressure on members of Congress. The president's hope is that high public approval will encourage members of Congress to cooperate with him because they fear the political consequences of challenging a popular president. Conversely, legislators may not perceive much political risk in obstructing the plans of a president with low approval.

Among recent presidents, Bill Clinton best exemplifies both ends of the spectrum. Following the 1994 election, with his approval ratings low, Clinton struggled to maintain visibility as media attention focused more on Congress—where both chambers were controlled by the Republican Party for the first time in 40 years. The brash, outspoken new Speaker of the House, Newt Gingrich, was promising "revolutionary" changes in American government. Clinton famously, and meekly, replied that the president was still "relevant." Republicans pushed ahead with their legislative plan with little concern for Clinton's views. Less than a year later, however, Clinton was riding a wave of public approval that resulted from his ability to portray himself as a reasonable moderate holding off the extremists in Congress. Finding that the public increasingly supported the president, congressional Republicans began to compromise with him more frequently.

Approval ratings tend to start high and drift down over time. During the early "honeymoon" period of a president's term, opposition to the president's plans has not yet solidified and the public is still likely to give him the benefit of the doubt. He will not likely be blamed, at least not immediately, for problems inherited from his predecessor. And usually, he has not had time to make any major mistakes. As these mistakes happen, and as it gets harder to blame the predecessor, people find reasons to criticize the president's performance.

Party identification is a key factor in approval ratings. Republicans are more likely to approve of a Republican president's job performance, Democrats are less likely, and independents are somewhere in-between. This does not mean that Republicans blindly approve of the president because of the party label. Rather, Republicans are more likely to agree philosophically with actions taken by a Republican president than are Democrats. Never have these party divisions been more pronounced than during George W. Bush's presidency, when Republicans overwhelmingly supported the president, and Democrats overwhelmingly opposed him.[25]

Approval ratings and the economy   The economy is the most important determinant of a president's job approval rating. The more positive people feel about the economy, the better the president's approval rating will tend to be. Presidents who fail to portray concern on economic issues face a tough road to reelection. George H. W. Bush is a classic example of this problem. The economy was in a downturn in 1991 and early 1992 as he prepared for the upcoming election. Democrats seeking their party's nomination hammered Bush incessantly on his economic record. The eventual nominee, Bill Clinton, promised if elected to "focus like a laser beam" on the economy. Although the economy started to improve in 1992, Bush's perceived economic failures left a stronger impression on the public than did the recovery. His efforts to show concern for the economy ended up as the butt of jokes on late-night television. These included the president purchasing socks at a Washington, D.C., area mall to demonstrate his confidence in the economy, and his seeming amazement at seeing grocery store price scanners, a technology that had been in stores for a decade. The image stuck of an aloof president out of touch with the economic concerns of average people, a perception that even pre-election economic improvement could not shake. George W. Bush, perhaps because of his father's experience, was keenly aware of the need to convey concern on economic matters. Speaking in Orlando in December 2001, Bush echoed Bill Clinton's empathetic "I feel your pain" when he told job-seekers, "I hurt, coming into the holiday season, that you're not working."

Approval ratings and rally events   **Rally events**, another factor in approval ratings, are short-term international events or military actions that tend to boost approval ratings in a "rally 'round the flag" effect. John F. Kennedy's rating surged 13 points in 1962 when the United States set up a blockade around Cuba after it was revealed that Soviet bases were being installed there. President George W. Bush's approval rating started out in the upper 50s and low 60s, substantially higher than his percentage of the vote in the 2000 election. It began drifting downward as perceived economic conditions deteriorated. Then, his approval rating rose enormously after the terrorist attacks on September 11, 2001 (see Figure 14-4). It also jumped sharply after the war with Iraq began in March 2003. Three days into the war, Bush's approval rating was 13 points higher than it had been before the war began. But by the summer of 2003, the president's approval rating was at about the level it was prior to September 11. After another short-lived rally

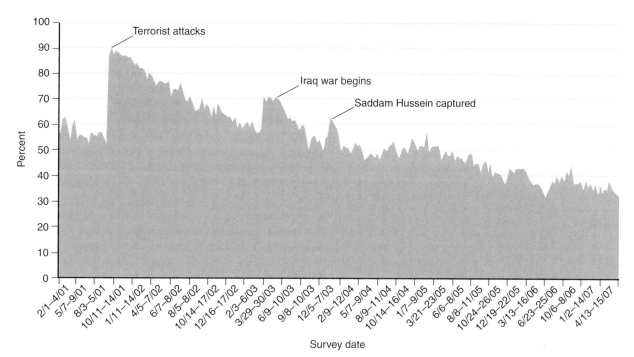

Figure 14-4. **Percent Approving of President George W. Bush's Job Performance, February 2001–May 2007.** President Bush's approval rating has been defined by sharp increases during rally events and gradual erosion due to public dissatisfaction with his handling of the economy, the war, and other matters.
Source: Gallup Poll.

event with the capture of Saddam Hussein, skepticism about the war in Iraq, the economy, and a series of missteps by the administration led to a steady decline in the president's approval rating.

Scandal and approval ratings As expected, scandals usually depress presidential approval ratings. During the Watergate investigation of the early 1970s, Richard Nixon's job approval plummeted. However, scandals do not always cause ratings to drop. Bill Clinton's approval ratings went up during the investigation of the Monica Lewinsky matter and his subsequent impeachment. Did scandal actually cause higher approval? Not really. Many people, especially Democrats, saw the investigation as a partisan effort to weaken the president rather than a serious scandal, so the investigation and impeachment had little effect on their approval of Clinton. The usual tendency of scandals to depress approval was therefore weakened. And at the same time this drama was unfolding, the economy—a powerful predictor of presidential approval—was growing rapidly. The public rewarded Clinton primarily for the economy, not for being impeached.

Presidents seek popular support by "going public."

When a president is **"going public,"** he engages in a highly visible campaign of trips, press conferences, interviews, speeches, and appearances designed to galvanize support around his agenda. These campaigns are precisely plotted, scripted, choreographed, and timed to elicit a favorable response from the public and the media. Every symbol and prop on the platform from which the president speaks is carefully chosen. Since World War II, presidents have gone public at an increasing rate. Dwight Eisenhower, in the 1950s, engaged in these activities about four times per month. The number forty years later, during Bill Clinton's presidency, was nearly thirty times per month.

In these public appeals, the president has strong advantages over Congress. Simply put, he is more likely to get access to the news media than are members of Congress. In part, the inherent significance of the presidency leads journalists to focus on this office. It is also due to the power of one—the president provides a single focal point that simplifies the task of presenting the news. Unlike 535 voting members of Congress, the president gives a journalist one story to tell.[26]

When President Bush was pushing his tax cut proposal in April 2003, he made a one-day visit full of speeches and photo opportunities in Ohio, the home state of Republican Senator George Voinovich. The trip received heavy media coverage. The president hoped that generating public support for his tax plan in Ohio would put pressure on the senator to support the president's plan. Despite the president's pressure, the senator would not agree to the president's proposed tax cut—but he provided Bush the vote he needed for a tax cut of $350 billion, half of the original proposal. The plan passed the Senate 51-50, with Vice President Dick Cheney casting the deciding vote. Although going public did not completely succeed in this case, careful observers noted that it was remarkable that the president managed to persuade Congress—and a reluctant Senator Voinovich—to pass a tax cut during a time of war, with the budget deficit expanding sharply, just one year after the president's first major tax cut.[27]

Sizable election victories lead presidents to claim they have a mandate.

Presidents elected to office with sizable victories, and who ran on a clear policy platform, are often in an advantageous position when dealing with Congress. These presidents can claim that they have received a **mandate** from the American people; that is, the public spoke clearly in the election about the direction in which it wanted the country to move. Of course, the more consistent the election results are nationally, the stronger the president's case. For example, if Republicans pick up many seats in the House and Senate formerly held by Democrats, win many governors' races, and win the presidency, the new Republican president is in a strong position to claim a mandate. It is a matter of perception: can the president convince the country, or more immediately, Congress, that he has a mandate? Most will try.[28]

Surprisingly, George W. Bush spent much of his first term governing as if he had received a strong conservative mandate from the public. Having won the presidency after a controversial Supreme Court decision brought him to office despite receiving fewer popular votes than Democrat Al Gore, many observers expected Bush to pursue a moderate agenda that would rely heavily on bipartisan coalitions. In some areas this turned out to be true, but in others the president pursued a more conservative tack that relied on almost unanimous support from congressional Republicans rather than a bipartisan coalition. The president made even stronger claims following his reelection in 2004, declaring explicitly that he had been given a mandate by virtue of his winning the popular vote and the Republicans picking up seats in the House and the Senate. Democrats, however, were unconvinced, and showed little inclination to cooperate with Bush on his major priorities, including judicial nominations and the reform of Social Security.

Presidents rely on fellow partisans to promote their policies.

Normally, the president can count on the members of his party in Congress to help him enact his policy ideas. The more members of the president's party elected to Congress, the better his chances are for legislative victories. This is a valuable electoral resource. The president still needs to persuade his fellow partisans to go along with him, but that task will usually be simpler than convincing members of the other party.

Unified and divided control of government Presidents, of course, do not get to choose the partisan balance in Congress, so they need to figure out how to work with the situation they face. Because the president and fellow partisans in Congress share many goals and were elected by similar constituencies, having his party in control of both houses is better than controlling one, and controlling one is better than controlling none. With his party in the majority in both houses, a situation known as **unified government,** the president is in a strong position to pass legislation to his liking. It is not a guarantee of success, however, because party members do not necessarily vote the same. Multiple factors affect whether legislators support the president on a vote. Constituency pressure, district economic interests, or other factors may cause a member of the president's party to vote against the president. President George W. Bush, for example, had great difficulty unifying fellow Republicans around a single plan for immigration reform after his reelection in 2004. On the other hand, significant accomplishments such as adding prescription drug benefits to Medicare were more popular among Democrats than Republicans.

In **divided government**, the party majority in one or both houses of Congress is held by a party different from the party of the president. If his party controls neither house, the president will typically face his most difficult challenges. Presidents may have some legislative success during this form of divided government, although less so than in unified government.[29] To succeed, the president needs to gain the support of a larger share of the opposition party by moving closer to their position, but without moving so far that he loses the support of his own partisans. The opposition party may want to deny the president victories, so it is likely to discourage its members from siding with the president. The president's success will be influenced by several factors, including how cohesive his party is, how cohesive the opposition party is, and the relative size of the two parties. The larger and more cohesive the opposition party is, the more difficult the president's legislative challenge (see Figure 14-5).

Political scientists researching leadership have found that party control of Congress complicates their analysis of presidential success. Politicians are strategic. In divided government, the president may have plans that he does not present to Congress because he believes they will have little chance at success. Or the president might offer a plan that he believes has as much or even more support in the opposition party than in his own. This was true for welfare reform during Bill Clinton's presidency and immigration reform during George W. Bush's. Similarly, during unified government, the president might offer bold legislative proposals that do not initially have strong support in the hope he can coax fellow partisans

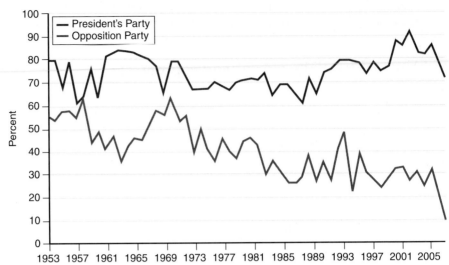

Figure 14-5. **Percent of House Roll-Call Votes On Which Party Members Supported the President's Position, 1953–2006.** Presidents get the greatest support from their fellow partisans in Congress. The growing gap in support between the president's party and the opposition party, represented by the shaded area, means presidents have increasingly had to rely on support from their own party.

Source: Source: Harold W. Stanley and Richard G. Niemi, *Vital Statistics on American Politics 2005-2006* (Washington, DC: CQ Press, 2006), pp. 260-61; Clea Benson, "CQ Vote Studies - Presidential Support: The Power of No," CQ Weekly, January 14, 2008, pp. 132-35.

to support him. Neither of these strategic actions change the overall pattern that presidents have more legislative success in unified government. But the net effect of these actions would be some additional wins when the opposition party controls Congress and some additional losses when his party controls Congress.

Differences between presidential and parliamentary systems These party dynamics make the president's relationship with Congress different from prime ministers' dealings with their legislatures in other countries. Whereas an American president is elected independently from Congress, and can serve even if his own party is a minority in Congress, a prime minister will be in office only if his party is the majority. A president is elected in a national election, but in a parliamentary system, constituents only elect legislators.[30] The prime minister is then selected by his or her party peers within Parliament.[31] If his party loses control of the legislature in the next election, he is guaranteed to lose his position as prime minister.

These differences make for significantly tighter ties between prime ministers and the legislators in their parties. Presidents Carter, Reagan, Clinton, and George W. Bush had all been state governors. Although somewhat familiar with national issues, they did not have strong ties with members of Congress. In contrast, prime ministers, as well as the heads of major government departments, emerge directly from Parliament. There is little need for "getting to know you" time. Not only do members of the party majority in Parliament know the prime minister, but they have *chosen* him as the person they wish to lead the country. Typically, they are ready to work with that person from day one.

Because parliamentary elections are not bound to a fixed schedule, the prime minister must make a determined effort to keep these ties strong. The relative independence from Congress that American presidents prize is less attractive in the case of prime ministers. Presidents rely heavily on their parties, but they also often need to forge some ties across party lines to enact parts of their agenda. In many parliamentary systems, by contrast, crossing party lines to support another party's position is very rare and heavily punished by the party whose member strayed. And while partisans in Congress may try to separate their electoral fate from the president's, partisans in Parliament know that if the prime minister is seen as a failure, their party is almost certain to be relegated to minority status in the next election. They therefore have an even stronger incentive than the president's fellow partisans in Congress to support their chief executive.

Popularity of current policies may affect presidential success.

Presidents can also draw on contextual resources. These are resources related to the nature of policy-making at particular points in time or in particular policy areas. Political time theory argues that the popularity of current policies, and whether the president's party supports or opposes those policies, will define presidential leadership potential.[32] The greatest opportunity to lead the country in a new direction occurs when a new president opposes existing policies that are widely considered to have failed, as Ronald Reagan did. However, relatively few presidents take office in a context open to such widespread policy change and bold presidential leadership. The most challenging situation faces the president who, like Jimmy Carter, wins office while his party's policies are perceived to be in crisis. Between these two extremes of leadership potential are those presidents who come to power when current policies are generally considered successful (Bill Clinton, George W. Bush). These presidents have more success in uniting people around a specific legislative plan when there is already some consensus for policy changes that are consistent in spirit with the current policies, rather than building a consensus for dramatic policy change.

Presidents may have some advantages in foreign policy.

The context of policy-making differs between foreign and domestic policy. In foreign policy, there are fewer interest groups, journalists, voters, and members of Congress who deeply care about these issues—a climate that gives the president a somewhat freer hand.[33] Because of this difference, the "two presidencies" theory argues that presidents exert significantly more influence over the writing and implementation of foreign policy than they do over domestic policy.

George W. Bush's tenure in office would appear to support the two presidencies theory. In waging wars against governments in Afghanistan and Iraq and against terrorist networks worldwide, the president has exerted his commander-in-chief authority, challenging the applicability of some U.S. laws and international treaties. But where these efforts have domestic implications, such as the trial and detention of terrorism suspects, Congress and the courts have tended to resist the president's authority. And his stiffest legislative challenges have been on domestic issues like Social Security reform.

Systematic evidence supports the two presidencies theory in some aspects of public policy-making but not in others. Presidential success on foreign policy votes in Congress has not been consistently better than in domestic policy votes. But more supportive of the theory, one analysis found that presidents are able to secure funding that better matches their budget priorities in foreign policy than in domestic policy. And when going public, presidents can sway public opinion more easily in foreign affairs than domestic affairs.

Windows of opportunity disrupt presidents' opponents.

Unique periods and events—"windows of opportunity"—provide another contextual resource important to presidential leadership. Opportunities emerge during these episodes because it may be harder for political opponents to defend the status quo and the public may be particularly receptive to presidential action. When Los Angeles erupted in riots in 1992, many observers concluded that President George H. W. Bush had—but failed to make the most of—a window of opportunity to exert leadership on domestic policy issues, an area in which he was viewed unfavorably by a majority of the public. In 2001, by contrast, the events of September 11 provided George W. Bush with the window to push for significant policy changes in domestic security, the fight against international terrorism, and foreign policy generally. Not only did September 11 provide a rally boost in the president's approval rating, but it created a willingness in Congress, the courts, and the public to entertain new policy initiatives. There is often an eagerness during these windows for the kind of leadership that only a president can provide.

CaseStudy: Passing the No Child Left Behind Act

During the lead-up to the 2000 election, Bush advocated major reforms for the balance of state and federal power in education policy, speaking from his experience as governor of Texas. As president, Bush then proposed that the federal government mandate that all students be tested in grades 3 through 8, that states and localities be held accountable to strict performance standards that would cover all students, and that schools failing to meet these standards be subject to sanctions. In January 2002, when the president signed the No Child Left Behind Act, he fulfilled one of his major campaign promises.[34] To do so, he needed to exercise many of the tools of leadership discussed in this section.

When President Bush came to office in 2001, the federal government's role in education had been on the national agenda for nearly two decades.[35] There was a substantial national consensus that the federal government needed to take a more active role in shaping K-12 education. One of the first necessary items of business was revising the Elementary and Secondary Education Act. The failure of the Republican Congress and Democratic President Clinton in 1999 to overcome their differences, provided Bush with a chance to lead in 2000 and 2001.

Although tradition and the president's party had long believed K-12 education to be an arena for the states and localities, the president positioned himself as the leading national figure in K-12 education reform. He was trying to claim an issue long associated with the Democratic Party. A national survey in 1999, for example, indicated that 52 percent of the public trusted Democrats to do a better job on education, while only 29 percent said they trusted Republicans to do a better job. But in the 2000 campaign Bush pushed harder on the issue than his Democratic opponent and touted his experience in reforming education while governor of Texas. And the public did broadly believe that standards, accountability, and improved performance were necessary for America's schools. He frequently drew upon beliefs in American political culture about individual opportunity and equality to make his arguments. When Bush talked about education reform, he often presented it as a civil rights issue to appeal to Democratic constituencies, put the "education establishment" on the defensive, and link himself to the federal government's longstanding interest in civil rights in education. Arguing against the "soft bigotry of low expectations," Bush insisted that education reform was particularly important for the nation's most disadvantaged and ill-served students.

Almost immediately after the Supreme Court certified his victory in December 2000, Bush held an education summit in Austin, Texas, featuring Republicans and centrist Democrats. He used personal persuasion skills to make Democratic legislators, in particular, feel like valued participants and new friends. Three days after the president's inauguration, the administration sent a legislative blueprint to Congress. This was not a proposed bill, but a statement indicating what the president would like to see in a bill. With this approach, Bush allowed Congress to work out the details, while making clear the basic principles he wished to see implemented. In this way, members of Congress could feel like full participants in the lawmaking process and could let their constituents know they had been vital in the reform of American education. The plan also borrowed from several ideas and proposals that had been circulating in Washington in the late 1990s, again allowing an array of participants to believe that the ultimate outcome would be shaped by their input.

With a House narrowly in Republican control and a Senate narrowly in Democratic control, the Republican president knew he would need some Democratic votes to pass a bill. The president went public to speak about his education plans, in an effort to raise the issue of educational accountability, to secure his position as the leading figure on the issue, and to pressure Congress to reach an agreement. Compromising on specific provisions, the president and administration staffers assembled a coalition of conservative Republicans, moderate and centrist Democrats, and traditional Democrats like Senator Ted Kennedy, who had invested much of his legislative career on the issue.

To build his coalition, Bush convinced Republicans to abandon their quests for education vouchers, limiting education spending, and giving states vast discretion over how to spend their federal funds.[36] Democrats, meanwhile, needed to accept annual state testing with sanctions for poor performing schools, a plan very unpopular with the teachers' unions that had often provided support for Democratic candidates. When the bills approved by the House and Senate went to conference committee, more than two thousand items remained unresolved. The president frequently reminded the committee members of his strong desire for a bill and relied on congressional heavyweights to push through the agreements. In the end, the signed legislation required all students, in all demographic groups, to reach proficiency in 12 years; monitored state, district, and school progress; allowed for student movement from weak performing schools; and threatened the reconstitution of persistently failing schools.

President Bush, with substantial help from key members of Congress and capitalizing on a 20-year legacy of federal government concern with K-12 education, managed to craft a bipartisan victory that put most of Washington on the side of reform. Democrats and Republicans alike could believe they got something from this deal in pursuit of school accountability—a goal that no one could oppose in the abstract. After all, who could argue that schools should *not* be able to demonstrate that their instruction is helping students' learn?

ThinkingCritically

1. What are the strategic challenges and opportunities facing a president who seeks to identify himself with an issue traditionally associated with the other major party?

2. President Bush chose to abandon some of his initial goals in pursuit of crafting bills that could win congressional approval. By what standards would you decide if such an action reflects pragmatic strategy or abandoning important principles?

Institutional Resources for Presidential Leadership

To improve their chances at leading successfully, presidents rely on the established agencies and offices of the executive branch; in addition, they may also create an array of new supporting institutions. Think of these institutions as concentric circles, with the president in the center. The outer ring consists of the Cabinet departments (discussed in further detail in Chapter 16). Closer in to the president is the Executive Office of the President, established during the presidency of Franklin Roosevelt. And closest to the president is the White House Staff. These institutions provide different kinds of resources for presidential leadership efforts. All have grown in size over time, especially since World War II.[37]

The Cabinet departments implement federal programs.

The outer ring of institutional resources, furthest away from the president, is the **Cabinet,** which includes departments that implement nearly all government programs and provide the vast majority of government services (see Figure 14-6). The Senate must approve the president's appointments to leadership positions in the 15 Cabinet departments. The heads of these departments are known as "secretaries" except for the Department of Justice, whose head is the attorney general. They are appointed, first, to run the major departments of the government and, second, to provide advice to the president and help him implement his agenda. The Cabinet meets with the president as a group; he can also call on their individual expertise. These departments, often in the news because they set important policies and run major programs, include Treasury, State, Defense, Justice, Housing and Urban Development, Health and Human Services, Transportation, Agriculture, and Education.

All department secretaries are permanent members of the Cabinet, but the president may also include other agencies that are not under the organizational control of any of the major departments. President Clinton, for example, included

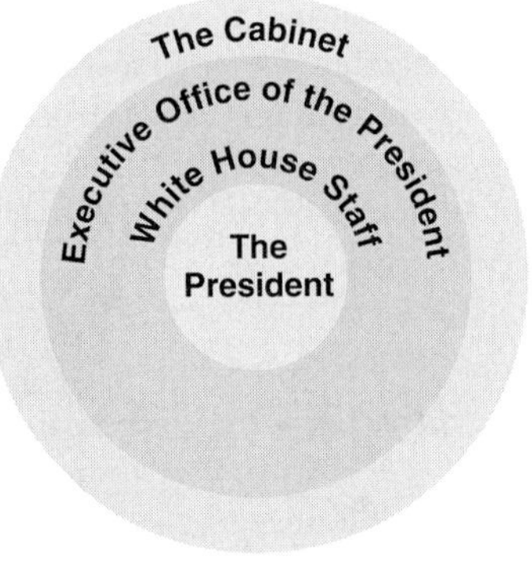

The Cabinet

Department Secretaries
State
Treasury
Defense
Justice
Health & Human Services
Labor
Commerce
Transportation
Energy
Housing & Urban Development
Veterans Affairs
Agriculture
Interior
Education
Homeland Security

Others Granted Cabinet Rank
Vice President
Administrator, Environmental Protection Agency
Director, Office of Management and Budget
U.S. Trade Representative
Director, Office of National Drug Control Policy

The Cabinet
Executive Office of the President
White House Staff
The President

White House Staff
Chief of Staff
Press Secretary
Legislative Affairs
Political Affairs
Public Liaison
Communications Director
White House Counsel
Intergovernmental Affairs
Policy Planning and Development
Cabinet Liaison
Domestic and Economic Affairs
Science and Technology Policy
National Security Affairs
Strategic Initiatives

Executive Office of the President
Council of Economic Advisors
Office of Management and Budget
Office of National AIDS Policy
Office of National Drug Control Policy
United States Trade Representative
Council on Environmental Quality
National Security Council
Domestic Policy Council
National Economic Council
Office of Administration
Office of Science and Technology Policy
President's Foreign Intelligence Advisory Board
Office of Faith-Based and Community Initiatives
Homeland Security Council
Privacy and Civil Liberties Oversight Board
USA Freedom Corps
White House Fellows Office
White House Military Office
Office of the First Lady

Figure 14-6. The Institutional Presidency, 2008. The president relies on the Cabinet departments to implement programs, the Executive Office of the President to provide policy advice, and the White House Staff to provide political advice.

the Environmental Protection Agency. Presidents will add these agencies to the Cabinet primarily because they genuinely want to hear the input of these agencies at Cabinet meetings, they want to make a symbolic show of support for a particular issue, or both.

From the president's point of view, there is always a risk that a department secretary will become so closely attached to the interests and perspectives of his or her department—become "captured"—that rather than communicating the president's viewpoint to the department, a secretary may push the department's views on the president. When the president's ideas meet resistance from department personnel, will the secretary support the president or will he or she obstruct the president's agenda? One notable case during the Bush presidency concerned Christine Todd Whitman, the administrator of the Environmental Protection Agency (who has Cabinet status). She resigned after a series of policy disagreements with the president and his closest advisers, including Vice President Dick Cheney, where the opinion of agency scientists was being overruled.

Because they are relatively high-profile figures, Cabinet officials also have the potential to put the president in the awkward situation of either defending or repudiating the Cabinet member. Statements by Defense Secretary Donald Rumsfeld, for example, created occasional controversy that forced a response from President Bush. In December 2004, Rumsfeld, hearing an American soldier's complaint that the military's vehicles in Iraq lacked adequate armor, replied that the Army was working as fast as it could to address the problem, but "you go to war with the Army you have. They're not the Army you might want or wish to have at a later time . . . . And if you think about it, you can have all the armor in the world on a tank and a tank can be blown up." Although in context Rumsfeld's comments expressed concern for the safety of troops, his seemingly aloof tone in the media's sound bites raised a firestorm of protest. White House officials found themselves defending the comments, and even the president was drawn into the fray in his press conference on December 20: "Listen, I know Secretary Rumsfeld's heart. . . . Beneath that rough and gruff no-nonsense demeanor is a good human being who cares deeply about the military and deeply about the grief war causes."[38]

One sign of the strain between presidents and the Cabinet is the large turnover of Cabinet officials in presidents' second terms. Although sometimes a Cabinet official simply wants to move on to a new challenge, obtain a more lucrative job in the private sector, or have a less hectic lifestyle, often the change in personnel is a direct result of presidential displeasure with the Cabinet official's performance. In the twentieth century, an average of about two Cabinet department heads served for both terms.[39] After being reelected in 2004, President George W. Bush replaced nine of fifteen department secretaries. Of the six who continued, four had taken their positions at the start of the president's first term. One of these was Rumsfeld, who, long under fire from both Democratic and Republican legislators, resigned shortly after the Republicans' loss of the House and Senate in the 2006 elections. Only three department heads have served for Bush's entire presidency.

The problems of directing department heads are more severe for the U.S. president than for prime ministers in European parliamentary systems. The U.S. president selects department heads from outside the legislature; the prime minister puts fellow legislators in charge of departments. The president cannot be sure that he or Congress will be able to work well with the heads of the Cabinet departments. Although the president appoints these officials, they are often people the president does not know well and has not worked with. The prime minister, on the other hand, chooses members of his party in Parliament to head the departments of his government. This would typically mean he has worked with these individuals and has confidence in them.

The agencies of the Executive Office of the President provide policy advice to the president.

The next closest concentric ring to the president is the **Executive Office of the President** (EOP), which consists of a number of policy-related groups that aid the president. Officials in these agencies generate policy alternatives and suggestions that are more faithful to the president's political agenda.[40] Their primary responsibility is to provide the president with trusted policy advice. Unlike Cabinet departments, Executive Office agencies generally do not administer programs, except in the sense of coordinating and directing the efforts of other federal agencies, and they do not have large staffs of career civil servants. Therefore, from the president's perspective, EOP officials do not have to wrestle with the pull of departmental loyalty that clouds the judgment of Cabinet secretaries. As Figure 14-6 indicates, the EOP provides advice and guidance across a number of policy areas, in some ways paralleling the areas covered by the Cabinet departments.

Probably the most important of the EOP agencies is the Office of Management and Budget (OMB). OMB enforces the president's budgetary priorities on the departments. OMB serves as a gateway through which departments must pass in making their budgetary requests, and it approves proposed regulations and testimony that a department wants to bring before Congress. In effect, OMB serves as a filter to make sure that departments are not seeking funds or regulations that are contrary to the president's program. Other particularly important EOP agencies are the Central Intelligence Agency, the Council of Economic Advisers, and the National Security Council.

The vice president is officially part of the EOP. Most vice presidents, however, are selected not for their policy expertise, but to provide the president with electoral advantages. A president with no Washington experience, for example, might select a vice president who has held office in the nation's capital. Or a vice president might be chosen because he increases the president's chances of winning a key state or region. The vice presidency is an often maligned institution, mostly because it has only two defined duties: to break tie votes in the Senate, and to succeed the president in case of the death, incapacity, or removal of the president from office. In some administrations, however, vice presidents do appear to play a greater role in policy-making. Bill Clinton delegated several significant policy tasks to Al Gore, especially in the area of reorganizing the federal bureaucracy, and George W. Bush relies heavily on the foreign policy advice of his vice president, Dick Cheney, a former secretary of defense.

The offices of the White House Staff provide political advice to the president.

The institutional circle closest to the president is the **White House Staff** (WHS) (sometimes referred to as the White House Office), a group of offices that provides the president with political advice, promotes the president's program with legislators and interest groups, and handles the president's public relations. With only about 420 employees in the Bush administration, the WHS is relatively small

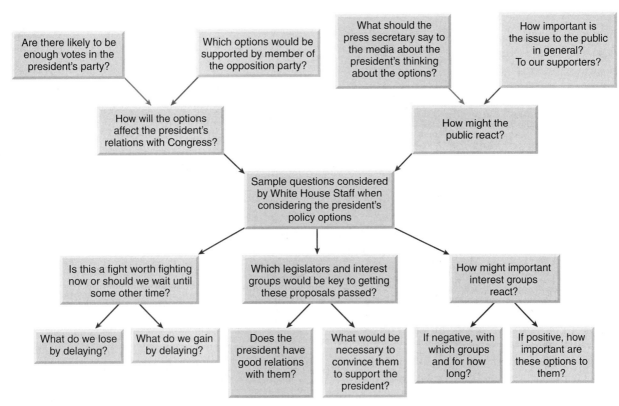

Figure 14-7. Types of Questions Asked by White House Staff. The White House Staff provides the president with political alternatives based on their analysis of the political environment.

compared to the EOP, which has about 1,800 employees, and the Cabinet departments, which total 1.7 million civilian employees. The WHS consists of small units such as the offices of the press secretary, legislative affairs, public liaison, and intergovernmental affairs, to name just a few. The primary concern of the WHS is the political well-being of the president. Whereas the EOP provides the president with policy advice and might be thought of as the president's policy filter, the White House Staff is the political filter. Figure 14-7 provides examples of the issues raised by the WHS when it considers policy proposals that emerge either from executive departments or Congress.

For President George W. Bush, Karl Rove was the key political confidante in the WHS. A senior adviser since Bush's Texas days, Rove headed the offices of Legislative Affairs, Political Affairs, and Strategic Initiatives. In the White House, he advised the president about how to advance his agenda, tend to important constituency groups, and increase his public approval. In his words, "my job is to pay attention to the things that affect his political future."[41] His knowledge of political history, and particularly his desire to cement Republican majorities for the long term, influenced the political advice he offered the president. For example, he is credited with being a chief advocate of fostering close ties between the president and evangelical Christians and in forging a mobilization drive to increase the turnout of evangelicals in the 2004 election. He also, however, came under fierce criticism in Bush's second term for the administration's political missteps concerning Hurricane Katrina, the war in Iraq, and allegations of government corruption.

SUMMARY

▶ Political institutions result from compromise and are crafted to solve particular governing problems, and that is certainly true of the U.S. presidency. The American presidency was an attempt by the Framers to balance many competing ideas about executive power. As a compromise, it contains some inherent contradictions. It is the office that Americans demand the most from, but its constitutional list of specific duties is relatively meager. The very vagueness of the job description has accommodated a historical expansion of the meaning and impact of the presidency from the time of the early republic to the present.

▶ Presidents have both formal and informal powers at their disposal in reaching their goals. Formal powers such as the veto, executive orders, and the role of commander-in-chief are specified in law or the Constitution, or are realized through independent executive initiative. The origins of informal powers are less easily identified. These powers include the president's skill at persuading others to do what he wants and the ability to tap into and strategically exploit the reservoir of support for basic values in American political culture. The manner in which presidents use their powers can be checked by the courts, which can declare presidential actions unconstitutional or inconsistent with law, and by Congress, which can use its legislative, budgeting, and, in extreme cases, impeachment powers to thwart presidents.

▶ Presidents draw on a variety of public and political resources to exercise leadership. The president's public approval receives substantial attention from politicians and political observers, and presidents devote significant amounts of time to appealing to the public to support their proposals. A president with a convincing election victory and his party in the majority in the House and Senate is in a strong position for successful leadership. Other factors that affect a president's success are the support for existing policies as well as differences between foreign and domestic policy.

▶ Presidents °also rely on institutional resources to exercise leadership. The Cabinet departments implement nearly all federal programs and are therefore crucial to the president's agenda. The Executive Office of the President provides the president with policy advice. And the White House Staff specializes in providing the president political advice and services.

KEY TERMS

approval rating, p. 000
Cabinet, p. 000
delegation, p. 000
divided government, p. 000
Electoral College, p. 000
executive agreement, p. 000
Executive Office of the President, p. 000
executive order, p. 000
executive privilege, p. 000
formal powers, p. 000
going public, p. 000

impeachment, p. 000
leadership, p. 000
line-item veto, p. 000
mandate, p. 000
necessary and expedient clause, p. 000
pocket veto, p. 000
take care clause, p. 000
rally event, p. 000
unified government, p. 000
veto, p. 000
White House Staff, p. 000

SUGGESTED READINGS

Edward Corwin. 1948. *The President, Office and Powers, 1787–1948: History and Analysis of Practice and Opinion.* New York: New York University Press. Classic treatment of the president's constitutional powers.

George Edward and Desmond King, eds. 2007. *The Polarized Presidency of George W. Bush.* New York: Oxford University Press. Collection of essays reflecting on Bush's presidency.

Marc Landy and Sidney Milkis. 2000. *Presidential Greatness.* Lawrence, KS: University of Kansas Press. Careful assessment of the elements of presidential greatness and the individuals who achieved it.

Sidney Milkis and Michael Nelson. 2003. *The American Presidency: Origins and Development 1776–2002.* Washington, D.C.: Congressional Quarterly Press. Thorough history of the evolution of the office of the presidency since the nation's founding.

Richard Neustadt. 1990. *Presidential Power and the Modern Presidents.* New York: Free Press. A highly influential analysis of the informal powers that presidents utilize to achieve their policy objectives in the modern era.

Richard Pious. 1995. *The Presidency.* New York: Longman. Overview of the office of the presidency, with special attention paid to historical developments.

Arthur M. Schlesinger, Jr. 2004. *The Imperial Presidency,* reprint ed. New York: Mariner Books. A careful documentation of the excesses of presidential power.

Stephen Skowronek. 2007. *The Politics Presidents Make: Leadership from John Adams to Bill Clinton.* Cambridge: Harvard University Press. A rich account of the various political environments facing presidents when they assume office and the limits and opportunities for leadership in those environments.

electoral college the meeting, in each state and the District of Columbia, of electors who cast votes to elect the president. In most states, electors are required by law to vote for the winner of the popular vote in that state.

necessary and expedient clause a clause in Article II, Section 3, of the Constitution that authorizes the president to recommend legislation to Congress.

take care clause the constitutional clause that grants the president the authority and leeway to determine if laws are being "faithfully executed" and to take action if in his judgment they are not.

executive privilege the idea that executive branch officials need to be able to advise president in confidence, and that the president has a right to prevent that advice from becoming public.

delegation the granting of authority by Congress to the president to be the first or main actor in a policy area, usually with implicit or explicit limits on actions that Congress would find acceptable.

leadership the ability to influence and guide others to achieve some desired policy or action.

formal powers specific grants of authority defined in the Constitution or in law.

veto the president's power to reject legislation passed by Congress. Congress can override a veto with a two-thirds vote in both the House and Senate.

pocket veto the president's veto of a bill without the opportunity for Congress to override the veto. It occurs if the president does not act on a bill within ten days after passage by Congress and Congress adjourns during that time.

line-item veto a form of veto power that allows the chief executive to veto portions of bills rather than entire bills. Over forty U.S. governors enjoy some form of line-item veto power, but presidents do not have this power.

executive agreement an agreement with a foreign country that does not require changes in U.S. law or congressional approval.

executive order a presidential directive or proclamation that has the force of law.

impeachment a vote in the House of Representatives that initiates a trial against the president in the Senate, alleging the president has committed "high crimes and misdemeanors," treason, or bribery. If convicted by the Senate, the president is removed from office.

approval rating the percentage of the public that approves of the job the president is doing overall.

rally event short-term international events or military actions that boost presidential approval ratings temporarily.

going public activities of presidents such as highly visible trips, press conferences, interviews, speeches, and public appearances in an attempt to raise public support for a policy agenda.

mandate the idea that the public provided clear policy guidance in the results of the prior election.

unified government a situation where the presidency and both houses of Congress are controlled by the same party.

divided government a situation where the presidency is held by one party and at least one house of Congress is controlled by a different party.

Cabinet a group of the top-ranking officials of every major federal department, plus other officials included by the president, who meet periodically with the president to discuss major administration priorities and policies.

Executive Office of the President a group of agencies in the executive branch that primarily generate policy alternatives for the president's consideration.

White House Staff a group of offices in the executive branch that provides the president with political advice, promotes the president's program with legislators and interest groups, and handles the president's public relations.

15 The Federal Court System

In the case of *Commonwealth of Massachusetts et al. v. Environmental Protection Agency*, the U.S. Supreme Court weighed in, for the first time, on the political debate over what should be done about global warming. The stakes could not have been higher. "This is the whole ball of wax," said Sierra Club attorney David Bookbinder about the Court's decision to take the case. "This will determine whether the Environmental Protection Agency is to regulate greenhouse gases from cars and whether EPA can regulate carbon dioxide from power plants."[1]

The seeds of *Massachusetts v. EPA* were planted in 1999. That year, a number of environmental groups petitioned the EPA to limit new motor vehicles' emissions of carbon dioxide (CO_2) and other greenhouse gases, which are produced by the burning of fossil fuels like gasoline.[2] Under the 1963 Clean Air Act and its subsequent amendments, the EPA is charged with setting emissions standards for air pollutants that harm the public's health. While the EPA under President Bill Clinton had formally

acknowledged that CO_2 was a pollutant that warranted regulation,[3] the EPA under President George W. Bush adopted the opposite position. In September 2003, the agency rejected the environmental groups' request to regulate CO_2. As justification, the EPA explained that it did not have the authority to regulate the gas because it is not explicitly classified as an air pollutant by the Clean Air Act. It also cited "scientific uncertainty" about whether global warming is truly harmful to human health.[4]

Environmental groups and a number of state government officials were outraged by the EPA's response. Massachusetts Attorney General Tom Reilly decided to sue the EPA. Joined by 11 other states and several environmental groups, Reilly brought the case to the U.S. Court of Appeals for the District of Columbia in October 2003.[5] Reilly argued that the EPA's failure to limit CO_2 emissions harmed his state of Massachusetts and the other states filing suit. CO_2 contributed to climate change, he said, which in turn caused rising sea levels and the erosion of his and other states' coastlines. By not regulating CO_2 emissions, Reilly argued, the EPA neglected its legal responsibility

to protect Americans from the harmful effects of air pollution.

Reilly also accused the EPA of tailoring environmental policy to President Bush's political preferences. Bush, after all, had expressed concerns about the potential negative economic effects of regulating CO_2 emissions.[6] "The vacuum of leadership on global warming by the Bush administration is a betrayal of the best interests of the American people," said New York Attorney General Eliot Spitzer, then a party to the suit, and one-time governor of the state of New York.[7] Spitzer, Reilly, and the attorneys general of the other states argued that just because the Clean Air Act did not explicitly identify CO_2 as an air pollutant does *not* mean that Congress intended for the EPA to avoid regulating it. Rather, Congress had purposely made the law flexible so that the experts at the EPA would be free to craft policy as scientists developed more knowledge about air pollution.

In a 2-1 decision, the U.S. Court of Appeals sided with the EPA, with only one judge voting in favor of the states. One of the judges claimed that the other side had not actually been harmed by the EPA and therefore had no reason to be in court. The other judge siding with the EPA argued that even if the agency did have the authority to regulate greenhouse gases, it was free to decide *not* to do so.[8]

The attorneys general appealed the case to the U.S. Supreme Court. On April 2, 2007, the Supreme Court justices voted 5 to 4 in their favor, reversing the decision from the lower court. The five-member majority ruled that CO_2 is an air pollutant under the Clean Air Act and therefore can be regulated by the EPA. Justice John Paul Stevens wrote, "EPA has offered no reasoned explanation for its refusal to decide whether greenhouse gases cause or contribute to climate change."[9] In the future, the majority said, if the EPA decides not to regulate greenhouse gases from new motor vehicles, it must provide a reasonable scientific explanation for that decision.[10]

The four dissenting justices argued that the Court had gone beyond its authority as a neutral decision-maker in classifying CO_2 as an air pollutant. They claimed that Congress and the executive branch—not the federal court system—should be responsible for addressing the global warming concerns raised by the plaintiffs.[11] In his dissenting opinion, Justice Antonin Scalia wrote, "this Court has no business substituting its own

desired outcome for the reasoned judgment of the responsible agency."[12]

Justices in the majority—the more liberal members of the Court—called their decision a check on executive power based on clear interpretation of the Clean Air Act. Dissenting justices—all originally appointed to the Court by Republican presidents—accused the majority of trying to make policy on global warming. Did the justices' own political leanings influence how they voted in *Massachusetts v. EPA*? Perhaps it was not a coincidence that the dissenting justices voted in favor of the Republican presidential administration and

the conservative EPA in a case brought by 12 attorneys general, all of whom were Democrats.[13] The timing of the decision was also quite convenient. Was the Court politically strategic in deciding its first ever global warming case in favor of environmentalists only five months after Democrats took control of Congress?[14] Congressional Democrats applauded the *Massachusetts v. EPA* decision as a call to action. Upon hearing of the decision, Rep. John Dingell (D-IL) stated, "Today's ruling provides another compelling reason why Congress must enact, and the President must sign, comprehensive climate change legislation."[15]

THIS CHAPTER WILL EXAMINE:

▶ the constitutional design of the federal judiciary

▶ the organization of the judiciary

▶ the kinds of cases that judges hear

▶ the ways in which judges decide cases that involve public policy

▶ the manner by which judges are appointed to office.

The Constitutional Design of the Federal Judiciary

At the nation's founding, the Framers sought to build a federal judiciary that would serve the federal government in much the same way that state judiciaries had done in state governments for years. A federal judiciary was needed to perform the core functions of: (1) interpreting the laws that Congress and the president enacted; (2) issuing rulings over disputes where no guiding legislation previously existed; (3) ensuring that individuals who violated these laws and rulings were appropriately punished; and (4) compensating (where possible) the victims of these violations.

The first three articles of the Constitution lay out the powers, resources, and responsibilities of Congress first (in Article I), then the president (in Article II), and finally the judiciary (in Article III). Last in order, Article III also is shortest in length. It establishes a "Supreme Court" and "inferior" courts operating underneath its jurisdiction; it recognizes a "judicial power" that applies to laws, treaties, and other formal acts of government; and it offers some brief guidelines about the prosecution of cases involving criminal behavior and treason. And that is all.

The Founders gave the judiciary a brief, and by and large vague, mandate. A complete system of courts did not appear until 1789, when Congress enacted the

Judiciary Act, which created a system of lower courts that would ease the workload of the one "Supreme Court." It should not come as a surprise, then, that most of the Founders expected that the judiciary would be the weakest of the three branches of government. According to Alexander Hamilton, the judiciary would be the "least dangerous branch." Whereas Congress had the power of the purse (that is, the power to levy taxes) and the president had the power of the sword (that is, control over the military), the judiciary had only its judgment. The ability of judges to exert political power, then, ultimately depended upon the persuasive appeal of the substantive rulings that it handed down. Recognizing its original design, the political scientist Robert Dahl concluded that the judiciary's "most important [base of power] is the unique legitimacy attributed to its interpretations of the Constitution."[16]

Consequentially, from the nation's beginning, judicial proceedings were structured to foster notions of respect and legitimacy. And so they are to this very day. Deliberations in courts are different from those in any other political institution. When judges enter courtrooms, everyone inside is required to stand. Judges are referred to as "your honor." And when serving on the bench, judges wear robes. All of this symbolic imagery is meant to increase the chances that citizens and other political actors will accept court rulings as binding—for again, lacking the powers of either the purse or sword, the courts have little means by which to independently ensure that others heed their orders.

Perhaps most importantly, judges do everything possible to exude the qualities of a trustworthy and independent arbiter of justice. Judges go out of their way to distinguish themselves from elected political actors, whose job it is to represent the interests of a diverse and often fickle public. In the tumult of daily political life, courts protect individual rights, constitutional principles, and time-tested legal doctrine against the "tyranny of the majority." Rather than engaging in politics, judges do their utmost to rise above it.

For the most part, such efforts of successive generations of judges seem to have borne fruit. Today, citizens hold the courts in higher regard than any other branch of government. According to one national public opinion poll conducted in January 2007, 72 percent of Americans expressed favorable views of the Supreme Court. By comparison, 53 percent of Americans had a favorable perception of Congress, and only 33 percent approved of the job George W. Bush was doing as president.[17] Even when public approval of the Supreme Court dips, it usually remains equal to or higher than support for the other branches. For instance, the Supreme Court's approval ratings fell to 57 percent in July 2007, following a series of controversial rulings. Yet, this number was still 16 percentage points higher than support for Congress and 24 percentage points higher than the president's job approval rating.[18]

With such strong public support, the courts stand at the center of some of the most pressing national controversies—about freedom of speech, reproduction, civil rights, the treatment of "enemy combatants," and the like. Failing to advance their preferred political reforms in the legislative and executive branches, interest groups often turn to the courts. Both state and federal law enforcement agencies prosecute criminal activities through the courts. And when individuals feel that their constitutional rights have been violated, they regularly seek redress in the judiciary.

As stated above, this chapter examines how the federal court system is structured, and how federal judges make decisions about cases. When analyzing the latter issue, though, it will not do to simply take the supposed impartiality of the judiciary at face value. Just because judges claim to operate outside of politics does not mean, as a matter of practice, that they do. In fact, politics plays an integral role in both the selection of judges and in judicial decision-making itself.

The Organization of the Federal Judiciary

The federal government supports many different types of courts. For example, the so-called Foreign Intelligence Surveillance Act Court reviews requests to track the behavior of suspected terrorists within the United States. The United States Territorial Courts operate within U.S. territories such as the Virgin Islands and Guam. And the Court of International Trade deals with cases involving trade and customs.

The core elements of the federal judiciary, however, consist of district courts, appellate courts, and the Supreme Court. These courts accept three kinds of cases: those in which the federal government is a party; those that involve a question about the U.S. Constitution, a federal law, or a federal treaty; and those involving a large civil suit between two parties from different states. In terms of sheer volume, district courts, appellate courts, and the Supreme Court collectively decide the vast majority of cases that come before the federal judiciary.

The federal judiciary is hierarchical.

Figure 15-1 shows the three tiers of the federal judiciary. The bottom tier consists of 94 **district courts**. Every state contains at least one district court, and the most-populated (California, Texas, and New York) contain as many as four. Individual judges oversee district court proceedings, and a single judge (or a jury) renders the verdict. In 2006, a total of 678 full-time federal judges worked in district courts.

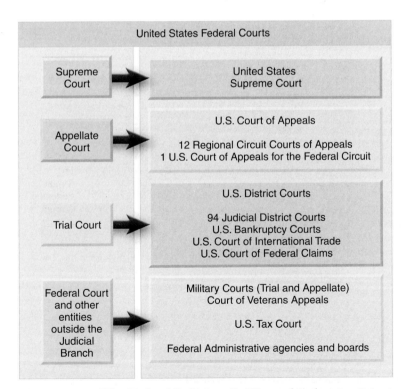

Figure 15-1. The Federal Judiciary Is Hierarchical. Most federal cases are decided in district courts. A portion of them are then appealed to appellate courts. And a tiny fraction of these make it to the Supreme Court, which has final say over the outcome.

Source: http://uscourts.gov/outreach/structure.jpg.

These judges are appointed by the president and can hold office for as long as they are alive. These life-term judges then have the power to appoint **magistrate judges**, who serve either four- or eight-year terms. By hearing and deciding minor cases, and by overseeing the early stages of major cases, magistrate judges help reduce the caseload of district court judges. In 2006, 550 magistrate judges worked in district courts around the nation.[19]

The second tier of the federal judiciary consists of **appellate courts**. Appellate courts, as discussed further below, primarily consider challenges to cases that have already been decided at the district level. Appellate courts are organized into 13 circuits. As shown in Figure 15-2, 12 circuits have regional jurisdictions; that is, the rulings of courts within these circuits are legally binding within a specified geographic area. Eleven of these circuits are referred to by number, and one is referred to as the District of Columbia Circuit. There is also a federal circuit, which accepts cases based on subject matter rather than regional location. In 2006, a total of 179 appellate judges worked in the federal circuit courts. Typically, panels of three judges hear cases at the appellate level. To win a case, therefore, a party must secure the support of either two or three of the judges.

Standing atop the federal judiciary is the **Supreme Court**, which is the only court that is explicitly identified in Article III of the Constitution. While there are many district and appellate courts, there is just one Supreme Court, which is located in Washington, D.C. In any given year, the Supreme Court considers only a small fraction of the cases that have proceeded through the district and appellate

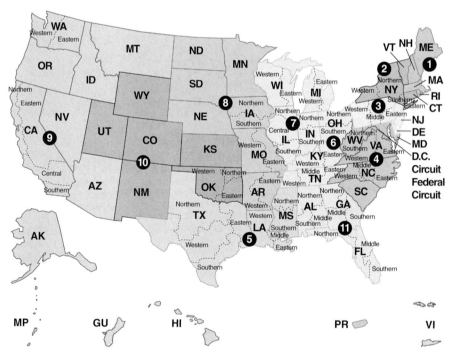

Figure 15-2. U.S. Federal Courts Are Divided into Circuits. Circuits serve different geographic regions, which vary dramatically in size. The first circuit includes only the northeastern portion of the country. The ninth, by contrast, includes the entire West, along with Alaska and Hawaii.

Source: http://www.uscourts.gov/courtlinks/.

courts. Between 2004 and 2006, the Supreme Court never heard more than 87 cases per year, and it never offered a decision on more than 85.[20] Though the Supreme Court decides far fewer cases than the other courts, those that it does decide tend to have the biggest impact on society. Some of the most important have included *Brown v. Board of Education* (1954), which struck down state-mandated segregation in public schools; *Gideon v. Wainwright* (1963), which required the government to ensure that all individuals charged with criminal acts were granted adequate legal representation; *U.S. v. Nixon* (1974), which forced President Nixon to turn over White House audio recordings that would ultimately lead to his resignation from office; and *Bush v. Gore* (2000), which put George W. Bush into the White House.

In the United States, the three tiers of state-level courts mirror (in name and function) the three tiers of federal-level courts. Other countries, however, have structured their systems rather differently. In Israel, for example, religious courts—which deal with disputes about Jewish dietary laws, the necessary qualifications to become a rabbi, and other matters relating to religious law and customs—co-exist with secular magistrate, district, and supreme courts that focus on civil and criminal proceedings. Portugal's Supreme Court is at the top of a tiered system that handles civil and criminal cases, but a separate Constitutional Court is responsible for judging the constitutionality of legislative acts and international agreements. Finland has created special courts to handle certain types of civil cases, such as land, water, or labor disputes. Clearly, there is no single template for how a judicial system ought to be structured. Instead, countries tend to develop legal systems that reflect their political histories and cultural norms, and that best suit the particular kinds of local cases that require resolution.[21]

District and appellate rulings can be appealed to the next level.

Almost all federal court cases start at the district level. District judges, though, do not have the final say about a case's outcome. The losing side always has the option of appealing to the appellate court, which can affirm the district court's decision, reverse it, or refuse to take the case—in which case the district ruling stands. Whatever the outcome at the appellate level, the losing side has yet another opportunity to appeal—this time to the Supreme Court. The highest court to issue a ruling has the final say on the outcome of the case.

The vast majority of cases terminate at the district court, and therefore it is the district court's judgment that usually settles the matter. The high costs of litigation, combined with the fact that higher courts usually come to the same judgment as lower courts, generally convince the losing side to accept defeat. Trying cases, additionally, can take an extraordinary amount of time. It can take years for a case to wind its way through the federal judiciary.

The Supreme Court is especially choosy about which cases it will hear. Historically, the Supreme Court has accepted—or, to use the technical term, granted a **writ of certiorari** to—around 5 percent of petitions for appeals. Given the astronomical rise of cases filed with the Supreme Court in the last half-century, this number has dwindled down to about 1 percent. In 1945, just over 1,000 cases were appealed to the Supreme Court. By 2000, the number surpassed 9,000 cases.

The Supreme Court is the only judicial body that grants "cert," short for *writ of certiorari*. Doing so requires the support of four Supreme Court justices, the so-called "rule of four." Typically, the Court grants cert when either an important legal or constitutional issue is at stake, or when lower courts in different circuits came to different conclusions about a particular issue.[22] Such was the case in 2005 when the Court chose to hear two cases dealing with the display of the Ten Commandments on government property. In *McCreary County v. ACLU of Kentucky*, the Sixth Circuit ruled that two Kentucky counties' displays of the Ten Commandments on the walls of their courthouses violated the establishment clause of the First Amendment. Around the same time, the Fifth Circuit in *Van Orden v. Perry* ruled that the display of the Ten Commandments on the grounds of the Texas State Capitol *was* constitutional. The Supreme Court intervened, clarifying that the intended purpose of such displays—whether purely religious or partially secular—must be taken into account in deciding matters of constitutionality with regards to the establishment clause.

Though most cases start at the district level, some go straight to the Supreme Court. Article III of the Constitution, for instance, stipulates that "all Cases affecting Ambassadors, other public Ministers and Consuls, and those in which a State shall be Party" shall be decided by the Supreme Court. When the Supreme Court has **original jurisdiction**, it is the first and last court to hear a federal case. The most common instance of original jurisdiction is when two states are in conflict with one another. Kansas and Colorado, for example, have been arguing for decades over the rights to the upper waters of the Arkansas River. In 1985, Kansas accused Colorado of violating their mutual Arkansas River Compact, which led to a series of lawsuits that fell under the original jurisdiction of the Supreme Court. And most recently, in *Kansas v. Colorado* (2004), the Supreme Court denied Kansas's request that a River Master be appointed to settle all remaining disputes over the distribution of water rights between the two states.

Other cases bypass the federal district courts for other reasons. Challenges to actions taken by federal administrative agencies often begin in the D.C. Court of Appeals. This explains why the judicial history of *Massachusetts v. EPA* discussed at the outset of this chapter did not begin with a district court ruling. Similarly, as it did in *Bush v. Gore*, the U.S. Supreme Court directly receives appeals to state supreme court rulings.

Supreme Court proceedings are highly scripted.

Whereas judges serve on district and appellate courts, justices serve on the Supreme Court. And when a case makes it to the top of the federal judiciary, the nine justices who comprise the Supreme Court hear it. Once the Court has agreed to hear a case, both sides submit **briefs**, which contain legal arguments about the dispute at hand. These briefs discuss relevant past case law, outline the case's key facts, and present additional research that might bear on a particular policy issue. After they and their clerks have reviewed these briefs, the justices meet to hear **oral arguments** directly from the lawyers. During these sessions, the two lawyers are granted a half-hour each to make their arguments. Typically, though, the justices interrupt them, long before their time is up, to ask pointed questions.

Following oral arguments, the justices gather for **conference**, where they discuss their current thinking on the case and cast preliminary votes. This meeting provides each justice with some sense of where the other justices stand on the case. Conferences are completely confidential, however, and no formal record is kept of what is said or done during them.

The **chief justice**, who currently is John Roberts, presides over the conference and then selects which justice will write the majority opinion of the Court.[23] As its name implies, the **majority opinion** reflects the collective judgment of those justices—typically five or more—who are on the majority side of the vote.[24] The majority opinion represents the final determination of the Court. Whoever has the job of writing this opinion will do so, typically, with great care. It is not uncommon for justices to compose multiple drafts of an opinion. Usually, these drafts are written in ways that intentionally curry the support of every individual member of the majority.

In addition to the majority opinion, some members of the majority may decide to write **concurring opinions**, which outline additional considerations that they think are important and provide alternative rationales for the majority opinion. Members of the minority typically write **dissenting opinions**, which outline their reasoning on the case and often identify the flaws that they perceive in the majority or concurring opinions. Concurring and dissenting opinions are elements of the final record of the Court, but only the majority opinion is officially binding. Lawyers and judges in subsequent court cases, nonetheless, may cite elements of concurring and dissenting opinions to justify their positions. In fact, the most influential element of a court case can sometimes be a passing reference or footnote found in a concurring or dissenting opinion. Rather than the Court's majority opinion in *Youngstown Sheet and Tube Co. v. Sawyer* (1953), for instance, it was Justice Robert Jackson's concurring opinion that established an influential framework for subsequent courts to evaluate challenges to executive authority.

Having issued its decision, the Supreme Court typically sends a case back to a lower court for implementation. The justices tend to see their job as establishing broad principles that are meant to guide judicial decision-making at the district and appellate levels. As a consequence, the justices tend not to become especially involved in the details of the cases that come before them. Instead, having resolved the largest points of contention in a dispute, the justices rely upon district and appellate judges to make sure that their ruling is appropriately implemented.

The Amount and Types of Cases That Courts Process

As should now be clear, the primary responsibility of judges is to resolve disputes. Judges play the role of referee both in society and, as we'll soon see, in politics as well. They identify when an individual, a group of individuals, or an organization has suffered because of actions that are either unlawful or that violate established agreements; judges then determine the appropriate course of action. They take cases that determine whether one person stole money from another person, who was at fault in a car accident, and whether a business unlawfully fired an employee. And in each instance, judges then decide the appropriate remedy—whether it be time spent in prison, financial compensation for automobile damages, or financial compensation for lost wages.

In an adversarial system, judges decide criminal and civil cases.

U.S. courts have a rather peculiar way of resolving disputes. Rather than encouraging the two parties in the dispute to behave cooperatively, U.S. courts encourage the parties to behave adversarially. The legal counsel of each side independently decides what arguments and evidence to put forward. They do so, moreover, in an explicit effort to advance their own interests and undermine those of their adversary. This system sharply differs from the approach used in some European countries. In Germany and France, for example, judges lead the investigation, unearthing evidence and questioning witnesses. Lawyers, by contrast, play a relatively passive, supporting role.[25] The adversarial and inquisitorial systems derive from very different legal traditions. The former find its historical roots in English common law, and the latter in Roman law.

In U.S. court cases, the **plaintiff** brings the case before the court and, usually, makes accusations of wrong-doing. The **defendant** is the person or institution against whom the complaint is made. In a trial, both sides offer arguments and evidence to support their positions. A judge presides over the deliberations, deciding what kinds of evidence and arguments can be presented. At the end of a trial, a court ruling is made about which side made the strongest case and what should happen as a consequence.

The power to issue a court ruling is given to judges and juries. In the pages that follow we will have much more to say about the ways in which judges go about making their decisions on matters of law. **Juries**, meanwhile, render decisions on matters of fact. Hence, juries typically decide whether the facts best support one party or another, and judges then determine the appropriate outcome of the case. Juries consist of private citizens who are selected to listen to the trial and as a group offer a final verdict. In the lead-up to a trial, lawyers for both the plaintiff and defendant select members of the jury by questioning candidates to ascertain which are most free from any bias or prejudice that may impair the jury's judgment. Lawyers tend to reject those who they think will rule unfavorably. Juries are meant to provide an impartial judgment about a defendant's actions by his or her peers. Whether the practice of jury trials reaches this objective, though, is the subject of considerable controversy.[26]

Judges issue rulings on two kinds of cases: criminal and civil. **Criminal cases**, as the name implies, involve violations of the criminal code—that is, those statutes that are intended to protect the public's health, order, safety, and morality. In criminal cases, the plaintiff (also called the prosecutor) is always the government, and the defendant is the individual accused of committing a crime—whether it involves using illegal drugs or robbing a store or conducting fraudulent business practices. If the evidence suggests "beyond a reasonable doubt" that the defendant is guilty of committing a crime, then he or she faces punishments ranging from fines, probation, imprisonment, and even execution. The severity of the punishment, which is the purview of the judge, depends upon the severity of the crime. If the jury decides that the evidence is not sufficiently strong, however, then the defendant may avoid punishment altogether.

Civil cases concern violations of the civil code, which summarizes the legal rights and obligations that individuals have toward one another. When an individual slips and falls in a grocery store, he might sue the owner for negligence; when a husband and wife get divorced, they might fight over the fair division of belongings; or when a stock holder loses money from an investment, he might sue the corporation for bad business practices. In civil cases, the plaintiff is not the government, but instead a private individual, group of individuals, or institution. To win a case, the plaintiff in a civil trial needs only show that most—or more technically, a "preponderance"—of the evidence supports his or her position. If a jury finds in favor of the plaintiff, he or she does not confront many of the punishments that accompany criminal violations. Rather, the defendant has to pay damages (typically monetary in nature) to the plaintiff. Occasionally, the defendant must also take certain corrective actions that reduce the chances that other individuals or groups will suffer similar harm.

In some instances, multiple individuals come together to bring a civil case to trial. In these **class action suits**, the plaintiff typically consists of a group that suffered a common injury. Examples might include residents of a small town whose water is polluted, members of a minority group who have been discriminated against, or parents of children who have been injured by a dangerous toy. If successful, the financial rewards of a class action suit are divided among the members of the group.

The 2000 movie *Erin Brockovich*, for which Julia Roberts won a Best Actress Oscar, is based on a large class-action lawsuit that was settled in California in 1996. The case dates to the 1950s and 1960s, when the chemical chromium was used in a Pacific Gas and Electric (PG&E) pumping station and then leaked into the local groundwater. Over the next several decades, residents and visitors to the nearby town of Hinckley complained of serious illnesses that they believed were the result of drinking contaminated well water. Los Angeles lawyer Thomas Girardi, with the spirited assistance of his legal clerk, Erin Brockovich, represented 650 plaintiffs in their lawsuit against PG&E, who admitted the leakages but denied that the contamination was responsible for the complainants' problems. Following two years of negotiations, the utility company settled the dispute by agreeing to pay $333 million to a fund that would be distributed among the hundreds of plaintiffs.[27]

Courts do not resolve all disputes.

Not everyone can bring a civil case to trial. To do so, one must have **standing**— that is, one must personally have suffered a well-defined injury because of actions that violate the civil code. A pedestrian who watches two cars crash into one another from the safety of a nearby restaurant cannot sue the owners of the vehicles for reckless driving; and citizens who are outraged but personally unaffected by a business's hiring and firing decisions cannot sue for discrimination. To bring a case, the plaintiff must have experienced personal harm.

Even if an individual has standing, a judge may decide to dismiss a case on other grounds. A case, for instance, may not be "ripe" for consideration if an actual harm has not yet arisen. The **ripeness doctrine** is intended to "prevent the courts...from entangling themselves in abstract disagreements over administrative policies."[28] Before agreeing to accept a case, the ripeness doctrine says, judges must determine that a tangible harm has been inflicted upon an individual or group. So, for example, a citizen cannot sue a city for a poorly drafted law if that law has not been enforced, and a corporation cannot take another corporation to court for actions that it merely anticipates.

Many civil cases do not make it to trial because the two parties resolve their differences out of court. The plaintiff and defendant may decide that the costs of going to trial and the uncertainty of the outcome are too great, and they may negotiate a settlement. In these instances, the two parties are not required to disclose the terms of the settlement to the court or the public.

Most criminal cases are also decided without going to trial because the prosecutor and the defendant's lawyer reach a deal outside of court. In such **plea bargains**, both parties agree to a specified crime and punishment. A judge must approve the terms of plea bargains, which are then put into the public record. The prosecutor benefits from plea bargains by locking in a conviction; the defendant benefits by typically receiving a lesser punishment; and the court system benefits by avoiding the considerable costs of holding a trial.

Today, the vast majority of criminal cases are resolved through plea bargains. In 1989, according to one report, 84 percent of federal criminal cases were settled via plea bargains. By 1995, the figure had risen to 90 percent, and by 2001 it had reached 94 percent. By the end of the twentieth century less than 6 percent of federal criminal cases went to trial.[29]

Federal courts process hundreds of thousands of cases each year.

Despite the fact that many cases don't make it to court, federal judges around the nation face massive caseloads. Each year from 1998 to 2004, for instance, about 65,000 criminal cases were filed in federal district courts.[30] During the same time period, litigants filed approximately 262,000 civil cases per year in federal district courts.[31] In an average year, these cases came before just over 1,000 full-time and magistrate federal district judges. As a consequence, each judge processed an average of several hundred criminal and civil cases each year.

The total number of federal court cases was not always so large. In fact, caseloads have trended steadily upwards in recent decades. From 1960 to 1995, federal district court filings more than tripled, and appeals to higher courts grew by more than 13 times over.[32] These trends have multiplied court costs and delayed the implementation of government policy. For example, the amount of money annually spent on legal services in the United States increased from $9 billion in 1960 to $54 billion in 1987.[33] Additionally, the budget of the judicial branch skyrocketed from $57 million in 1962 to $5.4 billion in 2004.[34]

Federal appeals judges now must read 1,500 to 2,000 new opinions per year to remain up-to-date with legal developments.[35] Facing such a heavy workload, judges often have a difficult time keeping track of goings-on within their own courtrooms. Consider the experience of appellate judge Donald Lay: "A few months ago I was reading an opinion from our court; after reading several pages on a certain point, I wondered who wrote it. I was amazed to find that I had authored the opinion some 10 years before. The point is we read so much that we can no longer even recognize—let alone remember—our own opinions."[36]

The "litigation explosion" has led some observers to assert that "litigation has become the nation's secular religion."[37] Former Supreme Court Chief Justice Warren E. Burger warned in the late 1970s, "we may well be on our way to a society overrun by hordes of lawyers."[38] During his 1992 presidential campaign, George H. W. Bush claimed that Americans were "suing each other too much and caring for each other too little."[39] Similarly, President George W. Bush commented in 2003, "We're a litigious society. Everybody is suing, it seems like."[40] He also stated in 2004, "I'm deeply concerned about a legal system that is fraught with frivolous and junk lawsuits."[41]

Is the United States more litigious relative to other countries? The question has unleashed significant debate. Numerous studies conducted in the 1980s found that Americans were more likely than citizens of other democracies to bring disputes to court.[42] More recent scholarship, however, questions this view. One study concluded that the total volume of litigation in United States was actually comparable to that in Germany and Britain.[43] Like their counterparts in America, British government officials have expressed fears that Britain is developing a "compensation culture" in which "people with frivolous and unwarranted claims bring cases to court with a view of making easy money."[44] So while it is unclear whether American legal culture is unusually litigious compared to other countries, it certainly is more litigious now than it was 40 years ago.

The Judiciary Makes and Interprets the Law

In two ways, judges can influence public policy. The first is through actually making law. When no legislation exists, judges can develop rules that dictate how certain disputes are to be resolved. In these instances, judges create **common law** that becomes binding in future cases. For instance, most rulings in cases involving contracts, property, and personal injuries are based upon common law.

Judges also resolve political disputes about **public law**, which deals with the statutes that presidents and Congress write and that bureaucrats implement. Sometimes judges help interpret the correct meaning of a statute; other times they determine whether statutes are consistent with basic constitutional provisions; other times they step in when state or local laws conflict with national laws; and other times, such as with the EPA case that began this chapter, judges intervene because bureaucrats failed to implement congressional statutes. Collectively, these cases provide judges with considerable influence over the policy-making process.

Through the power of **judicial review**, judges interpret and, when necessary, overturn actions taken by the legislative and executive branches of government. Unlike many of the court's other powers, however, this one cannot be found in Article III of the Constitution. It is a power, instead, that the judiciary claimed for itself in a landmark 1803 court case called *Marbury v. Madison*. The case is sufficiently important to warrant recounting in some detail. After losing the 1800 election, President John Adams quickly appointed 42 individuals to the federal judiciary before his term expired. In the confusion of changing presidential administrations, however, the official commissions were never delivered to the new appointees. And when the newly elected president, Thomas Jefferson, took office, he refused to do so. As a consequence, these individuals could not assume their new posts in the judiciary.

What recourse was available to these appointees whose commissions were never delivered? According to the Judiciary Act of 1789, the appointees could request that the federal courts issue an order forcing Jefferson and his secretary of state, James Madison, to finalize the appointments. One of the appointees, William Marbury, did so, which put the newly formed federal judiciary in a difficult spot. On the one hand, the Supreme Court was being asked to take on a popularly elected president who might well ignore a court order that he opposed. On the other hand, if it did not force the president to deliver the commissions, the Court might appear weak and ineffectual.

In a brilliant move, the Supreme Court managed to assert its own power without offending the new presidential administration. Rather than demand that the president appoint Marbury to his office, as the Judiciary Act seemed to require, the Supreme Court ruled that portions of the act itself were unconstitutional. In so doing, the judiciary claimed the power of deciding which laws were constitutional and which were not—transforming it from the weakest of the three branches of government to, perhaps, equal footing with the other branches. As Chief Justice John Marshall stated in the Supreme Court's opinion, "it is emphatically the province and duty of the judicial department to say what the law is." And when judges determine that a law enacted by Congress conflicts with the Constitution, they are obligated to rule that the law either be amended or stricken from the books.

With the power of judicial review, the judiciary established a place for itself in the policy debates that would preoccupy the national government over time—debates about such issues as slavery, labor–management relations, racial and gender discrimination, and federalism. With the power of judicial review, the courts claimed the authority to have the final say about which laws violated the Constitution, and which did not. But how would it use this power? How, exactly, would judges determine when a law was unconstitutional, and when it was not? Political scientists have identified three models of judicial decision-making: legal, attitudinal, and strategic. And as the discussion that follows makes plain, each model casts the courts in a very different light.

Judges develop and apply legal principles in the legal model.

The Constitution is a notoriously vague document. As a consequence, it is not always obvious whether a particular law does or does not violate it. According to the **legal model** of judicial decision-making, to which most constitutional law scholars adhere, judges rely upon their judgment and expertise to decipher the correct interpretation of a law, the relevant portion of the Constitution, and whether there is any conflict between the two.

Different judges interpret the Constitution in different ways. Some pay careful attention to the intentions of those who wrote and ratified the document. For these judges, the Constitution can only be understood by reference to its historical record. Other judges think of the Constitution as a document that changes over time. For these judges, the Constitution has no fixed or final meaning. Rather, the correct meaning depends upon the context in which it is applied. Still other judges prefer to concentrate on a literal reading of the Constitution's text. For them, neither the intentions of the Constitution's authors nor the changing historical norms are relevant. Instead, they focus on the actual words of the Constitution and what implications they have for the dispute at hand.

Although judges may rely upon different ways of interpreting the Constitution, they all try to apply basic principles of jurisprudence. The most important of these is **stare decisis**, which literally translates into "to stand by things already decided." According to this principle, judges deciding cases today must carefully weigh the decisions made by their predecessors in similar cases. And if the basic elements of the case are the same, they come to the same decision about a law's constitutionality.

Of course, the principal of *stare decisis* is not a hard and fast rule. And different judges appear more or less willing to overturn established precedent. Advocates of **judicial restraint** insist that judges should almost never overturn past decisions; when they must, they should do so on the narrowest possible grounds. Advocates of **judicial activism**, by contrast, suggest that judges have considerably more leeway when deciding whether or not to abide by past court decisions. They suggest that the principle of *stare decisis* should not force judges to repeat mistakes from the past or apply the Constitution in ways that plainly are at odds with the dominant political culture at the time. Advocates of judicial restraint argue that the Supreme Court should stand by its ruling in *Roe v. Wade* (1973), which affirmed a woman's right to obtain an abortion. Advocates of judicial activism, by contrast, encourage the Court to abandon its previous position, which they view as legally flawed, and re-impose restrictions on a woman's right to have an abortion. At times, though, the differences between advocates of judicial restraint and activism are not altogether clear. For instance, some people claim that *Roe v. Wade* itself was the product of judicial activism, and that legal restraint requires that the ruling be overturned to honor earlier precedent.

Evidence in support of the legal model would appear plentiful. Judges, after all, routinely cite legal principles and the relevant case law when making their arguments. Beyond *stare decisis*, judges apply many other principles to the cases that come before them. Some we have already discussed, such as standing and ripeness, which concern decisions about whether to hear a particular case. Others are developed to help guide judicial decision-making in particular areas of the law, such as employment, contracts, or copyright. It is extremely difficult, though, to show that such principles and precedents alone cause judges to rule as they do. Judges, after all, have a tremendous amount of discretion to choose which cases they want to cite, and how they want to cite them. Perhaps judges first figure out how they want to rule on a case, and then search existing case law for cases that best support their position. If true, then the observed relationship between past and present rulings misleads proponents of the legal model into thinking that the principle of *stare decisis* causes judges to rule as they do.

Judges have their own policy preferences in the attitudinal model.

Many other political scientists argue that the legal principles that judges use to justify their rulings constitute nothing more than convenient fiction. Though judges try to project an image of neutrality and objectivity, they still use their powers to advance their policy preferences. According to the **attitudinal model** of judicial decision-making, courts "are not importantly different than legislatures and judges are no different than elected politicians."[45]

To justify their claims, political scientists have developed a variety of ways to measure judges' policy preferences. The most common of these is the party identification of the president who appointed the judge. Judges appointed by Republicans tend to be conservative, and judges appointed by Democrats tend to be liberal. Moreover, the great majority of judicial appointees identify with the same political party as the president who nominated them. Over the past 30 years, roughly 90 percent of district and appellate court appointees were members of the president's party. This pattern held for Republican and Democratic administrations alike. These judicial nominees, moreover, were not passive party members. Most of them actively supported their political parties in the past. In fact, more than 66 percent of appellate court appointees and 57 percent of district court appointees over this period had a record of party activism.[46]

Political scientists also have found an extremely strong relationship between judges' ideologies and the decisions they make—a fact that should not hold if judges are merely applying well-established legal principles to the cases that come before them. According to one study, judges rule on civil liberties cases in ways that are consistent with their ideological preferences roughly 80 percent of the time. And even after accounting for a wide range of other influences on judicial decision-making, judges' personal ideologies appear to be far and away the most important determinant of ruling outcomes.[47] As one political scientist notes, "even critics of the attitudinal model have conceded [the] exceptional explanatory ability" of judges' policy preferences.[48]

Conservative and liberal critics of the court system regularly accuse judges of projecting their own policy preferences onto the cases that come before them. "We still see judges ruling far too often on the basis of their personal opinions or their view of the good society," wrote Edwin Meese III and Todd Gaziano of the conservative Heritage Foundation.[49] Adam Cohen, assistant editor for the liberal leaning *New York Times* editorial board, expressed dismay that many of the Supreme Court's decisions in 2006 were driven by ideology: "The most basic charge against activist judges has always been that they substitute their own views for those of the elected branches. The court's conservative majority did just that this term."[50]

The fact that judges' ideology is such a powerful predictor of case outcomes does not mean that ideology is the only, or even the most important, causal factor in the outcome of every case. Political scientists generally concede, for instance, that ideology plays little role in determining the outcome of criminal cases. And even among civil cases, ideology may not be the only relevant factor. For instance, if public opinion strongly leans in one direction or another, or if the nation is at war, or if the president indicates that he will ignore an objectionable court ruling, then judges may be persuaded to set aside their own policy preferences when formulating their decision.

Just the same, it is worth underscoring how radical the attitudinal model really is. In law schools, students spend years learning about the principles that are supposed to guide judicial decision-making; law journals are filled with articles about how the Constitution is appropriately interpreted; and when advancing arguments, both lawyers and judges constantly pay tribute to the relevant case law at hand. If the attitudinal model is correct, then all of this amounts to little more than theater, merely dressing up what are, at their heart, political motivations and interests.

Judges pay attention to politics in the strategic model.

Most political scientists agree that judges issue rulings that are consistent with their policy preferences. Advocates of the **strategic model** of judicial decision-making, however, argue that judges also keep an eye to the long-term integrity of their rulings. Justices are strategic actors who recognize that their own ability to advance their policy preferences depends upon the larger political environment in which they work.[51] Justices see that their word is not final on any policy matter. And they understand that other political institutions (most notably Congress and the presidency) may subsequently reverse or ignore their rulings. Where resistance is imminent, therefore, justices may craft opinions that do not perfectly reflect their policy preferences in order to avoid a clash with either adjoining branch of government.

There is a fair amount of evidence that judges do monitor the political context in which they issue their rulings. Consider, for instance, the impact of the **solicitor general**, who is appointed by the president and who represents the interests of the executive branch in the Supreme Court. The solicitor general's influence with the Supreme Court is so great that the position is sometimes referred to as "the tenth justice." The Court accepts only about 5 percent of all cases, but it accepts over 70 percent of the cases in which the solicitor general's office is the petitioning party.[52] And among those accepted cases, the office maintains an impressive record. According to one study, the executive branch won more than 60 percent of its cases in the nineteenth century and almost 70 percent from 1953 to 1983.[53] During his 2001–2002 and 2002–2003 terms, Solicitor General Theodore Olson's win rate hovered around 80 percent. The government's success is notable even when it is not a party to the case. According to some estimates, the side of a case that receives the endorsement of the solicitor general wins upwards of 87 percent of the time.[54]

Courts also pay attention to the arguments made by relevant interest groups. Individuals and organizations that are not party to a court case may nonetheless express their opinions through **amicus curiae**, which literally translates into "friend of the court." The practice of *amicus curiae* allows arguments to be presented by groups that may not have standing, and hence may not be able to bring a case forward themselves. One study of court challenges to executive orders found that courts were more likely to rule against the president when *amicus curiae* briefs were filed in opposition.[55]

Political scientists have generated a substantial body of evidence suggesting that judges are sensitive to the content of public opinion. When the public overwhelmingly supports a particular policy, judges are less likely to overturn it; when the public opposes the policy, judges are more likely to do so. There probably is no starker example of the Supreme Court setting aside legal and constitutional principles in order to cater to public opinion than the 1944 case, *Korematsu v. United States*. As described in Chapter 6, during World War II, President Franklin Roosevelt unilaterally decided to place 120,000 Japanese Americans into internment camps. In the aftermath of the Japanese attack on Pearl Harbor, Roosevelt argued, Japanese Americans represented a latent security threat. The president's only cause of action, however, was their national origin. These individuals had done nothing at all to warrant their forced removal from their homes. The Supreme Court nonetheless ruled in favor of Roosevelt's policy. When the nation stood on a war footing, and the public stood squarely behind its president, the justices dared not intervene, even though the president's actions were unconstitutional.[56]

Studies of public opinion, in particular, require special sensitivity to issues of causation. It is not always clear, after all, whether the courts are following the public, or the public is following the courts. A number of scholars have shown that public opinion changed in the direction of court rulings in the aftermath of important desegregation and abortion cases.[57] It is possible, though, that judges sensed or anticipated these shifts in public opinion, in which case the public may have influenced the court ruling.

Was *Bush v. Gore* a Political Decision?

A full month after the 2000 presidential election, the United States still had not declared a new president. The race between George W. Bush and Al Gore had been so close that determination of a winner rested entirely on which candidate was to receive Florida's 25 electoral votes. The day after the election, Florida had announced that Bush had won by a mere 1,784 votes out of almost 6 million ballots cast. A statewide machine recount revealed that Bush's victory margin was even smaller.[58]

With the presidency hanging by a thread, Gore requested manual recounts of ballots in four Florida counties. Two of the four counties, however, did not complete the recounts by the deadline established under Florida state law. Moreover, each of the counties used different procedures to process ballots that the machines had failed to read. Despite the fact that the recounts turned up a few hundred additional votes for Gore, Florida Secretary of State Katherine Harris rejected the new figures from the two tardy counties. She declared Bush the winner on November 26, 2000.[59]

Gore next contested the election in the Florida state court system. The Florida Supreme Court ruled in his favor: the recount votes for Gore from the two tardy counties were to be added to his total, and all Florida counties were to conduct their own manual recounts. Bush immediately appealed this decision to the U.S. Supreme Court. Within days, a five-member majority of the Court ruled that the manual recounts were unconstitutional. The vote tallies announced by Harris on November 26 therefore became final.[60]

As a direct result of the Court's decision, George W. Bush became president of the United States. Unsurprisingly, Bush followers praised the Court, while Gore supporters were outraged. Was *Bush v. Gore* a political decision? How do we know?

Judges' decisions can have extremely important consequences: in *Bush v. Gore*, justices decided who would be president for the next four years. Because of their immense importance to society, we expect judges to be neutral and open-minded, free of all the influences of political bargaining and allegiance. But politics often seems to intrude. It is important, then, to understand how judges make decisions that give shape, meaning, and force to the nation's law and politics.

The legal underpinnings of any Supreme Court decision can readily be found in the arguments made, the *amicus* briefs filed, and the opinions written in a case. A political scientist applying the legal model to a case would therefore want to determine whether the precedent the Court used was appropriate and whether the Court's interpretation of the law made sense. In deciding *Bush v. Gore*, the Supreme Court relied upon the equal protection clause of the Fourteenth Amendment, discussed in greater detail in Chapter 5. Seven of the nine justices agreed that the use of different standards to recount votes violated Floridians' right to have their votes count equally. Two of these seven wanted to give the counties a chance to come up with a uniform method of recounting that would guarantee voters equal and fair treatment. The remaining five, however, opted to stop the recounting entirely. They cited the Florida Supreme Court's earlier decision that the state would abide by a federal law that required presidential election disputes to be settled by December 12, 2000. The U.S. Supreme Court decision was handed down that very day, leaving no time for additional recounts.

A political scientist applying the attitudinal model would argue that these legal explanations simply provided cover for the *real* reasons justices voted the way they did. Rather than analyzing the written opinions for a particular case, an attitudinalist typically uses data on many court decisions to show how often conservative judges make conservative choices, how often liberal judges make liberal choices, and how closely judges adhere to precedent. Jeffrey Segal and Harold Spaeth, for example, analyzed 40 years of Supreme Court justices' votes and found that justices who dissented in important cases rarely changed their stance when the same issue came up in later cases. If those justices had truly been abiding by *stare decisis*, Segal and Spaeth argued, they would have changed their stance in respect for precedent.[61] Segal and Spaeth later said of the *Bush v. Gore* decision, "Never in its history has a majority of the Court behaved in such a blatant *politically* partisan fashion."[62] The five most conservative justices, all appointed to the Court by Republican presidents, joined together in a decision that handed the presidency to the Republican candidate, while the Court's most liberal members dissented.[63]

The strategic model highlights the political context in which justices consider a case. The Supreme Court was under a great deal of pressure to hear and decide the case of *Bush v. Gore*. Many Americans worried that the impasse would raise doubts about the legitimacy of American government.[64] At the time, outgoing President Clinton felt the need to assure world leaders that there was "nothing to worry about."[65] In deciding the case, was the Court responding to a nationwide desire to have the matter resolved? The issue was so politically-charged that the majority decided to hand down a *per curiam* decision, one that is not signed by any justice, suggesting that no justice wanted to be associated with its authorship, perhaps for fear the author would be a target for intense personal criticism.

So which view of the courts is correct? In a researcher's ideal world, a political scientist would be able to interview the justices and ask them directly. She might even conduct a survey of federal judges to ask about their true motivations in deciding cases. In the American political system, however, judges tend to stay out of the public eye. They conduct their deliberations in secret. When they finally reveal a decision, it is *always* grounded in legal reasoning. The legitimacy of the entire federal court system rests on the neutrality of the judges, and most judges would not admit to being influenced by politics.

Although conservative judges consistently vote conservatively and liberal judges vote liberally, this trend may not reveal *political* motivation. Perhaps conservative and liberal judges just use different methods of interpreting the Constitution. In other words, maybe judges divide not on political lines but on beliefs about interpreting the law. To test this proposition, one would ideally like to replay history and allow Gore to have a slight lead in Florida and Bush to call for a manual recount. If the attitudinal model is correct, this basic fact would cause the justices to rethink their positions. If the legal model is right, the underlying principles would stand and the votes would remain the same.

The Bottom Line

Though judges go to great lengths to justify their opinions, it is extremely difficult to identify their true motivations. Taken at face value, the written record that judges leave behind suggests that legal and constitutional issues are paramount. But the inescapable fact is that judges' partisan identification is a powerful predictor of the votes they cast. This is abundantly clear in *Bush v. Gore*, where the selection of the next president was at stake. The conservative justices sided with the Republican candidate, and the liberal justices sided with the Democratic candidate. On this case in particular, then, judges' political views probably did influence the court's ruling.

Judicial Appointments

The Constitution gives the president the power to appoint judges and justices with "the advice and consent" of the Senate. Because judges hold office for life, these appointments enable presidents to have a lasting impact on the workings of government long after they have left office. And because of the stakes involved, presidents take great care when selecting individuals for federal judgeships.

Over the last half-century, each president has appointed scores of individuals to the federal judiciary. Recent presidents have had the opportunity to appoint even more. Every president since World War II appointed more than 100 judges and justices (except Gerald Ford, who failed to do so only because he held office for just two years). Ronald Reagan and Bill Clinton, both of whom served two consecutive terms, appointed upwards of 400 individuals to the bench. In the first three years of his first term, George W. Bush appointed no less than 170, more than Truman, Kennedy, or Johnson did in their entire times in office. The power to appoint so many federal judges gives presidents some control over the policy preferences and priorities of those individuals who wield the extraordinary power of judicial review.

In terms of race and gender, judges look more and more like a cross section of America. Among Ronald Reagan's appointments, only 8 percent were women; 2 percent, African-American; and 4 percent, Hispanic. Among George W. Bush's appointments, by contrast, fully 21 percent were women; 7 percent, African-American; and 11 percent, Hispanic. In terms of other demographics, however, nominees to the federal judiciary continue to look very different from the rest of the population. Over 50 percent of both Bill Clinton's and George W. Bush's nominees, for instance, had a net worth over $1 million. The average age of a nominee has remained steady at about 50 years. And not surprisingly, almost all nominees worked in politics as either elected or appointed officials or as lawyers before being nominated to a judgeship.[66]

Confirmation hearings for district and federal courts are political.

Presidents try to appoint individuals who are competent at what they do, who have legal expertise, and who have a strong record of accomplishment. But politics also looms large in judicial appointments. Presidents regularly appoint judges who share their partisan affiliation. No less than 91 percent of Carter's appointments were Democrats, as were 88 percent of Bill Clinton's. Similarly, 92 percent of Ronald Reagan's appointments were Republicans, as were 89 percent of George H.W. Bush's and 85 percent of George W. Bush's during his first term in office.[67]

Despite this political favoritism, most lower-court nominees are confirmed. Take a look at Figure 15-3. In the 1980s and early 1990s, Congress confirmed the appointments of roughly four in five district and appellate nominees. With the Republican takeover of the 104th Congress, however, and the advent of divided government, nominees for appellate courts were significantly less likely to be confirmed than nominees for district courts. By the 107th and 108th Congresses, confirmation rates of appellate judges were half as large as confirmation rates among district judges.

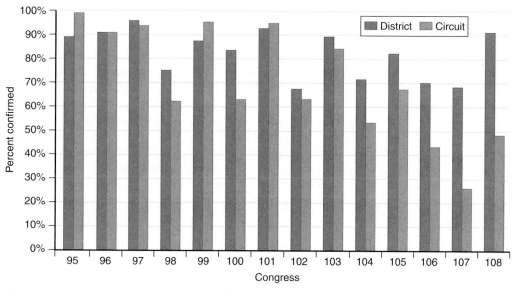

Figure 15-3. District and Appellate Judges Are Usually Confirmed. The number of district court nominees ranges from 51 to 168 per congress with an average of 95. The number of circuit court nominees ranges from 13 to 60 per congress with an average of 30.

Source: Wendy L. Marinek, "The Lower Federal Court Confirmation Database, 1977–2004," Center on Democratic Performance, August 22, 2005.

Part of the reason why most district nominees are confirmed is that senators themselves play an important role in their selection. When choosing a judicial nominee for a district court, the president will often seek the approval of the senior senator from the president's party who represents the state where the court is located. This norm, known as **senatorial courtesy**, tends to hasten the process of selecting and confirming district court judges around the nation.

Things get more complicated, however, when moving to the appellate levels. For starters, senatorial courtesy only applies to district-court appointments. Moreover, appellate-court judges tend to be subject to greater scrutiny by both the president and the Senate. As a consequence, there are some individuals who are easily confirmed at the district level, but who are denied assignment to an appellate judgeship.

The saga of Judge Charles Pickering is a case in point. In 1990, George H.W. Bush appointed Pickering to a federal district court in Southern Mississippi. Twelve years later, George W. Bush nominated Pickering for a position on the Fifth Circuit court of appeals. At the time, the Democrats controlled the Senate, and they refused to confirm Pickering's nomination. Democrats levied a variety of charges against Pickering, including racial insensitivity and political views that were "out of step" with mainstream America. The next year, when the Republicans regained control of the Senate, Bush re-nominated Pickering for the position. This time Democrats filibustered the nomination, and the Republicans lacked the needed votes to cut off debate—a parliamentary procedure discussed in greater detail in Chapter 13. Not to be outdone, when the Senate was not in session in early 2004, Bush granted Pickering a **recess-appointment**. This allowed him to hold the position until the end of the Congress's next session, which ended on December 8, 2004. When Congress got around to formally considering Pickering's case, concerns about his political positions were once again raised. Rather than drag the confirmation out any longer, Pickering withdrew his name from consideration and retired from the federal judiciary.

In this confirmation process, it is difficult to figure out just how much influence the president and the Senate wielded. On the one hand, the fact that most presidential nominees are appointed would appear to be a clear testament to the president's influence. If the president were weak, the Senate might decide to block a greater number of his nominees. On the other hand, the fact that most nominees are confirmed might instead indicate congressional influence. Fearing that the Senate will refuse to confirm them, the president might not even nominate certain individuals—even though he would like them to serve on the bench. Instead, the president might nominate only those individuals who he thinks stand a good chance of being confirmed. And as a consequence, senators may approve nominees not because the president is strong, but because the president has chosen candidates that are to the senators' liking.

Confirmation hearings for the Supreme Court are extremely political.

If the stakes involved in district and appellate court nominations are high, those in Supreme Court nominations are off the charts. Norms of senatorial courtesy play no role in Supreme Court appointments. Instead, presidents consult directly with their closest advisors and heed the demands of different political constituencies. The trick is to find an individual with just the right mix of judicial experience, expertise, and policy preferences. And occasionally, presidents also find it advantageous to select a candidate with a particular socioeconomic background. For example, George H.W. Bush in 1991 nominated Clarence Thomas to the Court. Thomas was a strong conservative who did not have a wealth of judicial experience.[68] Some political observers argued, however, that by selecting an African American, Bush managed to mute some liberals' criticisms of the nomination.

Once the president comes up with a potential Supreme Court nominee, he asks the Federal Bureau of Investigation to conduct a full background check on the individual. This check is intended to identify any evidence of unlawful behavior that a nominee might have engaged in. Recent presidents also have sent the names of prospective nominees to the American Bar Association (ABA), an interest group that represents the legal profession and that provides ratings of the qualifications of candidates. The ABA's Standing Committee on the Federal Judiciary typically rates nominees as either "well qualified," "qualified," or "not qualified." George W. Bush, however, opted not to ask the ABA to rate his candidates before they were publicly announced. Instead, he relied more upon the Federalist Society, a politically conservative organization of students and faculty at law schools around the nation.

If a presidential nominee survives these background checks, he or she then must face the public. From the moment that the president announces a name, there follows a torrent of media scrutiny. Interest groups take out radio and television advertisements in order to highlight the candidate's strengths and foibles. Legal scholars write opinion pieces in the nation's newspapers about the candidate's qualifications and judicial philosophies. Journalists investigate the candidate's personal and professional histories. When an individual is being considered for appointment to the Supreme Court, no element of his or her past is considered off-limits. During the 1991 Senate confirmation hearings for Supreme Court Justice Clarence Thomas, for instance, the media and politicians fixated on accusations that he had sexually harassed prior co-worker Anita Hill. The hearings became so personal and accusatory, in fact, that Thomas argued that he was the victim of a "high-tech lynching" by the U.S. Senate.[69]

The real action of the judicial appointment process occurs during the confirmation hearings, which are open to the public. Members of the Senate Judiciary Committee have the opportunity to directly interrogate a nominee about decisions he made as a lawyer or lower-court judge. They may ask about his views on issues ranging from abortion to the legal status of enemy combatants. And given that they may eventually issue rulings that fundamentally alter these public policies, it is perfectly appropriate that these nominees be interrogated on their views. Whether the nominees are completely forthcoming in their answers, however, is another matter.

When he came before the Judiciary Committee in 2006, Samuel Alito was grilled about his views on the proper role of presidential power. Democratic senators hoped to put Alito on the defensive by pulling quotes from briefs that he wrote as a deputy assistant to the U.S. attorney general in the Reagan administration and from opinions he wrote as an appellate judge on the Third Circuit. Like most Supreme Court nominees, however, Alito deflected many of the accusations made about his ideological views. He also refused to answer specific legal questions on the grounds that a similar case might soon come before the Supreme Court, and that therefore it would be inappropriate to stake out a position one way or another.

The Senate ultimately confirmed Alito by a vote of 52 to 48. In general, however, the Senate is less likely to confirm Supreme Court nominees than appellate or district court nominees. Since the nation's founding in 1789, presidents have formally submitted 158 nominations to the Court, including those for chief justice. Of these, the Senate confirmed 122, and 115 actually took office.[70]

As Table 15-1 shows, dissenters can be found in all of the recent Supreme Court confirmation hearings. And in some cases, such as Clarence Thomas's, full blown controversies can erupt. Of late, however, nothing compares to the confirmation hearings of Robert Bork, whom Reagan nominated to the Supreme Court in 1987. No less than 86 different interest groups testified at his confirmation hearings.[71] Critics focused not on Bork's knowledge of the law—the ABA rated

Table 15-1. **Supreme Court Nominations Since World War II**

PRESIDENT	NOMINEE	SENATE VOTE DATE	VOTE COUNT	CONFIRMATION
G. W. Bush	Samuel Alito	January 31, 2006	58–42	Yes
	John Roberts	September 29, 2005	78–22	Yes
	Harriet Miers	None	None	**No**
Clinton	Stephen Breyer	July 29, 1994	87–9	Yes
	Ruth Bader Ginsburg	August 3, 1994	96–3	Yes
G. H. W. Bush	Clarence Thomas	October 15, 1991	52–48	Yes
	David Souter	October 2, 1990	90–9	Yes
Reagan	Anthony Kennedy	February 3, 1988	97–0	Yes
	Robert Bork	October 23, 1987	42–58	**No**
	Antonin Scalia	September 17, 1986	98–0	Yes
	Sandra Day O'Connor	September 21, 1981	99–0	Yes
Ford	John Paul Stevens	December 17, 1975	98–0	Yes
Nixon	William Rehnquist	December 10, 1971	68–26	Yes
	Lewis Franklin Powell Jr.	December 6, 1972	89–1	Yes
	Harry Blackmun	May 12, 1970	94–0	Yes
	G. Harrold Carswell	April 8, 1970	45–51	**No**
	Clement Haynesworth	November 21, 1969	45–55	**No**
	Warren E. Burger	June 9, 1969	74–3	Yes
L. Johnson	Homer Thornberry	None	None	**No**
	Thurgood Marshall	August 30, 1967	69–11	Yes
	Abe Fortas*	August 11, 1965	—	Yes
Kennedy	Arthur Goldberg	September 25, 1962	—	Yes
	Byron White	April 11, 1962	—	Yes
Eisenhower	Potter Stewart	May 5, 1959	70-17	Yes
	Charles E. Whittaker	March 19, 1957	—	Yes
	William J. Brennan Jr.	March 19, 1957	—	Yes
	John M. Harlan	March 16, 1955	71-11	Yes
	Earl Warren	March 1, 1954	—	Yes
Truman	Sherman Minton	October 4, 1949	48-16	Yes
	Tom C. Clark	August 18, 1949	73-8	Yes
	Fred M. Vinson	June 20, 1946	—	Yes
	Harold H. Burton	September 19, 1945	—	Yes

* Sitting justice also nominated in 1968 to be chief justice, but nomination was withdrawn.

Where no vote count is listed, confirmation was by voice or otherwise unrecorded.

Source: David G. Savage, Guide to the U.S. Supreme Court, 4th ed., vol. II (Washington, DC: CQ Press, 2004), pp. 1186–89

him "well qualified"—but on his political views on abortion, civil rights, and civil liberties. Less than an hour after Reagan announced Bork's nomination, Senator Edward Kennedy declared, "Robert Bork's America is a land in which women would be forced into back alley abortions, blacks would sit in segregated lunch counters, rogue police could break down citizens' doors in midnight raids."[72] And for the next three and a half months, an avalanche of criticism fell upon the nominee. On October 23, 1987, the Senate rejected Bork's confirmation by a vote of 58 to 42.

CaseStudy: The Abandoned Nomination of Harriet Miers

Sandra Day O'Connor's retirement announcement presented President George W. Bush with a unique opportunity. Justice O'Connor was a pivotal member of the Supreme Court, casting the tie-breaking vote in many important social policy cases. Whoever replaced her would have a significant impact on the Court. Bush wanted a replacement who was conservative, preferably a woman, and someone whom the Republican-controlled Senate would confirm with minimal opposition.[73] On October 3, 2005, the president nominated his White House counsel and former corporate attorney, Harriet E. Miers.

Reaction to the nomination was swift and negative. To Bush's surprise, however, many of the attacks came from members of his own party. Conservative activists from groups like Concerned Women for America and Operation Rescue had expected Bush to appoint someone with a strong conservative record on contentious issues like abortion—someone like Justices Antonin Scalia or Clarence Thomas. Instead, Bush selected a longtime colleague who had a thin employment history and absolutely no prior experience as a judge.

Miers attended church regularly, and she once made a donation to an anti-abortion organization. These facts suggested that she might be a social conservative. On the other hand, she also had made donations to the Democratic National Committee and Democratic candidates. In a 1993 speech to a Dallas women's group, Miers said she supported "self-determination" on abortion. As president of the Texas Bar Association, she also had approved of judges who had used their position to address social issues. These facts did not help Miers's standing with conservative activists, who worried that Miers could become "another David Souter," the justice who George H.W. Bush had appointed but who turned out to be a more reliable member of the Court's liberal voting bloc.[74]

Just as conservatives were gearing up to fight the nomination, Senate Minority Leader Harry Reid praised Miers on the Senate floor. As it turned out, Reid, a Democrat, had recommended her for the appointment. Other Senate Democrats, however, expressed skepticism of Miers's qualifications. In hopes of getting more information about the nominee, they called on the White House to release documents that would shed light on her five years of service to the president. Bush, however, refused to hand over the documents.[75]

The Bush administration initially dismissed the criticism pouring in from conservative groups and tried to reassure Republican senators that Miers was a good choice. Miers, however, failed to temper the concerns of key Republican senators. Judiciary Committee Chairman Arlen Specter reported to the press that Miers had told him she believed in a constitutional right to privacy, a controversial notion that establishes strict limits on government intrusions into the personal lives of citizens. Later that day, Miers denied this and asked Specter to correct his statement. Specter issued the correction but maintained that his recollection remained unchanged.[76] When Miers turned in her responses to a Judiciary Committee questionnaire, Specter rejected them as inadequate and ordered her to redo them.[77] He said Miers could use a "crash course in constitutional law."[78]

Meanwhile, several Republican senators joined Democrats in a call for the White House to produce documents on Miers's work.[79] "They're going to have to try and err as much as they can on the side of openness in furnishing that information, because there are so many questions," said Republican Senator John Thune. "The paper trail's very thin, and more is better."[80] The Bush administration again refused, dealing a critical blow to the nomination.[81]

On October 26, Senate Majority Leader Bill Frist (R-TN) informed Bush that his nominee was in trouble. The following day, Miers formally withdrew her name from consideration, a decision that Bush supported.[82] After 24 days of attack from both the right and the left, Miers returned to her job as White House counsel, and Bush returned to his short list of Supreme Court nominees. He selected Samuel Alito, a federal appellate judge with strong conservative credentials, and the Senate confirmed his appointment in short order.

ThinkingCritically

1. Which played a bigger role in derailing Miers's confirmation, her lack of judicial experience or concerns that she was not sufficiently conservative?

2. Would Miers have stood a better chance of being confirmed if she had been nominated for a district or appellate judgeship?

SUMMARY

▶ When originally constructed, many anticipated that the federal judiciary would be the weakest of the three branches. Lacking the powers of both the sword and the purse, judges were left merely with the persuasive appeal of their judgment. From the nation's beginning, therefore, judges worked hard to promote the legitimacy of their institution. And over time, the public learned to hold the courts in high regard.

▶ The federal judiciary is organized hierarchically, with district courts at the bottom, appellate courts in the middle, and a Supreme Court on top. Most decisions are decided at the district court level. The losing party to a case, however, has the option of appealing the decision to the appellate and Supreme courts. Decisions made by higher courts are binding for lower courts.

▶ In civil and criminal cases, the judiciary resolves disputes among individuals, organizations, and the government. Though many cases are settled before ever going to trial, federal courts nonetheless process hundreds of thousands of cases each year.

▶ With the power of judicial review, judges exert considerable influence over the interpretation and implementation of laws. When deciding a case, judges rely upon a variety of different considerations. They attempt to correctly interpret the Constitution and apply legal principles to the case at hand. They turn to their own political preferences and ideas about what constitutes good public policy. And they pay attention to politics more generally, trying to steer clear of certain decisions that are likely to evoke widespread opposition.

▶ Politics, in varying degrees, intrudes upon the process of appointing judges to the federal judiciary. Presidents have strong incentives to select individuals who share their views, and will advocate on behalf of these views long after the president has left office. As a consequence, the Senate confirmation process can be highly contentious. Nominees to the Supreme Court, in particular, face an extraordinary amount of public scrutiny. And occasionally, these nominees fail to be confirmed, either because the Senate votes against them or because the president withdraws the nominee.

KEY TERMS

amicus curiae, p. 000
appellate courts, p. 000
attitudinal model, p. 000
briefs, p. 000
chief justice, p. 000
civil case, p. 000
class action suit, p. 000
common law, p. 000
concurrent opinion, p. 000
conference, p. 000
criminal case, p. 000
defendant, p. 000

dissenting opinion, p. 000
district courts, p. 000
judicial activism, p. 000
judicial restraint, p. 000
judicial review, p. 000
jury, p. 000
legal model, p. 000
magistrate judges, p. 000
majority opinion, p. 000
oral argument, p. 000
original jurisdiction, p. 000
plaintiff, p. 000

SUGGESTED READINGS

Lawrence Baum. 2004. *The Supreme Court*, 8th ed. Washington, D.C.: Congressional Quarterly Press. A useful overview of the Supreme Court.

Cornell Clayton and Howard Gillman (eds.). *Supreme Court Decision-Making: New Institutionalist Approaches.* Chicago: University of Chicago Press. A collection of essays on different aspects of the strategic model of judicial decision-making.

Lee Epstein and Jeffrey Segal. 2005. *Advice and Consent: The Politics of Judicial Appointments.* New York: Oxford University Press. A contemporary look at the politics of judicial appointments.

Herbert McCloskey. 2000. *The American Supreme Court*, 3rd ed. Chicago: University of Chicago Press. A careful analysis of the relationship between Supreme Court rulings and public opinion.

Shep Melnick. 1994. *Between the Lines: Interpreting Welfare Rights.* Washington, D.C.: The Brookings Institution. Analysis of the ways in which judges interpret (and re-interpret) congressionally enacted laws.

H.W. Perry. 1994. *Deciding to Decide: Agenda Setting in the United States Supreme Court*, reprint ed. Cambridge, MA: Harvard University Press. A classic examination of the criteria used by the Supreme Court when deciding whether or not to grant cert.

Jeffrey Segal and Harold Spaeth. 2002. *The Supreme Court and the Attitudinal Model Revisited.* New York: Cambridge University Press. A thorough examination of the attitudinal model of judicial decision-making.

district courts the first tier of the federal judiciary where most cases are decided.

magistrate judges judges who support federal district judges by hearing and deciding minor cases at the district court level.

appellate courts the second tier of the federal judiciary, which is primarily responsible for reviewing the decisions rendered by the first tier of district courts.

Supreme Court the highest court in the land, where all decisions are final.

writ of certiorari a formal acceptance by the Supreme Court to review a decision of a lower court.

original jurisdiction the right of a court to be the first to hear a case rather than simply review the decision of a lower court.

briefs documents that contain the legal arguments of a dispute.

oral argument a lawyer's spoken presentation of the legal reason she thinks her side should prevail.

conference the confidential gathering of justices in which they discuss their thoughts about the case and cast preliminary votes.

chief justice the presiding member of the Supreme Court who serves as chair of the conference and selects the justice who will write the majority opinion of the court.

majority opinion the written document that reflects the collective judgment of the justices who are on the majority side of a ruling.

concurring opinion a document written by a justice on the majority side of a ruling which outlines additional considerations she thinks are important.

dissenting opinion a document written by a justice on the minority side of a ruling which outlines her own reasoning on the case and identifies the flaws that she perceives in the majority opinion.

plaintiff the party who initiates a lawsuit by filing a complaint.

defendant the party being sued or accused of a crime.

jury a group of private citizens selected to listen to a trial and issue a final verdict.

criminal case a case that involves a violation of the statutes that are intended to protect the public's health, order, safety, and morality.

civil case a case that concerns a violation of the legal rights or obligations of one individual toward another.

class action suit a lawsuit in which the plaintiff is a group of individuals who have suffered a common injury.

standing the requirement establishing that for a plaintiff to bring a case to court, he or she must have suffered a well-defined injury that is a result of violation of the civil code.

ripeness doctrine principle by which the courts will only accept cases where the actual harm has already taken place.

plea bargain an agreement between the prosecutor and the defendant in a criminal case through which the parties agree to a specified crime and punishment.

common law law made by judges when no legislation currently exists.

public law those laws enacted by presidents and Congress that define the relationship between individuals (and organizations) and the state.

judicial review the power of the judiciary to interpret and overturn actions taken by the legislative and executive branches of government.

legal model a theory of judicial decision-making that judges make decisions by deciphering the correct interpretation of the law and the relevant portion of the Constitution, and determining whether there is a conflict between the two.

stare decisis the principle that judges deciding a case must carefully weigh the decisions of their predecessors in similar cases and come to the same decision if the basic elements of the case before them are the same.

judicial restraint the practice judges engage in when they limit the exercise of their own power by only overturning past decisions when they are clearly unconstitutional.

judicial activism the tendency of judges to give themselves leeway in deciding whether to abide by past court decisions or not, which allows them to consider possible outcomes, public opinion, and their own preferences before issuing a ruling.

attitudinal model the theory of judicial decision-making that judges use their own policy preferences in deciding cases.

strategic model the theory of judicial decision-making that judges consider their own policy preferences as well as the possible actions of the other branches of government when making decisions.

solicitor general the individual who represents the federal government in the Supreme Court.

amicus curiae a brief written by someone who is not a party to a case but who submits information or an argument related to the dispute at hand.

senatorial courtesy the custom by which the senior senator from the state in which there is a district court vacancy assists the president in selecting a replacement for that seat.

recess-appointment the appointment of a federal judge during the Senate's recess; such an appointment allows the president to temporarily fill a vacant judgeship without the Senate's consent.

16 The Bureaucracy

Building a Bureaucracy to Combat Terrorism

Less than a month after the terrorist attacks of September 11, 2001, newly appointed presidential advisor Tom Ridge reminded fellow Homeland Security Council members about the dangers of political infighting. "The only turf we should be worried about protecting is the turf we stand on," he warned.[1] Ridge was rightly concerned, for observers increasingly suspected that certain departments of the federal government had jealously guarded information that might have prevented the attacks. Initiatives to prevent such turf battles included coordinating various agencies under a single homeland security umbrella, while also expanding the federal government's efforts to protect the country against terrorism. Ironically, however, early efforts not only failed to eliminate interagency squabbles but in fact fueled even more infighting: between the executive and legislative branches, and between Republicans and Democrats.

The seeds of the controversy were sown on September 21, when Senate Intelligence Committee Chairman Bob Graham (D-FL) and several other Democrats introduced a proposal to create a National Office for Combating Terrorism. The new body would be charged with developing a comprehensive counterterrorism budget and coordinating different intelligence agencies. It was to be lodged within the Executive Office of the President. The office's director, however, would require Senate confirmation and its activities would be subject to congressional oversight.

White House officials balked at this perceived intrusion by lawmakers. The Bush administration supported the creation of an organizational structure that would perform this task, but the president wanted to ensure that he, rather than Congress, would be in charge. Accordingly, on October 8 Bush preempted congressional action by issuing an executive order that created an Office of Homeland Security (OHS) within the Executive Office of the President. Pennsylvania governor Tom Ridge, a longtime Bush ally, agreed to head the new body. The president's proposal differed from the Senate proposal in two important ways. Its director would be a special assistant to the president and thus would not be subject to Senate confirmation. And its activities would not require congressional oversight.

Many worried that the new agency, with only a small staff, few resources, and no clear authority over cabinet-level partners, faced a challenge that would quickly overwhelm it. A few days later, Senators Arlen Specter (R-PA) and Joseph Lieberman (D-CT) issued a counter-proposal. They introduced in the Senate a bipartisan bill that would establish a cabinet-level position, subject to congressional confirmation and oversight. The White House opposed the Senate bill. And at the time, members of Congress lacked the votes needed to override a possible presidential veto.

The conflict between Capitol Hill and the White House intensified a few months later, when President Bush asked for an additional $38 million from Congress for his OHS. The legislators seemed prepared to fulfill the request but insisted that Ridge publicly and formally testify before Congress about the office's activities to date. The administration refused, insisting that Ridge's responsibility was to advise the president, and the president alone. Later when facing the threat of a subpoena, though, the administration relented and sent the homeland security advisor to provide informal testimony to the House Government Reform Committee.

After months of resisting congressional efforts to create a cabinet-level position, on June 7 the administration blind-sided legislators from both political parties by announcing a plan to create a Department of Homeland Security (DHS). The proposed DHS would have four divisions, responsible for border security, emergency preparedness, weapons of mass destruction, and intelligence. It would combine no less than 22 federal agencies, programs, and research centers into a single organization. Importantly, though, it would not affect the Central Intelligence Agency and the

Federal Bureau of Investigation. And because DHS would be a department rather than an office, it incorporated many elements from the bipartisan Specter-Lieberman bill that the president previously had opposed.

For the most part, Capitol Hill welcomed the White House proposal. Senator Charles Schumer (D-NY) went so far as to say that any executive initiative to enhance Ridge's authority would "pass the House and Senate like a hot knife through butter."[2] But because the new DHS would incorporate portions of no fewer than eight current cabinet-level departments, it fell under the authority of 88 congressional committees and subcommittees. Soon the proposal was mired in yet another political battle.

"Flexibility" proved to be the main sticking point in the deliberations that followed. The Bush administration wanted to be able to transfer money freely between homeland security accounts, to reorganize departmental operations without congressional approval, and to reduce the influence of labor unions on hir-

ing practices. And for the most part, Republicans in Congress supported these initiatives, while also admitting the need for traditional job protections for DHS staff. Democrats, however, were intent on further limiting the president's control over personnel matters. The job security of DHS employees stood out as one of the largest federal issues during the 2002 midterm elections.

As it turned out, Democrats lost control of the Senate after these elections, and they quickly saw fit to give the president most of what he wanted. On November 25, President Bush signed into law a bill that created the DHS, and he nominated Tom Ridge as its first secretary. The Senate confirmed the appointment, and Ridge took office in January 2003. And thus was born the first executive department since 1988, when President Reagan created the Department of Veterans Affairs to replace the Veterans Administration.

The power struggles surrounding the birth of the DHS reveal the stumbling efforts of a federal government to more effectively address a pressing

social need—in this case, the development of new, and the consolidation of existing, antiterrorism initiatives. Most everyone agreed on the importance of creating a federal organization that would serve this goal. Nonetheless, deep concerns about how the organization would be structured and who would control it fueled drawn-out and highly charged political battles between the president and Congress, Republicans and Democrats.

This is the stuff of bureaucratic politics. On the one hand, people recognize the extraordinary importance of experts who perform vital tasks, whether it means the protection of our environment, the education of our children, the enforcement of the nation's laws, the assurance of citizens' health and social welfare, or, in this instance, the protection of our nation against terrorist attacks. On the other hand, serious disputes can rage over who is charged with overseeing the agencies that perform these activities, and the amount of independence that is granted to them.

IN THIS CHAPTER WE WILL EXAMINE:

- ▶ the kinds of functions that federal bureaucrats perform
- ▶ the growth and organization of the bureaucracy
- ▶ the challenges that bureaucrats face
- ▶ different approaches to overseeing and, in some instances, reforming the bureaucracy.

What Bureaucrats Do

What do bureaucrats do? The staggering number of functions that government bureaucracies perform might instead raise the question: What *don't* bureaucrats do? Bureaucrats, the individuals who work within a **bureaucracy**, run the nation's prisons and schools, collect garbage, maintain job-training programs, write social security checks, monitor the pollution of our rivers, pave highways, patrol streets, regulate industries, put out fires, issue drivers' licenses, and so much more besides. When we experience government in our daily lives, we typically interact with employees of one or another local, state, or federal bureaucracy—teachers, police and parole officers, prison guards, firefighters, garbage collectors, auditors, inspectors, customer service representatives. Such interactions, however, reflect just a small portion of the things that bureaucrats actually do.

Bureaucrats interpret and implement laws.

When Congress enacts a law, when the president issues a unilateral directive, or when the court issues a decree of one sort or another, somebody must figure out what exactly these policies require in practice, and then they must ensure that the government actually takes the steps needed to realize them. Both of these tasks fall to bureaucrats. And both are remarkably difficult.

Laws, after all, are often quite vague. Take, for example, the Full Employment Act, which Congress enacted after World War II. Facing the transition from a wartime to peacetime economy, and anticipating the return of hundreds of thousands of discharged veterans, Congress sought to encourage the development of broad economic policy for the country. With the Full Employment Act, Congress mandated certain actions. It required the president to submit an annual economic report along with his proposed budget. It created the Council of Economic Advisors, an appointed board to advise and assist the president in formulating economic policy. And it established the Joint Economic Committee, composed of members of Congress and charged with reviewing the government's economic policy at least annually. The overriding purpose of the law, meanwhile, was to ensure that federal policies "promote maximum employment, production, and purchasing power."

What does this mean? Consider the first clause: "promote maximum employment." What is maximum employment? Is 95 percent enough? How about 99 percent? Or does it require the employment of every single healthy adult who would like to work? And whatever the amount, is the specified goal of maximum employment fixed for all times? Or does the law allow for different objectives depending, for example, upon whether the nation is at war or whether the economy is experiencing a downturn? And what, then, does it mean to "promote" maximum employment? Are any means justified? Or should the government weigh the objective of maximizing employment against other objectives, such as reducing deficits or encouraging private enterprise?

There are no easy answers to these questions. It falls upon bureaucrats, though, to formulate answers. And they must do so in every imaginable policy domain. Either when the language of a statute is vague, or when Congress expressly delegates the responsibility to them, bureaucrats must decipher the exact meaning of broad legislative pronouncements. They must determine the exact number of pollutants that an industry can release into the air, the precise number of questions that students must answer correctly on standardized tests in order to graduate from high school, the particular design of highway exit signs, and the regularity with which such signs must be replaced.

Having deciphered the meaning of laws, bureaucrats then are charged with putting them into practice—that is, with implementing them. The **implementation** of public policy, in fact, constitutes the single biggest task assigned to bureaucrats. Laws, after all, constitute nothing more than words on paper until bureaucrats put them into practice. The implementation of public policy is where the "rubber hits the road."

Just as bureaucrats have considerable discretion to interpret laws, they also have considerable discretion when implementing them. Imagine, for example, a hypothetical agent working for the U.S. Drug Enforcement Administration (DEA) whose job is to enforce the nation's drug laws. This agent receives a tip that drugs are being sold out of an abandoned house on the outskirts of town. When he goes to investigate, he finds a teenage girl selling small amounts of cocaine. After arresting her, though, he learns that this teenager works for a well-known drug dealer in the region. To capture this dealer, the DEA agent will need the teenager's cooperation. To secure her cooperation, can the DEA promise not to prosecute her? Or must he enforce the law every time that he observes a violation?

The laws that DEA agents are sworn to uphold provide little guidance on the matter. Instead, DEA agents—and bureaucrats everywhere—must draw upon their expertise, their common sense, and whatever recommendations their superiors provide in order to determine the best way to enforce the laws of the land. Bureaucrats, ultimately, decide how the objectives identified in federal statutes are to be served.

Bureaucrats make rules.

One of the principal ways in which bureaucrats flesh out the meaning of congressional statutes, presidential directives, and court orders is by issuing **rules**. Rules typically provide more specific directions about how policy is to be interpreted and implemented. Moreover, once rules are issued, they take on the weight of law. For this reason, political scientists sometimes refer to bureaucratic rules as "quasi-legislation."[3]

Rules have a dramatic effect on a vast array of policies—environmental, worker safety, food safety, to name only a few. They influence the kinds of things we watch on television most everyday. Consider, for example, the efforts of the Federal Communications Commission (FCC) to regulate television and radio under the Communications Acts of 1934, the Communications Satellite Act of 1962, and the Telecommunications Act of 1996. The FCC is charged with "promoting safety of life and property and for strengthening the national defense." Part of this duty is the oversight of "obscene" and "indecent" programming. But exactly what kind of programming qualifies as obscene or indecent? Does it matter whether the programming is aired when children are likely to be watching television? And what, exactly, is to be done about violations? None of the three acts listed above provide clear answers to these questions. The FCC, therefore, has had to issue rules that clarify the original laws enacted by Congress.

Through such rules, the FCC has decided to forbid the airing of "obscene" programming at any time and the airing of "indecent programming" or "profane language" during certain hours. The FCC defines "obscene" material according to a three-pronged standard: (1) an average person, applying contemporary community standards, must find that the material, as a whole, appeals to prurient interests; (2) the material must depict or describe, in a patently offensive way, sexual conduct specifically defined by applicable law; and (3) the material, taken as a whole, must lack serious literary, artistic, political, or scientific value.[4] The FCC defines "indecent programming" as "language or material that, in context, depicts or describes, in terms patently offensive as measured by contemporary community standards for the broadcast medium, sexual or excretory organs or activities." It defines "profanity" as "language so grossly offensive to members of the public who actually hear it as to amount to a nuisance."[5] The FCC has further decided that neither indecent programming nor profanity can be aired between 6 a.m. and 10 p.m., when there is a reasonable risk that children may be in the audience.

Having developed these guidelines, the FCC's work is still not complete. It must then ensure that media outlets abide by the rules. The FCC does so by

monitoring the content of programming, and then punishing infractions by issuing warnings, imposing fines, or revoking station licenses.

The specific rules that the FCC developed are intended to guide bureaucrats
who do the everyday work of implementing public policy. Obviously, though,
these rules alone do not resolve the matter entirely. Considerable judgment is
required to figure out whether a specific word or image on a television show meets
the FCC's definitions of obscene, indecent, and profane, and if so, to decide what
kind of punishment, if any, should apply. Such judgments involve norms, which
are especially important when an agency's stated goals are vague. Norms come
from an organization's culture and sense of mission. They are informal expressions
of the customs, attitudes, and expectations put before people who work within a
bureaucratic agency. Within the FCC, for example, norms help employees determine which specific words ought to be deemed indecent. They also play an important role in deciding how aggressively to prosecute violations.

In contrast to norms, rules emerge from a well-defined process. The 1946
Administrative Procedures Act lays out the specific steps that agencies must follow
when they issue rules. To begin, rules are offered as proposals, allowing interested
parties an opportunity to express their opinions. Agencies, then, must respond to
each of the issues raised during the public comment period, which varies in length
depending upon the complexity of the rule. Further, the agency may be required
to issue formal reports to Congress and the president to identify how, for instance,
a rule will impact the economy. Final rules then are published in the *Federal Register*, a compendium of government rules, proposed rules, and notices. As agencies
have issued increasing numbers of rules over the last 60 years, the *Federal Register*
has grown longer and longer. To provide some indication of the volume of rules
that the federal bureaucracy produces each year, Figure 16-1 shows the number of
pages included in the *Federal Register* each year from 1945 to 2006. Note that
whereas rules, notices of rules, and other executive-branch policies required fewer
than 8,000 pages in 1949, they now take up about 80,000 pages each year.[6]

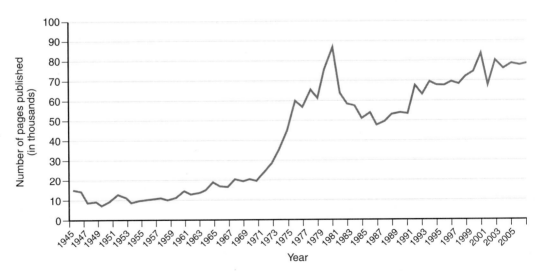

Figure 16-1. **The Size of the Federal Register.** During the past half-century,
the federal bureaucracy has issued more and more rules.

Source: Office of the Federal Register, National Archives and Records Administration, *"The
Federal Register*, vols. 1–71." Available online at: http://www.heinonline.org/ (accessed June
18, 2007).

Bureaucrats provide expert advice.

Bureaucrats in a particular area typically know a great deal more about the specifics of public policy than do members of Congress or the president. This should come as no surprise, for bureaucrats usually are experts who have devoted their professional lives to a specific policy issue, while paying considerably less attention to most other issues. By contrast, members of Congress and presidents are policy generalists who have collected relatively small amounts of information on a multitude of issues.

When determining which public policies are most in need of change, and then figuring out how best to change them, members of Congress and presidents regularly consult bureaucrats. The main responsibility of the Government Accounting Office (GAO), for example, is to provide formal reports to members of Congress about specific policy issues. When a lawmaker wants to learn more about the test score achievement gap between blacks and whites or the threat of terrorism to our nation's seaports, she can request that GAO investigate the issue. The GAO, then, consults with non-government experts, reads the relevant scholarship, and communicates with bureaucratic agencies that deal with the particular policy domain. Having completed its investigation, the GAO reports back to the lawmaker, who is then better equipped to address the issue at hand.

Often, though, members of Congress and presidents consult with bureaucrats through less formal means. Either through testimony in congressional hearings, advisory meetings, or simple conversations, bureaucrats provide lawmakers with vital information about how policies are affecting citizens, which policies seem to be working, which are not, and what should be done about it. Indeed, it is their expertise that makes bureaucrats so useful to lawmakers trying to figure out how best to solve the problems of the day.

Bureaucrats resolve disputes.

Just as bureaucrats serve core executive functions by implementing laws and core legislative functions by issuing rules and providing expertise, so too do they serve core judicial functions by resolving disputes. The National Labor Relations Board, for instance, regularly hears cases involving the unionization of workers and unfair labor practices. Similarly, the Social Security Administrations has a well established process by which citizens who are denied disability payments can appeal their cases. In these processes, both agencies act very much like a court, holding formal hearings, listening to testimony, evaluating evidence, and ultimately making a decision one way or another.

The FCC also resolves disputes. If a radio or television station wishes to challenge a punishment administered by the FCC for having violated its obscenity standards, it can appeal the matter directly to the agency's five commissioners. CBS Corporation did exactly this when the FCC fined the company $550,000 after the 2004 Super Bowl half-time performance, during which singer Janet Jackson's breast was briefly exposed to approximately 89.8 million television viewers. The FCC said that CBS had violated its rule governing the broadcast of indecent material. CBS appealed to the commission twice, arguing that the partial nudity was an accident, that Jackson was exposed for less than a second, and that the incident did not violate the FCC rule on indecency. On two separate occasions, the FCC rejected the appeals, saying that the incident was in fact indecent according to its rule and that CBS was at fault for not taking proper precautions to prevent it from happening. CBS, however, continues to insist that the indecency rule is vague.[7] Other networks have also challenged FCC policies on indecency, claiming that they are inconsistent. While CBS has exhausted its options for appealing directly to the FCC, it could still challenge the fine in the federal court system.[8]

Growth and Organization of the Bureaucracy

Most of the federal bureaucracy is located within the executive branch of government. But the bureaucracy is not a unitary body operating in a single building down the street from Congress and the president. Rather, it is spread out all over the country and consists of many different units, some more independent than others. The type and number of those units, as well as the kinds of people who work within them, have evolved over time.

The bureaucracy has changed dramatically over the nation's history.

In most of Western Europe, national political systems were bureaucratized long before they were democratized. Particularly in France and Germany, bureaucracies served kings and emperors before they did presidents and prime ministers. With bureaucratic organizations already in place when these countries became democracies, elected officials merely had to redirect administrative activities to serve popular ends. Today, European executive and legislative branches utilize bureaucrats much more extensively in the policy-making process, with civil servants regularly serving in the British prime minister's office and cabinet office, the French president's Secretariat and prime minister's cabinet office, and the office of the German chancellor.[9]

The evolution of the U.S. bureaucracy looks quite different. In the United States, democratic political institutions were in place prior to the development of a fully fledged bureaucracy. In fact, America's Founders, disgusted by the British government's abuse of the colonies, intentionally restricted the size and powers of the bureaucracy. In the early years of the Republic, Congress assumed responsibility for most administrative decisions in the new nation. Although the legislature later recognized the need for a fully functional bureaucracy, members of Congress outnumbered civil servants in Washington until the 1820s.[10]

The modest beginnings of the U.S. bureaucracy should not come as a great surprise. The federal government in the nineteenth century, after all, was dramatically smaller than it is today. Its involvement in the daily lives of citizens was minimal by twenty-first century standards. It produced and implemented far fewer policies than today. It provided little or no regulation of business practices. And it assumed very little responsibility for the welfare of average citizens.

Nineteenth century federal bureaucrats, therefore, had relatively little to do. Furthermore, they tended to be hired not for their expertise, but for their political allegiance to the party in power. The **spoils system**, as it came to be known, defined the common practice of handing out government jobs, contracts, and other favors not on the basis of merit, but on the basis of political friendships and alliances. When a new president was elected and a different political party assumed control of the executive branch, it would promptly fire most bureaucrats then in office and replace them with its own loyalists.

The spoils system served the political needs of people in power. Most obviously, it provided a basis upon which to reward individuals for their political support. And with a growing number of citizens gaining the right to vote, it became more and more important to reward political activists who got people to the polls. Politicians also could raise money for their campaigns by promising jobs. By delivering jobs to key political allies, and thereby shoring up their own electoral fortunes, politicians could often secure the passage of a favorite law.

The spoils system had disadvantages as well. Because bureaucrats tended to remain employed only as long as their party remained in office, turnover tended to be quite high. Rather than devoting their lives to a particular policy, bureaucrats often worked for just a few short years. This turnover, in combination with the fact that bureaucrats were selected on the basis of their party support rather than their skills, education, or experience, meant that agencies were less professional and often unable to furnish much-needed expertise about public policy.

During the latter half of the nineteenth century, increasing pressure emerged to replace the spoils system with a **civil service system**, which awarded jobs primarily on the basis of merit. Decrying the abuses and waste of a bureaucracy filled with partisan hacks, a diverse group of professional elites pushed for reform. And when President James Garfield was assassinated by a disgruntled (and mentally ill) office seeker in 1881, Congress finally saw fit to address their concerns. In 1883, Congress enacted the Pendleton Act, which established the Civil Service Commission (later the Office of Personnel Management). The Civil Service Commission oversaw the hiring and firing of federal bureaucrats on the basis of new procedures, examinations, and qualifications. Merit, rather than party allegiances, constituted the employment qualification that mattered most.

For the most part, though, the transition from the spoils system to a fully developed civil service was gradual. Since politicians still had incentives to reward their partisan backers with jobs, the spoils system was not eliminated overnight. Indeed, the spoils system's final death knell was not heard until 1939, when the vast majority of bureaucrats could fairly be called civil servants, and when Congress enacted the Hatch Act, which forbade federal employees from engaging in blatantly partisan political activities like campaigning and fund-raising.

During the same time period that the management of federal bureaucracy personnel experienced dramatic reform, the size of the federal bureaucracy began to grow rapidly. Figure 16-2 tracks the growth in the number of executive branch employees from 1816 to 2005. As the government took on greater and greater

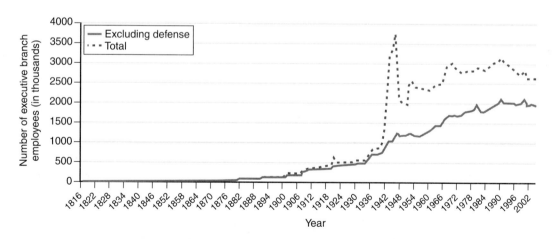

Figure 16-2. **The Size of the Federal Bureaucracy.** During the past century, the number of employees in the federal bureaucracy has increased dramatically. The dotted line includes all civilian executive branch employees. The solid line represents that total minus the number of civilian defense employees.

Sources: U.S. Bureau of the Census, *Historical Statistics of the United States: Colonial Times to 1970* (Washington, DC: Government Printing Office, 1975), 1102–03, series 312–314; U.S. Bureau of the Census, *Statistical Abstract of the United States: 2006* (Washington, DC: Government Printing Office, 2006), 330, table 481.

responsibility, it needed more agencies and employees to administer public policy. In the late nineteenth and early twentieth centuries, the federal government created agencies to establish and enforce rules on industry, trade, commerce, and transportation so that it could keep pace with the expanding American economy.[11] In 1871, the entire executive branch had only about 50,000 employees. Fifty years later, it had more than 400,000 employees.

But the expansion of the federal bureaucracy did not stop there. In the 1930s, Franklin D. Roosevelt created several new agencies through his "New Deal" program in an effort to lift the nation out of the Great Depression. The size of the bureaucracy skyrocketed when the U.S. became involved in World War II. Since 1946, the total number of executive branch employees has remained fairly stable. However, the number of non-defense employees has continued to grow throughout the last 60 years.

The bureaucracy today consists of many different units.

Since the end of World War II, the size of the federal bureaucracy has leveled off. In 1946, roughly the same number of bureaucrats worked for the federal government as today: slightly over 2 million.[12] These bureaucrats work within very different kinds of governing structures: departments, independent agencies and regulatory commissions, and government corporations.

Departments Most bureaucratic agencies are housed in a **department**, which is the largest organizational unit in the federal bureaucracy. Departments address broad areas of government responsibility, and the head of each department is appointed by the president to serve in his cabinet.

Today, there are 15 departments. The Department of Homeland Security, discussed at the beginning of this chapter, is the latest addition to the list. As Table 16-1 shows, at the nation's founding, George Washington oversaw only three departments: Treasury, War (now Defense), and State. During the nineteenth century, three more departments were added to the list: Interior, Justice, and Agriculture. But during the twentieth century, especially during the latter half, the number of departments really expanded. As the public expected the federal government to do more and more on its behalf, departments were created to help write and implement policy. Health and Human Services, Housing and Urban Development, Transportation, Energy, Education, Veterans Affairs, and finally Homeland Security were all created to confront problems ranging from the mental and physical health of citizens to the looming threat of terrorism.

Now take a look at Figure 16-3, which shows the amount of money spent by each of the departments in fiscal year 2005. Among the groups, the department that spends the most annually is Health and Human Services, which spent more than $580 billion in 2005. These costs covered such massive entitlement programs as Medicaid and Medicare, which are discussed at length in Chapter 17, as well as such prominent agencies as the Food and Drug Administration, the National Institutes of Health, and the Center for Disease Control and Prevention. Together, the two departments that employ the largest numbers of people, Defense and Veterans Affairs, spent more than $500 billion. Many of these funds covered the costs of ongoing wars in Afghanistan and Iraq. Education, Housing and Urban Development, and Energy, by contrast, are the three smallest agencies in terms of the number of people they employ. Combined, they spend about $136 billion each year and have fewer than 35,000 employees.

Table 16-1. Founding Data and Purpose of Federal Departments

DEPARTMENT	YEAR FOUNDED	RESPONSIBILITIES
War Department, renamed Department of Defense in 1949	1789	Coordinates and oversees the U.S. Army, the U.S. Navy, and the U.S. Air Force as well as smaller agencies that are responsible for national security.
Department of the Treasury	1789	Manages the government's money; prints paper currency, mints coins, and collects taxes through the Internal Revenue Service.
Department of State	1789	Develops and executes the president's foreign policy agenda. The department head, the Secretary of State, is the chief foreign policy advisor to the president.
Department of the Interior	1849	Conserves land owned by the federal government; manages cultural and natural resources like national parks, dams, wildlife refuges, and monuments.
Department of Justice	1870	The U.S. legal department that houses several law enforcement agencies, including the Federal Bureau of Investigation, the Drug Enforcement Administration, and the Federal Bureau of Prisons. Its lawyers represent the government in court. The chief lawyer of the federal government is the Attorney General.
Department of Agriculture	1889	Develops policy to protect farmers, promote agricultural trade, and alleviate hunger in the U.S. and abroad. It also inspects food to ensure that it is safe to consume.
Department of Labor, reconstituted in 1913	1903	Oversees labor practices in the U.S.; makes sure that workplaces are safe, enforces a minimum wage, and provides unemployment insurance.
Department of Commerce, reconstituted in 1913	1903	Works to maintain the health of the U.S. economy; supports businesses, promotes the creation of jobs, gathers and provides economic data, and issues patents and trademarks.
Department of Health and Human Services	1953	Administers more than 300 federal programs to protect the health and safety of Americans; provides health insurance to the elderly and disabled, offers immunization services and treatment for substance abuse, and inspects drugs to ensure their safety.
Department of Housing and Urban Development	1965	Works to increase homeownership in the U.S. It also helps low-income individuals to secure affordable housing.
Department of Transportation	1966	Ensures the safety, accessibility, and efficiency of air travel, the national highway network, railroads, and public transportation systems.
Department of Energy	1977	Oversees domestic energy production and conservation. It also manages the nation's nuclear weapons and reactors as well as the disposal of radioactive waste.
Department of Education	1980	Provides funding to education programs and enforces federal education laws such as "No Child Left Behind."
Department of Veterans Affairs	1988	Provides a wide array of benefits to war veterans, including general compensation, health care, education, life insurance, and home loans.
Department of Homeland Security	2002	Responsible for protecting the U.S. from terrorist attacks and responding to natural disasters.

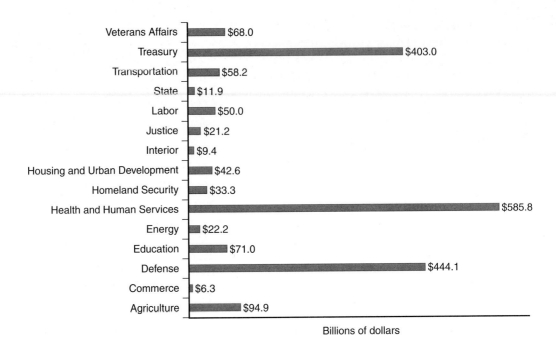

Figure 16-3. Department Spending in 2005. The sizes of the departments that make up the federal bureaucracy vary dramatically.

Source: U.S. Bureau of the Census, *Statistical Abstract of the United States: 2006* (Washington, DC: Government Printing Office, 2006), 318, table 462.

Independent agencies and regulatory commissions Not all agencies operate within a department. Many **independent agencies and commissions**, instead, operate outside of departments. These agencies and commissions are directed by administrators or boards who are appointed by the president, subject to Senate confirmation. The heads of these organizations, however, do not serve in the president's cabinet. And unlike department heads, whom the president can select freely and who can be fired at any time, heads of independent agencies and regulatory commissions must meet well-defined qualifications, and they hold office for fixed periods. These restrictions on the hiring and firing of agency leaders tend to protect them from the efforts of presidents and members of Congress to meddle in their affairs—a topic we discuss further below.

Independent agencies perform all sorts of functions. They manage national museums like the Smithsonian Institution. Through the Peace Corps, they send college graduates to volunteer in countries all over the globe. The National Aeronautics and Space Administration sends men and women into space, the Social Security Administration writes millions of checks each year, and the United States Postal Service delivers the mail. Recently, still more agencies have been created, which, as their names imply, serve an equally diverse array of responsibilities. As Table 16-2 shows, standouts include the Office of the Federal Coordinator for Alaska Natural Gas Transportation Projects, the U.S. Election Assistance Commission, and the Office of the National Counterintelligence Executive.

The first regulatory commission was the Interstate Commerce Commission, created in 1887 to regulate railroads. The nation subsequently experienced a rapid rise of commissions with the Administrative Procedures Act, which, as previously noted, established the governing framework for administrative agencies in the modern era. These commissions regulate all kinds of industries and organizations,

Table 16-2. Founding Date and Purpose of Select Independent Agencies, Regulatory Commissions, and Government Corporations The federal bureaucracy contains over 100 independent agencies and government corporations. The lists here contain some highlights.

INDEPENDENT AGENCIES AND REGULATORY COMMISSIONS	YEAR FOUNDED	RESPONSIBILITIES
United States Postal Service (USPS), became an independent agency in 1971	1775	Delivers all first and third class mail. Was a department for almost 200 years before it was reorganized as an independent agency. It is the only organization that can deliver mail to private mailboxes.
Board of Governors of the Federal Reserve System	1913	Governing body of the Federal Reserve System, which is the central bank of the U.S. Manages the nation's money supply, working to control inflation and maintain economic growth.
Federal Trade Commission (FTC)	1914	Created to protect consumers from deceptive and anti-competitive business practices; ensures that businesses advertise truthfully and provide buyers with adequate information about their products and services.
Securities and Exchange Commission (SEC)	1934	Enforces laws against insider trading and accounting fraud; created to regulate the stock market after the stock market crash of 1929 that led to the Great Depression.
Federal Communications Commission (FCC)	1934	Regulates radio and television broadcasting as well as interstate wire, satellite, and cable telecommunications. Governed by five commissioners who are appointed by the President and confirmed by the Senate.
Social Security Administration, reinstated as an independent agency in 1995	1935	Manages Social Security, the nation's social insurance program that delivers benefits to the elderly and disabled.
Central Intelligence Agency (CIA)	1947	Provides national security information on foreign governments, people, and corporations to senior officials in the federal government. Its secret operations are directed by the President and overseen by Congress.
National Aeronautics and Space Administration (NASA)	1958	Responsible for the nation's space program, including space exploration and scientific research.
Environmental Protection Agency (EPA)	1970	Protects Americans from the harmful health effects of air, water, and land pollution. Safeguards the natural environment by establishing and enforcing emissions standards for various types of pollutants.
Government Corporations		
Tennessee Valley Authority (TVA)	1933	A federally-owned power company that provides electricity to the Tennessee Valley, an area that includes most of Tennessee and parts of six other states in the region.
Federal Deposit Insurance Corporation (FDIC)	1933	Created during the Great Depression to promote confidence in the U.S. banking system; insures the money people deposit into checking and savings accounts in banks.
Corporation for Public Broadcasting	1967	Private, non-profit corporation that distributes funding for public television and radio programming, including programming made available through the Public Broadcasting Service (PBS) and National Public Radio (NPR). Funded almost entirely by the federal government.

(Continued)

Table 16-2. Founding Date and Purpose of Select Independent Agencies, Regulatory Commissions, and Government Corporations (*Continued*)

GOVERNMENT CORPORATIONS	YEAR FOUNDED	RESPONSIBILITIES
Amtrak (National Railroad Passenger Corporation)	1971	Provides passenger train service between U.S. cities. Receives funding from both the federal government and from ticket sales. Members of its board of directors are appointed by the President and confirmed by the Senate.
Overseas Private Investment Corporation (OPIC)	1971	Assists American businesses when they make investments abroad; helps companies manage the risk involved in overseas investments and promotes economic development in emerging markets. It gets most of its revenue from fees for its products.
Millennium Challenge Corporation (MCC)	2004	Provides funding to poverty-stricken countries in order to promote economic growth, infrastructure investment, and good government.

ranging from toy manufacturers to stock markets to television stations. Among the more important regulatory commissions are the Consumer Product Safety Commission, the Securities and Exchange Commission, the Federal Trade Commission, and, as previously discussed, the Federal Communications Commission.

Government corporations Even more removed from presidential and congressional control are **government corporations**.[13] These organizations most closely resemble private companies. Unlike private companies, however, government corporations receive government funding and are subject to modest oversight. In most cases, Congress or the president has decided that the private marketplace does not provide sufficient monetary incentives to provide these services (especially to low-income individuals). As shown in Table 16-2, prominent examples of government corporations include the National Railroad Passenger Corporation (Amtrak) and the Federal Deposit Insurance Corporation. These corporations take citizens to work and ensure the safety of their bank deposits. The most recent government corporation to come into existence is the Millennium Challenge Corporation, which promotes economic development projects around the globe.

Challenges of Bureaucracy

Bureaucrats provide vital services in an increasing number of policy areas. Indeed, hardly a day passes when we fail to interact with a bureaucrat of one type or another. But bureaucracy is not without its problems, which partially explains why so many politicians call for its reform. Sometimes bureaucrats attend to their own private interests or those of a narrow band of citizens rather than to the interests of the broader public. And sometimes the organizations in which bureaucrats work are extraordinarily inefficient. As a result, the services that the government bureaucracy provides are often more expensive and less effective than we might like.

Bureaucrats have their own interests.

In principle, bureaucrats are supposed to implement the policies written by their political superiors. When needed, bureaucrats are also supposed to clarify the meaning of laws, either through rules or norms. In practice, though, bureaucrats have their own interests, which may or may not align with those of the president or Congress. And because bureaucrats tend to have more expertise, they enjoy considerable discretion to pursue these ends, sometimes at a cost to the larger public.

To understand the problem of different interests, imagine that while driving home one day your car suddenly breaks down. What do you do? If you are like most Americans, you do not have a clue how to fix the car yourself. Underneath the hood, as far as you are concerned, lies nothing but a tangled mess of wires and pipes. So you have the car towed to the local mechanic to have it fixed. At this point, the interests of two people become involved. You need the mechanic for her expertise; the mechanic needs you for your money. The subsequent exchange, then, would appear perfectly straightforward. The mechanic fixes your car in exchange for a mutually agreed upon price.

But therein lies the rub. Precisely because you do not understand what is wrong with your car, you have little ability to determine how much it ought to cost to fix it. This would not ordinarily be a problem, at least not if the mechanic was honest and forthcoming. The trouble is that the mechanic's interests are different from yours. You want to pay the least amount of money for the most amount of work using the best possible parts. The mechanic, by contrast, wants to receive the most amount of money for the least amount of work using the least expensive parts. And because she knows more than you about what is wrong with your car and what is needed to fix it, the mechanic is often able to win out in this exchange.

The resulting inefficiencies are an example of what is commonly referred to as a **principal-agent problem**. In this example, you are the principal, and the mechanic is the agent. Both individuals are made better off by having the work done to the car at a fair price. But because the mechanic, as the agent, has private information that you, as the principal, cannot know, the mechanic is made even better off, and you worse off—either because the mechanic charges you for services that your car does not really need, or because she does not do as good a job as promised on the work order.

This principal-agent problem fundamentally defines the relationship between Congress and the president (the principals), on the one hand, and the bureaucracy (the agent), on the other. Congress and the president, as policy generalists, need bureaucrats for their expertise. Bureaucrats, however, do not necessarily share the same interests as Congress and the president.[14] Bureaucrats may not want to work as hard as Congress and the president would like them to—generating what political scientists refer to as **slack**. Anyone who has stood for hours at the local post office can attest to its frustrations. Alternatively, bureaucrats may be perfectly willing to work hard, but they choose to do so in the service of objectives that Congress and the president oppose—generating what political scientists refer to as **drift**. Examples of drift include the district attorney who aggressively pursues white-collar criminals but prefers not to prosecute federal drug offenses, or the park ranger who uses funds to purchase new computers for his staff rather than to clean campgrounds, or the teacher who decides to stick with her tried and true lesson plans rather than teach a new state-mandated curriculum.

An essential element of what makes slack and drift possible is the principal's difficulty of monitoring the agent. Congress and the president cannot personally watch every decision of a district attorney, a park ranger, or a teacher. Moreover, outcomes are often hard to measure. All of the available measures of criminal activity, park cleanliness, and student learning are imperfect, making it exceedingly difficult for Congress and the president to know for sure whether bureaucrats are working as effectively as they can in the service of their formal goals and responsibilities. Moreover, because there are so many contributors to each of these outcomes—what bureaucrats do, or do not do, is only part of the equation—bureaucrats can often explain away any observed failures to achieve stated objectives as being beyond their control. After all, as agents they are the ones who are experts, while Congress and the president, as principals, are not.

The troubles, though, do not end there. In the example of the broken car, there is but one agent and one principal. In government, by contrast, at any given moment there are many principals and many agents. And the interests of each do not perfectly overlap. When Congress and the president disagree about a policy issue, as they typically do during periods of divided government, agents may be able to play off one principal against the other. And when multiple agents are responsible for a particular policy issue, each can attempt to blame the others when failures are observed.

Consider the extraordinary efforts of the federal government to monitor and improve student learning in public schools. Under the recently enacted No Child Left Behind Act, discussed at length in Chapter 17, students are regularly evaluated on newly developed state tests; depending on student performance, schools may face consequences ranging from funding cuts to restructurings. Bureaucrats in local school districts, state education departments, and the federal government all work hard to implement the law. But given the stakes involved, and the controversies that surround standardized tests, these bureaucrats occasionally work at cross purposes: federal bureaucrats may blame state and local officials for refusing to fully incorporate the provisions of No Child Left Behind; local and state officials, meanwhile, blame the federal government for imposing undue burdens on schools without providing sufficient funding.

Compounding the principal-agent problem is the fact that in government, the preferences of the principals change every two or four years. A coalition within Congress may set a bureaucratic agency's official mandate one year, but following an election the individuals who comprised this coalition may no longer be in power. Those individuals who replaced them, meanwhile, may have very different ideas about what bureaucrats ought to be doing. When the new Congress and presidential administration assume office in 2009, No Child Left Behind may be radically altered: new state tests may be developed; the standards for evaluating student progress may shift; a new array of punishments for school failure may be introduced; and altogether new monitoring devices may be developed. For obvious reasons, such changes can place incredible burdens on those bureaucrats charged with interpreting and implementing a continually changing legislative mandate.

Bureaucrats sometimes serve the interests of unelected groups.

Bureaucrats occasionally stray from their mandate not in the pursuit of their own interests, but rather in the pursuit of someone else's. Sometimes it is a well-funded special interest group. Other times it is a highly mobilized segment of the population. Or it might be the industry that a bureaucratic agency is supposed to be regulating. In any one of these instances, bureaucrats would appear to be taking their cues not from their political superiors, but instead from individuals and organizations that operate outside of government entirely.

Political scientists use the term **agency capture** to describe the situation when an agency primarily serves the interests of a non-governmental group rather than those of elected officials. The possibility of agency capture is especially high under two conditions.[15] The first is when the benefits of agency actions are concentrated on a few individuals or organizations, while the costs are spread more or less evenly throughout society. Consider, for example, bureaucratic agencies that direct financial subsidies to farmers. These subsidies, which are discussed at the outset of Chapter 17, are not especially large. For the farmers who benefit from them, however, they mean a great deal. As such, these farmers will work hard to ensure that the agency continues to dole out these benefits year in and year out, regardless of whether they serve a larger public purpose.

Agency capture also occurs when the costs of policy implementation fall on a small group of individuals or organizations, but the social benefits are more diffuse. Consider, for example, an agency that is charged with monitoring the air pollutants produced by an industry on the edge of a large city. If the agency vigorously enforces rules that limit pollution, the industry will incur the high costs of compliance. These costs include both the fines it may have to pay for violating clean air rules and the new machinery it may need to purchase in order to comply with the law. From the perspective of each city resident, though, the benefits of the agency's actions are relatively small. They certainly prefer that the industry produce less waste, but their daily lives are probably not deeply affected by the agency's efforts to reduce industrial pollutants. Consequentially, the regulated industries have strong incentives to influence agency behavior, while the general public does not. The resulting mismatch between highly mobilized and organized interest groups and a less attentive public invites agency capture.

Some have argued that the Food and Drug Administration (FDA) has been captured by pharmaceutical companies, which help fund FDA activities, lobby members of Congress, and launch major public relations campaigns.[16] Pharmaceutical companies stand to make massive amounts of money when a drug is approved for public consumption. As a result, companies with existing drugs sometimes encourage raising the standards of evaluations, thereby reducing the opportunities for new treatments to enter the market. Other times companies pressure the FDA to approve drugs before the safety of those drugs has been conclusively established.

Such accusations came to a head in 2004, when members of Congress harshly criticized the FDA for failing to withdraw the popular arthritis drug Vioxx from the market, even after multiple studies linked it to an increased risk of heart attack or stroke. FDA whistleblower David Graham, who claimed the agency ignored his warnings about the drug's potential dangers, estimated that 88,000 to 139,000 Americans experienced heart attacks or strokes because of Vioxx, and as many as 55,000 may have died.[17] Asserting that this "profound regulatory failure" resulted from an inappropriately cozy relationship between FDA officials and pharmaceutical companies, Graham contended, "the FDA as currently configured is incapable of protecting America against another Vioxx."[18]

It is worth noting, though, that the FDA often is placed in an impossible position. If they do not approve drugs fast enough, they appear to be ignoring the needs of citizens in need of new treatments; but if they approve drugs hastily, they risk exposing the public to unsafe drugs. It often is difficult, therefore, to know whether the actions that the FDA takes are an attempt to balance these competing considerations, or whether the agency is ultimately guided by the very drug companies it is supposed to regulate.

Bureaucrats can be inefficient.

The most common complaint about bureaucrats is not that they serve their own interests or those of a narrow band of the U.S. public. Rather, it is that they do not do a good job of serving anyone's interest. For some, the very word *bureaucracy* has come to imply inefficiency, waste, and **red tape**.

Every few months, it seems, a story breaks in the news about a $1,000 hammer purchased by the federal government, a half-built bridge that never seems to be completed, a dozen agencies that are all supposed to be doing the same thing, piles of mail that sit for weeks in warehouses, or bureaucrats paid large amounts of money to do little but sit. A predictable set of charges follow: bureaucrats waste public funds, fail to complete their tasks, ignore pressing public needs, and live off the public's dole without any apparent justification.

Boston's "Big Dig" project stands out as one of the more recent and alarming examples of bureaucratic waste and mismanagement. Intended to reduce traffic in the downtown area and clear space for parks, the public works project was officially launched in 1991, when Congress appropriated funds for the project over a presidential veto. Early plans for the project suggested an official price of $2.5 billion. In less than a decade, though, costs rose to $7.5 billion, and by 2006 costs reached an astronomical $14.6 billion. For all the money spent, the project has been awash (literally) in scandal. Since the tunnels opened in January 2006, hundreds of water leaks have sprung; multiple investigations have uncovered the use of faulty materials; falling ceiling tiles have killed a commuter, attracting national media attention; and charges of corruption and waste have been leveled against both the companies who undertook the work and the government agencies charged with overseeing them.[19]

Some blame this state of affairs on a culture of inertia that exists within the government's bureaucracy. Culture, in this instance, emerges from worker incentives. Bureaucrats have strong job protections—a product of the civil service reforms previously discussed. And they are not driven by the profit motive; they do not need to work hard or reduce waste in order to remain employed. Quite the contrary. The culture of bureaucracy sometimes rewards individuals not for the impact that their labor has had on the lives of citizens, but rather for their faithful adherence to a stated process for how things ought to be done. Indeed, it was not until Massachusetts's governor and attorney general stepped in that the head of the Massachusetts Turnpike Authority was fired, companies were sued for "shoddy work," and responsibility for the project shifted to state government.

Although the waste and mismanagement of the Big Dig project was extreme, smaller versions of such failures are reasonably common. Moreover, they are entirely predictable. The bureaucracy, after all, is not designed merely for the sake of efficiency. It also is supposed to promote notions of fairness and equity. And to ensure that individual bureaucrats follow these directives, politicians have insisted that bureaucrats follow painstaking procedures for even the simplest of tasks.

Take, for example, the job of purchasing a new computer. An individual working in the private industry needs only to find the company that will provide the best possible machine that suits his individual needs for the lowest price. In a government agency, by contrast, bureaucrats must solicit bids from government-approved vendors, choose from a select group of machines, and maintain careful documentation of all transactions made. In this way, the public can rest assured that the companies that supply computers to the federal government do not discriminate against their workers, that bureaucrats are not spending lavish amounts of money, and that all monies are accounted for. The process is long and costly, but exists to promote the important goals of fairness and equality.

Moreover, there are political explanations for certain bureaucratic failures or inefficiencies. Congress and the president often oversee agencies whose activities they would just as soon reduce, or even eliminate. So rather than appoint individuals who will vigorously pursue an agency's mission, they choose people who will take a more lax approach to regulatory enforcement. James Watt's tenure as Secretary of the Interior under President Reagan and Gale Norton's under President Bush (43) were both marked by such charges. Critics claimed that both Reagan and Bush were less interested in protecting federal lands and more interested in developing housing and increasing energy production. Accordingly, these presidents deliberately chose secretaries whom they knew would take a rather restricted (some would argue, balanced) view of their duties to secure the well-being of the nation's parks and lands. Thus their choices for Interior Secretary were two former attorneys for the Mountain States Legal Foundation, an organization whose mission is to provide a "strong and effective voice for freedom of enterprise, the rights of private property ownership, and the multiple use of federal and state resources."[20]

Some political scientists argue that the very design of our system of governance undermines opportunities for effective bureaucracy. They claim that regular elections, multiple principals, and political compromise lend themselves to inefficiencies and mismanagement, even in domains that everyone agrees are essential to the nation's well-being. One political scientist, for instance, argues that the core agencies charged with intelligence-gathering—the Central Intelligence Agency, the Joint Chiefs of Staff, and the National Security Council—are "flawed by design."[21] The Joint Chiefs of Staff (JCS), for instance, emerged from "a brass-knuckle fight to the finish" between President Truman and the War Department, who sought to bring the military services under one umbrella, and the Department of the Navy, which fiercely guarded its independence.[22] The resulting structure of the JCS pleased few, and did little to quell inter-service rivalry. Bureaucratic in-fighting during the Korean War, for instance, was bitter enough that it "extended to conflicts over which service would operate a laundry in Alaska." More serious failures of the JCS included its approval of Kennedy's disastrous Bay of Pigs invasion, as well as coordination problems during interventions in Iran, Grenada, and Beirut.[23]

Even the redundancy that pervades so much of the federal bureaucracy has a certain inherent political logic. Imagine the challenge faced by a president who assumes office after a long stretch of control by the opposition party. Should the newly elected president rely upon individuals appointed under the former administrations to formulate his policy agenda? Or, after recognizing the awesome challenges of dismantling existing agencies, might he instead construct altogether new ones? Both options have advantages and disadvantages. Hence, when advancing a new policy initiative, presidents often spread out responsibilities across multiple new agencies while also creating new ones. This, in fact, is exactly what President George W. Bush did when launching his "Faith-Based Initiative," a key plank in his 2000 campaign platform. In an effort to support social programs run by private and religion-based charities, Bush created five new centers in existing cabinet departments (Justice, Housing and Urban Development, Health and Human Services, Labor, and Education), as well as a White House Office of Faith-Based and Community Initiatives.[24]

Did the Federal Bureaucracy Fail to Protect the City of New Orleans After Hurricane Katrina?

The Question

In August 2005, Hurricane Katrina tore through the Gulf Coast, devastating the city of New Orleans and other coastal areas in Louisiana, Mississippi, and Alabama. The collapse of several levees in New Orleans submerged much of the city under water. Survivors in the most ravaged sections of the city had no electricity, no way to communicate by telephone or radio, no roads or bridges on which to escape, and no functioning law enforcement to protect them from theft and violence. The disaster overwhelmed the response systems of the federal, state, and local bureaucracies. Thousands of residents who had not evacuated were left stranded on their rooftops for days without food or water, waiting to be rescued. More than 1,300 people died in the storm and its aftermath.

Americans were appalled by the slowness and inadequacy of the government's response to the disaster. In the months following, many questioned the effectiveness of multiple government agencies, especially the Federal Emergency Management Agency (FEMA), which had been moved into the Department of Homeland Security in 2003 after previously operating as an independent agency. Did the federal bureaucracy fail to protect the city of New Orleans after Hurricane Katrina? How do we know?

By objectively analyzing the effectiveness of the federal bureaucracy, we may contribute to policy discussions about what could be done better. These discussions shape decisions that affect us every time we take a prescription drug approved by the FDA, eat chicken inspected by the Department of Agriculture, or send a piece of mail through the U.S. Postal Service. Because we both consume those services and pay for them through taxes, we must think critically about whether our money is being spent well and whether the services provided by the bureaucracy meet our expectations.

In the U.S. federalist system, power is shared among the federal government and 50 state governments. The state governments bear a great deal of responsibility for designing and implementing policy, and the executive branches of the state government have their own bureaucracies with many of the same problems as the federal bureaucracy. Moreover, within the states, city and county governments have their own responsibilities. To evaluate the performance of the federal government, then, it is also important to account for the performance of state and local governments in the complex web of federalism.

Cities, states, and the federal government share the responsibility of responding to natural disasters. Technically, it is the job of counties and cities to respond first. Only after local resources have been exhausted do the governor and the state bureaucracies provide further disaster assistance. The governor can call in the federal government to help if the state cannot handle the situation. Even when federal assistance is called upon, however, federal agents must work with state and local agents to carry out relief. The shared nature of disaster relief makes it extremely difficult to sort out which level of government is most to blame for a poorly conducted relief effort.

The extent of damage wrought by Katrina clearly overwhelmed the disaster relief agencies of the city of New Orleans and state of Louisiana. Can we then pin blame on the federal bureaucracy? Perhaps. By media accounts, after all, it performed exceptionally poorly during and after Hurricane Katrina. The U.S. Army Corps of Engineers was criticized for not having detected a flaw in the designs of the 17th Street and London Avenue levees, a flaw that most likely caused the levees' collapse and the subsequent flooding of the city. A panel of engineers investigating the levee breaches, however, blamed budget cuts for the insufficiency of scientific expertise within the Army Corps of Engineers and the failure to identify the relatively simple flaw.[25] Should the Corps be blamed for building flawed levees, or should Congress be blamed for cutting the Corps' budget? Can we really say that the Corps failed simply because the levees it had built collapsed after a Category 3 hurricane? After all, prior to Katrina, the levees had held up quite well. How strong a storm would the levees have to withstand before the Corps could be commended for its performance?

FEMA also came under heavy fire for its failure to respond to the crisis speedily and effectively. The catastrophe made clear that FEMA was entirely unprepared to handle the large-scale rescue operation. The competence and credentials of then-FEMA director Michael Brown were called sharply into question after the agency's inadequate response. And the preponderance of evidence suggests that FEMA failed miserably in its responsibilities as a federal agency. Still, the devastation left by Hurricane Katrina was unprecedented. Even the most efficient, most effective federal agency might have struggled to deal with a catastrophe of such magnitude.

It also is worth noting that other federal agencies, by everyone's account, performed well during Katrina's aftermath. The U.S. Coast Guard was praised for rescuing people who were stranded on their rooftops due to the flooding of their homes. The National Weather Service had provided accurate predictions of the hurricane's intensity and path. But how do we know that those agencies were performing as well as they usually do? Wouldn't we need to know that before judging their performance during Katrina?

The circumstances surrounding Katrina, clearly, were far from typical. To evaluate the general effectiveness of bureaucracies, then, it might make more sense to examine their handling of multiple events. One way to do so is to use "organizational report cards." An organizational report card uses clearly defined measurements to determine the impact individual organizations have on the outcomes they were created to produce. The measurements are collectively translated into a "grade" that can be easily interpreted.[26]

To begin, the researcher must recognize that the outcome—disaster relief—is a combination of many things that may or may not be easily measured. For example, a researcher might calculate the speediness of an agency's response. How long did it take the first truck of supplies to arrive at the scene of the natural disaster? How long did survivors wait for food and water to be provided? The researcher might also try to find out the number of people the agency assisted. Better yet, she might measure the percentage of all survivors the agency assisted within a certain number of hours. It is also important to account for the context of the disaster relief. What was the extent of the damage? If the natural disaster destroyed the infrastructure of a large area, the agency could be expected to take longer to respond to the crisis. Also, the researcher would take note of the resources available to the agency. An emergency response agency working with a few trucks and a budget of $100,000 per year could not be expected to accomplish as much as a larger agency. All of these inputs would have to be measured in order to give an agency a grade for its performance.

The Bottom Line

The devastation wrought by Hurricane Katrina would seem to speak for itself. Clearly the government had failed to protect its citizens from the consequences of natural disaster. Assigning blame, though, is complicated by the fact that multiple levels of government, and multiple agencies within any given level, are responsible for disaster relief. Moreover, political scientists recommend that analysts examine agency responses to multiple disasters, rather than trying to prescribe reforms on the basis of one example, especially when it is atypical. Given the inherent challenges of a bureaucratic system, the response of the government as a whole may not have been as bad as the horrifying images of the hurricane's aftermath would imply.

Controlling and Reforming the Bureaucracy

Reformers have long sought solutions to the various problems of bureaucratic drift, slack, agency capture, and inefficiency. None works perfectly. But each manages to give the president, Congress, and the larger public somewhat more influence over the bureaucracy than would otherwise occur. These reforms generally fit into one of three categories: those that focus on the bureaucrats who work within agencies; those that focus on the structural relationship between agencies and their political superiors; and those that attempt to promote market forces of competition.

Presidents and Congress exercise control through appointments.

The secretaries of all cabinet-level departments are appointed by the president, subject to Senate confirmation. The president is free to choose whomever he likes to fill these positions. The president also can select the individuals and boards that govern independent agencies, regulatory commissions, and government corporations. These appointments are more constrained, often requiring a balance of Republicans and Democrats. Nonetheless, the president and Congress still have considerable opportunities to determine the leadership of these agencies and commissions. Indeed, in 2001 Bush made no less than 3,361 appointments to agencies and departments scattered throughout the executive branch.[27]

When making their selections, what criteria might Congress and the president consider? Plainly, both want to appoint individuals who are well-qualified, who have expertise and experience in the given policy arena, and who are likely to inspire their workforce. All of these characteristics reflect the civil service reforms of the early twentieth century. The appointment process, however, remains deeply political. Precisely because bureaucrats have a tendency to drift away from their given mandate, Congress and the president have strong incentives to choose leaders on the basis of their expressed ideological views and policy commitments. In other words, Congress and the president try to solve the principal-agent problem by selecting agents who share their worldview, and who appear committed to seeing it realized by the department or agency that they will eventually run.

Political scientists call this phenomenon the **politicization** of the bureaucracy.[28] Presidents and Congress select individuals they can trust, those they believe will faithfully implement their wishes and ensure that their staff will follow suit. And they do so for good reason. What is the point, after all, of appointing someone who is highly skilled and experienced, but who has no interest in following your wishes? Competence is important, but in politics, it is not enough. Presidents and Congress also need to know that those under their command will work hard on behalf of their interests, even when (especially when) these individuals are not being watched.

Of course, presidents and members of Congress themselves may disagree about the kinds of policies that bureaucratic agencies ought to implement. And in these instances, the appointment process can be highly controversial. Take, for example, Clinton's decision to appoint California attorney Bill Lann Lee to head the Civil Rights Division of the Department of Justice. When Clinton first nominated Lee for the position in 1997, the Republican-controlled Senate Judiciary Committee balked. Contrary to the praise Lee received from civil rights groups and Democrats in Congress, Republicans argued that the former NAACP lawyer was far too liberal, particularly on the issue of affirmative action. Clinton tried to re-nominate Lee, but the Senate continued to deny Lee the position.[29]

When the Senate will not confirm a president's appointment, the president has two choices. First, he can withdraw the nomination and offer up an entirely new candidate. Alternatively, he can issue what is known as a **recess-appointment**. Historically, presidents relied upon recess-appointments to ensure that the government continued to function when the Senate adjourned for longer periods of times. Increasingly, though, presidents have relied upon recess-appointments to circumvent political opposition within Congress, as Clinton did in the case of Lee.[30] Recess-appointments can be used only under very specific conditions. Each year after the Senate term ends, the president may appoint individuals who immediately assume their positions of leadership in the federal bureaucracy. When Congress reconvenes, the Senate may choose whether to formally confirm these candidates. If a confirmation vote is not held, the candidate can remain in office, at least until the end of Congress's session. Formally, presidents can repeatedly appoint the same individuals during Congress's recess. In practice, though, they tend not to do so.

Whether the result of presidents acting on their own or with Congress, the politicization of the bureaucracy has invited much criticism. Grumblings turned to heated condemnations when President Bush selected Michael Brown to help run the Federal Emergency Management Agency. Brown, a former commissioner for the International Arabian Horse Association, had no prior experience running a major disaster relief organization. Many argued that Brown was selected because of his political allegiance to the president rather than on the basis of merit. And when he failed to demonstrate clear leadership during the lead-up to and aftermath of Hurricane Katrina—a topic we discuss in the *How Do We Know?* section—many called for his resignation and attacked the Bush administration for having placed a purely political appointee in a position of such responsibility.

The politicization of the bureaucracy, however, concerns more than just the decision to hire individuals. It also relates to the decision to fire them. Here again, the Bush administration is illustrative. When it came to light in 2006 that Attorney General Alberto Gonzalez dismissed eight U.S. attorneys for political reasons, a firestorm erupted in Washington, D.C., with Democrats leading the charge.[31] The attorneys had solid reputations and positive job evaluations. They purportedly clashed with the administration, however, on such issues as immigration and capital punishment. Many argued that these disagreements lead to their dismissals. Because the attorney general was seen to be politicizing the Justice Department—a charge he vehemently denied[32]—Democrats and even some Republicans saw fit to call for his resignation. According to one particularly harsh op-ed piece, "Gonzales, the nation's highest legal officer, has been point man for serial assaults against the rule of law, most recently in the crude attempt to politicize criminal prosecutions. Obstruction of a prosecution is a felony, even when committed by the attorney general."[33]

Note, though, that the threat of firing individuals who do not share the president's mission helps address the basic problems of drift, slack, and agency capture. One could argue that if presidents (or their cabinet secretaries) discover that bureaucrats are not working hard or are implementing their own policies or those of an unelected subset of the population, the administration has cause to fire them. One might go so far as to argue that the attorney general has every right, and even the responsibility, to ensure that those individuals working within the Justice Department share the president's priorities about the prosecution of different crimes.

Of course, the high levels of turnover that result from all of these hirings and firings can create problems of their own. The election of each new president brings an entirely new set of appointments. Though the vast majority of workers within the bureaucracy enjoy strong job protection—the core result of the switch from the spoils system to the civil service system—many agency heads leave office at the end of a presidential term.[34] Such short tenures can diminish their ability to learn the culture of their agencies, to secure the trust of their subordinates, and to see through lasting policy changes.

In other countries, by contrast, a much more stable supply of policy experts runs the administrative apparatus. Take, for example, Canada. Whereas about 20 percent of American public servants leave their jobs in a typical year, only 4 percent of Canadian civil service employees do so.[35] One reason for this difference may be that the Canadian bureaucracy is comprised almost entirely of career civil servants (who serve for decades) rather than political appointees (who tend to serve shorter terms). In Canada, non-partisan career civil servants occupy all Canadian bureaucratic positions from the rank of deputy minister down the chain. Indeed, only the cabinet-level ministers, of which there are about 30, can be appointed by the prime minister based on their partisan affiliation.[36] By contrast, in the United States the president chooses roughly 3,000 political appointees to serve in the bureaucracy.[37] Although comprising less than 1 percent of the total civilian workforce, these partisan appointees dominate the highest echelons of agency management. Moreover, more than half of the 2.5 million American civil servants are "excepted" from the traditional merit-based guidelines, serving instead under agency-specific personnel systems.[38] While these systems officially operate under the merit scheme, the flexibility they give to managers makes it easier to circumvent merit rules in hiring and promotion.[39] As a result, agency-based personnel systems "blur the line between appointees and careerists."[40] For all of these reasons, the U.S. civil service may not possess the same level of stability, independence, and expertise found in Canada and elsewhere.

Presidents and Congress use money, rules, and structure to control bureaucracies.

Between the hiring and firing of individuals who run the federal government's agencies, the president, Congress, and the courts have further opportunities to influence bureaucratic behavior. Agencies, after all, do not run on their own. They require money to pay their employees; they must regularly report to their political superiors; they are situated within a larger bureaucratic structure; and their very survival often depends upon continued political support. Each of these facts allows for even further control over the federal bureaucracy.

Budgets Every year, the president must propose a budget, and Congress must enact it. (See Chapter 13 for a more thorough discussion of this process.) The budget process gives both an opportunity to reflect upon the performance of each bureaucratic agency, and to punish or reward it accordingly. When agencies are doing well, Congress can reward them with higher budgets; when agencies are not performing effectively, Congress may decide to slash their budgets. With control of the purse strings, Congress can create strong incentives for agencies to abide by their interests.

Beyond adjusting the amount of money granted to different agencies, Congress can attach any number of stipulations on how these monies are to be spent.

Rather than give each agency a lump-sum payment, which its employees then decide how to spend, Congress may write detailed instructions about which projects an agency should pursue and which it should abandon. In 2006, for instance, Congress required NASA to allocate $568.5 million of its budget for 198 special-interest items. A decade earlier, Congress had required that NASA devote just $74 million for 6 items.[41]

Oversight In a principal-agent relationship, you will recall, the agent's great advantages are information and expertise. So it is with the bureaucracy. Agencies, and the individuals who work within them, are great reservoirs of expertise about a vast array of public policies. They know what should be done, what is being done, and what plans are in place for the future. As policy generalists, the principals (Congress and the president) to some extent must rely on that knowledge for their decisions and directives.

Given this state of affairs, Congress and the president often seek to extract the private information that gives bureaucratic agencies such influence. One of the best ways to do so is through **hearings**. Should an issue or a problem come to light, committees and subcommittees can call upon bureaucrats to testify in formal settings. Though members of Congress often use these opportunities to show off before the television cameras, they also can direct pointed questions about agency actions, policies, and procedures. Moreover, members of Congress may choose to bring in outside experts and former agency employees in order to verify or dispute the claims made by current bureaucrats. With the information that they gather, members of Congress are in a better position to decide whether agency budgets need to be adjusted, whether their legislative mandates need to be revised, and sometimes whether criminal charges need to be brought forward.

In any given congressional session, literally thousands of hearings are held on topics ranging from the conduct of foreign wars to the collapse of domestic companies. Between the early 1950s and early 1990s, the number of biennial hearings held by the Senate almost doubled, rising from 704 hearings in 1951–1952 to 1,480 in 1993–1994.[42] The number has since fallen, in part due to reforms instituted in 1995 that reduced the number of staff available to congressional committees. Nonetheless, public hearings remain a critical means by which members of Congress can monitor activities in the federal bureaucracy.

In addition to hearings, members of Congress can choose to launch their own investigations into perceived abuses of power. And a number of agencies have the specific responsibility of monitoring other agencies and reporting their findings back to Congress. The General Accounting Office, the Congressional Research Service, and the Congressional Budget Office all provide independent sources of information about public policy and agency behavior. Often, this information comes in the form of reports about specific issues that individual members request. With this information, members of Congress can further influence agency behavior and reduce any problems that might arise from principal-agent relations.

Congress also has enacted a number of laws intended to make bureaucratic behavior more transparent. The 1976 Sunshine Law, for instance, requires that agency meetings be held in public, unless classified information is being discussed. Similarly, the 1967 Freedom of Information Act enables members of Congress (as well as all citizens) to inspect a wide variety of government documents. If agencies raise concerns about releasing these documents to the public, they must state their case before a federal judge. Both of these laws are designed to open to public scrutiny the federal government in general, and the bureaucracy in particular.

Centralization Left to their own devices, bureaucrats may wander from their policy mandate. This is especially true when their agencies are shielded from media scrutiny, and when Washington elites have few ways of directly monitoring their behavior. These bureaucrats may well be advancing policies that improve the public's welfare. But what are political superiors to do when these bureaucrats resist their orders? One solution: round them up and bring them closer to home.

Political scientists have made much of presidents' efforts to **centralize** the bureaucracy—that is, to move key functions from the departments to the Executive Office of the President (EOP), sometimes referred to as the presidential branch. The core administrative structures in the EOP consist of the White House, the Office of Management and Budget, and the Council of Economic Advisors. It also contains the Office of National Drug Control Policy, the Office of Science and Technology Policy, the United States Trade Representative, the President's Foreign Intelligence Advisory Board, and many other units. And throughout the EOP are people working on every imaginable policy. By relying upon these individuals, the president can more easily monitor their behavior and ensure that they are advancing his core interests.[43]

When do presidents rely upon individuals within the EOP for policy advice, and when do they turn to bureaucrats employed in the departments? The choice, some argue, comes down to the perceived costs and benefits of loyalty and expertise. Individuals within the EOP are more likely to follow the president's lead, but they tend to know less about policy issues. By contrast, employees in the departments typically have extensive expertise about policy, but they cannot so easily be trusted to promote the president's interests. According to one study, presidents tend to worry more about the importance of expertise when an issue is either new or very complex; in these instances, the president turns to department bureaucrats when developing his policy agenda.[44] When large numbers of people from the opposition party hold seats in Congress, however, presidents worry more about loyalty; under these conditions, presidents are more likely to depend upon EOP staffers.

Interestingly, this same study finds that the president's legislative initiatives are less likely to be enacted when the president centralizes authority. It is not clear why this is the case. Perhaps members of Congress are less likely to trust the president when he forsakes the expertise located in the departments in favor of the judgments of loyalists in the EOP. Alternatively, presidents may choose to centralize when they anticipate a difficult legislative road ahead. If so, then causality would appear to be reversed—expectations about legislative failure promote centralization, rather than centralization leading to legislative breakdown.

Beyond its impact on the likelihood of enacting presidential initiatives, centralization creates other problems. With increasing numbers of individuals and organizations working on any particular policy issue, lines of responsibility begin to blur. And as the EOP grows, some argue that there emerges "an unwieldy, tower hierarchy in which accountability is diffuse at best and the president is sometimes the last to know."[45] With the passage of time, one can well imagine presidents opting to centralize authority still further within the EOP—with loyalists working close by, and experts toiling away in the outer reaches of the presidential branch.

Agency eliminations If all else fails, Congress and the president can eliminate an agency outright. Contrary to conventional wisdom, agencies are not immortal. In fact, agencies are eliminated with a fair amount of frequency.[46] According to one analysis, fully 60 percent of all agencies created between 1946 and 1997 had been eliminated by 2000. When President Nixon assumed office after eight years of Democratic control, for instance, he eliminated the Office of Economic Opportunity, which was then responsible for administering many of the social welfare programs created under President Johnson. In an effort to reduce the ability of the Environmental Protection Agency to regulate industries, President Reagan eliminated the Office of Enforcement.

Different kinds of agencies tend to survive for different amounts of times. Government corporations and independent agencies and commissions, which are intentionally given more autonomy, tend to live longer than do agencies located within the Executive Office of the President, which are subject to more presidential control. Congress and the president also have a more difficult time eliminating an agency when they are more constrained in their ability to hire and fire agency heads, either because these heads must be from a specific party or because they serve for fixed terms.

Politics also appears to contribute to the lifespan of different agencies. Agencies are more likely to be eliminated when the current president is of the opposite party of the president who was in power when the agency was created. It is unclear, though, what exactly to make of this finding. Perhaps presidents tend to kill programs that they oppose, and these programs tend to be created by predecessors from the opposition party. On the other hand, a switch from one party to another in the presidency may reflect broader changes in the public's spending priorities. If true, then the fact that agencies tend to die when a new party takes control of the White House has less to do with the independent policy agenda of the president and more to do with the efforts of elected officials to keep pace with public opinion.

CaseStudy: Tying the Hands of the Environmental Protection Agency

Sometimes, efforts by presidents and Congress to control the bureaucracy do not result in a more effective institution. Instead, such efforts undermine the work of an agency that is, by all accounts, faithfully attending to its mandate. The resulting problem has less to do with slack or drift, and more to do with political interference. The recent history of the Environmental Protection Agency (EPA) is a case in point.

Upon signing the first act of Congress of his administration, President Richard Nixon in 1969 declared that the 1970s would be the "environmental decade." The new law, the National Environmental Policy Act, was the first of several to dramatically expand the role of the federal government in protecting the environment. At the time, the president and Congress were eager to respond to a widely publicized environmental movement and a growing number of powerful environmental interest groups.[47]

In 1970, Congress established the EPA, whose most important responsibility was implementing the Clean Air Act. Under the act, EPA officials were charged with setting limits for the amount of pollution that could be emitted by steel mills, chemical plants, motor vehicles, and other sources. As Congress passed more and more environmental legislation, the EPA saw its budget grow from $500 million in 1973 to $1.3 billion in 1980. Bureaucrats within the agency worked hard to implement and enforce the new environmental policies. During the first ten years of its existence, emissions of the five major air pollutants—particulates, nitrogen oxides, sulfur oxides, carbon monoxide, and hydrocarbons—decreased by 21 percent. By 1980, the EPA had 10,600 full-time employees who were committed to strict enforcement of the nation's clean air laws.[48]

When he won the presidential election in 1980, Ronald Reagan set out to change all that. During his campaign, Reagan had promised to address the nation's economic problems and drastically reduce the size of the federal government. He interpreted his victory against Jimmy Carter as a mandate to cut domestic program budgets and push business-friendly policies. One of his first targets was the EPA, an agency not well liked by business and industry leaders.[49]

Reagan started by filling EPA leadership positions with loyalists. Unlike President Carter, whose EPA appointees had mostly come from environmental organizations, Reagan appointed lobbyists, lawyers, and scientists who were closely tied to the very business interests the

EPA was supposed to regulate.[50] In May 1981, he appointed Anne Gorsuch to run the EPA. Gorsuch did not try to conceal her plan to ease enforcement of the Clean Air Act.[51] She assured small oil refineries that they did not have to worry about her enforcing the EPA's lead-in-gasoline regulations.[52] She disbanded the agency's Office of Enforcement and then re-created it with a smaller staff.[53] The decisions she made in the name of "administrative efficiency" outraged environmentalists, who accused her and Reagan of intentionally sabotaging the EPA.

Reagan did not stop with a few personnel replacements. He also pursued an aggressive legislative strategy through proposed budget cuts. During his first year in office, Republicans controlled the Senate, and few of the Democrats who held the majority in the House were willing to stand up against a president who had just won office with such a large victory margin.[54] As a consequence, the EPA operating budget was reduced by 24 percent in 1982. Funding for air pollution enforcement alone dropped by 42 percent between 1980 and 1983, and the number of EPA employees assigned to clean air responsibilities fell by 31 percent.[55]

Many believed that the combination of drastic budget and staff cuts and Gorsuch's leadership would be the EPA's undoing. In the short run, Reagan's budget cuts produced the desired result—not a stronger, more effective organization, but a weaker, less effective one. The EPA conducted 41 percent fewer inspections and compliance tests of air pollution sources in 1982 than it had in 1981, and it took 69 percent fewer enforcement actions to rein in over-polluters. His initial personnel changes, however, did not appear to affect the enforcement activity of the EPA. When Gorsuch was first appointed, the agency's monitoring activities actually *increased*. EPA employees continued to do their jobs as they had before Reagan came into office. If anything, they increased the intensity of their enforcement activity, remaining committed to faithful implementation of the clean air policies of the 1970s.[56]

Reagan's attempts to curtail EPA enforcement ultimately failed. By the end of 1982, it had become clear that the public did not want federal clean air regulations to be relaxed: 48 percent of Americans thought the EPA's old air pollution policies were fine as they were, and 38 percent wanted the Clean Air Act to be made stricter.[57] In another blow to Reagan's agenda, the 1982 congressional elections brought more pro-environment Democrats to the House. They cited Gorsuch (then using her married name of Burford) for contempt of Congress for her mismanagement of the EPA hazardous waste program. Representative John Dingell, who had earlier supported Reagan's failed effort to revise the Clean Air Act, led a full investigation of the EPA, which resulted in Burford's resignation in March 1983.[58]

Immediately after, EPA employees renewed their previous levels of enforcement activity. Even before its budget was restored, the EPA's pollution monitoring and abatement activity recovered to levels *higher* than during the Carter administration of the late 1970s. By May, Reagan had replaced Burford with the original EPA administrator of the 1970s, William D. Ruckelshaus. Congress restored much of the EPA budget in 1983.[59]

Ultimately, Reagan was not able to reverse the tide of the "environmental decade." From its beginning, the EPA had been staffed with experts committed to the enforcement of federal environmental laws. In the early years of his administration, Reagan discovered that the culture of the EPA and its attentive environmentalist constituency could not be easily undone.

Reagan was not the last president to attempt to curb the EPA. President George W. Bush attempted to ease air pollution restrictions and relax enforcement of emissions standards. His proposed policies led to clashes with EPA leaders—even with his own appointee, former EPA Administrator Christine Todd Whitman.[60] The Environmental Integrity Project, an organization founded by former EPA Regulatory Enforcement Director Eric Schaeffer, reported in 2007 that enforcement of environmental standards declined substantially during Bush's time in office in comparison to enforcement during the years of Clinton's presidency.[61] Whether this decline in enforcement represents a short-term or long-term trend remains to be seen.

ThinkingCritically

1. From the perspective of Reagan, were the EPA's activities examples of slack, drift, or something else entirely?

2. Is it necessarily a bad thing when bureaucrats do things that Congress and the president oppose?

Reformers seek to introduce market forces.

All of the above methods that presidents and Congress use to control the bureaucracy represent efforts to reform the existing system of bureaucratic governance. Increasingly, though, reformers are suggesting that the problems of bureaucracy, especially those that involve inefficiencies, are best solved by looking beyond the individuals and agencies that work within the federal government. These reformers suggest that increased effectiveness and efficiency can only come about through deregulation or privatization.

Deregulation Some argue that the best way to deal with the bureaucracy is to temper its impulse to regulate more and more areas of business activity. Claiming that government regulations cripple the entrepreneurial spirit of private industries, reformers argue that rather than restructuring these agencies or introducing better oversight mechanisms, political leaders ought to scale back their activities altogether.

Through **deregulation**, the government reduces the workload of bureaucrats. It cordons off certain areas of business activity, insisting that bureaucrats not interfere with market forces of supply and demand. During the 1970s and '80s, substantial efforts were made to deregulate the airline, trucking, telecommunication, and financial services industries. Through these efforts, the government encouraged new companies to form, providing more choices and cheaper services to consumers. For example, the deregulation of the telecommunications industry made possible the emergence of companies like Sprint and MCI (and later, Verizon, T-Mobile, and others).

Occasionally, though, deregulation can backfire. When the government deregulated the financial services industry in the early 1980s, savings and loan companies suddenly had many of the powers of traditional banks—such as the ability to issue credit cards, borrow money from the Federal Reserve, and make commercial loans—without the regulations of traditional banks. With their new powers, savings and loan companies began to invest large amounts of money in highly risky ventures. Not surprisingly, many of these ventures failed, leaving savings and loan companies without the money needed to pay back their investors. In total, these defaults cost the federal government (and the taxpayers) over $100 billion. Congress responded in 1989 by enacting the Financial Institutions Reform Recovery and Enforcement Act, which re-introduced many of the regulations that had been eliminated earlier in the decade.

Privatization While deregulation concerns the relaxation of bureaucratic oversight of different industries, **privatization** concerns the transfer of government functions from the federal government to private companies. Rather than government bureaucrats providing certain services, private companies do so. In communities around the country, private contractors have replaced government agencies to run prisons, provide security services, and manage hospitals. As we discuss in Chapter 17, some people call for the privatization of public schools as well.

Note that privatization is not an all-or-nothing arrangement. Many bureaucratic agencies turn to private companies to perform selected tasks. The military, for instance, pays billions of dollars each year to private contractors that build parts, conduct research, and provide strategic advice. And even when it decides to hand over complete responsibility for a certain public service to private companies, the government may continue to fund their work. When writing contracts with these companies, moreover, the government may introduce any number of requirements about how they conduct their business. The key question, then, is not whether a government service has been privatized, but how much it has been privatized.

SUMMARY

▶ Bureaucrats serve a wide variety of vital functions for the American public. They implement the policies that Congress and the president write; they write rules that clarify these policies; they provide expert advice to their political superiors; and they help resolve disputes. Thus the bureaucracy serves quasi-legislative, executive, and judicial functions.

▶ During much of the nineteenth century, the bureaucracy was quite small and tended to employ individuals better known for their political ties than for their experience or expertise. At the turn of the twentieth century, however, the nation witnessed the transformation of the spoils system into a merit-based system. During this period, the federal bureaucracy also expanded dramatically. Today, the bureaucracy consists of cabinet departments, independent agencies, regulatory commissions, and government corporations.

▶ Though the bureaucracy serves important functions, it also presents serious challenges. Because bureaucrats

know more about the policy issues that they oversee, they can act in ways that do not always represent the interests of Congress, the president, the courts, or the American public. Sometimes bureaucrats act on behalf of their own policy interests, sometimes they serve the interests of other unelected officials, sometimes they do not work especially hard, and often they are less efficient that the public would like.

▶ Congress and the president have devised a number of ways to address the problems of bureaucracy. Through appointments, they put like-minded individuals in charge of federal agencies. Through budgets, oversight hearings, and centralization efforts, Congress and the president reshape the incentives of bureaucrats and monitor their actions. And when all else fails, Congress and the president can eliminate agencies, substantially reduce their regulatory powers, and/or turn to the private marketplace for help in providing public services.

KEY TERMS

agency capture, p. 000
bureaucracy, p. 000
centralization, p. 000
civil service system, p. 000
department, p. 000
deregulation, p. 000
drift, p. 000
government corporation, p. 000
hearings, p. 000
independent agencies and commissions, p. 000

implementation, p. 000
politicization, p. 000
principal-agent problem, p. 000
privatization, p. 000
recess-appointment, p. 000
red tape, p. 000
rules, p. 000
slack, p. 000
spoils system, p. 000

SUGGESTED READINGS

Peri Arnold. 1998. *Making the Managerial Presidency: Comprehensive Reorganization Planning, 1905–1996,* 2nd ed. Lawrence, KS: University Press of Kansas. A comprehensive summary of presidents' efforts to reorganize the federal bureaucracy during the twentieth century.

Anthony Downs. 1966. *Inside Bureaucracy.* Boston: Little, Brown. Examines how the structure of bureaucracies affects the strategic decisions that are made within them.

Herbert Kaufman. 2006. *The Forest Ranger: A Study in Administrative Behavior,* special reprint ed. Washington, D.C.: Resources for the Future. A classic study of how top-level managers within the bureaucracy maintain control over lower-level bureaucrats whose day-to-day activities are not easily monitored.

Michael Lipsky. 1983. *Street Level Bureaucracy.* New York: Russell Sage Foundation Publications. A bottom-up approach to studying the bureaucracy, with special attention paid to lower-level bureaucrats.

James Q. Wilson. 1991. *Bureaucracy: What Government Agencies Do and Why They Do It.* New York: Basic Books. A contemporary classic that examines how politics contributes to bureaucratic organization and behavior.

bureaucracy a group of departments, agencies, and other institutions that for the most part are located in the executive branch of government and that develop and implement public policy.

implementation the process by which policy is executed.

rules administrative determinations about how laws will be interpreted and implemented.

spoils system a system of government in which a presidential administration awards jobs to party loyalists.

civil service system a system of government in which decisions about hiring, promotion, and firing are based on individuals' work experience, skills, and expertise.

department a major administrative unit that is composed of many agencies serving many policy functions, and that is headed by a secretary, who serves in the president's cabinet.

independent agencies and commissions bureaucratic organizations that operate outside of cabinet-level departments and are less subject to congressional or presidential influence.

government corporation a corporation created and funded by the government to provide some public service that would be insufficiently provided by the private sector.

principal-agent problem the problem that occurs when one person (the principal) contracts with another person (the agent) to provide a service and yet cannot directly observe what the agent is actually doing; the agent, meanwhile, is motivated to take advantage of the principal.

slack a situation in which bureaucrats do not work as hard as Congress or the president would like.

drift a situation in which bureaucrats create policy that does not match the policy preferences of Congress or the president.

agency capture the condition under which an agency primarily serves the interests of a non-governmental group rather than those of elected officials.

red tape the inefficiency and waste that results from excessive regulation and overly formal procedures.

politicization a phenomenon that occurs when Congress and the president select bureaucracy leaders who share their political views.

recess-appointment the means by which the president fills a vacant position in the bureaucracy when Congress is not in session, thus avoiding the need for prior congressional approval.

hearing a formal process in which committees in Congress call upon bureaucrats and other experts to help them understand and oversee a particular agency.

centralization the method of increasing the president's power by moving key administrative functions from the departments to the Executive Office of the President.

deregulation the process of decreasing the number of agency rules that apply to a particular industry or group of industries so as to introduce market forces to their operations.

privatization the transfer of government functions from the federal government to private companies.

17 Economic and Social Policy

Farm Subsidies

Each year, the federal government gives American farmers billions of dollars in aid.[1] Farmers who make their living planting corn, cotton, rice, soybeans, or wheat, get a good portion of their income in the form of government assistance. Indeed, farmers receive more direct aid from the federal government than most other workers in America.

The roots of modern farm assistance programs stretch back seven decades to the Dust Bowl and the Great Depression, when long droughts destroyed crops and the U.S. economy was in shambles. During this period, agricultural prices dropped by more than 50 percent, farm revenues fell by two-thirds, and farmers' per capita incomes were well below non-farm incomes.

President Franklin Roosevelt worried that overproduction had contributed to the farmers' problems. In 1933, therefore, he signed the Agricultural Adjustment Act, which authorized the government to pay farmers to limit planting. The act was meant to be a "temporary solution to deal with an emergency," but the aid continued long after the crisis had ended.[2] Interest groups and politicians raised concerns about wild swings in commodity prices, American dependence on imported food, and the impact of weather fluctuations on the nation's food supply. And so they kept the federal aid flowing to the nation's farmers.

Over the last 70 years, federal aid to farmers has increased dramatically. Converted to constant 2007 dollars, yearly direct payments grew from $2.1 billion in 1933, to $4.9 billion in 1960, to $14.9 billion in 1990.[3] By 2005, direct payments reached no less than $24.4 billion.[4] The variety of government assistance has multiplied as well. Contemporary farm bills offer a dizzying array of conservation incentives, disaster relief measures, guaranteed government purchases of surplus production, import tariffs, crop insurance, research funds, tax breaks, and irrigation projects.

While aid to farmers has increased significantly over the last seven decades, farmers now constitute a much smaller portion of the U.S. population. In Roosevelt's time, 1 in 5 Americans was a farmer. Today, only 1 in 150 is a farmer.[5] Furthermore, farmers as a group are significantly better-off today than they once were. Growing demand for corn-based ethanol is one factor that has propelled the average income of farm households past that of their non-farm peers in recent years.[6]

Moreover, federal aid does not always flow to independent farmers struggling to support themselves and their families. The vast majority of government assistance goes to large farms and agribusinesses. Indeed, two-thirds of farmers collect no subsidies at all.[7] In 2005, about 10 percent of the nation's farms received more than 50 percent of all payments, and the operators of those farms had an average household income of $200,000.[8] Perhaps most disturbingly, the Government Accountability Office recently reported that $1.1 billion in subsidies had been directed to deceased people.[9] Notes Ken Cook, president of the Environmental Working Group, "You don't have to sit on a tractor seat, visit the tractor seat, you don't even have to be alive to get a fixed payment. . . . It's ridiculous."[10]

In 2007, President George W. Bush set about reducing the inequity and waste of federal farm aid. The Bush administration and the Department of Agriculture unveiled a sweeping proposal, described by some observers as "perhaps the most reform-minded farm bill in decades."[11] Interest groups such as the American Heart Association, Taxpayers for Common Sense, Environmental Defense, and Grocery Manufacturers/Food Products Association joined in an effort to redirect federal aid to small farms, conservation, and fruit and vegetable cultivation. Portraying the central issue as food rather than farming, Senator Tom Harkin (D-IA), chair of the Senate Agriculture Committee, confidently proclaimed, "Americans who eat want a stake in it."[12]

Congress, however, did not see fit to drastically reduce federal aid to farmers. The House Agriculture Committee's bill retained most commodity subsidies, while also offering $4.7 billion for nutrition, $4.5 billion for conservation, and $1.6 billion for fruit and vegetable growers. "That was 'game over' right there," explained Representative Ron Kind (D-WI), whose proposal to cut "no-strings-attached" subsidies was defeated 309 to 117.[13] Speaker Nancy Pelosi applauded the Committee's bill—which required country-of-origin labeling for meat, closed a loophole that allowed some farmers to exceed subsidy limits, and implemented a $1 million income cap for recipients—as a "good first step to reform."[14] But the core elements of the farm subsidies remained very much intact. Indeed, President Bush cited a lack of adequate reform as cause for vetoing Congress's bill.[15]

Why is emergency aid so difficult to suspend once the crisis that prompted it has passed? For one thing, the current agricultural system rests on justifiable concerns about preserving America's self-reliance and addressing domestic inequalities. Furthermore, the distribution of costs and benefits of federal farm aid gives unique advantages to interest groups lobbying against roll-backs. While the costs are distributed widely among taxpayers, consumers, and foreign competitors, most of the outlays go to a relatively small yet powerful segment of society. As noted above, fewer than 2 percent of Americans are farmers and only about one-third of them collect subsidies.[16] These beneficiaries have organized persistently to maintain this aid, and interest groups including the American Farm Bureau Federation spent $135 million on lobbying and political donations in 2006 alone.

Robert Samuelson, a contributing editor for the *Washington Post*, observes that government programs often "start for good cause or with good intentions, then perpetuate themselves by creating a protective web of interests—constituents who believe that they have property rights in benefits, politicians whose power derives from renewing or expanding the benefits, and lobbies that exist to influence crucial politicians."[17] This explains much about the history of farm subsidies in America. But similar patterns arise in other social programs as well—social security, welfare, education, and healthcare. In each instance, the federal government intervened in a moment of crisis, establishing a new program intended to improve the lives of U.S. citizens. These programs almost always live longer than the crisis they were meant to solve. And usually, but not always, they increase in size and cost.

This chapter examines domestic policies supported by the federal government. While domestic policy covers issues ranging from environmental protectionto patent law, there we focus on economic policy and social programs—programs purposefully designed to enhance the well-being of U.S. citizens.

THIS CHAPTER WILL EXAMINE:

▶ the conditions under which policy innovations are created

▶ efforts by the federal government to manage the domestic economy

▶ the largest program, which assists the elderly

▶ the federal government's changing commitments to the poor

▶ the federal government's expanding involvement in education

▶ federal healthcare programs for the poor and aged.

When Economic and Social Policies Are Made

What prompts the federal government to create new public policies? Detailed histories of individual policy interventions often highlight the idiosyncrasies that lead to public policy-making. In retrospect, major policy innovations often appear to arise from chance meetings between key politicos or a particularly well-timed protest in Washington, D.C. For such chance occurrences to bear fruit, however, at least three factors must converge: a problem warranting a governmental response must be identified; a solution to the problem must be articulated; and some kind of focusing event must prod politicians into action. This section reflects upon each of these ingredients to domestic policy-making.[18]

Identifying a problem is the first step in developing a policy.

There are lots of facts about the world that we may wish were not true. Apple Computers' iPods are more expensive than we would like. Our friends do not always act like friends. When the economy hits a rough spot, some relatives lose their jobs. Our grandparents have a difficult time paying for their medication. And when droughts persist for years, as they did during the Dust Bowl, farmers can lose their livelihood.

It is difficult to imagine the federal government passing a law that requires Apple Computers to lower the price of iPods, or that requires friends to be more responsive to one another's needs, but what of the other problems? Which of them warrant government action? Much depends upon public opinion, which varies over time and across the country. Historically, though, those problems that appear to violate basic elements of the American creed or that threaten the nation's security have stood the best chance of attracting the attention of politicians in Washington, D.C.

The American creed Problems are especially likely to attract the attention of the federal government when they violate elements of the American creed. Concerns about equity stand out in this regard. Many social programs funded by the government aim to reduce long-standing inequities—whether they involve access to sports programs among men and women, the relative incomes of the rich and poor, or the test scores of white and black school children. Of course, certain inequalities are inevitable. Some are even desirable. But the federal government is especially likely to enact social programs designed to reduce gross and persistent inequalities that systematically limit the life chances of certain citizens. While the federal government may accept a certain amount of inequality of outcomes, it often intervenes into the lives of citizens in order to promote a base level of equality of opportunities.

In the modern era, concerns about equity were never more prominent than during Lyndon Johnson's presidency in the 1960s. Johnson sought to create a **Great Society** "where the demands of morality, and the needs of the spirit, can be realized in the life of the Nation."[19] He called upon the nation to tackle the problems of poverty, racial discrimination, environmental degradation, and urban decay. Only by doing so, Johnson argued, could the ideals of the Founders, enshrined in the Declaration of Independence and U.S. Constitution, be realized. With strong Democratic support within Congress, Johnson managed to enact more large-scale social programs than any other president since Franklin Roosevelt. Many of these programs are described in this chapter.

National security Above all else, the federal government's fundamental objective is to protect its citizens from foreign harm. Military threats, terrorist activity, the proliferation of nuclear weapons, and the like rise to the top of governmental concerns. Domestic problems that potentially link into U.S. security interests, either directly or indirectly, gain an important advantage in the contest to attract the attention of federal politicians.

To see this, recall the impetus for federal farm subsidies. It was not mere sympathy that prompted concern for farmers. When farmers could no longer support themselves, the nation's food supply appeared imperiled. And according to many politicians, dependence on foreign nations for food threatened U.S. security interests. As Representative Marion Berry (D-AR) contended in 2007, "If you can't feed and clothe yourself, your nation's at risk. Farming is a dadgum hard life, and we need folks to keep doing it."[20] By connecting economic hardships felt by a small portion of the U.S. population to national security concerns, farming interests have effectively made the case that farming problems demand government action.

Farming, of course, is not unique in this regard. As we shall soon see, national security interests spurred the federal government's initial foray into public education. Additionally, advocates for immigration reform to stem the flow of undocumented workers across U.S. borders, as well as advocates for more robust drug interdiction programs, regularly invoke national security. Presidents Lyndon Johnson and Ronald Reagan did not merely support anti-poverty and anti-drug programs—they waged self-declared "wars" against these looming threats. For example, in a 1988 ceremony honoring slain drug-enforcement officers, President Reagan drew vivid parallels between the War on Drugs and the American Revolution: "America's liberty was purchased with the blood of heroes [and] our release from the bondage of illegal drug use is being won at the same dear price. The battle is ultimately over what America is and what America will be. At our founding, we were promised the pursuit of happiness, not the myth of endless ecstasy from a vial of white poison."[21] In the aftermath of September 11, President George W. Bush framed energy policy in national security terms, advocating reduced oil imports from the Middle East and South America and increased domestic oil production. At every step, each president justified the importance of deploying significant resources to combat a perceived security problem.

Identifying a government solution is the next step in developing policy.

For social legislation to emerge, problems must suggest solutions. Lacking solutions, politicians can offer little more than their sympathies for those who suffer from society's ailments and injustices.

Policy entrepreneurs play an important role in identifying solutions, linking their solutions to observed problems.[22] These individuals work in think tanks, universities, lobbying organizations, unions, and interest groups, and, backed by data, conviction, and persuasive skills, they design solutions for the many problems facing the federal government. Often, like-minded entrepreneurs form networks that operate at the local, state, and federal levels of government. These entrepreneurs coordinate with one another, with the intention of convincing politicians to adopt their solutions.

Take, for example, the activities of the American Federation of Teachers (AFT) and the National Education Association (NEA), the two largest teachers' unions in the nation. Both advocate policies to support teachers, such as higher pay and fewer restrictions on how they perform in the classroom. Lobbyists for both unions work at all levels of government to convince politicians about the merits of their preferred policies, emphasizing the ways they will solve problems in education. Higher pay, for instance, is seen as a solution to problems ranging from teacher supply shortages to poor test scores in urban schools.

In most areas of life, there is a logical ordering of problems and solutions. We devise solutions for problems, not the other way around. And when the problems disappear, the solutions usually are discarded. In politics, though, things do not always work this way. If one day the nation no longer suffered from a shortage of public school teachers, the NEA and AFT, like all policy entrepreneurs, would look for other problems to attach their solutions to—higher salaries, for instance, might also attract better teachers. In this sense, solutions in politics can arise independently of problems and often outlive the problems they were intended to solve.

Focusing events spark government action.

At any given moment, many domestic problems demand government action. Many solutions also float about the corridors of Congress. Bringing problems and solutions together often requires some kind of focusing event. In the case of farm subsidies, the combination of the Dust Bowl and Great Depression put the plight of farmers—and the nation's food supply—in stark relief. These events infused the issue with a newfound sense of urgency, to which politicians felt compelled to respond.

Focusing events can take many forms. Sometimes human tragedy serves the role. In the aftermath of the killing spree at Virginia Tech University in 2007, for instance, advocates demanded that politicians pass new gun-control legislation. On April 16, 2007, student gunman Cho Seung Hui killed 33 faculty members and students, including himself, in the deadliest school shooting in American history. Hui's record of mental illness should have prevented him from obtaining handguns, yet he purchased his weapons legally because his information failed to show up in the national background-check database. The rampage led to the first new gun-control legislation in over a decade, a measure that encouraged states to report people prohibited from buying firearms to federal authorities. Upon President Bush's signing of the bill in January 2008, White House spokesman Tony Fratto declared, "We saw with the terrible shootings at Virginia Tech last year that an incomplete system can have tragic consequences."[23]

Other times, a particularly powerful report that documents a problem can move politicians to act. In 2007 former Senate Majority Leader George Mitchell released a report on steroid use in professional baseball. The so-called Mitchell Report sent shock waves through the sports community. Accusing a number of famous baseball players of using steroids or human growth hormones, the report underscored just how widespread illicit drug use in sports had become. Immediately after the report's release, the players' union and the baseball commissioner agreed to develop new drug-testing programs, in part to forestall government action. Nonetheless, Congress promptly launched formal hearings into the matter, and a number of its members introduced legislation to limit access to performance-enhancing drugs.[24]

Even the weather can act as a focusing event. As discussed in Chapter 16, the devastation wrought by Hurricane Katrina exposed the deep problems of poverty, crime, and corruption in New Orleans. Policy entrepreneurs descended upon the region, insisting that they could assist the government's efforts to solve these problems. And the images of families stuck on rooftops days after the levees broke infused the ensuing deliberations with a genuine sense of urgency. In Chapter 16, we considered whether the responses of local, state, and federal governments effectively solved the problems surrounding Hurricane Katrina. That the hurricane itself was a focusing event, though, is undeniable.

Among twentieth-century focusing events, nothing had more impact than the **Great Depression**. As indicated at the beginning of the chapter, the Great Depression was a period of unprecedented economic hardship for the nation. The stock market collapse in 1929 led to the utter devastation of the domestic economy. When Roosevelt took office four years later, the banks in 32 states had been closed by state-government edict, and bank operations in the remaining 16 states remained severely curtailed. No fewer than 15 million Americans—roughly 25 percent of the total workforce at the time—were unemployed. The gravity of the nation's problems spurred the federal government into action like never before. As many of the social policies described in this chapter attest, the federal government assumed altogether new responsibilities for the welfare of its citizens.

Economic Policy

More than any other factor, the domestic economy determines the well-being of a citizenry. The ability of farmers and manufacturers to sell their goods at a profit, the ability of consumers to purchase them, and the willingness of intermediaries to facilitate the exchange critically depend upon a healthy domestic economy.

Economists monitor different aspects of the domestic economy.

When gauging the health of the economy, people tend to monitor three main indicators. First, they focus on unemployment trends, which reveal the percentage of people who would like to work, but who do not have a job. Typically, the unemployment rate vacillates between 4 and 6 percent. In the early 1990s, though, it reached as high as 8 percent; and in the early 1980s, it reached double digits.

In addition to unemployment, people also monitor inflationary trends, which concern how the costs of basic goods and services change over time. When inflation is high, the costs increase at a rapid rate; when inflation is low, costs increase at a more moderate pace. The government tends to measure inflation through the Consumer Price Index (CPI), which tracks the costs of food, clothing, medical services, and other essential items from year to year. For all goods and services, the annual CPI in December 2007 was 4.1 percent, which somewhat higher than the annual average of 2.8 percent recorded between 1913 and 2007.

Third, and finally, people monitor the overall growth of the economy. A prime indicator to do so is the **Gross Domestic Product** (GDP), which is a statistic that measures all goods and services produced by U.S. individuals and businesses.[25] Between 2003 and 2005, GDP hovered around $13 trillion, which surpasses any other country. Indeed, the U.S. GDP constitutes almost 20 percent of all spending worldwide. Economists, though, tend to focus on annual changes in GDP, which in recent history have ranged between 2 and 4 percent. Between 2006 and 2007, however, GDP increased by less than 1 percent, raising concerns about a steep economic downturn.

Economists have different ideas about how to improve the economy.

How might the government respond to fluctuations in the economy, as reflected in changes in unemployment, inflation, or GDP? The first option is to do nothing—or at least very little—at all. This is the governing philosophy of **laissez faire economics**. According to this theory, the private marketplace experiences natural periods of expansion and decline, and the best thing for the government to do, by and large, is to stay out of the way. When the government tries to regulate the otherwise free exchange of goods and services between private parties, this theory suggests, fundamental distortions and inefficiencies are introduced. In the long run, the public benefits most by minimal government involvement in the economy.

Most economists, however, admit that a vibrant economy requires at least some government intervention. The government, for instance, might alter the supply of money in the marketplace, which is the central objective of **monetary policy**. The national bank system, called the Federal Reserve, retains the power to set interest rates, which affect the flow of money in the domestic economy. By increasing interest rates, the Federal Reserve can restrain economic growth and inflationary pressures. By decreasing interest rates, the Federal Reserve can stimulate economic activity, though at the risk of increasing inflation rates. The president has the power to appoint the chairman of the Federal Reserve, who currently is Ben Bernanke. For the most part, though, the Federal Reserve is kept independent from the political pressures that weigh upon the legislative and executive branches of government.

Finally, the government directly intervenes into the economy through taxing and spending, the central elements of **fiscal policy**. The government can stimulate economic activity either by spending in the marketplace or decreasing taxes. Conversely, in more prosperous times, when inflationary trends may need to be curbed, the government may opt to cut spending or increase taxes.

When the government spends less than it recovers through taxes, it incurs a surplus. More commonly, though, the government spends more than it recovers through taxes. In so doing, it contributes to the annual **deficit**, which represents the total amount of money that the federal government had to borrow from U.S. citizens and foreign governments in order to meet its spending obligations. President Bush assumed office in 2001 after four consecutive years of surpluses. Tax cuts, a declining economy, and foreign wars, however, have reinstated deficits on the order of several hundred billion dollars each year.

Over time, of course, these deficits mount. The **public debt** refers to the total amount of money that the federal government owes. As of 2007, the public debt surpassed a whopping $9 trillion. The debt constituted no less than 60 percent of the nation's GDP. Just to finance the interest on the debt, the federal government had to pay over $300 billion. And by some estimates, the debt increases by roughly $1.4 billion each day.[26]

The federal government, of course, does not have to choose between monetary and fiscal policies. It regularly implements both. In early 2008, economists worried about the onset of a **recession**, which exists when the GDP declines for two successive quarters. To encourage economic growth, the Federal Reserve decreased interest rates by 0.75 points. Shortly thereafter, Congress enacted an economic stimulus package that disbursed funds to individuals and families around the country, in the hopes of jumpstarting the economy. The tax rebates, the president promised, would give the economy a much-needed "shot in the arm."[27]

Different people, however, are affected by the economy in different ways. In the pages that follow, therefore, we examine a variety of social programs that are designed to address the specific challenges facing different populations within the United States.

Social Security

Think what it must have been like for the elderly during the Great Depression. After working for decades and putting money aside for their eventual retirement, they watched as their savings vanished overnight, often through no fault of their own. The collapse of the banking system drained the money they expected to live on during their golden years. And unlike some younger people, the elderly could not readily start over again and recover what they had lost. Often infirm, the elderly appeared consigned to spend their last years in poverty.

The **Social Security Act**, enacted in 1935, attempted to correct this state of affairs. The act established the framework for the Social Security Administration (SSA), charged with providing a reliable income stream for the elderly.[28] Social Security is best thought of as an insurance program against poverty in retirement. Today, most individuals qualify for social security benefits either when they turn 67 or when they become disabled and cannot work.[29] The benefits come in the form of a monthly check, the size of which varies according to the amount of money that the individual paid into the Social Security fund.

Funding for Social Security looks quite a bit different from other social programs, such as farm subsidies. During the course of their working lives, employees pay a portion of their income into a fund, which the SSA maintains. These payments, however, are not like deposits in a bank. A worker's contributions do not sit in the fund until he or she wishes to withdraw them. Rather, most of the contributions made today are promptly paid out to today's beneficiaries. This "pay-as-you-go" system means that funds flow into and out of the Social Security fund at a continual rate.

Social security benefits are **entitlements**—benefits that all qualifying individuals have a legal right to obtain. Social Security beneficiaries include anyone who is above a certain age and has paid into the system (or, if they are deceased, their survivors). Consequently, to receive Social Security benefits, one does not need to demonstrate financial need. Indeed, the size of the payments is completely unrelated to the amount of private savings an individual has upon retirement. Consequently, Social Security checks are an essential form of income for some people, and a welcome supplementary income for others.

Social Security benefits have expanded since 1935.

Since its enactment in 1935, Social Security has grown from a modest insurance program to a massive government infrastructure. Originally, the Social Security Act excluded many different types of workers, including farm workers, government employees, the self-employed, and individuals working for small businesses. Indeed, roughly one-half of the civilian labor force was excluded from the Social Security system. In 1950, though, farmers became qualified for Social Security. And, since then, virtually all industry restrictions have been lifted. In 2006, almost 50 million individuals received Social Security benefits in the United States.[30]

The size of the benefits has also increased. In part, this reflects the natural maturation of the program. During the program's early years, retired workers had paid into the system for relatively short periods of time. Upon retirement, therefore, these individuals qualified for relatively small payments. As their total contributions increased, however, workers stood to receive larger benefits when they retired. And workers who have contributed into the system over their entire working lives can expect to receive, on average, around $1,000 each month.[31]

The government itself also contributed to increases in Social Security benefits. The most important action occurred in 1975, when Congress revised the act to account for changes in the cost of living. Automatic increases in the size of benefits—so-called COLAs, short for "cost of living adjustments," were mandated. However, the COLAs eventually exceeded inflation, so that average benefits in

2006 were roughly 25 percent larger than they were in 1975, even after accounting for inflation.[32]

It should not come as a great surprise, then, that total Social Security outlays have increased dramatically over the past 70 years. In its first year (1935), Social Security expenditures hovered at around $1 million. They broke the $1 billion mark in 1950, and the $100 billion mark in 1980. In 2007, the Social Security system paid out over $495 billion in benefits.[33]

The future of Social Security is uncertain.

Changing demographics in the United States have introduced new challenges to the Social Security system. Recall that the system critically depends upon the ability of today's workers to fund the payments to today's elderly. The balance of workers to beneficiaries, however, has changed markedly over time. When the Social Security Act went into effect, roughly nine workers supported each elderly beneficiary. Today, just over three workers support each beneficiary. And by some projections, this number will drop to only two workers per beneficiary by 2030.[34]

Because workers dramatically outnumbered the elderly for so long, Social Security managed to build up substantial reserves, known as Old-Age, Survivors, and Disability Insurance (OASDI) trust funds. As Figure 17.1 shows, though, these reserves will begin to fall in the not-too-distant future. And by some projections, Social Security expenditures will exceed both receipts and available reserves by as soon as 2037. The combination of a large Baby Boom generation entering retirement, COLAs that mandate higher payments each year, and longer life expectancies are straining the Social Security system. Some leaders, such as Vice President Dick Cheney, warned the program is heading for a "financial train

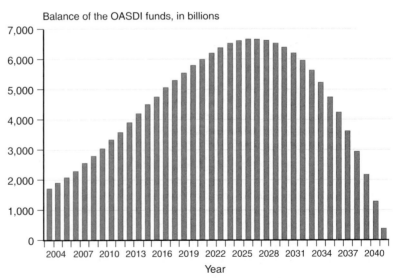

Balance of the OASDI funds, in billions

Figure 17-1. **Social Security Reserves Are Predicted To Decline.** Based upon the current policy and the best available information about the size of the contributing working force and the number of retired individuals, Social Security reserves will continue to increase until approximately 2028, at which time they will begin to rapidly decline.

Source: Gary Sidor, "Social Security: Brief Facts and Statistics," *CRS Report for Congress*, January 26, 2006, http://price.house.gov/issues/uploadedfiles/socialsecurity2.pdf.

wreck."[35] Or as President Bush put it, "If you're 20 years old, in your mid-twenties, and you're beginning to work, I want you to think about a Social Security system that will be flat bust, bankrupt, unless the United States Congress has got the willingness to act now."[36]

Plainly, something needs to be done. But what? The government has a variety of options. For instance, it can reduce the size of Social Security benefits doled out each year. To do this, it could raise the age at which individuals qualify for benefits—thereby reducing the number of beneficiaries. Alternatively, the government could decrease the benefits that it gives to each individual. Neither option, though, is especially attractive. Having paid into the Social Security system throughout their working lives, the elderly rightly expect to receive their due. And should they feel slighted, they will likely punish the offending politician at the next election. So charged is the issue of Social Security reform, in fact, that it is referred to as the "third rail" of American politics—should you touch it, you can fully expect to be zapped.

Although cutting Social Security benefits is difficult, it is not impossible. In 1983, after several years of stagflation—periods of high unemployment and high inflation—the federal government decided to reduce Social Security outlays. Such periods take an especially heavy toll on Social Security because high inflation triggers larger COLAs than normal and high unemployment means that fewer workers are paying into the Social Security system. To ensure the program's solvency, the government for the first time began to tax Social Security benefits, increased the eligible age for full benefits from 65 to 67, and added federal civil employees to the workers who could contribute to Social Security. As we discuss below, however, these amendments may not solve the longer-term challenges facing the program.

Another way to protect Social Security would be to increase taxes. Historically, this has been the approach most commonly adopted. When the Social Security Act was enacted in 1935, the Social Security tax was set at 1 percent of the first $3,000 earned. Over the next 65 years, both the tax rate and the maximum taxable earning were increased 20 times. In 2008, the rate for individuals who are not self-employed was 6.2 percent of the first $102,000 earned.[37] Of course, there are political costs associated with increasing taxes, which is why both political parties at the national level tout their records at cutting taxes, not raising them.

Finally, a number of politicians have recommended the adoption of private investment accounts. Rather than depositing funds into a general reserve account, which typically receives a low yield, workers under this scheme could invest a portion of their Social Security contributions into government-approved stocks and bonds. This reform represented the core innovation in President George W. Bush's 2005 effort to shore up Social Security. Under Bush's plan, workers could direct up to 5 percent of their Social Security taxes into private accounts. Ultimately, however, Bush's plan flopped. Worried about the risks of private investments, members of Congress proved unwilling to fundamentally restructure the largest and most popular domestic social program. Social Security reform constituted the single most important domestic policy in the president's 2005 State of the Union Address, but Congress never voted on his plan.

Earlier in this chapter, we suggested that a focusing event is often needed to propel government action. We now see that this event needs to underscore a problem that the American public faces in the here and now. From the vantage point of most politicians, several decades—the time when Social Security reserves are expected to run out—is a virtual eternity. Consequently, and perhaps unfortunately, these politicians are likely to shift their attention to other, more immediate problems.

Welfare

The federal government supports a wide range of programs designed to assist the poor. Collectively, these public assistance programs are often referred to as "welfare." However, the government assists the poor in many different ways. Some programs involve direct cash transfers to the poor; others provide the equivalent of food vouchers; and others supply modest income subsidies. In one way or another, though, all attempt to alleviate the hardships experienced by the poor.

Who are the poor?

All of the programs described in this section are **means tested**—that is, they target those who demonstrate a lack of means. To qualify for benefits, individuals must prove either that they are unemployed or that their income falls below a certain level. Means-tested programs are quite different from Social Security, which distributes benefits to all who have paid into the fund, no matter how well off they might be.

To ascertain eligibility for welfare programs, the federal government has developed a standard measure for identifying the poor: the poverty level. The poverty level varies according to a family's size: the larger the family, the higher the threshold. The precise level is calculated according to the costs of a family's basic needs. Specifically, it equals three times the cost of a minimally nutritious diet for a family of a given size. In 2006, the federal government calculated that a family of four would need to pay a minimum of $6,871 for food. For such a family, therefore, the pre-tax poverty threshold was set at $20,614.[38] This way of calculating poverty does not do a good job of accounting for unreported incomes, which often include earnings from tips or domestic work.[39]

Figure 17.2 shows the percentage of the U.S. population in poverty since 1960. The number peaks early and then steadily declines. Indeed, poverty rates

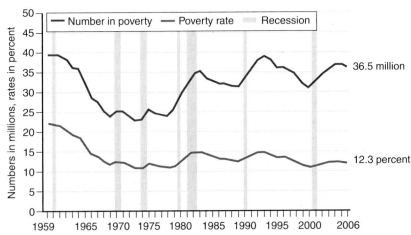

Figure 17-2. Number and Percentage of U.S. Population in Poverty.
Though the percentage of Americans in poverty declined during the 1960s, it has remained steady every since. Due to population increases, meanwhile, the number of individuals in poverty since 1970 has increased by over 10 million.

Note: The data points are placed at the midpoints of the respective years.

Source: U.S. Census Bureau, "Current Population Survey, 1960–2007," Annual Social and Economic Supplements.

continued to drop until the early 1970s, when they leveled off at roughly 12 percent. As the U.S. population has increased in size, however, the number of people living in poverty has steadily increased since the early 1970s.

The poor do not represent a random sample of U.S. adults. Young people, non-white adults, and single parents are disproportionately represented among the poor. No less than 18 percent of those under the age of 18 live in poverty, as compared to 10 percent of adults over the age of 65. Roughly 1 in 4 African Americans and Hispanics are poor, as compared to 1 in 10 whites. Five percent of married couples live in poverty, as compared to 13 percent of male single parents and 29 percent of female.[40]

The federal government supports a variety of welfare programs.

The federal government has devised a variety of ways to help the poor. Historically, the most significant effort was **Aid to Families with Dependent Children** (AFDC). Enacted in 1935 as part of the Social Security Act, this program provided assistance to needy children whose mother or father was missing from the home, physically handicapped, deceased, or unemployed. In 1950, the program was expanded to direct benefits to the parents of children in need as well. Not surprisingly, this reform lead to a marked rise in expenditures. By 1962, AFDC distributed upwards of half a billion dollars in benefits nationwide. Expenditures continued to steadily rise through the 1970s. The Reagan administration cut AFDC benefits slightly, but by the mid-1990s the program was distributing over $16 billion to citizens living in poverty around the nation.[41]

Throughout its history, AFDC attracted considerable controversy. Critics charged that it discouraged parents from working and staying together.[42] In 1996, therefore, the federal government replaced AFDC with a new program entitled **Temporary Assistance for Needy Families** (TANF). This program, as will be discussed in the *Case Study*, imposed considerably more restrictions on benefits than did its predecessor. In particular, TANF established new work requirements and firm limits on the number of years that any individual could receive welfare benefits. As a consequence, the number of citizens receiving this form of welfare benefit has dropped by more than 60 percent since the mid-1990s.[43]

Other programs, such as Supplemental Security Income (SSI), focus on those who are having an especially difficult time. The program's origins lay in a section of the 1935 Social Security Act that provided for cash payments to the poor elderly and the blind. In 1950, however, the program was expanded to include individuals who suffered from severe and permanent disabilities. The Social Security Administration administers the program, but aid comes from general tax revenues rather than Social Security contributions. To qualify for SSI support, individuals must demonstrate not only that they are poor, but also that they have few possessions. To qualify in 2006, a single individual usually could not own in excess of $2,000 worth of goods, and married couples could not own more than $3,000. SSI is really directed toward reaching the destitute.[44] In 2006, SSI disbursed a total of $34 billion in aid.[45]

Other federal programs assist the poor in obtaining specific necessities. The federal government supports a variety of food programs for the needy, including a nutritional program for women, infants, and children (WIC) and a school breakfast and lunch program. The largest, though, is the Food Stamp Program. After operating briefly in the late 1930s and early 40s, the program became a permanent component of the welfare landscape in 1964. Administered by the Department of Agriculture, it provides the poor with coupons that can be redeemed at local grocery stores to purchase approved food items. The income restrictions for the Food Stamp Program are not quite as strict as those for AFDC, TANF, or SSI. Consequently, the program benefits more U.S. residents. Over the last 40 years, the program has grown dramatically. In 1969, 3 million individuals received food stamps whose costs totaled $250 million. By 2007, 26 million people received them at a total cost of $35 billion.[46]

Other programs are designed expressly to support the working poor. The Earned Income Tax Credit (EITC), created in 1974, subsidizes the wages of low-income individuals. Specifically, it reduces the amount of income taxes they must pay; for some individuals, the EITC results in a government refund. Throughout its history, the EITC has received bipartisan support, largely because it encourages work, unlike other welfare programs (notably AFDC). EITC eligibility requirements have both an income ceiling and a floor. While the ceiling is as much as twice the poverty threshold for a household, the floor requires that families have a non-zero income. Consequentially, individuals who are unemployed for the entirety of a year cannot receive EITC benefits. When filing their taxes in 2006, upwards of 22 million individuals claimed EITC benefits that totaled $39 billion.[47]

CaseStudy: Welfare Reform in 1996

Welfare reform was one of the most contentious political issues of the 1990s. President Bill Clinton's 1992 campaign pledge to "end welfare as we know it" reflected growing popular concerns that the current system had become dysfunctional. Instead of lifting children out of poverty as originally intended, many feared that welfare had created a culture of dependency on government among the poor. By the mid-1990s, politicians on both sides of the aisle broadly agreed that reform was necessary.

The fact that both parties agreed that change was needed, however, does not mean that they agreed on the nature of the change. Clinton's original proposal called for a $10 billion increase in funding to pay for education and job-training programs designed to help welfare recipients find steady employment.[48] Republicans in Congress, by contrast, sought overall cuts, stricter time limits on benefits, and the delegation of authority to state governments to determine policy as they saw fit. As a result, the first two bills passed by the Republican-controlled Congress drew vetoes from the President.

Facing election-year pressure to fulfill his earlier pledge, Clinton signed the Personal Responsibility and Work Opportunity Reconciliation Act on August 22, 1996. The resulting law, known popularly as "welfare reform," went into effect the next year. This landmark piece of legislation instituted unprecedented changes in government aid to the poor and caused considerable backlash against Clinton from members of his own party. Senator Christopher Dodd (D-CT), for instance, decried the

law as an "unconscionable retreat," while Senator Paul Simon (D-IL) lamented, "This isn't welfare reform, it's welfare denial." Senator Daniel Patrick Moynihan (D-NY) labeled the bill "the most brutal act of social policy since Reconstruction."[49]

The final bill replaced the 1935 Aid to Families with Dependent Children (AFDC) program, a product of Franklin Roosevelt's "New Deal," with a program known as Temporary Assistance to Needy Families (TANF). Many of the provisions originally proposed by Republicans made it into the bill, including a five-year lifetime limit on aid per family and a requirement that recipients find full-time work within two years of receiving support. Whereas AFDC had guaranteed unlimited cash assistance to all qualifying citizens, under TANF, participants failing to find work within the two-year time frame stood to lose their benefits. The bill also contained a $55 billion cut in spending and delegated significant freedom to state governments to run their own programs. Nevertheless, the welfare bill also fulfilled some of Clinton's requests, including new money for daycare and demands that state governments maintain existing levels of welfare spending.

Thus far, the effects of the 1996 welfare bill remain controversial. Proponents note that the bill decreased the welfare rolls from 12.8 million recipients in 1996 to 4.4 million in 2003, increased the number of employed single mothers, and doubled child-support payments—that is, payments by a divorced parent to a child's primary caretaker.[50] Some evidence also suggests that welfare reform has lead to a decrease in teen pregnancies and an increase in two-parent households.[51] "We have been vindicated by the results," Representative E. Clay Shaw Jr. (R-FL) claimed, while President Clinton concluded that "the bill has done far more good than harm."[52]

Not everyone, though, has benefited from welfare reform. One Brookings Institution study concluded that as many as 10 percent of those previously on welfare were worse off because of low wages or a lack of any income.[53] State studies in New Jersey, Utah, and South Carolina have found that in some of the direst cases, the incomes of former welfare recipients were cut in half, leaving families to live on less than $500 a month.[54] Critics also pointed out that employment increases may have been attributable to the 1990s economic boom rather than welfare reform. If correct, this suggests economic downturns could expand welfare rolls in the future.[55]

ThinkingCritically

1. How did the federal government succeed in cutting welfare in the 1990s, when it failed to cut farm subsidies in 2007 and failed to privatize Social Security in 2005?

2. Do the interest groups that support welfare differ in important respects from those that support farm subsidies or Social Security?

3. Why wasn't a clear, focusing event necessary for the government to enact welfare reform?

U.S. welfare programs are small by international standards.

By European standards, the U.S. welfare system is quite young. Whereas most U.S. welfare programs were created in the 1930s and '60s, many European programs trace back to the nineteenth century. Germany pioneered early welfare efforts, enacting laws in the 1880s to aid poor people who could not work because of industrial accidents, illness, or old age. Other countries soon followed. These programs mainly resulted from the dramatic socioeconomic changes going on in Europe at the time. The emergence of factories, the rise of the working classes, and massive migration from rural areas into cities brought new social problems to the fore and exacerbated the hard conditions facing workers. Welfare assistance served as a way of quelling discontent among the working classes, who many feared might rise up against their governments. By the eve of World War I in 1914, Austria, Belgium, Britain, Denmark, Finland, France, Germany, Italy, the Netherlands, Norway, Sweden, and Switzerland all had some form of welfare in place. These programs expanded greatly in the years between the World Wars, and then again after World War II.[56]

The American welfare system is also smaller than that in other countries. The amount of money the U.S. government devotes to social programs lags far behind the sums spent in Western Europe, Australia, and Canada. In 1995, the United States ranked last out of 11 Western democracies in public welfare expenditures, contributing 17 percent of its national income to government social programs. This amounted to little more than half of the average expenditure of the other Western democracies.[57]

Scholars continue to debate the causes of the differences between U.S. and European welfare systems. Some have argued that American political culture, which prizes individualism and personal responsibility, is less amenable to social welfare programs than European cultures, which stress collective values. Others contend that the American system of checks and balances makes it harder to enact major social legislation. Both of these explanations, however, have obvious limitations. Programs like Social Security, which provides government support for all older Americans, remain wildly popular despite the individualistic culture of the United States. And sweeping anti-poverty measures such as Lyndon Johnson's Great Society initiative managed to overcome both cultural and institutional hurdles.[58]

Education

The U.S. Constitution does not discuss the education of children. The obligation to educate, therefore, fell upon state and local governments. Since the nation's founding, public schools in this country have been locally controlled. Starting in New England and then spreading south and west, town selectmen and then local school boards directed the financing, building, and governing of public schools. Localism thrived during this period. The goals of schooling, the investment of public funds, even the languages of instruction, were locally determined. And what held true for Chicago, Illinois, did not necessarily apply to Madison, Wisconsin, just 150 miles away.

As public education took hold in the United States, school boards contended with a loosely knit assembly of schools whose principals and teachers retained considerable freedom to do as they pleased. As the education historian David Tyack notes, public education constituted "more a miscellaneous collection of village schools than a coherent system."[59] Metaphorically, public schools around the nation looked less like peach trees in an orchard, and more like brightly colored and misshapen stones in a mosaic.

During the nineteenth century, the federal government granted public lands to states for educational use, but it had little say over what happened within the newly constructed schoolhouses. The Office of Education, established in 1870, collected descriptive statistics on public schools but otherwise rarely interfered. More than half a century later, though, all of this would change, and the federal government burst onto the education scene.

On October 4, 1957, the Soviet Union stunned the world with its successful launch of Sputnik I, the first satellite to circle the globe. The feat left many Americans deeply concerned about their ability to compete with the communist regime. Within a few months, President Dwight Eisenhower responded by outlining education reforms designed to improve U.S. schools. "As never before," he warned, "the security and continued well-being of the United States depend on extension of scientific knowledge."[60] Concerns about national security spurred the federal government's entry into the business of education.

On September 2, 1958, Eisenhower signed the National Defense Education Act into law. The act, the president declared, would "do much to strengthen our American system of education so that it can meet the broad and increasing demands imposed upon it by considerations of basic national security."[61] Most of the aid went to science, math, and foreign language training, though smaller amounts went to school construction and low-interest loans. Though the act did not change the curriculum or method of instruction of any public school, it opened the door for increased federal involvement in public education.

The federal government seeks to equalize education funding.

In principle, states and municipalities were supposed to provide a basic education to all children. For much of U.S. history, however, they did not. Boys had greater opportunities to join sports teams than girls. The amount of money spent on schools varied dramatically across school districts and states. And the educational options granted to white citizens were usually superior to those of African Americans, Latinos, and other ethnic minorities. Testifying before a Senate subcommittee in 1963, Commissioner of Education Frances Koppel cited a troubling statistic:

whereas nearly 75 percent of the young white population had completed high school, only 40 percent of non-whites had done so. Such inequalities in education, moreover, perpetuated inequalities in the workplace as well. For example, although African Americans then comprised 11 percent of the total population, they made up only 3.5 percent of all professional workers.[62]

During the 1960s and '70s, the federal government sought to redress such inequalities. Most importantly, in 1965 it enacted the **Elementary and Secondary Education Act** (ESEA), which provided direct aid to local school districts with large concentrations of poor residents. The original law and its subsequent amendments funneled additional assistance to Native Americans and to students whose primary language was not English.

In the 1970s, the federal government turned its attention to the educational needs of the physically handicapped. In 1975, Congress enacted what is now called the Individuals with Disability Education Act (IDEA). The act proclaimed that all citizens are entitled to a "free appropriate public education." It then mandated public schools to make the accommodations needed to ensure that students with physical disabilities received this. As a consequence, public schools needed to change their buildings, alter their curricula, and introduce classes that would suit the needs of disabled students. However, the federal government covers just a fraction of these costs. As a consequence, the IDEA is often referred to as an **unfunded mandate**.

Today, educational inequities persist. For example, high school drop-out rates for the 2003–2004 academic year hovered around 3 percent for whites but ranged between 5 and 8 percent for blacks.[63] In 2003, Hispanics constituted 18 percent of elementary school students but less than 11 percent of college students.[64] Among college graduates who obtained bachelor's degrees in computer science or engineering during the 2004–2005 school year, men outnumbered women by about 4 to 1.[65] The educational opportunities granted to certain segments of the population—especially women, African Americans, students for whom English is a second language, and the disabled—exceed what they were a half-century ago, but inequalities remain.

The federal government attempts to impose standards.

In the early 1980s, concerns about the ability of U.S. citizens to compete with others around the globe again intensified. In an influential report entitled *A Nation at Risk*, a panel of education experts complained about the "rising tide of mediocrity" infecting U.S. schools. International comparisons of student achievement, which had been completed a decade earlier, revealed that "on 19 academic tests American students were never first or second and, in comparison with other industrialized nations, were last seven times."[66] At the turn of the millennium, lackluster performance remained an issue. In a test administered in 2000 to 15-year-olds in 31 countries, the United States ranked 15th in science, 16th in reading, and 20th in mathematics. And as Table 17.1 shows, when averaging across the three subjects, the United States ranked 14th. Increasingly, it seemed, states and local districts could not be counted on to provide the level of excellence required to keep pace with students abroad.

The demand for standards and accountability came to a head in 2001, when Congress enacted the **No Child Left Behind Act** (NCLB).[67] For the first time, the federal government assumed the responsibility of monitoring individual schools and doling out punishments and rewards on the basis of their performance. Specif-

Table 17-1. U.S. Students Lag Behind Their International Counterparts on Standardized Tests

	AVERAGE SCORE
Japan	544.67
Korea, Republic of	535.33
Canada	526
United Kingdom	522.67
Australia	521.67
Austria	519
Sweden	518.67
Finland	517.67
New Zealand	516.33
France	515.33
Ireland	512.67
Iceland	511.67
Switzerland	510.67
United States	506.67
Belgium	503.33
Norway	501.33
Czech Republic	500.67
Poland	499.67
Germany	494
Lichtenstein	491
Denmark	488.33
Spain	486.33
Hungary	475
Italy	474
Portugal	470
Russian Federation	466.67
Latvia	460.33
Luxembourg	456.33
Greece	443.33
Mexico	427.67
Brazil	368.33

Source: National Center for Education Statistics, *Outcomes of Learning: Results from the 2000 Program for International Student Assessment of 15-Year-Olds in Reading, Math, and Science Literacy* (NCES Report 2002-115, December 2001)

ically, NCLB requires states to establish a testing regime that evaluates student learning trends from year to year. Furthermore, states must identify the percentage of students who perform at a certain level each year. Schools that fail to meet designated benchmarks are deemed "in need of improvement." If a public school fails to attain testing standards for two years, its attendees may transfer to higher-performing schools within their district. After three years, students qualify for supplemental tutoring services. Schools that fail for longer periods of time face harsher sanctions still.

Some have argued that NCLB is an unfunded mandate. Here, though, the case is not quite so clear. NCLB provides more than enough money for states to develop tests and for schools to administer them, and it has increased the funding for "Title I" schools, which the poor attend in large numbers. Even though NCLB provides insufficient funds for schools to make all the necessary reforms to improve their students' test scores, the lack of consensus on the amount of funding required makes the "unfunded mandate" charge difficult to sustain.

No Child Left Behind has not yet produced dramatic improvements in American students' rankings compared to their peers abroad. On tests administered in 2006 to 15-year-olds in 57 countries, the United States again delivered middling results, ranking 25th in science and 32nd in math.[68] However, NCLB has still had a dramatic effect on the U.S. education system. Two consequences are especially noteworthy. First, the federal government has become an important agenda setter in public education. Rather than merely providing support services and ensuring a roughly even playing field, the federal government now plays an important role in determining the curricula of schools around the nation. Second, NCLB has raised the stakes of standardized testing dramatically. Never before has so much ridden on children's performance on state-mandated standardized tests.

Reformers challenge the "public school monopoly."

During the last two decades, reformers have launched a series of challenges against public schools. According to these reformers, public schools fail to perform well because they are not subject to competition. For the most part, government-run schools can count on a steady supply of students, even when these schools perform quite poorly. As a result, public schools lack the competitive incentive to improve that drives most industries in the private marketplace.

These reformers have proposed two policy innovations to increase the schooling options available to parents, especially those in urban settings. The first concerns **charter schools**, which are public schools that are exempted from many rules and regulations faced by traditional public schools. For instance, when hiring teachers and choosing their curriculum, charter schools tend to have greater freedom than do traditional public school. Charter schools are directly responsible to a chartering board, which oversees their operations. Though their character varies from school to school, and from state to state, most charter schools focus on a particular population of students (such as those with special needs) or offer a distinctive curriculum (such as one that emphasizes science).

In 1991, the first charter school opened in Minnesota. Since then, over 40 states have enacted charter school legislation. The highest concentration of such schools is in Washington, D.C., where almost 20 percent of children attend a charter school. The devastation wrought by Hurricane Katrina created new opportunities to replace many of the affected region's traditional public schools with charter schools. Since 2005, roughly half of the schools reopening in New Orleans are charter schools.[69] And as Figure 17.3 shows, over 4,000 charter schools now serve upwards of one million students around the country.[70]

The second innovation is school **vouchers**, which are tuition subsidies that reduce the costs of sending a child to a private school. The first voucher experiment in the United States began in 1990 in Milwaukee, which offered tuition subsidies of (initially) up to $2,500 to low-income families. For the first eight years, the program could legally serve no more than 1.5 percent of the city's public-school population (approximately 1,700 students) and only secular schools were allowed to participate. In 1996, the state of Wisconsin permitted up to 15 percent of the public-school population to participate in the program, expanded the menu

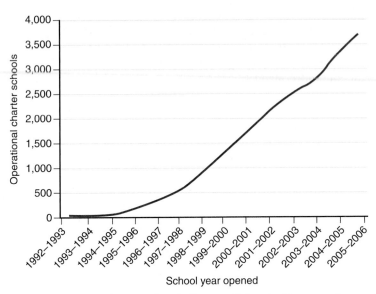

Figure 17-3. **Thousands of Charter Schools Operate Around the Nation.** Since the early 1990s, the number of charter schools has steadily risen.

Source: The Center for Education Reform, www.edreform.com.

of private schooling options to include religious institutions, and increased the monetary value of the vouchers.

Other publicly funded voucher programs now operate in Ohio, Florida, and Washington, D.C. Vermont and Maine have voucher-like programs that assist children in rural districts to attend either a secular private school or a public school in another district. In the 2005–2006 school year, thousands of non-special education students made use of the voucher program: roughly 14,200 in Milwaukee; 5,700 in Cleveland; 733 in Florida; 1,090 in Washington D.C.; 5,450 in Vermont; and 6,250 in Maine. That same year, tens of thousands more received scholarships, roughly equivalent to vouchers, through tax credit programs in Arizona, Pennsylvania, and Florida.[71] And thousands more pupils have enrolled in privately funded voucher programs. Such efforts include a national program operated by the Children's Scholarship Fund, as well as local initiatives in Washington, D.C., New York City, Dayton, Indianapolis, and San Antonio.

While controversial within the United States, vouchers have attracted widespread support in other nations. In 1980, the country of Chile enacted the equivalent of a national voucher program. Private schools in Chile are fully subsidized, while public schools face significantly fewer regulations than their U.S. counterparts. As a result, almost 40 percent of students in Chile attend private schools, as compared to just 10 percent in the United States. Whether Chilean students have benefited from these new educational opportunities, however, remains a subject of continued academic debate. Some scholars have found that the private-school students outperform their public-school peers, while others argue that the differences are negligible.[72]

Note a crucial difference between vouchers and charters, on the one hand, and NCLB, on the other. Vouchers and charters are intended to reduce the role of the government in the administration of schools. In both instances, participating students attend schools with considerably less oversight than traditional public schools. NCLB, on the other hand, increases the government's involvement in schools. Because of NCLB, schools must regularly test children, report their results, and then be graded accordingly. Moreover, a central premise of NCLB is that principals and teachers in failing schools will change their behavior because of the law's direct intervention into their schools.

Are Private Schools Better Than Public Schools?

The Question

There is overwhelming consensus that the federal government should support the education of children. A vibrant economy and a functioning democracy, after all, depend upon an educated citizenry. Less clear is whether the government should be in the business of actually running the schools. Currently, roughly 90 percent of children attend public schools, most of which serve children within well-defined neighborhood boundaries. The remaining 10 percent of children, however, attend a variety of private schools. Numerically, most of these schools are Catholic, but others adhere to different religious denominations, and many are secular. Do these students perform better on standardized tests than their public-school peers? How do we know?

Why It Matters

Local, state, and federal governments contribute a total of $9,762, on average, to educate a public-school student.[73] Most private schools charge parents approximately $3,000 a year to send a child to school. Private schools also are not subject to the kinds of rules and regulations that govern public schools. Private schools, for instance, do not participate in any of the NCLB testing regimes. If private-school students perform as well as or better than comparable public-school students, then one way to increase student performance may involve increasing the educational options available to parents, especially those who cannot currently afford the cost of a private education. Moreover, there may be substantial savings associated with doing so.

Investigating the Answer

The most straightforward way of assessing the relative quality of public and private schools would seem to involve simply comparing the test scores of a random sample of students in each sector. If private-school students score higher, one might conclude that private schools do a superior job of educating students. Unfortunately, things are not nearly so simple.

There is good reason to expect that private-school students differ systematically from public-school students. Private schools, after all, charge tuition, while public schools are nominally free. Moreover, private schools enjoy considerable discretion to select which students to admit. Traditional public schools, by contrast, typically accept all students within a defined geographic region. Given these facts, it is extraordinarily difficult to know whether observed differences between public- and private-school students arise from differences in the quality of education, or from differences in student backgrounds that influence whether they attend private or public school in the first place.

How might one go about distinguishing between these two possibilities? One option involves carefully controlling for a wide range of background characteristics when comparing public and private school test scores. Pursuing this approach, scholars have built large datasets and employed complex statistical techniques that allow them to account for differences in students' family backgrounds. These studies attempt to hold constant a wide range of observable qualities, such as race and ethnicity, parental involvement, and family education and employment levels.

The trouble with these studies, however, is that one can never be entirely sure that the analyst has correctly accounted for and measured all relevant characteristics. In surveys, for instance, people regularly misreport their income. Studies that rely upon survey income data, then, may not effectively control for this dimension. Moreover, such research could omit other important background characteristics, such as a parent's commitment to education. In either case, these studies may generate biased estimates of the quality of public and private schools.

The most effective way to solve these selection problems, then, is to randomly assign students to public and private schools. By conducting a randomized field trial, one could ensure that the two populations before the education intervention are exactly alike in all respects, both observable and unobservable. Subsequently, differences that arise between the two populations could be attributed to the education experience, and not to the children's backgrounds.

Randomized field trials are commonplace in medical studies, in which subjects are randomly assigned to receive a pill or placebo. In the last decade, this approach to studying the effectiveness of a policy intervention has come to education. As mentioned above, private philanthropists launched school voucher programs in New York City, Dayton, Ohio, and Washington, D.C., during the 1990s. Rather than give out the vouchers on a first-come-first-serve basis, however, the administrators conducted lotteries. Among qualified applicants, some students were randomly offered a voucher and some were not. As a consequence, the only thing that distinguished the "treatment" and "control" groups was the opportunity to attend a private school. By tracking the performance of these two groups over time, then, one stood the best chance of overcoming the self-selection problems described above.

What did these three programs teach us about the quality of public and private schools? Interestingly, the answer very much depends upon the ethnicity of the students. Across the three cities, white students who attended private schools did not score any higher than white students who attended public schools. The performances of Latino students in the two sectors also appeared indistinguishable from one another. However, private schools did seem to benefit African-American students. After three years, African-American students in private schools scored significantly higher on standardized tests than African Americans in public schools.[74]

Though randomized field trials are the gold standard of social research, one still needs to be careful when interpreting their results. For starters, it is not always clear that the observed findings from one study apply to a larger population. Randomized field trials of voucher programs in other cities, for instance, might yield very different results. Additionally, the private school advantage remains unclear. What is it about private schools that disproportionately benefits African-American students? The mere documentation of the private school effect does not explain what caused the effect.

The Bottom Line

In this instance, there appears to be a fair amount of consensus.[75] In both randomized field trials and observational studies, the test-score advantages of attending a private school appear to be concentrated among African Americans. Policymakers interested in improving the educational lives of African-American children, then, would do well to consider expanding the array of public and private schooling options available to them.

Healthcare

In addition to attending to the elderly, the poor, and the young, the federal government also assists the infirm. Many U.S. citizens receive private health insurance for themselves and their families through their workplace. Millions, though, rely upon the two largest government insurance programs: Medicare, which assists the elderly, and Medicaid, which assists the poor.

Medicare and Medicaid provide coverage to the elderly, poor, and disabled.

Though Lyndon Johnson's Great Society legislation tackled poverty, education, and discrimination, its most sweeping achievements were reserved for the infirm. Through two programs enacted in 1965, Johnson put the government into the healthcare business like never before. **Medicare** provided government health insurance to the elderly, and **Medicaid** did so to the poor and disabled.[76]

When originally enacted, Medicare covered physicians' fees and the costs of compulsory hospitalization for citizens over the age of 65. Over time, though, the program has expanded dramatically. Today it allows the elderly to secure a wide range of services including inpatient hospital care, certain kinds of home healthcare, hospice assistance, and outpatient hospital care. In 2003, the government added prescription drug benefits to Medicare. These benefits constitute the single largest expansion of Medicare in decades. Though they still must pay an annual deductible and a percentage of a prescription's costs, the elderly now pay less for their medicine than they did before.

By any calculation, Medicare is a massive government program. In 2007, Medicare assisted 42 million citizens at a total cost of $430 billion—almost as much as all Social Security outlays, and far more than any other federal education or welfare program.[77] Medicare is financed through a variety of means. As with Social Security, workers must pay a Medicare-specific tax. Additionally, for those receiving such medical services as x-rays, laboratory and diagnostic tests, and influenza and pneumonia vaccinations, the federal government deducts a portion of their Social Security payments, then covers the remaining costs with general revenues.

In many ways, though, Medicaid is even bigger than Medicare. In 2006, Medicaid provided health insurance to 54 million low-income and disabled citizens. It also assumed responsibility for providing a larger proportion of healthcare services. For instance, Medicaid now covers one-third of the nation's childbirths, nearly 40 percent of long-term care expenses, and more services for AIDS patients than any other provider in the country.[78]

Medicaid expenditures, however, are slightly lower than those of Medicare. In 2006, Medicaid cost federal and state governments a total of $325 billion, roughly $100 billion less than Medicare. Two primary reasons explain why Medicaid today is less expensive than Medicare, even though it provides more services to more people. First, Medicaid does not offer as generous a prescription drug benefit program. Indeed, before Medicare's 2003 drug benefit enhancement, the costs of the two programs tracked one another quite closely. Second, the costs of attending to the elderly have steadily increased over time. Today, the elderly are living eight years longer, on average, than they did when Medicare began. The elderly, moreover, typically require more expensive medical procedures than does the rest of the citizenry. And Medicare is picking up most of these extra costs.

Certain populations—such as the disabled and poor seniors—qualify for both Medicare and Medicaid. And because the two programs cover different kinds of medical services, these individuals draw benefits from both. In important respects, though, the two programs operate very differently from one another. Whereas Medicare is an entitlement program for the elderly, Medicaid is a means-tested program for the needy. And whereas Medicare is run exclusively by the federal government, Medicaid receives funding from the federal government and the states. The federal government contributes more to poorer states than it does to richer states. Nonetheless, because they are responsible for paying a substantial amount of the program's costs, state governments have some discretion in setting eligibility requirements and determining types of services provided. So while Medicare looks exactly the same across the country, Medicaid programs differ markedly from state to state.[79]

U.S. healthcare and health are poor by international standards.

Despite massive government programs like Medicare and Medicaid, as well as the patchwork of private insurance plans, many Americans lack health insurance. In every year between 1995 and 2005, more than 15 percent of U.S. citizens lacked any health insurance. Every other major industrialized nation in the world, by comparison, has some form of universal health care. The United Kingdom was the first nation to offer universal medical coverage. In 1948, it established the National Health Service, which uses general tax revenue to support hospitals that serve all citizens. Thus far, over 30 other European countries have followed suit with universal programs of their own, as have tens of other countries, including Israel, Uruguay, India, and Japan.

U.S. coverage rates are all the more troubling given the extraordinary costs of its healthcare. In 2003, the United States spent close to 16 percent of its Gross National Product on health costs. As a percentage of their economies, this proportion is higher than any other advanced industrialized nation. Indeed, U.S. costs are 50 to 80 percent higher than those in Germany, Canada, the United Kingdom, and France, all of which provide universal healthcare to their citizens.

Though they pay a great deal for healthcare, U.S. citizens remain comparatively unhealthy. Consider, for example, the number of years that people in different nations can expect to live. In 2004, the life expectancy of U.S. citizens trailed that of 24 other major industrialized nations. Ranking just above citizens of Poland, Mexico, and the Czech Republic, U.S. men live an average of 75 years, and U.S. women, 80. Both figures trailed those of every nation in Western Europe.[80] American citizens also have much less healthy lifestyles than their international counterparts. In 2005, for instance, U.S. obesity rates eclipsed those of every other industrialized nation in the world. Fully 32 percent of U.S. citizens were deemed obese, as compared to just 3 percent of the Japanese, 8 percent of the Swiss, 10 percent of the French, and 23 percent of the English.[81]

Given international differences in coverage rates and lifestyles, it is difficult to assess the overall quality of different healthcare systems. Those who have tried to do so, however, have not given the United States high marks. Table 17.2 ranks the quality of healthcare systems in the top 50 countries. According to the World Health Organization (WHO), the United States ranks 37th in the world for the overall performance of its healthcare system. This places the American system behind those of all Western European countries, as well as Canada, Australia, and

Table 17-2. Overall Health System Performance, World Health Organization Estimates (1997)

RANK	COUNTRY	RANK	COUNTRY
1	France	26	Saudi Arabia
2	Italy	27	United Arab Emirates
3	San Marino	28	Israel
4	Andorra	29	Morocco
5	Malta	30	Canada
6	Singapore	31	Finland
7	Spain	32	Australia
8	Oman	33	Chile
9	Austria	34	Denmark
10	Japan	35	Dominica
11	Norway	36	Costa Rica
12	Portugal	**37**	**United States of America**
13	Monaco	38	Slovenia
14	Greece	39	Cuba
15	Iceland	40	Brunei Darussalam
16	Luxembourg	41	New Zealand
17	Netherlands	42	Bahrain
18	United Kingdom	43	Croatia
19	Ireland	44	Qatar
20	Switzerland	45	Kuwait
21	Belgium	46	Barbados
22	Colombia	47	Thailand
23	Sweden	48	Czech Republic
24	Cyprus	49	Malaysia
25	Germany	50	Poland

Source: World Health Organization, "The World Health Report 2000: Health Systems: Improving Performance," http://www.who.int/whr/2000/en/whr00_en.pdf

Japan. Even some developing countries, including Colombia, Chile, and Costa Rica, outperform the United States by this measure.

The United States healthcare system would appear mediocre at best in comparison to those offered by other countries. Nevertheless, overall system performance is just one of many ways to evaluate national healthcare quality. The WHO report, for instance, bases its rankings on a composite measure that includes factors such as the health of a nation's citizens, the responsiveness of a healthcare system to patient's non-health concerns, and the extent to which healthcare systems accommodate patient's financial limitations. Although the United States performs poorly on financing, ranking 54th, it comes in at 24th in health attainment and 1st in system responsiveness.[82]

Moreover, ranking a nation's healthcare system based partly on the wellness of its population, as the WHO does, can be tricky. On the one hand, a healthy citizenry could indicate that the system is working effectively. Residents may be living longer and healthier lives due to good preventive medicine or access to excellent doctors and facilities. On the other hand, it could reflect considerations that have little to do with its healthcare system, such as culture, the environment, or economic development. For instance, people may live longer in a nation where the traditional diet consists of low-fat foods like fish, fruits, and vegetables. Conversely, populations of developing countries may be exposed to higher levels of pollution, which can trigger a variety of ailments. These examples illustrate the difficulty in measuring the effects of a country's healthcare system on the well-being of its citizens.

Comprehensive healthcare reform is extraordinarily difficult.

Everyone agrees that something needs to be done about the state of U.S. healthcare. It is too costly. Too many people are uninsured. And for many, the quality of care is unacceptable. What people cannot agree about is the right way to go about improving this state of affairs. Some suggest that allowing U.S. citizens to purchase prescription drugs from foreign countries might drastically reduce costs. Others push for closer regulation of the pharmaceutical industry. The most ambitious, however, advocate government-provided healthcare that covers every U.S. citizen.

Advocates of universal healthcare are generally liberals. They couch their arguments in terms of traditional American values about fairness and equity, asking, "Isn't health the most basic right?" Indeed, doesn't the exercise of all other rights depend upon citizens being healthy? And if so, how can we deny health insurance to millions of U.S. citizens?[83] Advocates also note that the United States is the only major industrialized nation in the world not to offer healthcare to all of its citizens.

There are powerful opponents, however, to universal healthcare. Most conservatives are deeply suspicious of what they call "socialized medicine."[84] Libertarian organizations, such as the Cato Institute, oppose reforms that would increase federal regulations of hospitals. And the American Medical Association is wary of any plan that would reduce the role of private insurance. Moreover, critics insist, government-provided healthcare threatens to reduce the number of hospital and doctor options available to the public. And in this sense, universal healthcare violates other basic tenets of the American creed, notably individualism and freedom of choice. These individuals do not dispute the importance of decreasing the number of uninsured individuals around the country. But they insist that private insurers, rather than the federal government, should assume primary responsibility for achieving this important goal.

The last big push for anything resembling universal healthcare occurred when Bill Clinton was in the White House. Early in his first term, Clinton established the Task Force on National Health Care Reform, which was charged with designing a comprehensive universal healthcare program. Hillary Clinton spearheaded the endeavor. In the fall of 1993, the Clintons introduced the Health Security Act, which would require employers to provide health insurance to all of their workers through carefully regulated health maintenance organizations.[85] The bill also represented the most ambitious attempt to reform Medicare and Medicaid. Politically, though, it ran into the equivalent of a buzz saw. Libertarians, conservatives, and physicians' groups rallied to kill the initiative, insisting that it was a colossal unfunded mandate that did more to increase healthcare costs than to expand coverage. The following fall, the bill died. Weeks later, the Republican Party won enough seats in the midterm election to take over both chambers of Congress for the first time in 40 years, effectively derailing an opportunity for comprehensive healthcare reform.[86]

While universal healthcare has proved difficult at the national level, advocates have made some headway at the state and local levels. In the summer of 2007, the

Commonwealth of Massachusetts began implementing a healthcare policy that provided coverage to nearly all of its residents. Governor Mitt Romney signed the bill into law and subsequently touted the policy as a crowning achievement of his time in office when he ran for president in 2008. In 2007, the city of San Francisco also launched a program that provides primary and preventive care to the city's estimated 82,000 uninsured residents.

That healthcare reform is difficult, therefore, does not mean that it is impossible. It is an area, after all, where two of the three preconditions for policy-making always exist. Though disagreements linger about their precise nature, problems clearly abound. And though disputed, solutions are hardly in short supply. To spur federal reform of the most expensive—and many would say most dysfunctional—of the nation's social programs, what may be needed most is a focusing event.

SUMMARY

▶ For social policies to be enacted, problems must be identified, solutions must be suggested, and a focusing event must propel action. Problems are most likely to attract government attention when they raise concerns about national security or equity. Politically viable solutions typically require the backing of organized interest groups. And focusing events can take a wide range of forms, ranging from environmental disasters to high-profile government reports.

▶ As the backbone of the modern welfare state, Social Security provides a steady income stream to the nation's elderly. During their working lives, individuals pay into the system with the expectation that they can draw from it when they retire. Over the past 70 years, the number of people paying into the system has increased markedly, but so has the amount of the benefits paid out. This, in combination with recent demographic changes, has raised deep concerns about the program's long-term sustainability.

▶ The U.S. welfare system consists of a patchwork of programs, each of which directs benefits to a different segment of the U.S. population. These programs provide varying levels and types of support, including direct cash transfers and subsidies for life necessities. Whereas most social programs expand over time, welfare has experienced some cutbacks. In 1996, Clinton fulfilled his campaign promise to "end welfare as we know it" by replacing AFDC with the more restrictive TANF.

▶ Historically, state and local governments assumed primary responsibility for the education of their residents. And though these governments continue to cover the vast majority of education expenses, over the last half-century the federal government has increased both its aid to public schools and its regulatory demands on them. Contemporary efforts to reform public schools focus on raising standards and increasing accountability, which further augment the federal government's involvement in public education, and expanding choice and competition, which reduces government regulations over where children attend school.

▶ More money is spent on healthcare than any other social program. Total expenditures of the two largest programs, Medicare and Medicaid, reached upwards of $800 billion in 2007. Run exclusively by the federal government, Medicare provides medical insurance to the elderly. A joint venture of federal and state governments, Medicaid assists the poor and disabled. Unlike all other major industrialized nations, however, the United States does not provide universal healthcare. Consequently, approximately 15 percent of the U.S. population lacks any medical coverage.

KEY TERMS

Aid to Families with Dependent Children (AFDC), p. 000

charter schools, p. 000

deficit, p. 000

Elementary and Secondary Education Act (ESEA), p. 000

entitlements, p. 000

fiscal policy, p. 000

Great Depression, p. 000

Great Society, p. 000

Gross Domestic Product (GDP), p. 000

laissez faire economics, p. 000

means-tested program, p. 000

Medicaid, p. 000

Medicare, p. 000

monetary policy, p. 000

No Child Left Behind Act (NLCB), p. 000

policy entrepreneurs, p. 000

public debt, p. 000

recession, p. 000

Social Security Act, p. 000

Temporary Assistance for Needy Families (TANF), p. 000

unfunded mandate, p. 000

vouchers, p. 000

SUGGESTED READINGS

Nancy Altman. 2005. *The Battle for Social Security: From FDR's Vision to Bush's Gamble.* Hoboken, NJ: Wiley. Reviews the history of Social Security, while offering a spirited critique of recent efforts to privatize the program.

John Chubb and Terry Moe. 1990. *Politics, Markets, and America's Schools.* Washington, DC: Brookings Institution Press. A probing and controversial account of how politics undermines the nation's public schools and of how markets might improve the educational lives of children.

Martin Gilens. 2001. *Why Americans Hate Welfare: Race, Media, and the Politics of Antipoverty Policy.* Chicago: University of Chicago Press. Examines the foundations of public attitudes toward welfare policy and welfare recipients.

Jeffrey Grogger and Lynn Karoly. 2005. *Welfare Reform: Effects of a Decade of Change.* Cambridge, MA: Harvard University Press. A careful assessment of how the poor have fared under the 1996 welfare reforms.

Jacob Hacker. 2002. *The Divided Welfare State: The Battle over Public and Private Social Benefits in the United States.* New York: Cambridge University Press. Surveys the historical roots of welfare programs, searching to explain why the U.S. welfare state is smaller than its European counterparts.

John Kingdon. 1995. *Agendas, Alternatives, and Public Policies,* 2nd ed. New York: HarperCollins College Publishers. Surveys the preconditions needed for major policy change.

Jonathan Oberlander. 2003. *The Political Life of Medicare.* Chicago: University of Chicago Press. A study of the politics of Medicare and the possibilities for comprehensive healthcare reform.

Great Society a set of large-scale social initiatives proposed by President Lyndon Johnson in the 1960s to reduce poverty, racial discrimination, environmental degradation, and urban decay.

policy entrepreneurs professionals working in think tanks, universities, lobby groups, unions, and interest groups, who propose solutions to policy problems and persuade politicians to adopt them.

Great Depression a period of severe economic recession in the United States precipitated by the stock market crash in October 1929.

Gross Domestic Product (GDP) a statistic that measures all goods and services produced by a nation's economy.

laissez faire economics a theory that discourages the government from becoming involved in the economy.

monetary policy policies designed to improve the economy by controlling the supply of available money.

fiscal policy policies designed to improve the economy through spending and taxation.

deficit the amount of money a government spends in a year, above and beyond what it brings in through taxation and other means.

public debt the total amount of money that the federal government owes.

recession an economic downturn, which technically exists when the Gross Domestic Product drops in size for two successive quarters.

Social Security Act a 1935 law that established Social Security, an entitlement program providing retirees with a monthly income in order to reduce poverty among the elderly.

entitlements benefits that all qualifying individuals have a legal right to obtain.

means-tested program any program that targets the poor and for which eligibility is based on financial need.

Aid to Families with Dependent Children (AFDC) a federal program in effect from 1935 to 1996 that provided assistance to households with needy children.

Temporary Assistance for Needy Families (TANF) a program replacing AFDC in 1996 that established new work requirements for welfare recipients and limits on the number of years an individual can receive assistance.

Elementary and Secondary Education Act (ESEA) a federal law passed in 1965 designed to reduce educational inequities by directly aiding school districts with large numbers of poor citizens.

unfunded mandate a law requiring certain actions without appropriating the necessary funds to carry them out.

No Child Left Behind Act (NCLB) a 2001 federal law that rewards public schools for meeting certain educational benchmarks and punishes schools that fail to do so.

charter schools public schools administered by chartering boards that are exempt from many rules and regulations applicable to traditional public schools.

vouchers tuition subsidies that reduce the costs of sending children to private schools.

Medicare a federally funded entitlement program that offers health insurance to the elderly.

Medicaid a means-tested program funded by federal and state governments that extends health insurance to the poor and disabled.

18 Foreign Policy

In the fall of 1986, two foreign policy incidents provoked a struggle between the executive and legislative branches that nearly brought down a popular president. On October 5, 1986, Nicaraguan troops shot down a suspicious cargo plane flying over their country. The plane and its American crew were carrying weapons and supplies to the *contras*, a Nicaraguan rebel group fighting the Sandinista regime, which was backed by the Soviet Union, then the main adversary of the United States. Nicaraguan officials accused the American government of aiding the *contra* insurgency, a charge the Reagan administration vehemently denied. Although the Central Intelligence Agency under Reagan had supported the *contras* in the early 1980s, Congress had barred the government in 1984 from providing any further assistance to the group. Reagan's team insisted they had complied with the law and halted aid to the *contras*. "It was, for all we know, a plane hired by private people, apparently some of them American," claimed Secretary of State George P.

Shultz. "They had no connection with the U.S. Government at all."[1]

The next month, a Lebanese newspaper revealed that the U.S. government had been secretly selling arms to Iran in exchange for the release of American hostages taken by Iranian-allied groups in Lebanon. At the time, Iran was one of the United States' most bitter enemies. In early 1979, Islamic hardliners had ousted its pro-U.S. government, led by Shah Mohammed Reza Pahlavi, and replaced it with a regime under the Ayatollah Khomeini. Later that same year, an Iranian mob stormed the U.S. Embassy in Tehran, taking 66 hostages. Many remained captive for over a year. The Iran hostage crisis of 1979–1981 created great hostility between Khomeini's regime and the United States. It also prompted a congressional embargo of Iran, making arms sales to the Islamic Republic illegal.

These two 1986 incidents touched off a media storm and an investigative frenzy on Capitol Hill. Each raised the possibility that the president had broken the law, deceived Congress, and lied to the American public. Moreover, the Reagan administration's activities in Iran and Nicaragua

appeared to be linked—two sides of a convoluted scheme that became known as the Iran-Contra Affair. Over the next several months, Congress, the Justice Department, and even the White House set up a slew of official committees to determine the facts. These inquiries quickly focused on members of Reagan's National Security Council (NSC).

The events that unfolded over months of hearings resembled the plot of a spy novel. The cast of characters parading before the investigative committees captivated Americans. Television networks even bumped their daytime soap opera schedule to cover the hearings. At the center of the storm sat Lieutenant Colonel Oliver L. North, a Marine and NSC staffer accused of managing the Iran-Contra operation. North's testimony to Congress made him a hero to some, as he portrayed his involvement as a dilemma between "lies and lives."[2]

North said he and others within the administration were concerned about both the American hostages in Lebanon and the *contras*. They concocted a scheme whereby the United States pledged to sell weapons and parts at a marked-up price to Iran for use in its war with Iraq. In return, Iranian moderates promised to use their influence with the Lebanese hostage-takers to broker the safe return of the American captives. North and his crew then diverted the proceeds from the Iranian weapons sales to provide assistance to the Nicaraguan *contras*. They then attempted to cover up their illegal actions by shredding official documents and lying to Congress.

In time, President Reagan reversed his initial denials that the administration participated in any illicit activities. On March 4, 1987, he took "full responsibility" for the weapons-for-hostages deal. In a televised speech, Reagan admitted, "A few months ago,

I told the American people I did not trade arms for hostages. My heart and my best intentions still tell me that's true, but the facts and evidence tell me it is not."[3] However, Reagan maintained he knew nothing about the diversion of funds to the *contras*. On that aspect of the affair, the White House claimed, Oliver North was acting alone. The extent of Reagan's knowledge of what transpired in his own administration remains hotly debated by scholars.

At the time, the Iran-Contra affair created significant political fallout. Reagan's approval ratings plummeted by 21 points when the scandal first broke and stayed low throughout the scandal.[4] And the final report of the House and Senate investigation panels in November 1987 ripped Reagan's White House to shreds

rhetorically. It accused administration officials of "secrecy, deception and disdain for the rule of law," "contempt for the democratic process," and evasion of the law "in letter and spirit."[5]

From a legal perspective, however, Congress let the president and his staff off the hook. North and his co-conspirators had already resigned or been fired; those convicted of wrong-doing were later pardoned by President George H.W. Bush. Reagan pledged to keep Congress informed in the future, and Congress did not press the issue of his involvement. After the report's release, committee member Senator George J. Mitchell (D-ME) expressed his belief that it was time to move forward: "It's important now to go on to the nation's business."[6]

Scandals like the Iran-Contra affair, of course, are not a regular occurrence. Nonetheless, the incident illustrates a number of enduring themes of American foreign policy: presidents and Congress often battle for supremacy in the making of foreign policy; parts of the bureaucracy involved in foreign affairs often do not know what the other parts are doing; and controversy surrounds the question of the United States' proper role in the world.

This chapter examines the key players in U.S. foreign policymaking. Like domestic policy, foreign policy consists of a diverse set of issues, such as trade, foreign aid, and even war. Throughout this chapter, we offer examples of these policies and the domestic political struggles that they engender.

THIS CHAPTER WILL EXAMINE:

▶ the history of U.S. foreign policy

▶ the powers of the president to direct foreign policy and the executive agencies that support the president

▶ congressional efforts to shape foreign policy

▶ the role of interest groups in foreign policymaking

▶ the foreign policy challenges that face the U.S. today.

A Brief History of U.S. Foreign Policy

Since its founding, the United States has formulated **foreign policies** that define its political and economic relationships with other states. At the heart of foreign policy debates lie concerns about the nation's **grand strategy**, the larger, organizing principles that define national interests, outline possible threats to those interests, and recommend military and diplomatic policies to protect those interests.

Until the 20th century, the United States followed a grand strategy of **isolationism**, a policy of minimizing the nation's involvement in world affairs. The alternative policy, **internationalism**, is based on the belief that intervention in the affairs of other nations is sometimes necessary to protect one's own interests. The founding fathers, however, feared that alliances with European countries could entangle the nation in overseas wars—or even worse, draw European wars to the North American continent. As a result, early American leaders sought to distance the country from European politics and its continuous conflicts. President George Washington set the tone for this policy, famously urging the country to avoid the "mischiefs of foreign intrigue" in his farewell address.[7]

Although subsequent presidents stayed out of European affairs, they actively intervened in the Western Hemisphere throughout the 19th century. "Manifest Destiny," the belief that the United States should expand across the continent, took hold of the nation. In pursuit of this goal, the United States purchased large portions of land from Spain, France and Britain. It fought a war with Mexico from 1846 to 1848, which resulted in the gain of California and other territory in the southwest. It tried to seize Canada from Britain in the War of 1812, although this attempt failed. And, in December of 1823, American leaders issued the Monroe Doctrine, a policy statement that warned European countries not to meddle in the Western Hemisphere. By 1900, the United States had become the most powerful country west of the Atlantic.[8]

In the early 20th Century, U.S. involvement in world politics is sporadic.

At the dawn of the 20th century, internal and external pressures were forcing American leaders to reconsider their grand strategy of isolationism. Industrialization and the expansion of the financial sector led to increased trade and investment abroad.[9] Economic ties to Europe then grew exponentially with the onset of World War I in 1914. The United States lent money and supplies to Britain and France as they fought Germany in one of the bloodiest wars in modern times. As a result, exports as a share of American national income doubled from 6% in 1914 to 12% in 1916. In 1916, fully 83% of those exports were bound for Britain, France, Italy, and the Russian Empire.[10]

Ultimately, concerns about trade with European allies convinced the United States to enter World War I. The German decision to launch unrestricted submarine warfare in January 1917 jeopardized American shipments to Britain and France. In April, the United States declared war on Germany.[11] The vast resources the United States brought to the war effort sealed the victory over Germany, Austria-Hungary and the Ottoman Empire in 1918.

World War I officially concluded with the Treaty of Versailles in 1919. Believing that the United States and its allies should use the historic occasion to reshape the world political order, President Woodrow Wilson urged acceptance of his "Fourteen Points" proposal for peace. Wilson called for a new international system based on the principles of democracy, self-determination, and the rule of law. He also championed the establishment of the League of Nations, a collective security institution designed to uphold European peace.

This brief turn towards internationalism in American foreign policy, however, did not last. Although Wilson's ideas received support in Europe, they foundered back home. The American public and many of its leaders were unwilling to give up their vision of a United States that remained apart from European power struggles. In the biggest defeat of his presidency, Wilson failed to secure Senate approval of accession to the League of Nations, and a spirit of isolationism once again infused U.S. foreign policy.[12]

The next 25 years, later called the "interwar period," saw great political and economic instability in Europe. The Great Depression, discussed in Chapter 17, devastated European economies. Hyperinflation brought ruin to the Weimar Republic, the weak democratic government established in Germany after WWI. Ultimately, the Weimar government could not survive the turmoil unleashed by the Depression, and the ultra-nationalist Nazi party under Adolf Hitler came to power in 1933. Around the same time Italy descended into fascism under Benito Mussolini and Spain became engulfed in civil war. The United States, however, remained largely distant from these developments as it dealt with its own economic difficulties.

As the 1930s wore on, an increasingly aggressive Japan, Germany, and Italy brought Europe and Asia to the brink of war. Japan's invasion of China, Italy's invasion of Ethiopia and Albania, and German expansion into Austria and Czechoslovakia raised serious concerns in the United States. Yet many hoped that a strong coalition of Russia, France, and Great Britain could contain Germany, Italy, and Japan.

This hope, however, did not materialize. World War II officially began on September 1, 1939, when Germany invaded Poland, provoking a declaration of war from Britain and France. Hitler's forces quickly overran France in 1940, "divert[ing] the flow of history into darker channels."[13] British forces then departed from the continent at Dunkirk, leaving Western Europe to Hitler's devices. To humiliate the French, who had lost to the Nazis despite superior manpower and materiel, Hitler forced the country's leaders to formally capitulate in the same railcar in which the Germans had surrendered in 1918.[14] The following year, Nazi armies invaded deep into the Soviet Union.

The U.S. president, Franklin Roosevelt, was highly sympathetic to the plight of the British, French, and Soviets.[15] He recognized that a Europe dominated by Hitler posed a great threat to American national security. If Hitler conquered all of Europe, he could readily secure the resources needed to challenge U.S. supremacy in North America. Still, the American public had little appetite for war. Roosevelt was able to assist the allies through his lend-lease program, which provided war materiel to the British, and eventually, the Soviets and the Chinese. But even this aid faced resistance in Congress. Many representatives feared being dragged into a war in which they felt America had few interests at stake.

This all changed with the Japanese surprise attack on Pearl Harbor in the early morning hours of December 7, 1941—a day that President Roosevelt said would "live in infamy." During the battle, Japanese planes damaged or destroyed 347 of the roughly 400 American aircraft stationed on Oahu. In all, 2,400 American servicemen and women were killed and 1,200 were injured. Most of the destruction had occurred within a scant 30 minutes.[16]

The attack on Pearl Harbor catapulted the United States into World War II. The United States spent the next four years fighting Germany, Italy, and Japan. Yet, the impact of Pearl Harbor reached far beyond American entry into the war. It ushered in a new era of American leadership in world affairs.

The United States enters the world stage for the long term.

In 1945, the United States and its allies emerged victorious after years of war in Europe and Asia. The war transformed American foreign policy. Politically, isolationism was no longer generally viewed as a viable option. Even though the United States and the Soviet Union had collaborated to defeat Hitler, goodwill between the countries quickly evaporated after the war. The looming presence of the Soviet army in Europe raised fears that an American departure from the continent could lead to Soviet domination. Economically, the United States was the only country to survive the war with its major industries intact. World War II had reduced Europe to shambles. Through the **Marshall Plan**, the United States supported vast reconstruction efforts in Western Europe, helping its worn-torn allies to rebuild their economies, with an eye towards bolstering their security against the Soviet communist threat.

Over time, a new type of conflict emerged which divided Europe along ideological lines. In the East, the Soviet Union established communist satellite governments in Bulgaria, Romania, Yugoslavia, Hungary, Poland, East Germany and Czechoslovakia.[17] This alliance was formalized by the Warsaw Pact. In Western Europe, the United States constructed a web of democratic allies, including Great Britain, France, the Netherlands, Italy, and West Germany. In 1949, the United States and its allies created the **North Atlantic Treaty Organization (NATO)** to solidify their common defense. Signatories to the NATO treaty pledged to come to each other's aid if attacked by the Soviet Union. Through NATO, the United States maintained a strong combat presence in Europe for over 40 years.

In the late 1940's the United States adopted a grand strategy of **containment**, which is a particular type of internationalism, and is meant to counter the threat the Soviet Union posed to Europe and America. Hitler's near takeover of Europe convinced Washington that the United States could not afford the rise of a hostile power that spanned the Eurasian continent. Such a country would possess vast economic resources and could threaten the American homeland. Advocated by State Department diplomat George F. Kennan, containment therefore sought to guard against Soviet expansion by adopting policies that checked Soviet power. Kennan thought that the Soviets could not be negotiated with, but that the Soviet economic system bore within itself "the seeds of its own decay, and . . . the sprouting of these seeds is well advanced." The United States needed only to bide its time until the Soviet system of government inevitably faltered. So, while the United States would not directly confront the Soviets or their allies, American foreign policy would meet Soviet challenges at every turn.[18]

Tensions ran high between America and the Soviet Union for the better part of 40 years, from the end of WWII until the revolutionary year of 1989. This period has been dubbed the **Cold War**. The name signified a state of diplomatic and economic hostility between the superpowers, but not open, "hot" warfare. Both sides consistently accused the other of unprovoked aggression as they competed for allies and influence throughout the world. This competition, however, never erupted into direct military confrontation.[19] After nearly 50 years of political upheaval, the continent returned to an era of stability not seen since the early 19th century.[20]

While Europe remained in a state of fragile peace, the rest of the world was not so fortunate. Indeed, the first major conflict between the East and West arose in Korea in 1950, when the Soviet-backed government of North Korea invaded South Korea, an American ally. The Korean War, which lasted from 1950 to 1953, confirmed the fears of many Americans that the Soviet Union was determined to spread its power and ideology across the globe. From the standpoint of American foreign policy, the Korean War was the final nail in the coffin of isolationists. Containment was widely viewed as a necessary policy that would require an extensive investment of American blood and treasure.

The United States vastly expanded its involvement in international affairs over the next several decades. The government sponsored coups in Iran (1953), Guatemala (1954), and the Dominican Republic (1956). It aided governments fighting communist insurgencies in the Philippines (1954), Chile (1964), and El Salvador (1980s). And, it funded anti-communist insurgencies in Chile (1973), Ghana (1961), Cuba (1960s), and Nicaragua (1980s). American policymakers viewed nearly every problem through the lens of the Cold War. International politics became a zero-sum game between Soviet interests and American ones.

The largest and most extensive conflict in the developing world would unfold in Vietnam, a former French colony. Throughout the late 1950s and early 1960s, the United States sent military aid to South Vietnam in an effort to curb the influence of North Vietnam, the Soviet Union, and an insurgency group called the National Front for the Liberation of South Vietnam. So doing, South Vietnam's leaders became completely dependent on American military support for their power. This turned much of the population of South Vietnam against its own government. In 1964, after a purported attack by the North on American military personnel known as the Gulf of Tonkin incident, President Lyndon Johnson asked Congress for the authority needed to conduct "all necessary action to protect our Armed Forces."[21] Congress granted Johnson's request and the Vietnam War began in earnest. At its height, the war would involve over half a million American troops and last until 1973.

The Vietnam War was a watershed event for American foreign policy. It is, after all, the first major war that the United States is perceived to have lost. Many Americans questioned the strategic interests in sending young men and women to fight and die in a distant land. And with television crews showing the carnage wrought by the war, protests mounted against the emergence of an "imperial presidency" in foreign affairs.[22] Congress, the media, and the public sought ways to restrict the president's foreign policy powers, lest America find itself mired in another unpopular, seemingly unwinnable war.[23]

In the aftermath of Vietnam, both the Soviet Union and the United States started to rethink whether fighting wars in far-off lands was worth the steep costs in money and lives. Many in the United States began to question whether the Soviets presented such a large threat. Meanwhile, the financial costs of the Cold War were taking their toll on the Soviet economy. In response to these changes in both states, a move towards more peaceful relations took place. This period of easing of tensions, known as **détente**, fostered Soviet-American cooperation on issues ranging from agricultural trade to space exploration.

While the 1970s were marked by declining tensions between the Soviet Union and the United States, the era of cooperation would not last forever. The 1979 Soviet invasion of Afghanistan soured relations between the two superpowers. American leaders, especially President Ronald Reagan, viewed the Soviets as aggressively pursuing expansion at the expense of the United States and its allies. Referring to the Soviet Union as the "evil empire," Reagan's administration launched a military buildup that nearly doubled Pentagon spending from 1980 to 1985.[24] This resurgence of Cold War hostilities, however, did not last long.

The Cold War ends, but new conflicts surface.

Nearly as quickly as détente faded, the Cold War came to a close. In 1985, a young reform-minded leader named Mikhail Gorbachev took over as Soviet premier. Over the next four years, Gorbachev passed numerous political and economic reforms intended to shore up the flagging Soviet economy. He withdrew Soviet troops from Afghanistan, agreed to arms control with the United States, and permitted democratic reform in the member states of the Warsaw Pact. By the end of 1989, the Berlin Wall, which had long divided communist East Berlin from capitalist West Berlin, was crumbling. And by the end of 1991, East and West Germany re-united and the Soviet Union dissolved.

Scholars continue to debate why the Cold War ended in the way that it did. Some, echoing Kennan, argue that the demise of the Soviet Union was inevitable. A system of centralized government and tight economic controls simply was not sustainable. Others argue that the inability of the Soviet Union to keep pace with

American ingenuity proved decisive. According to this line of argumentation, left to its own devices the Soviet Union might have persisted indefinitely. Competition from the West, however, provided the needed pressure to topple the communist regime. Whatever the precise cause, the peaceful revolutions of 1989–1991 were the most important international events since Pearl Harbor. For four decades, American foreign policy had focused almost exclusively on the Soviet threat. Now the United States was suddenly the world's lone superpower.

The dramatic end of the Cold War spurred a vigorous debate among scholars and policymakers over what America's new grand strategy should be. Four options arose from this debate. Some proposed a return to isolationism, arguing that the United States' geography and nuclear arsenal made it secure enough to disengage from Europe. Others advocated a strategy of *selective engagement*, whereby the U.S. would monitor Europe and the Middle East and intervene only if a clear threat emerged. A third option was *cooperative security*, which envisioned the United States as the leader of a "new world order" that would check aggression anywhere in the world. Finally, some recommended a strategy of American *primacy*, designed to maintain America's overwhelming military and economic power advantage.[25]

In practice, the American grand strategy during the 1990's consisted of a mix of all these policies. The First Gulf War, for instance, combined elements of selective engagement and cooperative security. In 1990, Iraq, then led by President Saddam Hussein, invaded and occupied oil-rich Kuwait. The invasion surprised the international community and drew criticism from nearly every country in the world. By conquering Kuwait, Hussein controlled 20% of the world's oil reserves. If he conquered Saudi Arabia next, that number would jump to 40%—allowing Hussein to manipulate world oil prices and threaten American interests.[26] The invasion also constituted an act of naked aggression, setting a troubling precedent for the post-Cold War world.

In response to the invasion, the United States led a United Nations-sponsored military force to liberate Kuwait and drive back Hussein's Iraqi forces. For many, this successful military campaign signaled the beginning of a new collective security system led by the United States and the United Nations. Japan, Russia, and European Union members all participated in some fashion. Many hoped that a newly empowered United Nations could put a stop to territorial aggression, civil wars, and humanitarian disasters. This had been the organization's founding purpose, and in the First Gulf War it succeeded.

Unfortunately, cooperative security proved to be short lived. For decades, tensions between the Soviet Union and the United States had kept regional conflicts in check. Local populations dared not provoke either superpower in their desire for independence or domination over other populations. With the Cold War's demise, however, these tensions quickly flared, and the United States found itself involved in regional wars in Somalia, Haiti, Bosnia, Serbia, Croatia, and Kosovo.

It was not until September 11, 2001, however, that U.S. foreign policy would fundamentally redefine its grand strategy. The simultaneous attacks on Washington, D.C., and New York that day changed the course of American foreign policy—focusing attention on terrorist groups and non-state actors as never before. Turning away from the previous strategy of collective security, the president announced a series of principles that collectively would become known as the **Bush Doctrine**. When formulating foreign policy, the president said, the United States would treat nations that harbored terrorists the same as they treated the terrorists themselves. The United States would no longer wait for terrorists activities to occur, but instead would launch preemptive strikes (military and otherwise) against emergent threats. And finally, the United States would not allow the

United Nations or any other international organization to dictate when the U.S. would flex its military muscle. If need be, the United States would wage unilateral wars to protect its interests at home and abroad.

In the immediate aftermath of the attacks, the United States began a war to evict al-Qaeda from its safe haven in Afghanistan. Osama bin Laden and his followers had benefited from ties to the Taliban government, which sympathized with their cause. The Taliban allowed the terror group to recruit and train members, as well as plan attacks, from their bases in the country. America's allies and the U.S. public strongly supported the war in Afghanistan, which they saw as a necessary response to September 11.

America's next choice of target, however, stirred controversy. In the spring of 2003, President Bush launched a war against the Saddam Hussein regime in Iraq. The Bush administration based its case for war on intelligence suggesting that Hussein had weapons of mass destruction (WMDs) and ties to al-Qaeda operatives. The president and his advisors raised the possibility that Saddam could hand off nuclear weapons to terrorists, leading to a deadlier version of the September 11 attacks. In an October 2002 speech, Bush warned that a preventive war against Iraq was necessary, claiming, "we cannot wait for the final proof—the smoking gun—that could come in the form of a mushroom cloud."[27] Critics argued that the administration was manipulating intelligence, that Hussein had no relationship with al-Qaeda, and that he could be contained.[28]

The initial invasion of Iraq went quite well for the Americans. However, the process of rebuilding the country and achieving political stability there proved far more difficult. Over the first four years of occupation, American forces suffered nearly 4,000 casualties—this after suffering only 138 during the initial invasion.[29] Moreover, extensive investigations failed to find any evidence of WMDs in Iraq, suggesting that the rationale for the invasion was misguided. The lack of WMDs and the struggle to stabilize Iraq led to dissatisfaction with the Bush administration over the war. In January 2008, polls showed that only 30% of the American public approved of Bush's handling of Iraq.[30]

Even as the United States continues its efforts to stabilize Iraq, new threats and challenges have emerged. These include domestic instability in Pakistan, a nuclear nation and a major American ally in the "war on terror;" concerns over the rising power of a non-democratic China; the ongoing hostilities in Afghanistan; Russia's backsliding toward totalitarianism; and continued violence between Israelis and Palestinians. These are all examples of the daunting challenges that continue to face the United States.

The Role of the Foreign Policy Bureaucracy

No other individual dominates U.S. foreign policymaking as much as the president. As discussed in Chapter 14, presidents exercise extraordinary power in foreign affairs. As commander-in-chief, the president decides when troops will be deployed, for how long, and what their mission will be. As chief diplomat, the president often holds summits with foreign heads of state about the major issues of the day. And as chief administrator, the president appoints many of the individuals who are charged with developing and implementing foreign policy. Serving the president in these various roles is a massive foreign policy bureaucracy. This bureaucracy plays crucial roles in both the definition of grand strategies and the development of particular policies that dictate U.S. relations with particular nations.

The National Security Council advises the president.

Thousands of individuals within the executive branch oversee foreign affairs, as discussed in the chapters on the presidency and bureaucracy. In many ways, the executive agency closest to the president on issues of foreign policy is the **National Security Council (NSC)**. Formed in 1947, the NSC coordinates the activities of the armed forces and other executive agencies (e.g., State, Defense, the CIA) to increase national security cooperation. The NSC assists the president in gathering advice from various agencies and departments.

By law, the NSC must include the vice president, the National Security Advisor (NSA), the Secretary of State, the chairman of the Joint Chiefs of Staff, and the Secretary of Defense. In practice, most presidents have chosen to include more individuals than these. In addition to the formal council, the NSC also includes staff assistants, whose roles have grown in size and importance over the years. Indeed, over time, the formal decision-making council of the NSC has declined in importance, while the staff's centrality to the decision-making process has grown. Recall that it was members of the NSC staff, including Oliver North, who were the focus of the Iran-Contra scandal.

Stephen Hadley served as National Security Advisor under President Bush. It was his job to mediate discussions within the NSC and to personally advise the president about foreign policy matters. As a close confidant of the president, Hadley communicated between the conflicting interests of various parts of the government. He then provided advice to the president on issues of national security.

The State Department oversees U.S. diplomacy.

At its core, foreign policy is about **diplomacy**—that is, the ongoing negotiation of economic and political relationships between different countries. Historically, the

State Department has held primary responsibility for U.S. diplomacy. The **State Department** is the agency home of diplomats, embassies, and most foreign aid programs run by the U.S. government. The primary job of the State Department is to represent U.S. interests overseas and in various international organizations. In so doing, it communicates with foreign governments and publics, and it provides analysis on events abroad and their implications for American foreign policy. The State Department also negotiates treaties and agreements, makes policy recommendations, and takes steps to implement them. Finally, the Department coordinates with the Agency for International Development (USAID) to oversee American foreign aid.

As Figure 18.1 highlights, State operates hundreds of foreign embassies and consulates all over the globe. Roughly thirty thousand employees, of which 3,500 are Foreign Service Officers (FSOs) or diplomats, work in these outposts. These FSOs work alongside personnel from other federal departments and agencies including Defense, Commerce, Agriculture, Homeland Security, USAID, and the Peace Corps.[31] Other employees include support staff, like security officers, secretaries, and drivers, many of whom are foreign nationals. Many FSOs work in foreign embassies, which serve as outposts for U.S. diplomacy efforts abroad.

State is very hierarchical. The Secretary of State leads the State Department, and is the most visible and notable figure of American diplomacy. Beneath the Secretary is the Deputy Secretary and then several Undersecretaries in charge of planning and coordination. State Department bureaus are organized in two ways: by issue and by region. Some bureaus focus on particular regions, while others are tasked with particular issues cutting across regions (such as AIDS policy or counterterrorism). Bureaus charged with regions then coordinate desk officers and personnel who focus on particular countries.

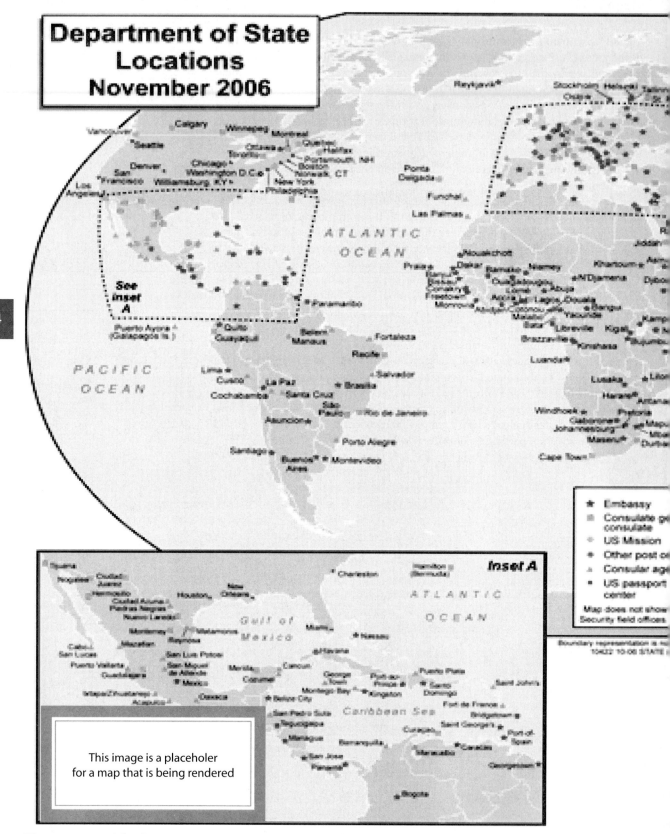

Figure 18-1. **The State Department Maintains Diplomatic Outposts Worldwide**. To come

Source: U. S. Department of State, available online at: http://www.state.gov/cms_images/fy2006par_DoS_LocationsMap.gif. Accessed March 6, 2008.

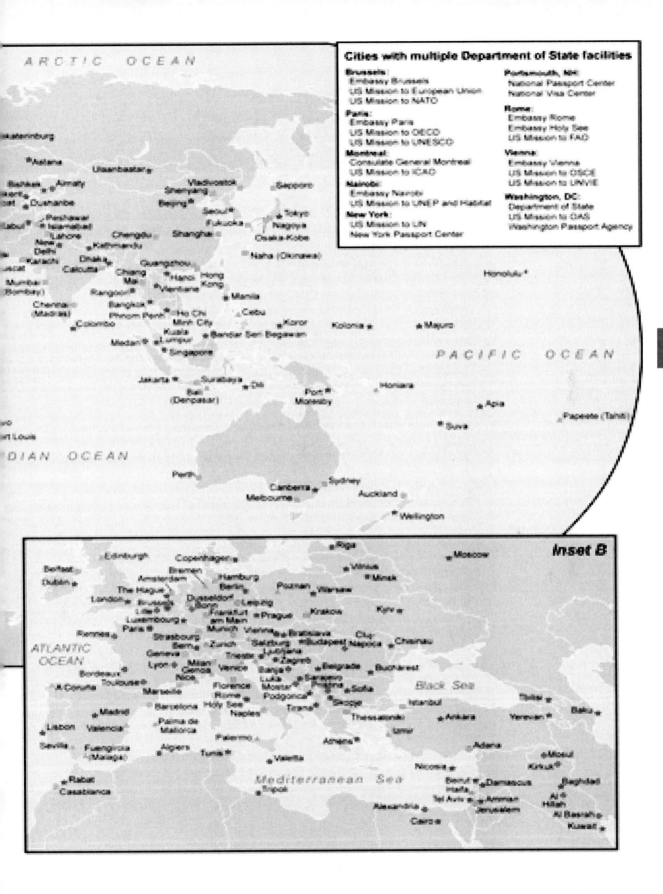

Cities with multiple Department of State facilities

Brussels:
Embassy Brussels
US Mission to European Union
US Mission to NATO

Paris:
Embassy Paris
US Mission to OECD
US Mission to UNESCO

Montreal:
Consulate General Montreal
US Mission to ICAO

Nairobi:
Embassy Nairobi
US Mission to UNEP and Habitat

New York:
US Mission to UN
New York Passport Center

Portsmouth, NH:
National Passport Center
National Visa Center

Rome:
Embassy Rome
Embassy Holy See
US Mission to FAO

Vienna:
Embassy Vienna
US Mission to OSCE
US Mission to UNVIE

Washington, DC:
Department of State
US Mission to OAS
Washington Passport Agency

Inset B

Do Economic Sanctions Work?

The Question

Effective diplomacy includes the right blend of carrots and sticks. Carrots typically consist of things like foreign aid, preferential trade agreements, and promises of military assistance that are meant to reward other governments for doing things that the United States supports. Sticks, by contrast, consist of various forms of punishment that are meant to discourage certain kinds of behaviors and policies.

In foreign affairs, economic sanctions are one of the most frequent sticks employed by the U.S. government against either single countries or groups of countries. Common sanctions include trade blockades, taxes placed on imports, and quotas on the amounts of goods that are traded between countries. Through sanctions, the State Department can pursue objectives ranging from signaling its displeasure toward other countries to undermining domestic support for another government. But while sanctions have a long history, do they achieve their intended goals? How do we know?

Why It Matters

During the 1990s and 2000s, the United States levied sanctions against countries ranging from Iran to Cuba to Iraq to India. And as we discuss in further detail below, in 2002 the George W. Bush Administration imposed tariffs on imported goods from China and India, leading the World Trade Organization to organize sanctions of its own against the United States. If sanctions are ineffective, though, then other more aggressive tactics might be called for, at the expense of U.S. lives and treasure. One goal of sanctions is to avoid military action.

Investigating the Answer

How might we determine whether sanctions are an effective tool of foreign policy? Scholars began to assess the effectiveness of sanctions by building a large data set that cataloged incidents of sanctions, their goals, and their effects. This initial work, by Gary Hufbauer, Jeffrey Schott, and Kimberly Elliot, found 116 episodes of economic sanctions placed by all states in the world from World War I to 1990.[32] These scholars concluded that sanctions could be effective as long as the goals were modest. Sanctions that were designed to change aspects of a foreign government's trade policies, for instance, stood some chance at success. But sanctions put in place to achieve more difficult goals, such as unseating stable regimes, have not performed as well. Moreover, Hufbauer and his colleagues argued that more recent sanctions have been less successful overall—likely owing to increasing globalization and the ease with which states can find new trade partners to replace those cut off by sanctions.

Numerous scholars, however, have questioned these conclusions. Daniel Drezner has argued that the key to sanctions success is the expectations of future conflict between the sanctioner and the sanctioned.[33] If sanctions are part of a larger pattern of conflict between states (that is, they are placed after a war or years of disagreements), they are unlikely to work. Drezner used the Hufbauer et al. data set to show that allies, who are unlikely to have a long history of differences, were more likely to successfully sanction each other and that sanctions were rarely successful when the opposing states were adversaries before the sanctions episode.

Later, Dean Lacy and Emerson Niou challenged the idea that the sanctions data used by these earlier scholars was complete.[34] They argued that potential targets of sanctions, hoping to prevent damage to their economy, may give in to international pressure prior to sanctions' taking effect. If this is common, then we are likely to see sanctions levied only in the most difficult cases, when the target state does not back down on the threat of sanctions. Because unneeded sanctions are never levied, they are not cataloged in the sanctions data set. Lacy and Niou therefore used several historical case studies to show how foreign governments, anticipating future sanctions, might change their behavior; and so doing, these governments made the actual imposition of sanctions unnecessary.

Even if a complete dataset of sanctions were assembled, though, challenges to a scholar interested in evaluating their success would persist. How, after all, should one go about determining whether sanctions achieved their stated goals? On the one hand, this seems straightforward—states adopt sanctions to force other states to change their behavior in reasonably clear ways. And scholars can observe whether target states change their behavior or not. Things are more complicated, however.

For starters, sanctions are often multilateral—that is, they are levied by multiple states, and different states may have different goals. For example, were the sanctions placed on Iraq after its 1990 invasion of Kuwait successful? They did not bring about a withdrawal from Kuwait—that took a war led by the United States and a large coalition of states. After the war, many states continued the sanctions in order to pressure Saddam Hussein to not attack Kurds and Shiites, to undermine his ability to rebuild his army, and to unseat him. While states differed in their justifications for the sanctions, they also differed in their assessments of whether the sanctions were working, leading some to lift sanctions against Iraq long before others were willing to do so. Much of the existing scholarship on sanctions has not dealt with this complication. Rather, most continue to use the Hufbauer et al. data, which treats each sanction episode as one unified sender and target, even if multiple states are senders or targets.

The Bottom Line

The debate over the effectiveness of economic sanctions is complex, but important. Given the frequent use of sanctions by foreign policymakers, it is crucial to be able to evaluate their effectiveness. The general conclusion is that, under certain circumstances, sanctions can be effective: namely, when the goals are modest, when the sanctions are against an ally, and when the costs to the sanctioned state are very high. Research continues in this area and future studies will no doubt further refine our knowledge of the conditions under which economic sanctions are likely to be successful.[35]

The Defense Department focuses on the military.

The primary responsibility of the **Defense Department** is to defend the nation from external attack. Increasingly, though, the United States has relied upon the Defense Department to pursue a wide variety of other objectives. In just the last two decades, the military has conducted counterterrorism efforts in the Middle East, provided assistance to war-torn areas in Africa, enforced peace agreements as peacekeepers in Eastern Europe, and trained other militaries for anti-drug operations in South America. This expansive set of missions has increased the importance of the American military and raised conflicts between the military and its civilian leaders over the appropriate uses of American military personnel.

As shown in Figure 18.2, expenditures by the Department of Defense far eclipse expenditures by the Department of State. Although Defense spending has varied with historical events—such as the escalation of the Vietnam War in the mid-1960s and the Reagan buildup of the 1980s—it trends clearly upwards. State Department spending has also grown over time, but at a much slower rate. As a result, these two agencies' budgets have increasingly diverged over the past several decades.

At the end of the Cold War, military spending fell significantly, creating a small "peace dividend" brought by declining superpower tensions. This trend, however, quickly reversed with the terrorist attacks of 2001. Military expenditures now outstrip even those observed during the Cold War, surpassing $400 billion annually, not even counting the costs of wars in Afghanistan and Iraq. In 2006, the United States accounted for 46 percent of the world's total military expenditures. Indeed, America spends more on its military than the next 14 states combined.[36]

Despite its size, the Defense Department is relatively young. It was created in 1947 to replace the Department of War, a weak institution that did not include the U.S. Navy and usually lay dormant until a major conflict arose. In the Cold War era, when the United States sought to meet any threat presented by the Soviet Union, a more permanent military establishment was needed. Thus began the growth of the Department of Defense into the largest executive branch agency—an agency that employed over 35 percent of all federal government workers in 2007.[37]

Various Secretaries of Defense have had smaller or larger roles in shaping the military as an institution. One of the most influential Secretaries of Defense was Robert McNamara, who served under presidents Kennedy and Johnson. As the former head of Ford Motor Company, McNamara brought a business mentality to the Defense Department. He cut waste, streamlined information systems, and introduced cost-benefit analysis into the budgetary process. Although he attracted internal criticism for treating Defense like a business and external criticism for escalating the Vietnam War, many consider McNamara one of the most influential Secretaries in modern times.

A more recent but no less controversial Secretary was Donald Rumsfeld, who served under George W. Bush. Rumsfeld argued that recent changes in military technology made large armies less important to military victory. He thus pressured the military to give up its conception of war as battles of attrition and instead to focus on becoming a smaller, more mobile, but highly lethal fighting force. Military leaders resisted this goal, as well as Rumsfeld's tendency to micromanage. Rumsfeld resigned in November 2006, the day after Democrats regained control of Congress in that year's midterm election.

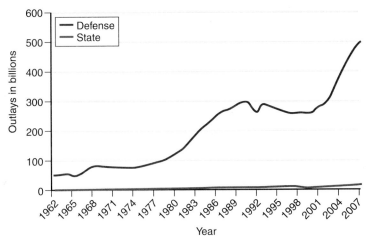

Figure 18-2. **The Defense Department Has Always Been Bigger Than the State Department.** Shown here are the annual defense and state department outlays between 1962 and 2006. The Defense Department has always had a larger budget than the State Department, but Defense Department spending increased substantially during the Reagan administration.

Source: *Historical Tables: Budget of the United States Government: Fiscal Year 2008*, pp. 73–78. Available online from: http://www.gpoaccess.gov/usbudget/fy08/browse.html. Accessed February 8, 2008.

A wide variety of executive agencies provide intelligence services.

To formulate U.S. foreign policy, the government needs reliable information about goings-on around the globe—about the activities and objectives of other states, the creation of new alliances between states and the dissolution of old ones, possible threats to U.S. economic and political interests, and many other things besides. This "intelligence" crucially facilitates the State Department's diplomatic efforts and the Defense Department's war planning.

Since World War II, the **Central Intelligence Agency (CIA)** has had primary responsibility for collecting and analyzing foreign intelligence. The CIA is fairly large organization, although the size of its budget and staff are classified. The popular conception of the CIA depicts the Agency's employees as shadowy figures staging cloak-and-dagger operations to overthrow foreign governments. This reputation is not altogether undeserved. In the immediate aftermath of World War II, for instance, the CIA engaged in activities as diverse as influencing election outcomes, sponsoring coups, and assassinating foreign leaders. The CIA's success in these endeavors led to its increased use as an operational foreign policy tool, sometimes replacing traditional military forces.

For the most part, though, CIA employees undertake far more mundane operations—monitoring overseas news for signs of crises, reading and analyzing reports from field offices abroad, briefing executive branch members or Congress of looming threats to American interests, or simply distilling the massive amounts of information it gathers. Historically, the CIA has enjoyed tremendous power and latitude to conduct such operations. Yet, it is subject to considerable scrutiny and occupies a challenging role. When a surprise event occurs, Congress often holds the CIA accountable for neglecting to anticipate it. If the CIA fails, all Americans see the outcome—a revolution, bombing, or other incident that harms American interests. Yet, when the agency succeeds in thwarting secret threats, it receives no public accolades. The CIA must walk a fine line between "crying wolf" too often and keeping the White House prepared for potential problems.

It is not surprising, then, that the agency received substantial blame for failing to foresee the September 11 terrorist attacks in New York and Washington, D.C. Some of these criticisms, though, may not have been warranted. After all, the CIA had been taking steps since the late 1990s to capture al-Qaeda ringleader Osama bin Laden. According to journalist Bob Woodward, CIA Director George J. Tenet worried obsessively about the prospect of a major terrorist attack on the homeland. During the summer of 2001, American intelligence had intercepted 34 al-Qaeda messages referencing an upcoming event. This "chatter" indicated something was brewing, but did not provide the date or location of the attack.[38]

The CIA, however, is not the only agency charged with collecting and analyzing national security intelligence. In fact, a veritable alphabet soup of agencies has such responsibilities. The National Security Agency (NSA) is one of the more prominent ones. Formed in 1952, the NSA monitors communications coming into and out of the United States. For decades, its existence was denied by the U.S. government, leading many to quip that NSA stood for "No Such Agency." The NSA also specializes in cryptography—the making and breaking of secret codes. It is probably the largest intelligence agency in terms of personnel.[39]

The Defense Department operates the Defense Intelligence Agency (DIA). Founded in 1961, the DIA is supposed to supply intelligence and analysis to the Secretary of Defense and the Joint Chiefs. Similarly, each military service branch conducts its own intelligence activities. The Army, Navy, Air Force, and Marines, accordingly, regularly contribute to the development of foreign policy strategies. In the State Department, the Bureau for Intelligence and Research (INR) does not gather intelligence directly, but creates intelligence reports for the Secretary of State based the knowledge of its area experts. Even the Federal Bureau of Investigation (FBI), which is supposed to focus on domestic security issues, is involved in intelligence. FBI tracks international terror suspects who travel to the United States, and keep tabs on any terrorist group that may attempt to find resources in America.

With so many different agencies pursuing overlapping mandates, the foreign policy bureaucracy is neither as efficient nor as effective as many would like. In the aftermath of September 11, therefore, the Office of National Intelligence (ONI) was created to oversee the many intelligence agencies in the federal government. In theory, the ONI coordinates the analysis of intelligence from *all* sectors of the intelligence community, including the CIA, FBI, INR, and all Defense agencies. In practice, this is difficult since each agency attempts to protect its turf (and thereby its budget). After all, if one agency could claim to have stopped a September 11th-type incident, it would stand to gain tremendous prestige and resources. Although the Office of National Intelligence has worked hard to coordinate the activities of all these executive branch agencies, it continues to encounter significant resistance.

The **Department of Homeland Security (DHS)** was also created in the aftermath of September 11. Like the ONI, DHS coordinates the work of agencies involved in preventing and responding to attacks on the United States. The Director of Homeland Security is a cabinet-level official who, in theory, has the power to coordinate intelligence, analysis, and response to strikes against the United States. Creation of the DHS merged 22 agencies with over 177,000 employees. It combined agencies as varied as the Secret Service, U.S. Customs, the Immigration and Naturalization Service (INS), the Federal Emergency Management Agency (FEMA), and the Coast Guard. It has yet to be seen whether ONI and DHS, in combination, can effectively coordinate the efforts of their respective agencies charged with collecting the information needed to formulate U.S. foreign policy.

The Role of Congress

Presidents stand front-and-center in debates about foreign policy. Congress, nonetheless, plays an important role. True, legislators may be less involved in foreign policy than in domestic policy, but it would be incorrect to claim, even during the Cold War, that Congress has sat silently by, ceding all authority to the president. As we survey the various foreign policy powers of Congress, we will highlight historical examples of Congress attempting to check presidential influence over foreign policy.

Congress enacts foreign policy statutes.

Congress legislates on a variety of foreign policy topics: weapons programs, foreign aid, environmental standards, and numerous other issues. Sometimes Congress wields influence by crafting legislation. The energy bill that became law in December 2007, for instance, sought to reduce America's dependence on foreign oil by mandating conservation measures, greater fuel efficiency in vehicles, and funding for alternative energy sources. At other times, Congress uses appropriations bills to provide more or less funding than the president has requested for specific projects, ranging from military operations in the Middle East to humanitarian ventures in the Southeast Asia.

Members of Congress tend to pay special attention to foreign trade, for it has immediate implications for the nation's economic growth, unemployment, and the cost of goods to the average citizen. The key issue in trade policy concerns **tariffs**, which are taxes upon goods exchanged between nations. As you might expect, high tariffs tend to discourage trade, while lower tariffs tend to promote it.

The most significant trade agreement in recent history is the **North American Free Trade Agreement (NAFTA)**. NAFTA's roots lie in the 1988 Canada-U.S. Free Trade Agreement, which aimed to steadily decrease tariffs and non-tariff barriers to trade and investment between the two countries. In the early 1990s, Mexican President Carlos Salinas expressed strong interest in extending the agreement to his own country. Salinas, U.S. President George H.W. Bush, and Canadian Prime Minister Brian Mulroney worked to build domestic support for the trilateral measure, and the three executives signed NAFTA in December 1992. Bush's failed re-election bid could have derailed congressional ratification, but instead the incoming president, Bill Clinton, took up the cause in 1993. In November 1993, NAFTA passed in both the House and the Senate.[40]

Some areas of the country benefit from freer trade because their industries produce goods that are export-oriented—that is, most of the goods made are sold overseas. Given that free trade agreements also mean that the other countries in the agreement will cut their own tariffs, this decreases the price of American goods overseas, leading to more sales. This can increase revenue, create jobs, and cut the costs of goods to consumers. Other industries, though, may suffer from free trade. Factories that are not efficient may close, jobs may be lost, and economic growth may falter. Different countries and districts have different specializations. Thus, free trade can be seen as good or bad, depending on the particular district in question and the country with which the United States is signing the agreement.

Congress also influences the foreign policymaking process through procedural legislation—that is, legislation that changes how institutions in the executive branch are structured or operate on a day-to-day basis. For example, after a number of high-profile military operations were carried out in a haphazard manner, Congress passed the Goldwater-Nichols Act, which mandated that the Chairman of the Joint Chiefs of Staff be the primary military advisor to the president and be in charge of long-range military planning and budget coordination. It also required that the staff of the Joint Chiefs serve only the Chairman, rather than the commanders of the individual service branches. With this Act, members of Congress hoped to give the Chairman more institutional powers, thereby reducing inter-branch competition for budget and operations and leading to better military advice and performance.

Finally, Congress occasionally enacts symbolic resolutions that may have implications for foreign policy. In the fall of 2007, the House passed a resolution labeling the killing of thousands of Armenians in Turkey during World War I a "genocide." Normally, such resolutions turn few heads. This resolution, however, came at a time when the Bush Administration was attempting to secure Turkish cooperation in the northern regions of Iraq, where Kurdish guerillas were operating. Insisting that Armenians had died as a part of the war and not as a result of systematic killing, Turkey responded to the resolution by recalling its ambassador and threatening to stop cooperation with the United States. Though eventually tabled before going to the Senate, the proposed resolution caused quite a diplomatic row.

Congress retains the power to declare war.

Congress's constitutional authority to declare war places it in the middle of debates over proposed uses of force by the American military. Perhaps no area of congressional-presidential politics has received more attention than the question of who has the ultimate authority to initiate and oversee the conduct of war.[41] One reason for the pitched debate is that the Constitution is vague by design: while Congress is given the power to declare war, the president is the commander-in-chief of the military. Consequentially, leadership of the military and its mission is divided. By constitutional design, Congress and the president must share the power to initiate and sustain armed conflict against an adversary.

Undoubtedly, the president maintains important advantages over Congress in the realm of military policy. For example, while Congress can call hearings to gather information about a potential or actual military conflict, the president has the NSC, including all the major military and civilian figures, at his or her beck-and-call in a moment's notice. As a result, the president often is able to respond more quickly—and with more information—than Congress.

Congress, however, occasionally challenges the president's war powers. In response to what many argued was a failed deployment in Vietnam, Congress passed the War Powers Act in 1973. The law, passed over Nixon's veto, placed several legal constraints on the executive's ability to initiate international conflict. First, the president must consult with Congress *before* committing armed forces into hostile situations. Second, the president must report to Congress within 48 hours after troops are introduced into an area where hostilities exist or are imminent. Third, and most important, the troops must be withdrawn within 60 days unless Congress authorizes them to stay longer.[42]

On paper, the War Powers Act would appear to be a significant constraint on executive authority. In practice, though, the Act has constrained the president less than its designers had hoped. Never has the Act been used to end a military venture. Indeed, the 60-day clock has been started only once, after the 1983 invasion of Lebanon. But in that case, Congress immediately approved an 18-month extension. The infrequency of its use has led some scholars to condemn the Act as "a sellout, a surrender."[43] Other scholars, however, argue that the Act has persuaded at least some presidents to limit military actions to shorter, smaller campaigns.[44]

Congress confirms nominees for foreign policy positions.

As explained in Chapter 13, the Senate has the power to confirm individuals nominated to various cabinet-level and ambassadorial posts. Although the vast majority is confirmed, the hearings often reveal pointed debates over aspects of foreign policy. Controversy is especially likely when a nominee seems underqualified or substantially diverges from the policy positions held by members of the Senate Committee on Foreign Relations, which must first approve the nomination in committee hearings.

Occasionally, a high-profile nominee is rejected or held up to such scrutiny that a president opts to withdraw the nomination. In 1989 President George H.W. Bush withdrew the nomination of John Tower as Secretary of Defense, and in 1997 President Clinton withdrew the nomination of Anthony Lake as director of the CIA. In August 2005 President George W. Bush took advantage of a congressional recess to appoint John Bolton as ambassador to the United Nations until the sitting Congress concluded in January 2007. Bolton had faced five months of strong opposition from Senate Democrats, who expressed concern over his confrontational temperament and allegations that he had manipulated intelligence while working at the State Department. The Bush administration cited the large number of recess appointments made by other presidents and portrayed the Bolton decision as a necessary move to avoid further "partisan delaying tactics."[45] Nevertheless, recess appointments for such high-level positions have been rare. Foreign states and international organizations, after all, want to have assurances that the U.S. officials with whom they negotiate have the full backing of the U.S. government.

Congress provides "advice and consent" on international treaties.

The Senate also has the power to ratify **treaties** signed by the President. There have been several high profile instances of the Senate rejecting treaties signed by the president, thus dealing a blow to the ongoing conduct of foreign policy. In the most famous instance, as mentioned earlier, the Senate rejected American involvement in the League of Nations after World War I, returning the United States to a course of isolationism for another two decades. In 1999, the Comprehensive Test Ban Treaty (CTBT) was rejected by the U.S. Senate after Republicans objected to several provisions.

Rejection is quite rare, however. In fact, the Senate itself reports that the full body voted to reject only 21 of the approximately 1,500 treaties it has considered since 1789.[46] Still, if they are worried about Congress's reaction, presidents can bypass the treaty ratification process by signing an **executive agreement**, which automatically is binding on state signatories. Indeed, of the 18,000 international agreements entered into by the U.S. between 1789 and 2000, only 2,000 have been in the form of a treaty requiring consent of the Senate.[47] As discussed in Chapter 14, the ratio of executive agreements to treaties has steadily increased during the past half century. Presidents have made executive agreements involving alliances, trade, finance, and a variety of other areas.

Executive agreements, however, do not allow presidents to do exactly as they please. Congress may pass a law that rescinds an executive agreement, or it may refuse to appropriate the funds needed to implement it. In addition, executive agreements tend to survive for shorter periods of time, as future presidents are free to overturn them unilaterally.

Congress oversees foreign policy bureaucracies.

Congress also influences foreign policy through oversight. At any point, either chamber can convene hearings on topics related to the conduct of foreign policy. While legislation may or may not result from these fact-finding exercises, the hearings themselves sometimes generate tremendous publicity about issues. This power of investigation can be powerful in setting the stage for new laws or simply bringing the public's attention to a particular issue.

In September 2007, for example, General David Petraeus and Ambassador Ryan Crocker provided much-anticipated testimony concerning the ongoing war in Iraq. Democrats and Republicans alike used the hearings to trumpet their positions. Ike Skelton (D-MO), chair of the House Armed Services Committee, complained that the troops in Iraq "are not available to go into Afghanistan to pursue Osama bin Laden and other Al Qaeda leaders who ordered an attack on us one day short of six years ago."[48] Meanwhile, Ileana Ros-Lehtinen (R-FL), the senior Republican on the House Foreign Affairs Committee, decried the differences between "those of us who are inspired by this new 'greatest generation' and believe that we should confront and defeat Al Qaeda and other jihadists on the Iraqi battlefield, and those of us who believe that we should simply retreat."[49] Through the hearings, the American public also learned of some nagging uncertainties. Asked whether ethnic reconciliation in Iraq appeared likely, Ambassador Crocker pointed to encouraging signs but admitted, "How long that is going to take and . . . whether it will succeed, I can't predict."[50] When Senator John Warner (R-VA) inquired whether Petraeus's proposed troop surge would make the U.S. safer, the general replied, "Sir, I don't know, actually."[51]

The Role of Interest Groups

The federal government does not determine foreign policy in a vacuum. Indeed, numerous interest groups weigh in with advice of their own. Domestic policy certainly attracts a great number of interest groups—but the groups that focus on foreign policy tend to be particularly well funded, well organized, and influential. They include three major types: ethnic lobbies, business groups, and think tanks.

Ethnic lobbies advocate foreign policies that concern a specific country.

Some of the most prominent foreign policy interest groups are **ethnic lobbies**. These groups advocate policies that focus on specific foreign states. In some instances, ethnic lobbies encourage great U.S. assistance to a foreign state. In other instances, they pressure the federal government to take a hard line against the foreign state's governing regime.

One of the more controversial interest groups in American foreign affairs is the American-Israeli Public Affairs Committee (AIPAC). Founded in 1953, AIPAC promotes close ties between Israel and the United States. Detractors have long criticized it for pressuring American decision-makers to support and aid Israel even when its policies cause difficulties in American relations with other Middle Eastern countries. However, the close relationship between the United States and Israel would likely have developed and prospered without AIPAC. After all, the United States began sending large quantities of weapons to Israel in the mid-1960s. Even then, U.S. decision-makers saw Israel as one of the few stable, pro-Western allies in a hostile region. The Soviet Union had garnered staunch allies such as Syria and Egypt, and other pro-Western states such as Lebanon and Jordan faced consistent internal threats.

Cuban-Americans make up another powerful ethnic lobby. Following Fidel Castro's 1959 communist revolution, many Cubans fled to the United States, particularly to Florida. Initially, the exiles hoped to return to their homeland once democracy had been restored. As Castro solidified one-party communist rule, however, the focus turned to isolating Cuba. By 1962, the U.S. had enacted an economic embargo against its neighbor to the south, and in 1996 the embargo was bolstered by the Helms-Burton Act, which placed even more stringent restrictions on Cuba-U.S. relations.

To be sure, the Cuban-American ethnic lobby exhibits a number of characteristics that could contribute to foreign policy influence: it is well-organized, geographically concentrated, well-funded, and motivated by involuntary exile.[52] However, in light of the anti-communism atmosphere of the Cold War, one could question whether the lobby was decisive in the United States' efforts to isolate Cuba. The key pitfall in considering the role of interest groups is witnessing the outcome of a foreign policy decision and assuming the process. Just because American foreign policy choices support the interests of a pressure group does not mean the pressure group was effective. Consider the classic political science definition of power paraphrased from the political scientist Robert Dahl: power is the ability to convince others to do things they would otherwise not do.[53] To show an interest group has power or influence, one must show that a policy would have been different without the group's pressure. This is difficult to determine. After all, how do we know what would have happened if it did not?

Business groups increasingly attempt to influence foreign policy.

Perhaps the most powerful set of foreign policy pressures arises from multinational business and defense firms. Traditionally, some of the more powerful lobby groups in America have been those involved in the production and sales of military goods. In his farewell address, President Eisenhower warned against "the acquisition of unwanted influence, whether sought or unsought, by the military-industrial complex."[54] The "military-industrial complex" has become a pejorative catch-phrase used by those who oppose the influence of big business, especially in the realm of national security policy.

The phrase suggests a handful of business and military elites conspiring to drive up (possibly unnecessary) defense spending. The fact is, though, that numerous segments of American society—including Congress, academia, business, and the military establishment—have aligned interests concerning defense spending. Various interests clearly benefit from defense spending: the military can be ready to defend the national interest, businesses can make money and spur economic growth, individuals can find and keep jobs, and each of these benefits helps members of Congress get re-elected. One analysis of defense spending during the Cold War concluded that 1 in 10 jobs in the U.S. relied, either directly or indirectly, on federal defense spending.[55] At a time when defense budgets are nearing $500 billion, the dependence of many businesses on defense spending is clearly enormous.

Other businesses lobby the government on a host of foreign policy issues, but perhaps no issue is more common than trade. As previously discussed, because so many individuals benefit *and* suffer from trade, thousands of industry-based groups have formed to lobby Congress and the president for more or less protection. Each time free trade discussions begin with a new country, lobbying groups support or oppose the proposals, based on whether their industries will be helped or harmed. In 2002, for example, while the United States and Chile haggled over free trade proposals, the National Association of Manufacturers estimated that the lack of an agreement had resulted in a total $800 million in foregone exports to Chile. U.S. farm lobbies, on the other hand, insisted that the negotiations should not affect American agricultural subsidies. The resulting bilateral agreement, which was ratified in July 2003, greatly reduced tariffs on tractors and other machinery items, while leaving agricultural subsidies intact.[56]

Think tanks offer foreign policy advice.

Think tanks support and publicize the work of scholars, many of whom have significant foreign policy expertise. Drawing on their government experience or academic research, these scholars contribute to newsletters, magazines, journals, and opinion pieces advocating particular policies. And under certain circumstances, their opinions resonate widely.

One of America's most prominent think tanks is contained within the New York-based Council on Foreign Relations (CFR), which publishes the influential journal *Foreign Affairs*. Founded in 1921, the CFR grew out of an informal band of foreign policy experts who advised President Woodrow Wilson toward the end of World War I. In planning for a post-war world, this group helped to formulate Wilson's Fourteen Points, planting the seed for the United Nations system and other innovations in international relations. Following World War II, the CFR again demonstrated its influence. In an anonymous *Foreign Affairs* article, George Kennan—a Council member and State Department official—made the case that the United States should limit the Soviet Union's expansionist tendencies.[57] Containment, as discussed above, became the key American grand strategy during the Cold War.

The Council on Foreign Relations is not alone in offering foreign policy insights. In July 2007, two members of the Brookings Institution, a left-of-center think tank based in Washington, D.C., published a striking op-ed in the *New York Times*. Following an eight-day visit to Iraq, Michael O'Hanlan and Kenneth Pollack praised the "surge" in U.S. troop levels and chided opponents for ignoring encouraging changes. "We are finally getting somewhere in Iraq, at least in military terms," they declared. "We were surprised by the gains we saw and the potential to produce not necessarily 'victory' but a sustainable stability that both we and the Iraqis could live with."[58] The opinion piece drew attention to improvements that numerous observers had overlooked. And because it was written by critics of George W. Bush's prior handling of the Iraq War, the opinion piece had a dramatic influence on Washington debates about the war.

CaseStudy: Interest Groups Call for Funds to Combat AIDS in Africa

In early 2003, President George W. Bush announced a major effort to fight AIDS overseas. The President's Emergency Plan for AIDS Relief focused on 15 countries: Botswana, Cote d'Ivoire, Ethiopia, Kenya, Mozambique, Namibia, Nigeria, Rwanda, South Africa, Tanzania, Uganda, Zambia, Haiti, Guyana, and Vietnam. The initiative, which called for $15 billion over five years to fund prevention, treatment, and orphan care, surpassed the aid of any previous administration.[59] Five years later, in 2008, Congress enthusiastically exceeded Bush's request by another $4 billion.[60]

Congress is not always so eager to provide such generous allotments of foreign aid. Only a few years earlier, the Clinton administration fought with Congress to secure just $225 million in global AIDS spending.[61] What explains such a remarkable turn of events? Interest groups, it seems, put pressure on the president and congressional leaders to do something about the spread of AIDS in developing countries. The most prominent of these interest groups, however, did not consist of ethnic lobbies, business groups, or think tanks. Rather, they consisted of Christian organizations and an especially entrepreneurial rock star.

In February 2002, Franklin Graham—the son of evangelist Billy Graham and founder of the charity Samaritan's Purse—sponsored the first "international Christian conference on HIV/AIDS." Graham announced that it was his Christian duty to "bring healing, to bring love, to bring compassion" to the sick and dying.[62]

The Irish rock star Bono subsequently advocated for combating AIDS, framing the issue as a moral imperative for Christians. In a meeting with conservative Senator Jesse Helms (R-SC), Bono pointed out that 2,103 verses of Scripture pertain to the poor, but Jesus mentions judgment only once.[63] Helms was moved by such arguments. In March, the influential senator published an op-ed piece in the *Washington Post* renouncing his lifelong skepticism of foreign aid and arguing for increased federal government spending on programs to combat AIDS abroad. This development was "like Nixon going to China," according to Patrick Cronin, a former assistant administrator at the Agency for International Development.[64]

Other conservative politicians also played instrumental roles. Senator Jeff Sessions (R-AL) held two congressional hearings about the role of unsafe healthcare in spreading the disease.[65] Senator Bill Frist (R-TN), a physician, co-sponsored a bill offering millions of dollars to prevent mother-to-child transmissions. In addition, key members of the Bush administration embraced the issue.

Chief-of-staff Josh Bolten and National Security Advisor Condoleeza Rice supported expanding foreign aid to fight AIDS.[66] Treasury Secretary Paul O'Neill ended his fact-finding trip to Africa by concluding that "there could no longer be any excuse for failure to address the basic needs of the world's poorest people."[67] President Bush himself compared AIDS to genocide, implying that fighting it was a moral imperative.[68] Expressing solidarity with his religious constituents, he declared that "everybody has worth, everybody matters, everybody was created by the Almighty."[69]

The president also had strategic reasons for backing the policy. In 2002, Bush highlighted the danger of allowing Africa to become a devastated region that would produce terrorists.[70] Bush further hoped that AIDS relief would improve America's tarnished international reputation. Among members of the Organization for Economic Cooperation and Development, the United States had ranked last or near last in terms of foreign development aid as a percentage of gross national income (GNI) for many years. While countries such as Denmark, the Netherlands, Sweden, Norway, and Luxembourg donated around 1 percent of their GNI, the United States contributed only about *one-tenth of* 1 percent.[71]

The administration and its congressional allies brought more than rhetoric to the table. Republican leaders introduced an ambitious 5-year, $15 billion plan that moved beyond mother-to-child transmission and the traditional focus on prevention. The resulting legislation—the U.S. Leadership against HIV/AIDS, Tuberculosis, and Malaria Act of 2003—allocated 55 percent of the funds to treatment, 20 percent to prevention, 15 percent to care for the dying, and 10 percent to orphans.[72] It aimed to treat 2 million people, provide care for 10 million, and prevent 7 million new infections.[73]

The increase in foreign assistance to combat AIDS shows how the preferences of an interest group can align with broader strategic goals held by the executive or legislative branch. Would AIDS have become a major issue without pressure from religious organizations? Possibly. But this pressure certainly helped.

ThinkingCritically

1. What other opportunities are there for religious organizations to join forces with other interest groups in order to further influence U.S. commitments of foreign aid?

2. What are some other ways in which religious organizations affect U.S. foreign policy?

Contemporary Foreign Policy Challenges

The United States continues to face extraordinary foreign policy challenges. It oversees an extraordinarily complex and dangerous international environment. And because the United States is the world's only superpower, foreign nations regularly look to it to formulate solutions. This section highlights recent efforts of presidents, the foreign policy bureaucracy, Congress, interest groups, and other domestic political actors to confront three important foreign policy challenges: how to reduce the threats of a North Korean nuclear program; how to balance the costs and benefits of free trade; and how to handle individuals who are suspected of terrorist activities.

Diplomatic efforts to halt North Korea's nuclear program, thus far, have failed.

On August 6, 1945, an atomic bomb code-named "Little Boy" leveled the Japanese city of Hiroshima, killing tens of thousands almost immediately. The United States had become the first—and to date, the only—country to use a nuclear weapon against another country. The demonstration of such weapons' devastating strength, coupled with the crystallizing Cold War, fuelled an international race for nuclear weapons. In 1949, the Soviet Union tested bombs of its own. By 1964, the United Kingdom, France, and the People's Republic of China acquired nuclear capabilities. Developments in rocket science made the specter of nuclear-armed states, able to project their power to far corners of the globe, much more real. And U.S. foreign policy needed to contend not only with the ramifications of America's own nuclear capability, but also that of its allies and rivals.

Some observers saw this as a benefit for U.S. foreign policy. Perhaps the overwhelming might of nuclear weapons actually made them integral for *deterring* open hostilities between the East and the West. By pursuing certain tactics—such as dividing up arsenals and placing warheads in underground facilities—nuclear powers could maintain second-strike capabilities. Thus, states would think hard about offensive moves, for while the instigator might wreak havoc on its enemy, it would bring similarly devastating retaliation upon itself. This notion of "mutually assured destruction" may be one of the key reasons why the Cold War remained cold.

Diplomatic efforts to stem the proliferation of nuclear weapons were codified in the Nuclear Non-Proliferation Treaty, which opened for signature in 1968. The United States, United Kingdom, and Soviet Union signed almost immediately. The treaty stipulates that non-nuclear countries will not seek nuclear capabilities, pre-existing nuclear states will not facilitate proliferation to more states, countries can acquire nuclear technology for peaceful uses such as energy, and all will work toward a somewhat vague disarmament goal. Currently, 189 different countries are signatories.[74]

Still, considerable uncertainties persisted. Miscalculations, laxity, or accidents in *any* of the five nuclear-capable states promised dire consequences. Moreover, non-nuclear countries reacted strongly. While some called for total disarmament, others were eager to obtain this kind of power and leverage for themselves. During the 1970s, 80s, and 90s, countries—including South Africa, Libya, and Iraq—launched, and then subsequently abandoned, efforts to acquire nuclear weapons. But more recently, others—such as Iran and North Korea—have been accused of concealing weapons development behind civilian energy programs.

Since the end of the Cold War, concerns about nuclear proliferation have only intensified. The break-up of the USSR scattered a massive stockpile among the newly independent countries. Even though much of the arsenal has been returned to Russia, part remains missing. And ensuring the stability of nuclear states such as Pakistan, as well as ascertaining the motivations "rogue states," are key priorities in U.S. foreign policy.

North Korea represents a key challenge for U.S. efforts to hinder the proliferation of nuclear weapons. Since the Korean War, relations between the United States and North Korea have vacillated between strained to non-existent. In 1990, satellite photos revealed a facility that appeared capable of producing weapons-grade plutonium from fuel rods. North Korea refused to cooperate fully with inspectors from the International Atomic Energy Agency (IAEA). Deeply concerned, the United States, South Korea, and a number of other countries pushed for United Nations sanctions. The Clinton Administration also engaged North Korean president Kim Il-Sung diplomatically, reaching a pact called the "Agreed Framework" in late 1994. North Korea promised to dismantle its weapons program and comply with IAEA inspectors. In exchange, the U.S. pledged to provide light-water reactors (which could not produce plutonium), oil for interim energy supplies, and later, humanitarian assistance.[75]

Neither side, however, fulfilled all of its obligations. In the aftermath of the terrorist attacks of September 11, 2001, new intelligence indicated that North Korea was still pursuing a nuclear weapons program. In his 2002 State of the Union Speech, Bush denounced the developments, and designated North Korea and Iran and Iraq (which also were suspected of developing nuclear weapons) as the lynchpins of an "Axis of Evil."[76] A year later, North Korea announced its withdrawal from the Nuclear Non-Proliferation Treaty, declaring that it needed nuclear weapons even more than before, to protect itself from Washington's "hostility."[77]

The country, by then led by Kim Il-Sung's son Kim Jong-Il, demanded a dialogue with the United States, even while issuing threats against America and its regional allies, Japan and South Korea. Disappointed by the diplomatic approaches embodied in the Agreed Framework, Bush refused. Instead, he insisted on multilateral discussions in which North Korea and the United States would be joined by China, Japan, Russia, and South Korea. Eventually, Kim relented. The Six-Party Talks commenced in August 2003 and continue to this day.

Although underway for nearly five years, the Six-Party talks—like the Nuclear Non-Proliferation Treaty and the Agreed Framework before them—have not compelled North Korea to wholly abandon its weapons program. In October 2006, North Korea detonated a nuclear bomb in an underground test. The issue became even more urgent in September 2007, when Israel conducted a strike against a Syrian facility that may have received nuclear material from North Korea. The following month, in return for 950,000 metric tons of fuel oil or its financial equivalent, North Korea agreed to dismantle its facilities and disclose all past and present nuclear programs by the end of the year. In December, President Bush held out the prospect of normalized relations with the United States, and with it the possibility of open trade and political engagement, if the country upheld its promise.[78]

On January 4, 2008, however, North Korea rejected Bush's offer. At the time, some observers suspected that Kim hoped to wait out the Bush administration in the hopes of a sweeter agreement with the next president. For its part, though, the Bush administration appeared divided on how best to respond. Secretary of State Condoleezza Rice, along with lead negotiator Christopher Hill, expressed interest in continuing the Six-Party talks. Vice President Dick Cheney and former UN ambassador John Bolton, however, condemned what they saw as a conciliatory stance. "They're in the classic North Korean role of deception," Bolton asserted.

"It's like groundhog day; we've lived through this before." It is not clear what the United States will do. As Hill, the negotiator, explained, "People lambaste the six-party process, and sure, it offers no refuge for those in need of instant gratification. But when asked for alternatives even the noisiest critics fall silent."[79]

Domestic lobbying groups push for protective tariffs.

International trade affects every one of us in material ways. Chances are that the clothes you are wearing now, the meal you ate a few hours ago, and the vehicle that you drove to school this morning became available to you with the aid of inputs from other countries. And foreign materials and labor contribute to much more than consumer goods—they are used in every part of society, from military deployments to domestic businesses to government offices.

The United States has been a vocal advocate of "free trade" in the world. This involves lowering or eliminating tariffs and other mechanisms that impede the movement of goods and services. Certainly, freer trade increases consumer choices, but there is a precise economic rationale as well. In his 1776 book *The Wealth of Nations*, the economist Adam Smith argued that countries should export according to their absolute advantage. Thus, if Britain was the lowest-cost producer of wool while Portugal was the lowest-cost producer of port wine, then the former should export wool in exchange for the latter's wine, and both parties would better for it.

As Smith makes clear, free trade has a powerful economic justification. But political realities complicate matters. For one thing, it may be difficult for a country to transfer inputs from one use to another. A worker who is proficient in painting automobiles, for example, may need to be retained in order to sell insurance. In addition, widespread exchange involves reliance on other countries. Some sectors raise security concerns, prompting governments to entertain less-efficient domestic production in order to avoid such dependence. Furthermore, even when gains from trade outweigh losses, those gains and losses may not be equally distributed across different populations. Widespread unemployment in a particular part of the country, for instance, can affect everything from crime rates to electoral fortunes. And when politically connected groups sustain significant losses, they make sure that politicians take notice.

As a result, even countries that advocate free trade may pursue selective **protectionism**—that is, the imposition of specific tariffs to protect the interests of domestic industries. The case of U.S. steel tariffs illustrates this well. In the late 1990s, a number of countries in Asia and elsewhere suffered financial crises that diminished the value of their currencies. The devaluation made exports from those countries relatively cheap and encouraged companies to sell their products quickly before their home currencies fell even further. Many tried to sell to the world's largest economy, the United States, which relies upon steel to manufacture all sorts of products. This abundance drove down steel prices, benefiting steel consumers but hurting U.S. steel producers.

Economists estimated that low steel prices resulted in higher gains than losses for the economy as a whole. Lots of consumers enjoyed small gains, but a reasonably small, but well organized, group of producers suffered substantial losses. Labor (represented by unions) and capital (represented by producers' associations) in the steel sector teamed up to petition the Clinton administration for help. They accused South Korea, Russia, and others of "dumping," an outlawed practice in which countries sell exports for less than their production cost or home-market price.[80] Politicians from steel-producing states also joined the chorus, frequently advancing concerns about national security. "This is an industry that has significant national security implications," declared Senator Rick Santorum (R-PA). "Allowing the industry to be liquidated would put this country on a path to overdependence, similar to oil, on foreign sources." Senator Carl Levin (D-MI) agreed, telling a cheering crowd of steelworkers: "We go to war with what you make."

The president, however, remained unconvinced that the steel producers had a strong legal case, and he declined to take action. Given traditional alliances between blue-collar labor and the Democratic Party, many lobbyists felt betrayed by Clinton and his vice president, Al Gore. In the closely contested 2000 presidential election, some citizens used their vote to punish the Democrats. The Republican candidate, George W. Bush, defeated Gore in steel-producing states such as Indiana, Ohio, and West Virginia.

In the spring of 2001, just months after Bush took office, the lobbyists launched another political offensive. The lobbyists demanded protection from imports, federal aid in paying workers' health and pension benefits, and assurances that the government would not challenge proposed industry mergers.[81] This time, the lobbyists met with greater success. The Bush administration anticipated political payoffs from siding with steel-producers—including inroads with traditionally Democratic voters and 2002 midterm election support in key states such as Pennsylvania and Ohio.

In June, the president initiated a case under Section 201 of U.S. trade law, claiming that a glut of foreign steel was injuring domestic producers. This move gave the International Trade Commission, an independent American panel, six months to investigate the allegations and provide recommendations to the White House.[82] The president also sent Treasury Secretary Paul O'Neill on an international trip to convince countries such as Russia, South Korea, China, and Japan to reduce global output by removing their subsidies for steel-producers.

In December, the American steel production was still hemorrhaging. Prices had dropped by about one-third during 2001, and numerous companies were declaring bankruptcy.[83] The International Trade Commission, having determined that imports had injured the U.S. industry, recommended that the president impose import quotas, as well as tariffs ranging from 15 to 40 percent.[84]

The administration, however, struggled to determine its course of action. Commerce Secretary Donald Evans and senior advisor Karl Rove backed higher tariffs, while chief economic advisor Lawrence Lindsey advocated free-trade principles. Additionally, a number of high profile members of Congress (including John McCain) railed against protectionism. In March 2002, the president finally decided on three-year tariffs as high as 30 percent (depending on the type of steel) against countries such as Japan, China, South Korea, Russia, Ukraine, and Brazil. He asserted that the action was within the World Trade Organization (WTO) allowance for temporary "safeguard provisions" and exempted many developing nations, in addition to NAFTA trading partners Canada and Mexico.[85]

This action, however, did not permanently resolve matters. In fact, an all-out trade war loomed. Almost immediately, China—the world's largest steel producer—filed a complaint with the World Trade Organization. Then the European Union, Japan, and China threatened to impose tariffs on other U.S. goods without waiting for the WTO's ruling, accurately pointing out that U.S. steel imports had in fact declined rather than risen over the past three years. Russia hinted that the tariffs would reduce its willingness to cooperate in the war on terror.[86]

In November 2002, the WTO rejected the U.S. government's protectionist policies, and it authorized other countries to impose countervailing tariffs as punishment. The following month, the Bush administration relented. Facing a full-blown trade war, Bush repealed the tariffs 15 months before their scheduled expiration. In an effort to save face, though, the president noted that: "I took action to give the industry a chance to adjust to the surge in foreign imports and to give relief to the workers and communities that depend on steel for their jobs and livelihoods. These safeguard measures have now achieved their purpose, and as a result of changed economic circumstances it is time to lift them."[87]

This episode reveals important lessons about the politics of trade. Despite the economic rationality of free trade, political realities may lead to selective protectionism. The steel case highlights a number of reasons for this: national security concerns, the difficulties of transferring workers from one industry to another, concentrated injury from trade, and powerful interest groups. As Gary Hufbrauer of the Institute for International Economics points out, a free-trade president who seeks quotas and tariffs may be anomalous, "but it's a way of trying to keep moving on the bigger goal while dealing with the truly squeaky wheels—and steel is truly a squeaky wheel."[88]

The president and civil liberties organizations disagree about the legal status of "enemy combatants."

The September 11 terrorist attacks spurred the Bush administration into a new kind of war, the ongoing "global war on terrorism" (GWOT). President Bush has called GWOT "a different kind of conflict with a different kind of enemy," a war "without battlefields or beachheads."[89] As a multi-faceted and broad initiative, GWOT has included diplomatic efforts to freeze terrorist assets overseas, tougher law enforcement at home and abroad, and heightened homeland security.

Many aspects of GWOT have garnered broad public support. A few, however, have provoked significant controversy. Among the most heated debates concerns the legal rights that should be afforded to U.S. citizens who are accused of plotting attacks or fighting with al Qaeda. The Bush administration contends that these individuals should be recognized as "enemy combatants." As such, they can be detained indefinitely without trial under the auspices of military law. Critics of the Bush administration, however, claim that the "enemy combatant" designation deprives suspects of their civil rights to due process. Instead, they argue, terror suspects should be tried in civilian courts of law under the U.S. criminal justice system.

The debate came to a head in with the case of *Hamdi v. Rumsfeld*, with members of the president's administration, the foreign policy bureaucracy, and numerous interest groups all weighing in. At issue was the fate of Yaser Esam Hamdi, an American citizen who was captured in Afghanistan in November 2001. Hamdi was born in Louisiana but raised in Saudi Arabia. Government officials claim he was carrying an assault weapon when he surrendered to the Northern Alliance, an ally of the United States. But his father, Esam Fouad Hamdi, insisted that his son traveled to Afghanistan only for religious study and humanitarian work.

Originally sent to the U.S. Navy base in Guantanamo Bay, Cuba, Hamdi was transferred to a military brig in Norfolk, Virginia upon confirmation of his U.S. citizenship. There he was held for years without any charges filed against him. Hamdi's case entered the U.S. court system when his father filed a petition for a writ of habeas corpus on his behalf, requesting a chance for Hamdi to contest his designation as an "enemy combatant" in court. Hamdi was appointed a lawyer, but the government barred him from communicating with his client. In 2004, the case came before the Supreme Court.[90]

The administration's case rested on a few key claims. First, government lawyers insisted that the president's constitutional war powers gave Bush the right to declare citizens as "enemy combatants" and detain them. Second, the 2001 congressional Authorization on the Use of Military Force (AUMF) explicitly delegated authority to the president to exercise "all necessary and appropriate force" against "persons" and organizations involved in terrorist actions against the United States. The government counsel claimed the AUMF authority included the detention of citizens. Finally, the administration and its supporters insisted that national security concerns dictated the selective use of military detentions. Paul Clement, a government counsel, complained it was "remarkable that we have to confront this question when our troops are still on the ground in Afghanistan."[91]

Hamdi's public defender bristled at the administration's claims that an American citizen could be denied both access to an attorney and a habeas review simply by being declared an "enemy combatant." He further argued that if the AUMF permitted the president to hold suspects without trial indefinitely, "we could have people locked up all over the country tomorrow without any due process, without any opportunity to be heard. There is no indication that Congress intended any such thing."[92] Several civil liberties groups and lawyers' organizations also backed Hamdi. In an amicus brief to the Court, the American Bar Association called the administration's arguments "circular and unprecedented. In Hamdi's case, where the deprivation of liberty is complete, ongoing, potentially without end, and based entirely upon a secret record, the need for counsel could not be more compelling."[93]

Ultimately, the Court ruled against the administration. The justices ruled that suspects retained the right to contest the charges against them before a "neutral decision maker." However, the Court largely ducked deeper questions about the limits of presidential power in wartime. It argued that AUMF did in fact permit the president to detain enemy combatants, but said nothing about whether that authority held in absence of an explicit congressional authorization. Hamdi, however, never got his day in court. Following the Supreme Court ruling, the administration released Hamdi to Saudi Arabia in exchange for renouncing his U.S. citizenship.[94]

The appropriate tradeoff between national security and civil liberties continues to attract widespread attention in the war on terror. The Court's ambivalence, coupled with the long period the United States expects to be engaged in GWOT, nearly guarantees the question of legal status of detainees will loom large for some time to come. And we can expect members of all three branches of government, as well as a wide variety of organized interest groups, to participate in the ongoing debate.

SUMMARY

- Throughout the 19th century, U.S. foreign policy was guided by a grand strategy of isolationism. After fighting two world wars in the first half of the 20th Century, the country was gripped by a new spirit of internationalism. During the Cold War, the United States sought to contain the spread of communism, but it never fought directly against the Soviet Union. Since the Cold War ended in 1989, the United States has been the world's only superpower, with economic and military interests that span the globe.

- As commander-in-chief, chief diplomat, and chief administrator, the president has extraordinary powers and responsibilities in foreign policy. Moreover, a vast network of agencies and departments assist the president in formulating and implementing his foreign policy agenda.

- Congress has a variety of means at its disposal to influence U.S. foreign policymaking. By enacting statutes, retaining the power to declare war, confirming bureaucratic nominees, ratifying treating, and exercising its oversight responsibilities, Congress can influence U.S. foreign policy in important ways.

▶ A variety of interest groups also contribute to foreign policy. Business groups, ethnic lobbies, and think tanks, in particular, can provide important insights. They also can shape national conversations about particularly pressing foreign policy issues; and so doing, they occasionally put pressure on members of Congress to challenge presidential powers in foreign policy.

▶ Presidents, officials in the State and Defense Departments, Congress, and a wide variety of interest groups all participate in ongoing foreign policy debates, which center on issues ranging from the spread of nuclear weapons to the protection of U.S. industries against foreign competition to the conduct of the ongoing war against terrorism.

KEY TERMS

Bush Doctrine, p. 000
Central Intelligence Agency (CIA), p. 000
Cold War, p. 000
containment, p. 000
Defense Department, p. 000
Department of Homeland Security (DHS), p. 000
détente, p. 000
diplomacy, p. 000
ethnic lobby, p. 000
executive agreement, p. 000
foreign policy, p. 000

grand strategy, p. 000
isolationism, p. 000
Marshall Plan, p. 000
National Security Council (NSC), p. 000
North American Free Trade Agreement (NAFTA), p. 000
North Atlantic Treaty Organization (NATO), p. 000
protectionism, p. 000
State Department, p. 000
tariff, p. 000
treaty

SUGGESTED READINGS

William Howell and Jon Pevehouse, *While Dangers Gather: Congressional Checks on Presidential War Powers*, Princeton University Press, 2007. The authors examine the proposition that the president has become all-powerful in the formation of policies concerning the use of military force. They show that Congress has a definite, if circumscribed, influence over decisions involving troop deployments abroad.

Graham Allison and Philip Zelikow, *Essence of Decision*, 2nd ed., AB Longman, 1999. An updated edition of the classic study of the Cuban Missile Crisis. Three models (rational actor, organizational processes, bureaucratic politics) are developed to explain foreign policy decision-making and the behavior that results from the process.

Stephen Hook and John Spanier, *American Foreign Policy Since World War II*, 17th ed., Congressional Quarterly Press, 2007. A classic book that traces all of the major phases of American foreign policy since World War II through the events of September 11th. The volume pays special attention to the political process and context in which decisions were made.

James F. Hoge and Gideon Rose, eds., *America and the World: Debating the New Shape of International Politics*, Foreign Affairs Press, 2003. This book contains a compendium of arguments about the role of American primacy, the clash of civilizations, and the future of democracy.

Amy Zegart, *Flawed by Design: The Evolution of the CIA, JCS, and NSC*, Stanford University Press, 1999. Reviewing the creation and evolution of several executive branch agencies, Zegart argues that pressures from Congress, the White House, and even the voting public have undermined the effective operation of certain security institutions. Meanwhile, bureaucratic politics work to limit the sharing of expertise and coordination of actions across various agencies.

David A. Welch, *Painful Choices: A Theory of Foreign Policy Change*, Princeton University Press, 2005. This book outlines both organizational and psychological theories about when foreign policy decision-makers attempt to make major changes in policy. Several historical case studies are then used to examine the ability of each theory.

foreign policy the mix of military, diplomatic, and economic policies that define U.S. relations with other nations around the world.

grand strategy a plan that determines American national security interests, outlines possible threats to those interests, and recommends military and diplomatic policies to attain them.

isolationism the grand strategy of minimizing a nation's involvement in world affairs.

internationalism the grand strategy of actively engaging in world affairs.

Marshall Plan a program that provided aid to rebuild Western European economies after the Second World War.

North Atlantic Treaty Organization (NATO) established in 1949, a military alliance of the United States and its European allies that pledged to join forces against an attack by any external threat.

containment the strategy of guarding against Soviet expansion by adopting policies that limited the geographic expansion of Soviet power.

Cold War the period, from the late 1940s to the late 1980s, in which the United States and the Soviet Union engaged in diplomatic and economic hostility but not full-fledged war.

détente a period of reduced Cold War tensions in the 1970s.

Bush Doctrine a grand strategy pursued after September 11, 2001, that emphasized an aggressive posture towards those nations that provide safe haven for terrorists, preemptive action, and a willingness to unilaterally launch military actions.

National Security Council (NSC) an advisory body, formed in 1947 by the National Security Act, that assists the President in gathering information from military services and other security-related executive agencies.

diplomacy the peaceful negotiation of economic and political relationships between different countries.

State Department the agency home of diplomats, embassies, treaty negotiators, and most foreign aid programs run by the U.S. government.

Defense Department an executive-branch agency that was created by the National Security Act in 1947 and replaced the Departments of War and the Navy.

Central Intelligence Agency (CIA) the cornerstone of U.S. efforts to gather and analyze data in order to confront America's real and potential enemies.

Department of Homeland Security (DHS) an executive-branch agency that was created in the aftermath of September 11 to coordinate the work of agencies involved in preventing and responding to attacks on the United States.

tariff a tax upon goods exchanged between nations.

North American Free Trade Agreement (NAFTA) an agreement, signed in 1992, to reduce tariff and non-tariff barriers to trade and investment among Canada, Mexico, and the United States.

executive agreement an international agreement in which the U.S. becomes a party once the president has signed, without requiring approval from two-thirds of the Senate.

ethnic lobby an interest group that advocates policies focusing on specific foreign states.

protectionism the practice of imposing selective tariffs on trade in an effort to protect specific domestic industries from international competition.

19 State and Local Governments

Nestor and his guidance counselor at South High School in Denver were frustrated and angry. It didn't seem fair. Nestor had worked diligently to pursue a college bound track of courses and earn a 3.5 grade point average. Teachers all agreed he was a bright, responsible, and highly motivated person who was bound to do well at a good university. But Nestor faced hurdles having nothing to do with academics or with choices that he had made.

When Nestor was 5 years old, his parents moved to Colorado from Guatemala to seek refuge from political turmoil and to take advantage of employment opportunities in the state. They did not go through the required immigration procedures, however. Nestor's dad had a job arranging and removing tables and chairs people rented for parties, and his mother worked at a candy store. They could not afford to pay for him to go to college. Nestor worked summers and did odd jobs during the school year, but his savings were only a little over $12,000. The lack of resources was especially important

because even though Nestor had been in Colorado since he was 5 years old and was graduating from a public high school in Colorado, he did not qualify for resident tuition at the state's public universities. The reason was that his parents were illegal immigrants. The federal government makes the determination of which immigrants are in the country legally and which are not. But state governments set policies about who has resident status for public universities and about eligibility for state programs providing students with loans and scholarships.

As of early 2008, ten states, in contrast to Colorado, allowed any student graduating from a state high school to pay resident tuition rates, regardless of their immigration status or that of their parents. Colorado, Georgia and Arizona, however, explicitly ban in-state tuition for undocumented students. In April 2008, the General Assembly (like the U.S. House of Representatives) of Virginia debated six different proposals, ranging from considering children of illegal immigrants as eligible for financial aid to prohibiting state universities from even admitting these students. Bob McDonnell, Virginia's

Attorney General, issued a legal opinion that fueled some of the debate. He noted some ambiguities in the state's current law and then told public university officials that they should presume that children of undocumented immigrants are legally not residents of Virginia, but allowed the universities to make exceptions on a case-by-case basis. The opinion was controversial because it was a response to the plea of a student who was born in Virginia. Anyone born in Virginia is a citizen of that state and of the United States, regardless of whether the parents entered the country legally. According to the Attorney General, it was the status of the boy's parents that mattered.

Educational opportunities and illegal immigrants are both emotional issues. During times of economic hardship, those who are unemployed or underemployed sometimes resent the presence of immigrant workers, especially those who are not in the country legally. Some employers rely heavily on workers from other countries who will work for relatively low wages, and employers are more concerned about having these workers than about whether they entered the country legally or have a visa that is still valid.

In addition, some citizens object to paying for public services for undocumented workers and their families. However, many undocumented workers pay income taxes and all pay sales taxes.

A complicating concern regarding tuition for public universities is that children, who obviously do not control the decisions of their parents, are affected. It seems more appropriate to penalize those who are guilty of negligence or malfeasance than those who played no role in the decision. The counter argument is that states can provide a disincentive for parents to be in the country illegally by denying resident status to their children.

Commonly, states that do grant children of illegal immigrants resident status for tuition require these students to become U.S. citizens, if they are not already. Students who do not become citizens within five years of qualifying for resident status must pay the state the difference between resident and nonresident tuition. This approach aims at increasing the country's pool of highly educated people and thereby helping the economy.

The states also differ in defining residence for circumstances other than immigration. Relationships between students and their parents are a general concern. What if, for example, a high school graduate leaves the state for a few years before going to college? Are they still a resident? Does that depend on where their parents are living? If the parents live apart, is one parent still in the state enough? States not only differ on how they answer these very basic questions, but also on whether someone becomes a resident through marriage or civil union. In some states, marriage works for getting resident fees for state parks, hunting and fishing licenses, and the like, but not for tuition to colleges or universities. Same sex marriages or civil unions affect eligibility in some states, but not others. States like California are generally very generous in granting residency status. One qualifies by showing financial independence and demonstrating intent to make California home by getting a drivers license, registering to vote, listing the state as residence on official records, or some similar act. At the other extreme are states like Wisconsin, which has a policy that assumes anyone who comes into the state to get a college degree as a nonresident regardless of financial independence or where they vote or get their drivers license.

State differences on higher education and residency generally or immigrant status specifically do not follow any particular patterns. Southern border states like California, Arizona, New Mexico and Texas have the largest number of immigrants from Mexico and Central America. Of these, Arizona has passed the most restrictive laws providing services to those who are not citizens. Other states with policies similar to those in Arizona are scattered around the country and include some that are highly urbanized and others that are very rural, some controlled by Republicans and some by Democrats.

There are a number of states with relatively large recent immigrants—legal and illegal—from parts of the world other than Mexico and Central America. Florida has a large contingent of migrants from Cuba. The West and some Midwestern states have Hmong, and recent newcomers from Somalia, Ethiopia, and eastern European countries are found in large cities primarily on the coasts. The immigration population in states like Colorado and Virginia is as varied as in other states, and states that confer residency on anyone who graduates from one of their high schools have no set or consistent immigration patterns. Differences in state policies are sometimes only understood by the politics and personalities that dominate individual state governments.

Not only do state policies vary, but also the ways states establish these policies. All states have legislatures that pass bills and present them to a governor for approval or veto. In addition, Arizona, California, and seventeen other states enact laws through the direct initiative, in which voters can get a proposal on a statewide ballot without any involvement of their legislature or governor. In eight states, legislatures place proposals on the ballot and laws are created without governors participating. These processes allow ad hoc groups and organized interest groups energized by a particular concern to influence decisions on tuition and admission policies in higher education in a state that otherwise would probably not give serious consideration their ideas. The point is not that legislatures and governors are likely to act one way and citizen initiatives and referenda another, but that states offer advocates a number of arenas for pursuing their ideas. Understanding state policies requires knowledge of the actors and the avenues for achieving change.

This chapter describes how state and local governments function. Most of the public policies that directly affect us are made and implemented by state and local governments. The notable exception in the federal government is the post office. Street maintenance, park services, garbage collection, police and fire protection, education from Kindergarten through college, marriage and divorce, highway safety, and the many other critical, daily governmental services and regulations we experience are all the products of state and local governments. Policies in arenas like the environment, energy, and commerce are typically made by the federal government, but then implemented by state and local agencies. When the federal government does not resolve issues like health care and climate change, state and even city governments have stepped in. In short, to understand the roles government plays in our lives requires an appreciation of the nature of politics and governance in the 50 states and over 87,000 local governments in the United States.

The Making of State and Local Governments

As the national Congress that existed under the Articles of Confederation adjourned to allow the writing of the Constitution, it passed the **Northwest Ordinance of 1787**, which was critical in shaping the United States and the state governments. In Article 5 of the Ordinance Congress provided for the admission of additional states to the Union with the full status of the first thirteen. This meant that all states would have the same rights and privileges:

> Article 5
> ... And, whenever any of the said States shall have sixty thousand free inhabitants therein, such State shall be admitted, by its delegates, into the Congress of the United States, on an equal footing with the original States in all respects whatever, and shall be at liberty to form a permanent constitution and State government: Provided, the constitution and government so to be formed, shall be republican, and in conformity to the principles contained in these articles; and, so far as it can be consistent with the general interest of the confederacy, such admission shall be allowed at an earlier period, and when there may be a less number of free inhabitants in the State than sixty thousand.

The other major provision of Article 5 was the requirement that new states have constitutions acceptable to Congress. Thus, territories petitioning for statehood had an incentive to adopt constitutions similar to those of the states already in the Union. The five states that were carved out of the Northwest Territory—Ohio, Indiana, Illinois, Michigan and Wisconsin—submitted constitutions almost identical to those of New York and Massachusetts, the states from which most of the initial U. S. settlers in the Territory had originated. The strategy of each of the territories was to present Congress with proposed constitutions that members of Congress would recognize. Ohio was the first to joined the Union (in 1803) and Wisconsin the last of the Northwest Territories (1848). States that emerged out of the Louisiana Purchase also modeled their governments and constitutions on those of existing states.

State constitutions primarily limit the power of government.

State constitutions differ fundamentally from the U.S. Constitution in that they were meant to *limit* government while the federal Constitution is meant to *empower* government. When delegates from the states met in Philadelphia at the Constitutional Convention, one of their charges was to be sure that they gave the national government enough power to operate effectively on behalf of the country as a whole. In contrast, when the authors of state constitutions began their work, their primary concern was to make certain that state governments did not have the power and discretion of their colonial predecessors. The founders had what they regarded as the tyranny of the British crown in mind as they formed the successors to Colonial governors. The Revolution was about providing power to the governed and limiting that of the government. As new states formed, they drafted constitutions that responded to the conditions facing them. And as new policy issues emerged over time, states have amended their constitutions to address them.

Evolution of the state constitutions Constitutions of the first thirteen states preceded the U.S. Constitution. The state constitutions included clauses that limited officials from placing restrictions on an individual's speech and assembly, participating in unreasonable searches and seizures, and using cruel and inhuman punishment. New Hampshire's constitution even makes clear that citizens have a right to revolt. The major limiting clauses of the U.S. Constitution are the first ten amendments, the Bill of Rights, which were added as a condition for ratification by the first thirteen states. The states considered individual liberties and limits on government power important enough to include in the national as well as the state constitutions.

The first state constitutions designed weak government institutions to prevent the kind of government tyranny that characterized colonial rule.[1] Legislatures were part-time and governors served only two-year terms. Governors of the new states had nothing close to the authority and discretion of colonial governors. State constitutions stipulated that these offices be primarily ceremonial and made legislatures the primary center of decision-making and authority. Initially only South Carolina, New York and Massachusetts allowed their governors to veto legislation.

The tradition of weak state governments continued with the adoption of constitutions in the aftermath of the Civil War and as the country expanded westward.[2] Former Confederate states had to write new constitutions that did not include the right of individuals to own slaves. However, following Reconstruction, formal power shifted from former slaves and carpetbaggers (the term used to refer to Northerners who moved to the former Confederate states and secured government posts) to white Southern economic and social elites. Individual southern states adopted and repealed as many as four different constitutions between 1865 and 1880. The end results were state constitutions severely limiting the power and role of government, allowing economic and social elites to govern informally.

When western states joined the Union, the **Progressive Movement** attempted to prevent the emergence of political machines by again limiting the authority of state governments. Progressives added new techniques: empowering voters with the **initiative,** which allows voters to enact new laws by putting a proposal on the ballot if enough people sign a petition, and the recall, which allows for the removal of elected officials through popular vote rather than impeachment. Although these mechanisms of direct democracy are most common in western states, nine states in other regions eventually adopted them.

It has only been with constitutional changes adopted in the 1960s and 1970s that state institutions have increased in power.[3] As discussed below, a U.S. Supreme Court ruling in 1962 mandating legislative redistricting in the states made state governments more relevant and important to policy making. This prompted reforms to enhance the power of state governments and to make them more active. Governors have veto authority and, except for New Hampshire and Vermont, now serve four-year terms. Legislatures increasingly are full-time, and state courts have become more streamlined and professional. But the historic distrust of powerful government continues and state constitutions still include many restrictions. In contrast to many countries in Asia and Europe, the political culture in the United States is generally cynical and cautious about government. The initial distrust towards state governments, specifically, is still reflected in constitutions since reforms have tended to focus on specific issues rather than wholesale re-writings.

Other attributes of state constitutions State constitutions do more than protect the rights of individual citizens and establish the institutions of state governments. Constitutions are meant to deal with basic functions of government. However, almost all state constitutions include a potpourri of policies and details that are more appropriate as laws and regulations, not constitutional provisions. Arkansas specifies in its constitution that registration forms must be completed in quadruplicate and each copy must be on a different color paper. California has a clause that dictates the length of a wrestling match. California led the way in embedding into state constitutions limits and formulas that restrict government taxing and spending patterns. In some states, farmers and ranchers have protected their special interests in constitutions. In others, the oil and mining industries have embedded their concerns.[4]

In part because of the inclusion of policy and administrative detail, state constitutions are lengthier than the U.S. Constitution. The average length of state constitutions is over 27,000 words, while the U.S. Constitution is 8,700 words. Unlike the U.S. Constitutions, it is relatively easy to amend most state constitutions. In 40 of the states a constitution can be changed by the legislature in just one session, while ten states require the proposed amendment to pass two legislatures. Twenty states require only a majority vote for approval, while the others require a super-majority, usually two-thirds. In all states, proposals for constitutional amendments must be submitted to voters for ratification.

Charters authorize local governments to make and enforce laws.

Alex de Tocqueville, a popular 19th century French philosopher and historian of early America, is widely cited as capturing the spirit and principles of early American democracy. He conveyed, however, a romantic but misleading picture of the place of local governments in the United States. He wrote that individuals established social contracts to formulate the basic terms and conditions of government and that "the township was organized before the county, the county before the state, the state before the union."[5]

In fact, local governments are not the building blocks of states, they are the creatures of the states. Judge John F. Dillon articulated this doctrine in 1868, when he ruled in a case that raised the question of whether there was an inherent requirement that all governments in the United States must have separate and balanced executive, legal and judicial branches. The case challenged whether Iowa violated a constitutional principle when it established local commissions that both applied regulations to railroads and then ruled on appeals from the railroads objecting to the ways in which they were regulated. Dillon stated that according to the U.S. Constitution and the state constitution of Iowa, local governments did not enjoy sovereignty or inherent powers or have to conform to a basic set of characteristics, such as separation of powers. **Dillon's rule** summarizes the legal status of local governments in all fifty states. He said:

The true view is this: Municipal corporations owe their origins to and derive their power and rights wholly from the (state) legislature. It breathes into them the breath without which they cannot exist. As it creates, so it may destroy. If it may destroy, it may abridge and control.6

State governments recognize the existence of local governments by granting them **charters**, which are similar to constitutions. Charters may be found in a state statute that relates to cities, counties, school districts, and the like or they may be written by a community and submitted for approval by the state legislature. Charters describe the institutions of government, the processes used to make legally binding decisions, the scope of issues and services that will be provided, and the ways in which the expenses of government will be funded.

Some local governments are created top-down. A legislature will divide the state into counties, for example, and write a charter that guides how they will operate. States use **counties** as basic administrative units for welfare and environmental programs, courts and law enforcement, registering land, births, and deaths, and for holding elections (see Table 19.1). All states except Connecticut and Rhode Island have counties, although in Louisiana they are called parishes and in Alaska they are called boroughs. County boundaries are arbitrary and have no relation necessarily to where people live, which sometimes requires counties to cooperate to provide effective governance to a community. There are, for example, some cities in which the boundaries of as many as three different counties converge. Since counties are typically responsible for 9-1-1 emergency services, cooperation is essential.

Local governments can also be created by a bottom-up process. When businesses and families locate in a particular area or when a city grows in land and population, residents must petition the state legislature to be recognized as a legal entity with powers to pass and enforce laws, collect taxes and fees, and provide services. Such a petition must include either a standard charter available from the state or a charter written for that proposed government. Municipal governments, which include towns, villages, and cities, emerge from this process. States typically distinguish between these governments based on the size of the population, but provide more authority in charters to cities than in charters for towns and villages. The Northwest Ordinance of 1787 attempted to export the model of the New England **town** by creating a grid of **townships** over the territories. Townships are geographic entities six miles by six miles. When people settled in a township, they usually, but not always, formed a town government and petitioned for a charter. The former Northwest Territories still have some townships or parts of townships, but as urban areas have emerged, cities and villages have acquired authority over much of the areas that had belonged to a township.

Most local governments are **special districts**, which mean they focus on a particular function or service. The most common special district is a school dis-

Table 19-1. Types and Numbers of Local Governments

TYPES OF LOCAL GOVERNMENTS	NUMBER
County	3,034
Townships and towns	16,504
Municipalities	19,429
Special districts	35,183

Source: Bureau of the Census, *Statistical Abstract of the United States, 2006* (www.census.gov/prod/2005pubs/06statab/stlocgov.pdf), 273 and 309

trict. Other examples are water districts, sewerage districts, park districts, and lake districts.[7] Not only are these governments restricted in what they control or provide, but they are also limited in how they may get revenue. Often special districts rely on a fee, like a charge for using water, or on grants from other governments. School districts typically may levy a tax on property and otherwise rely on state and federal funds. Municipal and county governments also rely heavily on property taxes. This source of revenue was originally to pay for services, such as police and fire protection, street repair, and the like, that benefited property owners. Since not all property owners have school-age children, there is some controversy about whether it is appropriate to fund public education through property taxes.

Other local governments, like counties, towns and cities, have a wide scope of responsibilities. Almost all states offer **home rule** charters to these jurisdictions.[8] These charters allow local governments to make and enforce public policy on any issue not under the mandate of a special district or explicitly prohibited under state law. Traditional charters itemized what kinds of policies municipalities were authorized to develop and enforce. Home rule uses the approach that anything goes unless it is prohibited.

School districts are special districts, and are created to divide an entire state into smaller educational units, and boundaries can be arbitrary. Again, there are cities and towns in which neighbors send their children to different schools simply because a street in the neighborhood is the boundary between two different school districts. Whereas counties have a general set of responsibilities, school districts are established by state legislatures to deal only with public education.

In 1991, Minnesota's state government passed a law allowing the creation of **charter schools**. By 2008, thirty-nine other states, plus the District of Columbia and Puerto Rico, followed this lead. School districts are, as discussed above, governed in accordance with charters. These districts—or in a few cases, a state agency—may, in turn, charter individual public schools to operate independently as public schools but within the school district. Usually these charters are for a three- to five-year period. Parents, teachers, or even entrepreneurs, when allowed by state law, may propose a charter that provides for a special approach to education or exempts a school from certain standard regulations. Some charter schools rely exclusively on computer-based instruction or emphasize the arts in all their courses or focus primarily on skills and crafts. Most, but not all, states require that teachers meet state certification requirements and states like Minnesota insist that charter schools have the same diversity among their students as exists in other public schools. Educators and parents tend to propose the establishment of a charter school because they favor a particular approach to learning or because they want to escape what they regard as defective public schools or both. If the school district or state approves a proposal, the school receives public funding and is in other ways a public school, but has authority to operate in accordance with its own, unique charter.

Executives and Legislatures

State and local governments make laws and implement them through enforcing regulations and providing services. To accomplish this, state governments generally follow the model of the federal government by having separate branches for making laws on the one hand and implementing them on the other. This separation includes checks, such as the authority of the executive to veto legislation and the administrative oversight responsibilities of the legislature. In local governments, however, executive and legislative responsibilities are not always separate, and the structures of these institutions take a variety of forms.

Governors are the chief elected executive in state governments.

The primary role of a **governor** is to set the agenda for state governments. Even when the office in all states was weak and largely ceremonial, governors were the most visible elected officials in state governments. Even the most flamboyant or outrageous legislator could not command the attention of a governor. From the time they campaign until the time they leave office, governors speak to and for statewide audiences. If a governor declares there is an urgent energy problem or a crisis in public schools, the focus inevitably will turn to those issues. Setting the agenda is not the same as solving a problem, but it is a good first step. Other gubernatorial roles, such as budgeting, appointments to administrative agencies, and modifying court actions, allow governors to go beyond agenda setting.

Budget authority Budgets provide governors with an opportunity to set agendas and move towards solutions. Until the 1920s, state legislative committees, not governors, initiated the budget process and then the legislature as a whole presented a budget bill to the governor for approval or veto. As discussed below, when the U.S. Supreme Court issued a mandate in 1962 that state legislatures had to use districts representative of the population, state governments became more relevant and important policy makers. This led to efforts to strengthen the powers of governors. Important among these efforts was making the governor the initiator of the budget, and the important decisions about how to generate revenues and allocate funds.[9] Legislators can amend what the governor submits, but debates begin with the governor's ideas. Moreover, state budgets in the 21st century commonly consist of hundreds of pages of detail. Inevitably most of that detail will escape scrutiny and change, and thus governors tend to get most of what they want.

The authority to veto enhances the role of the governor in the budget process considerably. Like presidents, governors have **package or general veto** authority, allowing them to reject an entire bill. Governors of 43 states also have the authority to exercise a **line-item veto** over bills that affect taxing and spending, an authority the president does not have. This allows governors to balance budgets by revising financially relevant legislation without rejecting it wholesale. Both numbers and words may be eliminated in a line-item veto. Although general and line-item vetoes can be overridden by the legislature, that usually takes a two-thirds majority in both houses and thus happens very rarely.[10]

Wisconsin's governors have exercised their line-item veto authority to go beyond simply eliminating parts of a bill. They illustrate what governors can do and increasingly are doing with the line-item veto. This power of governors also explains why U.S. presidents have perennially sought line-item veto authority. Governors in Wisconsin and elsewhere have at times reversed the intent of legislation by strategically vetoing the word "not" in a sentence. When Tommy Thompson was elected governor of Wisconsin in 1986, he began vetoing letters and numerals and created entirely new words and numbers, establishing state law that had never been considered or debated in the legislature. Voters rebelled in 1993 and passed the "Vanna White amendment" to the state constitution, prohibiting governors from striking letters within words and numerals within numbers. Governor Thompson responded by crossing out numbers and writing in a different number. The state supreme court approved of this as long as the new number was not larger than the one vetoed. In yet one more maneuver, Governor Jim Doyle crossed out words in several paragraphs and created new sentences. When he did this and created a law that a majority of legislators in one of the houses had explicitly rejected during the budget debate, voters again reacted. In 2008 they passed the "Frankenstein amendment" and took away the authority to use the partial veto to create new sentences.

Appointment powers Most agency heads are appointed by governors and serve at their pleasure. This allows a governor to prioritize state programs and to delay initiatives that he or she opposes.[11] Most state employees have job security that provides them with careers that can span many different governors. But as professionals they generally follow the lead of whomever is appointed to head their agency.

While the appointment powers of governors provide direction and control over administrative agencies, limits to this power reflect the legacy of historic efforts to check the authority of governors. Unlike the federal government, most states fill a number of agency head positions through statewide elections rather than gubernatorial appointment. Agency heads may be from a party other than the governor's and may even be planning to run against the governor. The most common and significant elected agency head is the attorney general. Forty-three states elect their attorneys general. Other elected positions include secretary of state, treasurer, heads of education, labor and agriculture departments, and even commissioner of charities.[12] Reforms to enhance gubernatorial powers have left largely untouched the process of selecting or appointing heads of state agencies.

Role in the judicial system Governors are also major actors in the judicial system, although again with limited powers. Only the governors of California, Maine and New Jersey appoint judges in a way similar to the president. Judges in other states are elected, but governors generally may appoint someone to complete a term when a judge leaves the bench. Because an incumbent judge running for reelection has considerable advantages over an opponent, the power to appoint an interim judge can be valuable.

The most substantial power of governors in the judicial system applies after someone is convicted of a crime. A governor has the authority to **pardon** someone, thereby voiding a conviction in court and eliminating all penalties that an individual was sentenced to pay. Governors also have the option of leaving the conviction in place and reducing sentences. They may **parole** prisoners who have served part of their term, releasing them from behind bars but keeping them under supervision, or **commute** all or part of a sentence, releasing someone from both prison and supervision. Governors may also commute a death penalty and replace it with life in prison. Governors may not, however, increase the severity of a sentence. They may not, for example, put someone serving a life sentence on death row.

The power to pardon has sometimes been abused by governors. For example, some governors of Texas used pardons as part of political wheeling and dealing and as a way of augmenting their state salaries. Governor James E. Ferguson granted 2,253 pardons between 1915 and 1917 for gubernatorial bargains.[13] When his wife, Miriam "Ma" Ferguson, took office two years later, she granted almost 3,800. In response, Texas voters amended the state constitution and placed authority for granting pardons in the hands of a board, thus making the Lone Star governor weaker in this arena than any other governor in the country.

The U.S. Constitution provides governors with the discretion to **extradite** individuals, that is, deliver an individual to a state where he or she is wanted for a particular crime. Extradition is not routinely granted and frequently highlights differences in how governors and states treat criminal justice issues, especially the death penalty. In December 2007, Governor Matt Blunt of Missouri asked Governor Rod Blagojevich of Illinois to extradite Timothy Krajcir, who was in prison in Illinois for rape and murder. Missouri wanted Krajcir to stand trial for raping and murdering five women in that state. Governor Blagojevich, however, had serious misgivings about the death penalty and was concerned that extraditing Krajcir might lead to his execution in Missouri. The issue was resolved when Krajcir, who was 63 in 2007, pled guilty to the Missouri murders and yet another in Illinois and was sentenced to serve consecutively two 40-year terms.

Between 1945 and 1990, Democrats usually had about 10 percent more governors than Republicans. Since 1990, however, governors have been relatively evenly split between Republicans and Democrats. After the 2008 elections, as shown in Figure 19.1.

State legislatures pass laws and monitor the activities of state agencies.

As explained above, the power and authority of governors has generally and substantially increased since the 1960s. In turn, state legislatures have seen their powers decrease. As mentioned above, the nation began with state legislatures that were very strong and governors that were primarily ceremonial. Legislatures formulated budgets, appointed judges and agency heads, and even elected U.S. Senators.

Figure 19-1. Political Party of State Governors, 2008. To come.

Source: http://www.ncsl.org/statevote2002/govParty_post2002.htm, and updates by the authors.

These legislators were initially true citizen policymakers, farmers and lawyers who traveled to the state capitol for several weeks each year to do their work.

Representation In the first half of the 20th century, population shifted from rural to urban areas, but the boundaries of districts from which legislators were elected did not change to reflect this shift. As a result, state legislatures were increasingly unrepresentative. In the same state legislature, one legislator could represent 50,000 people while another had 500,000 constituents. Not surprisingly, over-representation of rural areas led to a neglect of the issues and concerns of urban areas.

In the 1960s, a number of Supreme Court rulings began to address the imbalance of representation. In 1962, the Court ruled in *Baker v. Carr* that all legislative districts in a state had to have the same number of constituents. This ruling prompted significant efforts to make state legislatures more representative and state governments more competent. In 1964, the Court made clear that this decision applied to elections generally. *Reynolds v. Sims* (1964) prohibited states from following the federal model in which one legislative house is based on population and another on geography. Areas within a state do not have the same sovereignty that states within the federal system have, and so, the Court ruled, each chamber in a state legislature must be based on the one-person-one-vote principle. In *Westbury v. Sanders* (1964), the Court ruled that districts for the U.S. House of Representatives and local governments must also be based on population.

The one-person-one-vote principle articulated in *Baker v. Carr* led to policy agendas more relevant to the needs and opportunities of the entire state. Political scientists have examined the changes that occurred in policy agendas, state budgets, and legislative actions with the re-drawing of districts to implement the Court's ruling.[14] They found that an increased willingness to address the concerns of growing urban areas, as the voices of urban constituents reflected more effectively their presence in the state. The growth of urban areas requires major investments in water and sewerage systems, streets, schools, and parks. This requires not only some state funding, but changes in state laws authorizing municipalities to generate their own revenues. Issues of police and fire protection, public health, and traffic congestion also are special to urban areas. States almost inevitably have to allow cities to expand their jurisdiction over larger areas and to encourage regional forms of government. Legislatures ignored these issues until *Baker v. Carr* provided more urban representation.

The legislators The increased relevance of state legislatures has had an effect throughout state governments. Ironically, one of the major effects was to enhance the authority of governors and the executive branch, sometimes at the expense of legislative control. Legislatures, however, also have increased their activity and the amount of time they devote to lawmaking. In 1960, only eighteen states met annually. In 2008, all but seven met every year. In most states, floor sessions are longer, there is more committee work on proposed legislation, task forces examine issues in greater depth, and legislators and their committees have more staff to help with constituent services and legislative research than prior to 1960.[15] State administrative agencies as well as legislatures generally attract people who are more professional and eager to play a meaningful role in public problem solving.[16]

State legislatures, in contrast with Congress, are still primarily part-time citizen bodies. Some states, like Alabama and Montana, do not pay their legislators any salary but instead pay travel expenses and a set fee for every day the legislator meets either in committee or in a floor session. States with salaries for legislators pay from $8,000 in Texas to $120,000 a year in California.[17] Even in states where legislators have floor sessions and committee meetings throughout the year, compensation is usually set as a percentage of the salaries of senior administrators, and legislators receive reimbursement or special allowances for every time they leave home and travel to the state capitol. States explicitly recognize that their legislators typically have jobs in addition to their positions as representatives or senators, and have issued guidelines to avoid a conflict of interest when a legislator faces issues that affect his or her business or employment in the private sector. The most common approaches to conflicts of interest are to require disclosure of the sources of income for individual legislators and to encourage legislators from abstaining from votes on legislation that might affect their private income.[18]

Terms of office In the 1980s and 1990s, twenty states adopted **term limits** for their legislators limiting the number of years someone might serve as a state legislator. The argument fueling the drive for term limits was that individuals who made a career of elective politics amassed powers and advantages that made it difficult for someone to challenge them successfully in the polls. Representation, it was argued, would be enhanced by a regular rotation of people in and out of elective office. Some argued that limiting terms would weaken legislatures by decreasing institutional memory and policy expertise, and lobbyists and career administrators would gain influence.[19] The counterargument prevailed in five states, where state supreme court rulings and changes in political sentiment led to the abandonment term limits. Table 19.2 lists the states that still have term limits with the years that apply to each house. All of the states that adopted term limits either did so through the direct initiative process or in response to a direct initiative petition. States that adopted and then dropped term limits did so because their courts found the action conflicted with their state constitution.

All states except Nebraska have two legislative chambers. The state senate usually has fewer members than the "house" or "assembly." The most common ratio

Table 19-2. Term Limits for State Legislators

STATE	YEAR ENACTED	HOUSE LIMIT	SENATE LIMIT
Arkansas	1992	6	8
Arizona	1992	8	8
California	1990	6	8
Colorado	1990	8	8
Florida	1992	8	8
Louisiana	1995	12	12
Maine	1996	8	8
Michigan	1992	6	8
Missouri	1992	8	8
Montana	1992	8	8
Nebraska	2000	n/a	8
Nevada	1996	12	12
Ohio	1992	8	8
Oklahoma	1990	12	12
South Dakota	1992	8	8

Source: National Council of State Legislatures, www.ncsl.org

of members between the two chambers is 1:3, although New Hampshire has one senator for every 16 representatives. Thirty-four states have set four-year terms for senators and two-year terms for representatives. The other sixteen states have the same length of terms for all state legislators: eleven have two-year terms for everyone and the other five, including Nebraska, have four-year terms.

Partisan control Nebraska's legislature is also unique in that elections to its senate are **nonpartisan**, which means candidates do not run as nominees of any party. Some states and regions of the country have historically been dominated by one political party. Democrats, for example, controlled southern states from after the Civil War until the 1990s, while Republicans were predominant in New England states. Utah is an example of a Western state that has been and continues to be dominated by the Republican Party, which historically has been more conservative in Western states than it is in New England. Minnesota and Wisconsin once had very strong third parties—the Farm Labor Party in the former and the Progressive Party in the latter—that eventually merged with the Democratic Party.

The Democratic Party generally controlled substantially more state legislatures from 1952 to 1992, but Republican gains in the 1990s, especially in the South, have led to a much more competitive picture. White southerners had supported the Democratic Party since the presidency of Franklin D. Roosevelt, but started abandoning the party when it supported the civil rights movement in the 1960s. When the Republican Party shifted to the right with the election of Ronald Reagan, many white southern Democrats felt comfortable with the GOP and helped that party become more competitive in what had been a solidly Democratic region. In 2004 Republicans had a majority in both houses in 21 of the 49 bicameral state legislatures, Democrats in 17, and in 11 states party control was split. However, in 2006 Democrats gained control of both houses in 23 states, in contrast to 15 for Republicans and split control in 11 states. As Figure 19.2 shows, after the 2008 elections Democrats controlled both houses in XX states, Republicans in XX, and the parties split in XX.

As with Congress, party control of a state legislative chamber is critical to determining who will chair committees and control the agenda. Defining which issues have priority and how concerns are framed depends on who is in charge. Most states reflect the increasingly partisan nature of conflict and deliberation over policies that has characterized the federal government. Being in the minority party means being unable to achieve passage or even consideration of a proposal. Leaders of the majority party are likely to ignore and exclude legislators from the minority. Winners, of course, have always had the advantages in policy making, which is what representative democracy is all about. The partisan divide in state legislatures has, however, become so wide and bitter at times that the potential for stalemate and unresolved problems is causing increased concern.[20]

Local government executives and legislatures enact and implement public policies for communities.

Local governments follow a variety of patterns and, except for the largest cities and counties, are even more part-time than their state counterparts. Local government legislators in particular are friends and neighbors of their constituents, and have full-time jobs. They meet once a week or once a month, depending on community issues. They serve primarily out of civic duty or interest in a particular set of issues.

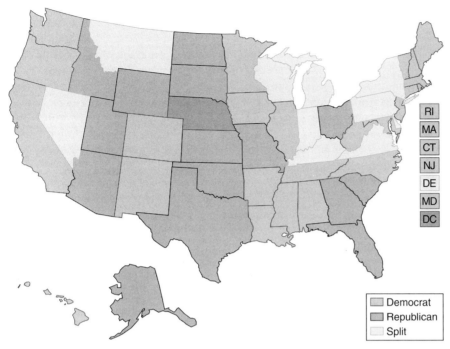

	Democrat
	Republican
	Split

Figure 19-2. **Party Control of State Legislatures, 2008.** To come.
Source: to come.

The institutions of local governments do not always follow the principles of separation of powers or checks and balances that we associate with the federal government or state governments. A single body, like a school board or village board, can have legislative, executive and even judicial powers. For example, school boards commonly adopt rules on student conduct and adjudicate any conflicts or appeals when a student is disciplined for not following those rules. School boards hire and fire administrators and, in many cases, teachers.

The composition of local governments can vary greatly, but generally will include an elected executive, such as a mayor, village president, or county executive; an elected council, such as a city council, school board, or county board; and an appointed manager, such as a city manager or school superintendent.

Elected executives Executives may be elected by voters in a community or be chosen by other council members. Almost three-fourths of the cities have a directly elected mayor. The common pattern among towns and villages is to have a mayor or president elected from among council members. Mayors of cities are usually full-time positions, while elected executives in smaller municipalities are part-time.

Most local government executives are elected in nonpartisan contests. Although, by definition, party identification is not on the ballot in nonpartisan elections, candidates in fact may be linked to a political party. In some cases, political parties make clear who their preferred candidate is in a nonpartisan election. Campaign managers and political consultants that work for candidates of a particular political party may run campaigns in nonpartisan as well as partisan elections. Individuals and organizations providing financial support to candidates may have a history of funding those using a given party label.

Like governors, local government executives have an opportunity to set the agenda since they are the most visible figures in their jurisdictions, but they do not have many of the powers of a governor. They do not, for example, have authority to amend or nullify court actions and most do not have veto powers. Some city charters explicitly provide for a **weak mayor** system by establishing two-year terms, no veto authority, and no authority to appoint the heads of administrative agencies. Mayors in such systems have, in short, little more than a ceremonial role. Other charters, primarily in large municipalities, have a **strong mayor,** with four-year terms, veto authority, and the opportunity to hire and fire top administrators. Strong elected executives may also have the power to appoint members of the legislative council to committees, thereby influencing what kinds of proposals are likely to be successful. Committee assignments, especially to committees that deal with issues critical to voters, are often extremely important to council or board members. Someone who ran to lower taxes will want to be on a budget committee and someone who argued for solutions to traffic congestion will want to be on a transportation committee. Those who identify themselves as crime fighters will want to be on a criminal justice or safety committee.

Elected councils Communities can elect representatives to a city council, school board or other local government legislative body by using geographically defined districts or as a whole. Local council elections are also usually nonpartisan.[21] **District-based elections** have the advantage of reflecting the needs and concerns of the different neighborhoods or areas in a community. People who live in apartments in densely populated areas are likely to have different concerns from those in single-family residences. Neighborhoods commonly differ from one another in ethnicity, income, and age. Boundaries can be drawn to reflect these differences, or they can fragment a particular ethnic group so that it becomes a minority in several districts and a majority in none. The Progressive movement sought to avoid district-based councils as a way of breaking up political machines based on wards with white ethnic bloc voting. The more contemporary concern is with the impact of district boundaries on African American, Hispanic, Asian American and other non-European ethnic groups. Like with the earlier white ethnic groups, one can ensure the election of an African American or Hispanic, for example, by designing districts that have substantial majorities of those groups, or one can fragment these groups into several districts so that they are minorities in each one. Ethnic representation is valued both symbolically and because it makes public policies more responsive to the needs of minorities.[22]

The alternative to district-based elections is **at-large elections**. Here candidates run to represent the city or school district or other jurisdiction as a whole, rather than a specific part of the city or school district. In some communities there are designated—usually numbered—positions so that candidates are running against one or more opponents for specific at-large positions. In other communities the election is more of a free-for-all in which the top vote getters fill whatever positions are available. Ethnic minorities are, of course, minorities in every contest in at-large elections.

Almost 3 percent of communities have a **commission** form of government, with at-large elections for positions that have both legislative and administrative responsibilities.[23] Voters elect commissioners for transportation, finance, economic development, and social services, for example. These commissioners form the equivalent of a city council and each commissioner is the head of a city agency. The commission form of government first emerged in Galveston as a response to a hurricane in 1900 that devastated southern Texas and killed almost 10,000 people.

Prominent business owners formed a task force that was formalized into a commission. The model received positive reviews and by 1917 almost 500 cities around the country adopted this form of government. Gradually a number of communities, including Galveston, abandoned the commission because agency heads ideally should be selected based on their expertise and managerial background, while elections are fundamentally about which candidate is most popular. In 2008, 176 cities had a commission. Portland, Oregon is the largest city that still has the commission form of government.

Appointed managers In part because the elected executives and legislators in most local governments serve part-time, many cities, counties, school boards, and the like hire full-time, professional managers. Progressive reformers advocated using appointed managers as part of their efforts to destroy political machines, which are built on providing jobs and services in return for electoral support. Progressives felt that having professionals in charge of providing services and hiring employees would reduce the patronage upon which machines depended. Typically city or village managers and school superintendents initially gain employment in a relatively small community and then move to larger jurisdictions. Some large and troubled school districts have contracted with national firms that specialize in the management of educational institutions and programs.

CaseStudy: Shootings on Campus

On Valentine's Day, 2008, at Northern Illinois University, a graduate returned to campus dressed in black, stepped from behind a curtain on a stage in a lecture hall, and opened fire. About 150 students were in the class, taking notes. Steven Kazmierczak, armed with a shotgun hidden in a violin case and 3 handguns concealed under a coat, shot 23 people, killing 5. He then turned one of his handguns on himself and committed suicide.[24]

Less than a year earlier, on April 16, 2007, Seung-Hui Cho had killed 32 people on the campus of Virginia Polytechnic Institute and State University (Virginia Tech), before killing himself. In the decade prior to the Northern Illinois tragedy, there were 38 school shootings in 24 states.[25] The incident at Virginia Tech was the deadliest—and it also was the deadliest shooting rampage by a single person in U.S. history.

The responsibility for maintaining safety on campuses and for responding to emergencies like school shootings falls on local government and state officials. Police at Virginia Tech and Northern Illinois were the first responders. Area police and medical personnel went into action as soon as 9-1-1 was called. Governors in both states declared official emergencies, thereby making counseling and recovery services available to the injured victims and to others affected by the incidents. State governments also reimbursed Blacksburg and DeKalb for some of the expenses they incurred in responding to the shootings.

Northern Illinois, like universities and colleges across the country, had reexamined and refined its emergency response plans in the light of lessons learned at Virginia Tech. Kazmierczak entered the lecture hall at 3:06 p.m. Police responded within 3 minutes after the shooting began. At 3:20 the campus was notified via email, text messages, the university website, and other warning systems of a gunman on campus and everyone was told to seek safety. At 3:40 the campus was locked down—no one other than emergency and law enforcement personnel were allowed on campus and classes and all other events were cancelled.

In contrast, the response at Virginia Tech had been criticized by a state-appointed task force for missing opportunities that might have saved some lives.[26] Cho's first three victims were shot in a dormitory about 7:15 a.m. Cho then went back to his dorm room, changed out of his blood-stained clothes, deleted his email, and filled his backpack with guns, ammunition and other supplies. Then he went to a post office and mailed a package of writings and video recordings to NBC News. About 2 hours after the initial shootings, Cho entered Norris Hall and chained the three main entrance doors shut. He placed a note on the barricaded entrance saying that a bomb would explode if the doors were opened. A faculty member found the note and notified the school's administration, but no one called 9-1-1. Cho went from one classroom in

Norris Hall to another, shooting students and faculty. In a 12 minute period, he fired at least 174 rounds, killing 29 and wounding 17. It took police almost 5 minutes to enter the barricaded building once they arrived on the scene.

The task force that reviewed the shootings at Virginia Tech faulted not only the response, but also the failures of state and university officials to heed signs that Seung-Hui Cho was troubled. In middle school he had been diagnosed with a severe anxiety disorder. He continued therapy until his junior year in high school. While in college a judge declared him mentally ill and ordered therapy. In part, the court action was a response to accusations in 2005 that he was stalking two female students. Because state authorities thought federal laws protecting the privacy of the mentally ill kept them from notifying gun dealers, Cho was able to purchase the guns and ammunition he used in the shootings. Similarly, university officials were not informed about his past. The shooter at Northern Illinois University also suffered from mental illness, although he did not have a history similar to Cho and there were no warning signs of the danger he posed.

Prompted by the Virginia Tech shootings, the federal government tightened its gun control laws and the U.S. Department of Education issued regulations so that the privacy rights of students would not trump the sharing of information vital to public safety. On the other hand, some state legislators in Virginia and elsewhere and the National Rifle Association argued for allowing students and faculty to carry concealed weapons on campuses, contending an armed student could have shot Cho or Kazmierczak and prevented further carnage.

ThinkingCritically

1. What, if anything, can be done to reduce the likelihood of shootings at schools and college campuses?

2. What should local police forces, hospitals, and trauma counselors do to be prepared for the shootings that might occur?

3. Should state and local governments allow individuals to carry concealed weapons on college campuses?

Forms of municipal government Municipal government may take various forms using some or all of the components just described. As Table 19.3 shows, almost 56 percent of municipalities use the combination of a mayor and an elected council. This is the most traditional form of city, town and village government. Of the mayors, 72 percent are directly elected and the others are council members who have been elected by their peers. Mayors and councils are common in the smallest and largest municipalities.

A majority of cities with populations between 25,000 and 250,000 have the council-manager form of government, in which there either is no mayor or only a weak ceremonial mayor. Elected councils hire professional managers to run their governments in this form. With very few exceptions, school districts follow the council-manager model, that is, elected school boards hire a superintendent to manage the schools.

In New England and the Midwest, most of the smallest municipalities have **town meetings** to consider budgets and laws. All voters are invited to attend a meeting, which might be annual or monthly, and conduct the public business of the community. Whoever attends determines the fate of the town. Frequently, very few actually take advantage of this opportunity for direct democracy.

A very small number of communities have **representative town meetings**. In these communities, located primarily in New Hampshire, Massachusetts, Connecticut and Vermont, voters choose representatives by precinct or district to participate in the town meeting. This form of government differs from the open town meeting in that not all voters are allowed to attend and vote. It differs from an elected council because no one serves a term of office. The representatives simply go to the meeting, deliberate, and return home as citizens without a title or set of ongoing responsibilities.

Informal power The most powerful and influential people in a community are not necessarily those who hold offices in government. Especially in small to

Table 19-3. Major Forms of Municipal Government, 2008

FORM OF GOVERNMENT	NUMBER	PERCENT
Mayor-Council	3,686	55.8
Council-Manager	2,290	34.7
Commission	176	2.7
Town Meeting	370	5.6
Representative Town Meeting	81	1.2

Source: International City/County Management Association, The Municipal Year Book 2008 (Washington, DC: ICMA, 2008), 39–45
Note: Only those municipalities with populations of at least 2,500 are included.

medium-sized communities, a single family or employer can commonly be the major decision maker, whether or not the family or the company holds a formal position such as mayor or president of the city council or chair of the county board.[27] Social and economic elites in these communities typically need to support changes in police procedures, efforts to attract new businesses, or other policy initiatives if they are to succeed. A newly elected mayor or village president would be naïve to think that he or she could govern as if the informal sources of power did not exist. When the informal and formal powers are in alignment on policies, those policies are likely to be adopted and implemented. If someone in a formal position of authority wants to oppose a family or company with informal power, he or she had better be prepared for a battle.

Ad hoc, issue-specific organizations are also important and relatively frequent sources of power at local levels of government. Individuals may, for example, come together to oppose a particular road project or to promote a program in the public schools. Their activity may be quite intense and visible as they advocate their cause. Once the decision has been made and the issue resolved—win or lose—then this ad hoc organization will generally disband and no longer exert influence on local officials.

Informal power is also important when certain personalities play a role that exceeds their formal position. This happened, for example, in San Diego in the 1970s when Pete Wilson was mayor. San Diego has a council-manager form of government, with a weak, ceremonial mayor. The city manager had been an advocate for rapid growth, but Mayor Wilson was opposed. He provided effective leadership in the community and on the City Council and was able to stop the manager.[28] Pete Wilson used his political skills, not the powers of his office. In fact, he gained attention outside the San Diego area and went on to become a U.S. Senator and then governor of California.

State Courts

Almost everyone will be in a courtroom at some point. It may be as a judge, a juror, a litigant, an attorney, or a witness. A dispute may bring us to court or an administrative function, such as the processing of a will, a name change, or an adoption. Most likely, these events will take place in a state or local court, not a federal court. The notable exception is for people who live in Washington, D.C. where all courts are federal.

The primary function of courts is to settle disputes and to enforce laws. Most disputes involve state laws, which cover criminal behavior, family matters such as divorce or child custody, business issues such as contracts, liability and land use, and, of course, traffic, parking, and speeding citations.

State and federal courts are separate but sometimes overlap.

Federal and state laws may sometimes be inter-related and federal courts may be involved in what would otherwise be a state issue. In contradictions between federal and state laws, federal law usually prevails. Through a rule known as **inclusion**, state courts are obliged to enforce the prevailing federal law. Federal courts resolve any disputes about the application of federal law. Occasionally federal and state laws apply to the same crime or acts, as is the case in most states regarding drug use and drug trafficking. These situations are called **dual jurisdiction**, which means the individual could be brought before both a state and a federal court. On these occasions, federal and state prosecutors generally agree to bring the accused to one of the two courts for trial and sentencing. Such agreements may well be based on whether the state or the federal government has the harsher penalties.

Since the 1970s, the U.S. Supreme Court has generally taken the position that state courts should regard its rulings regarding individual rights, such as freedom of speech and protection from unreasonable search and seizure, as minimums that might be enhanced by state governments. If, for example, a state law required officers making an arrest to remind the accused not only that they have a right to remain silent and have representation by an attorney, but that they also could call a friend or employer to post bail (something not guaranteed by federal law), then the extra requirement must be honored. If, on the other hand, a state did not require arresting officers to say anything about a right to remain silent, then the federal protection—known here as Miranda rights—must be applied by state courts.

Court structures in states provide routes for appeals.

States reorganized their courts in the 1970s to follow a model that simplified the handling of cases and appeals and allowed state supreme courts to refuse to take certain cases so that they had manageable workloads. Prior to these reforms, cases commonly took years, even decades, to resolve.[29] In some cases, parties to litigation about wills or land died before the courts resolved the disputes. Figure 19.3 presents the structure that describes almost all state courts since the simplification of the 1970s.

Urban areas typically have courts that handle traffic and parking citations, small claims (disputes seeking damages less than a certain sum—commonly $5,000), family issues, and probate (wills). Small towns and rural areas usually do not have their own courts, but if they do, the judges are generally part-time. Cases in these communities are heard in a county court. Municipal courts and courts that specialize in something like probate or small claims do not have juries. A single judge hears the cases. When a judge hears a case without a jury, it is referred to as a **bench trial**.

Most cases in state courts begin in county or circuit courts. These courts may also hear appeals from municipal or specialized courts. The trials in county or circuit courts are what most people envision when they think of what happens in a courtroom. In most states, either party to a dispute has the right to ask for a jury to deliberate and lawyers make arguments, call witnesses, and present evidence to the jury, with the judge presiding and ruling on whether the lawyers are following the rules in presenting evidence and questioning witnesses. The main role of the jury (or judge if the parties do not want a jury) is to evaluate the credibility of witnesses and evidence and then determine guilt, innocence, and liability, if any.

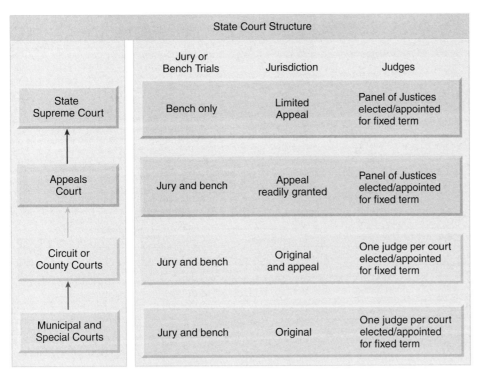

Figure 19-3. **State Court Structure.** To come.
Source: to come.

In the common state model, appeals courts are panels of several judges. Appeals courts typically must take all cases presented to them. There are no juries at this level. Appellate courts do not second guess the judges and juries that actually saw the witnesses and evidence regarding credibility. Instead, they hear arguments of lawyers about whether proper procedures were followed and whether laws and court precedents were properly applied.

State supreme courts are also appellate courts, but subsequent to the reforms of the 1970s, they can select which cases they will hear. This allows them to consider a manageable number of cases and to focus on cases where appeals courts rulings on similar issues disagree with one another or where major constitutional and legal issues are raised. If the supreme court decides not to hear a case, then the appeals court ruling stands.

Selection of judges and justices   Most state judges and **justices** (the term for members of state supreme courts) are elected to their positions for a specific term. This, of course, is different from the pattern in the federal government, where judges are appointed by the President, confirmed by the Senate, and serve indefinitely. The first states had their legislatures place judges and justices on the bench for fixed terms of 6 to 10 years. That is still the case in South Carolina and Virginia (Table 19.4). Governors in Maine and New Jersey appoint judges, subject to legislative confirmation, for 7-year terms. When a term expires, the governors may reappoint for another 7-year term. California's governor appoints appellate judges and supreme court justices for 12-year terms. When a term expires, the judge or justice must be elected for another 12 years.

Table 19-4. Judicial Selection Patterns

PARTISAN ELECTION	NONPARTISAN ELECTION	ELECTION BY LEGISLATURE	APPOINTMENT BY GOVERNOR	MISSOURI OR MERIT PLAN
Alabama	Arkansas	South Carolina	California	
Illinois	California	Virginia	Maine	
Indiana	Florida		New Jersey	
Kansas	Georgia			
Louisiana	Idaho			
Missouri	Indiana			
New York	Kentucky			
Ohio	Michigan			
Pennsylvania	Minnesota			
Tennessee	Mississippi			
Texas	Montana			
West Virginia	Nevada			
	North Carolina			
	North Dakota			
	Oregon			
	South Dakota			
	Utah			
	Washington			
	Wisconsin			
				Alaska
				Arizona
				Colorado
			Connecticut	
				Delaware
			Florida	
				Hawaii
				Indiana
				Iowa
				Kansas
				Maryland
				Massachusetts
				Missouri
				Nebraska
				New Hampshire
				New Mexico
				New York
				Oklahoma
				Rhode Island
				South Dakota
				Tennessee
				Utah
				Vermont
				Wyoming

Source: Adapted from *The Book of the States 2008* (Lexington, Ky.: Council of State Governments, 2008), pp. 251–254

Note: Some states use different selection systems for different courts.

Nineteen states elect their judges and supreme court justices on nonpartisan ballots. As with nonpartisan races for local government positions, party identification and support may be linked to candidates even though party labels do not appear on the ballot. In twelve states, judicial elections are in fact explicitly partisan and nominees may have to win a party primary just like candidates running for other, non-judicial offices (See *How Do We Know? Do Campaign Supporters Influence Decisions by Judges?*).

Concerned about the possibility of partisanship in judicial elections compromising the role and prestige of the court, 24 states use the **merit plan**, sometimes called the Missouri Plan, to select judges. In this system the governor appoints a committee of judges, attorneys and citizens to nominate individuals they consider highly qualified for a judicial position. The governor then selects someone from the list of nominees. That person serves for one year and then voters are presented with the question: "Shall Judge (name of the judge who had been serving) be retained in office?" If the majority says yes, the judge serves a full term. If the majority says no, then the governor must select someone else from the original list of nominees, who then serves a year before being subject to voter approval.

Another response to concerns about the possibility of elections compromising the impartiality of courts is to treat campaign support as a conflict of interest issue. Frequently one party in a case has a business or personal link to a judge that might rule on it. Judicial codes of conduct in all states stipulate that in such a situation the judge should make sure both sides know about the ties and can object to the judge continuing to handle the case. Moreover, judges are themselves encouraged to **recuse** themselves from the case, that is, voluntarily abstain or excuse themselves and let other judges or justices decide. Some judges recuse themselves from cases involving those who contributed substantially to their campaigns.

Recusal was a key issue in West Virginia in 2008 when Chief Justice Elliott E. Maynard received financial support for his reelection campaign and was photographed vacationing with Don L. Blankenship, chief executive of a coal company that was a litigant in cases before the state's Supreme Court. Justice Maynard voted with the majority in a 3-to-2 decision favoring Blankenship's company and only recused himself after publicity about the conflict of interest prompted the Court to reconsider the case. Voters regarded the recusal too late and too reluctant and Justice Maynard was defeated in the Democratic primary in his bid for a new term. His opponents ran heavily on the need to restore confidence in the integrity of the state's highest court.

States prohibit judicial candidates from indicating how they would rule in a pending or likely lawsuit. All states have such prohibitions. The U.S. Supreme Court in *Republican Party of Minnesota v. White* (2002) ruled that states cannot prohibit candidates for positions on the bench from discussing substantive issues or telling voters how they would handle certain types of cases or legal issues, but the Court agreed it was inappropriate to make promises about specific cases.

HOW DO WE KNOW?

Do Campaign Supporters Influence Decisions by Judges?

The Question

When judges are elected rather than appointed, they need financial and other forms of support in their campaigns. If special interest groups or wealthy individuals support a judicial candidate, they might expect that they will be treated favorably by the judge once he or she is elected. This expectation can threaten public confidence in the fairness of judicial decisions. Do campaign supporters influence decisions by judges? How do we know?

Why It Matters

Ideally, judges are regarded as neutral, third party arbiters of disputes. Unlike legislators or governors, judges are not considered to have constituents that they serve, because they serve society as a whole. Judges are to interpret and apply the law to specific cases, not reward supporters. The functioning of the court depends heavily on a general sense that *everyone* is treated fairly and impartially. Like in an athletic contest, it is important that referees or umpires are not blamed for being biased and ruling for one side because of that bias.

Even with attempts to distance judges from their campaign supporters that we discussed, the potential for bias remains. In fact, one might interpret these attempts as an acknowledgement of the power behind the notion that campaign supporters influence judges. Political scientists have addressed this issue in a number of studies, using different research designs.

Investigating the Answer

Stuart Nagel focused on states with a partisan election process for judicial selection. He then identified which state courts were dominated by Republicans, which by Democrats, and which were fairly even. Then he looked at whether decisions made by these courts favored criminal defendants, corporations, government agencies, and poor people.[30] He hypothesized that courts dominated by Republicans tended to favor corporations and rule against criminal defendants, government agencies and poor people; courts dominated by Democrats would have the opposite tendencies; and evenly split courts would be mixed. He found no significant correlations between the partisan character of a court and its judicial decisions.

Madhavi McCall, however, used a similar but more detailed approach in a study of the Texas supreme court. Texas uses partisan elections to select members of its supreme court. McCall correlated campaign contributors with the decisions of specific judges. Although there were some notable exceptions, McCall found a clear and systematic pattern in which the judges ruled in favor of groups who had made significant contributions to their campaigns.[31] The McCall study was about just one state, but it had the advantage of looking closely at the votes of individual justices and at their respective supporters.

Medina Gann Hall completed a comprehensive study of the influence of elections and campaign contributions on the behavior of state supreme court justices. Her study included states using different selection processes and, like McCall, analyzed the relationships between the decisions of individual justices and the groups providing campaign support. She, too, found a pattern suggesting that campaign contributions matter.[32] Justices rarely recused themselves from cases in which groups that had made substantial contributions had an interest. Moreover, they generally ruled in favor of those groups. The pattern in partisan elections was stronger than that for nonpartisan elections, but the relationship between contributions and rulings was evident in both systems.

Hall also compared what happens in states in which justices are elected and those in which they are appointed. This is important because the appointments are made by elected governors and legislators who usually draw support from particular sets of interest groups. Hall found that appointed justices tended to rule in favor of the groups who supported the governors and legislators responsible for their appointment. This was even somewhat the case with states that use the merit (or Missouri) plan. The degree to which appointed justices favored the groups who supported those who appointed them, however, was considerably less than occurred for elected justices, where the relationship to campaign contributors was more direct.[33]

The studies cited above examined state supreme courts. Many critical decisions are, of course, made at the appellate and trial court levels. It is reasonable to infer that the patterns discovered in looking at supreme courts also applies to other courts, but we do not know that for certain. Given the number of judges and decisions below the supreme court level, conducting a comparable study of the relationships between campaign contributions and the behavior of all these judges would be a Herculean task.

Another difference between the decisions of state supreme court justices and those of appellate and trial judges is that the reasoning provided in the written opinions of supreme court justices is typically more detailed. In large part, this is because state supreme courts set precedents that are supposed to be followed by other courts in their respective states. The issue of judicial reasoning also raises another caveat in the studies done by political scientists—and by those engaged in judicial campaigns. Disputes typically raise several important legal issues, and characterizing a justice as being for business interests or biased towards defendants in criminal cases is sometimes misleading. A vote that results in a victory for an insurance company may be based on how a state statute is written, rather than on a bias in favor of companies who made campaign contributions. What appears to be a ruling freeing a convicted criminal or reducing a sentence may be based on procedures that were not followed, not sympathy for someone who has had a rough life.

Finally, and importantly, determining whether or not campaign contributions influence judicial decisions almost inevitably involves making reasonable interpretations of why a correlation does or does not exist. We simply do not have emails or taped conversations between justices and their campaign contributors that reveal negotiations or motivations for particular decisions. If there was a pattern of justices ruling in favor of their supporters, we can conclude that there may be influence. However, it may also be that interest groups make contributions to candidates who would rule in their favor even if no contribution were made. The contribution, in other words, is designed to get a sympathetic candidate elected.

The Bottom Line

The most comprehensive, systematic research does show a positive relationship between campaign contributions to judicial candidates and the decisions those candidates make if they get on the bench. This finding is especially important because the relationship is stronger than that between the rulings of justices who are appointed to state supreme courts and the campaign supporters of those who appoint them. Even though we lack direct evidence of motivation or negotiation, it is reasonable to be concerned that elected justices seem to act like other elected officials, for whom we expect and accept constituent relations.

Direct Democracy

Some state and local governments provide their citizens with opportunities for participating directly in public policy making, rather than relying solely on elected representatives. The town meetings in small communities in New England and Midwestern states, discussed earlier, are one form of direct democracy. However, there are several other forms as well, which we will examine here.

Initiatives allow voters to enact laws. In nineteen states, most of them in the West, citizens can use the **direct initiative** to enact state laws (Table 19.5). Western states wrote their constitutions and were admitted to the United States at the height of the Progressive movement, which sought to empower voters rather than bosses of political machines. The direct initiative is also available at the local government level in twenty-eight states. Under this procedure, if enough citizens sign a petition supporting a particular proposal, that idea will be placed on a ballot and will become law if approved by a majority of those voting. The governor and legislature are not involved in direct initiatives.

The number of signatures required to get a measure on a ballot varies by state but is typically 8–10 percent of the number of people who voted in the most recent gubernatorial election. Wyoming requires 15 percent. North Dakota places the minimum at 2 percent of the voting age population.

The direct initiative was one of the reforms that came out of the Progressive Era. The idea was that, to combat political machines and special interest groups that might control governors or legislators, direct democracy would enable people to take action by themselves. However, special interest groups still have an impact. For example, business groups, labor unions, and single-issue advocacy organizations pay individuals as much as $5 for every signature they get on a petition to put a proposal on a ballot. As pointed out in Chapter 9, political advertising is key to campaigning and this applies to campaigns for and against ballot initiatives as well as candidates. Ideally, the advertisements inform the electorate, but unequal access to funds may mean that one side cannot get its message out to voters as effectively as the other.[34] In some states, like California, each side commonly spends about $35 million on ballot initiatives. Despite the drawbacks, the direct initiative has been widely used to enact legalizing medical use of marijuana, physician-assisted suicide, property tax limits, life terms for repeat offenders, and a ban on confining pregnant pigs.

One concern about the direct initiative is that it provides no opportunity for the kind of deliberation and amendment of proposals that occurs in a legislature. Voters have to accept or reject the proposal as presented on the ballot. When issues like the status of children of illegal immigrants described in the opening vignette are dealt with in an initiative, there are no opportunities for dealing with subtleties or complexities through debate and amendment. The **indirect initiative**, available in eight states—including five that also have the direct initiative—addresses this concern. This process starts with action by the legislature, which introduces, debates, amends and passes a proposal just like any other bill. However, instead of sending the bill to the governor for approval, the legislature puts the measure on the ballot for approval by voters.

Referenda allow voters in states to veto legislation and authorize borrowing money.

Another form of direct democracy is the **popular referendum**, sometimes called the direct referendum. Using a popular referendum, voters can veto actions by the

Table 19-5. Authority for Instruments of Direct Democracy

STATE	DIRECT INITIATIVE	INDIRECT INITIATIVE	POPULAR REFERENDUM	RECALL
Alabama				X
Alaska	X		X	X
Arizona	X		X	X
Arkansas	X		X	
California	X		X	X
Colorado	X			X
Florida	X			
Georgia				X
Idaho			X	X
Illinois	X			
Kansas				X
Kentucky			X	
Louisiana				X
Maine		X	X	
Maryland			X	
Massachusetts		X	X	
Michigan	X	X	X	X
Minnesota				X
Missouri	X		X	
Montana	X		X	X
Nebraska	X		X	
Nevada	X	X	X	X
New Mexico			X	
North Dakota	X		X	X
Ohio	X	X	X	
Oklahoma	X		X	
Oregon	X		X	X
Rhode Island				X
South Dakota	X		X	
Utah	X	X	X	
Washington	X	X	X	X
Wisconsin				X
Wyoming		X	X	

Source: Based on *The Book of the States, 2008* (Lexington, Ky.: Council of State Governments, 2008), 308–327

legislature and governor. Voters in twenty-four states may circulate a petition objecting to a bill passed in a recent legislative session, and if enough people sign the petition, the question of whether to uphold or veto the bill will appear on the ballot. For example, in North Dakota in 2007 the legislature and governor agreed on an abortion bill that was designed to bring the question before the U.S. Supreme Court of whether states could ban abortions. The governor and a majority of legislators felt that two new appointments to the Court by President George W. Bush probably meant that *Roe v. Wade* would be overturned. Voters in North

Dakota objected, however, to what they felt were excessive restrictions on the privacy rights of women and used the popular referendum to veto the law and keep it from becoming the basis of a test case in court.

When governments have to borrow money to complete a project like a new school or a bridge, they often have to get voter approval in a **bond referendum**. This is especially true for local governments. The debates about whether to approve the issuance of bonds include not only whether the project is needed but also how much taxpayers will be billed to pay back the loans and interest.

Sometimes legislators place an **advisory referendum** on the ballot. As the term implies, the results of an advisory referendum are not binding. Legislators may genuinely want to test voter sentiment before deciding whether or not to initiate a change in a law. Another reason for having an advisory referendum is political. An issue may be placed on the ballot to mobilize some voters to go to the polls in the hopes that they will support certain candidates as well as vote on the referendum. Such a strategy was used in advisory referenda on ending the United States involvement in Iraq in 2006 in over 2,500 local and state elections. Obviously cities and states have no control over U.S. military and foreign policy. The referenda were designed to mobilize anti-war sentiment and advantage certain candidates.

Recall allows voters in some states to remove elected officials from their positions before their terms expire.

Finally, most states allow their citizens to **recall** elected local government officials and 18 states allow state officials such as judges, legislators and governors to be recalled. A recall is a procedure in which an elected official is voted out of office before his or her term expires. In 11 of the 17 states that allow recall, a recall does not require any particular grounds, such as a crime or scandal. In Alaska, Georgia, Kansas, Minnesota, Montana, Rhode Island, and Washington, specific grounds are required and a judge determines whether the alleged misconduct or malfeasance is serious enough to warrant a recall. The judge makes the determination after a hearing in which both sides are able to make arguments and offer evidence. But in all situations, the issue of guilt or innocence and the decision whether to retain or remove the official are up to voters. State legislators have been recalled for raising taxes and supporting subsidies for professional baseball teams. Judges have been recalled for blaming victims of rape for the assault they suffered, rather than those who committed the crime. Only two governors have been recalled: North Dakota's Lynn Frazier in 1921 and California's Gray Davis in 2003.

Governor Davis did not enjoy a high level of popularity but nonetheless defeated a Republican candidate in 2002. A Republican group immediately began a recall effort. In California, a recall ballot has two parts. Part one asks voters if the person in office should or should not be recalled and part two presents candidates for the office should the majority favor recall. Of those voting, 54 percent indicated that they wanted Governor Davis to be recalled. Part two listed 134 candidates to replace Davis. Arnold Schwarzenegger, who had the advantage of widespread recognition because of his career as an actor, garnered 46.9 percent of the votes cast in part two, and thus took office.

In most other states a person must serve for one year in the office before he or she can be recalled and there are separate ballots and times to decide to recall someone and then choose a replacement. The more common process is first to decide whether or not to recall someone. If a majority favors recall, voters go to the polls three to four weeks later for a primary election to determine which names will be on the final ballot. After another three to four weeks, voters choose between winners of the primary.

The irony of all forms of direct democracy is that enhanced access to government does not translate into higher rates of participation. Even in visible, colorful recall elections like the one in California in 2003, less than half of eligible voters tend to go to the polls. This difference between opportunity and reality applies generally to state and local governments. School board members, city council members, mayors, and state legislators are approached with suggestions, complaints, and concerns when they shop for groceries, go for a walk, or attend church. They are contacted by phone and by email. But those who make the effort to express themselves in these ways and to attend meetings and hearings are small percentage of those who could participate in grassroots governance.

SUMMARY

▶ State constitutions and local government charters provide frameworks in much the same way that the U.S. Constitutions guides the federal government. The constitutions specify individual rights that state governments must respect and describe the basic institutions and processes for selecting officials and enacting public policies. In large part because territories that petitioned to join the Union as states had to have a constitution acceptable to Congress, states have borrowed from one another and their constitutions are generally similar. Local governments do not inherently have a right to exist or a responsibility to follow certain principles. State governments use charters to authorize specific local governments and determine the extent of their authority and what, if any, taxation or enforcement powers they might have.

▶ Like the federal government, states have separate legislative and executive branches each with distinct powers. Since the application in the 1960s of the one-person-one-vote principle for determining the boundaries of legislative districts, state governments have become more relevant and more competent. Governors, in particular, but have emerged as very powerful institutions. State legislatures are more representative of a state's population, have professional staff, and are increasingly becoming full-time. Local governments may have executive and legislative responsibilities located in the same offices and institutions. Most local governments are still run by individuals who serve part-time as elected leaders, and community leaders are important decision makers, even when they hold no public office. Any specific local government is likely to have one or more of the following: elected executive, elected council, and appointed manager.

▶ Most legal disputes are settled in state courts. Federal courts and federal laws have some impact on what happens in state courts, but only where federal and state laws converge. Unlike the federal pattern, most of the states elect their judges for specific terms of office. Campaigns have the potential for compromising the fair and impartial role that judges are supposed to play in deciding cases.

▶ Some states allow voters to place on the ballot proposals to enact laws or to veto recently passed legislation. When local governments borrow money, they generally have to seek voter approval. Another form of direct democracy is the opportunity voters have to remove an elected official from office before his or her term expires. In most cases, there does not have to be any specified grounds for a recall and in the seven states that do require that there be grounds, it is still up to voters rather than jurors to decide whether to retain or recall the official. While direct democracy is not the norm for governance, ballot initiatives and recall can and are used to pursue policy and political objectives.

KEY TERMS

advisory referendum, p. 000
at-large election, p. 000
bench trial, p. 000
bond referendum, p. 000

charter, p. 000
charter school, p. 000
commission, p. 000
commute, p. 000

SUGGESTED READINGS

Cronin, Thomas E. *Direct Democracy: The Politics of Initiative, Referendum, and Recall.* (Cambridge, MA: Harvard University Press, 1999) An examination of the origins and development of the major instruments of direct democracy.

Dresang, Dennis L. and James J. Gosling. *Politics and Policy in American States and Communities*, 6th edition (New York: Pearson Longman, 2008). A textbook covering the institutions, processes and major public policies of state and local governments.

Rosenthal, Alan. *Heavy Lifting: The Job of the American Legislature* (Washington, DC: Congressional Quarterly Press, 2004) A critique of the challenges faced by state legislatures and recent trends towards partisanship.

Wright, Ralph G. *Inside the Statehouse: Lessons from the Speaker* (Washington, DC: Congressional Quarterly Press, 2005). Reflections of the former Speaker of the Vermont General Assembly, both on dynamics within the legislature and relations with governors.

Northwest Ordinance of 1787 law passed by Congress under the Articles of Confederation that established the process by which the territories of Ohio, Indiana, Illinois, Michigan, and Wisconsin would be governed and admitted as states.

Progressive movement advocated measures to destroy political machines and instead have direct participation by voters in the nomination of candidates and the establishment of public policy.

initiative a process in which a proposal for legislation is placed on the ballot and voters can either enact or reject the proposal without further action by the governor or legislature.

Dillon's rule principle articulated in a court ruling that local governments do not have any inherent sovereignty but instead must be authorized by a state government.

charter a document that, like a constitution, specifies the basic policies, procedures, and institutions of a local government.

county a district created by state government for establishing a local government responsible for implementing a variety of state laws and for providing general governmental services.

town a local government with general responsibilities for order and services in a medium-sized community.

township a six-mile by six-mile area created by the Northwest Ordinance of 1787 to be used for local governance in the territories of Ohio, Indiana, Michigan, Illinois, and Wisconsin.

special district a local government created for a narrowly defined purpose and with a restricted source of revenue.

home rule a local government with authority to pass laws and provide services as long as those laws or services are not provided by a special district or otherwise prohibited under state law.

charter school schools that are within the public school system that operate in accordance with a charter approved by a school district or state agency to follow an individually designed program.

governor the chief elected executive official in state governments.

package or general veto the authority of a chief executive to void an entire bill that has been passed by the legislature.

line-item veto the authority of a chief executive to delete part of a bill passed by the legislature. This authority is limited to bills involving taxing or spending.

pardon the authority of a governor to cancel someone's conviction of a crime and eliminate all sanctions and punishments.

parole the authority of a governor to release a prisoner before his or her full sentence has been completed. A parole is for a specific period and includes restrictions and supervision.

commute the action of a governor to cancel all or part of a sentence while keeping a conviction on the record.

extradite the action of a governor to send someone against his or her will to another state to face criminal charges.

term limits restrictions that exist in some states about how long an individual may serve in an elected office.

nonpartisan an election in which candidates run without formal identification or association with a political party.

weak mayor a governance system in which the elected chief executive has little formal authority to veto legislation or appoint administrators.

strong mayor a governance system in which the elected chief executive has significant authority to veto legislation and appoint administrators.

district-based election election in which candidates run for an office that represents only the voters of a specific district within the jurisdiction.

at-large election election in which candidates for office must compete throughout the jurisdiction as a whole.

commission form of local government in which voters elect individuals to act as legislators and to head an administrative agency.

town meeting form of local government in which all eligible voters are invited to attend a meeting to pass budgets and ordinances.

representative town meeting form of local government in which voters select someone from their precinct or district to participate in a meeting that considers and approves budgets and ordinances. Representatives do not hold an office or serve a term after the meeting adjourns.

inclusion the principle that state courts will apply federal laws when those laws directly conflict with state laws.

dual jurisdiction when two different courts (state, tribal, federal) have the authority to try someone for crimes committed in the same incident.

bench trial a court trial in which a judge hears and rules on a case without a jury.

justice the term used to refer to a member of a state supreme court.

merit plan a method of selecting judges in wich a governor must appoint someone from a list provided by an independent panel. Judges are then kept in office if the get a majority of "yes" votes in general elections. Also called Missouri plan.

recuse the act of abstaining or not participating in a decision. This applies primarily to judges who avoid a conflict of interest by not participating in cases where they have a personal or financial interest.

direct initiative a process in which voters can place a proposal on a ballot and enact it into law without involving the legislature or governor.

indirect initiative a process in which the legislature places a proposal on a ballot and allows voters to enact it into law, without involving the governor or further action by the legislature.

popular referendum a process by which voters can veto a bill recently passed in the legislature by placing the issue on a ballot and expressing disapproval. Also called direct referendum.

bond referendum a process of seeking voter approval before a government borrows money by issuing bonds to investors.

advisory referendum a process in which voters cast non-binding ballots on an issue or proposal.

recall a process in which voters can petition for a vote to remove officials between elections.

NOTES

CHAPTER ONE

1. White House press release, February 24, 2004.
2. Election 2004: Key ballot measure results by state. http://www.usatoday.com/news/politicselections/vote2004/KeyBallotInitiativesByState.aspx?rti=G&cn=1&tf=l accessed on August 1, 2007.
3. Cecilia Le, "No 'Monopoly on Morality'" *Utica Observer Dispatch Web Edition.* November 10, 2004. Accessed at http://www.uticaod.com/archive/2004/11/10/news/12337.html on August 1, 2007.
4. Robert Shrum, *No Excuses: Concessions of a Serial Campaigner.* (New York: Simon and Schuster, 2007); Dana Hull, "Gay Marriage Opposition Seen as a Factor Aiding Bush." *San Jose Mercury News.* November 2004 accessed at http://www.tampabaycoalition.com/files/DATBRobinGayMarriageOpposition FactorAidingBushNov4.htm on August 1, 2007.
5. Walter Shapiro, "Presidential election may have hinged on one issue: Issue 1" *USA Today*, November 4, 2004 accessed at http://www.usatoday.com/news/opinion/columnist/shapiro/2004-11-04-hype_x.htm on August 1, 2007.
6. http://encarta.msn.com/text_761572095_1/Federalism.html accessed on August 1, 2007.
7. Thomas Hobbes, *Leviathan.* Edited by Richard Tuck. (New York: Cambridge University Press, 1996).
8. See Thomas Hobbes, *Leviathan*; John Locke, *Second Treatise on Government.* Edited by C. B. Macpherson (Indiana Publishing Company, 1980); and Jean-Jacques Rousseau. *Basic Political Writings.* Edited by Donald A. Cress. (Indianapolis: Hackett Publishing Company, 1987).

CHAPTER TWO

1. Because the creed is grounded in the "classical liberal" political theory of the seventeenth and eighteenth centuries, it is sometimes referred to as the liberal tradition, American creed, or classical liberalism. Although a difficult read, the chief source of the argument is Louis Hartz, *The Liberal Tradition in America: An Interpretation of American Political Thought Since the Revolution* (New York: Harcourt Brace, 1955). See also David F. Ericson and Louisa Bertch Green, eds., *The Liberal Tradition in American Politics: Reassessing the Legacy of American Liberalism* (New York: Routledge, 1999). The term "American creed" has a long history. One of its more famous scholarly proponents is sociologist Seymour Martin Lipset. See *American Exceptionalism: A Double-Edged Sword* (New York: W. W. Norton, 1997).
2. Peter A. Morrison, "A Demographic Perspective on Our Nation's Future," RAND Report, 2001. http://www.rand.org/publications/DB/DB320/.
3. Werner Sombart's argument was published in German in 1905. It appears in English as *Why Is There No Socialism in the United States?*, translated by Patricia M. Hocking (Armonk, NY: M.E. Sharpe, 1976).
4. See Theda Skocpol, "The Origins of Social Policy in the United States: A Polity-Centered Analysis," in Lawrence C. Dodd and Calvin Jillson, eds., *The Dynamics of American Politics: Approaches & Interpretations* (Boulder, CO: Westview Press, 1994); Adam Przeworski, "The Material Bases of Consent," in Adam Przeworski, *Capitalism and Social Democracy* (New York: Cambridge University Press, 1985); Hartz, *The Liberal Tradition in America.*
5. Edward S. Herman and Noam Chomsky, *Manufacturing Consent: The Political Economy of the Mass Media* (Pantheon, 2002); Robert Justin Goldstein, *Political Repression in Modern America: From 1870 to 1976* (Champaign: University of Illinois Press, 2001); Victoria Hattam, *Labor Visions and State Power: The Origins of Business Unionism in the United States* (Princeton, NJ: Princeton University Press, 1992).
6. See Michael Lind, "The American Creed: Does It Matter? Should It Change?" *Foreign Affairs*, March/April 1996; and Forrest Church, "The American Creed," *The Nation*, September 16, 2002. Property rights and religious freedom can be considered parts of liberty, but because of their historic significance and prominence in the way Americans think about politics and government, we present them as separate beliefs in the creed.

7. Richard M. Merelman, *Partial Visions: Culture and Politics in Britain, Canada, and the United States* (Madison: University of Wisconsin Press, 1991), 20.

8. Pew Research Center for the People & the Press and Pew Forum on Religion and Public Life, Religion and Public Life Survey, 2002. See http://people-press.org/reports/display.php3?PageID=388.

9. Equal opportunity poll data: Pew Values Update, 1998, question 15c.

10. Lars Osberg and Timothy Smeeding, "An International Comparison of Preferences for Leveling," October 3, 2003, http://www-cpr.maxwell.syr.edu/seminar/fall03/osberg.pdf; Lars Osberg and Timothy Smeeding, "'Fair' Inequality? An International Comparison of Attitudes to Pay Differentials," November 2, 2004, http://www.cpr.maxwell.syr.edu/faculty/smeeding/selectedpapers/Economicaversion27October2004.pdf.

11. *In The Democratic Wish: Popular Participation and the Limits of American Government*, revised edition (New Haven, CT: Yale University Press, 1998), James Morone discusses different perspectives on democracy in American history.

12. John Locke, a famous and influential political philosopher during America's colonial period, made the point that the "social contract" between government and the people required this escape hatch. Without the ability to disband and reformulate government, his theory suggests, the idea of consent would be very thin. John Locke, *Two Treatises of Government*, originally published in 1689.

13. Pew Values Update, 1998, question 14O.

14. Anne Norton, *Republic of Signs: Liberal Theory and American Popular Culture* (Chicago: University of Chicago Press, 1993).

15. On the intersection of Christianity and political culture in America, see James T. Kloppenberg, "The Virtues of Liberalism: Christianity, Republicanism, and Ethics in Early American Political Discourse," *Journal of American History* 74 (1987): 9–33.

16. "My position on these issues is shaped by deeply held beliefs. I'm a strong supporter of science and technology, and believe they have the potential for incredible good—to improve lives, to save life, to conquer disease...I also believe human life is a sacred gift from our Creator. I worry about a culture that devalues life, and believe as your President I have an important obligation to foster and encourage respect for life in America and throughout the world." "President Discusses Stem Cell Research," Office of the Press Secretary, August 9, 2001. http://www.whitehouse.gov/news/releases/2001/08/20010809-2.html.

17. Pew Center for the People and the Press surveys.

18. Pew Research Center for the People and the Press and Pew Forum on Religion & Public Life, August 2004 News Interest Index.

19. Pew Center for the People and the Press surveys.

20. Richard J. Ellis, *American Political Cultures* (New York: Oxford University Press, 1993).

21. Daniel J. Elazar, *American Federalism: A View from the States*, 3rd ed. (New York: HarperCollins, 1984). A map is available at http://www.valpo.edu/geomet/pics/geo200/politics/elazar.gif.

22. Daniel T. Rodgers, *Contested Truths: Keywords in American Politics Since Independence* (Cambridge, MA: Harvard University Press, 1998).

23. There have been multi-legislator districts in some states at some times, but they have been a very small share of the total.

24. *Vieth v. Jubilerer.*

25. Four cases were consolidated as *League of United Latin American Citizens v. Perry.*

26. Communitarianism is a modern version of a political philosophy known as classical republicanism. As the name suggests, the classical republican ethos harkens back to the politics, structure, and beliefs of the republics of antiquity, particularly Rome. This ethos was particularly prominent in the Revolutionary era. Although there are some distinctions between communitarianism and classical republicanism, they are similar enough for us to use the single label in this discussion.

27. Cited in Gordon S. Wood, *The Creation of the American Republic, 1776–1787* (New York: W.W. Norton, 1969), 61.

28. Wood, *The Creation of the American Republic, 1776–1787*; Bernard Bailyn, *The Ideological Origins of the American Revolution* (Cambridge, MA: Harvard University Press, 1992).

29. In the words of a colonist in 1776, "No man is a true republican that will not give up his single voice to that of the public." Cited in Wood, *The Creation of the American Republic, 1776–1787*, 61.

30. One of the best-known popularizers of communitarian ideas is Amitai Etzioni. See, for example, his *The Spirit of Community: The Reinvention of American Society* (New York: Touchstone, 1993).

31. For a classic statement of the political difficulties of the self-regulating market, see Karl Polanyi, *The Great Transformation: The Political and Economic Origins of Our Times*, 2nd ed. (Boston: Beacon Press, 2001).

32. Carmen DeNavas-Walt, Bernadette D. Peters, and Cheryl Hill Lee, United States Census Bureau, "Income, Poverty, and Health Insurance Coverage in the United States: 2004," 60–229, August 2005; Kate Bundorf and Victor Fuchs, "Who Favors National

Health Insurance? Who Opposes It? And Why?" talk delivered at the Center for Health Policy and Center for Primary Care and Outcomes Research, Stanford University, March 8, 2006. http://chppcor.stanford.edu/events/4436.

33. Francesca Colombo and Nicole Tapay, "Private Health Insurance in OECD Countries: The Benefits and Costs for Individuals and Health Systems," OECD Health Working Paper no. 15, 2004, 11–12.

34. See polls at http://www.pollingreport.com/health3.htm.

35. See Sven Steinmo and Jon Watts, "It's the Institutions, Stupid! Why Comprehensive National Health Insurance Fails in America," n.d., http://stripe.colorado.edu/~steinmo/stupid.htm.

36. See Colin Gordon, *Dead on Arrival: The Politics of Health Care in Twentieth-Century America* (Princeton, NJ: Princeton University Press, 2003); Jacob S. Hacker, "The Historical Logic of National Health Insurance: Structure and Sequence in the Development of British, Canadian, and U.S. Medical Policy," *Studies in American Political Development* 12, 1 (Spring 1998), 57–130.

37. See the case study in Chapter 8 for a discussion of the politics surrounding President Bill Clinton's health care plan.

38. Kate Bundorf and Victor Fuchs, "Who Favors National Health Insurance? Who Opposes It? And Why?" talk delivered at the Center for Health Policy and Center for Primary Care and Outcomes Research, Stanford University, March 8, 2006. http://chppcor.stanford.edu/events/4436.

39. See Rogers M. Smith, "Beyond Tocqueville, Myrdal, and Hartz: The Multiple Traditions in America," *American Political Science Review* 87, 3 (1993): 549–66, for an excellent discussion of discrimination as part of American political culture. Survey data in this paragraph is from the General Social Survey.

40. The case of Chicanos in the United States is discussed in Maria Hsia Chang, "Multiculturalism, Immigration and Aztlan," paper presented at the Second Alliance for Stabilizing America's Population Action Conference, Breckenridge, CO, August 6, 1999. http://www.diversityalliance.org/docs/Chang-aztlan.html

41. Doriane Lambelet Coleman, "Individualizing Justice Through Multiculturalism: The Liberals' Dilemma," *Columbia Law Review* 96, 5 (1996): 1093–1167.

42. Susan Moller Okin, "Is Multiculturalism Bad for Women?" In *Is Multiculturalism Bad for Women?*, eds. Joshua Cohen and Matthew Howard (Princeton, NJ: Princeton University Press, 1999). In Okin's view, "Despite all this evidence of cultural practices that control and subordinate women, none of the promi-

nent defenders of multicultural group rights has adequately or even directly addressed the troubling connections between gender and culture, or the conflicts that arise so commonly between multiculturalism and feminism." See also Cynthia Lee, "Cultural Convergence: Interest Convergence Theory Meets the Cultural Defense?" *Arizona Law Review* 49, 4, (2007).

CHAPTER THREE

1. "Dewine, Graham, Hagel & Snowe Introduce the Terrorist Surveillance Act of 2006," Office of Senator Mike DeWine, Ohio, http://dewine.senate.gov/pressapp/record.cfm?id=252819.

2. Eric Lichtblau, "Bush Would Let Secret Court Sift Wiretap Process," *New York Times*, July 14, 2006; Charles Babington and Peter Baker, "Bush Compromises On Spying Program," *Washington Post*, July 14, 2006.

3. Bernard Bailyn, *The Ideological Origins of the American Revolution* (Cambridge, MA: Harvard University Press, 1967), 160.

4. Bailyn, *Ideological Origins*, x.

5. "It seemed indeed to be a peculiar moment in history when all knowledge coincided, when classical antiquity, Christian theology, English empiricism, and European rationalism could all be linked....However imprecise, confused, and eclectic the colonists' gleanings from history and quotations from philosophers may seem to us, they represented to eighteenth-century Americans the experience and reason of the Western world." Gordon S. Wood, *The Creation of the American Republic, 1776–1787* (New York: W. W. Norton, 1969), 7–8.

6. Edmund S. Morgan, *Inventing the People: The Rise of Popular Sovereignty in England and America* (New York: W. W. Norton, 1989).

7. Bailyn, *Ideological Origins*, 173.

8. All colonies except Georgia sent representatives to the Congress.

9. Social scientists label this the "state," but that terminology is complicated by the fact that in the United States the word "state" is most often used in reference to state governments.

10. See Merrill Jensen, *The Articles of Confederation* (Madison: University of Wisconsin Press, 1970).

11. On the despair of the 1780s, see Wood, *Creation of the American Republic*, chap. 10.

12. He is also famously, or infamously, known for losing his life in a duel with Aaron Burr.

13. For an overview, see Michael Kammen, *The Origins of the American Constitution: A Documentary History*

(New York: Penguin Books, 1986); Catherine Bowen, *Miracle at PhiladelphiaThe Story of the Constitutional Convention, May - September 1787* (Boston: Little, Brown, 1966); Jack Rakove, *Original Meanings: Politics and Ideas in the Making of the Constitution* (New York: Alfred A. Knopf, 1996).

14. Some historians believe that the Framers were influenced by the governing practices of the Six Nations, known more commonly as the Iroquois Confederacy, which included the Cayuga, Mohawk, Oneida, Onondaga, Seneca, and Tuscarora tribes. Certainly many of the features of U.S. government were present in the Confederacy: checks and balances, federalism, participation, and civil liberties protections. The preamble to the Constitution echoes the language in a 1520 Iroquois treaty: "We the people, to form a union, to establish peace, equity, and order." The Iroquois occupied territory now in New York State. Members of the Iroquois visited the Continental Congress in June 1776. See Bruce E. Johansen, *Forgotten Founders: Benjamin Franklin, the Iroquois and the Rationale for the American Revolution* (Ipswich, MA: Gambit, 1982).

15. Randolph presented a resolution at the outset of the Convention that served, in effect, as a draft for a new system of government. Influenced by the thinking of James Madison, who would later play a key role in the ratification process as well as serve as secretary of state under Thomas Jefferson and be elected president in 1808, it would serve as a point of departure for debate over the next several months.

16. The New Jersey Plan was geared more toward revising the Articles rather than discarding them. By the time it was introduced, however, delegates had already gravitated toward the idea that a new system was needed.

17. The three-fifths calculation would also apply for federal taxation purposes as well.

18. Informally, it is reasonable to refer to the United States as having a democratic form of government, and this is more common than saying it has a republican form of government. In everyday language, when people think "democracy" they are thinking along the lines of republican government. "Direct democracy" is often used to describe democracy in which the people themselves make law. Another way to think about this is that there is a democratic continuum in which direct democracy is at one end and some form of republicanism is at the other; many different forms of democratic institutions can be scattered along the continuum between these two endpoints.

19. In *Federalist 51*, Madison notes that "it is not possible to give to each department an equal power of self-de-

fense. In republican government, the legislative authority necessarily predominates. The remedy for this inconveniency is to divide the legislature into different branches; and to render them, by different modes of election and different principles of action, as little connected with each other as the nature of their common functions and their common dependence on the society will admit."

20. *Federalist 51*.

21. *Federalist 51*.

22. The Supreme Court verified national supremacy on this issue in its decision in *Lorillard Tobacco Company v. Reilly* (2001): "Congress enacted a comprehensive scheme to address cigarette smoking and health in advertising and pre-empted state regulation of cigarette advertising that attempts to address that same concern, even with respect to youth. The First Amendment also constrains state efforts to limit advertising of tobacco products....To the extent that federal law and the First Amendment do not prohibit state action, States and localities remain free to combat the problem of underage tobacco use by appropriate means."

23. Iain McLean, "William H. Riker and the Invention of Heresthetic(s)," *British Journal of Political Science* 32 (2002), 535–58.

24. These names are misnomers. Federalism connotes a sharing of power across the national and state governments, and while both sides supported this idea, it was the Antifederalists who more ardently advocated this position.

25. Herbert Storing, *What the Anti-Federalists Were For: The Political Thought of the Opponents of the Constitution* (Chicago: University of Chicago Press, 1981).

26. Political scientist William Riker is especially prominent in arguing for the military incentive behind federalism generally, not just in the United States. See *Federalism: Origin, Operation, Significance* (Boston: Little, Brown, 1964).

27. Charles A. Beard, *An Economic Interpretation of the Constitution of the United States* (New York: Macmillan, 1913). For a contemporary account that reinforces and goes beyond Beard's analysis, see Jerry Fresia, *Toward an American Revolution: Exposing the Constitution and other Illusions* (Boston: South End Press, 1988).

28. Karen Orren and Stephen Skowronek, *The Search for American Political Development* (New York: Cambridge University Press, 2004), 53–54.

29. John P. Roche, "The Founding Fathers: A Reform Caucus in Action," *American Political Science Review* 55, 4 (1961): 799–816; Calvin C. Jillson and Cecil L. Eubanks, "The Political Structure of Constitution

Making: The Federal Convention of 1787," *American Journal of Political Science* 28, 3 (1984): 435–58.

30. Robert E. Brown, *Charles Beard and the Constitution: A Critical Analysis of "An Economic Interpretation of the Constitution"* (Princeton, NJ: Princeton University Press, 1956).

31. Colleen A. Sheehan, "Madison v. Hamilton: The Battle Over Republicanism and the Role of Public Opinion," *American Political Science Review* 98, 3 (2004): 405–20.

32. David Brian Robertson, "Madison's Opponents and Constitutional Design," *American Political Science Review* 99, 2 (2005): 405–20.

33. Keith L. Dougherty and Jac C. Heckelman, "A Pivotal Voter from a Pivotal State: Roger Sherman at the Constitutional Convention," *American Political Science Review* 100, 2 (2006): 297–302.

34. John R. Vile, "The Long Legacy of Proposals to Rewrite the U.S. Constitution," *PS: Political Science and Politics*, June 1993, 208–11, discusses the importance of societal consensus in the case of major restructuring of the Constitution.

35. Christopher P. Manfredi, "Institutional Design and the Politics of Constitutional Modification: Understanding Amendment Failure in the United States and Canada," *Law & Society Review* 31, 1 (1997): 111–36.

36. The discussion in this case study draws extensively on Alexander Keyssar, *The Right to Vote: The Contested History of Democracy in the United States* (New York: Basic Books, 2000). Many other Western countries also adapted the 18-year-old voting age in the early 1970s. As in the United States, many of these countries had significant youth movements in the 1960s and early 1970s challenging key aspects of economic, social, and foreign policy, but without any way to participate formally in the electoral process.

37. *Oregon v. Mitchell* (1970).

38. See Gregory A. Caldeira, "Constitutional Change in America: Dynamics of Ratification under Article V," *Publius* 15, 4 (1985): 29–49, for a discussion of various processes by which amendment ratification proceeds chronologically across the states.

39. Caldeira, "Constitutional Change in America: Dynamics of Ratification under Article V."

40. State constitutions provide a contrast to the federal Constitution. The average length of state constitutions is about three times that of the federal document, and the average number of amendments is over four times that of the U.S. Constitution. Alabama is the high end for length and amendments, at 310,000 words (the U.S. Constitution is about 8,700) and 740 amendments.

CHAPTER FOUR

1. A detailed timeline of the events in this case is at http://www.miami.edu/ethics2/schiavo/timeline.htm.

2. Pew Research Center survey conducted by Princeton Survey Research Associates International. Nov. 9–27, 2005. 1,500 adults nationwide surveyed. Margin of error is plus or minus three percentage points.

3. Nullification made its first appearance in 1798 when Virginia and Kentucky nullified the Alien and Sedition Acts. These acts will be discussed in detail in Chapter 5.

4. The situation differs for residents of the District of Columbia. The District is a "creature" of the federal government and has no separate status as a state, nor a constitution. The District has been given some state-like features, such as votes in the Electoral College, but it does not have formal voting representation in the House and Senate.

5. *United States v. E. C. Knight Co. et al.*, 1895.

6. The Court's language is clearly that of dual federalism: "It cannot be denied that the power of a state to protect the lives, health, and property of its citizens, and to preserve good order and the public morals, 'the power to govern men and things within the limits of its dominion,' is a power originally and always belonging to the states, not surrendered by them to the general government, nor directly restrained by the constitution of the United States, and essentially exclusive. The relief of the citizens of each state from the burden of monopoly and the evils resulting from the restraint of trade among such citizens was left with the states to deal with, and this court has recognized their possession of that power. . . . On the other hand, the power of congress to regulate commerce among the several states is also exclusive. The constitution does not provide that interstate commerce shall be free, but, by the grant of this exclusive power to regulate it, it was left free, except as congress might impose restraints."

7. Specifically, the law forbade the interstate transport of a product from a factory that, within the previous 30 days, had employed children under the age of 14 or permitted children ages 14 through 16 to work more than eight hours in a day, more than six days a week, after 7pm, or before 6am.

8. *Hammer v. Dagenhart* (1918).

9. Some scholars have argued that the programs geared toward the most vulnerable sections of the population at the time, especially women and blacks, tended to be structured to allow significant variation from one state to another. See Suzanne Mettler, *Dividing Citizens: Gender*

and Federalism in New Deal Public Policy (Ithaca, NY: Cornell University Press, 1998).

10. Any employee working for a business involved in interstate commerce is covered, as is any employee working for a business with sales volume exceeding $500,000.

11. *United States v. Darby* (1941). The case concerned the Fair Labor Standards Act (1938), which introduced national standards on the minimum wage, maximum weekly work week, mandatory overtime pay, and child labor restrictions. For a skeptical view of the attempt to sort out which level of government should do what, see Donald F. Kettl, "Real-Life Federalism," *Governing Magazine*, August, 2001.

12. *United States v. Mazurie* (1975).

13. See U.S. Department of Energy, Office of Environmental Management, "American Indian Executive Orders (1994 to Present)," http://web.em.doe.gov/public/tribal/orders.html; U.S. Department of Justice, Office of Tribal Justice, "Department of Justice Policy on Indian Sovereignty and Government-to-Government Relations with Indian Tribes," http://www.usdoj.gov/otj/sovtrb.htm.

14. For a journalist's account of the rise of the Foxwoods casino, see Kim Isaac Eisler, *Revenge of the Pequots: How a Small Native American Tribe Created the Worlds Most Profitable Casino* (New York: Simon and Schuster, 2001).

15. Generally speaking, state criminal law is considered binding on the reservations, but gambling law is considered to be regulatory rather than criminal. The exception to this rule is the Organized Crime Control Act of 1970, which provides federal criminal prosecution against certain gambling activity.

16. *Washington v. Confederated Tribes of Colville Indian Reservation* (1980).

17. Recall that the Supreme Court concluded in *McCulloch v. Maryland* that the power to tax was the power to destroy—the first assurance of sovereignty is that one political entity cannot destroy another.

18. Douglas Roger Nash, "Indian Gaming," FindLaw, 1999, http://library.findlaw.com/1999/Jan/1/241489.html.

19. For an argument supporting less state control over tribal gaming, see Steven Andrew Light and Kathryn R. L. Rand, *Indian Gaming and Tribal Sovereignty: The Casino Compromise* (Lawrence: University Press of Kansas, 2007).

20. Fox Butterfield, "Indian Casino Revenues Grow to Sizable Segment of Industry," *New York Times*, June 16, 2005, p. A18.

21. See Patrick Marshall, "Gambling in America," *CQ Researcher*, 13, 9 (March 7, 2003): 201–24, for an overview of Indian gaming as well as gambling generally.

22. Robert L. Fischman, "Cooperative Federalism and Natural Resources Law," *NYU Environmental Law Journal* 14 (2005): 179–231.

23. Angela Antonelli, "Promises Unfulfilled: Unfunded Mandates Reform Act of 1995," *Regulation* 19, 2 (1996); David S. Broder, "Those Unfunded Mandates," *Washington Post*, March 17, 2005, A25.

24. James Dao, "Rebellion of the States: Red, Blue, and Angry All Over," *New York Times*, January 16, 2005. See also http://www.ncsl.org/standcomm/scbudg/manmon.htm.

25. For data, see U.S. Census, *Statistical Abstract of the United States, 2004–05* (Washington: Government Printing Office, 2004), sections 8 and 9.

26. Paul Peterson, *The Price of Federalism* (Washington, DC: Brookings Institution Press, 1998).

27. Adeed I. Dawisha and Karen Dawisha, "How to Build a Democratic Iraq," *Foreign Affairs* 82, 3 (May/June 2003).

28. Nancy Bermeo, "Position Paper for the Working Group on Federalism, Conflict Prevention and Settlement," n.d.

29. Dean E. McHenry Jr., "Federalism in Africa: Is it a Solution to, or a Cause of, Ethnic Problems?" Paper presented at the annual meeting of the African Studies Association, Columbus, Ohio, November 1997.

30. Wisconsin officials working on the state budget for 2005–06, for instance, were concerned that the state was becoming a magnet for out-of-state parents seeking educational and medical services for their autistic children.

31. The race-to-the-bottom research and findings are discussed in William D. Berry, Richard C. Fording, and Russell L. Hanson, "Reassessing the 'Race to the Bottom' in State Welfare Policy," *Journal of Politics* 65, 2 (2003): 327–49; Michael A. Bailey, "Depressing Federalism: Re-Assessing Theory and Evidence on the 'Race to the Bottom,'" manuscript, April 2002; and Jan K. Brueckner, "Welfare Reform and the Race to the Bottom: Theory and Evidence," manuscript, March 1999.

32. Alfonso Lopez Jr. was a twelfth-grade student at Edison High School in San Antonio. In March 1992, he brought a concealed handgun and ammunition to school. Acting on an anonymous tip, school officers questioned Lopez and he acknowledged carrying the ammunition and weapon. He was charged with violating state law, but this charge was dropped the following day when federal agents charged him with violating the Gun-Free School Zone Act.

33. Section 5 of the Fourteenth Amendment provides the authority to override this immunity.

34. *Alden v. Maine* (1999); *Gregory v. Ashcroft* (1991); *Kimel v. Florida Board of Regents* (2000); *Board of Trustees of the University of Alabama v. Garrett* (2001), and *Seminole Tribe v. Florida* (1996).

35. Keith E. Whittington, "Taking What They Give Us: Explaining the Court's Federalism Offensive," *Duke Law Journal* 51, 1 (2001): 477–520.

36. Christine Vestal, "States Try New Approaches, Feds Cool," Stateline.org.

37. United States House of Representatives, Committee On Government Reform—Minority Staff Special Investigations Division, "Congressional Preemption Of State Laws And Regulations," June 2006.

38. http://www.ncsl.org/realid/.

39. Ben Arnoldy, "Resistance Rises to US Law that Requires Stricter ID Standards," *Christian Science Monitor*, February 9, 2007, 1; Leslie Miller, "States Following Maine's Lead to Fight National Driver's License," *Boston Globe*, February 5, 2007, B8; Spencer S. Hsu, "Homeland Security Retreats From Facets of 'Real ID,'" *Washington Post*, November 4, 2007, A7.

40. Paul Posner, "The Politics of Coercive Federalism in the Bush Era," *Publius* 37, 3 (2007): 390–412.

41. For an appraisal of current trends that suggests the change in federalism has been less seismic than is sometimes suggested, see Martha Derthick, "American Federalism: Half- Empty or Half-Full?" *Brookings Review*, 18, 1 (Winter 2000): 24–27.

42. Barry Rabe, "Environmental Policy and the Bush Era: The Collision Between the Administrative Presidency and State Experimentation," *Publius* 37, 3 (2007): 413–31; Posner, 390–412.

43. In *Nevada Department of Human Resources v. Hibbs* (2003).

44. Marci Hamilton, "The Supreme Court's Federalism Cases This Term: A String of Decisions Upholding Federal Power Show the Portrayal of the Court as Extreme Is a Caricature," FindLaw, June 3, 2004, http://writ.news.findlaw.com/hamilton/20040603.html.

45. *American Insurance Association v. Garamendi* (2004).

CHAPTER FIVE

1. Congress added the pledge to the United States Code in 1942. The relevant section in the Code currently reads as follows: The Pledge of Allegiance to the Flag, "I pledge allegiance to the Flag of the United States of America, and to the Republic for which it stands, one Nation under God, indivisible, with liberty and justice for all.", should be rendered by standing at attention facing the flag with the right hand over the heart. When not in uniform men should remove their headdress with their right hand and hold it at the left shoulder, the hand being over the heart. Persons in uniform should remain silent, face the flag, and render the military salute."

2. *West Virginia State Board of Education v. Barnette* (1943).

3. Newdow also objected to the constitutionality of the California law that required schools to start the day with patriotic activities and Elk Grove's policy that the Pledge would be used to fulfill this state requirement.

4. Newdow had also challenged the constitutionality of Congress's 1954 addition of the "under God" language. Originally, the appeals court declared the words "under God" in the Pledge to be unconstitutional, but in a revised decision it pulled back from this declaration and considered only the public school aspect of Newdow's complaint.

5. *Elk Grove v. Newdow* (2004).

6. We discuss freedom of the press in Chapter 10 (Media).

7. Where rights come from is a matter of philosophical dispute. Some view them as inherent in humans; they are part of what makes up human nature. To others, rights result from politics—there is nothing "natural" about them. They are what governments say they are, what the political culture of a country says they are, or what have resulted after determined efforts by those willing to fight and sometimes die to achieve them. And to a third group, and as stated in the Declaration of Independence, rights are seen as God-given.

8. *Kelo v. City of New London* (2005).

9. See, for example, the twin studies by Robert Barro, "Determinants of Democracy," *Journal of Political Economy* 107, 6 (1999); and *Determinants of Economic Growth: A Cross-Country Empirical Study* (Cambridge, MA: MIT Press, 1997).

10. Freedom House, Freedom in the World 2005, http://www.freedomhouse.org/research/freeworld/2005/table2005.pdf. For civil liberties, Freedom House assesses a country's freedom of expression and belief, association and organization rights, rule of law and human rights, and personal autonomy and economic rights.

11. Seventeen amendments had been adopted in the House of Representatives; twelve of these were accepted by the Senate. Ten were ratified by the states in December 1791.

12. Two cases kicked off the incorporation process. The first of the two cases, decided in 1897, concluded that the Fifth Amendment's property takings clause applied

to state governments. The second, decided in 1925, concluded that the free speech protections of the First Amendment applied to the actions of state governments. Although the decision was not immediately a victory for free speech—the Supreme Court concluded the state restriction on speech was valid—it did mark another step toward pulling state governments under the orbit of the Bill of Rights. The cases are *Chicago, Burlington, and Quincy Railroad Company v. Chicago* (1897) and *Gitlow v. New York* (1925), respectively.

13. The language of the due process clause in the Fourteenth Amendment is based on a nearly identically worded clause in the Fifth Amendment. The clause in the Fifth Amendment, however, does not specifically mention the states.

14. *Chicago, Burlington, and Quincy Railroad v. Chicago* (1897); *Gitlow v. New York* (1925).

15. One federal circuit court of appeals—the final level of appeals in federal cases prior to the Supreme Court—has embraced the view that the Second Amendment is a guarantee of individuals' right to keep and bear arms, so it is possible that court opinions could shift in that direction. As the circuit court noted in its decision, however, "none of our sister circuits has subscribed to this model." *U.S. v. Emerson* (2001), Fifth U.S. Circuit.

16. *Palko v. Connecticut* (1937).

17. See Lawrence Baum, "Membership Change and Collective Voting Change in the United States Supreme Court," *Journal of Politics* 54, 1 (1992): 3–24.

18. Although usually reluctant to agree to prior restraint, the Court in 1990 let a lower court ruling stand that prohibited the cable network CNN from airing a conversation between former Panamanian dictator Manuel Noriega and his attorney, arguing that this possibly affected his ability to get a fair trial. In 1979 a federal district court prohibited *Progressive Magazine* from publishing an article that the judge concluded might help a medium-sized country build a nuclear bomb more quickly than it would otherwise.

19. Arati Korwar, *War of Words: Speech Codes at Public Colleges and Universities.* Nashville, Tennessee: The Freedom Forum First Amendment Center, 1994.

20. *R.A.V. v. City of St. Paul* (1992).

21. The speech in question in this case is symbolic speech, rather than the actual utterance or writing of words. In recent decades the Supreme Court has tended to consider symbolic speech and actual speech to be deserving of the same protection. The Court has also been generally protective of "speech plus"—the combination of speech and some activity like picketing or a demonstration. Governments can regulate the nature of these activities by requiring permits, but it must be content neutral toward what it allows. It cannot constitutionally allow a rally by pro-choice individuals but deny one by pro-life individuals, nor can it make the requirements for one group notably more onerous than for the other.

22. *Virginia v. Black* (2003).

23. See Jon B. Gould, *Speak No Evil: The Triumph of Hate Speech Regulation* (Chicago: University of Chicago Press, 2005); Martin P. Golding, *Free Speech on Campus* (Lanham, MD: Rowman Littlefield, 2000).

24. See Geoffrey R. Stone, *Perilous Times: Free Speech in Wartime from the Sedition Act of 1798 to the War on Terrorism* (New York: W. W. Norton, 2004).

25. Darren W. Davis and Brian D. Silver, "Civil Liberties vs. Security: Public Opinion in the Context of the Terrorist Attacks on America," *American Journal of Political Science* 48, 1 (2004): 28–46. Another study, although not looking specifically at civil liberties, found that the more a person thinks his racial or ethnic group is superior to others, the greater the support for an aggressive war on terrorism. Whether these findings would extend to limitations on civil liberties is unclear. See Cindy D. Kam and Donald R. Kinder, "Terror and Ethnocentrism: Foundations of American Support for the War on Terrorism," *Journal of Politics* 69, 2 (2007): 320–38.

26. For example, see Thomas E. Nelson, Rosalee A. Clawson, Zoe M. Oxley, "Media Framing of a Civil Liberties Conflict and Its Effect on Tolerance," *American Political Science Review* 91, 3 (1997): 567–83; W. Kip Viscusi and Richard J. Zeckhauser, "Sacrificing Civil Liberties to Reduce Terrorism Risks," *Journal of Risk and Uncertainty* 26, 2–3 (2003): 99–120.

27. CBS News Poll. April 13–16, 2005.

28. Studies have differed on whether politically attentive Americans are more likely to be strong supporters of protecting civil liberties and discouraging government from taking restrictive measures. At the very least, this politically attentive group is not homogeneous, so it matters which part of the group has government's ear at any particular time. See, for example, Herbert McClosky, "Consensus and Ideology in American Politics," *American Political Science Review* 58, 2 (June 1964): 361–82; Herbert McClosky and John Zaller, *The American Ethos* (Cambridge: Harvard University Press, 1984); Herbert McClosky and Alida Brill, *Dimensions of Political Tolerance* (New York: Russell Sage, 1983); and Shmuel Lock, *Crime, Public Opinion, and Civil Liberties: The Tolerant Public* (Westport, Connecticut: Praeger Publishers, 1999). For

competing views, see Paul Sniderman, Joseph Fletcher, et al., *The Clash of Rights: Liberty, Equality, and Legitimacy in Pluralist Democracy* (New Haven: Yale University Press, 1996); and Robert W. Jackman, "Political Elites, Mass Publics, and Support for Democratic Principles," *Journal of Politics* 54 (Aug. 1992): 753–73.

29. George E. Marcus, John L. Sullivan, and Elizabeth Theiss-Morse (*With Malice Toward Some: How People Make Civil Liberties Judgments*; New York: Cambridge University Press, 1995) argue that civil liberties positions are determined by a combination of "predispositions" based in personality and general outlook, "standing decisions" that may include views on a related particular issue or set of issues, and "contemporary information" related to the specific situation at hand.

30. Researchers can infer support for these measures from public opinion surveys or, for times prior to polling, letters in newspapers, election results, and policy statements by organized groups with large memberships.

31. In *Terminiello v. Chicago* (1949), the Court declared that speech should be punished only when it creates a clear and present danger of a "serious substantive evil that rises far above public inconvenience, annoyance, or unrest."

32. *American Communications Association v. Douds* (1950); *Dennis v. United States* (1951).

33. See *Konigsberg v. State Bar of California* (1961), where the Supreme Court upheld the California State Bar's refusal to allow Raphael Konigsberg to practice law because of his refusal to answer questions about membership in the Communist Party.

34. *Palko v. Connecticut* (1937).

35. *Chaplinsky v. New Hampshire* (1942).

36. *Beauharnais v. Illinois* (1952).

37. *New York Times Co. v. Sullivan* (1964); *Gertz v. Robert Welch, Inc.* (1974), *Milkovich v. Lorain Journal Co.* (1990).

38. *Valentine v. Chrestensen* (1942); *Greater New Orleans Broadcasting Association v. United States* (1999); *Lorillard Tobacco v. Reilly* (2001).

39. *Morse v. Frederick* (2007).

40. *Roth v. United States* (1957).

41. In 2002, the Supreme Court overturned the Child Pornography Prevention Act of 1996. The act forbade "any visual depiction, including any photograph, film, video, picture, or computer or computer-generated image or picture . . . [that]is, or appears to be, of a minor engaging in sexually explicit conduct." It also prohibited sexually explicit images that are "advertised, promoted, presented, described, or distributed in such a manner that conveys the impression" that they de-pict "a minor engaging in sexually explicit conduct." The Court concluded that the act was overly broad in that it attempted to restrict materials that were not necessarily obscene as defined in previous court decisions. Also, with terms such as "appears to be" and "conveys the message," the law included materials in which no children were actually involved, such as computer generated and digitally manipulated graphics.

42. *Jacobellis v. Ohio* (1964).

43. *Reno v. American Civil Liberties Union* (1997).

44. *Ashcroft v. American Civil Liberties Union* (2004).

45. *United States et al. v. American Library Association, Inc., et al.* (2003).

46. David M. O'Brien, *Constitutional Law and Politics: Civil Rights and Civil Liberties*, 5th ed. (New York: W.W. Norton, 2003), 506.

47. As noted above, Article VI of the Constitution prohibits religious tests or oaths for public office.

48. Frank Lambert, *The Founding Fathers and the Place of Religion in America* (Princeton, NJ: Princeton University Press, 2003).

49. Article 11 of the 1797 Treaty with Tripoli reads: "As the government of the United States of America is not in any sense founded on the Christian Religion—as it has in itself no character of enmity against the laws, religion or tranquility of Musselmen—and as the said States never have entered into any war or act of hostility against any Mehomitan nation, it is declared by the parties that no pretext arising from religious opinions shall ever produce an interruption of the harmony existing between the two countries." Although there is substantial dispute about precisely how and when this article was inserted into the treaty, this text was approved unanimously by the Senate and signed into law by President John Adams.

50. *Aguilar v. Felton* (1985).

51. This does not mean the Court would be tolerant of public employees inculcating religion in the religious schools. Instead, the Court was saying there is no reason to presume that they would, so the need for extensive monitoring did not exist. "There is no suggestion in the record that the system New York City has in place to monitor [remedial education teachers] is insufficient to prevent or to detect inculcation." If improper behavior by a teacher was discovered, the school could react or a case could be brought to court.

52. *Engale v. Vitale* (1962); *Abington School District v. Schempp* (1963); *Lee v. Weisman* (1992); *Wallace v. Jaffrie* (1985); *Santa Fe Independent School District v. Doe* (2000).

53. *County of Allegheny v. ACLU Greater Pittsburgh Chapter* (1989). The Texas case is *Van Orden v. Perry* (2005); the Kentucky case is *McCreary County v. A.C.L.U. of Kentucky* (2005).

54. O'Brien, 782–85.

55. *Wisconsin v. Yoder* (1971) illustrates the application of the test particularly well. Jonas Yoder, a member of the Amish religion, and two other Amish men refused to send their eighth-grade children to high school through the age of 16, as required by Wisconsin law, because it conflicted with their religious beliefs. The Supreme Court determined that their religious exercise was indeed burdened by Wisconsin's requirement, noting that the secondary school experience and its accompanying values were "in sharp conflict with the fundamental mode of life mandated by the Amish religion." The Court also concluded that because the state's interest in demanding another one or two years of school attendance was not compelling enough to justify the burden on Yoder's religious practice, Wisconsin had violated his First Amendment free exercise rights.

56. The Supreme Court ruled that Quakers and Amish could not withhold portions of their federal income tax because of their religious objection to federal policies (*United States v. American Friends Service Committee*, 1974; *United States v. Lee*, 1982). Congress has on occasion allowed exemptions from the law based on religious beliefs. For example, drafts for military service have included provisions to allow those who object to war on religious grounds to be exempt from combat.

57. The Court's decision noted that the laws did not make clear why the Santeria practice should be treated differently from other practices, including kosher slaughter of animals, slaughter primarily for food (hunting, fishing), hunting and fishing for sport, euthanasia, insect eradication, and the use of live rabbits for training greyhound racing dogs for racing, nor did the laws attempt to regulate disposal of carcasses from hunting, fishing, and restaurant garbage.

58. The Archbishop of San Antonio had been thwarted in his efforts to enlarge a church because of a Boerne, Texas, law limiting construction in a historic preservation district. He challenged the city's action, noting that in RFRA Congress had intended to carve out a protection for religious institutions unless the city could demonstrate a significant compelling interest in rejecting the church expansion. The Court rejected the Archbishop's arguments in its decision in *City of Boerne v. Flores* (1997).

59. *Gonzales v. O Centro Espírita Beneficente União do Vegetal* (2006).

60. The law also granted churches great leeway in building projects, which had been the subject matter in the case that overturned RFRA. This aspect of the law will likely appear before the Court soon.

61. *California v. Greenwood* (1988).

62. *Michigan Department of State Police v. Sitz* (1990).

63. *Illinois v. Caballes* (2005); *Kyllo v. United States* (2001).

64. *Mapp v. Ohio* (1961).

65. *Davis v. United States* (1994). In *Arizona v. Fulminante* (1991), the Court ruled that a conviction need not be overturned because of an improperly obtained confession if the other evidence was strong enough to convict. An attempt by Congress to restore the status of voluntary confessions to their pre-*Miranda* status was struck down by the Court in *Dickerson v. United States* (2000). In the decision, the Court once again reminded Congress that it is the Court's job to interpret the Constitution and decide what it requires.

66. *Atkins v. Virginia* (2002) concerns the mentally retarded. *Roper v. Simmons* (2005) overturned the Court's *Stanford v. Kentucky* (1989) decision on capital punishment for minors.

67. *Rompilla v. Beard* (2005).

68. When Timothy McVeigh, one of the bombers of an Oklahoma City federal building in 1995, was executed in 2001, it was the first execution by the federal government in nearly forty years.

69. Death Penalty Statistics, Amnesty International, http://web.amnesty.org/pages/deathpenalty-statistics-eng.

70. See http://thomas.loc.gov/cgibin/bdquery/z?d107:HR03162:@@@L&summ2=m& for a brief description of the sections of the act.

71. Harris Poll, 1,015 adults nationwide, June 7–12, 2005, and September 19–24, 2001.

72. For a timeline of events, see http://www.bespacific.com/mt/archives/cat_patriot_act.html.

73. Sherly Gay Stolberg, "Senate Passes Legislation to Renew Patriot Act," *New York Times*, March 3, 2006, A14.

74. The anti-obscenity law was known as the Comstock Act. In 1938, a federal appeals court decision struck down the federal ban on the importation of birth control materials by physicians. In practical terms, this ended the federal government's surveillance of the use of birth control information and materials.

75. *Eisenstadt v. Baird* (1972).

76. The Court's opinion famously stated that "specific guarantees in the Bill of Rights have penumbras, formed by emanations from those guarantees that help

give them life and substance." Penumbras are partial shadings or shadows that are cast on outlying regions or peripheries.

77 The Court considered the question of whether a fetus was a "person." The majority concluded it was beyond the Court's ability to determine the answer and that medical, philosophical, and theological opinion was mixed. It noted that "person" in the U.S. Constitution seemed in each instance to assume post-natal life, not fetal life. And the majority noted that throughout the early nineteenth century, "prevailing legal abortion practices were far freer than they are today, persuad[ing] us that the word 'person,' as used in the Fourteenth Amendment, does not include the un-born."

78. In *Webster v. Reproductive Health Services* (1989), the Court declared constitutional a Missouri law outlawing abortions in public hospitals and prohibiting public employees from being involved in abortion services.

79. *Washington v. Glucksberg* (1997); *Vacco v. Quill* (1997); *Gonzales v. Oregon* (2006).

80. The relevant cases are, respectively, *NAACP v. Roberts*; *Boy Scouts of America v. Dale*; *Barnette v. West Virginia*; *Peirce v. Society of Sisters*; *Miranda v. Arizona*; and *Skinner v. Oklahoma*. The authors thank Howard Schweber for his comments on this topic. The Court's opinion in *Washington v. Glucksberg* (1997) provides a good discussion of substantive due process.

81. *Palko v. Connecticut* (1937) and *Moore v. East Cleveland* (1977), respectively.

82. Note the Court's comment in *Roe*: "This right of privacy, whether it be founded in the Fourteenth Amendment's concept of personal liberty and restrictions upon state action, as we feel it is, or, as [others have] determined, in the Ninth Amendment's reservation of rights to the people. . . ."

83. *Collins v. Harker Heights* (1992); *Sacramento County v. Lewis* (1998). In another case, the Court rejected by a 5-4 vote a substantive due process claim that would have, on the basis of the Fourteenth Amendment's protection of liberty, not allowed government to institutionalize sexual predators for monitoring and medical treatment after they had served their sentence (*Kansas v. Hendricks*, 1997).

84. For example, the Court concluded in *Troxel v. Granville* (2000) that a law in the state of Washington that allowed "any person" "at any time" to petition for visitation rights with children violated the parents' "fundamental right to rear children," a right previously established by substantive due process.

CHAPTER SIX

1. *Korematsu v. United States* (1944).

2. This discussion is based on Steven Kelman et al., "Against All Odds: The Campaign in Congress for Japanese-American Redress," Case Program, Kennedy School of Government, C16-90-1006.0.

3. Article I, Section 2; I, 9; and IV, 2, respectively.

4. This position was consistent with the stance of the northern states that considered slaves to become free when they traveled in free states.

5. The act guaranteed blacks the rights "to make and enforce contracts, to sue, be parties, and give evidence, to inherit, purchase, lease, sell, hold, and convey real and personal property, and to full and equal benefit of all laws and proceedings for the security of person and property, as is enjoyed by white citizens, and shall be subject to like punishments. . . ." These restrictions on blacks were not unique to the South, as several northern states had passed similar restrictions up through 1860 to regulate free blacks and in some cases deny blacks the ability to immigrate into a state.

6. Because Congress defeated President Johnson's veto narrowly, and fearing that the act might be declared unconstitutional, supporters moved quickly to include its major provisions in the Fourteenth Amendment.

7. Eric Foner, *A Short History of Reconstruction, 1863–1877* (New York: Harper and Row, 1990).

8. The Thirteenth Amendment was particular to slavery, not private racial discrimination in general, the Court ruled, so it could not be pointed to as justification for the act.

9. "There were thousands of free colored people in this country before the abolition of slavery, enjoying all the essential rights of life, liberty, and property the same as white citizens; yet no one, at that time, thought that it was any invasion of their personal status as freemen because they were not admitted to all the privileges enjoyed by white citizens, or because they were subjected to discriminations in the enjoyment of accommodations in inns, public conveyances, and places of amusement. Mere discriminations on account of race or color were not regarded as badges of slavery."

10. Plessy was one-eighth black, so one issue in the case was whether he should be considered white or black. The Supreme Court concluded that what constitutes "black" or "white" should be determined by the laws of each state, so on those grounds Louisiana could consider Plessy to be black.

11. Executive Order 8802. The hiring issue was brought to Roosevelt's attention by A. Philip Randolph, the president of the Brotherhood of Sleeping Car Porters; Walter White, the executive secretary of the National

Association for the Advancement of Colored People; and Mary McLeod Bethune, the minority affairs director of the National Youth Administration (a federal government agency created by Roosevelt). Randolph indicated that action to prohibit discrimination in the military and in the defense industry could halt the plans for a civil rights rally. Executive Order 9346 expanded the FEPC's budget and enforcement power. See Kevin J. McMahon, *Reconsidering Roosevelt on Race: How the Presidency Paved the Road to* Brown (Chicago: University of Chicago Press, 2004).

12. *State of Missouri ex rel. Gaines v. Canada* (1938).

13. In the Texas decision, *Sweatt v. Painter*, the Court noted "In terms of number of the faculty, variety of courses and opportunity for specialization, size of the student body, scope of the library, availability of law review and similar activities, the University of Texas Law School is superior. What is more important, the University of Texas Law School possesses to a far greater degree those qualities which are incapable of objective measurement but which make for greatness in a law school. Such qualities, to name but a few, include reputation of the faculty, experience of the administration, position and influence of the alumni, standing in the community, traditions and prestige."

14. "[The student] is handicapped in his pursuit of effective graduate instruction. Such restrictions impair and inhibit his ability to study, to engage in discussions and exchange views with other students, and, in general, to learn his profession." *McLaurin v. Oklahoma State Regents for Higher Education* (1950).

15. Seventeen states required segregation; another four allowed it as a local option.

16. The timetable applied to the District of Columbia also. On the same day as *Brown I*, the Court ruled that segregated schools in the District violated the Fifth Amendment's guarantee of due process in *Bolling v. Sharpe* (1954). The Court reached to the Fifth Amendment rather than the Fourteenth because the District of Columbia is a federal entity, not a state.

17. Gary Orfield and Chungmei Lee, "Racial Transformation and the Changing Nature of Segregation," The Civil Rights Project at Harvard University, January 2006, http://www.civilrightsproject.ucla.edu/research/deseg/Racial_Transformation.pdf.

18. *Green v. County School Board of New Kent County* (1968).

19. *Milliken v. Bradley* (1974).

20. The two cases were consolidated as *Parents Involved in Community Schools v. Seattle School District No. 1* (2007).

21. Erica Frankenberg and Chungmei Lee, "Race in American Public Schools: Rapidly Resegregating School Districts," The Civil Rights Project at Harvard University, August 2002. See also the document submitted to the Supreme Court in the Seattle and Louisville case by a group of social scientists: "Brief Of 553 Social Scientists As Amici Curiae In Support Of Respondents," October 2006.

22. The use of Congress's commerce clause and spending powers in the Civil Rights Act of 1964 was upheld by the Supreme Court in *Heart of Atlanta Motel v. United States* (1964) and *Katzenbach v. McClung* (1964).

23. The Voting Rights Act of 1965 was upheld by the Supreme Court in *South Carolina v. Katzenbach* (1965).

24. *Harper v. Virginia Board of Elections* (1966).

25. Executive Orders 10925 (Kennedy); 11246 and 11375 (Johnson); 12106 (Carter); 13087 and 13152 (Clinton).

26. Executive Orders 10925 (Kennedy), 11246 (Johnson), 11375 (Johnson), and 11478 (Nixon).

27. John David Skrentny, *The Ironies of Affirmative Action: Politics, Culture, and Justice in America* (Chicago: University of Chicago Press, 1996).

28. Vincent L. Hutchings and Nicholas A. Valentino, "The Centrality of Race in American Politics," *Annual Review of Political Science* 7 (2004): 383–408 provides an excellent overview of the literature.

29. Ibid., 389.

30. The pivotal figures in the debate have been Paul Sniderman and Donald Kinder. See Paul M. Sniderman and Edward G. Carmines, *Reaching Beyond Race* (Cambridge: Harvard University Press, 1997); Sniderman and Thomas Piazza, *The Scar of Race* (Cambridge: Harvard University Press, 1993); and Donald R. Kinder and Lynn M. Sanders, *Divided by Color: Racial Politics and Democratic Ideals* (Chicago: University of Chicago Press, 1996).

31. A number of alternative terms have been employed, including new racism, symbolic racism, and covert racism.

32. See Stanley Feldman and Leonie Huddy, "Racial Resentment and White Opposition to Race-Conscious Programs: Principles or Prejudice?" *American Journal of Political Science* 49, 1 (2005): 168–83 for a skeptical analysis of racial resentment. A more supportive account is found in Christopher Tarman and David O. Sears, "The Conceptualization and Measurement of Symbolic Racism," *Journal of Politics* 67, 3 (2005).

33. Robert C. Lieberman, *Shaping Race Policy: The United States in Comparative Perspective* (Princeton: Princeton University Press, 2005); Erik Bleich, *Race Politics in*

Britain and France: Ideas and Policymaking Since the 1960s (New York: Cambridge University Press, 2003).

34. See Richard M. Valelly, *The Two Reconstructions: The Struggle for Black Enfranchisement* (Chicago: University of Chicago Press, 2004).

35. King was arrested at the protest and it was at this time that he penned his famous essay, "Letter from Birmingham Jail, 1963." The essay appeared originally in the June 12, 1963, issue of *Christian Century*. King included it in his book, *Why We Can't Wait* (New York: Harper Collins, 1964).

36. Mark I. Lichbach, "Where Have All the Foils Gone? Competing Theories of Contentious Politics and the Civil Rights Movement," in Anne N. Costain and Andrew S. McFarland, eds., *Social Movements and American Political Institutions* (Lanham, MD: Rowman and Littlefield, 1998).

37. *Smith v. Allright* (1944).

38. Alan Ware, *The Democratic Party Heads North, 1877–1962* (New York: Cambridge University Press, 2006).

39. Edward G. Carmines and James A. Stimson, *Issue Evolution: Race and the Transformation of American Politics* (Princeton, NJ: Princeton University Press, 1990).

40. Lieberman, *Shaping Race Policy: The United States in Comparative Perspective*.

41. Bruce J. Dierenfield, *The Civil Rights Movement* (Harlow, England: Pearson, 2004), 104.

42. The argument is most forcefully made in Paul Frymer, *Uneasy Alliances: Race and Party Competition in America* (Princeton, NJ: Princeton University Press, 1999).

43. *Shaw v. Reno* (1993); *Miller v. Johnson* (1995); *Hunt v. Cromartie* (2001).

44. Hutchings and Valentino, "The Centrality of Race in American Politics," 383–408.

45. David Epstein and Sharyn O'Halloran, Columbia University, "The Voting Rights Act: Here Today, Gone Tomorrow?" manuscript, 2005.

46. *United States v. Carolene Products* (1938), footnote 4.

47. *Nordinger v. Hahn* (1992): "In general, the Equal Protection Clause is satisfied so long as there is a plausible policy reason for the classification, the legislative facts on which the classification is apparently based rationally may have been considered to be true by the governmental decisionmaker, and the relationship of the classification to its goal is not so attenuated as to render the distinction arbitrary or irrational."

48. *Reed v. Reed* (1971); *Craig v. Boren* (1976).

49. In 1961, the Supreme Court ruled in *Hoyt v. Florida* that Florida could exclude women from jury service.

50. *Meritor Savings Bank FBD v. Vinson* (1986).

51. Gohar Grigorian, "Women and the Law in Comparative Perspective," UCLA International Institute, July 4, 2004, http://www.international.ucla.edu/article.asp?parentid=13036.

52. Mark R. Daniels and Robert E. Darcy argue that the states that did not ratify the amendment disproportionately tended to be slow to adopt innovations generally and had a greater likelihood, historically, of opposing amendments. They were promising targets for opponents of the ERA. See "As Time Goes By: The Arrested Diffusion of the Equal Rights Amendment, *Publius* 15, 4, (1985): 51–60.

53. *Gregory v. Ashcroft* (1991).

54. A Supreme Court decision in 2000 (*Kimel v. Florida Board of Regents*) narrowed the law by stating that it did not apply to state government employees. The Court concluded that the law violated state sovereignty by allowing employees to use the federal courts to sue the states against their consent. However, the decision ruled that state employees could file cases in state courts if they believed that their state's law against age discrimination—which most states have enacted—was violated.

55. Samuel R. Bagenstos, "Comparative Disability Employment Law from an American Perspective," *Comparative Labor Law and Policy Journal* 24 (2003): 650.

56. This discussion relies heavily on Bagenstos, "Comparative Disability Employment Law from an American Perspective."

57. *Yick Wo v. Hopkins* (1886).

58. Gary M. Segura and Helena Alves Rodrigues, "Comparative Ethnic Politics in the United States: Beyond Black and White," *Annual Review of Political Science* 9 (2006): 375–95.

59. *Elks v. Wilkins* (1884).

60. *Oncale v. Sundowner Offshore Services* (1998)

61. *Boy Scouts of America v. Dale* (2000).

62. Helen Dewar and Alan Cooperman, "Senate Scuttles Amendment Banning Same-Sex Marriage," *Washington Post*, July 14, 2004. This article provides a good sense of the political calculations on this issue. President Bush indicated that he supported the proposed federal amendment, but he has argued that states should be free to come up with other legal arrangements such as civil unions that confer some of the benefits and responsibilities of marriage. The president's comments are at http://www.whitehouse.gov/news/releases/2004/02/20040224-2.html.

63. *Ward's Cove Packing Co. v. Atonio* (1989).

64. *St. Mary's Honor Center v. Hicks* (1993).

CHAPTER SEVEN

1. Excerpted, with edits, from James Surowiecki, *The Wisdom of Crowds* (New York: Random House, 2004).

2. Kevin Drum, "The Problem with Polls," *Washington Monthly Online,* April 23, 2004, http://www.washingtonmonthly.com/archives/individual/2004_04/ 003762. php.

3. Quoted in Ryan Lizza, "The Ad War '04," *New York Magazine*, April 19, 2003, http://newyorkmetro.com/nymetro/news/politics/national/2004race/adwars/n_10182/.

4. Robert S. Erikson and Kent L. Tedin, *American Public Opinion* (New York: Pearson Education, 2005), 6.

5. ABC News/ *Washington Post* Poll, December 16–19, 2004. "Do you think abortion should be legal in all cases, legal in most cases, illegal in most cases, or illegal in all cases?"; "How important is it to you that the next person nominated to join the U.S. Supreme Court agrees with your position on abortion—is that extremely important to you, very important, somewhat important, or less important than that?" December 21, 2004, http://www.washingtonpost.com/wp-srv/politics/polls/polltrend_122104.html.

6. David Easton and Jack Dennis, *Children in the Political System* (Chicago: University of Chicago Press, 1969), 236.

7. Ibid., 115.

8. Ibid., 146; and Fred Greenstein, *Children and Politics* (New Haven, CT: Yale University Press, 1965), 58–59.

9. Greenstein, *Children*, 58–59; and Easton and Dennis, *Children*, 138.

10. Easton and Dennis, *Children*, 254–70.

11. Ibid., 256.

12. M. Kent Jennings and Richard G. Niemi, *The Political Character of Adolescence* (Princeton, NJ: Princeton University Press, 1974), 274; and Greenstein, *Children*, 55.

13. Robert W. Connell, *The Child's Construction of Politics* (Melbourne: Melbourne University Press, 1971), 46–49, 59, 62.

14. Robert D. Hess and Judith V. Torney, *The Development of Political Attitudes in Children* (Chicago: Aldine Publishing Company, 1967), 215.

15. Connell, *Child's Construction*, 58.

16. Greenstein, *Children*, 68, 73.

17. Connell, *Child's Construction*, 50.

18. Jennings and Niemi, *Political Character*, 266.

19. Ibid., 271.

20. Ibid., 275–76.

21. Roberta S. Sigel, *Learning About Politics* (New York: Random House, 1970), 103.

22. Kenneth P. Langton, *Political Socialization* (New York: Oxford University Press, 1969), 53.

23. M. Kent Jennings and Richard Niemi, *Generations and Politics* (Princeton, NJ: Princeton University Press, 1981), 90.

24. Hess and Torney, *Development*, 134–37; Frank J. Sorauf and Paul Allen Beck, *Party Politics in America* (New York: Harper Collins Publishers, 1988), 180–82.

25. Sigel, *Learning*, 412.

26. Hess and Torney, *Development*, 137–43; Erikson and Tedin, *American Public Opinion*, 127–28.

27. For an overview of the role of school and education in the socialization process, see Hess and Torney, *Development*, 120–32.

28. Edward Greenberg, "Black Children in the Political System," *Public Opinion Quarterly* 34 (1970): 335–48; Chris F. Garcia, *Political Socialization of Chicano Children* (New York: Praeger, 1973); Dean Jaros, Herbert Hirsch, and Frederick Fleron, "The Malevolent Leader: Political Socialization in an American Sub-Culture," *American Political Science Review* 62 (June 1968): 564–75; and Erikson and Tedin, *American Public Opinion*, 121; but see also 122.

29. M. Kent Jennings, "Residuals of a Movement: The Aging of the American Protest Generation," *American Political Science Review* 81 (June 1987): 365–81.

30. William G. Mayer, *The Changing American Mind* (Ann Arbor: University of Michigan Press, 1992), 247.

31. Ibid., 252–54.

32. Erikson and Tedin, *American Public Opinion*, 142.

33. Ibid., 140.

34. Judge Learned Hand, "We Seek Liberty," address in Central Park, New York, May 21, 1944.

35. The ANES Guide to Public Opinion and Electoral Behavior, http://www.electionstudies.org/nesguide/toptable/tab5a_1.htm.

36. Joseph S. Nye Jr., Philip D. Zelikow, and David C. King, eds., *Why People Don't Trust Government* (Cambridge, MA: Harvard University Press, 1997); and Pew Research Center for People and the Press, "How Americans View Government: Deconstructing Distrust," March 10, 1998, http://people-press.org/reports/print.php3?ReportID=95.

37. Russell J. Dalton, "The Social Transformation of Trust in Government," unpublished manuscript, 5, http://www.worldvaluessurvey.org/.

38. Marc J. Hetherington, "The Political Relevance of Political Trust," *American Political Science Review* 92, 4 (December 1998): 791–808.

39. Pew, "How Americans View Government."

40. We have rounded up from a 1998 estimate of $1.9 billion in United States General Accounting Office,

"Supporting Sugar Prices Has Increased Users' Costs While Benefiting Producers," June 2000, Appendix II.

41. See, for example, Herbert McClosky, "Consensus and Ideology in American Politics," *American Political Science Review* 58, 2 (June 1964): 361–82; McCloskey and Zaller, *American Ethos*; Herbert McCloskey and Alida Brill, *Dimensions of Political Tolerance* (New York: Russell Sage, 1984); and Shmuel Lock, *Crime, Public Opinion, and Civil Liberties: The Tolerant Public* (Westport, Connecticut: Praeger Publishers, 1999).

42. See, for example, Paul Sniderman, Joseph Fletcher, et al., *The Clash of Rights: Liberty, Equality, and Legitimacy in Pluralist Democracy* (New Haven: Yale University Press, 1996); and Robert W. Jackman, "Political Elites, Mass Publics, and Support for Democratic Principles," *Journal of Politics* 54 (August 1972): 753–73.

43. Michael X. Delli Carpini and Scott Keeter, *What Americans Know About Politics and Why It Matters* (New Haven, CT: Yale University Press, 1996), 101–02.

44. Ibid., 101–02.

45. Phillip Converse, "The Nature of Belief Systems in Mass Publics," in David E. Apter, *Ideology and Discontent* (New York: Free Press, 1964), 206–61.

46. Donald R. Kinder, "Diversity and Complexity in American Public Opinion," in Ada W. Finiter, ed., *Political Science: The State of the Discipline* (Washington, D.C.: American Political Science Association, 1983), 397.

47. John Zaller and Stanley Feldman, "A Simple Theory of the Survey Response: Answering Questions Versus Revealing Preferences," *American Journal of Political Science* 36, 3 (August 1992): 379.

48. George F. Bishop, Robert W. Oldendick, and Alfred J. Tuchfarber, "Pseudo-Opinions on Public Affairs," *Public Opinion Quarterly* 51 (Summer 1980): 198–209.

49. Data from the Gallup Organization, in response to the question, "What do you think is the most important problem facing this country today," December 5–8, 2004 and February 7–10, 2005.

50. The question asked by Gallup was, "Next, thinking about the issue of global warming, sometimes called the 'greenhouse effect,' how well do you feel you understand this issue—would you say very well, fairly well, not very well, or not at all?"

51. See also Jim Yang and Gerald Stone, "The Powerful Role of Interpersonal Communication in Agenda Setting," *Mass Communications and Society* 6, 1 (2003): 57–74; and Hans- Bernd Brosius and Gabriel Weimann, "Who Sets the Agenda?" *Communication Research* 23, 5 (October 1996): 561–80.

52. Benjamin I. Page and Robert Y. Shapiro, *The Rational Public* (Chicago: University of Chicago Press, 1992), 341–48.

53. One of the most important and influential discussions of the role of party identification in shaping Americans' thinking about politics appears in Angus Campbell, Philip E. Converse, et al., *The American Voter* (New York: Wiley, 1960). See especially chap. 6.

54. Campbell, Converse, et al., *American Voter*, 201. Reference is to 1980 re-print.

55. For a discussion of this phenomenon as applied to presidential economic performance, see Campbell, Converse, et al., *American Voter*, chap. 14.

56. Stimson, *Tides of Consent*, 163.

CHAPTER EIGHT

1. Alabama Department of Archives & History, "Application for Registration," 1965, http://www.alabamamoments.state.al.us/sec59pstrans.html (accessed March 17, 2005).

2. Steven F. Lawson, *Black Ballots: Voting Rights in the South, 1944–1969* (New York: Columbia University Press, 1976).

3. Sidney Verba, Kay Shlozman, and Henry Brady, *Voice and Equality* (Boston: Harvard University Press, 2006), 127.

4. Anthony Downs, *An Economic Theory of Democracy.* (New York: Harper, 1957), 267–68.

5. It was political scientist Mancur Olson who introduced the idea of selective benefits, which he called "selective incentives," in another classic work: *The Logic of Collective Action*. We have much more to say about this book in Chapter 12 on interest groups.

6. Riker and Ordeshook elaborated on this article in a 1973 book entitled *Introduction to Positive Political Theory*. Their logic does not apply as well to other forms of political behavior—writing a letter to a member of Congress, for example, or gathering signatures on a petition. The concept of "civic duty" does not apply as well to such activities. To cover these other kinds of participation, therefore, political scientists have tended to talk about their "psychic benefits." "Psychic benefits" is just another way of saying that people derive satisfaction from participating in politics, regardless of whether or not their participation has any effect on relevant political outcomes.

7. Verba, et al., *Voice and Equality*, 115, 550.

8. Michael McDonald and Samuel Popkin, "The Myth of the Vanishing Voter." *American Political Science Review* 95 (2001).

9. Shirley Zilberstein, "Ballot, Machine Problems to Blame for Uncounted Votes in 2000 Election," CNN, July 17 2001, http://archives.cnn.com/2001/ALLPOLITICS/07/16/voting.problems/index.html.

10. Verba, et al., *Voice and Equality*, 349.

11. Some states allowed women and those aged 18 to 20 to vote prior to these amendments.

12. Clegg, Roger, "Felon Disenfranchisement Is Constitutional, And Justified," National Constitution Center, http://www.constitutioncenter.org/education/ForEducators/Viewpoints/FelonDisenfranchisementIsConstitutional,AndJustified.shtml.

13. United States Federal Election Commission, "Executive Summary of the Federal Election Commission's Report to the Congress on the Impact of the National Voter Registration Act of 1993 on the Administration of Federal Elections," June 1997, http://www.fec.gov/votregis/nvrasum.htm.

14. See Stephen Knack, "Drivers Wanted: Motor Voter and the Election of 1996," *PS: Political Science and Politics* 32, 2 (June 1999): 237–43; and Michael D. Martinez and David Hill, "Did Motor Voter Work?" *American Politics Quarterly* 27, 3 (July 1999): 296–315.

15. See Knack, "Drivers Wanted," 239.

16. Mark A. Smith, "The Contingent Effects of Ballot Initiatives and Candidate Races on Turnout," *American Journal of Political Science* 45 (2001): 700–06; Caroline Tolbert, John Grummel, and Daniel Smith, "The Effects of Ballot Initiatives on Voter Turnout in the American States," *American Politics Review* 29 (2001): 625–48; and Caroline Tolbert, Ramona McNeal, and Daniel A. Smith, "Enhancing Civic Engagement: The Effect of Direct Democracy on Political Participation and Knowledge," *State Politics and Policy Quarterly* 3 (2003): 23–41.

17. *State of Discipline*, 448; Robert A. Jackson, "The Mobilization of State Electorates in the 1988 and 1990 Elections," *Journal of Politics* 59 (1999): 520–37; Richard W. Boyd, "The Effects of Primaries and Statewide Races on Voter Turnout," *Journal of Politics* 51 (1989): 730–39.

18. Priscilla L. Southwell, "Voter Turnout in the 1986 Congressional Elections: The Media as a Demobilizer?" *American Politics Quarterly* 19 (1991): 96–108; and Dean Lacy and Barry C. Burden, "The Vote-Stealing and Turnout Effects of Ross Perot in the 1992 U.S. Presidential Election," *American Journal of Political Science* 43 (1999): 233–55.

19. Gary W. Cox and Michael C. Munger, "Closeness, Expenditures, and Turnout in the 1982 U.S. House Elections," *American Political Science Review* 83 (1989): 217–31; Mark N. Franklin and Wolfgang P. Hirczy de Mino, "Separated Powers, Divided Government, and Turnout in U.S. Presidential Elections," *American Journal of Political Science* 42 (Jan, 1998): 316–26; and Gregory A. Caldeira and Samuel C. Patterson, "Getting Out the Vote: Participation in Gubernatorial Elections," *American Political Science Review* 77 (1982): 675–89.

20. The American National Election Studies, "The NES Guide to Public Opinion and Electoral Behavior," The American National Election Studies, http://www.electionstudies.org/nesguide/gd-index.htm#6.

21. Steven J. Rosenstone and John M. Hansen, *Mobilization, Participation, and Democracy in America*, (New York: Macmillan, 1993), 29.

22. Ibid., 44.

23. "Voter Turnout: An International Comparison," *Public Opinion Quarterly* (1984).

24. National Center for Education Statistics, Digest of Education Statistics. http://nces.ed.gov/pubs2002/digest2001/tables/dt008.asp.

25. Steven J. Rosenstone and John M. Hansen, *Mobilization, Participation, and Democracy in America*, (New York: Macmillan, 1993), 215.

26. Ibid.

27. M. Margaret Conway, *Political Participation in the United States* (Washington, D.C.: CQ Press, 1991), 171.

28. Steven J. Rosenstone and John M. Hansen, *Mobilization, Participation, and Democracy in America*, (New York: Macmillan, 1993), 163.

29. Paul R. Abramson, John H. Aldrich, and David W. Rohde, *Change and Continuity in the 2004 Elections*, (Washington, D.C.: CQ Press, 2006), 85.

30. For a review of the existing literature and a report on some new research findings, see Alan S. Gerber and Donald P. Green, "The Effects of Canvassing, Direct Mail, and Telephone Contact on Voter Turnout: A Field Experiment," *American Political Science Review* 94 (2000): 653–63.

31. Rui Texeira, *The Disappearing American Voter* (Washington DC: Brookings Institution Press, 1992), 7, 36.

32. Steven J. Rosenstone and John M. Hansen, *Mobilization, Participation, and Democracy in America*, (New York: Macmillan, 1993), 156.

33. As quoted in Kenneth M. Goldstein, *Interest Groups, Lobbying, and Participation in America* [New York: Cambridge University Press, 1999].

34. We derived this discussion from Conway, *Political Participation*, 108–11, and Nancy E. McGlen and Karen O'Connor, *Women, Politics, and American Society* (Englewood Cliffs, NJ: Prentice Hall, Inc., 1995), chap. 1.

CHAPTER NINE

1. D.W. Miller, "Election Results Leave Political Scientists Red-Faced over Their Forecasting Models," *The Chronicle of Higher Education*, November 8, 2000.
2. Ibid.
3. Robert G. Kaiser, "Gore to Win Election?" *Washington Post*, May 26, 2000, A1.
4. This isn't so in two states: Louisiana and Washington both use a "top two" system in which the two final candidates (if no candidate receives over 50 percent in the first round) could both be Democrats or both be Republicans.
5. "New Hampshire Primary," Wikipedia, http://en.wikipedia.org/wiki/New_Hampshire_primary#Democrats.
6. Ron Gunzburger, publisher, "Presidency 2000: Arizona Primary Results," Politics 1, http://www.politics1.com/vote-az.htm.
7. Lawrence D. Longley and Neal R. Peirce, *The Electoral College Primer 2000* (New Haven and London: Yale University Press, 1999), 18–19.
8. Gary L. Gregg II, *Securing Democracy: Why We Have an Electoral College* (Wilmington, DE: ISI Books, 2001), 6.
9. Ibid., 7, 8.
10. Ibid., 27–29. Originally the second-place finisher became the vice president. This was changed by constitutional amendment in 1804 so that electors cast votes separately for president and vice president. By awarding the vice presidency to the second place finisher, the previous system set up the possibility for severe disharmony in the executive branch.
11. "U.S. Electoral College," Wikipedia, http://en.wikipedia.org/wiki/U.S._Electoral_College#Maine-Nebraska_method.
12. "US President, National, Exit Poll," CNN, http://www.cnn.com/ELECTION/2004/pages/results/states/US/P/00/epolls.0.html.
13. William H. Flanigan and Nancy H. Zingale, *Political Behavior of the American Electorate* (Washington, DC: CQ Press, 2002), 93.
14. Michael Gant and Norman Luttbeg, "The Cognitive Utility of Partisanship," *Western Political Quarterly* 40 (1987): 499–517.
15. Flanigan and Zingale, *Political Behavior of the American Electorate*, 78.
16. Michael R. Alvarez, *Information and Elections* (Ann Arbor, MI: University of Michigan Press, 1998), 8.
17. V.O. Key, *The Responsible Electorate, Rationality in Presidential Voting, 1936–1960* (Cambridge, MA: Belknap Press of Harvard University Press, 1966); Gregory B. Markus and Philip Converse, "A Dynamic Simultaneous Equation Model of Electoral Choice," *American Political Science Review* 73 (1979).
18. Edward G. Carmines and James A. Stimson, *Issue Evolution: Race and the Transformation of American Politics* (Princeton, NJ: Princeton University Press, 1989).
19. Donald E. Stokes, "Some Dynamic Elements of Contests for the Presidency," *The American Political Science Review* 60 (1966): 19–28.
20. Controversies, 90–91.
21. Larry M. Bartels, "Impact of Candidate Traits in American Presidential Elections," in *Leaders' Personalities and the Outcomes of Democratic Elections*, Anthony King (ed.) (Oxford and New York: Oxford University Press, 2002), 46.
22. Angus Campbell et al., *The American Voter* (Chicago and London: University of Chicago Press, 1980), 44–45.
23. Markus and Converse, "A Dynamic Simultaneous Equation Model of Electoral Choice."
24. Classics, 120, which is drawn from Page and Jones.
25. Angus Campbell et al., *The American Voter*; Stanley Kelley Jr. and Thad W. Mirer, "The Simple Act of Voting," *American Political Science Review* 68 (1974): 572–91; Markus and Converse, "A Dynamic Simultaneous Equation Model of Electoral Choice"; Warren E. Miller and J. Merrill Shanks, *The New American Voter* (Cambridge, MA: Harvard University Press, 1996), chap. 17.
26. Kelley and Mirer, "The Simple Act of Voting."
27. Kelley and Mirer, "The Simple Act of Voting"; Markus and Converse, "A Dynamic Simultaneous Equation Model of Electoral Choice."
28. Markus and Converse, "A Dynamic Simultaneous Equation Model of Electoral Choice."
29. Larry M. Bartels, *Presidential Primaries and the Dynamics of Public Choice* (Princeton, NJ: Princeton University Press, 1998).
30. Randall E. Adkins and Andrews J. Dowdle, "The Money Primary: What Influences the Outcome of Pre-Primary Presidential Nomination Fundraising?" *Presidential Studies Quarterly* 32, 2 (2002): 256–75.

31. James E. Campbell, "Forecasting the Presidential Vote in the States," *American Journal of Political Science* 36 (1992): 386–407.

32. Randall J. Jones Jr., *Who Will Be in the White House: Predicting Presidential Elections* (New York: Longman, 2002), 31.

33. Ibid.

34. Morris P. Fiorina, "Parties and Partisanship: A 40-Year Retrospective," *Political Behavior* 24 (June 2002): 93–115.

35. Ibid.

36. Ibid.

37. Dan Balz, "Bad Signs for Bush in History, Numbers Approval Rating Is Lowest of His Term, *Washington Post*, May 13, 2004.

38. Jimmy Carter, "Remarks Accepting the Presidential Nomination at the 1980 Democratic National Convention," August 14, 1980, *Public Papers of the Presidents of the United States: Jimmy Carter: 1977–1981*, 9 vols. (Washington, DC: Government Printing Office, 1977–1982), http://www.4president.org/speeches/carter1980convention.htm.

39. Stan Greenberg and Jim Gerstein, "Focus Group Report: Findings from Recent Discussions with Voters," April 9, 2004, Democracy Corps, http://archive.democracycorps.com/focus/Democracy_Corps_April_2004_Focus_Group_Report.pdf.

40. "Banking on Becoming President," OpenSecrets, http://www.opensecrets.org/pres08/index.php?sort=E.

41. "Stats at a Glance," OpenSecrets, http://www.opensecrets.org/overview/index.php.

42. "Political Actors and Their Activities: National Party Committees," The Campaign Legal Center, http://www.campaignfinanceguide.org/guide-108.html.

43. "Most Expensive Races," OpenSecrets, http://www.opensecrets.org/bigpicture/topraces.asp?cycle=2004.

44. "Congressional Candidates Spend $1.6 Billion During 2003–2004," June 9, 2005, Federal Election Commission, http://www.fec.gov/press/press2005/20050609candidate/20050609candidate.html.

45. http://www.opensecrets.org/pressreleases/2004/04results.asp

46. "Top Soft Money Donors," OpenSecrets, http://www.opensecrets.org/bigpicture/softtop.php?cycle=2002.

47. John McCain, "Ban the Soft Money," January 9, 2000, http://mccain.senate.gov/public/index.cfm?FuseAction=PressOffice.OpEds&ContentRecord_id=l04456b96-c05c-4bfd-8482-a6e32808a61f&Region_id=&Issue_id=.

48. Deborah Beck, Paul Taylor, Jeffrey Stanger and Douglas Rivlin, *Issue Advocacy Advertising During the 1996 Campaign*, (State College, PA: University of Pennsylvania Annenberg Public Policy Center, 1997), 56, http://www.annenbergpublicpolicycenter.org/Downloads/Political_Communication/Advertising_Research_1997/REP16.pdf.

49. "Presidential Public Funding System: Primary Election," The Campaign Legal Center, http://www.campaignfinanceguide.org/guide-50.html.

50. R. Lawrence Butler, *Claiming the Mantle: How Presidential Nominations Are Won and Lost Before the Votes Are Cast* (Cambridge, MA: Westview Press, 2004), 53.

51. "Presidential Public Funding System: General Election," The Campaign Legal Center, http://www.campaignfinanceguide.org/guide-51.html.

CHAPTER TEN

1. "Prosecute Kerry," http://johnkerry-08.com/ (accessed January 17, 2008).

2. "The 1,712th CyberAlert," 2004, http://www.mrc.org/printer/cyberalerts/2004/cyb20040505pf.asp (accessed January 17, 2008).

3. Interview with John O'Neil, 2005, http://goliath.ecnext.com/coms2/gi_0199-3933841/John-O-Neil-Live-with.html (accessed February 5, 2008).

4. "Swift Boat Veterans for Truth, 2004 Election Cycle," 2004, http://www.opensecrets.org/527s/527events.asp?orgid=61 (accessed January 17, 2008).

5. Interview with John O'Neil.

6. Kate Zernike and Jim Rutenberg, "Friendly Fire: The Birth of an Attack on Kerry," National Desk Page, *New York Times*, August 20, 2004, late edition.

7. F. Newport, *Questions and Answers with the Editor in Chief*, 2004, http://www.gallup.com/poll/12895/Questions-Answers-Editor-Chief.aspx (accessed February 6, 2008).

8. Ibid.

9. D.C. Hallin and R. Giles, *Presses and Democracies*, in *The Press*, G. Overholser and K. Hall Jamieson, eds. (New York: Oxford University Press, 2005), 7.

10. S. Djankov, et al., *Who Owns the Media?*, 2001, http://siteresources.worldbank.org/INTWDR2002/Resources/2423_djankov.pdf (accessed February 5, 2008).

11. Hallin and Giles, *Presses and Democracies*.

12. BBC England, *Annual Review 2006–2007*, 2007, http://www.bbc.co.uk/england/ace/bbc_england_annual_review.pdf (accessed February 6, 2008).

13. T. Patterson, "Political Roles of the Journalist," in *The Politics of News: The News of Politics*, D.A. Graber, D. McQuail, and P. Norris, eds. (Washington, DC: CQ Press, 2007); R.E. Horn, *Visual Language: Global Communication for the 21st Century.* 1999.

14. Hallin and Giles, *Presses and Democracies,* 8–9.

15. Hallin and Giles, *Presses and Democracies,* 10.

16. Patterson, "Political Roles of the Journalist," 22, table 1.1.

17. Ibid., 23.

18. Poynter Forums, *Afflicting the Comfortable,* 2008, http://www.poynter.org/forum/?id=16725, (accessed January 17, 2008).

19. F. Esser and B. Pfetsch, eds., "Comparing Political Communication: Theories, Cases, and Challenges," *Communication, Society and Politics* (New York: Cambridge University Press, 2005); Graber, et al., *The Politics of News: The News of Politics.*

20. *New York Times Co. v. United States,* 403 U.S. 713 (1971).

21. http://www.law.ou.edu/hist/sedact.html.

22. Margaret A. Blanchard, "Freedom of the Press," in W. David Sloan and Lisa Mullikin Parcell, *American Journalism: History, Principles, Practices* (Jefferson, North Carolina: McFarland and Co., 2002), 127.

23. Richard W. T. Martin, *The Free and Open Press* (New York: New York University Press, 2001), 132.

24. W.D. Sloan and L.M. Parcell, eds., *American Journalism: History, Principles, Practices* (New York: McFarland & Company, 2002); R. Martin, *The Free and Open Press: The Founding of American Democratic Press Liberty* (New York: NYU Press, 2001).

25. Samuel D. Warren and Louis D. Brandeis. "The Right to Privacy," *Harvard Law Review* 4, 5 (1890): 195.

26. W. Overbeck, *Major Principles of Media Law* (Wadsworth Publishing, 2007).

27. Patterson, "Political Roles of the Journalist," 22, table 1.1.

28. Ibid.

29. Margaret A. Blanchard, "Freedom of the Press."

30. "Press Freedom Day by Day," http://www.rsf.org/article.php3?id_article=11715 (accessed January 17, 2008).

31. "Periodicals," http://encarta.msn.com/encyclopedia_761567699/Periodicals.html?partner=orp (accessed January 17, 2008).

32. "Radio and Television Broadcasting," http://encarta.msn.com/encyclopedia_761566157_2/Broadcasting.html (accessed January 17, 2008).

33. "Infinity Chief Executive Farid Suleman Says, 'Infinity Stations Won't Begin Streaming Content Until We Figure Out How To Make Money From It,'" http://www.radioink.com/HeadlineEntry.asp?hid=47048&pt=archive (accessed January 17, 2008).

34. M. Stephens, *History of Television,* http://www.nyu.edu/classes/stephens/History%20of%20Television%20page.htm (accessed January 17, 2008).

35. "United States: Cable Television," 2008, http://www.museum.tv/archives/etv/U/htmlU/unitedstatesc/unitedstatesc.htm (accessed February 6, 2008).

36. H.W. Stanley and R.G. Niemi, eds., *Vital Statistics on American Politics 1999-2000* (Washington, DC: CQ Press, 1999).

37. *The State of the News Media in 2004: An Annual Report on American Journalism,* 2004, http://www.stateofthenewsmedia.org/ (accessed February 6, 2008).

38. M. Schudson and S.E. Tifft, "American Journalism in Historical Perspective," in *The Press,* 32.

39. *The Right Talk,* Online NewsHour, 2003, http://www.pbs.org/newshour/bb/media/july-dec03/righttalkradio_10-13.html (accessed January 17, 2008).

40. Schudson and Tifft, "American Journalism in Historical Perspective," 33.

41. J. Robinson, "The Story of How CBS Was Caught Perpetrating a Hoax on the American People," 2004, http://www.freerepublic.com/focus/f-news/1219050/posts (accessed January 17, 2008).

42. "Bush Guard Documents: Forged," 2004, http://littlegreenfootballs.com/weblog/?entry=12526_Bush_Guard_Documents-_Forged (accessed January 17, 2008).

43. "The Sixty-First Minute," 2004, http://www.powerlineblog.com/archives/007760.php (accessed January 17, 2008).

44. Ibid.

45. M. Halperin, et al., "Playing for Harvard: The Second Draft of History Is Usually Better Than the First," 2004, http://www.abcnews.go.com/sections/politics/TheNote/TheNote_Sept1004.html (accessed January 17, 2008).

46. Transcript of Statements by CBS News President Andrew Heyward and Anchor Dan Rather, 2004, http://www.freerepublic.com/focus/f-news/1221463/posts (accessed January 17, 2008).

47. D. Thornburgh and L.D. Boccardi, *Report of the Independent Review Panel: Concerning President Bush's Texas Air National Guard Service,* 2005, http://wwwimage.cbsnews.com/htdocs/pdf/complete_report/CBS_Report.pdf (accessed January 17, 2008).

48. Ibid.

49. Ibid.

50. S. Robert Lichter and Patricia McGinnis. "Government In and Out of the News" *The Public Manager* 32 (2003): 48.

51. Ibid, 49.

52. Schudson and Tifft, "American Journalism in Historical Perspective," 33.

53. Ibid.

54. T. Patterson, *Out of Order: An Incisive and Boldly Original Critique of the News Media's Domination of America's Political Process* (New York: Vintage, 1994).

55. J.N.Cappella and K.H. Jamieson, *Spiral of Cynicism: The Press and the Public Good.* (Oxford University Press, 1997).

56. J.T. Hamilton, "The Market and the Media," in *The Press*, 358.

57. ABC News Transcript, "Democrats Plan a Media Attack on President Bush's Budget," August 20, 2001.

58. Lichter and Mcginnis, "Government In and Out of the News," 32.

59. Ibid.

60. Albert Hunt, "Tension in Hillaryland Grows as Plan Goes Awry," http://www.bloomberg.com/apps/news?pid=newsarchive&sid=anRcoLyfN0VM (accessed April 14, 2008).

61. S.J. Farnsworth and S.R. Lichter, *The Nightly News Nightmare: Network Television's Coverage of U.S. Presidential Elections, 1988–2000* (New York: Rowman & Littlefield, 2002).

62. S. R. Lichter, *Good Intentions Make Bad News: Why Americans Hate Campaign Journalism* (New York: Rowman & Littlefield, 1996).

63. T. Patterson and P. Seib, "Informing the Public," in *The Press*, 194.

64. Ibid., 195; Patterson, *Out of Order: An Incisive and Boldly Original Critique of the News Media's Domination of America's Political Process.*

65. Center for Media and Public Affairs, http://www.cmpa.com/studies.html (accessed February 13, 2008).

66. Kaplan, Goldstein, Hale, *Local News Coverage of the 2004 Election Campaigns*, Lear Center Local News Archive, 2004.

67. M. Dolny, "Right, Center Think Tanks Still Most Quoted," 2004, http://www.fair.org/index.php?page=2534 (accessed February 13, 2008).

68. Center for Media and Public Affairs, http://www.cmpa.com/studies.html (accessed February 13, 2008).

69. S. Tiner, "Why Editors Are Dumber Than Mules," 1999, http://www.asne.org/kiosk/editor/97.jan-feb/tiner1.htm (accessed January 17, 2008).

70. R. Parry, "Media Mythology: Is the Press Liberal?" 1997, http://www.consortiumnews.com/archive/story21.html (accessed January 17, 2008).

71. D. D'Alessio and M. Allen, "Media Bias in Presidential Elections: A Meta-Analysis," *Journal of Communication* 50, 4 (2000): 148.

72. Ibid., 145.

73. Ibid.

74. J. Bryant and D. Zillman, eds., *Media Effects: Advances in Theory and Research*, Lea's Communication Series (Lawrence Erlbaum, 2002).

75. Ibid.

76. Angus Campbell, Philip E. Converse, Warren E. Miller, and Donald Stokes, *The American Voter* (New York: Wiley, 1960).

77. John Zaller, "The Myth of Massive Media Impact Revived: New Support for a Discredited Idea," in Diana C. Mutz, Paul M. Sniderman, and Richard A. Brody, eds., *Political Persuasion and Attitude Change*, 17.

78. Larry Bartels, "Messages Received: The Political Impact of Media Exposure," *American Political Science Review* 87, 2: 267.

79. S. Iyengar and D.R. Kinder, *News That Matters: Television and American Opinion*, American Politics and Political Economy Series (Chicago: University of Chicago Press, 1989).

80. C. Trumbo, *Longitudinal Modeling of Public Issues: An Application of the Agenda-Setting Process to the Issue of Global Warming*, Journalism and Communications Monographs, 1995, 152; Larry Bartels, "Politicians and the Press: Who Leads, Who Follows?" in *Annual Meeting of the American Political Science Association* (San Francisco, CA: 1996).

81. *Time of Presidential Election Vote Decision 1948–2004*, 2005, http://www.electionstudies.org/nesguide/toptable/tab9a_3.htm (accessed February 6, 2008).

82. L. Festinger, *Theory of Cognitive Dissonance* (Stanford University Press, 1957).

83. John Zaller, *The Nature and Origins of Mass Opinion* (New York: Cambridge University Press, 1992).

84. Ibid.

85. Ibid.

86. Ibid.

87. Bartels, "Politicians and the Press: Who Leads, Who Follows?"; T. Patterson, *Mass Media Election* (New York: Praeger Publishers, 1980); S.J. Farnsworth and S.R. Lichter, "No Small Town Poll: Network Coverage of the 1992 New Hampshire Primary," *Harvard International Journal of Press/Politics* 4 (1999): 51–61.

88. Bartels, "Politicians and the Press: Who Leads, Who Follows?"; John Zaller, *The Nature and Origins of Mass Opinion*, 23, 37, 48.

89. Patterson, *Out of Order: An Incisive and Boldly Original Critique of the News Media's Domination of America's Political Process.*

CHAPTER ELEVEN

1. Adam Nagourne, "A Referendum on Iraq Policy," *New York Times*, August 9, 2006; Rick Klein, "Lieberman Crafts Backup Plan," *Boston Globe*, July 4, 2006; Shailagh Murray, "Lieberman Wins Republican Friends, Democratic Enemies With Support for War," *Washington Post*, December 10, 2005; Meryl Gordon, "Joe Lieberman's War," *New York*, July 31, 2006.

2. There are many different definitions of political parties. The one offered here is based on the definitions provided by William Chambers (p. 5) and Leon Epstein (Mold p 18-19).

3. See, for example, Marty Cohen, David Karol, Hans Noel, and John Zaller, "Political Parties in Rough Weather," *The Forum* 5, 4 (2008), article 3.

4. John Aldrich, Why Parties. Note parties can arise for other reasons also.

5. The best known argument against this conclusion is offered in David R. Mayhew, *Divided We Govern* (New Haven, CT: Yale University Press, 1991). However, since the publication of Mayhew's work, a number of studies have shown that unified and divided government do in fact produce different results. See COLEMAN<HOWELL<ANYONE ELSE>

6. Cite Goldstein.

7. McGerr book, on minimizing immigrant influence.

8. Harold W. Stanley and Richard G. Niemi, *Vital Statistics on American Politics, 2007-08* (Washington, DC: CQ Press, 2008), pp. 43–43.

9. It is also worth noting that Candidates of third parties that are relatively large, such as the People's Party of the 1890s or the Progressive Party of the early 20th century, eventually absorb back into the major parties and can work to change the major parties' positions from within.

10. Cite Burden on Nader.

11. 873 cites on two party system.

12. In most systems, a party with 40% of the vote would actually win a larger share of seats than 40%, because the rules require parties to reach a threshold of votes to elect legislators, which denies seats to very small parties.

13. 873 cite.

14. Aldrich cite. Downs parties find folks as they take them.

15. Cite Disch book.

16. *Timmons v. Twin Cities Area New Party* (1997). The seven states are Connecticut, Delaware, Idaho, Mississippi, New York, South Carolina, and Vermont.

17. Cite Rosenstone on third parties.

18. A number of alternative systems is discussed at the website for the advocacy group FairVote (www.fairvote.org).

19. Designed for use in multi-member districts, cumulative voting could be modified for single-member district use. In this method, voters are allowed to cast more than one vote and distribute those votes across the candidates as they wish, meaning they could, for example, give one candidate three votes, or divide their votes 2-1 across two candidates, or vote for three candidates with one vote each. In a multi-member district, the number of votes given to each voter would equal the number of seats being elected. In a single-member district, an appropriate number would have to be determined. The logic is that a voter could indicate some strong support for a third party candidate, while also casting support for a preferred major party candidate. Its use in the United States currently is at the local level in about fifty jurisdictions, in elections featuring multi-member boards like city councils, school committees, or county commissions. It has been used successfully as a way to increase minority representation on these boards.

20. Burnham, Mayhew, Beck, others.

21. Mayer 1998.

22. (Abramowitz and Saunders 1999; Bartels 1998)

23. Rise of majority Republican coalition
   - "In the public perception, all these things merged. Ghetto riots, campus riots, street crime, anti-Vietnam marches, poor people's marches, drugs, pornography, welfarism, rising taxes, all had a common thread: the breakdown of family and social discipline, of order, of concepts of duty, of respect for law, of public and private morality."
   - "[Liberalism came to mean that] you take the side of blacks, no matter what; dismiss middle class complaints as racism; handcuffing the police; transferring resources and sympathy from a vulnerable middle class to minorities; rationalizing rioting and dependency and other moral afflictions as 'caused' by the environment or as a justifiable response to oppression."

24. Cite Burnham on Reagan.

25. Democrats controlled the Senate from mid-2001 until the end of 2002 when James Jeffords, a Republican Senator from Vermont, declared himself an Independent and aligned with the Democrats.

26. Cite Gerring.

27. (Carmines and Layman 1997; Layman 1997).

28. David Wright, Andy Fies, and Sunlen Miller, "Obama: 'Old Politics Just Won't Do'—Democratic Contender Frames Race Against Clinton as 'Past Versus the

Future,'" January 30, 2008, http://www.abcnews.go.com/Politics/Vote2008/story?id=4215588&page=1; Associated Press, "McCain Outlines Vision of Iraq Victory, Reduced Partisanship," May 15, 2008, http://elections.foxnews.com/2008/05/15/mccain-outlines-vision-of-iraq-victory-reduced-partisanship/.

29. The "two Americas" label was used by Democratic presidential candidate John Edwards; the "50/50 nation" (or 49/49) by *National Journal* writer Michael Barone; "red and blue America" by a number of observers, including *New York Times* columnist David Brooks; and "culture war" by author and media personality Bill O'Reilly and former Republican presidential candidate Patrick Buchanan.

30. Morris P. Fiorina, Samuel J. Abrams, and Jeremy C. Pope, *Culture War? The Myth of a Polarized America*, 2nd ed. (New York: Longman, 2005).

31. Paul DiMaggio, John Evans and Bethany Bryson, "Have Americans' Social Attitudes Become More Polarized?" *American Journal of Sociology* 102, 3 (1996): 690-755.

32. Marjorie Randon Hershey, *Party Politics in America*, 13th ed. (New York: Longman, 2009), p. 187.

33. For a selection of these studies, see Marc J. Hetherington, "Resurgent Mass Partisanship: The Role of Elite Polarization," *American Political Science Review* 95, 3 (2001): 619-31; Geoffrey C. Layman and Thomas M. Carsey, "Party Polarization and 'Conflict Extension' in the American Electorate," *American Journal of Political Science* 46, 4 (2002): 786-802; Nolan McCarty, Keith T. Poole, and Howard Rosenthal, *Polarized America: The Dance of Ideology and Unequal Riches* (Cambridge: MIT Press, 2006); Mark D. Brewer and Jeffrey M. Stonecash, *Split: Class And Cultural Divides in American Politics* (Washington, DC: CQ Press, 2006); Gary C. Jacobson, "Party Polarization in National Politics: The Electoral Connection," in Jon R. Bond and Richard Fleisher, eds., *Polarized Politics: Congress and the President in a Partisan Era* (Washington, DC: Congressional Quarterly Books, 2000); Richard Fleisher and Jon R. Bond, "Evidence of Increasing Polarization Among Ordinary Citizens," in Jeffrey E. Cohen, Richard Fleisher, and Paul Kantor, eds., *American Political Parties: Decline or Resurgence?* (Washington, DC: CQ Press, 2001); Barbara Sinclair, *Party Wars: Polarization and the Politics of National Policy Making* (Norman, OK: University of Oklahoma Press, 2006).

34. In *Culture War?*, Fiorina, Abrams, and Pope argue that voters have had little choice but to vote more ideologically and more consistent. Imagine a voter who is slightly to the left of center. This voter might be open to voting for a mildly conservative Republican at some times and a mildly liberal Democrat at others. However, if the choices for this voter are between a strong liberal and a strong conservative, he will vote for the strong liberal consistently, even though that candidate's views do not reflect his own very well.

35. Frymer.

36. Green and herrsnson book, coleman article, apsa report

37. Klinkner out party.

38. McGerr on miliatriaistic campaigns

39. This is true almost by definition: if turnout is 80 percent or more, class skew in turnout is less likely to be present.

40. Cite Ware on primaries.

41. Cite Epstein.

42. This discussion borrows heavily on Herrnson.

43. California Democratic Party v. Jones (2000). Tashjian v. Connecticut (1986).

44. Hershey p. 76

45. The discussion in this case study relies extensively on Marjorie Randon Hershey, *Party Politics in America*, 13th ed. (New York: Pearson Longman, 2009), pp. 205–06, and Matthew J. Burbank, Ronald J. Hrebenar, and Robert C. Benedict, *Parties, Interest Groups, and Political Campaigns* (Boulder CO: Paradigm Publishers, 2008), pp. 148–51.

46. Hershey, *Party Politics in America*, p. 205.

47. David Paul Kuhn, "DNC blunts GOP microtargeting lead," www.politico.com, May 23, 2008.

48. Cited in Burbank, Hrebenar, and Benedict, *Parties, Interest Groups, and Political Campaigns*, p. 149.

49. Hershey p. 80

50. Coleman orthodoxy.

CHAPER TWELVE

1. Adapted from Conway, *Political Participation*, pp.108–111, and Nancy E. McGlen and Karen O'Connor, *Women, Politics, and American Society* (Englewood Cliffs, NJ: Prentice Hall, Inc., 1995), Chapter 1.

2. http://www.census.gov/hhes/www/hlthins/hlthin06/hlth06asc.html

3. http://www.pollingreport.com/health3.htm

4. (Latham's phrase—1965, p.221.)

5. (p.507 of Truman, plus)

6. A critique, p.289.

7. http://www.census.gov/Press-Release/www/releases/archives/income_wealth/010583.html

8. Nelson W. Polsby, "How to Study Community Power: The Pluralist Alternative," in Roderick Bell, David V.

Edwards, and R. Harrison Wagner, editors, *Political Power: A Reader in Theory and Research* (New York: The Free Press, 1969), p.33. Excerpted from *Journal of Politics* 22 (1960), pp.474–84; and Nelson W. Polsby, *Community Power and Political Theory* (New Haven: Yale University Press, 1980), p.116.

9. That quote is from Schlozman p. 1029. The numbers are from 1013.

10. Two Faces of Power

11. Peter Bachrach and Morton S. Baratz, "Decisions and Nondecisions: An Analytical Framework," American Political Science Review, Vol.57, No.3, September 1963, pp.632–42.

12. p.71

13. Truman 1951 p.31,2.

14. http://ivaw.org/about

15. p.2.

16. p.16.

17. Olson p.51 coined "selective incentives".

18. Light, Artful Work, p.76.

19. This is from ASQ, September 1961, p.134.

20. "Social distinction" comes from ASQ p.135.

21. ASQ, p.7.

22. http://www.exploreveg.org/help/volunteer-testimonials

23. Salisbury, exchange theory of interest groups

24. http://www.vpc.org/nrainfo/chapter1.html

25. http://www.campaignfinancesite.org/structure/opinions16.html; http://www.mdfva.org/2004News/Washtimes041018_041024.html#M041020%20%20%20Soros-supported%20voter-registration%20drive

26. http://www.naco.org/Content/NavigationMenu/About_NACo/Membership/Membership.htm; http://congressional.energy.gov/state_local.htm

27. *The Business History Review*, Vol. 52, No. 3, Corporate Liberalism. (Autumn, 1978), pp.321–341.

28. http://www.opensecrets.org/bigpicture/pac2cands.asp?cycle=2006

29. http://www.opensecrets.org/bigpicture/elec_stats.asp?Cycle=2006#house

30. http://www.opensecrets.org/527s/527cmtes.asp?level=C&format=&cycle=2004

31. http://www.opensecrets.org/527s/527cmtes.asp.

32. http://www.opensecrets.org/527s/527cmtes.asp?level=C&format=&cycle=2004

33. http://horse.he.net/~swiftpow/article.php?story=2004092911015589

34. http://www.factcheck.org/article294.html

35. http://www.barackobama.com/issues/ethics/

36. 12/11/2007 LEAnet alert.

37. http://www.avma.org/onlnews/javma/mar04/040301j.asp

38. http://www.nytimes.com/2005/11/14/politics/politicsspecial1/14progress.html?pagewanted=print

39. http://www.washingtonpost.com/wp-dyn/articles/A18417-2004Nov28.html Jeffrey Birnbaum, Returning to the Game he Started

40. http://www.porternovelli.com/pnwebsite/pnwebsite.nsf/SiteSearch/812B28D17826E47C85256C0C006ECA31?OpenDocument&Tab=1

41. Darrell M. West, Diane Heith and Chris Goodwin. "Harry and Louise Go to Washington: Political Advertising and Health Care Reform." *Journal of Health Politics, Policy and Law*, .vol. 21. no. 1. spring 1996.

42. HW, p.802.

43. http://72.14.253.104/search?q=cache:nartLRj_rsYJ:www.politicalscience.uncc.edu/godwink/RecentPublications/What%2520Corporations%2520Really%2520Want%2520from%2520Government.pdf+%22what+corporations+really+want+from+government%22&hl=en&ct=clnk&cd=1&gl=us

44. http://72.14.253.104/search?q=cache:nartLRj_rsYJ:www.politicalscience.uncc.edu/godwink/RecentPublications/What%2520Corporations%2520Really%2520Want%2520from%2520Government.pdf+%22what+corporations+really+want+from+government%22&hl=en&ct=clnk&cd=1&gl=us

45. Walker, Jack L, Mobilizing Interest Groups in America: Patrons, Professionals and Social Movements. University of Michigan Press. 1991.

46. Totals include subsidiaries and affiliated PACs, if any. The names used in this stable are those of the organization connected with the PAC, rather than the official PAC name.

47. Anthony Nownes' *Total Lobbying: What Lobbyists Want (and How They Try to Get it).*

CHAPTER THIRTEEN

1. Shawn Reese, Congressional Research Service Report for Congress, *Fiscal Year 2005 Homeland Security Grant Program: State Allocations and Issues for Congressional Oversight* (Washington, DC: Congressional Research Service, 2004).

2. Kathleen Hunter, "Per Capita, New Anti-terror Funds Still Favor Wyoming," Pew Research Center, December 16, 2004, http://www.stateline.org.

3. Reese, *Fiscal Year 2005 Homeland Security Grant Program.*

4. The remaining 60% of the funds are distributed by formula according to population.

5. "U.S. Not 'Well-prepared' for Terrorism," December 5, 2005, http://www.cnn.com.

6. Judy Holland, "Anti-terror Funding Open to 'Pork Barrel' Politics," *Milwaukee Journal Sentinel*, August 22, 2004, 18A.

7. Kathleen Hunter, "Budget Would Revise Antiterrorism Funding," Pew Research Center, February 8, 2005, http://www.stateline.org.

8. Veronique de Rugy, "Homeland-Security Scuffle," *National Review*, October 15, 2004, http://www.nationalreview.com/comment/rugy200410150840.asp.

9. The Homeland Security Grant Program, however, has gradually reduced the total amount of money distributed through SHSP and has increased the amount of antiterrorism funding awarded through another of its programs, the Urban Areas Security Initiative, which is relatively free to distribute federal antiterrorism funding to the cities that need it most. U.S. Department of Homeland Security, Office of Grants and Training, *Overview: FY 2007 Homeland Security Grant Program*, January 5, 2007.

10. Non-voting members come from the District of Columbia, American Samoa, Guam, Puerto Rico, and the Virgin Islands.

11. At the nation's founding, state legislatures appointed senators to office. In 1913, however, the states ratified the Seventeenth Amendment, which required the direct election of senators. Representatives in the House have always been popularly elected.

12. Max Farrand ed. *The Records of the Federal Convention of 1787* (New Haven: Yale University Press, 1966), 151.

13. David Mayhew, *The Electoral Connection* (New Haven, CT: Yale University Press, 1974).

14. Mayhew, *The Electoral Connection*, 16.

15. Brandice Canes-Wrone, David Brady, and John Cogan, "Out of Step, Out of Office: Electoral Accountability and House Members' Voting," *American Political Science Review* 96, 1 (2002): 127–40.

16. Edmund Burke, "Speech to the Electors of England" in *The Works of the Right Honorable Edmund Burke, Vol. II.* (New York: Oxford University Press, 1774 [1907]). Also available online at http://oll.libertyfund.org/Texts/LFBooks/Burke0061/SelectWorks/HTMLs/0005-04_Pt02_Speeches.html#c_burkeelectors.nt9.

17. Based on figures from fiscal year 2000. Congressional Budget Office, "Federal Spending on the Elderly and Children," July 2000, http://cbo.gov/ftpdocs/23xx/doc2300/fsec.pdf.

18. Gary Jacobson, *The Politics of Congressional Elections*, 6th ed. (New York: Longman, 2003).

19. Brody Mullins, "Growing Role for Lobbyists: Raising Funds for Lawmakers," *Wall Street Journal*, January 27, 2006, 1.

20. Kenneth Goldstein, *Interest Groups, Lobbying, and Participating in America* (New York: Cambridge University Press, 1999); John Mark Hansen, *Gaining Access: Congress and the Farm Lobby, 1919–1981* (Chicago: University of Chicago Press, 1991).

21. Keith T. Poole and Thomas Romer, "Ideology, 'Shirking', and Representation," *Public Choice* 77 (1993): 185–96.

22. Kenneth N. Bickers and Robert M. Stein, "The Congressional Pork Barrel in a Republican Era," *Journal of Politics* 62, 4 (November 2000): 1070–86.

23. For more on descriptive or numerical representation, see Jane Mansbridge, "Should Blacks Represent Blacks and Women Represent Women? A Contingent 'Yes'," *Journal of Politics* 61, 3 (August 1999): 628–57.

24. Michele Swers, *The Difference Women Make* (Chicago: University of Chicago Press, 2002).

25. Ebonya Washington, "Female Socialization: How Daughters Affect Their Legislator Fathers' Voting on Women's Issues," *American Economic Review*, Forthcoming.

26. These states include Connecticut, Colorado, Florida, Iowa, Indiana, Louisiana, Minnesota, Missouri, Nebraska, New Mexico, Nevada, Ohio, Oregon, Pennsylvania, South Dakota, Virginia, and Vermont. Two of the states (Connecticut and Vermont) elected a Democrat and Independent. All the other states elected a Democrat and Republican.

27. For more on this particular example, see Barry Burden, *The Personal Roots of Representation* (Princeton, NJ: Princeton University Press, 2007).

28. Because of its small population, Alaska has just one House representative.

29. Daniel Gitterman. *The Politics of Increasing Our Take-Home Pay in America* (Washington, DC: Brookings Institution Press, Forthcoming.)

30. For one study of the role of information in Congress, see Keith Krehbiel, *Information and Legislative Organization* (Ann Arbor, MI: University of Michigan Press, 1992).

31. Kenneth Shepsle, *The Giant Jigsaw Puzzle: Democratic Committee Assignments in the Modern House* (Chicago: University of Chicago Press, 1978).

32. Robert C. Albright, "Two-Stage Battle, If Necessary, Planned for Urban Affairs Unit," *The Washington Post, Times Herald*, January 24, 1962, A2; Russell Baker, "Kennedy Accused on Urban Moves: G.O.P Sees Racism in Plan to Create Cabinet Post," *The New York Times*, January 26, 1962, 14; Richard L. Lyons, "House

Kills Urban Plan by 262-150." *The Washington Post, Times Herald*, February 22, 1962, A1; Chalmers M. Roberts, "Anguish in Urban Affairs: Kennedy Nudges GOP Into Own Booby Trap," *The Washington Post, Times Herald*, January 26, 1962, A2; and House of Representatives Committee on Rules, "Committee on Rules: A History," http://www.rules.house.gov/archives/rules_history.htm (accessed October 25, 2007).

33. Gary Cox and Mathew McCubbins, *Setting the Agenda: Responsible Party Govern ment in the U.S. House of Representatives.* (New York: Cambridge University Press, 2005).

34. See, for example, Keith Krehbiel, "Where's the Party?" *British Journal of Political Science* 23 (1993): 235–66.

35. Since the Civil War, Southern politicians retained strong loyalties to the Democratic Party. Ideologically, however, they had more in common with Northern Republicans. Beginning in the 1970s, over a century after the Civil War's end, Southern Democrats began to abandon their former partisan commitments in order to join the ranks of the Republican Party.

36. Nolan McCarty, Keith Poole, Howard Rosenthal, *Polarized America: The Dance of Ideology and Unequal Riches* (Cambridge, MA: MIT Press, 2005).

37. For a profile of congressional staffers in 2007, see "The Hill People 2007: A Special Report," *National Journal*, June 23, 2007.

38. By declaring war, Congress asserts that a state of war currently exists. By authorizing war, Congress typically grants the president the authority to decide whether to respond militarily to a perceived foreign crisis.

39. Louis Fisher, *Congressional Abdication on War and Spending* (College Station, TX: Texas A&M University Press, 2000), 65.

40. William Howell and Douglas Kriner, "Political Elites and Public Support for War," University of Chicago typescript, 2007.

41. William Howell and Jon Pevehouse, *While Dangers Gather: Congressional Checks on Presidential War Power* (Princeton, NJ: Princeton University Press, 2007). See also: William Howell and Jon Pevehouse, "When Congress Stops Wars," *Foreign Affairs* 86, 5 (2007): 95–108.

42. Barbara Sinclair, *Unorthodox Lawmaking: New Legislative Processes in the U.S. Congress* (Washington, D.C.: Congressional Quarterly Press, 1997).

43. It is possible to bypass the Rules Committee. With a two-thirds vote, members can send a bill directly to the floor, where only 40 minutes of debate are allowed and all amendments are forbidden. To enact the bill under this fast-track procedure, though, supporters must garner the support of two-thirds of the House. Typically, only those bills that are either trivial in importance or that enjoy widespread support are thus considered.

44. The Senate also offers its members several other ways of prolonging the legislative process. For instance, senators can place anonymous holds on bills, which prevent them from moving forward. Additionally, senators have more opportunities to introduce amendments to bills than do representatives in the House, where the party leadership exercises more control over deliberations.

45. It is worth noting, though, that floors have some powers to check such tendencies—for example, the discharge petition allows a majority of floor members to force a committee to release a bill for a floor vote.

46. Norman Ornstein, Thomas Mann, and Michael Malbin, *Vital Statistics on Congress, 1995–1996* (Washington D.C.: Congressional Quarterly Press, 1996), 169.

47. Howard E. Shuman, legislative and administrative assistant to Senator Paul Douglas, interviewed by Donald A. Ritchie, August 13, 1987, United States Senate Historical Office, Oral History Project, 134–88, http://www.senate.gov/artandhistory/history/resources/pdf/Shuman_interview_3.pdf (accessed July 16, 2007).

48. Gregory Wawro and Eric Schickler, *Filibuster: Obstruction and Lawmaking in the U.S. Senate* (Princeton, NJ: Princeton University Press, 2006).

49. The two exceptions: Franklin Pierce, who ranks near the bottom of most ratings of presidential greatness; and Andrew Johnson, who ranks no higher and who the House went on to impeach. See Lyn Ragsdale, *Vital Statistics on the Presidency* (Washington, D.C.: Congressional Quarterly Press, 1998), 27–28.

50. Rachel L. Swarns, "Split Over Immigration Reflects Nation's Struggle," *New York Times*, March 29, 2006, A17; Robert Pear, "Bush Ties Drop in Illegal Immigration to His Policies," *New York Times*, April 10, 2007, A18; and Robert Pear, "Many Employers See Flaws as Immigration Bill Evolves," *New York Times*, May 27, 2007, 1.23.

51. Julia Preston, "Grass Roots Roared, and an Immigration Plan Fell," *New York Times*, June 10, 2007, 1.1.

52. Jeff Zeleny, "Immigration Bill Prompts Some Menacing Responses," *New York Times*, June 28, 2007, A18.

53. David Rogers and Sarah Lueck, "Immigration Bill Might Be Dead After Failing Pivotal Senate Test; Barring White House Push, Political Climate May Halt Overhaul Effort for Now," *Wall Street Journal*, June 8, 2007, A3; David Rogers, "Politics & Economics: White House Courts Kyl To Back Immigration Bill," *Wall Street Journal*, April 30, 2007, A4.

54. June Kronholz and Sarah Lueck, "State of the Union: Immigration Proposals Reverse Party Loyalties," *Wall Street Journal*, January 24, 2007, A2.

55. Carl Hulse, "An Immigration Compromise Divides Republican Senators," *New York Times*, June 7, 2007, A31.

56. Jonathan Weisman, "Immigration Bill Dies in Senate; Bipartisan Compromise Fails To Satisfy the Right or the Left," *Washington Post*, June 29, 2007, A1.

57. Peter Baker, "Bush May Be Out of Chances For a Lasting Domestic Victory," *Washington Post*, June 29, 2007, A1.

58. Sandy Streeter, CRS Report 97-684, *The Congressional Appropriations Process: An Introduction* (Washington, DC: Congressional Research Service, 2006), 4.

59. Allen Schick and Felix LoStracco, *The Federal Budget: Politics, Policy, and Progress* (Washington, DC: Brookings Institution Press, 2000), 235, 236, 238.

60. See http://appropriations.senate.gov/budgetprocess.cfm (accessed March 27, 2008).

61. Streeter, *The Congressional Appropriations Process*, 17.

62. See Taxpayer's for Common Sense website: http://www.taxpayer.net (accessed March 28, 2008).

63. Bennet Roth and Patrick Brendel, "Texas Reaps $2.2 Billion in Earmarks," *Houston Chronicle*, March 23, 2008, http://www.chron.com/disp/story.mpl/headline/metro/5641050.html (accessed March 28, 2008).

64. See http://appropriations.house.gov/ (accessed March 27, 2008).

65. Streeter, *The Congressional Appropriations Process*, 14.

66. Ibid., 6.

CHAPTER FOURTEEN

1. Ford Fessenden and John M. Broder, "Examining the Vote; The Overview: Study of Disputed Florida Ballots Finds Justices Did Not Cast the Deciding Vote," *New York Times*, November 12, 2001. "A close examination of the ballots found that Mr. Bush would have retained a slender margin over Mr. Gore if the Florida court's order to recount more than 43,000 ballots had not been reversed by the United States Supreme Court.... But the consortium, looking at a broader group of rejected ballots than those covered in the court decisions, 175,010 in all, found that Mr. Gore might have won if the courts had ordered a full statewide recount of all the rejected ballots.... The findings indicate that Mr. Gore might have eked out a victory if he had pursued in court a course like the one he publicly advocated when he called on the state to 'count all the votes.'"

2. See Richard Pious, *The Presidency* (New York: Longman, 1995).

3. For an analysis of the president's place in the American political system, see Charles O. Jones, *The Presidency in a Separated System* (Washington, DC: Brookings Institution Press, 1994).

4. The Twenty-second Amendment, a reaction to Franklin Roosevelt's four-term presidency, limited the president to two terms in office.

5. Technically, Lincoln suspended the writ of habeas corpus. A defendant can request a writ of habeas corpus, which is a court order that requires a government official to explain to a judge why an individual is incarcerated.

6. Roosevelt proposed that for every justice over the age of 70, the president could nominate one additional justice until the Supreme Court reached a maximum size of 15. The plan would have allowed Roosevelt to offset older, more conservative justices with those more likely to accommodate his proposals.

7. The scandal was so-named because of the break-in at the Democratic National Committee's headquarters at the Watergate Hotel in Washington, D.C., on June 17, 1972. The president's aides were responsible for arranging the break-in, and the president engineered a cover-up designed to keep the truth from coming out. The discovery of that break-in prompted investigations that revealed a wide range of White House abuses of power, ultimately leading to Nixon's resignation in August 1974.

8. *Walker v. Cheney* (2002).

9. On different leadership styles, see Fred I. Greenstein, *The Presidential Difference: Leadership Style from FDR to George W. Bush* (Princeton, NJ: Princeton University Press, 2004).

10. On public opinion and the president, including the issue of homosexuals in the military during the Clinton administration, see Jeffrey E. Cohen, *Presidential Responsiveness and Public Policy Making: The Publics and the Policies That Presidents Choose* (Ann Arbor: University of Michigan Press, 1999).

11. For a skeptical view of the president's ability to change public opinion, see George Edwards, *On Deaf Ears: The Limits of the Bully Pulpit* (New Haven, CT: Yale University Press, 2003).

12. Isaiah J. Poole, "Two Steps Up, One Step Down." *CQ Weekly*, January 9, 2006, 80.

13. Harold W. Stanley and Richard G. Niemi, *Vital Statistics on American Politics 2005–2006* (Washington, D.C.: CQ Press, 2006), 260–61; Jill Barshay, "Popularity Not Required," *CQ Weekly*, January 1, 2007, 44–53.

14. Whether the bill was originally one of interest to the president or not, to become law both the Congress and the president must approve of the legislation.

15. Charles M. Cameron, *Veto Bargaining: Presidents and the Politics of Negative Power* (New York: Cambridge University Press, 2000).

16. William G. Howell, *Power without Persuasion: The Politics of Direct Presidential Action* (Princeton, NJ: Princeton University Press, 2003).

17. Craig Crawford, "Stubborner Than a Donkey," *CQ Weekly*, May 28, 2007, 1638.

18. See Richard Neustadt, *Presidential Power and the Modern Presidents: The Politics of Leadership from Roosevelt to Reagan* (New York: Free Press, 1991).

19. United States Government Accountability Office, "Presidential Signing Statements Accompanying the Fiscal Year 2006 Appropriations Acts," June 18, 2007, http://www.gao.gov/decisions/appro/308603. pdf. The investigation looked at appropriations bills only. Of the 12 bills, the president questioned a total of 160 provisions in 11 of the bills. The investigation tracked 19 of these and found noncompliance on 6 of those 19.

20. Jeffrey K. Tulis, *The Rhetorical Presidency* (Princeton, NJ: Princeton University Press, 1988); Martin J. Medhurst, *Beyond the Rhetorical Presidency* (College Station: Texas A&M Press, 2004).

21. *Rasul v. Bush* (2004); *al Odah v. United States* (2004); *Hamdi v. Rumsfeld* (2004).

22. Congress can also impeach other executive branch officials or members of the judiciary.

23. Tyler was the first vice president to assume the office of president, and his tenure was uncertain: the Constitution did not make it clear whether he should be an acting president until another was chosen or whether he was in fact president. A former Democrat, he was elected to the vice presidency as a member of the Whig party, but he soon antagonized the Whigs, leading to the resignation of his entire Cabinet and heated battles with Congress. After a series of controversial vetoes, an attempt was made to impeach him for misusing his power and not taking care to pass legislation fundamental to the government's operation. The failure of this attempt led to his censure by the Senate.

24. George Edwards, *At the Margins: Presidential Leadership of Congress* (New Haven, CT: Yale University Press, 1990).

25. Gary Jacobson, *Divider, Not a Uniter: George W. Bush and the American People* (New York: Longman, 2006).

26. Samuel Kernell, *Going Public: New Strategies of Presidential Leadership*, 3rd ed. (Washington, DC: CQ Press, 1997).

27. The bill achieved the $350 billion figure by assuming that some tax cuts would be phased out after a few years, but it was widely expected that Congress, fearful of appearing to increase taxes, would vote to extend the cuts when the time came, resulting in a cost closer to $1 trillion. This made the achievement even more remarkable given rising concerns over deficits.

28. Patricia Heidotting Conley, *Presidential Mandates: How Elections Shape the National Agenda* (Chicago: University of Chicago Press, 2001).

29. See John J. Coleman, "Unified Government, Divided Government, and Party Responsiveness," *American Political Science Review* 93, 4 (1999): 821–35, for an overview of literature on lawmaking during unified and divided government.

30. As was demonstrated in 2000, the presidential election is not technically a national election in which the candidate receiving the most popular votes nationally wins. Instead, it is 51 separate elections—each state and the District of Columbia—selecting electors to the Electoral College, and the candidate amassing a majority of electoral votes might not be the one who received a majority of the popular vote. The election is national in the sense that voters from around the country will be voting for president.

31. Although still distinctive from the presidential system, recent elections in Great Britain have had the appearance of presidential races, with the faces and words of the leading contenders for prime minister plastered around the country, even though the population at large is unable to vote for these candidates.

32. The discussion in this section is based on Stephen Skowronek, *The Politics Presidents Make: Leadership from John Adams to Bill Clinton* (Cambridge: Harvard University Press, 1997). The majority might actually be a coalition rather than just one political party. After the 1980 election, for instance, the Republicans controlled the Senate and held the presidency. The House, however, was held by the Democrats. President Reagan, however, had a working majority in the House on many issues, as he gathered the support of Republicans along with conservative Democrats.

33. Representative Tammy Baldwin of Wisconsin expresses this sentiment in these remarks: "I think one of the challenges I've had as I've moved from working on domestic issues to now having a vote and a say on international issues is, I would say, a frustration with the limits to your information sources. If I look at almost any domestic issues imaginable, I can easily obtain information from a variety of perspectives and weigh the pros and cons of most policy decisions. It's much more difficult on a wide range of international issues, be

they trade issues, global environmental issues, issues of war and peace. The information that's easiest to obtain is usually through the filter of the State Department, the military, or an agency of the United States government. It has been a real challenge for me to try to get information from a broader array of resources." *Badger Herald*, 1999.

34. This case study relies heavily on Andrew Rudalevige's "The Politics of No Child Left Behind," http://www.educationnext.org/20034/62.html.

35. The publication of the report *A Nation at Risk* in 1983 kick-started the standards and testing movement, followed by a major education summit attended by the nation's governors and the first President Bush in 1989 in Charlottesville, Virginia. The *America 2000* report emerging from the summit included a call for voluntary national tests linked to standards. And in 1994, President Clinton signed the Goals 2000 legislation, which would financially assist states as they developed academic standards. Clinton would also sign into law a reauthorization of the Elementary and Secondary Education Act in 1994 that required states to develop K-12 standards and to make consistent progress toward student proficiency, but did not provide any timetable for achieving these goals or punish school districts that failed.

36. Vouchers would provide students a financial stipend that they could use to attend the private school of their choice.

37. John P. Burke, *The Institutional Presidency: Organizing and Managing the White House from FDR to Clinton* (Baltimore: Johns Hopkins University Press, 2000).

38. Department of Defense, "News Transcript: Secretary Rumsfeld Town Hall Meeting in Kuwait," December 8, 2004, http://www.dod.mil/transcripts/2004/tr20041208-secdef1761.html; Richard Tomkins, "Analysis: Bush Cheerleads Iraq, Rumsfeld," *Washington Times*, December 20, 2004, http://www.washtimes.com/upi-breaking/20041220-040901-4646r.htm; CNN, "Troops Put Thorny Questions to Rumsfeld," December 9, 2004, http://www.cnn.com/2004/WORLD/meast/12/08/rumsfeld.troops/.

39. Charles O. Jones, "Clinton's Cabinet: Stability in Disorder," *PRG Report* 24, 1 (2001): 13–16.

40. Like the secretaries of Cabinet departments, the president's appointments of the heads of the various EOP offices must be confirmed by the Senate.

41. James Carney and John F. Dickerson, "The Busiest Man in the White House," *Time*, April 22, 2001, Time Online Edition, (http://www.time.com/time/nation/article/0,8599,107219,00.html).

CHAPTER FIFTEEN

1. H. Josef Hebert, "Supreme Court Will Hear Important Environment Case," *Associated Press State & Local Wire*, June 26, 2006.

2. Beth Daley, "High Court Tells EPA to Rethink Policy on Emissions; Mass. Led Case Against Agency," *Boston Globe*, April 3, 2007.

3. Noreen Gillespie, "Three States File EPA Carbon Dioxide Lawsuit," *Associated Press State & Local Wire*, June 4, 2003.

4. Robert Barnes and Juliet Eilperin, "High Court Faults EPA Inaction on Emissions," *Washington Post*, April 3, 2007, A1.

5. Gillespie, "Three States File EPA Carbon Dioxide Lawsuit"; John Heilprin, "Court Rejects Effort by States to Force Bush Administration to Regulate Greenhouse Gases," *Associated Press State & Local Wire*, July 15, 2005.

6. J.R. Pegg, "U.S. Supreme Court Agrees to Hear Global Warming Case," *ENS Newswire*, June 27, 2006, http://www.ens-newswire.com/ens/jun2006/2006-06-26-10.asp (accessed June 25, 2007).

7. Noreen Gillespie, "States Go to Court to Force Carbon Dioxide Regulation," *Associated Press State & Local Wire*, October 23, 2003.

8. Heilprin, "Court Rejects Effort by States to Force Bush Administration to Regulate Greenhouse Gases."

9. Daley, "High Court Tells EPA to Rethink Policy on Emissions; Mass. Led Case Against Agency."

10. Joan Biskupic, "Stricter Emission Limits Get a Boost," *USA Today*, April 2, 2007; Jennifer Parker, "Supreme Court Rejects Bush in Global Warming Debate," *ABC News*, April 2, 2007, www.abcnews.go.com (accessed June 25, 2007).

11. Daley, "High Court Tells EPA to Rethink Policy on Emissions; Mass. Led Case Against Agency."

12. Parker, "Supreme Court Rejects Bush in Global Warming Debate."

13. Gillespie, "States Go to Court to Force Carbon Dioxide Regulation."

14. Parker, "Supreme Court Rejects Bush in Global Warming Debate"; Barnes and Eilperin, "High Court Faults EPA Inaction on Emissions."

15. Ibid.

16. Robert A. Dahl, "Decision-Making in a Democracy: The Supreme Court as a National Policy-Maker," *Journal of Public Law* 6, 2 (1957): 279–95. Quote on p. 293.

17. Pew Research Center for People and the Press, "Clinton Widens Lead, Giuliani Slips: A Summer of Discontent in Washington," August 2, 2007, 2,

http://people-press.org/reports/display.php3?
ReportID=345.

18. Ibid. When it comes to the judicial branch as a whole, Americans hold similarly positive views. Over the past 25 years, a majority of Americans have reported a "great deal" or "fair amount" of confidence in the courts. From 1973 to 2005, levels of public trust ranged from a low of 63 percent in 1976 to a height of 80 percent in 1999. Confidence in the judiciary was consistently higher than trust in either the executive branch or the legislative branch during the same period. See: Joseph Carroll, "Slim Majority of Americans Approve of the Supreme Court: Approval Rating Still Lower Following Partial-Birth Abortion Ban Earlier This Year," *Gallup News Service*, September 26, 2007, http://www.gallup.com/poll/28798/Slim-Majority-Americans-Approve-Supreme-Court.aspx.

19. See table 1.1 at http://www.uscourts.gov/judicialfactsfigures/2006.html (accessed August 8, 2007).

20. "Workload of the Courts," *The Third Branch* 39, 1 (January 2007), http://www.uscourts.gov/ttb/2007-01/workload/index.html (accessed August 9, 2007).

21. U.S. Library of Congress, Federal Research Division, "Country Studies," http://lcweb2.loc.gov/frd/cs/.

22. Strictly speaking, appellate court rulings in one circuit are not binding for appellate courts in other circuits. As a result, different circuits can produce different appellate rulings on similar cases.

23. This last responsibility only applies when the chief justice is in the majority.

24. If a justice recuses himself or herself from a case, a majority can be achieved with less than five supporters.

25. Timothy L. Hall (ed.), *The U.S. Legal System* (Pasadena, CA: Salem Press, 2004).

26. For a sampling of the arguments made for and against jury trials, see Jeffrey Abramson, *We, the Jury: The Jury System and the Ideal of Democracy* (Cambridge, MA: Harvard University Press, 2000); William Dwyer, *In the Hands of the People: The Trial Jury's Origins, Triumphs, Troubles, and Future in American Democracy* (New York: St Martin's Griffin, 2004); Stephen Adler, *The Jury: Trial and Error in the American Courtroom* (New York: Times Books, 1994).

27. Frank Clifford, "Utility to Pay $333 Million to Settle Suit," *Los Angeles Times*, July 3, 1996, 3.

28. *Abbott Laboratories v. Gardner*, 387 U.S. 136 (1967), at 148.

29. George Fisher, *Plea Bargaining's Triumph: A History of Plea Bargaining in America.* (Stanford, CA: Stanford University Press, 2003), 222.

30. See tables 2.1 and 3.1 at http://www.uscourts.gov/judicialfactsfigures/2006.html (accessed August 8, 2007). During the same period, fully 7.7 million criminal cases were filed in state trial courts.

31. See table 6.1 at http://www.uscourts.gov/judicialfactsfigures/2006.html (accessed August 8, 2007). During the same period, nearly 11 million civil cases were filed per year in state trial courts. State trial court data includes limited and general jurisdiction courts. Sources: *Judicial Business of the United States Courts*, vols. 2001, 2002, 2003, 2004, and 2005 (Washington, DC: Administration of the United States Courts); *Examining the Work of State Courts: A National Perspective from the Court Statistics Project*, vols. 1999, 2000, 2001, 2002, 2003, 2004, 2005, 2006 (Washington, DC: Administration of the United States Courts), http://www.ncsconline.org/D_Research/csp/CSP_Main_Page.html.

32. Richard A. Posner, *The Federal Courts: Challenge and Reform* (Cambridge, MA: Harvard University Press, 1996), 59–61.

33. Figures are in constant 1983 dollars. Source: Robert A. Kagan, "American Lawyers, Legal Cultures, and Adversarial Legalism," in Lawrence M. Friedman and Harry N. Scheiber, *Legal Culture and the Legal Profession* (Boulder: Westview Press, 1996), 13–14.

34. These figures are in current dollars. In constant FY 2000 dollars, the amounts would be about $316 million in 1962 and $5 billion in 2004. Office of Management and Budget, "Historical Tables, Budget of the United States Government, FY 2006," 25–26, 71, 76, http://www.whitehouse.gov/omb/budget/fy2006/.

35. David M. O'Brien, "The Dynamics of the Judicial Process," in David M. O'Brien (ed), *Judges on Judging: Views from the Bench* (Chatham, NJ: Chatham House Publishers, 1997), 34.

36. Quoted in O'Brien, "The Dynamics of the Judicial Process," 34.

37. Quoted in Jethro K. Lieberman, *The Litigious Society* (New York: Basic Books, 1981), xi.

38. Quoted in Lieberman, *The Litigious Society*, 8.

39. Quoted in Thomas F. Burke, *Lawyers, Lawsuits, and Legal Rights: The Battle over Litigation in American Society* (Berkeley, CA: University of California Press, 2002), 171.

40. "President Calls for Medical Liability Reform," White House Press Release, January 16, 2003, http://www.whitehouse.gov/news/releases/2003/01/20030116-1.html.

41. "President Outlines Path for Lasting Prosperity in Wednesday Speech," White House Press Release, April

21, 2004, http://www.whitehouse.gov/news/releases/2004/04/20040421-5.html.

42. Kagan, "American Lawyers, Legal Cultures, and Adversarial Legalism," 8–10.

43. The only notable difference was the rate of tort filings, which was much lower in Britain. The British filed 1,200 tort claims—which concern personal injuries to one's property, body, or rights—for every million of the British population, while Americans filed 3,750 suits per million and Germany, 3,278. See: Basil S. Markensinis, *Foreign Law and Comparative Methodology: A Subject and a Thesis*, (Oxford, UK: Hart Publishing, 1997), 452. Herbert M. Kritzer similarly shows that the British are no less likely to litigate than Americans, except in cases of personal injury torts. Herbert M. Kritzer, "Courts, Justice, and Politics in England," in Herbert Jacob et al., eds., *Courts, Law, and Politics in Comparative Perspective* (New Haven: Yale University Press, 1996), 125–35.

44. Catherine Elliot and Frances Quinn, *English Legal System*, 7th ed. (Harlow, UK: Pearson Education Limited, 2006), 474. See also Martin Partington, *Introduction to the English Legal System*, 3rd ed. (Oxford, UK: Oxford University Press, 2006), 206–07.

45. John Ferejohn and Barry Weingast, "A Positive Theory of Statutory Interpretation," *International Review of Law and Economics* 12 (1992): 265.

46. Averages calculated from data found in Sheldon Goldman, Elliot Slotnick, Gerard Gryski, and Sara Schiavoni, "W. Bush's Judiciary: The First Term Record," *Judicature* 88, 6 (May-June 2005): 269, 274.

47. Jeffrey Segal, Lee Epstein, Charles Cameron, and Harold Spaeth, "Ideological Values and the Votes of U.S. Supreme Court Justices Revisited," *Journal of Politics* 57, 3 (1995): 812–23.

48. Jeffrey Segal, "Separation-of-Powers Games in the Positive Theory of Congress and Courts," *American Political Science Review* 91 (1997): 33.

49. Edwin Meese III and Todd Gaziano, "Restoring the Proper Role of the Courts," *Issues 2006: The Candidate's Briefing Book* (Washington, DC: Heritage Foundation, 2006), http://www.heritage.org/research/features/issues/index.cfm (accessed August 22, 2007).

50. Adam Cohen, "Last Term's Winner at the Supreme Court: Judicial Activism," *New York Times*, July 9, 2007.

51. See: Lee Epstein and Jack Knight, *The Choices Justices Make* (Washington, DC: CQ Press, 1998); Forrest Maltzman, James Spriggs, and Paul Wahlbeck, "Strategy and Judicial Choice: New Institutionalist Approaches to Supreme Court Decision Making," in Cornell W. Clay-

ton and Howard Gillman, eds., *Supreme Court Decision-Making: New Institutional Approaches* (Chicago, IL: University of Chicago Press, 1999).

52. For more on the solicitor general, see: Rebecca Mae Salokar, *The Solicitor General: The Politics of Law* (Philadelphia: Temple University Press, 1992).

53. Lincoln Caplan, *The Tenth Justice: The Solicitor General and the Rule of Law* (New York, NY: Knopf, 1987), 295.

54. David G Savage, *Guide to the U.S. Supreme Court*, 4th ed., vol. II. (Washington, DC: Congressional Quarterly Press, 2004), 809.

55. See chapter 6 of William Howell, *Power Without Persuasion: The Politics of Direct Presidential Action* (Princeton: Princeton University Press, 2003).

56. Decades later, the U.S. government would officially apologize for the internment of Japanese Americans and pay upwards of $1 billion in reparations to their families. In 1998, President Bill Clinton selected Fred Korematsu as a recipient of the Presidential Medal of Freedom.

57. Timothy Johnson and Andrew Martin, "The Public's Conditional Response to Supreme Court Decisions," *American Political Science Review* 92 (1998): 299–309; Jennifer Hochschild, *The New American Dilemma: Liberal Democracy and School Desegregation* (New Haven: Yale University Press, 1984).

58. Abner Greene, *Understanding the 2000 Election* (New York: New York University Press, 2001).

59. Ibid.

60. Ibid.

61. Jeffrey A. Segal and Harold J. Spaeth, "The Influence of Stare Decisis on the Votes of United States Supreme Court Justices," *American Journal of Political Science* 40, 4 (1996): 971–1003.

62. Jeffrey A. Segal and Harold J. Spaeth, *The Supreme Court and the Attitudinal Model Revisited* (New York: Cambridge University Press, 2002), 171.

63. Ibid., 172–74.

64. See, for example: Richard Z. Chesnoff, "Europe Worries as U.S. Re-Counts," *Daily News*, November 12, 2000; No Author, "The Nation's Mood: Get It Resolved, but Get It Right; Americans Express Faith in the Electoral System, but Many Say, 'We Need to Move On,'" *Grand Rapids Press*, November 12, 2000.

65. Terrence Hunt, "Election Impasse 'Nothing to Worry About,' Clinton Tells Putin," *Star-Ledger*, November 15, 2000, 11.

66. Goldman et al., "W. Bush's Judiciary: The First Term Record," 269.

67. Ibid. See also tables 9-4 and 9-5 in Lyn Ragsdale, *Vital Statistics on the Presidency* (Washington, DC: Congressional Quarterly Press, 1998), 432–33.

68. The ABA refused to give Thomas a "well qualified" rating.

69. "Hearing of the Senate Judiciary Committee on the Nomination of Clarence Thomas to the Supreme Court," Electronic Text Center, University of Virginia Library, October 11, 1991, http://etext.lib. virginia.edu.

70. Seven justices who were confirmed nonetheless declined to serve, the most recent being Roscoe Conkling in 1882. Data available online at http://www.senate. gov/pagelayout/reference/nominations/ Nominations.htm.

71. Karen O'Connor, Alixandra Yanus, and Linda Mancillas Patterson, "Where Have All the Interest Groups Gone? An Analysis of Interest Group Participation in Presidential Nominations to the Supreme Court of the United States," in Allan Cigler and Burdett Loomis (eds.), *Interest Group Politics*, 7th ed. (Washington, DC: Congressional Quarterly Press, 2007).

72. Manuel Miranda, "The Original Borking: Lessons from a Supreme Court Nominee's Defeat," *Wall Street Journal*, August 24, 2005, http://www.opinionjournal.com/nextjustice/?id=11000 7149 (accessed August 14, 2007).

73. Peter Baker and Amy Goldstein, "Nomination Was Plagued by Missteps from the Start," *Washington Post*, October 28, 2005, A1.

74. Michael A. Fletcher, "White House Counsel Miers Chosen for Court; Some Question Her Lack of Experience as a Judge," *Washington Post*, October 4, 2005, A1; Charles Babington and Thomas B. Edsall, "Conservative Republicans Divided Over Nominee," *Washington Post*, October 4, 2005, A11.

75. Peter Baker and Shailagh Murray, "Bush Defends Supreme Court Pick; President Reassures Conservatives on a Range of Issues," *Washington Post*, October 5, 2005.

76. David S. Broder, "Bush and Miers: A Tale of Missteps," *Washington Post*, October 23, 2005, B7.

77. Baker and Goldstein, "Nomination Was Plagued by Missteps from the Start."

78. David D. Kirkpatrick, "More Republican Senators Voice Doubts About Miers," *New York Times*, October 27, 2005, 5.

79. Baker and Goldstein, "Nomination Was Plagued by Missteps from the Start."

80. Rick Klein, "Senators Press Bush for Data from Miers White House Stint," *Boston Globe*, October 26, 2005.

81. Ibid.

82. Baker and Goldstein, "Nomination Was Plagued by Missteps from the Start."

CHAPTER SIXTEEN

1. Elizabeth Becker and Elaine Sciolino, "A Nation Challenged: Homeland Security; A New Federal Office Opens Amid Concern That Its Head Won't Have Enough Power," *New York Times*, October 9, 2001, B11.

2. Bill Miller, "Ridge Lacks Power to Do His Job, Says Panetta at Hearing; Cabinet Rank, Budget Clout Urged," *Washington Post*, April 18, 2002, A19.

3. Cornelius Kerwin, *Rulemaking: How Government Agencies Write Law and Make Policy* (Washington, DC: Congressional Quarterly Press, 2003).

4. The FCC adopted its three-prong definition of obscenity from a 1973 U.S. Supreme Court case, *Miller v. California*.

5. FCC rules can be found at: http://ecfr.gpoaccess. gov/cgi/t/text/text-idx?c=ecfr&tpl=/ecfrbrowse/ Title47/47tab_02.tpl (accessed July 25, 2007).

6. Some of the increase in the length of the *Federal Register* can be explained by the introduction of stricter requirements for publication of final rules. In 1973, the Administrative Committee of the Federal Register decided that every rule must include a summary of its subject matter in its preamble. As of 1977, the preamble of a rule must also include a summary of public comments about the rule as well as the agency's answers to questions raised by the public.

7. Federal Communications Commission, Order on Reconsideration, May 31, 2006.

8. No Author, "FCC Reaffirms Its Indecency Fine for CBS," *Wall Street Journal*, June 1, 2006; No Author, "FCC Rebuffs Second CBS Appeal for Super 'Wardrobe Malfunction'," *Houston Chronicle*, June 1, 2006.

9. James Fesler, "The Higher Public Service in Western Europe," in Ralph Clark Chandler (ed.), *A Centennial History of the American Administrative State* (New York, NY: The Free Press, 1987).

10. Michael Nelson, "A Short, Ironic History of American National Bureaucracy," *The Journal of Politics* 44, 3 (1982): 747–78. See also William Nelson, *The Roots of American Bureaucracy, 1830–1900* (Cambridge, MA: Harvard University Press, 1982).

11. Stephen Skowronek, *Building a New American State: The Expansion of National Administrative Capabilities, 1877–1920.* (New York: Cambridge University Press, 1982).

12. The number of bureaucrats working for state and local government, however, has increased dramatically. At the local level, there were approximately 3 million bureaucrats in 1946. By 2003, that number climbed to upwards of 14 million. During the same period state bureaucrats grew from less than one million to over five. Source: U.S. Bureau of the Census, *Historical Statistics of the United States: Colonial Times to 1970* (Washington, DC: Government Printing Office, 1975); *Statistical Abstract of the United States, 2006* (Washington, DC: GPO, 2006).

13. All in all, the 2006–2007 edition of the *U.S. Government Manual* lists 110 independent agencies and government corporations. However, the actual number may be larger than 110. It is particularly difficult to determine the number of government corporations in operation; actual counts vary significantly. National Archives and Records Administration, Office of the Federal Register, *U.S. Government Manual 2006–2007*. (Washington, DC: Government Printing Office, 2006), 361–554. Available online at http://www.gpoaccess.gov/gmanual/browse-gm-06.html. See also General Accountability Office, *Government Corporations: Profiles of Existing Government Corporations* (GAO/GGD-96-14). (Washington, DC: General Accounting Office, 1995.) Available online at: http://www.gao.gov/archive/1996/gg96014.pdf.

14. For a classic treatment of this topic, see Max Weber, "Bureaucracy," in H.H. Gerth and C. Wright Mills (eds.), *From Max Weber: Essays in Sociology* (New York, NY: Oxford University Press, 1946).

15. This idea was developed most fully by the Nobel Prize–winning economist George Stigler. See, for example, *Citizen and the State: Essays on Regulation* (Chicago: University of Chicago Press, 1975).

16. John Carey, "A Shot at Making Drugs Safer: Congress Could Revamp the Cozy Ties Between Drugmakers and the FDA. Will It?" *Business Week*, May 21, 2007, 71.

17. Gardiner Harris, "F.D.A. Failing in Drug Safety, Official Asserts," *New York Times*, November 19, 2004, 1.

18. Marc Kaufman, "FDA Officer Suggests Strict Curbs on 5 Drugs; Makers Dispute Claims About Health Risks," *Washington Post*, November 19, 2004, A1.

19. Michael Powell, "Boston's Big Dig Awash in Troubles: Leaks, Cost Overruns Plague Project." *Washington Post*, November 19, 2004, A3; Elizabeth Taurasi, "Boston's Big Dig: One of Engineering's Biggest Mistakes?" *Design News*, July 28, 2006, http://www.designnews.com/index.asp?layout=article&articleid=CA6357443.

20. See http://www.mountainstateslegal.org/mission.cfm.

21. Amy Zegart, *Flawed by Design: The Evolution of the CIA, JCS, and NSC* (Stanford, CA: Stanford University Press, 1999).

22. Ibid., 57.

23. Ibid., 159–60.

24. See Dana Milbank, "Bush Unveils 'Faith-Based' Initiative; Effort Will Team Agencies, Nonprofits on Social Issues," *Washington Post*, January 30, 2001, A1.

25. John Schwartz, "Panelist on Levees Faults Army Corps Budget Cuts," *New York Times*, October 19, 2005, A18; No Author, "Experts: Levees Were Faulty," *Grand Rapids Press*, October 24, 2005.

26. William T. Gormley Jr. and David L. Weimer, *Organizational Report Cards*. (Cambridge, MA: Harvard University Press, 1999.)

27. By comparison, Kennedy in 1961 made just 286 appointments. "Urgent Business for America: Revitalizing the Federal Government for the 21st Century," Report of the National Commission on the Public Service, January 2003, http://www.brook.edu/gs/cps/volcker/reportfinal.pdf.

28. Thomas Weko, *The Politicizing Presidency: The White House Personnel Office, 1948–1994*. (Lawrence, KS: University Press of Kansas, 1995); Terry Moe, "The Politicized Presidency," in John Chubb and Paul Peterson (eds.), *New Directions in American Politics* (Washington, DC: Brookings Institution Press, 1985); David Lewis, *The Politics of Presidential Appointments: Political Control and Bureaucratic Performance* (Princeton, NJ: Princeton University Press, 2008).

29. Mark Johnson, "Rights Lawyer Faces New Senate Showdown," *Tampa Tribune*, March 14, 1999, 6; John C. Henry, "President Resubmits Nomination; Choice for Civil Rights Post Rejected by GOP," *Houston Chronicle*, March 6, 1999, 10.

30. Randall Mikkelsen, "Clinton Shuns the GOP in Naming Lee as Civil Rights Enforcer," *Star-Ledger*, August 4, 2000, 15; Christopher Marquis, "Clinton Sidesteps Senate to Fill Civil Rights Enforcement Job," *New York Times*, August 4, 2000, A14.

31. Dan Eggen, "Justice Department Fires 8th U.S. Attorney: Dispute over Death Penalty Cited," *Washington Post*, February 24, 2007, A2; Richard Schmitt, "Gonzales Gets Rare Rebuke from Bush," *Los Angeles Times*, March 15, 2007, A14.

32. Richard Serrano, "Gonzales to Admit Mistakes in Firings," *Los Angeles Times*, April 16, 2007, A1.

33. Robert Kuttner, "Gonzales Should Be Impeached," *Boston Globe*, March 24, 2007, A11.

34. See Lewis, *The Politics of Presidential Appointments*.

35. United States Office of Personnel Management, *Federal Civilian Workforce Statistics: The Fact Book,*

2005 Edition, p. 23, http://www.opm.gov/FedData/ factbook/index.asp (accessed April 30, 2008); Government of Canada Privy Council Office, *Fifteenth Annual Report to the Prime Minister on the Public Service of Canada*, March 31, 2008, p. 33, http://www.pco-bcp.gc.ca/index.asp?lang=eng&Page=information& Sub=publications&Doc=ar-ra/15-2008/table_e.htm (accessed April 30, 2008).

36. See Donald J. Savoie, *Breaking the Bargain: Public Servants, Ministers and Parliament* (Toronto: University of Toronto Press, 2003), 28, 136.

37. Lewis, *The Politics of Presidential Appointments*, 98.

38. Ibid., 20–21.

39. Ibid., 25.

40. Ibid., 218.

41. No Author, "NASA's Greedy Overseers," *New York Times*, April 30, 2006.

42. The data on congressional hearings are available through the Center for American Politics and Public Policy at the University of Washington and the Department of Political Science at Penn State University. Hearing data for the House of Representatives (not shown) does not account for significant numbers of unpublished hearings, most notably between 1957 and 1972. The number of unpublished Senate hearings during this time period is much smaller.

43. John Hart, *The Presidential Branch: Executive Office of the President from Washington to Clinton*, 2nd ed. (Chatham, NJ: Chatham House Publishers, 1995); Matthew Dickinson, *Bitter Harvest: FDR, Presidential Power, and the Growth of the Presidential Branch* (New York: Cambridge University Press, 1997).

44. Andrew Rudalevige, *Managing the President's Program: Presidential Leadership and Legislative Policy Formation* (Princeton, NJ: Princeton University Press, 2002).

45. Paul Light, *Thickening Government: Federal Hierarchy and the Diffusion of Accountability* (Washington, DC: Brookings Institution Press, 1995), 1.

46. David Lewis, *Presidents and the Politics of Agency Design: Political Insulation in the United States Government Bureaucracy, 1946–1997* (Stanford, CA: Stanford University Press, 2003); David Lewis, "The Adverse Consequences of the Politics of Agency Design for Presidential Management in the United States: The Relative Durability of Insulated Agencies," *British Journal of Political Science* 34 (2004): 377–404.

47. Norman J. Vig and Michael E. Kraft, "Environmental Policy from the Seventies to the Eighties," in Norman J. Vig and Michael E. Kraft (eds.), *Environmental Policy in the 1980s: Reagan's New Agenda* (Washington, DC: CQ Press, 1984), 3–26.

48. Ibid.

49. Michael E. Kraft, "A New Environmental Policy Agenda: The 1980 Presidential Campaign and Its Aftermath," in Vig and Kraft (eds.), *Environmental Policy in the 1980s*, 29–50.

50. Norman J. Vig, "The President or the Environment: Revolution or Retreat?" in Vig and Kraft (eds.), *Environmental Policy in the 1980s*, 77–95.

51. J. Clarence Davies, "Environmental Institutions and the Reagan Administration," in Vig and Kraft (eds.), *Environmental Policy in the 1980s*, 143–60.

52. Richard J. Tobin, "Revising the Clean Air Act: Legislative Failure and Administrative Success," in Vig and Kraft (eds.), *Environmental Policy in the 1980s*, 227–49.

53. Davies, "Environmental Institutions and the Reagan Administration."

54. Kraft, "A New Environmental Policy Agenda"; Henry C. Kenski and Margaret Corgan Kenski, "Congress Against the President: The Struggle Over the Environment," in Vig and Kraft (eds.), *Environmental Policy in the 1980s*, 97–120..

55. B. Dan Wood, "Principals, Bureaucrats, and Reponsiveness in Clean Air Enforcements," *American Political Science Review* 82, 1 (1988): 213–34; Kenski and Kenski, "Congress Against the President."

56. Wood, "Principals, Bureaucrats, and Reponsiveness in Clean Air Enforcements."

57. Tobin, "Revising the Clean Air Act: Legislative Failure and Administrative Success."

58. Davies, "Environmental Institutions and the Reagan Administration."

59. Wood, "Principals, Bureaucrats, and Reponsiveness in Clean Air Enforcements."

60. See Joel A. Mintz, "'Treading Water': A Preliminary Assessment of EPA Enforcement During the Bush II Administration," *Environmental Law Institute*, 2004, http://www.eli.org (accessed July 19, 2007).

61. Eric Schaeffer, "Paying Less to Pollute: Environmental Enforcement Under the Bush Administration," Environmental Integrity Project, May 23, 2007, http://www.environmentalintegrity.org/pub443.cfm (accessed July 20, 2007).

CHAPTER SEVENTEEN

1. Andrew Martin, "Lean Crop of Dollars," *New York Times*, October 4, 2007, C1.

2. Michael Grunwald, "Why Our Farm Policy Is Failing," *Time*, November 2, 2007.

3. U.S. Department of Agriculture, 1933–1995, 1996–2006 farm income data, http://www.ers.usda.gov/briefing/farmincome/data/GP_T6.htm (accessed

January 31, 2008). Total direct payments in non-constant dollars were $131 million in 1933, $703 million in 1960, and $9,298 million in 1990. Conversion to constant 2007 dollars was done using the U.S. Department of Labor's Consumer Price Index Inflation Calculator at http://www.bls.gov/cpi/ (accessed January 31, 2008).

4. U.S. Department of Agriculture, 2003–2007 farm income data, http://www.ers.usda.gov/briefing/farmincome/data/GP_T6.htm (accessed January 31, 2008).

5. Grunwald, "Why Our Farm Policy Is Failing."

6. Editorial, "Plowing Old Ground; Congress Gets Ready to Flub Farm Subsidy Reform Again," *Washington Post*, October 23, 2007, A18.

7. Grunwald, "Why Our Farm Policy Is Failing."

8. Editorial, "Plowing Old Ground; Congress Gets Ready to Flub Farm Subsidy Reform Again."

9. Grunwald "Why Our Farm Policy Is Failing."

10. Marian Burros, "The Debate Over Subsidizing Snacks," *New York Times*, July 4, 2007, F1.

11. Alexei Barrionuevo, "Agriculture Dept. Urges Big Overhaul in Farm Policy," *New York Times*, February 1, 2007, A20.

12. Burros, "The Debate Over Subsidizing Snacks."

13. Grunwald, "Why Our Farm Policy Is Failing."

14. David M. Herszenhorn, "Farm Subsidies Seem Immune to an Overhaul," *New York Times*, July 26, 2007, A1.

15. Dan Morgan, "Senate Passes Huge Farm Bill; Citing Inadequate Reforms, White House Issues Veto Threat," *Washington Post*, December 15, 2007, A2.

16. From 1995 to 2005, for example, the top 5 percent of farm subsidy recipients obtained well over half of total payments, and these recipients tended to control large businesses with substantial resources. Leslie K Paige, "Reining in Farm Subsidies." *The Washington Post. .* June 27, 2007, p. A18.

17. Robert J. Samuelson, "A Bumper Crop of Inertia," *Washington Post*, September 12, 2007, A19.

18. For further reading on this topic, see John Kingdon, *Agendas, Alternatives, and Public Policies*, 2nd ed. (New York: Harper Collins, 1995).

19. The full text of Johnson's University of Michigan speech on the Great Society is available in *Public Papers of the Presidents of the United States: Lyndon B. Johnson, 1963–64*, vol. I, entry 357, 704–07 (Washington, DC: Government Printing Office, 1965).

20. Grunwald, "Why Our Farm Policy Is Failing."

21. Public Papers of the President, "Remarks at a White House Ceremony Honoring Law Enforcement Officers Slain in the War on Drugs, April 19, 1988," http;//www.presidency.ucsb.edu/ws/index.php?pid=35 698&st=war+on+drugs&st1= (accessed January 15, 2007).

22. In our own lives, we typically devise solutions after having recognized the existence of a specific problem. In politics, though, policy entrepreneurs often advocate on behalf of specific policies that they deem solutions to a wide variety of problems.

23. Richard Simon, "Bush Signs Bill to Tighten Gun-Buyer Screening," *Los Angeles Times*, January 9, 2008.

24. Associated Press, "Congress Comes Calling Again," http://sportsillustrated.cnn.com/2007/baseball/mlb/12/18/congress.steroids.ap/index.html (accessed December 19, 2007).

25. More specifically, GDP is the sum of all domestic consumption spending, investment spending, government spending, and the differences between export and import spending.

26. Associated Press, "U.S. Debt: $30,000 Per Person," *USA Today*, December 3, 2007, http://www.usatoday.com/news/washington/2007-12-03-debt_N.htm (accessed February 1, 2008).

27. Associated Press, "Bush Calls for $145 Billion Stimulus Package," January 18, 2008, http://www.msnbc.msn.com/id/22725498/ (accessed February 1, 2008).

28. The Social Security Act also provided grants-in-aid and health and welfare services to states. The most important elements of the act, though, concern the establishment of a retirement account, which we focus on here.

29. Individuals born after 1938 qualify for full benefits at the age of 67.

30. Figures available at http://www.ssa.gov/OACT/STATS/OASDIbenies.html (accessed December 24, 2007).

31. Figures available at http://www.ssa.gov/cgi-bin/awards.cgi (accessed December 24, 2007).

32. Figures available at http://www.ssa.gov/cgi-bin/awards.cgi (accessed December 24, 2007).

33. Figures available at http://www.ssa.gov/OACT/STATS/table4a1.html (accessed December 24, 2007).

34. Social Security Administration, *The 2007 Annual Report of the Board of Trustees of the Federal Old-Age and Survivors Insurance and Federal Disability Insurance Trust Funds*, http://www.ssa.gov/OACT/TR/TR07/ (accessed December 23, 2007).

35. White House Press Release, "Vice President and Chairman Thomas' Remarks at a Town Hall Meeting on Social Security," March 21, 2005, http://www.whitehouse.gov/news/releases/2005/03/20050321-14.html (accessed January 10, 2008).

36. Michael A. Fletcher, "Bush Promotes Plan for Social Security," *Washington Post*, January 12, 2005, A4.

37. Tax rates available at http://www.ssa.gov/OACT/ ProgData/taxRates.html. Maximum taxable earning available at http://www.ssa.gov/OACT/COLA/cbb. html#Series (accessed December 24, 2007).

38. Figures available at http://www.census.gov/hhes/www/ poverty/threshld/thresh06.html (accessed December 24, 2007).

39. These problems have led some scholars to conclude that poverty rates should be calculated on the basis of consumption patterns rather than reported income. See, for example, Bruce Meyer and James Sullivan, "Measuring the Well-Being of the Poor Using Income and Consumption," *Journal of Human Resources* 38 (2004): 1180–1220.

40. Figures available at http://www.census.gov/hhes/www/ poverty/poverty06/table3.pdf (accessed December 24, 2007).

41. Figures available at http://aspe.hhs.gov/hsp/AFDC/ baseline/4spending.pdf (accessed December 24, 2007).

42. For an especially influential critique, see Charles Murray, *Losing Ground: American Social Policy, 1950–1980* (New York: Basic Books, 1984).

43. Figures available at http://www.acf.hhs.gov/ programs/ofa/caseload/2007/tanf_family.htm (accessed December 24, 2007).

44. Additional information on SSI eligibility requirements are available at http://www.socialsecurity.gov/ssi/index. htm (accessed December 24, 2007).

45. See Table 8.5 of *The Budget for Fiscal Year 2008, Historical Tables*, http://www.whitehouse.gov/omb/ budget/fy2008/pdf/hist.pdf (accessed December 24, 2007).

46. Figures available at http://www.fns.usda.gov/pd/ fssummar.htm (accessed December 24, 2007).

47. Figures available at http://www.cbpp.org/eic2007/ EIC_Participation.pdf (accessed December 24, 2007).

48. Peter T. Kilborn and Sam Howe Verhovek, "Clinton's Welfare Shift Ends Tortuous Journey," *New York Times*, August 2, 1996, A1.

49. Ibid.; Francis X. Clines, "Clinton Signs Bill Cutting Welfare; States in New Role," *New York Times*, August 23, 1996.

50. Robert Pear, "Clinton to Sign Welfare Bill That Ends U.S. Aid Guarantee and Gives States Broad Power," *New York Times*, August 1, 1996, A1; Robert Pear and Erik Eckholm, "A Decade After Welfare Overhaul, a Fundamental Shift in Policy and Perception," *New York Times*, August 21, 2006, A12.

51. Leslie Kaufman, "Are Those Leaving Welfare Better Off Now? Yes and No," *New York Times*, October 20, 2003, B1.

52. Pear and Eckholm, "A Decade After Welfare Overhaul, a Fundamental Shift in Policy and Perception."

53. Ibid.

54. Kaufman, "Are Those Leaving Welfare Better Off Now? Yes and No."

55. Pear and Eckholm, "A Decade After Welfare Overhaul, a Fundamental Shift in Policy and Perception."

56. For the origins of European welfare programs, see Peter Flora and Jens Alber, "Modernization, Democratization, and the Development of Welfare States in Western Europe," in Peter Flora and Arnold J. Heidenheimer, eds., *Development of Welfare State in Europe and America* (New Brunswick: Transaction Books, 1981); and Philip Manow, "Germany: Co-operative Federalism and the Overgrazing of the Fiscal Commons," in Herbert Obinger, Stephan Leibfried, and Francis G. Castles, eds., *Federalism and the Welfare State: New World and European Experiences* (Cambridge, UK: Cambridge University Press, 2005).

57. Jacob S. Hacker, *The Divided Welfare State: The Battle over Public and Private Social Benefits in the United States* (Cambridge, UK: Cambridge University Press, 2002), 13–15.

58. Hacker, *The Divided Welfare State.*

59. David Tyack, *The One Best System: A History of American Urban Education* (Cambridge, MA: Harvard University Press, 1974).

60. Bess Furman, "President to Give Education Plans: Will Forward His Message to Congress Tomorrow on Spurring Science Study," *New York Times*, January 26, 1958, 60.

61. Public Papers of the President, American Presidency Project, "President Eisenhower's Statement upon Signing the National Defense Education Act," September 2, 1958, http://www.presidency.ucsb.edu/ws/ (accessed January 31, 2008).

62. Marjorie Hunter, "More School Aid for Negro Urged," *New York Times*, June 26, 1963, 21.

63. National Center for Education Statistics, "Numbers and Rates of Public School Dropouts: School Year 2004–05," December 2007, http://nces.gov.edu/ pubs2008/hsdropouts/tables/table_7.asp (accessed January 16, 2008).

64. National Center for Education Statistics, "Race/ Ethnicity of Students," October 2003, http:// nces.ed.gov/programs/youthindicators/Indicators. asp?PubPageNumber=10&ShowTablePage= TablesHTML/10.asp (accessed January 16, 2008).

65. National Center for Education Statistics, "Bachelor's, Master's, and Doctor's Degrees Conferred by Degree-granting Institutions, by Sex of Student and Field of Study: 2004–05," July 2006, http://nces.ed.gov/

programs/digest/d06/tables/dt06_258.asp (accessed January 16, 2008).

66. U.S. Department of Education, *A Nation at Risk*, http://www.ed.gov/pubs/NatAtRisk/risk.html (accessed January 10, 2008).

67. Frederick Hess and Michael Petrilli, *No Child Left Behind: A Primer* (New York: Peter Lang Publishing, 2006).

68. OECD Program for International Student Assessment, *PISA 2006 Science Competencies for Tomorrow's World*, December 2007, http://www.pisa.oecd.org/document/2/0,3343,en_32252351_32236191_39718850_1_1_1_1,00.html (accessed January 15, 2008).

69. Joseph Berger, "A Post-Katrina Charter School in New Orleans Gets a Second Chance," *New York Times*, October 17, 2007.

70. For more figures, see www.edreform.com.

71. For a survey of tax credit programs, see William Howell and Mindy Spencer, "Choice without Vouchers: Expanding Education Options through Tax Benefits," a Pioneer Institute White Paper, October 2007, http://www.pioneerinstitute.org/pdf/wp41.pdf (accessed December 27, 2007).

72. See Patrick McEwan and Martin Carnoy, "The Effectiveness and Efficiency of Private Schools in Chile's Voucher System," *Education Evaluation and Policy Analysis* 22, 3 (2000): 213–39; Gregory Elacqua, Dante Contreras, and Felipe Salazar, "The Effectiveness of Private School Franchises in Chile's National Voucher Program," Princeton University Typescript, 2007.

73. National Center for Education Statistics, *The Condition of Education Annual Reports 2000–2007*, http://nces.ed.gov/programs/coe/2007/section4/table.asp?tableID=733 (accessed January 13, 2008).

74. William G. Howell and Paul E. Peterson, *The Education Gap: Vouchers and Urban Schools*, rev. ed. (Washington, DC: Brookings Institution Press, 2006).

75. See, for example, Jeffrey Grogger and Derek Neal, "Further Evidence on the Effects of Catholic Secondary Schooling," in *Brookings-Wharton Papers on Urban Affairs: 2000* (Washington, DC: Brooking Institution Press, 2000).

76. In addition to the elderly, Medicare also provides some assistance to the disabled.

77. Figures available at http://www.cms.hhs.gov/DataCompendium/17_2007_Data_Compendium.asp (accessed December 26, 2007).

78. Alan Weil, "There's Something About Medicaid," *Health Affairs* 22, 1 (2003), http://content.healthaffairs.org/cgi/reprint/22/1/13.pdf (accessed December 26, 2007).

79. Centers for Medicare and Medicaid Services, United States Department of Health and Human Services, *Medicaid At-a-Glance, 2005*, http://www.cms.hhs.gov/MedicaidDataSourcesGenInfo/Downloads/maag2005.pdf (accessed December 26, 2007).

80. Figures available at http://caliban.sourceoecd.org/vl=2555969/cl=18/nw=1/rpsv/health2007/g2-1-02.htm (accessed December 26, 2007).

81. Figures available at http://masetto.sourceoecd.org/vl=4048346/cl=15/nw=1/rpsv/health2007/g3-3-01.htm (accessed December 26, 2007).

82. World Health Organization, "The World Health Report 2000: Health Systems: Improving Performance," 176–84, 189, http://www.who.int/whr/2000/en/whr00_en.pdf (accessed January 14, 2008).

83. See, for example, Center for Economic and Social Rights, "The Right to Health in the United States of America: What Does it Mean?" October 29, 2004, http://cesr.org/ushealthright?PHPSESSID=91 . . . a78f9969da61bd9 (accessed December 27, 2007).

84. See, for example, John Goodman, "Five Myths of Socialized Medicine," Cato Institute: *Cato's Letter*, Winter 2005, http://www.cato.org/pubs/catosletter/catosletterv3n1.pdf (accessed December 27, 2007).

85. The full text of the bill is available at http://thomas.loc.gov/cgi-bin/query/z?c103:H.R.3600.IH: (accessed December 27, 2007).

86. For a fascinating study of these events, see Haynes Johnson and David Broder, *The System: The American Way of Politics at the Breaking Point.* (Boston: Little Brown and Company, 1996).

CHAPTER EIGHTEEN

1. Richard Halloran, "American Is Captured Atfer Plane Is Downed In Nicaragua Territory," *The New York Times*, October 8, 1986, p. A1.

2. Congressional Quarterly, Inc., *The Iran Contra Puzzle,*" p. 3.

3. President Ronald Reagan, quoted from "The Reagan White House; Transcript of Reagan's Speech; 'I Take Full Responsibility for My Actions," *The New York Times*, March 5, 1987, p. A18.

4. E.J. Dionne, Jr., "Poll Shows Reagan Approval Rating at 4-Year Low," *The New York Times*, March 3, 1987.

5. John Felton, "Report Deals Another Blow to Reagan Record," *Congressional Quarterly Weekly*, November 21, pp. 2847–53.

6. Felton, "Report Deals Another Blow to Reagan Record."

7. *Washington's Farewell Address*, 1796; available at http://www.yale.edu/lawweb/avalon/washing.htm. Accessed 1/29/2008.

8. John J. Mearsheimer, *The Tragedy of Great Power Politics* (New York: W. W. Norton & Company, 1999), pp. 236–249.

9. Jeff Frieden, "Sectoral Conflict and Foreign Economic Policy: 1914–1940," *International Organization*, Vol. 41, No. 2 (Winter 1988), p. 63.

10. Benjamin O. Fordham, "Revisionism Reconsidered: Exports and American Intervention in World War I," *International Organization*, Vol. 61, (Spring 2007), p. 286.

11. Fordham, "Revisionism Reconsidered."

12. For more on World War I, see Donald Kagan, *On the Origins of War and the Preservation of Peace*, (New York: Anchor Books, 1996).

13. Williamson Murray and Allan R. Millet, *A War to Be Won: Fighting the Second World War* (Cambridge, MA: Harvard/Belknap Press, 2000), p. 75.

14. Williamson Murray and Allan R. Millet, *A War to Be Won*, p. 82.

15. For World War II, the Allied nations were Great Britain, France, the Soviet Union, and eventually, the U.S. The Axis nations were Germany, Italy, and Japan.

16. Williamson Murray and Allan R. Millet, *A War to Be Won*, pp. 177–178.

17. Williamson Murray and Allan R. Millet, *A War to Be Won*, p. 82.

18. George F. Kennan, "The Sources of Soviet Conduct," in *American Diplomacy*, Expanded ed. (Chicago: University of Chicago Press, 1984), pp. 115–120, 125.

19. The Cold War has also been called the "Long Peace." Coined by Yale historian John Lewis Gaddis, the Long Peace referred to the prolonged lack of war in Europe. John Lewis Gaddis, "The Long Peace: Elements of Stability in the Postwar International System," *International Security*, Vol. 10, No. 4 (Spring 1986), pp. 99–142.

20. For an overview of Cold War history, see John Lewis Gaddis, *The Cold War: A New History*, (New York: Penguin Books, 2005).

21. President Johnson's message to Congress, August 5, 1964. Available online at: http://www.mtholyoke.edu/acad/intrel/tonkinsp.htm. Site accessed February 29, 2008.

22. Arthur Schlesinger Jr, *The Imperial Presidency*. (Mariner Books, 2004)

23. For more on the war in Vietnam, see George C. Herring, *America's Longest War: the United States and Vietnam, 1950–1975*, 3rd ed. (New York: McGraw-Hill, 1996), and Leslie H. Gelb and Richard K. Betts, *The Irony of Vietnam: The System Worked* (Washington, DC: Brookings Institution Press, 1979).

24. Gaddis, *The Cold War*, p. 225.

25. For the post-Cold War grand strategy debate, see Michael E. Brown et. al. eds., *America's Strategic Choices*, revised edition, (Cambridge, MA: MIT Press, 2000).

26. Robert A. Pape, *Bombing to Win: Air Power and Coercion in War* (Ithaca, NY: Cornell University Press, 1996), p. 214.

27. President George W. Bush, "President Bush Outlines Iraqi Threat," White House Press Release, October 7, 2002. Available online at: http://www.whitehouse.gov/news/releases/2002/10/20021007-8.html. Accessed February 2, 2008.

28. John J. Mearsheimer and Stephen M. Walt, "An Unnecessary War," *Foreign Policy*, Jan/Feb 2003, Issue 134, pp. 51–59.

29. Data on U.S. Casualties in Iraq available online at: http://www.globalsecurity.org/military/ops/iraq_casualties.htm. Accessed February 2. 2008.

30. Michael Abramowitz, "Economy, War to Dominate State of the Union; Bush's Challenge May Be Getting People to Listen," *The Washington Post*, January 28, 2008, p. A1.

31. Consulates can be thought of as "sub-embassies", usually located in large non-capital cities abroad to help American citizens or support the main embassy). Many employees of foreign embassies and consulates are foreign nationals providing support for American personnel.

32. Gary Hufbauer, Jeffrey Schott, and Kimberly Elliot. *Economic Sanctions Reconsidered: History and Current Policy*, Peterson Institute, 1990.

33. Daniel Drezner, *The Sanctions Paradox: Economic Statecraft and International Relations*, Cambridge University Press, 1999.

34. Dean Lacy and Emerson M. S. Niou, Theory of Economic Sanctions and Issue Linkage: The Roles of Preferences, Information, and Threats, Journal of Politics, Vol. 66, No. 1, February 2004, pp. 25–42.

35. For additional reading, see: David Baldwin, *Economic Statecraft*, Princeton University Press, 1985; Robert Pape, "Why Economic Sanctions Do Not Work," *International Security*, Vol. 22, No. 2, Autumn 1997, pp. 90–136; A. Cooper Drury, "Sanctions as Coercive Diplomacy: The U. S. President's Decision to Initiate Economic Sanctions," *Political Research Quarterly*, Vol. 54, No. 3, September 2001, pp. 485–508.

36. Stockholm International Peace Research Institute (SIPRI), "The Fifteen Major Spenders in 2006," available online from http://www.sipri.org/contents/milap/milex/mex_trends.html. Accessed February 8, 2008.

37. This number excludes U.S. Postal Service employees, as well as those working for the CIA, NSA, Defense Intelligence Agency (DIA) and the National Imagery and Mapping Agency. These latter four agencies do not make their employment figures public for national security reasons. Source: *Career Guide to Industries: Federal Government, Excluding the Postal Service.* United States Department of Labor, Bureau of Labor Statistics. Available online from http://www.bls.gov/oco/cg/cgs041.htm. Accessed February 8, 2008.

38. Bob Woodward, *Bush at War* (New York: Simon & Schuster, 2002), pp. 3–4.

39. The National Reconnaissance Office (NRO) is also in charge of data monitoring, but its tools are spy aircraft and reconnaissance satellites. Also unacknowledged for many years, the NRO operates under the cover of the Air Force.

40. Destler, I.M. 1995. *American Trade Politics*, 3rd ed. Washington, DC: Institute for International Economics.

41. See, for example, Louis Fisher, 2004, *Presidential War Power, 2nd Edition.* (Lawrence, KS: University of Kansas Press).

42. This 60-day clock can be extended for another 30 days if the President certifies that the time is necessary for the troops' safety.

43. Louis Fisher, *Congressional Abdication on War and Spending.* (College Station: Texas A&M University Press, 2000, p. 65).

44. David Auerswald and Peter Cowhey. 1997. "Ballotbox Diplomacy: The War Powers Resolution and the Use of Force." *International Studies Quarterly.* 41(3): 505–28.

45. VandeHei, Jim, and Colum Lynch. August 2, 2005. *The Washington Post.* "Bush Names Bolton U.N. Ambassador in Recess Appointment." Page A01.

46. Figures available at: http://www.senate.gov/artandhistory/history/common/briefing/Treaties.htm. Site accessed February 5, 2008.

47. Rosati and Scott, *The Politics of United States Foreign Policy*, p. 333.

48. Hulse, Carl. September 11, 2007. "Political Fault Line Emphasized by Timing of Hearings." *New York Times.* Page A.18.

49. Hulse, Carl. September 11, 2007. "Political Fault Line Emphasized by Timing of Hearings." *New York Times.* Page A.18.

50. Strobel, Warren P. September 11, 2007. "Two Days of Iraq Testimony, but No Answer to 'How this Ends,'" *Knight Ridder Tribune News Service.* Page 1.

51. Strobel, Warren P. September 11, 2007. "Two Days of Iraq Testimony, but No Answer to 'How this Ends,'" *Knight Ridder Tribune News Service.* Page 1.

52. Lindsay, James M. Winter 2002. "Getting Uncle Sam's Ear: Will Ethnic Lobbies Cramp America's Foreign Policy Style?" Washington, DC: Brookings Institution. http://www.brookings.edu/articles/2002/winter_diplomacy_lindsay.aspx. Site accessed February 5, 2008.

53. Robert Dahl, 1961. *Who Governs? Power and Democracy in an American City.* (New Haven, CT: Yale University Press).

54. As quoted in Alan Curtis (ed), 2005. *Patriotism, Democracy, and Common Sense.* (New York: Rowman & Littlefield Publishers, p. xii).

55. Rone Tempest, "Servants or Masters? Revisiting the Military-Industrial Complex," LA Times, July 10, 1983, p. H1.

56. Becker, Elizabeth, and Larry Rohter. December 12, 2002. *New York Times.* "U.S. and Chile Reach Free Trade Accord." Page C.1.

57. Council on Foreign Relations: History. http://www.cfr.org/about/history/cfr/index.html. Accessed February 5, 2008.

58. O'Hanlon, Michael E., and Kenneth M. Pollack. July 30, 2007. "A War We Just Might Win." *New York Times.* Page A.17.

59. McNeil, Donald G. March 31, 2007. "Audit Finds Bush's AIDS Effort Limited by Restrictions." *New York Times.* Page A12.

60. Stolberg, Sheryl Gay. January 5, 2008. "In Global Battle On AIDS, Bush Creates Legacy." *New York Times.* Page A1.

61. Stolberg, Sheryl Gay. February 2, 2003. "Getting Religion on AIDS." *New York Times.* P. 4.1.

62. Stolberg, Sheryl Gay. February 2, 2003. "Getting Religion on AIDS." *New York Times.* P. 4.1.

63. Sandalow, Marc. April 1, 2002. "Jesse Helms, Global AIDS Activist." *San Francisco Chronicle.* http://www.sfgate.com/cgi-bin/article.cgi?f=/c/a/2002/04/01/ED2779.DTL Site accessed January 9, 2008.

64. Becker, Elizabeth. December 7, 2003. "With Record Rise in Foreign Aid Comes Change in How It Is Monitored." *New York Times.* Page 1.10.

65. Burkhalter, Holly. 2004. "The Politics of AIDS: Engaging Conservative Activists." *Foreign Affairs* Vol. 83, No. 1, p. 10.

66. Stolberg, Sheryl Gay. January 5, 2008. "In Global Battle On AIDS, Bush Creates Legacy." *New York Times.* Page A1.

67. Stevenson, Richard W. June 9, 2002. "Middle Path Emerges In Debate On Africa Aid." *New York Times*. Page 3.4.

68. Kahn, Joseph. March 15, 2002. "A Star Close to the Heart of Aid Policy." *New York Times*. Page A.8.

69. Stolberg, Sheryl Gay. February 2, 2003. "Getting Religion on AIDS." *New York Times*. P. 4.1.

70. Becker, Elizabeth. December 7, 2003. "With Record Rise in Foreign Aid Comes Change in How It Is Monitored." *New York Times*. Page 1.10.

71. Stevenson, Richard W. June 9, 2002. "Middle Path Emerges In Debate On Africa Aid." *New York Times*. Page 3.4.

72. McNeil, Donald G. March 31, 2007. "Audit Finds Bush's AIDS Effort Limited by Restrictions." *New York Times*. Page A12.

73. Stolberg, Sheryl Gay. January 5, 2008. "In Global Battle On AIDS, Bush Creates Legacy." *New York Times*. Page A1.

74. United Nations NPT Treaty Status. http://disarmament.un.org/TreatyStatus.nsf/NPT%20(in%20alphabetical%20order)?OpenView&Start=1. Accessed February 27, 2008.

75. Carnegie Endowment for International Peace. Non-proliferation: Agreed Framework. http://www.carnegieendowment.org/static/npp/agreed_framework.cfm. Accessed February 26, 2008.

76. The American Presidency Project. "George W. Bush: Address Before a Joint Session of the Congress on the State of the Union, January 29, 2002." http://www.presidency.ucsb.edu. Accessed February 26, 2008.

77. CNN. January 6, 2004. "Timeline: North Korea's Nuclear Weapons Development." http://www.cnn.com/2003/WORLD/asiapcf/east/08/20/nkorea.timeline.nuclear/ Accessed February 26, 2008.

78. Cooper, Helene. January 19, 2008. "U.S. Sees Stalling by North Korea on Nuclear Pact." *The New York Times*. Page A.3.

79. Cooper, Helene. January 19, 2008. "U.S. Sees Stalling by North Korea on Nuclear Pact." *The New York Times*. Page A.3.

80. The lobbyists themselves disagreed about which remedy they desired under U.S. trade law. Some called for anti-dumping measures, which required minimal evidence of injury but could be applied only against specific products and countries. Others wanted to pursue a "Section 201" complaint, which would offer more comprehensive protection to the sector, but only if a much higher burden of proof was met.

81. Stevenson, Richard W. December 11, 2001. "Big Steel: An Invalid that Can Roar in Washington." *The New York Times*. Page C.1.

82. Blustein, Paul. June 6, 2001. "Bush to Seek Protection for U.S. Steel Firms; President Yields to Industry Pressure." *The Washington Post*. Page E.01.

83. Andrews, Edmund L. December 18, 2001. "To Little Avail, U.S. Presses for Steel Output Cut Abroad." *The New York Times*. Page C.2.

84. Perlstein, Steven, and Mike Allen. February 28, 2002. "Bush Faces Tough Choices on Steel Imports; Under Lobbying Pressure, President Must Decide by Wednesday whether To Act to Aid U.S. Industry." *The Washington Post*. Page A.04.

85. Allen, Mike, and Steven Perlstein. March 5, 2002. "Bush Settles on Tariff for Steel Imports." *The Washington Post*. Page A.01.

86. Blustein, Paul. April 18, 2002. "U.S. Indignant Over EU Threat; Retaliatory Tariffs Would Be 'Hypocritical,' Official Says." *The Washington Post*. Page E.02.

87. Weisman, Jonathan. December 5, 2003. "Bush Rescinds Tariffs on Steel; Trade War Averted; Industry Angry." *The Washington Post*. Page A1.

88. Blustein, Paul. June 6, 2001. "Bush to Seek Protection for U.S. Steel Firms; President Yields to Industry Pressure." *The Washington Post*. Page E.01.

89. Transcript of George W. Bush's address to the nation on September 15th, 2001. See "AFTER THE ATTACKS; The President's Message: A Different Battle Awaits," *The New York Times*, September 16, 2001. Available online at: http://query.nytimes.com/gst/fullpage.html?res=9C0CE3D9163BF935A2575AC0A9679C8B63. Accessed February 25, 2008.

90. Katharine Q. Seelye, "THREATS AND RESPONSES: THE DETAINEE; Court to Hear Arguments in Groundbreaking Case of U.S. Citizen Seized with Taliban," *The New York Times*, October 28, 2002. Available online at: http://query.nytimes.com/gst/fullpage.html?res=9802E4DA173FF93BA15753C1A9649C8B63&sec=&spon=&pagewanted=1. Accessed February 27, 2008.

91. Linda Greenhouse, "Court Hears Case on U.S. Detainees," *The New York Times*, April 29, 2004, p. 1.

92. Greenhouse, "Court Hears Case on U.S. Detainees."

93. American Bar Association brief to the Supreme Court, quoted in Linda Greenhouse, "The Imperial Presidency and the Constraints of the Law," *The New York Times*, April 18, 2004, p. 7.

94. Noah Feldman, "Who Can Check the President?" *The New York Times*, January 8, 2006, p. 52.

CHAPTER NINETEEN

1. G. Alan Tarr, *Understanding State Constitutions* (Princeton, NJ: Princeton University Press, 1999).

2. Albert L. Sturm, "The Development of State Constitutions," *Publius* 12 (Winter 1982), 60–67.

3. Albert L. Sturm, *Thirty Years of State Constitutions-Making 1938–1968* (New York: National Municipal League, 1970).

4. David C. Nice, "Interest Groups and State Constitutions—Another Look," *State and Local Government Review* 20 (Winter 1988), 21–29.

5. Alexis de Tocqueville, *Democracy in America*, ed. Phillips Bradley (New York: Knopf, 1945), 40.

6. *City of Clinton v. Cedar Rapids and Missouri River Railroad Co.* (Iowa, 1868)

7. Kathryn A. Foster, *The Political Economy of Special Purpose Government* (Washington, DC: Georgetown University Press, 1997) and Nancy Burns, *The Formation of American Local Governments: Private Values in Public Institutions* (New York: Oxford University Press, 1994).

8. Dale Krane, Platon N. Rigos, and Melvin B. Hill, Jr., *Home Rule in America: A Fifty State Handbook* (Washington, D.C.: Congressional Quarterly Press, 2001).

9. Dall Forsyth, *Memos to the Governor: An Introduction to State Budgeting* (Washington, D.C.: Georgetown University Press, 1997).

10. Alan Rosenthal, *Governors and Legislators: Contending Powers* (Washington, D.C.: Congressional Quarterly Press, 1990).

11. Norma M. Riccucci and Judith R. Saidel, "The Demographics of Gubernatorial Appointees: Toward an Explanation of Variation," *Policy Studies Journal* 29 (January 2001), 11–22; and Thad L. Beyle, "Enhancing Executive Leadership in the States," *State and Local Government Review* 27 (Winter 1995), 18–35.

12. Council of State Governments, *The Book of the States 2008* (Lexington, KY: Council of State Governments, 2008), 201–206. www.csg.org

13. Leon W. Blevins, *Texas Government in National Perspective* (Englewood Cliffs, NJ: Prentice-Hall, 1987), 169.

14. Ann O'Bowman and Richard C. Kearney, "Dimensions of State Government Capability," *Western Political Quarterly* 41 (June 1988), 341–62 ; Timothy G. O'Rourke, *The Impact of Reapportionment* (New Brunswick, NJ: Transaction Books, 1980); and David M. Hedge, *Governance and the Changing American States* (Boulder, CO: Westview Press, 1998).

15. Council of State Governments, *The Book of the States 2008* (Lexington, KY: Council of State Governments, 2008), 145–176. www.csg.org

16. Glenn Abney and Thomas P. Lauth, *The Politics of State and City Administration* (Albany: State University of New York Press, 1986), 65–89.

17. Council of State Governments, *Book of the States 2008* (Lexington, KY: Council of State Governments, 2008) 142–145. www.csg.org

18. National Conference of State Legislatures, "Dual Employment" www.ncsl.org/programs/pubs/summaries/08LBFeb_Dual-sum.htm

19. For a discussion of the effects of term limits, see Karl T. Kurtz, Bruce Cain and Richard G. Niemi, eds., *Institutional Change in American Politics: The Case of Term Limits* (Ann Arbor: University of Michigan Press, 2007) and Rick Farmer, John David Rausch, Jr., and John C. Green, eds. *The Test of Time: Coping with Legislative Term Limits* (Lanham, MD: Lexingon Books, 2008).

20. Alan Rosenthal, *Heavy Lifting: The Job of the American Legislature* (Washington, DC: Congressional Quarterly Press, 2004).

21. Kimberly L. Nelson, *Elected Municipal Councils: Special Data Issue* (Washington, DC: International City/County Management Association, 2002); and Brian F. Schaffner, Gerald Wright and Matthew Streb, "Teams Without Uniforms: The Nonpartisan Ballot in State and Local Elections," *Political Research Quarterly* 54 (March 2001), 7–30.

22. Susan Welch, "The Impact of At-Large Elections on the Representation of Blacks and Hispanics," *Journal of Politics*, 52 (November 1990), 1050–1057 and Susan A. MacManus and Charles S. Bullock III, "Women and Racial/Ethnic Minorities in Mayoral and Council Positions," in *Municipal Year Book, 1993* (Washington, DC: International City/County Management Association, 1993), 57–69.

23. www.census.gov/govs/cog/GovOrgTab03ss.html

24. Stories, video, timeline and photographs are archived by *Northwest Herald*, www.nwherald.com under "Tragedy on Campus."

25. Complete coverage of the shootings and their aftermath is available from the Chronicle of Higher Education, www.chronicle.org under Virginia Tech shootings.

26. The state-appointed Virginia Tech Review Panel's report and background material is available at www.vtreviewpanel.org/

27. Floyd Hunter, *Community Power Succession* (Chapel Hill, NC: University of North Carolina Press, 1980) and Robert Dahl, *Who Governs?* (New Haven, CT: Yale University Press, 1961).

28. Glen Sparrow, "The Emerging Chief Executive: The San Diego Experience," *National Civic Review* 74 (December 1985), 538–547.

29. American Bar Association, *Standards Relating to Court Organization* (New York: American Bar Association, 1974).

30. Stuart Nagel, "Unequal Party Representation in State Supreme Courts," *Journal of the American Judicature Society* (September 1961), 62–65.

31. Madhawi McCall, "The Politics of Judicial Elections: The Influence of Campaign Contributions on the Voting Patterns of Texas Supreme Court Judges," *Politics and Policy* 31 (June 2003), 314–333.

32. Medina Gann Hall, "Justices as Representatives: Elections and Judicial Politics in the American States," *American Politics Quarterly* 23 (October 1995), 427–446.

33. Melinda Gann Hall, "Electoral Politics and Strategic Voting in State Supreme Courts," *Journal of Politics* 54 (Fall, 1992), 508–518 and Melinda Gann Hall, "Toward an Integrated Model of Judicial Voting Behavior," *American Politics Quarterly* 20 (March 1992), 147–168.

34. Elisabeth R. Gerber, Arthur Lupia, Matthew D. McCubbis, and D. Roderick Kiewiet., *Stealing the Initiative: How State Government Responds to Direct Democracy* (Upper Saddle River, NJ: Prentice-Hall, 2001).